SOUTHEAST ASIA

SOUTHEAST ASIA

A Historical Encyclopedia, from Angkor Wat to East Timor

EDITED BY OOI KEAT GIN

A B C 🌐 C L I O

Santa Barbara, California · Denver, Colorado · Oxford, England

Copyright © 2004 by Ooi Keat Gin

Library of Congress Cataloging-in-Publication Data
Southeast Asia : a historical encyclopedia from Angkor Wat to East Timor /
edited by Ooi Keat Gin.
p. cm.
Includes bibliographical references and index.
ISBN 1-57607-770-5 (hardcover : alk. paper); 1-57607-771-3 (e-book)
1. Asia, Southeastern—History—Encyclopedias. I. Ooi, Keat Gin, 1959–
DS524.S68 2004
959'.003—dc22
2004004813

07   06   05   04   10 9 8 7 6 5 4 3 2 1

This book is also available on the World Wide Web as an eBook.
Visit http://www.abc-clio.com for details.
ABC-CLIO, Inc.
130 Cremona Drive, P.O. Box 1911
Santa Barbara, California 93116-1911
This book is printed on acid-free paper.
Manufactured in the United States of America

CONTENTS

VOLUME II: H–Q

Volume III: R–Z

Y

Z

FOREWORD

History in Southeast Asia's Regional Future

WANG GUNGWU

The task of providing exhaustive information about any subject is a daunting one, but it is a measure of maturity when a group of scholars believe they are ready to produce an encyclopedia about their field of knowledge. When that field concerns Southeast Asia, the challenge is all the greater. Although various parts of the region can claim a recorded history of some two thousand years, Southeast Asia is one of the most fragmented regions in the world. Its maritime links stretch outward in at least three directions—toward the Indian Ocean and the West, toward the China Seas and eastern Asia, and toward the Polynesian-Melanesian world of the Pacific. In addition, it has strong overland and riverine bonds with continental China and the highlands of Tibet and eastern India. Partly because of these many-directional ties, there have not been pivotal centers that help to define a region, and it has taken a long time for the divided lands and strung-out islands to be recognized as having a significant identity as a region in its own right.

How the Story Began

Once, however, the imaginative leap was made to view the area between the imperial powers of the Chinese and Indian subcontinent as one that needed a name and to be given a more precise shape, the geographers and historians got to work. But as long as their vision was colored by rival European colonial boundaries, they used different criteria for their studies and were not able to sustain an integrated picture of the region. Names like Malaisie, Malaysia, Indonesie, and Indo-China show that only certain parts of the region were included, while those like Greater India, the Hinduized states, and the Far East were so vague that they could encompass somewhat larger areas but gained little credibility. Nevertheless, the foundations of a regional grouping were laid during the late nineteenth and early twentieth centuries. But it was not until the region faced a common enemy, imperialist Japan in 1941, with its call for a Greater East Asia Co-prosperity Sphere, that a collective response could take shape. The strategic needs of a hard-fought war drove the Western allies to find a common name for a South-East Asia Command (SEAC) based in Ceylon (now Sri Lanka) for the final stage of that campaign. Winning the war ensured that the name would stand. Although the idea of a strategic region was externally determined, it became part of the countervision of an economic and political identity that could be nurtured after the colonial powers had departed. This gave fresh impetus after 1945 to Anglo-American scholars to find an identity that would distinguish the region from China and Japan on the one hand, and from the Indian subcontinent on the other. The other powers of the time—notably the two other former empires, France and The Netherlands, and the short-lived empires of Japan and Germany, as well as the weak new nations of China and India and the emerging Russian superpower—were all in no position to prevent Britain and the United States from carving out a distinct space for their postcolonial relationships. All that remained was to wait for the peoples and states within the region to accept this new identity for themselves.

This latter recognition was far from being straightforward. The return of Western, largely Anglo-American, power met with strong opposition from anticolonial, anti-imperialist, and nationalist forces that were supported by an international communist movement. The region was freshly divided along new faultlines. Anglo-American forces provided support for nationalist elites who rejected communism in order to match the Soviet and Chinese assistance being given to socialists who sought total independence from a capitalist West. For at least three decades, from the late 1950s to the end of the 1980s, there was a deadly struggle by political leaders both inside and outside to define whose Southeast Asia the region should eventually be. But, for different reasons among the various protagonists, the region was being steadily defined. Even those on opposing sides came to accept the redrawn map of Asia as they fought for the hearts and minds of the peoples in the region. The final triumph came after the collapse of Soviet power and the end of the Cold War. After that dramatic end, all the four anticapitalist states of Vietnam, Laos, Myanmar (Burma), and Cambodia had agreed to join the Association of Southeast Asian Nations (ASEAN), thus establishing the boundaries of a region that historians and strategists had worked hard to affirm. That was a significant marker of success when it is borne in mind that ASEAN had been created thirty years earlier by anticommunist states that supported the American superpower in the Vietnam War (1964–1973)

against Soviet Russia and the People's Republic of China (PRC).

The Role of Historians

Throughout this period, historians played a vital part in shaping the image of a unified region. They were backed first by Anglo-American agencies and institutions, and then by scholars in other disciplines. They were among the earliest whose imaginations were stimulated by the possibilities of a synchronic reinterpretation of the great diversities that characterized the region. It was a challenge that two British historians, Brian Harrison and D. G. E. Hall, took up when they wrote the first histories of Southeast Asia. These were the first attempts to outline a postcolonial view of the region. They were assisted in this task by Victor Purcell, who offered a perspective of Southeast Asia that was colored by the Sino-Japanese concept of the Nanyang (Chinese) or Nanyo (Japanese; the South Seas area), one that included a similar geographical area. Two institutions, the University of London (notably the School of Oriental and African Studies and the London School of Economics) and Cornell University, then led the way to consolidate the vertical and horizontal representations of the region. During the decade of the 1950s, a new generation of scholars was trained to define its borders. They also dug deep into the region's history to refine our understanding of the region's commonalities so that they would eventually suffuse the minds and perceptions of everybody concerned.

The course of political changes, supported by continuous efforts by dedicated scholars, has now made Southeast Asia a discrete region, one that can hope to survive the pressures from powerful interests that still wish to manipulate regions in different ways. These interests have conflicting agendas. Some to the region's east and south would like to combine the region with East Asia or the Asia-Pacific, while others on its western flank would stress what it has in common with South and West Asia. Yet others would want to dilute such regional groupings in order to accommodate the expansive future of a truly globalized world. Thus the battles won so far to establish the historical validity of the region may yet be short-lived, especially if the political leaders fail to strengthen the region's defenses against future change. The ten members of ASEAN may wish to find more muscle power in their unity, but they have yet to prove that they can bury their historical differences effectively and act together no matter what threatens them.

This brings us back to the contributions of the art of history to this encyclopedia. They remind us of the divergent ways that history has been used to meet the needs of newly established nation-states in a newfound region. The most important, of course, have been the efforts to project the region as having common roots in its past. This has been easier for historians outside the region than for those within it because the postcolonial nations that had recently emerged all needed to examine their own state histories afresh. Thus, this encyclopedia is not a work done essentially within the region so much as the culmination of the achievements of several generations of historians from many parts of the world. What they have achieved was encapsulated by the essays in *The Cambridge History of Southeast Asia,* edited by Nicholas Tarling and published in 1992, in which fewer than a quarter of the twenty contributors have their roots within the region itself. All the same, that was the strongest demonstration yet that the region's time has come. The analyses and narratives published there confirm the value of the scholarly work accumulated since the 1950s. The historians do not argue that the region's borders are perfect or unchangeable. But they have moved forward more convincingly than other, earlier attempts to do so, including the pathbreaking volume *In Search of Southeast Asia,* edited by David J. Steinberg and his colleagues in 1971. Twenty years afterward, the case for a better understanding of Asian, if not world, history through a holistic view of the region has become more difficult for anyone to refute.

For a better appreciation of the value of this encyclopedia, however, we need to take into account the parallel but opposite tendency within the region for the historians of each country to write their national histories by assuming that the modern borders that mark out their states are permanent and are deeply rooted in the past. Here most historians in each Southeast Asian country began by following the prevailing methods of writing national history as practiced in Europe. This was particularly true during the decades of the 1950s and the 1960s. Was it unavoidable?

How History Shaped the Future

The historians at the time felt that they too were bound to perform civic duties for their respective countries. The past in each of the ten countries (it is too early to speak of the national history of East Timor) could not be left unwritten. The political leaders could not afford not to ask their historians to reexamine, if not repackage, the past to strengthen the weak foundations that their countries have inherited. Each country had to live with new boundaries that included minority peoples, whether indigenous or not, who did not necessarily share the same inherited value systems. It was understandable that these leaders expected their historians to perform a nation-building role. However, the task of these historians, if they were serious about their profession, would still have to be to ensure that what they wrote conformed to high standards of scholarship. The historians had to show their governments and peoples that reliable accounts of the past would make for a better future and that the credibility of their nation itself was invariably at stake.

This was an awesome responsibility. It was not only that the historians had to deal with strident calls for unity and conformity by minimizing internal differences and conflicts in the country's past, but that they also had to resist the urge to depict the quest for peace and harmony with its neighbors in the region as the historical norm. This difficult path between two extremes has often led national historians to favor less controversial topics and avoid those that are politically sensitive. But without doubt the most successful local historians did succeed in overcoming the narrow confines of national history and making significant contributions to the history of the region. A few notable examples would suffice here. For Indonesia, there have not been many who have dedicated their lives to the study of history. Of these, there is general agreement that Sartono Kartodirdjo, Onghokham, and Taufik Abdullah have made valuable contributions. There have been more professional historians in Malaya/Malaysia. Of these, the writings of Wong Lin Ken, Khoo Kay Kim, and Cheah Boon Kheng have made an impact on a wider historiography. As for the Philippines, Horacio de la Costa, Cesar Majul, and Teodoro Agoncillo had earned wide respect for their writings and, among the younger historians, Reynaldo Ileto has gained an international reputation. On the mainland of Southeast Asia, historians have not fared as well, but the work of Charnvit Kasetsiri for Thailand, Michael Aung-Thwin for Burma, and Hue-Tam Ho Tai for Vietnam has received the recognition that they deserved.

But the reality is that, where the history of the region as a whole is concerned, local historians have shown less interest because priority has had to be given to national history. In contrast, scholars from outside the region could avoid the pressures to perform patriotic duties on behalf of each country's past. Their freedom and capacity to think of common regional themes have been, therefore, that much greater. In time, however, they have become more understanding about the constraints that their local counterparts have had to face and less inclined to criticize them either for their timidity or their bias where their own histories are concerned. If the views of earlier colonial historians, who showed scant respect for local attitudes toward the past, are compared with those of the major contributors in the 1990s to *The Cambridge History of Southeast Asia,* it will be clear how much the advent of professional history-writing during the closing decades of the twentieth century has changed our perspectives.

Taking the long view, it has to be acknowledged that the story of how Southeast Asia's past has been reconstructed as regional history has owed much to contributions made from outside. The epigraphic and archaeological record was largely put together by scholars from India and the West; the main traces of early economic activity have been kept by Chinese scholars and officials; and the earliest indigenous annals and chronicles of Vietnam, Java, Thailand, Melaka, and Myanmar, not prominent until after the twelfth century, have been influenced by models from outside the region. During the nineteenth and twentieth centuries, the tools of historical inquiry were augmented by European classical scholars who introduced new methods of research. They were followed by Japanese, Indian, and Chinese historians before local scholars found their own voices. It is no wonder, therefore, that the regional history of Southeast Asia remains one that displays very strong external perspectives. Indeed, that was an inevitable result of the region's fragmentation throughout most of recorded history and the weak traditions of indigenous historical writing.

Now that the region has surfaced and the depths of its historical record are being systematically explored, this dominance of external scholarship may be replaced by a more balanced contribution from local historians. This encyclopedia represents the *first* effort to demonstrate a growing self-consciousness within the region. Although international contributions are still clearly very much stronger than regional ones, the leadership of the editor, Dr. Ooi Keat Gin from Penang in Malaysia, has been decisive in bringing forth the fresh perspectives that modern national scholarship within Southeast Asia can offer. The process of change in that balance has begun, and further changes are bound to come. At this stage of our understanding of how a new region has taken its place in world history, this encyclopedia is an event to be celebrated. It gives me great pleasure to congratulate the editor and his advisory board for the steps taken to advance a cause that has taken centuries to mature. It is time for exhaustive information to be displayed for all to see.

PREFACE

Morning Coffee

The idea for an encyclopedia of Southeast Asian history came to the fore in the spring of 2000. It was through a conversation between Dr. Bob Neville (senior acquisition editor, ABC-CLIO) and me in his office in Oxford, England, that the idea of this project was first proposed. I was spending a research sojourn in Oxford and decided one morning to drop by Bob's office for a social visit. Over coffee, Bob inquired about new proposals for publications, and I casually suggested an encyclopedia of the historical development of Southeast Asia. Nicholas Tarling's two-volume *Cambridge History of Southeast Asia* (Cambridge, 1992) was the major work to date. But that series of long essays by renowned scholars appeared to be rather intimidating for nonspecialist readers, and perhaps inaccessible to a younger audience such as high school students. An encyclopedia format of alphabetically arranged entries of various lengths (the longest not exceeding 3,000 words) might have wider readership appeal. I myself thought that smaller articles written in an easily accessible style would be more appropriate than Tarling's volumes. Then the question of editorship came up. I named several senior scholars as potential candidates; Bob interrupted and proposed that my name be added to the list. It was flattering to be considered but at the same time rather daunting to think of embarking on such a major project. Eventually, however, I agreed to proceed with the project, working in cooperation with an advisory board of senior scholars.

The Work

Southeast Asia: A Historical Encyclopedia from Angkor Wat to East Timor is intended to be the authoritative reference work on Southeast Asian history, catering to users of high school, public, and university libraries. This encyclopedia will serve as a reliable source of information and a quick reference guide to high school and college students, researchers, academicians, and others who want a better understanding of the intricate historical development of Southeast Asia, one of the fastest growing regions in the world.

A pioneering work, this user-friendly, dictionary-style encyclopedia has over 800 entry-articles contributed by more than 130 specialists worldwide, offering in-depth coverage of a wide range of topics including archaeology and prehistory, political history, cultural heritage, economic and social transformation, and ethnohistory of ethnic minorities. Also featured are historical periods and eras, concepts and ideas, institutions and organizations, wars and conflicts, personalities, religions and popular beliefs, constitutional developments and legislation, and historical geography and the environment. Complementing the large number of historians, the international panel of contributors includes archaeologists, sociologists, political scientists, anthropologists, ethnographers, geographers, economists, and demographers.

The geographical coverage encompasses the contemporary nation-states of Myanmar (Burma prior to 1989), Thailand (Siam prior to 1939), Laos, Cambodia, Vietnam, Malaysia, Singapore, Brunei, Indonesia, the Philippines, and East Timor (since 2002). Owing to the interconnectedness of their historical relations, influences, and developments, India and Sri Lanka (Ceylon) of South Asia, and China, Taiwan (Formosa), and Japan of East Asia are each given appropriate focus and emphasis. The time frame traces the historical development of Southeast Asia from the period of "Java Man" (ca. 500,000 B.C.E.) to the declaration of independence by East Timor (August 2002).

Arranged alphabetically, entry-articles range in size from a brief entry of some 300 words to long essays of 3,000 words. Brief entries generally focus on concepts, ideology, and terminology, whereas medium and long entries represent thematic essays and feature articles. Whether long or short, each entry balances descriptive narrative with in-depth analysis, interpretation, and commentary designed for a general readership. Each entry-article contains three components: textual content, cross-referencing, and a list of references for further reading. Cross-referencing allows the reader to have a follow-up, thereby building a secure understanding of historical knowledge and the appreciation of the interrelationships and linkages of events, phenomena, and personalities. A list of readings (books and journal articles) accompanies each entry-article, to cater to those who intend to explore the subject further or in more detail. Although the references recommended are mainly academic-oriented works, care has been taken to select books and journal articles that are easily accessible (in most public libraries) and congenial for a general audience. Despite advances in electronic information technology, the print media have been given priority in the reference listing; some more permanent websites and WebPages are recommended. Non-English titles of books and journal articles have been rendered in English in parentheses to give readers an idea of their contents; they do not imply that there is an English version available.

The selection process is, to say the least, a tedious and unenviable task. A balancing act and coordination effort must be exercised to ensure that all the territories and areas are given equal focus in accordance with their historical importance. The same attention is given to events, personalities, phenomena, wars, organizations and movements, concepts, and ideologies of Southeast Asia's past. No encyclopedia can be entirely comprehensive. Omissions are inevitable because of time and word constraints.

Maps, tables, and photos are designed to supplement the text. The majority of the illustrations come from the contributors. However, not all the proposed illustrations could be accommodated within these pages.

Explanatory Notes
Alphabetical Order
The order of entry-articles is alphabetical, in accordance with the rules of letter-by-letter alphabetization.

Entry-articles
There are four types of entry-articles based on word length: brief (300 words), short (800 words), medium (1,800 words), and long (3,000 words). Irrespective of its length, the textual content of every entry-article has three parts. The first part primarily defines the entry and explains its historical significance vis-à-vis Southeast Asia. The second part provides the basic information of the entry. The concluding section places the subject matter into perspective in the overall historical development. Moreover, it offers the current historiographical insights on the subject matter.

Cross-references
Each entry-article is cross-referenced to others of close or related interest. Many entry-articles are interrelated, and cross-referencing provides the reader a better and clearer picture of a particular subject matter.

References
For further or more detailed study, the reader should explore the readings listed under "References." As far as possible, English-language books and journal articles have been recommended.

In-text Citation

In-text citation is used in lieu of footnotes or endnotes. It is also utilized to indicate the source for quotations and statistical data.

Terms and Alternative Spellings

Preference has been given to the common usage of a term, word, place-name, title, or the names of individuals that are generally recognized. The alternative or other term is given in parentheses—for example, Sri Lanka (Ceylon), Melaka (Malacca), Beijing (Peking), Burma (Myanmar), Siam (Thailand)—upon first mention. The Hanyu-Pinyin system of transliteration is generally preferred, with the Wade-Giles version in parentheses upon first mention—for instance, Qing (Ch'ing/Manchu). Where appropriate, however, the Wade-Giles transliteration of certain words and names has been retained where it is widely known—for instance: Chiang Kai-shek (Jiang Jieshi) and Admiral Cheng Ho (Zheng He). Likewise, spelling variations abound owing to the transliteration of indigenous languages into the Roman alphabet. Hence Ayutthaya, Ayuthaya, Ayudhya, or Ayuthia, and Yogyakarta or Jogjakarta. Similarly, popular usage is adopted: Suharto over Soeharto.

Non-English Words/Phrases

Terms, words, phrases, and titles of reference materials in languages other than English are given their English translation in parentheses.

Life Dates

The lifespan of an individual, institution, or organization is indicated in parentheses, if available. Abbreviations are used: "r." = reign; "b." = birth; "d." = death; "t." = tenure of office.

Family and Personal Names

Southeast Asians, including the Chinese community, have their own format for writing their names. In the Western style, personal names precede family names—for example, Dwight David Eisenhower; among Southeast Asians, only those of Christian Philippines and East Timor follow this format: Sergio Osmena, José Rizal, Rogerio Lobato, José Ramos Horta.

Other Southeast Asians possess their own style of address.

For Brunei, Malaysia, and Singapore, the main ethnic groups are Malays, Chinese, Indians including Sikhs, and various ethnic minorities in the East Malaysian states of Sabah and Sarawak. Malays do not have family names, therefore their personal name is used in lieu as a form of formal address—for example, Abdullah bin Haji Ahmad Badawi is addressed as Encik (Mr.) Abdullah; Rafidah Aziz as Puan (Mrs.) Rafidah. Family names precede personal names for the Chinese, and rarely is hyphenation used in personal names, such as is the practice among the mainland Chinese and Taiwanese—thus Tan Cheng Lock, Lee Hau Shik. Some Indians do display their family or clan names following their personal names, as in Dharma Raja Seenivasagam and Selvakumar Ramachandran, Seenivasagam and Ramachandran being family names; but Anthony s/o (son of) Andiappen must be addressed as Mr. Anthony. "Singh" and "Kaur" are not family names of Sikhs; the former denotes male and the latter, female. The Sikhs do possess family or clan names, such as Kernial Singh Sandhu, Harcharan Singh Khera; others, however, do not insert the family/clan name in their names—thus Amarjit Kaur. For the Iban, Sarawak's largest ethnic group, family names often do not appear—for example, Leo Moggie anak (son of) Irok and Peter Tinggom anak Kamarau. Therefore they would be addressed as Mr. Leo Moggie and Mr. Peter Tinggom. Among the Kadazan-Dusun, personal names precede family names as in the Western style: Joseph Pairin Kitingan, James Ongkili.

Discerning family names in Indonesia is at best problematic. Apparently for Muslims, like their counterparts in Malaysia, Brunei, and Singapore, there are no family names, and the initial name is taken for addressing purposes—for instance, Tan Malaka, Kahar Muzakkar, and Abdurrahman Wahid. However, it seems that there is a preference for addressing Sekarmadji Maridjan Kartosuwiryo and Bacharuddin Jusuf Habibie as Kartosuwiryo and Habibie respectively. On the other hand, there are communities possessing family/clan names—for instance, among the Bataks and Mandailings of Sumatra, names like Lubis and Nasution are prominent. Then there are the single-word names such as Semaun, Soekarno, and Suharto. Amid these divergences, Indonesian names are presented in their popular usage, with apologies for any inconsistency.

In Myanmar (Burma), there are apparently no family names. Often the initial name is assumed as the "family name" or name to address. Thus Kyaw Thet, Maung Maung, and Thant Myint U are referred to as Mr. Kyaw, Mr. Maung, and Mr. Thant, respectively. U, as in U Thant, is an honorific denoting an individual of standing.

In the case of Thailand (Siam), the personal name precedes the family name: Kukrit Pramoj, Thanom Kittikachorn, Prem Tinsulanond. But the bibliographic reference for them is listed under "K," "T," and "P," respectively, as convention dictates.

Similar to Chinese names in Brunei, Malaysia, and Singapore, the Vietnamese family name precedes the given name—for example, Nguyễn Long Thanh Nam and Ngô Đình Diệm.

In Cambodia an individual's personal name precedes the family/clan name: Norodom Sihanouk, Ieng Sary, Heng Samrin. But often, as in the case of the latter two personalities, they are addressed in full as Ieng Sary and Heng Samrin; likewise with Pol Pot, or when using his real name, Saloth Sar.

Laotians such as Katay Don Sasorith, Khammao Vilay, and Nhouy Abhay are addressed as Messrs. Katay, Khammao, and Nhouy.

Research/Study Aids

In addition to helping readers to select topics from the pool of entry-articles, the Topic Finders and Index are designed to assist the reader in identifying and locating particular themes, issues, and facts. Furthermore, the Chronology offers the flow of historical development through the ages and highlights significant events, incidents, and happenings coupled with concise explanatory notes.

Acknowledgments

This three-volume work is the result of teamwork by contributors, members of the advisory board, and the publisher (from acquisition to production). I have thanked each and every one of the more than 130 contributors for their diligence, cooperation, and patience, as well as for the sacrifice of their time and energy. Moreover, I am grateful and deeply touched by several contributors who, despite their own tight schedules, went the extra mile during critical stages in the encyclopedia's development. All of the contributors are specialists in their fields of study and research.

Members of my advisory board were most helpful and displayed great tolerance, despite their heavy schedules and commitments, in affording me advice, recommendations, and guidance throughout the preparation of this encyclopedia. I greatly appreciate that all of them also contributed entry-articles.

I am very much obliged to Professor Wang Gungwu, who not only happily penned the Foreword but who also wrote several entry-articles.

I wish to thank all personnel of ABC-CLIO who directly or indirectly were involved in the production of this encyclopedia: I congratulate you for the exceptional quality of your work and your professionalism. I reserve especial mention of appreciation and gratitude for Ms. Karna Hughes, development editor, ABC-CLIO, Santa Barbara. Karna's assistance, initiative, patience, diplomacy, and perseverance saw me through various difficulties. Dr. Robert Neville, senior acquisitions editor, ABC-CLIO, Oxford, is also the recipient of my especial gratitude. Likewise to Anna Kaltenbach, production editor, ABC-CLIO, Broomfield, Colorado.

To my longtime friend Teoh Boon Hoe, I acknowledge and appreciate your constructive criticisms, arguments, and analytical thoughts on several issues that I raised during the early stages of the present work. Dr. Ann Heylen deserves an accolade of thanks for her assistance in myriad forms.

To my mother, Tan Ai Gek, and sisters Saw Lian and Saw Ean, your love and support are priceless. Here is another addition to your bookshelf.

And to my dearest wife, Swee Im, I am grateful for your helping hand, patience, and tolerance, and most of all thank you for your love and emotional sustenance.

Ooi Keat Gin
The Pongo, Island Glades
Penang, Malaysia
May 2004

INTRODUCTION

The term "SOUTHEAST ASIA" is a recent construct that came into use during the Pacific War (1941–1945) to designate the area of operation for Anglo-American forces under ADMIRAL LORD LOUIS MOUNTBATTEN (1900–1979) and SOUTH-EAST ASIA COMMAND (SEAC). While American GENERAL DOUGLAS MACARTHUR (1880–1964) focused on fulfilling his promise of retaking the Philippines, the reoccupation of the rest of the region was entrusted to the British and their Australian and New Zealand partners. Subsequently, in the aftermath of the sudden Japanese surrender in early August 1945, BRITISH MILITARY ADMINISTRATION (BMA) IN SOUTHEAST ASIA held sway for several months (except in the kingdom of Siam/Thailand and the Philippines) until the reinstatement of civilian government.

The lands of Southeast Asia comprise what are today Myanmar (Burma), Thailand (Siam), Laos, Cambodia, Vietnam, Malaysia, Singapore, Brunei, the Philippines, Indonesia, and East Timor, possessing a long and complex historical development dating back to the first millennium C.E. Known human habitation in the region is believed to date from 500,000 to 1,000,000 years ago. The region is indeed ancient. Over the centuries, Southeast Asia has been known by numerous designations. SUVARNABHUMI (LAND OF GOLD) was what Indians during the early centuries C.E. called the lands of Southeast Asia, often referring to the island of SUMATRA and the Malay Peninsula (present-day West/Peninsular Malaysia). ARABS and Persians referred to Southeast Asia as the "lands below the winds,"

acknowledging the fact that the seasonal MONSOONS—namely, the prevailing winds from the northeast and southwest—brought their sailing trading vessels to the region. *NANYANG* ("South Seas") to the Chinese and *Nanyo* to the Japanese were references to the region denoting the seas to the south of China and Japan.

The Environment

Lying between the Indian subcontinent (South Asia) to the west and the Chinese mainland (East Asia) to the east, Southeast Asia's strategic position had from earliest times played a pivotal role in seaborne East-West trade and commerce, as well as communication and interaction. The monsoonal winds from the northeast (November–February) and the southwest (June–August) not only facilitated shipping and trading but also dictated the agricultural cycle. RICE IN SOUTHEAST ASIA has long relied on the seasonal rainfall; the northeast monsoon ushers in the wet season, whereas the reversed winds of the southwest monsoon offer lesser precipitation, hence the drier season. The characteristically hot, wet, and humid equatorial conditions throughout the year are prevalent to maritime Southeast Asia—namely, Malaysia, Singapore, Brunei, Indonesia, East Timor, and central and southern Philippines. Mainland Southeast Asia—Myanmar, Thailand, Laos, Cambodia, and Vietnam—and the northern Philippines experience tropical conditions with a more distinct wet and dry season. The greater part of the region receives an annual average rainfall of more than 1,500 millimeters. With the notable exception of northern parts of Vietnam, which experience a lower temperature (that is, 23° C/74° F), the yearly average temperatures throughout Southeast Asia hover around 27° C (80° F).

The ECOLOGICAL SETTING OF SOUTHEAST ASIA is dictated by tropical and equatorial climatic characteristics coupled with the monsoon patterns. The imaginary WALLACE LINE, named after the nineteenth-century British botanist and explorer Alfred Russel Wallace (1823–1913), divides the biogeographical zone of Asia from Australasia, with the Philippines straddling a transitional zone. Those regions of Southeast Asia situated west of the divide possess a distinctively Asian pattern of flora and fauna: tropical rainforests supporting tigers, elephants, rhinoceros, and orangutan.

The HISTORICAL GEOGRAPHY OF MAINLAND SOUTHEAST ASIA portrays the major river systems—the Irrawaddy, Salween, Chao Phraya, Mekong, and Red—which have a great influence on the demographic pattern, economic activities, and sociocultural characteristics of the land and peoples. On the other hand, the HISTORICAL GEOGRAPHY OF INSULAR SOUTHEAST ASIA is shaped by the shared similar tectonic characteristics of volcanic activities and fertile lava-based soils. The surrounding seas and the strategic STRAITS OF MELAKA play a prominent role in the lives and history of the inhabitants, dispersed over the myriad spread of thousands of islands. Bridging continental and maritime Southeast Asia is the ISTHMUS OF KRA, which had a long history of international trade.

Southeast Asia Today

Contemporary Southeast Asia is best identified and better known to the international community by the regional grouping known as the ASSOCIATION OF SOUTHEAST ASIAN NATIONS (ASEAN) (1967). From the time of its founding with only five members, today ASEAN has doubled its membership to ten: Brunei, Cambodia, Indonesia, Laos, Malaysia, Myanmar, Singapore, Thailand, the Philippines, and Vietnam. Including the non-ASEAN, newly independent East Timor, Southeast Asia today comprises eleven sovereign nation-states.

Officially known as Negara Brunei Darussalam ("Abode of Peace"), this small (5,765-square-kilometer) Malay Islamic sultanate perched on the northeast coast of BORNEO once claimed suzerainty over the entire island. A protectorate of Britain since 1888, Brunei gained independence in 1984. BRUNEI MALAYS constituted close to 67 percent of the estimated total population of 358,098 (July 2003 est.); Chinese constituted about 15 percent, and the remainder was BRUNEI ETHNIC MINORITIES (Daniel 2002: 208). Bandar Seri Begawan is the administrative capital of this Malay Islamic monarchy.

The state of Cambodia (Roat Kampuchea), occupying the southwestern part (181,035 square kilometers) of the Indochinese peninsula, once hosted the kingdoms and empires of Southeast Asia during the early centuries C.E. Following a long period of French colonial rule since the late nineteenth century, Cambodia became independent in 1953. Thereafter followed a complicated unfolding of events intertwined with developments in neighboring Laos and Vietnam, as well as decisions undertaken in Washington, Bangkok, Moscow, and Beijing. The majority of the 13,124,764 population (July 2003 est.) were KHMERS, with sizable communities of Vietnamese and Chinese (ibid.: 241). The capital city of PHNOM PENH bears witness to the KHMER ROUGE regime, Vietnamese invasion, the intervention by the United Nations, and the political fortunes of NORODOM SIHANOUK (1922–).

Stretching from ACEH (ACHEH) in the west to IRIAN JAYA (West Irian) in the east, more than 13,000 islands compose the archipelago of "INDONESIA," making the republic of Indonesia (Republik Indonesia) the largest country in Southeast Asia, covering an area of nearly 2 million square kilometers. The prominent islands include SUMATRA, JAVA, the southern half of BORNEO (named Kalimantan), and the chain of islands from MADURA, BALI, and LOMBOK to West TIMOR. In the eastern part of the archipelago lie SULAWESI (Celebes), MALUKU (THE MOLUCCAS), ROTI (ROTE), SAVU (SABU), and IRIAN JAYA (West Irian). Equally diverse is the population of an estimated 234,893,453 (July 2003 est.) that comprised a wealth of ethnic communities (ibid.: 520). Better known ethnic groups are the Javanese, Madurese, Sundanese, Balinese, BATAKS, MINANGKABAU, DAYAKS, and BUGIS (BUGINESE). Others are REJANGS and TORAJAS. The varied EAST INDONESIAN ETHNIC GROUPS add to the complexity and multicultural characteristics of present-day Indonesia. Fittingly adopted is BHINNEKA TUNGGAL IKA ("UNITY IN DIVERSITY") as the national motto since 1950. Composed of the former NETHERLANDS (DUTCH) EAST INDIES or DUTCH EAST INDIES, Indonesia gained its independence in 1945. Jakarta on the island of Java had since the early seventeenth century—at which time it was known as BATAVIA (SUNDA KELAPA, JACATRA, DJAKARTA/JAKARTA)—played the role of administrative center of this far-flung country.

Indonesia's affair with democracy has gone through various metamorphoses, from the GUIDED DEMOCRACY (*DEMOKRASI TERPIMPIN*) of SOEKARNO (SUKARNO) (1901–1970) to the *ORDE BARU* (NEW ORDER) of SUHARTO (1921–). Post-Suharto governments have to struggle to balance an array of diverse elements—namely, a powerful and politicized military, a growing and influential Islamic popular movement, and a liberal and Western-leaning intellectual elite—while addressing separatists and regional aspirations, economic decline, and the increasingly widening gulf between the haves and have-nots.

Laos, or officially the LAO PEOPLE'S DEMOCRATIC REPUBLIC (LPDR) (Sathalanalat Pasathipatay Pasason Lao), is a narrow, landlocked country occupying an area of 236,800 square kilometers in the Indochinese peninsula. Sparsely populated (5,921,545 [July 2003 est.]), the country's predominant ethnic group is LAO; numerous ethnic minorities are dispersed in the hilly countryside. Contested by Siam and France during the late nineteenth century and early twentieth century, Laos was under French colonial domination until 1954. The post-French period witnessed the struggle for ascendancy between royalist elements and communist groups, with the latter establishing the LPDR in 1975. VIENTIANE is the seat of this socialist-based government.

The Federation of MALAYSIA (1963), constituted in 1963, is composed of two parts. It encompasses a total land area of 329,750 square kilometers, and the South China Sea separates West or Peninsular Malaysia (the former BRITISH MALAYA) from East Malaysia (the former BRITISH BORNEO less Brunei). The former consisted of the WESTERN MALAY STATES (PERAK, SELANGOR, NEGRI SEMBILAN, AND PAHANG), MELAKA,

PENANG (1786), SINGAPORE (1819), the SIAMESE MALAY STATES (KEDAH, PERLIS, KELANTAN, TERENGGANU), and JOHOR. The former British Crown colonies of SARAWAK AND SABAH (NORTH BORNEO), components of BRITISH BORNEO, and SINGAPORE (1819) gained their independence through MALAYSIA (1963). SINGAPORE (1819), however, moved out of the federation in 1965. There is a unique system of CONSTITUTIONAL MONARCHY (MALAYA/ MALAYSIA), whereby the position of the Malaysian king is rotated among the nine Malay sultans. A Westminster style of democracy is practiced by successive governments based on a coalition of the major ethnic groups in the country—namely, MALAYS, Chinese, Indians, IBAN, and KADAZAN-DUSUN. KUALA LUMPUR (KL) is the capital city, but the administrative center is the newly planned city of Putrajaya. The population of the country is estimated to be 23,092,940 (July 2003 est.), the bulk of which is in West Malaysia.

The republic of Singapore, a city-state (692 square kilometers) on the southern tip of West Malaysia, gained independence from Britain through joining the Federation of Malaysia in 1963; this island republic, however, separated itself from the federation in 1965. Chinese formed the bulk of the 4,608,595 (July 2003 est.) population, along with minorities of Malays and Indians. Parliamentary democracy is practiced, but since independence a one-party government has been the norm.

The Union of Myanmar (Pyidaungzu Myanma Naingngandaw) replaced the Union of Burma in 1989. With a land area of 678,500 square kilometers, Myanmar's political and international boundaries coincided with those of the former BRITISH BURMA with Bangladesh and INDIA to the west and northwest, respectively; China to the north and northeast; Laos to the east; and Thailand to the southeast. Since independence from Britain in 1948, the country has experimented with parliamentary democracy, dictatorship, and military junta government. The country's population was officially estimated as 42,510,537 (July 2003 est.), with a diversity of ethnic groups: BURMANS, CHINS, KACHINS, KARENS, MONS, PYUS, and SHANS. There are small enclaves of Chinese and Indians, particularly in urban areas including the capital city of RANGOON (YANGON).

The kingdom of Thailand (Muang Thai) was formerly known as the kingdom of Siam. The name Thailand (Land of the Free) was adopted in 1939 to reflect its independent status, unshackled by foreign domination vis-à-vis its neighbors, which were all under Western colonial rule. Moreover the name change was an assertion of the ethnic T'AIS, who shared linguistic similarities with LAO, SHANS, and other minorities in northern Vietnam and south and southwest China. Situated in the heartland of mainland Southeast Asia, Thailand's overall land area is 514,000 square kilometers including the extension southward, where it shares the ISTHMUS OF KRA with Myanmar. Ethnic T'AIS composed the majority of the inhabitants of 64,265,276 (July 2003 est.). The Chinese, though an urban minority, had long been and continue to be a significant and influential economic player. MUSLIM MINORITIES (THAILAND) dominated peninsular or southern Thailand. Civilian parliamentarians jostled for power with the military, the latter an ever influential party to the political landscape. The CONSTITUTIONAL (BLOODLESS) REVOLUTION (1932) (THAILAND) replaced absolutist monarchical rule with a constitutional monarchy.

Named after the Spanish monarch Philip II (r. 1556–1598), the Republic of the Philippines (Republika ng Pilipinas) comprises an archipelago of more than 7,000 islands. The Philippines possesses a total area of 300,000 square kilometers surrounded by the South China Sea to the west and north, the Philippine Sea to the east, and the Celebes Sea to the south. The three major island groupings are, from north to south, LUZON (Luzon, Mindoro, and Palawan), VISAYAN ISLANDS (BISAYAN ISLANDS, THE BISAYAS, THE VISAYAS) (Bohol, Cebu, Leyte, Masbate, Negros, Panay, and Samar), and MINDANAO. Filipinos whose ancestors were MALAYS composed the main ethnic group of a population estimated at 84,619,974 (July 2003 est.). Consequent of MISCEGENATION, there emerged MESTIZO minorities of Sino-Filipino, Spanish-Filipino, and American-Filipino descent. In the southern Philippines are found ILANUN AND BALANGINGI, MOROS, Sulus, and Tausugs. The Philippines declared its independence from Spain in 1898; however, the United States assumed colonial rule from that year and granted independence only in 1946. The Philippines adopted the U.S. political system of a presidency and a congress. MANILA served as the national capital of the country.

The Socialist Republic of Vietnam (Cong Hoa Xa Hoi Chu Nghia Viet Nam), with an area of 329,560 square kilometers hugging the eastern hump of the Indochinese peninsula, was established in mid-1976. Out of a population of 81,624,716 (July 2003 est.), VIETS composed the predominant ethnic group; minorities include HMONG and MONTAGNARD, as well as Chinese enclaves in urban localities particularly in SAIGON (GIA DINH, HỒ CHÍ MINH CITY). Under French colonial rule since the last quarter of the nineteenth century, Vietnam gained its independence in 1954. The country, however, was partitioned at 17° north latitude into NORTH VIETNAM (POST-1945), comprising TONKIN (TONGKING) and ANNAM, and SOUTH VIETNAM (POST-1945), covering COCHIN CHINA and surrounding provinces. Reunification was achieved a year following the conclusion of the SECOND INDOCHINA WAR (VIETNAM WAR) (1964–1975), and since then Vietnam has been governed along socialist-communist principles. HANOI (THANG-LONG) is the capital city of the country.

The Democratic Republic of East Timor gained its independence in 2002. The eastern portion of the island of TIMOR, East Timor, once declared its independence in 1975, following the end of Portuguese colonial rule. Shortly afterward, however, Indonesia annexed the territory. A 1999 plebiscite witnessed an overwhelming majority of Timorese opting for independence rather than remaining within the Republic of Indonesia. With a total area of 15,007 square kilometers, the country has a population of 800,000 (July 2003 est.). A democratic system of government is gradually evolving. Dili is the capital of the country.

The Peoples

Toward the closing years of the twentieth century, Southeast Asia's population was close to half a billion, with Indonesia, Vietnam, and Thailand the most populous countries. A predominantly rural-based settlement pattern is the norm, although some metropolitan centers, such as BANGKOK and metropolitan MANILA, have huge concentrations of people—6.3 million (2000 census) and 1.5 million (2000 census), respectively (Daniel 2002: 1392, 1255).

Ethnohistories

In a region where the monsoons meet, Southeast Asia is host to a rainbow spread of ethnic groups. Southward migration from the Asian interior brought settlers to the region. Subsequent waves of migrants displaced or settled with earlier arrivals, resulting in the emergence of a complex ethnic pattern. The ETHNOLINGUISTIC GROUPS OF SOUTHEAST ASIA reflect the multiethnic and multicultural characteristics that the region has nurtured since earliest times.

The ethnic tapestry of Myanmar comprised the majority BURMANS and minorities of CHINS, KACHINS, KARENS, MONS, PYUS, and SHANS. T'AIS predominate in Thailand's population, while KHMERS predominate in Cambodia. In Laos the main ethnic group is LAO. VIETS are an overwhelming majority in Vietnam, with HMONG and MONTAGNARD minorities. MUSLIM MINORITIES (THAILAND) are found in peninsular Thailand.

MALAYS are spread over large areas of insular Southeast Asia, encompassing the Indonesian archipelago, the Malay Peninsula (West Malaysia), and the Philippines. The aboriginal inhabitants of West Malaysia are the ORANG ASLI, a collective term representing more than a dozen small ethnic groups. The ORANG LAUT have settlements on both shores of the STRAITS OF MELAKA and the Riau-Lingga archipelago. The IBANS are predominant in Sarawak, while KADAZAN-DUSUNS predominate in neighboring Sabah. Besides the minority BAJAUS, there are a host of other EAST MALAYSIAN ETHNIC MINORITIES. BRUNEI MALAYS are the largest group in this small kingdom. Although small in numbers, the varied BRUNEI ETHNIC MINORITIES add color to the demographic composition.

The inhabitants of the Philippines are of MALAY stock. In the southern provinces there are the Muslim ILANUN AND BALANGINGI, and the MOROS. Other Muslim groups are the SULU AND THE SULU ARCHIPELAGO and TAUSUG AND THE SULU SULTANATE.

Diversity characterizes Indonesia's ethnic map. SUMATRA is the heartland of the BATAKS, MINANGKABAU, and REJANGS. The DAYAKS are the predominant group in Kalimantan Borneo, while BUGIS (BUGINESE) and TORAJAS inhabit SULAWESI (CELEBES). EAST INDONESIAN ETHNIC GROUPS further contribute to the rich diversity.

Owing to the marketplace position of Southeast Asia from the dawn of historical times, the region has witnessed the congregation of traders and merchants from Europe, West Asia, the Indian subcontinent, and East Asia. Scholars, missionaries, pilgrims, soldiers, adventurers, and a host of other foreigners over the centuries decided to settle rather than to sojourn. INDIAN IMMIGRANTS ranged from Brahmin priests, wealthy merchants, and professionals (doctors, lawyers) to prisoners, soldiers, and coolies. Distinct communities of CHETTIARS (CHETTYARS) and GUJARATIS are found in Myanmar and Malaysia. ARABS and other West Asians initially came as traders but later decided to call Southeast Asia home, often settling in Malaysia, Brunei, or Indonesia. The CHINESE IN SOUTHEAST ASIA are generally urban based, although farming communities are found in Malaysia and Indonesia. SINGAPORE (1819) is reputed to be the largest city of Chinese outside of China. "Chinatowns" flourished in RANGOON (YANGON), BANGKOK, SAIGON (GIA DINH, HÔ CHÍ MINH CITY) PENANG (1786), KUALA LUMPUR (KL), Medan, SURABAYA, and MANILA. While they represent a small minority in most nations of Southeast Asia, the Chinese in MALAYSIA form close to a third of the total population.

Statistical Sources

http://www.cia.gov/cia/publications/factbook/index.html.

Daniel, Lynn. (ed.). 2002. *The Far East and Australasia 2002*. 33rd ed. London: Europa Publications.

Enkelaar, Karen, Susan Page, Penny Martin, and Caroline Hunter, eds. 2001. *Geographica's Pocket World Reference*. Hong Kong: Periplus Editions.

In the Beginning
Human Existence and
Prehistoric Cultures

The HUMAN PREHISTORY OF SOUTH-EAST ASIA dates back to some 1 million years ago, with finds in Java of human existence as exhibited by the skeletal remains of "JAVA MAN" AND "SOLO MAN." The former (representing *Homo erectus*) and the latter (*Homo sapiens soloensis*) are believed to be from 500,000 to 1,000,000 years old, and 100,000 years old, respectively.

HOABINHIAN, the hunter-gatherer culture of Southeast Asia, became evident around 16,000 B.C.E. The term derives from Hoa Binh, the province in northern Vietnam where there is evidence of an occupied cave or rock shelter with findings of stone tools. Other, similar discoveries have been uncovered in cave sites throughout Southeast Asia—namely, in central Vietnam, various parts of Thailand, Burma, Cambodia, and Malaysia. An excavation in central Perak, Peninsular Malaysia, uncovered a Paleolithic human skeleton, "PERAK MAN," estimated to be 10,000 to 11,000 years old. Apparently these hunter-gatherers had their counterparts in Indonesia and the Philippines as well, and also in southern China.

The NEOLITHIC PERIOD OF SOUTH-EAST ASIA denotes the practice of crop cultivation or agriculture prior to the advent of metal. The period is also referred to as the New Stone Age, in which adzes, pestles, mortars, and other polished stone implements were used in the labors of forest clearance, planting, harvesting, and processing of food crops. Representative of this period is the BAN KAO CULTURE, named after the site in Kanchanaburi province, south-central Thailand. It has been dated to between 1300 and 2000 B.C.E. Early Ban Kao pottery includes the characteristically narrow-stemmed cups, three-legged bowls (tripods), and vases with a wide foot-ring and funnel-shaped mouth.

The DONG-SON best reflect the METAL AGE CULTURES IN SOUTHEAST ASIA. This 2,000-year-old culture from northeast Vietnam is particularly famous for its bronze kettledrums. Inscriptions on the drums depict the society that was in existence then. Bronze, TIN, lead, iron, GOLD, and silver were important metals used in METALSMITHING.

Archaeological Sites

Current work at ARCHAEOLOGICAL SITES OF SOUTHEAST ASIA is increasingly uncovering new discoveries and fresh interpretations that challenge past analyses of the prehistoric period of the region. Despite controversies and differing claims, archaeological finds in the past several decades have added to the understanding of Southeast Asia's distant and elusive past. Further complementing land sites are contributions drawn from UNDERWATER/MARITIME ARCHAEOLOGY IN SOUTHEAST ASIA.

As early as the 1860s the NIAH CAVES (SARAWAK) attracted the attention of scholars, and their curiosity and labors have been amply rewarded; this immense cavernous complex displays the longest continuous sequence of human existence in Southeast Asia, dating from 2,000 to 40,000 years ago. Situated about 110 kilometers from the oil-rich town of Miri, Sarawak, the caves at Niah offer a wide range of artifacts including human skeletons, animal bones, CERAMICS, shells, and botanical remains. Moreover, there are more than 200 burial sites and numerous wall paintings depicting paddled boats and dancing human figures.

Across the Balabac Straits to the western coast of Palawan in the southern Philippines is series of caves collectively known as the TABON CAVES (PALAWAN). The discovery of Pleistocene fossil *Homo sapiens* established the presence of human habitation in the Philippine archipelago. It is believed that the caves continuously hosted human dwellers from about 9,000 to about 30,000 years ago.

BAN CHIANG, together with its related sites such as Non Nok Tha and Ban Na Di, situated in Thailand's Khorat Plateau in the northeast, is known for its bronze artifacts and painted ceramic wares. Continuous occupation is estimated between about 3,500 B.C.E. and 500 C.E.

In the lower reaches of the Mekong River in Vietnam, between the delta area and the Gulf of Thailand (Siam), lies OC ÈO, an archaeological site generally believed to be FUNAN, a kingdom that flourished in the third through seventh centuries C.E., hitherto known only through written source materials. The phrase "Culture of Oc Èo" is used to denote the culture that emerged and developed in this delta area throughout the first half of the first millennium C.E., as exhibited by the uncovering of more than 300 sites.

The Story Unfolds
The Religious Legacies

RELIGIOUS DEVELOPMENT AND INFLUENCE IN SOUTHEAST ASIA witnessed the propagation, adaptation, and impact of the world's religious traditions on the multiethnic and multicultural peoples. Out of the complexity and diversity that characterized Southeast Asia, some form of division could be discerned along lines of religious adherence. BUDDHISM holds sway over mainland Southeast Asia: THERAVADA BUDDHISM in Myanmar, Thailand, Cambodia, and Laos; and MAHAYANA BUDDHISM in Vietnam. Vietnam, which possesses a Sinicized tradition, upholds tenets of CONFUCIANISM and Taoist beliefs that have served to complement Buddhist teachings. ISLAM IN SOUTHEAST ASIA presented an alternative to Hindu–Buddhist traditions in island Southeast Asia, gradually displacing the latter from the thirteenth to fourteenth centuries C.E. The island of BALI alone withstood the influence of Islam and continues to this day to strongly embrace HINDUISM. The city-state of SINGAPORE (1819), with an overwhelming Chinese majority, along with the Chinese in Malaysia, practice the traditional Chinese beliefs of an eclectic combination of CONFUCIANISM, MAHAYANA BUDDHISM, and Taoism. CATHOLICISM accompanied Spanish annexation of the Philippines, spreading rapidly throughout the archipelago except in MINDANAO and other southern islands in the Sulu Sea, which remained Muslim. Despite the spread of established world religions over the centuries, there have remained in Southeast Asia pockets of communities that abide by *ADAT* and other animistic beliefs and practices. Likewise, FOLK RELIGIONS abound in modern, contemporary Southeast Asia.

Hindu-Buddhist Influences

The HINDU-BUDDHIST PERIOD OF SOUTHEAST ASIA introduced to the region HINDUISM and BUDDHISM from INDIA and SRI LANKA (CEYLON). Initially, INDIAN IMMIGRANTS composed of Brahmin priests and members of the upper caste acquainted the Southeast Asian ruling class with the intricacies and influential utilization of Hindu practices to further enhance their political status and power. INDIGENOUS POLITICAL POWER demonstrate the apparent interrelationship between religion and the reins of political control. The INDIANIZATION process witnessed the adoption of concepts and ideologies by the indigenous elite in sustaining and expanding their power over lands and peoples. The erection and architectural design of the royal palace adhere to traditional Hindu cosmological precepts of replicating the universe on earth. Identifying themselves as the Hindu *DEVARAJA* or the Buddhist *CAKKAVATTI/SETKYA-MIN* (UNIVERSAL RULER), Southeast Asian rulers exerted a powerful and influential hold on the minds of their subjects.

Kingdoms and empires that were established and flourished during the HINDU-BUDDHIST PERIOD OF SOUTHEAST ASIA were FUNAN, CHAMPA, CHENLA, ANGKOR, and PAGAN (BAGAN) on the mainland. SRIVIJAYA (SRIWIJAYA), LANGKASUKA, SAILENDRA, and MAJAPAHIT (1293–ca. 1520s) were all prominent powers in insular Southeast Asia, each in its own heyday.

Further perpetuating HINDUISM and BUDDHISM were the temples and monasteries that undertook the task of transmitting TRADITIONAL RELIGIOUS EDUCATION to the subject class. The Buddhist *SANGHA* preserved the sanctity of the monarch; the ruler in turn supported the clergy and their institutions. A symbiotic relationship persisted that sustained the TEMPLE POLITICAL ECONOMY as demonstrated in Burma.

Literary works played an important role in religious and sociocultural influences, as shown by the Indian epics *MAHÂBHÂRATA* AND *RÂMÂYANA,* and by the *JATAKAS,* Buddhist moral stories based on the historical Buddha. The MONUMENTAL ART OF SOUTHEAST ASIA reflects Hindu-Buddhist influences as depicted in the celebrated ANGKOR WAT (NAGARAVATTA) and the awe-inspiring BOROBUDUR. Other equally impressive structures can be found in the MALANG TEMPLES, BLITAR, and PRAMBANAN.

Buddhist organizations like Burma's YOUNG MEN'S BUDDHIST ASSOCIATION (YMBA) (1920) and the GENERAL COUNCIL OF BURMESE ASSOCIATIONS (GCBA) (1919), Cambodia's BUDDHIST INSTITUTE OF PHNOM PENH, and Vietnam's UNIFIED BUDDHIST CHURCH (1963) were involved in political struggles. Burma attempted to create BUDDHIST SOCIALISM as a political philosophy and a form of governance.

Confucian and Chinese Heritage

The CHINESE IN SOUTHEAST ASIA practiced an eclectic system of beliefs combining MAHAYANA BUDDHISM with a measured dose of CONFUCIANISM peppered with a host of Taoist tenets. This seeming hotchpotch that represents Chinese popular religion is both adaptable and accommodating of other beliefs and practices. For instance, Malay holy men who were venerated after their passing as *keramat* (saints) often received *halal* offerings of dishes such as chicken curry served with glutinous rice as a thanksgiving offering from Chinese patrons at small shrines along roads or under trees. The philosophical as well as religious principles of CONFUCIANISM were perpetuated through OVERSEAS CHINESE EDUCATION whereby schools were organized wherever a Chinese community emerged.

Owing to the Chinese occupation of Vietnam of some 1,000 years (111 B.C.E. to 968 C.E.), SINO-VIETNAMESE RELATIONS prior to Vietnamese independence in the tenth century C.E. were cultivated on political, economic, and sociocultural foundations. The Chinese colonial period, or *Thoi Bac-Thuoc*, saw the introduction of *TAM GIAO*, which denotes the three traditional religions of Vietnam: BUDDHISM (THERAVADA and MAHAYANA), Taoism, and CONFUCIANISM.

Vietnam inherited the Chinese model of political economy and administrative structure, which was steeped in Confucian doctrines. The Chinese tradition of the scholar-bureaucrat selected on the basis of academic merit through a system of public civil service examination was adopted in governing even independent Vietnam. Like their Chinese counterparts, the Vietnamese elite were conversant in the Confucian classics and possessed a reverence for history and a faith in BUDDHISM; in addition, they appreciated Taoist traditions and practices. Chinese heritage with a basis in *TAM GIAO* was preserved and transmitted from generation to generation through TRADITIONAL RELIGIOUS EDUCATION.

Much emphasized and adopted as the basic ruling theory of feudal absolutism of Vietnamese dynasties was *TAM CUONG*, the sociopolitical relationships of CONFUCIANISM—namely, ruler-subject, father-son, and husband-wife. The basic principle of observance is the unquestionable obedience and loyalty of subject, son, and wife to ruler, father, and husband, respectively; conversely, the revered ruler, father, and husband should be exemplary and virtuous models.

Islamic and Christian Impact

The coming of ISLAM IN SOUTHEAST ASIA from the thirteenth to fourteenth centuries was an inevitable development owing to the close trading and commercial ties between the region and the Indian subcontinent. Just as INDIA played a prominent role in the introduction of HINDUISM and BUDDHISM more than ten centuries ago, when Islam gradually spread it was Indian traders and merchants who had brought along their new faith to Southeast Asia. Continental Southeast Asia was less receptive to Islamic influence, but maritime Southeast Asia readily welcomed it. In the latter, conversion of the ruling elite often was repeated among the common people.

The north Sumatran city-ports of PASAI and ACEH (ACHEH) adopted Islam to their economic advantage. SPICES AND THE SPICE TRADE, Southeast Asia's prized commodity, were much sought after by Europe; ARABS and Indian merchants served as the intermediaries. From the tenth to eleventh centuries the carrying trade of the Arabian Sea and the Indian Ocean was in the hands of Muslims from West Asia and South Asia. Prudently, the fifteenth-century Malay port of call of MELAKA, strategically situated midway in the STRAITS OF MELAKA, converted to Islam, further enhancing its economic prowess. The savvy Malay sultans of MELAKA transformed the city-port into a religious center where Islamic scholars and missionaries congregated. Territorial expansion covering SUMATRA and the Malay Peninsula, coupled with expansive trading relations, spread throughout the Malay archipelago (encompassing present-day Malaysia, Indonesia, and southern Philippines). MELAKA was credited with the Islamization of the greater part of insular Southeast Asia, particularly the *PASISIR* polities of JAVA.

DEMAK, BANTEN (BANTAM), and later MATARAM in Java and BRUNEI in northwest BORNEO received the patronage of Muslim traders who avoided MELAKA, which had from 1511 become a part of the PORTUGUESE ASIAN EMPIRE. ACEH (ACHEH), commanding the northern entrance to the STRAITS OF MELAKA, profited the most as the new spice entrepôt (for PEPPER in particular) and the focus of Islamic teachings and scholarship. Sufi scholarship, for instance, is the much richer for the contributions of HAMZAH FANSURI, SHAMSUDDIN AL-SUMATRANI (d. 1630), and NURUDDIN AL-RANIRI (d. 1658).

In JAVA, Islamic influence impacted unevenly on the inhabitants. The *ABANGAN*, though embracing the new religion, continued to retain Hindu-Buddhist practices and indigenous Javanese beliefs. On the other hand, the *SANTRI* were more steadfast to principles of the faith such as the obligatory five daily prayers and the observance of the fast during Ramadan. In the Javanese context, a *KIAI* is a religious leader whose knowledge of Islamic doctrines is generally acknowledged. The concept of the *RATU ADIL* (RIGHTEOUS KING/PRINCE) that emerged in PEASANT UPRISINGS AND PROTEST MOVEMENTS IN SOUTHEAST ASIA reflects an example of the combination of Islamic deliverance with traditional Javanese messianic expectations. DIPONEGORO (PANGERAN DIPANEGARA) (ca. 1785–1855) of the JAVA WAR (1825–1830) and HAJI OEMAR SAID TJOKROAMINOTO (1882–1934) both were said to be the *RATU ADIL* (RIGHTEOUS KING/PRINCE), who would deliver the people from the Dutch colonial rulers.

SUMATRA posed as a hotbed of Islamic movements, from the PADRI MOVEMENT that sparked the PADRI WARS (1821–1837) to the DARUL ISLAM MOVEMENT (DI) of the twentieth century. The ACEH (ACHEH) WARS (1873–1903) used Islam as a bulwark against Dutch IMPERIALISM and COLONIALISM.

Similarly Islam pervaded the Indonesian nationalist struggle. SAREKAT ISLAM (1912) utilized the faith as a rallying point as well as a defense against socialism and COMMUNISM. NAHDATUL ULAMA and MUHAMMADIYAH had Islam as their guiding principle. Similarly, PERSATUAN ULAMA-ULAMA SELURUH ACEH (PUSA), or the Association of Aceh *Ulama,* utilized Islam in its anticolonial struggle.

ISLAMIC RESURGENCE IN SOUTHEAST ASIA (TWENTIETH CENTURY) witnessed the emergence of a gulf of divergence between the traditionalist and the reformist. In Indonesia, the formation of the MADJLISUL ISLAMIL A'LAA INDONESIA (MIAI) (GREAT ISLAMIC COUNCIL OF INDONESIA) was an attempt to resolve differences and unite the faithful. SYED SHAYKH AL-HADY (1867?–1934), who was based in PENANG (1786) during the early decades of the twentieth century, was a prominent leader in Islamic modernism.

During the JAPANESE OCCUPATION OF SOUTHEAST ASIA (1941–1945), the MADJELIS SJURO MUSLIMIN INDONESIA (MASJUMI) (COUNCIL OF INDONESIAN MUSLIM ASSOCIATIONS) was established in Indonesia to garner Muslim support. After the Pacific War (1941–1945), Islam continued to have an important influence in the unshackling of colonial domination and nation-building. PARTAI ISLAM SE MALAYSIA (PAS) was at the forefront in the fight for independence for BRITISH MALAYA. In the early 1970s the ANGKATAN BELIA ISLAM MALAYSIA (ABIM) (MALAYSIAN ISLAMIC YOUTH MOVEMENT) sought to champion the Islamic resurgence in Malaysia. Brunei adopted the concept of MELAYU ISLAM BERAJA (MIB, MALAY ISLAMIC MONARCHY).

MUSLIM MINORITIES (THAILAND) of South/Peninsular Thailand had long resisted the authority of the Buddhist central government in BANGKOK. More akin to the neighboring peninsular Malay States of West Malaysia, the Muslim descendants of the SUL-

TANATE OF PATANI (PATTANI) preferred cession to assimilation into the Buddhist Thai polity and identity.

MINDANAO and most of the islands of the southern Philippines resisted Spanish colonization and HISPANIZATION, the latter including Christianization. They remained Muslim and defended their faith and land in a protracted struggle against the Spanish colonial regime. In that centuries-old conflict, the MOROS took center stage during the 1970s when the revolutionary MORO NATIONAL LIBERATION FRONT (MNLF) launched a separatist struggle. The issue of a separate homeland for the Muslims of the Philippines remained unresolved—a blemish on the Christian Philippine government that had inherited this legacy from the past.

In the sixteenth century, CATHOLICISM made rapid advances in tow with the HISPANIZATION of the Philippines following the establishment of Spanish colonial rule over the islands. Among SPANISH FRIARS (THE PHILIPPINES) of various denominations, the Dominicans were especially dominant, possessing spiritual as well as temporal influence over the Filipinos. The fear of God made excommunication a decidedly powerful instrument of control over the masses. Besides amassing great material wealth in the form of land and property, the Catholic Church wielded tremendous influence in secular state affairs. The FRIAR-SECULAR RELATIONSHIP was often strained. Dissatisfaction was even more rife among Filipino clergy, as racism was the norm in the hierarchical Catholic establishment.

Elsewhere throughout Southeast Asia, CHRISTIAN MISSIONARIES made little headway. A small Christian community can be found in SAIGON (GIA DINH, HỒ CHÍ MINH CITY). The city-state of SINGAPORE (1819) has a growing Christian following. Outside the Philippines, indigenous ethnic communities in SARAWAK AND SABAH (NORTH BORNEO) account for the greatest number of Christian converts to CATHOLICISM and Protestantism (Anglican, Methodist, Adventist, and Borneo Evangelical Mission). The majority of IBANS and KADAZAN-DUSUNS and some groups of EAST MALAYSIAN ETHNIC MINORITIES embraced Christianity. Others, like the BAJAUS and Melanau of the coastal areas, turned to Islam, whereas those in the interior kept to ADAT and animistic practices.

Despite the propagation of the world religions and modernity from without, a variety of FOLK RELIGIONS remained vibrant and continued to be practiced among the peoples of Southeast Asia. ADAT, "custom," or "customary law" remained the spiritual compass for a great many ethnic groups from the Chin Hills of western Myanmar to the Maoke Mountains of IRIAN JAYA to the Sierra Madre of LUZON. Notwithstanding formal acknowledgment of the world religions, many Javanese are followers of KEBATINAN MOVEMENTS, indigenous Javanese spiritual movements based on ancestral culture that predate Hindu-Buddhist influences. CAO DAI is an indigenous Vietnamese religion that drew its inspiration from a host of other religious philosophies—namely, from CONFUCIANISM, BUDDHISM, Taoism, CATHOLICISM, and others. HOA HAO, a South Vietnamese indigenous religion, is a variant of BUDDHISM with messianic overtones.

RELIGIOUS SELF-MORTIFICATION IN SOUTHEAST ASIA is a phenomenon that both fascinates and intrigues observers as to the motives and inspirations that result in the performance of such rituals in the name of a faith. Examples could be found throughout the region, from crucifixion by nailing during Holy Week in central LUZON to body piercing with spears and lances during the Thaipusam procession in PENANG (1786). In the latter a Hindu devotee carries a *kavadi,* a fancifully decorated wooden or steel frame with skewers literally supported by his body, representing the burden of the carrier by way of paying penance.

Hindu-Buddhist Kingdoms and Empires

The HINDU-BUDDHIST PERIOD OF SOUTHEAST ASIA from around the first century B.C.E. to the thirteenth century C.E. saw the growth, development, expansion, and decline of numerous political centers throughout the region.

Chinese records noted a maritime kingdom situated on the lower reaches of the Mekong that flourished from the third to seventh centuries C.E. Referred to as FUNAN, this polity is believed to be the intermediary of the seagoing trade between IMPERIAL CHINA to the east and INDIA to the west. During its heyday during the mid-third century, FUNAN dominated modern-day southern Vietnam, Cambodia, central Thailand, and northern West Malaysia. It was also a reputable center of Buddhist scholarship during the latter part of the fifth and early sixth centuries. The CHINESE TRIBUTE SYSTEM was imposed on FUNAN from the fourth century until its demise in the latter half of the sixth century. The archaeological site of OC ÈO is generally believed to be the uncovering of the kingdom of FUNAN.

The name CHAMPA refers to a series of small kingdoms situated on the coastline of today's central Vietnam. A contemporary of FUNAN, the first of these kingdoms was established toward the end of the second century C.E., located in the vicinity of modern HUÉ. Maritime commerce with southern China was the lifeblood of CHAMPA. During the early seventh century, Hindu-Buddhist culture blossomed. CHAMPA continually had to defend itself from attacks by IMPERIAL CHINA, VIETS, KHMERS, and Mongols. The last of the kingdoms fell to Vietnam in the early nineteenth century.

Akin to the MONS of Burma, the KHMERS established CHENLA, which encompassed modern Cambodia and northeast Thailand. Originally a vassal of FUNAN, CHENLA during the seventh century not only asserted its independence but also dominated its former overlord. Chinese records spoke of Land CHENLA and Water CHENLA, the former accessible overland and the latter reached by sea. Like FUNAN and CHAMPA, CHENLA maintained tributary relations with China and conducted a lucrative trade along the maritime silk route. The division of CHENLA weakened the KHMERS, and their power dissipated in the ninth century when rivals from island Southeast Asia began to encroach on the East-West trade.

The MALAYS established the greatest maritime power in insular Southeast Asia, that of ŚRIVIJAYA (ŚRIWIJAYA), which flourished during the seventh to thirteenth centuries. The fall of FUNAN, which had played such a prominent role in the carrying trade between IMPERIAL CHINA and INDIA, created a vacuum without a worthy successor on mainland Southeast Asia. Based in southern SUMATRA, with its fortified city-port of PALEMBANG possessing a strategic command of the STRAITS OF MELAKA, ŚRIVIJAYA (ŚRIWIJAYA) rose to the challenge and cornered the lucrative East-West trade. Its mighty fleet enforced its monopolistic will, demanding that all vessels call at its ports to partake of their facilities and pay dues. ARABS, both traders and chroniclers, spoke of the power and influence of ŚRIVIJAYA (ŚRIWIJAYA), which extended throughout SUMATRA, the Malay Peninsula, and the western part of JAVA. I-CHING (I-TSING) (635–713 C.E.), the Chinese pilgrim, wrote of PALEMBANG as a significant center of Buddhist learning, with monasteries accommodating more than a thousand students.

Envious and determined to reap the fabulous wealth and impose their hegemony, the Cholas of southern India sacked and occupied large parts of ŚRIVIJAYA (ŚRIWIJAYA) on either side of the STRAITS OF MELAKA for two decades following 1025 C.E. Overstretched in their commitments, however, the Cholas withdrew; ŚRIVIJAYA (ŚRIWIJAYA) nonetheless wisely accepted Chola overlordship.

Also challenging the political and economic power of ŚRIVIJAYA (ŚRIWIJAYA) were the SAILENDRAS, toward the end of the tenth century. The SAILENDRAS were Buddhist monarchs whose kingdom lay in MATARAM in east-central JAVA during the eighth to mid-ninth centuries. The SAILENDRAS harbored imperialistic ambitions to expand their power, not only in insular but also in mainland Southeast Asia. Accordingly, a Javanese force defeated Water CHENLA. The KHMERS rallied to the aid of JAYAVARMAN II (r. 770/790/802?–834 C.E.) to expel the invaders. Credited as the builders of the BOROBUDUR, the SAILENDRAS left behind numerous Buddhist temples and monuments. The association of SAILENDRAS with the SUMATRA-based maritime power of ŚRIVIJAYA (ŚRIWIJAYA) is unclear; some sources point to their rivalry for the Sino-Indian trade.

The KHMERS rejuvenated their power in the founding of ANGKOR. Shifting from the delta area to northwest Cambodia, ANGKOR was the dominant power in mainland Southeast Asia from the ninth to the fifteenth centuries. Water control and architectural prowess in temple building were the twin Angkorian legacies. The crowning achievement is the imposing ANGKOR WAT (NAGARAVATTA). During the reign of SURYAVARMAN II (r. 1113–1145?), the power of ANGKOR extended to modern Burma and Vietnam. Angkorean kings utilized the concept of DEVARAJA to enhance their power and establish legitimacy. Temple building and maintenance of monuments, large numbers of state-supported Buddhist clergy, and punitive wars, coupled with the more egalitarian characteristics of THERAVADA BUDDHISM and the rise of the T'AIS, contributed to the decline of ANGKOR.

The kingdom of NAM VIET (NAN YUE) was mentioned in Chinese records at the early part of the first century B.C.E., encompassing a territory that included present-day Guangdong/Guangxi province, Hainan Island, and the northern portion of Vietnam. This early kingdom had five rulers, a century of independence, and then was under Chinese domination for a millennium from 111 B.C.E. Sinicization took root during this Chinese colonial period. Scholars and officials who fled the mainland crossed over to the Red River delta following the demise of the Imperial Han dynasty (202 B.C.E.–220 C.E.); this elite arrival contributed tremendously to the Sinicization process in language, political philosophy, social etiquette, and religious adherence.

The VIETS successfully shook off Chinese colonial rule with the establishment of the Early Ly dynasty in 980 C.E. For the next millennium Vietnam enjoyed its independence and adopted the term DAI VIET, or Great Viet, implying the rule of all VIETS. Interestingly, all the indigenous dynasties resisted Chinese reoccupation, but their politico-administrative structure and sociocultural norms imitated the Chinese model. During the period of DAI VIET, which lasted to the early nineteenth century, SINO-VIETNAMESE RELATIONS were maintained on the basis of the CHINESE TRIBUTE SYSTEM. The rulers of DAI VIET sent tributes to IMPERIAL CHINA acknowledging the overlordship of the latter. But at the same time in relations with neighboring kingdoms, DAI VIET assumed the status of a Chinese-styled empire to which all others had to owe subservience.

During DAI VIET the nomenclature of Vietnamese dynasties included the Early Ly dynasty (980–1009), LY DYNASTY (1009–1225), Tran dynasty (1225–1400), Ho dynasty (1400–1407), and LE DYNASTY (1428–1527; 1533–1789). The Tran repulsed a Mongol offensive in the mid-thirteenth century. Between 1407 and 1418, China once again asserted domination over the VIETS, instituting a harsh and repressive rule with an accelerated dose of Sinicization. This Chinese interregnum ended with the establishment of the LE DYNASTY (1428–1527; 1533–1789).

Beginning in the fourteenth century, DAI VIET expanded southward over the next two centuries at the expense of CHAMPA and the KHMERS to reach the Mekong Delta. This southern migration, NAM TIEN, was spurred by overpopulation as well as Trinh-Nguyễn rivalry. The Nguyễn family actively pursued this policy of expansion that finally established the NGUYỄN DYNASTY (1802–1945), which occupied ANNAM and COCHIN CHINA, modern central and southern Vietnam, respectively. Meanwhile the TRINH FAMILY ruled over TONKIN (TONGKING) in the name of the greatly weakened LE DYNASTY.

Migrating southward from southwest China, the PYUS entered Burma in the third century C.E. and established a capital city in the area of modern Prome. The PYUS embraced HINDUISM and both MAHAYANA and THERAVADA BUDDHISM, the latter being dominant from the seventh century C.E. Meanwhile the MONS, akin to the KHMERS, around the first century C.E. moved from central Burma (Dry Zone) to Lower Burma. The MONS in Lower Burma came into contact with Indian traders and Buddhist missionaries, facilitating the process of INDIANIZATION in Burma. THERAVADA BUDDHISM was particularly strong among the MONS. In the eighth century, the MONS drove the PYUS away; the latter fled to the north and came under the T'AIS, then established at NAN CHAO (NANCHAO) (DALI/TALI). The MONS established themselves at Thaton, PEGU, and Martaban.

Originating from northern China, the BURMANS migrated through Tibet and then YUNNAN PROVINCE into the Kyaukse plain in central Burma during the seventh to tenth centuries C.E. They displaced the PYUS in Upper and central Burma. The BURMANS founded their capital city of PAGAN (BAGAN), which developed into the first Burmese empire (ca. 850–1287 C.E.), attaining its apex during the eleventh and twelfth centuries and expanding as far southward as TENASSERIM. One of the renowned rulers of PAGAN (BAGAN) was ANAWRAHTA (ANIRUDDHA) (r. 1044–1077), who expanded the rule of the BURMANS over the area coinciding with the contemporary Union of Myanmar in the process of defeating the MONS and seizing Thaton. The name "Myanmar" has been used for the country during the PAGAN (BAGAN) period from around the thirteenth century. The BURMANS adopted THERAVADA BUDDHISM, which was derived from SRI LANKA (CEYLON), as the predominant religious tradition that spurred the erection of fabulous temples, mural paintings, and other visual arts. The BURMANS also embraced the Indianized high culture of the MONS, including the concept of kingship and divine political power.

The T'AIS, the main ethnic group in modern Thailand, originated from southern China and later moved southward and westward into mainland Southeast Asia. The T'AIS established the kingdom of NAN CHAO (NANCHAO) (DALI/TALI); that contention, however, has been disputed. NAN CHAO (NANCHAO) (DALI/TALI) proved to be the "back-door" trade passage to IMPERIAL CHINA, and the T'AIS profited from that position from the eighth century C.E. onward. The Mongol invasions of the thirteenth century drove the T'AIS southward into the upper Menam Valley. It turned out to be a fortunate move, as RAMA KAMHAENG (r. 1279–1298) seized the opportunity in capturing SUKHOTAI (SUKHODAVA), then an outpost of ANGKOR that was fast declining following the demise of JAYAVARMAN VII (r. 1181–1220?). The SUKHOTAI (SUKHODAVA) period from the thirteenth to fifteenth centuries witnessed the effervescence of the arts and culture of the T'AIS. Two *muang* (principalities) of the T'AIS were CHIANG RAI and CHIANG MAI, both established in the second half of the thirteenth century.

RAMATHIBODI (r. 1351–1369) in 1351 C.E. established the KINGDOM OF AYUT-THAYA (AYUTHAYA, AYUDHYA, AYUTHIA) (1351–1767 C.E.). THERAVADA BUDDHISM and the Hindu-Buddhist concept of kingship reigned supreme. The capital city of the same name situated at the confluence of the Chao Phraya, the Pasak, and the Lopburi was sufficiently strategic to command the central floodplain, the major rice-producing heartland. Situated close to the Gulf of Siam and the ISTHMUS OF KRA, the KINGDOM OF AYUTTHAYA (AYUTHAYA, AYUDHYA, AYUTHIA) (1351–1767 C.E.) profited from international maritime commerce and an agriculturally rich hinterland.

AIRLANGGA (r. 1019–1049), of Javanese-Balinese parentage, was a ruler of the eastern part of JAVA who attempted in vain to subdue the declining ŚRIVIJAYA (ŚRIWIJAYA). From his capital at Kahuripan, he ruled over the Brantas Valley as a divine ruler. Despite the division of his kingdom into the southern part—Pangjalu or KADIRI (KEDIRI), with the capital at Daha—and the northern half—Janggala—to forestall disputes between his two sons, war broke out between the heirs. KADIRI (KEDIRI) finally won after more than half a century of conflict. It was not long before rebellions broke out within KADIRI (KEDIRI). Ken Arok or Angrok (r. 1222–1227) established the kingdom of SINGHÂSÂRI. SINGHÂSÂRI was the first Javanese kingdom that had pretensions of achieving *NUSANTARA,* an archipelagic empire outside Java. KERTANAGARA (r. 1268–1292), ruler of SINGHÂSÂRI, prepared the way for the achievement of *NUSANTARA* by the rulers of MAJAPAHIT (1293–ca. 1520s).

MAJAPAHIT (1293–ca. 1520s) was born out of several factors: the arrogance of KERTANAGARA (r. 1268–1292), a Mongol invasion, a usurper who seized the throne of SINGHÂSÂRI, and a dispossessed heir apparent. The latter, Wijaya, finally prevailed, establishing the new kingdom of MAJAPAHIT (1293–ca. 1520s) and assuming the name Kertarâjasa Jayawardhana (r. 1294–1309). The reign of HAYAM WURUK (RÂJASANAGARA) (r. 1350–1389) and the tenure of the celebrated *patih* (grand vizier) GAJAH MADA (t. 1331–1364) witnessed the attainment of *NUSANTARA*, which covered most of contemporaneous Indonesia. MAJAPAHIT (1293–ca.

1520s) was the greatest and last of the Hindu-Buddhist polities prior to the advent of ISLAM IN SOUTHEAST ASIA.

Buddhist Polities, Confucian Dynasties, and Islamic City-Ports

From the fifteenth century, Islamized city-ports in island Southeast Asia took center stage as the main players in the East-West trade. Meanwhile, Buddhist-based polities and Confucian Vietnam on the mainland attempted to consolidate their power amid contentions and conflicts. The BURMA-SIAM WARS that began in the early sixteenth century were the singularly disruptive element in mainland Southeast Asia.

The KINGDOM OF AYUTTHAYA (AYUTHAYA, AYUDHYA, AYUTHIA) (1351–1767) successfully weakened ANGKOR with offensives launched in the mid-fourteenth and early fifteenth centuries; ANGKOR was sacked, and the KHMERS fled to PHNOM PENH. To the north, SUKHOTAI (SUKHODAVA) was absorbed into the realm. CHIANG MAI remained independent. In the south, LIGOR/NAKHON was incorporated, as well as some parts of the northern Malay Peninsula. The rise of MELAKA in the early fifteenth century was seen as a threat, and two offensives were launched on the city-port; both failed. Relations with IMPERIAL CHINA were ordered on the CHINESE TRIBUTE SYSTEM; despite paying tribute and acknowledging the suzerainty of IMPERIAL CHINA, Ayutthaya made much profit from transactions in Chinese products (such as silk and CERAMICS). Trading relations were established with Japan beginning in the fifteenth century and lasting till the mid-seventeenth century, including the settling of a Japanese mercantile community. This East Asian trade, coupled with that of insular Southeast Asia, made the KINGDOM OF AYUTTHAYA (AYUTHAYA, AYUDHYA, AYUTHIA) (1351–1767) fabulously prosperous.

Meanwhile the demise of PAGAN (BAGAN) in the early part of the fourteenth century witnessed a power vacuum until the ascension of the FIRST AVA (INWA) DYNASTY (1364–1527 C.E.). In terms of size, wealth, power, and influence this new kingdom with its capital at Ava (situated 128 kilometers inland from its predecessor) was a smaller replica of PAGAN (BAGAN). Ava's legacy lay in the sociocultural traditions that had their roots in PAGAN (BAGAN) that was preserved and developed during the two centuries of the FIRST AVA (INWA) DYNASTY (1364–1527 C.E.) and continues to be evident to the present day.

The sixteenth century witnessed increasing tension between the BURMANS and the T'AIS. Contention over the control of the polities of the MONS along the northern parts of the ISTHMUS OF KRA, such as Tavoy, Mergui, and TENASSERIM, and of CHIANG MAI with the BURMANS subsequently led to the destruction of the KINGDOM OF AYUTTHAYA (AYUTHAYA, AYUDHYA, AYUTHIA) (1351–1767) in 1767. It was one of the most significant events in the protracted BURMA-SIAM WARS.

The establishment of the TOUNGOO DYNASTY (1531–1752) saw the acceleration of the BURMA-SIAM WARS. TABINSHWEIHTI (r. 1531–1550) launched offensives against the SHANS and the T'AIS/Siamese. Under the reign of BAYINNAUNG (r. 1551–1581), the empire surpassed that of PAGAN (BAGAN), extending westward to Manipur and eastward to Cambodia, often sacking the LAO and the KINGDOM OF AYUTTHAYA (AYUTHAYA, AYUDHYA, AYUTHIA) (1351–1767). In the Buddhist tradition, BAYINNAUNG (r. 1551–1581) became a *CAKKAVATTI/SETKYA-MIN* (UNIVERSAL RULER). Partial to the MONS, PEGU in Lower Burma was made the capital city and flourished from foreign trade. But PHRA NARET (KING NARESUAN) (r. 1590–1605) of PITSANULOK (PHITSANULOK) regained Siamese pride and independence in defeating the Burmese Crown prince in a duel on ELEPHANTS at Nong Sarai in 1593.

The Restored Toungoo Dynasty (1597–1752) revived its former strength and reconquered polities like CHIANG MAI that had asserted their independence. The capital city had shifted to Ava in Upper Burma. But after the reign of King Thalun (r. 1629–1648), internal court struggle greatly weakened the empire. The MONS seized the opportunity and revolted in the mid-eighteenth century; again PEGU became their rallying point. Into this chaotic situation of a declining dynasty arose a champion of the BURMANS, ALAUNGHPAYA (r. 1752–1760), who defeated the MONS and regained and reunited the whole country with the establishment of the KONBAUNG DYNASTY (1752–1885).

The third ruler of the KONBAUNG DYNASTY (1752–1885), HSINBYUSHIN (r. 1763–1776), repeated the feat of BAYINNAUNG (r. 1551–1581) in dominating mainland Southeast Asia from Manipur to the Lao regions. His generals sacked the KINGDOM OF AYUTTHAYA (AYUTHAYA, AYUDHYA, AYUTHIA) (1351–1767) in 1767.

After the fall of the KINGDOM OF AYUTTHAYA (AYUTHAYA, AYUDHYA, AYUTHIA) (1351–1767) the empire fragmented, with each polity asserting its freedom and independence. PHYA TAKSIN (PHYA TAK [SIN], KING TAKSIN) (r. 1767–1782), a Sino-Thai provincial governor, emerged to defeat the BURMANS, regain lost territories, and reunify the realm, which approximated contemporary Thailand. Key areas for safeguarding Siam's independence were seized, including CHIANG MAI and the Cambodian provinces of BATTAMBANG and SIEM REAP. Also conquered was the city-port polity of HATIEN on the Cambodian coast, made into an economic powerhouse during the reign of MAC THIEN TU (1700–1780); it controlled the Mekong hinterland. A new capital, Thonburi, was built across the Chao Phraya opposite modern BANGKOK—hence the Thonburi period.

In Vietnam, although the LE DYNASTY (1428–1527; 1533–1789) reigned, real power rested with two parties: the TRINH FAMILY and the Nguyễn. A stalemate ensued as neither was able to subdue the other. The TAY-SON REBELLION (1771–1802) broke this impasse in defeating the TRINH FAMILY and almost wiping out the entire Nguyễn clan. The country was apportioned among three brothers: Van-Hue ruled TONKIN (TONGKING) in the north, Van-Nhac controlled ANNAM in the center, and Van-Lu occupied COCHIN CHINA in the south. One surviving Nguyễn prince, NGUYỄN ANH (EMPEROR GIA LONG) (r. 1802–1820), managed to rally his forces and to defeat and reunite Vietnam under the NGUYỄN DYNASTY (1802–1945).

The advent of ISLAM IN SOUTHEAST ASIA gradually began in the thirteenth century, making inroads in the conversion of the city-ports of northern SUMATRA. Two centuries later emerged the greatest of the Islamic city-ports of the MALAYS, that of MELAKA.

By the beginning of the fifteenth century, MAJAPAHIT (1293–ca. 1520s), although in existence, was an emaciated kingdom. Into this vacuum emerged a prince from PALEMBANG, PARAMESWARA (PARAMESHWARA, PARAMESVARA) of the ŚRIVIJAYA (ŚRIWIJAYA) line, who fled his father-in-law's kingdom and sought refuge in TEMASIK (TUMASIK). In attempting to seize control, he killed the local ruler and fled northward up the Malay Peninsula. At a small fishing village on the western coast settled by ORANG LAUT, the prince decided to establish his kingdom. Named after a local tree, MELAKA was established around 1400. Conversion to Islam followed and brought many Muslim traders to that strategically located city-port at the narrowest part of the STRAITS OF MELAKA, where it could command the sea traffic of this international waterway. Acknowledging the Chinese MING DYNASTY (1368–1644) as its suzerain power and cordially receiving ADMIRAL CHENG HO (ZHENG HE) (1371/ 1375–1433/1435) was another prudent and calculated move by its Malay rulers. Through trading relations, MELAKA propagated Islam throughout island Southeast Asia; Muslim clerics and scholars congregated at the city-port to teach and to learn. Under the able leadership of TUN PERAK (d. ca. 1498), the *bendahara* (chancellor/chief minister), the empire of MELAKA, which encompassed large parts of central and southern SUMATRA and most of the Malay Peninsula, further enriched the flourishing entrepôt city-port.

The fabulous success and prosperity of MELAKA was its undoing, as foreign eyes covetously lusted for possession. In Portuguese plans for creating a maritime PORTUGUESE ASIAN EMPIRE, MELAKA featured as one of several key strategic city-ports stretching from the Arabian Sea to the South China Sea.

ACEH (ACHEH) and BRUNEI (SIXTEENTH TO NINETEENTH CENTURIES) were contemporaneous with MELAKA but remained as secondary Muslim city-ports, dealing in specialized local products, the former in PEPPER and the latter in JUNGLE/FOREST PRODUCTS. In JAVA the *PASISIR* city-ports were quick in seeing the economic advantages of conversion to Islam.

DEMAK in north-central JAVA embraced Islam through one of the *WALI SONGO* shortly after the collapse of MAJAPAHIT (1293–ca. 1520s). Establishing close alliance through trade and religious relations with other *PASISIR* city-ports along the northern and eastern Javanese coast, including BANTEN (BANTAM) (1526–1813), made DEMAK a strong Islamic polity in the sixteenth century, largely between 1518 and 1550. DEMAK also nurtured cordial contacts with MALUKU (THE MOLUCCAS) and southern SULAWESI (CELEBES), as well as with the influential and powerful ACEH (ACHEH) and PALEMBANG of northern and southern SUMATRA, respectively.

BANTEN (BANTAM) (1526–1813) began as a Hindu kingdom around the twelfth century, controlling the ports of Sunda Kelapa and Banten. Having command of the Sunda Strait, the kingdom was strategically placed to be a major entrepôt for PEPPER from southern SUMATRA and western JAVA. Conversion to Islam attracted Muslim traders from INDIA and across the archipelago.

Hindu-Javanese MATARAM emerged around the fourth century C.E. in western JAVA; it then shifted to the central part of the island, where a high culture flourished from around 732 C.E. to 918 C.E. It is highly probable that MATARAM was absorbed into the great realm of MAJAPAHIT (1293–ca. 1520s). The ascendancy of Islamic MATARAM was contemporaneous with that of BANTAM (BANTEN) (1526–1813). Amid the political chaos following the decline of DEMAK in the mid-sixteenth century, Panembahan Senapati (r. 1582–1601), a vassal ruler of the kingdom of Pajang in south-central JAVA, successfully rebelled against his overlord to establish MATARAM. In the reign of Krapyak (r. 1601–1613) the foundations of a great Islamic-Javanese empire were laid and reached their zenith during the tenure of Rangsang, who assumed the title of AGUNG, SULTAN OF MATARAM (r. 1613–1645).

China and Southeast Asia

Apart from imposing its imperialistic will and implementing the process of Sinicization over Vietnam, IMPERIAL CHINA pursued a lord-vassal relationship with the territories of *NANYANG* (South Seas)—that is, Southeast Asia. This relationship was structured in accordance with the CHINESE TRIBUTE SYSTEM. The Chinese world order admitted no equals; all external relations were conducted on the basis of IMPERIAL CHINA as the overlord and others in subordinate positions paying tribute to the Chinese emperor, the "Son of Heaven."

The CHINESE TRIBUTE SYSTEM demanded of vassal rulers that they personally journey to Beijing to perform the *kow-tow* (act of obeisance) and present a tribute to the emperor, acknowledging him as suzerain lord. Exhibiting his benevolence and the abundance of the wealth of IMPERIAL CHINA, the emperor bestowed Chinese products upon the vassal ruler several times the value of the tribute that was originally given. Thereafter some form of limited trading transaction was allowed for the foreign entourage; in this sense the tribute mission was in fact also a trading expedition, and much profit was gained for the vassal party returning home with invaluable Chinese goods, such as silks and CERAMICS. In fact, the tribute missions from various corners of Southeast Asia around the seventh century C.E. recorded the heyday of the *Nanhai* or *NANYANG* (South Seas) trade. Consequently, the office of the superintendent of the shipping trade was established at Guangzhou (Canton) in the early part of the eighth century to oversee that lucrative enterprise.

IMPERIAL CHINA under the Song (Sung) dynasty (960–1279 C.E.) had good relations with ŚRIVIJAYA (ŚRIWIJAYA); it encouraged foreign and tributary trade with the region. Taking this official cue and on their own initiative, Chinese private traders embarked on commercial expeditions to Southeast Asia, ushering in the age of the Chinese junk trade, which flourished over the next 200 years.

The YUAN (MONGOL) DYNASTY (1271–1368) asserted the CHINESE TRIBUTE SYSTEM as a means to gain submission of Southeast Asia. Meanwhile, trade was left to private enterprise—not only to Chinese merchants but also to others such as ARABS, Persians, and Europeans—for example, the Italian MARCO POLO (1254–1324). Expeditionary forces to punish recalcitrant kingdoms were launched against the VIETS, KHMERS, BURMANS, and Javanese in not always successful attempts to bring them into line.

Fearing subversion from within and from without, possibly funded by the profits gained from maritime commerce, the MING DYNASTY (1368–1644) placed an embargo on foreign overseas trade. Politics and security were prioritized in tributary relations, leading to the various expeditions of ADMIRAL CHENG HO (ZHENG HE) (1371/1375–1433/1435), which reasserted the CHINESE TRIBUTE SYSTEM and announced that all trade be officially regulated with Guangzhou as the designated port. This format and related regulations were in force until the early nineteenth century, and several Southeast Asian polities such as Vietnam, Laos, and Siam continued to send tribute missions on a regular basis.

The European "Age of Discovery"

While the MING DYNASTY (1368–1644) was regulating formal tributary relations with Southeast Asia, a far-reaching agreement was reached between two powers of CATHOLICISM—Portugal and Spain. Mediated and decreed by the Holy See in the Vatican, the TREATY OF TORDESILLAS (1494) divided the non-Christian world into two halves designated by an imaginary line some 370 leagues west of the Cape Verde Islands in the east Atlantic Ocean. Lands to the east were the Portuguese sphere, and those to the west the Spanish. Two years prior to this agreement, Christopher Columbus (1451–1506), an Italian in the patronage of Spain, had reached the Bahamas in the Caribbean claiming it to be INDIA—hence the "West Indies." In order to avoid disputes over territories, the Catholic powers signed the TREATY OF TORDESILLAS (1494), which set in motion the beginning of European IMPERIALISM and COLONIALISM in Southeast Asia.

By the mid-thirteenth century, Portugal and Spain had managed to drive the Muslim Moors out of their peninsula; the last Moorish stronghold, Granada, was regained only in 1492.

Spurred on by "God, Gold, and Glory," the Catholic Iberian powers of Portugal and Spain embarked on the "Age of Discovery" from the early fifteenth century. From 1420, Prince Henrique "The Navigator" (1394–1460), son of John I (r. 1385–1433) of Portugal, gave patronage to geographers, cartographers, and sailors to explore the west coast of Africa; they reached as far south as the Gambia River, the Azores, and the Cape Verde Islands. Prince Henrique's sponsoring of expeditions was an attempt to strike at the erstwhile Muslim enemies of Portugal. Greater success in reaching INDIA followed, with Bartholomeu Diaz (1450–1500) rounding the Cape of Good Hope, the southern tip of Africa, in 1487, and the celebrated voyage of VASCO DA GAMA (1459–1524), who landed at Calicut, India, in 1498.

The Portuguese threefold ambition of eliminating Muslims and spreading CATHOLICISM, securing SPICES AND THE SPICE TRADE, and establishing a PORTUGUESE ASIAN EMPIRE for the glory of Portugal laid plans to capture various strategic city-ports. Having defeated a confederation of Muslims at the Battle of Diu (1509), Viceroy Dom Francisco d'Almeida (t. 1505–1509) launched the imperialistic grand plan. It was to the credit of his successor, ALONSO DE ALBUQUERQUE (ca. 1462–1515), that Goa was secured in 1510, MELAKA in 1511, and Ormuz in 1514. MACAU (MACAO) was captured in 1556 to serve as the foothold to IMPERIAL CHINA.

Ferdinand Magellan (ca. 1480–1521), a Portuguese navigator in the service of Spain, reached MALUKU (THE MOLUCCAS) in 1511. Starting out in 1519, he sailed an alternative route that reached South America, rounded the Strait of Magellan, and crossed the Pacific Ocean to reach the Philippines in 1521, where he was killed in a clash with natives. Four decades later the Spaniard CAPTAIN GENERAL MIGUEL LOPEZ DE LEGAZPI (1500–1572) colonized the Philippines for Philip II (r. 1556–1598).

Trade Patterns and Economic Transformation

Witnessing the development of the ECONOMIC HISTORY OF EARLY MODERN

SOUTHEAST ASIA (PRE-SIXTEENTH CENTURY), we have had some inkling of the gradual changes taking place. But a century prior to the coming of the Europeans and the widespread Islamization of insular Southeast Asia in the sixteenth century, apparent changes were in motion.

Until the mid-fifteenth century, the commodities from Southeast Asia that featured in the commercial transaction list of the East-West trade comprised exotic JUNGLE/ FOREST PRODUCTS and MARINE/SEA PRODUCTS. Apparently, the cloves and nutmegs from MALUKU (THE MOLUCCAS) were collected from the wild. But a change began to be apparent from the mid-fifteenth century that witnessed the emergence of commercial agriculture, intraregional trade, and the growth of large urban centers. The period from that time to the seventeenth century was described as the AGE OF COMMERCE, whereby coastal areas throughout Southeast Asia were increasingly active in participating in the global economy, resulting in the growth of city-port polities.

Cash cropping was intensified for the global market with PEPPER, a major Southeast Asian export commodity. Other SPICES AND THE SPICE TRADE flourished, and production in MALUKU (THE MOLUCCAS), known as the "Spice Islands," was undertaken on a systematic, commercial basis. Cloves, nutmegs, mace, and the fabulous PEPPER fetched lucrative profits. SUGAR, produced largely by the CHINESE IN SOUTHEAST ASIA, featured as a major export in the seventeenth century. Grown generally by immigrant Teochew (Teochiu), one of the CHINESE DIALECT GROUPS, sugar was produced for the Japanese market from central Vietnam, Siam, Cambodia, and BANTAM (BANTEN). TIN exports were also important in the sixteenth and seventeenth centuries, largely derived from the Malay Peninsula and JUNK CEYLON (UJUNG SALANG, PHUKET). The export boom stimulated the import of consumption products, particularly Indian textiles. SHIPBUILDING also intensified, in the production of vessels for trade goods.

The boom period of the AGE OF COMMERCE was from the last quarter of the sixteenth century to the mid-seventeenth century, spurred by rising prices for most Southeast Asian commodities, abundant flow of silver, and keen competition among the many players. Urbanization was another consequence, and by the sixteenth century, cities such as HANOI (THANG-LONG), Ayutthaya, ACEH (ACHEH), BANTEN (BANTAM), MATARAM, and Makassar supported populations of more than 100,000, comparable to their European counterparts. The large urban cosmopolitan centers relied on imported foodstuffs. RICE IN SOUTHEAST ASIA, the staple food, was increasingly produced on an export-oriented basis, focusing more on the intraregional market than world export.

A global crisis during the mid-seventeenth century of climatic variations and the decline in output of silver hurt Southeast Asia. The advent of Europeans with technologically advanced FIREARMS tipped the balance of power toward European superiority by the early eighteenth century. Southeast Asian city-ports that relied on trade for economic and political power were steadily eclipsed by European might. As trade declined and wealth dissipated, the urban population increasingly receded into the hinterland.

The Dutch, the English, and Southeast Asia (ca. 1600–ca. 1800)

When in 1594 Philip II (r. 1556–1598) of Spain (who also ruled Portugal from 1580) closed Lisbon to the Dutch, they were forced to venture directly to Southeast Asia for SPICES AND THE SPICE TRADE. The Dutch had been the main distributor for northern Europe of spices that had been brought by Portuguese carracks from MALUKU (THE MOLUCCAS) via MELAKA. The action of Philip II was designed to destroy the economic base of the Protestant Dutch, who had revolted against Catholic Spain's rule over The Netherlands.

Under the aegis of the Compagnie van Vere (1595), Cornelius de Houtman headed the first Dutch expedition to Southeast Asia. Rounding the Cape of Good Hope, the expedition made for Madagascar, then across the Indian Ocean to the west coast of SUMATRA to BANTAM (BANTEN), avoiding the STRAITS OF MELAKA and the Portuguese at MELAKA. De Houtman was well received by local rulers, as European rivalry translated into higher prices.

After achieving their national independence in 1598, the Dutch ambitiously planned to oust all competitors and to monopolize SPICES AND THE SPICE TRADE in Southeast Asia. The formation of the VEREENIGDE OOST-INDISCHE COMPAGNIE (VOC) ([DUTCH] UNITED EAST INDIA COMPANY) (1602), as a single umbrella enjoining several small Dutch companies with total support from The Netherlands government, was to spearhead the Dutch offensive. By the mid-seventeenth century the Dutch had established factories (outposts) at several vital points in Southeast Asia, such as Banda and Ternate in MALUKU (THE MOLUCCAS), ACEH (ACHEH), and BANTEN (BANTAM), and had driven the Portuguese out of Amboina and Tidore. MELAKA fell to the Dutch in 1641 with the assistance of the JOHOR-RIAU EMPIRE. SPANISH PHILIPPINES, with MANILA as the base of operations, failed in their attempts to halt the Dutch advance in maritime Southeast Asia. But the major threat to Dutch monopolistic practices came from the English.

ANGLO-DUTCH RELATIONS IN SOUTHEAST ASIA (SEVENTEENTH TO TWENTIETH CENTURIES) were highly complex, conditioned by the geopolitical situation in Europe, which often was incongruent with the economic conditions and realities in Southeast Asia. English COUNTRY TRADERS were an irritant to the enforcement of Dutch monopoly. But the greater threat was that posed by the ENGLISH EAST INDIA COMPANY (EIC) (1600), an ardent exponent of FREE TRADE that was diagonally opposed to Dutch VOC monopolistic policy and trading modus operandi of "buying cheap and selling dear." Their opposing trading practices created intense conflicts between them. Unable to make much headway or profits in SPICES AND THE SPICE TRADE, the EIC decided to withdraw and focus more of their undertakings in INDIA. The AMBON (AMBOINA/AMBOYNA) MASSACRE (1623) hastened this decision. The EIC, however, still maintained commercial relations with BANTAM (BANTEN) from 1628 until the Dutch conquest in 1682. Thereafter the EIC built Fort Marlborough on BENGKULU (BENCOOLEN, BENKULEN) in 1685, which remained the sole British outpost in Southeast Asia until the establishment of PENANG (1786).

European Imperialism and Colonialism

Southeast Asia from the mid-sixteenth century to the early twentieth century was partitioned into European spheres of influence that subsequently led to colonization. European IMPERIALISM entered into an earnest stage in the nineteenth century whereby the whole region, with the notable exception of the kingdom of Siam, was territorially colonized. Overall the metropolitan powers centered in Lisbon, Madrid, London, The Hague, Paris, and Washington dictated the political, economic, social, and to a lesser extent the cultural development and norms of their respective colonies and protectorates in Southeast Asia.

In establishing their far-flung PORTUGUESE ASIAN EMPIRE stretching from Ormuz to MACAU (MACAO), the Portuguese in 1520 moved into the Spice Islands with an outpost at Oekusi on TIMOR trading in sandalwood. The Portuguese Dominican Order operated a base on Solor Island around 1561. A half-century later the VOC opened a trading post, ousting the Dominicans. Following a peace between the Dutch Republic and Portugal in 1641, TIMOR was partitioned: the West was under the Dutch while East Timor became a Portuguese enclave.

Meanwhile, their Iberian neighbor was preoccupied with the creation of SPANISH PHILIPPINES. PRE-HISPANIC PHILIPPINES comprised a string of independent BARANGAY of some 30 to 100 families headed by a *datu* (chief). Animists, and ethnically MALAYS, the decentralized *BARANGAY* had a sociopolitical structure that could easily be dominated by the Spanish conquistadors numbering fewer than a thousand men. Colonizing the entire Philippine archipelago was in line with an economic-cum-religious design for the SPANISH EXPANSION IN SOUTHEAST ASIA—namely, a share in the lucrative SPICES AND THE SPICE TRADE, and the Christianization of the islands. Moreover, the islands would be convenient as a base of operations for the various CHRISTIAN MISSIONARIES laboring in East Asia (China and Japan), as well as for tapping the China trade. In fact, from Madrid's viewpoint the Philippines were an extension of the Spanish empire of the Americas—namely, Peru and Mexico; they served the fabulously profitable GALLEON TRADE with the international linkage of Madrid-Acapulco-MANILA-MACAU (MACAO).

Spanish conquest was not difficult, beginning with the taking of Cebu (1565), a major island in the VISAYAN ISLANDS (BISAYAN ISLANDS, THE BISAYAS, THE VISAYAS), and MANILA (1571) in LUZON. The lands were apportioned to Spanish colonists under the *encomienda* system adopted from Mexico. Claiming to be the patrons of the Filipinos, the Spanish *encomenderos* (landowners) also had rights over the labor services of the *BARANGAY*. The Filipinos as clients had to pay tribute (*tasacion*) to Spanish patrons. In return the *encomenderos* were responsible for protecting and defending the Filipinos and instructing them in CATHOLICISM with a view toward conversion. The PATRON-CLIENT RELATIONS were often lopsided to the advantage of the former; however, overly harsh or oppressive means were eschewed. Initially the SPANISH FRIARS (THE PHILIPPINES) defended the Filipinos from harsh treatment by their Spanish patrons.

The HISPANIZATION process, largely referring to the Christianization of the lowland tribute-paying inhabitants, was moderately successful. HISPANIZATION failed, however, to penetrate the highland ethnic groups (Bontocs, Igorots, Ilocanos, Ilocanos) of northern LUZON, or the Muslims of the south in MINDANAO such as the MOROS, SULU AND THE SULU ARCHIPELAGO, and TAUSUG AND THE SULU SULTANATE. Spanish CHRISTIAN MISSIONARIES of various denominations (Augustinians, Dominicans, Franciscans) spread CATHOLICISM among the hitherto animistic Filipinos. Awed by the rich ritual and pageantry, the recipients were, however, at best nominal converts, with a superficial understanding of the religion. The Filipinos, in fact, combined pagan practices and beliefs with CATHOLICISM, a blending that by the nineteenth century was the religious norm.

In the adjoining archipelago of modern Indonesia, the creation of the NETHERLANDS (DUTCH) EAST INDIES, commonly referred to simply as DUTCH EAST INDIES, was under way, with the VOC consolidating its economic monopoly complemented by political and military domination. The Dutch empire builder was JAN PIETERSZOON COEN (1587–1629), who captured BANTEN (BANTAM) and in 1619 converted one of its two ports into the main base of operations of the VOC, renaming it BATAVIA (SUNDA KELAPA, JACATRA, DJAKARTA/JAKARTA). But it was not until the early 1920s that the DUTCH EAST INDIES became a reality: JAVA (1830), SUMATRA (1904), Riau Archipelago (1911), DUTCH BORNEO (1911), SULAWESI (1907), MALUKU (THE MOLUCCAS) (1907), and IRIAN JAYA (1921).

Starting with a monopolistic control of SPICES AND THE SPICE TRADE for the greater part of the seventeenth and eighteenth centuries, a trade based largely on treaty engagements with local rulers, the Dutch shifted their policy as a result of the acquisition of a territorial empire coupled with the ECONOMIC TRANSFORMATION OF SOUTHEAST ASIA (ca. 1400–ca. 1800). Following the NAPOLEONIC WARS IN ASIA, whereby Dutch possessions came under temporary British tutelage (1811–1815), JAVA came under a LIBERAL EXPERIMENTAL PERIOD (1816–1830). The financially devastating JAVA WAR (1825–1830), led by the charismatic DIPONEGORO (PANGERAN DIPANEGARA) (ca. 1785–1855), resulted in a revision of policy to ensure that the colonial possessions were not a drain on the metropolitan treasury and should instead bring in wealth. COUNT JOHANNES VAN DEN BOSCH (1780–1844) designed the highly profitable CULTIVATION SYSTEM (*CULTUURS-TELSEL*), which focused on JAVA. With the connivance of the Javanese *bupati* (regents) and *camat* (district heads), as well as the Dutch *controleur,* this systematic program of forced cultivation by Javanese peasant farmers of export crops (COFFEE, SUGAR, tea) reaped fabulous returns. The metropolitan government was the main benefactor. The Nederlandsche Handelmaat-Schappij (Netherlands Trading Company) handled the shipping of the export crops from JAVA to Amsterdam.

Eager to secure bigger profits, the Dutch and Javanese overseers of the CULTIVATION SYSTEM (*CULTUURSTELSEL*) disregarded the built-in safeguards; abuses set in, as poignantly demonstrated in prose by Edward

Douwes Dekker's *MAX HAVELAAR* (1860) or *The Coffee Auctions of the Dutch Trading Company*. Liberals in The Netherlands from the 1860s began to voice criticisms of this system of FORCED DELIVERIES of export crops by Javanese peasants, and a more liberal approach was proposed to rectify the appalling situation. In the next decade efforts were under way to gradually phase out the CULTIVATION SYSTEM (*CULTUURSTELSEL*). In its place a policy shift encouraged participation and investment of Dutch private enterprise on the basis of free competition. During this period of economic liberalization (1870–1900), new cash crops were introduced, notably RUBBER. TIN production surged rapidly, oil exploration and exploitation were undertaken, HIGHWAYS AND RAILWAYS were constructed, communications were improved, and WESTERN SECULAR EDUCATION was introduced. However, instead of government-sponsored oppression of the indigenous Indonesians during the phase of the CULTIVATION SYSTEM (*CULTUURSTELSEL*), the liberalization period witnessed the exploitation of the local peasantry by Dutch and Chinese capitalists in their pursuit for greater profits.

Perplexed by two successive failures of the unresolved equation of Dutch profits versus Indonesian welfare, the metropolitan government swung full circle to lay emphasis on native welfare; thus the ETHICAL POLICY (*ETHISCHE POLITIEK*), introduced in 1901. Advancement in social services, native welfare, and the promotion of democratic self-government were characteristics of this new approach to the colonial question. The lack of sincerity on the part of the Dutch and the high expectations of the Indonesians worked against the success of the ETHICAL POLICY (*ETHISCHE POLITIEK*). A conspicuous outcome was the beginning of Indonesian NATIONALISM AND INDEPENDENCE MOVEMENTS IN SOUTHEAST ASIA.

Unable to compete profitably with the Dutch VOC, the English EIC retreated to INDIA, where it carved out an empire on the subcontinent. Meanwhile, enterprising English COUNTRY TRADERS utilizing their wit and native network crisscrossed maritime Southeast Asia, penetrating the VOC monopoly to pursue their fortune. The GOVERNMENT OF BRITISH INDIA, besides benefiting from

the Indian cotton textile industry that supplied the Manchester looms with raw materials, visualized a lucrative area of investment that awaited just over the horizon in IMPERIAL CHINA. Long before the mission of Lord Macartney in 1793 to IMPERIAL CHINA of the isolationist QING (CHING/MANCHU) DYNASTY (1644–1912), many an English capitalist was fully convinced that the "end of the rainbow" lay in the China trade of silk, tea, and CERAMICS. After a century of closed-door policy on foreign maritime trade, IMPERIAL CHINA allowed restricted trade at Guangzhou in 1751.

Between INDIA and IMPERIAL CHINA there was no friendly port of call for the shelter and repair of the East Indiamen of the EIC. These ships made use of the MONSOONS, and Southeast Asia was the halfway point where they would await the next favorable winds. The EIC's sole outpost was BENGKULU (BENCOOLEN, BENKULEN) on the northwestern coast of SUMATRA. Furthermore, the Anglo-French struggle over the subcontinent often resulted in battles in the Bay of Bengal. While the French could retire to their base in Mauritius or at ACEH (ACHEH) under treaty agreements, the English had to brave the MONSOONS, because they had only Bombay. On the basis of both economic and military concerns, it was imperative to the GOVERNMENT OF BRITISH INDIA that a viable outpost be established on the eastern shores of the Bay of Bengal that could serve as both a naval base and an entrepôt for Southeast Asian products.

Against this scenario emerged the ambitious CAPTAIN FRANCIS LIGHT (1740–1794), an English COUNTRY TRADER who had for decades traded along the ISTHMUS OF KRA and the northern parts of the Malay Peninsula from his base at JUNK CEYLON (UJUNG SALANG, PHUKET). Acting as the intermediary between the GOVERNMENT OF BRITISH INDIA and the Kedah ruler, who had offered the island of PENANG (1786) in return for military protection against his Siamese overlord, Captain Light secured for the former an outpost on PENANG (1786). He, however, was less than explicit on the question of military assistance. PENANG (1786) became a naval base and entrepôt for the EIC's China trade. In 1800 the strip on the mainland opposite the island was acquired from Kedah and named Province Wellesley.

When in 1821 the ruler of LIGOR/ NAKHON attacked and overran Kedah on orders from BANGKOK, the British in PENANG (1786) remained uncommitted, though Sultan Ahmad Tajuddin (r. 1797–1843) was given shelter. The British did not want to risk Anglo-Siamese relations over Kedah, as there were imminent developments intimating the outbreak of the ANGLO-BURMESE WARS (1824–1826, 1852, 1885). A Burmese-Siamese alliance would have been detrimental to British ambitions in Burma.

The NAPOLEONIC WARS IN ASIA caused a chilling of ANGLO-DUTCH RELATIONS IN SOUTHEAST ASIA (SEVENTEENTH TO TWENTIETH CENTURIES). In accordance with the KEW LETTERS penned by the Dutch monarch in exile in England, the British temporarily administered the DUTCH EAST INDIES. SIR (THOMAS) STAMFORD BINGLEY RAFFLES (1781–1826) became lieutenant governor of JAVA from 1811 to 1816. During his tenure he instituted liberal reforms (TAXATION, SLAVERY) that were retained during the Dutch LIBERAL EXPERIMENTAL PERIOD (1816–1830). Similarly, MELAKA came under British occupation.

The British victory at the Battle of Trafalgar (1805) over the Franco-Spanish invasion fleet established its supremacy at sea. PENANG (1786) as a naval base became irrelevant. Its status as an entrepôt supplying the China trade was at best fair in tapping the products of northern SUMATRA, southern Siam, and the northern peninsular Malay States. And as an outpost for checking Dutch activities, its location on the northern part of the STRAITS OF MELAKA proved inconvenient. The drawbacks of PENANG (1786) led to the search for a more strategically located base farther south that could be in a better position not only to procure a wider range of Southeast Asian products but also to monitor DUTCH INTERESTS IN SOUTHEAST ASIA FROM 1800.

SINGAPORE (1819), formerly TEMASIK (TUMASIK), proved to be the ideal British base that possessed all the qualities that PENANG (1786) lacked. The visionary SIR (THOMAS) STAMFORD BINGLEY RAFFLES (1781–1826) executed some sleek maneuvering to take possession of the island for the EIC at the southern tip of the Malay Peninsula. With its free port status, natural, sheltered harbor, and British rule, SINGAPORE (1819) within a short period was a booming port. The Dutch protested over the controversial ownership of the island, which they claimed was part of the JOHOR-RIAU EMPIRE, with which the Dutch had treaty relations. Nonetheless the GOVERNMENT OF BRITISH INDIA stood firm over SINGAPORE (1819), having witnessed its impressive performance.

Meanwhile in Europe, the Battle of Waterloo (1815) changed the balance of power and improved ANGLO-DUTCH RELATIONS IN SOUTHEAST ASIA (SEVENTEENTH TO TWENTIETH CENTURIES). Britain wanted an ally in an economically strong Netherlands to avoid a repeat of the latter's being used as a launching base for the invasion of the British Isles. The DUTCH EAST INDIES was a vital key to this resurgence. Therefore the Anglo-Dutch Treaty of London (1824) apportioned the Malay archipelago with the Straits of Singapore as the division between two spheres of influence: the Dutch to the south of the straits and the British to the north. BENGKULU (BENCOOLEN, BENKULEN) was exchanged for MELAKA. This agreement effectively chartered the fate of modern Indonesia in Dutch hands, and Malaysia under the British.

In 1826 the STRAITS SETTLEMENTS (1826–1946) were constituted, comprising PENANG (1786), SINGAPORE (1819), and MELAKA, further strengthening the British command of the STRAITS OF MELAKA in protection of the EIC's all-important China trade from PIRACY. The ENTREPÔT TRADE AND COMMERCE OF SINGAPORE (NINETEENTH CENTURY TO 1990s) developed rapidly. The STRAITS SETTLEMENTS (1826–1946) served as a platform for the British entry into the WESTERN MALAY STATES (PERAK, SELANGOR, NEGRI SEMBILAN, AND PAHANG) in the last quarter of the nineteenth century.

BRITISH BORNEO was created when Britain in 1888 granted protectorate status over the Malay sultanate of BRUNEI (SIXTEENTH TO NINETEENTH CENTURIES) and the oddities of SARAWAK

AND SABAH (NORTH BORNEO). Theoretically, BRUNEI (SIXTEENTH TO NINETEENTH CENTURIES) claimed possession of BORNEO—at least the northwestern portion of the island. The DAYAKS and the IBANS in particular and the EAST MALAYSIAN ETHNIC MINORITIES in general paid little attention to the suzerainty of this Bornean Malay kingdom. However, an anti-Brunei revolt (1836–1841) broke out in the northwest corner, owing to oppressive treatment of the local inhabitants. A visiting English gentleman-adventurer was invited to intervene; he succeeded and was consequently rewarded with a fiefdom by the sultanate. JAMES BROOKE AND SARAWAK is the romantic tale of an English white raja who ruled over a multiethnic, multicultural population; he (and his heirs) practiced a consistently paternalistic policy of championing the interests and welfare of the native inhabitants. The second white raja, SIR CHARLES ANTHONI JOHNSON BROOKE (1829–1917), expanded the fiefdom to the borders of contemporary Brunei and laid the foundations of a modern state. From the mid-nineteenth century a series of speculators had secured rights from BRUNEI (SIXTEENTH TO NINETEENTH CENTURIES) and the sultanate of Sulu for the territory encompassed by the present-day East Malaysian state of Sabah. In the early 1880s an Anglo-Austrian private partnership was in possession of these territorial rights and successfully gained a royal charter from Britain in establishing the BRITISH NORTH BORNEO CHARTERED COMPANY (1881–1946). The Austrian interests withdrew, and the solely BRITISH NORTH BORNEO CHARTERED COMPANY (1881–1917) administered what became known as British North Borneo. Owing to the increasing encroachment on BRUNEI (SIXTEENTH TO NINETEENTH CENTURIES) by the respective regimes of SARAWAK AND SABAH (NORTH BORNEO), Britain granted the protectorate to ensure the integrity of the Malay kingdom.

Britain in the mid-1870s intervened in the affairs of the TIN-producing WESTERN MALAY STATES (PERAK, SELANGOR, NEGRI SEMBILAN, AND PAHANG) (in the 1880s) established the RESIDENTIAL SYSTEM (MALAYA), ushering in the beginnings of British COLONIALISM that subsequently created BRITISH MALAYA by the first decade of the twentieth century. A succession dispute over the Perak throne, intertwined with clashes between rival Chinese *HUI* squabbling over mining territories, PIRACY in Selangor, and civil war in Sungai Ujong (later to become Negri Sembilan), created a most untenable situation in these TIN-producing Malay States, disrupting production and trade.

TIN, which does not rust, was in high demand for the tin-plate industry. Several *TOWKAY* from the STRAITS SETTLEMENTS (1826–1946), some of whom headed the *HUI*, invested heavily in the lucrative TIN industry. The EUROPEAN AGENCY HOUSES also had a stake in the TIN of the WESTERN MALAY STATES (PERAK, SELANGOR, NEGRI SEMBILAN, AND PAHANG) as the increasing demand pushed up ore prices.

In a high-handed manner, SIR ANDREW CLARKE (1824–1902), governor of the STRAITS SETTLEMENTS (1826–1946), executed a fait accompli by intervening and settling the disputes and wars in the WESTERN MALAY STATES (PERAK, SELANGOR, NEGRI SEMBILAN, AND PAHANG) through the terms of the PANGKOR ENGAGEMENT (1874), which introduced the RESIDENTIAL SYSTEM (MALAYA). Excluding Islam and Malay customs and practices, the resident was the de facto administrator possessing legislative, judicial, and executive power, but in the eyes of the *rakyat* (masses) he appeared to rule in the name of the Malay sultan.

As a means of achieving administrative centralization, the WESTERN MALAY STATES (PERAK, SELANGOR, NEGRI SEMBILAN, AND PAHANG) were combined into the FEDERATED MALAY STATES (FMS) (1896). Through the Treaty of Bangkok (1909), Britain acquired the SIAMESE MALAY STATES (KEDAH, PERLIS, KELANTAN, TERENGGANU), among other privileges from the kingdom of Siam. These northern peninsular Malay States had been acknowledging Siamese suzerainty through the periodic tribute of the *BUNGA EMAS* to BANGKOK. Under the British fold, each of the Malay rulers had in his royal court a British adviser, no different in function from the RESIDENTIAL SYSTEM (MALAYA). ABU BAKAR (r. 1862–1895),

SULTAN OF JOHOR, the far-sighted Anglophile ruler, had succeeded in delaying the imposition of British COLONIALISM by building his kingdom as a modern, Westernized state. Through the Chinese *KANGCHU SYSTEM*, his father and predecessor had encouraged cash cropping of PEPPER and gambier. Nonetheless, Ibrahim (r. 1895–1959), son and successor of ABU BAKAR (r. 1862–1895), SULTAN OF JOHOR, had little choice in 1914 but to tolerate a British adviser. By means of the system of indirect rule through British residents and advisers, BRITISH MALAYA became a reality from 1914.

The expansionist designs of the KONBAUNG DYNASTY (1752–1885) under Bodawpaya (r. 1782–1819), who conquered ARAKAN in 1784, brought about the sharing of a common border with the GOVERNMENT OF BRITISH INDIA. But ARAKAN was far from subdued and regularly staged futile revolts against Burmese authority, with the defeated rebels crossing into Chittagong as refugees. Attempts were made to annex Manipur, Assam, and Cachar in eastern Bengal, bringing them under the KONBAUNG DYNASTY (1752–1885). Maha Bandula, the ambitious general of Bagyidaw (r. 1819–1838), harbored plans for the annexation of eastern Bengal. Fearing increasing French influence over Konbaung rulers, the GOVERNMENT OF BRITISH INDIA used the disputed possession of the island of Shahpuri as a pretext for war.

KONBAUNG RULERS AND BRITISH IMPERIALISM witnessed the clash of two proud, imperialistic powers that erupted into the ANGLO-BURMESE WARS (1824–1826, 1852, 1885), which subsequently led to the emergence of BRITISH BURMA. The hurriedly concluded TREATY OF YANDABO (1826), lest British forces violate the capital city of Amarapura during the first conflict of 1824–1826, was in itself the bone of contention that resulted in the second war, in 1852, and the acquisition of PEGU. The issues of the British annexation of ARAKAN, TENASSERIM, and PEGU and the acceptance of a British resident on a diplomatic basis at the Burmese royal court created a quagmire of problems that soured Anglo-Burmese relations. The reign of MINDON (r. 1853–1878) was a respite in the troubled relationship between the KONBAUNG RULERS AND BRITISH IM-PERIALISM. But Thibaw (r. 1878–1885) lacked the finesse of MINDON (r. 1853–1878) in playing off the British against the French, with fatal consequences. THE "SHOE ISSUE" was another touchy matter that effectively led to the complete breakdown of diplomatic intercourse between the two parties. Sensing the ascendancy of French influence over MANDALAY, the British unfairly seized the transgression case of the BOMBAY BURMAH TRADING CORPORATION (BBTC) as a pretext for the third and final war, in 1885. Following the Burmese defeat, Upper Burma was annexed in 1886 and Thibaw was exiled to INDIA, hence bringing an end to the KONBAUNG DYNASTY (1752–1885).

At the same time attempting to assert their influence over the KONBAUNG DYNASTY (1752–1885) in Burma, FRENCH AMBITIONS IN SOUTHEAST ASIA were also focused on the Indochinese peninsula, which subsequently led to the creation of FRENCH INDOCHINA in the last quarter of the nineteenth century. Anglo-French concern over Burma and the Indochinese peninsula, particularly Vietnam, focused on the possibility of accessing the Irrawaddy and Mekong in order to reach YUNNAN PROVINCE in China's southwest, rumored to possess vast commercial potential. This "back door" to IMPERIAL CHINA to a large extent played a significant role in influencing the relationship between the KONBAUNG RULERS AND BRITISH IMPERIALISM, especially from the mid-nineteenth century; likewise the NGUYỄN EMPERORS AND FRENCH IMPERIALISM.

In 1867, steamers were permitted accessibility to the Irrawaddy by MINDON (r. 1853–1878), as far north as Bhamo. The British were keen to uncover a trade route to YUNNAN PROVINCE, with the thought of annexing Upper Burma. The LAGRÉE-GARNIER MEKONG EXPEDITION (1866–1868) revealed to the French the unsuitability of the Mekong as a back-door route; subsequently, it led the French to earnestly press for the acquisition of TONKIN (TONGKING) so as to facilitate exploration of the Red River.

Unofficial French involvement in Vietnam began with the assistance rendered by PIERRE JOSEPH GEORGES PIGNEAU DE BEHAINE, BISHOP OF ADRAN (1741–1799) to NGUYỄN ANH (EMPEROR GIA

LONG) (r. 1802–1820), who reunified the country and established the NGUYỄN DYNASTY (1802–1945). For the sake of his beloved bishop, the first emperor tolerated CHRISTIAN MISSIONARIES in his realm. The NGUYỄN DYNASTY (1802–1945) in fact adopted a closed-door policy to all Europeans, in the hope that the Western powers would leave the country alone; the same was the case in IMPERIAL CHINA. Despite the humiliating lessons of the so-called Opium Wars (1839–1842, 1856–1860), Thieu-tri (r. 1841–1847) not only enforced the disastrous closed-door policy but also began persecuting CHRISTIAN MISSIONARIES, in an attempt to eject both them and CATHOLICISM from Vietnam. Minh Mang (r. 1820–1841) had set the persecution policy with edicts from the mid-1820s without any adverse effect, but his successors Thieu-tri (r. 1841–1847) and Tu-duc (r. 1848–1883) faced an aggressive France bent on securing its "place in the sun" vis-à-vis their erstwhile rival, the British.

The story of the NGUYỄN EMPERORS AND FRENCH IMPERIALISM is a tale of arrogance, stubbornness, and pursuit of an unrealistic policy by the former in the face of an ambitious, prestige-conscious Napoleon III (r. 1852–1870) of the Second Empire.

French IMPERIALISM in Vietnam, which was initially an attempt to defend and protect CHRISTIAN MISSIONARIES from persecution, began to feature an economic angle in securing overseas markets for manufactured goods. Furthermore, French prestige and honor were emphasized, particularly during the reign of Napoleon III. After 1860, *MISSION CIVIL-ISATRICE* ("CIVILIZING MISSION") was an added motive for France's aggressive attitude toward Vietnam. FRANCIS GARNIER (1839–1873), a naval officer and colonial official, was a vocal advocate of France's adopting *MISSION CIVILISATRICE;* also influential was Justin Napoleon Samuel Prosper, Count de Chasseloup-Laubat (t. 1859–1867), French minister of marine and colonies in Paris. Therefore the annexation of Vietnam was a foregone conclusion.

The French conquest of Vietnam and Indochina began as follows: Tourane (1858), COCHIN CHINA (1858–1862, 1867), SAIGON (GIA DINH, HỒ CHÍ MINH CITY) (1862), CAMBODIA (EIGHTEENTH TO NINETEENTH CENTURIES) (1863), ANNAM and TONKIN (TONGKING) (1883). By 1887, when COCHIN CHINA, ANNAM, and TONKIN (TONGKING)—modern Vietnam—succumbed to French IMPERIALISM and COLONIALISM, the FRENCH INDOCHINESE UNION (UNION INDOCHINOISE FRANÇAISE) (1887) came into existence. Then in classic gunboat-diplomacy style, AUGUSTE PAVIE (1847–1925), French consul in BANGKOK, forced the Siamese through the PAKNAM INCIDENT (1893) to return the provinces of BATTAMBANG and SIEM REAP to CAMBODIA (EIGHTEENTH TO NINETEENTH CENTURIES), and to hand over LAOS (NINETEENTH CENTURY TO MID-1990s) to the French. The creation of FRENCH INDOCHINA was completed with COCHIN CHINA as a colony, and protectorates over ANNAM, TONKIN (TONGKING), CAMBODIA (EIGHTEENTH TO NINETEENTH CENTURIES), and LAOS (NINETEENTH CENTURY TO MID-1990s).

King Chulalongkorn (Rama V) (r. 1868–1910) of Siam had no room for maneuver during the PAKNAM INCIDENT (1893) when faced with a determined AUGUSTE PAVIE (1847–1925). But like his father and predecessor, Mongkut (Rama IV) (r. 1851–1868), Chulalongkorn knew that his priority was the PRESERVATION OF SIAM'S POLITICAL INDEPENDENCE. Mongkut had observed the humiliation suffered by IMPERIAL CHINA and the neighboring KONBAUNG DYNASTY (1752–1885) in the face of Western IMPERIALISM and COLONIALISM. The closed-door policy was suicidal in the face of aggressive Western powers bent on exploiting weaknesses and engineering any pretext for imposing COLONIALISM on unreceptive regimes. Therefore Mongkut practiced an open-door policy and at the same time set in motion the process of REFORMS AND MODERNIZATION IN SIAM that were brought to their fruition by Chulalongkorn. Having concluded a cordial and satisfactory treaty agreement with the British government's representative SIR JOHN BOWRING (1792–1872) in 1855, Mongkut signed similar treaties with other Western nations. Modeled after the treaty with Britain, agreements were made with France and the United States (1856), Denmark (1858), Portugal (1859), The Netherlands (1860), Prussia (1862) (later with a unified Germany in 1872), and Belgium, Italy, Norway, and Sweden (1868). The treaties in effect opened Siam to Western trade and commerce under favorable terms; a consul was to reside in BANGKOK, and extraterritorial rights were granted to Westerners. Although the agreements largely favored the Western nations, Siam swallowed its pride to ensure the PRESERVATION OF SIAM'S POLITICAL INDEPENDENCE.

Colonial Southeast Asia

COLONIALISM paid handsome dividends for the metropolitan powers, largely as a result of the exploitation of natural resources (TIN, GOLD, OIL AND PETROLEUM, and timber) and commercial agriculture (ABACA [MANILA HEMP], PEPPER, COFFEE, SUGAR, TOBACCO, RUBBER, and RICE IN SOUTHEAST ASIA). EUROPEAN AGENCY HOUSES, Western joint stock companies, Chinese TOWKAY entrepreneurs, CHETTIARS (CHETTYARS), and most of the indigenous elite of Southeast Asia who collaborated with the colonial regimes reaped financial benefits from their capital investments in the mining industry or plantation agriculture.

Toward the close of the nineteenth century, RICE IN SOUTHEAST ASIA was increasingly cultivated for the export market in the spacious floodplains and deltas of the mainland—namely, Lower Burma, the Menam central plain, COCHIN CHINA, and the Red River delta. Production of RICE IN SOUTHEAST ASIA largely catered to the vast workforce in mines and plantations throughout the region. No other food crop—SAGO, tapioca—could match this staple food of monsoon Asia. The CHINESE IN SOUTHEAST ASIA in various corners of the region produced PEPPER and gambier, SUGAR, and RUBBER in smallholdings for the export market. Western capital and enterprise relying largely on immigrant labor managed vast plantations of COFFEE and TOBACCO, and in the early twentieth century, the fortune maker, RUBBER. The peasantry in JAVA was the most hard-pressed in the FORCED DELIVERIES of export crops;

likewise their Burmese, Vietnamese, and Filipino counterparts.

The exploitation of TIN, initially for the greater part of the nineteenth century a Chinese-dominated industry with capital from TOWKAY entrepreneurs and imported labor from southern China, was transformed toward the last quarter of the century. By the first decades of the twentieth century, the TIN industry of the WESTERN MALAY STATES (PERAK, SELANGOR, NEGRI SEMBILAN, AND PAHANG) was a highly capitalized, technology-driven sector monopolized by Western joint stock companies registered in London, Paris, and Amsterdam. Processing and smelting plants and shipping of the ore were in the hands of Western companies. Likewise, the labor-intensive, sluggish mining methods in GOLD exploitation as undertaken by the Chinese were outpaced by Western technical advancement utilizing machinery and huge capital outlays. OIL AND PETROLEUM—whether in THE NETHERLANDS (DUTCH) EAST INDIES, BRITISH BURMA, or BRITISH BORNEO—from the outset was dominated exclusively by Western companies. For instance, the BRUNEI OIL AND GAS INDUSTRY from the outset was a British enterprise. Similarly the mining of iron and coal enjoyed profitable returns by Western enterprise.

Colonial regimes invested in the provision of HIGHWAYS AND RAILWAYS to facilitate the transportation needs of mining and commercial agriculture linking producing areas to the ports for shipment to markets abroad. BRITISH BURMA, BRITISH MALAYA, JAVA, and Vietnam possessed a purpose-built, fairly efficient network of HIGHWAYS AND RAILWAYS. Intraregional shipping was in indigenous hands and those of the Chinese, while Western shipping lines plied international routes to West Asia and Europe. The SUEZ CANAL (1869) immeasurably improved East-West trade and commerce. By the early twentieth century the bane of PIRACY was generally under control.

The complementing equation of Western capital and Asian immigrant labor (namely Chinese and Indian) fueled the exploitation of minerals and development of export agriculture in colonial Southeast Asia. Dire conditions in IMPERIAL CHINA and INDIA during the second half of the nineteenth century, coupled with a resource-rich but labor-deficient Southeast Asia, resulted in the immigration of Chinese and Indians to the region. BRITISH MALAYA in particular was the major recipient of these waves of immigration; the Chinese surge began in the 1840s, whereas mass INDIAN IMMIGRANTS came in the early decades of the twentieth century.

Accompanying economic development, progress and expansion of social services (public health and education) were undertaken by colonial regimes. The promotion of Western medical care, the provision of hospitals in urban centers and clinics in rural areas, and public health campaigns to eradicate malaria, tuberculosis (TB), and other tropical DISEASES AND EPIDEMICS were emphasized to ensure that the workforce was not delinquent in its contribution to the colonial economy. In 1900 the INSTITUTE FOR MEDICAL RESEARCH (IMR) was established in KUALA LUMPUR (KL). The colonial period assisted THE DEMOGRAPHIC TRANSITION IN SOUTHEAST ASIA. Investments in public health showed apparent results as the mortality rate commenced to dip from the early part of the twentieth century, accelerating from the 1950s. At the same time there was a high increase in the birth rate.

CHRISTIAN MISSIONARIES initiated the introduction of Western-style schooling and education in place of TRADITIONAL RELIGIOUS EDUCATION. The apparent intention of mission schools was to infuse religious doctrines among their charges. Schools, orphanages, and hospitals were the vehicles of proselytization by the CHRISTIAN MISSIONARIES. The UNIVERSITY OF SANTO TOMAS, reputedly the oldest existing tertiary institution in the Philippines and Asia, began as a boarding novitiate in 1611, then became a university in 1645. The Catholic Christian Brothers and the Sisters of St. Maur established Brothers' schools for boys and convent schools for girls, respectively, throughout BRITISH MALAYA, BRITISH BORNEO, and BRITISH BURMA. Often boarding was provided to further facilitate proselytization. Anglicans and U.S. Methodists emulated the strategy of their Catholic counterparts in the provision of schools and Western-style education, which used one of the Western languages as a medium of instruction: Spanish in the Philippines and English in the British-dominated territories.

Alongside the mission schools, WESTERN SECULAR EDUCATION employing Western languages as the medium of instruction, without the religious aspect, was popular and much sought after by the indigenous elite, including the PERANAKAN community and the BABA NYONYA in the DUTCH EAST INDIES, BRITISH MALAYA, and BRITISH BORNEO. The "Free" in the PENANG FREE SCHOOL (1816) meant that this secular English-language school was open to all pupils irrespective of their ethnicity, creed, or religion. Other similar "free" schools were established in the STRAITS SETTLEMENTS (1826–1946). Modeled after the British public school, the MALAY COLLEGE, KUALA KANGSAR (MCKK) was purpose-built for the provision of English-language WESTERN SECULAR EDUCATION for the sons of Malay sultans and chiefs. Its graduates proceeded to Britain for tertiary studies, to return as middle-ranking officers in the colonial bureaucracy. The clamor for higher education locally led to the establishment in SINGAPORE (1819) of the KING EDWARD VII COLLEGE OF MEDICINE and RAFFLES COLLEGE in 1905 and 1929, respectively.

British colonial officials who combined their administrative duties with scholarly pursuits—the latter out of genuine interest in the MALAYS and the Malay archipelago, in the footsteps of SIR (THOMAS) STAMFORD BINGLEY RAFFLES (1781–1826)—established in 1877 the STRAITS/MALAYAN/MALAYSIAN BRANCH OF THE ROYAL ASIATIC SOCIETY (MBRAS). It published a scholarly journal that continues to be undertaken from its original base in KUALA LUMPUR (KL). SIR R[ICHARD] O[LAF] WINSTEDT (1878–1966), a colonial officer who had contributed much to MALAYAN/MALAYSIAN EDUCATION, was a staunch supporter of the society and wrote many articles in its journal.

The SARAWAK MUSEUM, established in Kuching in 1870 by the second white raja, SIR CHARLES JOHNSON ANTHONI BROOKE (1829–1917), features the flora and fauna of BORNEO. The collection expanded from the nucleus of exhibits collected by the English naturalist and botanist Alfred Russel

Wallace (1823–1913), who spent a sojourn in Sarawak in the 1860s as a guest of Sir James Brooke (1803–1868), the first white raja. (The WALLACE LINE, a biogeographical divide, was named after this English scientist who formulated the evolutionary theory independently of Charles Robert Darwin [1809–1882].) The SARAWAK MUSEUM published the multidisciplinary *Sarawak Museum Journal* from 1911 to the present.

Under the ETHICAL POLICY (*ETHISCHE POLITIEK*), an expansion of education particularly at the elementary level was featured. In the urban centers, particularly in JAVA and SUMATRA, schools using Dutch as the language of instruction serviced mainly PERANAKAN and the indigenous middle and upper classes. BRITISH BURMA also emphasized English-language WESTERN SECULAR EDUCATION, but that policy harmed the Buddhist monastic order. In Burma the *SANGHA* had for centuries been the custodian of TRADITIONAL RELIGIOUS EDUCATION; the latter's displacement by WESTERN SECULAR EDUCATION created a vacuum in their ranks. Moreover, the demise of the monarchy that had been the patron of THERAVADA BUDDHISM and the *SANGHA,* coupled with the colonial government's total indifference, saw members of the *SANGHA* sliding into disarray; some even transformed into antigovernment activists.

In Vietnam, when the French colonial policy of "assimilation" replaced "association" at the turn of the twentieth century, French education pushed aside the traditional, heavily Sinicized Confucian system of education that gave undue emphasis to history, morality, and the Chinese language. The latter was abolished, and in its place *QUỐC NGỮ,* the romanization of Vietnamese script, was promoted. French culture and civilization consistent with the objectives of *MISSION CIVILISATRICE* ("CIVILIZING MISSION") dominated the curriculum, with French as the language of instruction. The French-language schools laid emphasis on critical and analytical thought in place of the traditional Confucian rote learning. Such a pedagogical shift had dire consequences for the colonial regime in the long run. Although WESTERN SECULAR EDUCATION was introduced and greatly encouraged in COCHIN CHINA, AN-

NAM, and TONKIN (TONGKING), the TRADITIONAL RELIGIOUS EDUCATION of the Buddhist monastic school system was retained in the French protectorates of CAMBODIA (EIGHTEENTH TO NINETEENTH CENTURIES) and LAOS (NINETEENTH CENTURY TO MID-1990s). The *SANGHA* of both territories remained intact and continued to be the custodian of Buddhist learning and scholarship despite the impotent monarchies.

The immigrant communities of CHINESE IN SOUTHEAST ASIA emphasized the importance of book learning and literacy, reflecting upon the traditional social hierarchy of the elite scholar-bureaucrat. Every Chinese, whether a penniless coolie or a wealthy *TOWKAY,* harbored the passionate desire that the next generation be literate as a means of moving up the social ladder. Therefore Chinese communities throughout Southeast Asia set up their schools, often community funded and managed, with curricula, books, and teachers imported from IMPERIAL CHINA. The orthodox Confucian repertoire of learning to mold the Chinese gentleman and scholar-bureaucrat was the basic content of OVERSEAS CHINESE EDUCATION.

Throughout colonial Southeast Asia, government-sponsored, elementary vocational-type education in the vernacular was promoted. Some basic literacy was deemed essential for the indigenous population to understand the dictates of the colonial authorities. Instruction in Western languages was limited to the training of subordinate, clerical personnel to staff the colonial bureaucracy and European capitalist establishments. The fear of creating an army of "B.A.s" without appropriate employment, as was the case in British India, was an ever-present concern among official colonial circles in Southeast Asia.

The REFORMS AND MODERNIZATION IN SIAM were undertaken in earnest under Chulalongkorn. The formulation and successful implementation of this forward policy were largely due to the cooperation, support, and capable assistance of the royal princes, notably PRINCE DEWAWONGSE (1858–1923) and PRINCE DAMRONG (1862–1943), and members of The Bunnag Family. The act of prostration to the monarch was abolished, likewise SLAVERY and compulsory labor. A decree of 1878 forced all nobles to send their sons to Europe for WESTERN SECULAR EDUCATION; the royal princes also had their schooling abroad, particularly in Britain. The REFORMS AND MODERNIZATION IN SIAM covered fiscal, administrative (centralization and local administration), judicial, and educational concerns (English-language schools were emphasized). The development of HIGHWAYS AND RAILWAYS was an important component in the modernization program. From 1915, BANGKOK was linked by rail to KUALA LUMPUR (KL). The policy of engaging Western technocrats in various fields, as begun by Mongkut, continued during the reign of Chulalongkorn. Notwithstanding the pursuit of REFORMS AND MODERNIZATION IN SIAM, the traditional institution of absolute monarchy remained unquestioned.

While Chulalongkorn's REFORMS AND MODERNIZATION OF SIAM were being implemented and the ETHICAL POLICY (*ETHISCHE POLITIEK*) was under way in the DUTCH EAST INDIES, BRITISH BURMA was grappling with moving colonial policy from a laissez-faire approach to an active, committed administration beginning in the late 1890s. Dictated by the GOVERNMENT OF BRITISH INDIA, as BRITISH BURMA was a part of British India, a British system of administration was adopted after 1826 with priority placed on maintaining law and order. However, after 1897 a more active role was played by the colonial administration, attending to socioeconomic problems and infrastructural development. All vestiges of the traditional administrative structure of the KONBAUNG DYNASTY (1752–1885) were eliminated, retaining only the *thugyis,* or headmen, at the village level. The age-old institution of the HLUTDAW, an advisory council of ministers (*wungyis*) to the monarch, was dispensed with like other traditional officials. British colonial officials assumed the role of tax collectors, magistrates, school inspectors, and welfare officers. Although it was undeniable that the colonial administration was efficient, the cold and impersonal nature of British officers created a conspicuous gulf between ruler and ruled.

British and Indian private enterprise was given a free hand in the economic develop-

ment of BURMA UNDER BRITISH COLONIAL RULE, which by the early decades of the twentieth century had transformed Lower Burma into a major rice-producing and -exporting region of the world and RANGOON (YANGON) into an international port. INDIAN IMMIGRANTS were a cheap and plentiful pool of labor (both skilled and unskilled) that dominated the export sector of the economy. Indian laborers were engaged for public works, while Indian clerks attended to the paperwork of the Western (mostly British) commercial firms. Indians also dominated the medical profession, the railways, and postal and telegraph services. Chinese vied with Indians as shopkeepers, retailers, and middlemen in the profitable rice trade. CHETTIARS (CHETTYARS), the Indian money-lending clan, exploited the ignorance of illiterate indigenous farmers of the British credit facilities that provided much-needed capital for rice cultivation; the farmers pledged their rice fields as collateral on their loans. Crop failures or a dip in rice prices meant the foreclosure of the land by the CHETTIARS (CHETTYARS). Absentee-landlordism, peasant indebtedness, and the phenomenon of the landless indigenous farmer were widespread, especially in Lower Burma where commercial monoculture of rice was the norm.

The absence of the Burmese monarchy meant a loss in patronage of the arts (literature, music, and dance), and consequently cultural decay set in. Together with the moral decline of the *SANGHA,* the sociocultural and religious landscape of BRITISH BURMA appeared desolate and impoverished. Notwithstanding the establishment of the BURMA RESEARCH SOCIETY (1909) to study, preserve, and promote the country's history and sociocultural heritage, it had scant impact on the overall situation.

The plural population phenomenon consequent of BURMA UNDER BRITISH COLONIAL RULE was replicated in BRITISH MALAYA. In fact the bulk of the CHINESE IN SOUTHEAST ASIA settled in BRITISH MALAYA, with PENANG (1786), SINGAPORE (1819), and KUALA LUMPUR (KL) possessing overwhelming Chinese majorities. The TIN industry of the WESTERN MALAY STATES (PERAK, SELANGOR, NEGRI SEMBILAN, AND PAHANG) ushered in large waves of Chinese immigrants (mostly Cantonese) from the 1840s. INDIAN IMMIGRANTS started to arrive in huge numbers in the early years of the twentieth century in response to the high demand for labor on the RUBBER estates. Public works in HIGHWAYS AND RAILWAYS also relied heavily on Indian labor. But the socioeconomic problems arising in BRITISH BURMA were largely avoided in BRITISH MALAYA. Nonetheless the emergence of a plural school system—English, Chinese, Malay, Tamil—sowed the unhealthy seeds of separatism among the various ethnic groups.

The PHILIPPINES UNDER SPANISH COLONIAL RULE (ca. 1560s–1898) witnessed the process of HISPANIZATION. SPANISH FRIARS (THE PHILIPPINES) became increasingly influential and repeatedly intervened in administrative matters, consequently straining the FRIAR-SECULAR RELATIONSHIP. The traditional administrative structure of PRE-HISPANIC PHILIPPINES was retained with the *datu* (non-royal chiefs) overseeing village administration and the BARANGAY as the smallest political unit. The *adelantado* (governor-cum-captain-general) headed an oligarchical form of government whereby power lay in a few hands, be it at the level of the *BARANGAY, pueblo* (group of *BARANGAY*), or *provincia* (province). The *CACIQUES* (the indigenous class of chieftains), together with Spanish colonial officials and SPANISH FRIARS (THE PHILIPPINES), oppressed and exploited the Filipino peasantry, exacting from them tribute (*vandala*) and labor (*polo*).

The teaching and use of Spanish were restricted; Tagalog, the language of the lowlands of LUZON, was the preferred choice for the indigenous inhabitants. SPANISH FRIARS (THE PHILIPPINES) used Tagalog in their pastoral work.

The Spanish introduced a monetized economy of using silver for transactions of goods and services. Silver from the mines of Spanish Mexico was plentiful. Chinese luxury products such as silk and CERAMICS were bought with silver, and MANILA facilitated this highly lucrative trade. Chinese traders soon became residents, and a quarter in MANILA designated the Parian housed the Chinese community. As elsewhere in MELAKA, PENANG (1786), and BATAVIA (SUNDA KELAPA, JACATRA, DJAKARTA/JAKARTA), MISCE-GENATION produced a PERANAKAN community in MANILA.

MANILA was an important port of call of the fabulously rich GALLEON TRADE, which operated from 1593 to 1815. Chinese junks brought the highly prized silk and CERAMICS to MANILA. Spanish galleons with cargoes of silver bullion from Mexican and Peruvian mines sailed transpacific from Acapulco to MANILA. The junks, laden with silver, journeyed home, while the galleons returned to Acapulco with Chinese luxury goods. From Mexico the Chinese cargo crossed the Atlantic to Madrid, where it fetched high prices in the European market. The Filipinos were mere bystanders to this profitable transcontinental trade operating from their doorstep.

The Filipino peasant farmers were forced through *polo* labor to work on the government-owned plantations of commercial crops that enriched the colonial regime. The most successful export crops undertaken in the SPANISH PHILIPPINES were TOBACCO, ABACA (MANILA HEMP), and SUGAR.

VIETNAM UNDER FRENCH COLONIAL RULE was administratively structured under a French residential system headed by a governor-general responsible to the ministry of marine and colonies in Paris. A lieutenant governor administered COCHIN CHINA, while a *resident particulier* (senior resident) was appointed for the protectorates of ANNAM and TONKIN (TONGKING), as well as for CAMBODIA (EIGHTEENTH TO NINETEENTH CENTURIES) and LAOS (NINETEENTH CENTURY TO MID-1990s). French control over the colony of COCHIN CHINA was far more penetrating under direct rule to the village level than in the protectorates, where a less regimented, semiautonomous state of affairs existed. In fact, CAMBODIA UNDER FRENCH COLONIAL RULE was described as a "painless colonialism." Governor-General Paul Doumer (t. 1897–1902) resolved various difficulties, such as making the colony and protectorates profitable concerns through fiscal and economic reforms. HIGHWAYS AND RAILWAYS linked SAIGON (GIA DINH, HỒ CHÍ MINH CITY) to HANOI (THANG-LONG) and the port of Haiphong to Kunming in YUNNAN PROVINCE. French capitalists, the Banque de l'Indochine (Bank of Indochina), and a handful of Vietnamese landowners benefited from the export-oriented cultivation of rice and RUBBER on vast plantations. The majority of the Vietnamese peasantry suffered from indebtedness; others were landless tenant farmers, and those who drifted to the towns subsisted as lowly paid coolies or seasonal laborers.

A middle class emerged as a result of VIETNAM UNDER FRENCH COLONIAL RULE. The redistribution of land benefited some quarters of the peasantry who prudently leased out their land to tenant farmers, making a small fortune from land rent. Those Vietnamese who possessed a smattering of the French language and who held subordinate, clerical appointments in the lower rungs of the colonial administrative machinery joined the ranks of the middle class. The middle class sent their children to French-language schools to earn the recognized paper qualifications for a civil service appointment. Students who performed well at the *lycées* (French secondary schools) with financial support from their middle-class parents could pursue tertiary education in one of the universities in France. But frustrations set in upon their return home, as they were denied appointments commensurate with their French-earned qualifications. Regardless of the policy of "assimilation," discrimination in position and salary persisted against the Vietnamese in spite of their French education.

In line with the introduction of WESTERN SECULAR EDUCATION, the French established the prestigious ÉCOLE FRANÇAISE D'EXTRÊME-ORIENT as a research center for the study of Asia. Such an elitist institution was meaningless to the illiterate Vietnamese coolie; likewise the modern HIGHWAYS AND RAILWAYS to the rural peasant farmer tilling his rice field of less than an acre. Small sections of the indigenous population of Southeast Asia reaped benefits during the colonial period. The vast majority of the inhabitants, however, suffered under the colonial yoke.

Struggle for Freedom

Protracted struggles resisting the advancement of colonial domination were exemplified in the case of the MOROS in MINDANAO and the southern Philippines against Spanish IMPERIALISM and COLONIALISM. Similarly, the Dutch fought the long and arduous ACEH (ACHEH) WARS (1873–1903). But once colonial rule had been imposed, the avenues and possibilities for resistance became more restrictive. The ANTI-SPANISH REVOLTS (THE PHILIPPINES) were sporadic, parochial, and isolated—hence their easy suppression; likewise the Vietnamese and Javanese peasant uprisings against French and Dutch colonial authorities, respectively. On the other hand the JAVA WAR (1825–1830), and to a lesser extent the MAT SALLEH REBELLION of 1894 to 1905 and the Saya San Rebellion (1930–1931), revealed the vulnerability and rejection of the established colonial regime.

Oppression, exploitation, discrimination, and downright bullying characterized the colonial experience in Southeast Asia. The peasant farming masses across the region were the hardest hit because of their small, insignificant voice. To be sure, precolonial Southeast Asia was no peasant paradise; on the contrary, indigenous rulers were rapacious, ruthless, and even cruel in the treatment of the masses. But the peasants could move en masse, depriving the potentate of tributes, foodstuffs, and labor if treatment was deemed too harsh. The colonial period, with clear-cut, designated territorial boundaries marked out by the rival Western powers, formed a kind of cage for all inhabitants, restricting freedom of movement from one colonized country to its colonized neighbor. With nowhere to run or hide, the peasantry of Southeast Asia bowed to the demands of their colonial masters.

PEASANT UPRISINGS AND PROTEST MOVEMENTS IN SOUTHEAST ASIA represented bottled-up frustrations, dissatisfactions more often than not economic in origin. Millenarian beliefs of a "golden age," often translated as a return to precolonial times, propagated by a charismatic individual, brought hope to the weary peasant masses that willingly climbed on the bandwagon. Millenarianism, usually with a religious twist, could invoke a huge following among the people. What is more, a *jihad,* or holy war of Islamic tradition, declared on the infidel colonial regime could swell the ranks of a rebel army.

It would be naive to assume that the various PEASANT UPRISINGS AND PROTEST MOVEMENTS IN SOUTHEAST ASIA were nationalistic expressions. Whether they were based on economic or religious grounds, or the ushering in of some millenarian golden age, there was scant thought of the idea of a united struggle for a nation-state. Ironically, it was during the colonial period that Southeast Asia possessed fixed political boundaries of nation-states mirroring the European continent. WESTERN SECULAR EDUCATION was the second irony. Introduced and promoted by the colonial regimes, the liberal education exposed Southeast Asians to the ideals of the French Revolution (1789–1799): *Liberté, Fraternité,* and *Egalité* (Liberty, Fraternity, and Equality). These liberal aspirations, combined with the sense of belonging to a nation-state, gradually instilled among the inhabitants of Southeast Asia a nationalistic consciousness. Furthermore, during the colonial period ethnic differentiation became increasingly apparent, thereby creating the identification of ethnicity and country, indigenous and immigrant.

Moreover, NATIONALISM AND INDEPENDENCE MOVEMENTS IN SOUTHEAST ASIA received impetus from the international arena. Japan's humiliating defeat of IMPERIAL CHINA and czarist RUSSIA in the Sino-Japanese War (1894–1895) and Russo-Japanese War (1904–1905), respectively, was a flowering tribute to the grand achievements of Japan's modernization program following the Meiji Restoration (1868). Japan's entry into the GREAT WAR (1914–1918) on the side of Britain and France signaled the equality of an Asian nation with the Western powers. To many Southeast Asians, Japan was a role model for emulation. During the early decades of the twentieth century the tumultuous events on the Chinese mainland were observed closely, thanks to NEWSPAPERS AND MASS MEDIA IN SOUTHEAST ASIA. DR. SUN YAT-SEN (1866–1925) and his revolutionary ideology *sanmin zhuyi* (Three Principles of the People—namely, Nationalism, Democracy, and People's Livelihood) impacted positively on the region. More inspiring were the unfolding of events: the CHINESE REVOLUTION (1911), the collapse of the QING (CHING/MANCHU) DYNASTY (1644–1912), and the emergence of NATIONALIST CHINA. The Russian Bolshevik Revolution (1917) introduced to the world the first nation to embrace COMMUNISM. The ISLAMIC RESURGENCE IN SOUTHEAST ASIA (TWENTIETH CENTURY) was a wake-up call to Muslims for self-evaluation and making Islam relevant to the modern world.

Within Southeast Asia the Filipino experience in nationalist awakening was inspiring, despite witnessing the closure of one colonial chapter (PHILIPPINES UNDER SPANISH COLONIAL RULE [ca. 1560s–1898]) only to open another colonial era (PHILIPPINES UNDER U.S. COLONIAL ADMINISTRATION [1898–1946]). While the various localized ANTI-SPANISH REVOLTS (The PHILIPPINES) had little bearing or significance, recalcitrant behavior on the part of certain Filipinos during the course of the nineteenth century had a great influence on the national psyche, leading eventually to the PHILIPPINE REVOLUTION (1896–1898).

Two events greatly spurred the growth of Filipino nationalism. In 1841, Spanish soldiers massacred hundreds of members of the *Cofradia de San José,* an *indios* (indigenous Filipino) religious organization headed by APOLINARIO DE LA CRUZ (1814/1815–1841). Then, in 1872, the Spanish colonial government ordered the execution by garroting of three prominent Filipino priests accused of conspiracy in the CAVITE MUTINY. But the reformers, rather than the revolutionaries, took the initiative.

Filipino students studying in Europe, including JOSE RIZAL (1861–1896), joined the PROPAGANDA MOVEMENT. Through its newsletter *LA SOLIDARIDAD,* the PROPAGANDA MOVEMENT during the 1880s and 1890s sought to convince the Spanish public and in turn the government in Madrid that reforms were needed in the Philippines. In line with this strategy were the publications of *NOLI ME TANGERE* (1887) AND *EL FILIBUSTERISMO* (1891), two novels by JOSÉ RIZAL (1861–1896) that exposed the defects of the Spanish colonial administration and the frightful and intolerable conditions of the Filipino peasantry. Neither the Spanish public nor the Madrid government gave any serious attention to the PROPAGANDA MOVEMENT.

The revolutionary phase began with the establishment of LA LIGA FILIPINA by JOSÉ RIZAL (1861–1896) in 1892, which aimed at the improvement of the lot of the Filipinos. Shortly thereafter Rizal was arrested and deported to Dapitan, MINDANAO. The suppression of LA LIGA FILIPINA led to a split: those who remained convinced of the reformist line continued contributing to *LA SOLIDARI-DAD*, whereas others joined the revolutionary KATIPUNAN.

Under the leadership of ANDRES BONI-FACIO (1863–1897), the KATIPUNAN spearheaded the PHILIPPINE REVOLU-TION (1896–1898), which broke out prematurely in August 1896. In December 1896, JOSÉ RIZAL (1861–1896) was executed by firing squad, accused of conspiring in the uprising. In death Rizal became even more potent in inspiring the nationalist struggle for independence.

Rivalry within the KATIPUNAN between ANDRES BONIFACIO (1863–1897) and EMILIO AGUINALDO (1869–1964) resulted in the execution of the former under orders from the latter. In January 1899 the revolutionary government declared the Philippines an independent republic with a written constitution. APOLINARIO MABINI (1864–1903) was the prime composer of the constitution.

While the PHILIPPINE REVOLUTION (1896–1898) was under way, the SPANISH-AMERICAN WAR (1898) broke out. COM-MODORE GEORGE DEWEY (1837–1917) destroyed the Spanish fleet in Manila Bay. The Americans supported EMILIO AGUINALDO (1869–1964) in his revolutionary struggle. With better arms supplied by their U.S. ally and support from all strata of Filipino society, the revolutionaries managed to bring most of LUZON under their control. In June 1898 the revolutionary government confidently declared the Philippines independent from Spain. Allowing the Americans to take MANILA, however, EMILIO AGUINALDO (1869–1964) and his followers were cheated of their freedom. The SPANISH-AMERICAN TREATY OF PARIS (1898) ceded the sovereignty of the Philippines from Spanish hands to the United States.

The PHILIPPINE WAR OF INDEPEN-DENCE (1899–1902) was basically a guerrilla war fought between a bitter and betrayed EMILIO AGUINALDO (1869–1964) and his revolutionary militia and the disciplined, well-equipped army of the United States. The Americans were determined to secure the Philippines, invoking a MANIFEST DES-TINY. Following the surrender of EMILIO

AGUINALDO (1869–1964), the struggle against the United States rapidly subsided.

The PHILIPPINES UNDER U.S. COLO-NIAL ADMINISTRATION (1900–1941) witnessed CONSTITUTIONAL DEVELOP-MENTS IN THE PHILIPPINES (1900–1941), preparing the Filipinos and the country for self-rule and eventual independence. The pace of progress seesawed between U.S. Republican and Democrat administrations. U.S. administrators who played prominent roles in preparing the country for self-government were WILLIAM HOWARD TAFT (1857–1930) and FRANCIS BURTON HARRI-SON (1873–1957). On the Filipino side MANUEL LUIS QUEZON (1878–1944) and SERGIO OSMENA SR. (1878–1961) were leading figures. FILIPINIZATION of the administration was carried out. In the economic field, the Filipinos were given preferential access to U.S. markets and benefited from this closer relationship, often referred to enviously as the PHILIPPINES–U.S. "SPECIAL RELA-TIONSHIP," which also extended to the political sphere. Landmark legislation, the Tydings-McDuffie Act of 1934, established the Commonwealth of the Philippines in 1935, and within a decade the Philippines would be granted independence. But the JAPANESE OCCUPATION OF SOUTHEAST ASIA (1941–1945) disrupted the independence timetable of the Philippines.

BURMA UNDER BRITISH COLO-NIAL RULE nurtured anti-British and anti-Indian feelings among the indigenous Burmese population, the former resented as colonial political masters and the latter as economic oppressors. Burmese nationalistic consciousness manifested in political, economic, and religious terms all targeted toward the British colonial administration at RANGOON.

The early expression of Burmese nationalism was in the cultural field. Among the organizations aimed at resuscitating Buddhist traditions and cultural heritage were the YOUNG MEN'S BUDDHIST ASSOCIATION (YMBA) (1906) and the BURMA RESEARCH SOCI-ETY (1909).

THE GREAT WAR (1914–1918), which disrupted and curtailed shipping, exacerbated the dire situation of the Burmese peasantry with the halt to the export of rice, the staple income earner. This economic disaster added to the bitterness of the Burmese toward the colonial regime, as well as toward the CHETTIARS (CHETTYARS) and Indian absentee landlords. But ironically, the Burmese gained inspiration from the nationalist movement of "Mahatma" Gandhi (1869–1948), particularly the potency of "civil disobedience," boycotts, and strikes. On the other hand, members of the dispirited SANGHA led violent mobs in unruly antigovernment demonstrations.

From the 1920s, aggressive, violent, and politically motivated nationalist activities became the norm. The opening of the UNIVERSITY OF RANGOON in 1920 witnessed a massive student strike objecting to colonial education policy. As BRITISH BURMA was considered a part of INDIA, CONSTITUTIONAL DEVELOPMENTS IN BURMA (1900–1941) mirrored those of the subcontinent. In 1923 the GENERAL COUNCIL OF BURMESE ASSOCIATIONS (GCBA) (1920) opposed through boycott and violence the implementation of dyarchy government in the country. The GREAT DEPRESSION (1929–1931) devastated the lives of the Burmese peasantry, while rice stocks stood idle in the RANGOON (YANGON) docks, as all export shipments were canceled owing to the absence of buyers. The Hsaya San Rebellion (1930–1931) capitalized on the dire economic situation in garnering support that swelled its rebel ranks. In attempting a monarchical restoration, the uprising injected a large dose of Burmese pride into their traditional institutions, further boosting nationalistic consciousness. DR. BA MAW (b. 1893) gained prominence as Hsaya San's defense attorney.

From the 1930s, Burmese nationalists began to append THAKIN to their names to declare that they and not the British were the rightful masters in Burma. A constitution was granted in 1935. In 1937, Burma was separated from INDIA and came directly under the British Parliament in London. A Westminster-style parliamentary government was introduced with DR. BA MAW (b. 1893) as prime minister. He had the support of the THAKIN, the most prominent being AUNG SAN (1915–1947). Not satisfied with the CONSTITUTIONAL DEVELOPMENTS IN BURMA (1900–1941), DR. BA MAW (b. 1893) and the THAKIN turned to Japan for assistance.

Indonesian nationalism aimed at political independence as the ultimate goal but also strove for socioeconomic reforms to improve the livelihood and welfare of the population. The PRIYAYI, Java's traditional aristocratic-bureaucratic elite, had benefited from the fruits of Dutch colonialism, serving as subordinate administrators alongside Dutch officials; they now began to reevaluate their role. Younger members of the PRIYAYI, products of Dutch-language schools and higher education, increasingly rejected appointments in the lower rungs of the colonial bureaucracy mainly as clerical staff, positions once held by their grandfathers and fathers. Instead, many aspired to professional careers as doctors, engineers, and schoolteachers, but there were few such openings under colonial rule. Nevertheless, having themselves benefited from WESTERN SECULAR EDUCATION, they argued for the wider provision of Dutch-language schools and higher educational institutions accessible to all Indonesians and not only the privileged few. WESTERN SECULAR EDUCATION was seen as the passport to freedom, as well as a means of improving their socioeconomic status.

RADEN AJENG KARTINI (1879–1904), a Javanese princess of the royal family of Japara and reputedly the first Indonesian feminist, promoted female education as a means of emancipation. Using a curriculum of Dutch and local subject matter, she established "Kartini Schools" throughout JAVA. Kartini was an inspiration to the early awakening of Indonesian nationalistic consciousness. Dr. Wahidin Soedirohoesodo, who had assisted Kartini in her educational crusade, established BOEDI OETAMA (BUDI UTOMO) (1908). Basically an intellectual, PRIYAYI-dominated organization, it attempted a cultural renaissance of Javanese aristocratic culture and a synthesis of Asian and European culture. At the same time, BOEDI OETAMA (BUDI UTOMO) (1908) promoted the spread of WESTERN SECULAR EDUCATION.

Within a short period, the Javanese-based, elitist PRIYAYI organization that had education and sociocultural issues as its priority was taken over as a politicized organization with mass support. In the early part of this political phase in Indonesian nationalism, socioeconomic and religious aspirations were prominent.

SAREKAT ISLAM (1912), originating with Sarekat Dagang Islam (1909), promoted the economic progress of Indonesians. Its highly respected leader, HAJI OEMAR SAID

TJOKROAMINOTO (1882–1934), relied effectively on Islam as the rallying point for garnering members and supporters numbering in the thousands, with branches throughout JAVA and beyond. In 1916 cries for self-government were heard, alarming the Dutch colonial government. Fearing a concerted challenge, the Dutch denied recognition of a central body of SAREKAT ISLAM (1912), instead giving official sanction only to its branches. Even more demanding was the PERANAKAN National Indische Partij (National Indies Party) (1912), which argued for socioeconomic equality and political independence. Highly vocal, the leaders of the Indische Partij demanded that the DUTCH EAST INDIES belong to those who had permanently settled and made it their home.

In response to the clamor from various quarters for a say in the administration, as well as the overall decentralization and democratization process under the ETHICAL POLICY (*ETHISCHE POLITIEK*), the VOLKSRAAD (PEOPLE'S COUNCIL) (1918–1942) was constituted. The membership of this unicameral parliament was along ethnic lines—namely, Dutch, Indonesians, and "foreign Orientals" (usually Chinese). The Indonesian members tended to be conservative, and not highly nationalistic. HAJI AGUS SALIM (1884–1954) was the representative of SAREKAT ISLAM (1912) between 1921 and 1924. Despite moving from an advisory role to acquiring limited legislative powers in the mid-1920s, and even sanctioning the budget in the early 1930s, the VOLKSRAAD (PEOPLE'S COUNCIL) (1918–1942) did not satiate nationalist aspirations for greater command of their destiny.

Attending to the challenges of the ISLAMIC RESURGENCE IN SOUTHEAST ASIA (TWENTIETH CENTURY), religious parties such as MUHAMMADIYAH and NAHDATUL ULAMA emerged. Nonpolitical and modernist in outlook, the MUHAMMADIYAH, established in 1912, aimed at improving the welfare and religiosity of the Muslim community through Islamic-based education and social programs. Defending the orthodox view, NAHDATUL ULAMA, set up in 1926, was an influential bastion of traditionalism. Opposing the modernist emphasis on the sole authority of the Qur'an and Hadiths, the traditionalists relied on the teaching authority of the *ulama* (Islamic scholars) and their diversity of thought. NAHDATUL ULAMA propagated their thought through the *KIAI* (Islamic teachers) and their *pesantren* (religious boarding schools). Members of NAHDATUL ULAMA undertook social welfare work in eastern rural JAVA. MUHAMMADIYAH and NAHDATUL ULAMA, each in its own sphere of influence—cities and urban areas and rural communities, respectively—brought about an awakening and pride in Islam vis-à-vis the Protestant Dutch colonial masters.

Alongside the Islamic resurgence, KEBATINAN MOVEMENTS emerged in the early 1900s. Their members practiced indigenous Javanese ancestral culture that predated Hindu-Buddhist influences. It was a wholly indigenous spiritual movement that gave Indonesians—the Javanese in particular—a sense of identity and pride in their ancient culture. Rejecting both Western and Islamic modernist influences was the TAMAN SISWA (1922). A homegrown educational association, its string of schools focused on promoting indigenous (mainly Javanese) social values and cultural heritage. The contribution of TAMAN SISWA (1922) to the nationalist cause was in its inculcation of an Indonesian sociocultural identity that made the people proud to be "Indonesian."

PARTAI KOMUNIS INDONESIA (PKI) (1920) was by far the most radical nationalist movement, with COMMUNISM as its ideological engine. SEMAOEN (SEMAUN) (1899–1971) and IBRAHIM DATUK TAN MALAKA (1897?–1949), both communists who became leaders of PARTAI KOMUNIS INDONESIA (PKI) 1920, attempted to infiltrate and seize control of SAREKAT ISLAM (1912). They, however, failed. Within a short time of its emergence, the Dutch colonial government proscribed the party, forcing PARTAI KOMUNIS INDONESIA (PKI) (1920) to operate underground for the greater part of its existence throughout the 1920s. Full political independence, adopting COMMUNISM as the national ideology, was the ultimate objective of the PARTAI KOMUNIS INDONESIA (PKI) (1920), which garnered the bulk of support from the urban proletariat and some peasantry. But PARTAI KOMUNIS INDONESIA (PKI) (1920) tended to portray an internationalist outlook rather than an Indonesian nationalistic struggle. The communists swerved the nationalist movement into revolutionary, militant gear.

Having captured large sections of mostly urban proletariat, PARTAI KOMUNIS INDONESIA (PKI) (1920) launched a series of strikes between 1923 and 1926 as a strategy to cripple the Indonesian economy and bring down the Dutch colonial government. Into this orchestrated chaos, the communists would seize control of the country and establish a communist regime under its leadership. In an ambitious plan in 1926, a full-scale revolution erupted in SUMATRA and BANTEN (BANTAM).

Repression was swift and harsh throughout the archipelago. Thousands were arrested and faced imprisonment; suspected leaders and hard-core elements were deported to internment camps in Papua New Guinea. The Dutch colonial government effectively crushed the communists, and PARTAI KOMUNIS INDONESIA (PKI) (1920) was dealt a severe blow that it never recovered from during the remainder of Dutch rule.

Like their Filipino counterparts abroad, Indonesian students studying in The Netherlands organized into the Perhimpunan Indonesia (Indonesian Union), which demanded outright independence. Although formed in 1922, it came into prominence only in 1927, after the failed communist putsch. Returned students set up study clubs as a means of organizing support. The major contribution of the Perhimpunan Indonesia was in its emphasis on Indonesian independence above all other concerns.

In this spirit, SOEKARNO (SUKARNO) (1901–1970), who was a member of the Bandung study club, together with others, founded the PERSERIKATAN NASIONAL INDONESIA (PNI) (1927). Its strategy was to unite all Indonesians under the umbrella of secular nationalism and to achieve independence through a policy of noncooperation with the colonial authorities. The fiery speeches of the gifted SOEKARNO (SUKARNO) (1901–1970) were like a beacon, attracting huge popular support from the masses. The PNI's unity plan attained some success in the formation of Permuafakatan Perhimpunan Politiek Kebangsaan Indonesia (Union of National Political Associations of Indonesia). But the arrest of the charismatic SOEKARNO (SUKARNO) (1901–1970) in late 1929 doomed the PNI, which folded in 1931.

MINANGKABAU nationalists such as SUTAN SJAHRIR (1909–1966) and MOHAMMAD HATTA (1902–1980) formed the socialist Club Pendidekan Nasional Indonesia in 1932, aimed at educating the people in nationalist principles. For their efforts, both were deported to Papua New Guinea in 1934.

AMIR SJARIFUDDIN (1907–1948), together with R. M. Sartono, formed Partai Indonesia (Partindo) in 1931. Its objectives mirrored those of the PNI. Upon release from prison in 1931, SOEKARNO (SUKARNO) (1901–1970) joined Partai Indonesia (Partindo) and was made its chairman. Thanks to his inspiring speeches, membership rapidly surged and branches were set up in most urban centers of JAVA. Realizing the potential danger that SOEKARNO (SUKARNO) (1901–1970) posed, the Dutch authorities had him arrested in 1933. The next time he stepped out of prison was to witness the raising of the Japanese *hinomaru* (red rising sun against a white background, the flag of Imperial Japan) over Indonesia.

The colonial Dutch government had by 1935 silenced all dissenting voices to its rule. The term "INDONESIA" was proscribed, as its increasingly subversive use among nationalists crystallized their aspirations of an independent, multiethnic polity to replace the DUTCH EAST INDIES. Organizations that then survived were those focusing on social and Islamic concerns (MUHAMMADIYAH and NAHDATUL ULAMA) or educational issues (TAMAN SISWA [1922]). Even the mild proposal of the SOETARDJO PETITION (1936) requesting a discussion of the constitutional position of Indonesia was given an outright rejection. However, when a similar proposal was voiced in the WIWOHO RESOLUTION (1940), a commission of inquiry was initiated. Then the Pacific War (1941–1945) broke out.

VIETNAM UNDER FRENCH COLONIAL RULE sparked opposition that initially came from members of the NGUYỄN DYNASTY (1802–1945) and the scholar-gentry class, which primarily sought the restoration of the traditional rule of the emperor; later, from the 1920s, it came from moderate intellectuals, and throughout the 1930s, radical revolutionaries led by the communists. The French colonial administration eliminated the traditional group with ease and brushed aside reform-minded Vietnamese intellectuals. Repressive offensives were launched against the communists but failed to extinguish their influence.

CAN VUONG (AID THE KING) MOVEMENT was an attempt to garner support for the restoration of the young emperor Hàm-Nghi, who had fled in 1885. It invoked patriotism, attracting peasant support mainly from the provinces of ANNAM—Nghe An, Hà Tinh, and Thanh Hóa. By 1897 French forces had snuffed out those uprisings that took the form of guerrilla-style opposition. The mandarin class at the beginning of the twentieth century was in despair, having witnessed the failure of opposition and the impotence of the monarchy in the face of French IMPERIALISM and COLONIALISM. A feeling of uselessness and hopelessness became pervasive among the scholar-gentry class, and also trickled down to the peasantry, becoming associated with the term MAT NUOC (LOSING ONE'S COUNTRY). It was coined by the Vietnamese intellectual PHAN BÔI CHÂU (1867–1940), who in his essays argued that if the Vietnamese did not improve themselves, the result would be annihilation by the French. It was therefore imperative to set in motion a sociopolitical revolution that was aimed not only at rejecting French rule but also at rejuvenating Vietnamese society. PHAN BÔI CHÂU (1867–1940) looked to emulate Japan, which had succeeded marvelously in modernization (equated with Westernization) but at the same time had retained much of Japanese tradition and culture. He journeyed to Japan to seek assistance; several Vietnamese students followed in his footsteps.

PHAN CHAU TRINH (1872–1926) agreed that revitalizing Vietnamese society was essential to unshackle the country from foreign rule. To him the monarchical system was outdated; he firmly advocated Western republicanism. The strategy he proposed was to embark on reforms and the process of modernization, based on the Western model. The caveat, however, was not to rely exclusively on foreign assistance, as advocated by his fellow reform-minded activists. At the same time he opposed the mindset that considered the force of arms as the only way of attaining freedom from COLONIALISM. Instead he favored moderate means and proposed that a series of reforms be gradually introduced into the French colonial system in Vietnam. A keen supporter of Đông

Kinh Nghia Thuc (Free School of the Eastern Capital [Hanoi] for the Just Cause), a patriotic educational organization that utilized QUÔC NGÙ (romanized script of the Vietnamese language) in teaching Western science and technology, he fervently believed this approach would provide the much-needed sociopolitical change.

The first Vietnamese political organization, Viet Nam Quang Phuc Hoi (Association for the Restoration of Vietnam), the brainchild of PHAN BÔI CHÂU (1867–1940), was clandestinely and illegally established in 1913. Within a short time, the French colonial authorities suppressed it and imprisoned its founder.

Advocates of the line of thought of PHAN CHAU TRINH (1872–1926) established political organizations that cooperated with the French colonial administration—namely, the Constitutional Party (1923) and the Viet Nam People's Progressive Party (1926). Little, however, was achieved. He was enthroned as the Nguyễn emperor BÅO ĐAI (VĨNH THỤY) (1913–1997) in 1926; his return in 1932 following studies in France saw the young monarch attempting to effect reforms and modernization from the imperial court at HUE. Proposals for greater autonomy and for self-government mooted by BÅO ĐAI (VĨNH THỤY) (1913–1997) were flatly rejected by the French.

Failure of the moderate, collaborationist group led to the ascendancy of radical nationalists that favored revolutionary and militant methods in the struggle for freedom. Although the CAO DAI was a religious organization, its adherents were reactionaries that sought the overthrow of the French and the restoration of Prince Cuong De. But a more formidable revolutionary force was the VIET NAM QUOC DAN DANG (VNQDD) (VIETNAMESE NATIONALIST PARTY). Modeled on the KUOMINTANG (KMT) of DR. SUN YAT-SEN (1866–1925), this revolutionary organization sought the overthrow of the French colonial regime and its replacement with a Chinese-style republican government. The clandestinely established VNQDD built up a following from a cross section of Vietnamese society: the landed gentry, civil servants, soldiers, schoolteachers, and students. But a botched assassination of French officials and betrayal led to the ruthless suppression of this foremost noncommunist revolutionary organization in 1930.

Into this vacuum came the communists under the leadership of HỒ CHÍ MINH (1890–1969). He established the INDOCHINA COMMUNIST PARTY (JUNE 1929), which later was renamed the VIETNAMESE COMMUNIST PARTY (VCP) in 1930. ANNAM and especially TONKIN (TONGKING) were communist strongholds. The communists were equally successful in organizing the urban proletariat and the rural peasantry. The NGHE TINH SOVIETS (1930–1931) were set up in the provinces of Nghe An and Ha Tinh in ANNAM, representing model communist states. Terrorist tactics were employed in their attempt to cripple the economy. As with all opposition and subversive activities, the French colonial administration swung into swift and merciless repression.

From 1936 the communists in COCHIN CHINA, in accordance with a COMINTERN directive, adopted a "united front" strategy against fascism. The Popular Front government (t. 1936–1937) of Leon Blum (1872–1950) provided a conducive environment for the Vietnamese communists to operate in—but not so much anticolonialist as anti-Fascist. But toward the late 1930s, the French colonial authorities took repressive action against the communists consequent of an uprising.

In the face of an uncompromising French colonial government in Vietnam and harsh suppression of any semblance of challenge, the Vietnamese nationalist struggle, from reformers to revolutionaries, faced a dead end. The changing geopolitical situation ushered in by the outbreak of the Pacific War (1941–1945) offered a new dawn for Vietnamese patriots of various persuasions.

Anticolonial revolts in BRITISH BORNEO and BRITISH MALAYA in the nineteenth century were generally localized though protracted, offering little threat to the respective colonial regimes. RENTAP, the Iban warrior who opposed the rule of the white raja, staged a stout resistance that finally ended with the storming of his jungle fort atop a hill in 1857. He and some of his followers apparently escaped into the jungle in the area of the headwaters of the Skrang, Katibas, and Kanowit Rivers. His ability to rally supporters in opposition to Brooke rule made him a hero of the upriver IBANS. RENTAP represented a struggle against change to the traditional Iban way of life instituted by Rajah Brooke's regime. Likewise, the decade-long MAT SALLEH REBELLION against the administration of the BRITISH NORTH BORNEO CHARTERED COMPANY (1881–1946) between 1894 and 1905 resembled a traditional type of opposition to change from without.

The assassination of the British resident to Perak, J. W. W. BIRCH (1826–1875), at the hands of local Malay chiefs led by the Maharaja Lela in November 1875 was a response to the loss of traditional status and privileges of the Malay elite. Haste to effect reforms and introduce changes to the traditional administrative structure where the Malay chiefs were major players brought the British resident to a head-on collision with the chiefs. Local opposition in PAHANG in the late 1880s was instigated by chiefs who had lost political power, social status and prestige, and economic privileges. TO' JANGGUT (1853–1915), who led a brief uprising in Kelantan in 1915, fought for the return of the traditional way of life; the introduction of a new land tax provoked the rebellion.

The foregoing opposition to the implementation of colonial rule had scant hint of a nationalistic struggle. Neither was any millenarian or religious element present. Basically, the resistance resembled the response of traditional societies to change from without, resulting in the loss of freedom, power, status, and privileges by certain quarters and resort to arms and violence.

Malay nationalism began to manifest during the early decades of the twentieth century; the struggle was undertaken by three groups, each with its own agenda—namely, Muslim reformists, secular revolutionaries, and English-educated nationalists. SYED SHAYKH AL-HADY (1867?–1934), of Arab descent, was a reformist who maintained that the basic doctrines of Islam were in tune with modern, secular knowledge such as science and constitutional law. Female education was also stressed. Representing the *Kaum Muda* (modernist) against the *Kaum Tua* (traditionalists), he argued for the benefits of modern secular education, including the teaching of English to complement Islamic schooling, which emphasized religious doctrines. Through the influential *Al-Imam,* SYED SHAYKH AL-HADY (1867?–

1934) and his fellow reformists sought to win over the Malays to their progressive line of thought, which had some measure of success among urban Malays in the STRAITS SETTLEMENTS (1826–1946). The Arab reformists, despite having scant influence over the bulk of the Malay population in the peninsular Malay States, caused small ripples in Malay consciousness.

The formation of the KESATUAN MELAYU MUDA (KMM) (YOUNG MALAY UNION) in 1938 under the presidency of IBRAHIM YAACOB (1911–1979) galvanized the aspirations of the Malay-educated revolutionary group. It drew most of its membership from alumni of the SULTAN IDRIS TRAINING COLLEGE (SITC) and civil servants; the main objective was to overthrow the British colonial regime, including the Malay sultanates, and thereafter effect union with neighboring Indonesia. This revolutionary group failed to gain support from the conservative and parochial Malay peasantry. With only a handful of members, the KESATUAN MELAYU MUDA (KMM) (YOUNG MALAY UNION) awaited the entry of Japanese forces into BRITISH MALAYA at the outbreak of the Pacific War (1941–1945).

English-educated Malay nationalists were particularly conscious of Malay rights, special privileges, and unity of the community vis-à-vis other communal groups—namely, the British, Chinese, ARABS, and Indians. Alien domination in all sectors of the economy was apparent in the STRAITS SETTLEMENTS (1826–1946), and the clamor of the Chinese for equal rights as citizens of BRITISH MALAYA aroused the members of this group, who were from the aristocracy and high-ranking civil servants. Notwithstanding their stance in protecting Malay rights, the English-educated Malay nationalists were staunchly loyal to Britain, and nothing in their numerous discourses in the Malay press, in periodicals, or in speeches at the various Malay associations and clubs gave any hint of their questioning the presence of the British and colonial rule. They were to play prominent roles in the negotiations toward independence in the post-1945 period.

VAJIRAVUDH (RAMA VI) (r. 1910–1925) ascended the throne as the sixth ruler of the Chakri line of absolute monarchs. Even more Westernized in outlook than his father, Chula-

longkorn, as a result of his British education, his reign achieved remarkable success. In the field of education, recognized as an important component in the modernization process, VAJIRAVUDH (RAMA VI) (r. 1910–1925) instituted compulsory elementary education and the establishment of CHULALONGKORN UNIVERSITY in 1917. His reign saw an abrogation of extraterritoriality, acceded to by his successors so as to avoid any pretexts that might be used by the Western powers to compromise Siam's political independence. It was a significant diplomatic coup, as now the kingdom of Siam was in theory accorded equal standing with the Western powers.

"THE JEWS OF THE ORIENT," penned by VAJIRAVUDH (RAMA VI) (r. 1910–1925), offered a caveat to his fellow countrymen regarding the threat posed by the immigrant Chinese in the kingdom. This article, published in mid-1914, compared the Chinese to the Jews of Europe. The Chinese, he wrote, possessed three adverse characteristics: nonassimilation in their host society, superiority of attitude and contempt toward non-Chinese, and a highly mercenary approach to business. "THE JEWS OF THE ORIENT" cast aspersions on the Chinese community in Siam, and that prejudicial attitude persisted for a long time.

The extravagance, the nepotism, and the controversial lifestyle of VAJIRAVUDH (RAMA VI) (r. 1910–1925) were shortfalls that marred a remarkable reign. "THE JEWS OF THE ORIENT" stirred a national consciousness among the indigenous T'AIS.

PRAJADHIPOK (RAMA VII) (r. 1925–1935) inherited a serious deficit in the royal treasury and a contempt for the throne among the kingdom's emerging middle class. This Anglo-French-educated monarch created a supreme council of state to temper the excesses of absolutism by devolving power to a larger group of political leaders. All major decisions had to be a consensus among the monarch and all five members of the council, thus reducing arbitrariness and favoritism. The GREAT DEPRESSION (1929–1931), which hit Siam in 1930, seriously affecting rice, the major export earner, forced the government to implement drastic budgetary cuts to alleviate the fiscal situation. Then in 1932 a major crisis with long-term impact for the political landscape broke out.

THE CONSTITUTIONAL (BLOOD-LESS) REVOLUTION (1932) (THAILAND) ended 150 years of Chakri absolute monarchism. Within a brief three hours, the People's Party, comprising junior military officers and civilians, engineered a coup and instituted a constitutional monarchy. PRIDI PHANO-MYONG (1900–1983), a law instructor at CHULALONGKORN UNIVERSITY and a prime coup plotter, set about to draft a constitution based on the principle of popular sovereignty. The seeds of this revolution were sown toward the end of Chulalongkorn's reign, ironically as a result of the successes attained in the REFORMS AND MODERNIZATION IN SIAM. Social equality and justice were, however, overlooked in the modernization program, and princes and members of the nobility continued to wield power and influence. Centralization of the administration concentrated all power in the throne and the bureaucracy at BANGKOK. Republicanism then became an inviting alternative to the educated of common birth who held subordinate appointments in the military and civil administration. Little headway could be achieved during the reigns of Chulalongkorn and VAJIRAVUDH (RAMA VI) (r. 1910–1925). But the besieged reign of PRAJADHIPOK (RAMA VII) (r. 1925–1935), appearing always on the defensive, seemed the opportune time to launch the CONSTITU-TIONAL (BLOODLESS) REVOLUTION (1932) (THAILAND).

The first constitutional government established THAMMASAT UNIVERSITY in 1934 as the second public university aimed at teaching law and politics. The brainchild of PRIDI PHANOMYONG (1900–1983), THAM-MASAT UNIVERSITY was to embody the future of a democratic country, the engine of democratic thought and institutions for the people.

The success of the CONSTITUTIONAL (BLOODLESS) REVOLUTION (1932) (THAILAND) brought to the fore FIELD MARSHAL PLAEK PHIBUNSONG-KHRAM (1897–1964), who was credited with bringing the military into politics. (MILI-TARY AND POLITICS IN SOUTHEAST ASIA became a major theme in post-1945 developments.) As a member of the People's Party and the leading military officer in the

government, he further established his position following the failed Boworadet Rebellion of October 1933, when royalist-conservative elements attempted to overthrow the constitutional government. His first premiership (t. December 1938–July 1944) covered most of the period of the Pacific War (1941–1945). In June 1939 the kingdom of Siam became the kingdom of Thailand, emphasizing the nation as the "Land of the Free," the only country that retained its political independence while the rest of the neighboring territories in Southeast Asia were under Western colonial rule. In his characteristic authoritative style, FIELD MAR-SHAL PLAEK PHIBUNSONGKHRAM (1897–1964) attempted to instill a Thai identity and consciousness through language, appearance and mannerism, and a strong patriotic zeal and nationalism. His attitude and relations with the monarchy were at best lukewarm, which subsequently hurt his political survival. FIELD MARSHAL PLAEK PHIBUN-SONGKHRAM (1897–1964) brought Thailand into the Pacific War (1941–1945) as an ally of Imperial Japan.

Wars and Conflicts

The first half of the 1940s was dominated by the Pacific War (1941–1945) and the JAPA-NESE OCCUPATION OF SOUTHEAST ASIA (1941–1945). The second half of the decade witnessed the DECOLONIZATION OF SOUTHEAST ASIA, beginning with the Philippines (1946), Burma (1948), and Indonesia (1949). The following decade saw the attainment of independence for Cambodia (1953), Laos (1953), Vietnam (1954), and BRITISH MALAYA (1957). Some achieved their freedom peacefully, while others paid a high price in blood and tears; still others had a long, torturous path to freedom. Japanese fascism reigned over Southeast Asia from 1941, and after 1945 a battle for the "hearts and minds" between the Western democracies and the communist bloc ensued. Virtually all of Southeast Asia became a set piece in the COLD WAR. The two decades of the mid-twentieth century were filled with modern wars and conflicts, some extending to the last quarter of the century.

Prior to the military push to the south in late 1941, there was already a peaceful migration of

Japanese to Southeast Asia, beginning with the Meiji period (1868–1910). The early immigrants were peasant farmers followed by professionals (doctors, dentists), photographers, barbers, and prostitutes. The traffic of young women and girls from poor peasant families to supply inmates of brothels in the urban centers of Southeast Asia was a common phenomenon from the late nineteenth century. Japanese investment in mineral extraction and commercial agriculture (ABACA [MANILA HEMP], RUBBER) began to flow into the region in the early twentieth century. Cordial relations existed between JAPAN AND SOUTHEAST ASIA (PRE-1941). Western colonial regimes across the region welcomed Japanese immigrants and investments. The Japanese community largely kept to themselves and mostly assumed a low profile. Indigenous Southeast Asians viewed Japan and the Japanese with admiration and respect, an Asian model to emulate. The CHINESE IN SOUTHEAST ASIA were the only group who harbored reservations about the Japanese.

Japan's phenomenal achievement in modernization and proven military prowess over IMPERIAL CHINA (1894–1895) and Tsarist Russia (1904–1905) made it inclined to assume the leadership role over all of Asia. Besides providing a safe haven and providing military training and higher studies for nationalists from IMPERIAL CHINA, Japan also accommodated nationalists from Vietnam, Burma, and other Southeast Asian countries.

Southeast Asia, as the supplier of raw materials (OIL AND PETROLEUM, RUBBER, TIN, rice and other foodstuffs) to Japan and a market for its manufactured goods (mainly textiles), was economically vital. When denied access to the region by the Anglo-Americans in the late 1930s, Japan adopted the forward policy of annexing Southeast Asia. While the United States Pacific Fleet at Pearl Harbor in Hawai'i was being crippled on 8 December 1941, simultaneous amphibious landings of Japanese troops were under way in HONG KONG and on the beaches of Kota Bahru on the northeastern coast of the Malay Peninsula. Swift landings in other key points throughout Southeast Asia followed thereafter. MANILA was occupied on 2 January 1942, and in less than three months following the Kota Bahru landings, "FORTRESS SINGAPORE" surrendered to GENERAL YAMASHITA TOMOYUKI (1885–1946), dubbed the Tiger of Malaya, on 15 February 1942. By early March BATAVIA (SUNDA KELAPA, JACATRA, DJAKARTA/JAKARTA) and RANGOON (YANGON) had fallen. The military takeover of all of Southeast Asia was accomplished by the end of May 1942.

The situation in FRENCH INDOCHINA and Thailand was slightly different from that in the rest of Southeast Asia. Prior to hostilities, Japan, through arrangement with the French Vichy regime, had occupied the northern part of Indochina on 23 September 1940 and the southern portion on 29 July 1941. The government of FIELD MARSHAL PLAEK PHIBUNSONGKHRAM (1897–1964) (t. December 1938–July 1944) concluded the Pact of Alliance with Japan on 11 December 1941, which effectively sanctioned the de facto occupation of Thailand.

The overall military command of the Philippines was entrusted to U.S. GENERAL DOUGLAS MACARTHUR (1880–1964). The swift Japanese offensive launched from their base in occupied Vietnam caught the U.S. forces unprepared, and they began to retreat to the Bataan Peninsula and Corregidor. Lacking naval support and with the destruction of Clark Field depriving them of air support, there was little hope for the besieged Americans. Bataan surrendered on 9 April 1942, followed a month later by Corregidor on 6 May. The BATAAN DEATH MARCH consumed the lives of more than 10,000 U.S. and Filipino prisoners of war during the 120-kilometer, nine-day ordeal in early April 1942, their deaths brought about by malnutrition, disease, harsh treatment, and outright murder.

Prior to the surrender some U.S. and Filipino soldiers had fled to the jungles and highlands, where they conducted a guerrilla war against the Japanese. LUIS TARUC (1913–) organized the HUKBALAHAP (HUKBO NG BAYAN LABAN SA HAPON) (PEOPLE'S ANTI-JAPANESE ARMY) (1942), an anti-Japanese guerrilla band of peasant irregulars that operated in Central Luzon. Its strategy was aimed at depriving the enemy of food supplies and other essential resources and eliminating collaborators, mainly members of the landowning class and those who served in the constabulary that cooperated with the Japanese. Although the core members of the HUKBALA-HAP (HUKBO NG BAYAN LABAN SA HAPON) (PEOPLE'S ANTI-JAPANESE ARMY) (1942) were communists, many non-communists joined its struggle. The guerrillas could readily tap the peasantry for foodstuffs and information on enemy movements in the locality. While undertaking efforts at sabotaging the Japanese, LUIS TARUC (1913–) implemented land reforms and distributed land to the landless peasants, a classic communist strategy of winning over the peasantry to their cause.

The United States had promised independence to the Philippines scheduled for 4 July 1946. Therefore, despite the Japanese offer of an earlier date of independence if the Filipinos cooperated, there was little enthusiasm. However, although GENERAL DOUGLAS MAC-ARTHUR (1880–1964) had encouraged the people to wage guerrilla warfare prior to his return, Commonwealth of the Philippines president MANUEL LUIS QUEZON (1878–1944) urged his fellow countrymen, in particular the civil servants, to remain at their posts and accommodate the Japanese in order to lessen the burden of the common people. Taking this cue, many Filipino civil servants served in the wartime regime under Japanese superiors.

In October 1943 the Japanese declared the Philippines independent, with JOSE PACIANO LAUREL (1891–1959) as president overseeing a Republic of the Philippines with executive, legislative, and judicial powers. Nonetheless no one was the least convinced of Japanese sincerity; what was declared and set up was a "hollow," independent republic in which the Japanese continued to hold the reins of power.

The greatest irony was that the successes gained by the Anglo-American forces in the Pacific theater in destroying Japanese naval power and eliminating most of its merchant marine fleet led to the disruption and almost total halt of essential goods to the civilian population of Southeast Asia after 1944. In the Philippines starvation was rife, despite rationing. The countryside faced harsh reprisals consequent of Japanese offensives against the HUKBALAHAP (HUKBO NG BAYAN LABAN SA HAPON) (PEOPLE'S ANTI-JAPANESE ARMY) (1942) and other resistance groups.

Preparedness in gathering reliable intelligence of British defense arrangements, coupled with the high morale of Japanese troops, paid handsome dividends as the Japanese swept down in a two-pronged offensive on both sides of the Malay Peninsula. The defenders—British, Australian, New Zealand, and Indian—were unprepared for a northern invasion; some of the troops were inexperienced vis-à-vis the Japanese veterans of the Manchurian campaign. Victory was swift.

Based in BANGKOK, the Japanese military intelligence network, FUJIWARA KIKAN (F. KIKAN), headed by Major Fujiwara Iwaichi (1908–1986), was from September 1941 gathering support and cooperation from the nationalist movements in Southeast Asia—Indian, Malay, Indonesian, and Chinese. The Japanese scored the most success with the Indian Independence League (IIL), the organization headed by SUBHAS CHANDRA BOSE (1897–1945). Members of the IIL accompanied the Japanese army in the invasion of BRITISH MALAYA and succeeded in persuading Indian soldiers in the British Army to desert to the Japanese side. In this manner those who switched allegiance were gathered to form the INDIAN NATIONAL ARMY (INA), the military arm of the IIL.

BRITISH BORNEO offered even less resistance to the Japanese invaders; only one Punjab regiment was deployed to protect the petroleum industry in Miri and Lutong and the airfield outside Kuching. There was little fighting, and on Christmas Eve 1941, Kuching was in Japanese hands. Unlike the formation of resistance groups in the Philippines and the MALAYAN PEOPLE'S ANTI-JAPANESE ARMY (MPAJA) and WATANIAH, SARAWAK AND SABAH (NORTH BORNEO) and Brunei had none. Toward the end of the war in 1945, the Australian SERVICES RECONNAISSANCE DEPARTMENT (SRD) operated behind enemy lines in the highland areas of north-central BORNEO preparing the groundwork for the reoccupation of northwest BORNEO in June of that year. Besides Australians, there were British and New Zealand operatives. They organized resistance groups among the Kayans, Kenyahs, Kelabits, Muruts, and IBANS.

In the Malay Peninsula the MALAYAN PEOPLE'S ANTI-JAPANESE ARMY

(MPAJA) and WATANIAH were active, although overall they had little impact on the Japanese occupying forces. The Chinese-dominated MALAYAN COMMUNIST PARTY (MCP), headed by CHIN PENG (ONG BOON HUA/HWA) (1922–), was the architect of the MALAYAN PEOPLE'S ANTI-JAPANESE ARMY (MPAJA), which drew most of its members from the Chinese community with a sprinkling of Malays and Indians. The Malays of PAHANG organized the resistance group WATANIAH, which, like the MALAYAN PEOPLE'S ANTI-JAPANESE ARMY (MPAJA), cooperated with FORCE 136. The latter, set up by the British under the SOUTH-EAST ASIA COMMAND (SEAC) based in SRI LANKA (CEYLON), undertook the task of sending its members (mostly British) to occupied Southeast Asia to promote indigenous armed resistance by training and arming those local groups.

Under the Japanese, SINGAPORE (1819) was renamed SYONAN-TO ("Lighting up the South" or "Light of the South"). The occupation years were characterized by deprivation of daily necessities and acute shortages of foodstuffs, particularly rice, the staple diet of the multiethnic population. Conscious that the Chinese might organize resistance to the occupation forces based on their prewar vociferous support for the KUOMINTANG-sponsored CHINA RELIEF FUND and other national salvation movements, the Japanese singled out this community for harsh treatment in order to preempt their threat. *SOOK CHING,* or "cleansing," was carried out in SINGAPORE (1819) and PENANG (1786) to weed out suspected or potential anti-Japanese elements (read Chinese); consequently, thousands of Chinese men were victims of massacres by the Japanese army. The KEMPEI-TAI, the Japanese military police, through their local informers weeded out subversives; their modus operandi was arrest, torture, then questioning, and thereafter, killing and disposal. For the Chinese in Brunei, SARAWAK AND SABAH (NORTH BORNEO), *SOOK CHING* took the form of exorbitant monetary demands as a means of redeeming themselves for their prewar anti-Japanese activities—such as contributing to the CHINA RELIEF FUND and the British war effort. Furthermore, Chinese women were singled out as "COMFORT WOMEN" for the

Japanese soldiers; women from other ethnic groups, including Europeans (Dutch), were also recruited into "comfort stations" (military brothels) throughout Southeast Asia. Fear and hatred toward the Japanese were dominant thoughts among the Chinese in BRITISH MALAYA and BRITISH BORNEO during this period of occupation.

The peninsular Malay aristocracy and the English-educated Malay elite were unharmed; not having any option, both groups collaborated with the Japanese military administration. Likewise, Malay members of the lower rungs of the bureaucracy and police personnel remained at their prewar jobs and bowed to Japanese superiors. While the townspeople suffered food and material deprivation, the Malay peasantry in the rural areas were in less dire straits, as they bravely stowed away rice and other foodstuffs from requisitioning by the Japanese. The indigenous peoples of BRITISH BORNEO reacted similarly to Japanese demands. Initially Japanese-indigenous relations were cordial. The Malays initially viewed the Japanese as liberators. However, the harshness of Japanese soldiers toward the Malays and other native peoples created resentment. The IBANS were particularly offended by the public face slappings meted out by the Japanese for slight delinquent behavior, such as forgetting to bow to a sentry.

Their harsh behavior notwithstanding, Japanese propaganda of "ASIA FOR THE ASIATICS" and their grand economic design of the GREATER EAST ASIA CO-PROSPERITY SPHERE had little impact on the Chinese, Malays, or other native EAST MALAYSIAN ETHNIC MINORITIES. Certain quarters of the Indian community might have been swayed, likewise the radical Malay groups—both parties that looked to Japan and the Japanese for deliverance.

The Indian community in BRITISH MALAYA was split: one group remained steadfastly loyal to the British, whereas another supported the Japanese, riding on the promise of the liberation of INDIA. The latter group swelled the branches of the IIL that were set up in all major towns and enthusiastically jumped on the bandwagon of the INDIAN NATIONAL ARMY (INA).

In fact, members of the KESATUAN MELAYU MUDA (KMM) (YOUNG MALAY UNION) assisted the Japanese with intelligence during the initial landings and the southward advance down the peninsula. Imprisoned by the British in August 1941 for spreading anti-British propaganda, IBRAHIM YAACOB (1911–1979) was released by the Japanese in February 1942. Despite its assistance, the KMM was proscribed. Instead the Japanese elevated IBRAHIM YAACOB (1911–1979) to the rank of lieutenant colonel to head the Pembela Tanah Ayer (PETA, Defenders of the Fatherland), a Japanese-sponsored Malay militia, as a means of garnering support in anticipation of an Anglo-American reoccupation. Then in June 1945, another Japanese ploy to win over Malay support was the establishment of Kesatuan Raayat Indonesia Semenanjung (KRIS, Union of Peninsular Indonesians). IBRAHIM YAACOB (1911–1979) was keen on independence together with Indonesia; however, when SOEKARNO (SUKARNO) (1901–1970) announced independence on 17 August 1945, BRITISH MALAYA and BRITISH BORNEO were not mentioned.

In general most Indonesians welcomed the Japanese as liberators and as ushering in a new dawn. The Japanese on their part encouraged Indonesian nationalism, which was consistent with their "ASIA FOR THE ASIATICS" policy, with Japan as the leader of the "New Asia." The red-and-white Indonesian flag fluttered in public for the first time alongside the singing of *Indonesia Raya,* the nationalist anthem. Educated Indonesians were given the golden opportunity of filling in middle and even top positions in the civil administration, as Dutch and Eurasians were behind the wire in internment camps. While the Japanese sought to utilize the influence of SOEKARNO (SUKARNO) (1901–1970) to garner support for their cause, the wily nationalist in turn used the opportunity in his public speeches to awaken the masses to Indonesian nationalism and independence. His adroitness in exploiting Javanese language and symbolism couched his anti-imperialistic messages under the nose of the Japanese imperialist. While SOEKARNO (SUKARNO) (1901–1970) and MOHAMMAD HATTA (1902–1980) seemingly appeared to be collaborating with the Japanese, SUTAN SJAHRIR (1909–1966) headed an underground resistance movement aimed at sabotage. Both groups— "collaborators" and the "resistance"—possessed

common objectives—namely, Indonesian independence at all costs. They cooperated and coordinated their plans and actions.

PUSAT TENAGA RAKJAT (PUTERA) (CENTRE OF PEOPLES' POWER) was aimed at mobilizing the inhabitants of JAVA for the Japanese war effort through an aggressive propaganda campaign. SOEKARNO (SUKARNO) (1901–1970) and MOHAMMAD HATTA (1902–1980) were chairman and vice chairman, respectively. The Japanese promise of self-government attracted much mass support. Together with the Central Advisory Board under the presidency of SOEKARNO (SUKARNO) (1901–1970), large numbers of Indonesians lent their support. The Pembela Tanah Ayer (PETA, Defenders of the Fatherland), a Japanese-sponsored militia similar to the organization that was established in the Japanese-occupied Malay Peninsula, was the most significant of all organizations, as it formed the core of the republican army that played a pivotal role in the INDONESIAN REVOLUTION (1945–1949). In efforts to win over Islamic elements, the Japanese created the MADJELIS SJURO MUSLIMIN INDONESIA (MASJUMI) (COUNCIL OF INDONESIAN MUSLIM ASSOCIATIONS), which brought together all Muslim groups and organizations. (It succeeded the MADJLISUL ISLAMIL A'LAA INDONESIA [MIAI] [GREAT ISLAMIC COUNCIL OF INDONESIA], which was established in 1937.) Both the MUHAMMADIYAH and NAHDATUL ULAMA were participants, a coup for Muslim solidarity. The exalted status of the Showa emperor alienated the *KIAI,* who withdrew their support.

Japanese sincerity in granting Indonesian independence was demonstrated by the establishment of a preparatory committee for Indonesian independence (January 1944) and the Badan Penjelidik Usaha Persiapan Kemerdekaan (Research Body for the Preparation of Independence) (March 1945), both entrusted with the task of preparing a draft constitution. FIELD MARSHAL COUNT TERAUCHI HISAICHI (1879–1946), Japanese supreme commander of Southeast Asia, on 7 August 1945 ordered the setting up of a Panitia Persiapan Kemerdekaan Indonesia (Preparatory Panel for Indonesian Independence) and promised to grant independence to Indonesia on 24 August 1945. Events escalated rapidly—the U.S. atomic bombings of Hiroshima (6 August) and Nagasaki (9 August), Japan's unconditional surrender (15 August)—and SOEKARNO (SUKARNO) (1901–1970) was strongly urged to declare the independence of Indonesia. He procrastinated. Then, on 17 August 1945, he finally proclaimed Indonesian independence.

Looking to Japan for assistance in their nationalistic aspirations, the group calling themselves THAKIN, led by AUNG SAN (1915–1947), formed the THIRTY COMRADES; they underwent military training on Hainan Island under the Japanese. The THIRTY COMRADES was the nucleus of the BURMA INDEPENDENCE ARMY (BIA). Like their Indonesian counterparts, AUNG SAN (1915–1947) and his fellow nationalists were pragmatic strategists, Machiavellian in character and with the dedicated objective of attaining independence for Burma by any means. Therefore, if the situation suited them to be pro-Japanese, they allied with the Japanese; conversely, when it became prudent to be pro-British, they aligned themselves with their former colonial masters.

BURMA DURING THE PACIFIC WAR (1941–1945) was the only country in Southeast Asia to suffer the ravages of war twice over. Through the Three Pagoda Pass the Japanese invaded the country from the south, advancing northward until halted on the borders of British India. Then British forces under ADMIRAL LORD LOUIS MOUNTBATTEN (1900–1979), supreme commander of the SOUTH-EAST ASIA COMMAND (SEAC), pushed the Japanese southward in his reoccupation campaign. Prior to the reoccupation, an Anglo-American guerrilla force, the CHINDITS, who were trained and led by Major General Orde Charles Wingate (1903–1944), undertook sorties in occupied Burma from 1943. Burma proved to be a vital funnel for supplies via the BURMA ROAD to southwest China, fueling the KUOMINTANG-led Chinese fight against the Japanese in besieged NATIONALIST CHINA.

As in Indonesia, the Japanese promised to grant independence to the civilian administration of DR. BA MAW (b. 1893) if Burma declared war on the Anglo-American powers. Accordingly, on 1 August 1943, Burma was proclaimed independent and thereafter declared war on Britain and the United States. DR. BA MAW (b. 1893) assumed the position of *Adipati*, or head of state, as well as prime minister.

The Japanese defeat at the BATTLE OF IMPHAL-KOHIMA (1944) halted their westward advance and signaled the turn of their military fortunes. The INDIAN NATIONAL ARMY (INA), which had had a part in the battle, was annihilated, to a large extent dashing the aspirations of the IIL and SUBHAS CHANDRA BOSE (1897–1945).

Meanwhile, in March 1945, the THAKIN (LORD, MASTER) nationalists had switched allegiance, becoming anti-Japanese. AUNG SAN (1915–1947) and GENERAL NE WIN (1911–2002) transformed the Burma Defence Army (previously the BURMA INDEPENDENCE ARMY [BNA]) into the Burma National Army (BIA) in 1943. The THAKIN (LORD, MASTER) organized the ANTI-FASCIST PEOPLE'S FREEDOM LEAGUE (AFPFL). In early 1945 the Burma National Army (BIA) launched attacks on the Japanese. By the time ADMIRAL LORD LOUIS MOUNTBATTEN (1900–1979) reoccupied RANGOON (YANGON) in mid-1945, the ANTI-FASCIST PEOPLE'S FREEDOM LEAGUE (AFPFL), under the leadership of AUNG SAN (1915–1947), was the most influential and powerful nationalist force agitating for full independence.

Neighboring Thailand, under the premiership of FIELD MARSHAL PLAEK PHIBUN-SONGKHRAM (1897–1964) (t. December 1938–July 1944), entered the Pacific War (1941–1945) as a Japanese ally, declaring war on Britain and the United States. But the Thai minister plenipotentiary to the United States, M. R. SENI PRAMOJ (1905–1997), held back the delivery of the declaration of war to Washington. Instead he organized a chapter of the FREE THAI MOVEMENT in the United States. In Thailand itself members of the FREE THAI MOVEMENT led by PRIDI PHANOMYONG (1900–1983) went underground and undertook sabotage activities against the occupying Japanese forces and infiltrated the pro-Japanese Thai administration. The ultimate objective of the FREE THAI MOVEMENT was to negotiate favorably with the Anglo-American powers regarding the ambivalent status of Thailand in the war to ensure that the country's sovereignty and independence remained intact.

The Japanese rewarded the collaborationist government of FIELD MARSHAL PLAEK PHIBUNSONGKHRAM (1897–1964) by transferring the northern peninsular Malay States, formerly the SIAMESE MALAY STATES (KEDAH, PERLIS, KELANTAN, TERENGGANU), Laotian territory west of the Mekong River, and the Cambodian provinces of BATTAMBANG and SIEM REAP to Thai authority. (After the war all those territories were returned.)

In order to facilitate the transportation of troops and supplies to Burma, the Japanese undertook the construction of a 415-kilometer rail link connecting Kanchanaburi in Thailand to Thanbyuzayat in Burma, across difficult terrain. Work on this arduous task (mid-1942 to late 1943) was undertaken by hundreds of thousands of conscripted laborers—British, Australian, New Zealand, Dutch, and Indian prisoners of war, alongside Thais, Burmese, Indians, Chinese, and Malays. The death rate was frighteningly high, hence it was dubbed the DEATH RAILWAY (BURMA-SIAM RAILWAY). Death resulted from tropical diseases (malaria, beriberi), overwork, malnutrition, and harsh treatment by the Japanese.

INDOCHINA DURING WORLD WAR II (1939–1945) was a curious anomaly, in that for a greater part of the war years, the colonial French administration continued to function and remain intact while Japanese troops were garrisoned in the territory with freedom of mobilization. French governor-general Jean Decoux (t. 1940–1945) administered FRENCH INDOCHINA for the Vichy government and accommodated or bowed to the Japanese as the situation developed.

When ominous war clouds gathered, most of the Vietnamese nationalists took flight and regrouped in southern NATIONALIST CHINA, close to the border with TONKIN (TONGKING). They received support from the KUOMINTANG (KMT) government of NATIONALIST CHINA. HỒ CHÍ MINH (1890–1969) and his communists reevaluated their struggle and decided to postpone the class struggle and instead to strive for the independence of Vietnam. A "united front" organization, VIỆT MINH (VIỆT NAM ĐỘC LẬP ĐỒNG MINH HỘI, LEAGUE FOR THE INDEPENDENCE OF VIETNAM), was set up in 1941 under the leadership of HỒ CHÍ MINH (1890–1969). Its main objective was to solicit mass support of all Vietnamese in the nationalist struggle against France and Japan. In 1944 the VIỆT MINH (VIỆT NAM ĐỘC LẬP ĐỒNG MINH HỘI, LEAGUE FOR THE INDEPENDENCE OF VIETNAM) returned to Vietnam, where they orchestrated sabotage operations against the Japanese military.

In a sudden and swift manner the Japanese executed the takeover of the FRENCH INDOCHINESE UNION (UNION INDOCHINOISE FRANCAISE) (1887) on 9 March 1945, catching Decoux and his administration by surprise. The following day the Japanese requested that Emperor BẢO ĐẠI (VĨNH THỤY) (1913–1997) proclaim the independence of Vietnam (less COCHIN CHINA), likewise the monarchs SISAVANG VONG (r. 1904–1959) of Laos and NORODOM SIHANOUK (1922–) of Cambodia. Despite independence and the setting up of the ineffectual collaborationist government of Tran Trong Kim (t. April–August 1945), the Japanese remained in control, concentrating their military forces in and around SAIGON (GIA DINH, HỒ CHÍ MINH CITY). Seizing this opportunity, the communist-dominated VIỆT MINH (VIỆT NAM ĐỘC LẬP ĐỒNG MINH HỘI, LEAGUE FOR THE INDEPENDENCE OF VIETNAM) entrenched itself in TONKIN (TONGKING) and the greater part of NORTH VIETNAM (POST-1945).

During the war years two movements emerged in occupied LAOS (NINETEENTH CENTURY TO MID-1990s), one anti-Japanese and another anti-French. The royal court of LUANG PRABANG led the former, whereas the latter, the LAO ISSARA (ISSARAK), was headed by PHETSARATH (1890–1959), based in VIENTIANE. No parallel resistance movement arose in neighboring Cambodia. After the Japanese-impelled proclamation of independence by the young NORODOM SIHANOUK (1922–) in March 1945, SON NGOC THANH (1907–1976?) headed an impotent government as the Japanese remained in control.

In an unprecedented manner the Japanese Showa emperor Hirohito (r. 1926–1989) announced in a radio broadcast to the Japanese nation the unconditional surrender of Japan on 15 August 1945. This event broke all traditions. No Japanese emperor had ever given public speeches—in fact, no one outside the inner palace in Kyoto had ever heard the august voice or seen this god-king. The sudden Japanese surrender was generally though reluctantly accepted by Japanese commanders and their troops in the empire stretching from Manchuria in northeast Asia to Papua New Guinea to Guadalcanal in the southwest Pacific. Opportunities immediately arose, conflicts erupted, and chaos and relief intermingled in the aftermath of the surrender.

The BRITISH MILITARY ADMINISTRATION (BMA) IN SOUTHEAST ASIA faced the seemingly insurmountable task of addressing the urgent issues of food and nationalists. Food shortages, especially of rice, reigned throughout the region. The distribution of supplies was hampered by the lack of ships. Equally daunting were nationalist demands for independence. Securing the release of thousands of European prisoners of war and civilian internees, who spent the war years in prisons and internment camps where malnutrition and harsh treatment killed many, was a race against time. There was a real fear of the recurrence of tragedies like the SANDAKAN DEATH MARCH in northwest BORNEO, where thousands of mostly Australian prisoners of war were force-marched from the prison camp at Sandakan to Ranau in the interior during the closing months of the war. Thousands perished, and only a handful of survivors (those who managed to escape) lived to tell the horrifying tale. It was feared that the Japanese in their humiliation and shame of defeat might vent their anger and vengeance on European prisoners of war and internees.

As supreme commander of SOUTH-EAST ASIA COMMAND (SEAC), which was responsible for the BRITISH MILITARY ADMINISTRATION (BMA) IN SOUTHEAST ASIA, ADMIRAL LORD LOUIS MOUNTBATTEN (1900–1979) managed to establish fairly effective and efficient short-lived military governments throughout the region. A sticky question faced by the brief military administration was the COLLABORATION ISSUE IN SOUTHEAST ASIA. In order not to jeopardize the delicate situation in British India, where nationalist agitation for independence had reached a near-explosive level, prosecution was limited to those "collaborators" whose actions had directly led to the deaths of their fellow countrymen. The postwar Anglo-American military tribunals pronounced the death sentence on FIELD MARSHAL COUNT TERAUCHI HISAICHI (1879–1946), Japanese supreme commander of Southeast Asia, and GENERAL YAMASHITA TOMOYUKI (1885–1946), commander of Japanese forces in the Philippines toward the end of the war.

Amid the rubble of war and the efforts at reconstruction and rehabilitation, the United States kept its promise, and the Philippines was granted independence on 4 July 1946. In Burma the situation was less straightforward in the attainment of independence; similarly with Indonesia.

Governor SIR REGINALD DORMAN-SMITH (t. 1941–1946) and his administration, which had spent the war years in INDIA, were critical of AUNG SAN (1915–1947) and the ANTI-FASCIST PEOPLE'S FREEDOM LEAGUE (AFPFL). But ADMIRAL LORD LOUIS MOUNTBATTEN (1900–1979), who had retaken Burma in May 1945, was cautious in the treatment of the powerful, influential, and popular AUNG SAN (1915–1947). Sir Hubert Rance, who had headed the military administration, was appointed civilian governor (t. 1946–1948). Talks regarding a peaceful transfer of power commenced thereafter and concluded in early 1947, when Britain agreed to Burma's independence. Interestingly, the conservative faction led by U Saw and the communist wing of the ANTI-FASCIST PEOPLE'S FREEDOM LEAGUE (AFPFL) was dissatisfied with the negotiated agreement. U SAW AND THE ASSASSINATION OF AUNG SAN was an event of tragic proportions for Burmese politics. Fired with ambition and thirst for power, U Saw ordered the killing of AUNG SAN (1915–1947), his arch political rival. AUNG SAN (1915–1947) and members of his cabinet were gunned down during a meeting on 19 July 1947. The British invited U NU (1907–) to form a new government and to draft a new constitution. On 4 January 1948, Burma became independent, and unlike other former British colonies, it left the Commonwealth.

The INDONESIAN REVOLUTION (1945–1949) was a protracted struggle colored by bloodshed, insincerity, bitterness, and hatred.

It was only with the intervention of the United Nations (UN), the first test of the UNITED NATIONS AND CONFLICT RESOLUTION IN SOUTHEAST ASIA, that The Netherlands finally recognized an independent Indonesia in December 1949.

Lieutenant Governor-General DR. JOHANNES HUBERTUS VAN MOOK (1894–1965) faced a very different DUTCH EAST INDIES when he returned in 1945. The British who reoccupied the country before the arrival of the Dutch faced stiff, armed opposition from the Indonesian republican forces in BATAVIA (SUNDA KELAPA, JACATRA, DJAKARTA/JAKARTA), Bandoeng, Semarang, and SURABAYA. Negotiations interspersed with DUTCH POLICE ACTION (FIRST AND SECOND) were the strategy employed by the Dutch in an attempt to reinstate their prewar colonial authority over Indonesia. Two efforts at a peaceful resolution failed—namely, the LINGGADJATI (LINGGAJATI) AGREEMENT (1947) and the RENVILLE AGREEMENT (JANUARY 1948).

Then, suddenly, the MADIUN AFFAIR (SEPTEMBER 1948) broke out. It was an attempt by the lower-echelon members of the PARTAI KOMUNIS INDONESIA (PKI) (1920) to wrest power from the republican government. The MADIUN AFFAIR (SEPTEMBER 1948) put the PARTAI KOMUNIS INDONESIA (PKI) (1920) in a very bad light; while the republican government of Prime Minister MOHAMMAD HATTA (1902–1980) was battling the Dutch, the communists were trying to undermine him. Consequently, the Indonesian republican armed forces virtually annihilated the entire leadership of the communist movement. Musso, AMIR SJARIFUDDIN (1907–1948), and IBRAHIM DATUK TAN MALAKA (1897?–1949) were killed. The Dutch seized the opportunity to launch an offensive in December 1948 but failed.

The republican government benefited from the unsuccessful communist putsch in that it gained a supporter in the United States for its anti-leftist stance. Finally in December 1949, with pressure from Britain and the United States coupled with the intervening role of the United Nations, The Netherlands at The Hague agreed to transfer sovereignty to an independent United States of Indonesia. In August 1950 the unitarian Republic of Indonesia came into being with SOEKARNO (SUKARNO) (1901–1970) as president. Indonesia at last achieved its *MERDEKA* (FREE, INDEPENDENT) following a prolonged *PERJUANGAN* (*PERDJUANGAN*).

A Cambodian nationalist movement, the KHMER ISSARAK (FREE KHMER), emerged in June 1945 in BANGKOK and soon had units in the country, especially in the southeast. The objective of the movement was to eject the French from Cambodian soil. In addition to Thai backing, the KHMER ISSARAK (FREE KHMER) received support from the VIỆT MINH (VIỆT NAM ĐỘC LẬP ĐỒNG MINH HỘI, LEAGUE FOR THE INDEPENDENCE OF VIETNAM).

Then in October 1945, the French reoccupied Cambodia and deposed the government of SON NGOC THANH (1907–1976?). The Cambodian nationalist groups split into communist and noncommunist camps. The communists with Vietnamese support waged an anti-French guerrilla war in the countryside. SON NGOC THANH (1907–1976?) led the noncommunist Khmer Serei in opposition. But NORODOM SIHANOUK (1922–) upstaged both parties. In June 1952 he took over the reins of government. Through his visits to the Western democracies to garner support for his government and country, his diplomacy won him support. Even the French were won over and consequently granted independence to Cambodia in 1953. This independence was confirmed in the GENEVA CONFERENCE (1954) when the government of NORODOM SIHANOUK (1922–) was acknowledged as the sole legitimate authority over Cambodia.

Upon the reemergence of the French in LAOS (NINETEENTH CENTURY TO MID-1990s) in the early months of 1946, the LAO ISSARA (ISSARAK) fled to Thailand. The French recognized the internal autonomy of the country under SISAVANG VONG (r. 1904–1959), king of LUANG PRABANG. In 1949 the French granted limited self-government. This government was dominated by radical figures, notably SOUPHANOUVONG (RED PRINCE) (1911–1995), who assumed the presidency. In 1950 the PATHET LAO (LAND OF LAOS), an anti-French, procommunist movement, emerged with close ties to the

VIỆT MINH (VIỆT NAM ĐỘC LẬP ĐỒNG MINH HỘI, LEAGUE FOR THE INDEPENDENCE OF VIETNAM). It was particularly strong in the northeast of the country bordering Vietnam. In October 1953 the French granted independence to the country.

The day after the Japanese surrender was announced, a People's National Liberation Committee under the presidency of HỒ CHÍ MINH (1890–1969) was constituted by the VIỆT MINH (VIỆT NAM ĐỘC LẬP ĐỒNG MINH HỘI, LEAGUE FOR THE INDEPENDENCE OF VIETNAM). The committee refused to acknowledge the Japanese puppet government in SOUTH VIETNAM (POST-1945) under Tran Trong Kim. A communist-orchestrated general uprising was staged. To resolve the impasse, Emperor BẢO ĐẠI (VĨNH THỤY) (1913–1997) abdicated in August 1945. A week later, on 2 September 1945, HỒ CHÍ MINH (1890–1969) proclaimed the independence of the Democratic Republic of Vietnam (DRV).

The drama unfolded when the French with the assistance of British forces reoccupied COCHIN CHINA. The lines were drawn with a communist-dominated NORTH VIETNAM (POST-1945) and a noncommunist, French-controlled SOUTH VIETNAM (POST-1945). The stage and the props were ready for the players to act out the FIRST INDOCHINA WAR (1946–1954).

In the initial stage in early 1946, there was an agreement between HỒ CHÍ MINH (1890–1969) and the French; the latter recognized the communist government and the promise that French troops would remain on Vietnamese soil awaiting a gradual withdrawal over a five-year period. However, it was apparent that both sides possessed objectives that were poles apart: a united Vietnam with complete, full independence against the reinstatement of a colonial regime. In November the first shots were fired in the FIRST INDOCHINA WAR (1946–1954).

The French through force of arms reunited the country to create the Associated State of Vietnam in 1949 with former emperor BẢO ĐẠI (VĨNH THỤY (1913–1997) as the head of state. No Vietnamese, whether communist or noncommunist, was amused. The guerrilla war conducted by the VIỆT MINH (VIỆT NAM ĐỘC LẬP ĐỒNG MINH HỘI, LEAGUE

FOR THE INDEPENDENCE OF VIETNAM) was under way and increasingly moving toward a victory for the communist regime in HANOI (THANG-LONG). The conflict begun to resemble a proxy struggle between adversaries of the COLD WAR. Mao Zedong (1893–1976) and the newly proclaimed People's Republic of China (PRC) were funneling supplies to their brother communists across the border to TONKIN (TONGKING). U.S. president Dwight D. Eisenhower (1890–1969) was justifying his support to the French with the term DOMINO THEORY; if Indochina became communist, the rest of Southeast Asia would follow suit like falling dominoes.

The BATTLE OF DIEN BIEN PHU (MAY 1954), though a heroic stand on the part of the French forces, was not only a military victory for GENERAL VO NGUYỄN GIAP (1911–) but more significantly a political triumph for HỒ CHÍ MINH (1890–1969). The GENEVA CONFERENCE (1954), originally intended to resolve the KOREAN WAR (1950–1953), ended the FIRST INDOCHINA WAR (1946–1954)—but at the cost of the partitioning of Vietnam at the 17° N parallel, officially creating NORTH VIETNAM (POST-1945) and SOUTH VIETNAM (POST-1945). There was also the provision (the Final Declaration) for an election to unify the country, scheduled for July 1956, to be conducted under an international commission. In order to deny an almost certain election victory for the VIỆT MINH (VIỆT NAM ĐỘC LẬP ĐỒNG MINH HỘI, LEAGUE FOR THE INDEPENDENCE OF VIETNAM), the United States and the regime of SOUTH VIETNAM (POST-1945) refused to pen their signature to the Final Declaration in the Geneva Accords. Hence the elections were never held.

The Democratic Republic of Vietnam (DRV) under the supreme leadership of HỒ CHÍ MINH (1890–1969) governed NORTH VIETNAM (POST-1945). Both the Union of the Soviet Socialist Republics (Soviet Union) and the PRC were staunch supporters of this newly emerging communist state. A socialist program of agricultural collectivization and industrialization was implemented with financial, material, and technical aid from Moscow and Beijing. The leadership of the DRV included personalities such as PHAM VAN DONG

(1906–2000), TRUONG CHINH (1907–1988), LE DUAN (1907–1986), and LE DUC THO (1911–).

In SOUTH VIETNAM (POST-1945), a noncommunist regime, the Republic of Vietnam, was set up in October 1955 under the presidency of NGÔ ĐÌNH DIỆM (1901–1963). By April 1956 the last detachment of the French military finally left. U.S. influence and presence became increasingly apparent in supporting the government of NGÔ ĐÌNH DIỆM (1901–1963). In fact, since 1950 a U.S. military mission had been set up in SAIGON (GIA DINH, HỒ CHÍ MINH CITY) as U.S. involvement in the Vietnam conflict began to escalate.

The fortnight interregnum between the Japanese surrender (mid-August 1945) and the arrival of British forces under ADMIRAL LORD LOUIS MOUNTBATTEN (1900–1979) (September 1945) witnessed revenge killings and murders of individual collaborators, but more serious were the Sino-Malay clashes in several places in the peninsular Malay States. The harsh wartime treatment of the Chinese and the seemingly cozy existence of the sultans and Malay civil servants who collaborated with the Japanese military administration sparked a racial hatred of one community accusing the other of being traitors. Aggravating the Sino-Malay tensions was the emergence from the jungle of the MALAYAN PEOPLE'S ANTI-JAPANESE ARMY (MPAJA), which was dominated largely by the Chinese-based MALAYAN COMMUNIST PARTY (MCP) claiming to be the liberators of the country.

The announcement of the British postwar political and administrative setup known as the MALAYAN UNION (1946) to replace the varied structure of BRITISH MALAYA sparked Malay opposition. Led by the English-educated Malay nationalist group headed by ONN BIN JA'AFAR (1895–1962), the MALAYS rejected the proposed MALAYAN UNION (1946), which they claimed was too liberal in granting citizenship to immigrant groups (mainly Chinese), and because of the abrogation of Malay special rights and privileges. The high-handed manner employed by the special representative of the British government, Sir Harold MacMichael, in securing the royal assent of the nine Malay rulers was an-other sore point with the MALAYS. In May 1946 forty-one Malay organizations from all the peninsular Malay States came together to inaugurate the formation of the UNITED MALAYS NATIONAL ORGANIZATION (UMNO), which spearheaded Malay opposition after the MALAYAN UNION (1946) came into force on 1 April 1946.

Bowing to Malay demands, a revised constitution and political-cum-administrative setup—the FEDERATION OF MALAYA (1948)—replaced the MALAYAN UNION (1946). SINGAPORE (1819) was retained as a British Crown colony for geopolitical reasons. Certain quarters within the Chinese community were dissatisfied with the FEDERATION OF MALAYA (1948). The English-educated BABA NYONYA of PENANG (1786) refused to participate in the new setup, citing anticipated economic losses and political subservience. The PENANG SECESSIONIST MOVEMENT (1948–1951) campaigned for PENANG (1786) to remain as a British Crown colony of the STRAITS SETTLEMENTS (1826–1946), with close ties to the British Empire. Petitions to the British government failed because London, after having successfully ridden the storm of Malay protest and winning them over to a new setup, had no intention of again rattling Malay sensitivity by acceding to English-educated Chinese professionals and businessmen.

Meanwhile the MALAYAN COMMUNIST PARTY (MCP), led by CHIN PENG (ONG BOON HUA/HWA) (1922–), launched an attempt to overthrow the colonial regime and to attain independence for BRITISH MALAYA less the "British." The strategy employed was to cripple the economy and in the ensuing socioeconomic chaos seize power. The MALAYAN COMMUNIST PARTY (MCP), through "united front" tactics, infiltrated labor and labor unions, and strike action was commonplace in SINGAPORE (1819) and other urban centers. Sabotage of dredges and other machinery, the destruction of rubber trees, and burning of workers' quarters on estates were undertaken to terrorize Chinese and Indian workers in the TIN and RUBBER industries, the backbone of the colonial economy. Then came the murders of European planters. In mid-1948 the MALAYAN EMERGENCY (1948–1960) was declared.

Combating the MALAYAN COMMUNIST PARTY (MCP) was done on several levels: military, political, psychological, and socioeconomic. Troops from the British Commonwealth (largely from Britain, Australia, New Zealand, and Fiji) conducted search and pursuit operations against the communist terrorists (CTs), a term attributed to members of the MALAYAN COMMUNIST PARTY (MCP). On the political front, local elections were under way as a preparation for eventual self-government, countering the communist assertion that they alone were fighting for independence. The psychological warfare of winning the "hearts and minds" of the multiethnic population, but mainly targeting the Chinese community, was most challenging. The resettlement of Chinese communities that had established villages on the fringe of the jungle during the Japanese occupation to avoid recruitment into labor gangs and harsh treatment was another daunting but highly effective strategy. Dubbed the BRIGGS PLAN after Lieutenant General Sir Harold Briggs, the director of operations (t. 1950–1952), it witnessed the transfer of nearly half a million Chinese squatters from the jungle fringes to "NEW VILLAGES" (MALAYA/MALAYSIA). A helping hand for the newly settled inhabitants came from members of the MALAYAN/MALAYSIAN CHINESE ASSOCIATION (MCA) (1949), which was established from among the *TOWKAY* led by SIR TAN CHENG LOCK (1883–1960). Initially a welfare organization, the MALAYAN/MALAYSIAN CHINESE ASSOCIATION (MCA) (1949) was to be to the Chinese inhabitants an alternative to the MALAYAN COMMUNIST PARTY (MCP). This resettlement campaign succeeded in its primary objective of cutting off the supply line of the CTs in food, recruits, and intelligence. Deprived of their support and supplies, the CTs moved farther into the jungle; in some instances they enlisted the assistance of the ORANG ASLI for food and safe havens. The British colonial government on its part wooed the ORANG ASLI, accommodating them in improving their socioeconomic conditions.

The MALAYAN COMMUNIST PARTY (MCP) scored a major victory when CTs ambushed and shot dead Sir Henry Gurney (t. 1948–1951), British high commissioner of the FEDERATION OF MALAYA (1948), at

Fraser's Hill in October 1951. Morale then was at the lowest ebb on the government side. The appointment of GENERAL SIR GERALD TEMPLER (1898–1979) as Gurney's replacement, however, turned the tide against the CTs. Implementation of the BRIGGS PLAN continued in earnest. The number of special constables and home guards was increased. Much to Malay distress, he relaxed citizenship requirements to increase the number of Chinese as citizens as one of the ways of winning over the community. Collective punishment was meted out to whole villagers if found assisting the CTs. "Black Areas" faced around-the-clock curfews and rationing (food, water, and electricity).

The road to independence for BRITISH MALAYA by the early 1950s was clearly marked out. In the effort to resolve the MALAYAN EMERGENCY (1948–1960), steps toward self-rule were hastened: village and municipal council elections in 1952, as well as elections to the federal Legislative Council in 1955. In the latter, TUNKU ABDUL RAHMAN PUTRA AL-HAJ (1903–1990), the second president of the UNITED MALAYS NATIONAL ORGANIZATION (UMNO), struck an alliance with the MALAYAN/MALAYSIAN CHINESE ASSOCIATION (MCA) (1949)—hence the birth of the ALLIANCE PARTY (MALAYA/MALAYSIA)—to sweep 51 out of 52 contested seats. (PARTAI ISLAM SE MALAYSIA [PAS] won 1 seat.) British fears of Sino-Malay problems drastically subsided. It was amply clear that the newly elected chief minister, TUNKU ABDUL RAHMAN PUTRA AL-HAJ (1903–1990), could lead the country to *MERDEKA* (FREE, INDEPENDENT).

Riding on his success, TUNKU ABDUL RAHMAN PUTRA AL-HAJ (1903–1990) agreed to the request by CHIN PENG (ONG BOON HUA/HWA) (1922–) to negotiate a peaceful settlement to the hitherto "undeclared war." But the BALING TALKS (1955), which brought together the top leadership of the MALAYAN COMMUNIST PARTY (MCP) led by CHIN PENG (ONG BOON HUA/HWA) (1922–) and the government headed by TUNKU ABDUL RAHMAN PUTRA AL-HAJ (1903–1990), came to nothing. The latter refused to recognize the MALAYAN COMMUNIST PARTY (MCP); CHIN

PENG (ONG BOON HUA/HWA) (1922–) and his colleagues Chen Tien and Abdul Rashid Mahideen would not agree to the dissolution of their party and to giving up their struggle. TUNKU ABDUL RAHMAN PUTRA AL-HAJ (1903–1990) argued that independence was imminent and graciously granted amnesty to all surrendered CTs; few took up the offer.

On 31 August 1957, TUNKU ABDUL RAHMAN PUTRA AL-HAJ (1903–1990) proclaimed *MERDEKA* (FREE, INDEPENDENT) for Malaya and became its first prime minister, with the ALLIANCE PARTY (MALAYA/MALAYSIA) as the ruling party. The MALAYAN/MALAYSIAN INDIAN CONGRESS (MIC) had by then joined the ALLIANCE PARTY (MALAYA/MALAYSIA), making it truly representative of the three main ethnic groups of the country—namely, Malay, Chinese, and Indian.

SINGAPORE (1819) was again excluded from the independence granted to Malaya in 1957. Elections for a limited self-government as recommended by the Rendel Constitution (1955) brought to the fore DAVID SAUL MARSHALL (1908–1995), the leader of the Labour Front, as the city-state's first chief minister (t. 1955–1956). Having failed to attain full internal self-government in talks in London, he resigned. LIM YEW HOCK (1914–1984) assumed the chief ministership (t. 1956–1959). The talks in London in March 1957 led by LIM YEW HOCK (1914–1984) were successful and resulted in the elections of May 1959. LEE KUAN YEW (1923–), who led the PEOPLE'S ACTION PARTY (PAP) to victory, became the prime minister. He pledged independence through merger with Malaya.

The PEOPLE'S ACTION PARTY (PAP) government faced a series of communist-instigated strikes by labor unions, and infiltration of the Chinese schools. A prime target for the communists was the NATIONAL TRADES UNION CONGRESS (NTUC). Leftist elements also worked their way into the PEOPLE'S ACTION PARTY (PAP) itself. As in Malaya and BRITISH BORNEO, the English-educated Chinese of SINGAPORE (1819) eschewed COMMUNISM; the ideology attracted the Chinese-educated Chinese. The latter, owing to their Chinese school education (teachers, curriculum, and textbooks all imported and highly oriented toward IMPE-RIAL CHINA, then after 1911, NATIONALIST CHINA, and from the 1920s, COMMUNISM), looked to China for inspiration and sustenance. They became particularly patriotic when a resurgent China emerged in 1949 under Mao Zedong (1893–1976) and the People's Republic of China (PRC).

The leftist elements within the PEOPLE'S ACTION PARTY (PAP) attempted to topple the English-educated leadership of LEE KUAN YEW (1923–). But he outmaneuvered them, forcing their expulsion to form the BARISAN SOSIALIS (SOCIALIST FRONT) in mid-1961. The following year the PEOPLE'S ACTION PARTY (PAP) received the mandate from the electorate for merger with Malaya, together with SARAWAK AND SABAH (NORTH BORNEO), to form MALAYSIA (1963).

Through MALAYSIA (1963), SINGAPORE (1819) and SARAWAK AND SABAH (NORTH BORNEO) gained their independence. TUNKU ABDUL RAHMAN PUTRA AL-HAJ (1903–1990) mooted the idea of a greater federation in May 1961 as a means of preventing a communist takeover of SINGAPORE (1819); the indigenous inhabitants of SARAWAK AND SABAH (NORTH BORNEO) would offset the racial balance, favoring a non-Chinese majority.

Following the Japanese surrender, momentous events unfolded in BRITISH BORNEO. Despite Sarawak Malay opposition to cession, SARAWAK AND SABAH (NORTH BORNEO) were transformed in mid-1946 into British Crown colonies following the transfer of sovereignty to Britain from Rajah Charles Vyner Brooke (r. 1917–1941, 1946) and the BRITISH NORTH BORNEO CHARTERED COMPANY (1881–1917), respectively. Brunei remained a British protectorate. Much investment in development projects was under way in SARAWAK AND SABAH (NORTH BORNEO), as the years of neglect in the former and the ravages of war in the latter required energetic efforts at reconstruction and rehabilitation. Notwithstanding the commendable input by the British colonial government, the formidable physical terrain seriously hampered progress.

ANGLO-BRUNEI RELATIONS (NINETEENTH CENTURY TO 1980s) were on a secure footing. British technical assistance and investment had benefited the BRUNEI OIL

AND GAS INDUSTRY. OMAR ALI SAI-FUDDIN III, SULTAN OF BRUNEI (1914–1986), who came to the throne in June 1950, was ambivalent over the MALAYSIA (1963) proposal. However, the staunchly anti-MALAYSIA (1963) PARTAI RAKYAT BRUNEI (PRB) led by SHEIKH AZAHARI BIN SHEIKH MAHMUD (1928–2002) perceived the palace as keen on the wider federation. SHEIKH AZAHARI BIN SHEIKH MAHMUD (1928–2002) had alternative aspirations—namely, the idea of Kalimantan Utara (Northern Borneo) encompassing Brunei, SARAWAK AND SABAH (NORTH BORNEO), with the sultan as head of state and him as prime minister. Despite having won the election in 1962, PARTAI RAKYAT BRUNEI (PRB) remained powerless in the legislative and executive councils that were dominated by nominated members and officials.

The outbreak of the BRUNEI REBELLION (DECEMBER 1962), led by PARTAI RAKYAT BRUNEI (PRB), was a debacle that sealed the fate of the party. Within a week British troops rushed over from SINGAPORE (1819), crushing the uprising. Whether this failed BRUNEI REBELLION (DECEMBER 1962) had any influence on the decision of OMAR ALI SAIFUDDIN III, SULTAN OF BRUNEI (1914–1986), not to participate in MALAYSIA (1963) remains unanswered.

In the meantime, across the border in SARAWAK AND SABAH (NORTH BORNEO), British administrators were encouraging the native inhabitants to view MALAYSIA (1963) in a positive light. The Chinese community in both territories favored the wider federation that they anticipated would widen the economic scope. After all, most of the trade, commerce, and shipping—including also capital flow of Chinese undertakings—were from SINGAPORE (1819). MALAYSIA (1963) increased political consciousness among the non-Malay indigenous population of SARAWAK AND SABAH (NORTH BORNEO). But to be sure, apart from the few native leaders, each with his own personal agenda, the majority of the indigenous peoples had little inkling of what MALAYSIA (1963) entailed. Apart from the Chinese, left-leaning Sarawak United People's Party (SUPP), the newly formed political parties of SARAWAK AND SABAH

(NORTH BORNEO) favored independence through MALAYSIA (1963). But as the findings of the British-sponsored Cobbold Commission (August 1962) showed, and as confirmed by the United Nations Commission (August 1963), more than three-quarters of the inhabitants in both territories were approving of MALAYSIA (1963), but with certain built-in safeguards (immigration, labor, education).

Despite the SABAH CLAIM from the Philippines and *KONFRONTASI* ("CRUSH MALAYSIA" CAMPAIGN) launched by Indonesia, on 16 September 1963 MALAYSIA (1963) was inaugurated with TUNKU ABDUL RAHMAN PUTRA AL-HAJ (1903–1990) as prime minister. British commitments continued as obligated in the ANGLO-MALAYAN/MALAYSIAN DEFENCE AGREEMENT (AMDA) that ran from 1957 to 1971.

Post-Independence Developments

By 1963 only Brunei and East Timor remained under a colonial arrangement, to British and Portuguese, respectively. The unshackling of independence in other Southeast Asian countries brought in different challenges and struggles. All the newly independent states faced the uphill task of nation-building, but for some the process had to be postponed, as other pressing, more urgent matters awaited resolution. Wars and conflicts continued to plague several territories, while in others the search for an appropriate system of government, economic setup, and sociocultural policy appeared illusive. Various "isms," including attempts to draw sustenance from religious traditions, were undertaken with varied outcomes.

The first president (t. 1946–1948) of the independent Republic of the Philippines was MANUEL ROXAS (1892–1948). He defeated SERGIO OSMENA SR. (1878–1961) in the presidential elections of April 1946. The PHILIPPINES–U.S. "SPECIAL RELATIONSHIP," particularly in the economic and military sphere, established a firm footing during this period. U.S. investments and business enterprises were accorded preferential status in the Philippines. Among U.S. MILITARY BASES IN SOUTHEAST ASIA, Subic Bay Naval Base and Clark Air Base on LUZON were the most important, after Cam Ranh Bay in Vietnam. U.S. military bases functioned as an *imperium in imperio;* they, however, were economic assets in terms of providing employment, businesses, and commercial opportunities to the surrounding local community. MANUEL ROXAS (1892–1948) faced an insurgency launched by the HUKBALAHAP (HUKBO NG BAYAN LABAN SA HAPON) (PEOPLE'S ANTI-JAPANESE ARMY) (1942) that demanded agrarian reform. The government's response to this rural-based, communist-led uprising was the banning of the organization in 1948.

Philippine president ELPIDIO QUIRINO (1890–1956) (t. 1948–1953) took a reconciling stance toward the HUKBALAHAP (HUKBO NG BAYAN LABAN SA HAPON) (PEOPLE'S ANTI-JAPANESE ARMY) (1942): a truce with the rebels. He allowed their leader, LUIS TARUC (1913–), to take the seat in the Philippine Congress that he won in 1946. But abruptly LUIS TARUC (1913–) left MANILA and in April 1949 publicly declared that the HUKBALAHAP (HUKBO NG BAYAN LABAN SA HAPON) (PEOPLE'S ANTI-JAPANESE ARMY) (1942) aimed to overthrow the government. To combat this threat, RAMON MAGSAYSAY (1907–1957) accepted the presidential appointment as secretary of national defense. Combining a new tenancy reform program with the rehabilitation of surrendered rebels, as well as eschewing military excesses that were driving peasants to the rebel cause, RAMON MAGSAYSAY (1907–1957) succeeded in ending the insurgency that came about with the surrender of LUIS TARUC (1913–) in mid-1954.

The presidency (t. 1953–1957) of RAMON MAGSAYSAY (1907–1957) witnessed the further strengthening of the PHILIPPINES–U.S. "SPECIAL RELATIONSHIP." The U.S. parity with Filipinos in the exploitation of natural resources was expanded to encompass all economic activities (the Laurel-Langley Agreement). An aggressive rural development program focusing on agrarian reform was implemented, aimed at improving the livelihood and welfare of the rural poor. RAMON MAGSAYSAY (1907–1957) made the Philippines a founding member of the U.S.-mooted military pact of the SOUTHEAST ASIA TREATY ORGANIZATION (SEATO) (1954). His sudden death in an air accident in March 1957 saw the beginning of a loosening of the ties in the PHILIPPINES–U.S. "SPE-CIAL RELATIONSHIP." His successor, President Carlos P. Garcia (t. 1957–1961), embarked on a "Filipino First" policy that asserted the country's economic nationalism with the objective of reducing dependence on the United States.

Economic reforms funded by foreign sources, mainly from the United States and the International Monetary Fund (IMF), characterized the presidency (t. 1961–1965) of DIOSDADO MACAPAGAL (1910–1997). His MAPHILINDO CONCEPT, which that mooted the creation of a regional organization of territories of the MALAYS, comprising the Philippines, Malaysia, and Indonesia, was realized in August 1963. MAPHILINDO succeeded the Association of Southeast Asia (ASA) and was a forerunner of the ASSOCIATION OF SOUTHEAST ASIAN NATIONS (ASEAN) (1967). But when MALAYSIA (1963) finally came into being in September despite the SABAH CLAIM by the Philippines, diplomatic relations were severed with KUALA LUMPUR.

The SABAH CLAIM was the sovereignty dispute over the East Malaysian state of Sabah (previously North Borneo). The Philippines argued that the territory of North Borneo formed part of the Sulu sultanate. Since the latter had become a part of the Republic of the Philippines, all territories of the sultanate rightly belonged to the Philippines. MANILA formally protested the sovereignty claim in June 1963 to KUALA LUMPUR (KL), when SARAWAK AND SABAH (NORTH BORNEO) were planning to join MALAYSIA (1963).

Besides the SABAH CLAIM, Prime Minister TUNKU ABDUL RAHMAN PUTRA AL-HAJ (1903–1990) of the newly inaugurated MALAYSIA (1963) faced cross-border military raids in SARAWAK AND SABAH (NORTH BORNEO) from Indonesian Kalimantan as part of *KONFRONTASI* ("CRUSH MALAYSIA" CAMPAIGN). SOEKARNO (SUKARNO) (1901–1970) viewed the formation of MALAYSIA (1963) as a neocolonial ploy by the British imperialists to prolong their control and influence in Southeast Asia despite independence for its former colonies of SINGAPORE (1819), SARAWAK AND SABAH (NORTH BORNEO). With the assistance of Commonwealth troops, the Malaysian armed forces managed to contain these military incursions. By 1966, KUALA LUMPUR (KL) had resumed relations with both Indonesia and the Philippines.

The PEOPLE'S ACTION PARTY (PAP) led by LEE KUAN YEW (1923–) sought the creation of a "Malaysian Malaysia" that represented a direct challenge to the "special rights and privileges" of the MALAYS that were enshrined in the Malaysian constitution. The PEOPLE'S ACTION PARTY (PAP) undermined the position of the MALAYAN/ MALAYSIAN CHINESE ASSOCIATION (MCA) (1949) in competing for the Chinese electorate. The divisive policy pursued by LEE KUAN YEW (1923–) that might lead to interethnic clashes subsequently brought about the expulsion of SINGAPORE (1819) from MALAYSIA (1963).

The "Malaysian Malaysia" concept pursued by LEE KUAN YEW (1923–) disrupted the consensual agreement between the leaders of the UNITED MALAYS NATIONAL ORGANIZATION (UMNO) and the MALAYAN/ MALAYSIAN CHINESE ASSOCIATION (MCA) (1949), as well as the MALAYAN/ MALAYSIAN INDIAN CONGRESS (MIC). The consensus among the elite of the main ethnic groups was that the MALAYS held political predominance and that the Chinese continued in their control of the country's economy, with the Indians playing a lesser economic role. Gradually, but without a specific time frame, it was expected that a greater parity would evolve, with MALAYS sharing more of the economic pie and the Chinese and Indians partaking in some aspects of political power. The "Malaysian Malaysia" concept demanded that equal opportunities be given and be open to all, regardless of ethnic background. If it were adopted, the numerical advantage of the Chinese would have them seizing the political stewardship and at the same time dominating the economy. Consequently, the peninsular MALAYS and EAST MALAYSIAN ETHNIC MINORITIES would be in a completely subservient role.

TUNKU ABDUL RAHMAN PUTRA AL-HAJ (1903–1990) maintained close ties with Britain and the Commonwealth politically, economically, as well as militarily. The last mentioned was apparent when British and Commonwealth forces assisted the Malaysian military in facing KONFRONTASI ("CRUSH MALAYSIA" CAMPAIGN). In the COLD WAR, MALAYSIA (1963) stood solidly with the Western democracies; it supported the increasing involvement of the United States in Vietnam during the SECOND INDOCHINA WAR (VIETNAM WAR) (1964–1975). It effected no diplomatic relations with either the Soviet Union or the People's Republic of China (PRC). TUNKU ABDUL RAHMAN PUTRA AL-HAJ (1903–1990) was one of the major players in the formation of the ASSOCIATION OF SOUTHEAST ASIAN NATIONS (ASEAN) (1967).

SARAWAK AND SABAH (NORTH BORNEO) as East Malaysian states experienced glitches in federal-state relations. A political crisis led to the removal of the IBAN chief minister of Sarawak, Stephen Kalong Ningkan (t. 1963–1966), through the use of federal emergency powers by KUALA LUMPUR (KL). Similarly, Donald/Fuad Stephens, Sabah's chief minister (t. 1963–1967), who promoted the interests of the KADAZAN-DUSUNS and allegedly harbored separatist ambitions, was removed by the federal government.

"MAY 13, 1969" (MALAYSIA) was the date of the Sino-Malay riots in KUALA LUMPUR (KL) and in other urban centers; they rocked the entire country. The crisis brought to the fore the leadership of TUN ABDUL RAZAK (1922–1976), then the deputy prime minister, who immediately assumed control of the situation as director of the National Operations Council that governed the country by decree in lieu of a suspended parliament. Neglect of the Malay masses who stood by the sidelines while other ethnic groups—particularly the Chinese—forged forward created frustration and anger within the community. The MALAYAN/MALAYSIAN CHINESE ASSOCIATION (MCA) (1949), which was party to the consensual agreement, lost ground to the Chinese-dominated parties of the opposition that demanded a faster end to Malay political predominance. Gains by the opposition Chinese-dominated political parties—namely, Gerakan Rakyat Malaysia (Gerakan, Malaysian People's Movement) and DEMOCRATIC ACTION PARTY (DAP)—in the elections of May 1969 provoked a backlash from the Malays.

Consequent of "MAY 13, 1969" (MALAYSIA), sedition laws were passed that proscribed public discussion relating to sensitive subjects—namely, the powers and status of the Malay sultans, Malay special rights and privileges, statutes making Islam the official religion of the country, and citizenship rights. To nurture integration and solidarity among the multiethnic and multicultural population, a five-principle national ideology, the RUKUNEGARA, was promulgated. The implementation of *Bahasa Malaysia* (Malay language) as the language for education and administration was stepped up. The basic principles of the country's education policy, based on the Razak Report (1956), were aimed at national unity through a national school system using *Bahasa Malaysia* as the language of instruction, a national curriculum, locally recruited teaching staff, and textbooks oriented toward Malaya from 1957, then MALAYSIA (1963). MALAYAN/MALAYSIAN EDUCATION considered as the key to national integration was a minefield, especially over the issue of the language of instruction.

TUN ABDUL RAZAK (1922–1976), who assumed the premiership (t. 1970–1976), implemented the NEW ECONOMIC POLICY (NEP) (1971–1990). In two decades it was expected to eradicate poverty irrespective of ethnicity, extirpate the identification of economic activities along racial lines, and ensure a better distribution of the country's economic pie, as well as educational and employment opportunities. Also targeted were *BUMIPUTERA* (*BUMIPUTRA*), meaning MALAYS and EAST MALAYSIAN ETHNIC MINORITIES, ownership of 30 percent of the share capital in commercial and industrial concerns by 1990. The NEW ECONOMIC POLICY (NEP) (1971–1990) in its poverty-eradication program focused on rural development where the bulk of the poor—largely MALAYS—resided. DR. MAHATHIR BIN MOHAMAD (1925–) criticized the government of the aristocratic TUNKU ABDUL RAHMAN PUTRA AL-HAJ (1903–1990) in his book *The Malay Dilemma* (1970) for sidelining the development of the Malays vis-à-vis other communities.

In foreign relations TUN ABDUL RAZAK (1922–1976) moved the country out of the pro-Western camp to a neutral stance. In fact, he proposed that Southeast Asia be a ZONE OF PEACE, FREEDOM AND NEUTRALITY (ZOPFAN) (1971). Such a concept was consistent with the principles agreed to in the ASIAN-AFRICAN (BANDUNG) CONFERENCE (APRIL 1955), although then MALAYSIA (1963) was still under colonial rule. The NON-ALIGNED MOVEMENT (NAM) AND SOUTHEAST ASIA was increasingly relevant to avoid the flaring up of another conflict similar to the ongoing SECOND INDOCHINA WAR (VIETNAM WAR) (1964–1975). TUN ABDUL RAZAK (1922–1976) visited Beijing in 1974, establishing diplomatic relations with the People's Republic of China (PRC); assurance was given by the Chinese government of noninterference and nonsupport of the MALAYAN COMMUNIST PARTY (MCP).

The formation of the BARISAN NASIONAL (NATIONAL FRONT) (1974) was an attempt by the ALLIANCE PARTY (MALAYA/MALAYSIA) to encompass a wider membership of political parties that were established largely along ethnic lines. The intention was to lessen politicking among the multitude of parties and to channel all efforts to national development and nation-building.

The secular policies of TUN ABDUL RAZAK (1922–1976), despite the avowed acceptance of Islam as the country's official religion, were viewed with distrust and disappointment by certain quarters of the Malay Muslim community. The 1970s witnessed another wave of ISLAMIC RESURGENCE IN SOUTHEAST ASIA (TWENTIETH CENTURY). The *dakwah* movement began to impact on the Malay Muslims thanks to the influence of PARTAI ISLAM SE MALAYSIA (PAS) and ANGKATAN BELIA ISLAM MALAYSIA (ABIM), or the Muslim Youth Movement of Malaysia. The latter, led by the student leader Anwar Ibrahim (1947–), was highly critical of the UNITED MALAYS NATIONAL ORGANIZATION (UMNO)–led government for not implementing Islamic principles in governance. PARTAI ISLAM SE MALAYSIA (PAS), though a component of the BARISAN NASIONAL (NATIONAL FRONT) (1974) until it left in 1978, accused the government of being un-Islamic; it consistently sought the creation of an "Islamic State" but remained vague as to its structure and content. PARTAI ISLAM SE MALAYSIA (PAS) appealed to the rural, conservative MALAYS in Malay-dominated states such as Kedah, Kelantan, and Terengganu. As a response to the onslaught of modernization, globalization, and Western sociocultural influences, the MALAYS turned toward Islam for sustenance, identity, and belonging.

Hussein Onn (1922–1990), son of ONN BIN JA'AFAR (1895–1962), became prime minister on the sudden death of TUN ABDUL RAZAK (1922–1976) in London in 1976. In the domestic sphere, he successfully eliminated corruption involving key figures in the government, the most celebrated case being that of the *Menteri Besar,* or chief minister, of the state of Selangor, who commanded Malay grassroots support. He also neutralized the powerful Mustapha bin Datu Harun, the founding leader of the United Sabah National Organization (USNO), who apparently entertained ambitions of heading a new nation comprising Sabah and three southern provinces of the Philippines (Sulu, MINDANAO, and Palawan). The KUANTAN PRINCIPLE (1980), though not implemented, demonstrated the security concerns of Hussein Onn and Indonesia's president SUHARTO (1921–) over the increasing influence of the PRC and the Soviet Union on Vietnam, which had invaded and occupied Cambodia in late December 1978. The Malaysian-Indonesian statement urged the condemnation of Vietnam for its aggression over Cambodia. However, both Indonesia and MALAYSIA (1963) toed the ASEAN line and dropped the KUANTAN PRINCIPLE (1980).

DR. MAHATHIR BIN MOHAMAD (1925–) took over the premiership upon the retirement of Hussein Onn in 1981. DR. MAHATHIR BIN MOHAMAD (1925–) was of common parentage; as a locally trained medical doctor he differed from his predecessors, who had pedigreed backgrounds. Under his leadership the country entered a new era in its development, characterized by phenomenal economic growth throughout the 1980s and lasting till the mid-1990s. The country also enjoyed domestic political stability and became an increasingly important player in the international arena as a voice of the Third World, the South, and the global Muslim community.

Postindependence Burma was plagued with ethnic insurgency, separatist movements, and communist uprisings. Constitutional, civilian government under the ANTI-FASCIST PEOPLE'S FREEDOM LEAGUE (AFPFL) led by U NU (1907–1995) ruled the country until a coup engineered by GENERAL NE WIN (1911–2002) brought about a military dictatorship (1962–1974).

The government of U NU (1907–1995) faced revolts from virtually every known ethnic minority in the country. SHAN NATIONALISM provoked a struggle for a Shan state, and the SHAN UNITED REVOLUTIONARY ARMY (SURA) sought through the force of arms to attain that objective. The KACHIN INDEPENDENCE ORGANIZATION (KIO) championed the nationalist struggle of that hill minority, the KACHINS of northern Burma. Mostly Christianized, the KACHINS resented the policy of U NU (1907–1995) in making BUDDHISM the official religion of the country. The KAREN NATIONAL UNION (KNU), KAREN NATIONAL LIBERATION ARMY (KNLA), and KAREN NATIONAL DEFENCE ORGANIZATION (KNDO) pursued the separatist aspirations of the KARENS through armed insurgency against the central government. Meanwhile, members of the BURMA COMMUNIST PARTY (BCP) sought the overthrow of the government through revolutionary means.

Under the leadership of GENERAL NE WIN (1911–2002), the army undertook a ruthless clampdown on all recalcitrant groups. By the early part of the 1950s most of the country had come under the control of the central government of U NU (1907–1995) at RANGOON (YANGON). Pockets of insurgency remained in the hill regions.

In 1958 schism in the ruling party of the ANTI-FASCIST PEOPLE'S FREEDOM LEAGUE (AFPFL) led U NU (1907–1995) to invite GENERAL NE WIN (1911–2002) to head a "caretaker" government. Meanwhile preparations were made to hold the forthcoming election scheduled for 1960. The military administration sufficiently quelled most insurgencies, fostered economic growth, and weeded out corruption in the public sector. In the 1960 elections, U NU (1907–1995) won under the banner of his Union Party, the so-called Clean faction of the ANTI-FASCIST PEOPLE'S FREEDOM LEAGUE (AFPFL). BUDDHIST SOCIALISM that envisaged a Buddhist welfare state was the prime objective of U NU (1907–1995). But in declaring BUDDHISM to be the state religion. he antagonized non-Buddhist ethnic groups, notably the SHANS and KACHINS; likewise the MONS and the KARENS also displayed dissatisfaction. The communists were undoubtedly opposed to such a policy. Amid intense opposition toward the central government, with revolts flaring up in the regions of the SHANS and KACHINS, GENERAL NE WIN (1911–2002) seized control through a coup and instituted military rule from 1962.

A revolutionary council consisting of a handful of senior officers headed by GENERAL NE WIN (1911–2002) ruled the country by decree; one of the first decrees was the abolition of BUDDHISM as the state religion. GENERAL NE WIN (1911–2002) transformed the political landscape that accommodated a single-party government; the BURMA SOCIALIST PROGRAM PARTY (BSPP) was created in June 1962 to fulfill that end. Its political philosophy was spelled out in its manifesto, "The Burmese Way to Socialism," which was composed of a concoction of Marxism and THERAVADA BUDDHISM. The registration of all members of the *SANGHA* was made mandatory, to preempt any attempt by that influential group to rally against the military government. An isolationist policy was adopted. Educational reform was implemented, including the monastic schools replacing the TRADITIONAL RELIGIOUS EDUCATION with a curriculum designed to inculcate the state ideology in the younger generation. The process of Burmanization was undertaken in earnest (1963–1971), embracing economic, social, and cultural aspects of the country and affecting the inhabitants in virtually all ways. In a single stroke of the brush, Burmanization eliminated Indian, Chinese, and Western (mostly British) trading and commercial interests that had long dominated the country's economy during the period of BURMA UNDER BRITISH COLONIAL RULE.

The Burma of GENERAL NE WIN (1911–2002) was characterized by a stagnating economy, an increasingly flourishing black market, net imports of rice, abuse of power and corruption among the ruling military junta, and an administration staffed by senior military officers. Then in mid-1971, a new constitution and a civilian government assumed power from the military. The civilianization of the government began with the resignation of GEN-

ERAL NE WIN (1911–2002) and twenty of his colleagues to become ordinary citizens who continued to hold the reins of power. The revolutionary council disbanded. Elections held in 1974 in accordance with the new constitution ushered in a council of state under the chairmanship of GENERAL NE WIN (1911–2002), who assumed the presidency of the new, civilian government (1974–1988).

As intended, one-party rule was achieved with the civilian government of the BURMA SOCIALIST PROGRAM PARTY (BSPP). A policy reversal was adopted toward the *SANGHA* and BUDDHISM; the civilian government set up the Ministry of Religious Affairs to offer administrative and financial support. Religious courts were revived to further monitor recalcitrant elements within the Buddhist order. Indians and Chinese were accorded "associated" or "naturalized" categories of citizenship that came with restricted rights in politics and the economy; they were barred from the armed forces.

Notwithstanding the granting of amnesty to U NU (1907–1995) and the release of thousands of political prisoners, the civilian government of the BURMA SOCIALIST PROGRAM PARTY (BSPP) faced civil unrest, with riots in late 1974 caused by rice shortages. Student riots broke out in 1976 to protest declining educational quality standards. Without prior approval from GENERAL NE WIN (1911–2002), the BURMA SOCIALIST PROGRAM PARTY (BSPP) government implemented several liberal policies in response to the social turmoil: foreign aid and investment were encouraged, and the disclosure of assets by public servants and politicians was made mandatory.

GENERAL NE WIN (1911–2002) reacted with a policy reversal and undertook a series of purges (1976, 1977, 1978) of the BURMA SOCIALIST PROGRAM PARTY (BSPP). He replaced the top positions of the party with serving as well as retired military officers. In 1981, GENERAL NE WIN (1911–2002) officially stepped down as president. San Yu assumed the presidency, but it was apparent that his predecessor still held the reins of power behind the scenes. For the next decade (the 1980s), socialist principles were adhered to under the leadership of military personnel.

A combination of adverse weather, mismanagement in rice and other agricultural production and distribution, and escalating inflation resulted in appalling poverty throughout the country. Publicly admitting errors on the part of the government in August 1987, GENERAL NE WIN (1911–2002) implemented various reforms to alleviate the situation. State control over basic food items including rice was lifted; likewise the government monopoly on rice exports in 1988. Devaluation of the *kyat,* intended to undermine the black market, effectively limited the flow of money in the country, prompting student protests in RANGOON (YANGON) and elsewhere. Police reprisals were brutal; universities and schools were closed, and curfew was imposed in most regional centers as unrest spread nationwide.

In response to the national crisis, GENERAL NE WIN (1911–2002) and San Yu stood down from their positions in July 1988. Both the chairmanship of the ruling party and the presidency of the Socialist Republic of the Union of Burma (as the country was then officially designated) passed to the hands of Sein Lwin, a known hardliner. Not surprisingly, protests by reform groups in August were brutally suppressed; it was alleged that thousands were killed.

Under Dr. Maung Maung the situation was stabilized. Martial law was lifted, political prisoners were released, and there were promises of reforms, including elections within three months. Political parties were permitted, hence the emergence of the NATIONAL LEAGUE FOR DEMOCRACY (NLD), which subsequently became the main opposition party. Its leaders included former colleagues and associates of GENERAL NE WIN (1911–2002) such as Brigadier General Aung Gyi and General U Tin Oo. Undoubtedly the most high-profile and most popular leader of the NATIONAL LEAGUE FOR DEMOCRACY (NLD) was the daughter of the slain AUNG SAN (1915–1947), DAW AUNG SAN SUU KYI (1945–).

Anticipating a landslide victory for the NATIONAL LEAGUE FOR DEMOCRACY (NLD) in the forthcoming elections, in September 1988 General Saw Maung, who headed the armed forces, launched a coup. Citing his intention to ensure public order in the followup to the elections, he instead established a new military junta, the STATE LAW AND ORDER RESTORATION COUNCIL (SLORC), with himself as chairman. All governmental institutions and bodies were abolished, demonstrations were proscribed, and a dusk-to-dawn curfew was imposed throughout the country. The army was accused of massacring several hundred protestors following the coup.

SOEKARNO (SUKARNO) (1901–1970) was the first president (t. 1945–1967) of an independent Indonesia. In June 1945 he introduced PANCASILA (PANTJA SILA), the philosophical principles that he hoped would be adopted for an independent Indonesia. The five principles were "belief in one God," "nationalism," "humanitarianism," "democracy," and "social justice." PANCASILA (PANTJA SILA) was incorporated in the preamble of the 1945 constitution and subsequently in the 1949 and 1950 versions. These national principles were intended to act as a unifying set of noble values amid the diversity of the land and the people. The principle of "A belief in one God" was intended to deflect any demands for an Islamic state and at the same time to reject COMMUNISM as the state ideology. Furthermore, BHINNEKA TUNGGAL IKA ("UNITY IN DIVERSITY"), Indonesia's national motto adopted in August 1950, encapsulated the multiethnic, multicultural population spread over 13,000 islands.

The experiment with parliamentary democracy between 1950 and 1957 under the figurehead presidency of SOEKARNO (SUKARNO) (1901–1970) and several brief governments, where prime ministers and cabinets had to resign owing to lack of support, was at best ineffective in attending to the multitude of challenges. The rapid succession of governments of no fewer than five prime ministers and their respective cabinets and governments created disillusionment and lack of confidence.

Disparity and conflicts arose between the heavily populated JAVA and the resource-rich SUMATRA and the Outer Islands. During this period rebellions were aplenty, from the secessionist REPUBLIK MALUKU SELATAN (RMS, REPUBLIC OF THE SOUTH MOLUCCAS) to the Islamic DARUL ISLAM MOVEMENT (DI) in JAVA, SUMATRA, and SULAWESI (CELEBES). The latter sought the establishment of an Islamic state.

One significant achievement that raised the country's standing on the world stage was the hosting of the ASIAN-AFRICAN (BAN-DUNG) CONFERENCE (APRIL 1955), which gave voice to the dilemmas faced by small countries caught in the COLD WAR. The NON-ALIGNED MOVEMENT (NAM) AND SOUTHEAST ASIA offered an alternative, that of neutrality: nations in the region could adopt a neutral stance instead of being manipulated into one of the contending camps—namely, Western democracies versus the communist bloc.

On the domestic front, the elections of 1955 proved the ascendancy of four leading political parties: PARTAI KOMUNIS INDONESIA (PKI) (1920), MADJELIS SJURO MUS-LIMIN INDONESIA (MASJUMI) (COUN-CIL OF INDONESIAN MUSLIM ASSOCI-ATIONS), PERSERIKATAN NASIONAL INDONESIA (PNI) (1927), and NAHDATUL ULAMA. In terms of support, there was a JAVA predominance among the parties except for MADJELIS SJURO MUSLIMIN IN-DONESIA (MASJUMI) (COUNCIL OF IN-DONESIAN MUSLIM ASSOCIATIONS), which possessed strongholds in western SUMATRA, southwestern SULAWESI (Celebes), and among the Sundanese of eastern JAVA. Cleavages were also drawn between the *SANTRI* (devout Muslims), staunch supporters of NAHDATUL ULAMA, and ABANGAN (pre-Islamic syncretism) that provided sustenance to MADJELIS SJURO MUSLIMIN INDONESIA (MASJUMI) (COUNCIL OF INDONESIAN MUSLIM ASSOCIATIONS).

SOEKARNO (SUKARNO) (1901–1970) became restless holding an impotent presidency. In early 1957, with backing from GENERAL ABDUL HARIS NASUTION (1918–2000), the chief of staff of the army, SOEKARNO (SUKARNO) (1901–1970) demanded a return to the 1945 constitution whereby the president was not only the ceremonial head of state but also invested with executive power to govern.

Having straddled himself with executive power, SOEKARNO (SUKARNO) (1901–1970) introduced GUIDED DEMOCRACY (*DEMOKRASI TERPIMPIN*), which drew sustenance from indigenous concepts and indigenous styles of decision-making. *Musyawarah* and *mufakat* were two procedures commonly practiced at the village level that were adopted at the national level. The former refers to prolonged discussions before arriving at a consensual (*mu-fakat*) decision. He proposed the inclusion of functional groups besides political parties to compose the Majelis Permusyawaratan Rakyat (MPR, People's Consultative Assembly). Overall, GUIDED DEMOCRACY (*DEMOKRASI TERPIMPIN*) represented a retreat toward authoritarianism, the curtailment of democracy and at the same time increased authoritarian rule with SOEKARNO (SUKARNO) (1901–1970) as supreme dictator. SOEKARNO (SUKARNO) (1901–1970) sought self-glorification and embarked on a grandiose campaign with symbols of greatness reflected in national monuments and impressive public buildings matched by equally impressive slogans to make his fellow countrymen proud to be Indonesians and of their independence.

More concerned with showmanship and his oratorical skills, SOEKARNO (SUKARNO) (1901–1970) was uninterested in day-to-day administration and attending to real issues facing his regime. On the economic front GUIDED DEMOCRACY (*DEMOKRASI TERPIMPIN*) was a national calamity. The country suffered from high inflation, declining exports, and a massive foreign debt. Nationalization of Western, mainly Dutch, enterprises, with a military that lacked managerial and technical expertise assuming control, led to neglect, decline, and waste. The land reform program, though commendable, faced bureaucratic inertia as well as resistance from vested local interests.

SOEKARNO (SUKARNO) (1901–1970), acting like the Javanese *dalang* ("puppeteer"), orchestrated a balancing act between the armed forces and PARTAI KOMUNIS INDONESIA (PKI) (1920), often playing one against the other. He consistently shielded the communists from attacks by the army and increasingly made use of communist rhetoric—for example, emphasizing the continuing revolution for the poor and the oppressed. SOEKARNO (SUKARNO) (1901–1970) used the PARTAI KOMUNIS INDONESIA (PKI) (1920) in mobilizing popular support. By the mid-1960s the PARTAI KOMUNIS INDONESIA (PKI) (1920) claimed to receive support from more than one-third of the country's population. Although Indonesia adopted a neutralist stance following the ASIAN-AFRICAN (BAN-DUNG) CONFERENCE (APRIL 1955), SOEKARNO (SUKARNO) (1901–1970) progressively moved against the Western democracies (Oldfos, Old Established Forces, as against Nefos, New Emerging Forces). The army and Muslim groups were concerned about the potential threat of the communists, though none held power; some quarters even speculated about a coup by the PARTAI KOMUNIS INDONESIA (PKI) (1920) following the death or sickness of SOEKARNO (SUKARNO) (1901–1970).

Therefore, during the second half of the 1950s there emerged the Pemerintah Revolusioner Republik Indonesia (PRRI, Revolutionary Government of the Republic of Indonesia), a right-wing uprising of the military in response to GUIDED DEMOCRACY (*DEMOKRASI TERPIMPIN*). The intention was to establish a conservative national government with a more balanced representation than the JAVA-based, increasingly left-leaning central administration, which apparently sidelined the Outer Islands. PRRI was confined to western parts of SUMATRA and northern SULAWESI (CELEBES). The recalcitrant army units that set up PRRI were crushed within four months in 1958; remnants of the rebel force, however, continued their struggle until 1961.

The parochial and staunchly Islamic ACEH (ACHEH) began in the early 1950s to resent the JAVA-based central government that from the vantage point of faraway northern SUMATRA was corrupt, un-Islamic, and nonchalant regarding affairs of the provinces. Daud Beureu'éh (1906–1987) led a rebellion in ACEH (ACHEH) in the latter part of 1953 that subsequently merged into the wider DARUL ISLAM MOVEMENT (DI), which aimed at the creation of an Islamic state of Indonesia. As a peace settlement, ACEH (ACHEH) was accorded the status of *Daerah Istimewa* ("Special Territory") in 1959, which allowed it greater autonomy over religious and educational affairs.

In foreign relations SOEKARNO (SUKARNO) (1901–1970) won genuine support among Indonesians when IRIAN JAYA (WEST IRIAN) was recovered in 1962. (The Dutch retained the territory in 1949.) *KONFRONTASI* ("CRUSH MALAYSIA" CAMPAIGN) was launched in 1963 in response to SOEKARNO (SUKARNO) (1901–1970) perceiving MALAYSIA (1963) as a British strategy to retain its influence in Southeast Asia. The In-

donesian armed forces launched cross-border incursions into SARAWAK AND SABAH (NORTH BORNEO) with inconsequential results. In protest against the appointment of MALAYSIA (1963) as a member of the UN Security Council, Indonesia withdrew from the world body.

The GESTAPU AFFAIR (1965) on 30 September witnessed the kidnapping and killing of six generals by a group of allegedly left-wing junior army officers. Then a full-scale attempt at seizure of power was launched, despite the poor preparation for such a major undertaking. The backlash was spearheaded by SUHARTO (1921–), then deputy to the army chief of staff and commander of KOSTRAD (Army Strategic Reserve Command). The communists were blamed for the coup attempt. The PARTAI KOMUNIS INDONESIA (PKI) (1920) was proscribed. The ensuing witch hunt claimed, it was believed, the deaths of half a million party members and communist sympathizers, mainly at the hands of the army. Another 1.5 million were detained for various periods.

Between October 1965 and March 1966 SOEKARNO (SUKARNO) (1901–1970) was increasingly eased out of power. Initially elected as acting president by the MPR in March 1967 and as president in March 1968, SUHARTO (1921–) was cautious not to provoke the supporters of the charismatic and still-popular SOEKARNO (SUKARNO) (1901–1970). The latter moved off center stage and remained under house arrest until his death in 1970.

ORDE BARU (THE NEW ORDER) was the regime ushered in by SUHARTO (1921–) when he assumed the reins of power. First and foremost, in external relations, he terminated *KONFRONTASI* ("CRUSH MALAYSIA" CAMPAIGN) and by 1966 attained normalization with KUALA LUMPUR (KL). Likewise Indonesia rejoined the United Nations. In 1967, Indonesia became one of the founding members of the ASSOCIATION OF SOUTHEAST ASIAN NATIONS (ASEAN) (1967). ADAM MALIK (1917–1984), architect of the foreign policy of *ORDE BARU* (THE NEW ORDER), played a significant role in rehabilitating Indonesia's international standing. Besides ADAM MALIK (1917–1984), the *ORDE BARU* (THE NEW ORDER) regime incorporated civilian leaders such as Sultan Hamengkubuwono IX of YOGYAKARTA

(JOGJAKARTA). The armed forces allied with the civil administration to support a basically authoritarian form of government headed by SUHARTO (1921–) at the apex of its power structure.

Political groups were amalgamated with Muslim-based parties coming under the umbrella of the United Development Party, whereas non-Muslim parties joined the Indonesian Democratic Party. Then there was the Joint Secretariat of Functional Groups, or GOLKAR, a nonpartisan government-sponsored organization comprising the functional groups (similar to those of the MPR). In reality, GOLKAR was a government party with full support of the incumbent during elections.

The regime of the *ORDE BARU* (THE NEW ORDER) adopted the PANCASILA (PANTJA SILA) as the national ideology. It was vigorously promoted during the first two decades of SUHARTO's (1921–) 30-year presidency.

Dwifungsi, or dual function, the idea that the military undertook the dual roles of national defense and ensuring a stable and efficient government, guaranteed the prominent place of the military in the *ORDE BARU* (THE NEW ORDER) setup. Operating on this concept, members of the Indonesian armed forces (serving and retired personnel) took on the task of becoming village heads, factory managers, and chief executive officers (CEOs) of corporations to cabinet ministers.

The *ORDE BARU* (THE NEW ORDER), in contrast to its predecessor, was fully committed to economic recovery. A group of U.S.-trained economists was entrusted to effect the turnaround of the deteriorating economy. Their efforts bore fruit. Within a decade the economy not only recovered but also was rapidly developing, with impressive growth rates. Inflation was reduced and the *rupiah* stabilized. Adoption of new techniques in rice cultivation improved production to the extent that by the early 1980s the country had become self-sufficient in rice, the staple food. Foreign direct investments (FDIs) paid handsome returns, especially conspicuous in oil and natural gas exploration and exploitation (through Pertamina, the state oil corporation), forestry, and the manufacturing sector. FDIs benefited the Outer Islands, specifically northern SUMATRA, Riau, IRIAN JAYA (WEST IRIAN), and eastern Kaliman-

tan. Profits from the oil industry underwrote a massive program of infrastructure development that was viewed as the basis for growth. Military entrepreneurs drawing from a younger generation with business savvy, coupled with managerial skills, brought success and profits to military-managed enterprises.

Economic development and the successes gained brought about the emergence of an Indonesian middle class. A cross-sectional profile of its components ranged from rural small-time traders to big-time capitalists, top bureaucrats to clerical personnel, military officers, professionals, and Chinese entrepreneurs (from retail shop owners to wealthy industrialists). The booming economy helped to spur rapid population growth. A decade of the vigorous implementation of the transmigration scheme (transferring inhabitants from densely populated regions like JAVA and BALI to sparsely populated areas like BORNEO and SUMATRA) succeeded to some extent in lessening population pressure, especially in JAVA. The social consequences of transmigration and the blossoming middle class began to be felt toward the third decade of SUHARTO's (1921–) rule.

The transmigration program in the 1970s that brought other Indonesians to ACEH (ACHEH) was greatly resented by the highly provincial Acehnese, who felt that their autonomy was being compromised. Furthermore, the exploitation of natural resources such as natural gas and coal by the central government, with few of the profits being plowed back to the province, angered the locals. The general feeling was that the autonomy granted in the late 1950s was being eroded. Exploiting the widespread resentment, Hasan di Tiro established the Gerakan Aceh Merdeka (GAM, Free Aceh Movement) in 1976; he boldly declared the independence of ACEH (ACHEH) in 1977. When the military suppressed the rebellion, Hasan di Tiro formed a government-in-exile in Sweden, where he and several others were granted political asylum.

Dictatorship was in the making when in November 1965 constitutionally elected FERDINAND MARCOS (1917–1989), shortly after his second term as Philippine president, declared MARTIAL LAW (1972–1981) (THE PHILIPPINES). During his first term, Marcos faced serious opposition: student activism, a renewed leftist insurgency by the NEW

PEOPLE'S ARMY (NPA), and secessionist movements from Muslims in MINDANAO. From 1969, student demonstrations increased in frequency, demanding social justice and economic sovereignty. The latter referred to the preferential status accorded foreign, particularly U.S., businesses and investments. The gap between the rich and the poor was rapidly widening; the flawed distribution of the country's economic pie made the rich richer and the poor poorer, forcing the latter to seek revolutionary solutions to their predicament. The frustration and dissatisfaction of the lower classes resulted in their swelling the ranks of the NEW PEOPLE'S ARMY (NPA), the military arm of the Communist Party of the Philippines (CPP), led by Jose Maria Sison (1939–). While the Partido Komunista ng Pilipinas (PKP, Philippines Communist Party) preferred the constitutional and parliamentary way to redress grievances and condemned violence, Sison and the CPP turned to armed revolutionary means. The Muslim MOROS of the southern Philippines had long resented the rule of the Christian central government of MANILA and sought cession. The MORO NATIONAL LIBERATION FRONT (MNLF), headed by NUR MISUARI (1940–), launched an armed struggle to break away from the Republic of the Philippines.

The presidency (t. 1965–1986) of FERDINAND MARCOS (1917–1989) witnessed a mounting foreign debt brought about by massive public expenditure on infrastructure, largely financed by foreign loans. Critics accused the Marcoses—the president and the first lady, Imelda Romualdez Marcos (1930–)—of having amassed a huge personal fortune allegedly plundered from the country; likewise their associates (cronies), who had benefited enormously from government contracts involving corruption and plunder. Conspicuous consumption by the first family further fueled rumors of personal aggrandizement. Key wealthy landowning families and political figures kept private armies.

Against this volatile backdrop and as a means not only to secure but also to strengthen Marcos's position, MARTIAL LAW (1972–1981) (THE PHILIPPINES) was imposed from September 1972. Under a new constitution, FERDINAND MARCOS (1917–1989) was both president and prime minister, possessing far-reaching executive and legislative powers. He was empowered to dictate the convening of the National Assembly (Batasang Pambansa). In 1978 he formed the NEW SOCIETY MOVEMENT (KILUSANG BAGONG LIPUNAN, KBL), created specifically to keep him in power. Not surprisingly, the KBL won in the elections to the National Assembly in April 1978 as well as in local polls held in January 1980.

Under MARTIAL LAW (1972–1981) (THE PHILIPPINES), which ran until January 1981, the country returned to authoritarian dictatorial rule. The justification for declaring MARTIAL LAW (1972–1981) (THE PHILIPPINES) was the deteriorating law-and-order situation in the country, which was rapidly sliding into anarchy with antigovernment demonstrations and a declining economy, in addition to a growing Muslim secessionist movement in the southern provinces. All protests and dissents were violently suppressed; democracy was suspended. Opposition politicians, including Benigno ("Ninoy") Aquino Jr. (1932–1983), were held in detention. Large hoards of firearms were confiscated from the general public, and private militias were disbanded. Owing to these high-handed measures, there was a temporary lull in antigovernment protests during the mid-1970s.

In the Tripoli Agreement brokered by Muammar al-Qaddafi (1942–) of Libya in the late 1970s, the Philippines government agreed to grant regional autonomy to the Muslim areas in the southern provinces. It was alleged that leaders of the MORO NATIONAL LIBERATION FRONT (MNLF) were bought over with large monetary handouts.

Despite repressive measures, from the late 1970s, antigovernment protests were again active and highly vocal. Under pressure from the international community and especially from Washington, MARTIAL LAW (1972–1981) (THE PHILIPPINES) was lifted in early 1981. Earlier, several political detainees had been released. Upon his leaving detention in May 1980, Aquino left for the United States for medical treatment.

Three years later, in August 1983, Aquino returned home from self-exile in the United States. Among the leaders of the opposition, Aquino appeared to be the most viable alternative to FERDINAND MARCOS (1917–

1989). Upon alighting from the aircraft, Aquino was shot by one Rolando Galman, who in turn was killed by military guards. According to the published report (October 1984) of an independent commission of inquiry, a military conspiracy had engineered the assassination. Twenty-five officers, including General Fabian Ver, commander of the armed forces, were tried for the murder.

By the mid-1980s the Philippines was racked with daily demonstrations, faced with a massive foreign debt, and suffering a tottering economy close to collapse. The disparate opposition prudently decided to combine under the United Nationalist Democratic Organization (UNIDO). When presidential elections were announced for early 1986, CORAZON CO-JUANGCO AQUINO (1933–), Aquino's widow, and Salvador Laurel became presidential and vice presidential candidates, respectively, on the UNIDO ticket. Just prior to the elections, General Ver and others were acquitted of murder charges; many believed that FERDINAND MARCOS (1917–1989) had had a hand in the verdict.

In the presidential elections on 7 February 1986, FERDINAND MARCOS (1917–1989) claimed victory. The government's Commission on Elections (Comelec) authenticated this claim, and the National Assembly endorsed Marcos as president. Meanwhile, the National Movement for Free Elections (Namfrel), an election watchdog organization financed by the National Endowment for Democracy based in the United States, declared CORAZON CO-JUANGCO AQUINO (1933–) president. The influential Catholic Church of the Philippines led by Cardinal Jaime Sin declared the elections a fraud; several foreign observers concurred. A week later Aquino launched a nonviolent civil disobedience campaign to protest the election results.

Thereafter a military coup by right-wing reformist army officers (Reform the Armed Forces Movement, RAM) occurred on 21 February. The following day saw the minister of national defense, Juan Ponce Enrile, and the deputy chief of staff of the armed forces, Lieutenant General FIDEL VALDEZ RAMOS (1928–), seeking refuge in Camp Aguinaldo; both had renounced their support for FERDINAND MARCOS (1917–1989). Within the next two days Enrile and Ramos received support from Cardinal Jaime Sin and the United States. Led by CORAZON COJUANGCO AQUINO (1933–), more than a million Filipinos from all walks of life gathered peacefully at EDSA (Epifanio De los Santos Avenue—henceforth the EDSA REVOLUTION [1986]) to lend their support to the duo. Under pressure from Washington, on 25 February FERDINAND MARCOS (1917–1989) reluctantly left the presidential Malacanang Palace for Hawai'i on board a U.S. Air Force plane. The EDSA REVOLUTION (1986) of "people power" had brought about the presidency of CORAZON COJUANGCO AQUINO (1933–) (t. 1986–1992).

Following the partition, SOUTH VIETNAM (POST-1945) came under a noncommunist regime headed by former emperor BẢO ĐAI (VĨNH THỤY) (1913–1997). In June 1954, NGÔ ĐÌNH DIỆM (1901–1963), with backing from the United States, became prime minister. In October 1955 through a government-orchestrated referendum, BẢO ĐAI (VĨNH THỤY) (1913–1997) was removed as head of state and replaced by NGÔ ĐÌNH DIỆM (1901–1963), who also assumed the premiership. Together with his brother, Ngo Dinh Nhu (d. 1963), who operated a pervasive secret security force, NGÔ ĐÌNH DIỆM (1901–1963) attempted through totalitarian methods to eliminate all opposition. His pro-Catholic regime alienated the majority Buddhist population—particularly his repressive campaigns against members of the Buddhist clergy. Apart from plans for land reform that failed to materialize owing to resistance from vested interests, NGÔ ĐÌNH DIỆM (1901–1963) expanded resources in building up the ARMY OF THE REPUBLIC OF VIETNAM (ARVN). The communists, referred to as VIET CONG, were the main enemy, as they sought to overthrow the regime and reunify the country. NGÔ ĐÌNH DIỆM (1901–1963) rejected the all-Vietnamese elections as provided for by the Final Declaration consequent of the GENEVA CONFERENCE (1954).

In NORTH VIETNAM (POST-1945), the Democratic Republic of Vietnam (DRV) under HỒ CHÍ MINH (1890–1969) launched a land reform program (1953–1956) designed to eliminate as a class rich peasants and landlords. The lands thus confiscated were redistributed to landless farmers. Cooperatives were established in the late 1950s; another energetic drive, by TRUONG CHINH (1907–1988), commenced a decade later. The less conservative LE DUAN (1907–1986) replaced TRUONG CHINH (1907–1988) as party secretary in 1959. In order to assess the situation himself, LE DUAN secretly toured SOUTH VIETNAM (POST-1945) in 1956 and again in 1958. He was responsible for designing a new strategy (1959) for the armed struggle undertaken by the VIET CONG. Courted by both Moscow and Beijing with material support and technical assistance, LE DUAN (1907–1986) was treading on delicate ground against the backdrop of the SINO-SOVIET STRUGGLE in the late 1950s and early 1960s.

In 1960 the National Front for the Liberation of South Viet Nam, popularly known as the National Liberation Front (NLF), was established to challenge the SAIGON (GIA DINH, HỒ CHÍ MINH CITY) regime. At this time U.S. president John Fitzgerald Kennedy (t. 1961–1963) was convinced of the DOMINO THEORY, first advanced by his predecessor Dwight David Eisenhower (t. 1953–1961); he therefore determined to contain the spread of COMMUNISM. A contingent of U.S. Army personnel (about 8,000) were stationed in SOUTH VIETNAM (POST-1945) as advisers to the ARMY OF THE REPUBLIC OF VIETNAM (ARVN). In mid-1963 the VIET CONG launched an offensive and through guerrilla tactics managed to control several rural areas. Then in November 1963, apparently with U.S. approval, elements within the ARMY OF THE REPUBLIC OF VIETNAM (ARVN) ousted NGÔ ĐÌNH DIỆM (1901–1963), who was killed together with Ngo Dinh Nhu. Following the coup, two more military seizures of power occurred before NGUYỄN VAN THIEU (1923–2001) became head of state and Nguyễn Cao Ky his prime minister. (Under the new constitution in 1967, NGUYỄN VAN THIEU [1923–2001] was elected president [t. 1967–1975], and Nguyễn Cao Ky, vice president.)

The GULF OF TONKIN INCIDENT (AUGUST 1964), the naval exchange between U.S. warships and naval units of NORTH VIETNAM (POST-1945), was the pretext used by President Lyndon Baines Johnson (t. 1963–1969) to commence the involvement of the United States in Vietnam on a massive scale.

The U.S. Congress had given the president carte blanche authority to address the situation in Vietnam without any formal declaration of war. The number of U.S. combat troops rose rapidly; by early 1968, U.S. military forces stood at more than half a million men. The naval firefight in the GULF OF TONKIN INCIDENT (AUGUST 1964) was the first salvo in the SECOND (VIETNAM WAR) INDOCHINA WAR (1964–1975), commonly referred to as the Vietnam War.

The increasing presence of U.S. combat troops as well as contingents from the Philippines, Thailand, Australia, and the Republic of Korea (South Korea) witnessed the escalation of the conflict. Aerial bombardment over NORTH VIETNAM (POST-1945) commenced in March 1965. Although no regular DRV troops were deployed at this juncture (mid-1960s), the VIỆT CONG through the NLF received supplies from NORTH VIETNAM (POST-1945). The HỒ CHÍ MINH TRAIL, a complex network of hidden and camouflaged tracks through jungles traversing southern Laos and northeastern parts of Cambodia, was the main supply conduit between NORTH VIETNAM (POST-1945) and SOUTH VIETNAM (POST-1945). Military aid from the Soviet Union to the DRV increased proportionally to the escalation of this undeclared war.

The TET OFFENSIVE (1968), though a military defeat for the VIỆT CONG that launched a major offensive, including attacks on SAIGON (GIA DINH, HỒ CHÍ MINH CITY), was a political triumph. The offensive was coupled with domestic mass demonstrations in the United States, and Washington was forced to reevaluate its Vietnam policy. Informal peace talks began in Paris; then in early 1969, President Richard Milhous Nixon (t. 1969–1974) converted that informal discussion into a peace conference involving all parties concerned. The PARIS PEACE AGREEMENT (1968, 1973) (VIETNAM) at this stage came to nothing. Nixon commenced troop withdrawals, as domestic pressure was mounting for disengagement.

Notwithstanding the PARIS PEACE AGREEMENT (1968, 1973) (VIETNAM), the years from 1969 to 1970 saw the intensification of the war. In April 1970 the Americans launched an invasion of Cambodia to unseat

NORODOM SIHANOUK (1922–). The following year they made incursions into Laos in an attempt to destroy the HỒ CHÍ MINH TRAIL. The early part of 1970 witnessed the entry of regular troops of the DRV.

The year 1972 was a turning point in the SECOND (VIETNAM WAR) INDOCHINA WAR (1964–1975). By the early part of the year the number of U.S. combatants stood at about 95,000, following withdrawals since 1969. The VIET CONG launched a new offensive. The U.S. response was the massive bombardment of NORTH VIETNAM (POST-1945), including HANOI (THANG-LONG) and the mining of Haiphong and other harbors. By September a deadlock in the conflict was apparent.

Meanwhile, on the outskirts of Paris, secret discussions were held (starting in 1969) between LE DUC THO (1911–), a senior figure of the DRV, and Dr. Henry Kissinger (1923–), chief presidential adviser on foreign policy and national security. In order to force the communists to the negotiating table following the collapse of secret talks, December 1972 witnessed the heaviest bombing raids on NORTH VIETNAM (POST-1945), including on HANOI (THANG-LONG). The following January a ceasefire agreement was secured in Paris. In the PARIS PEACE AGREEMENT (1968, 1973) (VIETNAM), the United States agreed to a complete withdrawal and the DRV reciprocated by the return of U.S. prisoners of war.

As far as the U.S. government was concerned, the war had ended. The issue of MIAs (MISSING IN ACTION) remained unresolved, and MY LAI and similar incidents continued to haunt the U.S. conscience. The Vietnam War was a war that Washington and the U.S. public would prefer to forget.

LE DUAN (1907–1986) lent his support to a new offensive in early 1975, one aimed at toppling the government of NGUYỄN VAN THIEU (1923–2001). To the delighted surprise of the campaign's planners, the ARMY OF THE REPUBLIC OF VIETNAM (ARVN), without their U.S. allies, offered scant resistance, and within two months (instead of the anticipated two years), the regime collapsed. SAIGON (GIA DINH, HỒ CHÍ MINH CITY) was captured on 30 April 1975 without much fighting.

The two decades following Cambodia's independence in 1953 witnessed challenges to the political ascendancy of NORODOM SIHANOUK (1922–) from virtually all shades of the political spectrum. Feeling restricted as a constitutional monarch, he stood down from the throne to establish the SANGKUM REASTRE NIYUM (PEOPLES' SOCIALIST COMMUNITY) (MARCH 1955), a mass political movement. (His father, Norodom Suramarit [t. 1955–1960], succeeded to the throne.) The SANGKUM REASTRE NIYUM (PEOPLES' SOCIALIST COMMUNITY) (MARCH 1955) defeated the Democrats in the polls held in late 1955 and dominated the National Assembly. Styled as Prince NORODOM SIHANOUK (1922–), he was prime minister until he ascended the throne upon his father's death in 1960. His authoritarian rule limited all forms of political activity; the state police clamped down on all opposition. A handful of Cambodian communists fled to the northeast forest fringe of the country bordering Vietnam; in that isolated refuge, POL POT (SALOTH SAR) (1925–1998) and his comrades built up the KHMER ROUGE, or Red Khmer.

In foreign relations NORODOM SIHANOUK (1922–) adopted a nationalist stance opposing in general the U.S. INVOLVEMENT IN SOUTHEAST ASIA (POST-1945) and in particular the U.S. role in SOUTH VIETNAM (POST-1945) and in the SECOND (VIETNAM WAR) INDOCHINA WAR (1964–1975). U.S. MILITARY BASES IN SOUTHEAST ASIA, especially those established in SOUTH VIETNAM (POST-1945) and Thailand, were viewed with misgivings. But at the same time, NORODOM SIHANOUK (1922–) was not in favor of a communist victory in the Vietnam conflict and the threat of a unified Vietnam under HỒ CHÍ MINH (1890–1969). Publicly Cambodia then adopted a neutrality position on the international stage. In 1965, however, convinced of Washington's attempt through the regime of NGÔ ĐÌNH DIỆM (1901–1963) to topple his government, NORODOM SIHANOUK (1922–) broke off diplomatic relations with the United States. To counter the U.S. threat, he allowed the VIỆT CONG to operate on Cambodian soil; secret agreements with HANOI (THANG-LONG) protected a communist offensive against PHNOM PENH. At the same time, he also moved closer to Beijing when the Vietnam War escalated from the mid-1960s.

Domestically, NORODOM SIHANOUK (1922–), though revered by the masses, faced serious opposition from both the conservative right and the radical left. The former resented his break with Washington while the latter was indignant over the shackles placed on political dissent. Furthermore, the non-state-orchestrated elections of 1966 brought members to the National Assembly who were not particularly pro-Sihanouk. Drawn from the small Cambodian intelligentsia, these members voiced their opposition to the authoritarian regime. The prince responded with even more severe repression against the opposition forces. The pro-U.S. Khmer Serei headed by SON NGOC THANH (1907–1976?) received the brunt of the prince's wrath, including public executions of its members (or Thanists). Notwithstanding his clandestine arrangements with the VIỆT CONG, POL POT (SALOTH SAR) (1925–1998) and his comrades increasingly engaged the Cambodian army in skirmishes in the northeast of the country. Rapprochement with Washington increased domestic communist opposition. There had been a deteriorating economic situation since the mid-1960s, and by 1969 NORODOM SIHANOUK (1922–) found himself caged in on all sides; he had failed in his juggling act to play off one enemy against the other.

In March 1970, LON NOL (1913–1984), the prime minister of Cambodia and commander of the armed forces, together with anti-communist elements such as SON NGOC THANH (1907–1976?), engineered a bloodless coup that ousted NORODOM SIHANOUK (1922–) from power. The prince was in Moscow when the plotters announced the establishment of the Khmer Republic headed by LON NOL (1913–1984). The coup leaders justified their action by arguing that NORODOM SIHANOUK (1922–) had compromised the country's sovereignty and permitted a threat to its independence by allowing the VIET CONG sanctuary on Cambodian soil. LON NOL (1913–1984) assumed the presidency, while SON NGOC THANH (1907–1976?) became the prime minister of the new government.

From Moscow, NORODOM SIHANOUK (1922–) proceeded to Beijing. Convinced of U.S. involvement in his ouster, he readily agreed with his Chinese host to head a united front government-in-exile that incorporated the KHMER ROUGE and was allied with the People's Republic of China (PRC) and the Democratic Republic of Vietnam (DRV), then headed by LE DUAN (1907–1986). The prince thereupon entered the socialist camp in the COLD WAR.

The formation of the Khmer Republic of LON NOL (1913–1984) brought the country into the SECOND (VIETNAM WAR) INDOCHINA WAR (1964–1975). Opposition to the new government in the form of mass demonstrations by NORODOM SIHANOUK (1922–) loyalists and communists prompted an invasion by a joint U.S. and ARMY OF THE REPUBLIC OF VIETNAM (ARVN) force in May 1970. Ironically, the invasion, which was meant to eliminate the VIỆT CONG in eastern Cambodia, instead drove them farther inland. The Vietnamese communists assisted the KHMER ROUGE in training and organization, provision of military supplies, and recruitment. With Vietnamese support the KHMER ROUGE was in a stronger position to play a greater role in the United National Front of Cambodia (FUNC), led by NORODOM SIHANOUK (1922–) in exile. LON NOL (1913–1984) on his part launched two unsuccessful offensives against the VIET CONG and KHMER ROUGE.

Notwithstanding massive U.S. military and economic aid, the corrupt Khmer Republic was crumbling. The armed forces of LON NOL (1913–1984) suffered defeat toward the close of 1972. The Vietnamese presence was most unpopular among the population, and the government's inability to eject them encouraged opposition demanding its removal. The saturation bombing undertaken by the U.S. Air Force over Cambodia for the greater part of 1973 was inconsequential. But the PARIS PEACE AGREEMENT (1968, 1973) (VIETNAM) resulted in the withdrawal of the VIET CONG from Cambodia. Toward the end of 1973, LON NOL (1913–1984) controlled only the capital city, PHNOM PENH, parts of the northwest region, and several provincial towns; the rest of the country was under the KHMER ROUGE.

The ascendancy of the KHMER ROUGE was apparent when they occupied ministerial portfolios in the government-in-exile styled as the Royal Government of National Union of

Cambodia, led by the then-powerless NORO-DOM SIHANOUK (1922–). Despite past assistance and collaboration, the KHMER ROUGE always viewed the Vietnamese communists as a threat and began to eliminate (mainly killed) pro-Vietnamese elements within their ranks. KHMER ROUGE forces rapidly closed in on PHNOM PENH. In early April 1975 the Khmer Republic collapsed; the KHMER ROUGE captured PHNOM PENH on 17 April. Earlier, LON NOL (1913–1984) was airlifted by the Americans to Hawai'i.

Within weeks of their victory and entry into PHNOM PENH, the KHMER ROUGE removed all inhabitants to the countryside, leaving behind ghost towns. The high death toll from the hurried forced evacuation was the prelude to four horrifying years when Cambodia was transformed into *THE KILLING FIELDS*, which consumed an estimated 1.7 million lives, or about 15 percent of the country's population. (Some estimates place the death toll at more than 2 million.)

DEMOCRATIC KAMPUCHEA (DK) was a radical Marxist-Leninist regime set up by the KHMER ROUGE headed by the little-known former schoolteacher POL POT (SALOTH SAR) (1925–1998). Among his more prominent comrades were IENG SARY (1927–), CHEA SIM (1932–), KHIEU SAMPHAN (1931–), HENG SAMRIN (1934–), and HUN SEN (1951–). Drawing inspiration from Maoist China, the leadership believed in the peasantry as the vanguard of the revolution, and that revolutionary will alone could overcome all obstacles and attain the utopia outlined by COMMUNISM. Money, markets, and private property were abolished; likewise, schools, hospitals, shops, and monasteries were closed. Publication of books and newspapers was proscribed. Everyone was to don peasant clothing (which was dull and formless), not unlike the population in Maoist China. The attempt at achieving total collectivization of the country and doubling the rice output witnessed the emptying of the towns and removal of the entire population to the rural areas, where they became an army of slave laborers. Overwork, disease, malnutrition, starvation, and execution drove the death toll to horrific figures.

The paranoia that engulfed POL POT (SALOTH SAR) (1925–1998) and the handful of cadres led to the torture and execution of thousands of so-called traitors in the notorious interrogation facility of the regime in PHNOM PENH. Party members were continuously purged to weed out "traitors." This untenable situation drove many, such as HENG SAMRIN (1934–), HUN SEN (1951–), and CHEA SIM (1932–), to defect to the Vietnamese.

Elections were held in March 1976 for the People's Representative Assembly, a legislative body. The restricted electorate, limited to supporters of the KHMER ROUGE, elected KHIEU SAMPHAN (1931–) as chairman and the relatively unknown POL POT (SALOTH SAR) (1925–1998) as prime minister. NORODOM SIHANOUK (1922–), by then in PHNOM PENH, declined the role as the head of state. In 1977, POL POT (SALOTH SAR) (1925–1998) publicly declared that the Communist Party of Kampuchea (CPK) was the ruling party of the country.

Then on Christmas Day 1978, a huge Vietnamese force invaded Cambodia, and within weeks, DEMOCRATIC KAMPUCHEA (DK) collapsed. POL POT (SALOTH SAR) (1925–1998) and the KHMER ROUGE fled to Thailand. A Vietnamese-sponsored regime, the People's Republic of Kampuchea (PRK), was inaugurated. Accompanying the Vietnamese military force were HENG SAMRIN (1934–), HUN SEN (1951–), and CHEA SIM (1932–), who formed the leadership of the KAMPUCHEA UNITED FRONT FOR NATIONAL SALVATION (KUFNS).

According to the GENEVA CONFERENCE (1954), instead of partition like neighboring Vietnam, an armistice was declared in LAOS (NINETEENTH CENTURY TO MID-1990s). The northeastern provinces of Xam Neua and Phongsali were allocated to the procommunist PATHET LAO (LAND OF LAOS), led by SOUPHANOUVONG (RED PRINCE) (1911–1995), and the rest of the country to the Royal Lao Government (RLG) based in VIENTIANE. Furthermore, elections were to be held as a means of effecting the unification of the country. Having failed to agree on the electoral process, the RLG proceeded with elections in regions under its jurisdiction. Heading the newly formed government was SOUVANNA PHOUMA (1901–1984), younger brother of PHETSARATH (1890–1959) and the half-brother of SOUPHANOUVONG (RED PRINCE) (1911–1995).

By the mid-1950s, the United States had replaced France as the major Western power in Indochina supporting the Republic of Vietnam or SOUTH VIETNAM (POST-1945) and the government of SOUVANNA PHOUMA (1901–1984) in Laos. As in Vietnam, the major concern of the Americans in Laos was to prevent a communist takeover. SOUVANNA PHOUMA (1901–1984), on the other hand, possessed a nationalist agenda—namely, the unification of Laos, and a neutralist stance lest the country be dragged into the COLD WAR. Under an agreement with SOUPHANOU-VONG (RED PRINCE) (1911–1995), SOU-VANNA PHOUMA (1901–1984) accepted two representatives of the PATHET LAO (LAND OF LAOS) in the coalition in order that national unity be achieved with the inclusion of the two provinces.

The Americans retaliated by cutting off aid to the country, which succeeded in bringing down the coalition government of SOU-VANNA PHOUMA (1901–1984). From 1958 to 1960, right-wing elements and the military (Lao National Army [LNA]) took turns dominating the government; the United States resumed its support. In the early part of 1961, amid the clash between the neutralist party led by SOUVANNA PHOUMA (1901–1984) and the PATHET LAO (LAND OF LAOS), headed by SOUPHANOUVONG (RED PRINCE) (1911–1995), the Americans pursued a policy for the neutralization of Laos. A second coalition government including representatives from the PATHET LAO (LAND OF LAOS) declared the neutralization of Laos in July 1962.

SOUVANNA PHOUMA (1901–1984), one of the powerless neutralists in the second coalition government, was able neither to achieve unification nor to prevent the country from being drawn into the conflict in Vietnam. All hope rapidly dissipated following the assassination of the foreign minister in April 1963 in VI-ENTIANE. PATHET LAO (LAND OF LAOS) representatives in the government hurriedly left the capital.

When the SECOND (VIETNAM WAR) INDOCHINA WAR (1964–1975) broke out, Laos became a pawn between the United States and the DRV. The strategic Plain of Jars and the HỒ CHÍ MINH TRAIL that passes through southern and eastern parts of Laos were vital to the DRV. The former could be used for launching an offensive on the DRV and the latter was the lifeline for supplies from the DRV to support the VIET CONG in SOUTH VIETNAM (POST-1945). The Americans recruited the HMONG to wrest the Plain of Jars while massive aerial bombings sought to destroy the HỒ CHÍ MINH TRAIL.

A major casualty of the SECOND (VIET-NAM WAR) INDOCHINA WAR (1964–1975), Laos suffered more than 200,000 killed and twice that number wounded. The U.S. aerial bombing of the country was considered the worst in history.

When the third coalition government was constituted in April 1974, it was apparent that the PATHET LAO (LAND OF LAOS) held the upper hand. SOUVANNA PHOUMA (1901–1984) again headed the government; he was the sole neutralist. In LUANG PRA-BANG, the royal capital, SOUPHANOU-VONG (RED PRINCE) (1911–1995) chaired the National Political Consultative Council (NPCC). The following year the die was cast: PHNOM PENH fell to the communist KHMER ROUGE, followed by SAIGON (GIA DINH, HỒ CHÍ MINH CITY) to the VIET CONG. Then on 23 August, VIEN-TIANE was symbolically "liberated" without a shot being fired. King Savang Vatthana (t. 1959–1975) abdicated on 2 December, and the LAO PEOPLE'S DEMOCRATIC RE-PUBLIC (LPDR) was proclaimed with SOU-PHANOUVONG (RED PRINCE) (1911–1995) as president.

The major concern facing the government of postwar prime minister M. R. SENI PRAMOJ (1905–1997) of Thailand in September 1945 was to rehabilitate its wartime alliance with Japan and return to the good graces of the Anglo-American powers. Thanks to his prudent wartime action in refusing to deliver FIELD MARSHAL PLAEK PHIBUN-SONGKHRAM's (1897–1964) declaration of war on the United States, and instead establishing a chapter of the FREE THAI MOVE-MENT in Washington, the Americans sided with the Thais against British demands for war reparations. Moreover, all territories seized by Thailand with Japanese support were returned—namely, territories west of the Mekong River to Laos; the provinces of BAT-TAMBANG and SIEM REAP to Cambodia;

the northern peninsular Malay States of Kedah, Perlis, Kelantan, and Terengganu to Malaya; and the Shan States to Burma.

During the period of civilian governments from 1945 to 1948, constitutional democracy was restored and political parties were established. KHUANG APHAIWONG (1902–1968) formed the Democrat Party (DP, Prachatipat), reputedly the only civilian political party to ride successfully the series of coups during the late 1940s and the 1950s. The party owed its survival to its conservative, proroyalist stance, which gained staunch support from the urban electorate, especially of BANGKOK. Corruption and mismanagement among civilian politicians marred their reputations and created resentment from the military. King Ananda Mahidol (Rama VIII) (1935–1946) died from a gunshot wound in the palace in BANGKOK. His mysterious death was blamed, though unsubstantiatedly, on the prime minister, PRIDI PHANOMYONG (1900–1983), by his political rival FIELD MARSHAL PLAEK PHIBUNSONGKHRAM (1897–1964). The incident forced the resignation of PRIDI PHANOMYONG (1900–1983), who went into exile.

Sensing the geopolitical situation to be conducive for his return, a military coup seized power in the later part of 1947, which paved the way for FIELD MARSHAL PLAEK PHIBUNSONGKHRAM (1897–1964) to return to power as prime minister in April 1948. Against the COLD WAR scenario, with mainland Southeast Asia in turmoil, Thailand alone appeared to be a reliable ally to the Western democracies, especially to the Americans. From the late 1940s and the early 1950s it became apparent that U.S. INVOLVEMENT IN SOUTHEAST ASIA was steadily accelerating vis-à-vis the Soviet Union and the People's Republic of China (PRC).

During his second dictatorship, FIELD MARSHAL PLAEK PHIBUNSONGKHRAM (1897–1964) set aside the constitution, proscribed all political parties and activities, and clamped down on all opposition; radical elements faced imprisonment or the death sentence. Adopting a staunch anticommunist stance, he made Thailand a devoted ally of the United States; in return, U.S. military and economic aid flowed into the country. BANGKOK became the headquarters of the SOUTHEAST ASIA TREATY ORGANIZATION (SEATO) (1955), aimed at the collective security of the region against COMMUNISM.

Pragmatism persuaded FIELD MARSHAL PLAEK PHIBUNSONGKHRAM (1897–1964) to soften his stance on economic nationalism and to establish mutually beneficial alliances with Chinese entrepreneurs in exploiting the economic boom consequent of the KOREAN WAR (1950–1953) and the increasing U.S. presence. Powerful figures within the military emerged to challenge him, the most prominent being General Sarit Thanarat (t. 1958–1963), who later presided over an authoritarian government during his fourteen-year premiership.

Sarit's military dictatorship was characterized by rapid economic modernization opening the country to FDIs, and a boom consequent of the deep involvement of the United States in the SECOND (VIETNAM WAR) INDOCHINA WAR (1964–1975). While BANGKOK was the mecca of entertainment for U.S. troops on rest and relaxation (R&R) sojourns, the countryside benefited from road-building schemes and improvements in communications funded mainly by the U.S. military for security ends. Local businesses prospered in supplying the U.S. bases. The construction sector in BANGKOK and in other provincial towns enjoyed a boom as buildings sprang up to accommodate new businesses. Labor came from the rural areas, lured by the comparatively attractive wages.

Against this background of economic prosperity, traditional values and sociocultural norms and practices were sidelined. The money economy that rapidly engulfed the rural farming communities undermined the traditional social structure that was far more apparent in BANGKOK and other towns. Sarit stepped in to arrest the erosion and sought to restore traditional values. After the CONSTITUTIONAL (BLOODLESS) REVOLUTION (1932) (THAILAND), Sarit reestablished reverence, respect, and loyalty to the Thai throne—BHUMIBOL ADULYADEJ (RAMA IX, r. 1946–). His predecessor, FIELD MARSHAL PLAEK PHIBUNSONGKHRAM (1897–1964), during neither his prewar government nor his postwar administration, paid any particular attention to the monarchy.

But the obverse side to development and prosperity was the greater tightening of the political reins. Owing to obsession with security, the inhabitants in the rural areas—particularly in ISAN, the northeast, bordering Laos and Cambodia—came under greater direct control. Resentment drove many to join the communist insurgents operating along the borderlands. The MUSLIM MINORITIES (THAILAND) in southern Thailand harbored secessionist tendencies and rebellions flared up continually. Despite his authoritarian rule, Sarit failed to contain the numerous uprisings throughout the country; beyond the Thai heartland of the central plain there was little security for life and property.

FIELD MARSHAL THANOM KITTIKA-CHORN (1911–) and General Praphat Charusathien held the reins of power (t. 1963–1973) following Sarit's death in 1963. For the rest of the decade, the new regime rode the crest of prosperity thanks in large part to the escalation of the SECOND (VIETNAM WAR) INDOCHINA WAR (1964–1975). FDIs, mainly Japanese, invested in manufacturing, trade, and agribusiness. Consequent of Washington's decision to negotiate an honorable disengagement from the Vietnam conflict and Nixon's historic visit to Beijing in 1972, followed by the thawing of Sino-American relations, adverse ripples were felt throughout the Thai economy. Cutbacks were made in both the public and private sectors, resulting in widespread resentment. Within the military among those outside the inner circle, there was dissatisfaction with corrupt practices and personal enrichment of the chosen few.

The STUDENT REVOLT (OCTOBER 1973) (THAILAND) that originated from the campus of THAMMASAT UNIVERSITY in BANGKOK was soon replicated on provincial campuses. Students criticized the government for the economic woes and demanded social reforms, besides voicing a multitude of grievances. The National Student Centre of Thailand (NSCT) played a decisive role in organizing the protests. King BHUMIBOL ADULYADEJ (RAMA IX) (r. 1946–) decided to withdraw support for the military government; henceforth the options for survival were narrowed. Then when armed action against the student demonstrators backfired—the soldiers refused to shoot the students—FIELD MAR-SHAL THANOM KITTIKACHORN (1911–) and General Praphat Charusathien went into exile.

The period from 1973 to 1976 in the aftermath of the STUDENT REVOLT (OCTOBER 1973) (THAILAND) saw the comings and goings of a series of short-lived, ineffectual civilian governments. This period was characterized by a markedly conservative attitude among the urban electorate (largely the middle class) and an escalation in insurgency in the northeast and peninsular Thailand. Unwavering loyalty to BHUMIBOL ADULYADEJ (RAMA IX) (r. 1946–) remained strong. There was little progress in economic development, while instability reigned in the countryside. At the same time Thailand sought to disentangle its ties with the United States relating to the military bases.

Between 1976 and 1988 military rule was reinstated. In fact, the urban middle class regarded authoritarian rule as a probable panacea to Thailand's stagnating economy and the increasing instability. But the harshness of Thanin Karivixien's government (1976–1977) through the military-dominated National Administrative Reform Council (NARC)—which undertook severe reprisals to dissent, particularly from leftist elements—alienated the majority of the middle class. The clampdown on all opposition drove numerous student leaders, leftist activists, labor leaders, and peasant organizers (from farmers' associations) to the jungle to join the communist insurgents. The NARC apparently went overboard; the repressive actions marred the country's international standing. General Kriangsak Chomanan's government (1977–1980) offered a reprieve. His regime scaled down censorship, allowing limited activity by political parties, and released detainees. But like that of his predecessor, his three-year rule was unable to address the deteriorating economic situation.

PREM TINSULANOND (1920–) assumed control, and his military-dominated government (t. 1980–1988) received increasing support from center-right politicians who were the vital linkages among the powerful groups—namely, the military, civilian (politicians), civil service, and business interests. The discovery and exploitation of petroleum and natural gas in the Gulf of Thailand toward the end of the 1970s and increasing FDIs (largely from Japan) revived economic growth and hastened development. Expansion occurred in the industrial, construction, manufacturing, and agribusiness sectors. The robust economy perked up the middle class, and the working class assumed a new importance. The new emerging urban centers in the provinces began to gradually erode the political primacy of BANGKOK.

The political landscape experienced a transformation that saw the shifting of power bases from the traditional PATRON-CLIENT RELATIONS and revolving around personalities to the forging of smart partnerships between interest groups and political ideals. Bankers, industrialists, and other captains of capitalist enterprises began to become involved with political parties, while within the military, groups emerged based on shared political objectives rather than personalities. But political impasse was not uncommon among the various military and civilian groups. The revered monarch BHUMIBOL ADULYADEJ (RAMA IX) (r. 1946–) increasingly assumed a legitimizing role in Thai politics; often a royal pronouncement would resolve a seemingly insurmountable political deadlock.

In the international arena, Thailand under PREM TINSULANOND (1920–) benefited from the adversarial developments in SINO-VIETNAMESE RELATIONS that on the domestic front meant the drastic reduction in material and moral support from its two patrons for the Communist Party of Thailand (CPT), the major force of the insurgency in ISAN. Students and others who had fled to join the communists in the north and northeast provinces became disillusioned with the CPT's continuous strategy of protracted peasant warfare. The amnesty offered by the government in 1982–1983 witnessed mass defections. Coupled with earlier successful military campaigns undertaken by General Chavalit Yongchaiyudh (later the supreme commander of the armed forces from 1985), the CPT-led insurgency came close to defeat. Thailand opposed the Vietnamese invasion of Cambodia and the Vietnamese-sponsored regime of HENG SAMRIN (1934–) and urged its fellow members in the ASSOCIATION OF SOUTHEAST ASIAN NATIONS (ASEAN) (1967) to be firm in their stance on the Cambodian issue. Closer military-based ties were forged with the United States, including joint military exercises and military aid projects.

In contrast to Thailand's seesawing trend between parliamentary democracy and authoritarian military rule, SINGAPORE (1819) maintained a stable civilian, paternalistic-style government following its expulsion from MALAYSIA (1963) in 1965. Separation was not unduly problematic; there was little change either constitutionally or administratively. Challenges came in terms of defense and the economy. The British continued their military commitment to SINGAPORE (1819) through the ANGLO-MALAYAN/MALAYSIAN DEFENSE AGREEMENT (AMDA), which operated from 1957 to 1971. (Besides Britain, Australia and New Zealand were members.) Nonetheless, in 1966, Britain announced its military withdrawal "east of Suez" over a ten-year period. Such a move directly affected SINGAPORE'S (1819) position as one of the prime British bases in Southeast Asia. Compulsory national service was introduced to prepare and bolster SINGAPORE'S (1819) defenses. The British intention to bring forward its withdrawal to 1971 sent shock waves through the city-state, as close to one-fifth of its economy was dependent on the British base. Efforts to promote a mixed economy to attract FDIs went hand in hand with promoting export-oriented industrialization. Fortunately for an island republic that historically thrived on trade and commerce, the mid-1960s to the early 1970s saw a global boom. Industrialization and the service sector came to the forefront as significant contributors to the economy. The U.S. INVOLVEMENT IN SOUTHEAST ASIA had a positive effect on SINGAPORE (1819), which, like neighboring Thailand, Malaysia, and the Philippines, furnished an array of supplies to the U.S. military.

The PEOPLE'S ACTION PARTY (PAP) government of LEE KUAN YEW (1923–) adopted a national policy aimed at increasing living standards but eschewed creating a welfare state. Full employment was one of their principles, in addition to subsidization in housing, public health, and high-quality education (elementary to tertiary). The school curriculum stressed technical skills and English, the language of modernization. Government-built and -subsidized high-rise apartments housed virtually all the population, each family owning its own home. Hospitals both public and private offered unparalleled health care. A single-child family and a strict immigration policy were aimed at capping population growth.

But LEE KUAN YEW (1923–) governed the island republic with a firm hand, emphasizing political stability as the vital prerequisite for economic prosperity. His government's track record for stability was unrivaled in the highly volatile region. There was little room for dissent. The Internal Security Act (ISA), an inheritance from the British colonial period, allowed indefinite detention without trial of anyone deemed by the government to be a security risk.

SINGAPORE (1819) participated in the formation of the ASSOCIATION OF SOUTH-EAST ASIAN NATIONS (ASEAN) (1967). Only in the mid-1970s did the city-state begin to forge closer links with its regional neighbors, in particular with Malaysia. SINGAPORE-MALAYA/MALAYSIA RELATIONS (ca. 1950s–1990s), often strained, began to thaw in the early 1970s; cooperation was established in combating leftist subversion and in curbing narcotics trafficking. A member of the United Nations and the British Commonwealth since 1965, SINGAPORE (1819) maintained cordial and diplomatic relations with all countries in the world, including Israel and FORMOSA (TAIWAN).

The PEOPLE'S ACTION PARTY (PAP), led by LEE KUAN YEW (1923–), had been unchallenged for more than two decades in the parliament and the government. The 1981 electoral triumph of J. B. Jeyaretnam of the Workers' Party, followed by Chiam See Tong of the Singapore Democratic Party (SDP) in 1984, was a wake-up call to the incumbent PAP. Although inconsequential, the two seats in a parliament dominated by the PEOPLE'S ACTION PARTY (PAP) showed that their once-invincible armor was now dented. Nevertheless, the opposition's victories did not lead to the emergence of a credible alternative, and none seemed to appear in sight.

Following the election of 1984, Prime Minister LEE KUAN YEW (1923–) decided to hand over the task of day-to-day administration to a younger set of ministers, notably GOH CHOK TONG (1941–), the first deputy prime minister.

The New Population Policy of 1987 encouraged early marriages and the promotion of the three-child family, consequent of a decline in fertility. Immigration of talented Asians to work and settle in the city-state was another strategy to attain the targeted 4 million by the year 2010.

The uncovering of the so-called Marxist network in 1987, alleged to have members in the opposition Workers' Party and among student and Christian groups, led to the arrest of several activists under the ISA. The following year the ISA was further strengthened in that detention was beyond the review of the law courts, closing virtually all avenues for redress.

Reluctant Sultanate and Blood for Freedom: Independence for Brunei and East Timor

OMAR ALI SAIFUDDIN III, SULTAN OF BRUNEI (1914–1986), and his son and successor, HASSANAL BOLKIAH, SULTAN OF BRUNEI (1946–), were determined that Brunei remain under Britain's protective umbrella lest the wealthy but vulnerable sultanate be absorbed by its ambitious neighbors. In contrast, blood and tears lined the long road to independence for the East Timorese as they became victims of the COLD WAR politics of the 1970s.

Following the abortive BRUNEI REBELLION (DECEMBER 1962) and the banning of the PARTAI RAKYAT BRUNEI (PRB), voices supporting entry into MALAYSIA (1963) from the Brunei Alliance Party were wholly ignored by OMAR ALI SAIFUDDIN III, SULTAN OF BRUNEI (1914–1986). MALAYSIA (1963) came into being without Brunei.

During the latter half of the 1960s the main political party in the sultanate was the PEOPLE'S INDEPENDENCE FRONT (BARISAN KEMERDEKAAN RAKYAT, BAKER) (1966). It sought independence through peaceful, constitutional means, pledging complete loyalty to the palace. Nonetheless, several of its members were from the proscribed PARTAI RAKYAT BRUNEI (PRB). In 1968 the party failed to gain support in the district council elections.

In 1967, HASSANAL BOLKIAH, SULTAN OF BRUNEI (1946–), ascended the throne upon the retirement of his father. ANGLO-BRUNEI RELATIONS (NINETEENTH CENTURY to 1980s) entered a new level with the signing of a treaty in 1971 that gave the sultan full control of internal administration, while

Britain handled the sultanate's foreign relations. In a separate treaty, a Ghurkha battalion maintained by Britain was stationed in the sultanate.

HASSANAL BOLKIAH, SULTAN OF BRUNEI (1946–), and his father, the former sultan, were both reluctant about independence from Britain. They were suspicious of the intentions of neighboring MALAYSIA (1963) and Indonesia. Relations were strained with Malaysia, as it had not only harbored fugitive members of the PARTAI RAKYAT BRUNEI (PRB) and the establishment of an office in KUALA LUMPUR (KL) but also in 1975 sponsored a delegation to the United Nations presenting its case for independence. Two years later the UN General Assembly sanctioned a Malaysian-sponsored resolution that called for free elections in Brunei, lifting of the ban on political parties, and the return home without prosecution of all exiles.

Having failed to further delay the granting of independence, HASSANAL BOLKIAH, SULTAN OF BRUNEI (1946–), and the former sultan reluctantly penned an agreement pronouncing 1 January 1984 as the date on which Brunei would become a sovereign nation. In 1983 an Anglo-Brunei defense agreement allowed the continuing presence of the Ghurkha battalion, maintained by the sultanate.

The strategic location of TIMOR, literally on the doorstep to Australia, witnessed the landings of Australian troops in Dili in East Timor in mid-December 1941, despite Portugal's declaration of its neutrality in the war in Europe and in the Asia-Pacific region. Notwithstanding the stiff resistance they offered the invading Japanese, the Australians were eventually evacuated in early 1943. As with others throughout Southeast Asia, privation to near starvation engulfed the hitherto impoverished inhabitants of East Timor through the war years.

DECOLONIZATION OF SOUTHEAST ASIA was gaining pace in the late 1940s and 1950s, and Portugal was under international pressure to give up its colony of East Timor. The belief then was that East Timor—like Goa and MACAU (MACAO), components of the PORTUGUESE ASIAN EMPIRE—would be absorbed by powerful neighbors; Brunei shared that fear. No move on the part of SOEKARNO (SUKARNO) (1901–1970) or SUHARTO (1921–) showed any indication of annexation at this juncture.

The coup in April 1974 in Lisbon offered some hope of possible independence for Portugal's far-flung colonies. Responding to such indications, three East Timorese political organizations emerged. Advocating democratization and eventually independence was the Uniao Democratica Timorense (UDT, Timorese Democratic Union). Its supporters were senior civil servants of the colonial administration in league with plantation owners. The Associacao Social Democratica Timorense (ASDT, Timorese Social Democratic Association), composed of intellectuals and Portuguese-trained professionals, insisted on a faster pace to independence and strongly emphasized the implementation of social reforms. (Consequent of colonial neglect, the majority of East Timorese were illiterate, eking out a bare subsistence existence.) Opposing independence—and favoring integration with Indonesia—was the Associacao Popular Democratica Timorense (Apodeti, Timorese Popular Democratic Association). It was believed that this group was supported by Indonesia's intelligence organization, which unofficially and clandestinely was working toward annexation of East Timor. The radical stance of ASDT was appealing, and the organization gained widespread support. Later in that year ASDT acquired the new identity of FRETILIN (FRENTE REVOLUCIONARIA DO TIMOR-LESTE INDEPENDENTE), or Revolutionary Front for an Independent East Timor. Riding on its popular support, the left-leaning FRETILIN assumed the role of the voice of the East Timorese.

ADAM MALIK (1917–1984), Indonesia's minister of foreign affairs (t. 1966–1977), in June 1974 formally announced that Indonesia respected the self-determination of the East Timorese and had no intention of annexing the territory. But within Indonesia's military and intelligence circles, annexation was the solution, considering the leftist profile of FRETILIN; a "Cuba" on Indonesia's back door was unpalatable to the staunchly anticommunist Indonesian armed forces. The DOMINO THEORY added to the concerns of the military as events in the Indochina peninsula foresaw an eventual communist victory. Therefore the Indonesian military prepared for imminent annexation.

In 1975 events moved rapidly. To forestall possible Indonesian intervention, colonial officials in January proposed that UDT and FRETILIN form a coalition as a national transitional government to independence scheduled by Lisbon to eventuate in the latter part of 1976. The MACAU (MACAO) conference for the decolonization of East Timor took place in May. FRETILIN refused to participate; it opposed the presence of Apodeti, but, more important, objected to Lisbon's taking the leading role in the discussion. Then UDT withdrew from the coalition in May and on 11 August launched a coup, capturing Dili. FRETILIN retook Dili later that month. Meanwhile Indonesian forces moved stealthily into East Timor. By the latter part of November Indonesian intentions were apparent. In response FRETILIN on 28 November declared independence and the establishment of the Democratic Republic of East Timor under the presidency of Francisco Xavier do Amaral. An all-out invasion was under way, apparently with U.S. blessing. On 17 December, Apodeti headed a provisional government of East Timor. Then, in mid-July 1976, East Timor officially was incorporated as Indonesia's twenty-seventh province.

FRETILIN, which continued to maintain wide support, resisted the Indonesian military occupation through guerrilla warfare. Adopting a strategy similar to that of the BRIGGS PLAN, which successfully implemented positive outcomes in the MALAYAN EMERGENCY (1948–1960), Indonesia embarked (1977–1979) on the resettlement of villages into strategic hamlets. Although successful from a military perspective, it was a social calamity. Mismanagement and flawed planning resulted in famines that claimed more than 100,000 lives.

Numerous UN resolutions (1975–1982) calling for Indonesia's withdrawal and respect for the self-determination of the East Timorese went unheeded by Indonesia, the United States, and Australia.

Notwithstanding Indonesia's investments, which achieved rapid advances in communications and education, the harsh suppression of dissent, including torture and massacres, alienated the East Timorese. Economic development in commercial agriculture (mainly COFFEE), and the service and construction sectors benefited Indonesian entrepreneurs and the military but not the majority of the East Timorese population, who remained at the poverty line.

In the mid-1980s, Jose Alexandre "Xanana" Gusmao assumed the leadership of FRETILIN.

A new impetus to the East Timorese struggle came from Portugal. Lisbon, with support from the United Nations, reasserted its claim as the legitimate governing power of East Timor. Through the European Union, Portugal sought the support of the international community for the plight of East Timor. In 1990, Indonesia began negotiations with Portugal through the office of the UN secretary-general to resolve the issue; Indonesia sought international recognition as the legal administering power for East Timor.

The focus of the international community was brought to bear on the massacre in Dili on 12 November 1991. Perpetrators of the killings, Indonesian military personnel, were court-martialed, resulting in dismissal and sentences of varying periods of imprisonment. The following year Gusmao was captured in Dili and incarcerated in Cipinang prison in Jakarta.

The downfall of SUHARTO (1921–) in mid-1998 was a harbinger of positive developments in East Timor. President Bucharuddin Jusuf (B. J.) Habibie (t. 1998–1999), in an unprecedented announcement in January 1999, stated that in the event that East Timor was not keen on autonomy, Indonesia would allow it to be independent. Furthermore, it was agreed that a referendum (for autonomy or independence) under the auspices of the United Nations would be held in August. Intimidation and violence erupted to coerce the population away from voting.

On 30 August 1999 the referendum was undertaken, and an overwhelming majority rejected autonomy and voted for independence. Indonesia ratified the result of the referendum in October. At the same time the UN Transitional Administration in East Timor (UNTAET) was formed to oversee the transition to independence. In August 2002, East Timor became a sovereign, independent nation with Gusmao as president.

Some Recent Developments (1980s–2000)

The last two decades of the twentieth century saw a lesser degree of upheaval in Southeast Asia than the previous decades. Vietnam and Laos, together with Thailand, Malaysia, Brunei, and Singapore, steadily progressed, registering healthy signs of economic growth and overall development. In fact, Singapore was accorded "developed nation" status, while Malaysia and Thailand were dubbed potential "economic tigers." Indonesia entered a new era with the end of *ORDE BARU* (THE NEW ORDER), whereas the Philippines continued with the search for a viable and stable government. The impasse between prodemocracy groups led by DAW AUNG SAN SUU KYI (1945–) and the military junta of Myanmar (prior to 1989, called Burma) remained unresolved. With the intervention of UN peacekeepers, the volatile situation in Cambodia achieved some semblance of stability and optimism. The ASSOCIATION OF SOUTHEAST ASIAN NATIONS (ASEAN) (1967) expanded its membership to include Brunei (1984), Vietnam (1995), Laos and Myanmar (1995), and Cambodia (1999). A challenging and long road lies ahead for the newly independent (2002) East Timor.

Following independence in 1984, Brunei introduced the state ideology MĚLAYU ISLAM BERAJA (MIB, MALAY ISLAMIC MONARCHY). Emphasis was on the upholding and promotion of Islamic values, the sociocultural heritage of the BRUNEI MALAYS, and the Brunei sultanate. BRUNEI MALAYS as *BUMIPUTERA* (*BUMIPUTRA*) took precedence over other BRUNEI ETHNIC MINORITIES by means of preferential treatment. The Chinese community, constituting about one-third of the total population, was classified as noncitizens, deprived of any state benefits. Their economic role was limited to the private sector. MELAYU ISLAM BERAJA (MIB, MALAY ISLAMIC MONARCHY) was the bulwark against modernization, globalization, and other non-Islamic influences. The 1990s witnessed an intensification of Islamization in banking, education, and the mass media.

HASSANAL BOLKIAH, SULTAN OF BRUNEI (1946–) since 1967, and the royal family monopolized power in Brunei. The sultan assumed the portfolios of prime minister and minister of defense; his brother Mohamed held the portfolio of foreign affairs, while broher Jefri undertook that of finance. Jefri was chairman of both the Brunei Investment Agency (BIA) and the Amedeo Development Corporation, the largest investment and construction firm in the sultanate.

During the mid-1980s political parties were permitted to function, though under strict surveillance. The BRUNEI NATIONAL DEMOCRATIC PARTY (BNDP) (1985–1988), supported by Malay professionals and the corporate sector, sought democratization and equitable distribution of the economic pie and administrative power. A breakaway faction formed the BRUNEI NATIONAL SOLIDARITY PARTY (BNSP) (1985), but it was dissolved in less than a year following the publication of its "radical" demands: removal of the sultan as the head of government, an end to the state of emergency (imposed in 1962), and free elections. In 1996 all members of the proscribed PARTAI RAKYAT BRUNEI (PRB) were allowed to return home from exile, but they had to pledge noninvolvement in political activity.

The sultanate suffered undisclosed financial losses in the last quarter of the 1990s, brought about by a combination of developments: plummeting global petroleum prices; haze pollution from forest fires in Kalimantan caused by SWIDDEN AGRICULTURE and logging activities, which harmed tourism; and the collapse of the Amedeo Development Corporation owing to mismanagement.

Following independence Brunei established diplomatic links with numerous countries in the region and beyond. It also joined the ASSOCIATION OF SOUTHEAST ASIAN NATIONS (ASEAN) (1967), the Organization of Islamic Conference (OIC), the Commonwealth, the World Bank, and the International Monetary Fund (IMF). Brunei retained its traditional defense with related ties with Britain and Singapore, and in the 1990s it forged military relations with Australia and the United States. The sultanate attended a conference at Bandung, Indonesia, in 1991 together with other claimants over the SPRATLY AND PARACEL ARCHIPELAGOS DISPUTES. Closer ties with Malaysia in 1993 saw bilateral discussions over the Limbang issue, the territory in the East Malaysian state of Sarawak adjacent to Brunei.

To what extent MELAYU ISLAM BERAJA (MIB, MALAY ISLAMIC MONARCHY) can withstand the onslaught of increasing globalization, information technology (IT), modernization, and secularization is a question for this sultanate in the twenty-first century. Moreover, the sustainability of the BRUNEI OIL AND GAS INDUSTRY is in question, according to the Brunei Darussalam Economic Council (BDEC) in its evaluation report of February 2000.

GOH CHOK TONG (1941–) assumed the premiership of Singapore when LEE KUAN YEW (1923–) stepped down in November 1990. The latter became senior minister in the cabinet as well as secretary-general of the ruling PEOPLE'S ACTION PARTY (PAP). Ong Teng Cheong, secretary-general of the NATIONAL TRADES UNION CONGRESS (NTUC), and Lee Hsien Loong, the son of LEE KUAN YEW (1923–), were elevated as deputy prime ministers; the latter became acting premier in the absence of the prime minister, clearly indicating the hierarchical power structure.

The changing of the guard did little in terms of policy direction. Authoritarian and paternalistic rule continued to be the norm, creating the reputation of a "nanny state." Like his predecessor, GOH CHOK TONG (1941–) emphasized diligence, meritocracy, quality education, and steady economic growth; he eschewed a welfare state. Although public criticism—albeit constructive criticism—was welcomed and even encouraged, proposals for radical change were unacceptable. The draconian Internal Security Act (ISA), a legacy from the British colonial period, continued to be invoked when and if the need arose. All dissenting voices were silenced; only the elected leadership could determine the country's political agenda.

GOH CHOK TONG (1941–) faced several challenges. One major concern was the difficulty in attracting capable and willing candidates for public office, especially as ministers of state. Even the increase in ministerial remuneration on a par with the private sector did not prove successful. A declining birth rate and an increasingly aging population were prime concerns for the leadership. Inculcating a sense of nationhood and belonging, patriotism, and multiethnic and multicultural integration occupied the social policy agenda. Efforts were undertaken to stem the brain drain and immigration abroad; foreign skilled professionals were welcomed.

Singapore continued to be the financial hub of Southeast Asia. Possessing a strong economic infrastructure, a huge foreign exchange reserve, and unparalleled political stability, the city-state could ride out the repercussions of the financial crises of the 1990s—namely, the collapse of Barings PLC, the British banking giant in 1995; and the Asian Financial Crisis (1997–1998). Prudent measures were rapidly taken to shield the republic from the adverse impact of the latter. Singapore was elevated to the status of "more advanced developing country" by the Organization for Economic Co-operation and Development (OECD) in 1996, the first to attain that rank in Southeast Asia. The gains from economic successes were plowed back into the population in terms of housing subsidies, tax rebates, education, and public health. Incidences of corruption, mismanagement, and abuse of power were virtually nonexistent in tightly controlled Singapore.

In the regional arena Singapore supported the ASEAN Free Trade Area (AFTA) proposed in 1992; the entry into the ASSOCIATION OF SOUTHEAST ASIAN NATIONS (ASEAN) (1967) of Vietnam, Myanmar, Laos, and Cambodia; and the so-called policy of constructive engagement in relations with Myanmar. Singapore was the prime mover in reestablishing the strength of the ASSOCIATION OF SOUTHEAST ASIAN NATIONS (ASEAN) (1967), which had failed to contain the Asian Financial Crisis (1997–1998) that crippled many economies of the region. Boosting intraregional trade and attracting the return of FDIs to Southeast Asia were main priorities in the rehabilitation program. Apart from the occasional minor hiccups, SINGAPORE-MALAYA/MALAYSIA RELATIONS (ca. 1950s–1990s) were more cordial and intimate throughout the 1990s. GOH CHOK TONG (1941–) struck a good working relationship with Malaysia's DR. MAHATHIR BIN MOHAMAD (1925–), resolving disputes and issues through bilateral negotiations.

Despite the successes, GOH CHOK TONG (1941–), like Senior Minister LEE KUAN YEW (1923–), repeatedly emphasized the city-state's vulnerability and the fact that political stability was a pivotal ingredient for continuous and dynamic economic prosperity. The Singapore government is ever vigilant toward changes in the global economic barometer, the adverse effects of globalization, terrorism, and the geopolitical situation, particularly in the Southeast Asian context.

Toward the end of the 1980s, Thailand experienced parliamentary rule (1988–1991) interspersed with a brief return to military domination (1991–1992) and back to civilian government (from 1992). The political climate was marred by the phenomenon of vote-buying and by violence during the electoral period; military-dominated regimes when in power tended to be harsh and repressive, whereas civilian governments were plagued with corruption, abuse of power, incompetence, and infighting among coalition members.

Following the 1988 elections, General Chatichai Choonhavan, the leader of Chart Thai, became prime minister (t. 1988–1991). Leading a political party like Chart Thai, which drew its support from the business sector, Chatichai was partial to policies that benefited the Thai private sector. He turned to Thailand's mainland neighbors as potential marketplaces and as a field for economic exploitation. He sought from Myanmar fishing rights, timber concessions, and mining contracts (gems). In turn Thailand was keen to supply consumer necessities to the isolated regime. ISAN, Thailand's northeast, was to serve as the country's springboard for economic penetration into Laos, Cambodia, and Vietnam.

Chatichai's rapprochement with the Indochinese states was viewed with disaffection within the Thai military. The military was staunchly anticommunist and continuously fighting a protracted leftist-led insurgency in the borderlands. Chatichai entrusted General Chavalit Yongchaiyudh, supreme commander of the armed forces and commander of the army, with a free hand in senior military appointments. Chavalit used his prerogative to promote members of the Class 5 Group, the graduating class of 1958 of Chulachomklao Military Academy. Its leader, General Suchinda Kraprayoon, was elevated to deputy commander of the army in 1989. Chavalit, who harbored political ambitions, resigned from the military in 1990 to form the New Aspiration Party (NAP). Into his shoes stepped General Sunthorn Kongsompong, to become supreme commander of the armed forces, and Suchinda, as commander of the army. Sunthorn was known to be supportive of the Class 5 Group. Chatichai failed to learn from his predecessors PREM TINSULANOND (1920–) and Kriangsak Chomanan in not allowing the domination by any single faction in the military.

It was too late for Chatichai to make amends when in February 1991 a bloodless coup was staged that brought the military to power. Sunthorn headed a NATIONAL PEACE KEEPING COUNCIL (NPKC) (THAILAND) that governed the country under martial law. The military chose Anand Panyarachun, president of the Federation of Thai Industries, reputedly an honest and capable captain of industry, to be prime minister (t. 1991–1992). Although nonmilitary technocrats dominated his cabinet, the legislature was controlled by the military. Suchinda took over from Sunthorn as supreme commander of the armed forces and promoted his brother-in-law, General Issarapong Noonpakdi, to the position of commander of the army. Interestingly, Anand's military-backed government allowed political parties to function. A new constitution was proclaimed in December 1991.

The March 1992 elections witnessed a weak coalition forming the government. Apparently no one in particular was suited to be prime minister; instead, Suchinda assumed the premiership. His action sparked widespread demonstrations against a nonelected prime minister, despite the provision in the new 1991 constitution. When a violent backlash from the military resulted in about 100 deaths in BANGKOK, BHUMIBOL ADULYADEJ (RAMA IX) (r. 1946–) stepped in to resolve the crisis. Suchinda resigned in May. In his place the palace recalled Anand to be interim prime minister. The National Assembly amended the constitution, stipulating that only an elected member of the legislature could hold the post of prime minister; at the same time it trimmed the powers of the nonelected senate.

The Democrat Party (DP) won the September 1992 polls, and its leader, Chuan Leekpai, became prime minister (t. 1992–1995). Chuan's agenda was threefold: stamping out corruption, decentralization of power from BANGKOK to the provinces, and rural development. He was not very successful on any count, as he lacked strong leadership qualities.

In February 1993, Thailand, Vietnam, Cambodia, and Laos agreed to jointly develop the "Greater Mekong Sub-Region." Nevertheless, the socialist states were not exactly welcoming of Thailand's initiative. For instance, Cambodia preferred investments from Malaysia and Singapore to those from Thailand. Likewise, Myanmar was partial to investments from Singapore in preference to its immediate neighbor. Laos sought to balance Thailand's influence with that of the People's Republic of China (PRC) and Vietnam. Moreover, Laos insisted that the Mekong River Commission be shifted to VIENTIANE from its base in BANGKOK. Thailand also sought to transform centrally located BANGKOK as an investment and financial hub for mainland Southeast Asia and southern and southwestern China. Furthermore, to spur economic growth Chuan's government signed an agreement in July 1993 with Malaysia and Indonesia to establish a "growth triangle" (Indonesia-Malaysia-Thailand Economic Triangle) that encompassed northern SUMATRA, Peninsular Thailand, and northwestern Peninsular Malaysia.

Chart Thai, with its recourse to huge campaign funds furnished by business concerns, was able to "buy over" the electorate, especially in the provinces during the July 1995 elections that swept it to power. Banharn Silipa-Archa, leader of Chart Thai, assumed the premiership (t. 1995–1996). Patronage replaced expertise as the qualification for ministerial positions in Banharn's cabinet; consequently, incompetence ruled. Even BHUMIBOL ADULYADEJ (RAMA IX) (r. 1946–) voiced his concern over government incompetence. Money politics and blatant corruption were the norm during this period.

The November 1996 elections brought in a coalition government led by Chavalit as prime minister (t. 1996–1997) as well as minister of defense. Two major events marked Chavalit's tenure—namely, the drafting of a new constitution (promulgated in October 1997) and the Asian Financial Crisis (1997–1998), which severely crippled the Thai baht (currency) and economy. The Constitutional Drafting Assembly chaired by Uthai Pimchaichon, a respected political activist, was given the mandate to draft a constitution that would enable the functioning of a genuine democratic system of government. Significant provisions included composition and membership of the Senate (reduced to 200 members, all elected), the requirement that cabinet members (the executive) resign from the National Assembly (legislature), and making a university degree necessary for membership in the National Assembly. The electorate (a minimum of 50,000) could initiate investigations into corruption charges against a member of the National Assembly. A proposal for fewer restrictions on the mass media was also included.

The inability to resolve the economic crisis led to Chavalit's resignation in November 1997. Chuan of the Democrat Party was able to convene a viable coalition to form a new government. Like his predecessor, Chuan became prime minister (t. 1997–2001) and minister of defense. In tackling the economic crisis, Thailand adopted the IMF rescue package of U.S.$17,200 million, accompanied by mandatory macroeconomic reforms. Although the IMF rescue plan achieved success, the implementation of austerity measures as part of the rescue package resulted in criticisms of Chuan's government. Despite various accusations and resentments toward the government in handling the economic crisis, Chuan was able to ride out the storm. In August 1998, Queen Sirikit commended the premier and urged public support for the government's efforts to stabilize the economy and at the same time to revitalize it.

Chuan's meetings with Malaysian prime minister DR. MAHATHIR BIN MOHAMAD (1925–) in April 1998 led to an agreement whereby the latter guaranteed that no assistance would be rendered to the Muslim separatists of southern Thailand. Furthermore, Malaysia would cooperate in suppressing the Muslim separatists and in apprehending those operating within its borders. Both countries also agreed to develop the gas reserves in the Thai-Malaysian Joint Development Area, a part of the Indonesia-Malaysia-Thailand Economic Triangle.

Relations between Thailand and Myanmar were strained over numerous issues, such as narcotics trafficking, separatist groups, and refugees. Also unpopular among its neighbors was Thailand's participation in the UN International Force for East Timor (INTERFET) in 1999. Similarly, Thailand's initiative to convert "constructive engagement" to "flexible engagement" as a new approach to interrelationships among members of the ASSOCIATION OF SOUTHEAST ASIAN NATIONS (ASEAN) (1967) was rejected. Mooted in mid-1998 by Surin Pitsuwan, the Thai minister of foreign affairs, "flexible engagement" made possible discussion of domestic matters of another member country if such matters went beyond the country's borders. The traditional policy of noninterference in domestic affairs was upheld.

Membership in the newly elected senate (March 2000) under the provision of the 1997 constitution saw increasing representation of the media, academia, and nongovernmental organizations (NGOs) vis-à-vis the military and civil service. The new composition ushered in a new era for this upper house.

By the time of the January 2001 election for the House of Representatives (formerly the National Assembly), the main rival of Chuan's ruling Democrat Party was Thai Rak Thai, which was established in 1998, led by Thaksin Shinawatra. Thai Rak Thai won overwhelmingly. Thaksin successfully forged a merger with the Seritham Party; consequently, Prime Minister Thaksin headed a government that commanded an absolute majority. Finally, the days of coalition government were over. Later in the year, Thaksin barely escaped imprisonment for violation of assets disclosure.

When the LAO PEOPLE'S DEMOCRATIC REPUBLIC (LPDR) was established in 1975, the PATHET LAO (LAND OF LAOS) assumed the new name of Lao People's Revolutionary Party (LPRP), led by Kaysone Phomvihane, its powerful secretary-general. The first decade of the LPDR was a disastrous period. In 1985, Laos was one of the world's poorest nations. The comforting fact was that at least the country was self-sufficient in rice, the staple food. Owing to repressive totalitarian rule, it was estimated that more than 10 percent of the population had fled abroad; of that, some 90 percent constituted the educated elite. This emigration of talent and expertise was a major loss to nation-building.

The economy was severely crippled through socialist policies of nationalization of industry, collectivization of agriculture, and restriction on domestic trade. The establishment of agricultural cooperatives, unpopular among the farming population, drove many to flee across the border into Thailand. Likewise, the detention of persons in reeducation (imprisonment) camps for long periods (even years) deprived many families of breadwinners; once released many fled to Thailand. The Lao National Revolutionary Front subsequently emerged from the refugee camps in Thailand; small groups returned to Laos to spread antigovernment propaganda and to undertake sabotage operations. By the early 1990s there were some 60,000 refugees remaining in Thai camps; most of them were HMONG.

In 1977 the royal family, including the Crown prince, were arrested and exiled to Xam Neuea, where it was believed they were all killed. The communist authorities feared that the royal personages would rally opposition to their rule following an incident in northern Laos when a group of HMONG briefly held a village near LUANG PRABANG, the royal capital.

By 1979 there was realization among the leadership circle that adherence to dogmatic socialist policies was problematic. A reevaluation of policy resulted in preparation of plans to gradually return to a market economy. In this context the first five-year economic development plan was designed (1981–1985); none of the objectives were attained, however, largely consequent of the dire need of expertise and for want of basic infrastructure. By 1985 it was again necessary to rethink the economic plan. A second five-year plan (1986–1990) adopted the so-called new economic mechanism policy, which basically endorsed a market economy and began the dismantling of the centralized socialist economic system. Relations with foreign capitalist countries were encouraged to woo FDIs.

The LAO PEOPLE'S DEMOCRATIC REPUBLIC (LPDR) had historical ties with Vietnam, which had been a major ally, mentor, and aid donor. Likewise Laos also relied on the Soviet Union for ideological, economic, and military support. Relations with the PRC were rather problematic. In the SINO-SOVIET STRUGGLE, Laos chose Moscow over Beijing.

Local elections were held in April 1988, the first since 1975, followed by national elections in March 1989. A Constitution Drafting Committee set to work on the historic task of producing a constitution for the country. Rapprochement with the PRC was achieved in 1988, and by the early 1990s, Laos had established good ties with Myanmar, Thailand, Vietnam, and Cambodia. In cooperation with Thailand and the UN High Commissioner for Refugees (UNHCR), Laos sought the resettlement of Laotian refugees who were in Thai camps. Repatriation or resettlement in third (mainly Western) countries led to the closure of the refugee camps and the reduction of insurgency along the Thai-Laotian border. Cooperation with Thailand achieved much in reducing the activities of the insurgents. Laos also cooperated with the United States on two major issues: the search for U.S. MIAs (MISSING IN ACTION) from the SECOND (VIETNAM WAR) INDOCHINA WAR (1964–1975), and combating the narcotics trade. Northwestern Laos, with northern Thailand and northeastern Myanmar, formed the infamous "Golden Triangle," in which private militias coerced the hill people to grow poppy and set up makeshift "factories" to produce heroin, cocaine, and other drugs. The trafficking in illegal narcotics, undoubtedly a lucrative enterprise, involved separatist movements (drugs for arms) and corrupt officials.

During the Fifth Congress of the LPRP in 1991, the new constitution was endorsed, together with economic reforms based on free-market principles. In August the National Assembly (formerly the Supreme People's Assembly) adopted the new constitution, which ensured basic freedoms and private ownership of property. Kaysone was named president of the LAO PEOPLE'S DEMOCRATIC RE-PUBLIC (LPDR), and Khamtay Siphandone was prime minister. The following year when Kaysone died, Nouhak Phoumsavanh, chairman of the National Assembly, was elevated to the state presidency. Khamtay retained the premiership and also became president of the LPRP. Saman Vignaket assumed the chairmanship of the National Assembly. Surprises were in store at the Sixth Congress of the LPRP in 1996, when a power shift occurred with the military dominating the party lineup, although Khamtay retained the presidency.

Laos became a member of the ASSOCIATION OF SOUTHEAST ASIAN NATIONS (ASEAN) (1967) in 1997. Sharing a common mistrust of Thailand, Laos moved closer to Myanmar and Cambodia. Strong ties were maintained with Vietnam. Meanwhile, Laos continued to nurture friendly relations with the PRC.

FDIs flowed into Laos with Thailand heading the list; others included the United States, Australia, France, and the PRC. Japan led as the main foreign aid donor, followed by Germany, Sweden, France, and Australia. During the latter part of the 1990s, tourism became an important foreign exchange earner. In 1998 the UN Educational, Scientific, and Cultural Organization (UNESCO) accorded LUANG PRABANG the status of a World Heritage site, further spurring the influx of foreign visitors to this royal capital city and boosting the tourist industry.

The fortunate policy shift from a dogmatic socialist stance to more liberal "open-door" approach marked a significant reorientation of the LAO PEOPLE'S DEMOCRATIC REPUBLIC (LPDR). The replacement of the red star of COMMUNISM with a silhouette of That Luang stupa in the national crest might be the harbinger of further sociocultural reevaluation, even a reinstatement of traditional values and norms. Meanwhile the country faced numerous challenges, such as drugs (addiction, trafficking, and trade), prostitution, HIV (human immunodeficiency virus) and AIDS (acquired immune deficiency syndrome), and environmental degradation (dam construction, logging, SWIDDEN AGRICULTURE). HMONG insurgency continued to be a thorn in the side of the VIENTIANE regime.

The establishment in January 1979 of the People's Republic of Kampuchea (a Vietnamese-sponsored regime dominated by the KAMPUCHEA UNITED FRONT FOR NATIONAL SALVATION [KUFNS] headed by HENG SAMRIN [1934–]) as the government replacing DEMOCRATIC KAMPUCHEA (DK) did not win international acceptance. Both the PRC and the ASSOCIATION OF SOUTHEAST ASIAN NATIONS (ASEAN) (1967) strongly objected to the invasion by the communist HANOI (THANG-LONG) regime. In February–March the PRC clashed with Vietnam in the latest of the SINO-VIETNAMESE WARS, and the Vietnamese ejection of the Beijing-supported DEMOCRATIC KAMPUCHEA (DK) was viewed by the Chinese as a Vietnamese hegemonic design over mainland Southeast Asia. The invasion was seen by the ASSOCIATION OF SOUTHEAST ASIAN NATIONS (ASEAN) (1967) as a threat to its security.

Through the 1980s the Cambodian situation hogged the headlines of the international media and posed another major challenge to the capabilities and resources of the UNITED NATIONS AND CONFLICT RESOLUTION IN SOUTHEAST ASIA. By the early part of the decade the various antagonistic camps were outlined. The PRK was led by HENG SAMRIN (1934–) based in PHNOM PENH, with Vietnam and the Soviet Union as its main support (moral, military, and economic). Opposing the PRK was the Coalition Government of Democratic Kampuchea (CGDK), presided over by NORODOM SIHANOUK (1922–). CGDK comprised the Party of Democratic Kampuchea (PDK, formerly the Communist Party of Kampuchea [CPK]), led by KHIEU SAMPHAN (1931–) and POL POT (SALOTH SAR) (1925–1998) and others in the shadows; FUNCINPEC (a French acronym for United National Front for an Independent, Neutral, Peaceful and Co-operative Cambodia), led by NORODOM SIHANOUK (1922–) and later his son, Prince Ranariddh; and the KHMER PEOPLE'S NATIONAL LIBERATION FRONT (KPNLF) under Son Sann. The PRC provided military supplies to all three factions of the CGDK. FUNCINPEC and the KPNLF received nonmilitary aid (mainly humanitarian and medical) from the ASSOCIATION OF SOUTHEAST ASIAN NATIONS (ASEAN) (1967), the United States, Britain, and France.

The armed conflict between the CGDK and PRK was of low intensity; both parties, willingly or reluctantly, looked to a political settlement. Non-Cambodian players and events from without appeared to be more influential in dictating the situation within. First, in 1983, Vietnam began to withdraw its troops; this unilateral action intensified the international desire to resolve the Cambodian issue. Vietnam's action of scheduling a complete withdrawal by the latter part of 1989 was consequent of the pressure from Moscow. The Soviet Union had reduced aid (military and economic) to Vietnam since 1987. The rapprochement in 1988 with Beijing had replaced decades of SINO-SOVIET STRUGGLE, prompting Moscow to demand a settlement to the Cambodian impasse.

The ruling party of the PRK, Kampuchean People's Revolutionary Party (KPRP), in PHNOM PENH appealed to all nationalist groups to effect a "national reconciliation" based on a broad coalition comprising all parties except the PDK. Domestically the KPRP began to "liberalize" its state-controlled economy, including implementation of a partial form of private ownership of property (land, housing). A name change was also made, with the PRK becoming the State of Cambodia (SOC) in 1989.

Again events from without initiated a step forward in resolving the Cambodian issue. The worldwide retreat of COMMUNISM with the disintegration of the Soviet Union in 1989–1990 prompted the convening of the PARIS CONFERENCE ON CAMBODIA (PCC) (1989, 1991). Coupled with the decisions reached at the UN Security Council in 1990, a comprehensive political settlement was finally signed in Paris in 1991. A UNITED NATIONS TRANSITIONAL AUTHORITY IN CAMBODIA (UNTAC) (1992–1993) would undertake to create a conducive and neutral condition in which free elections could be held in the country.

In October 1991, the KPRP had a makeover. First, it abandoned the one-party state and supported the establishment of a multiparty democracy. Second, a name change took place from KPRP to the Cambodian Peoples' Party (CPP), and at the same time it announced the renunciation of COMMUNISM. HENG SAMRIN (1934–) was relegated to an honorary role in the CPP; CHEA SIM (1932–) assumed the chairmanship of the Central Committee with HUN SEN (1951–) as deputy chairman and party spokesman.

The UNITED NATIONS TRANSITIONAL AUTHORITY IN CAMBODIA (UNTAC) (1992–1993), the largest peacekeeping operation undertaken by the United Nations, formally assumed responsibility from February to March 1992, headquartered in PHNOM PENH. Akashi Yasushi was named the special representative of the UN secretary-general in Cambodia and chief of the UNITED NATIONS TRANSITIONAL AUTHORITY IN CAMBODIA (UNTAC) (1992–1993); Australian major general John Anderson headed the 16,000-strong international military force.

On 23–28 May 1993 the anticipated elections were carried out, with close to 90 percent of the registered voters participating. The FUNCINPEC Party edged the CPP with fifty-eight seats (48.5 percent of the votes) to fifty-one seats (38.2 percent of the votes). In mid-July HUN SEN (1951–) and Prince Ranariddh would share the chairmanship of the Provisional National Government of Cambodia, while a new constitution was being drafted. In September the new constitution was adopted, proclaiming the kingdom of Cambodia, a constitutional monarchy advocating a multiparty liberal democracy. NORODOM SIHANOUK (1922–) acceded to the throne as the king of

Cambodia; the seventy-one-year-old monarch had come full circle since relinquishing the throne in 1955. The Royal Government of Cambodia (RGC), a CPP-FUNCINPEC coalition, was headed by Prince Ranariddh as the first prime minister and HUN SEN (1951–) as the second prime minister.

Although most of the country was under the control of the RGC, the PDK still held sway over some 10 percent of the territory and the population. CHEA SIM (1932–), with support from the FUNCINPEC Party, was elected chairman of the National Assembly and in mid-1994 legislated the proscription of the PDK.

The CPP-FUNCINPEC coalition managed, through a series of rather undemocratic methods (for example, the new press law of 1995), to eliminate all other political parties and possible opposition. At the same time, within the CPP-FUNCINPEC coalition itself things were rather stormy, with each party attempting to consolidate its power and position. Interestingly, in the early days (around 1994), Ranariddh and HUN SEN (1951–) agreed to eliminate Sam Rainsy, the FUNCINPEC Party member who was appointed minister of finance in the RGC, as his policies geared toward economic growth (free markets, independent system of assessing customs duties, close relationship with foreign donors, review of past business contracts) intruded on party patronage and vested interests. But from 1995, Ranariddh–HUN SEN (1951–) relations turned from strained to a fallout in mid-1997. Accusing Ranariddh of attempting to bring KHIEU SAMPHAN (1931–) of the PDK and other KHMER ROUGE leaders back into the political mainstream, HUN SEN (1951–) in a series of calculated moves forced Ranariddh to leave the country for France in early July. The removal of the first prime minister undoubtedly strengthened HUN SEN's (1951–) hand, and the CPP rapidly seized the initiative in establishing pivotal control over the power structure in the civil service, the armed forces, and the police, sidelining their FUNCINPEC Party partners in the process.

On 26 July 1997 news over PDK radio announced the denunciation and trial of POL POT (SALOTH SAR) (1925–1998) by the KHMER ROUGE, which sentenced him to life imprisonment at the Anlong Veng guerrilla enclave in the northwest of the country on treason charges. It was, however, difficult to ascertain whether the event was a show trial or a genuine purge.

The need for international recognition and foreign aid forced HUN SEN (1951–) to request a full pardon from King NORODOM SIHANOUK (1922–) for Ranariddh, who was sentenced in absentia to a total of thirty-five years' imprisonment on a variety of charges, mainly complicity with the KHMER ROUGE and causing instability in the country.

Opposition parties, including the FUNCINPEC Party, entered the elections of July 1998 at a disadvantage following the events of July 1997. Name changes were effected: the Khmer Nation Party (KNP) (formed in 1995) became the Sam Rainsy Party (SRP), and the Buddhist Liberal Democratic Party (BLDP) (formed by the KHMER PEOPLE'S NATIONAL LIBERATION FRONT [KPNLF]) became the Son Sann Party. In elections said to be "free and fair" by the UN Joint International Observation Group, the CPP won a majority (sixty-four seats), but shy of the two-thirds required to form a government. Offers for a CPP-led coalition were rejected by both the FUNCINPEC Party (forty-three seats) and the SRP (fifteen seats). A political impasse thus resulted.

King NORODOM SIHANOUK (1922–), through tireless efforts in the course of 1998, finally breached the stalemate in October: HUN SEN (1951–) became prime minister, Ranariddh president of the National Assembly, and CHEA SIM (1932–) chairman of a yet-to-be-established senate and acting head of state in the absence of the monarch. The senate was created the following year.

Meanwhile, the KHMER ROUGE was disbanded when large numbers defected to HUN SEN (1951–) in March 1998. Many were reintegrated into the ranks of the Royal Cambodian Armed Forces. On 14 April, POL POT (SALOTH SAR) (1925–1998) died, apparently of suicide. Several of the KHMER ROUGE leaders—Noun Chea, KHIEU SAMPHAN (1931–), and IENG SARY (1927–)—reentered society. Others, such as Ta Mok and Duch (Kang Khek Ieu), were in government custody.

The HUN SEN (1951–) government opposed the trial of KHMER ROUGE leaders that might provoke the rank and file to return to the jungle and relaunch the insurgency. King NORODOM SIHANOUK (1922–) shared that view. National reconciliation, peace, and stability overrode justice when framing the tribunal law that maintained the maximum penalty of life imprisonment for convicted KHMER ROUGE leaders.

The issue of the trial of KHMER ROUGE leaders was a sore point for Cambodia in the international arena, particularly in relations with the United Nations and the United States. Cambodia was able to secure financial assistance from the IMF and the World Bank in 1999–2000. In the regional context, Cambodia did fairly well. Eager for bilateral trade relations, Malaysia had long lobbied for Cambodia's entry into the ASSOCIATION OF SOUTH-EAST ASIAN NATIONS (ASEAN) (1967); Cambodia finally gained membership in April 1999. Relations with the PRC and Vietnam remained cordial and close throughout the turmoil of the 1990s.

Consequent of national elections held in 1976, a single National Assembly came into being in April; in its inaugural seating in July it proclaimed the Socialist Republic of Vietnam with HANOI (THANG-LONG) as its capital. The ruling party, the Communist Party of Vietnam (formerly the Vietnam Workers' Party), dominated the political leadership and the government of the country. During 1976–1977, agriculture and light industry were emphasized; then from 1977, in line with the practice in other socialist countries—namely, the Soviet Union—all capitalist enterprises were proscribed: agricultural cooperatives were created, private industry was nationalized, and labor was sent from the urban areas to the NEW ECONOMIC ZONES (NEZs) (VIETNAM). The last mentioned was a program to forcefully reverse the rural-urban migration—in short, to repopulate the countryside where labor was much needed in the agricultural sector.

In an attempt to attract FDIs in its industrialization program, especially from the West, Vietnam joined the IMF and the World Bank in 1976. The following year Vietnam gained membership in the United Nations. At the same time Vietnam moved closer to the Soviet Union and joined the Soviet trading bloc. Intimacy with Moscow was viewed with suspicion by Beijing. At this juncture SINO-VIETNAMESE RELATIONS were highly strained. Vietnam visualized a leadership position in an "Indochinese Federation"; close ties therefore needed to be fostered with both Cambodia and Laos. The PRC viewed the situation in the context of the SINO-SOVIET STRUGGLE: by establishing direct ties with PHNOM PENH and VIENTIANE independent of HANOI (THANG-LONG), Beijing sought to eliminate the influence of the Soviet Union in the region.

Then, in December 1978, Vietnam, together with the KAMPUCHEA UNITED FRONT FOR NATIONAL SALVATION (KUFNS), invaded DEMOCRATIC KAMPUCHEA (DK). PHNOM PENH fell to the invaders. In January 1979 the People's Republic of Kampuchea (PRK), a Vietnamese-sponsored regime, was established, headed by HENG SAMRIN (1934–). The Cambodian invasion brought untold problems for Vietnam.

SINO-VIETNAMESE RELATIONS were on the downturn, mainly as a result of the Vietnamese invasion, which toppled the Beijing-backed DEMOCRATIC KAMPUCHEA (DK), and partly because of the treatment of the Chinese inhabitants in Vietnam. The Chinese community played a major role in the economy of Vietnam—particularly in the southern provinces and in SAIGON (GIA DINH, HỒ CHÍ MINH CITY)—as traders and entrepreneurs, traditionally dominating trade and commerce. The centralization of the state-controlled economy harmed the Chinese, which drove many to leave the country. Unable to flee overland to the PRC, as the borders were closed, the Chinese turned to the South China Sea for escape. The phenomenon of the BOAT PEOPLE was to dominate world headlines for the next decade, bringing adverse publicity to Southeast Asian countries, notably Malaysia. It was estimated that by the first half of 1979, more than 200,000 BOAT PEOPLE had braved the precarious journey to Southeast Asia, HONG KONG, FORMOSA (TAIWAN), and as far as Australia. Vietnamese officials exploited the plight of these Chinese in demanding gold or Western currencies in exchange for exit papers. Unknown numbers, perhaps thousands, lost their lives on board unseaworthy vessels. This human tragedy prompted the UNHCR, in agreement with Vietnam, to arrange and underwrite an Orderly Departure Program (ODP).

Soured SINO-VIETNAMESE RELATIONS slipped into another SINO-VIET-

NAMESE WAR. In February 1979, the PRC launched an offensive. Beijing claimed to have captured several provincial capitals (Cao Bang, Lang Son, and Lao Cai) in the border provinces. Following a month of fierce battles, the Chinese forces withdrew in March. The peace negotiations thereafter did not produce any settlement, apart from the exchange of prisoners of war.

A new constitution was adopted in 1980, consequent of four years of debate. In addition to the National Assembly, there were the State Council and a Council of Ministers (cabinet). TRUONG CHINH (1907–1988) was the president of the State Council, hence head of state, whereas PHAM VAN DONG (1906–2000) was the chairman (prime minister) of the Council of Ministers. LE DUAN (1907–1986) remained a dominant figure in the Communist Party of Vietnam as general secretary. After his passing in 1986, TRUONG CHINH (1907–1988) took over as general secretary while at the same time retaining his governmental appointments.

Reforms were under way, particularly in the economy, from the mid-1980s. Modeled after the Soviet Union of Mikhail Gorbachev (t. 1985–1991), a restructuring of the economy (termed "renovation" [doi moi]) was under way in Vietnam that aimed at reducing centralized planning and state subsidies. But progress in carrying out the reforms was sluggish, owing to opposition from the traditionally dogmatic factions in the party and the government.

The Cambodian issue created a serious rift between Vietnam and Thailand. Thailand and its partners in the ASSOCIATION OF SOUTHEAST ASIAN NATIONS (ASEAN) (1967) supported the Coalition Government of Democratic Kampuchea (CGDK), headed by NORODOM SIHANOUK (1922–). All three members of the coalition had resistance forces operating from camps in Thailand that launched attacks on Vietnamese forces inside Cambodia. In 1985, Vietnamese offensives eliminated the base camps of these resistance groups on Thai soil, much to the anger of BANGKOK and other supporters of the CGDK—notably the PRC, the United States, and the ASSOCIATION OF SOUTHEAST ASIAN NATIONS (ASEAN) (1967).

It became imperative for Vietnam to withdraw its troops from Cambodia as a prerequisite to the receipt of foreign aid. It was duly emphasized that the lifting of the trade embargo imposed on Vietnam by the United States, Japan, the European Community (currently the European Union, EU), and the ASSOCIATION OF SOUTHEAST ASIAN NATIONS (ASEAN) (1967) consequent of its invasion would take place only if Vietnam agreed to withdraw. Even the Soviet Union exerted pressure on Vietnam to disengage from Cambodia. Vietnam promised to commence the withdrawal of troops in mid-1988, to be completed by the end of 1989.

The retreat of COMMUNISM and the disintegration of the Soviet Union (which became the Russian Federation in 1991) prompted a rapprochement in SINO-VIETNAMESE RELATIONS. Of help in this quest was the comprehensive settlement of the Cambodian question as outlined in the PARIS CONFERENCE ON CAMBODIA (PCC) (1989, 1991). Subsequently, in November 1991 following secret talks, Vietnam and the PRC resumed political relations. But the unresolved territorial issue of the SPRATLY AND PARACEL ARCHIPELAGOS DISPUTE remained a thorn in SINO-VIETNAMESE RELATIONS. For instance, in 1995, Vietnam, not yet a member, showed solidarity with the ASSOCIATION OF SOUTHEAST ASIAN NATIONS (ASEAN) (1967) in protesting the Chinese occupation of Mischief Reef in the Spratlys, claimed by the Philippines.

Vietnam's foreign policy from the early 1990s placed scant emphasis on ideological considerations and began to establish relations with all, including former foes. Relations with the Russian Federation were dramatically established in 2001. During a visit to Vietnam in February, Russian president Vladimir Putin slashed the country's outstanding debt to the former Soviet Union from U.S.$11 billion to U.S.$1.6 billion, including an extension to a twenty-three-year repayment schedule. The Russian lease on Cam Ranh Bay as a military facility would be renewed upon expiration in 2004.

In June 1991 the Communist Party of Vietnam adopted a decade-long program for economic liberalization and for upholding the socialist political system. The April 1992 inauguration of the new constitution stressed the pivotal role of the Communist Party of

Vietnam and that it had to abide by the country's laws. Notwithstanding the socialist economic system, the constitution guaranteed FDIs in the country. Furthermore, Vietnamese were allowed to invest abroad as well as permitted to travel overseas. In September the National Assembly elected General Le Duc Anh and Nguyễn Thi Binh to the posts of president (head of state) and vice president, the latter being the first woman to enjoy senior standing. Under the new constitution President Anh appointed, with approval from the National Assembly, Vo Van Kiet as prime minister. In an unprecedented move the National Assembly in June 1994 gave assent to a labor law that gave workers the right to undertake strike actions. Taking the cue, workers in some of the southern provinces went on strike. This new labor law was part of Vietnam's open-door strategy to woo FDIs.

Diplomatic relations were reestablished between Vietnam and Japan in September 1993. Japan proved a dynamic economic catalyst in becoming not only the largest foreign aid donor but also a major trading partner to Vietnam. Japanese "soft" loans for infrastructure development undoubtedly were a vital prerequisite to spurring economic growth and development. Even prior to the conclusion of the PARIS CONFERENCE ON CAMBODIA (PCC) (1989, 1991), Australia, confident of a settlement to the Cambodian question, restored direct developmental aid to Vietnam. Australia numbered among the most important FDIs to the country.

Political dissent continued to be proscribed, and throughout the 1980s and 1990s, recalcitrant elements—opposition voices, critics of the government or of the ruling party, advocates of organized religious groups—were imprisoned while others were executed. Officials of the UNIFIED BUDDHIST CHURCH (1963) who opposed the government's intolerance of organized religions were tried and imprisoned. Dissenters within the Communist Party of Vietnam itself were silenced through incarceration.

By the mid-1990s there were concerns from the leadership about the continued existence of widespread poverty and the increasing rate of corruption and crime. The national education system also came under scrutiny for its flaws and weaknesses. The rising disparity between the urban and rural economies was another source of concern. Social evils attributed to foreign (Western) influences, such as drug addiction, gambling, prostitution, and pornography, were targeted in a government campaign in 1996.

In July 1995, Vietnam was admitted into the ASSOCIATION OF SOUTHEAST ASIAN NATIONS (ASEAN) (1967). Trade and investment in Vietnam from the member states of ASEAN increased considerably during the 1990s (prior to the onset of the Asian Financial Crisis of 1997–1998).

The Eighth Congress of the Communist Party of Vietnam in mid-1996 reaffirmed the position of senior leaders—namely, Do Muoi as party secretary-general, Le Duc Anh as state president, and Vo Van Kiet as prime minister. The concept of multiparty democracy was strongly rejected. Economic modernization was the short-term objective, while industrialization (particularly in heavy industries) was the long-term aim of the socialist economic policy. Although the private sector was permitted to function alongside state enterprises, the unquestioned dominance of the latter was emphasized. FDIs continued to be encouraged in line with the country's open-door policy.

Elections to the expanded National Assembly (from 395 to 450 seats) in mid-1997 brought in a legislature with members drawn from a younger generation and with a comparatively higher level of education. Women and representatives from ethnic minorities were conspicuous. But more important was the presence of nonparty deputies and independent candidates. To a certain extent this new National Assembly ushered in some form of political liberalization. The newly elected leadership lineup was as follows: Tran Duc Luong as state president, Nguyễn Thi Binh as vice president, and Phan Van Kai as prime minister.

In combating the Asian Financial Crisis (1997–1998), Vietnam undertook the mobilization of domestic capital to counter the retraction and poor performance of FDIs. Priority was also given to promote labor-intensive, export-oriented processing industries. In mid-1998 a securities market was created subsequent to the establishment of a stock exchange.

Toward the end of the 1990s the protracted debate between conservative hardliners and reformists over the issue of the pace and extent of economic reform was aimed at growth and development. In October 1998, Prime Minister Phan Van Kai concurred with his Chinese counterpart, Zhu Rongji, who prioritized "socialist stability" over economic reforms. This pronouncement undoubtedly strengthened the hardliners' argument for restraining the pace of economic reforms, lest they compromise and threaten the political stability of the country and the monopolistic power of the Communist Party of Vietnam. Also of concern in this ongoing debate were the adverse effects of Western influences and globalization vis-à-vis the preservation of indigenous culture, values, and identity.

In 1998, Vietnam, together with the majority, opposed the Thai proposal of "flexible engagement" in place of the long-held principle of nonintervention in domestic affairs of member countries in the ASSOCIATION OF SOUTHEAST ASIAN NATIONS (ASEAN) (1967). Surin Pitsuwan, the Thai minister of foreign affairs, justified his "flexible engagement" concept, which sanctioned discussion of the internal affairs of another member country if such affairs had an impact beyond the country's borders—with examples of recent developments that had affected the region. They included the haze pollution in Indonesia, human rights issues in Myanmar, and the violence in Cambodia in July 1997.

Relations with the United States were commendable, beginning with joint missions seeking U.S. MIAs (MISSING IN ACTION) starting in 1986, the lifting of the economic embargo (February 1994), and the establishment of full diplomatic relations (July 1994). Furthermore, the United States was one of the major FDIs (by the mid-1990s). In July 2000, Vietnam was accorded normal trade relations, which drastically reduced tariff rates on its exports entering the United States from 40 percent to 3 percent. But more important, it was a step in enabling Vietnam to gain membership in the World Trade Organization (WTO). Despite these breakthroughs achieved in Vietnam-U.S. relations, President Bill Clinton's November 2000 visit was coldly received by his Vietnamese counterpart.

The baneful repercussions of resettlement programs in the second half of the 1970s returned when massive peasant rebellions erupted in the Central Highlands in the early months of 2001. Antagonisms between the ethnic minori-ties of the hill regions played themselves out, in particular between the HMONG and the immigrant VIETS. Coincidentally, the HMONG and the MONTAGNARD once collaborated with the U.S. military during the SECOND (VIETNAM WAR) INDOCHINA WAR (1964–1975), and afterward had grudgingly accepted the communist government of HANOI (THANG-LONG).

The clampdown on organized religion continued against Catholics and the UNIFIED BUDDHIST CHURCH (1963). Religious leaders and their organizations apparently were viewed with suspicion and even as a threat to the government. Curiously, however, Evangelical Protestantism was legalized and given official status. In a dramatic protest against religious suppression, a Buddhist nun committed self-immolation in March 2001.

Beginning in the late 1990s, tourism became an increasingly important foreign exchange 'earner for Vietnam. Europeans and Americans have been contributing valuable tourist dollars and boosting the service sector; the learning of English was encouraged and officially promoted for greater interaction with foreigners.

Indonesia during the late 1980s and the 1990s witnessed some turbulent developments that at times made it appear that the far-flung country of more than 13,000 islands might disassociate. From 1998 to 2001 the country witnessed widespread street demonstrations, riots, anti-Chinese retributions, secessionist movements, and ethnic-related violence in the wake of three regime changes. At the same time rapprochement with the PRC beginning in 1985 led to the reestablishment of full diplomatic relations in August 1990.

In 1989 a flare-up was again apparent in ACEH (ACHEH), which had long harbored secessionist tendencies and strongly resented the central government. The National Liberation Front of Aceh Sumatra led an uprising that, like previous rebellions, sought the independence of ACEH (ACHEH). The SUHARTO (1921–) government responded by declaring this province in northern SUMATRA a "military operations zone" in 1990; it meant that the military was given a free hand in suppressing the insurrection. Independent reports revealed that excessive force was used by the Indonesian military in swiftly clamping down on the uprising. By mid-1991 several thousands were killed and many more had "disappeared"; there were also reported atrocities committed by the military on the civilian population.

But unlike the pogroms following the fall of SOEKARNO (SUKARNO) (1901–1970) in 1965, the collapse of the *ORDE BARU* (THE NEW ORDER) of SUHARTO (1921–) did not mass massacres or witch hunts. Amid street violence that rocked the capital city of Jakarta, peaking in mid-May 1998, came a late-night visit on 20 May to the presidential palace by the armed forces chief of staff, General Wiranto, informing President SUHARTO (1921–) that the military was unable to guarantee security in Jakarta if he did not step down. It was a clear signal that the military had deserted him. Then on the following morning, President SUHARTO (1921–) announced his resignation to the nation. Vice President B. J. Habibie (1936–) took the oath of office as Indonesia's third president.

Reflecting on the last decade of SUHARTO (1921–) rule, few would have dared to venture that he would ever leave the scene except through death, as developments in the 1990s gave little indication of an exit for the aging but still formidable leader. Ironically, the successes achieved during ORDE BARU (THE NEW ORDER) led to the emergence of a new middle class with higher education and possessing higher expectations and aspirations—demanding *keterbukaan,* or "openness"—that subsequently exerted pressure on the government for more liberal and democratic changes. By the mid-1990s the Majelis Permusyawaratan Rakyat (MPR, People's Consultative Assembly) was engaged in debate aimed at terminating government-controlled news services and a possible reduction of parliamentary seats held by the military from 100 to 75 at the forthcoming election. Even the PANCASILA (PANTJA SILA), which was rigorously adhered to in the 1970s, was less stringently emphasized during the 1990s. There was a growing perception, particularly among the middle class, that a more liberal political order was gradually emerging in place of the *ORDE BARU* (THE NEW ORDER). That was reflected in the mushrooming of independent political organizations. Two intellectual organizations in particular were especially prominent. The first was Ikatan Cendekiawan Muslim In-

donesia (ICMI, Association of Muslim Intellectuals), established in 1990 and headed by B. J. Habibie, a protégé of SUHARTO's (1921–) who held the governmental appointment of minister of state for research and technology. The other was the Democracy Forum, founded in 1991 by a well-known *KIAI*, Abdurrahman Wahid (1940–), popularly known as "Gus Dur." Another was the revitalized Partai Demokrasi Indonesia (PDI, Indonesian Democratic Party); in 1993, Megawati Sukarnoputri (1947–), a daughter of SOEKARNO (SUKARNO) (1901–1970), assumed its chairmanship. The Partai Uni Demokrasi Indonesia (United Democratic Party of Indonesia) was founded by Sri Bintang Pamungkas in mid-1996.

Despite the economic successes of *ORDE BARU* (THE NEW ORDER), the seemingly liberal relaxation in the political arena was insufficient to satiate the appetite of *keterbukaan*. In addition there was the increasing public perception that SUHARTO (1921–) intended not only to entrench the economic position of his children but also to hand down political power to his family and friends. One clear indication was the high possibility of the promotion of General Prabowo Subianto, his son-in-law, to head KOSTRAD (Army Strategic Reserve Command). This move, it was believed, was intended to ensure the family's position and fortunes following the demise of the president.

In the follow-up to the parliamentary elections of May 1997, religious and ethnic strife erupted in various corners of the country. Targeting the Chinese Indonesian community, mobs of Muslim youths burned and looted churches, temples, and trading establishments in JAVA. In West Kalimantan, indigenous DAYAKS launched a reign of terror (including massacres) in an attempt to forcibly evict the immigrant Madurese from the province. (In the 1970s, under the transmigration program, several thousand Madurese were resettled in parts of Kalimantan where they became prominent in trade and commerce.)

GOLKAR was victorious in every province in the May 1997 parliamentary elections, with a voter turnout of close to 94 percent. SUHARTO (1921–) emerged from the polls in a strong political position and was prepared to commence his seventh presidential term. But developments from without that impacted adversely on the country were to create a situation in which his options to maneuver were closing in.

The Asian Financial Crisis (1997–1998), which saw the rapid devaluation of the Indonesian *rupiah*, exacerbated the country's massive foreign indebtedness. There appeared little choice but to turn to the IMF for assistance. Cost-cutting measures in the IMF package impinged into the realms of the sources of patronage—notably of family members of SUHARTO (1921–) and his cronies.

The downward plunge of the *rupiah* resulted in the closure of many industries, with layoffs of labor numbering in the hundreds of thousands nationwide. The price of imported goods, including such staples as wheat flour, shot up, aggravating the dire situation of the impoverished working class. The army of the poor and unemployed took to the streets in demonstrations, rioting, and even killings, with the ethnic Chinese community as the prime target. Arson of Chinese businesses and looting of shop houses were carried out, as the Chinese were generally (though unfairly) perceived as being responsible for the hike in prices. The crisis worsened when it became apparent that the regime had little intention of implementing the IMF rescue package. There were calls from respected individuals that strongly appealed to SUHARTO (1921–) to relinquish his hold on power. The value of the *rupiah* further plummeted toward the end of January 1998, when SUHARTO (1921–) made known that Habibie was his intended choice for vice president. Habibie was reputed to be an advocate of economic nationalism with a taste for highly expensive technological projects with doubtful returns. It did not bode well for the austerity program put forth by the IMF.

SUHARTO (1921–) formally began his seventh term as president in March 1998, when he was elected by the MPR with Habibie as vice president. Having his father-in-law at the helm confirmed General Prabowo's position as head of KOSTRAD. In a move to further consolidate his power, SUHARTO (1921–) had a cabinet that comprised his family members and close associates, sidelining all others including Habibie's supporters.

The blatant nepotism exhibited in the cabinet lineup sparked increasing student demonstrations and riots throughout the country, with urban centers seeing the worst of the public disorder. *Reformasi* (reform) was the united opposition's slogan, aimed at ousting SUHARTO (1921–).

The final straw was the announcement in early May of a 70 percent increase in fuel prices in accordance with an IMF strategy to cut state subsidies. Street demonstrations immediately escalated and violence against the ethnic Chinese community forced many to flee to neighboring Malaysia and Singapore. By mid-May the situation had reached a climax. The once-undisputed strongman of Indonesia, the seventy-seven-year-old SUHARTO (1921–), left the stage without applause.

The late 1990s witnessed uneasy relations between Indonesia and its neighbors Malaysia and Singapore. The haze pollution as a result of man-made forest fires in Indonesia disrupted communications and air transport, hurting the trade and tourism sectors of Malaysia and Singapore. Consequent of the Asian Financial Crisis (1997–1998), Malaysia deported several thousand Indonesian workers from the early part of 1998. Earlier in 1993 there had been friction between Indonesia and Malaysia over the disputed islands of Ligitan and Sipadan, situated offshore from the East Malaysian state of Sabah. On the international platform, East Timor was the contentious issue of Indonesia's relations with the West.

Habibie's brief tenure as president (t. 1998–1999) saw the revision of election laws in preparation for the June 1999 elections. There were also attempts to launch investigations into the family wealth of the deposed SUHARTO (1921–). Habibie lent his support to General Wiranto when the latter dismissed General Prabowo as head of KOSTRAD. He also released several notable political prisoners, including Sri Bintang Pamungkas, leader of the Partai Uni Demokrasi Indonesia. In a well-publicized gesture, Habibie not only visited the homes and shops of ethnic Chinese damaged in Jakarta as a result of the racial riots of May 1998 but also expressed sympathy for the plight of the victims.

Meanwhile, owing to internal struggles within the PDI, Megawati's faction became PDI-Perjuangan (PDI-P, Struggle of PDI). Abdurrahman Wahid established the Partai Kebangkitan Bangsa (PKB, National Awakening Party), which drew its main support from conservative Muslim communities of eastern JAVA.

Partai Amanat Nasional (PAN, National Mandate Party), led by Amien Rais, also vied for the electorate.

Ethnic- and religious-based violence erupted in various parts of the country, witnessing clashes between Muslims and Christians in MALUKU (THE MOLUCCAS), the unresolved murder of hundreds of Muslim clerics and others, and DAYAKS with support from the Malay community clashing with immigrant Madurese in West Kalimantan. In ACEH (ACHEH) secessionist elements began to be active.

In June 1998 the status of ACEH (ACHEH) as a "military operations zone" was revoked, and shortly thereafter troop withdrawals from the province began. General Wiranto even publicly apologized for past military excesses. But when antigovernment riots erupted in September, a halt was made to troop withdrawals. The general feeling among the Acehnese was complete independence. Guerrillas from the Gerakan Aceh Merdeka (GAM) engaged in a protracted war against the Indonesian military.

A 91 percent voter turnout in a relatively fair election in June 1999 brought victory for Megawati's PDI-P (34 percent), with GOLKAR (20 percent) coming in second. The main Muslim party of the ORDE BARU (THE NEW ORDER) era, Partai Persatuan Pembangunan (PPP, United Development Party), secured third place (11 percent). The PKB, as expected, scored promising support from its stronghold of eastern JAVA. PAN, however, had a poor showing.

The election of Indonesia's president was scheduled for deliberation in the MPR in November 1999 from the nominees that had been submitted by the political parties prior to the June polls. The two front-runners were Megawati and Habibie. In an impressive rebound from the disastrous showing in the polls, Amien Rais managed to bring about a coalition of Muslim parties (with the notable exception of the PKB) to form Poros Tengah (Central Axis); his intention was to ensure a strong Islamic voice in the next government. Habibie's prospects began to dwindle owing to several of his actions, the most prominent being the general perception that he had mishandled the East Timor issue. The overwhelming rejection by the East Timorese of integration and the vote for independence in the referendum of August 1999 were considered by many in Indonesia as a slap in the face, especially within the military. Megawati's aloofness, the fact that female leaders were not generally favored among Muslims, and the alleged "money politics" of her PDI-P put Megawati at a disadvantage despite her pedigreed background.

At the eleventh hour Habibie withdrew his candidacy. GOLKAR and Poros Tengah immediately swung their support to Abdurrahman Wahid, who subsequently won the presidency in an MPR election on 20 October 1999, garnering 373 votes to Megawati's 313. The following day Megawati was sworn in as vice president.

With a "rainbow" cabinet drawn from a multitude of political parties and led by a KIAI who was partially blind and in deteriorating health (he suffered a severe stroke in early 1998), the twenty-two-month presidency of Abdurrahman Wahid did not exude much confidence. The new government had little impact on the country's deteriorating economic situation; likewise the religious strife in MALUKU (THE MOLUCCAS), which subsequently developed into an all-out civil war with local army units backing the Muslims and the police supporting the Christians. Elsewhere, violence persisted in West Kalimantan between DAYAKS and Madurese. A standoff between the president and General Wiranto in the early part of 2000 ended in the latter's handing in his resignation in mid-May. (The Human Rights Commission of Indonesia implicated General Wiranto in the postreferendum [August 1999] violence in East Timor.) The investigation into the accumulated personal wealth of former president SUHARTO (1921–) was resumed. (SUHARTO [1921–] suffered a stroke in 1999.) Hutomo "Tommy" Mandala Putra, the youngest son of SUHARTO (1921–), was accused of a series of bombings in August and September of 2000; but the lack of evidence failed to convict him. He was, however, handed eighteen months' imprisonment for corruption by a Jakarta judge, but he evaded arrest. Gunmen assassinated the presiding judge in July 2001; they later confessed to police that Hutomo ordered the killing.

In his effort to garner support and recognition for his government and to restore confidence among the international business community, President Abdurrahman Wahid, despite his ill health, undertook a series of visits to foreign countries in late 1999 and early 2000. His foreign tours took him to thirty-four national capitals. But the persistent instability, widespread unrest, and violence in Indonesia worked against the president's efforts abroad.

In ACEH (ACHEH) President Abdurrahman Wahid, when he initially came to power, hinted at a referendum on independence. A proreferendum rally was immediately organized in Banda Aceh in early November 1999. But a referendum like the one in East Timor was strongly opposed by the military. But in his characteristic indecision, President Abdurrahman Wahid by the early months of 2000 had apparently backtracked on his referendum proposal. He instead stressed the granting of wider autonomy, with a greater share of revenue derived from the province's natural resources, and some concessions in the introduction of some aspects of Islamic law. Few were convinced, and the campaign for independence continued. By mid-2000 GAM claimed to control almost half of all the villages in the province. Talks between the government and the secessionists in Geneva in May 2000 resulted in a three-month ceasefire. Although extended to January 2001, the ceasefire was at best on paper while violence reigned in the province.

As early as mid-2000 there was dissatisfaction with the performance of Abdurrahman Wahid, and he was ordered to explain his actions to the MPR in August. At this juncture no action against him was taken, in the fear that his supporters might retaliate with violence and unrest. A year later, despite being cleared of corruption charges, the president faced impeachment by the MPR on the basis of unsatisfactory performance. A standoff occurred between Abdurrahman Wahid and the MPR on 23 July. In the afternoon the MPR unanimously voted for the dismissal of Abdurrahman Wahid as president. Megawati assumed the presidency, with Hamzah Has of the PPP as vice president.

In Myanmar the STATE LAW AND ORDER RESTORATION COUNCIL (SLORC) was established in 1988, with Saw Maung assuming three portfolios concurrently as minister of defense and foreign affairs, and as prime minister. The country became known officially as the Union of Burma. Despite the abrogation of the single-party law and the registration of

political parties for the 1990 election, martial law restricted virtually all types of political activities—for example, gatherings were limited to five persons, and there were various restrictions on publications, public meetings, and travel. The BURMA SOCIALIST PROGRAM PARTY (BSPP) was renamed the National Unity Party (NUP) under the chairmanship of U Tha Kyaw. Following his expulsion from the NATIONAL LEAGUE FOR DEMOCRACY (NLD) over a clash with DAW AUNG SAN SUU KYI (1945–), Aung Gyi established the Union National Democracy Party (UNDP). Although elections were scheduled for mid-1990, the STATE LAW AND ORDER RESTORATION COUNCIL (SLORC) declared that it would continue to be the government even after the elections until a new constitution was drafted and accepted by the elected legislative assembly. Until then, martial law remained in force.

In order to avoid identification with the majority BURMANS and to reflect multiethnic composition, another name change was effected in June 1989, from the Union of Burma to the Union of Myanmar (Myanma Naingngan). BURMANS acquired the new term Bamars, KARENS became Kayin, and Karenni became Kayinni.

The NATIONAL LEAGUE FOR DEMOCRACY (NLD) scored an overwhelming victory in the May 1990 elections, winning 392 seats out of the total 485 seats. The NUP managed 10 seats. The remainder, 83 seats, were shared among twenty-three political parties. Ethnic-based parties received much support from the electorate. A coalition was formed of non-BURMANS, calling itself the United Nationalities League for Democracy (UNLD). When all opposition parties combined, they dominated 95 percent (461 of 485 seats) in the legislative assembly.

Then in July 1990, the STATE LAW AND ORDER RESTORATION COUNCIL (SLORC) issued Order 1/90, which declared the STATE LAW AND ORDER RESTORATION COUNCIL (SLORC) as the de facto government, as it had international legitimacy recognized by the United Nations and other countries. Until a new constitution accepted by all ethnic groups in the country came into being, political power was to rest with the STATE LAW AND ORDER

RESTORATION COUNCIL (SLORC) as a safeguard to national solidarity. It further reiterated that the May 1990 elections were aimed not at forming a new government but at providing an assembly that was to draft a new constitution under the auspices of a national convention to be constituted by the STATE LAW AND ORDER RESTORATION COUNCIL (SLORC) in due course.

In April 1991, Lieutenant General Than Shwe, the vice chairman of the STATE LAW AND ORDER RESTORATION COUNCIL (SLORC) and the deputy commander of the armed forces, announced that there would not be any transfer of the reins of power to those elected representatives of the May 1990 polls. He accused the political parties of being subversive. In March–April 1992, Than Shwe became both minister of defense and prime minister when Saw Maung stepped down. Despite that change, many still regarded Khin Nyunt, the first secretary of the STATE LAW AND ORDER RESTORATION COUNCIL (SLORC) and head of the military intelligence service, to be the principal influence in the government.

Throughout the 1990s, tension and strained relations occurred between the opposition, led mainly by the NATIONAL LEAGUE FOR DEMOCRACY (NLD) in the persona of DAW AUNG SAN SUU KYI (1945–), and the de facto government of the STATE LAW AND ORDER RESTORATION COUNCIL (SLORC). The latter in fact waged a war of attrition with DAW AUNG SAN SUU KYI (1945–), whose struggle for democracy gained international support when she became a recipient of the Nobel Peace Prize in October 1991.

The National Convention—which had a six-year life span from 1993 until it went into indefinite recess in 1996—was a pathetic showcase of a rubber-stamp assembly. Some 80 percent of the delegates were appointed by the STATE LAW AND ORDER RESTORATION COUNCIL (SLORC), while the NATIONAL LEAGUE FOR DEMOCRACY (NLD) had a 13 percent representation of the overall total of 702 delegates. The major contention of the opposing groups was the demand by the STATE LAW AND ORDER RESTORATION COUNCIL (SLORC) to provide a central role to the military. Nonetheless, following the arrest and intimidation of

the opposition, the sitting of the National Convention in September 1994 emphasized the pivotal role of the Tatmadaw (armed forces), which was subsequently incorporated in the new constitution.

Paralleling the military-dominated STATE LAW AND ORDER RESTORATION COUNCIL (SLORC) was its civilian front, known as the Union Solidarity and Development Association (USDA). It was established in 1993 and not registered as a political party but as an "association" under the purview of the ministry of education; civil servants were encouraged to be members with promises of privileges. There was little doubt that the military junta fully controlled the USDA; Than Shwe was its patron.

DAW AUNG SAN SUU KYI (1945–), under house arrest beginning in 1989, was released on 10 July 1995. Prior to this unexpected event, there were some indications of such a possibility. A year earlier, Khin Nyunt had stated the willingness on the part of the STATE LAW AND ORDER RESTORATION COUNCIL (SLORC) to hold talks with DAW AUNG SAN SUU KYI (1945–). In mid-September 1994 she had talks with Than Shwe and Khin Nyunt; a second meeting took place in October. In November she was granted permission to meet Tin Oo and Kyi Maung, leaders of the NATIONAL LEAGUE FOR DEMOCRACY (NLD) serving prison sentences. In February 1995 the UN assistant secretary-general Alvaro de Soto held talks with leaders of the STATE LAW AND ORDER RESTORATION COUNCIL (SLORC). The following month Tin Oo and Kyi Maung, together with several political detainees, were released.

There was apparently some relaxation of the ban on gatherings of more than five individuals, as crowds easily numbering more than a thousand wellwishers and enthusiastic supporters congregated outside the house of DAW AUNG SAN SUU KYI (1945–) in RANGOON (YANGON) to see and hear her public speeches. On 19 July 1995 she was shown on state television laying a wreath on the grave of her father, AUNG SAN (1915–1947), in a Martyrs' Day ceremony in RANGOON (YANGON). The foreign media were allowed access to her. In interviews with foreign journalists she appealed to the STATE LAW AND ORDER RESTORA-

TION COUNCIL (SLORC) for the release of all political prisoners and the gradual lifting of martial law. She requested that the ruling junta officially sanction the May 1990 election result and convene a discussion with opposition groups with national reconciliation as the priority agenda. In mid-November the NATIONAL LEAGUE FOR DEMOCRACY (NLD) reinstated DAW AUNG SAN SUU KYI (1945–) as general secretary. Aung Shwe retained the chairmanship, and Tin Oo and Kyi Maung both remained as vice chairmen.

But in the latter part of 1995, subtle signs of restrictions were beginning to be imposed on DAW AUNG SAN SUU KYI (1945–). For instance, she was strongly advised by the military authorities that for her own personal safety she should refrain from leaving the compound of her house in RANGOON (YANGON). After her talks in September and October 1994, no further dialogue had developed; it appeared that DAW AUNG SAN SUU KYI (1945–) was being shunned by the military junta.

Nonetheless, in July 1997, Khin Nyunt held talks with Aung Shwe. But the NATIONAL LEAGUE FOR DEMOCRACY (NLD) refused to attend the scheduled second meeting in September, as the military junta barred the participation of DAW AUNG SAN SUU KYI (1945–). In fact, her reinstatement as general secretary of the NATIONAL LEAGUE FOR DEMOCRACY (NLD) was considered illegal by the STATE LAW AND ORDER RESTORATION COUNCIL (SLORC).

In a surprise move in November 1997, the STATE LAW AND ORDER RESTORATION COUNCIL (SLORC) was replaced by a State Peace and Development Council (SPDC). It was mere window dressing, however, as the principal players remained: Than Shwe as chairman (concurrently prime minister, minister of defense, and commander of the army), Maung Aye as vice chairman, and Khin Nyunt as first secretary (and head of military intelligence). The second and third secretaries were Lieutenant General Tin Oo (different from the NLD's Tin Oo) and Lieutenant General Win Myint (also the adjutant-general), respectively. In fact, the entire nineteen-member SPDC consisted of serving military officers. Besides the premiership, civilians drawn largely from the USDA held ministerial portfolios in the cabinet.

Beginning in 1998, the SPDC stepped up its efforts at clamping down and ultimately eliminating the NATIONAL LEAGUE FOR DEMOCRACY (NLD) with arrests, imprisonment, and the forced resignation of several thousand of its members. Several of its regional centers were forced to close. Paralleling this development was the SPDC's continuous refusal to allocate any role for DAW AUNG SAN SUU KYI (1945–) in national politics. The military leadership persistently questioned her nationality, whether British or Myanmar, as she was married to a British academic, Michael Aris, and her children held British passports.

By a combination of military offensives, diplomacy, and negotiations with individual groups, the military regime by 1998 was able to eliminate most of the ethnic insurgencies and separatist movements in Myanmar. Only the KAREN NATIONAL UNION (KNU) under the leadership of Saw Ba Thin continued to challenge the SPDC. However, in early 2000 the KAREN NATIONAL UNION (KNU) announced its willingness to negotiate a political settlement with the SPDC, and reportedly there were a series of talks between them in February and March.

The international community, including the ASSOCIATION OF SOUTHEAST ASIAN NATIONS (ASEAN) (1967), possessed two major concerns relating to Myanmar—namely, democracy and narcotics. Having failed to bring the ruling military junta and the NATIONAL LEAGUE FOR DEMOCRACY (NLD) to the negotiating table despite five attempts, Alvaro de Soto was replaced in April 2000 by the Malaysian diplomat Razali Ismail as UN Special Envoy to Myanmar. Razali brokered the commencement of secret talks between the two parties. He himself, however, was barred from entering the country in 2001. But in mid-2003 Razali resumed his efforts; there was apparently little headway.

Equally frustrating was the fight against narcotics production and trafficking in the notorious "Golden Triangle." In the mid-1970s, Burma (Myanmar) participated with the United Nations and the United States in a campaign to suppress the cultivation of opium in the northeastern part of the country. All joint efforts were, however, suspended following the 1988 military coup. Despite Myanmar's being a signatory to the UN Vienna Convention against trafficking in illegal drugs, it was believed that during the 1990s the country's export earnings were derived largely from the narcotics trade. Provincial military commanders were directly or indirectly involved in this lucrative narcotics business. Likewise, ethnic insurgent groups conducted a "drugs-for-arms" deal to bolster their armaments in their struggle against the central regime in RANGOON (YANGON).

Myanmar became a member of the ASSOCIATION OF SOUTHEAST ASIAN NATIONS (ASEAN) (1967) in July 1997. Thailand, Singapore, and Malaysia were keen on the potential economic opportunities that Myanmar might offer. From the political perspective, Indonesia in particular and the ASSOCIATION OF SOUTHEAST ASIAN NATIONS (ASEAN) (1967) in general were concerned to ensure that Myanmar not come under the influence of the PRC. In the 1990s a policy of "constructive engagement," which meant nonintervention in domestic affairs of individual countries, was the policy adopted by the ASSOCIATION OF SOUTHEAST ASIAN NATIONS (ASEAN) (1967) toward Myanmar's military regime. As a goodwill gesture Myanmar's foreign minister, U Ohn Gyaw, was invited to BANGKOK in July 1994 as a guest in the opening and closing ceremonies of the ASSOCIATION OF SOUTHEAST ASIAN NATIONS (ASEAN) (1967) yearly meeting of ministers for foreign affairs. Meanwhile, trade relations between Myanmar and its regional neighbors steadily increased. Prior to full membership Myanmar had concluded a treaty of friendship and cooperation in 1995, and the following year it was granted observer status to witness the July 1996 ASSOCIATION OF SOUTHEAST ASIAN NATIONS (ASEAN) (1967) meeting in Jakarta. Myanmar also qualified in becoming a full member of the ASEAN Regional Forum (ARF).

Prior to Myanmar's entry into the ASSOCIATION OF SOUTHEAST ASIAN NATIONS (ASEAN) (1967), the latter had shown solidarity and support for it. For example, in 1991 the ASSOCIATION OF SOUTHEAST ASIAN NATIONS (ASEAN) (1967) refused demands by the United States that it use its influence to pressure Myanmar to end human rights violations and restore democratic government. Then in 1999, an ASEAN-EU meeting planned for February was postponed indefi-

nitely over the issue of Myanmar's presence, which was strongly objected to by the EU while vigorously defended by ASEAN. There was optimism in the region that the efforts of Razali Ismail, UN special envoy to Myanmar, would achieve significant breakthroughs in the near future.

DR. MAHATHIR BIN MOHAMAD (1925–), Malaysia's fourth prime minister, was the most controversial, characterized by his outspoken style in speaking his mind, whether at the meeting of his UNITED MALAYS NATIONAL ORGANIZATION (UMNO) (1946)—the leading component in the BARISAN NASIONAL (NATIONAL FRONT) (1974) coalition government—or while addressing the UN General Assembly in New York. Abiding by his publicly declared intention to step down in October 2003, Dr. M (as he is popularly known) completed twenty-two years as prime minister, almost equivalent to the combined tenures of his three predecessors. When, true to his word, he retired as Malaysian prime minister in October 2003, the premiership passed to his deputy, Abdullah Ahmad Badawi (1939–), who also concurrently held the finance and home affairs portfolios. Of commoner background and a medical practitioner by profession, Dr. M differed from the aristocratic lineage of previous prime ministers. He in fact represented a new generation of Malays determined to assert their position vis-à-vis the other ethnic groups in a multiracial country. His emphasis on meritocracy was a bitter pill to swallow within the Malay community, which had hitherto enjoyed a "helping hand" from the government primarily through the NEW ECONOMIC POLICY (NEP) (1971–1990).

Determined that Malaysia be a modern and developed nation, Dr. M embarked on a modernization program that earmarked industrialization as the engine of economic growth and development. The exploitation of natural resources (oil, natural gas, timber) and the promotion of export agriculture (mainly palm oil extraction) paralleled industrialization (electronics to car manufacturing). East Asian work ethic models, particularly those of the Japanese and the South Koreans, were encouraged and energetically emphasized in Dr. M's "Look East Policy" of the 1980s. For the 1990s there was "Vision 2020," his ambitious foresight that by the year 2020, Malaysia would attain the status of a "fully developed" nation. Outlining its objectives in February 1991, he envisaged not only material gains (the public health care system, quality education, advanced infrastructure facilities) but also harmony in a dynamic, just, and democratic multiethnic society.

Meanwhile, the NEW ECONOMIC POLICY (NEP) (1971–1990) was replaced in June 1991 with the New Development Policy (NDP). Economic growth and the eradication of poverty were the twin foci of the NDP, with "Vision 2020" as its ultimate objective. By 1997, Malaysia was confidently on the path to attaining the Newly Industrialized Country (NIC) status and becoming another promising Asian "economic tiger."

Within the Malay community, three groups challenged Dr. M. There was the conservative, religious PARTAI ISLAM SE MALAYSIA (PAS), which aimed at transforming Malaysia into an Islamic state. It was particularly strong in the Malay heartlands of Kelantan and Terengganu, with growing influence in Kedah (once its stronghold in the 1960s and 1970s) among the rural Malay population. The royal authority of the Malay sultans, some of whom were known to intervene in political matters in transgression of the federal constitution, posed another challenge to Dr. M's government. But the most dramatic opposition came from within the UNITED MALAYS NATIONAL ORGANIZATION (UMNO) (1946) when in April 1987, Tengku Razaleigh Hamzah (1937–) vied for the party's presidency. Dr. M, the incumbent, narrowly won, and the deep schism within the party appeared irreparable. But by a twist of fate in 1988, the UNITED MALAYS NATIONAL ORGANIZATION (UMNO) (1946) apparently violated the Societies Act and was declared technically illegal, thus forcing it to dissolve. Dr. M formed a new party, UMNO Baru (New UMNO), which inherited the assets of its predecessor, and a reregistration of members was undertaken; Razaleigh and his supporters were denied membership. Razaleigh established Semangat '46 (Spirit of '46), which claimed to capture the essence of the Malay struggle as originally defined in 1946 when the UNITED MALAYS NATIONAL ORGANIZATION (UMNO) (1946) was constituted.

With the ruling coalition of Dr. M's BARISAN NASIONAL (NATIONAL FRONT) (1974) holding the two-thirds of the parliamentary seats in the Dewan Rakyat (Lower House of Representatives) required for any constitutional amendment, the aim of the diverse opposition was to deny that advantage. The most unlikely political partnerships were struck among the opposition parties for the 1990 elections. Despite their animosity in Kelantan, the secular Semangat '46 and PARTAI ISLAM SE MALAYSIA (PAS) became political bedfellows, forming an alliance called Angkatan Perpaduan Ummah (APU, Muslim Unity Movement). Semangat '46 also allied with the Chinese-dominated DEMOCRATIC ACTION PARTY (DAP); this alliance was termed the Gagasan Rakyat (People's Concept). Through these alliances, PARTAI ISLAM SE MALAYSIA (PAS) ended as a political ally of the DEMOCRATIC ACTION PARTY (DAP); from the start it was apparent that they had nothing in common except to deny the "two-thirds" to the BARISAN NASIONAL (NATIONAL FRONT) (1974). Few could envisage the formation of a government in the event of an opposition-upset electoral victory. Dr. M's BARISAN NASIONAL (NATIONAL FRONT) (1974) comfortably retained its "two-thirds" in the 1990 elections.

Two years into his premiership Dr. M proposed to remove the right of the nine hereditary Malay sultans to withhold assent to legislation. Although theoretically the BARISAN NASIONAL (NATIONAL FRONT) (1974) government could push through such amendments with its two-thirds majority, a compromise was struck between the parties involved. The Malay aristocrats began to view Dr. M with mistrust. In mid-1992 the government issued a code of conduct for the Malay sultans that restricted their role in any political process. Furthermore, in early 1993 the legislature removed the personal legal immunity of the sultans. And in May 1994 a constitutional amendment removed the sultans' right to withhold assent to legislation. In 1997, Islamic jurisprudence, hitherto the purview of the individual sultan as the head of the faith in his own state and of the state religious authorities, was centralized and controlled from the federal government in KUALA LUMPUR (KL). The intention was not particularly to target the Malay rulers but more to control the conservative state religious authorities that allegedly impeded national development with various religious injunctions, or *fatwa*.

Turning to the judiciary, several changes were effected in the late 1980s. The controversial removal of Tun Salleh Abbas, lord president of the Supreme Court, on charges of "misbehavior" in August 1987, followed by the suspension of the remaining five judges of the Supreme Court, of whom two were dismissed, shocked the nation and the British Commonwealth. (The Malayan/Malaysian bench was highly regarded within the Commonwealth.) The following year the powers of the judiciary to interpret laws were curtailed through a constitutional amendment. In 1994 the government outlined a mandatory code of ethics for judges; moreover, the Supreme Court became the Federal Court and the lord president was renamed chief justice.

Not only was the Internal Security Act (ISA) retained, it was strengthened in June 1988 in that detainees were denied appeals to the court. The sale of political parties' newspapers was limited to within the party itself. That was directed specifically at opposition groups, notably PARTAI ISLAM SE MALAYSIA (PAS) and the DEMOCRATIC ACTION PARTY (DAP), and to a lesser extent, the social reform organization ALIRAN Malaysia.

Just prior to the 1990 elections the Christian-dominated Partai Bersatu Sabah (PBS, Sabah United Party), led by Joseph Pairin Kitingan, disengaged itself at the eleventh hour from the BARISAN NASIONAL (NATIONAL FRONT) (1974) to ally with the opposition, Semangat '46. Although Kitingan won and led as chief minister a PBS state government in Sabah, he was excluded from decision-making meetings in KUALA LUMPUR (KL), and development funds for Sabah were deliberately delayed or withheld. Attempts were made to remove Kitingan from office, including court cases brought against him over corruption charges. Furthermore, in February 1991, the UNITED MALAYS NATIONAL ORGANIZATION (UMNO) (1946) established a branch in Kota Kinabalu, Sabah. In the 1994 state elections PBS narrowly won; shortly thereafter there were several defections from PBS to various splinter parties. The UNITED MALAYS NATIONAL ORGANIZATION (UMNO) (1946) was able to create a coalition with a Chinese-based party and with the KADAZAN-DUSUNS. The coali-

tion members agreed that the three major communities (Malay, Chinese, and KADAZAN-DUSUNS) should take turns providing a chief minister.

Malaysia under Dr. M's government created currents in the international arena. For instance, Dr. M's idea of an East Asia Economic Caucus (EAEC), a trade group that excluded the United States, Australia, and New Zealand, was strongly objected to by Washington. The Americans were keen to promote the Asia Pacific Economic Cooperation Organization (APEC), a grouping that they initiated. In mid-1993 it was agreed that EAEC would be a component championing East Asian interests within APEC. EAEC was formally established in the latter part of 2000; a Malaysian proposal for a trans-Asian railway to enhance economic integration was accepted.

Dr. M played a pivotal role in environmental issues. The Kuala Lumpur Declaration (April 1992) demanded that the developed West cease criticizing issues such as logging in developing countries, and at the same time that the rich nations should review their consumption and production patterns in order to lessen the adverse impact on the environment. This Kuala Lumpur Declaration was brought to the UN Conference on Environment and Development in Rio de Janeiro, Brazil, in June 1992.

In the run-up to the polls of 1995, the already uneasy alliance of the opposition parties that formed the Gagasan Rakyat was aggravated by the announcement of the intention of PARTAI ISLAM SE MALAYSIA (PAS) to introduce *hudud* (Islamic criminal code) in Kelantan, which would include jurisdiction over non-Muslims. Regardless of the fact that such a move contravened the federal constitution that guarantees freedom of worship, PARTAI ISLAM SE MALAYSIA (PAS), which ruled Kelantan, passed the legislation; it was adopted in 1993. Not surprisingly the Chinese-based DEMOCRATIC ACTION PARTY (DAP) withdrew from the Gagasan Rakyat just prior to the general elections.

Notwithstanding several embarrassments to the government—allegations of corruption and serious offenses such as statutory rape leveled against senior political figures, which received extensive coverage in the local media—Dr. M's BARISAN NASIONAL (NATIONAL FRONT) (1974) again won a convincing victory in the 1995 elections. Of the opposition parties only PARTAI ISLAM SE MALAYSIA (PAS) managed a fair showing. In alliance with Semangat '46, it managed to retain Kelantan. Following the polls there was a concerted effort on the part of PARTAI ISLAM SE MALAYSIA (PAS) to maneuver Semangat '46 out of Kelantan, leading to the end of the APU. Its poor showing in other parts of the country forced Razaleigh to dissolve Semangat '46; many of its members rejoined the UNITED MALAYS NATIONAL ORGANIZATION (UMNO) (1946). The DEMOCRATIC ACTION PARTY (DAP) suffered a devastating defeat, largely because of its association with PARTAI ISLAM SE MALAYSIA (PAS), that appalled many of the non-Muslim, urban electorate.

In the aftermath of his 1995 triumph, Dr. M faced the perplexing question of his successor. Past practices in Malaysia witnessed the smooth leadership succession process. There was little doubt that Anwar Ibrahim (1947–), deputy president of the UNITED MALAYS NATIONAL ORGANIZATION (UMNO) (1946), deputy prime minister, and minister of finance, should step into Dr. M's shoes upon his retirement. But events in the second half of the 1990s unfolded in a manner that few observers would have anticipated back in 1995. The Asian Financial Crisis (1997–1998) played a decisive role in the succession stakes.

Meanwhile, smoke from the open burnings in the rain forests of Indonesia, particularly of Kalimantan and SUMATRA, harmed Malaysia's trade and commerce, in particular the tourist industry. In the spirit of the ASSOCIATION OF SOUTHEAST ASIAN NATIONS (ASEAN) (1967), Malaysia was less critical of Indonesia. Moreover, Malaysian firefighters assisted their counterparts in alleviating the situation.

SINGAPORE-MALAYA/MALAYSIA RELATIONS (ca. 1950s–1990s) became strained in the mid-1990s consequent of some remarks from Singapore's senior minister, LEE KUAN YEW (1923–). In 1994 he touched a highly sensitive note when he proposed that a merger between Singapore and Malaysia was possible, even desirable, if only the latter abandoned its affirmative BUMIPUTERA (BUMIPUTRA) policy. In 1997, LEE KUAN YEW (1923–) made disparaging remarks about the city of Johor Bahru, where an opposition Singapore

politician sought refuge to escape arrest; he later apologized. Then in his published memoirs, he criticized several Malay leaders of Malaysia. Disputes over the island of Batu Putih (Pedra Branca) again soured relations between the neighbors.

Conflicting sovereignty claims over the islands of Sipadan and Ligitan between Malaysia and Indonesia were brought to the International Court of Justice (ICJ), The Hague. The ICJ ruled against Indonesia in its verdict, announced in 2003. The repatriation of thousands of unskilled Indonesian laborers from Malaysia in the aftermath of the Asian Financial Crisis (1997–1998) created unease between the governments. Malaysia-Thailand relations were strained over the issue of MUSLIM MINORITIES (THAILAND) and their separatist aspirations. In 1998, Malaysia-Thailand agreed to jointly develop an offshore oil field and natural gas in a disputed area in the Gulf of Thailand. KUALA LUMPUR (KL)–MANILA ties became strained over the kidnap-ransom issue in Sipadan in April 1998, as well as President Joseph Estrada's comments on the Anwar case.

In mid-May 1997, Anwar became acting prime minister while Dr. M was abroad. In mid-July the *ringgit* (currency) began to slide consequent initially of the disastrous situation in neighboring Thailand, but increasingly exposing structural problems in the Malaysian economic system. By October the *ringgit* lost 40 percent of its value, which hit companies and investors that had borrowed from foreign sources particularly hard. Rejecting assistance from, and henceforth the intervention of, the IMF, Dr. M decided to impose capital controls to arrest the *ringgit*'s downturn by pegging it at a fixed RM3.80 to U.S.$1.00. Acceptance of an IMF rescue package might involve the abandonment of large, prestigious infrastructure projects and scaling down or even ending the policy of affirmative action in the economy for Malays and other BUMIPUTERA (BUMIPUTRA). Anwar as minister of finance favored implementing an austerity program that appeared to be more in tune with IMF proposals, but such a view was opposed to Dr. M's plan.

Taking a cue from events in neighboring Indonesia when SUHARTO (1921–) was forced to step down in May 1998 amid allegations of ill-gotten family fortunes, cronyism, nepotism, and corruption, in June at the annual conference of the UNITED MALAYS NATIONAL ORGANIZATION (UMNO) (1946), an Anwar supporter delivered a strongly worded speech condemning corruption and implicating the party leadership. The distribution among delegates of the pamphlet *Lima puluh dalih mengapa Anwar tidak akan menjadi perdana mentri* ("Fifty Reasons Why Anwar Cannot Become Prime Minister") presented the conspiracy of Anwar to seize power and his various sexual misdemeanors (homosexuality and sodomy). Furthermore, Anwar's cronies who benefited from his patronage were exposed. Apparently Dr. M asked Anwar to resign; if not he would be dismissed in disgrace and criminal charges would be brought against him.

On 2 September 1998, Dr. M sacked the deputy prime minister, citing his corruption and sexual impropriety as unsuitable for a leader of Malaysia. The following day Anwar was expelled from the UNITED MALAYS NATIONAL ORGANIZATION (UMNO) (1946). Daim Zainuddin, a corporate figure and a former minister of finance in the late 1980s, was recalled to oversee the economy. Dr. M himself assumed the post of minister of finance.

Again looking toward Indonesia, Anwar expected a groundswell of public support. Exploiting his oratorical skills, Anwar portrayed himself as a victim of a political conspiracy and denied all the allegations of homosexual relations and sodomy. (Homosexuality and sodomy are serious offenses punishable under Malaysia's penal code; Islam condemns such practices as "unnatural acts.") His supporters, numbering a few thousand, held peaceful demonstrations in KUALA LUMPUR (KL), uttering the adopted Indonesian slogan of *reformasi* (reform). Invoking the ISA, Anwar and a handful of supporters were arrested on 20 September. Nine days later a badly bruised Anwar appeared in court, where he was charged with five counts of corruption and five counts of unnatural sexual acts. Investigations revealed that Abdul Rahim Noor, inspector-general of police, was responsible for assaulting Anwar during his detention; as a result he tendered his resignation and later was sentenced to a brief jail term and a small fine.

The trial of Anwar Ibrahim went through several twists and turns with amended charges and appeals; finally in April 1999 he was convicted of four charges of corruption and received a six-year imprisonment term. This con-

viction automatically disqualified him from public office. Then in early August 2000, he was convicted of sodomy and was sentenced to nine years' imprisonment, to commence only after the completion of his earlier six-year prison term. As early as May 1999, Dr. M already had made it clear to delegates of the UNITED MALAYS NATIONAL ORGANIZATION (UMNO) (1946) at its yearly conference that there was no reconciliation with Anwar.

In January 1999, Abdullah Ahmad Badawi (1939–), the minister of foreign affairs, was appointed deputy prime minister and minister of home affairs; Daim was appointed minister of finance. While Dr. M consolidated his hold on power, Anwar's supporters, rallying under his wife, Dr. Wan Azizah Wan Islamil, formed the Partai Keadilan Nasional (PKN, National Justice Party) in April 1999. Although the PKN claimed to be multiethnic and multireligious, it was undeniably predominantly a Malay Muslim party. In June, the PKN allied with the DEMOCRATIC ACTION PARTY (DAP) and PARTAI ISLAM SE MALAYSIA (PAS) to create the Barisan Alternatif (BA, Alternative Front) to run in the June 2000 election.

But the election was brought forward to November 1999. As expected, Dr. M's BARISAN NASIONAL (NATIONAL FRONT) (1974) again retained its two-thirds majority. However, besides continuing its hold on Kelantan, PARTAI ISLAM SE MALAYSIA (PAS) seized Terengganu. Abdul Hadi Awang became chief minister of Terengganu and embarked on an Islamization program. Fadzil Mohamed Nor (1937–2003), the president of PARTAI ISLAM SE MALAYSIA (PAS), became the opposition leader in the Dewan Rakyat. The PKN and the DEMOCRATIC ACTION PARTY (DAP) had a lackluster showing. But a year later in a by-election for the Lunas seat in Kedah (Dr. M's home state), BA scored a major victory in denying the BARISAN NASIONAL (NATIONAL FRONT) (1974) a two-thirds majority in the Kedah state legislature. Such inroads in Malay-dominated Kedah became a major concern for the UNITED MALAYS NATIONAL ORGANIZATION (UMNO) (1946).

The Philippine presidency (t. 1986–1992) of CORAZON COJUANGCO AQUINO (1933–) began on a high note, but by the early 1990s it became apparent that little was achieved, owing to the continuous threat of real and rumored military coups. The president often appeared to be in a perpetually besieged situation, faced with a restive military and ministers with personal political agendas.

Shortly after her inauguration, CORAZON COJUANGCO AQUINO (1933–) created the Presidential Commission on Good Government and the presidential Commission on Human Rights. The former was entrusted with the difficult mandate to recover the huge fortune of former president FERDINAND MARCOS (1917–1989), alleged to have been plundered from the country during his long tenure. The task of the second commission was to undertake investigation of alleged human rights abuses during the previous regime. A generous number of political detainees—about 500—were released from detention, including communist leaders such as Jose Maria Sison.

A national referendum in February 1987 gave resounding approval to the new constitution. It provided for an executive presidency and a bicameral legislature: a House of Representatives of 250 (200 elected, 50 presidential appointees), and a 24-seat Senate (directly elected). It also stipulated that there should not be any foreign military bases or nuclear weapons on Philippine soil after 1991; that clause undoubtedly referred to the U.S. military bases in the country.

In the latter part of the 1980s, the controversial issues surrounding the U.S. military bases in the Philippines invoked a nationalistic consciousness that preferred to see the closure of those foreign installations, which many believed contained nuclear weapons. The six U.S. military bases provided both employment and government revenue (from the lease). Under the October 1988 agreement to extend the lease another two years after its expiration in 1989, the Philippines gained more than twice in yearly military and economic aid from the United States. In return the Americans were allowed to use the facilities without having to disclose whether nuclear weaponry was present. In 1990 it was announced that all U.S. military planes and personnel would vacate the Philippines by the end of 1991. But in August 1991 a new ten-year lease was signed for Subic Bay Naval Base, with generous compensation; the Senate, however, voted against it.

An ambitious Comprehensive Agrarian Reform Program (CARP) was launched in June 1988 that attempted to address the perennial problem of land shortages and landlessness among the farming population. CARP was a ten-year agricultural land redistribution scheme for untenured farmers. Implementation of the program was an onerous task, as opposition came from vested interests, notably the landowning class (disproportionately occupying the majority of seats in the House of Representatives). Overall little was accomplished despite the noble intentions.

The Philippine government in July 1987 initiated legal proceedings against FERDINAND MARCOS (1917–1989), his family, and his cronies (associates). By the time the first of the numerous civil suits was served on the former president in September 1989, in an attempt to recover his ill-gotten wealth, he died in his home in Hawai'i. His body, however, was denied burial in the Philippines in the interest of national security.

Despite formal talks with communist rebels (NEW PEOPLE'S ARMY [NPA]) and Muslim secessionist groups (MORO NATIONAL LIBERATION FRONT [MNLF] and Moro Islamic Liberation Front [MILF]), there was no permanent solution to the insurgency. Although a ceasefire was agreed upon in the mid-1980s between the NEW PEOPLE'S ARMY (NPA) and the government, pessimism and insincerity on either side rendered the peace process meaningless. In 1986, while the government in negotiations with the MORO NATIONAL LIBERATION FRONT (MNLF) agreed to the autonomy of four Muslim-dominated provinces in MINDANAO, the MILF, which was not party to the talks, rejected the government's offer. The MILF commanded a wider support base than the MORO NATIONAL LIBERATION FRONT (MNLF), led by NUR MISUARI (1940–). Ultimately, little was accomplished.

By early 1987 it became apparent that, for want of resources, the armed forces were unable to contain both the communist insurgents and Muslim secessionists. Talks brokered by the OIC resulted in the MORO NATIONAL LIBERATION FRONT (MNLF) agreeing to autonomy and to discarding demands for independence. Again the MILF stressed that it would not recognize any agreement over MINDANAO between the government and the MORO NATIONAL LIBERATION

FRONT (MNLF). MILF forces clashed with government troops in western MINDANAO, where fierce fighting flared up. Nevertheless talks continued sporadically between NUR MISUARI (1940–) and the government; there was hope that a joint commission could be formed to undertake the task of drafting an autonomy plan for MINDANAO.

President CORAZON COJUANGCO AQUINO (1933–) faced no fewer than seven military coups to oust her government. If not for the support from FIDEL VALDEZ RAMOS (1928–), the chief of staff of the armed forces, in executing fast action to diffuse the critical situation, there was likely to be massive unrest or even civil war. Some quarters in the military expressed dissatisfaction with the president's accommodating approach toward the leftist insurgents and Muslim secessionists demanding that a tougher line be adopted. In fact, within her cabinet the president faced challenges to her authority from Juan Ponce Enrile, the minister of national defense, and Salvador Laurel, the vice president, to the extent that those individuals directly engineered attempts to topple the government and seize power for themselves.

For instance, in October 1986, Enrile and Laurel, with support from Ramos (later withdrawn), demanded that new presidential elections be held and that the government adopt a tough stance toward the insurgents. The following month Enrile and some factions in the military staged a coup in various military camps. President CORAZON COJUANGCO AQUINO (1933–) took immediate steps in sacking Enrile as minister of national defense; her entire cabinet was ordered to hand in their resignations. Then in August 1987, Colonel Gregario Honasan, a close associate of Enrile's, seized Camp Aguinaldo, the headquarters of the Philippine Army. In the ensuing exchanges more than fifty people died; Honasan and his colleagues escaped. (They were finally apprehended in December.) It was Enrile again and Laurel who were behind the coup attempt staged by the Marines and the Scout Rangers, the elite units of the army in cohort with pro-Marcos officers in December 1989. The rebel soldiers managed to seize the headquarters of the Philippine Air Force and a military base. The president turned to the U.S. Air Force, which scrambled several jets in the skies over MANILA and over the presidential Malacanang Palace as a deterrent to rebel aerial attacks. In February 1990, Enrile was arrested for treason and also for harboring the rebel Honasan.

Following a plebiscite held in November 1989 in thirteen provinces and nine cities in MINDANAO for a government-proposed autonomy plan, four provinces agreed to the option of having direct elections to a unicameral legislature in each province. Therefore Lanao del Sur, Maguindanao, Tawi-Tawi, and Sulu formed the Autonomous Region of Muslim Mindanao (ARMM).

The three-year trial over the assassination of Benigno Aquino and Rolando Galman (the supposed assassin) ended in September 1990 with the conviction of sixteen members of the military; twenty others were acquitted. It was, however, believed that the real perpetrators escaped justice. In mid-1991 the government announced that Imelda Marcos, the former first lady, and her family were allowed to return to the Philippines to face charges of tax evasion and fraud. A year earlier a New York court had acquitted Imelda Marcos of charges of fraud and illegal transfer of stolen funds into the United States. Then in October 1991, President CORAZON COJUANGCO AQUINO (1933–) granted permission for the remains of FERDINAND MARCOS (1917–1989) to be brought back for burial in his home province of Ilocos Norte. Imelda Marcos returned home to stand trial on more than eighty civil and criminal charges.

Negotiations over the SPRATLY AND PARACEL ARCHIPELAGOS DISPUTE among rival claimants were held in January 1990, July 1991, and mid-1992. The PRC, Taiwan, Vietnam, Brunei, Malaysia, and the Philippines agreed in principle to settle the disputed sovereignty issue peacefully and to jointly develop the natural resources of the archipelagos (which were believed to possess vast oil and natural gas reserves).

In the presidential elections of May 1992, President CORAZON COJUANGCO AQUINO (1933–) supported the candidacy of FIDEL VALDEZ RAMOS (1928–), whose running mate was Joseph Ejercito Estrada. FIDEL VALDEZ RAMOS (1928–) won to become the first Protestant president of the mainly Catholic Philippines. Shortly following his inauguration in June, President FIDEL VALDEZ RAMOS (t. 1992–1998) announced his government's intention to resolve the insurgencies by the communists, Muslim secessionists, and rebels within the Philippine armed forces.

Although during the 1987 OIC-brokered talks the MORO NATIONAL LIBERATION FRONT (MNLF) agreed to drop its demands for independence and accept autonomy, it again demanded that the 1976 Tripoli Agreement be reinstated. This demand for the creation of an independent Islamic state in the southern Philippines was emphasized during formal negotiations with the government of President FIDEL VALDEZ RAMOS (1928–) in Jakarta in October 1993. The second round of talks at the same venue was convened in April 1994. In June a military offensive was launched against the Abu Sayyaf, a Muslim secessionist organization alleged to have links with Osama bin Laden's Al-Qaeda international terrorist network. The modus operandi of the Abu Sayyaf was the kidnap and ransom of Westerners and others and various terrorist activities, including wholesale killings. In April 1995, for instance, the Christian town of Ipil in MINDANAO witnessed the massacre of more than fifty civilians allegedly by the Abu Sayyaf; some quarters, however, blamed it on the Islamic Command Council, a splinter group of the MORO NATIONAL LIBERATION FRONT (MNLF). In June 1996 it was announced that a proposal by President FIDEL RAMOS (1928–) to create a transitional administrative council—the Southern Philippine Council for Peace and Development (SPCPD)—was agreed to by the MORO NATIONAL LIBERATION FRONT (MNLF). The establishment of the SPCPD was in preparation for a referendum on an expanded autonomous region in MINDANAO to be added to the existing ARMM. In September 1996, NUR MISUARI (1940–) became governor of Muslim MINDANAO when he was unopposed in the elections; the following month he assumed the chairmanship of the SPCPD.

Meanwhile, the Abu Sayyaf and MILF refused to abide by any negotiations or concessions resulting from talks between NUR MISUARI (1940–) and the government. But in August 1996 the MILF agreed to hold preliminary talks with the government. The Abu Sayyaf remained recalcitrant, refusing to support any talks with the government and MILF. Clashes broke out in Cotabato and Maguindanao involving the MILF and government forces. Despite the fighting, a second round of MILF-government peace talks proceeded in January 1997. In an attempt to derail the peace process the following month, the Abu Sayyaf assassinated a Catholic bishop in Jolo. Curiously, the MILF was suspected to be responsible for the kidnapping of forty workers from the Philippine Oil Company in June. Not surprisingly, the peace talks collapsed.

The peace process with the communists similarly faced a multitude of obstacles. In August 1992, talks were held in The Netherlands with leaders of the National Democratic Front (NDF, an umbrella organization including the CPP, formed in the early 1970s) such as Sison and Luis Jalandoni. Other communist leaders, such as Saturnino Ocampo and Romulo Kintanar, were released from detention to enable them to participate in the discussion. Manuel Romero, head of the NDF, agreed to negotiate for a settlement of the protracted insurgency. Owing to demands and counterdemands, the peace talks in The Netherlands between the government and the NDF reached an impasse with little prospect for progress. Sison then announced the postponement of peace negotiations to be suspended until the end of the tenure of FIDEL VALDEZ RAMOS (1928–) in 1998. Meanwhile, in October 1992, following several rounds of secret talks with military rebel leaders such as Jose Maria Zumel and Honasan, they too agreed to discuss a negotiated settlement with the government.

By September 1992 the Americans had completed their withdrawal from the Subic Bay Naval Base and formally handed over the facility to the Philippine government. The Subic Bay Metropolitan Authority was created to undertake the conversion of the 56,000-hectare area to commercial use.

In July 1993, President FIDEL VALDEZ RAMOS (1928–) reiterated his predecessor's permission for the remains of former president FERDINAND MARCOS (1917–1989) to be brought back from Hawai'i for burial in his home province of Ilocos Norte, without state or military honors. In September only a few thousand supporters paid their last respects at the funeral, and no incidents were reported. In the same month Imelda Marcos was sentenced to eighteen years' imprisonment for corruption.

In December 1993 the Philippines agreed to cooperate over fishing rights with Malaysia in

the SPRATLY AND PARACEL ARCHIPEL-
AGOS DISPUTE areas that were not claimed
by the other four countries—namely, the PRC,
Taiwan, Brunei, and Vietnam. President FIDEL
VALDEZ RAMOS (1928–) made a historic
visit to Vietnam and appealed to all claimants to
remove any military installation or personnel
from the disputed archipelagos. The Philippine
government authorized petroleum exploration
by a U.S. company off southwestern Palawan,
which was within the SPRATLY AND
PARACEL ARCHIPELAGOS DISPUTE
perimeter. The PRC lodged an official com-
plaint, but in a deft move Jose de Venecia,
trusted envoy of President FIDEL VALDEZ
RAMOS (1928–) and speaker of the House of
Representatives, invited Beijing to join the
project as a partner.

In March 1994, in an attempt to reconvene
peace talks with military rebels, President FI-
DEL VALDEZ RAMOS (1928–) announced
an amnesty for all rebels as well as government
soldiers who were charged with offenses during
counterinsurgency operations, except for those
involved in serious crimes (torture, wanton
killings, rape, and robbery). RAM (Reform the
Armed Forces Movement) rejected the presidential gesture, saying that the root causes of
the rebellions had not been addressed. Ocampo
accused the government of discrimination in
that the pardon was not applicable to large
numbers of communists who were charged
with common crimes that were beyond the
purview of the amnesty.

Meanwhile, the East ASEAN Growth Area
(EAGA) was formally established in March 1994.
It was an attempt to promote joint ventures and
economic cooperation in the area comprising the
East Malaysian states of SARAWAK AND
SABAH (NORTH BORNEO), Brunei, the
southern Philippines, and the east Indonesian is-
lands of SULAWESI (CELEBES) and MALUKU
(THE MOLUCCAS).

The high incidence of serious crime, in particular kidnapping for ransom, was dissuading
foreign investments in the country. The formation in July 1992 of the Presidential Anti-
Crime Commission (PACC) under the over-
sight of Vice President Estrada was an attempt
to address this problem. The following year
rampant corruption was uncovered in the
Philippine National Police (PNP), leading to
the removal of hundreds of personnel including several senior officers. By the extended
deadline of November 1993, efforts to disarm
private armies had made little headway. Estrada
apparently failed in his task in the PACC; from
October 1995, President FIDEL VALDEZ
RAMOS (1928–) took personal charge to
eradicate serious offenses and organized crime,
which more often than not exposed collusion
with members of the PNP. The worsening
crime situation was a damaging blot on the
presidency of FIDEL VALDEZ RAMOS
(1928–).

The SPRATLY AND PARACEL ARCHI-
PELAGOS DISPUTE again occupied the
agenda in February 1995, when the PRC occupied and established permanent structures on
Mischief Reef, which was claimed by
MANILA. Discussions in August made little
headway in terms of resolving the overlapping
claims, but a significant breakthrough was accomplished: for the first time Beijing agreed to
settle the issue in accordance with international
law and not by invoking the principle of the
precedence of historical claims. Thereafter a
code of conduct was agreed to by both parties
to ensure that a military confrontation was
avoided. Likewise the Philippines contracted a
similar agreement with Vietnam in November
1995. In March 1996 both the Philippines and
the PRC agreed to cooperate in eliminating
PIRACY. Following a series of military moves
from the PRC and the Philippines over the
SPRATLY AND PARACEL ARCHIPELA-
GOS DISPUTE, in August 1997 both parties
agreed to put aside their territorial claims and
instead to focus on strengthening economic cooperation.

Attempts to amend the constitution to grant
FIDEL VALDEZ RAMOS (1928–) a second
presidential term failed. Sensing such efforts on
the part of the supporters of FIDEL VALDEZ
RAMOS (1928–), the highly respected Cardinal
Jaime Sin of the influential Catholic Church,
together with former president CORAZON
COJUANGCO AQUINO (1933–), orchestrated a peaceful demonstration in September
1997 displaying displeasure and rejection of a
second term for the incumbent. FIDEL
VALDEZ RAMOS (1928–) backed down.

The May 1998 presidential elections
brought to power the flamboyant Estrada (t.
1998–2001), a former popular film actor. Consistently identifying himself with the lower

strata of society despite his middle-class background, Estrada not surprisingly drew the bulk of his support from among the working class or the *masa* (the masses).

Estrada's "pro-poor" platform faced an uphill challenge, owing to the Asian Financial Crisis (1997–1998). The focus of his policy was to ensure "food security" for the lower socioeconomic strata of society. Various mechanisms and pieces of legislation were put in place to achieve these goals—notably the National Anti-Poverty Commission, CARP, and the Agricultural and Fisheries Modernization Act. The last mentioned ensured that government funding was allocated to projects such as rural credit and the improvement of infrastructure (irrigation, roads). For the urban poor, rehousing under a state-sponsored mortgage scheme made available homes for more than 25,000 of the lower income group in MANILA. In addition, the Subic Bay Metropolitan Authority was engaged in reorienting its development to accommodate the needs of its depressed surrounding areas—for instance, by providing employment opportunities and other economic benefits. But overall the "pro-poor" policy was a disappointment, partly because of the economic downturn during its initiation and partly because of vested interests with strong political influence.

The Philippine secretary of foreign affairs, Domingo Siaszon Jr., supported his Thai counterpart's proposal that flexible engagement replace the traditional nonintervention policy of the ASSOCIATION OF SOUTHEAST ASIAN NATIONS (ASEAN) (1967). Curiously, while it was generally believed that President Estrada was opposed to "flexible engagement," he publicly criticized the government of DR. MAHATHIR BIN MOHAMAD (1925–) in the arrest and assault of the former deputy prime minister, Anwar Ibrahim. KUALA LUMPUR (KL) was not the least amused at such unwarranted comments.

Ironically, when Estrada headed the PACC in the early 1990s, the results were far from satisfactory in addressing the high crime rate. But during his presidency serious crimes such as kidnapping for ransom were sharply reduced. It was apparent that preventive measures worked out between the government and the Chinese community, and with the close cooperation of the PNP, had made promising

progress. Surprisingly, in April 2000, while a climate of dissatisfaction with the government's performance was gaining momentum, significant improvements were made in tax collection.

President Estrada was unsuccessful in the peace process with the various antigovernment groups. The NDF withdrew talks with the government in May 1999 when the Senate ratified a defense treaty with the United States—namely, the Visiting Forces Agreement (VFA). (The VFA permitted joint military operations between Philippine and U.S. forces.) Its military wing, the NEW PEOPLE'S ARMY (NPA), was actively tapping for recruits from among the increasing numbers who were greatly disillusioned with the political leadership, which was blamed for the plethora of social and economic inequalities in the country. The government's inability to address the needs of the rural poor in the southern Philippines, in particular among Muslim constituencies, led to the growth of secessionist groups such as the MILF and the MORO NATIONAL LIBERATION FRONT (MNLF), as well as radicals such as the Abu Sayyaf. Government military offensives against Muslim secessionists further alienated the entire community, which was weary of the Christian administration in faraway MANILA. Consequent of the fighting, thousands were displaced, and they were potential recruits in the drawn-out struggle.

During the early part of 2000 there was an escalation of hostilities, engineered in particular by the MILF. An olive branch with development grants on the one hand, and an automatic gun on the other, were the symbols of President Estrada's stance toward the troubled areas of the Muslim southern provinces. But the gun became dominant when in February the Philippine Air Force bombed Camp Omar, a prominent base of the MILF; government troops succeeded in overcoming a secondary facility of the MILF. By the middle of the year, government forces retook sections of a highway that for a long time had been under the MILF owing to its proximity to the headquarters of Camp Abubakar, Maguindanao. In July, Camp Abubakar itself fell to government forces. Despite President Estrada's offer of amnesty, MILF leaders instead appealed to their supporters and all Muslims, saying that the struggle was a *jihad*, or holy war. It was not surprising that such a declaration occurred: besides the government offensive, Christian vigilante groups had been terrorizing and even killing ordinary Muslims. Both the amnesty offer and the promise to reconvert the area of Camp Abubakar into a special economic zone for the Muslims were shunned by the MILF, which remained steadfast in its demands for an independent Islamic state.

The Abu Sayyaf, which had long opposed any negotiations or compromise with the government and demanded nothing less than complete independence, continued its terror campaign and its trademark activity of kidnapping for ransom. In March 2000 about thirty students and teachers were kidnapped and ransom was demanded. Then in April the Abu Sayyaf kidnapped twenty-one tourists—mainly Western vacationers—on Sipadan Island, off the East Malaysian state of Sabah. They were held hostage on Jolo Island, the headquarters of the organization, awaiting the payment of a huge ransom. It was uncertain whether the release of the foreign hostages in late September was a result of the payment of the demanded ransom or a political compromise. Later reports revealed that the ransom, millions of U.S. dollars, was paid in the form of "development aid" by the Libyan government in securing the release of the citizens of South Africa, France, Germany, Finland, and Malaysia who had been seized as hostages from Sipadan Island.

As early as the latter half of 1999 dissatisfaction, disappointment, and outright disgust with Estrada's government were increasingly voiced, not only by the political opposition but also by ordinary citizens. Peaceful expressions in the form of large rallies and demonstrations were organized, such as the one on 21 September 1999 led by Cardinal Jaime Sin and former president CORAZON COJUANGCO AQUINO (1933–), and the march by farmers on the presidential palace in October, protesting the proposed constitutional amendment that would make possible foreign ownership of land. Opposition also came from trade unions and teachers over wages; the Makati Business Club protested the slowness of economic liberalization and reforms, and legislation that allowed foreign interests to enter the retail industry and buy into local banks.

Although President Estrada seemingly appeared to be popular, the urban and rural poor were increasingly disillusioned with government efforts and the abysmal implementation of the "pro-poor" program. Even Karina Constantino-David, the head of the government's mass housing scheme, tendered her resignation in October 1999 over the sluggish pace of housing reform and the influence exerted by developers with political connections that opposed such reform. It was therefore not surprising that the NEW PEOPLE'S ARMY (NPA) was able to increase substantially the number of armed guerrillas, which were estimated at about 6,000 in 1994 and swelled to close to 9,500 by mid-2000, largely as a result of disaffected rural and urban youth.

In the international arena the Philippines supported the efforts of the UNITED NATIONS AND CONFLICT RESOLUTION IN SOUTHEAST ASIA. For example, the Philippines participated in the peacekeeping force INTERFET in East Timor prior to its becoming independent in August 2002. Malaysia and especially Indonesia were not pleased at the involvement of the Philippines in East Timor.

On the domestic front, however, the proverbial beginning of the end for President Estrada was in October 2000, when an estranged former supporter, Luis Singson, the governor of Ilocos Sur, accused the president of accepting bribes from illegal gambling businesses as well as from provincial tobacco taxes. Vice President Gloria Macapagal Arroyo, in an attempt to distance herself from Estrada, announced her resignation from the cabinet in which she had served as secretary for social welfare and development. Arroyo, however, retained her vice presidency. Notwithstanding repeated denials by Estrada, the opposition parties began impeachment proceedings in the latter part of the month. In November, Estrada faced impeachment charges of bribery, corruption, culpable violation of the constitution, and betrayal of public trust. No vote was taken, as a petition endorsing impeachment had been signed by one-third of members of the House of Representatives. Speakers of both the Senate and the House of Representatives stepped down, having simultaneously tendered their resignations from the ruling coalition.

Since the time of Singson's accusations, street demonstrations had been under way demanding Estrada's removal. Anti- and pro-

Estrada groups clashed in the streets. A fortnight into the impeachment trial, on 30 December 2000 five separate bomb explosions shook MANILA, resulting in at least twenty-two fatalities and many more injured. Speculation was rife as to the real perpetrators, despite official blame being leveled on opposition parties or Muslim separatists. Many, however, believed that pro-Estrada supporters were the real culprits; their action was designed to intimidate witnesses to the ongoing trial or to create an untenable situation in which martial law could be declared by the government.

When the pro-Estrada Senate blocked prosecutors from opening an envelope that many believed contained damning evidence of Estrada's corrupt banking practices as alleged by a bank officer, the prosecutors resigned in protest. More and more of Estrada's supporters deserted him, including the military and the police, as street protests gained momentum mirroring the EDSA REVOLUTION (1986), when FERDINAND MARCOS (1917–1989) was toppled.

On 20 January 2001, Estrada finally decided to leave Malacanang Palace. Arroyo was immediately sworn in as president. The removal of Estrada reinforced the earlier precedent of the so-called People Power Revolution, which undoubtedly further weakened the process of electoral democracy and its institutions.

On Storytelling

Modern historical works on Southeast Asia as a region in its own right appeared in the mid-1950s with Brian Harrison's *South-East Asia: A Short History* (London: Macmillan, 1954), followed by D. G. E. Hall's *A History of South-East Asia* (London: Macmillan, 1955; 2nd ed., 1964, 3rd ed., 1968, 4th ed., 1981). While the former was composed for a general readership, the latter was a scholarly volume with a specialist audience in mind. Despite not offering any innovative conceptual framework or introducing new methodological approaches, Hall's single-volume work was a watershed achievement. "What is attempted here," as Hall explained in the preface (1955), "is first and foremost to present South-East Asia historically as an area worthy of consideration in its own right, and not merely when brought into contact with China, India or the West. Its history cannot be safely viewed from any other perspective until seen from its own." John R. W. Smail embraced this approach, putting forth his persuasive argument in his paper "On the Possibility of an Autonomous History of Modern Southeast Asia," *Journal of Southeast Asian Studies* 2, no. 2 (1961): 72–102. Taking the cue, several notable works of scholarship appeared in the 1960s—namely, John F. Cady's *Southeast Asia: Its Historical Development* (New York: McGraw-Hill, 1964) and Nicholas Tarling's *South-East Asia: Past and Present* (Melbourne: F. W. Cheshire, 1966).

While historical works in the years prior to the outbreak of the Pacific War (1941–1945) and the Japanese occupation of Southeast Asia (1941–1945) were largely the work of European and U.S. colonial scholar-administrators, the immediate postwar decades witnessed the predominance of Western professional historians. It was only from the late 1960s and early 1970s that professional historians of Southeast Asian heritage began to chart the history of the region and of its constituent parts. Again the majority of these indigenous historians were trained abroad, particularly in Europe, the United States, and Australia and New Zealand. While prewar works were accused of being biased and sympathetic to the Western colonial regimes, nationalist historians of the postwar era turned the tables, in being partial to the indigenous viewpoint and exhibiting their patriotism. As two wrongs do not make a right, the contentious issue of perspective should be amicably resolved by producing a balanced, objective history.

The postwar era, which was an eyewitness to tremendous changes in the geopolitical and regional sphere, required a paradigm shift in approach to historical works. H. J. Benda in "The Structure of Southeast Asian History: Some Preliminary Observations," *Journal of Southeast Asian History* 3, no. 1 (1962): 103–108, argued convincingly that historians should also be social scientists. The trend of historians to draw on the methods and the findings of other disciplines—political science, economics, anthropology, sociology, archaeology, demography, and others—is increasingly common and acceptable. More often than not, history merged with politics when in dealing with more contemporary political developments, and history combined with ethnography and anthropology in detailing the past and present situation of ethnic minorities.

The literature on the writing of Southeast Asian history is a recent development. Some of the more notable works on historiography are listed in the recommended readings. These works on historiography focus on the major characteristics of historical writing and outline the principal shifts in orientation and emphasis. In addition, some of these works debated issues, discussed emerging trends, and even set future directions. For instance, in the last quarter of the twentieth century there was an increasing concern among historians over several issues—namely, the overnationalistic content of school textbooks, "national history" versus "regional (Southeast Asian) history," and the predominance of political history with lesser emphasis on other foci (economic, social, cultural, religious, ethnohistory, etc.). Furthermore, there appeared to be a lacuna in historical works on indigenous ethnic minorities, marginalized groups, and women. Also, many Southeast Asian historians have published in their native language; consequently their works are less known or available to the international scholarly community.

Suggested Readings

No reading list can claim to be definitive or exhaustive, but what is attempted here is to offer some suggested works that are useful for a greater understanding of the historical development of Southeast Asia, from prehistory to the early 2000s. The following list is meant to complement the references that appear under each entry-article in the *Encyclopedia*. Six categories of works are identified to facilitate ease of selection—namely, Historiography of Southeast Asia; Southeast Asia—General Overview; Anthologies of Travelers' Accounts; Thematic Works on Southeast Asia; Country Focus—General; and Country Focus—Themes and Topics. The brackets indicate when the work was first published.

Historiography of Southeast Asia

Abu Talib Ahmad and Tan Liok Ee, eds. 2003. *New Terrains in Southeast Asian History.* Research in International Studies Southeast Asia Series no. 107. Athens: Ohio University Press; Singapore: Singapore University Press.

Benda, Harry J. 1972. *Continuity and Change in Southeast Asia: Collected Journal Articles of Harry J. Benda.* Southeast Asian Studies Monograph Series no. 18. New Haven: Yale University.

Cowan, D. E., and O. W. Wolters, eds. 1976. *Southeast Asian History and Historiography: Essay Presented to D. G. E. Hall.* Ithaca, NY: Cornell University Press.

Legge, J. D. 1992. "The Writing of Southeast Asian History." Pp. 1–50 in *The Cambridge History of Southeast Asia.* Vol. 1: *From Early Times to c. 1800.* Edited by Nicholas Tarling. Cambridge: Cambridge University Press.

McVey, Ruth T., ed. 1978. *Southeast Asian Transitions: Approaches through Social History.* New Haven: Yale University Press.

Reid, Anthony, and David Marr, eds. 1979. *Perceptions of the Past in Southeast Asia.* Singapore: Heinemann Educational Books for Asian Studies Association of Australia (ASAA).

Reynolds, Craig J. 1995. "A New Look at Old Southeast Asia." *Journal of Asian Studies* 54, no. 2: 419–446.

Sears, Laurie J., ed. 1993. *Autonomous Histories, Particular Truths: Essays in Honor of John R. W. Smail.* Monograph 11. Madison: University of Wisconsin Center for Southeast Asian Studies.

Wyatt, David K., and Alexander Woodside, eds. 1982. *Moral Order and the Question of Change: Essays on Southeast Asian Thought.* Southeast Asia Studies no. 24. New Haven: Yale University.

Southeast Asia—General Overview

Cady, John F. 1964. *Southeast Asia: Its Historical Development.* New York: McGraw-Hill.

Daniel, Lynn, ed. 2002. *The Far East and Australasia 2002.* 33rd ed. London: Europa.

Hall, D. G. E. 1981 [1955]. *A History of South-East Asia.* 4th ed. London: Macmillan.

Heidhues, Mary Somers. 2000. *Southeast Asia: A Concise History.* London: Thames and Hudson.

Kundstadter, Peter, ed. 1967. *Southeast Asian Tribes, Minorities, and Nations.* 2 vols. Princeton: Princeton University Press.

Osborne, Milton. 1995. *Southeast Asia: An Introductory History.* St. Leonards, NSW: Allen and Unwin.

Sardesai, D. R. 1997 [1989]. *Southeast Asia: Past & Present.* Boulder, CO: Westview.

Steinberg, David J., ed. 1985 [1971]. *In Search of Southeast Asia.* 2nd ed. New York: Praeger.

Tarling, Nicholas, ed. 1992. *The Cambridge History of Southeast Asia.* Vol. 1: *From Early Times to c. 1800;* Vol. 2: *The Nineteenth and Twentieth Centuries.* Cambridge: Cambridge University Press.

Wolters, O. W. 1982. *History, Culture, and Region in Southeast Asia.* Singapore: Institute of Southeast Asian Studies.

Anthologies of Travelers' Accounts

Barwise, J. M., and N. J. White. 2002. *A Traveller's History of South East Asia.* London: Windrush Press, in association with Cassell and Co.

Bastin, John, ed. 1994. *Travellers' Singapore: An Anthology.* Kuala Lumpur: Oxford University Press.

Gullick, J. M., ed. 1993. *They Came to Malaya: A Travellers' Anthology.* Singapore: Oxford University Press.

King, Victor T., ed. 1993. *The Best of Borneo Travel.* Singapore: Oxford University Press.

Maugham, W. Somerset. 1994. *The Gentleman in the Parlour: A Record of a Journey from Rangoon to Haiphong.* New York: Marlowe and Co.

Miller, George. 1996. *To the Spice Islands and Beyond: Travels in Eastern Indonesia.* Kuala Lumpur: Oxford University Press.

Murphy, Dervila. 1999. *One Foot in Laos.* London: John Murray.

Reid, Anthony. 1995. *Witness to Sumatra: A Travellers' Anthology.* Singapore: Oxford University Press.

Rush, James R. 1996. *Java: A Travellers' Anthology.* Kuala Lumpur: Oxford University Press.

Vickers, Adrian. 1994. *Travelling to Bali: Four Hundred Years of Journey.* Kuala Lumpur: Oxford University Press.

Thematic Works on Southeast Asia

Ahmad Ibrahim, Sharon Siddique, and Yasmin Hussain, eds. 1985. *Readings on Islam in Southeast Asia.* Singapore: Institute of Southeast Asian Studies.

Anderson, Benedict. 1998. *The Spectre of Comparison: Nationalism, Southeast Asia and the World.* London: Verso.

Blusse, Leonard. 1986. *Strange Company: Chinese Settlers, Mestizo Women and the Dutch in VOC Batavia.* Dordrecht, The Netherlands: Foris.

Coedes, George. 1969. *The Making of South East Asia.* Berkeley: University of California Press.

Hall, Kenneth. 1985. *Maritime Trade and State Development in Early Southeast Asia.* Honolulu: University of Hawai'i Press.

Hewison, Kevin, Richard Robison, and Garry Rodan, eds. 1993. *Southeast Asia in the 1990s: Authoritarianism, Democracy and Capitalism.* St. Leonards, NSW: Allen and Unwin.

Higham, Charles. 1989. *The Archaeology of Mainland Southeast Asia: From 10,000 BC to the Fall of Angkor.* Cambridge: Cambridge University Press.

———. 1996. *The Bronze Age of Southeast Asia.* Cambridge: Cambridge University Press.

Kershaw, Roger. 2001. *Monarchy in South-East Asia: The Faces of Tradition in Transition.* London and New York: Routledge.

Keyes, Charles F. 1977. *The Golden Peninsula: Culture and Adaptation in Mainland Southeast Asia.* New York: Macmillan. Reprinted in 1977 by University of Hawai'i Press, Honolulu.

Laothamatas, Anek, ed. 1997. *Democratization in Southeast and East Asia.* Singapore: Institute of Southeast Asian Studies.

Li Tana. 1998. *Nguyễn Cochinchina: Southern Vietnam in the Seventeenth and Eighteenth Centuries.* Ithaca: Cornell University Press.

Marr, David G., and A. C. Milner, eds. 1986. *Southeast Asia in the 9th to 14th Centuries.* Singapore: Institute of Southeast Asian Studies; Canberra: Research School of Pacific Studies, Australian National University.

Reid, Anthony. 1988. *Southeast Asia in the Age of Commerce.* Vol. 1: *The Lands below the Winds.* New Haven: Yale University Press.

———. 1993. *Southeast Asia in the Age of Commerce.* Vol. 2: *Expansion and Crisis.* New Haven: Yale University Press.

Rigg, Jonathan. 1997. *Southeast Asia: The Human Landscape of Modernization and Development.* London and New York: Routledge.

Scott, James C. 1976. *The Moral Economy of the Peasant: Rebellion and Subsistence in Southeast Asia.* New Haven: Yale University Press.

Tarling, Nicholas. 1998. *Nations and States in Southeast Asia.* Cambridge: Cambridge University Press.

———. 2001. *Imperialism in Southeast Asia: "A Fleeting, Passing Phase."* London and New York: Routledge.

Taylor, Jean. 1983. *The Social World of Batavia: European and Eurasian in Dutch Asia.* Madison: University of Wisconsin Press.

Wheatley, Paul. 1960. *The Golden Khersonese: Studies in the Historical Geography of the Malay Peninsula before AD 1500.* Kuala Lumpur: University of Malaya Press.

———. 1983. *Nagara and Commandery: Origins of Southeast Asian Urban Traditions.* Research Paper nos. 207–208. Chicago: University of Chicago Department of Geography.

Wolters, O. W. 1967. *Early Indonesian Commerce: A Study of the Origins of Śrivijaya.* Ithaca: Cornell University Press.

———. 1970. *The Fall of Śrivijaya in Malay History.* Ithaca: Cornell University Press.

Woodside, Alexander B. 1971. *Vietnam and the Chinese Model.* Cambridge: Harvard University Press.

Wurfel, David, ed. 1996. *Southeast Asia in the New World Order: The Political Economy of a Dynamic Region.* London: Macmillan.

Country Focus—General

Andaya, Barbara Watson, and Leonard Y. Andaya. 2001 [1982]. *A History of Malaysia.* 2nd ed. London: Palgrave.

Chandler, David. 2000 [1983]. *A History of Cambodia.* 3rd ed. Boulder, CO: Westview.

Lee, E., and C. T. Chew, eds. 1991. *A History of Singapore.* Singapore: Oxford University Press.

Sardesai, D. R. 1998. *Vietnam: Past and Present.* 3d ed. Boulder and Oxford: Westview.

Saunders, Graham. 1994. *A History of Brunei.* Kuala Lumpur: Oxford University Press.

Steinberg, David J. 1994. *The Philippines: A Singular and a Plural Place.* Boulder and Oxford: Westview.

Stuart-Fox, Martin. 1997. *A History of Laos.* Cambridge: Cambridge University Press.

Taylor, Keith W. 1983. *The Birth of Vietnam.* Berkeley: University of California Press.

Taylor, Robert H. 1987. *The State in Burma.* Honolulu: University of Hawai'i Press; London: C. Hurst.

Turnbull, C. M. 1989 [1977]. *A History of Singapore 1819–1988.* 2nd ed. Singapore: Oxford University Press.

Wyatt, David K. 1984. *Thailand: A Short History.* New Haven: Yale University Press.

Country Focus—Themes and Topics

Ang Cheng Guan. 2002. *The Vietnam War from the Other Side: The Vietnamese Communists' Perspective.* London: RoutledgeCurzon.

Aung-Thwin, Michael. 1985. *Pagan: The Origins of Modern Burma.* Honolulu: University of Hawai'i Press.

Carey, Peter, and G. Carter Bentley, eds. 1995. *East Timor at the Crossroads: The Forging of a Nation.* London: Cassell.

Cribb, Robert, and Colin Brown. 1995. *Modern Indonesia: A History since 1945.* London and New York: Longman.

Crouch, Harold. 1978. *The Army and Politics in Indonesia.* Ithaca: Cornell University Press.

Duiker, William J. 1996. *The Communist Road to Power in Vietnam.* Boulder, CO: Westview.

Girling, John. 1996. *Interpreting Development: Capitalism, Democracy, and the Middle Class in Thailand.* Ithaca: Southeast Asia Program, Cornell University.

Goodno, James B. 1991. *The Philippines: Land of Broken Promises.* London and Atlantic Heights, NJ: Zed.

Jesudason, James V. 1989. *Ethnicity and the Economy: The State, Chinese Business, and Multinationals in Malaysia.* Singapore: Oxford University Press.

Kahin, George McTurnan. 1952. *Nationalism and Revolution in Indonesia.* Ithaca: Cornell University Press.

Kamm, Henry. 1998. *Cambodia: Report from a Stricken Land.* New York: Arcade.

Kerkvliet, Benedict J., and Resil B. Mojares, eds. 1991. *From Marcos to Aquino: Local Perspectives on Political Transition in the Philippines.* Honolulu: University of Hawai'i; Manila: Ateneo de Manila Press.

Kiernan, Ben. 1996. *The Pol Pot Regime: Race, Power, and Genocide in Cambodia under the Khmer Rouge, 1975–1979.* New Haven: Yale University Press.

Kratoska, Paul H. 1997. *The Japanese Occupation of Malaya 1941–1945.* London: C. Hurst; Honolulu: University of Hawai'i Press.

Marr, David G. 1995. *Vietnam 1945: The Quest for Power.* Berkeley: University of California Press.

Milne, R. S., and Diane Mauzy. 1999. *Malaysian Politics under Mahathir.* London and New York: Routledge.

Ooi Keat Gin. 1999. *Rising Sun over Borneo.* London: Macmillan; New York: St. Martin's Press.

Porter, Gareth. 1993. *Vietnam: The Politics of Bureaucratic Socialism.* Ithaca: Cornell University Press.

Ramage, Douglas E. 1995. *Politics in Indonesia: Democracy, Islam, and the Ideology of Tolerance.* London: Routledge.

Reid, Anthony J. S. 1974. *The Indonesian National Revolution 1945–1950.* Hawthorn: Longman Australia.

Ruane, Kevin. 1998. *War and Revolution in Vietnam 1930–1975.* London: University College Press.

Schwarz, Adam. 1994. *A Nation in Waiting: Indonesia in the 1990s.* St. Leonards, NSW: Allen and Unwin.

Shiraishi Takashi. 1990. *An Age in Motion: Popular Radicalism in Java, 1912–1926.* Ithaca: Cornell University Press.

Tai, Hue Tam Ho. 1983. *Millenarianism and Peasant Politics in Vietnam.* Cambridge, MA, and London: Harvard University Press.

Tambiah, S. J. 1976. *World Conqueror and World Renouncer: A Study of Buddhism and Polity in Thailand against a Historical Background.* Cambridge: Cambridge University Press.

Taylor, John G. 1991. *Indonesia's Forgotten War: The Hidden History of East Timor.* London: Zed.

———. 1999. *East Timor: The Price of Freedom.* London and New York: Zed; Annandle, NSW: Pluto Press Australia; Bangkok: White Lotus.

Woodside, Alexander B. 1976. *Community and Revolution in Modern Vietnam.* Boston: Houghton Mifflin.

Wurfel, David. 1991. *Filipino Politics: Development and Decay.* Quezon City: Ateneo de Manila University Press.

Wyatt, David K. 1994. *Studies in Thai History: Collected Articles.* Chiang Mai: Silkworm.

Closing Remarks

It is hoped that this encyclopedia will promote a wider and deeper understanding of the historical development of the region and offer some cognizance of the lessons of the past. If so, the time and energy expended will have been more than worthwhile, and we as scholars have made a difference, however modest.

Ooi Keat Gin

A

ABACA (MANILA HEMP)

Abaca is the name given to the fiber of the plant botanically known as *Musa textilis,* a member of the *Musa* genus (to which the banana tree also belongs). Technically, the name *Manila hemp* is incorrect because, properly speaking, hemp is a bast fiber extracted from the bark of the plant *Cannabis sàtiva,* whereas abaca fiber is obtained from the leaf sheath. *Musa textilis* is a treelike herb growing to heights of 5 to 10 meters. Abaca is a hard fiber that does not absorb moisture, is resistant to water (even saltwater), and can be made into excellent cordage, particularly naval cordage and binding twine. Early in the nineteenth century, its qualities were recognized as superior to those of other natural fibers, such as sisal and maguey. Because of its lightness and strength, abaca can also be used as a raw material for clothing, rugs, paper, and other items.

Musa textilis is indigenous to the Philippines, where both climatic and soil conditions are conducive to its growth. The plant requires a humid environment and rainfall throughout the year, is susceptible to drought, and can be damaged by severe winds during typhoons. The most favorable locations for the plant are along the eastern and southern coasts in the Philippines. The Philippines have had the natural monopoly of this product.

The fiber is obtained from the leaf petioles, which are peeled from the stalk with a knife. The extraction of fiber can be done either by hand stripping or by using stripping machines. The oldest method in the Philippines is hand stripping, a labor-intensive and burdensome process whereby the laborer uses a knife blade to strip the fiber. It was only in the 1920s and 1930s that properly functioning fiber-extracting machinery was introduced.

Although its qualities had been noticed in previous centuries, abaca did not become an export product of the Philippines until the 1820s. American and British merchant houses established themselves in Manila, engaging in the exportation of abaca, sugar, tobacco, and other products. Abaca exports increased over the years, from about 26,000 metric tons in the 1860s to more than 100,000 tons in the early 1900s, 130,000 in the 1920s, and 140,000 in the 1930s; they fell back to a level of less than 100,000 tons in the 1960s. During the first two decades of the U.S. colonial administration of the Philippines, abaca was the leading export product of the islands, accounting for more than 50 percent of total export earnings. Between 1875 and 1900, most of the exports went to Great Britain, with the United States being the second largest buyer. When the United States assumed sovereignty of the islands in 1898, the market switched to America, and Great Britain became the second largest buyer. In the second half of the 1930s, Japan emerged as an important buyer.

The greatest percentage of abaca exports has always been in the form of raw fiber, for processing in cordage factories in the United States and Great Britain. In the 1930s, a somewhat greater part of the exports consisted of manufactured cordage, but this trend did not continue after the Pacific War (1941–1945). In the 1930s and during the Pacific War, the shortage of natural fibers had stimulated the development of synthetic fibers as a replacement. As a consequence, abaca exports declined significantly after the war.

The area of abaca production has changed over the years. During the nineteenth century, the Bicol region in southern Luzon (the provinces of Albay, Sorsogon, and Camarines) was the main production area, followed by the eastern Visayan Islands (Leyte and Samar). In the 1920s and 1930s, the island of Mindanao (particularly the province of Davao) became an important producer of abaca, as a result of the efforts of Japanese settlers who had established large plantations in the Philippines. They formed production and marketing associations, introduced fiber-stripping machinery that allowed them to produce quality fiber, and used auctions to market their produce—in short, they operated with modern methods. In 1934, Japanese producers in Davao contributed almost 45 percent to the national abaca output. After the Pacific War, though the Japanese had been forced to leave the country, the province of Davao remained an abaca-producing area.

Abaca prices have always fluctuated in accordance with the international conjuncture. During the last decades of the nineteenth century and the early years of the twentieth, until about 1918, abaca brought relative prosperity to the prime abaca-producing region, the Bicol area. But during the economic depression in the first half of the 1930s, abaca prices in the world market dropped dramatically, exports fell, and the production areas suffered widespread poverty. Economic historian Norman Owen (1984) has drawn attention to the fact that, although abaca has brought prosperity during periods of economic upswing, the Bicol region ultimately has not made the transition to self-sustaining economic growth. Apparently, its people have been unable to convert periodic wealth into sustainable economic activities.

WILLEM WOLTERS

See also Great Depression (1929–1931); Japan and Southeast Asia (pre-1941); Philippines under Spanish Colonial Rule (ca. 1560s–1898); Philippines under U.S. Colonial Administration (1898–1946); Philippines–U.S. "Special Relationship"; Shipbuilding

References:
Owen, Norman G. 1984. *Prosperity without Progress: Manila Hemp and Material Life in the Colonial Philippines.* Quezon City, the Philippines: Ateneo de Manila University Press.

ABANGAN

Abangan, from the word *abang* (red), originally meant "worldly" or "'profane." This term was first used in East Java as a pejorative designation in contrast to *putihan,* from *putih* (white), which was applied to the more piously Islamic segment of the population, many of whom adopted white garb. The formation of a putihan group in East Java was associated with the spread of Islamic schools (*pesantren*) during the nineteenth century. In the 1950s, abangan acquired political connotations in association with both the communist and nationalist parties that adopted red as their group color. In his influential book entitled *The Religion of Java* (1960), based on fieldwork in East Java in the 1950s, the anthropologist Clifford Geertz used the term *abangan* to designate a significant segment of the Javanese population whose "syncretic" religious traditions featured extensive spirit beliefs; were centered on a ritual feast called *slametan;* and involved a set of theories and practices of curing, sorcery, and magic. He used abangan as a sociological contrast term to *santri,* which he defined as a subvariant of the Javanese villagers who espoused a "purer Islam" and had strong associations with trade. Whereas santri originally referred to students and graduates of a pesantren and was, indeed, another expression for the so-called putihan, in Geertz's discussions it came to refer to pious Muslims in general. Geertz's sociological characterizations have been widely criticized as overly simplistic and lacking in adequate historical comprehension. Generalizing such historical contrasts to the whole of the Javanese population proved particularly difficult. After the destruction and banning of the Parti Komunis Indonesia in 1965, the social use of the term *abangan* declined in East Java, and it now no longer retains popular currency except among scholars influenced by Geertz.

JAMES J. FOX

See also Islam in Southeast Asia; Islamic Resurgence in Southeast Asia (Twentieth Century); Partai Komunis Indonesia (PKI) (1920); Perserikatan Nasional Indonesia (PNI) (1927); *Santri*

References:
Bachtiar, H. W. 1973. "The Religion of Java: A Commentary." *Madjalah Ilmu-Ilmu Sastra Indonesia* 5: 85–115.
Geertz, Clifford. 1960. *The Religion of Java*. Glencoe, IL: Free Press.
Koentjaraningrat. 1985. *Javanese Culture*. Singapore: Oxford University Press.

ABDUL RAHMAN PUTRA AL-HAJ, TUNKU (1903–1990)
Nationalist Prince

Officially addressed as Tunku Abdul Rahman Putra Al-Haj and more popularly known by the royal designation "Tunku," this first prime minister of independent Malaya and later Malaysia is designated *Bapa Merdeka* (Father of Independence) in Malaysian school textbooks.

Born in Alor Setar of a Siamese mother, on 8 February 1903, Tunku was the twentieth child of Sultan Abdul Hamid Halim Syah (1881–1943) of the Malay state of Kedah in Peninsular Malaysia. Educated in Alor Setar, Bangkok, and Penang, Tunku later attended St. Catherine College (1920) in London and then Cambridge University, where he obtained a B.A. degree in law and history in 1925. After three attempts to commence studies in order to qualify as a barrister-at-law, Tunku resumed his studies at the Inner Temple in 1946 and was called to the English bar in 1949.

In 1926, together with some fellow students and future leaders of independent Malaya, Tunku formed the Malay Society of Great Britain, which soon became the nucleus of the social, intellectual, and, to some extent, political activities of Malay students in Great Britain. Another Malay prince and his namesake, Tengku Abdul Rahman (1895–1960)—later the first Yang Di Pertuan Agung (King) of independent Malaya—became the society's first president and Tunku the honorary secretary. Tunku headed the society a number of times and after

the Pacific War (1941–1945) had the experience of working with younger colleagues such as Abdul Razak Hussein (1922–1976) and Muhammad Suffian Hashim (b. 1917).

Back in Kedah in 1931, Tunku was appointed assistant district officer of Kulim, and having passed the cadet's law exam of the Kedah Civil Service, he was promoted to district officer (DO) and served in various districts. A naturally sociable and caring man, Tunku soon became famous, and his "abduction" of his father, the sultan, from the retreating British convoy in December 1941 enhanced his reputation. During the war, Tunku led or participated in relief efforts for the distressed and poor, including the setting up of the Poor Men's Home in Alor Setar. Toward the end of the war and immediately after, by virtue of his royal descent and popularity, Tunku became involved in politically motivated organizations such as Saberkas and Persatuan Melayu Kedah (Kedah Malay Association). When he moved to Kuala Lumpur as assistant public prosecutor in 1949, he became involved in the wider pan-Malaya organizations, and following the resignation of Dato' Onn bin Jaafar (1895–1962), he was appointed the second president of the United Malays National Organization (UMNO) in 1951.

Contrary to Dato' Onn's hasty endeavor to create a multiracial party, Tunku kept UMNO as an exclusively "Malay" organization but began to foster ties with organizations representing other communities, in particular the Malayan Chinese Association (MCA). Following the success of the UMNO-MCA cooperation in the Kuala Lumpur municipal election in February 1952, the Alliance Party was officially formed in 1954, consisting of UMNO, MCA, and the Malayan Indian Congress (MIC). Tunku's stature rose when the Alliance won fifty-one of the fifty-two seats contested in the first ever general election in July 1955. Appointed as chief minister, Tunku led the negotiations for self-government and played a major role in the Baling Talks with the Malayan Communist Party (MCP) in December of the same year. After his country achieved independence from Britain on 31 August 1957, Tunku contributed significantly to the formation of the bigger Federation of Malaysia in 1963, encompassing the eleven states of Malaya, Singapore, and the British territories of North Borneo and Sarawak.

While facing Filipino claims over Sabah as well as Sukarno's "Crush Malaysia" policy (*Konfrontasi*), Tunku had to deal with the communal politics engendered by the People's Action Party (PAP), which formed the government in Singapore. Communal politics, which persisted even after the Singapore separation from Malaysia (in 1965), took a turn for the worse in the May 13, 1969 incident. The communal clashes that erupted in and around Kuala Lumpur three days after the 10 May general elections forced Tunku to the background. The day-to-day running of the country was handed over to Tun Abdul Razak, the deputy prime minister and director of the newly formed National Operations Council. Parliament was suspended, and measures were taken to reduce sources of conflict between the various communities. When Parliament reconvened on 22 September 1970, Tunku tendered his retirement to the fifth Yang Di Pertuan Agung, who, coincidentally, was also his nephew.

Shortly after his retirement, Tunku became secretary-general of the Organization of Islamic Conference (OIC) and was instrumental in setting up the Islamic Development Bank. Returning from Jeddah in 1974, he wrote his reminiscences in *The Star,* a national English daily. The articles were later compiled into volumes entitled *Looking Back* (1977), *View Points* (1978), *As a Matter of Interest* (1981), *Lest We Forget* (1983), *Something to Remember* (1983), *Challenging Times* (1986), and *Political Awakening* (1987). Tunku died on 6 December 1990, and his remains were laid to rest at his family's royal mausoleum in Langgar, Alor Setar.

ABDUL RAHMAN HAJI ISMAIL

See also Abdul Razak, Tun (1922–1976); Alliance Party (Malayan/Malaysian); Baling Talks (1955); Konfrontasi ("Crush Malaysia" campaign); Malayan/Malaysian Chinese Association (MCA) (1949); Malayan/Malaysian Indian Congress (MIC); Malaysia (1963); "May 13, 1969" (Malaysia); *Merdeka* (Independence); Onn bin Jaafar (1895–1962); People's Action Party (PAP); Sabah Claim; United Malays National Organization (UMNO) (1946)

References:

Healy, A. M. 1982. *Tunku Abdul Rahman.* St. Lucia, Australia: University of Queensland Press.

Miller, H. 1959. *Prince and Premier.* London: Harrap.

Sheppard, Mubin. 1995. *Tunku, His Life and Times: An Authorized Biography of Tunku Abdul Rahman Putra al-Haj.* Kuala Lumpur: Pelanduk Publications.

ABDUL RAZAK, TUN (1922–1976)
Champion of the Rural Peasantry

Tun Abdul Razak, more popularly known as Tun Razak, was a prominent Malay administrator and politician who played a major role in the United Malays National Organization (UMNO) and the Alliance Party as well as the negotiations that led to Malaya achieving independence from Britain in 1957. The 1956 Razak Report, issued one year after he became minister of education, would be the blueprint for the national education policy for Malaya and later Malaysia. When Malaya achieved independence, Razak was appointed deputy prime minister and minister of defense in the Tunku Abdul Rahman cabinet. In 1961, he was also entrusted with the national and rural development portfolio, which endeared him to the rural Malays. His efforts to improve and modernize rural life by bringing amenities such as electricity, clean water, health care, education, and economic projects to the rural areas changed the socioeconomic landscape of the country, and as a result, he is regarded as *Bapa Pembangunan* (Father of Development). His contributions were recognized internationally when he received the Magsaysay Award in 1967.

When another senior minister, Dr. Ismail Datuk Haji Abdul Rahman (1915–1973), resigned in 1967, Razak also became responsible for the Ministry of Home Affairs, and following the May 13, 1969 incident, he was made director of the National Operations Council and minister of finance. Razak's experience was greatly enriched in 1959 when he served as prime minister of Malaya for more than four months (from 21 April to 7 August) after Tunku Abdul Rahman resigned temporarily in order to devote his time to campaigning for the

Alliance Party in the first general election after independence.

In addition to his other responsibilities, Razak often served as a roving envoy representing Malaya/Malaysia at international meetings and conferences. He played a major role in the negotiations leading to the end of the Indonesian *Konfrontasi* against Malaysia in 1966. He strongly propagated the Zone of Peace, Freedom and Neutrality (ZOPFAN) concept as well as regional cooperation, which finally materialized in the form of the Association of Southeast Asian Nations (ASEAN) in 1967. Having such a wide exposure in politics and administration, Razak was well prepared for the job when Tunku retired on 22 September 1970. It was under Razak's guidance that the new national ideology, the Rukunegara (lit. State Doctrine), and the New Economic Policy (NEP) were promulgated to foster unity and a more equitable distribution of resources and wealth among all Malaysians, regardless of ethnicity. As prime minister, Razak successfully changed Malaysia's strongly pro-West foreign policy to one of nonalignment. His visit to Beijing in 1974 made him the first Southeast Asian leader to establish diplomatic relations with the People's Republic of China (PRC).

Born in Pekan in the eastern Malay state of Pahang on 11 March 1922, Razak was the first child of a prominent Pahang aristocrat, Dato' Hussein Mohd. Taib. Razak entered the elite Malay College at Kuala Kangsar in 1934 before enrolling at Raffles College in Singapore in 1940 to study economics, law, and history. In 1946, he embarked for London to study law, and he entered Lincoln's Inn in October 1947. He was called to the English bar in May 1950 and returned to Malaya immediately after his father's death.

Active in the Malay Society of Great Britain, Razak became its president when Tunku returned to Malaya in 1949. Back in Malaya in 1950 and still a bachelor at the age of twenty-eight, Razak was installed as Orang Kaya Indera Syahbandar (a traditional chieftainship title), and about three months later, he was nominated as a member of the Federal Legislative Council, a position held by his late father. In June 1951, he became assistant state secretary of Pahang, and he assumed the post of state secretary the following January. About three years

later, at the young age of thirty-two, he became the *menteri besar* (chief minister) of Pahang.

Razak's rise in politics was rapid. Shortly after joining UMNO in 1950, he was chosen as the organization's youth chief; in August 1951, he became its deputy president. By that time, he was second only to Tunku, the president of UMNO, whom he had earlier invited to join UMNO in anticipation of Dato' Onn's resignation. Being number two in UMNO and deputy head of the Alliance Party, he was pivotal in the success of the Alliance. After Tunku's retirement and learning from past mistakes, Razak worked toward political conciliation and merger with former adversaries, such as the Gerakan Party and the Pan-Malaysia Islamic Party (PAS), which led to the formation of an even bigger organization known as the Barisan Nasional (National Front) in 1974. Although PAS was expelled from the Barisan Nasional in 1978, the membership of the Barisan Nasional had grown to more than a dozen communal-based parties by 2003.

In 1952, Razak married Rahah, the daughter of a senior officer in Johor, Noh Omar, who later became speaker of the Malaysian House of Representatives. Razak died suddenly of mononucleosis on 14 January 1976 and was laid to rest at the National Mausoleum in Kuala Lumpur.

ABDUL RAHMAN HAJI ISMAIL

See also Abdul Rahman Putra Al-Haj, Tunku (1903–1990); Alliance Party (Malaya/Malaysia); Association of Southeast Asian Nations (ASEAN) (1967); Barisan Nasional (National Front) (1974); Konfrontasi ("Crush Malaysia" campaign); Malay College, Kuala Kangsar (MCKK); "May 13, 1969" (Malaysia); New Economic Policy (NEP) (Malaysia) (1970–1990); Non-Aligned Movement (NAM) and Southeast Asia; Parti Islam Se Malaysia (PAS); Raffles College; Rukunegara; Zone of Peace, Freedom and Neutrality (ZOPFAN) (1971)

References:
Paridah Abd. Samad. 1998. *Tun Abdul Razak: A Phenomenon in Malaysian Politics—A Political Biography.* Kuala Lumpur: Affluent Master.
Shariff Ahmad. 1999. *Tun Razak: Putera Titiwangsa* [*Tun Razak: Prince of Titiwangsa*]. Kuala Lumpur: Utusan Publications.

Shaw, William. 1976. *Tun Abdul Razak: His Life and Times.* Kuala Lumpur: Longman Malaysia.

ABDULLAH BIN ABDUL KADIR, MUNSYI (1797–1854)
Modern Malay Writer

Better known as Munsyi Abdullah, Abdullah bin Abdul Kadir was the foremost modern Malay writer. Indeed, his writings represented a radical departure from traditional works of Malay literature. Recognized as a pioneer and innovator, he introduced a refreshing trend that not only enriched and popularized Malay literary works but also contributed to Malay historiography.

Born in 1797 in Melaka of Indian-Arab-Malay parentage, Abdullah had an early education that comprised traditional Koranic teachings, as well as the reading and writing of Jawi (Malay script), Tamil, and Arabic under the tutelage of his father. He moved to the newly established British outpost of Singapore, and his fluency in Malay enabled him to teach the language to the Indian soldiers, or *sepoy,* of the British garrison in exchange for acquiring Hindi from them. The sepoy respectfully addressed him as *munsyi,* meaning "teacher." From 1823, Abdullah diligently learned English from Christian missionaries; he in turn taught them Malay.

Because of his proficiency in Malay in particular and his knowledge of English, he served well as a copywriter for the colonial government. He benefited from working in a European printing and publishing firm and briefly was the acting head of the Anglo-Chinese College in Singapore when the Reverend G. H. Thompson was on furlough in England. He also served as letter writer to Stamford Raffles (1781–1826), governor of Singapore from 1819–1823, the "Tuan Raffles" mentioned in his writings. Raffles had an immense interest in the history and cultural heritage of the Malay world; he undoubtedly tapped Abdullah's knowledge and experience.

Abdullah's memoirs, *Kisah Pelayaran Abdullah* (1838) and *Hikayat Abdullah* (1848), broke new ground in Malay literature. Unlike their predecessors, these writings were printed, not handwritten, and they were published commercially.

Moreover, their authorship was prominently displayed. The pronoun *I* was used, and the contents were conveyed in simple, contemporary Malay. Fantasies and legendary stories and characters were absent; Abdullah's writings dealt with realism. He presented ideas, opinions drawn from personal experiences, observations, and reflections. In relating the activities of the T'ien Ti Hui (Heaven and Earth Society), a clandestine Chinese organization in Singapore, Abdullah employed elements of investigative journalism. Departing from past practices of utilizing symbolism and incredible tales as means of criticism, he used straightforward language in his critiques of Malay rulers, officials, and the establishment as well as the ordinary Malay peasant. Although he mainly wrote in prose, he also composed verses, as in *Syair Singapura Terbakar* (1830).

Straddled between the traditional, insular, and conservative world of Malay aristocracy and the ignorant and illiterate *rakyat* (masses), on the one hand, and the modern, cosmopolitan, and progressive world brought by European colonialism and its attendant influences, on the other, Abdullah attempted to use his pen to raise Malay consciousness and awaken his people from their prolonged slumber. Abdullah died during his pilgrimage to Mecca in 1854. His son, Mohamed Ibrahim, followed in his footsteps as a scribe to Sultan Abu Bakar (t. 1862–1895) of Johor.

OOI KEAT GIN

See also Malays; Raffles, Sir (Thomas) Stamford Bingley (1781–1826); Siamese Malay States (Kedah, Perlis, Kelantan, Terengganu); Singapore (1819); Western Malay States (Perak, Selangor, Negri Sembilan, and Pahang)

References:
Abdullah bin Abdul Kadir. 1970. *The Hikayat Abdullah: The Autobiography of Abdullah bin Abdul Kadir (1797–1854).* Translated and annotated by A. H. Hill. Kuala Lumpur: Oxford University Press.
Abdullah bin Abdul Kadir, Munshi. 1967. *The Voyage of Abdullah (Pelayaran Abdullah); Being an Account of His Experiences on a Voyage from Singapore to Kelantan, A.D. 1838.* Translated by A. E. Coope. Kuala Lumpur: Oxford University Press.

Mohamed Ibrahim bin Abdullah Munshi. 1975. *The Voyages of Mohamed Ibrahim Munshi.* Translated, with an introduction and notes, by Amin Sweeney and Nigel Phillips. Kuala Lumpur: Oxford University Press.

Siti Aisah Murad. 1996. *Abdullah Munsyi dan Masyarakat Melayu* [*Munsyi Abdullah and Malay Society*]. Kuala Lumpur: Dewan Bahasa dan Pustaka.

ABU BAKAR, SULTAN OF JOHOR (r. 1862–1895)
Father of Modern Johor

Abu Bakar is considered the founder of modern Johor and was the first of the new-model Malay princes in British Malaya. His ancestors included Sultan Abdul Jalil of Johor (r. 1699–1719) and Daing Parani, one of the Bugis chiefs who seized power in Riau during the early eighteenth century. Abu Bakar was the eldest son of Daing Ibrahim (r. 1825–1862), *temenggong* (state minister of defense and justice) of Johor, and the grandson of Temenggong Abdul Rahman (r. 1806–1825), the Malay chief who had permitted the settlement of Thomas Stamford Raffles (1781–1826) at Singapore in 1819. Raffles was lieutenant governor of Java (1811–1816), governor of Benkulen (1816–1819), and governor of Singapore (1819–1823), which he was instrumental in establishing as a British outpost in 1819. Abu Bakar grew up in colonial Singapore in his father's kampong at Teluk Belanga and attended the Malay school of the Reverend Benjamin Peach Keasberry. He was thus one of the first Malay rajas to receive an English education.

Temenggong Ibrahim had made a start at settling Chinese pepper and gambier planters on the mainland of Johor and had continued to play a role in the politics of the nearby Malay States. Abu Bakar, in his turn, pursued these initiatives with ambition and skill.

As soon as he succeeded his father, he established a capital at Tanjong Putri (now Johor Bahru), and in close partnership with a clique of Chinese merchants in Singapore, he introduced large numbers of planters into the virgin jungles of Johor. Calling upon his siblings and other Malays who had once been his classmates, he built up a state administration based at his new capital. With reliable revenue from the Chinese planters and well-ordered government in his own state, he was hailed by British administrators and merchants in Singapore as an enlightened ruler.

Abu Bakar also continued to seek a place for himself in the politics of nearby Malay States, becoming involved in the Pahang civil war in the 1860s and in the affairs of nearby, Dutch-controlled Riau. He overshadowed the heirs of Sultan Hussain (r. 1819–1835), claimants to the Johor crown. He was also a presence in conflicts that later arose in Negri Sembilan, Perak, Selangor, and Terengganu. Although British governors and Singapore merchants were concerned about his ambitious schemes, he ultimately was able to establish an acceptable balance between his goals and British sensibilities. For the most part, the colonial officials found him a useful ally whose own power was never allowed to threaten the stability of prosperous Singapore.

In 1865, he traveled to England and was presented to Queen Victoria (r. 1837–1901), thus establishing a connection that significantly boosted his status not only among his fellow rajas but also in Europe. He dropped the title of temenggong and adopted that of maharaja (the original Malay title had been *temenggong sri maharaja*), a term more recognizable in Europe. Throughout his life, he remained a close friend of the British monarch, and through her, he gained a privileged entry into the world of European aristocracy. He spent much time during the 1880s and 1890s traveling in Europe, entertaining and being entertained by the crowned heads of the Continent. At the same time, he constructed European-style palaces in Johor Bahru and at his Singapore estate at Tyersall, where he entertained a procession of global dignitaries, including the Duke of Buckingham and General Arthur MacArthur, among many others.

His wealth and status were reinforced by his ability to understand and compete with Europeans on their own ground. Early on, he made use of the services of European lawyers in Singapore, and he maintained close commercial relations with a number of the main European agency houses as well as with the key Chinese *towkay* (merchants, entrepreneurs) in the town. Colonial authorities were forced to recognize the sovereignty of his state, and the British government ultimately acknowledged him as sultan of the state and territory of Johor in 1885.

His relations with colonial governors and the Colonial Office in London were not always smooth, as British officials and mercantile factions in Singapore found much to criticize in his independence and his sometimes extravagant lifestyle. Ultimately, his son was forced to yield to British pressures in 1914 and submit to colonial status. Abu Bakar made a significant impact, however, not only in creating a viable state but also in finding a path for educated and progressive Malays in his administration. They and their immediate descendants were important figures in establishing Malaysia's first political parties and its federal administration.

CARL TROCKI

See also Agency Houses, European; British Malaya; Bugis (Buginese); Chinese in Southeast Asia; Johor; Johor-Riau Empire; Pahang; Siamese Malay States (Kedah, Perlis, Kelantan, Terengganu); Singapore (1819); *Towkay;* Western Malay States (Perak, Selangor, Negri Sembilan, and Pahang)

References:

Ahmad Fawzi Basri. 1988. *Johor, 1855–1917: Pentadbiran dan Perkembangannya [Johor, 1855–1917: Its Administration and Development]*. Siri Sejarah Fajar Bakti series. Petaling Jaya, Malaysia: Penerbit Fajar Bakti.

Gullick, J. M. 1992. *Rulers and Residents: Influence and Power in the Malay States, 1870–1920.* Kuala Lumpur: Oxford University Press.

Thio, Eunice. 1969. *British Policy in the Malay Peninsula, 1880–1910.* Vol. 1, *The Southern States.* Singapore: University of Malaya Press.

Trocki, Carl A. 1979. *Prince of Pirates: The Temenggongs and the Development of Johor and Singapore, 1785–1885.* Singapore: Singapore University Press.

Winstedt, Richard O. 1992 [1932]. *A History of Johor.* MBRAS Reprint no. 6. Kuala Lumpur: Malaysian Branch of the Royal Asiatic Society. First published in 1932 in *Journal of the Malayan Branch of the Royal Asiatic Society* (JMBRAS) 10, no. 3.

ACEH (ACHEH)

Banda Aceh, the present-day capital city of the province of Aceh, Indonesia, lies strategically in the northwestern tip of the island of Sumatra.

From the early sixteenth century, Banda Aceh developed as the capital of a great and powerful Islamic kingdom. Foreign accounts as well as local chronicles and legends point to the existence of small kingdoms (Lamuri or Ramni and various others—Lambri, Lan-li, Lan-wu-li) prior to the emergence of Banda Aceh. In Chinese and Arab sources, mention was made of several exported items, including brazilwood, camphor, coral, cranes' nests, gold, ivory, rattan, tin, turtle shells, and lignal-oes (the resinous wood of various tropical trees, from which oil is extracted for use as an ingredient in soaps, perfumes, and foods).

Chau-Ju-Kua (1225) mentioned that Lan-wu-li (Lamri) was under the control of Śriwijaya, which annually sent tribute to San-fo-chi, and the Javanese chronicle *Nâgarakertâgama,* written by Prapanca (1365), mentioned Perlak, Samudra, and Lamuri among the Sumatran states that recognized the supreme authority of Majapahit's king, Hayam Wuruk (Râjasanagara, r. 1350–1389).

From the early part of the sixteenth century, Lamuri was apparently subjected to the king of Aceh, as mentioned by Tome Pires in his *Suma Oriental* (1512–1515). The well-known king who strengthened Aceh was Sultan Ali Mughayat Shah (r. 1496–1530); he was mentioned in the Malay literatures—particularly in the *Hikayat Bustan as-Salatin,* written in the seventeenth century by Nuruddin Al-Raniri (d. 1666). Sultan Ali Mughayat Shah was identified as Raja Ibrahim in the Portuguese account. In 1511, the Portuguese conquered Melaka, the very important international trading center in Southeast Asia. Consequently, the Islamic kingdom of Demak avoided the Straits of Melaka and utilized the trade route through the Strait of Sunda and the Indian Ocean along the western coast of Sumatra. This diversion benefited Aceh. Sultan Ali Mughayat Shah began to expand his power and proclaimed Aceh's independence from Pedir in 1520. Daya was annexed in 1520; four years later, the kingdoms of Pedir and Samudra-Pasai were conquered. Both Pedir and Pasai were pepper ports with a flourishing trade with Gujerat and China. In 1528, despite the opportunity, Sultan Ali Mughayat Shah failed to capture the Portuguese fleet commanded by Simao de Souza Galvao, which was sheltering from a storm off the port of Aceh. One year later, the sultan's plans to attack

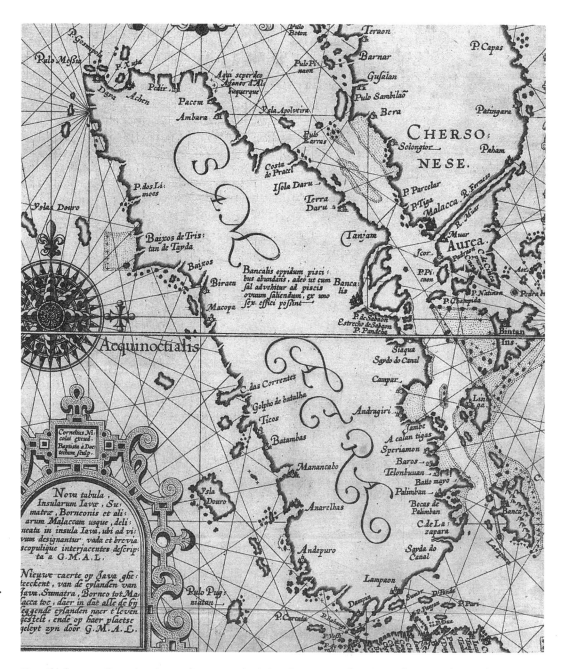

Detail of a map from the sixteenth century depicting Sumatra and regions of present-day Aceh Province in Indonesia. (James Ford Bell Library, University of Minnesota)

the Portuguese in Melaka also failed to materialize. He died in the following year and was buried at Kandang XII in Banda Aceh.

Sultan Alauddin Riayat Shah al-Khahar (r. 1537–1568) was another great ruler of Aceh. He expanded the armed forces, developed trade, and established close relations with Islamic powers in the Middle East (West Asia), especially with Turkey, and in Africa, namely with Abyssinia and Egypt. In 1563, he sent an envoy to Constantinople requesting assistance against the Portuguese. Two years later, Turkey dispatched two ships with supplies and military technicians to Aceh. Therefore, with his strong military forces, the sultan conquered Batak, Aru (Deli), and Barus. Johor and Melaka were attacked in 1537, 1547, and 1568 by large forces of the Acehnese armada, equipped with Turkish-manned artillery pieces.

The political expansion of the Acehnese sultanate was continued by his successors, who attacked Melaka in 1573 and conquered the rich tin-producing state of Perak in the Malay Peninsula two years later. Meanwhile, Aceh struck an alliance with the Javanese kingdom of Japara under Ratu Kalinyamat.

When Aceh overran Perak in 1575, its ruler, Sultan Ahmad, died; his wife and his son, Mansur, were taken to Aceh. The Acehnese sultan married his daughter to Mansur; the latter succeeded his father-in-law as Sultan Alauddin Mansur Shah (r. 1579–1585). After that time, a foreign sultan ruled Aceh. According to the *Hikayat Bustan as-Salatin,* Sultan Alauddin Mansur Shah was a very virtuous and just king, and he supported religious scholars. During his reign, Aceh was visited by many *'ulamas* (religious teachers), such as Syekh Abulkhaer ibn Syekh ibn Hajar. In 1582, he was teaching *sufism* (mysticism), *fikh* (law), and *tauhid* (knowledge on the unity of God). In the same year, Syekh Muhammad Jamani, an expert in *usul addin* (basis of religion), arrived in Aceh; he was followed by the famous ulama Syekh Jailani ibn Hasan ibn Muhammad Hamid.

The chronicles say that Sultan Alauddin Mansur Shah died in 1585 and was succeeded by Sultan Alauddin Riayat Shah ibn Sultan Munawar Shah, who reigned until 1588 and in turn was succeeded by Sultan Alauddin Riayat Shah ibn Firman Shah (r. 1589–1604). During the latter's reign, the Europeans, notably the English East India Company (EIC) under James Lancaster in 1599 and in 1602, visited Aceh and presented a letter from England's Queen Elizabeth I (r. 1558–1603). The Dutch ships commanded by Cornelis de Houtman anchored in the Bay of Aceh on 30 June 1599. De Houtman and Lancaster were given a friendly reception and permitted to buy pepper.

When Sultan Alauddin Riayat Shah died in 1604, the throne of Aceh was in the hands of a very weak ruler, Sultan Muda, also known as Sultan Ali Riayat Shah, who reigned until 1607. His successor was the famous Sultan Iskandar Muda (Mahkota Alam, r. 1607–1636). He reigned over a prosperous city and a strong kingdom that thrived because of his achievements in the development of international trade and commerce, political expansion, and the establishment of close relations with foreign Islamic kingdoms that not only strengthened Aceh's military forces but also intensified the kingdom's Islamic faith. The regions along the western and eastern coasts of Sumatra acknowledged the power of Aceh. Johor, in the Malay Peninsula, was forced to acknowledge the authority of the Acehnese sultanate. Aceh's international trade networks encompassed England, France, India, Africa, Egypt, Turkey, Arabia and the Middle East, China, and Japan. The port of Aceh hosted foreign merchants armed with foreign commodities: porcelain, cloth, carpet, silk, fine chintz, butter, rice, wheat, and lacquerware. The export commodities from Aceh itself and from the other countries included pepper, silk, benzoin, pitch, lignal-oes, camphor, sulphur, petroleum, gold, tin, lead, ivory, sandalwood, cinnamon, and other spices. Of all of the native products, pepper was the most important export commodity. The total amount of pepper produced annually on the western coast of Sumatra at the time was about 40,000 bags, and the sultan of Aceh handled about 16,000 bags, so the total amount for the kingdom was about 56,000 bags (Dasgupta 1962). Through the mercantilist system, many noblemen and aristocrats became much richer than the sultan himself. Sultan Iskandar Muda was said to be the richest king in the region, with his large income derived from trade revenues and customs duties. He created an efficient bureaucratic system and codified the basic law of the sultanate, known as *Adat Meukuta Alam* or *Kanun Meukuta Alam.* Iskandar Muda also supported the development of Islam. The teaching of the heterodox Sufism, or *Wihdatul Wujud,* of Hamzah al-Fansuri and Shamsuddin al-Sumatrani (d. 1630) was protected, and their influence spread over the kingdom and even to the Malay Peninsula. After Sultan Iskandar Muda died in 1636, Nuruddin al-Raniri (d. 1658) returned to Aceh and undertook a reformation against the teaching of Hamzah al-Fansuri and Shamsuddin al-Sumatrani. Al-Raniri was an expert not only in theology and history but also in neo-Sufism (orthodox Sufism), or *Wihdatul Shuhud,* and his teachings were supported by Sultan Iskandar Thani (r. 1636–1641), the successor of Iskandar Muda. The historical books *Bustan as-salatin* and *Taj as-salatina* were written by Nuruddin al-Raniri. His follower in Aceh was also a famous ulama, named Abdurraf as-Singkili or Syekh Kuala.

The news of the fall of Melaka to the Dutch East India Company (VOC) in 1641 had spread, but it had little impact on the sultanate. After the demise of Iskandar Thani in 1641, the sultanate of Aceh was ruled by queens (from 1641 to 1699): Taj al-Alam Safiatuddin Shah, Sri Sultan Nur al-Alam Nakiat ad-din Shah, Inayat Shah Zakiat ad-din Shah, and Ratu Kamalat Shah. Thereafter, rulers of Arab descent reigned: Sultan Badr al-alam Syarif Hasyim Jamal ad-din (r. 1699–1702) and Sultan Perkasa Alam Syarif Lamtui Ibn Syarif Ibrahim (r. 1702–1703). There were also rulers who descended from the Buginese dynasty, namely, Sultan Ala ad-din Ahmad Shah or Maharaja Lela Melayu (r. 1727–1735). The political situation and economic condition of the Acehnese sultanate apparently began to decline from the end of the seventeenth century and continued to do so throughout the eighteenth century.

In the nineteenth century, the sultanate of Aceh was threatened by Dutch political expansion. As in other regions in Indonesia, there was resistance to Dutch colonialism. The Aceh Wars (1873–1903) represented the most intense and protracted struggle. Because the spirit of war was stimulated by religious motivation—the so-called *perang sabil* (holy war)—the opposition against the establishment of Dutch hegemony was intense. The roots and passion of the conflict could be traced to the early nineteenth century.

From the time of Sultan Alauddin Muhammad Daud Shah's reign (1823–1838), the prestige of Aceh as an Islamic kingdom was strong and constantly promoted. Meanwhile, Dutch political control, reaching to Sibolga and the interior of Tapanuli and Batak in 1830, threatened the freedom of Aceh. The regions along both the western and the eastern coasts of Sumatra began to be influenced by the political power of the Netherlands Indies. In February 1858, the Dutch subjugated Siak, followed by Deli, Asahan, Kampar, and Indragiri. These kingdoms were directly and indirectly under the protection of the sultanate of Aceh. The subjugation of these kingdoms by the Dutch,

strengthened by the Sumatra Treaty of 1871 between The Netherlands and Great Britain, directly threatened the sovereignty of Aceh. Preparations for war with the Dutch were made, and the sultan sent Habib Abdurrakhman to Turkey to seek assistance. When the delegation returned and visited Singapore, agreements regarding aid to Aceh were made with the consuls of the United States and Italy.

In March 1873, Sultan Muhammad Daud Shah refused to submit to the authority of the Netherlands Indies, and military campaigns were launched in April and again in December. By mid-January 1874, Aceh Besar also came under the authority of the Netherlands Indies. But it took another thirty years before Acehnese opposition was finally subdued. The *uleëbalangs* (provincial chiefs) and the 'ulamas provided the leadership in this protracted armed struggle. The government of the Netherlands Indies gradually realized that military action was not the key to overcoming Acehnese recalcitrance. The Dutch government engaged Christiaan Snouck Hurgronje (1857–1936), who was an expert on Islam and had conversed with the 'ulama of Aceh while in Mekka (Mecca). Hurgronje proposed that the unity of the 'ulama and the aristocrats had to be broken. Further, the Netherlands Indies government had to offer civil service appointments to aristocrats and their sons.

However, the military campaign continued under the civil and military governor, J. B. van Heutsz, who led a major offensive against Pedie (Pedir) in March 1898. Acehnese resistance slowly crumbled with the deaths and surrender of the leadership: Teungku Cik Di Tiro and Muhammad Syaman died in 1891; Panglima Polem and his wife were captured in 1903; and Teuku Umar was killed in February 1899 and his wife, Cut Nya' Din, was captured and exiled to Sumedang in 1906. By the September 1904 decree of the Netherlands Indies government, van Heutsz was appointed as governor-general of the Netherlands Indies, and General J. C. van der Wijck was appointed as governor of Aceh.

UKA TJANDRASASMITA

See also Aceh (Acheh) Wars (1873–1903); Darul Islam Movement (DI); Demak; Economic Transformation of Southeast Asia (ca. 1400–ca. 1800); Hamzah Fansuri; Hayam Wuruk (Rajasanagara) (r. 1350–1389)

Iskandar Muda, Sultan (Mahkota Alam)
(r. 1607–1636); Islam in Southeast Asia;
Johor-Riau Empire; Melaka; Nurud-din
al-Raniri (d. 1658); Pepper; Persatuan Ulama
Seluruh Aceh (PUSA); Portuguese Asian
Empire; Snouck Hurgronje, Professor
Christiaan (1857–1936); Sumatra; Van Heutsz,
General Joannes Benedictus (1851–1924)

References:

Azra, Azyumardi. 1994. *Jaringan Ulama Timur
Tengah dan Kepulauan Nusantara Abad, XVII
dan XVIII* [*'Ulama Networks of the Middle East
and the Malay Archipelago, 17th and 18th
centuries*]. Bandung, Indonesia: Penerbit Mizan.

Cortesao, Armando. 1967. *The Suma Oriental of
Tome Pires: An Account of the East, from the Red
Sea to Japan, Written in Malacca and India in
1512–1515*. Liechtenstein: Kraus Reprint.

Dasgupta, A. K. 1962. *Acheh in Indonesian Trade
and Politics, 1600–1641*. Ann Arbor, MI:
University Microfilm.

Djajadiningrat, Hoesein R. 1911. "Critiesch
overzicht van de in Malaische Werken
vervatte Gegegevens over de Geschiedenis
van het Soeltanaat van Atjeh" [Critical
Review on the Malay Literatures containing
evidences on the history of the Sultanate of
Aceh]. *Bijdragen van het Koninklijk Instituut
voor de Taal-Land-en Volkenkunde* 65: 135–265.

Lombard, Denys. 1967. *Le sultanat d'Atjeh au
temps D'Iskandar Muda, 1607–1636* [*The
Sultanate of Aceh during the Reign of Iskandar
Muda, 1607–1636*]. Paris: École Française
d'Extrême-Orient.

Marwati Djoened Poesponegoro-Nugroho
Notosusanto. 1994. *Sejarah nasional Indonesia.
4, Abad kesembilanbelas* [*National History of
Indonesia. Vol. 4, Nineteenth Century*]. Special
edition by F. A. Sutjipto. Jakarta: Departmen
Pendidikan Dan Kebudayaan, PN. Balai
Pustaka Jakarta.

McKinnon, Edwards E. 1988. *Beyond Serandib:
Note on Lambri at Northern Tip of Aceh*. Ithaca,
NY: Cornell Southeast Asia Program.
Reprinted from *Indonesia* 46 (October):
103–121.

Mukti, Ali A. 1970. *An Introduction to the
Government of Acheh's Sultanate*. Jogjakarta:
Jajasan Nida.

Pusat Dokumentasi dan Informasi Aceh. 1977.
*Perang Kolonial Belanda di Aceh: The Dutch
Colonial War in Aceh*. Bandung, Indonesia:
P. T. Harapan Offset.

Snouck Hurgronje, C. 1906. *The Achenese*.
Translated by A. W. S. O'Sullivan and
indexed by R. J. Wilkinson. Leiden, the
Netherlands: E. J. Brill; London: Luzac.

Zakaria Ahmad. 1972. *Sekitar Kerajaan Atjeh
Dalam Th., 1520–1675* [*An account of the Aceh
Government, 1520–1675*]. Banda Aceh:
Monara.

ACEH (ACHEH) WARS (1873–1903)

Beginning in 1873, the contest for the former
sultanate of Aceh was emblematic of the struggle for Islamic independence in the Indonesian
archipelago. The Aceh Wars were the longest
conflict in which the Dutch became embroiled
in Indonesia and formally lasted until 1903, although fighting persisted well into the following decade.

Aceh had long served as one of the principal
centers for the study of Islam and as a gateway
for the pilgrimage to Mecca. By the late sixteenth century, it had become the most powerful state in Sumatra, reaching its apogee under
Sultan Iskandar Muda (r. 1607–1636). This state
exercised control over territories in the west of
present-day Indonesia and Malaysia and forged
formal links with the Ottoman Empire. The
following centuries, however, witnessed a decline in Acehnese fortunes, though the region
persisted as an independent kingdom.

The 1824 Treaty of London divided insular
Southeast Asia into British and Dutch spheres
while recognizing Acehnese sovereignty. Anxiety about the intervention of a third power in
the region led Great Britain and The Netherlands to conclude a new agreement in 1871,
allowing for Dutch intervention. The Dutch
alleged, with little evidence, that the Acehnese
were seeking to negotiate with the United
States, and on the pretext that the sultanate
was sponsoring piracy in the Straits of Melaka,
they sent an expedition to north Sumatra in
March 1873.

This poorly prepared force did not even locate the royal residence and was forced to retreat after the death of its commander, General
Köhler. A massive expedition, better planned
and equipped, was mounted in late 1873. This
time, the palace was captured and the sultanate
was declared at an end; on 31 January 1874,
General van Swieten proclaimed Aceh a part of
the Netherlands Indies. This proved to be a

hollow victory. The young successor to the throne, Muhammad Dawot (Muhammad Daud), was taken to safety while a key adviser to the late sultan, Habib 'Abd al-Rahman al-Zahir (1833–1896), continued to press for Ottoman aid from Istanbul. Such aid was not forthcoming, but the continuing resistance of the Acehnese served as a source of inspiration for many of the Muslims of the Netherlands Indies and the Malay Peninsula and among the Southeast Asian community in Mecca.

Effective resistance to Dutch incursions now passed briefly to the various petty lords (*uléëbalang*). Subsequently, opposition was undertaken by the religious leaders, the 'ulama. Key 'ulama such as Teungku di Tiro (1836–1891) enjoyed popular support bolstered by widely disseminated texts equating the struggle with a holy war, a *jihad* (Arab) or *perang sabi* (Aceh). In 1876 and after two years spent gathering support from the British port of Penang, 'Abd al-Rahman al-Zahir returned to Aceh to coordinate the resistance. He soon fell out with the local leadership and submitted to the Dutch in 1878 in exchange for a lifelong pension in Mecca. The war dragged on regardless.

With an uncertain foothold on the coast and beset regularly by cholera and dysentery, the Dutch would opt to fortify their position as a base from which to launch incursions into the surrounding territory. This state of affairs prevailed for several years, being formalized with the so-called line of concentration, inaugurated under General van Pel (d. 1876). Thereby, the capital was surrounded by a series of fortified posts connected by an armored tramway. This policy worked to the advantage of the Acehnese leadership. The vast majority of Greater Aceh was still impassable for the Dutch.

A third campaign to complete the pacification of the province was begun in 1884. But with the Indies in recession and the ongoing campaign causing substantial hardship in Java, where most colonial revenues were raised, the morass persisted. Criticism of the war from within Dutch and Indies society led to the appointment of an Aceh veteran, J. B. van Heutsz (1851–1924), as military governor in 1898. With the advice of Christiaan Snouck Hurgronje (1857–1936), whose studies had identified the uléëbalangs as potential clients and who counseled the vigorous prosecution of guerrilla tactics against the 'ulama, van Heutsz

engaged in a series of successful campaigns, advancing Dutch control across Pedir (1899–1901) and Daya (1898–1903) and pushing into the Gayo highlands by 1903. In each territory, the local uléëbalang, on submission, was obliged to sign "the short declaration," a document drafted by Snouck Hurgronje that pledged allegiance to the Dutch sovereign and her agents.

Victory finally seemed complete in 1903, with the submission of the aspirant sultan Muhammad Dawot. But the conflicts were by no means over: fighting continued until the taking of Alas (1907), and indeed scattered resistance occurred until as late as 1912. Furthermore, Dutch rule, as enforced under van Heutsz and his successor van Daalen, was barely accepted, being accomplished by the use of extreme violence. The Aceh campaign would continue to haunt the Dutch in Indonesia, and its incorporation within the Java-centered Netherlands Indies would be a source of instability in the future nation of Indonesia.

M. F. LAFFAN

See also Aceh (Acheh); Iskandar Muda, Sultan (Mahkota Alam) (r. 1607–1636); Islam in Southeast Asia; Netherlands (Dutch) East Indies; Penang (1786); Pepper; Short Declaration, Long Contract; Snouck Hurgronje, Professor Christiaan (1857–1936); Van Heutsz, General Joannes Benedictus (1851–1924)

References:
Alfian, Ibrahim. 1992. *Sastra Perang: Sebuah Pembicaraan Mengenai Hikayat Perang Sabil* [*Scripture of War: A Discussion of the Hikayat Perang Sabil*]. Jakarta: Balai Pustaka.
Reid, Anthony. 1969. *The Contest for North Sumatra: Aceh, the Netherlands and Britain, 1858–1898.* Kuala Lumpur: Oxford University Press.
Siegel, James T. 1969. *The Rope of God.* Berkeley: University of California Press.
Snouck Hurgronje, C. 1906. *The Achehnese.* Translated by A. W. S. O'Sullivan and indexed by R. J. Wilkinson. Leiden, the Netherlands: E. J. Brill; London: Luzac.

ADAT

Despite its probable Arabic origin, the term *adat* resonates deeply throughout the Malayo-Indonesian archipelago. Often defined as "custom" or "customary law," the word refers, broadly speaking, to the customary norms, rules, interdictions, and injunctions that guide an individual's conduct as a member of the community and the sanctions and forms of redress by which these norms and rules are upheld. *Adat* may also refer, more abstractly, to the natural order (for example, that the sun rises in the east and sets in the west) or to the ideal, in the sense of what is correct or proper.

Among Muslim societies in Southeast Asia, the concept of adat is generally distinguished from *ugama'* religion (which is separately concerned with the rules of religious observance) and from Islamic law. For most non–Muslim groups, this distinction between adat and religion is not recognized. Iban adat, for example, concerns not only social norms but also ritual procedures and rules of propitiation. For the Iban, the prime function of adat is to ensure harmonious relations among community members. At the same time, conduct in accordance with adat is believed to maintain the community in a state of ritual well-being in respect to the gods, ancestors, and spirits. The correct observance of adat is thought to result in a continuing state of spiritual well-being, demonstrated outwardly by the health, longevity, and material prosperity of community members. In this sense, the meaning of the word is not restricted to customary law but rather applies to the entire normative framework of traditional social and religious life.

The word *adat* means roughly what an English speaker means by *custom*. Thus, it describes the various things people customarily do and the ways in which they customarily do them. Like the English notion, it also covers personal habits. To have good adat implies that a person not only acts in accordance with the rules of adat but also that his or her conduct exemplifies more abstract ideals, such as generosity or personal courage. The notion of adat therefore also embraces more general values, moral ideals, and standards and so provides a measure against which a person's conduct may be judged.

In the early decades of the twentieth century in the Netherlands East Indies, the study of adat emerged as a specialized field of inquiry. Although associated with the needs of colonial administration, this study nevertheless gave rise to an active scholarly discipline that dealt with differing systems of adat comparatively, and many scholars were involved in compiling codes of adat from throughout the Indonesian archipelago. The massive literature that resulted remains, to this day, a major contribution to Indonesian ethnography and jurisprudence.

CLIFFORD SATHER

See also Brunei Ethnic Minorities; Brunei Malays; East Malaysian Ethnic Minorities; Iban; Kadazan-Dusuns; Malays; Orang Asli

References:

Haar, B. ter. 1948. *Adat Law in Indonesia*. Edited by E. A. Hoebel and A. A. Schiller. New York: Institute of Pacific Relations.

Hooker, M. B. 1976. *Adat Law in Modern Malaysia*. Kuala Lumpur: Oxford University Press.

Sandin, Benedict. 1980. *Iban Adat and Augury*. Penang: Penerbit Universiti Sains Malaysia.

Schlegel, Stuart. 1972. *Tiruray Justice: Traditional Tiruray Law and Morality*. Berkeley: University of California Press.

Warren, Carol. 1993. *Adat and Dinas: Balinese Communities in the Indonesian State*. Kuala Lumpur: Oxford University Press.

AGE OF COMMERCE

Anthony Reid first coined the phrase *age of commerce* in the late 1980s in his two-volume masterpiece *Southeast Asia in the Age of Commerce, 1450–1680* (1988, 1993). Since its publication, this pathbreaking work has become the most influential interpretation of early modern Southeast Asian civilization. With a focus on examining Southeast Asia in its relations with the rest of the world that shaped the region, it has entirely reconstructed the understanding of precolonial Southeast Asia.

In the historiography of the colonial era that dominated the field of Southeast Asian history up to the early 1960s, the region was studied in separate parts, as colonial dependencies of the West or as appendages of China and India. This view saw Southeast Asians as fundamentally lacking the impetus for internal change. Departing from this colonial stand, nationalist histories either treated Southeast Asians as powerless victims or attempted to correct this image by forging a more celebratory, empowering view of the region's past that emphasized the internal orientation of individual Southeast Asian countries. Ironically, this approach supported the colonial historiography in that it compartmentalized Southeast Asian history into separate national histories. This approach served to further isolate the study of the region from international forces and comparisons.

The publication of *Southeast Asia in the Age of Commerce* reflected the shifts in the political and academic climate during the late twentieth century and heralded a new trend of scholarship on Southeast Asian historiography. Reid sought to reposition the region back into a world historical process on which it had made an impact. Building on the achievements of postcolonial scholarship, he highlighted the region's interconnectedness to the world without displacing the Southeast Asians from the center of their own historical stage.

Carrying on the Annals School's tradition of rejecting events and great people as the simple causes of historical change, Reid focused on the daily life of ordinary peoples in Southeast Asia and organized his research along the themes of physical and material culture. In his first volume (1988), he dealt with Southeast Asian social structure, environment, diet, dress, and entertainment. He identified the cultural essence that made Southeast Asia one unit and distinguished it from the rest of Asia. In this grand historical investigation, Reid applied an interdisciplinary approach and built his strength on the scholarship of modern geographers, anthropologists, demographers, and environmental scientists. His grasp of the details in the lives of ordinary men and women and nonelite merchants permitted a remarkable departure from the elite-centered paradigm of political narrative that had dominated Southeast Asian historiography for centuries.

For Reid, the period between the fifteenth and seventeenth centuries, the age of commerce, was the major turning point in Southeast Asian history. This notion broke away from the conventional historiography that labeled the period as "early European contact," "Islamization," or simply according to the individual dynasties, such as Ayutthaya and Mataram. Such labels, Reid argued, obscured the underlying coherence of a period that brought profound and momentous changes to all of Southeast Asia, whereas the age of commerce theme enabled Reid to trace the longer-term shifts. Again he departed from the conventional historiography, which marked the arrival of Europeans in 1500 as the start of a new era in

Southeast Asian history. Reid's age of commerce starts in 1450, the initial impetus being the explosion of energy of the Ming dynasty (1368–1644) in China. The movement toward coastal areas and the rise of port polities marked this period. This followed the decline of the Indianized kingdoms that had been centered in dry, inland areas.

In his second volume (1993), Reid provided an economic analysis based on carefully derived statistics on the rapid growth of cash cropping, spice exports, indigenous intraregional trade, and urbanization. His intention in emphasizing the economic dimension of Southeast Asian history was to be able to compare it with other parts of the world. Commerce was taken as an index of change in order to demonstrate the important changes that took place in Southeast Asia before the colonial period. Reid traced the intense interaction with the world economy in the fifteenth and sixteenth centuries and the decline of trade from the mid-seventeenth century.

In this age of commerce, a significant portion of the Southeast Asian population was drawn into the international market economy. Pepper, the most important single export of Southeast Asia in the age of commence, was carried from India to Southeast Asia as a cash crop explicitly grown for the market. Reid argued that the involvement of hundreds of thousands of Southeast Asians in cultivating and marketing pepper in response to world demand was one of the most overt economic consequences of the trade boom. As such, Southeast Asia provided many of the goods that dominated global long-distance trade, the elements essential to the creation of merchant capitalism in Europe.

The boom in exports stimulated a rapid increase in imports of consumption products, most noticeably Indian cloth, at a value of about 40 ton silver equivalent per year, at the height of the age of commerce from 1620 to 1650 (Reid 1990: 22–23). This flourishing commerce enabled a large percentage of the population to live on food supplied not by local but by long-distance trade. This trade was carried out by thousands of Southeast Asian junks, a distinct type of vessel incorporating elements of Chinese and Southeast Asian traditions. In the sixteenth century, at least six cities in Southeast Asia (Thang Long, Ayutthaya, Aceh,

Banten, Makassar, and Mataram) had a population of 100,000, equivalent to most contemporary European cities except for Paris, London, and Amsterdam (Reid 1993: 72–73). As such, these cities were larger in 1600 than they were in 1850. Reid's finding overthrew the conventional view in which urbanization went hand in hand with colonization and the peasantry was placed at the heart of "traditional" Southeast Asia. He further argued that the region was, in the age of commerce, an intensely mobile society both horizontally and vertically, in which the functions of farmer, trader, warrior, and chief were often combined in one extended family or even one individual.

These multiethnic market cities witnessed the most intensive process of both Islamization and Christianization in Southeast Asia. More than half the population of the region adopted Islam or Christianity during the age of commerce, leaving a permanent impact on the course of Southeast Asian history. Ironically, Reid argued, the arrival of the Portuguese and Spaniards, who were determined not only to make Christian converts but also to destroy Muslim trading dominance, was a stimulus to the spread of Islam. Islam was still a minority coastal phenomenon when the Portuguese arrived in the early 1500s. Their takeover of Melaka in 1511 and their consequent expulsion of Muslim spice trade merchants created a diaspora of Muslim traders who established their trading centers in Aceh, Johor, Pahang, and Patani. Islam proliferated from these port towns to the hinterland, whereas Christianity quickly converted most Filipinos and large numbers of Vietnamese. Parallel to this was a marked shift to a more universalist and moralist emphasis of Theravada Buddhism in Burma, Siam, southern Vietnam, and Cambodia and an enforcement of neo-Confucian orthodoxy in northern Vietnam. All these changes fragmented Southeast Asian countries, on the one hand, but led them in a similar direction, on the other. They strengthened the appeal of universal moral codes, which were reinforced by written scriptures and a system of eternal rewards and punishments.

Scriptural religion and the enhanced prestige of the rulers in turn reduced the power of local nobility and helped in the formation of centralized states. These entities owed their power largely to the wealth and military expertise that came with international trade. The absolutist states being created in this age drastically changed the oligarchic style of governance commonly found in the island kingdoms in Southeast Asia in the beginning of the age of commerce. The necessity of trying to survive under the external pressure from the (Dutch) United East India Company (VOC) sped up this process. According to Reid, the shift toward centralized rule, the mobilization of huge armies, the royal monopoly of trade, and the codification of law were all consequences of the age of commerce. Kings, who by then considered themselves "universal" monarchs, recognized no real legal restraints on the royal will, and consequently, there were no clear safeguards for private property. Tensions developed between royal authority and the market as this lack of security undermined commercial initiative and profit accumulation.

At the peak of the age of commerce, Southeast Asia shared similarities with Europe and Japan in that it had advanced more rapidly than most parts of the world. This is evident in terms of the integration into world trade, the commercialization of production and consumption, the growth of cities, the specialization of economic functions, the monetization of taxation, and the rapid improvements in the military and transport technology. Yet Southeast Asia differed from Europe and Japan in terms of the accumulation and mobilization of capital in private and corporate hands. These characteristics became fatal when Southeast Asia was facing the aggressive European expansion into the region. Reid pinpointed 1650 as a turning point. In 1600, Southeast Asians interacted as equals with Europeans, but by 1700, the inequalities between them were clear. Europeans had altered the balance of power by their superior naval firepower, impregnable fortresses, and Asian allies. As a consequence, the states most dependent on trade wealth were the most vulnerable and the first to fall victim to European arms: Melaka (1511), Pegu (1600), Banda (1621), Makassar (1669), and Banten (1682). The prosperous indigenous ports of the fifteenth, sixteenth, and seventeenth centuries declined, and by the 1630s, Dutch Batavia and Spanish Manila became Southeast Asia's most important international ports.

Reid's work demonstrated that the age of commerce remade Southeast Asia and enabled it to play a leading role in global commerce. As commerce declined, so did the role of merchants, the growth of cities, and the cosmopolitan character of the society. The seventeenth century marked not only a retreat from reliance on the international market but also a greater distrust of external ideas. Reid's *Age of Commerce,* as pointed out by many in the field, raised early modern Southeast Asian historiography to a new level of sophistication and synthesis. For sheer originality, breadth of vision, and encyclopedic brilliance, these volumes have no equal.

LI TANA

See also Aceh (Acheh); Ayutthaya (Ayuthaya, Ayudhya, Ayuthia) (1351–1767 C.E.), Kingdom of; Banten (Bantam); Batavia (Sunda Kalapa, Jakatra, Djakarta/Jakarta); British Interests in Southeast Asia; Chinese in Southeast Asia; Dutch Interests in Southeast Asia from 1800; East India Company (EIC) (1602), English; Economic Transformation of Southeast Asia (c. 1400–ca. 1800); Hanoi (Thang-long); Islam in Southeast Asia; Melaka; Ming Dynasty (1368–1644); Pepper; Portuguese Asian Empire; Spanish Expansion in Southeast Asia; Spices and the Spice Trade; Vereenigde Ooste-Indische Compagnie (VOC) ([Dutch] United East India Company) (1602)

References:

Reid, Anthony. 1988. *Southeast Asia in the Age of Commerce, 1450–1680.* Vol. 1, *The Lands below the Winds.* New Haven, CT: Yale University Press.

———. 1990. "An 'Age of Commerce' in Southeast Asian History." *Modern Asian Studies* 24, no. 1: 1–30.

———. 1992. "Economic and Social Change, c. 1400–1800." Pp. 460–507 in *The Cambridge History of Southeast Asia.* Vol. 1, *From Early Times to c. 1800.* Edited by Nicholas Tarling. Cambridge: Cambridge University Press.

———. 1993. *Southeast Asia in the Age of Commerce, 1450–1680.* Vol. 2, *Expansion and Crisis.* New Haven, CT: Yale University Press.

AGENCY HOUSES, EUROPEAN

Agency houses were large European firms that dominated the economies of Southeast Asia in the colonial era (ca. 1800–ca. 1965). They became central to the region's economic growth because of their dual commercial role—first, as the agents for European manufacturers, shipping lines, and insurance companies, and second, as the managing agents of investments in primary production (for example, rubber estates). In these ways, the agency houses linked European financiers and manufacturers with investment and trading opportunities in Southeast Asia. Distant investors could relax in the knowledge that their capital was being managed "on the spot" by Europeans with local expertise. Manufacturers, meanwhile, avoided the need to set up their own sales branches, distributive networks, and factories.

The agency houses were predominantly British. Merchant firms—such as Guthrie & Company—set up in Singapore following British annexation in 1819. At first, they focused on trading activities, exchanging Straits produce for British goods. Toward the end of the nineteenth century, however, the agency houses took on new roles as promoters of fixed investments. Following the extension of British authority to the Malay States after 1874, the Singapore firms expanded into the peninsula through diversification into plantations and mines. In particular and from the 1900s, they channeled money from the city of London into rubber plantations. In being awarded managerial and secretarial functions as well as seats on boards of directors, the agency houses came to control clusters of companies they often did not own. By 1931, for example, Guthries was the managing agent for twenty-six planting companies with £6 million in capital, presiding over 52,800 hectares of rubber and 4,200 hectares of oil palms. The British houses also extended their trading and investment interests from Singapore into British Borneo. The Borneo Company Limited (BCL) exercised a virtual monopoly in Sarawak, and Harrisons & Crosfield became a major extractor of timber from North Borneo. In Burma, similar developments took place from the 1860s. Steel Brothers & Company built up a vast commercial portfolio encompassing rice, timber, oil, cotton, tin, imports, shipping, manufacturing, rubber, and insurance. The tentacles of the agency houses also spread into independent Thailand, where, for instance, the BCL had vast investments in the teak industry—British colonial rule was not essential for the success of the agency house.

Concurrently, the British firms played a central role in the economic development of the Netherlands (Dutch) East Indies (Indonesia). After 1906, Harrisons & Crosfield became a major promoter of rubber companies on Sumatra and tea companies on Java. Even so, there were four huge Dutch firms with wide-ranging activities that compared with the British agency houses and rose to prominence after the liberalization of Indies trade in the 1870s. The Borneo-Sumatra Company, for example, engaged in activities ranging from merchanting to mining. The Dutch specialist managing agencies (*administratie kantoors*) and agricultural finance corporations (*cultuurbanken*) also performed managerial and investment functions akin to those of the British agency houses. Dutch and, before the Great War (1914–1918), German merchants were also to be found in Singapore. But the British, Dutch, and German firms could not penetrate French Indochina, where the protectionist policies of the colonial administration ensured that about ten French import-export firms monopolized trade with France by 1914. In contrast to their British and Dutch equivalents, however, the French merchants tended not to venture into plantations or mines. Rather, the promotion of fixed investments, from the 1920s, was the role of giant finance corporations, or *banques d'affaires,* that directly owned and managed a number of subsidiaries.

The agency houses weathered the depression of the 1930s and returned to Southeast Asia after the Japanese occupation (1941–1945). Yet in the postwar era of decolonization and economic nationalism, it made sense to spread risks and diversify geographically. Most of the British houses established branches and investments in North America and Australasia. In independent Burma (Myanmar) and Indonesia, British and Dutch assets were nationalized. In Malaysia, the big British firms continued to operate after independence (1957) and diversified into local manufacturing. But the government's New Economic Policy (NEP) (1971–1990) forced the agency houses into Malaysian ownership and control during the 1970s and 1980s, and by that time, they had been superseded by Japanese capital.

Nevertheless, at their height in the late colonial period, the agency houses had proved to be the linchpins of modern capitalism in Southeast Asia, linking the region to the industrialized world. In recent scholarship, the British agency houses have been termed "investment groups"; they have been recognized as crucial to British economic expansion in Southeast Asia and beyond, and it is estimated that they commanded financial resources equivalent to those of some of the larger industrial firms in metropolitan Britain. The heads of the agency houses had close links with the city of London, but their influence over colonial administrations and imperial governments was limited. Despite the relative decline of the British economy, the agency houses remained dynamic and enterprising into the late twentieth century.

NICHOLAS J. WHITE

See also British Borneo; British Burma; British Malaya; Burma under British Colonial Rule; Decolonization of Southeast Asia; French Indochina; Great Depression (1929–1931); Guided Democracy *(Demokrasi Terpimpin);* Java; Netherlands (Dutch) East Indies; New Economic Policy (NEP) (1971–1990) (Malaysia); Rubber; Sarawak and Sabah (North Borneo); Singapore (1819); Singapore (Nineteenth century to 1990s), Entrepôt Trade and Commerce of; Sumatra; Tin; Vietnam under French Colonial Rule; Western Malaya States (Perak, Selangor, Negri Sembilan, and Pahang)

References:
Allen, G. C., and A. G. Donnithorne. 1957. *Western Enterprise in Indonesia and Malaya: A Study in Economic Development.* London: Allen & Unwin.
Drabble, J. H., and P. J. Drake. 1981. "The British Agency Houses in Malaysia: Survival in a Changing World." *Journal of Southeast Asian Studies* 12: 297–328.
Jones, G., and J. Wale. 1999. "Diversification Strategies of British Trading Companies: Harrisons & Crosfield, ca. 1900–ca. 1980." *Business History* 41, no. 2: 69–101.
Murray, Martin J. 1980. *The Development of Capitalism in Colonial Indochina (1870–1941).* Berkeley: University of California Press.
White, N. J. 1996. *Business, Government, and the End of Empire: Malaya, 1942–57.* Kuala Lumpur: Oxford University Press.
———. 1998. "The Diversification of Colonial Capitalism: British Agency Houses in

Southeast Asia during the 1950s and 1960s." Pp. 12–40 in *Dynamic Asia: Business, Trade and Economic Development in Pacific Asia*. Edited by Ian G. Cook, Marcus A. Doel, Rex Y. F. Li, and Yongjang Wang. Aldershot, England: Ashgate.

AGRICULTURAL INVOLUTION

The concept of involution was brought to prominence by the American anthropologist Clifford Geertz in his historical and ecological study of social, cultural, and economic changes among Javanese peasants under Dutch colonialism (Geertz 1963). He attempted to explain the reasons for Indonesia's failure to modernize and industrialize in comparison with Japan. He identified the obstacles to economic evolution or revolution in the particular kinds of colonial policies and practices that the Javanese experienced during the nineteenth and early twentieth centuries.

Geertz argued that with the introduction by the Dutch colonial state of the forced cultivation of cash crops such as sugar and coffee in 1830 and then the development of commercial, plantation agriculture from the 1870s, Javanese society was stifled; it turned in on itself and became internally so elaborate and complex that the villagers were locked into a "permanent transition." The Dutch did this by using Javanese land and labor for the cultivation of crops for the world market while confining the farmers to the rice subsistence sector. This dualism was made possible by the properties of irrigated agriculture, in contrast to the forest-based shifting cultivation practiced in Indonesia's Outer Islands. Wet-rice cultivation can support increasing population densities, and it responds to agricultural intensification. Therefore, the Javanese, without access to the Dutch-dominated cash crop sector, squeezed more and more of their number into the rice sector, dividing up and redistributing work and production. This resulted in a high level of peasant socioeconomic homogeneity, a large number of small rice farms, and what Geertz called "shared poverty."

Geertz's work has been the subject of much debate and criticism, particularly by historians such as Robert van Niel (1992). Geertz's critics draw attention to his oversimplified picture of the country's ecology; the evidence of marked inequalities in rural landownership, wealth, and power; the considerable variations among population density, rice cultivation, cash crop agriculture, and land tenure across Java; the dynamism rather than involution in Javanese rural areas; and the increase in rural prosperity in the nineteenth century, particularly among those who owned land. Geertz has also defended his thesis and responded to his critics (1984).

VICTOR T. KING

See also Cultivation System (*Cultuurstelsel*); Forced Deliveries; Java; Netherlands (Dutch) East Indies

References:

Geertz, Clifford. 1963. *Agricultural Involution: The Processes of Ecological Change in Indonesia.* Berkeley and Los Angeles: University of California Press.
———. 1984. "Culture and Social Change: The Indonesian Case." *Man* 19: 511–532.
van Niel, Robert. 1992. *Java under the Cultivation System: Collected Writings.* Verhandelingen van het Koninklijk Instituut voor Taal-, Land- en Volkenkunde, 150. Leiden, the Netherlands: KITLV Press.

AGUINALDO, EMILIO (1869–1964)
Filipino Revolutionary Leader

Emilio Aguinaldo y Famy was a general in the Philippine Revolution and the founder and president of the first Philippine republic. He led the fight against the Spanish colonial regime during the first phase of the revolution and the fight against the Americans during the second.

Aguinaldo was born in the town of Kawit, in the province of Cavite, on 22 March 1869, the son of a well-to-do family. He started his secondary schooling in Manila, but when his father died, he had to discontinue his studies for financial reasons. He then worked on the agricultural family holdings in his hometown. In 1895, he was elected municipal captain in Kawit. In that year, he also joined the Katipunan, the secret association founded and led by Andres Bonifacio (1863–1897) that strove to mobilize Filipinos against oppressive Spanish rule in the islands. In August 1896, the revolution started with uprisings in Manila, the capital, and in the nearby provinces. The Spanish colonial government was repressive in its clampdown. Spanish forces marched against the

Emilio Aguinaldo was a Filipino leader who fought first against Spain and later against the United States for the independence of the Philippines around the turn of the twentieth century. (Library of Congress)

ill-prepared rebels and defeated them in several places. However, in Cavite, the rebel troops, ably led by Aguinaldo, defeated the Spanish forces repeatedly and drove them out of the province.

The revolutionary movement in Cavite consisted of two rival factions. The Katipunan chapter in Kawit, which was given the symbolic name *Magdaló* (after Maria Magdalena) and was led by Aguinaldo, thought that the time had come to replace the Katipunan organization with a new revolutionary government. The council in the town of Noveleta, with the symbolic name *Magdiwang* and associated with the Katipunan *supremo* (supreme head) Bonifacio (1963–1897), opposed the move. In March 1897, the two councils convened in Tejeros,

Cavite, and a majority decided to elect a revolutionary government, with Aguinaldo as president. Andres Bonifacio, who attended the meeting, disagreed and opposed the new government. Aguinaldo then ordered the arrest of Bonifacio; he was charged with sedition and treason before a military court. Bonifacio was sentenced to death and executed on 10 May.

In June, a strong Spanish army defeated the rebel forces and regained control over Cavite. Aguinaldo moved the revolutionary government to the town of Biyak na Bato in the province of Bulacan. Negotiations started between the Spanish government and the revolutionary government. In December 1897, an agreement was reached—the Pact of Biyak na Bato—on the following terms: (1) 800,000 pesos would be paid to Aguinaldo and other revolutionary leaders, who would then go into voluntary exile in Hong Kong; (2) 900,000 pesos would be paid to other revolutionaries, who would remain in the Philippines; (3) the rebels would promise to surrender their arms; (4) a general amnesty for all would be granted; and (5) the Spaniards would verbally promise to institute reforms in the colony. With two Spanish generals as hostages, Aguinaldo and a number of revolutionary leaders then went to Hong Kong.

In the first half of 1898, a number of developments took place. The two parties to the agreement accused each other of breaking the pact. In April, war broke out between Spain and the United States, and the American fleet destroyed the Spanish fleet in Manila Bay. Aguinaldo returned to the Philippines and resumed the leadership of the revolutionary movement. On 12 June 1898, Aguinaldo proclaimed Philippine independence at his home in Cavite. In August, American forces seized Manila, and Spanish military and civil officials started to evacuate their positions throughout the country, which were quickly taken over by the revolutionaries. In November, a congress of representatives convened in Malolos adopted the Constitution of the Philippine Republic. In January 1899, Aguinaldo was inaugurated as president of the new republic, and he formed a cabinet, with Apolinario Mabini (1864–1903) as prime minister.

The U.S. government, having concluded the Treaty of Paris with Spain on 10 December 1898 and claiming jurisdiction over the Philippines, did not accept Philippine independence.

In February 1899, war broke out between the United States and the Philippine Republic, a conflict usually referred to in U.S. history textbooks as the Philippine Insurrection. Facing a strong American army, the revolutionaries resorted to guerrilla warfare. In June, a conflict erupted between Aguinaldo's staff and General Antonio Luna, leading to an incident in which Luna was killed. Under pressure from the bloody American campaign and confronted with overwhelming forces, Aguinaldo's troops retreated to the north. From June 1899 until March 1901, Aguinaldo and his dwindling group of followers succeeded in evading the U.S. military columns chasing them.

When he was finally captured in March 1901, Aguinaldo took an oath of allegiance to the United States and issued a manifesto urging the Filipinos to lay down their arms. After that, he retreated from public life to manage his farm in Cavite. In 1935, during the first elections of the Philippine Commonwealth, Aguinaldo ran for president, but he lost to Manuel Quezon (1878–1944). During the Japanese occupation of the Philippines (1942–1945), Aguinaldo was appointed a member of the Japanese-controlled Council of State, a move that postwar Filipino officials did not hold against him. In 1962, President Diosdado Macapagal (t. 1961–1965) officially proclaimed the date of 12 June as Philippine Independence Day, acknowledging Aguinaldo's proclamation of 1898. Emilio Aguinaldo died on 6 February 1964.

Filipino historians have portrayed him with some ambiguity. On the one hand, he was the leader of the revolution and the president of the first republic, but on the other, he was tainted by the fact that he ordered the execution of Andres Bonifacio and may have been involved in the murder of Antonio Luna. For some scholars (Constantino 1975), he epitomizes the leading role of the landowning elite in the revolution.

WILLEM WOLTERS

See also Collaboration Issue in Southeast Asia; *Ilustrados;* Katipunan; La Liga Filipina; Mabini, Apolinario (1864–1903); Philippine Revolution (1896–1898); Philippine War of Independence (1896–1902); Philippines under Spanish Colonial Rule (ca. 1560s–1898); Rizal, Jose (1861–1896); Spanish-American Treaty of Paris (1898); Spanish-American War (1898)

References:

Agoncillo, Teodoro A., and Milagros C. Guerrero. 1977. *History of the Filipino People.* Quezon City, the Philippines: R. P. Garcia Publishing.

Constantino, Renato C., with the collaboration of Letiza R. Constantino. 1975. *The Philippines: A Past Revisited.* Quezon City, the Philippines: Renato C. Constantino.

Corpuz, O. D. 1989. *The Roots of the Filipino Nation.* 2 vols. Quezon City, the Philippines: Aklahi Foundation.

AGUNG, SULTAN OF MATARAM (r. 1613–1645)
Javanese Imperialist

Sultan Agung, the son of Seda-ing Krapyak (r. 1601–1613) and grandson of Senapati (r. 1582–1601), is regarded as the greatest Indonesian conqueror since the fourteenth century. He did not formally assume the title of sultan until 1641.

Agung undertook expeditions to expand the boundaries of his kingdom of Mataram, beginning with attacks on the southern region of Surabaya in 1614. In 1615, he captured Wirasaba, a strategic city that guarded the entrance to the lower Brantas Valley. Next, Agung was able to attain temporary allegiance from Pajang, which proved crucial to his effective decimation of the Surabayan army sent to stall his progress in January 1616. Agung's victory over the Surabayan army paved the way for further successes in subjugating Javanese cities: Lasem in 1616, Pasuruhan in 1617, and Tuban in 1619. By 1620, only Surabaya remained. Mataram carried out a five-year siege that eventually led to Surabaya's surrender. By 1625, Mataram had become the sole sovereign power in central Java. Balambangan in the east and Banten in western Java remained autonomous, but these polities were incapable of challenging Agung's military prowess.

Early in Agung's reign, a new player began to establish its presence in Java. This new force was the Dutch East India Company (VOC), and it gained a foothold in West Java in 1619, which the company renamed Batavia. The VOC was able to establish a presence there because Agung was initially more interested in pacifying and bringing other Javanese rulers under his control than in challenging the strength of the Dutch.

His earlier neglect of the Dutch and the deeply entrenched distrust between Mataram and its coastal vassals allowed the opportunistic Dutch to wrench power from Sultan Agung's successors after his death in 1645.

Though Agung's success was based mainly on his military superiority, part of his authority was founded on his ability to establish a cult of personality that attracted other, lesser rulers to him. He was skilled at balancing centralized legitimacy and decentralized administration. Agung built a new capital at Kartasura between 1614 and 1622. Kartasura's palatial architecture utilized pre-Islamic iconography to symbolize the macrocosm. Agung's palace demonstrated a preference for the number four—for example, the presence of four high officials divided into two groups, two of the left and two of the right. The number nine—comprising the four cardinal directions, the four intermediate points, and the center—was also manipulated as a symbol of sacredness.

Agung reached the zenith of his power between 1625 and 1627, demonstrating his military superiority by engaging in constant wars against his lesser neighbors. His continued success in expanding his empire gave him an aura of invincibility. These repeated wars and resulting epidemics eventually took their toll on Agung's forces. Meanwhile, Agung began to turn his attention to the Dutch in Batavia, following his conquest of Surabaya in 1625. However, his forces did not set off until 1628. In fighting that continued over the course of a year, the Javanese suffered heavy losses. Agung's army was forced to retreat in 1629 after the Dutch withstood the Javanese siege, and the Javanese army began to suffer from diseases and starvation brought about by the refusal of another Javanese kingdom, Banten, to supply Agung with food. This defeat showed that Agung had overextended himself and overestimated his strength. Perhaps the greatest damage, however, was the destruction of the myth of Sultan Agung's invincibility.

The Mataram ruler had to continue to assert his authority by pursuing further campaigns of conquest. Between 1631 and 1636, he had to crush resistance from Sumedang and Ukur in West Java. The greatest threats, however, came from Central and East Java; these stemmed from religious authorities located in various pilgrimage sites. In 1630, Agung had to subdue opposition at Tembayat. He then erected a ceremonial gateway at the holy site, demonstrating his possession of spiritual as well as military prowess. In 1636, he subjugated Giri, another holy site. Giri, however, would only be completely overcome during the reign of Agung's grandson, Amangkurat II (r. 1677–1703). War continued to tear through the eastern half of Agung's empire from 1636 to 1640, when he finally conquered Balambangan.

In 1639, Agung sent an envoy to Mecca to request a new title in celebration of his impending victory over Balambangan. The ambassador returned in 1641 with authorization for a new title, Sultan Abdullah Muhammad Maulana Matarani. This move signaled the beginning of a period of peace. As the sultan neared the end of his life, he ordered the construction of a royal gravesite on top of a hill at Imogiri, which was to become the royal burial ground for many generations of kings. In 1646, Sultan Agung passed away; the probable cause of death was the epidemic that broke out in the city during the same year.

GOH GEOK YIAN

See also Amangkurat I (Sunan Tegalwangi) (r. 1645–1677); Amangkurat II (Adipati Anom) (r. 1677–1703); Banten (Bantam); Batavia (Sunda Kalapa, Jakatra, Djakarta/ Jakarta); Diseases and Epidemics; Mataram; *Pasisir;* Surabaya; Vereenigde Oost-Indische Compagnie (VOC) ([Dutch] United East India Company) (1602); *Wali Songo*

References:

De Graaf, H. J. 1958. "De regering van Sultan Agung, vorst van Mataram 1613–1645, en die van zijn voorganger Panembahan Seda-ing-Krapjak 1601–1613)" [The reign of Sultan Agung, king of Mataram 1613–1645, and that of his predecessor Penambahan Seda-ing-Krapjak 1601–1613]. *Verhandelingen van het Koninklijk Instituut voor Taal-, Land- en Volkenkunde,* vol. 23. Amsterdam: Koninklijk Instituut voor Taal-, Land- en Volkenkunde (KITLV).

Hall, D. G. E. 1981. *A History of South-East Asia.* 3d ed. New York: St. Martin's Press.

Ricklefs, M. C. 1974. *Yogyakarta under Sultan Mangkubumi, 1749–1792.* London: Oxford University Press.

———. 2001. *A History of Modern Indonesia since c. 1200.* Hampshire, UK: Palgrave.

AGUS SALIM, HAJI (1884–1954)
Modernist Muslim Nationalist

Haji Agus Salim was an Indonesian political leader and diplomat. He was born in Kota Gedang, Bukittinggi, in West Sumatra, the son of a government official and the cousin of Sutan Sjahrir (1909–1966). He studied at a Dutch secondary school in Batavia and was employed at the Dutch consulate in Jeddah from 1906 to 1909. He then worked in the public works department at Batavia before returning to his home village in Minangkabau to set up an elementary school, where he taught until 1915.

Salim first came into contact with Sarekat Islam (SI) in 1915 as a member of the political section of the police, sent to investigate rumors that the nationalist organization was planning a revolt supplied with German arms. Satisfied that the rumors were untrue, he left the police and joined SI. He subsequently played a prominent role in drafting the party's "Basic Principles" in 1921, becoming vice-president of the SI's central committee in 1923 and later chairman of the Dewan Partai (Party Council). He strongly backed the participation of SI in the *Volksraad* (People's Council), where he represented the party from 1921 to 1924 (and where he used the Indonesian language for the first time). Salim then turned his back on the *Volksraad* as a sham, recommending instead the adoption of Mohandas Gandhi's policy of noncooperation, which was refined into the Hidjrah policy (the noncooperation stance vis-à-vis the Dutch colonial government). During his years in SI, he was editor of a number of periodicals, such as *Bataviaasch Nieuwsblad, Neratja, Fadjar Asia,* and *Moestika.* In addition, he was active in the labor movement, in particular serving as secretary of the important pawnshop employees' union.

He visited Europe in 1929 as technical adviser to the Netherlands Trade Union Federation, and he attended an International Labor Organization (ILO) conference in Geneva. He also spent nearly a year in The Netherlands, where he met Dutch and Indonesian socialists and was particularly impressed by Mohammad Hatta (1902–1980). Despite his labor activities, he was strongly opposed to communist infiltration in SI and backed the expulsion of leftist elements from the party, believing they weakened its foundation in Islam (although one promi-

nent communist leader was his brother, Abdul Chalid). He was similarly wary of some of the forms of indigenous nationalism that were developing. For instance, in 1928, he warned that Sukarno (1901–1970) and others were elevating nationalism into a form of religion, and he pointed out the difference in principles between SI and Sukarno's Perserikatan Nasional Indonesia (PNI, Indonesian National Party). He also visited Mecca in 1927 as the SI representative to the abortive Second al-Islam Congress.

In 1936, Salim feared that stricter government regulations against noncooperating parties would leave the SI movement paralyzed, and he founded the Barisan Penjadar PSII (Partai Sarekat Islam Insaf) (meaning "Movement to Make the Sarekat Islam Conscious"), but his opposition to the party's policy of noncooperation led to his own expulsion from SI.

Although not involved in active politics in the following years, he did begin, in 1943, to provide linguistic and educational support to the Pembela Tanah Air (PETA, Defenders of the Fatherland)—the Indonesian voluntary army launched by the Japanese. In 1945, he played an important role in the Japanese-appointed Committee for the Preparation of Indonesian Independence. He was part of the subcommittee that drew up the Jakarta Charter, which, among other things, proclaimed the state was to be based upon "belief in God, with the obligation for adherents of Islam to carry out Islamic law."

In the following years, Salim served as the republic's deputy minister of foreign affairs and then as the principal foreign minister. He was the official chairman of the Indonesian delegation to the Asian Relations Conference convened by Indian prime minister Jawaharlal Nehru (t. 1947–1964) in India in 1947. This was followed by travels to the Middle East (West Asia), where he secured recognition of the new republic by a number of Arab countries and contracted important commercial treaties, most notably with Egypt. He was also a member of the republic's delegation that signed the Renville Agreement with the Dutch in January 1948. During the second Dutch "police action," he was arrested and imprisoned together with Sukarno and Sutan Sjahrir, in Brastagi and then in Prapat (near Lake Toba in Sumatra), before finally being taken to Bangka (off the east coast of Sumatra).

After 1950, Salim no longer held a cabinet post. In 1953, he went to the United States as a visiting professor at Cornell University and also addressed a colloquium at Princeton University. He died in November 1954.

Salim was one of the most prominent and respected figures in the new Indonesian republic, referred to fondly by his colleagues as "Indonesia's grand old man," and he was honored as a gifted linguist (fluent in nine languages) and a man of letters as well as a skilfull diplomat. Islam was central to his life and political vision, but he was also emphatic that democracy, socialism, and brotherhood lay at the heart of Islam. Writing in the periodical *Neratja* on 29 October 1921, he declared that the "aim of Islam is man's equality, complete and absolute justice, and the efforts and cooperation of all for the benefit of all." It was such convictions that made him a living symbol of the vital role of the modernist Muslim movement in Indonesian nationalism.

ANTHONY MILTON

See also Indonesian Revolution (1945–1949); Islamic Resurgence in Southeast Asia (Twentieth Century); Mohammad Hatta (1902–1980); Perserikatan Nasional Indonesia (PNI) (1927); Sarekat Islam (1912); Sjahrir, Sutan (1909–1966); Soekarno (Sukarno) (1901–1970); *Volksraad* (People's Council) (1918–1942)

References:

Agus Salim, Haji. 1954. *Djedjak langkah H. A. Salim: Pilihan karangan* [*In the Footsteps of H. A. Salim: Selected Essays*]. Jakarta: Tintamas.

Ingelson, J. E. 1979. *The Road to Exile: The Indonesian Nationalist Movement 1927–1934*. Singapore: Heinemann Education.

Kahin, George McT. 1952. *Nationalism and Revolution in Indonesia.* Ithaca, NY: Cornell University Press.

Noer, Deliar. 1973. *The Modernist Muslim Movement in Indonesia, 1900–1942.* Oxford: Oxford University Press.

Salam, Solichin. 1963. *Hadji Agus Salim: Pahlawan Nasional* [*Hadji Agus Salim: National Warrior*]. Jakarta: Djajamurni.

Seratus tahun Haji Agus Salim [*One Hundred Years of Haji Agus Salim*]. 1984. Jakarta: Sinar Harapan.

AIRLANGGA (r. 1019–1049)
King of Hindu-Buddhist Mataram

Airlangga was a king who reigned over mainly the eastern part of Java, Indonesia, in the eleventh century C.E. His distinction lies in the fact that during his reign, he ordered a project in dam construction along the course of the River Brantas, presumably guided by an integrated political and economic outlook. He emerged on the political scene within the context of a hegemonic rivalry over the control of trade between Śriwijaya in Sumatra and the prominent kingdoms in Java. The management of interstate trade relations and the issue of "political marriages" were central preoccupations of Airlangga's reign.

Airlangga's emergence appeared in his well-known bilingual (Sanskrit and Old Javanese) stone inscription of 963 śaka (the Burmese era beginning in 78 C.E.), now deposited at the Indian Museum of Calcutta, in which a reference was made to the mishap that befell Yawadwîpa, the kingdom ruled by his father-in-law. The mishap was called the *pralaya,* literally meaning "the end of the world." In Hindu cosmogony, the term means "the end of a cycle of creation," premeditated by the age of Kaliyuga in which all noble values have been disrupted. It is then to be followed by another cycle, beginning with very ideal conditions of virtue. The pralaya in 1016 C.E. referred to in the inscription was caused by an attack by the king of Wurawari, who until Ailangga had been considered an ally of Śriwijaya. The inscription further stated that, at that time, Airlangga (who was sixteen years old), together with Narottama (a faithful state dignitary), took refuge in the forests and lived with the hermits. He prepared himself spiritually and perhaps also physically. The fact is that he then became the king and restored the kingdom from the damaging pralaya.

Airlangga was born in the year 1000 C.E., and just before the tragedy, he married the daughter of King Dharmawangsa Tguh (r. 991–1007 C.E.), who reigned in Java before him. Airlangga himself was the son of Gunapriyadharmapatnî (also known as Mahendradattâ), who was possibly Dharmawangsa Tguh's sister and who married the Balinese king Udayana. It is important to note that the Java-Bali relation was accentuated by the use of Old Javanese script in Bali during Udayana's time.

As indicated by Balinese inscription, Udayana seemed to reign together with his consort, Mahendradattâ. Airlangga's marriage with Tguh's daughter could then be seen as a strengthening of the Java-Bali relation, which might have been not only political but cultural as well. Among the cultural reminiscences of Airlangga in Bali is the story of Calon Arang, a well-known narrative used for the ritual performance known by the same name: Calon Arang, or Barong-Rangda, enacts the perpetual battle between evil and virtue.

Between 1029 and 1037 C.E., Airlangga launched several campaigns to subdue his enemies and consolidate Java. The inscriptions noted that Wurawari, Wuratan, Lewa, Magĕhan, Hasin, and Wĕngkĕr resisted his advances. His sphere of influence extended over parts of West Java, as can be inferred from the use of the Old Javanese language (and not Old Sundanese) in the inscriptions of Jayabhupati, who reigned in West Java during Airlangga's time.

The first capital Airlangga established was at Wwatan Mas. But a siege forced him to abandon the place and move to Pâtakan. Then, in 1032 C.E., a new capital was erected at Kahuripan. An inscription of 1042 C.E., however, indicated that the capital at that time was Dahana (Daha or Dahanapura). His last capital was situated in the region of Pangjalu. The regions Pangjalu and Janggala were partitions of Airlangga's kingdom, later divided by him for the sake of his two sons.

Between 1035 and 1042, after the consolidation phase of his reign, Airlangga embarked upon programs that benefited agriculture and economics (primarily a river-control system) and cultural development (primarily in literature and architecture). His inscription of 959 śaka (1037 C.E.), found in Kelagen, East Java, mentioned the construction of a dam at Wringin Sapta in the area of the village of Kamalagyan. Taxes were reduced as a compensation for maintaining the dam, including security measures. With the River Brantas controlled, trading boats could travel farther upstream, all the way to Hujung Galuh.

Airlangga's inscriptions are known for the beauty of their language. Moreover, it was under his patronage that one of the two most beautiful Old Javanese poetical narratives was created, namely, the *Arjunawiwâha* written by Mpu Kanwa (the other one being the *Râmâ-yana*). This work is recognized as an original Javanese creation, using only the gist of the story gleaned from the Indian *Mahâbhârata*. In architecture, Airlangga is known for developing more specific traits of the house to indicate rank and privilege.

EDI SEDYAWATI

See also Bali; Hindu-Buddhist Period of Southeast Asia; Java; Kadiri (Kediri); Mataram; Srivijaya (Sriwijaya)

References:
Boechari. 1967–1968. "Rakryân Mahâmantri I Hino: A Study on the Highest Court Dignitary of Ancient Java up to the 13th Century A.D." *Journal of the Historical Society* (University of Singapore): 7–20.
———. 1968. "Srî Mahârâja Mapañji Garasakan: A New Evidence on the Problem of Airlangga's Partition of His Kingdom." *Majalah Ilmu-ilmu Sastra* 4, nos. 1–2: 1–26.
De Casparis, J. G. 1958. *Airlangga (Inaugural Speech).* Malang, Indonesia: University of Airlangga.
Sedyawati, Edi. 1998. "Architecture in Ancient Javanese Inscriptions." Pp. 72–73 in *Indonesian Heritage.* Vol. 8, *Architecture.* Edited by Gunawan Tjahjono. Singapore: Archipelago Press (Editions Didier Millet).
Sumadio, Bambang, ed. 1993. "Jaman Kuna." Pp. 157–314 in *Sejarah Nasional Indonesia.* Vol. 2. Edited by Marwati Djoened Poesponegoro. Jakarta: Balai Pustaka.
Tejowasono, Ninny Susanti. 2003. "Airlangga: Raja Pembaharu di Jawa pada abad ke-11 Masehi" [Airlangga: Innovative King in Java in the 11th century]. Ph.D. dissertation, University of Indonesia.

ALAUNG-HPAYA (r. 1752–1760)
Founder of the Konbaung Dynasty

After a period of severe disorder, Alaung-hpaya (r. 1752–1760) restored the hegemony of Upper Burma over western mainland Southeast Asia and founded Burma's last and most successful dynasty, that of the Konbaung kings.

In the 1730s and 1740s, the Restored Toungoo dynasty (1597–1752), which was based at Ava in Upper Burma, disintegrated through the combined effects of court factionalism, disorders in the military service system, price inflation, and imperial rebellions. Among the latter challenges, a revolt by the predominantly Mon population of Lower Burma, which seized Ava in 1752, was by far the most destructive, laying waste wide areas of the interior. Even before the capital fell, a number of bandit chiefs and strongmen in the north, many eager to supplant the stricken Toungoo house, built independent bases, and it was from the ranks of these contenders that Alaung-hpaya emerged. As hereditary headmen of Mok-hso-bo in the Mu Valley, Alaung-hpaya—or, as he was known originally, U Aung-zeya—was a member of the rural gentry and a man of relatively modest social station. But he capitalized on his extended family network, a nearly infallible strategic instinct, and a growing Burman-Mon ethnic polarization that he systematically nurtured. Insofar as self-identified Burmans were in a large majority in the Irrawaddy lowlands, ethnic opposition eventually proved fatal to the Mon-dominated Lower Burma kingdom.

Having proclaimed himself a royal "Embryo Buddha"—whence derived his posthumous name, Alaung [Embryo]-hpaya [Buddha]—the erstwhile headman began his reconquests. In early 1754, he expelled the southern garrison from Ava. In early 1755, the fall of Prome opened the way to the Irrawaddy Delta, where his armies seized a series of riverine towns, including Dagon, which he renamed Rangoon (meaning "the enemy is consumed"), and Syriam. Finally, in May 1757, he subjected Pegu, the last major Mon redoubt, to a horrific sack. In keeping with his universal religious claims, he presented his realm as a polyethnic domain, but in practice, his unabashed Burman partisanship and his sponsorship of Burman colonization hastened the collapse of Mon ethnicity and the forcible reintegration of Lower Burma into a Burman-led polity centered in the north. Reproducing arrangements started in the early seventeenth century, this geopolitical dispensation would continue until the British transferred the capital from Mandalay to Rangoon.

Following his southern victory, Alaung-hpaya devoted himself to administrative and religious affairs. He reorganized Toungoo military formations and founded de novo at least seventeen regiments, chiefly musketeers, composed of Upper Burmans with an enlivening influence or boost of Mons, French, Muslims, and Manipuris. To reverse the damage of recent decades, he gathered refugees and sponsored resettlement throughout the lowlands, appointed headmen, and strengthened fiscal administration. To provide his rough-and-ready court with suitable charters, he sponsored the best-known law code of the precolonial era, the Manu-kye Dhammathat, and a treatise on court punctilio.

Alaung-hpaya devoted the last two years of his life to attacking Shan principalities in the northeast, Manipur, and Siam. His Shan and Manipuri campaigns, both relatively successful, were defensive insofar as these areas had ravaged Upper Burma during the period of Toungoo debility. His grand invasion of Siam also had a defensive element because he feared Siam's support for renewed Mon disturbances, but in a broader sense, he sought to validate his increasingly strident millennial claims and to reproduce the Siamese triumphs of sixteenth-century Burman rulers. Yet ironically, his strategy of eschewing a north-south pincers attack defied the lessons of sixteenth-century campaigning. The invasion of Siam failed, and Alaung-hpaya himself died on the retreat, either from a war wound or from a venereal disease.

His sons were destined to subdue Siam (albeit temporarily), to strengthen their hold over the Shans, and to annex Arakan, but by the time of Alaung-hpaya's death, the essential achievements of early Konbaung rule had been realized. Whereas the Restored Toungoo court had been dominated by courtiers who were politically astute but militarily incompetent, the crisis of the mid-eighteenth century produced a new class of proven warriors. Expanding from Upper Burma to the coast and thence to the upland perimeter, Alaung-hpaya reversed the basic pattern by which the imperial territories had come apart. He also halted the loss of manpower to private networks, enlarged the royal service population, and created a more unified patronage system. In combination with a growing emphasis on commercial taxation under his sons, Alaung-hpaya's achievements would endure until the onset of the Anglo-Burmese Wars of the nineteenth century. In a broader sense, his work paralleled late-eighteenth-century, postcrisis consolidations in Siam and Vietnam and thus finalized an effective tripartite division of the mainland that would endure to the present.

VICTOR B. LIEBERMAN

See also Arakan; Burmans; Burma-Siam Wars;
First Ava (Inwa) Dynasty (1364–1527 C.E.);
Konbaung Dynasty (1752–1885); Mon;
Mons; Pegu; Rangoon (Yangon); Toungoo
Dynasty (1531–1752)

References:

Koenig, William. 1990. *The Burmese Polity,
1752–1819.* Ann Arbor: University of
Michigan Press.

Lieberman, Victor B. 1984. *Burmese
Administrative Cycles: Anarchy and Conquest,
c. 1580–1760.* Princeton, NJ: Princeton
University Press.

ALBUQUERQUE, AFONSO DE (ca. 1462–1515)

Portuguese Empire Builder

Afonso de Albuquerque was not the original
architect of the Portuguese Empire in Asia, but
he was chiefly responsible for laying its foundations by creating the chain of *fortalezas*
(fortresses) and *feitorias* (trading posts) in the Indian Ocean on which Lisbon's power came to
be based. Born around 1462 into a noble family
with royal blood and a long tradition of service
to the Portuguese Crown, he took part in military campaigns in Morocco and Castile and in
two expeditions in the Indian Ocean. In the
second of these campaigns, he captured Socotra
with Tristão da Cunha and invested Ormuz,
before being appointed governor of India in
1509. Earlier that year, his predecessor, Dom
Francisco de Almeida, had decisively defeated
an alliance of Mameluk Egypt and several Indian states at Diu, thus giving Albuquerque an
opportunity to achieve Portuguese dominance
of trade in the Indian Ocean.

In March 1510, Albuquerque captured Goa
and established his capital there. The previous
year, a Portuguese fleet commanded by Diogo
Lopes de Sequeira had been to Melaka and attempted to set up a feitoria but had been
thwarted by the hostility of the Muslim merchants. Therefore, in April 1511, Albuquerque,
with a force of only 800 Portuguese soldiers
and 200 Malabar mercenaries, sailed to Melaka;
on 25 July, he took the city and drove the sultan into exile. He spent five months in Melaka,
during which he built a fortress (A Famosa); established a Portuguese administration; minted a
coinage; and sent an embassy to Siam and an
expedition, led by António de Abreu, to

*Engraved portrait of Afonso de Albuquerque.
(Bettmann/Corbis)*

Maluku. After his return to India, Albuquerque
had to repossess Goa and Ormuz, and he attempted unsuccessfully to take Aden. He died
on 15 September 1515 within sight of Goa on
board the ship that was taking him there from
Ormuz.

JOHN VILLIERS

See also Melaka; Portuguese Asian Empire

References:

Birch, Walter de Gray. 1875–1884. *Commentaries
of the Great Afonso Dalbuquerque.* 4 vols.
London: Hakluyt Society.

Diffie, Bailey W., and George D. Winius. 1977.
*The Foundations of the Portuguese Empire,
1415–1580.* Minneapolis: University of
Minnesota Press.

Earle, T. F., and John Villiers. 1990. *Albuquerque, Caesar of the East: Selected Texts by Afonso de Albuquerque and His Son.* Warminster, UK: Aris and Phillips.

ALLIANCE PARTY (MALAYA/MALAYSIA)

The Alliance Party, or Perikatan, in Malay was initially a political organization composed of the three major political parties—the United Malays National Organization (UMNO), the Malayan Chinese Association (MCA), and the Malayan Indian Congress (MIC)—that formed the government of the Federation of Malaya between 1957 and 1963. The alliance was formed in Sabah in 1962 to forge a united force in negotiations related to the formation of Malaysia and was composed of organizations such as the United National Kadazan Organization (UNKO), the United Sabah National Organization (USNO), and the Sabah Chinese Association (SCA). In Sarawak, the Alliance was formed prior to the 1963 election, and it was composed of parties such as the Barisan Rakyat Jati Sarawak (BERJASA), the Parti Negara Sarawak (PANAS), the Sarawak National Party (SNAP), and the Sarawak Chinese Association (SCA). When Malaysia came into being in September 1963, the two Alliance parties in Sabah and Sarawak became closely linked to the Alliance of the Peninsula, thus facilitating the control of the two states from Kuala Lumpur.

Historically, the Alliance came into being rather accidentally. It began as an ad hoc and temporary electoral arrangement for the Kuala Lumpur municipal elections of 16 February 1952. It was fostered between the Kuala Lumpur branch of UMNO, headed by Dato Yahaya bin Dato Abdul Rahman, and the Selangor MCA, headed by the wealthy tin miner Lee Hao-shik (better known as Colonel H. S. Lee). Their joint announcement on 9 January came as a surprise to the headquarters of both parties, but the electoral pact was allowed to materialize nevertheless. The UMNO-MCA candidates won nine of the twelve contested seats, and the noncommunal Independence of Malaya Party (IMP), headed by Dato Onn bin Jaafar (1895–1962), secured only two. The success of the coalition in subsequent municipal elections cemented the UMNO-MCA "communal friendship."

When Dato Onn and the chief ministers of seven Malay states held a national conference in April 1953, UMNO-MCA boycotted it and organized its own national convention in August and October. The convention demanded more elected representatives in the federal and legislative councils and called for federal elections to be held no later than 1954. Toward the end of 1954, MIC, which had previously supported Dato Onn, left the national conference and joined the Alliance. Despite various communal and conflicting issues between them, the UMNO-MCA-MIC Alliance managed to enter the July 1955 federal election as one body, and it secured fifty-one of the fifty-two contested seats and 81 percent of the total votes. Guided by its election manifesto, *The Road of Independence,* the Alliance intensified its efforts toward ethnic conciliation and negotiation for political independence from Britain.

Due to the Alliance's overwhelming majority in the federal, state, and local councils, the Reid Constitutional Commission that was formed in 1956 to prepare the constitution for an independent Malaya afforded priority to the Alliance's representations. The commission's work was facilitated by prior agreements between the different communities within the Alliance.

Composed of three political parties representing three different communities with diverse ethnic and cultural backgrounds, the Alliance found that its stability was often threatened by internal disputes that were communal and partisan in nature. Extremists from each of the component parties frequently made demands that challenged the sensitivities and interests of other parties within the Alliance. However, the liberal attitude and exceptional ability of the top leadership, headed by Tunku Abdul Rahman Putra Al-Haj (1903–1990), managed to safeguard the continuity of the Alliance at least until 1969.

Externally, the Alliance had to face other political parties in the elections. It managed to chalk up victory after victory to form the government at the federal level and in most states. However, it was comparatively less successful in the overwhelmingly Malay-populated northeastern states of Kelantan and Terengganu and in the states populated by large numbers of non-Malays, such as Penang, Perak, and Selangor on the west coast of the peninsula. When Singapore was part of Malaysia from 1963 to 1965, it was ruled by the People's Action Party (PAP), which vigorously challenged the MCA for the leadership of the Chinese; after Singapore's separation, the Democratic Action Party (DAP) and the Gerakan Rakyat Malaysia (Gerakan) emerged to rival the MCA. In terms of the total votes at the federal level, the Alliance's performance in the various general elections is reflected in the following percentages: 81.7 percent (1955), 51.8 percent (1959), 58.4 percent (1964), and 48.4 percent (1969). Thus, by 1969, although still an overall winner, the Alliance garnered less than half of the total votes. At the state level, it secured only 47.95 percent that year, which was 10 percent less than in 1964. The mixed sense of anxiety within the Alliance and the uncontrolled jubilation among supporters of the non-Malay opposition parties contributed to the eruption of the 13 May 1969 disturbances, which led to the declaration of a state of emergency the following day.

After a series of negotiations following the reconvening of the Malaysian Parliament in February 1971, the Alliance was enlarged, and it was replaced in 1974 by the Barisan Nasional (BN, National Front), which saw former opposition parties such as the Pan-Malaysia Islamic Party (PAS), Gerakan, and the People's Progressive Party (PPP) as its components.

ABDUL RAHMAN HAJI ISMAIL

See also Abdul Rahman Putra Al-Haj, Tunku (1903–1990); Abdul Razak, Tun (1922–1976); Barisan Nasional (National Front) (1974); Malayan/Malaysian Chinese Association (MCA) (1949); Malayan/Malaysian Indian Congress (MIC); "May 13th, 1969" (Malaysia); Onn bin Jaafar (1895–1962); Parti Islam Se Malaysia (PAS); People's Action Party (PAP); United Malays National Organization (UMNO) (1946)

References:

Means, Gordon P. 1976. *Malaysian Politics.* London: Hodder and Stoughton.

Milne, R. S., and Diane K. Mauzy. 1980. *Politics and Government in Malaysia.* Singapore: Times Books International.

Vasil, R. K. 1980. *Ethnic Politics in Malaysia.* New Delhi: Radiant Publishers.

A. M. AZAHARI

See Azahari bin Sheikh Mahmud, Sheikh (1928–2002)

AMANGKURAT I (SUNAN TEGALWANGI) (r. 1645–1677)

A Murderous Reign

Amangkurat I was the son of Sultan Agung (r. 1613–1645) and the great-grandson of Senapati (r. 1582–1601). Amangkurat I assumed the throne during a trying time. The Javanese kingdom of Mataram was afflicted by epidemics, and the sudden nature of Sultan Agung's death in 1645 threatened to bring about chaos and succession disputes. The palace gates were secured during the coronation ceremony of Amangkurat I to avert a possible coup.

Amangkurat I was an ambitious ruler, much like Sultan Agung, but unlike his father, his attempts to unify the kingdom and bring about a centralized government were doomed to fail, due to two factors. The first was recorded in the Javanese chronicles known as the *Babad*. According to these sources, while Senapati was meditating at Sela Gilang, a falling star signified that Mataram would fall during Amangkurat I's reign. The second factor pertained to the conceited and designing nature of the sultan himself, for the arrogant Amangkurat I alienated many powerful people by his efforts to acquire absolute authority over all of Java. Unlike Sultan Agung, who was able to maintain a strong grip on his empire through military genius and prowess, Amangkurat I lacked fundamental military ability and leadership. He attempted to accumulate power either through coercion or by assassinating important nobles and military commanders.

Murder and tyranny characterized the almost macabre nature of Amangkurat I's reign. One of the sultan's victims was Tumenggung Wiraguna, whose wife was involved in a scandalous affair with the sultan when he was still the crown prince. In 1647, Amangkurat I sent Wiraguna to drive the Balinese forces from the Eastern Salient of Java; while there, the latter was conveniently disposed of. Other members of Wiraguna's family were subsequently killed as well. Amangkurat I's brother, Pangeran Alit, the patron of Wiraguna, feared for his life and assembled a force of devout Muslims to attack the royal palace. However, Amangkurat's troops repelled the assault, and the prince was killed in battle. Fearing further threats from the Islamic community, Amangkurat I ordered the massacre of all prominent Islamic leaders and their families, totaling approximately 5,000 to 6,000 people. Many of Sultan Agung's old associates were also murdered.

Amangkurat I's oppression extended to his immediate family as well. In 1659, the sultan ordered the killing of his own father-in-law, Pangeran Pekik of Surabaya, who was slaughtered together with most of his family. Even Amangkurat I's uncle was not exempted from his cruelty; he was, however, saved from the jaws of death by the timely intervention of the sultan's mother. Other nobles were not that lucky. Amangkurat I's period of rule can be characterized as a reign of terror during which the nobility and court officials lived in perpetual fear of the sultan's whimsical rages.

As Amangkurat I meted out terrible punishments to those he suspected of opposing his rule, he continued to alienate allies and vassals on the fringes of his empire. The 1647 expedition had failed to bring the Eastern Salient under Mataram's control, allowing the Balinese to raid the eastern coast. Two failed campaigns to Banten, in 1650 and 1657, by Mataram forces resulted in the estrangement of not only Banten but also Cirebon. By 1659 and 1663, Kalimantan and Jambi, respectively, had escaped from Mataram's control. Amangkurat I's desire to establish a centralized Mataram empire increasingly became a forlorn and unrealistic dream.

Amangkurat's lack of resourcefulness, compared with his father and the tyranny of his rule, led many vassals to reconsider the wisdom of maintaining allegiance to Mataram. Realizing that the sultan was not able to mobilize a large army, more and more vassals began to break away from the empire. Amangkurat also lacked foresight and charisma. He was an insecure man who lived in constant fear and distrust of his military officers and court officials, which contributed greatly to his failure to amass support, earn loyalty, and rule efficiently.

Amangkurat I also made another important mistake during his reign: he misconstrued the strength of the Dutch in Java. One of his greatest failings was his inability to recognize that not only did the Dutch East India Company (VOC) represent an important source of wealth, it was also an important political rival to his control over the peripheral areas of his now dwindling empire. His initially amicable relationship with the Dutch soon worsened, as the sultan's attempts to reestablish control over the north coast of Java repeatedly met with failure.

The oppressive rule of Amangkurat I eventually generated enough unhappiness and opposition to stimulate a rebellion, which broke out in 1675. This rebellion was part of a sequence of events that began with an attempted coup by the sultan's son, the crown prince, who eventually succeeded to the throne under the title Amangkurat II (r. 1677–1703). Even as the relationship between the father and the son became increasingly estranged, the crown prince began to cultivate the friendship of the Dutch. He also plotted with Raden Kajoran and Trunajaya to overthrow Amangkurat I. Trunajaya, a vassal ruler from the island of Madura, agreed to start a rebellion in favor of the crown prince. The rebellion reached its peak when Trunajaya's forces attacked the court of Amangkurat I at Plered in 1677. The *Babad* recounts that the rebel forces met little resistance at the court because the sultan allegedly had told his troops not to resist, as it was God's will that Mataram was to fall during his reign. Amangkurat I fled the court but did not survive long thereafter. He died a few months later and was buried at Tegalwangi on the northern coast of Java.

GOH GEOK YIAN

See also Agung, Sultan of Mataram (r. 1613–1646); Amangkurat II (Adipati Anom) (r. 1677–1703); Javanese Wars of Succession (1677–1703, 1719–1722, 1749–1755); Madura; Mataram; Vereenigde Oost-Indische Compagnie (VOC) ([Dutch] United East India Company) (1602)

References:
De Graaf, H. J. 1961–1962. *De Regering van Sunan Mangku-Rat I Tegal-Wangi, vorst van Mataram 1616–1677* [*The Reign of Sunan Mangku-Rat I Tegal-Wangi, King of Mataram 1616–1677*]. The Hague: M. Nijhoff.

De Graaf, H. J., and T. G. Th. Pigeaud. 1976. *Islamic States in Java, 1500–1700.* The Hague: M. Nijhoff.

Lombard, D. 1990. *Le Carrefour Javanais: Essai d'histoire globale* [*A Javanese Crossroad: Essay in World History*]. Paris: Éditions de l'École des Hautes Études en Sciences Sociales.

Ricklefs, M. C. 2001. *A History of Modern Indonesia since c. 1200.* Stanford, CA: Stanford University Press.

AMANGKURAT II (ADIPATI ANOM) (r. 1677–1703)
A Troubled Reign

Amangkurat II was the son of Amangkurat I (r. 1645–1677) and a Surabayan princess, the daughter of Pangeran Pekik. Adipati Anom, as he was known before his ascension to the throne as Amangkurat II, possessed an adversarial relationship with his father because of the murder of Pangeran Pekik and his family. However, Amangkurat II shared certain other interests with his father, the most prominent of which was a weakness for beautiful women. Ultimately, however, a contest for the affection of a woman between 1668 and 1670 led to a complete rupture between father and son. The crown prince had earlier attempted to overthrow his father in a failed coup in 1661. But that did not prevent Adipati Anom from hatching further plots to dethrone his father. A rebellion in 1675 eventually brought about the end of Amangkurat I's reign.

Adipati Anom grew up in a court marked by dissension, personal jealousies, and distrust, as various princes jostled for position. The Plered court was a dangerous place ruled by a tyrannical Amangkurat I, who did not tolerate mistakes. The crown prince learned at an early age that in order to succeed, he needed the support of parties from without, especially the powerful (Dutch) United East India Company (VOC, or *Kumpeni*). Adipati Anom was aware that the sultan was unpopular and realized that a successful rebellion might effectively oust him. He first attempted to gain the support of the Dutch by sending nine missions to Batavia. He next plotted with Raden Kajoran and Trunajaya, an alienated Madurese prince, to overthrow Amangkurat I. Trunajaya was more than willing to rebel against Amangkurat I: his own father had been murdered at court in 1656, and

his own life was threatened by the suspicious ruler.

In 1670, Adipati Anom and Trunajaya came to an agreement whereby Trunajaya was to start a rebellion against Amangkurat I; when the sultan was deposed, Adipati Anom would ascend the throne, and in return for his services, Trunajaya would be awarded control of Madura and part of East Java. Trunajaya gathered troops and successfully took control of Madura in 1671. Adherents flocked to his cause, and in 1675, the rebels carried out many attacks on the ports of East Java.

One year later, Adipati Anom was placed in charge of an army sent to suppress the rebellion. Amangkurat I might have arranged for the crown prince to be killed in battle, or perhaps the assignment was Adipati Anom's own idea, for he may have wanted to engage in a mock battle with Trunajaya to channel suspicion away from himself. In any case, Adipati Anom survived the battle, but a number of other princes were killed. In 1677, the rebels continued to expand the territory under their control. Most of Mataram's vassals succumbed to the demands of the rebels and ceased paying homage to Amangkurat I. Trunajaya enjoyed one success after another, and he began to entertain the ambition of seizing the throne for himself. Adipati Anom soon realized that he had lost control of the rebellion that he had incited.

In May 1677, the rebellion reached its peak when the forces of Trunajaya attacked and took the palace at Plered. Adipati Anom fled with his father, and his younger brother, Puger, was left to defend their retreat. Amangkurat I died a couple of months later, and the crown prince buried him at Tegalwangi. Armed with only the royal regalia, the crown prince began his reign as the new ruler, Susuhunan Amangkurat II. Without an army, a court, a treasury, or even a kingdom, the new ruler turned to the Dutch for assistance to fight the war and regain his throne.

In July 1677, Amangkurat II formed an alliance with the Dutch. He promised them the revenue from port duties, rice and sugar monopolies, land, and other rewards in return for help in regaining the throne. In 1678, the Dutch began expeditions to regain the ruler's territories. By late 1679, the rebels were in retreat. Trunajaya was captured and executed by Amangkurat II. With the assistance of the

Dutch, the ruler enjoyed a string of victories as more and more Javanese began to pledge allegiance to him. His younger brother, Pangeran Puger, still controlled the site of the old palace at Plered. Amangkurat II established a new court at Pajang, which he named Kartasura. But Puger and many other princes who survived the constant wars refused to recognize Amangkurat II's authority. Puger attacked Kartasura in 1681 but was defeated by the Dutch forces. His subsequent submission to Amangkurat II finally secured the latter's position.

As Amangkurat II's confidence grew, his relations with the Dutch cooled. He tried to renege on the concessions that he had promised the Dutch in 1677. And even as his relations with the Dutch gradually worsened, a rebellion against the Dutch broke out in West Java, led by a former slave of Balinese ancestry, Surapati. Surapati's forces also attacked a number of Dutch posts farther east, including Kartasura. Though the Dutch suspected the sultan of complicity, there is no evidence that he was directly allied with Surapati's cause. However, various members of the Kartasura court did supported the rebel leader, among them the crown prince, the son of Amangkurat II. The kingdom once again began to fall into disarray, as Surapati's power increased and competing factions within the court threatened the sultan's position. The Eastern Salient of Java was soon lost to the rebel. In a last bid for help, the king pleaded for reconciliation with the Dutch but was rejected. Amangkurat II died in 1703, throwing the Kartasura court into chaos as the crown prince, who was to become Amangkurat III (r. 1703–1704), competed with his uncle, Pangeran Puger, for the throne.

GOH GEOK YIAN

See also Amangkurat I (Sunan Tegalwangi) (r. 1645–1677); Javanese Wars of Succession (1677–1703, 1719–1722, 1749–1755); Madura; Mataram; Vereenigde Oost-Indische Compagnie (VOC) ([Dutch] United East India Company) (1602)

References:

Hall, D. G. E. 1981. *A History of South-East Asia.* 4th ed. New York: St. Martin's Press.

Raffles, Sir Stamford. 1965. *History of Java.* 2 vols., with an introduction by John S. Bastin. Kuala Lumpur and New York: Oxford University Press. First published in 3 vols. in 1817 and 1830 in London.

Reid, Tony, ed. 1995. *Indonesian Heritage.* Vol. 3, *Early Modern History.* Singapore: Archipelago Press (Editions Didier Millet).

Van Goens, Rijklof. 1956. *De vijf gezantschapsreizen van Rijklof van Goens naar het hof van Mataram, 1648–1654* [*The Five Missions of Rijklof van Goens to the Capital of Mataram, 1648–1654*]. The Hague: Martinus Nijhoff.

AMBON (AMBOINA/AMBOYNA) MASSACRE (1623)

The massacre at Ambon is one of the most notorious episodes in the turbulent history of Anglo-Dutch relations in the seventeenth century: indeed, it became the subject of a play, John Dryden's *Amboyna,* making propaganda in the Third Anglo-Dutch War (1672–1674). Yet the reasons for the massacre remain, even now, uncertain, and its impact on Anglo-Dutch relations has been a subject of controversy, too.

Ambon was a source of cloves, one of the fine spices so much sought after by the Europeans in a period when they were without effective food preservatives. The Dutch East India Company (VOC) was then far better capitalized than the English East India Company (EIC). Commercial competition in Asia was, however, accompanied by a political connection in Europe. In 1619, the EIC was allowed to establish factories alongside the Dutch ones in Maluku, in return for bearing one-third of the costs of the Dutch garrisons. That arrangement proved a burden that the English, enjoying only a limited share of the trade, could not bear. On 21 January 1623, the English council at Batavia (Jakarta) finally decided to withdraw from the eastern islands.

On 27 February, Gabriel Towerson, the chief English factor (merchant) at Ambon, was beheaded by order of the Dutch governor, Herman Van Speult, along with nine other Englishmen, ten Japanese, and a Portuguese. The charge was that they had planned to kill Van Speult and overwhelm the Dutch garrison as soon as an English ship arrived to support them. Some of the evidence came from a Japanese man under torture, and Towerson and his men confessed only under torture. Though Van

Speult may have been convinced, the conspiracy seems quite improbable: "The attempt had only been for Fools and Madmen," as Towerson says in Dryden's play (Dearing 1994: 71). There were only about twenty Englishmen at Ambon, and any ship that came was likely to be bringing instructions to leave. The letter of 21 January may not have arrived before the executions, but Van Speult acted with undue haste, given that the English were in alliance with the Dutch.

It is possible that the action was intended, in some measure, to set an example. In fact, historians have sometimes argued that the massacre prompted or at least confirmed the English decision to withdraw. They have gone on to argue that it marked the end of the EIC's commercial enterprise in the archipelago. The late David Bassett convincingly refuted both these points. Without at once dropping its trade in clove, the EIC built up its pepper trade from its factory in Bantam. It retreated to the western coast of Sumatra only in the 1680s.

NICHOLAS TARLING

See also Anglo-Dutch Relations in Southeast Asia (Seventeenth–Twentieth centuries); Banten (Bantam); Bengkulu (Bencoden, Benkulen); East India Company (EIC) (1600), English; Maluku (The Moluccas); Pepper; Spices and the Spice Trade; Vereenigde Oost-Indische Compagnie (VOC) ([Dutch] United East India Company) (1602)

References:

Bassett, David Kenneth. 1960. "The 'Amboyna Massacre.'" *Journal of Southeast Asian History* 1, no. 2: 1–19.

Dearing, Vinton A., ed. 1994. *The Works of John Dryden*. Berkeley: University of California Press.

ANAWRAHTA (ANIRUDDHA) (r. 1044–1077)

Founder of Pagan

Considered the first historical king of Pagan (Strachan 1996: 7), Anawrahta is credited with turning a small chieftainship in the dry zone of Upper Burma into the first Burman empire, which lasted until the Mongol invasions of 1287. Historical tradition also credits Anawrahta with an invasion of the Mon city of Thaton in 1057 that resulted in his deporting its Mon king Manuha, Theravada Buddhist priests and the Buddhist scriptures, and artisans and population to Pagan to inaugurate a renaissance in Buddhist culture in Pagan. It is said that prior to that point, the culture of Pagan was based on a mixture of *nat* (spirit) worship and elements of Mahayana Buddhism. Under the impact of the Theravada Buddhist culture, the literary life of eleventh-century Pagan flourished. Anawrahta and his chief priest, Shin Arahan, made Theravada Buddhism the official state religion of Pagan and commenced an era of monumental temple building, resulting, by the thirteenth century, in over 3,000 temples rising above the Pagan plain. Anawrahta's conquest of Thaton most likely had a strategic commercial motivation as well, for possession of this port gave him access to the lucrative international trade of the maritime provinces, an advantage later Pagan kings built on in establishing control over ports on the Tenasserim coast.

Pagan's economy became centered on temple building, thereby encompassing the means for its own demise (Aung-Thwin 1985). To escape the exactions of the king, well-to-do people donated wealth to the temples, constructed temples, and became temple slaves, thus denying resources to the Crown. This paradigm may have been repeated in successive Burmese empires.

The strength of Pagan's culture was undoubtedly its inclusiveness—its gift for syncretism that underpinned the development of its distinctive visual arts. Pagan culture was not distinctively Mon, as has been often supposed, but exhibited a Pyu base. Recently, Michael Aung-thwin (2001) questioned the entire legend of the conquest of Thaton and the import of Mon culture to Upper Burma, placing emphasis instead on the impact of the Pyu in the development of Pagan culture. He suggested that the technological, cultural, and political development in early Burma moved from the interior to the coasts rather than the other way around, and he considered the "Mon paradigm" a creation of colonial historians (Aung-thwin 2001).

HELEN JAMES

See also Buddhism; Buddhism, Mahayana; Buddhism, Theravada; Burmans; Mon;

Mons; Pagan (Bagan); Pyus; Temple
Political Economy

References:

Aung-thwin, Michael. 1985. *Pagan: The Origins of Modern Burma*. Honolulu: University of Hawai'i Press.

———. 2001. "The Legend That Was Lower Burma." Paper presented at the International History Conference "Texts and Contexts in Southeast Asia," Yangon University, December 2001.

Bode, Mabel Haynes. 1966. *The Pali Literature of Burma*. London: Royal Asiatic Society of Great Britain and Ireland.

Strachan, Paul. 1996. *Pagan: Art and Architecture of Old Burma*. 2nd ed. Arran, Scotland: Kiscadale Publications.

ANCIENT COINAGE IN SOUTHEAST ASIA

Prior to the rise of Melaka in the early fifteenth century, Southeast Asia possessed three distinct coin-producing subregions: (1) northern Vietnam; (2) a mainland zone extending from the Bay of Bengal through Burma (Myanmar), Thailand, Cambodia, and southern Vietnam; and (3) island Southeast Asia, including Indonesia, peninsular Thailand, Malaysia, and the Philippines.

In the late tenth century, the Dinh were the first independent Vietnamese rulers to issue their own coinage, consisting of square-holed, copper-alloy cast coins based upon the design of Chinese cash pieces that had circulated in the region for more than a millennium. Under the Dinh (968–980 C.E.), an inscription written in Chinese characters on the obverse included the reign title of the issuing monarch and the phrase *hungbao* (to prosper, precious); under the Early Ly dynasty (980–1009 C.E.), the secondary phrase became *tranbao* (to guard, precious). The dynastic name was often included on the reverse. This Chinese-inspired tradition of cast coinage was maintained by later Vietnamese dynasties, and it continued unabated through the nineteenth century.

The first coinage of mainland Southeast Asia proper had its origins in the coastal zone of Lower Burma. By the fifth century, the ancient Mon had initiated a silver Conch/Temple coin type that would influence numismatic productions on the mainland for nearly four hundred years. The ancient Pyu of central Burma issued an extensive series of struck silver coins derived from the Conch/Temple series—a Rising Sun type as well as a series impressed with an hourglass-drumlike design. Both were issued in multiple denominations. Central Thailand under Mon Dvaravati saw similar coinage issues, supplemented by an extraordinary series of rare, inscribed dedicatory medals. By the early ninth century, this diverse numismatic tradition was at an end. Subsequent coin production in Thailand, first under Sukhothai and later under Ayudhya (Ayuthia; Ayutthaya), took a unique form—small, elongated struck silver (and occasionally gold) pieces of globular shape commonly known as "bullet" coinage. Burma proper would not see coinage again until the eighteenth century.

Deva rulers in southeastern Bengal minted Gupta-style gold coinage for at least two hundred years following the latter's demise in the mid-sixteenth century. In neighboring Arakan (on Burma's west coast), Candra kings and their successors between the fifth and eleventh centuries struck a Southeast Asian–style silver Bull/Trident coinage, a type also favored by southeastern Bengal's Harikela rulers. This series continued through the eleventh century. Beginning in the thirteenth century, Turkic rulers established mints in Bengal and Assam as an explicit statement of Islamic control over the region.

Indigenous silver and gold coin issues first appeared in south-central Java at the end of the eighth century. This so-called Sandalwood Flower coinage—consisting of a simple, four-petaled design on the obverse of the coin and a single Devanagari letter opposite—eventually spread to Sumatra, the Malay Peninsula, Bali, and the Philippines. Derivative types included large slablike silver and gold stamped ingots and a nearly spherical gold series known in the Philippines as *piloncitos* (named after the conical shape of coarse brown sugar sold in the marketplace). By the end of the thirteenth century, this native tradition was supplanted by the widespread adoption of low-value imported Chinese copper cash.

The initial series of Islamic-style coinage in island Southeast Asia was a diminutive, epigraphic gold type containing (on the obverse) the phrase *malik al-zahir* (the victorious king) together with the name of the issuing ruler and (on the reverse) *al-sultan al-'adil* (the just sultan). These coins were first struck at Samudra/Pase in northern Sumatra in the late thirteenth century. Struck to the indigenous 0.60-gram *kupang* standard, north Sumatra gold under Samudra/Pase's successor, Aceh, became a staple in Southeast Asian commercial transactions.

Due to the difficulty of acquiring specimens from clearly defined archaeological contexts, the precise function of coinage in early Southeast Asia remains imperfectly understood. Rising Sun issues were often struck in multiple denominations and have been found over a large geographic area, an indication that they likely served an exchange function in the marketplace. Other types, such as Dvaravati medals, with a much more limited geographic distribution and no significant wear, were probably used chiefly in ritual deposits and for personal adornment.

One of the most intriguing problems facing the student of early Southeast Asian coinage is why some areas that displayed otherwise high levels of cultural achievement, maintained extensive commercial ties, and possessed relatively complex monetary systems based upon units of silver and cloth—areas such as ancient Cambodia under Angkor or Burma's Pagan—did not adopt coinage as a facilitator in monetary transactions.

ROBERT S. WICKS

See also Banks and Banking; Dvaravati; Ly Dynasty (1009–1225); Tun-sun

References:

Mitchiner, Michael. 1998. *The History and Coinage of South East Asia until the Fifteenth Century.* Sanderstead, England: Hawkins Publications.

Wicks, Robert S. 1992. *Money, Markets, and Trade in Early Southeast Asia: The Development of Indigenous Monetary Systems to AD 1400.* Ithaca, NY: Cornell Southeast Asia Program.

———. 1999. "Indian Symbols in a Southeast Asian Setting: Coins and Medals of Ancient Dvaravati." Pp. 8–18 in *Art from Thailand.* Edited by Robert L. Brown. Mumbai, India: Marg Publications.

ANDA Y SALAZAR, DON SIMON DE (1710–1766)
Spanish Patriot

Don Simon de Anda y Salazar was a Spaniard who distinguished himself in the service of the Spanish colonial government in the Philippines during the British invasion of the islands in 1762. He organized forces to resist the British and kept the Spanish administration functioning even as the British established their own government in Manila. He was recognized for his feats by being named governor-general in 1769. As governor-general, he sought to reduce the hold of the friars and implemented orders to shift power to secular priests.

Anda was born in 1710, and by 1761, he was an official in the Spanish colonial government in the Philippines. He was formally appointed a judge (*oidor*) in the Royal Audiencia in Manila in that year.

In 1762, the British invaded Manila as a consequence of the Seven Years' War (1756–1763) in Europe. The acting governor-general of the Philippines, Archbishop Manuel Antonio Rojo, seeing the imminent danger of Manila falling into the hands of the British, appointed Anda as lieutenant governor and captain general, making him the second-highest-ranking Spanish colonial official. When the British occupied Manila, Anda left the city and established the capital of the Spanish government in Bacolor, Pampanga, north of Manila. Anda proclaimed himself as the governor-general while the British were in Manila, and he led the anti-British resistance. The British attempted to crush Anda and his followers, but Anda was able to defend the province of Bulacan (between Manila and Pampanga) against the British who were out to capture him. The British declared Anda a rebel and offered a 5,000-peso reward for his apprehension. Anda, however, successfully eluded all attempts to capture him.

The Treaty of Paris in 1763 ended the war between Britain and Spain and provided for the return of the Philippines to Spain. In 1764, the British left Manila, and authority was returned to the Spaniards. Anda reclaimed Manila for Spain, keeping the title of governor-general. Since a new governor-general had been formally appointed, he surrendered his command to the incoming official. Because of his resistance against the British and his loyalty to

Spain, as well as his success in keeping other areas of the Philippines from being conquered by the British, Anda was considered a hero in his homeland. Spain recognized and rewarded him for his deeds by formally appointing him as governor-general in 1769.

In that post, Anda was given orders to turn over parishes from the friars to secular priests. The intent was to reduce the strength of the big religious orders in the Philippines; the secular priests, who did not belong to any of the orders, were believed to be more loyal to the Spanish Crown. Anda initially carried out these orders, but the friars complained and reminded him that they had supported him during the British invasion. Anda suspended implementation of the secularization of parishes partly because of the friars but also because he felt the secular priests (most of them Filipino) were not qualified. He also sought to reduce corruption in the government and filed suits against his predecessor and other corrupt officials. His enemies, however, were able to get the court decisions overturned, and Anda was charged with paying all the costs of the trials.

Anda died on 30 October 1776 in San Felipe, Cavite. It was said that the pressures from his enemies had hastened his death. The role he had played in keeping the Spanish flag flying during the British occupation of Manila was commemorated by the erection of a monument in his honor in Manila. The monument was damaged during the Pacific War (1941–1945) but was repaired in the 1950s. It still stands as a reminder of Anda's service to the Spanish colonial government in the Philippines.

RICARDO TROTA JOSE

See also Friars, Spanish (The Philippines); Manila; Philippines under Spanish Colonial Rule (ca. 1560s–1898)

References:
Escoto, Salvador P. 1973. "The Administration of Simon de Anda y Salazar, Governor General of the Philippines, 1770–1776." Ph.D. diss., Loyola, University, Chicago.
Manila Lions Club. 1957. *A Pledge and a Rededication to Simon de Anda.* Manila: privately printed.
Rodriguez, Felice Noelle R. 1998. "A British Interlude." Pp. 196–197 in *Kasaysayan: The Story of the Filipino People.* Vol. 3, *The Spanish Conquest.* Manila: Asia Publishing.

ANG CHAN (1781–1835)
Ruler amidst Powerful Neighbors

Ang Chan reigned over Cambodia as king from 1797 to 1835. As a child, he succeeded his father, Ang Eng (r. 1779–1796), and for several years thereafter, Thai officials who were sent to Cambodia from Bangkok closely supervised his kingship. Soon after he formally ascended the throne in 1806, he sought to weaken his dependency on the Thai court by forming an alliance with Vietnam. His efforts angered the Thai king and induced three of his brothers to seek refuge in Bangkok. Consequently, his alliance with Vietnam led in the 1830s to a de facto occupation of Cambodia by Vietnam. Chan's tactics vis-à-vis larger powers foreshadowed the maneuvers that would be pursued by his great-grandnephew Norodom Sihanouk (1922–) more than a century later. Both rulers sought a modicum of independence by playing larger powers off against one another.

When a Thai army invaded Cambodia in 1833, Chan was evacuated to Vietnam. The Thai forces eventually withdrew after sacking the Cambodian capital (Phnom Penh), burning Chan's palace, and driving the population into exile. Chan returned to Phnom Penh in 1834 and died soon afterward aboard his royal barge, moored in the Tonle Sap, opposite his gutted palace.

Little is known of Chan's personality, but he seems to have inspired little loyalty among his subordinates. The Vietnamese treated Chan with contempt, and his reign is dealt with fleetingly in Cambodian historiography, which often displays an anti-Vietnamese bias.

DAVID CHANDLER

See also Ang Duong (Ang Duang) (1796–1860); Ang Eng (ca. 1774–1797); Cambodia (Eighteenth to Mid-Nineteenth Centuries); Cambodia under French Colonial Rule; Nguyen Dynasty (1802–1945); Rama I (Chakri) (r. 1782–1809); Sihanouk, Norodom (1922–)

References:
Chandler, David. 1974. "Cambodia before the French." Ph.D. diss., University of Michigan, Ann Arbor.
———. 2000. *A History of Cambodia.* Boulder, CO: Westview Press.

ANG DUONG (ANG DUANG) (1796–1860)

Founder of Modern Cambodia

Ang Duang was king of Cambodia (r. 1848–1860), succeeding his niece Ang Mei (r. 1835–1847). Duang was the youngest brother of King Ang Chan (r. 1797–1835). Following a Vietnamese invasion of Cambodia in 1811, Duang fled with two other brothers to Bangkok, where he sought the protection of the Thai court. In 1835, following Chan's death and a Thai defeat inside Cambodia at the hands of the Vietnamese, the Thai placed Duang in charge of a formerly Cambodian province of Siem Reap, which had been administered by the Thai since 1794. Three years later, in an obscure incident that may have involved a Vietnamese offer to Duang of the Cambodian throne, the Cambodian prince was arrested by the Thai, taken to Bangkok, and forced to swear allegiance to Rama III (r. 1824–1851). In 1841, he was allowed to return to Cambodia, accompanying a powerful Thai army that aimed to remove the Vietnamese from Cambodia and to reestablish political influence in Vietnam. As fighting between the Thai and Vietnamese forces inside Cambodia dragged on, Duang struggled to enlist support from Cambodia's small and decimated elite in an attempt to rebuild the rudiments of national government. When the Vietnamese withdrew from Cambodia in 1847, the Thai placed Duang on the throne and established the Cambodian court in Udong, north of Phnom Penh, where Chan and Mei had once ruled with Vietnamese protection. The court remained there until 1866, when it was reverted to Phnom Penh.

Although Duang's activities were closely monitored by Thai officials, he has been treated respectfully by most Cambodian historians, who see him as the founder of a modern, independent nation that reemerged after decades of warfare, disorder, and Vietnamese control. Duang was an accomplished poet and a fervent Buddhist, who sought through his actions and his example to restore dignity to his kingdom. He welcomed several European visitors to his court, and toward the end of his reign, he successfully led Cambodian forces against Cham rebels. He also sought to lessen Thai political influence by secretly appealing to the French emperor Napoleon III (r. 1852–1870) for support. Accordingly, a French diplomatic envoy was sent to take up this offer, but Thai officials prevented him from proceeding to Udong, and Duang's initiative was effectively snuffed out. Norodom (1836–1904), Duang's son, revived the appeal for French assistance in 1863, which consequently ushered in almost a century of French protection. Under the Cambodian constitution, only Duang's descendants are eligible candidates for the throne.

DAVID CHANDLER

See also Ang Chan (1781–1835); Ang Eng (ca. 1774–1797); Cambodia (Eighteenth to Mid-Nineteenth Centuries); Cambodia under French Colonial Rule; Siem Reap; Sihanouk, Norodom (1922–)

References:

Chandler, David. 1974. "Cambodia before the French." Ph.D. diss., University of Michigan, Ann Arbor.

———. 2000. *A History of Cambodia.* Boulder, CO: Westview Press.

ANG ENG (ca. 1774–1797)

Impotent Ruler

Ang Eng reigned as king of Cambodia from 1794 to 1797 and founded the dynasty that ruled Cambodia from 1794 to 1970. The monarchy was restored in 1993. During Eng's boyhood, Cambodia was without a monarch; the country was fought over by Thai, Vietnamese, and local forces. Eng had been spirited out of the country in 1779 and spent his youth under the protection of the Thai court. He was crowned king of Cambodia by the Thai in 1794 and allowed to return to his country under Thai supervision. The Cambodian court *Chronicle,* celebrating his return after a time of kinglessness, boasted that when he entered the country, "the sky did not get dark, nor did rain fall, but thunder boomed in the noon sky, making the noise of a mighty storm" (Eng 1969: 1013). In reality, he was powerless, and soon afterward, without referring the matter to Ang Eng, the Thai assumed administrative control over two Cambodian provinces, namely, Battambang and Siem Reap (the latter containing the medieval ruins of Angkor). The provinces did not revert to Cambodia until 1907. Eng's brief reign, monitored by Thai advisers, was uneventful. According to the *Chronicle,* he built a new palace at Udong, north of Phnom Penh, and visited Bangkok in 1796 on a tributary mission.

DAVID CHANDLER

See also Ang Chan (1781–1835); Ang Duong (Ang Duang) (1796–1860); Battambang; Cambodia (Eighteenth to Mid-Nineteenth Centuries); Cambodia under French Colonial Rule; *Cambodian Chronicles;* Nguyen Dynasty (1802–1945); Phya Taksin (Pya Tak [Sin], King Taksin) (r. 1767–1782); Siem Reap

References:

Chandler, David. 1974. "Cambodia before the French." Ph.D. diss., University of Michigan, Ann Arbor.
———. 2000. *A History of Cambodia.* Boulder, CO: Westview Press.
Eng Sut. 1969. *Akkasar mahaboros khmaer* [*Documents about Khmer Heroes*]. Phnom Penh: n.p.

ANGKATAN BELIA ISLAM MALAYSIA (ABIM) (MALAYSIAN ISLAMIC YOUTH MOVEMENT)

Formed in 1972 in the wake of the worldwide Islamic resurgence, Angkatan Belia Islam Malaysia (ABIM, Muslim Youth Movement of Malaysia) was founded by a group of young Muslim students and intellectuals led by student leader Anwar Ibrahim (1947–). The primary aim of ABIM was to promote the true understanding of Islam and the realization of Islamic teachings as a complete and perfect way of life, particularly among Muslim youths and the public in general. It was essentially an educative and reformist organization that strove to propagate modern Islam through lectures, seminars, and publications. It started its own kindergartens and schools as an alternative to the existing mainstream educational institutions. Its members, numbering about 40,000 in 1986, consisted of religiously inclined, educated youths disenchanted with what they regarded as the decadent, secular, and imbalanced ways of the Western world. ABIM became a strong social critic and attacked policies and practices it deemed inhumane, unjust, and contrary to the teachings of Islam. During its heyday toward the end of the 1970s, ABIM was at the forefront of the struggle against oppressive laws such as the Internal Security Act (ISA) and the Universities and University Colleges Act.

Although not a political organization, ABIM was ideologically closer to the Pan-Malaysia Islamic Party (PAS, Parti Islam Se Malaysia), and many of its leaders, such as Fadzil Mohamed Noor (deputy president) and Abdul Hadi Awang (Terengganu commissioner), stood as PAS candidates in the elections. But when Anwar Ibrahim joined the United Malays National Organization (UMNO) to contest in the 1982 general elections, ABIM became seriously split, and its credibility and popular support began to wane. Anwar's participation helped to boost UMNO's image among some Malays, but it tainted and weakened ABIM's. ABIM became less critical of the government and often directly opposed PAS. But when Anwar was dismissed from UMNO and the government in 1998, ABIM-PAS relations resumed, albeit rather guardedly.

ABDUL RAHMAN HAJI ISMAIL

See also Islamic Resurgence in Southeast Asia (Twentieth Century); Parti Islam Se Malaysia (PAS); United Malays National Organization (UMNO) (1946)

References:

Chandra Muzaffar. 1987. *Islamic Resurgence in Malaysia.* Petaling Jaya, Malaysia: Penerbit Fajar Bakti.
Hussin Mutalib. 1990. *Islam and Ethnicity in Malay Politics.* Singapore: Oxford University Press.
Means, Gordon P. 1991. *Malaysian Politics: The Second Generation.* Singapore: Oxford University Press.
Nagata, Judith. 1984. *The Reflowering of Malaysian Islam: Modern Religious Radicals and Their Roots.* Vancouver: University of British Columbia Press.

ANGKOR
Cambodia's Cultural Heritage

Located in northwest Cambodia, Angkor was the capital of Khmer kings from the ninth to fifteenth centuries. Until the thirteenth century, it was a center for the building of hydraulic works and for an art and architecture that were unequaled in peninsular and insular Southeast Asia. The Angkorian landscape was marked by the building of reservoirs, canals, monuments, and cities displaying distinctive architecture and sculpture. In the capital and also in the kingdom's other cities, temples represented the spiritual consecration of achievements in the economic and social realms. At that time, the Khmer kingdom was the most prosperous and powerful in Southeast Asia.

The city of Angkor and its monuments, sanctuaries for the most part, rose from the center of a network of reservoirs and canals. Intimately linked with this network and lying at the heart of a systematic spatial organization, the capital was central both geographically and symbolically. The irrigation reservoirs, whose banks were dotted with monasteries, were also considered sacred ponds. Today, the Angkor plain is still punctuated by some fifty major temples and gigantic hydraulic works. In 1992, the UN Educational, Scientific, and Cultural Organization (UNESCO) paid recognition to the present-day archaeological park, covering 400 square kilometers. Art from the Angkorian period continues to be a reference point nationally, regionally, and internationally.

The Rise of a Kingdom

Following the decline of Funan sea power by about the sixth century, the Khmers turned inland, to the country's agricultural regions. Lying in the Cambodian floodplains, Angkor is well provided with water resources. Not only is it near Tonle Sap (lit. Great Lake), which practically becomes an inland sea with the yearly flooding of the Mekong River, it is also watered by rivers descending from the surrounding mountainsides. In this monsoon-affected area of Asia, the builders of Angkor learned how to control fluctuations in the water supply and adapt them for irrigation purposes.

Traditionally, the Angkorian period is said to have begun in 802, the year that Jayavarman II (r. 802–834) was crowned king. In a ritual evoking the mythology of Śiva and celebrated in the Phnom Kulen (Kulen Mountains), north of Angkor, he became the *cakravartin/cakkavatti* (universal monarch) of the new kingdom. The Khmer land had previously experienced an architectural and artistic flowering, and local hydraulic works had been built in small administrative units. However, with Jayavarman II, the founder of Angkor, there was a shift to centralization under royalty.

In the reign of Indravarman I (r. 877–889), whose capital, Hariharālaya (present-day Roluos),

stood about 20 kilometers from present-day Angkor, the scale of the hydraulic work undertaken was unprecedented. The first great reservoir, the Indratatāka (meaning "the reservoir of the god Indra"), measured 3,800 meters by 800 meters and could hold at least 10 million square meters of water, or 100 times more than any previously built reservoir. Indravarman's royal temple, Bakong, was similarly larger in volume than any other (Groslier 1974: 100). In this reign as well, the sequence for carrying out grand projects was clearly defined for the first time. A public foundation (a hermitage or reservoir) was built initially, followed by a temple consecrated to ancestors and then by a royal temple (Stern 1954: 684).

Yaśovarman I (r. 889–900) was the first king to establish his capital on the future site of Angkor (known then as Yaśodharapura). The most important monuments he had built were the Eastern Baray, a reservoir measuring 7 kilometers by 2 kilometers and capable of holding 42 to 70 million square meters of water, and the mountain temple of Phnom Bakheng, constructed on an elevation. The greatest of the kings who followed Yaśovarman I expanded the irrigated limits of Angkor, and each built a new royal temple, in the form of a mountain temple, to mark the center of the newly enlarged city.

The Temples

The mountain temple was not only the most prestigious institution that a Khmer king could build but also the most symbolically significant. This original architectural form began to emerge when Prasat Ak Yum was constructed in the eighth century, a short time before the founding of the Angkor royal line. A mountain temple was the royal foundation par excellence. It was shaped like a tiered pyramid surmounted by one or several sanctuaries. Organized around the six directions of space, it corresponded to a specific concept of the cosmos. The mountain temple structured and controlled the spatial order of the city of Angkor and the kingdom. Marking the center of the city, the kingdom, and even the entire universe, the mountain temple was built in the image of the sacred mountain Meru, which was the center of the gods' world. Symbolically, the purifying, fertilizing water of the sacred mountain's rivers streamed down from the summit of the temple and flowed into its moats before irrigating the land. The most famous of these temples are Bakong (ninth century), Phnom Bakheng (tenth century), Prè Rup (tenth century), Phimeanakas (early eleventh century), Angkor Wat/Angkor Vat (twelfth century), and Bayon (late twelfth century). Other religious monuments expressed the same principles of architectural composition but were built on the same level.

The temples of Angkor held images of Hindu deities. Foremost was Śiva, represented as a *linga* (phallus, symbol of creative power and pillar of the world); Viṣṇu, as well, was often found in temples throughout the Angkor period. Buddhist deities also appeared, particularly in the reign of Jayavarman VII (r. 1181–ca. 1220). Numerous sanctuaries dedicated to ancestor worship existed as well. These cults melded in various combinations and forms of syncretism. However, in the mythological universe of every cult, the sacred nature of the mountain was primordial. The mountain was both the source of fecundity and fertilizing, regenerative waters and a place of sacrificial offerings. It was also the axis of the world.

Angkorian temples expressed a strict order in their architectural composition and in their orientation. Whether the layout was built around an axis, a central point, or a combination of the two, the temple was aligned with the cardinal points and emphasized the east-west direction, which, with very few exceptions, was the direction from which the temple was entered. On either side of this main axis, architectural elements were organized in a symmetrical arrangement, although, on closer examination, this symmetry reveals elements of dissymmetry with a systematic pattern of their own. The whole might be organized in tiers or on the same level, but every component helped to accentuate the importance of the central sanctuary, which was necessarily lofty.

Visual considerations were also extremely important in these monuments. Perspective effects were sought, often based on proportion reduction. In the case of Angkor Wat, built in the reign of Sūryavarman II (r. 1113–ca. 1145), the entire planning of the monument was colored by this objective. To create viewpoints, the architect positioned elements so that they acted as screens between the visitor and certain parts of the structure. He also used changes in level to vary the angle of the visitor's gaze. The approach to the central sanctuary is thus punctuated with obstacles that provide unexpected views and make the monument into an architectural spectacle (Dumarçay and Royere 2001: 84). The architecture of the early twelfth century, when Angkor Wat was erected, achieved unprecedented grandeur through its innovation, daring, and tremendous scope.

Sculpted Decoration

Sculpted decoration also played a role in the strict spatial and visual organization of the temples. Ornamentation became richer and fuller over the centuries, adapting to various architectural elements such as pilasters, doors, abutments, column bases and arris, modenatures, and the now famous pediments, exemplified in particular by those of the temple of Banteay Srei (ninth century).

Certain temples are also decorated with bas-reliefs. At the beginning of the Angkor period, a frieze of little mythical scenes, ruined today, was sculpted on Bakong's fifth tier. At the great temple of Baphuon, groups of small scenes also frame the second-level *gopuras* (monumental entrances). But at Angkor Wat and Bayon (the center of the city now known as Angkor Thom), the galleried walls are covered with immense narrative bas-reliefs, some stretching for about 30 meters. They depict scenes of daily life, particularly at Bayon, as well as certain historical events and cosmological themes inspired by Indian literature. These included the Indian creation myth *The Churning of the Ocean of Milk,* as well as stories from the Indian epics, the *Râmâyana* and the *Mahâbhârata,* involving conflicts between gods and demons or battles between their representatives.

By the Angkorian period, the culture of India had been known in the Khmer land for centuries. Indians traveled to Cambodia, and the Khmers themselves, like other peoples of Southeast Asia, seem to have visited the subcontinent. They apparently brought back new ideas, which they adapted freely to local concepts. According to Michael Vickery (1998: 141), "Indigenous traits and institutions may lie under the Indic façade."

Angkor Today

Today, Angkor is the symbol of the Khmers' cultural heritage. It is given considerable importance not only culturally but also from a national perspective. Internationally as well, the archaeological site is a standard reference for the country. At present, efforts to develop Cambodian tourism are concentrated on Angkor, along with other archaeological sites such as Sambor Prei Kuk, Preah Vihear, and Angkor Borei.

From the early twentieth century until the tragic events of the 1970s in Cambodia, the École Française d'Extrême-Orient accomplished immense work on the history and art of the monuments. During that time, the French school's epigraphists, notably George Coedès, had translated the greater part of the Cambodian inscriptions (in the Khmer language and Sanskrit). These inscriptions represent the largest such collection in Southeast Asia. Since the 1980s and 1990s, when work recommenced on the site, other international teams have become involved. Since 1995, the Autorité pour la Protection du Site et l'Aménagement de la Région d'Angkor (APSARA), a Cambodian public establishment, coordinates all operations, overlooks the work of international agencies, and is responsible for the maintenance of the archaeological park. The French are now concentrating on four major projects: the restoration of Baphuon, the stratigraphic excavation of the city of Angkor Thom, a study of the urban margins of Angkor, and a study of the Marches of the Empire. Today, two Japanese teams and an American one, as well as teams from Italy, Germany, and China, are working on sites such as Angkor Wat, the Bayon, Suor Prat, the Preah Khan, Prè Rup, and Chau Say Tevoda. Part of the teams' mission is to train the Cambodians who will eventually take charge of the Angkor archaeological park. A training school with a similar goal has also been established at the little-visited ruins of the Ta Nei temple. Finally, the newly established Center for Khmer Studies (CKS), located inside the monastery walls of Wat Damnak at Siem Reap, is devoted to the promotion of international cooperation in the field of social and human sciences in relation to Khmer studies.

HÉLÈNE LEGENDRE DE KONINCK

TRANSLATED BY JANE MACAULEY

See also Angkor Wat (Nagaravatta); Archaeological Sites of Southeast Asia; *Cakkavatti/ Setkya-min* (Universal Ruler); L'École Française d'Extrême-Orient; Funan; Hindu-Buddhist Period of Southeast Asia; Hinduism; Indianization; Jayavarman II (r. 770/790/802?–834 C.E.); Jayavarman VII (r. 1181–1220?); ; *Mahâbâratha* and *Râmâyana;* Monumental Art of Southeast Asia; Sūryavarman I (r. ca. 1002–1049); Sūryavarman II (r. ca. 1113–1145?)

References:

Boisselier, Jean. 1989. *Trends in Khmer Art.* Ithaca, NY: Cornell Southeast Asia Program.

Dagens, Bruno. 1995. *Angkor: Heart of an Empire.* New York: Abrams.

Dumarçay, Jacques, and Pascal Royere. 2001. *Cambodian Architecture: Eighth to Thirteenth Centuries.* Translated and edited by Michael Smithies. Leiden, The Netherlands: Brill.

Groslier, Bernard Philippe. 1974. "Agriculture et religion dans l'Empire angkorien" [Agriculture and religion in the Angkorian empire]. *Études Rurales,* pp. 95–117.

Jessup, Helen I., and Thierry Zephir, eds. 1997. *Sculpture of Angkor and Ancient Cambodia: Millennium of Glory.* Washington, DC: National Gallery of Art, in association with the Réunion des Musées Nationaux, Paris.

Le Bonheur, Albert, and Jaroslav Poncar. 1995. *Of Gods, Kings, and Men: Bas-Reliefs of Angkor Wat and Bayon.* London: Serindia.

Legendre De Koninck, Hélène. 2001. *Angkor Wat: A Royal Temple.* Weimar, Germany: VDG.

Stern, Philippe. 1954. "Diversité et rythme des fondations royales khmères" (Diversity and rhythm of the foundations of royal Khmers). *Bulletin de l'École Française d'Extrême-Orient* 44, no. 2: 649–687.

Vickery, Michael. 1998. *Society, Economics, and Politics in Pre-Angkor Cambodia.* Tokyo: Toyo Bunko (Centre for East Asian Cultural Studies for UNESCO).

ANGKOR WAT (NAGARAVATTA)
Palladium of Cambodia

The temple of Angkor Wat (Angkor Vat), located in the Angkor Park near the city of Siem Reap, was built during the reign of King Sūryavarman II (r. ca. 1113–1145?). It was a funerary edifice meant to exalt the memory of a

Temple of Angkor Wat. (Corel Corporation)

deceased king whose statue, in the form of the god Viṣṇu, stood in the central cella.

This monument deviates in some respects from the architectural models that had previously guided the works of the Khmer builders; for instance, the perspective effects that had been used for several centuries were abandoned. Furthermore, for one of the first times in Cambodia, the personality of an architect was clearly visible, not only in the originality of the plan but also in the care devoted to the construction of the edifice, a factor that partly explains its present condition.

The placement of the temple was determined by previously existing structures and the main axis of the town, perpendicular to that of the temple, which merged with the western edge of its moat. The location that was chosen probably corresponded with a depression that significantly lessened the labor needed for the terracing involved in the construction of the 200-meter-wide moat that surrounds the temple grounds. The grounds are enclosed by a laterite wall that one passes through along the axes at entrance pavilions made of sandstone.

The main entrance to the complex is located on the west side and is marked by a causeway (there is also a causeway on the east, which was never finished) that allows visitors to cross the moat. This construction is faced with laterite and paved with sandstone, on each edge of which is a balustrade symbolizing a *naga* (serpent). The moat is bounded by terraces built of upper courses of sandstone on a laterite base; the construction of these was never completed. Visitors enter the interior of the complex through a very wide pavilion crowned by three towers; there is a gate for a cart at either end. Crossing the pavilion through the central door, one enters the temple itself by way of a path (faced with sandstone) raised above the surrounding ground level. Staircases along the sides of the path lead to structures that once stood nearby, to pavilions called "libraries" and built of standstone, or to pools reflecting the temple.

The monument is accessible via staircases on three sides of the building, but on the west is a special structure—a wide terrace that completely surrounds the structure and a cruciform terrace (a structure that was not part of the original design). From the latter, one enters the first gallery, comprising an interior wall bearing the famous narrative reliefs and on the exterior a colonnade of shorter pillars. The roof resting on these pillars evokes tiles on arches. Pavilions at the corners and axes adorn this gallery.

On the west upon exiting the entrance pavilion, one reaches a section now called "the gallery of the thousand Buddhas"; this consists of a cruciform gallery with, on its eastern aisle, three staircases that provide access to the second-story terrace. On the other three sides, one reaches the second story directly through a simple entrance pavilion. The first-story terrace comprises two libraries on the north and south of the main edifice. The second gallery, having neither reliefs nor a demigallery, completely surrounds the main edifice. At the corners, towers have been erected (partially in ruins today) resembling those on the pinnacle and, on the axes, simple pavilions on the north, east, and south but tripled on the east.

The second-story terrace is almost completely taken up by the very large base of the highest temple, each face of which is broken by three staircases. On the west, one can, however, discern two libraries of small dimensions. A gallery flanked on the interior by a demigallery surrounds the third story. At the corners of this complex are towers, and at the axes are pavilions that open on another gallery, flanked by a demigallery leading to the central tower, resembling those at the corners but on a larger scale.

The decoration, which plays a major role in the symbolism of the temple, is essentially of Viṣṇuite inspiration, illustrating the main scenes of the *Mahâbhârata* and *Râmâyana* episodes that have been sculpted on the wall of the first-story gallery. These do not consist of consecutive illustrations of the text but rather feature various prestigious scenes, perhaps organized parallel with the lives of the deceased king and of the heroes celebrated in the texts. The walls are covered with reliefs depicting feminine divinities, or *apsaras,* probably meant to evoke the heaven of Viṣṇu.

The monument was abandoned in the course of the fourteenth century, then transformed into a Buddhist temple. During the sixteenth century, King Satha undertook a complete restoration of the monument and had reliefs carved in the gallery of the first story (the northeast corner that had been left incomplete in the twelfth century). Finally, at the end of the nineteenth century, Angkor Wat became the palladium of the Cambodian kingdom. Thereafter, it was depicted on the state flag.

JACQUES DUMARÇAY
TRANSLATED BY JOHN N. MIKSIC

See also Angkor; Hindu-Buddhist Period of Southeast Asia; *Mahâbârata* and *Râmâyana;* Monumental Art of Southeast Asia

References:
Chandler, David. 2000. *A History of Cambodia.* 3rd ed. Boulder, CO: Westview Press.
Coedes, G. 1963. *Angkor: An Introduction.* Translated by E. F. Gardiner. Oxford: Oxford University Press.
Dagens, B. 1995. *Angkor: Heart of an Ancient Empire.* New York: Abrams.
Dumarçay, J., and P. Royere. 2001. *Cambodian Architecture, Eighth to Thirteenth Centuries.* Translated and edited by Michael Smithies. Leiden, The Netherlands: Brill.
Nafilyan, G. 1969. *Angkor Vat: Description graphique du temple* [*Angkor Vat: Graphic Description of the Temple*]. Paris: École Française d'Extrême-Orient.

ANGLO-BRUNEI RELATIONS (NINETEENTH CENTURY TO 1980s)

The United Kingdom was the key factor in Brunei's history during the nineteenth and twentieth centuries, but for the British, Borneo was never of central strategic importance. After 1945, the relationship between the two countries became more equal, as the British Empire was liquidated throughout the world and Brunei moved steadily toward full independence at the end of 1983.

British interest in Southeast Asia was based at Bantam (Java) from 1602 until 1682 and at Bencoolen (Sumatra) between 1685 and 1825. During the seventeenth century, the English East India Company (EIC) maintained an extensive trade in the East Indies, but it displayed scant interest in Brunei. Situations during times of war, such as the temporary British occupations of Manila (1762–1764) and Java (1811–1816), tended to be accompanied by closer British attention to Borneo and Sulu: desultory attempts were made to establish a station at Balambangan (1762–1763, 1773–1775, and 1803–1805). In 1775 and 1803, Brunei offered Labuan to Britain in return for protection against Sulu piracy.

The British, who succeeded in establishing flourishing settlements in the Malay Peninsula (Penang in 1786 and Singapore in 1819), regarded Borneo alternately as a nuisance and an irrelevance. Policy was driven not so much by the island itself as by the imperatives of European politics, the needs of the British Indian Empire, and the growing importance of the China trade. Interference by individuals (the Brooke family) or organizations (the British North Borneo Company) further complicated British policy due to the comparative weakness of indigenous regimes. The British government did not wish to become entangled in the island, contenting itself for decades (from 1846 to 1889) with Labuan as a coaling station and a base to fight piracy. Brunei, North Borneo, and Sarawak did become British protectorates in 1888, but all three territories retained considerable internal autonomy. The establishment of a British residency in Brunei (1906–1959) was a last resort, failing any better solution. Political stability in Brunei was necessary to avoid giving a rival European power a pretext for intervention. The possible existence of oil in Brunei was *not* a factor in British thinking at the time.

Brunei's primary concern was mere survival. It was difficult enough to resist Sulu, much less combat more powerful Western nations. In the latter part of the nineteenth century, Brunei also wanted some protection against encroachment by Sarawak and North Borneo. In the twentieth century, its concerns were to uphold the royal dynasty, the Muslim religion, and the Malay language. The United Kingdom could assist the sultanate in these goals.

The Treaty of London (17 March 1824), an Anglo-Dutch agreement regulating colonial expansion south of Singapore, was an effort by London to secure Dutch friendship in European affairs by ending the hostility of the two nations in the East. Amsterdam argued that the agreement applied to Borneo; Whitehall argued to the contrary.

James Brooke (1803–1868), an English gentleman-adventurer, arrived in Kuching in 1839 and assumed power in Sarawak two years later. During the next fifty years, the Brooke dynasty absorbed more and more Brunei districts, culminating in the annexation of Limbang in 1890, thereby splitting the sultanate into two parts. Meanwhile, Brunei had come under pressure from the northeast. The British North Borneo Company then governing the region acquired large swaths of territory in the closing two decades of the nineteenth century.

In view of threats to its security, Brunei accepted a treaty of friendship and commerce with Britain in 1847. Then, in 1888, in order to defend the existence of Brunei, Sultan Hashim Jallal (r. 1885–1906) agreed to a protectorate agreement with the United Kingdom. Brunei was to continue to be governed by the sultan as an independent state, and the British would have rights of interference only in certain specified instances. Under a further agreement concluded in 1905 and 1906, Brunei accepted "a British officer to be styled Resident," whose "advice must be taken and acted upon all questions in Brunei other than those affecting the Muslim religion" (*Brunei Annual Report 1946*: 82). The treaty placed Brunei under a residential system like that in the Federated Malay States. According to the treaty, the resident was to serve as an adviser to the sultan, but in reality, state administration was assumed by the colonial power.

When the Pacific War broke out in 1941, Japan expelled the British and placed Brunei under military administration for three and a half years. Australian forces liberated the sultanate in June 1945. A British Military Administration lasted until civil government was restored in July 1946. Once again, a British resident was appointed. A written constitution was proclaimed in 1959, when the residential system was abolished and Brunei regained responsibility for its internal affairs.

In the advance toward full independence, Sultan Hassanal Bolkiah (1946–) held a series of discussions with the British, and further treaties were signed in 1971 and 1979. The upshot was that on 1 January 1984, Negara Brunei Darussalam assumed full responsibility as an independent, sovereign, and democratic Islamic Malay monarchy. Before it could accept independence, Brunei needed a stable regional environment, which was lacking during the Cold War era. In effect, the British protective role was taken over by international organizations, such as the Association of Southeast Asian Nations (ASEAN), the Organization of Islamic Conference (OIC), the Commonwealth, and the United Nations.

A. V. M. HORTON

See also Ambon (Amboina/Amboyna) Massacre (1623); Anglo-Dutch Relations in Southeast Asia (Seventeenth–Twentieth Centuries); Association of Southeast Asian Nations (ASEAN) (1967); Banten (Bantam); Bengkulu (Bencoolen, Benkulen); Borneo; British Borneo; British Interests in Southeast Asia; British North Borneo Chartered Company (1881–1946); Brooke, Sir Charles Anthoni Johnson (1829–1917); Brooke, James, and Sarawak; Brunei (Sixteenth to Nineteenth Centuries); East India Company (EIC) (1602), English; Federated Malay States (FMS) (1896); Hassanal Bolkiah, Sultan of Brunei (1946–); Labuan (1847); *Melayu Islam Beraja* (MIB, Malay Islamic Monarchy); Piracy; Residential System (Malaya); Sarawak and Sabah (North Borneo); Singapore (1819); Sulu and the Sulu Archipelago; Vereenigde Oost-Indische Compagnie (VOC) ([Dutch] United East India Company) (1602)

References:

Bassett, D. K. 1960. "The Amboyna Massacre of 1623." *Journal of South-East Asian History* 1, no. 2: 1–19.

———. 1964. "The Historical Background, 1500–1815." Pp. 113–127 and 415–420 in *Malaysia: A Survey*. Edited by Wang Gungwu. London: Pall Mall Press.

Brown, Donald E. 1970. *Brunei: The Structure and History of a Bornean Malay Sultanate.* Monograph of the *Brunei Museum Journal*. Bandar Seri Begawan, Brunei: Brunei Museum.

Brunei Annual Report 1946. Brunei: Government Printing Press.

Hall, D. G. E. 1968. *A History of South-East Asia.* 3rd ed. London: Macmillan.

Mohd Jamil al-Sufri, Pehin Orang Kaya Amar Diraja Dato Seri Utama (Dr.) Haji Awang. 1990. *Latar belakang Sejarah Brunei* [*Historical Background to Brunei*]. Bandar Seri Begawan, Brunei: Jabatan Pusat Sejarah.

Saunders, Graham. 1994. *A History of Brunei.* Kuala Lumpur: Oxford University Press.

Tarling, Nicholas. 1971. *Britain, the Brookes & Brunei.* Kuala Lumpur: Oxford University Press.

ANGLO-BURMESE WARS (1824–1826, 1852, 1885)

The three Anglo-Burmese wars ended the independence of Konbaung Burma, for progressively more of the country was annexed to British India after each conflict concluded. The first war, from 1824 to 1826, was halted with the Treaty of Yandabo. This war was the result of a clash of different forms of imperialism resulting from the two very different political and administrative systems that prevailed in Europe and Southeast Asia at the end of the eighteenth century. To Burma's west was the growing empire of British India, which was expanding, seemingly inexorably, and absorbing Indian states one after another with apparent ease. In Manipur, the British came up against a Burmese assertion to suzerainty over the ruling prince there, who had been placed on the throne by the troops of the Konbaung King Hsinbyushin (r. 1763–1776) following their battles against the Chinese in the Shan states.

The Burmese court treated Manipur and Assam as their dependencies, but the British refused to accept such claims. The British refused to deal with the Burmese court as a legal equal but insisted on conducting negotiations with Burma through the instrument of the East India Company (EIC). The Burmese under Hsinbyushin's successor, King Bodawpaya (r. 1781–1819), found this attitude insulting and unacceptable. Contradictory concepts of sovereignty also created misunderstandings between the two imperial forces. The Burmese understood sovereignty to be a multilayered and imprecise set of relationships. The British, by contrast, believed they should have sole control over any territory where they felt their interests predominated.

The British were also concerned that their great European imperial rival, France, might be making inroads into Southeast Asia at their expense. War eventually broke out along the British-designated border at the River Naaf. Anti-Konbaung rebels, claiming to be fighting for the restoration of the Arakanese monarchy, repeatedly fled across the river, where they were pursued by the Konbaung forces. The British viewed these cross-border incursions as an unacceptable violation of sovereignty and insisted that such events cease. The British protest was unacceptable to the Burmese, who felt that they had every right to defend their territory against enemies of the throne by whatever means necessary. The British were also upset at the treatment that British traders received when they entered the Burmese port of Rangoon. From the king's perspective, however, these individuals were not mere traders but illegal usurpers of his own royal prerogative to monopolize trade in the kingdom in order to generate the revenues required to support the state and its activities. The continuing activities of Burmese armies in Assam and Manipur further whetted the appetite of the British for war with what they saw as a recalcitrant and unreasonable monarchy.

Diplomatic relations between the two sides terminated in 1811, and therefore, the ability of both sides to assess the power and intentions of their rivals deteriorated. The new king of Burma, Bagyidaw (r. 1819–1837), who succeeded to the throne in 1819, sent General Maha Bandoola (Bandula), as governor first of Assam and then of Arakan, to suppress the rebels operating in those territories. The British at this time began to assist the rebels in the hope of weakening Burmese influence in the area. Bandoola's forces began to threaten the British state of Cachar and also seized an island in the middle of the River Naaf that the British claimed in 1823. The result was war the following year, when the British dispatched a naval expedition to Rangoon in May 1824. They easily seized the city as well as the delta region. This success did not force the king to sue for peace, however, and the following year, the British Indian army began a slow and difficult march against the king's forces until they reached Yandabo, where the king agreed to end the conflict. Arakan and Tenasserim were thus lost from Burmese control. In this way, what had commenced as a minor irritant to a powerful kingdom ended in a humiliating defeat because of the faulty assessment of the strength and intentions of the new imperialist force to Burma's west.

The second war arose in 1852 as the result of another clash between Burmese administrative practices and state trading monopolies and British ideas about free trade in an age of liberal imperialism. In 1850, King Pagan (r. 1846–1853) appointed a new *myo-wun* (governor) of Rangoon. Named Maung Ok, he quickly developed a reputation among the foreign trading community for his arbitrary decisions as well as the exorbitant tax rates he applied. His extracting of fees to avoid prosecution and the various court fees designed to increase his personal income and that of his ruler were standard practice in Southeast Asian monarchies at the time. But such practices rankled British and other foreign traders, who sought low, regular, and predictable rates of taxation as a precondition for successful business. As the level of complaints going back to the EIC grew, the Indian government sent Commodore Lambert, known as "combustible Lambert," to investigate in November 1851.

Lambert, ignoring his instructions to merely investigate the cases of two British shipmasters imprisoned for failing to pay a fine, single-handedly precipitated a war. Using his three ships, he seized one of the king's vessels and sailed it out of Rangoon waters. This insubordinate behavior, however, fit with larger British intentions toward Burma, and a full-scale war was soon under way. The major ports of the country were seized quickly, and by July 1852, an army formed to march on the capital. Meanwhile, a palace revolt had taken place against King Pagan, and several princes deserted the throne, taking their troops with them. Pagan's brother, Mindon Min, organized against the king and soon entered the capital. By the time Pagan was ousted, the British had advanced north of Prome, thus seizing the best teak forests of Lower Burma. Mindon (r. 1852–1878), who was crowned king in February 1852, sued for peace, and though he refused to sign a peace treaty with the British, he tacitly acknowledged British possession of British Burma, to which were added Arakan and Tenasserim. By March of that year, following the initial intervention of two Italian priests, the war was over. The British had cut the territorial control of the Konbaung dynasty down to a mere rump of its former glories. All seaborne trade now had to pass through British territory, and river transport would quickly become a near monopoly for the British.

There are few examples of such naked imperialist ambition as the Second Anglo-Burmese

War. As the British liberal statesman Richard Cobden (1804–1865) wrote at the time:

> [The governor-general of India] begins with a claim on the Burmese for less than a thousand pounds; which is followed by an additional demand of an apology from the Governor of Rangoon for the insult offered to our officers; next, his terms are raised to one hundred thousand pounds, and an apology from the king's ministers; then follows the invasion of Burmese territory; when, suddenly all demands for pecuniary compensation and apology cease, and his lordship is willing to accept the cessation of [Lower Burma] as a compensation and reparation. (Htin Aung 1967: 230)

The Third (and final) Anglo-Burmese War was a short, sharp affair. Between the final two wars, the British had imposed a number of constraints on the capacity of the new monarch to reform his administration. With the financial base of the kingdom severely eroded, the fighting capacity of the king's army was much reduced. And though the British merchants in Rangoon continued to demand that the king's remaining monopolies be abolished for the greater good of free trade, the British became increasingly worried about the alleged threat of growing French influence in the king's court. The court was itself riven with factionalism, and two of the key princes had defected to the British; they, in turn, were plotting to put one of themselves on the throne in the place of Mindon's successor, Thibaw Min (r. 1878–1885).

In a failed attempt to gain some leverage over the British, Thibaw sent a delegation to Europe in 1884 to negotiate commercial treaties with France, The Netherlands, and Germany. This fueled speculation that there were secret military clauses negotiated in Paris, and though the French never ratified the agreement, it justified, in already suspicious minds, further arguments for finally annexing all of Burma. There were even rumors circulating at the time that the French had agreed to supply the king of Burma with arms or, alternatively, to organize an invasion from Vietnam via Siam to impose a new, pro-French king on the throne.

In this atmosphere of frenzied speculation, the Hlutdaw, the royal court at Mandalay, issued its decision on a long-standing case involving

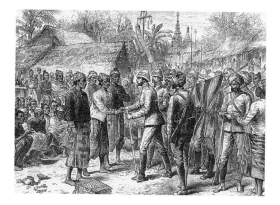

British troops with the officers and remnant of the Burmese Army in 1886 during the Third Anglo-Burmese conflict. (The Illustrated London News Picture Library)

the large, Indian-owned Bombay Burma Trading Corporation. Bombay Burma had a near monopoly over the export of timber from the king's forests. The case started as a suit by private individuals seeking compensation for logs supplied by them to the company, but when the records were examined, it was revealed the company had been underpaying the royalties due to the Crown. Under Burmese law, this required the company to pay twice what was owed as punishment. Though British officials accepted the justice of the decision, they felt the fine was excessive.

The governor-general of India, Lord Dufferin (t. 1884–1888), however, sought to use the case as the excuse for the imposition of a number of demands on the Burmese monarchy. In effect, these would have made the king a mere agent of the British in India, as most of his remaining limited authority would be severely constrained. Moreover, his political position at home would be gravely damaged, for granting such concessions would deliver a severe blow to his prestige. Without waiting for a reply to these demands, the British amassed troops at Thayetmyo in anticipation of a third invasion. The king's reply to the demands made upon him was deemed unsatisfactory and was rejected, and the British ordered their army to march.

The Burmese empire was too weakened to put up more than token resistance to the might of the British forces. When the king sought to conclude an armistice with the British commander, he in turn demanded complete surrender. The war was over in eleven days, as British troops surrounded the king's palace at Mandalay and took the king and his chief queen away to a life in exile in India. The last Burmese monarch made his final journey not as the Lord of Life in a royal procession with elephants and attendants, as all his predecessors had done, but as a virtual prisoner of war, riding in a common cart pulled by two oxen.

R. H. TAYLOR

See also Arakan; Bombay Burmah Trading Corporation; British Burma; British India, Government of; British Interests in Southeast Asia; East India Company (EIC) (1602), English; Free Trade; French Ambitions in Southeast Asia; Hlutdaw; Hsinbyushin (r. 1763–1776); Imperialism; Konbaung Rulers and British Imperialism; Mindon (r. 1853–1878); Tenasserim; Yandabo (1826), Treaty of

References:

Browne, Edmund C. 1924 [1988]. *The Coming of the Great Queen: A Narrative of the Acquisition of Burma.* London: n.p.

Cady, John F. 1960. *A History of Modern Burma.* Rev. ed. Ithaca, NY: Cornell University Press.

Htin Aung. 1965. *The Stricken Peacock: Anglo-Burmese Relations, 1752–1948.* The Hague: Martinus Nijhoff.

———. 1967. *A History of Burma.* New York: Columbia University Press.

Singhal, D. R. 1960. *The Annexation of Upper Burma.* Singapore: Eastern University Press.

Thant Myint-U. 2001. *The Making of Modern Burma.* Cambridge: Cambridge University Press.

Woodman, Dorothy. 1962. *The Making of Burma.* London: Cresset Press.

ANGLO-DUTCH RELATIONS IN SOUTHEAST ASIA (SEVENTEENTH TO TWENTIETH CENTURIES)

The English polity—and the larger British polity that succeeded it in the eighteenth century—shared a number of interests with the Dutch Republic, the United Provinces, and the Netherlands monarchy that was its successor in the nineteenth century. Their interests were not, however, identical: indeed, there were four

Anglo-Dutch wars. Moreover, the change in their relative strengths over time produced arrogance and resentment, admiration and envy, adding to the complexity of the connection between two states that faced each other over the narrow seas.

The Dutch polity emerged from a struggle with Hapsburg Spain, with which it fought a long war of independence between 1576 and 1648, broken only by a twelve-year truce from 1609 to 1621. With its cause, the England of Elizabeth I (1533–1603) and James I (1566–1625) found common interest: the independence of the Dutch was a guarantee of the security of England against a dominant power on the Continent. There was a common cause, too, in Protestant opposition to the Counter-Reformation, with which the Hapsburgs identified themselves. At this time, however, England was much weaker than Spain. Elizabeth's rhetoric was coupled with caution, and she intervened in the struggle only belatedly and without declaring war on Spain. James I was still more equivocal.

England and the United Provinces were, moreover, also commercial rivals. To ensure their survival, the Dutch pursued control of the European carrying trade that was the original source of their prosperity. Then, after the Crowns of Portugal and Spain were united in 1580, they sought to displace the trade of the Iberian powers by trading directly with Asia and displacing Iberian trade in Asia and elsewhere. In this case again, England was the weaker of the two powers. England's trade suffered, as did that of the enemies of the Dutch.

The mismanagement on the part of the Stuart monarchy, culminating in its overthrow and the execution of the king (Charles I) in 1649, prevented England from effectively mobilizing its power. The republic in England sought to put its relations with the Dutch Republic on a new basis. It directed the Navigation Act of 1651 against the Dutch carrying trade and asserted a right to search Dutch ships for contraband. At the same time—feeling politically insecure—it sought a "union" with the Dutch. Now no longer under threat from Spain, the Dutch saw no reason to respond, and the Dutch Reformed Church was incensed by the English treatment of the Presbyterians and by the invasion of Scotland. Clashes at sea developed into a naval war. That conflict showed the vulnerability of the Dutch in the narrow seas. But Oliver Cromwell (1599–1658)—anxious to reduce opposition to his regime—accepted a mild treaty. Though the Navigation Act remained and the Dutch had to pay reparations for the Amboyna massacre of 1623, no permanent damage was done to the Dutch system save in Brazil.

The restored Stuart monarchy renewed English pressure on the Dutch. It passed a strengthened Navigation Act and prohibited Dutch vessels from fishing in coastal waters. The king's brother, James, backed by junior ministers and courtiers, wanted to go further than Charles II (1630–1685) himself. He believed that the English would be victorious in a new war and that, adopting the prevailing "mercantilist" view of international trade, victory could lead to the annexation of the republic's trade and its wealth. Taking a share of the slave trade as an objective, the English attacked the ports of the Dutch West India Company in West Africa, and they seized New Netherland, renaming New Amsterdam as New York after the duke. In home waters, the battle off Lowestoft was a triumph for the English. The best-known event in the war, however, is the Dutch attack on the great English ships in the Medway in June 1667. That event and the king's reluctance to contact Parliament and secure funds led to the conclusion of a peace.

That, however, did not halt James's ambitions. He concluded that he could deal a decisive blow to the Dutch with the help of Louis XIV (1638–1715) and the French army. What resulted was the Third Dutch War, 1672–1674, which was very much, as J. R. Jones (1996) argued in his excellent study of the wars, the work of the court rather than of the anti-Dutch interest groups involved in making the first two wars. John Dryden's play *Amboyna* was part of the propaganda of the day. But the war became deeply unpopular, all the more so because of the alliance made with Catholic France. In the House of Commons, William Coventry declared that "the interest of the king of England is to keep France from being too great on the Continent, and the French interest is to keep us from being masters of the sea" (Jones 1996: 214).

The chief effect of the war was felt within English politics in the following decade. When James II (1633–1701) realized that William of Orange (1650–1702) was about to invade England, he tried to rally support by describing the Dutch as England's traditional enemy, but "his attempt failed abysmally." William could argue that now, as in the 1670s, the kings of England and France had allied not only against the republic "but also against the liberties and religion of England and Scotland" (Jones 1996: 216).

The Revolution of 1688 turned out to have yet larger effects. It produced a consensus on the political future of England and indeed of Britain and thus permitted the mobilization of resources that had evaded the Stuart monarchy and the Cromwellian Commonwealth. Britain became a major commercial and naval power, successfully contending with the French throughout the world. And that had its effect on the Dutch at home and overseas.

In Southeast Asia, the Vereenigde Oost-Indische Compagnie (VOC), or the (Dutch) United East India Company, had pursued its commercial objectives—monopoly of the fine spices of Maluku and then of the far more widely grown pepper and a share in the tin trade—with increasing determination, particularly during the recession in the latter half of the seventeenth century. As the Amboyna massacre suggested, they were no less ruthless toward the English than toward other rivals, European or Asian, and their policies took no account of what the two powers had in common, let alone their moments of collaboration. A burden- and trade-sharing agreement in 1619 worked to the disadvantage of the weaker company, the English East India Company (EIC). Even before Amboyna, the EIC had resolved to withdraw its factories from the eastern part of the archipelago. The EIC withdrew from Bantam in the 1680s, retreating on the pepper trade of the western coast of Sumatra.

Yet even before the revolution and reconstruction at home, England was securing advantages in the Asian trade, which the Dutch did not share. The VOC did not compete as successfully in the newer branches of that trade as in the old. Driven almost entirely from the archipelago, the English company dedicated itself to supplying the new European craze for Indian textiles and satisfying the new demand for Chinese tea. The VOC increasingly focused on the Indies rather than on Asia as a whole, with the introduction of coffee in Java being its major innovation. When Britain, in the pursuit of its rivalry with France, began to build a territorial dominion in India, the Dutch were further disadvantaged, for their factories there were more on sufferance and their access to opium was inferior. Increasingly, too, English "country traders" penetrated the archipelago, partly by contacting Bugis intermediaries. But the British government stopped short of issuing a political challenge to the Dutch in Asia because of their relationship in Europe. The ideas William Coventry had enunciated in the 1670s were no less true in the subsequent decades.

Joint Anglo-Dutch opposition to the French was a feature of the wars of the early eighteenth century—those of the Spanish succession (1701–1714) and the Austrian succession (1740–1748). At the end of the former, the Dutch gained the right to garrison fortresses in the southern Netherlands, which passed to Austria. In the latter, by which time the Dutch republic had become much weaker, the ruling oligarchy sought to pursue a cautious policy, even though that risked their relations with Britain. In 1744, however, the French invaded The Netherlands, and in 1747, they overran Dutch Flanders. Called to the Stadhouderate (the seat of government) during the crisis, William IV of Orange (1711–1751) told the British he could not continue without a loan. The following year, however, the peace treaty of Aix-la-Chapelle more or less restored the status quo.

The Stadhouder (governor) failed to effect the reforms that those in the Dutch Republic believed were necessary to restore the country's fortunes, much damaged by the wars and by economic competition, and to check the role of the old oligarchy. Calling themselves the "Patriots," opponents of the royal house of Orange looked to French ideas. But even more risky, they looked to French influence. They were joined by a section of the oligarchy mainly from Holland (the chief province, traditionally opposed to the Orange princes) and by some of the First Hand, or international merchants, who saw that Britain's commercial expansion divided its interests from theirs, though security interests might unite them. The British tried to avoid provoking a pro-French reaction and weakening the Anglophile Orange party. The American War of Independence (1775–1783) made that impossible. The British wanted to deny neutrals the ability to trade with the rebels and with their French and Spanish allies, but the First Hand wanted to retain that ability, and the Patriots sought to weaken the Stadhouder. Late in 1780, Britain declared war on the Dutch Republic to prevent it from joining the League of Armed Neutrality sponsored by Catherine II (1729–1796) of Russia.

In the seventeenth century, the VOC had pursued its commercial objectives without taking much account of the common interests—often obscured, if not displaced—of England and the Dutch Republic in Europe. The eighteenth-century policy of the EIC was, in this respect, a more restrained one. The British avoided recognizing the exclusive claim of the VOC to navigation in the archipelago, with which the VOC sought to back the numerous commercial privileges and monopolies it gained by treaties and contracts with Indonesian and Dutch rulers. Furthermore, though the British carried on what the VOC saw as a "smuggling" trade, they did not openly invade the Dutch sphere of influence. Their attempt to settle at Balambangan in the 1770s was, for example, more a challenge to Spain than to the republic.

Access to French influence in the republic undermined this approach. If it had been followed up in Asia, moreover, the French would have been in a stronger position to renew their challenge to the British in India, to command the Bay of Bengal, and to threaten the route to China. With the opening of the war in 1780, the British took preemptive measures, acquiring Trincomalee in Ceylon, for example, as well as Dutch settlements in India and Padang, neighbor of Benkulen in western Sumatra. At the end of a war that was, in general, far from glorious for the British—the Americans made good their independence—they hoped to secure at least some successes. Though the Dutch were still supported by the French, the British did secure their right to navigate in the eastern seas—namely, Southeast Asian waters—in the 1783 treaty that ended the Fourth Anglo-Dutch War.

The continued Franco-Dutch alliance was a factor in the British decision to occupy Penang in 1786, affording some access to the trade of the archipelago and some protection for the Bay of Bengal. However, by establishing themselves north of the main settlement of the Dutch in the Straits, Melaka, the British still avoided making a direct challenge to them. The following year, the pro-French Patriots were overthrown by a Prussian intervention, designed to protect the Stadhouder William V's (1748–1806) Prussian wife from Patriot insults but supported diplomatically and financially by the British. The latter now sought to put their relations with the republic on a more friendly footing. Their idea of a compromise—in which the Dutch would cede Trincomalee, as well as the recently acquired Riau at the tip of the Straits, in return for a guarantee of the spice monopoly—was quite unacceptable even to a friendly regime in the republic. No treaty was made, even though the British ambassador, Lord Auckland, argued in 1791 that "the general ferment in Europe" was a reason "for strengthening our union with the Republic both really and ostensibly" (Tarling 1962: 44).

French armies, penetrating the republic from late 1794, were not unwelcome, and the Patriots set up a "Batavian Republic" under their aegis, allied with the French republic from May 1795. In turn, the British took preemptive action in Asia, aided by a letter secured from William V, who had fled to England. A number of Dutch possessions were taken, usually, despite the Kew Letters (a document by William V instructing Dutch colonial governors not to resist British forces), as a result of some hostilities. They included the Cape Province, Trincomalee, settlements in India, Melaka, Padang, and Maluku. Java itself was occupied only in the second phase of the French wars. An interim administration was installed, headed by Stamford Raffles (1811–1814), who favored the creation of a British empire in the archipelago.

That was not, however, the course British policy took. The peace treaties included provisions designed to prevent a further French attempt to dominate the European continent. The establishment of the kingdom of The Netherlands, encompassing the Belgian provinces of the Hapsburgs as well as the old republic headed by the Orange prince as King William I (1772–1843), was one of the measures taken. The return of the majority of Dutch possessions overseas would help to sustain the new Netherlands kingdom and enable it to fulfill its role in Europe. That was Britain's priority. It retained the Cape and Ceylon but returned what it had taken in the Indies. "I still feel great doubts about the acquisition in sover-eignty of so many Dutch colonies," the British foreign secretary, Lord Castlereagh, wrote. "I am sure our reputation on the Continent, as a feature of strength, power and confidence is of more real value than an acquisition thus made" (Koebner 1961: 289).

In such a concept, the security of the route to China and access to the trade of the archipelago relied on the goodwill of the Dutch and their ability to exclude other powers. Neither Raffles nor his superiors in Bengal thought that the convention of 1814 was adequate. The result was the Anglo-Dutch Treaty of 1824, the kind of compromise with a friendly Dutch regime that the British had vainly sought during the prewar period. The essence of it was that the British should not offer a political challenge to the Dutch in the archipelago, whereas the Dutch would offer British traders fair opportunity in ports they possessed or in respect of which they had contracts with Indonesian rulers. There was also a kind of territorial division, though expressed in negative terms. The British transferred Benkulen and agreed not to make settlements in Sumatra in the future. The Dutch accepted the occupation of Singapore (accomplished by Raffles in 1819), transferred Melaka, and agreed to make no settlements on the peninsula.

The negative phrasing of much of the treaty was prompted by a recognition that the two powers were, as Robert Stewart Castlereagh's successor, George Canning, put it, "exclusive Lords of the East" (India Office Records 1824). Once it had been decided that the Dutch should predominate in the archipelago and so boost their strength in Europe, it was necessary to be sure that they could keep others out. Too clear an assertion of the deal might only encourage others to challenge it.

The policy was successful. No other powers seriously challenged the Dutch in the nineteenth century, all being aware of their relationship with the greatest power of the day. Secure in their ultimate claim, the Dutch were thus able to take their time in what they could regard as rounding out their empire. They therefore focused on the most profitable part of their domains, Java, before turning to the Outer Islands, and they established the "culture system," a revenue system that forced farmers to cultivate land for the production of cash crops, the sale of which solely to the Dutch colonial government would enable the farmers to pay land tax. The implementation of the culture system in Java was accelerated when William I made a bid to stop the Belgians from breaking away from his kingdom after the Revolution of 1830.

This is not, of course, to suggest that the Anglo-Dutch relationship was always smooth. Being patronized by a superior power is not always easy to bear. Nor was the patron ready to accept the measures the Dutch took—in apparent defiance of the treaty—to build up their commerce in the 1830s and 1840s. But though that led the British to offer some support for the Brooke venture, the appointment of an Englishman, James Brooke (1803–1868), as rajah of Sarawak in northern Borneo, they offered no overall challenge to the Dutch. It seemed, as Lord Wodehouse put it in 1860, "very advantageous to us that the Dutch should possess this Archipelago. If it was not in the hands of the Dutch it would fall under the sway of some other maritime Power, possibly the French unless we took it ourselves" (Memorandum, 18 August 1860, FO 12/28, Public Record Office, London).

In the Great War (1914–1918), the German Empire destroyed the neutrality of Belgium but respected that of the kingdom of The Netherlands. Its eastern possessions became a base for German-backed subversion of India, but the British Foreign Office rejected a suggestion from its consul general in Batavia that part of Netherlands India be given to Britain's ally, Japan. "If the Netherlands Indies are not too friendly they are harmless," wrote W. Langley at the Foreign Office. "It would be quite another matter if the islands were in the hands of the Japanese" (Minute, n.d., FO 371/2691 [235431/31446], Public Record Office, London).

The Japanese were seen to be the main threat to the future of colonial Southeast Asia, particularly after their conquest of Manchuria. Now much weakened, however, the British felt themselves unable formally to promise to aid the Dutch in the event of an attack, unless there was some undertaking from the United States as well. The Japanese did not move in 1940, when the Germans invaded The Netherlands and Belgium. Their move, prompted by the American embargoes, came in late 1941. Only at the last minute had the United States promised aid. The Japanese overthrew all the Western empires.

Following the Pacific War (1941–1945), the Europeans determined to return to Southeast Asia. The Dutch were all the more intent on doing so because they connected the possession of the Indies with their hopes of recovery in the postwar world. Their return, however, depended on the British, who were dominant in the Allies' South-East Asia Command (SEAC). The British saw no prospect of simply restoring the colonial structures in Southeast Asia: the powers had to come to terms with nationalism. That the Dutch found difficult to do, particularly in respect to nationalists whom they saw as Japanese collaborators or extremists, and they resented pressure from the British. Their "police actions" were, however, counterproductive. Indeed, the second action underlined their dependence in Europe, not on the British now but on the Americans.

NICHOLAS TARLING

See also Ambon (Amboina/Amboyna) Massacre (1623); Banten (Bantam); Bengkulu (Bencoolen, Benkulen); British Borneo; British India, Government of; British Interests in Southeast Asia; British Malaya; Brooke, James, and Sarawak; Bugis (Buginese); Coffee; Country Trader; Cultivation System (*Cultuurstelsel*); Dutch East Indies; Dutch Interests in Southeast Asia from 1800; Dutch Police Action (First, Second); East India Company (EIC) (1600), English; French Ambitions in Southeast Asia; Great War (1914–1918); Indonesian Revolution (1945–1949); Japan and Southeast Asia (pre-1941); Java; Kew Letters; Maluku (The Moluccas); Napoleonic Wars in Asia; Nationalism and Independence Movements in Southeast Asia; Netherlands (Dutch) East Indies; Penang (1786); Pepper; Raffles (1781–1826), Sir (Thomas) Stamford Bingley; Singapore (1819); South-East Asia Command (SEAC); Spices and the Spice Trade; Sumatra; Tin; Vereenigde Oost-Indische Compagnie (VOC) ([Dutch] United East India Company) (1602)

References:
India Office Records. 1824. "Note on Courtenay Memorandum of 15 January 1824." Dutch Records I/2/32, India Office Records, British Library, London.

Jones, J. R. 1996. *The Anglo-Dutch Wars of the Seventeenth Century*. London and New York: Longman.

Koebner, R. 1961. *Empire*. Cambridge: Cambridge University Press.

Tarling, Nicholas. 1962. *Anglo-Dutch Rivalry in the Malay World, 1780–1824*. London: Cambridge University Press; St. Lucia, Australia: University of Queensland Press.

ANGLO-DUTCH TREATY (1824)

See Anglo-Dutch Relations in Southeast Asia (Seventeenth to Twentieth Centuries)

ANGLO-FRENCH DECLARATION OF LONDON (1896)

Signed by Lord Salisbury, the British prime minister and foreign secretary, and by Alphonse de Courcel, the French ambassador in London, the Anglo-French Declaration penned on 15 January 1896 was intended to stabilize Anglo-French rivalries in Siam (Thailand) and in southwest China. Furthermore, it sought to resolve a series of smaller colonial irritations on the Lower Niger and in Tunis. Its principal clause effectively immunized central Siam from the threat of military invasion by France or Britain. Some historians attribute Siam's escape from European colonization to the barrier established by this arrangement to unilateral annexation by either power.

The declaration also reflected the pursuit of separate, as well as common, objectives by the British and French in Siam. For the British, the clauses relating to Siam were primarily intended to debar French colonialists from urging any future annexation. The French *parti colonial* tended to advocate westward encroachment into Siam from Indochina. The Paknam Incident of 1893, marked by the forcing of the Chao Phraya River defenses by two French gunboats, had sharpened British realization of the high influence enjoyed by the French colonial lobby over the making of French policy in Southeast Asia. Since British economic and political influence already predominated in Siam, the arrangement to preclude military intrusion worked mainly in favor of British local interests.

From the perspective of the French foreign ministry, the arrangement was entered into mainly to serve the broader purposes of France's continental diplomacy. Courcel hoped that it would open the way to a possible resolution of Anglo-French acrimony over the far greater problem of Egypt. French colonialists, for their part, chose to interpret the agreement as having established an "Anglo-French condominium" in Siam, an impression that the Siamese successfully worked to eliminate in the decade following the agreement by systematically blocking French investment in the kingdom's modernization.

PATRICK TUCK

See also British Interests in Southeast Asia; French Ambitions in Southeast Asia; Paknam Incident (1893); Preservation of Siam's Political Independence; Reforms and Modernization in Siam

References:

Jeshurun, Chandran. 1977. *The Contest for Siam, 1889–1902: A Study in Diplomatic Rivalry*. Kuala Lumpur: Penerbit Universiti Kebangsaan Malaysia.

Tuck, Patrick. 1995. *The French Wolf and the Siamese Lamb: The French Threat to Siamese Independence, 1858–1907*. Bangkok: White Lotus.

ANGLO-MALAYAN/MALAYSIAN DEFENCE AGREEMENT (AMDA)

The Anglo-Malayan/Malaysian Defence Agreement (AMDA) commenced on 12 October 1957 and ceased on 1 November 1971. Under AMDA, Britain would guarantee the external defense of Malaya/Malaysia. Australia and New Zealand joined AMDA in 1959, as did Singapore in 1961. AMDA also permitted British, Australian, and New Zealand forces to station armed troops in Malaya/Malaysia and Singapore. Because AMDA's viability depended on Britain's military commitments, however, AMDA's financial cost to Britain would eventually precipitate its demise.

For Malaya/Malaysia and Singapore, both newly independent and with nascent defense forces, AMDA was a guarantee of security in an unstable region. For Britain, AMDA expressed its commitment to Malaya and Singapore as former colonies. And for Australia and New Zealand, AMDA also guaranteed their own security by ensuring Britain's military presence in the region.

Britain's rapid and substantial military reaction to Indonesia's Confrontation (*Konfrontasi*, a campaign against British plans to create a new Federation of Malaysia) and Australia and New Zealand's military commitments demonstrated AMDA's viability. However, the economic impact on Britain was considerable at a time when economic crises in the homeland precipitated considerable defense cutbacks. Consequently, in 1967, Britain announced its intentions to end its defense commitments "East of Suez" by the mid-1970s. Australia and New Zealand, despite increased military commitments, could not fulfill Britain's pivotal role in AMDA, without which the agreement was not viable.

By 1971, despite their security and economic concerns at Britain's withdrawal, all parties agreed that AMDA was untenable. Subsequently, AMDA was replaced that same year by the more flexible Five-Power Defence Agreement, which facilitated the parties' adjustment to a post-AMDA world. The Five-Power Defence Agreement involved Australia, New Zealand, Great Britain, Malaysia, and Singapore.

IAN K. SMITH

See also Australia and Southeast Asia;
Cold War; Domino Theory; Konfrontasi ("Crush Malaysia" campaign); Malayan Emergency (1948–1960); U.S. Military Bases in Southeast Asia; Zone of Peace, Freedom and Neutrality (ZOPFAN) (1971)

References:
Chin Kin Wah. 1983. *The Defence of Malaysia and Singapore: The Transformation of a Security System, 1957–1971.* Cambridge: Cambridge University Press.

ANNAM

The term *Annam* was one of the traditional popular appellations of Vietnam when the country was a protectorate of T'ang China, which then covered present North Vietnam. The term is also the official name of Vietnamese (Dai Viet) dynasties as vassals of the Chinese Empire. During the nineteenth century, Annam referred to the French protectorate of Central Vietnam.

The Chinese term *Annam* (lit. pacification of the South) was originally employed during the Six Dynasties period (third to sixth centuries)

as part of a title of general usage conferred on Chinese officials or foreign kings (of Champa and Funan). During the T'ang period (618–907 C.E.), Annam became the name of one of the T'ang protectorates (*tu-hu-fu*) founded outside China to loosely control surrounding "barbarians." The An-nan (Annam) tu-hu-fu was established in 679 C.E. and covered provinces of the Red River delta (with the administrative center of Chiao-chou at present-day Hanoi) and the Thanh Hoa-Nghe Tinh region, as well as tribal chiefs in the surrounding mountains. The tu-hu-fu controlled mountainous chiefs only nominally, and the traditional assimilation policy enforced in the deltaic regions since the first century C.E. was abandoned gradually because of the persistent resistance of the indigenous people, including the rebellions led by Mai Hac De in 722 C.E. and Phung Hung in 791 C.E. The tu-hu-fu also suffered foreign invasions of Java (Sailendra-Śrivijaya) in 767 C.E., of Champa in 803 C.E., and of Nanchao (kingdom of Yunnan) in 860 C.E. and 862 C.E. The Chinese general Kao P'ien defeated Nanchao, but he himself established a semi-independent polity to put an end to China's direct rule in Vietnam.

After the tenth century, an indigenous polity that would call itself Dai Viet after 1054 ruled North Vietnam. Nevertheless, although the expeditions for reconquest by the Nan-han (in 923 C.E. and 938 C.E.) and the Sung (in 980 and 1075) were all unsuccessful, Chinese rulers still regarded former Annam as one of their provinces, conferring domestic official titles and peerage on its rulers. It was only in 1174 that China conferred the title "King of the Nation of Annam" on Ly Anh Tong, recognizing Annam as a foreign country, though it was still expected to send tribute to China. From then until the eighteenth century, Vietnam maintained a dual diplomacy: faced with China and other East Asian countries, it was the Chinese vassal state of Annam; with Southeast Asian neighbors such as Champa and Cambodia, it was the Chinese-styled empire of Dai Viet, to which all these countries were to be subject.

The Yuan (in 1258, 1284, and 1287), the Ming (from 1407 to 1427), and the Ch'ing (in 1789) dynasties also invaded Dai Viet in vain. Once they had driven back the Chinese armies, the rulers of Dai Viet resumed tributary relations with China for the purpose of national security and trade. However, not all of them could obtain the title "King of the Nation of Annam" because China often looked unfavorably upon "disobedient" vassal kings. For instance, the Yuan gave the title to three persons other than the ruling king, though none of the three could actually rule. The Ming only conferred lesser titles on the early Le rulers (regretting the defeat in 1427) and on the Mac rulers and then the restored Le rulers (first blaming the usurpation by the Mac). The Le rulers recovered the title "King of the Nation of Annam" only in 1647, when the Ming government in exile, seeking support for the resistance against the Ch'ing, promoted the status of the Le dynasty. The Ch'ing dynasty, for its part, confirmed the title after the exile Ming government perished.

The Tay Son rulers, who overthrew the Le and defeated the Ch'ing army, also managed to obtain the title "King of the Nation of Annam." Nguyễn Phuoc Anh, who defeated Tay Son and unified South and North Vietnam but never defeated the Chinese invasion, did not regard his polity as a mere successor of the dual state of Dai Viet–Annam. His first proposal to adopt the name Nam Viet (in Chinese, Nan-Yueh) was refused by the Ch'ing because it could imply that the polity should dominate not only Vietnam but also Kuang-tung and Kuang-hsi, as did ancient Nan-Yueh (203–111 B.C.E.). Then a compromise was made, and a new official name—Vietnam—was used after 1804, though Annam continued to be popular in unofficial expressions.

The French were deeply interested in Annam ever since they helped Nguyễn Phuoc Anh defeat Tay Son. In their French Indochinese Union, established in 1887, the core area of the Nguyễn dynasty—namely, Central Vietnam—was called Annam, despite the Nguyễn's official names of Vietnam and Dai Nam (the latter was also employed from 1838 on). In the protectorate of Annam, the French *résident supérieur* (resident general) exercised power, reducing the emperor and his imperial bureaucracy to honorific positions. In general, Annam and Tonkin (protectorate of North Vietnam) were left underdeveloped, whereas the French invested much in the development of Cochin China (the colony of South Vietnam).

MOMOKI SHIRO

See also China, Imperial; Dai Viet (939 C.E.–1407); French Indochinese Union *(Union Indochinoise Française);* Le Dynasty (1418–1527; 1533–1804); Ly Dynasty (1009–1225); Ming Dynasty (1368–1644); Nam Viet (Nam Yue); Nguyễn Dynasty (1802–1945); Qing (Ch'ing/Manchu) Dynasty (1644–1911); Vietnam under French Colonial Rule

References:
Ennis, Thomas E. 1973 [1936]. *French Policy and Developments in Indochina.* New York: Russell & Russell. First published in 1936 by the University of Chicago Press, Chicago.
Le Thanh Khoi. 1954. *Le Viet-Nam, l'histoire et civilisation* [*Viet-Nam, its History and Civilization*]. Paris: Les Éditions des Minuit.
Tarling, Nicholas, ed. 1992. *The Cambridge History of Southeast Asia.* 2 vols. Cambridge: Cambridge University Press.
Taylor, Keith W. 1983. *The Birth of Vietnam.* Berkeley and London: University of California Press.
Woodside, Alexander B. 1988. *Vietnam and the Chinese Model: A Comparative Study of Vietnamese and Chinese Government in the First Half of the Nineteenth Century.* 2nd ed. Cambridge, MA: Council on East Asian Studies, Harvard University.

ANTI-FASCIST PEOPLE'S FREEDOM LEAGUE (AFPFL)

Normally known by the acronym AFPFL (or, in Burmese, as Pa Has Pa Lat), the Anti-Fascist People's Freedom League was the major legal political organization in Burma (Myanmar) from the time of its formation in March 1945 until its final split in 1958. Organized in 1944 as the Anti-Fascist Organization (AFO), it was initially a coalition of the Burma Communist Party (BCP) led by Thakin Than Tun and Thakin Soe, the People's Party Revolution group led by U Ba Swe and U Kyaw Nyein, and Burmese army leaders, most importantly General Aung San. As implied by its original title, it sought an alliance with the British to drive the Japanese out of the country. However, that was only the first stage in its strategy to regain Burma's complete independence, as suggested by the league's revised name in 1945. At that time, it had cast its net even wider and incorporated a number of other political groups.

From 1945 through 1947, the AFPFL, led by Chairman Aung San and General Secretary Than Tun, provided the major opposition to the restored British colonial administration. However, the league began to disintegrate in 1946 over policy disagreements between its communist and noncommunist factions and, following the expulsion of the communist parties, became more narrowly based. But as the British changed their policies toward Burma, the AFPFL was included in the Governor's Executive Council (cabinet). When Burma regained independence on 4 January 1948, following the assassination of General Aung San and other Executive Council members in July 1947, the league, now led by U Nu, controlled the government.

Never tightly organized, the AFPFL had little ideological coherence and a poorly articulated organizational base. Although successful in returning to power in elections in 1952 and 1956, it never gained the support of half of the voters. Presided over by Prime Minister Nu, the league was split by rival factions of socialists and conservative interests, which made it difficult to form stable governments. In the 1950s, the league's principal constituent organizations included the Socialist Party and its affiliates—the Trades Union Congress-Burma (TUC-B) and the All Burma Peasants Organization (ABPO). Minority organizations were also included, such as the Burma Muslim Congress, the Kachin National Congress, the Union Karen League, the Chin Congress, and the United Hill People's Congress, as well as women's, youth, and trade associations and fire brigades and the St. John's Ambulance Corps. But the real power lay in the hands of many bosses who dominated parts of the countryside following the Pacific War (1941–1945).

Corruption spread, and in 1956, clashes of interests among the leaders threatened the league's coherence. Following elections in that year, Prime Minister Nu resigned from his government office to devote himself for one year to rebuilding the AFPFL and ridding it of corrupt elements. His action was a ploy in a rapidly developing rift within the leadership of both the AFPFL and the Socialist Party that had started before the 1956 elections. Nu's action had the effect of revealing to the public some of the abuses that made it possible for league officials to use the power and privilege of government for their own and their party's advantage. He could not push reform too far, however, since it might have undermined the entire structure of the league.

The overlapping authority of the government and the league ensured the election of AFPFL candidates by a variety of means. In addition to controlling the electoral machinery, some local league leaders had their own private or pocket armies to guard their positions. League affiliate ABPO saw to it that only league supporters had easy access to redistributed agricultural lands and annual government crop loans. The Union Military Police, a paramilitary force under the control of the home minister, was at the disposal of league members. As a front with no better justification than controlling the state, the AFPFL suffered from much bickering among its members over the spoils of office. These disputes were kept under control until 1958, when, following the league's first national congress since 1947, they became unmanageable and precipitated an open rift.

Conflicts within the political leadership then became so severe that the league and the government split, thus opening the way for the military "caretaker government" from 1958 to 1960. The AFPFL name continued to be used by the socialist faction that called itself the "Stable" AFPFL, but the party failed to win the elections of 1960; those were won by U Nu's faction, renamed the Union Party. The AFPFL never returned to power and was banned by the Revolutionary Council in 1964. The name "AFPFL," however, had a brief revival when a party contesting the elections in Myanmar adopted it in 1990.

R. H. TAYLOR

See also Aung San (1915–1947); Burma Communist Party (BCP); Burma during the Pacific War (1941–1945); Burma under British Colonial Rule; Dorman-Smith, Sir Reginald (t. 1941–1946); Military and Politics in Southeast Asia; Nationalism and Independence Movement in Southeast Asia; Nu, U (1907–1995); Suu Kyi, Daw Aung San (1945–); Thakin (lord, master)

References:

Callahan, Mary P. 1998. "The Sinking Schooner: Murder and the State in Independent Burma, 1948–1958." Pp. 17–38 in *Gangsters, Democracy, and the State in*

Southeast Asia. Edited by Carl A. Trocki. Southeast Asia Program Series no. 17. Ithaca, NY: Cornell University Southeast Asia Program.

Tinker, Hugh. 1967. *The Union of Burma: A Study of the First Years of Independence.* 4th ed. London: Oxford University Press.

Trager, Frank N. 1966. *Burma: From Kingdom to Independence.* London: Pall Mall Press.

ANTI-SPANISH REVOLTS (THE PHILIPPINES)

Throughout the Spanish colonial period in the Philippines, several revolts were launched by Filipinos against the Spanish rulers. Indeed, there was resistance against the Spaniards from the inception of their colonial rule. As the Spanish Empire consolidated its hold on the Philippines in the late 1500s and until the end of Spanish rule in 1898, Filipinos throughout the archipelago revolted due to various causes. Some of the revolts were small and very localized; others crossed provincial boundaries. By the late nineteenth century, the revolts came to have a more nationalistic character. They culminated in the Philippine Revolution of 1896.

When the crew of the first Spanish expedition, led by Ferdinand Magellan (1480–1521), arrived in the Philippines in 1521, they met opposition on the island of Mactan. In the resultant battle, Lapu Lapu led a group of men who killed Magellan. Subsequent voyages to assert Spanish control over the Philippines were likewise met with resistance, and the Spanish expeditions ended in failure. Then, in 1565, the colonizing mission headed by Miguel Lopez de Legazpi (1500–1572) arrived and claimed the Visayan Islands and Luzon for the Spanish king, Philip II (r. 1556–1598). The start of colonization and consolidation into the Spanish Empire, together with Christianization and Hispanization, the establishment of colonial government, and the galleon trade, brought Spanish policy and practices into conflict with existing traditional practices. In response to Spanish impositions, injustices, and control, various revolts broke out. Some lasted only a few days; the longest was crushed only after more than eight decades.

The early anti-Spanish uprisings were led by political and/or religious leaders who had lost their positions of authority as a consequence of the establishment of the Spanish colonial government; they attempted to recoup their losses by leading revolts. Although the Spaniards gave some of the chieftains and local leaders minor positions in government, the loss of power, influence, and prestige, as well as the failure of the Spaniards to keep their promises, prompted several of these chieftains to encourage popular uprisings against the colonizers. In 1574, Raja Lakandula and Raja Sulayman, chieftains in the newly established Spanish city of Manila, attacked Spanish positions to oppose Spanish rule and also because the Spaniards did not keep their promises to exempt them and their families from taxation. In 1589, descendants of Lakandula plotted to overthrow the Spanish in Luzon, aiming to regain the freedoms enjoyed by their forefathers.

Religious leaders also staged revolts, partly due to the loss of power they experienced but also in reaction to the spread of Christianity in the colonized areas. Native priests or religious elders enjoined their followers to reject Christianity and return to the old, traditional religion. Others reacted to impositions by the Spanish priests. Anti-Spanish movements of this sort were particularly common in the Visayan Islands. In 1621, a native priest named Tamblot led a revolt of hundreds on the island of Bohol; in the following year, a similar revolt led by Bankaw erupted on the island of Limasawa and spread to the larger island of Leyte.

Other revolts broke out in response to Spanish impositions, particularly forced labor, heavy taxes, mandatory payment of tribute and other fees, and forced sales of agricultural products at low prices. These uprisings took place throughout the colonized areas in Luzon and the Visayans. Other revolts resulted from unjust treatment by *encomenderos* (Spaniards who were given the privilege of administering property), high land rentals, and a variety of agrarian injustices. Still others were in response to government monopolies. The 1596 revolt of Magalat in Cagayan was one example of resistance against tribute and other Spanish impositions. The revolt led by Sumoroy in Samar in 1649 opposed conscription for forced labor; it eventually spread to neighboring islands and provinces in southern Luzon, the Visayans, and northern Mindanao. The Maniago revolt in Pampanga in 1660 similarly resisted forced labor and forced sales of agricultural produce.

With the British defeat of the Spaniards in Manila in 1762, Filipinos in Pangasinan demanded the abolition of tribute collection and the removal of the local Spanish official. Diego Silang, in the Ilocos provinces, revolted against Spanish rule and attempted to create a "kingdom," seeking British assistance. A Spanish mestizo assassinated him, but the revolt continued, led by his widow, Gabriela, until superior Spanish forces crushed it.

The longest revolt, which lasted for eighty-five years, took place on the island of Bohol. Initially led by Dagohoy, who was incensed when a Spanish priest refused to allow a Christian burial for his brother, the revolt underscored deep-seated grievances in the island's population in regard to colonial rule.

Most of the revolts were local in character, due to the Spanish policy of divide and rule, whereby travel from one town or province to another was discouraged. Linguistic differences were maintained, and the Spaniards were able to utilize drafted men from one region or province against those revolting in another. Through the use of spies and the church, some of the plots were uncovered in their early stages, resulting in the quick imposition of countermeasures. After a revolt was crushed, the leaders were usually executed in public or exiled to distant places in the Philippines or in Mexico. The Spaniards resorted to harsh penalties and the threat of torture as well as excommunication from the church to deter would-be rebels. Nonetheless, revolts continued to erupt throughout the Spanish colonial period.

RICARDO TROTA JOSE

See also Galleon Trade; Hispanization; Legazpi, Miguel Lopez de (1500–1572); Manila; Moros; Peasant Uprisings and Protest Movements in Southeast Asia; Philippines under Spanish Colonial Rule (ca. 1560s–1898)

References:
Blair, Emma H., and James A. Robertson, eds. 1903–1909. *The Philippine Islands, 1493–1898.* 55 vols. Cleveland, OH: Arthur H. Clark.

Corpuz, O. D. 1989. *The Roots of the Filipino Nation.* Quezon City, the Philippines: Aklahi Foundation.

ANWAR IBRAHIM
See Angkatan Belia Islam Malaysia (ABIM) (Malaysian Islamic Youth Movement)

AQUINO, CORAZON COJUANGCO (1933–)
Reinstating Democracy in the Philippines
Making history as the first woman president of Southeast Asia, Corazon Cojuangco Aquino was drawn into the vortex of Philippine politics by the overthrow of the Marcos regime (1965–1986) in a four-day "people power revolution" in February 1986, following fourteen years of Ferdinand Marcos's dictatorship, which began with his imposition of martial law on the Philippines in 1972. Widow of the assassinated opposition leader Benigno "Ninoy" Aquino Jr. (1932–1983), Cory Aquino became the rallying symbol for the struggle to restore democracy in the Philippines. What she lacked in political experience was more than made up for by her moral authority and widespread popularity as the logical leader for the opposition, making her the overwhelming choice of the people to replace Marcos. In the 1986 "snap election" that Marcos had called, Aquino was massively cheated, leading to a chain of events that culminated in the toppling of the dictator three weeks later.

Upon assuming office as the "transition president," Aquino convened a representative group of Filipinos to draft a new constitution. Ratified by a large majority, this constitution took effect in 1987, followed by the first national election since the Marcos overthrow; twenty-two of Aquino's candidates for twenty-four senatorial seats won.

Aquino's presidency (1986–1992) was wracked by a series of attempts to stage military coups or destabilize the government by disgruntled elements who had been plotting even against Marcos earlier. They thought Aquino was soft on the communists and unable to govern. They almost succeeded in removing the fledgling Aquino administration in 1987, and they were to strike again toward the end of 1989. In both cases, the Filipino tradition of civilian supremacy, the loyalty of Aquino's followers in the military, and U.S. assistance in fending off the plotters saved the day for Aquino. By the time she handed the presidential reins to Fidel Ramos (t. 1992–1998), the country had returned to political normalcy.

Aquino's principal contribution as president was the restoration of democratic institutions and civil liberties, which had been flagrantly violated during the Marcos regime. One of the most important developments during her tenure was the lifting of censorship over the media. But as was expected in a free society, the media later became Aquino's major critic, calling her term a presidency of "lost opportunities."

Aquino comes from the nation's wealthy landed elite and now devotes her time to family concerns and a foundation that she established in honor of her martyred husband. She remains a well-respected figure and now and then speaks her mind on current political issues. She was vocal during the so-called second people power revolution that toppled the presidency of Joseph Ejercito Estrada (t. 1998–2001).

BELINDA A. AQUINO

See also EDSA Revolution (1986); Marcos, Ferdinand (1917–1989); Martial Law (1972–1981) (The Philippines); New Peoples Army (NPA); Ramos, Fidel Valdez (1928–)

References:
Kerkvliet, Benedict J., and Resil B. Mojares, eds. 1991. *From Marcos to Aquino: Local Perspectives on Political Transition in the Philippines.* Honolulu, HI, and Manila: Ateneo de Manila University Press.

Swept to power in 1986 after the assassination of her husband, Benigno Aquino, Corazon Aquino served as president of the Philippines through six coup attempts and public unrest related to the slow pace of political and economic reform. (Embassy of the Philippines)

ARABS

Arabs may have traveled to Southeast Asia for spices as early as the beginning of the common era. Their role changed when some became missionaries of Islam, especially from the thirteenth century C.E. The sixteenth-century irruption of Europeans temporarily impaired links with Arabia but never completely severed them. As the Dutch grip faltered in the later eighteenth century, Arabs settled in growing numbers, as entrepreneurs, religious teachers, and political figures. The majority of this latest wave of migrants were Muslims from Hadhramaut (eastern Yemen), who went chiefly to Indonesia and Malaysia. In contrast, most of those entering the Philippines were Christians from Ottoman Syria. Despite marriages with local women and a sharp reduction in immigration

after 1941, Arab communities have retained their separate identity. Many captains of industry, religious leaders, civil servants, and even cabinet ministers in Indonesia and Malaysia have come from their well-educated ranks since independence.

Arabs first appeared in Southeast Asia as the spice trade gathered momentum. Those claiming descent from the prophet Muhammad (s.a.w.), bearing the title of "Sayyid" or "Sharif," are often credited with a major role in mass conversions to Islam from the late thirteenth century, for example, in Java and the southern Philippines. As Southeast Asian Muslims are overwhelmingly members of the Shafi'i legal school, contacts may have been strongest with southwestern Arabia and the Red Sea, although South India and pre-Shi'ite Persia are other possible origins of this legal school.

After a depressed period during the Dutch heyday, Hadhrami Sayyids immigrated to Southeast Asia from the mid-eighteenth century. Revered for their descent from the Prophet, they married into noble families and became senior religious figures, and their tombs sometimes became centers of pilgrimage. However, other Sayyids became pirates and then seized power, notably members of the Bin Shihab dynasty of Siak in Sumatra and the Algadri dynasty of Pontianak in West Kalimantan. Yet others became senior advisers to Europeans; Sayyid Hasan al-Hibshi, for instance, was entrusted by the Dutch with diplomatic missions to Thailand (Siam) and Bali. At the same time, they purchased square-rigged European vessels and temporarily dominated the regional sea-lanes of the archipelago, outstripping both European and Chinese competitors. Their main economic centers were in Surabaya, Semarang, Palembang, and Singapore.

Hadhramis were progressively eased out of shipping as sail gave way to steam from the 1860s, but they successfully diversified. They were among the wealthiest owners of urban real estate in Indonesia and Malaya, and they dominated the horse trade from the Lesser Sunda Islands to Java. They traded in a host of other products and became famous money-lenders as well as pioneer industrialists on Java in the 1930s. Their religious role grew to the point that the Dutch appointed Sayyid 'Uthman as the grand mufti of Indonesia in the late nineteenth century. Singapore's leading Sayyid families took turns in being honorary Ottoman consuls from the 1860s. Wealthy Arabs sent their children to European schools and universities, and they benefited from the relaxation of Dutch controls over "foreign Orientals."

Success did not, however, bring unity. Non-Sayyid Hadhramis were attracted to Southeast Asia in increasing numbers from the 1870s, together with a few Hijazis and Iraqis, and the community grew to around 75,000 at its height in the 1930s. Newcomers resented Sayyid pretensions, and a formal split occurred in 1914 over the question of Islamic modernism. Most non-Sayyids became members of al-Irshad, a charitable organization that concentrated on providing modern schooling in Arabic. This division was overlaid with another in the 1930s, when young locally born Arabs, Sayyid and non-Sayyid, threw in their lot with local nationalists, whereas their elders remained attached to Hadhramaut. The Sukarno regime (1947–1967) drove many of the latter back home or to Saudi Arabia after Indonesian independence.

A quite different stream of migration took Arabs to the Philippines. This community was smaller, peaking at around 10,000 in the late 1970s (Gleek 1975). The pioneers were probably Bethlehem Christians in the 1870s, but later, Lebanese dominated—mainly Maronite Christians but also Druze Muslims. In addition, there were Greek Orthodox and Jewish families, mainly from Syria proper. This migration was closely linked to large and influential Syrian communities in the Americas, and many took out U.S. citizenship after the U.S. takeover of 1898. They tended not to get involved in religion or politics but to stick to trade and, later, manufacturing.

The role of Arabs in Southeast Asia's history has been much less studied than that of the Chinese, yet their influence was felt across a wider spectrum of activities, at least in the Hadhrami case. Growing interest in the Arab case could usefully be extended to other Middle Eastern (West Asian) minorities in Southeast Asia, notably Iraqi Jews, Armenians, and Persians.

WILLIAM G. CLARENCE-SMITH

See also Economic Transformation of Southeast Asia (ca. 1400–ca. 1800); Islam in Southeast Asia; Miscegenation; Piracy; Plural Society; Spices and the Spice Trade; Trade and Commerce of Southeast Asia

References:
Algadri, Hamid. 1994. *Dutch Policy against Islam and Indonesians of Arab Descent in Indonesia.* Jakarta: Pustaka LP3ES.
Freitag, Ulrike, and William G. Clarence-Smith, eds. 1997. *Hadhrami Traders, Scholars and Statesmen in the Indian Ocean, 1750s to 1960s.* Leiden, The Netherlands: E. J. Brill.
Gleek, Lewis E., Jr. 1975. *American Business and Philippine Economic Development.* Manila: Carmelo and Bauermann.
Kroef, Justus van Der. 1953. "The Arabs in Indonesia." *Middle East Journal* 7, no. 3: 300–323.
Mobini-kesheh, Natalie. 1999. *The Hadrami Awakening: Community and Identity in the*

Netherlands East Indies, 1900–1942. Ithaca, NY: Cornell University Press.

Safa, Elie. 1960. *L'Emigration Libanaise* [*The Lebanese Emigration*]. Beirut: École Française de Droit.

Yoshihara Kunio. 1985. *Philippine Industrialization: Foreign and Domestic Capital.* Singapore: Oxford University Press.

ARAKAN

Situated on the southwestern coast of Burma (Myanmar) adjoining Bangladesh, Arakan, or Rakhine State, is some 36,760 square kilometers (14,200 square miles) in area. Its capital is Sittwe. It has a population of around 3 million (Hla Min 2001: 99). Since 1784 when the Konbaung monarch, King Bodawpaya (r. 1782–1819), conquered it, Arakan has been incorporated into Burma. Events in Arakan precipitated the First Anglo-Burmese War (1824–1826), in the course of which pestilence and fevers in Arakan accounted for the deaths of an entire British army.

Arakan has had a checkered history in modern times, and it had an illustrious autonomous history before its incorporation into monarchical Burma, when its kings and fleets influenced the course of events around the Bay of Bengal. Independent Arakan in the early centuries of the Christian era was centered at Dhanyawadi, the capital city in the fourth to sixth centuries C.E. and original home of the Buddhist Mahamuni Shrine, the palladium (state image) of Arakan. On the sixth-century stone stele, the Shit-thaung pillar, the early history of the kings of Arakan is inscribed. From the sixth to ninth centuries, the political center shifted to Vesali, a short distance south of Dhanyawadi. Archaeological remains have revealed an oval-shaped city of some 7 square kilometers (2.7 square miles) surrounded by a moat, similar to Dhanyawadi. The palace site, with its own moat and royal lake, was at the center of the city. There, the Candra kings ruled. A certain Anandracandra ruling at Vesali in the eighth century was a Buddhist monarch who endowed monasteries and gilded images. Early Arakan drew its wealth from the trade of the Bay of Bengal and kept close relations with the Pyu and Mon cities to the east. With the migration of the Tibeto-Burman peoples into the Pagan region from the eighth century, the population pool in Arakan received newcomers called Rakhaing, who then took over the country. On the Mrauk-U plain, in the tenth century, two new cities were built, one of which, Mrauk-U, became the capital center. Other cities arose at Sambawak, Hkrit, Launggret, and Parein west of the Le-mro River. The Vesali kings are thought to have founded Sambawak about 1018 C.E. A princess of Vesali is said to have been sent to King Anawrahta (r. 1044–1077) of Pagan as a peace offering. For a time in the mid-Pagan period, Arakan was a tributary state of Pagan, but it regained its independence as the power of Pagan faded. From the new capital at Launggret in 1237 C.E., Arakan again extended its influence around the Bay of Bengal up to Cape Negrais, and it maintained relations with the Buddhist cultural world of Ceylon (Sri Lanka).

In the fifteenth century, Arakan for a time had a precarious existence between the Islamic power taking hold in the Bengal sultanate to the west, the Burmese at Ava, and the Mons at Pegu in the east. For a period in 1404, the Burmese occupied Launggret. The king, Min Saw Mun, sought help from the sultan of Gaur in Bengal, and with his assistance, Min Saw Mun recaptured Arakan and founded Mrauk-U in 1433, destined, as the last capital of independent Arakan (1433–1784), to preside over the glory days of Arakan's dominance in the region. Tributary to Bengal for a century, the Buddhist kings at Mrauk-U used Muslim titles. Their coinage was inscribed with the *kalima,* the Islamic declaration of faith. At Ramoo, Min Saw Mun's brother, Ali Khan, was installed, and his son, Kalimah Shah, took Chittagong. Under Min Bin (r. 1531–1553), a contemporary of Tabinshweihti of Toungoo (r. 1553–1551), and aided by Portuguese mercenaries and munitions, Arakan asserted its power in the region. It possessed a navy of some 350 ships that raided the coasts, taking slaves, trading cotton and rice, and dominating the economy of the Kaladan and Le-mro Valleys. With civil war in Bengal after the arrival of the Mughals, Min Bin occupied eastern Bengal. Arakan maintained a viceroy at Chittagong until 1666. Min Bin held off the Burmese under Tabinshweihti in 1546 and 1547. In 1595, his successor, Raza-gri, with Portuguese allies, captured Pegu, then ruled by Nanda Bayin (r. 1581–1599). Along with a white elephant and a royal princess, Raza-gri's spoils of war included the thirty Buddhist images and bronze cannon that Nanda Bayin's father, Bayinnaung (r. 1551–1581), had captured at Ayutthaya in 1569.

Allied with the Portuguese Felipe de Brito at Syriam, Arakan's power extended along the Bay of Bengal up to Moulmein in Tenasserim Province. In the seventeenth century, King Sandathudamma provided additional support to Arakan's power based on the trading ventures of the Dutch, who were allowed to trade out of Mrauk-U. But King Sandathudamma's lust after the daughter of Shah Shuja, the former Mughal viceroy of Bengal who had taken refuge in Arakan after his defeat by his brother, Emperor Aurangzeb (r. 1659–1707), led to a crisis. Mughal retaliation for the death of Shah Shuja and his family destroyed Arakan's power in Bengal. Instability in Arakan for the rest of the century saw Arakanese power recede back to the environs of Mrauk-U. With the rise of the Konbaung dynasty in Burma, it was only a matter of time before Arakan attracted their imperial designs. In 1784, King Bodawpaya (r. 1782–1819) sent his crown prince to seize Arakan and to deport its royal family, 20,000 people, horses, munitions, and the great Mahamuni image, the palladium of Arakan, back to the Burmese capital at Amarapura (Koenig 1990: 22–23; Gutman 2001: 34, 39).

Arakan under the Konbaung dynasty was subjected to massive levies in 1790 and 1795 to support public building projects, notably the Meiktila irrigation system and the Mingun pagoda construction. The Burmese governor, Mingyi Mingaung-gyaw, appointed subordinates at Ramree, Sandaway, and Cheduba. Arakan was now administered as a province of Konbaung Burma. Arakanese refugees fled to Chittagong, then under the English East India Company (EIC). Border tensions in Arakan increased in 1811 with the rebellion of the Arakanese chief, Chin Pyan. The Burmese suspected the British of supporting his rebellion, a belief Chin Pyan encouraged. Such suspicions had not been allayed by the missions of Michael Symes (1795, 1802), Hiram Cox (1796), or Lieutenant (later Captain) John Canning (1803, 1809, 1811). Chin Pyan's death in 1815 and Bodawpaya's in 1819 did not reduce the tensions. From 1821 to 1822, the Burmese general Maha Bandula was stationed in Arakan, ready for the onset of hostilities with the British in 1824. His epic march from Arakan to Rangoon (Yangon) could not save the city. Arakan, with Tenasserim, was ceded to the British in accordance with the Treaty of Yandabo (1826) at the conclusion of the First Anglo-Burmese War.

After independence (1948), Arakan was the site of insurgencies by Muslim groups seeking autonomy. Suppression during the socialist and postsocialist era of modern Burmese history caused over 150,000 Rohingya (Muslim) refugees to seek safe haven in Bangladesh (Christie 1996: 170–171; *Guardian Weekly*).

HELEN JAMES

See also Anawrahta (Aniruddha) (r. 1044–1077); Anglo-Burmese Wars (1824–1826, 1852, 1885); East India Company (EIC) (1602), English; Konbaung Dynasty (1752–1885); Konbaung Rulers and British Imperialism; Pagan (Bagan); Sri Lanka (Ceylon); Tabinshweihti (r. 1531–1550); Yandabo (1826), Treaty of

References:
Charney, Michael W. 1998. "Rise of a Mainland Trading State: Rahkaing under the Early Mrauk-U Kings, c. 1430–1603." *Journal of Burma Studies* 3: 1–34.
Christie, Clive J. 1996. *A Modern History of Southeast Asia: Decolonization, Nationalism and Separatism*. London and New York: Tauris Academic Studies; Singapore: Institute of Southeast Asian Studies.
Collis, Morris. 1943. *The Land of the Great Image, Being Experiences of Friar Manrique in Arakan*. New York: Alfred A. Knopf.
Fraser-lu, Sylvia. 1994. *Burmese Crafts: Past and Present*. New York: Oxford University Press.
Guardian Weekly. 16 February 1992.
Gutman, Pamela. 2001. *Burma's Lost Kingdoms: Splendours of Arakan*. Bangkok: Orchid Press.
Hazra, Kanai Lal. 1982. *History of Theravada Buddhism in Southeast Asia*. New Delhi: Munshiram Manoharlal.
Hein, Don. 1996. "Ceramic Production in Myanmar—Further Evidence on Old Traditions." Pp. 179–205 in *Traditions in Current Perspective*. Yangon: Universities Historical Research Centre.
Hla Min. 2001. *Political Situation of Myanmar and Its Role in the Region*. 27th ed. Yangon: Office of Strategic Studies.
Koenig, William J. 1990. *The Burmese Polity, 1752–1819: Politics, Administration and Social*

Organization in the Early Konbaung Period. Ann Arbor, MI: Center for Southeast Asian Studies.

Strachan, Paul. 1989. *Pagan: Art and Architecture of Old Burma.* Aran, Scotland: Kiscadale.

Woodman, Dorothy. 1962. *The Making of Modern Burma.* London: Cresset.

ARCHAEOLOGICAL SITES OF SOUTHEAST ASIA

Archaeological sites are the physical register of past activity. Most archaeological remains are debris left behind at habitation abodes and task stations, along with the vestiges of dwellings and other facilities. A small proportion consists of useful artifacts that have been lost during use or when dropped underfoot. A very small proportion, usually involving the most spectacular and informative artifacts, comprises those goods intentionally buried in caches or in graves. The physical remains of burials and other customary treatments of the deceased are also considered part of the archaeological record. However, early *Homo* fossils fall within the domain of paleoanthropology because the dead were then, apparently, abandoned to the same physical processes that affected other animals, and when preserved, they turn up in fossil beds of general interest to paleontologists. Southeast Asia has a rich record essentially on a par with Northern Europe in terms of its paleontological beds with hominid fossils, rock shelters and caves, stone-tool and pottery scatters, mounds of kitchen waste (middens), wetland sites with a wide array of organic remains, old agricultural fields, megalith sites, temple monuments, historical urban complexes, and other sites.

Archaeologists use a wide range of skills to explore and understand their sites. Classification and comparison of artifacts remain important but have definitely taken the back seat compared with more scientifically oriented approaches. The study of faunal (nonhuman animal) and floral remains is critical for understanding the human ecology and subsistence economy of early Southeast Asians. The sediments that hold together or encase a site—and preserve it for the archaeological record—offer clues on water flow, erosion, and other environmental factors. Older sediments can often be dated in various ways, for instance, through correlation with the shifts and switches of the earth's magnetic field or through measuring the decay of radioactive isotopes. Materials within the sediments can also be dated, most notably through radiocarbon dates on organic items (going back some 40,000 years) but also thermoluminescence dates on ceramics and a host of other techniques.

Generally speaking, sites can be classified as closed sites (caves and rock shelters), open sites, and built sites (with imperishable structural remains). All have their advantages and drawbacks. Closed sites trap sediments and items taken inside the cavern, which can lead to continuous cultural sequences that may span 40,000 years or longer. However, by the same token, human burials and even mild forms of sediment disturbance can juxtapose objects that belong to intervals thousands of years apart. Deciphering closed sites in terms of which items belong to the same time band is a chronic problem. Some open sites also suffer from an admixture of objects from different periods, especially as the attractions of a location are likely to persist over time, but most open sites offer greater scope for catching a discrete episode of human activity. More problematic is the greater exposure of open sites to the elements and the large element of luck required for an open site to be sealed by protective sediments but then subsequently exposed to archaeological inquiry. (The greater visibility of closed sites has tricked many archaeologists into believing that cave-dwelling troglodytes held sway in times of yore.) Built sites provide a framework to trap sediments and objects, but in Southeast Asia, sites such as these date to the last two millennia. Also, as archaeologists move to a historical time scale, their research questions require an increasingly finer chronological resolution. Because built sites are particularly prone to various forms of earthworks, their digging, construction, and usage cycles demand close attention.

The oldest known hominid presence in Southeast Asia is found in Java, but there is much debate on whether the correct dating is closer to 1 million or 1.8 million years ago. A series of volcanic eruptions on Java has bequeathed layer upon layer of volcanic debris that potentially can be scientifically dated and so provide age brackets for any fossils, including *Homo erectus,* sealed between the layers. Unfortunately, Java's fossil beds have been subject to vigorous water action, and materials of very different antiquity have often been jumbled together. Although by no means a certainty, the 1.8-million-year dates would support other evidence that the direct ancestor of *Homo erectus,* not *Homo erectus* itself, left Africa at around 2 million years ago, before evolving into *Homo erectus* in Asia. Java has additionally yielded later *Homo erectus* skulls, dating through to about 300,000 years ago, but a lengthy gap in the fossil record immediately follows. Consequently, paleoanthropologists cannot determine whether *Homo sapiens* in Southeast Asia arrived from Africa between 60,000 and 100,000 years ago, as per the "out of Africa" theory on modern human origins, or else evolved at least partly from Southeast Asian *Homo erectus,* as claimed by the "multiregional continuity" theory.

Apart from tentatively identified *Homo erectus* specimens near the border between Vietnam and China, all of the human fossils found in Southeast Asia's closed sites clearly represent anatomically modern *Homo sapiens.* Hunter-gatherer burials are concentrated in the Malay Peninsula and at Niah Cave in Borneo, whereas smaller numbers are known in North Vietnam, the Philippines, and Indonesia. Even after the spread of farming across most of Southeast Asia and the establishment of permanent settlements, many communities continued to inter the deceased in caves. However, most preferred to establish open-air cemeteries or to bury the dead beneath their houses. Estimates of the number of burials can exceed a thousand in the largest sites, such as Khok Phanom Di (Thailand, Neolithic) and Gilimanuk (Bali, Iron Age). These large burial assemblages allow useful assessments of the residents' life expectancies and their susceptibility to infectious disease, trauma, genetic disorders, and dental problems. Broadly speaking, burials dating to the last 4,000 years resemble present-day Southeast Asians in their skeletal features, whereas more ancient skeletons suggest a larger people with more rugged and elongated skulls.

Apart from hominid fossils, stone artifacts are the oldest preserved reminder of humans in Southeast Asia. Dates on volcanic samples, meticulous study of the geomorphology, and correlations with ancient changes in the earth's magnetic field have shown that *Homo erectus* produced stone tools in Java by 800,000 years ago, in Flores by 700,000 years ago, and in North Thailand by 560,000 to 700,000 years ago. Remarkably, whereas *Homo erectus* would have been able to walk to Java in those days, further travel to Flores would have required at least one sea crossing. In the caves of South Java, a small number of stone artifacts may be up to 150,000 years old, even if most date to the last 16,000 years. Attempts to place early Southeast Asian stone tools on a timeline from early and crude to more evolved have never succeeded, and morphologically identical examples may be separated by hundreds of kilometers and tens of millennia.

A major concern is that where open and closed sites are believed to overlap in their chronology (and the dates exceed 10,000 years ago), the stone artifacts in these two contexts fail to match up. This problem affects the Malay Peninsula, Java, Sabah (northeastern Borneo), and southwestern Sulawesi. Hunter-gatherers evidently took an expedient approach to making stone tools, dictated more by the specifics of the raw material than by any attempt to produce standardized end products. It is true that in certain parts of Indonesia, well-defined types appeared in the last 10,000 years, such as bone points, stone arrowheads, and spear barbs with characteristic trimming along their backs. Further, a broad division can be made between mainland Southeast Asia (and northern Sumatra), where river pebbles tended to be utilized, and the usual pattern in island Southeast Asia of shaping blocks of stone into cores, knocking flakes off the cores, and trimming the flakes. However, generally speaking, stone tools in Southeast Asia resist classification into discrete, coherent cultures.

Economic information on Southeast Asia's earliest inhabitants is sparse. Where the fossils of extinct vertebrates are found in association with hominid remains or ancient stone artifacts, their main use is to help to date the materials of archaeological interest. It would be mere supposition that the early hominids preyed on the animals found in the same geological layer. The outlook is brighter for closed sites, where it is more likely that any faunal remains are scraps discarded from people's meals. Changes in hunting patterns spanning the last 40,000 years or so have been observed in the Malay Peninsula, Sarawak (Niah Cave), southwestern Sulawesi, and Java. Shellfish were, naturally enough, consumed from early times. The layers

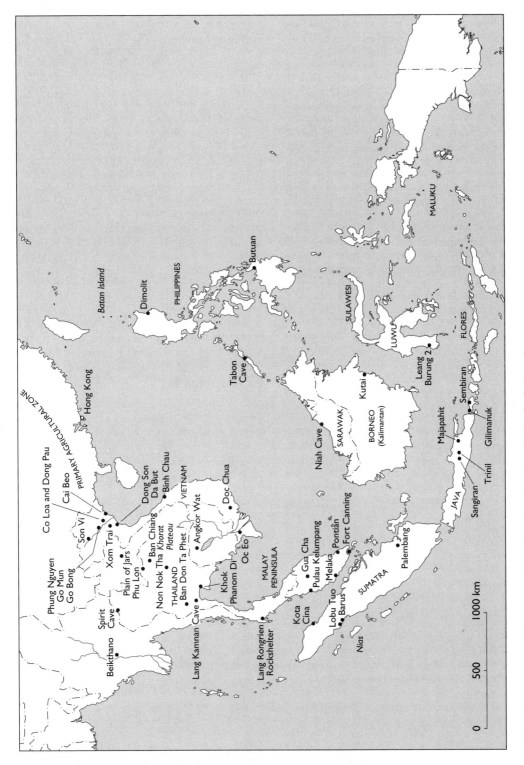

Archaeological sites of Southeast Asia. (David Bulbeck and Elizabeth Bacus)

deposited between 30,000 and 20,000 years ago at Leang Burung 2 in southwestern Sulawesi are thick with freshwater shell. Plant foods have always been important in Southeast Asia, and charred fragments of vegetation in closed sites provide some insight into that component of the diet, especially over the last 10,000 years. By then, people clearly exploited the whole range of edible resources, and a broad-spectrum economy is thought to be a useful defining feature, along with the inclination toward pebble tools, of the so-called Hoabinhian technocomplex of mainland Southeast Asia and North Sumatra.

Marine shellfish make up an abundant resource for communities based on the coast. Some Hoabinhian middens in Sumatra reached 12 meters in height from waste marine shells thrown upon the heaps. There is little reason to doubt that coastally oriented Southeast Asians have been consuming marine shellfish since time immemorial, but sea-level changes over the millennia mean that the oldest marine shellfish middens we know of date only to the last 4,000 to 9,000 years. The largest middens may have been deliberately built up as monuments and territorial markers and were often used as burial places, but the usual motivation was probably to keep the beaches free of dangerously sharp-edged litter. By themselves, middens need not imply a diet centered on shellfish, and indeed, they always preserve scraps from other animals discarded along with the masses of shell.

The oldest sites to give a well-rounded view on daily life are habitation mounds, which date back to 6,500 years ago in North Vietnam, 5,000 years ago in Thailand, and 3,000 years ago in Indonesia. These build up over time through the concentration of material brought into the settlement: timber, stone, clay, and other materials for building and craftwork; useful objects manufactured or obtained elsewhere; the day's catch or the season's harvest, including food that will be stored on site; dirt carried in on the body or clothes; and the excrement of humans and domestic animals. Even when preservation circumstances treat these sites unkindly and congeal them into one relatively homogeneous body, they at least have a coherence that forms a buffer against the rampant destruction that awaits most temporary, open-air encampments. On occasion, rapid buildup and positive conditions can bequeath a succession of discrete layers, which, through meticulous excavation, can be distinguished and interpreted in terms of a succession of phases spanning hundreds of years. The 12-meter-high mound of Khok Phanom Di is particularly exemplary; a series of monographs detail the information available on subsistence economy, handicrafts, mortuary practices, physical health, and so forth. In places where bronze and especially iron metallurgy was practiced, the masses of ore brought on site for processing could have led to an even more rapid accumulation of debris.

Archaeological remains from settlements built over oxygen-starved wetlands can be especially informative. Housing on wooden piles has undoubtedly been widespread in Southeast Asia since its first settlements were established, so waterlogged terrain has proved no barrier to permanent residency, especially when canoes can carry people over tides and swamps. Swampy and shallow marine conditions are responsible for the preservation of indigenous Southeast Asian watercraft between 2,000 and 1,000 years old at Butuan in the Philippines, Pulau Kelumpang and Pontian in the Malay Peninsula, and Palembang in southern Sumatra. At the 2-hectare village of Pulau Kelumpang, where residents made beads of glass and semiprecious stone, the estuarine mud reveals extraordinarily detailed information such as house piles, burials (sometimes contained in canoes), and traces of dammar resin. Food refuse includes rice, coconuts, crabs, marine fish and shellfish, whales and porpoises, monkeys, squirrels, deer, pigs, dogs, and chickens. In Luwu, Sulawesi, a Bugis palace center dated between the fifteenth and sixteenth centuries has been discovered in what used to be a sago swamp. An estimated 400 to 500 tons of cultural materials are sealed within its 3-hectare area, with earthenware pottery apparently the major class by weight, followed by timber and faunal fragments (especially water buffalo) and some plant remains (dammar gum, canarium nut, coconut husks).

Megaliths are a distinctive part of the landscape in the plateaus of southern Sumatra, Java, Sarawak, central Sulawesi, and the area known as the Plain of Jars in Laos. Here, we find boulders sculpted into human figures and other effigies, shaped into huge vats and other containers, or arranged into characteristic patterns of upright stones (menhirs) and lidded chambers (dolmens). Some of the megalith complexes of West Java are massive architectural works that resemble the Polynesian temples built of stone slabs and laid boulders. Excavations at the Plain of Jars suggest that the production of its massive vats and lid-shaped disks started in the last centuries B.C.E., whereas other Southeast Asian megaliths would date to the last two millennia. The most spectacular of Southeast Asia's megaliths are probably the enormous tombs constructed to this day in Sumba, as well as the stone villages of the Nias Islands, Sumatra, where the ancestors are placed in huge stone tables that skirt the central, paved plaza. Many megaliths, such as the boat-shaped altars of southern Maluku, seem to be aggrandized versions, in stone, of artifacts originally made in timber, and attempts to trace long-distance cultural relationships through shape similarities would be illusory. In other cases, particularly where the megaliths appear intrusive, formal similarities may reflect cultural connections. For instance, the megaliths of Malaya have probably derived from Sumatra but in two discrete episodes: the first involving slab-sided graves about 2,000 years ago and the second involving plain and carved menhirs at the time when Islam was spreading among the Malays.

Megaliths carry an implicit association with the indigenous Southeast Asian belief systems of animism and ancestor worship. These beliefs have obviously carried over into the various brands of Hinduism, Buddhism, Islam, and Christianity followed in later times, and the transition is evident in Southeast Asia's megaliths. One reason for dating Indonesia's early megaliths to the first millennium C.E. is the fifth-century dating of its oldest Sanskrit inscriptions on what would otherwise be considered standard megaliths, specifically, menhirs at Kutai in East Kalimantan, and boulders in West Java with carved impressions of the king's footprints. However, Southeast Asia's oldest stone inscriptions (fourth century C.E.) are actually found in the Cham area of central Vietnam, which lacks a megalith tradition. Hindu-Buddhist architectural complexes, with their origins dating back to the first millennium C.E., are widely known in Java, Sumatra, Malaya, southern/central Thailand, Cambodia, and Vietnam. The picture emerges of cosmopolitan centers espousing an Indic model of royal organization, located at nodes in the international trade routes and at certain hinterland locations of exceptional agrarian potential (especially in Java), surrounded by more traditional societies where people continued to erect megaliths and otherwise follow their ancestral ways.

The enormous potential of archaeology to illuminate Southeast Asia's historical period has already led to some major successes. Whereas early views on the "Indianization" of Southeast Asia presumed a socially undifferentiated world, in which visitors might as well choose one place as any other, we now know of sophisticated, stratified societies in certain locations with origins stretching back to 2000 B.C.E. A local view generated through archaeology strongly suggests that chiefly authority—and comparative security for the subjects—developed early where resources were concentrated and access to trade routes was optimal. These circumstances subsequently attracted traders, artisans, scribes, and priests to come from afar and set up shop. This is certainly the general impression to be gained in areas of secondary civilization, such as southwestern Sulawesi, where events unfolded more recently, allowing greater insight into the relevant processes. At the same time, archaeological evidence has dated the onset of Indianization further back in time than the historical records would have allowed. Sites such as Ban Don Ta Phet in Thailand and Sembiran in Bali trace Indian contacts back to the last centuries B.C.E.

The pivotal role that archaeological sites can play is well illustrated in their contribution to early Malay history. Based on its concentration of relevant inscriptions in Old Malay, Palembang has long been touted as the capital of the Hindu-Buddhist empire of Śrivijaya. This encouraged archaeologists to continue prospecting the area despite initially disappointing returns, until the expected tons of relevant cultural materials finally were unearthed beginning in the late 1980s. Further archaeological discoveries at Barus, Kota Cina, Lobu Tuo, and other coastal sites have provided additional insight into the complexities of early trade relations in Sumatra. Excavations at Fort Canning conclusively show that Singapore acted as an intermediary step in the movement of Malay imperial rule from Śrivijaya to Melaka. In addition, ongoing work at the late classical capitals of Angkor Wat in Cambodia and Majapahit in Java—cities whose sheer size seemingly defies the usual processes of urbanization, as observed elsewhere in the world—highlights the relevance of historical archaeology in Southeast Asia not only for the region but also for humanity as a whole.

The view of historical archaeology as the "handmaiden of history" still tends to prevail for the period when Europeans arrived in Southeast Asia and began keeping detailed records. Archaeological research is mainly used to confirm information from written accounts and maps or to highlight cultural resources such as the forts of indigenous rulers who faced off the European intruders. Theory lags behind that in other parts of the world where the archaeology of capitalism (broadly defined) is increasingly seen as the ideal opportunity to develop the full potential of archaeology. The rapid turnover of highly standardized, internationally marketed goods allows extremely fine chronological resolution, whereas textual accounts offer a "thick description" of the use of material culture in maintaining and negotiating social relations. Some Southeast Asian archaeologists are embarking on the critical use of material culture over the last few centuries to explore the nuances of change at a time of wide-scale social transformations and unprecedented new opportunities. The challenge remains to plumb Southeast Asia's "ghost towns" and other historical complexes for their insights into the region's economic, social, and religious history.

DAVID BULBECK

See also Ban Chiang; Ban Kao Culture; Hoabinhian; Human Prehistory of Southeast Asia; "Java Man" and "Solo Man"; Metal Age Cultures in Southeast Asia; Niah Caves (Sarawak); "Perak Man"; Tabon Cave (Palawan)

References:
Bellwood, Peter. 1997. *Prehistory of the Indo-Malaysian Archipelago.* Rev. ed. Honolulu: University of Hawai'i Press.
Bulbeck, David. 2001. "Island Southeast Asia Late Prehistoric." Pp. 82–116 in *Encyclopedia of Prehistory.* Vol. 3, *East Asia and Oceania.* Edited by Peter N. Peregrine and Melvin Ember. New York: Kluwer Academic/Plenum Publishers.
Bulbeck, David, and Ian Caldwell. 2000. *Land of Iron: The Historical Archaeology of Luwu and the Cenrana Valley.* Hull, England: University of Hull Centre for South-East Asian Studies.
Forrestier, Hubert. 2000. "De quelques chaînes opératoires lithiques en Asie du Sud-Est au Pléistocène Supérieur Final et au début de l'Holocène" [Some stone-working operational sequences in Southeast Asia at the end of the Upper Pleistocene and the beginning of the Holocene]. *L'Anthropologie* 104: 531–548.
Higham, Charles. 1989. *The Archaeology of Mainland Southeast Asia.* Cambridge: Cambridge University Press.
Manguin, Pierre-Yves. 1992. "Excavations in South Sumatra, 1988–90: New Evidence for Sriwijayan Sites." Pp. 63–73 in *Southeast Asian Archaeology, 1990.* Edited by Ian Glover. Hull, England: University of Hull Centre for South-East Asian Studies.
Miksic, John. 2000. "Heterogenetic Cites in Premodern Southeast Asia." *World Archaeology* 32, no. 1: 106–120.
Saya Vongkhamdy, Thongsa, and Peter Bellwood. 2000. "Recent Archaeological Research in Laos." *Bulletin of the Indo-Pacific Prehistory Association* 19: 101–110.
Simanjuntak, Truman. 2001. "New Light on the Prehistory of the Southern Mountains of Java." *Bulletin of the Indo-Pacific Prehistory Association* 21: 152–156.
Simanjuntak, Truman, Bagyo Prasetyo, and Retno Handini, eds. 2001. *Sangiran: Man, Culture, and Environment in Pleistocene Times.* Jakarta: Yayasan Obor Indonesia.
Sorenson, Per. 2001. "A Reconsideration of the Chronology of the Early Palaeolithic Lannathaian Culture of North Thailand." *Bulletin of the Indo-Pacific Prehistory Association* 21: 138–141.
Tayles, N. G. 1999. *The Excavation of Khok Phanom Di: A Prehistoric Site in Central Thailand.* Vol. 5, *The People.* London: Society of Antiquaries of London.
Van Heekeren, H. R. 1958. *The Bronze–Iron Age of Indonesia.* The Hague: Martinus Nijhoff.
Waterson, Roxana. 1990. *The Living House: An Anthropology of Architecture in South-East Asia.* Singapore: Oxford University Press.

ARCHITECTURE OF SOUTHEAST ASIA

Architecture depends on climate, topography, population, culture, history, ethnic composition, and religion. Southeast Asia was once the site of several great architectural civilizations. Indeed, the architectures of Pagan (Burma [Myanmar]), of Sukhothai (Siam [Thailand]), and of the Khmer of Cambodia are all significant landmarks in the architectural record.

The region's climate features heavy tropical rains, and seasonal monsoon winds predominate over most of the area. The population is unevenly distributed, with very high densities in many low and flatland areas. The chief crop is rice. Yet despite such commonalities, there is great diversity in terms of economic activities and other critical dimensions in the lives of the people of Southeast Asia.

From the late sixteenth century, Europeans began to colonize the whole of Southeast Asia, with the exception of Siam. The architecture designed by people who had a long tradition of adapting to climate and culture was abruptly stopped by colonization. The schools of thought in architecture developed in opposite directions. Newly developed or redeveloped schemes of architecture in the colonial period derived from Europe. Moreover, the architecture of Southeast Asia was brutally attacked in the course of heavy fighting during the Pacific War (1941–1945). After the war, most of the Southeast Asian countries achieved independence in terms of architectural thought, but weak economies and political turmoil, including violent conflicts between communist and noncommunist factions, have disrupted the history of architecture in the region. Nonetheless, as the historical record attests, the architecture of the region provides considerable evidence and even definite proof that the people of Southeast Asia have often lived in harmony.

From very early times, this region has ranked among the most important in regard to the architectural features of Asia. It is widely acknowledged that the development of Southeast Asian architecture in its unique form was influenced by the great civilizations of its two neighbors—India and China. However, there are few studies and little research on the early settlers of Southeast Asia and the settlements

and architecture they developed. For example, the Pyu, Kanyan, and Thet were the earliest settlers known in present-day Burma, a fact that was mentioned in the *Glass Palace Chronicle* (1828) but was almost unknown in other contexts. Among the three ancient settlers, the Pyu left the most significant architectural remains in their cities and towns. Their unique culture and lifestyle, dominant for about a millennium, presumably started in the first century B.C.E.

There can be no doubt that the enormous walls and broad moats of Pyu cities afforded stout defenses, and there were fortified rice fields, vegetable lands, and water tanks for urban dwellers within a broad architectural base. The largest architectural achievement of Pyu cities involved the irrigation systems inside the urban areas and across the surrounding territory. In most Pyu cities, the land area enclosed by the city walls was between 5 and 20 square kilometers and contained a significant proportion of cultivated land, tanks, canals, the royal palace, and urban settlements. Funeral halls, burial terraces, temples, stupas, monasteries, and nonfood production facilities lay beyond the cities' citadels. Blacksmiths, traders, potters, brick makers, jewelers, weavers, dancers, drummers, learned monks, and courtiers to the king and his family were graded in a hierarchical order within a well-organized society that evolved over many centuries. It is evident that Pyu architecture was unique and possessed its own principles and traditions.

These Pyu conceptions of architectural design in urban spaces are still evident in contemporary Mandalay, with its large royal territory surrounded by cultivated lands, the spacing between numerous monasteries, and the courtyards of craftspeople and business quarters with markets and waterways, which together formed the unique urban complex. Even modern Bangkok, with its Western architectural theories, still preserves many of the Southeast Asian values of architecture, including the historical Southeast Asian concept of space derived from the urbanization of traditional Pyu cities. This is not to say that Mandalay and Bangkok have direct connections with Pyu cities. However, the ancestral remains of their predecessors' cities reveal some traces of connections to the Pyu, as, for example, in Pagan in central Burma and Sukhothai in Siam.

Architecture of Pagan

The traditional architecture of Pagan is based on Pyu achievements, such as the system of city and palace planning, as well as the main type of Buddhist temples and the brick-building technology that employed radiating arches. At the beginning of the eleventh century, the town was under Burman control. Before that, no monumental buildings were erected inside or outside the city walls. Pagan was an ordinary feudal town, surrounded by villages and arable lands. The territory of the initial town was small (about 1.5 square kilometers), but its defensive system was strong, notably consisting of walls that were 4 meters thick and 10 meters high. It remains unclear who constructed the town—whether Pyu, Mon, or local people.

In 1044, the year the kingdom of Pagan was founded, King Anawrahta (r. 1044–1077) took the throne. He transformed the little principality into a mighty kingdom, embracing a territory at least as large as present-day Burma. Rich architectural monuments were constructed in the capital. Prisoners provided an unlimited source of cheap labor. These favorable conditions promoted enormous monumental buildings, which continued to be constructed until the end of the thirteenth century. Within Pagan's area of about 48 square kilometers, there stood some 5,000 monuments erected from the eleventh to thirteenth centuries. Today, 2,217 monuments are officially listed.

Siam's Golden Age of Architecture

Sukhothai, which means "dawn of happiness" in Thai, is the name of a city, a kingdom, and a historical landmark of architecture in Southeast Asia. The history of Sukhothai unveils the major achievements in art and architecture of the first kingdom of Siam, which flourished from the mid-thirteenth to mid-fifteenth centuries. The architects of Sukhothai studied a number of distinctive ideas from nearby kingdoms, including Mon, Khmer, and Pagan examples, and combined them in a way that formed a unique Sukhothai style of architecture. King Rama Kamhaeng (r. 1279–1298) had organized a writing system (the basis of modern Thai), and he also codified the Thai form of Theravada Buddhism, borrowed from the Sinhalese. Sukhothai architecture is considered to have

had great sentimental vision, representative of the golden age of Thai art and architecture. It lasted until the city was taken over by Ayutthaya in 1376, and by that time, a national architectural identity had started to emerge.

The T'ai kings of Ayutthaya became very powerful in the fourteenth and fifteenth centuries; they conquered former Khmer strongholds such as U'Tong (Udong) and Lopburi, then moved eastward in their conquests until Angkor was defeated in 1431. The Khmer court customs and language were assimilated into Ayutthayan traditions. Architecture of that period favored the Khmer style. In the early sixteenth century, Ayutthaya received European visitors, first the Portuguese in 1511, who set up an embassy, then the Dutch in 1605, the English in 1612, the Danes in 1621, and the French in 1662. Ayutthaya was one of the greatest and wealthiest cities in Asia, admired not only by the Burmese who periodically invaded but also by Europeans, who were in great awe of the city. Ayutthaya was the site of the first capital of the kingdom of Siam. The city was founded in about 1350 by King Ramathibodi (r. 1351–1369), and it remained the center of Thai power and culture until 1767, when the Burmese destroy it. Some of the architectural monuments still survive in Ayutthaya.

Angkor Wat

The history of Southeast Asian architecture would not be complete without mention of Angkor Wat. Angkor was the capital city of the Khmer Empire (present-day Cambodia) from the ninth to fifteenth centuries. According to Hindu cosmology, the original city was constructed around the Phnom Bahkeng Temple on a hill representing the center of the world. Utilizing architecture as a tool, the successive Khmer kings enlarged the city with new buildings devoted to the Hindu god Viṣṇu. The greatest and the most representative architecture in the Angkor dynasty was Angkor Wat, which was built by King Sūryavarman II (r. ca. 1113–1145?) in the thirteenth century. Angkor covered about 100 square kilometers and was one of the largest cities in the world. During the early decades of the fifteenth century, the Angkor Empire started to decline, and it fell to the Thai in 1431. The monuments and architecture of Angkor still survive, despite having witnessed various wars. At present, Angkor Wat is one of the world's largest religious buildings.

Borobudur: Buddha in a World of Emptiness

The Buddhist philosophy of "Nothingness" and its relation to the usage of space is reflected in the majestic Borobudur monument, with its horizontal lines and elegant relief. The monument is a masterpiece of Buddhist architecture: its layout concentrates spiritual energy in the center and a series of square terraces ascend toward its highest point. Undeniably, Borobudur is one of the greatest architectural marvels of Southeast Asia. Buddhism made its way along the trade routes to Java and found a firm settlement there; Buddhist monks and pilgrims traveled frequently through Indonesia during the seventh and eighth centuries. Borobudur was begun in the mid-eighth century, and construction continued for sixty years under an organized society. The architecture of Borobudur tells about the ancient civilization of the Javanese, and in turn Javanese history tells about Borobudur's architecture. Its construction utilized about 1 million stones (each weighing 100 kilograms), comprising a total of over 40,000 cubic meters, and several hundred men were engaged to complete the monument, working seasonally to accommodate the agricultural cycle. A century after its completion, the Javanese court civilization disappeared, and though Borobudur was not entirely forgotten, it faded away in history. Successive governments tried to rediscover the structure, and restoration attempts were made. Restoration work was finally completed in 1983, making Borobudur one of the best-preserved ancient monuments in the world today.

The monuments mentioned here are just some of the highlights of the history of architecture in Southeast Asia. Many more could be discussed, and some of the indigenous architecture in the remote areas has yet to be studied. The glories of Southeast Asian architecture developed under long-held traditional values. However, the twentieth century is likely to be viewed as a time in which architectural developments in Southeast Asia revolved around Western styles and values. Mechanization eventually created today's high-tech societies and made life more convenient and more financially rewarding for many. But we must not forget that the period of colonial domination by Western states and the struggles under a succession of indigenous governments during the postindependence period also caused an immense loss of cultural heritage in the countries of Southeast Asia. Postwar fluctuations of power, contested between democracies and military takeovers, pushed many citizens of Southeast Asia, particularly many minority groups, to the brink of annihilation, and countless invaluable cultural treasures were destroyed. In many instances, therefore, a succession of political, military, and economic catastrophes resulted in the devastation of an older and invaluable cultural heritage.

KOUNG NYUNT

See also Angkor Wat (Nagaravatta); Ayutthaya (Ayuthaya, Ayudhya, Ayuthia) (1351–1767), Kingdom of; Bangkok; Batavia (Sunda Kalapa, Jakatra, Djakarta/Jakarta); Borobudur; Buddhism, Theravada; Burmans; Hanoi (Thang-long); Hindu-Buddhist Period of Southeast Asia; Indianization; Islam in Southeast Asia; Kuala Lumpur; Luang Prabang; Malang Temples; Mandalay; Manila; Mons; Monumental Art of Southeast Asia; Pagan (Bagan); Penang (1786); Prambanan; Pyus; Rangoon (Yangon); Saigon (Gia Dinh; Hồ Chí Minh City); Singapore (1819); Sukhotai (Sukhodava); T'ais

References:
Aung Thaw. 1972. *Historical Sites of Burma.* Rangoon: Ministry of Culture, Union of Burma.

Aung-thwin, Michael. 1985. *Pagan: The Origins of Modern Burma.* Honolulu: University of Hawai'i Press.

Charpentier, Sophie Clement. 1996. "Rebirth of a Capital Which Was Deserted: The Case of Phnom Penh." *Journal of Southeast Asian Architecture* 1, no. 1: 27–45.

Coedes, G. 1963. *Angkor: An Introduction.* Translated by Emily Floyd Gardiner. Oxford: Oxford University Press.

Hall, D. G. E. 1968. *A History of South-East Asia.* London: Macmillan.

Luce, Gordon H. 1970. *Old Burma—Early Pagan.* 3 vols. New York: New York University Press.

An Army of the Republic of Vietnam (ARVN) patrol discovers a communist outpost with an improvised bulletin board in Tân Phuoc. Though some of its units were outstanding, as a whole the ARVN suffered from a lack of effective leadership and thorough training. (U.S. National Archives)

Pe Maung Tin and G. H. Luce. 1923. *Hmannan Yazawin: The Glass Palace Chronicles of the Kings of Burma.* London and Rangoon: Oxford University Press.

Popwel, Robert. 1996. "Urban Morphology: Values Embedded in the Singapore Landscape." *Journal of Southeast Asian Architecture* 1, no. 1: 46–59.

Quaritch-Wales, H. G. 1973. *Early Burma—Old Siam.* London: Bernard Quaritch.

Soekmono, J. G. de Casparis, and Jacques Dumarçay. 1990. *Borobudur: Prayer in Stone.* Singapore: Archipelago Press.

Stargardt, Janice. 1990. *The Ancient Pyu of Burma.* Cambridge: Cambridge University Press.

Stratton, Carol, and Mirian McNair Scott. 1987. *The Art of Sukhothai: Thailand's Golden Age.* Kuala Lumpur and New York: Oxford University Press.

ARMY OF THE REPUBLIC OF VIETNAM (ARVN)

The Army of the Republic of Vietnam (ARVN) (Saigon) lasted for only twenty-one years, between 1954 and its collapse in 1975. Yet despite the brevity of its existence, it played an important role in the history of South Vietnam.

The ARVN was heir to the National Army of Vietnam, which was built up with the help of France during the First Indochina War. The "associated state" of Vietnam (Bảo Đại) was recognized by Paris in 1949 in order to counter the Democratic Republic of Vietnam (DRV) under Hồ Chí Minh, which drew up its own army to fight on the side of the French expeditionary corps. Although the National Army was small at the beginning, there were already some 250,000 soldiers by 1954. The officers, of whom there was a shortage, were trained at the Military College of Dalat under French supervision.

Under Ngô Đình Diệm (t. 1955–1963), who overthrew Bảo Đại in 1954 and transformed the state of Vietnam into the Republic of Vietnam, south of the seventeenth parallel, the ARVN stood to benefit from U.S. military aid. Its soldiers would be trained and supplied with weapons from the United States. From 1961, American advisers were assigned to various units when the Kennedy administration (1961–1963) decided to provide Saigon with the means to contain the Viet Cong (Vietnamese communist) insurrection. In the context of the struggle against the communists, the ARVN became increasingly powerful: it had more than 600,000 men in 1965, the year of the American military intervention, when ARVN field officers had already assumed control of power. In November 1963, backed by Washington, a military putsch overthrew and killed President Ngô Đình Diệm and his brother and adviser Ngô Đình Nhu. In the ensuing confusion, General Nguyễn Van Thieu emerged as the head of state, remaining so until 1975.

The Tet offensive (1968) marked a turning point. Intending to withdraw troops progressively, President Richard Nixon (t. 1969–1974) encouraged the "Vietnamization" of the conflict through an enlarged South Vietnamese army that was more seasoned in combat. The army would exceed 1 million men in 1972 and should have been able to master the situation on the terrain, not only serve as a backup for American troops.

At the time (late 1960s to early 1970s), the South Vietnamese army was essentially composed of thirteen regular divisions divided into four army corps, each of which was further divided according to four military regions. In addition, the army had specialized units, such as parachutists, marines, and special forces. The army constituted the major component of Saigon's military force. The air force remained less than effective despite the panache of General Nguyễn Cao Ky (1930–). The South Vietnamese Air Force had undergone spectacular growth due to Vietnamization but, despite having some 50,000 men and thirty-nine operative fighter squadrons in 1972, it could not withstand the fierce conflict technically or on the level of organization or material. The navy, almost equally strong in manpower (42,000) and number of ships (albeit of small tonnage), was confined to river and coastal operations. Nonetheless, in 1974, it could not prevent the Chinese occupation of the Paracel Islands off the coast of Danang.

This military apparatus performed unevenly. Faced by regular enemy units, ARVN troops rarely displayed enough pugnacity, at least when fighting on their own. Deployed in the Mekong Delta, they performed poorly in offensive operations such as the 1971 Lam Son 719 operation in southern Laos on the Hồ Chí Minh Trail. Despite sufficient manpower, the South Vietnamese army suffered endemic problems that affected its strength: the soldiers' motivation was less powerful than that of the Viet Cong, and corruption was present at all levels. These shortcomings had repercussions on the supply of material, besides an almost total dependence upon support from the United States.

After the cease-fire agreement signed in Paris in January 1973 and the withdrawal of U.S. forces, the ARVN permitted South Vietnam to control the government area, while remaining dependent on American supplies. When supplies failed to materialize and despite battles in which it made a good impression (such as Xuan Loc), the ARVN collapsed like a house of cards in the spring of 1975, driven from the field by the last communist offensive. When the Popular Army entered Saigon on 30 April, except for a few pockets of resistance it did not encounter many members of the numerous units of the ARVN, whose commanding officer had already fled. Only their abandoned uniforms and shoes were seen in the streets. Soon afterward, "reeducation" would come for the soldiers and officers of the fallen republic. Thus, the ARVN would go down together with the regime with which it had progressively identified itself, in the inglorious end to South Vietnam.

HUGUES TERTRAIS

See also Bảo Đại (Vinh Tuy) (1913–1997); Hồ Chí Minh (1890–1969); Hồ Chí Minh Trail; Indochina War (1964–1975), Second (Vietnam War); Ngô Đình Diệm (1901–1963); Nguyễn Van Thieu (1923–2001); Paris Peace Agreement (1968, 1973) (Vietnam); Tet Offensive (1968); U.S. Involvement in Southeast Asia (post-1945); U.S. Military Bases in Southeast Asia; Viet Cong; Vietnam, South (post-1945)

References:

Fall, Bernard. 1963. *The Two Viet Nams: A Political and Military Analysis.* New York: F. Praeger Publications.

Karnow, Stanley. 1983. *Vietnam, a History: The First Complete Account of Vietnam at War.* New York: Viking Press.

Kissinger, Henry. 1979. *White House Years.* New York: Little, Brown.

Tran Van Don. 1978. *Our Endless War inside Vietnam.* San Rafael, CA, and London: Presidio Press.

"ASIA FOR THE ASIATICS"

"Asia for the Asiatics" was the slogan advocated by the Japanese Imperial government prior to and during the Pacific War (1941–1945). The objective was to garner Asian peoples' support for its policy of ousting the Western colonial powers from Asia. An Indian nationalist, it was said, originally inspired the Japanese to adopt this slogan in the mid-1910s. It embodied the idea of the Japanese Asianists who had emerged since the early Meiji era (1867–1912). The Japanese Asianists fundamentally fell into two schools. In order to liberate Asia, adherents of one school intended to cooperate with the Asians as an equivalent partner; adherents of the other school intended to unite the Asians, with Japan as a supreme leader. From the late 1880s, those in the latter school prevailed. In the earlier period, they mainly focused on East Asia. The Japanese Imperial government implemented this idea when it colonized Taiwan (1895) and Korea (1910), sent troops to China, and then established the Manchurian puppet government (1932). Southeast Asia became the focus after 1938 when the term *East Asia Co-Prosperity Sphere,* understood to include Southeast Asia, was first used in a military plan. In August 1940, the then foreign minister, Matsuoka Yosuke (1880–1946), announced the idea of the Greater East Asia Co-Prosperity Sphere. It was the first official proclamation that Southeast Asia was included in the area that would be liberated by Japan to realize the new order in Asia and bring to fruition the idea of Asia for the Asiatics.

HARA FUJIO

See also Greater East Asia Co-Prosperity Sphere; Japan and Southeast Asia (pre-1941); Japanese Occupation of Southeast Asia (1941–1945); Nationalism and Independence Movements in Southeast Asia

References:

Lebra, Joyce C., ed. 1975. *Japan's Greater East Asia Co-Prosperity Sphere in World War II: Selected Readings and Documents.* Kuala Lumpur and New York: Oxford University Press.

ASIAN-AFRICAN (BANDUNG) CONFERENCE (APRIL 1955)

The Asian-African Conference in the Indonesian town of Bandung on 18 to 24 April 1955 was an unprecedented meeting of political leaders from twenty-nine countries. The conference marked the first decisive step toward the independent cooperation of Third World countries and the later Non-Aligned Movement in a world that was becoming increasingly dominated by the contending Western and Eastern blocs.

The initiative for the conference had come from Indonesia at a much smaller gathering in Colombo, Sri Lanka, a year earlier. In Bandung, all Southeast Asian governments were represented except Malaya and British Borneo. The conference brought together the first generation of leaders of postcolonial Asian and African countries, with the dominant figures being Ahmed Sukarno (1901–1970) of Indonesia, Jawaharlal Nehru (1889–1964) of India, Zhou Enlai (1898–1976) of China, and Gamal Abdel Nasser (1918–1970) of Egypt. In its central communiqué, the conference declared basic principles of international relations, denouncing colonialism and alignment with one of the dominant blocs and advocating independence, a multilateral system of states under the United Nations, racial equality, and self-determination for all states. Of particular significance were the participation of China and its relations with India. In the years following the conference, China's clear commitment to communism and the deterioration of relations with India excluded it from the Non-Aligned Movement, whereas Indonesia emerged as the main advocate of nonalignment in Southeast Asia.

Although an attempt to convene a second Asian-African meeting in 1965 in Algeria did not materialize, the Bandung Conference remains a symbol of the emancipation process of the Third World. The event gave the newly independent states of the South—and Indonesia in particular—unprecedented visibility. However, it did not lead to the establishment of an institutionalized organization as a counterweight to the bipolar system of international relations.

STEFAN HELL

See also Anglo-Malayan/Malaysian Defence Agreement (AMDA); Association of Southeast Asian Nations (ASEAN) (1967); Cold War; Comintern; Non-Aligned Movement (NAM) and Southeast Asia; Soekarno (Sukarno) (1901–1970); Southeast Asia Treaty Organization (SEATO) (1954); U.S. Military Bases in Southeast Asia; U.S. Involvement in Southeast Asia (post-1945); Zone of Peace, Freedom and Neutrality (ZOPFAN) (1971)

References:
Kahin, George M. 1956. *The Asian-African Conference: Bandung, Indonesia, April 1955.* Port Washington, WA: Kennikat Press.
Romulo, Carlos P. 1956. *The Meaning of Bandung.* Chapel Hill: University of North Carolina Press.
Wright, Richard. 1994. *The Color Curtain: A Report on the Bandung Conference.* Jackson: University Press of Mississippi.

A-SO-YA-MIN

A-so-ya-min is a transliteration of an old Myanmar (Burma) word meaning "government"; it literally breaks down as "royal person who has authority over or rules." The traditional form of government in Myanmar, as in all Theravada Buddhist kingdoms in South Asia and Southeast Asia, was a monarchy that drew its legitimacy from certain theories of government that were commonly accepted by king and subject alike. The hereditary ruler, always the son of a king through a senior wife who was also descended from the royal clan, was the theoretical fount of all authority. All other members of the ruling classes, including ministers and chiefs, acted as his agents. Among his many titles was "Lord of Life," denoting his supreme authority.

The theory of Buddhist kingship that provided the legitimating myth for the monarchy began with the notion that the king was descended from the *Maha Thammada*, or "The Great Elected." In a variation of the social contract theory of government, the first king was said to have been chosen when people, then living in a degraded paradise, realized that greed was undermining the tranquillity of their society. They then chose one among them, the Maha Thammada, to have absolute power over them to keep order. He was elected in two senses. In one sense, the first king was the choice of the people, and his hereditary descendants shared his lineage. In another sense, he was special in that he could be trusted with all power because the king was a *Hpaya laung* (future Buddha). He had achieved this august status because of the merit derived from the good deeds he had performed in previous lives. The king thus ruled because of his ability to uphold the moral law as a *dhamma raja* (the Just King of Buddhist thought).

R. H. TAYLOR

See also Buddhism; Buddhism, Theravada; *Cakkavatti/Setkya-min* (Universal Ruler); *Devaraja;* Hindu-Buddhist Period of Southeast Asia; Hinduism; Indianization; Indigenous Political Power

References:
Heine-Geldern, Robert. 1942. "Concepts of State and Kingship in Southeast Asia." *Far Eastern Quarterly* 2 (November): 15–30.
Tambiah, S. J. 1976. *World Conqueror and World Renouncer: A Study of Buddhism and Polity in Thailand against a Historical Background.* Cambridge: Cambridge University Press.

ASSOCIATION OF SOUTHEAST ASIAN NATIONS (ASEAN) (1967)

Indonesia, Malaysia, the Philippines, Singapore, and Thailand established the Association of Southeast Asian Nations (ASEAN) on 7 August 1967. In the ASEAN Declaration, adopted on the same date, the organization's main goals were spelled out. The association was to promote regional collaboration in Southeast Asia and in so doing contribute to peace, development, and prosperity in the region. Relations among the member states were to be governed by two fundamental documents adopted in 1976: the Treaty of Amity and Cooperation in Southeast Asia (TAC, also known as the Bali Treaty) and the Declaration of ASEAN Concord.

Following a period of tension between ASEAN and the three Indochinese countries (Vietnam, Laos, and Cambodia) in connection with the Cambodian conflict between 1979 and 1991, the rest of the 1990s was characterized by a gradual process of ASEAN expansion, with Vietnam, Laos, Myanmar (Burma), and Cambodia becoming members of the association. The 1992 agreement to establish the ASEAN Free Trade Area (AFTA) within fifteen years marked an expansion of economic cooperation within the organization. This expansion was considerably slowed by the Asian Financial Crisis (AFC, 1997–1998), which had major negative impacts on the economies of the member states. The expansion of membership and the negative repercussions of the AFC posed major challenges for ASEAN to address in the late 1990s and into the early 2000s.

Establishment of ASEAN

ASEAN was established in 1967, but it was not the first subregional association to be set up in Southeast Asia. In 1961, the Association of Southeast Asia (ASA) was formed, bringing together what was then the Federation of Malaya, the Philippines, and Thailand. In 1963, Indonesia, the Federation of Malaya, and the Philippines established Maphilindo, in an attempt to promote cooperation among the three countries. But cooperation within both ASA and Maphilindo was seriously hampered by the conflicts between Malaysia and Indonesia and between Malaysia and the Philippines, respectively, over the formation of the Federation of Malaysia in 1963. In fact, ASA and Maphilindo proved to be inadequate for handling and containing the two conflicts, thus indicating that the two bodies could not be used to manage severe interstate conflicts among their members. The limitations and shortcomings of these organizations showed that there was a need for a broader and more efficient association to serve as a vehicle for regional cooperation and conflict management. The establishment of ASEAN can be seen as the result of efforts by some Southeast Asian states to create an association that could provide a framework for the successful management of disputes among member states. To bring about a broader membership base in the new association, all the major nonsocialist countries in Southeast Asia except the Republic of Vietnam joined ASEAN, together with Singapore, in 1967.

Regional Cooperation through ASEAN
Intra-ASEAN Dimension

Although ASEAN was created as part of a process aimed at peaceful management of conflicts among its members, the main goal expressed through the ASEAN Declaration in 1967 was to promote social and economic cooperation among the member states.

Through a system of informal and formal meetings between their leaders, ministers, and senior officials, the ASEAN states have managed to build confidence, familiarity, and an understanding of one another's positions on a range of issues. ASEAN is renowned for its decision-making process, which requires that all decisions be reached by consensus. Particular emphasis has been put on promoting and achieving regional resilience based on the internal resilience of each of the member states through economic development. This approach should result in greater political support for the governments and lead to enhanced political stability in the future.

Achieving a high level of interaction, cooperation, and understanding among the original member states was a gradual process influenced both by intra-ASEAN developments and by developments in the broader Southeast Asian region. Already by 1971, the ASEAN countries had responded to international developments by issuing the Kuala Lumpur Declaration on 27 November 1971, which called for the creation of the Zone of Peace, Freedom and Neutrality (ZOPFAN) in Southeast Asia. The next step came in 1976 with the signing of TAC and the Declaration of the ASEAN Concord on 24 February 1976 in connection with the first ASEAN Summit, in Bali.

The core element of the structure of formal collaboration within the organization is the annual ASEAN Ministerial Meeting (AMM), which was set up by the member states on a rotating basis at the establishment of the association. As collaboration within ASEAN has expanded, the number of meetings has increased considerably, and there are now hundreds of meetings each year in various fields of cooperation. It is notable that official and informal summits are held among the leaders of the member states on a regular basis. In 1981, the ASEAN Secretariat was established, and it has assumed a coordinating role within the association.

As the economies of the ASEAN member states developed, in particular from the late 1980 and into the 1990s, a process of expanding economic cooperation within the association took place. This development led to the establishment of subregional economic zones linking various regions in the member states. The early 1990s were also characterized by coordinated efforts to expand economic cooperation and integration. In 1992, an agreement was reached on the establishment of AFTA within fifteen years. The member states also signed an agreement on the Common Effective Preferential Tariff (CEPT), which is the key instrument in the process through which AFTA will be established. However, beginning in 1997, the expansion of economic cooperation was considerably slowed by the AFC, which caused a regionwide economic recession. The AFC has been a major issue of concern for the member states of ASEAN, and the early 2000s have shown that many countries (Indonesia in particular) are still facing continued economic problems coupled with political instability.

External Relations and the Expansion of ASEAN

In its foreign relations, ASEAN has generated strength from the fact that the member states have acted together as one political force by taking a collective stand on major foreign policy issues. The most obvious example is the ASEAN success in gaining widespread international support for its position on the Cambodian conflict. In the post–Cambodian conflict era (that is, since 1991), ASEAN has initiated two major foreign relations initiatives. First was the process of expanding membership in ASEAN within the Southeast Asian region. Second was the process leading to the establishment of the ASEAN Regional Forum (ARF).

The expansion of membership in ASEAN in the 1990s grew out of the rapprochement between ASEAN and Vietnam, Laos, and Cambodia, following the settlement of the Cambodian conflict in 1991, as well as the ASEAN policy of "constructive engagement" toward Myanmar. (Brunei had joined in 1984 after achieving independence from the United Kingdom.) These two processes led to the accession to the Bali Treaty by the four states. ASEAN observer status and membership in ARF for the four states followed. Finally, Vietnam (in 1995), Laos and Myanmar (in 1997), and Cambodia (in 1998–1999) acceded to full membership in ASEAN. The integration of the new members is a challenge to the organization and is leading to the gradual emergence of a more heterogeneous association.

The "political factor" seems to have been crucial in creating the necessary conditions for an expansion of membership in ASEAN. This refers to the fact that the founding members of ASEAN had, from the outset, formulated the vision and goal of "one Southeast Asia" with all ten Southeast Asian countries as members of the association. There was also a political interest among the other four Southeast Asian countries to improve relations with the ASEAN countries and to gradually integrate into the framework for regional cooperation. Changes within countries of the region, within the region, and within relations among the major outside powers contributed to create conducive conditions for rapprochement and gradual integration.

The "security factor" is also relevant in explaining the expansion of ASEAN, given the history of internal as well as interstate conflicts in the region. Expanding the acceptance of the Bali Treaty as a code of conduct for interstate relations and expanding ASEAN membership within the Southeast Asian region are processes designed to enhance the overall security in the region by promoting regional cooperation.

The "economic factor" does not seem to have been as crucial in explaining the urge to expand ASEAN membership within Southeast Asia, as seen from the perspective of the six original ASEAN members ("the ASEAN six"). However, it was of considerable importance for the four new members, as other ASEAN members were major foreign investors in and leading trading partners of those four countries.

The ARF grew out of an increased awareness among the ASEAN states that there was a need for a multilateral forum to discuss security issues within the broader Asian Pacific context following the end of the Cold War. The indications of a reduction in the U.S. military presence in and commitment to East and Southeast

Asia also influenced the ASEAN states. They reached a consensus on the need for such a forum at the ASEAN Summit in Singapore in January 1992. Australia had already expressed support for such an idea. Gradually, the major powers—notably China, Japan, and the United States—decided to give their support. This process led to the establishment of the ARF, with its first working session being held in connection with the AMM in Bangkok in July 1994. The founding members of the ARF were the six ASEAN members, the Dialogue Partners (Australia, Canada, the European Union, Japan, New Zealand, South Korea, and the United States) of ASEAN, the "consultative partners" of ASEAN at the time (China and Russia), and the ASEAN observers at the time (Papua New Guinea, Laos, and Vietnam). In all, there were eighteen founding members. The number of ARF members has since expanded to twenty-three.

Conclusion

Despite ASEAN's original goal of promoting social and economic cooperation among its member states, as expressed in 1967, it is generally recognized that ASEAN has achieved more in terms of cooperation in the political and security fields as compared with the economic field.

Some observers argue that ASEAN was a success story up to the mid-1990s but that its image was tarnished thereafter due to the challenges brought about by the expanding membership and the impact that would have on the coherence of the association, as well as the impact of the AFC that swept through the region from 1997. A more balanced assessment suggests that ASEAN was not such a success story by the mid-1990s and that cooperation within ASEAN has not been weakened to the extent argued by its critics. Nevertheless, ASEAN must address a number of difficult issues. Some of these relate to interstate relations, and others involve internal problems in the individual member states. One persisting challenge, both nationally and regionally, involves Indonesia, with its continued political instability and the questions that remain about its future as a unified nation given the armed secessionist movements in some parts of the country.

RAMSES AMER

See also Economic Development of Southeast Asia (post-1945 to ca. 1990s); Konfrontasi ("Crush Malaysia" campaign); Kuantan Principle (1980); Malaysia (1963); Maphilindo Concept; Paris Conference on Cambodia (PCC) (1989, 1991); Sabah Claim; Spratly and Paracel Archipelagos Dispute; Zone of Peace, Freedom and Neutrality (ZOPFAN) (1971)

References:

Acharya, Amitav. 1991. "The Association of Southeast Asian Nations: 'Security Community' or 'Defence Community'?" *Pacific Affairs* 64, no. 2: 159–177.

———. 1993. *A New Regional Order in South-East Asia: ASEAN in the Post–Cold War Era.* Adelphi Paper 270. London: International Institute of Strategic and International Studies.

Amer, Ramses. 1998. "Expanding ASEAN's Conflict Management Framework in Southeast Asia: The Border Dispute Dimension." *Asian Journal of Political Science* 6, no. 2: 33–56.

———. 1999. "Conflict Management and Constructive Engagement in ASEAN's expansion." *Third World Quarterly* (Special Issue on New Regionalisms) 20, no. 5: 1031–1048.

Aranal-Sereno, Lourdes, and Joseph Sedfrey S. Santiago, eds. 1997. *The ASEAN: Thirty Years and Beyond.* Quezon City: Institute of International Legal Studies, University of the Philippines Law Center.

ASEAN Secretariat. 1997. *ASEAN Economic Co-operation: Transition & Transformation.* Singapore: Institute for Southeast Asian Studies.

Boisseau du Rocher, Sophie. 1998. *L'ASEAN et la construction régionale en Asie du Sud-Est [ASEAN and the Regional Structure in South-East Asia].* Paris and Montreal: L' Harmattan.

Joyaux, François. 1997. *L'Association des Nations du Sud-Est Asiatique (ANSEA) [The Association of South-East Asian Nations (ASEAN)].* Que sais-je no. 3153. Paris: Presses Universitaires de France.

Kamarulzaman Askandar. 1994. "ASEAN and Conflict Management: The Formative Years of 1967–1976." *Pacifica Review* 6, no. 2: 57–69.

Narine, Shaun. 1998. "ASEAN and the Management of Regional Security." *Pacific Affairs* 71, no. 2: 195–214.

Suryadinata, Leo, ed. 1997. "Special Issue on ASEAN." *Asian Journal of Political Science* 5, no. 1 (June).

AUGUST REVOLUTION (VIETNAM, 1945)

See Hồ Chí Minh (1890–1969); Vietnam, North (Post-1945)

AUNG SAN (1915–1947)
Acclaimed Burmese National Hero

Aung San is the foremost national hero in modern Burma (Myanmar). His foreshortened political career, ended when he was assassinated by political rivals at the age of thirty-two, left a brief and ambiguous legacy that every political actor in Burma subsequently has claimed as his or her own. Held up as an example of fearless nationalist dedication and ultimate self-sacrifice for the good of the country, Aung San is championed by all who seek power in Burmese politics. A photograph of Aung San, ironically clad in the greatcoat of an English army officer (taken on his only visit to London in 1947), hangs in every schoolroom and office in Burma, reminding students and others of the traditions of Burmese politics that Aung San represented. His written legacy is sufficiently ambiguous that all—socialist, communist, liberal, civilian, or military—can claim to be carrying on Aung San's flame.

Born on 13 February 1915 in the small town of Natmauk in Burma's Magwe Division, he described himself as a descendant of prosperous rural gentry with distinguished patriotic forefathers. After schooling at Natmauk and the National High School in Yeinangyaung, he attended Rangoon University, where he studied English, history, and law and commenced postgraduate studies in law. He was twice suspended from the university because of his political activities. On one of these occasions, in 1936, his suspension prompted a nationwide strike of students from universities and high schools, leading to a revised universities act in 1938. Following his student days—during which he had been editor of the student newspaper and president of the student union, as well as cofounder and president of the All-Burma Students Union—he worked briefly on the editorial staff of the only Burmese-owned English-language newspaper in the capital.

In 1938, he joined the Dobama Asiayone (DAA), a fiery nationalist organization dominated by other young men determined to speed the achievement of self-government in Burma. Aung San assumed the title of "Thakin" (master) at that time. Thakin Aung San became the general secretary of the DAA and was arrested for subversion in 1939. At that point, the DAA was in alliance with Dr. Ba Maw's Hsinyeitha Party to form the Freedom Bloc, opposed to cooperation with Britain's war effort against Nazi Germany. In 1940, he went to India to attend a congress of the Indian National Congress before going underground to avoid rearrest. Fleeing Burma, he set off to the east in search of assistance for the Burmese nationalist cause. He was intercepted in Amoy (Xiamen) by the Japanese, who took him to Tokyo for discussions on Japan's support for Burma's independence. Aung San returned to Burma in 1941 with the outline of a plan to train the officer corps of a future Burmese national army. He then returned to Hainan with twenty-nine other young men for military training.

The famous Thirty Comrades then accompanied the Japanese as they invaded Thailand and Burma in 1942. Raising en route an army of more than 15,000 young men, known as the Burma Independence Army (BIA), General Aung San and his men became key figures in the establishment of the nominally independent but Japanese-sponsored state headed by Dr. Ba Maw (b. 1893) in 1943. However, Aung San and his fellow nationalists soon became disenchanted with the sham independence the Japanese allowed; in response, they joined the Anti-Fascist Organization (AFO), as well as the Burma Communist Party (BCP) led by his brother-in-law Thakin Than Tun and other groups. In March 1945, the BIA, which had been renamed the Burma National Army, turned against the Japanese, having assured the British in secret communications of its willingness to join forces against the common Japanese enemy.

After the defeat of the Japanese, General Aung San agreed with Adm. Lord Louis Mountbatten (1900–1979), who headed the

South-East Asia Command (SEAC), to merge his army, now renamed the Burmese Patriotic Forces, with the official British Burma army. Aung San then resigned from the army to pursue the goal of Burma's independence as a civilian politician. Many of his former troops, however, remained loyal to him. Eventually, the British government was forced to concede independence to the noncommunist nationalists that Aung San led. Aung San joined the colonial Governor's Executive Council as its deputy chairman—effectively becoming the prime minister of the preindependence government. In January 1947, he went to London, where he concluded the Aung San–Attlee Agreement that established the terms of Burma's independence a year later. Just six months later, however, in July 1947, Aung San was assassinated while chairing a meeting of the Governor's Council in the Secretariat Building in Yangon.

R. H. TAYLOR

See also Anti-Fascist People's Freedom League (AFPFL); Ba Maw, Dr. (b. 1893); Burma Communist Party (BCP); Burma during the Pacific War (1941–1945); Burma Independence Army (BIA); Burma under British Colonial Rule; Constitutional Developments in Burma (1900–1941); Mountbatten, Admiral Lord Louis (1900–1979); Nationalism and Independence Movement in Southeast Asia; Suu Kyi, Daw Aung San (1945–); Thakin (lord, master); Thirty Comrades; U Saw and the Assassination of Aung San

References:
King Oung. 1996. *Who Killed Aung San?* Bangkok: White Lotus.
Maung Maung, ed. 1962. *Aung San of Burma.* The Hague: Martinus Nijhoff.
Maung Maung and Mya Han, eds. 2000. *The Writings of General Aung San.* Yangon: Universities Historical Research Centre.
Suu Kyi, Aung San. 1984. *Aung San.* Brisbane, Australia: University of Queensland Press.

AUSTRALIA AND SOUTHEAST ASIA

For much of Australia's history, Asia was largely undifferentiated: it was a racially and culturally homogeneous entity within which only China and Japan possessed identifiable characteristics. Only in the mid-twentieth century did the term *Southeast Asia* begin to have a geographically precise definition. Today, it includes Brunei, Burma (Myanmar), Cambodia, East Timor, Indonesia, Laos, Malaysia, the Philippines, Singapore, Thailand, and Vietnam.

Before European settlement, trade in *trepang* (a type of sea slug) had developed between northern Australia and Macassar (Makassar) in the Celebes (modern Sulawesi). This trade, which continued throughout the nineteenth century, fostered close links between trepang fishermen and aboriginal people. Although Southeast Asia provided nineteenth-century Australians with foodstuffs and various manufactured goods, contacts were mediated through the colonial powers that controlled most of Asia. Australia viewed the region through the prism of European imperialism and race, and many Australians feared it would be the route for an invasion of their continent. This prompted the creation of a restrictive immigration policy, known as the White Australia Policy, that was intended to keep Australia socially harmonious and beyond Asia's influence.

Australian travelers rarely ventured to the region until the 1930s, when Batavia (Jakarta), Bali, and Singapore became, for wealthy citizens, exotic destinations in their own right and not simply ports of call en route to Europe and North America. For most Australians, however, Southeast Asia remained a romanticized, exotic area, found only in popular books, newspapers, journals, or art.

The Pacific War (1941–1945) and the threat of a Japanese invasion propelled Southeast Asia into the public imagination. Australia's first mass engagement in the region occurred when about 18,000 Australian troops faced the Japanese army in Singapore. Most of these men became prisoners of war (POWs), along with 4,000 other Australians. More than 8,000 died in prison camps across the region: in Java, Changi, Sandakan, Ranau, Ambon, Tol, Banka, and on the Burma-Thailand "Death Railway" (Beaumont 2001: 345).

After the war, decolonization, the ascendancy of Asian nationalism, and the Cold War impelled nervous Australian governments to protect their country from the region. Australia played the role of an armed frontier state, with a continuous military presence in Southeast Asia from 1941 until 1974. Public debate and the Australian government's approach to Southeast Asia were dominated by the so-called domino theory, a metaphor for the strategic consequences for the region if Indochina fell to communism: according to that theory, other Southeast Asian nations would tumble like a row of dominoes until communism reached Australia. The fear and misunderstanding that underpinned the theory, combined with memories of the Pacific War, influenced Australia foreign policy for decades. In the postwar years, Australia fought in Malaya (1950), Korea (1950–1953), and Indonesia (1964–1966). Then, in 1954, it became a founding member of the Southeast Asia Treaty Organization (SEATO); shortly thereafter, Australia stationed troops and naval vessels in Malaya as part of the Far East Strategic Reserve. The Australia, New Zealand and the United States Treaty (ANZUS) was intended to bolster Australia's "forward defense" policy. This policy culminated in an Australian commitment to support the United States in the Vietnam War (1964–1975).

Positive engagement with the region occurred in the areas of technical and economic assistance and diplomatic representation. By 1960, Australia's diplomatic service had expanded significantly, with permanent representatives in Indonesia, Malaya (after 1963, Malaysia), the Philippines, Singapore, Thailand, Portuguese Timor, South Vietnam, Laos, Cambodia, and Burma. Developmental aid under the Colombo Plan sponsored thousands of students for tertiary and technical education in Australia and sent Australian professionals to most countries in Southeast Asia. The students were the forerunners of thousands more self-funded Asian scholars who have gained tertiary qualifications in Australia. In 1956, the Australian government funded the creation of Indonesian departments at the Australian National University (ANU) and the Universities of Sydney and Melbourne. By the mid-1950s, the government's overseas radio service, Radio Australia, was broadcasting news commentaries in English, French, Indonesian, Thai, and Mandarin.

From the 1970s on, Australian prime ministers placed increasing emphasis on their nation's role in Southeast Asia and the Pacific. Australia's foreign relations were characterized by a commitment to regional economic cooperation and efforts to build multilateral regional institutions, such as the Asia Pacific Economic Cooperation Organization (APEC). Some setbacks occurred, such as Australia's failure to join the Association of Southeast Asian Nations (ASEAN).

There were few Southeast Asian migrants in Australia before the late 1970s and early 1980s, when thousands of refugees arrived from Vietnam and Cambodia. Of the 1 million Asian-born Australians in 2000, just over half (about 3 percent of the total population) were born in Southeast Asia. Their most common countries of birth were Vietnam (174,400), the Philippines (123,000), Malaysia and Brunei (97,600), and Indonesia (67,600) ("Australian Social Trends").

Although many Australians remain concerned about their place and responsibilities in the region, the country has taken a prominent role in some regional issues, helping facilitate a peace settlement in Cambodia (1989, 1991) and leading a multinational peacekeeping operation in East Timor (1999–2000). Australia continues to be concerned with refugees from Southeast Asia, human rights abuses, conflict between ethnic and religious groups, violations of territorial integrity, and acts of terrorism such as the October 2002 Bali bombings.

DANIEL OAKMAN

See also Association of Southeast Asian Nations (ASEAN) (1967); Batavia (Sunda Kalapa, Jakatra, Djakarta/Jakarta); Boat People; Cold War; "Death Railway" (Burma-Siam Railway); Domino Theory; "Fortress Singapore"; Indochina War (1964–1975), Second (Vietnam War); Japanese Occupation of Southeast Asia (1941–1945); Konfrontasi ("Crush Malaysia" Campaign); Korean War (1950–1953); Malayan Emergency (1948–1960); Marine/Sea Products; Paris Conference on Cambodia (PCC) (1989, 1991); Sandakan Death March; Services Reconnaissance Department (SRD); Timor; United Nations Transitional Authority in Cambodia (UNTAC)

References:
"Australian Social Trends." www.abs.gov.au.
Beaumont, Joan, ed. 2001. *Australian Defence: Sources and Statistics.* Melbourne, Australia: Oxford Univeristy Press.
Coughlan, James E., and Deborah J. McNamara, eds. 1997. *Asians in Australia: Patterns of*

Migration and Settlement. Melbourne: Macmillan Education Australia.

Goldsworthy, David, ed. 2001. *Facing North: A Century of Australian Engagement with Asia.* Vol. 1, *1901 to the 1970s.* Melbourne, Australia: Melbourne University Press.

Keating, Paul. 2000. *Engagement: Australia Faces the Asia Pacific.* Sydney, Australia: Macmillan.

Rickard, John. 1996. *Australia: A Cultural History.* New York: Longman.

Walker, David. 2000. *Anxious Nation: Australia and the Rise of Asia, 1850–1938.* Sydney, Australia: University of New South Wales Press.

AVA DYNASTY

See First Ava (Inwa) Dynasty (1364–1527 C.E.)

AYUTTHAYA (AYUTHAYA, AYUDHYA, AYUTHIA) (1351–1767), KINGDOM OF

Ayutthaya was the capital city of Siam for more than four hundred years. It was founded by King Ramathibodi I (U Thong) on 4 March 1351 and was destroyed by Burmese armies in the reign of King Ekathat on 7 April 1767. In all, thirty-four kings ruled there, from five different dynasties (U Thong, Suphanburi, Sukhothai, Prasat Thong, and Ban Phlu Luang). Hinayana Buddhism was the dominant religion throughout its territory, although generally mixed with elements of animism and Mahayana Buddhism. At the highest social level, the royal court, Hindu and Brahmanic rites were maintained to enhance the power and aura of the ruler, understood as a fusion of Dhammaraja (the Just King of Buddhist thought) and Devaraja (the God-King of Hindu tradition).

The royal capital was strategically located at the confluence of three big rivers (the Chao Phraya, the Pasak, and the Lopburi) and formed an island, secure all on its own. The road encompassing this island measured about 12 kilometers, and the city itself eventually contained about 190,000 people (Loubere 1693, vol. 1). The surrounding region was a flat plain perfectly adapted for wet-rice cultivation, while at the same time being sufficiently close to the sea to make external trade an easy matter. Hence, Ayutthaya had a double character, combining a land-based agricultural realm and another realm based on maritime commerce.

From the middle of the thirteenth to the middle of the fourteenth century, various Thai states came into being—Sukhothai, Lanna (Chiang Mai), Lanchang (Luang Phrabang), and others—but these kingdoms were still of a quite local and decentralized character, and they arose spontaneously on their own. None of them formed a true royal domain under strongly centralized power.

Ayutthaya had its origins in the union of Suphanburi and Lopburi, the two "local" powers dominant in the central region of today's Thailand. Suphanburi was overlord of the region to the west of the Chao Phraya River. It encompassed various ancient statelets, such as Nakhon Chaisi (later Nakhon Pathom), Ratburi, and Phetburi, and its influence probably extended as far south as Nakhon Srithamamarat. Lopburi, by contrast, dominated the region to the east of the Chao Phraya.

Both Suphanburi and Lopburi were the historical legatees of the kingdom of Dvaravati (sixth–eleventh centuries C.E.) and came under the influence of Angkor from the eleventh to thirteenth centuries, that is, in the reign of Sūryavarman I (ca. 1002–1049) and thereafter.

Three developments created the opportunity for the creation of various larger "local" powers in what is present-day Thailand. First, the power of Angkor began to decline after the reign of Jayavarman VII (1181–ca. 1220). Second, major alterations occurred in religious outlook, with a shift from Brahmanic Hinduism and Mahayana Buddhism to Hinayana Buddhism. And third, political transformations in Asia took place as a consequence of the dynastic change in Imperial China from the Sung (960–1279) to the Yuan (1271–1368) dynasties.

Therefore, in 1351, U Thong founded the new kingdom of Ayutthaya in the ancient city-state known as Ayodhaya, which lay between Suphanburi and Lopburi. The early political history of Ayutthaya was characterized by the rivalry beteen two dynastic families, that of U Thong himself and that of Suphanburi (represented by the family of U Thong's wife); the rivalry ended with the triumph of Suphanburi in 1409, in the reign of Intharacha I (1409–1424). The outcome was that in the first half of Ayutthaya's history (from 1351 to 1569, that is, until its first crushing defeat by the Burmese), only three of the seventeen rulers came from U Thong's direct line.

In the early period of Ayutthaya, efforts were made to expand the realm by attempting to seize the domain of Angkor in three successive wars—in 1369, 1388, and 1431. Angkor gradually grew weaker, and finally, the Khmer capital was sacked, forcing the rulers to move far away to Phnom Penh. At the same time, Ayutthaya also tried to expand to the north and successfully incorporated Sukhothai, although it failed to enforce permanent control of Chiang Mai. To the south, Ayutthaya established its authority over Nakhon Sri Thammarat and tried to achieve the same control over the peninsular Malay States.

Ayutthaya's favorable geographic location meant that maritime trade was a very important factor in its growth. The monarchs held a monopoly over this trade, and they used Chinese seamen to carry it on. From its earliest days, foreign commerce was vital to the royal revenues, no matter whether the court's dealings were with the Ming dynasty (1368–1644) or the Ch'ing (Qing) dynasty (1644–1911). The trade between the two states took the form of "gifts." The Ayutthayan court sent them as "tribute" to the Chinese emperor and in return was given special privileges in buying and selling Chinese goods. Usually, Ayutthaya's tribute consisted of forest products, such as sappanwood or other fragrant woods; from the Chinese, it obtained finished goods such as porcelain and silk (in this way, Ayutthaya became a station on the famous Silk Sea-Route).

Ayutthaya also had trade connections with states in today's Southeast Asia and beyond, especially on the Malay Peninsula, in the Indonesian archipelago, and in India, though these connections declined gradually after the Europeans started their incursions in the sixteenth century. In the fifteenth century, there were also commercial exchanges with Japan; one result of this traffic was that Japanese went to Ayutthaya, formed their own settlement there, and played an important role from the end of the sixteenth century to the middle of the seventeenth century. It was exactly in this period, however, that the Europeans began to seize control of the older Asian trade system, displacing the Indians, Arabs, and Chinese. Among these Europeans, who included the Portuguese, the English, and the French, it was the Dutch who were the most important (with their base/center on Java) in establishing a commercial presence and playing a significant role in Ayutthaya right up to its final destruction in 1767.

The ultimate outcome was that, at its peak, the Ayutthayan state encompassed a population of around 2 million people, including a mixture of Thais, Chinese, Mons, Malays, Cambodians, and even some foreigners from distant lands, such as Portugal and Japan (Loubere 1693, vol. 1; Reid 1988: 14).

The expansion of Ayutthaya's domain led to intensifying competition with Burma, especially for control over Chiang Mai and the kingdom of the Mon (which later became part of Burma). In the sixteenth century, Ayutthaya suffered a major defeat at Burmese hands (1569), but the setback was only temporary. In the seventeenth century, it managed to establish control over parts of the Mon kingdom, for example Tavoy, Mergui, and Tenasserim—port cities that gave Ayutthaya direct access to the Indian Ocean. But the endeavor to exercise control over Chiang Mai and the Mon realm caused continuous conflict with the Burmese and eventually led to Ayutthaya's destruction in 1767.

Ayutthaya's form of government was a monarchy, but it was not an absolutist monarchy. Although the king was the highest authority, there was as yet no sharp and clear division marking off the monarch and the nobility from everyone else, as would emerge in the middle of the Jakkri (Chakri) dynastic era. Ayutthaya's king, nobility, Buddhist monks, and commoners were organized in a graduated *sakdina* hierarchy, which was first clearly regulated by law in the reign of King Trailokanat (1448–1488). According to the letter of this law, every man had his own sakdina rank, and everyone had a given amount of land depending on this rank, running from 5 to 100,000 *rai* (2.5 rai is equal to 1 acre of land). For example, beggars, street musicians, slaves, and children of slaves were assigned 5 rai of paddy fields; low *phrai* (serfs) got 10 rai, middle phrai 15 rai, phrai with families 20 rai, phrai foremen 25 rai, low artisans 50 rai, taxmen and market chiefs 200 rai, ship captains 400 rai, elephant masters 600 rai, heads of the Muslim community and the Chinese population 1,400 rai, grandchildren of the king 1,500 rai, high nobles 10,000 rai, and the second king/heir apparent 100,000 rai. The *chao* (royalty) was divided into three ranks: *chao fa* (children of the king), *phraong chao* (grandchildren), and *mom chao* (great grandchildren).

According to the letter of Ayutthayan law, all land originally belonged to the King/Lord of the Land, who would then divide it up among his male subjects according to their status. But the general belief today is that there was no real division of land (even though the rulers held firmly to the principle that they owned all the land in the realm and could bestow it or take it back at will). In other words, sakdina actually functioned as a hierarchy of social status: it marked each individual off from others, in an order from high to low, thereby determining each person's means of livelihood, residence, and even clothes and type of housing. It was also used as an instrument of legal punishment.

The status division between royalty and nobility was neither absolute nor permanent. In succession crises, a nobleman might seize power and found a new dynasty, as happened, for example, in the case of Khun Worawongsathirat (1548) or the last two Aytthayan dynasties—Prasat Thong (1629–1688) and Ban Phlu Luang (1688–1767).

Commoners were divided mainly into two types of phrai (attached to lords, or *munnai*): the *phrai luang* and the *phrai som*. The phrai luang were directly attached to the monarch, whereas the phrai som "belonged" to the nobles. Both types of phrai were subject to corvée (unpaid labor) at the will of their respective lords, and they could be conscripted in times of war. A special group known as the *phrai suai* were free from corvée duties but were obliged to pay special taxes in kind. This kind of phrai typically lived in remote areas where forest and mineral resources were available.

In the seventeenth and eighteenth centuries, the phrai were liable for six months of corvée labor each year (in alternating months), but it was possible to buy remittance from this labor by making payments at the rate of about 2 baht a month or 12 baht a year. Ayutthayan society, however, also had a stratum of slaves. Most of these individuals became slaves as prisoners of war or as a result of unpaid debts. (The phrai-slave system only began to disappear in the later nineteenth century. Slavery was abolished in 1874, and corvée labor was replaced by general military service in 1905.) But the head tax (paid for remittance of corvée labor) was only completely abolished in 1939, well after the end of the absolutist monarchy in 1932.

So extensive and long-lasting was the realm of Ayutthaya that it continued to exert a powerful influence even after its final destruction by the Burmese in 1767. Following the disaster of 1767 (the sacking of Ayutthaya by the Burmese), a younger generation of Thai leaders, such as Phra Chao Taksin (r. 1767–1782) and Phra Phuttayotfajulalok (Rama I) (r. 1782–1809), endeavored in turn to build a new center of power on the banks of the Bangkok River by tracing their historical and cultural lineage back to Ayutthaya while at the same time constructing new traditions of their own.

CHARNVIT KASETSIRI

See also Angkor; Buddhism, Mahayana; Buddhism, Theravada; Burma-Siam Wars; Chiang Mai; Chinese Tribute System; *Devaraja*; Dvaravati; Economic History of Early Modern Southeast Asia (Pre-Sixteenth Century); Economic Transformation of Southeast Asia (ca. 1400–ca. 1800); Hinduism; Lopburi (Lawo); Mon; Phya Taksin (Pya Tak [Sin], King Taksin) (r. 1767–1782); Rama I (Chakri) (r. 1782–1809); Ramathibodi (r. 1351–1369); Slavery; Sukhothai (Sukhodava); T'ais; Taxation

References:

Breazeale, Kennon, ed. 1999. *From Japan to Arabia: Ayutthaya's Maritime Relations with Asia.* Bangkok: Toyota Thailand Foundation and the Foundation for the Promotion of Social Sciences and Humanities Textbooks Project.

Charnvit Kasetsiri. 1976. *The Rise of Ayudhya: A History of Siam in the Fourteenth and Fifteenth Centuries.* Kuala Lumpur: Oxford University Press.

Loubere, Simon de la. 1693. *A New Historical Relation of the Kingdom of Siam.* London: n.p.

Reid, Anthony. 1988. *Southeast Asia in the Age of Commerce, 1450–1680.* Vol. 1, *The Lands below the Winds.* New Haven, CT, and London: Yale University Press.

Wyatt, David K. 2001. *Thailand: A Short History.* Chiang Mai, Thailand: Silkworm.

AZAHARI BIN SHEIKH MAHMUD, SHEIKH (1928–2002)
Charismatic Brunei Politician

Sheikh Azahari, popularly known as A. M. Azahari, was perhaps the most charismatic Brunei political figure of the twentieth century. After building up his Partai Rakyat Brunei (PRB, Brunei People's Party) into a major political force (1956–1962) capable of winning a landslide victory at the general election of August 1962, he was forced into lifelong exile after the failure of the December 1962 uprising.

A political leader and businessman of mixed descent (Arab, Malay, Javanese, Sumatran, and European), Azahari was born at Brunei Town in 1928. Sent to Java by the Japanese in 1943 for training as a veterinary surgeon, he became a precocious participant in Indonesia's postwar independence struggles. In 1956, having returned to Brunei some years earlier, he emerged as leader of the newly established PRB. A *merdeka* (independence, freedom) mission to London in September 1957 ended in failure. His party's fortunes slumped, and its adherents were not galvanized until after Malaya's premier, Tunku Abdul Rahman (t. 1957–1970), called, on 27 May 1961, for the creation of "Greater Malaysia." The sultan, though he vacillated somewhat, appeared to favor the idea, and so did the British; the PRB, however, resolutely opposed the sultanate's inclusion in the proposed federation, preferring instead a union of Kalimantan Utara (Northern Borneo). The party won a decisive victory in the 1962 election, but it was still left in a minority position on the partially nominated legislative and executive councils. Frustration led to the disastrous uprising by the party's military wing in December 1962.

The exiled Azahari presided over the party again after it was revived under Malaysian patronage in 1974. He successfully lobbied the United Nations in 1975 and enjoyed the satisfaction of seeing the United Kingdom being pilloried by the international community. The irony is that those who fought hardest for Brunei's independence, such as Azahari, paid the highest price for the accomplishment of that goal, whereas those who did the least and indeed resisted independence for as long as possible garnered the most benefit from the sacrifices of others. Azahari died in Bogor on 30 May 2002.

A. V. M. HORTON

See also Brunei Rebellion (December 1962); Malaysia (1963); *Merdeka* (Freedom, Independence); Partai Rakyat Brunei (PRB)

References:

Anak Agung Gde Agung, Ide. 1973. *Twenty Years of Indonesian Foreign Policy, 1945–1965*. The Hague and Paris: Mouton.

Hussainmiya, B. A. 1995. *Sultan Omar Ali Saifuddin III and Britain: The Making of Brunei Darussalam*. Kuala Lumpur: Oxford University Press.

Poulgrain, Gregory John. 1998. *The Genesis of "Konfrontasi": Malaysia, Brunei, Indonesia, 1945–1965*. Foreword by Pramoedya Ananta Toer. Bathurst, England: Crawford House Publishing; London: C. Hurst.

B

BA MAW, DR. (b. 1893)
Prominent Burmese Nationalist

One of the dominant nationalist figures in late colonial British Burma, Dr. Ba Maw was the first premier of the colony following its separation from British India in 1937 (until 1939) and head of state during the nominal independence granted by Japan from 1943 to 1945. He made his mark initially as a barrister, defending the leader of the 1931 peasant revolt, Hsaya San. On the back of the fame he achieved as a politician who stayed within colonial law while defending the downtrodden, his small Hsinyeitha (Poor Man or Proletarian) Party was sufficiently popular to allow him to form a coalition government after the elections for the Legislative Assembly. Following his fall from office two years later, he began his political alliance with nationalist students, including Thakin Aung San and Thakin Nu, eventually gaining the backing of Imperial Japan both before and during the Pacific War (1941–1945).

Born in 1893, Ba Maw was a man of prodigious intellect. After an education that included studies at Rangoon College and Calcutta University, he was called to the bar at Grays Inn, London. While pursuing his legal studies at Cambridge University, he simultaneously earned a doctorate in literature from Bordeaux University in France. As a politician, he was most adept at developing strategies to achieve the most power for the Burmese under colonial rule. This approach often led to accusations that

he was inconsistent and lacked principle, but in the logic of colonialism, he was merely adopting the politician's adage of seeing his opportunities and taking them. Following the trial of Hsaya San, which first put his name before the public, Dr. Ba Maw became active in the popular campaign over whether Burma should be separated from India. He was publicly said to be on both sides of the question as he read the changing political mood of the electorate. Dr. Ba Maw first assumed public office in 1934 when he became education minister. An astute coalition builder, he managed to construct political machines with a combination of patronage, corruption, and financial backing from the Asian (mostly Indian) business community in prewar Burma.

The Government of Burma Act (1935) established an elected legislature and cabinet form of government under the colonial governor. Although the governor remained responsible for defense, finance, and foreign affairs, the elected Burmese ministers had extensive powers in all other areas of administration in central Burma. Dr. Ba Maw, despite the fact that his party had won only a minority of the seats in the previous elections, was able to form a government and became the first elected Burmese prime minister. His rise to power was greatly assisted by the financial support he received from the Indian business community, especially the powerful Chettiar caste of moneylenders who controlled much of the agricultural land

197

in Lower Burma. His government fell two years later in the face of opposition from students and workers who accused him of being proimperialist and aiding foreign capitalists. Inevitably, anyone in office under the British could have been similarly accused, and as radical nationalism grew in Burma in the late 1930s, the attacks on the government became fiercer still.

Out of office, Dr. Ba Maw joined with the student leaders who had helped oust him. Together with prominent students such as Aung San, who would become a national hero, and U Nu, the future prime minister, he helped organize a united front called the Freedom Bloc, which opposed continued British rule as well as Burmese cooperation in Britain's war against Nazi Germany. Arrested by the British, he was released by the invading Japanese in August 1942. Recognizing Dr. Ba Maw's popularity and his ability to work with the youthful nationalists of the country, the Japanese made him head of a newly proclaimed independent state. Taking the title of *adipati ashin minkyi* (head of state), a title with royalist pretensions, Dr. Ba Maw led a government that was recognized by only Japan and the Axis powers. His brother, Dr. Ba Han, helped draft a detailed planning document for the future of Burma under his supervision. Together with other prewar nationalists, Ba Maw founded the Maha Bama Asiayone (Greater Burma Association) as a nationalist front to rally support to his government and the faltering Japanese war effort.

At the end of the war, Dr. Ba Maw fled Burma with the retreating Japanese army. He was captured and held by the U.S. Army in Japan, then released after being considered for prosecution as a war criminal. The British authorities in London deduced that his wartime crimes were no more extensive than those of General Aung San and Dr. Ba Maw's prewar rival, U Saw. Returning to Burma, he attempted to reestablish a political career; however, by that time, he lost out to the former students he had both opposed and worked with in the previous decade. His waning influence was subsequently expressed through occasional newspaper articles. His memoirs, published in the United States in 1968, tell little of his experience of prewar politics but make much of his wartime exploits.

R. H. TAYLOR

See also Aung San (1915–1947); British Burma; British India, Government of; Burma during the Pacific War (1941–1945); Burma under British Colonial Rule; Chettiars (Chettyars); Constitutional Developments in Burma (1900–1941); Dorman-Smith, Sir Reginald (t. 1941–1946); Nationalism and Independence Movements in Southeast Asia; Nu, U (1907–1995); Peasant Uprisings and Protest Movements in Southeast Asia; Thakin (Lord, Master); U Saw and the Assassination of Aung San

References:

Ba Maw. 1968. *Breakthrough in Burma: Memoirs of a Revolution, 1939–1946.* New Haven, CT: Yale University Press.
Cady, John F. 1958. *A History of Modern Burma.* Ithaca, NY: Cornell University Press.
Taylor, Robert H. 1974. "The Relationship between Burmese Social Classes and British-Indian Policy on the Behavior of the Burmese Political Elite, 1937–1942." Ph.D. diss., Cornell University.

BABA NYONYA

The Baba Nyonya, a subgroup within the Chinese community, are the descendants of Sino-indigenous unions in Melaka and Penang. It was not uncommon among early Chinese traders to take "Malay" women of Peninsular Malay, Sumatran, or Javanese descent as wives or concubines. Consequently, the Baba Nyonya possessed a syncretic mix of Sino-Malay sociocultural traits.

The term *Baba,* derived from Hindustani (which has been strongly influenced by the Persian language), refers to an honorific of respect and was used to address men of Straits-born Chinese heritage. (Straits Chinese are Chinese people born in the British Straits Settlements, as opposed to Chinese born in China.) *Nyonya* (like its variants *Nyonyah, Nonya,* and *Nona*) refers to Straits Chinese women and is a traditional Malay form of address for non-Malay married women of standing; its etymological origin could be traced to the Portuguese word meaning "grandmother." The term *Nyonya,* although not commonly used in contemporary Malaysia, remained popular in neighboring Sumatra and in Java and had a similar meaning.

The term *Straits Chinese* is often used interchangeably with Baba Nyonya; there are, however, qualifications. As mentioned, Straits Chinese are those Chinese born and/or living in the Straits Settlements, a British-created administrative unit of Penang, Melaka, and Singapore that was constituted in 1826. But Straits-born Chinese or those living in the Straits Settlements were not regarded as Baba Nyonya unless they displayed certain unique characteristics. The term *Straits Chinese* was used to differentiate Chinese people who had long been settled in the Straits Settlements from those who had recently (from the mid-nineteenth century on) arrived from China, namely, the China-born, who were referred to as *Sinkheh* (lit. new arrivals).

The Malay term *peranakan* (lit. born of, children of), meaning "locally born foreigner," refers to people of mixed Malay and foreign ancestry but born in the region of present-day Malaysia and Indonesia. For instance, *Jawi Peranakan* denotes a Muslim of mixed South Indian–Malay descent born in Malaysia; also, there are Chinese communities in Medan (Sumatra) and Surabaya (Java) whose members are addressed as *peranakan*. Therefore, Baba Nyonya are peranakan, but not all peranakan are Baba Nyonya.

The Baba Nyonya possessed identifiable characteristics and traits that differentiate them from the China-born Chinese and their descendants who were born and raised in the Straits Settlements or in the Peninsular Malay States. Their unique characteristics were apparent in attire, food, language, educational background, occupation, religious adherence, and loyalties.

The Baba preferred Western suits and leather oxfords to Chinese attire. The Nyonya's clothing was akin to that of the Malay, typically featuring the *baju panjang* (lit. long dress), the *batik sarung* (wraparound), and the *kerongsang* (brooch) and other Malay-style jewelry. Home-cooked meals were an eclectic ensemble of Malay coconut-based curries, Chinese roast pork and braised duck and stir-fry vegetables, and English steak and kidney pie. Bread pudding and ice cream vied with Nyonya *kuih* (cakes) as desserts; there was also an assortment of teatime specialties collectively termed *th'ng chooi* (sweetened water/soup), such as *pungat* (sweet potatoes and yam boiled in sweetened

coconut milk), *bee-koh moi* (black glutinous rice cooked with sugar in porridge form and served with slightly salted coconut milk), *cendol* (stringy green stripes of rice flour in coconut-sugar syrup with ice shavings), and *thour tau th'ng* (peanut soup). The Penang Baba Nyonya spoke a jumbled admixture of Hokkien (Chinese dialect), English, and Malay. Baba Malay, a patois heavily based on Malay, remained the lingua franca of the community in Melaka and Singapore. English-medium education was the preferred choice for the children of Baba Nyonya families. The affluent sent their sons to Britain to study medicine and law. Others became clerks in the colonial civil service or in European firms or banks. Teaching and nursing were acceptable careers for a Nyonya.

Marriages within the community and between those of similar socioeconomic status were the norm during the prewar (pre-1941) period. The wealthy preferred to contract a *chin choay,* or matrilocal marriage, that is, the husband moved in with his wife's family following the wedding. Consequently, daughters in Baba Nyonya families were not considered liabilities. In fact, it was not uncommon for wealthy families to seek promising young bachelors of lesser socioeconomic standing for marriage to their daughters as a means of injecting "talent" into the family gene pool.

The Baba Nyonya subscribed to Chinese beliefs—Taoism, Confucianism, and Chinese Buddhism. But at the same time, true to their eclectic nature, they might pay homage to Malay *keramat* (deified holy man, saint), pray at Hindu temples, or offer candles in churches. Some embraced Christianity through marriage; a small minority converted to Islam when they married Muslims.

The Baba Nyonya of Penang shared similarities with counterparts in northern Sumatra (Medan) and southern Thailand (Songkhla, Pattani, Phuket). There are slight differences between members of the community of Penang and their brethren in Melaka, including its offshoot, Singapore. One apparent difference is in language usage.

Because of their inherited family wealth and their English-medium education, most Baba Nyonya families were economically better off than the China-born Chinese. Their fluency in English and their jobs in civil service or as professionals (doctors, lawyers), coupled with their family wealth and social connections, qualified them to form the Chinese elite. Being British subjects, their loyalty was to the British Crown. They established the Straits Chinese British Association (SCBA) and played leading roles in the postwar Penang Secession Movement (1948–1951). They also led in the establishment of the Malayan Chinese Association (MCA) in 1949, which fought for pan-Malayan Chinese rights.

In many cases, a lack of thriftiness and an ostentatious lifestyle among members of Baba Nyonya households gradually eroded their inherited wealth, built over generations. The depression (1929–1931) and the Pacific War (1941–1945) affected many families that had suffered reversals in fortune. Thus, by the 1950s and 1960s, there were but a handful of rich Baba Nyonya families. And by then, several of the China-born Chinese had managed to build empires in trading, mining, and commercial agriculture. The China-born also gradually displaced the Baba in political leadership of the Chinese community.

Today, the Baba Nyonya communities of Penang, Melaka, and Singapore are shrinking quickly; their way of life and material culture are disappearing. Efforts to revive the Baba Nyonya cultural heritage during the 1980s and the 1990s were commendable. But the heyday of the Baba Nyonya during the early decades of the twentieth century had long entered the annals of history.

OOI KEAT GIN

See also Malayan/Malaysian Chinese
Association (MCA) (1949); Melaka;
Miscegenation; Penang (1786); Penang
Secessionist Movement (1948–1951);
Peranakan; Straits Settlements (1826–1941)

References:
Chia, Felix. 1983. *Ala Sayang! A Social History of Babas and Nyonyas.* Singapore and Petaling Jaya, Malaysia: Eastern Universities Press.
Clammer, John R. 1980. *Straits Chinese Society: Studies in the Sociology of the Baba Communities of Malaysia and Singapore.* Singapore: Singapore University Press.
Heidhues, Mary F. Somers. 1974. *Southeast Asia's Chinese Minorities.* Hawthorne, Australia: Longman.
Khoo Joo Ee. 1996. *The Straits Chinese: A Cultural History.* Amsterdam and Kuala Lumpur: Pepin Press.
Vaughan, J. D. 1879. *The Manners and Customs of the Chinese of the Straits Settlements.* Singapore: Mission Press. Reprinted in 1971 by Oxford University Press, Kuala Lumpur and Singapore.

BAJAU

The term *Bajau* (also *Badjaw, Bajo,* and other variants) is applied to a diverse collection of Sama/Bajau-speaking peoples. They are spread over a vast area of islands and littoral, extending from the central Philippines through the Sulu Archipelago to the eastern coast of Borneo and from coastal Sulawesi southward through the Moluccas to western Timor. In the Philippines, most Sama speakers are referred to by others as *Samal,* whereas in eastern Indonesia, they are generally known by the Bugis term *Bajo.* Most refer to themselves as *Sama,* or *a'a Sama,* usually with an additional toponymic name to indicate geographic and/or dialect affiliation. The Sama are highly fragmented politically and were divided in the past among a number of maritime states, most of them dominated by other ethnic groups.

In all of Southeast Asia, Sama speakers number between 800,000 and 950,000. In 2001, the Bajau numbered 354,000 in Sabah (Malaysia), making them the second largest indigenous group in the state. No reliable population figures exist elsewhere, but recent estimates place their numbers at 400,000 in the Philippines and at between 150,000 and 230,000 in Indonesia. The Sama/Bajau language family belongs to the Hesperonesian branch of Austronesian and includes an estimated ten languages, most of them highly dialectalized.

Linguistic evidence suggests that the proto-Sama homeland was centered in the islands of the Basilan Strait. From there, Sama speakers spread generally south and westward, establishing themselves throughout the Sulu Archipelago. Although some groups, in reaching Borneo, settled along the western coast of Sabah, others moved eastward through the Straits of Makassar to southern Sulawesi. Their subsequent dispersal over much of eastern Indonesia was closely linked to the development of a *trepang* (sea slug) trade and, with it, the expanding commercial and political influence of Bugis and Makassarese traders. For almost three hundred years, the Bajau were the principal gatherers of trepang in eastern Indonesia and the Sulu region. With the rise of the Tausug sultanate as a major slave market, some Sama speakers, most notably the Balangingi, emerged for a time as major slave raiders.

Local communities take a wide variety of forms. Formerly, at one extreme were boat-dwelling groups—local communities that consisted of flotillas of boat-living families who regularly anchored at the same moorage site. Far more common, both in the past and today, are the pile-house or shoreline villages, typically aggregated settlements where houses are raised on piles above the sea or built along beaches or estuarine shorelines. At the opposite extreme are the land-based villages, with individual houses dispersed and surrounded by fruit trees and gardens.

In most shoreline settlements, fishing is a major source of livelihood. However, farming is also practiced, and in western Sabah, most Bajau settlements are located inland; there, most of the people farm (growing mainly rice) or engage in trade. In addition, some raise water buffalo, cattle, and horses. For centuries, trade has been a central part of the Bajau economy, and historically, Sama speakers have been valued by the traditional trading states of the region for their craft products, for their boatbuilding and seafaring skills, and as suppliers of marine produce.

Households are often large, frequently containing the families of one or more married children. Houses are typically grouped in clusters (*tumpuk* or *ba'anan/banan*). In daily life, household clusters form important support groups, with members lending help in farmwork, child care, and house building and in conducting village ceremonies. Kinship ties, which are traced through both men and women, tend to be heavily focused within these groups and are often reinforced by intermarriage. A cluster may coincide with a parish, a group of households affiliated with a single mosque, or a parish may contain more than one cluster, with one cluster's spokesperson acknowledged as the parish leader. In villages containing more than a single parish, one parish leader typically acts as village head. The latter administers village affairs and is empowered to convene face-to-face hearings in the event of village disputes.

Considerable respect is shown for age. In household clusters, elders, including cluster spokespeople, are invariably consulted when important decisions must be made. Responsibility for resolving disputes falls chiefly on the house elders and the parish and village leaders. Above the village level, factional rivalries tend to be pervasive. Vendettas occur, but endemic armed conflict, characteristic of other ethnic groups in the Sulu-Sulawesi region, is generally lacking. Political relations are organized primarily in terms of leader-centered coalitions. Locally, these coalitions coalesce around cluster, parish, and village leaders. In Sabah, in contrast to Indonesia and the Philippines, the Bajau have played a major role in state politics and today hold numerous public offices at all levels of state government.

The Bajau are Sunni Muslims. Religious piety and learning are important sources of prestige, and persons considered descendants of the Prophet (*salip* or *sharif*) are shown special deference. Every parish is served by a set of mosque officials, including an *imam* (leader in prayer), a *bilal* (he who calls the faithful to prayer), and a *hatib* (preacher). In addition to conducting mosque prayers, the imam officiates at life-transition rituals, counsels parish members in religious and legal matters, and leads them in prayer during household-sponsored rites. Those who are well versed in religious matters are known as *paki* or *pakil*. In times of misfortune, a variety of other religious practitioners may also be consulted, including midwives, herbalist-curers, spirit mediums, and diviners.

CLIFFORD SATHER

See also Borneo; Brunei (Sixteenth to Nineteenth Centuries); Brunei Ethnic Minorities; East Malaysian Ethnic Minorities; Iranun and Balangingi; Marine/Sea Products; Piracy; Sarawak and Sabah (North Borneo); Slavery; Sulu and the Sulu Archipelago; Tausug and the Sulu Sultanate

References:

Casino, Eric. 1976. *The Jama Mapun: A Changing Samal Society in the Southern Philippines.* Quezon City, the Philippines: Ateneo de Manila Press.

Nimmo, H. Arlo. 2001. *Magosaha: An Ethnography of the Tawi-Tawi Sama Dilaut.*

Quezon City, the Philippines: Ateneo de Manila University Press.

Sather, Clifford. 1978. "The Bajau Laut." Pp. 172–192 in *Essays on Borneo Societies*. Edited by Victor King. Hull Monographs on South East Asia. Oxford: Oxford University Press.

———. 1993a. "Bajau." Pp. 30–35 in *Encyclopedia of World Cultures*. Vol. 5, *East and Southeast Asia*. Edited by David Levinson. Boston: G. K. Hall.

———. 1993b. "Samal." Pp. 217–221 in *Encyclopedia of World Cultures*. Vol. 5, *East and Southeast Asia*. Edited by David Levinson. Boston: G. K. Hall.

———. 1997. *The Bajau Laut: Adaptation, History, and Fate in a Maritime Fishing Society of South-Eastern Sabah*. Kuala Lumpur: Oxford University Press.

BALI

Bali, an island of about 5,633 square kilometers, is located between Java and Lombok and bounded by the Bali Sea in the north, the Indian Ocean in the south, the Strait of Lombok in the east, and the Strait of Bali in the west. In the center of the island is a range of volcanic mountains; Mount Agung and Mount Batur are active volcanoes. Mountain ranges divide the island into the very narrow northern part and the wider southern part, where the population is concentrated; there are roughly 3 million people in Bali today, most of whom are Hindus. The mountain is very important in the Balinese cultural concept. It is considered the center of the world and the place of God, according to the cosmology and Mandala concept in Hindu mythology. Four lakes (sources of irrigation) are located in the center of the island: Tamblingan, Buyan, Beratan, and Batur.

According to the archaeological data, Bali has been inhabited at least since the Upper Pleistocene (60,000–50,000 years ago), as evidenced by the discovery of stone tools in Sembiran and Trunyan and the caves at Karang Boma and Selonding.

Bali might have received two cultural influences, from mainland Southeast Asia and from South Asia (India). The appearance of early metal (bronze) technology in Bali was considered as the influence of Dongson culture (Vietnam) or a local development, with artifacts at Manuaba and Sembiran. With neither tin nor copper available, Bali may have been involved in long-distance trade during prehistoric times. The economic surplus of Balinese society during the prehistoric period might have been based on rice cultivation, which has been practiced in Bali to the present.

Inscriptions dating from the ninth and tenth centuries C.E. mention *sawah* (wet-rice fields), *pagagan* (dry-rice fields), *parlak* (dry fields), *mmal* (garden), and *padang* (grasslands). The intensification of agriculture may have been facilitated through the construction of dikes and irrigation canals and also by the introduction of the plow. The terms *suwak* and *kasuwakan*, meaning an "irrigation system," were already being recorded in Balinese inscriptions dating from the eleventh century.

Archaeological evidence indicates that contacts between Bali and India might have started some two thousand years ago. The appearance of Indian pottery in North Bali might have stimulated the development of Hinduism in Bali. By the seventh century, Hinduism had been entrenched in the island; it remains speculative whether Hinduism derived directly from India or via Sumatra and Java.

The appearance of Balinese inscriptions in the late ninth century C.E. provides insight into the social and political units in early historical Bali. The oldest inscriptions, from 882–975 C.E., use the title *Sang Ratu* (Indonesian/Austronesian for "Maharaja") to refer to the highest political authority. The inscriptions also mention a king, Warmadewa. During the tenth century, it is believed that Hindus from East Java migrated to Bali, among them Mahendradatta, the mother of Airlangga (r. 1019–1049). She married Prince Udayana from the Warmadewa royal lineage. Thus, when Airlangga's half brother ascended the Balinese throne, he consummated the blood ties between the ruling houses of East Java and Bali.

The kingdoms of Singhasari and Majapahit in East Java attacked Bali in 1284 and 1343, respectively. Kĕrtanagara of Singhasari seized Bali in 1284 and held on to the island until his demise in 1292. The Balinese enjoyed a brief period of independence until Majapahit forces arrived in 1343. A Javanese nobleman, Sri Krisna Kepakisan, and his fellow nobles (*aryas*) from Majapahit in East Java reigned over Bali. The intense Javanization of Bali had begun, including the stratification of society into caste

Sunrise on Gunung Batur in Bali. (Corel Corporation)

groups, with the *satriya,* or warrior caste, presiding at Samprangan. Those who rejected this hierarchical society fled to the mountain regions; they came to be referred to as the Bali Aga (Bali Mula), the so-called original Balinese. The majority, however, bowed to Javanese domination to the extent that the contemporary Balinese commonly believed that their ancestors derived from Majapahit. Another wave of Javanese Hindus crossed over to Bali following the collapse of the Majapahit regime to the Muslim *pasisir* states (those on the northern coastal strip of Java) around the late 1520s. Thereafter, the narrow Strait of Bali separated Hindunized Bali from Muslim Java.

The focus of political power was initially centered at Samprangan; later, it shifted to Gelgel and then to Klungkung. Bali as a unified polity never existed; instead, the island was fragmented into numerous small kingdoms. Bali reached its zenith of political influence during the twenty-year reign of Batu Renggong (Waturenggong, r. 1550–1570), the ruler of Gelgel.

Then, Balinese hegemony encompassed Balambangan in East Java and Lombok and Sumbawa. During the seventeenth century, nine competing states coexisted: Klungkung, Karangasem, Mengwi, Badung, Bangli, Tabanan, Gianyar, Buleleng, and Jembrena. Slaves were Bali's only exportable commodity. Balinese slaves comprised a sizable portion of Batavia's population in the late seventeenth and early eighteenth centuries. South Africa received a considerable number of slaves bought and brought from Bali. Chinese traders prized female slaves for their diligence and beauty, and being Hindu, they had no aversion to having pork in the household.

Cornelis de Houtman led an unsuccessful Dutch expedition to Bali in 1597. But Dutch priorities were focused elsewhere (Maluku, Java, and Sumatra), and it took another two centuries before Bali came onto the Dutch agenda. In 1839, Mads Lange, a Danish "country trader," opened a trading post at Kuta, dealing with everything from luxury items to common trade goods. Kuta was a regular port of call until Lange's death in 1856.

Then, in the mid-nineteenth century, as a preemptive measure to exclude other Europeans, the Dutch adopted a forward policy toward Bali. Klungkung, Karangasem, Badung, and Buleleng acknowledged Dutch sovereignty in 1841. Military expeditions were launched in 1846, 1848, and 1849 to curb piracy, the plunder of shipwrecks, slavery, and the Hindu practice of *suttee* (the burning alive of a widow at her deceased husband's funeral pyre). In 1853, Buleleng and Jembrena were brought under direct Dutch control. The Dutch then subdued Karangasem and Gianyar in 1882. The looting of a Chinese-owned ship at Sanur in 1904 was utilized as a pretext for the final subjugation of Bali. A sizable Dutch force landed in September 1906 and marched toward Badung. More than 3,000 Balinese collectively committed ritual suicide (*puputan,* meaning "ending" in Balinese) amid the hail of gunfire from the Dutch troops. Likewise, in operations against Klungkung in 1908, puputan was again practiced.

The Bali who had remained relatively unchanged since the sixteenth century gradually slipped into the twentieth century with direct Dutch colonial rule. The Dutch took pride in not exposing the Balinese to foreign cultural influences. For instance, Christian missionaries were allowed access to the island only in the 1930s. In 1929, the Dutch restored the former kingdoms to their rulers and declared these territories as *zelfbesturen* (self-governing territories, under Dutch authority). But the period of Dutch colonial rule (1908–1942) witnessed one disaster after another: a devastating earthquake in 1917, a plague that killed off almost all of the island's rice crop, an influenza outbreak, and then the disastrous effects of the Great Depression (1929–1931).

Apart from shortages of food and other daily necessities, Bali experienced little change during the Japanese occupation (1942–1945). The hectic postwar period witnessed the Dutch creation of the Republic of East Indonesia, with Bali as one of its thirteen administrative constituencies. The republic lasted for seven months. In August 1950, Bali became part of the independent Republic of Indonesia.

The several thousand deaths recorded as a consequence of the eruption of Mount Agung in 1963 did not compare to the estimated 60,000 massacred as alleged communists during the bloodbath that took place from October 1965 to February 1966. The Partai Komunis Indonesia (PKI, Communist Party of Indonesia) had gained a reasonable footing in the early 1960s in local politics.

The last quarter of the twentieth century saw the flourishing of Bali's tourism industry. The island's rich, unique sociocultural heritage, exotic traditions and practices, and numerous colorful festivals complement the physical landscape of rugged mountains and beautiful sandy beaches, making Bali a visitors' haven. Germans, Australians, and Japanese made up the majority of tourist arrivals.

The Asian Financial Crisis of 1997–1998, followed by political instability in Indonesia, adversely affected Bali's economy, where tourism was a mainstay. Developments during the early 2000s, in particular the terrorist bombings of October 2002, were even more damaging to the tourism industry.

I. WAYAN ARDIKA

See also Airlangga (r. 1019–1049); Dong-son; Hindu-Buddhist Period of Southeast Asia; Hinduism; Indianization; Kĕrtanagara (r.1268–1292); Majapahit (1293–ca. 1520s); Mataram; Partai Komunis Indonesia (PKI) (1920); Rice in Southeast Asia; Singhasari

References:

Agung, Ide Anak Agung Gde. 1991. *Bali in the 19th Century.* Jakarta: Yayasan Obor Indonesia.

Boon, James A. 1990. *Affinities and Extremes: Crisscrossing the Bittersweet Ethnology of East Indies History, Hindu-Balinese Culture, and Indo-European Allure.* Chicago: University of Chicago Press.

Geertz, Hildred, ed. 1992. *State and Society in Bali: Historical, Textual and Anthropological Approaches.* Leiden, The Netherlands: KITLV Press.

Hobart, Angela, Urs Ramseyer, and Albert Leeman. 1996. *The Peoples of Bali.* Oxford: Blackwell Publishers.

Van der Kraan, Alfons. 1995. *Bali at War: A History of the Dutch-Balinese Conflict of 1846–49.* Monash Paper no. 34. Clayton, Australia: Centre of Southeast Asian Studies, Monash University.

Vickers, Adrian. 1989. *Bali: A Paradise Created.* Berkeley, CA: Periplus Editions.

BALING TALKS (1955)

The so-called peace talks at Baling in the northern Malay state of Kedah, close to the Thai border, were held on 28 and 29 December 1955. The participants were Tunku Abdul Rahman Putra Al-Haj (1903–1990), Malaya's chief minister at the time, and Chin Peng (1922–), the secretary-general of the Malayan Communist Party (MCP). Aimed at bringing an end to the Malayan Emergency—the communists' armed insurrection that began in 1948—the talks marked an important turning point in Malaya's independence struggle, although they ended in a stalemate. The Tunku (prince) went to the talks accompanied by David Marshall (1908–1995), Singapore's interim self-government chief minister, and Tun Tan Cheng Lock (1883–1960), president of the Malayan Chinese Association. Chin Peng attended with his colleagues Chen Tien and Rashid Mydin. In the midst of tight security, the communist leaders emerged from the jungles outside of Baling town and were escorted by British police officers to the schoolhouse where the talks took place. The talks received wide coverage from the local and international media.

Chin Peng's "unexpected" assurance that the communists would lay down their arms if the Tunku could secure powers in internal security and defense from Britain served to strengthen the latter's hand in the independence talks he held later with the British government in London in February 1956. Indeed, it hastened the end of British rule by at least three years. Chin Peng told the Tunku that he recognized that the people had elected the Tunku's UMNO-MCA-MIC Alliance government in the 1955 general elections, but internal security and defense were still in British hands. Anxious not to appear as a stumbling block in efforts to end the "shooting war," in which thousands of lives had been lost, the British government not only acceded to the Tunku's request for those powers but also agreed to his suggested date for independence—"if possible, by 31 August, 1957." Britain, however, secured an agreement with the Tunku that British military bases in Malaya would continue to operate for as long as it was mutually acceptable to both countries.

After independence had been secured, the communists failed to keep their promise: they did not lay down their arms until 1989. However, the Emergency was ended many years earlier, in 1960, as the government felt the communists no longer posed a threat. The Baling talks broke down over the Tunku's refusal to accept Chin Peng's demand that the MCP be allowed to exist as a legal organization and that the communist insurgents who laid down their arms were not to be detained and screened by the police authorities.

Malaya (the Malay Peninsula) is one of three territories that make up the present nation-state of Malaysia. The other two are the Borneo territories of Sarawak and Sabah. The MCP operated mainly in Malaya.

CHEAH BOON-KHENG

See also Abdul Rahman Putra Al-Haj, Tunku (1903–1990); Chin Peng (Ong Boon Hua/Hwa) (1922–); Malayan Communist Party (MCP) (1908–1995); Malayan Emergency (1948–1960); Marshall, David Saul; Nationalism and Independence Movements in Southeast Asia; Tan Cheng Lock

References:

Short, Anthony. 1975. *The Communist Insurrection in Malaya, 1948–60*. London: Muller.

Stockwell, A. J., comp. 1995. *Malaya*. Pt. 3, *The Alliance Route to Independence, 1953–1957*. British Documents on the End of Empire, vol. 3. London: Her Majesty's Stationery Office.

BAN CHIANG

Ban Chiang is one of Thailand's most famous archaeological sites, owing to its critical place in the well-publicized claims that there was an early Bronze Age in Thailand, as well as the exquisite antiques of painted pottery that had been buried by the inhabitants as grave goods. The site is a large mound, approximately 8 hectares in area and standing 5 meters above the surrounding rice fields, and takes its name from the modern village built over it. The prehistoric deposit was built up during the Neolithic, Bronze Age, and early Iron Age, during a period of occupation from approximately 3,500 B.C.E. until 500 C.E. In terms of continuity of occupation and preservation of ancient materials, it is arguably the best exponent of a group of related prehistoric sites, which include Non Nok Tha and Ban Na Di, located on the Khorat Plateau in Thailand's semiarid northeastern corner.

At the time of first occupation, Ban Chiang was a low mound of yellow soil. The inhabitants apparently built wooden houses on piles in small areas of habitation that shifted over time, and they buried their deceased in isolated graves or small cemetery areas. Reflecting the role of farming in the subsistence economy, rice chaff was used as a pottery temper from the outset, and the remains of domesticated pigs, dogs, cattle, and chickens from early times are still present. Hunting and gathering supplemented the diet significantly throughout the site's occupation. Ceramic crucibles for metal production are most common after 1000 B.C.E. but are reported throughout the sequence, and anvils attest to pottery manufacture on site. Differences in social status seem to have remained fluid, with no evidence for the imposition of a hierarchical society, and Ban Chiang seems to have remained one among a network of autonomous villages that participated in long-distance trade and exchange. Analysis of skeletons from the site has revealed little or no evidence for population change. Notwithstanding these continuities in the site's prehistoric character, significant changes in technology and mortuary practices allow archaeologists to recognize ten phases, grouped into three periods.

The Early Period (approximately 3500–1000 B.C.E.) is characterized by cord-marked and incised pottery, the appearance of bronze, and the largest range of burial modes. The mortuary pottery varies considerably in terms of whether curvilinear or parallel lines were incised, the location and extent of cord-markings and burnishing, the color of the jar, and the choice of a rounded base or a foot-ring to sit the vessel. On the basis of the detail of ceramic decorations and other stylistic markers, Joyce White (1997) divided the Early Period into five phases. The earliest dated bronze, a nodule from the base of a grave assigned to the junction between phases 2 and 3, is radiocarbon-dated to between 1500 and 2000 B.C.E. A spearhead, an adze head, and various bracelets and anklets of bronze were interred as grave goods during phases 3, 4, and 5 of the Early Period. Most of the adult burials were extended lying on their backs, including one apparently associated with a ca. 3500 B.C.E. radiocarbon date. Five adults (phases 2 to 4) were interred in a flexed position, with the oldest of these reliably dated to around 2000 B.C.E. Nine fetuses, newborns, and infants up to two

to three years of age were buried inside pots, perhaps symbolizing the concept of a womb, and one newborn and six children up to five years of age were buried in the usual manner for the adults. A four-year-old wore bronze anklets, which, given the scarcity of bronze at the time, is suggestive of an elevated status compared with most of the population. Radiocarbon dates of over 4500 B.C.E. (perhaps too early for any archaeologist to believe) and 1500–2000 B.C.E. have been obtained for the burials in jars. Flexed burials and jar burials fell out of practice after the Early Period's phase 4.

The Middle Period (approximately 1000–300 B.C.E.) witnessed an increase in local bronze working, the arrival of iron, and the earliest painted pottery at the site. Traces of bronze metallurgy include a casting hearth, the bulk of the crucibles and crucible fragments excavated at the site, and the recycling of slag (a by-product of smelting ore) as a temper occasionally added to the clay from which the crucibles were made. For reasons that are not clear, ornaments were found with most of the burials of children up to five years of age but with few of the remains of more mature persons. In any case, seven of the thirty-three burials assigned to this period were found wearing anklets or bracelets of bronze, and one of these also had iron bracelets, indicative of the increased availability of metal wares. Iron, following its appearance in the Middle Period's phase 7, evidently succeeded bronze as the preferred material for weapons. The earliest examples are two spearheads with bronze sockets and blades of forged iron. As similar spearheads have been found only in Dong-son sites, it is probable that these were not local products but had been traded in from the Red River area. An iron blade hafted to a wooden handle was found with one phase 8 burial. The mortuary pottery during the Middle Period was mostly dark brown to black in color, with incised decorations, often enhanced with an infill of red paint.

The final two prehistoric phases are assigned to the Late Period, ca. 300 B.C.E.–500 C.E. During this Late Period, red-on-buff mortuary vessels, which feature a range of spiral and curvilinear designs painted in red on a buff background, were often interred alongside the extended corpse. These exquisite and widely sought-after antiques, with which Ban Chiang is most often associated, had probably been made at specialist potting centers and exported to sites such as Ban Chiang. Ornaments and other artifacts of bronze from this Late Period often have a high percentage of tin, suggesting they, too, were imported from production sites located elsewhere, just as the glass beads found in some burials had certainly been imported. Cylindrical objects of clay, with a hole through the long axis and deeply carved designs circumscribing the external face, appeared concurrently at Ban Chiang and other sites in the vicinity. Their interpretation as seals for marking ownership or recording transactions would directly support other evidence for increased trade at around two thousand years ago, but even if they had had some other function, their sudden appearance at several sites would at least point to increased interaction between rural communities at that time. Iron knives and spear-blades, as well as axes of bronze or iron, are other noteworthy implements.

Late Period burials and mortuary goods dominated the discoveries made at Ban Chiang during the initial excavations, by Thai archaeologists, during the 1960s and early 1970s. But the Late Period was poorly represented, comparatively speaking, during the major season at the site in 1974 and 1975, with the excavation and subsequent analysis of finds dominated by U.S. researchers. Fieldwork at Ban Chiang has come full circle with the most recent excavation of an extensive, well-laid-out Late Period cemetery by the Thai archaeologists Bannanurag and Khemnark. The sheer size of the site and its independent investigation by several different teams have created some difficulties in delivering a final verdict on the site's interpretation. Technical advances in archaeological analysis, many of which are particularly germane to a site whose stratigraphic sequence is as long and as complex as Ban Chiang's, are still being applied to the 1974–1975 finds, and the chronological details described here are subject to revision.

The human remains from the 1974–1975 season have been fully described by Michael Pietrusewsky (1997) and Michele Douglas in a series of articles and a joint monograph (2002). Depending on the precise makeup of the comparative populations, skull measurements link Ban Chiang most closely to one of two sites: either the Neolithic skulls from the Neolithic site of Khok Phanom Di in central Thailand or the prehistoric and recent skulls representing the non-Japanese inhabitants of the main islands and the Ryukyu chain of Japan. In either case, as also indicated by study of the teeth, the Ban Chiang people seem to have been part of a broadly "Mongoloid" population whose roots in Southeast Asia appear older than those of the T'ais who now dominate Thailand demographically. The demographic profile of the Ban Chiang skeletal series is consistent with an essentially stationary population that could have remained in equilibrium with the available subsistence resources over several millennia. The lifestyle appears to have been rigorous but relatively free from chronic ill health or warfare. Many people wore their teeth down to stubs, and bouts of anemia (possibly associated with malarial infection) occurred at modest rates. Some of the more elderly (especially the males) were afflicted by osteoarthritis, and both men and women occasionally suffered bony fractures that are best attributed to accidents experienced during the course of daily activity.

In summary, Ban Chiang may be viewed as a major archaeological testament to the long-term history of the Mon-Khmer speakers who numerically dominated the Thailand region before the immigration of T'ai speakers in historical times. The continuities in cultural practices and economic pursuits agree with the biological evidence for occupation by essentially the same population throughout the site's prehistory. Cultural practices such as the preference to bury the dead as extended, supine inhumations with pots and other grave goods and a similar weight placed on farming, hunting, and gathering in the food quest support the biological evidence of a stable population. Complementing this basic stability, changes in material culture over time reflect a dynamic situation of trade and related interactions between the communities at Ban Chiang and other rural settlements on and near the Khorat Plateau. This network facilitated the flow of novel goods and technologies across the region during the Bronze Age and especially the Iron Age, without swamping the local identity that served as a key ingredient in the social reproduction of the communities and their web of communication.

DAVID BULBECK

See also Archaeological Sites of Southeast of
Asia; Ceramics; Dong-son; Human
Prehistory of Southeast Asia; Khmers; Metal
Age Cultures in Southeast Asia; Mons;
Neolithic Period of Southeast Asia; T'ais
References:
Bellwood, Peter. 2001. "Southeast Asia Neolithic
and Early Bronze." Pp. 287–306 in
Encyclopedia of Prehistory. Vol. 3, *East Asia and
Oceania.* Edited by Peter N. Peregrine and
Melvin Ember. New York: Kluwer
Academic/Plenum Publishers.
Higham, Charles. 1989. *The Archaeology of
Mainland Southeast Asia.* Cambridge:
Cambridge University Press.
———. 1996. *The Bronze Age of Southeast Asia.*
Cambridge: Cambridge University Press.
Pietrusewsky, Michael. 1997. "The People of
Ban Chiang: An Early Bronze Age Site in
Northeast Thailand." *Bulletin of the Indo-
Pacific Prehistory Association* 16: 107–110.
Pietrusewsky, Michael, and Michele Toomay
Douglas. 2002. *Ban Chiang, a Prehistoric
Village Site in Northeast Thailand.* Vol. 1,
The Human Skeletal Remains. Philadelphia:
University of Pennsylvania Museum of
Archaeology and Anthropology.
Stark, Miriam. 2001. "Mainland Southeast Asia
Late Prehistoric." Pp. 160–205 in *Encyclopedia
of Prehistory.* Vol. 3, *East Asia and Oceania.*
Edited by Peter N. Peregrine and Melvin
Ember. New York: Kluwer Academic/
Plenum Publishers.
Vernon, William W. 1997. "Chronological
Variation in Crucible Technology at Ban
Chiang: A Preliminary Assessment." *Bulletin
of the Indo-Pacific Prehistory Association* 16:
107–110.
White, Joyce C. 1997. "A Brief Note on New
Dates for the Ban Chiang Cultural
Tradition." *Bulletin of the Indo-Pacific Prehistory
Association* 16: 103–106.

BAN KAO CULTURE

Ban Kao is an ancient village mound in Kanchanaburi Province, in south-central Thailand,
with numerous burials preserved in the debris.
Apart from one flexed burial, all of the excavated human skeletons were found extended
on their backs, and all but two individuals had
pots placed at strategic points around the
corpses. Adzes of polished stone, of varied
shape, size, and cross-sectional geometry, were
common funerary gifts. Rings, beads, and other
jewelry of stone, bone, or shell often accompanied the dead. Two of the graves had iron rather
than stone adzes, and one of these included
ivory disks. This association of extended inhumations decked with earthen pots that conform
to certain canons of shape and decoration, polished stone adzes, and nonmetallic ornaments is
the distinguishing feature of the so-called Ban
Kao culture.

Per Sørenson (1967) originally nominated
the term *Ban Kao* to refer to the Neolithic
phase in southern Thailand and West Malaysia.
However, the chronology of Ban Kao has generated some controversy. Radiocarbon dates on
charcoal consistently date the early period of
habitation at the site to about 2000–1300
B.C.E., as would be entirely reasonable for Neolithic remains in central Thailand and the
Malay Peninsula. However, iron slag, fragments
of iron implements, and small pieces of bronze
occur in the upper layers of the site. The iron
demonstrates that occupation must have continued until at least 500 B.C.E. Most burials lie
beneath the layers with metal remains, but as
the excavation could not determine the levels
from which the graves had been cut, they could
be of either Iron Age or Neolithic antiquity.
The two graves with iron adzes are among the
deepest at Ban Kao, in support of an Iron Age
dating for the whole lot. However, these two
graves did contain pots that are thought to be
relatively late in the Ban Kao sequence, so the
burials with earlier pottery could be Neolithic.

The three most interesting of the early Ban
Kao pottery types are narrow-stemmed cups,
vases with wide foot-rings and funnel-shaped
mouths, and three-legged bowls called tripods.
Cups and vases such as these are extremely
scarce in Southeast Asia. Tripods like those at
Ban Kao are otherwise restricted to the Malay
Peninsula, notably the approximately four-
thousand-year-old examples from Jenderam
Hilir. Chronologically and geographically, the
Ban Kao culture would have a very narrow application if these distinctive vessels were included in its definition. So they do not particularly help Sørenson's cause when he
distinguished a Ban Kao culture to the exclusion of sites in Southeast Asia north and east of
Ban Kao. Yet all three vessel types can be found
in the "Lungshanoid" sites of China and Tai-

wan, which approximately date to between 4000 and 500 B.C.E. Perhaps early contact with China introduced these ceramic forms to the people of Ban Kao and some closely related groups.

Two other early Ban Kao pottery types are bowls on funnel-shaped stands and long-necked beakers and bowls with a carination at the midriff where the contour abruptly changes direction. Lungshanoid parallels for these forms are still apparent but now provide less precise matches than can be found in Southeast Asia. Bowls with funnel-shaped pedestals have been found at the base of Non Nok Tha in northeast Thailand and at Khok Charoen in central Thailand. Gua Cha, in the Malay Peninsula, yielded a few carinated, long-necked beakers. All of the burials with these vessels are Neolithic.

The later vessel forms at Ban Kao have the least number of Lungshanoid similarities and the greatest number of Southeast Asian parallels. These forms include saucers and bowls on trumpet-shaped stands, wide-necked carinated bowls, globular jars with necks of varying length, vases with funnel-shaped or trumpet-shaped mouths, and a wide variety of dishes and shallow bowls. Analogues of these forms have been illustrated for Non Nok Tha, Khok Charoen, and Gua Cha, as well as Khok Phanom Di in southeast Thailand, Gua Harimau and Bukit Tengku Lembu in the Malay Peninsula, and Sa Huynh sites on the central coast of Vietnam. Per Sørenson noted similar pottery at sites lying between Bukit Tengku Lembu and Ban Kao. The age span of these sites lies between about 2000 and 1 B.C.E., with Neolithic, early Bronze Age, and Iron Age associations.

The concept of a Ban Kao culture implies that the later Ban Kao forms would have evolved from the earlier ones. However, archaeologists now understand that the so-called later forms had appeared at some sites in Thailand before even the earliest funerary pottery was buried at Ban Kao. So the notion of an archaeological culture—a recurring association of distinctive artifact types—is difficult to sustain in the case of Ban Kao. Archaeologists now prefer to interpret the similarities of Ban Kao with other sites in Thailand and northern Malaya as evidence of a common tradition. They also recognize locally specialized craft practices based on the occurrence of vessel types peculiar to one or the other site (for example, Khok Charoen, Khok Phanom Di, and Non Nok Tha, as well as Ban Kao).

In addition to a similar repertoire of vessel forms, Neolithic to Iron Age pottery in Thailand and Malaya is similar in the common use of cord-marking as a decorative technique. This effect is achieved by wrapping a paddle in twine or cloth and beating it against the outside wall while a stone anvil takes the pressure on the inner wall. Refining a pot's shape with the paddle-and-anvil technique before firing the vessel is very widespread in Asia, and adding cord-marked decorations during the exercise is a truly ancient practice in mainland Southeast Asia. Where the surfaces of Ban Kao and related vessels are not cord-marked, they may bear types of geometric and curvilinear motifs that occur widely on Southeast Asian pottery dating to the same time frame. The mortuary practice of extended inhumations decked with adzes (bronze and iron, as well as stone) and jewelry, in addition to the funerary pots, is another shared characteristic of the Thailand and Malaya sites that partake of the same tradition as Ban Kao.

The types of sites where these extended inhumations occur illustrate a marked contrast between the Malay Peninsula and the main body of Thailand to the north of the peninsula. Almost all Ban Kao–related sites in the peninsula occur in rock shelters, and many are cemeteries of burials dug into more ancient deposits containing debris from Hoabinhian hunter-gatherers. In contrast, the sites located north of the peninsula are always mounds of varying size with traces of village occupation throughout the deposit. The burials were most likely interred beneath the villagers' houses (except at Khok Phanom Di, where designated cemetery areas have been discerned). The height and expanse of the mounds vary widely because of various factors, such as cycles of erosion, intentionally created layers of clay or shell, and the quantity of waste debris left by the residents. With an area of around 8,000 square meters and a depth of about 2 meters, Ban Kao is a smaller example of these mounds, as compared, for instance, with Khok Phanom Di (50,000 square meters in area and a height of up to 12 meters).

Despite the size of the Khok Phanom Di mound and its remains of domesticated rice, the excavator, Charles Higham (1989), is ambivalent on the degree to which the inhabitants practiced farming rather than a hunter-gatherer economy. In marked contrast, a farming subsistence is generally accepted for the occupants of other, related village sites in Thailand, which are now marked by mounds. The wealth of Khok Phanom Di, represented by its burial goods, is attributed by Higham to the bounty of natural resources in the immediate environment and a range of highly developed crafts, the products of which were traded with adjacent groups for exotic goods and agricultural produce. Actually, Higham's approach may apply with greater force to the burial grounds in rock shelters in the Malay Peninsula. Direct evidence of domesticated food is rarely forthcoming from these burial grounds, and the peninsula includes vast swaths of rain forest inhabited by hunter-gatherer groups to this day. Collection of rain forest produce to trade for manufactured goods is an ancient practice among Malaya's hunter-gatherers. Further, religious customs may be transmitted through trade relationships. This sort of interaction could conceivably account for the incorporation of Ban Kao–related funerary goods with the Neolithic extended burials in rock shelters in various parts of the peninsula.

Analysis of the burials also permits inferences on biological differences between the people in the peninsula and their counterparts to the north. The Neolithic burials at Gua Cha evidently represent a short people, with male and female stature estimated at 157 and 150 centimeters, respectively, compared with the sites of Ban Kao, Khok Phanom Di, and northeast Thailand, where both males and females were between 5 and 10 centimeters taller. The skulls in the Thailand sites are large by present Southeast Asian standards but clearly represent Mongoloid people with broad cranial vaults, flat faces, and shovel-shaped incisors. No such claims can be made for the Gua Cha Neolithic skulls, whose longer cranial vaults, short faces, and lack of Mongoloid dental features invite comparison with the earlier, Hoabinhian inhabitants of the area. The Ban Kao burials in particular have been viewed as forerunners of the T'ais, who constitute the dominant ethnic group in present-day Thailand. This claim emphasizes their Mongoloid affinities even if historical evidence and the location of present-day enclaves of Mon speakers make a Mon association far more likely. Almost certainly, the people of Ban Kao and related sites spoke languages belonging to the Mon-Khmer family, even in the Malay Peninsula, where the distribution of the indigenous "Aslian" branch of Mon-Khmer coincides with sites linked to the Ban Kao tradition.

Sørenson's nomination of a Ban Kao culture was a pivotal step toward the current archaeological understanding of a widespread tradition in Thailand and Malaya that bridged the Neolithic phase with the protohistorical phase of early, Iron Age civilization in the region, as best represented by the Mons. The common practice of extended burials furnished with pots of frequently exceptional quality, ornaments of fine production, and implements such as adzes, bark-cloth beaters, and pottery anvils points to a period of cultural integration, which underpinned early historical developments in the region. The expansion of trade relations, the local establishment of bronze metallurgy and other aspects of craft specialization, and the spread of farming practices are all linked to the extensive distribution of this shared tradition. Complementary economic specialization by the communities linked within this network and the emergence of incipient social stratification are other critical features of the period. Continued debate among archaeologists on the details of Ban Kao and its counterparts can be expected in the process of furthering our understanding of the long-term historical implications of these sites.

DAVID BULBECK

See also Archaeological Sites of Southeast of Asia; Hoabinhian; Human Prehistory of Southeast Asia; "Java Man" and "Solo Man"; Neolithic Period of Southeast Asia; "Perak Man"

References:
Bayard, Donn. 1996–1997. "Bones of Contention: The Non Nok Tha Burials and the Chronology and Context of Early Southeast Asian Bronze." Pp. 889–940 in *Ancient Chinese and Southeast Asian Bronze Age Cultures,* vol. 2. Edited by F. David Bulbeck and Noel Barnard. Taipei: Southern Materials Center.

Bellwood, Peter. 1997. *Prehistory of the Indo-Malaysian Archipelago.* Rev. ed. Honolulu: University of Hawai'i Press.

Bulbeck, David. 1996. "Holocene Biological Evolution of the Malay Peninsula Aborigines (*Orang Asli*)." *Perspectives in Human Biology* 2: 37–61.

———. 2000. "Dental Morphology at Gua Cha, West Malaysia, and the Implications for 'Sundadonty.'" *Bulletin of the Indo-Pacific Prehistory Association* 19: 17–41.

Hassan Zolkurnian. 1998. "Urutan kebudayaan prasejarah Lembah Lenggong, Hulu Perak, Perak pada zaman Holosen" [Details of the Prehistoric Culture of the Lenggong Valley, Upper Perak, Perak during the Holocene Period]. Master's thesis, Universiti Sains Malaysia, Penang.

Higham, C. F. W. 1996–1997. "The Social and Chronological Context of Early Bronze Working in Southeast Asia." Pp. 821–888 in *Ancient Chinese and Southeast Asian Bronze Age Cultures,* vol. 2. Edited by F. David Bulbeck and Noel Barnard. Taipei: Southern Materials Center.

Higham, Charles. 1989. *The Archaeology of Mainland Southeast Asia.* Cambridge: Cambridge University Press.

Loofs-Wissowa, Helmut. 1997. "'Hills of Prosperity': State-of-the-Art and the Publication of Khok Charoen Site, Lopburi Province, Thailand." *Bulletin of the Indo-Pacific Prehistory Association* 16: 199–211.

Macdonald, William K. 1978. "The Bang Site, Thailand." *Asian Perspectives* 21, no. 1: 30–51.

Pietrusewsky, Michael. 1997. "The People of Ban Chiang: An Early Bronze Site in Northeast Thailand." *Bulletin of the Indo-Pacific Prehistory Association* 16: 119–147.

Sørenson, Per. 1973. "Prehistoric Iron Implements from Thailand." *Asian Perspectives* 16, no. 2: 134–173.

Sørenson, Per, and Tove Hatting. 1967. *Archaeological Excavations in Thailand.* Vol. 2, *Ban-Kao Neolithic Settlements with Cemeteries in the Kanchanaburi Province,* pt. 1: *The Archaeological Material from the Burials.* Copenhagen: Munksgaard.

Tayles, N. G. 1999. *The Excavation of Khok Phanom Di, a Prehistoric Site in Central Thailand.* Vol. 5, *The People.* London: Society of Antiquaries of London.

BANDJARMASIN (BANJERMASIN), SULTANATE OF

Bandjarmasin was one of the most important Muslim states in Dutch Borneo. Like the sultanates of Brunei and Kutai, it had Hindu-Buddhist roots, and the chronicles of the kingdom indicate connections with the Javanese state of Majapahit. Its origins are given in the "Story of Lambu Mangkurat and the Dynasty of the Kings of Ban(d)jar and Kota Waringin" (Ras 1968). The early court and capital were apparently modeled on the Javanese style of palace (*kraton*) and on Javanese origin myths (Ras 1968: 182–200). Apparently, an "Indianized" kingdom called Negaradipa had been established in the hinterland region of present-day Bandjarmasin sometime before the middle of the fourteenth century. It came under the influence of the northern Javanese Muslim state of Demak in the early sixteenth century; the ruler of Bandjarmasin, Pangeran Samudra, converted to Islam along with his followers and became Sultan Surian Allah or Suriansjah, possibly around 1530 (Hudson 1968: 60–61).

Bandjarmasin witnessed an increase in trade after the fall of Melaka to the Portuguese in 1511 when more Chinese visited the port to trade in camphor, diamonds, and bezoar stones in return for Chinese ceramics. The capital was transferred from the interior to its present location in the Barito Delta in the mid-sixteenth century to facilitate trade. The Dutch then established a factory at Bandjarmasin in 1603 to develop the trade in pepper (Irwin 1955: 4). Javanese traders also settled at the port from the 1620s, fleeing conflicts in Java, and this gave a boost to commercial pepper cultivation that expanded rapidly in the hinterland regions in the seventeenth and eighteenth centuries. The need for greater quantities of pepper resulted in the expansion of Banjar Malay cultivators throughout the southeastern Barito River basin at the expense of the interior Dayak populations (Hudson 1968: 65). In the seventeenth century, Bandjarmasin was one of the principal Bornean states and counted among its clients all the Muslim kingdoms of the east coast, along with Kota Waringin, Sukadana, Landak, and Sambas in the southwest and west.

Although the Dutch attempted to establish a firmer presence in Bandjarmasin and set up a monopoly over the pepper trade in the seventeenth century, the Banjarese were still sufficiently strong militarily to resist the Dutch until well into the eighteenth century, and they played the Dutch off against English traders. The Dutch also had to deal with commercial competition from the Buginese and the Chinese, and their interest in Bandjarmasin dwindled from the 1670s until they reasserted their presence in the later eighteenth century. It was not until 1786 that the Dutch, intervening in a succession dispute, supported the usurper Pangeran Nata, and in 1787, they negotiated a treaty with him by which the control of most of the sultanate's possessions and rights over several trade items were ceded to the Dutch (Hudson 1968: 69–74). Further treaties followed in 1817, when Bandjarmasin ceded its claims to various east coast states (including Kutai), and in 1826, when additional concessions by Sultan Adam (r. 1825–1857) were made to the Dutch. In 1849, two administrative divisions were created in Dutch-controlled Borneo: the Western Division, with the seat of the Dutch resident at Pontianak, and the Southern and Eastern Division, with its capital at Bandjarmasin (King 1993: 147).

Following the Dutch interference in another succession dispute in 1857 after Sultan Adam's death, a major anti-Dutch rebellion, the so-called Banjar War, broke out in 1859. The Dutch then abolished the sultanate in 1860 and placed Bandjarmasin and its territories under direct colonial rule. Intermittent Banjarese struggles continued against the Dutch until 1905 when the last pretender to the throne, Mohammed Seman, died in the Upper Barito region (Avé and King 1986: 24).

Bandjarmasin continued to enjoy commercial prosperity in the twentieth century. The export of rubber increased rapidly, supported by the ongoing production of pepper and copra (Lindblad 1988: 178–179). It also retained its important administrative role during the remainder of the Dutch colonial period and into the period of Indonesian independence. It became the capital of the Indonesian province of South Kalimantan and now has a population, primarily of Banjar Malays, approaching half a million (King 1993: 4–6). Nevertheless, its economic importance has been eclipsed by the oil, gas, and timber industries of the Balikpapan-Tarakan-Samarinda region on Kalimantan's east coast.

VICTOR T. KING

See also Borneo; Brunei (Sixteenth to Nineteenth Centuries); Dayaks; Demak; Dutch Borneo; Kraton Culture; Kutai (Koetei); Oil and Petroleum; Pepper; Sambas and Pontianak Sultanates

References:
Avé, Jan B., and Victor T. King. 1986. *The People of the Weeping Forest: Tradition and Change in Borneo*. Leiden, The Netherlands: Rijksmuseum voor Volkenkunde.
Hudson, A. B. 1968. *Padju Epat: The Ethnography and Social Structure of a Ma'anjan Dajak Group in Southeastern Borneo*. Ann Arbor, MI: University Microfilms.
Irwin, Graham. 1955. *Nineteenth-Century Borneo: A Study in Diplomatic Rivalry*. The Hague: Martinus Nijhoff. Reprinted in 1965 by Donald Moore, Singapore.
King, Victor T. 1993. *The Peoples of Borneo*. Oxford: Blackwell.
Lindblad, J. Thomas. 1988. *Between Dayak and Dutch: The Economic History of Southeast Kalimantan, 1880–1942*. Verhandelingen van het Koninklijk Instituut voor Taal-, Land- en Volkenkunde, vol. 134. Dordrecht, The Netherlands, and Providence, RI: Foris Publications.
Ras, J. J. 1968. *Hikajat Bandjar: A Study in Malay Historiography*. Bibliotheca Indonesica, Koninklijk Instituut vor Taal-, Land- en Volkenkunde. The Hague: Martinus Nijhoff.

BANGKA AND BELITUNG (BILITON)
See Tin

BANGKOK
"City of Angels"
Founded in 1782 by Phya Chakri, King Rama I (r. 1782–1809) of the reigning Chakri dynasty, Bangkok is the capital of Thailand, home to a population of around 15 million people. Bangkok, or Ban Kok as it appeared in the description of Engelbert Kaempfer (1727) in 1690, was a small village. During the turbulent times at the end of the reign of King Narai (r. 1656–1688) in 1688, the French temporarily had a garrison of soldiers there before being forced to withdraw from the country.

Under the first three kings of the Chakri dynasty, the village was transformed into a flourishing city that thrived on international trade, the profits from which were used to erect magnificent temples and palaces. Some 2,000 Buddha images were carried from the countryside to temples built to adorn the new city. There, in 1826, King Rama III (r. 1824–1851) signed the first commercial treaty with the British envoy, Henry Burney.

During the reign of King Rama IV (r. 1851–1868), known as King Mongkut, Bangkok's importance as a center for international trade increased following the signing of the commercial treaty with Sir John Bowring in 1855. The opening of the country to British and international trade in this reign was further enhanced during the succeeding reign of Mongkut's son, King Chulalongkorn (Rama V, r. 1868–1910), when Siam was able to benefit from much British investment. Furthermore, Siam's security was ensured because its old rival, Burma, had been incorporated in the growing British overseas empire following the Third Anglo-Burmese War (1885). King Chulalongkorn employed foreign advisers from Western nations—Belgium, France, Germany, Denmark, the United States, and Britain—to revamp the administration in a far-reaching reform program designed to modernize Siam and strengthen its capacity to withstand the encroachments of imperialistic colonialism. King Chulalongkorn's astute domestic and foreign policies enabled him to play Britain and France off against each other during the dangerous decade of the 1890s when Siam's independence was in jeopardy, caught between British Burma and French Indochina. In the 1893 Paknam Incident, a French naval contingent forced Siam to cede territory along the Mekong in eastern Siam to France and paid an indemnity to hold off further French demands. The rivalry between Britain and France at this time was part of the broader competition for the trade and markets of Siam and potential access to the southwest "back-door" route to China. Bangkok was the backdrop to the events of these critical years.

At the heart of the old city encircled by the Banglamphu canal, or *khlong,* is the magnificent Grand Palace, which was enlarged and enhanced during the reign of King Rama V. The Chakri Maha Prasad throne hall was but one of the many official buildings in Bangkok in the

Detail of the ornate Grand Palace in Bangkok, Thailand. Construction began on the royal palace, also known as Wat Po, in 1782, after the capital of Siam moved from Ayutthaya to Bangkok. The palace was initially built in the style of the original ancient capital, and each subsequent ruler added to the impressive complex of buildings. (Corel Corporation)

late nineteenth century that featured the Italianate architectural styles. The Ananta Samakhom throne hall is another fine example. Near the Grand Palace is the most revered Temple of the Emerald Buddha, housing the palladium of the Chakri dynasty, said to have been brought originally from Laos, and Wat Po, famous for its large Reclining Buddha. A short distance away is the Palace of the "King to the Front," or the "Second King," as he was known to foreigners; this building currently houses the National Museum. The Wang Lang, or Palace at the Back, is across the Chao Phraya on which Bangkok stands, in Thonburi, seat of King Rama I's predecessor, the ill-fated King Taksin (r. 1767–1782). The twin cities (Bangkok-Thonburi), as they were once called, have now blended into a huge metropolis.

In the mid-twentieth century, as William Klausner (1998) described it, Bangkok still had the canals for which it was known as the Venice of the East. With the exception of the Phetburi canal, these are now mostly filled in to make way for roads for Bangkok's ever growing traffic. A maze of overpasses and freeways and a sky train attempt to ease the traffic flow. In the 1960s, Bangkok still had many traditional wooden houses, but high-rises of cement and blue glass now dot the skyline. Yet Bangkokians still love their markets and flock to the Pramane ground near the Grand Palace or to Chatuchak, looking for the coveted bargains.

Bangkok is home to many universities, both state and private. The oldest two, Chulalongkorn University (founded in 1917) and Thammasat University (founded in 1933), take their place in modern Thai history in connection with the student activist movement of the 1973–1992 period that ushered in Thailand's strengthening democracy and displaced its former military dictatorships. The student uprisings of 1973 and 1976 were centered on Thammasat University, founded by former prime minister and regent Pridi Phanomyong (1900–1983). From the Grand Palace past Thammasat University, the royal avenue, Rajadamnoen, runs down to the present monarch's home at Chitralada Palace. Here, King Bhumibol Adulyadej, the much loved and revered King Rama IX (1946–), has an experimental farm and carries out agricultural research in support of his many projects for the advancement of rural peoples.

From a small village on the banks of the Chao Phraya, Bangkok has grown to be one of the great conurbations of the world, at the crossroads of international transport. The city with the longest name in the world—the "City of Angels," whose shortened name is Daravati-SriAyuthiaKrungthepPrahaMahaNakorn, known to Bangkokians as Krungthep—is a cosmopolitan center of international trade and commerce, with a population hailing from all quarters of the world.

HELEN JAMES

See also Chulalongkorn University; Narai (r. 1656–1688); Paknam Incident (1893); Phya Taksin (Pya Tak [Sin], King Taksin) (r. 1767–1782); Preservation of Siam's Political Independence; Rama I (Chakri) (r. 1782–1809); Reforms and Modernization in Siam; Student Revolt (October 1973) (Thailand); Thammasat University

References:
Hoskin, J., and T. Chuawiwat. 1987. *Thailand.* Bangkok: Asia Books.
Kaempfer, Engelbert. 1727. *A Description of the Kingdom of Siam, 1690.* Reprinted in 1987 by White Orchid Press, Bangkok.
Klausner, W. J. 1998. *Thai Culture in Transition.* 2nd ed. Bangkok: Siam Society.
Smith, M. 1957. *A Physician at the Court of Siam.* Reprinted in 1982 by Oxford University Press, Singapore.
Wyatt, David K. 1984. *Thailand: A Short History.* New Haven, CT, and London: Yale University Press.

BANKS AND BANKING

As economies develop, they rely increasingly on money as the medium of exchange. Banks perform several roles that facilitate the use of money. For instance, they create money through lending. The supply of currency in Southeast Asia long depended on the development of foreign trade. A few banks were active, but mainly in facilitating payments, not lending. A consequence of the "gold-exchange standard" was that national currency systems emerged during 1870–1910, and data on money in circulation became available. The table suggests that the monetization rate was low. Per capita money supply in Southeast Asia was about one-third of levels in developed countries, except in Malaysia, where it was about half.

Most pre–Pacific War (1941–1945) money supply consisted of currency (banknotes and coins). Demand deposits became significant only in the 1930s, when they were about 10 to 15 percent of M_1 (a measure of the volume of money) in Burma, Thailand, and Indochina, and 25 to 30 percent in Indonesia and the Philippines, compared with, for instance, 70 percent in Japan (Mitchell 1995: 832–835). After the war, the share of demand deposits increased, as banks attracted more deposits to enhance their lending. The low rate of monetization implies a low usage of banking services and a small size of capital markets.

The first banks were established with share capital raised overseas, or were branch offices of foreign banks. During the nineteenth century, the number of such banks and their activities remained limited. They were most significant in Indonesia and the Philippines and later Malaya, where they catered to the needs of foreign firms. They mainly arranged overseas payments by discounting bills of exchange drawn on trusted institutions, generally banks. They also discounted promissory notes. For most domes-

Supply of Money, 1890–1999 (U.S. dollars per capita, ten-year averages)

	Burma (*)	Thai-land	Malaya/ Malaysia	Singa-pore	Indo-nesia	Indochina Total	Vietnam (**)	Cam-bodia	Laos	Philip-pines
A: Currency only										
1890s	0.1		3.3		1.6					
1900s	0.5	4.3	4.6		1.5					2.4
1910s	1.9	5.2	7.3		2.4	1.2				3.9
1920s	8.1	6.0	9.2		3.5	2.8				5.1
1930s	13.1	3.9	6.4		2.6	2.2				4.5
B: Currency plus demand deposits (M_1)										
1950s	5.6	13.9	58.7		5.6	9.4	11.7	7.7		16.9
1960s	5.6	20.6	47.9	165.6	6.1		19.8	13.1		20.5
1970s	6.1	43.1	154.6	609.3	21.1		23.9	18.4		31.9
1980s	9.3	82.3	371.9	1,678.0	55.1		20.1	10.8	5.1	45.4
1990s	34.3	208.6	802.1	4,203.5	96.1		67.8	11.9	12.9	90.4

NOTE: Black market exchange rates have been used after World War II where necessary to approximate the actual purchasing power of currencies.
* Prewar Burma banknotes only. No data available on Indian rupee coins circulating in Burma.
** South Vietnam 1955–1974, Vietnam 1986–1999.
SOURCE: Calculated/compiled by the author from various sources.

tic payments, cash rather than banknotes and bank transfers remained the main means of exchange.

Western enterprises in the region were generally financed with private investment capital, often raised overseas. Their expansion was financed by incorporating ventures and selling their shares on foreign stock markets or by reinvesting profits. Banks had a limited role in lending for the establishment of firms. As far as they were lending, it was on the basis of share capital and their own reserves, not on the basis of deposits. The most important lenders were trading houses that extended short-term self-liquidating loans for current operations of plantation companies, against the expected revenue of next year's crop. They were prominent in colonial Indonesia, where they were known as *kultuurbanken,* such as the Nederlandsche Handel-Maatschappij and the Nederlandsch-Indische Escompto Mij. Gradually banks and trading houses also provided working capital to ventures in other economic sectors, such as manufacturing. For instance, the Banque Franco-

Chinoise financed trade and industry ventures in Indochina. Toward 1900 the trading houses also offered services previously provided only by the exchange banks.

As countries in the region stabilized their currencies relative to gold, the reduced exchange risk encouraged foreign banks to establish branch offices in the region. For instance, European banks such as Lloyds Bank; the Mercantile Bank; the Chartered Bank of India, Australia and China; and the Hong Kong and Shanghai Banking Corporation established branch offices throughout the region. Banks from other countries followed, such as the U.S. National City Bank of New York, the Bank of China, and the Japanese Yokohama Specie Bank.

Foreign banks generally started with exchange banking and gradually provided short-term credit to foreign-owned ventures. They also provided long-term credit to a new generation of foreign companies in the region: large capital-intensive rubber and oil palm plantations and mining and petroleum companies that required sums of investment capital not available in Southeast Asia. Foreign banks acted as managing agents or brokers between such companies and overseas banks in international financial centers such as London, Amsterdam, and New York.

As banks increased their extension of credit, they also started to take deposits. Deposit banking was long restricted to high-income earners. Banks had little interest in small deposits, because of the high overhead costs. That changed after 1900 when foreign-owned banks in the region—although not all—expanded their banking services and started to accept checking and demand deposits in an effort to emulate the success of small-scale savings banks in attracting deposits.

Until then, people with lower incomes could not use bank accounts to accumulate savings. Many commonly saved in the form of accumulating nonproductive assets, such as gold and jewelry. Such assets could be turned into cash at pawnshops, which were significant institutions that required a license to operate.

Small Chinese banks and some local indigenous banks were at the forefront of deposit banking. Chinese traders had long been involved in moneylending, and in the organization of remittances of migrant workers to China, generally in an informal way based on trust. Those activities expanded, leading to the incorporation of such Chinese ventures as small banks. The first was the Kwong Yik Bank, established in 1903 in Singapore. Others soon followed in other urban centers. Chinese banks successfully tapped small savers. They used cost-effective ways of monitoring deposits and lending. The success of Chinese banks often depended on the support of wealthy Chinese businesspeople (*towkay*), which inspired confidence among small would-be depositors.

Until then, Western banks financed large Chinese commercial ventures through a Chinese *comprador* (agent on commission). In some cases *compradors* established banks themselves with the support of wealthy Chinese, attracting deposits and starting deposit-based lending. Deposit banking was initially an urban phenomenon of local importance, but gradually ethnic Chinese financial networks developed that spread from the cities into rural areas where Chinese traders had long been a source of credit.

This development enhanced concerns about the high interest rates that informal moneylenders generally charged and about the problems that indebtedness created in rural societies. Around 1900, colonial governments in the region considered steps to break the supposed grip of usurers on the rural economy. In Indonesia the government encouraged the establishment of small local credit institutions after 1900. Such local institutions were merged into a national organization, the Algemeene Volkscredietbank (AVB), with up to 5,000 village banks. Its impact was significant. In the 1920s and 1930s, AVB-provided credit was about half the total value of credit extended by the big four banks in Indonesia. The French colonial government emulated the system in Indochina as the *Crédit Agricole Mutuel*. Other government-sponsored facilities were post office savings banks and a government savings bank (1913) in Thailand. They took deposits but did not lend to private borrowers. A range of small, local, semi-incorporated cooperative banks or loan associations such as credit unions emerged. Although of regional significance, their overall impact was marginal.

A growing number of financial institutions started to accept demand deposits and to lend to the public. As their loan portfolios increased, banks added to the amount of money in circulation, because banks extend more credit than they have deposits. Gradually the volume of currency in circulation started to depend primarily on the money-creating role of banks, rather than the currency issued by central banks on the basis of export earnings. Still, the increase depended on whether people trusted the banks with their savings, and whether the banks offered high enough interest rates that made savings deposits worthwhile.

With the development of banking, the need for supervision increased. Supervision was left to central banks. In Southeast Asia, selected private banks acted to different degrees as central banks. For instance, they had a monopoly on the issuance of banknotes and acted as government banks in the region in brokering loans and setting discount rates, but they did not lend to other banks. The oldest of such banks was the Javasche Bank (1827) in colonial Indonesia, followed by the Banco Español Filipino (later the Bank of the Philippine Islands, 1851), and the Banque de l'Indochine (1875). These banks were different. For instance, the Banque de l'Indochine was also an investment bank, providing investment and operating credit to most foreign enterprises in Indochina.

The Japanese occupation of Southeast Asia (1941–1945) threw monetary and financial systems into disarray. Rampant inflation eroded the reserves of financial institutions. After the occupation, and after gaining independence, indigenous governments in the region set out to make the financial systems of their countries subordinate to the tenet of their economic policies. They established government-owned central banks and regulated financial sectors, in part to orchestrate lending toward favored sectors and enterprises.

Central banks were nationalized or newly established as government-owned banks. The Bank of Thailand was established in 1942, and the Central Bank of The Philippines in 1948. The Javasche Bank was nationalized in 1952 and became Bank Indonesia. The Union Bank of Burma was established as a private bank in 1948 and was nationalized in 1960 and renamed Central Bank of Myanmar in 1990. The Banque de l'Indochine lost its monopoly on the issuance of banknotes in 1947, after which government-owned central banks were established in North Vietnam in 1951 and in Cambodia, Laos, and South Vietnam in 1955. The government-owned Bank Negara Malaya (1959, Bank Negara Malaysia after 1963) and the Central Bank of Singapore (1970) were established as central banks and took over the issuance of currency notes from the Board of Commissioners of Currency. The new institutions took on tasks commonly associated with central banks: issuance of currency, supervision of the financial sector, acting as lenders of last resort, arranging the government's transactions, and discounting government bonds.

Postwar governments had a new array of monetary policy tools. Before the war, the main tool was keeping the exchange rate stable. But the 1930s had shown that exchange rates could be manipulated to discourage imports and encourage exports. The late 1940s had shown that foreign exchange and credit could be rationed to particular sectors or industries, at below-market interest rates. Throughout the region governments actively used such instruments.

Limitations were placed on the operations of foreign banks, and domestic banks were favored in all countries except Malaysia and Singapore. During the 1950s the number of domestic commercial banks increased quickly. In Indonesia and Burma hostility toward foreign banks was so strong that the largest commercial banks were nationalized in 1958 and 1963, respectively. Increasingly tight regulation of financial markets was used to channel credit to the industries or the special interest groups that governments supported. Interest rates were capped in order to stimulate borrowing. In the case of Indonesia in the 1960s, inflation was so high that real interest rates were negative, and credit rationing took place on the basis of political favors.

Banks increasingly became machines to lend to favored companies—be it state-owned companies in the case of state-owned banks (such as Bank Negara Indonesia), military-commercial ventures in the case of military-owned banks (such as the Thai Military Bank), or private firms. A growing number of private business groups were associated with banks (such as the Bank of the Philippine Islands and the Ayala Group).

Such policies did not always yield the most efficient allocation of finance or a guarantee that loans would be repaid. Except for Malaysia and Singapore, the supervisory role of central banks was lax. For instance, the rules that required banks to maintain minimum reserves against outstanding liabilities were not always strictly enforced, and supervision of the credit policies of commercial banks was poor, leading to increased exposure to bad debts. Poor supervision became a problem in the 1980s, when economic development in the Association of Southeast Asian Nations (ASEAN-4) countries increased the demand for finance and banking services that the tightly regulated government-dominated financial sectors could not provide. Governments acknowledged that financial services to customers had to improve in order to attract more deposits and allow services to diversify. In the late 1980s, financial systems were liberalized. Foreign banks were allowed back into the financial sector, new bank licenses were issued, and rules regarding the direction of lending were loosened. The financial sectors diversified significantly to encompass a greater range of nonbank institutions, such as finance and insurance companies. Only the financial sectors of Vietnam, Cambodia, Laos, and Burma remained restricted.

Liberalization and the increase in lending occurred faster than effective monitoring evolved. Owners of new banking licenses established banks whose main purpose was to lend to companies in their business groups. In the early 1990s, several private and state-owned banks experienced bad debt problems that were not acted upon. Countries opened their capital accounts, which allowed banks to take advantage of low international interest rates through international short-term borrowing. This development climaxed in mid-1997, when the poor state of the financial sectors in the ASEAN-4 countries was exposed, and each country was forced to address its bad debt problems by nationalizing some banks, pumping public funds into the financial system, and tightening supervision of the financial sector.

Throughout the development of the formal banking system, informal small-scale lending remained an important source of finance. Before the Pacific War, informal moneylending was dominated by ethnic Chinese and rich indigenous traders, and by Chettyars (Chettiars) who were mainly active in Burma, Malaya, and South Vietnam. Although governments sponsored various initiatives to provide small-scale formalized credit, informal small-scale lending continued to be very important, especially in rural areas. Lenders were often regarded as usurers, but recent research has indicated that high rates of interest were caused by the fact that credit was supplied on highly personalized terms, generally without collateral or means of foreclosing on collateral. The small amounts involved and the short duration of the loans also explain why interest rates tended to be high.

PIERRE VAN DER ENG

See also Agency Houses, European; Chettiars (Chettyars); *Towkay;* Trade and Commerce of Southeast Asia (ca. Nineteenth Century to the 1990s)

References:

Brown, R. 1990. "Chinese Business and Banking in South-East Asia since 1870." Pp. 173–190 in *Banks as Multinationals.* Edited by G. Jones. London: Routledge.

———. 1993. "Chettiar Capital and Southeast Asian Credit Networks in the Inter-war Period." Pp. 254–287 in *Local Suppliers of Credit in the Third World 1750–1960.* Edited

by A. Austin and K. Sugihara. London: Macmillan.

Choon Beng Liau, D. 1993. "Financial Development in Thailand." *Journal of Asian Business* 9, no. 4: 110–137.

Cole, D. C., and B. F. Slade. 1996. *Building a Modern Financial System: The Indonesian Experience.* Cambridge: Cambridge University Press.

Gonjo, Y. 1993. *Banque Coloniale ou Banque d'Affairs: La Banque de l'Indochine sous la IIIe République.* Paris: Ministères de l'Économie et du Budget.

Lee Sheng-yi. 1986. *The Monetary and Banking Development of Singapore and Malaysia.* Singapore: Singapore University Press.

Mitchell, B. R. 1995. *International Historical Statistics: Africa, Asia & Oceania.* London: Macmillan.

Skully, M. T., ed. 1984. *Financial Institutions and Markets in Southeast Asia.* London: Macmillan.

Van Laanen, J. T. M. 1990. "Between the Java Bank and the Chinese Moneylender: Banking and Credit in Colonial Indonesia." Pp. 244–266 in *Indonesian Economic History in the Dutch Colonial Era.* Edited by Anne Booth et al. New Haven: Yale University Southeast Asia Studies.

BANTEN (BANTAM) (1526–1813)

Banten most likely emerged out of the Hindu kingdom of Pajajaran in the twelfth century; the kingdom had two main ports: Kelapa (Jakatra/Jacatra; present-day Jakarta/Djakarta) and Banten. Even before the arrival of the Europeans, Banten was one of the busiest ports in the Malay Archipelago. After the Portuguese captured Melaka in 1511, Chinese, Arab, and Indian traders poured into Banten, turning it into the most important trading center in the Sunda Straits, an important entrepôt for pepper produced in South Sumatra and West Java.

In 1522, the Portuguese formalized trade relations with Banten. The ruler of Banten accepted Portuguese advances, which he took as support against the sultan of Demak, who intended to convert Banten to Islam. The Portuguese received unlimited access to the pepper supplies and were allowed to build a fort near Tangerang. The Portuguese returned in 1527, just after the sultan of Demak had seized most of Banten. They left without building their fort.

Under its first Muslim ruler, Mulana Hasanudin (r. ca. 1550–1570), Banten converted to Islam. Hasanudin conquered pepper-producing Lampung in South Sumatra and turned neighboring Jakatra into a vassal. Trade increased with the Chinese and Portuguese, who established a trading post in Banten. Trade strengthened Banten's economy and the growth of its port. Hasanudin's son, Pangeran Yusuf (r. 1570–1580), conquered Pajajaran in 1579. He also introduced irrigated rice agriculture in Banten to improve food production.

The first Muslim rulers of Banten remained subordinate to the sultan of Demak. When his sultanate weakened and ceded parts of its territory to the most powerful state in Java, Mataram, Banten broke away from Demak. Its ruler adopted the title of sultan. The rule of Hasanudin's grandson, Pangeran Mohamed (r. 1580–1596), marked a turning point in Banten's fortunes. Mohamed waged war against neighboring Palembang in 1596, but he died during the siege of the city. A political vacuum emerged when the Dutch arrived in the Indonesian archipelago.

The rulers of Banten were unsuccessful in withstanding the advance of the Dutch, who defeated the Portuguese fleet in a battle in 1601 in Banten harbor and dominated the pepper trade. The Dutch East India Company (VOC) established a trading post in Banten in 1610. When the sultan of Banten resisted the attempts of Governor-General Jan Pieterszoon Coen (t. 1618–1623, 1623–1629) to entirely control the pepper trade, Coen transferred the VOC's headquarters to neighboring Jakatra, where he established a fort in 1618.

When Coen left for the Maluku islands in 1619, the sultan of Banten seized Jakatra and besieged the VOC fort. Upon his return, Coen ended the siege and founded the city of Batavia on the ruins of Jakatra. He forced the sultan of Banten to surrender the city and its surroundings to the VOC. Coen moved all VOC trade from Banten to Batavia and demanded pepper deliveries. Although the English maintained a trading post in Banten, the sultanate lost its economic significance.

Subsequent rulers of Banten sought to extend their territory southward into the Priang-gan area, provoking unceasing conflicts with Mataram. In addition, Banten had to contend with the Dutch. The border between Banten and Batavia and its surroundings was established in a treaty in 1659. However, conflicts persisted because the VOC aimed to reduce the significance of Banten by redirecting all trade to Batavia.

Sultan Ageng tried to turn the tide, but he had to acknowledge the power of the VOC in a disadvantageous treaty in 1684. Thereafter, Banten's history was marked by futile attempts to withstand the mounting demands of the VOC in terms of claims to territory and deliveries of pepper. For instance, Banten gave up Pulau Panjang in 1731, and it gave Pulau Seribu to the VOC in 1776. In 1752, after the VOC's suppression of a general uprising in West Java, the sultan of Banten acknowledged subservience to the VOC.

In 1808, after the Dutch government had taken over the possessions of the VOC, Governor-General Herman W. Daendels (t. 1808–1811) led a military expedition to Banten and put its coastal areas under direct Dutch colonial rule, leaving only the interior to the sultan. The British lieutenant governor, Thomas Stamford Raffles (t. 1811–1816), ended the existence of the sultanate of Banten in March 1813 because he wanted to introduce the land tax in as large an area of Java as possible. Banten became a residency under direct colonial rule, and the sultan was banned from the area in 1832. However, effective colonial rule was introduced after 1846. By then, local colonial officials had ended the extortionist demands made by the nobility and the religious elite on the local population.

Banten experienced uprisings against Dutch colonial authority in 1849, 1888, and 1926. The first two incidents took place in Cilegon and were provoked in part by the high land tax, in part by religious chicanery and fanaticism, and in part by intrigue among the local nobility. The Partai Komunis Indonesia (PKI) instigated the 1926 uprising.

PIERRE VAN DER ENG

See also Batavia (Sunda Kalapa, Jacatra, Djakarta/Jakarta); Coen, Jan Pieterzoon (1618–1623, 1623–1629); Demak; East India Company (EIC) (1600), English; Economic Transformation of Southeast Asia (ca. 1400–ca. 1800); Islam in Southeast Asia; Java; Mataram; Palembang; Partai Komunis

Indonesia (PKI) (1920); Pepper; Raffles, (Thomas) Stamford Bingley, Sir (1781–1826);Vereenigde Oost-Indische Compagnie (VOC) ([Dutch] United East Indies Company) (1600)

References:

Guillot, C. 1990. *The Sultanate of Banten.* Jakarta: Gramedia.

Kathirithamby-Wells, J. 1990. "Banten: A West Indonesian Port and Polity during the 16th and 17th Centuries." Pp. 107–125 in *The Southeast Asian Port and Polity: Rise and Demise.* Edited by J. Kathirithamby-Wells and J.Villiers. Singapore: Singapore University Press.

BẢO ĐẠI (VĨNH THỤY) (1913–1997)
The Last Emperor of Vietnam

Born Prince Vĩnh Thụy on 21 October 1913, the last emperor of the Nguyễn dynastic line that had ruled Vietnam since 1802 was enthroned on 8 January 1926 under the imperial name Bảo Đại (meaning "Preservation of Grandeur"); he succeeded his father, Khải Định, who had died on 6 November 1925. While Bảo Đại continued his studies in France, a regency council back in Huế managed imperial duties. Those duties, however, had been reduced to purely ritual matters, for the convention imposed by the French colonial administration after Khai Đinh's death had taken away whatever political prerogatives were still left to the Vietnamese monarch.

In 1932, Bảo Đại returned to Huế and, despite the limitations of his authority, showed his determination to modernize the Vietnamese administration. He championed judicial, financial, and educational reforms and endeavored to do away with some of the more archaic practices of the court. He soon realized, however, that he had no real power, as the officials of the French protectorate were never eager to emancipate the functions of the imperial government. Consequently, Bảo Đại abandoned whatever desire he might have had for personal government and confined himself to being a figurehead.

After the Japanese unseated the French colonial regime on 9 March 1945, Bảo Đại declared the abolition of the 1884 protectorate treaty and Vietnam's independence under Japan's aegis. But because he was considered to be a king who reigned but did not govern, he could not possibly attract mass support. Following Japan's capitulation on 15 August 1945, the communist movement led by Hồ Chí Minh (1890–1969) proceeded to take control of the whole country. Bảo Đại readily agreed to step aside on behalf of the superior interest of the nation, and he affirmed through his edict of abdication, dated 25 August 1945, that he was voluntarily transmitting his mandate, thereby lending legitimacy to the regime that was to succeed him. He briefly accepted the position of supreme adviser to the new Democratic Republic of Vietnam (DRV), before going abroad to live in exile.

The outbreak of war between France and the DRV in December 1946 highlighted Bảo Đại's role as an alternative to Hồ Chí Minh. Once France had given way on the two issues of unification for the three regions of Viêt-Nam and complete self-determination, it proved possible to persuade Bảo Đại to return from his voluntary exile and preside over a *Quốc Gia Việt Nam* (State of Vietnam). Though retaining the appellation "His Majesty," he was no longer emperor but simply head of state (*Quốc Trưởng*). The autonomous Associated State of Vietnam within the framework of the French Union came into existence on 1 January 1950, but during its short life span, it won only limited recognition at home and abroad as the legitimate representative of the national aspirations of the Vietnamese people.

The Geneva Agreements in 1954 having resulted in the division of Vietnam into the North and the South, Bảo Đại and his advisers tried to assume true power in Saigon. But in 1955, his prime minister, Ngô Đình Diệm (t. 1955–1963), organized a referendum that deposed him and ended his long involvement with the history of the Vietnamese people. Bảo Đại chose not to contest the referendum and spent the rest of his life in France.

Having squandered most of his royal fortune, he lived out his final years in a modest Paris apartment. He passed away on 31 July 1997 at the age of eighty-three, leaving an ambiguous legacy. Reputedly a bon vivant, he was a reformer with enough intelligence to have foreseen the limits of the causes he could represent. He adapted to changes but without great conviction, and he apparently lacked the necessary motivation to abide by a long-lasting choice. He sincerely cared about the plight and future of his people—in 1972, in a rare public statement, he appealed to the Vietnamese for national reconciliation—but he did not seem to possess the necessary political skills to adequately fulfill the functions of a chief of state.

NGUYỄN THẾ ANH

See also French Indochinese Union *(Union Indochinoise Française)* (1887); Geneva Conference (1954); Hồ Chí Minh (1890–1969); Indochina during World War II (1939–1945); Indochina War (1946–1954), First; Ngô Đình Diệm (1901–1963); Nguyễn Dynasty (1802–1945);Vietnam under French Colonial Rule;Vietnam, North (post-1945); Vietnam, South (post-1945)

References:
Bảo Đại, S. M. 1980. *Le Dragon d'Annam* [*The Dragon of Annam*]. Paris: Plon.
Chapuis, Oscar. 2000. *The Last Emperors of Vietnam: From Tu Duc to Bao Dai.* Westport, CT: Greenwood Press.
Lockhart, Bruce M. 1993. *The End of the Vietnamese Monarchy.* New Haven, CT: Yale Southeast Asia Studies.
Nguyễn Thế Anh. 1985. "The Vietnamese Monarchy under French Colonial Rule, 1884–1945." *Modern Asian Studies* 19, no. 1: 147–162.

BARANGAY

Barangay (balangay, balangai, balanghai) is a native word in the Philippines with two meanings: first, a type of boat, and second, the basic sociopolitical unit of the pre-Spanish Tagalog society as well as the smallest unit of local government in the Philippines today. In the first context, the barangay was a rowed boat used widely in the Philippines prior to the arrival of the Spaniards; reputedly, it was also used by some settlers to reach the Philippines. In the second context, the barangay was an independent political, social, and economic unit in the Tagalog regions of the Philippines. Consisting of around 30 to 100 households, the barangay was under the leadership of a *datu* (chief), to whom all members owed allegiance. The residents of the barangay were generally related by blood, having originated from one family, and they lived together with their slaves and relatives. The various barangays traded and had

friendly relations with each other and were known to make alliances. On occasion, however, they went to war or raided other barangays.

The Spaniards retained the word *barangay* during the Spanish colonial period and incorporated the institution into their colonial government. The Spaniards used the barangay heads to collect taxes and tributes and maintain order. During the 1970s, the term was revived and used in reference to the basic unit of local government in the Philippines, replacing the word *barrio*.

RICARDO TROTA JOSE

See also Philippines under Spanish Colonial Rule (ca. 1560s–1898)

References:
Jocano, F. Landa, ed. 1975. *The Philippines at the Spanish Contact.* Manila: MCS Enterprises.
Scott, William Henry. 1994. *Barangay: Sixteenth Century Philippine Culture and Society.* Quezon City, the Philippines: Ateneo de Manila University Press.

BARISAN NASIONAL (NATIONAL FRONT) (1974)

Officially registered on 1 June 1974, Barisan Nasional (BN, National Front) was a confederation of political parties formed in Malaysia following the May 13, 1969 incident. The political parties that initially comprised BN were: United Malays National Organization (UMNO), Malaysian Chinese Association (MCA), Malaysian Indian Congress (MIC), Partai Islam Se Malaysia (PAS), People's Progressive Party (PPP), Gerakan Rakyat Malaysia (Gerakan), Sarawak United People's Party (SUPP), Partai Pesaka Bumiputera Bersatu (PBB), and Sabah Alliance. The overall aims of the coalition were to minimize politicking, to foster national unity, and to coordinate efforts toward national development and progress.

Started loosely in 1970 in the two Borneo states of Sabah and Sarawak, the idea for an organization of this type spread to the peninsula, leading to the Gerakan-Alliance coalition in Penang (February 1972), the Alliance-PPP coalition in Perak (1 May 1972), and the PAS-Alliance coalition agreement of 28 December 1972. Chaired by Tun Abdul Razak (1922–1976), then UMNO president and prime minister of Malaysia, BN was administered by a supreme committee composed of members from the component parties. Differences of opinion were to be settled through negotiations within BN, and decisions were to be arrived at by consensus.

The new political formula contributed significantly toward interparty political calm, lasting at least until 1978. The popular votes for the ruling coalition in Peninsular/West Malaysia immediately swelled from 48.4 percent to 84.6 percent, a figure never to be attained thereafter. Although UMNO had to accommodate PAS in its effort to remain influential among the Malays, MCA and MIC leaders had to share their role as spokespeople for the Chinese and Indians in the government with representatives from other non-Malay parties.

BN won 135 (87.7 percent) of the 154 parliamentary seats in the 1974 general election and formed governments in all thirteen states. Intraparty disputes within PAS and its continued challenge to UMNO resulted in PAS being expelled from BN. Consequently, BN lost Kelantan in 1978. With UMNO as its backbone, BN membership grew to fourteen in 2002, and it continues to enjoy a two-thirds majority in the Malaysian Parliament.

ABDUL RAHMAN HAJI ISMAIL

See also Abdul Razak, Tun (1922–1976); Alliance Party (Malaya/Malaysia); Mahathir bin Mohamed, Dr. (1925–); Malayan/ Malaysian Chinese Association (MCA) (1949); Malayan/Malaysian Indian Congress (MIC); "May 13th 1969" (Malaysia); Partai Islam Se Malaysia (PAS); United Malays National Organization (UMNO) (1946)

References:

Case, William. 1996. *Elites and Regimes in Malaysia: Revisiting a Consociational Democracy.* Clayton, Australia: Monash Asia Institute.

Crouch, Harold, Lee Kam Heng, and Michael Ong. 1980. *Malaysian Politics and the 1978 Election.* Kuala Lumpur: Oxford University Press.

Mauzy, Diane K. 1983. *Barisan National: Coalition Government in Malaysia.* Kuala Lumpur and Singapore: Marican & Sons.

Means, Gordon P. 1991. *Malaysian Politics: The Second Generation.* Singapore: Oxford University Press.

Milne, R. S., and Diane K. Mauzy. 1978. *Politics and Government in Malaysia.* Singapore: Times Books International.

BARISAN SOSIALIS (SOCIALIST FRONT)

Barisan Sosialis, formed in July 1961, was the foremost opposition party in Singapore in the early 1960s, but it faded into political obscurity by the latter half of the decade. It had come into being as a result of a split within the ruling People's Action Party (PAP), precipitated by the prospect of Singapore gaining independence through merger with a wider Malaysian federation that would include Malaya and the British Borneo territories. Though the PAP government welcomed the scheme, the procommunist faction within the party opposed it, and thirteen of its parliamentarians crossed the floor and went on to form the Barisan Sosialis, with Lee Siew Choh (1917–2002) as chairman and Lim Chin Siong (1933–) as secretary-general. The split had seriously hurt the PAP, leaving it with only a fragile parliamentary majority of one and with the Barisan firmly in control of a far superior grassroots and party network.

In February 1963, however, Barisan suffered a major setback after the Internal Security Council launched a preemptive security operation, code-named Operation Cold Store, and made 113 arrests, including 24 of the Barisan's ablest nonparliamentary leaders. Two months later, a belated protest march over the detention turned into a riot and led to further arrests of Barisan leaders, including 10 assemblymen. Though the Barisan retained its 13 seats in the September 1963 elections, it was now bereft of its top leadership and was a party on the wane. After Singapore gained its independence in August 1965, upon its separation from Malaysia, Lee Siew Choh announced in December the party's decision to boycott Parliament. With the resignation and walkout of its remaining parliamentarians ten months later, the Barisan ended its days at the front line of Singapore politics. It failed to contest the 1968 elections and failed to win any seats in the elections in which it subsequently participated. Though it still exists as a registered political party, it has long ceased to have any political significance.

ALBERT LAU

See also British Borneo; British Malaya;
Communism; Labor and Labor Unions in
Southeast Asia; Lee Kuan Yew (1923–);
Malaysia (1963); People's Action Party (PAP);
Singapore-Malaya/Malaysia Relations (ca.
1950s–1990s)
References:
Lee Ting Hui. 1996. *The Open United Front: The
Communist Struggle in Singapore, 1954–1966.*
Singapore: South Seas Society.

BATAAN DEATH MARCH

The Bataan Death March was a forced march
of some 80,000 Filipino and American prisoners of war who surrendered in the Bataan
Peninsula on 9 April 1942. The march covered
some 120 kilometers and was characterized by
extremely brutal and barbaric treatment meted
out by the Japanese guards. Around 10,000 Filipinos and at least 650 Americans are confirmed to have died during the nine-day
march, due to malnutrition, disease, torture, or
murder.

The march was initially disorganized, with
the Filipinos and Americans being made to
travel to collection points on their own and
without guards; the Filipinos were even told
that they could go home. Many soldiers became victims of Japanese lootings, but otherwise, the Filipinos and Americans were left
alone. However, as the prisoners approached
the town of Balanga, the Japanese soldiers became increasingly cruel toward them. Men
were deprived of food and water, were beaten
by rifle butts or poles, or were run down by
tanks or trucks. From Balanga, they were made
to march in the hot sun in groups of 100; the
prisoners had been on short rations and with
little medicine for over three months, and those
who were so weakened by hunger or disease
that they could not keep up were beaten or
killed outright. Conditions worsened as the
march moved northward. They were jammed
into enclosures during rest stops and were
given scarcely any food or water. The prisoners
of war were forced to board boxcars in San
Fernando, Pampanga, and were taken to the
town of Capas, Tarlac, in the hottest part of the
day; many suffocated in the airless cars. From
Capas, the prisoners were made to march a final stretch to the concentration camp, where
thousands more died.

*U.S. prisoners of war in the Philippines use
improvised litters to carry their comrades who,
from the lack of food or water on the march from
Bataan, fell along the road. (U.S. National
Archives)*

The Bataan Death March was one of the
worst atrocities in the Philippines during the
Pacific War (1941–1945), and Lieutenant General Homma Masaharu, commander-in-chief of
the invading Japanese forces, was subsequently
tried and executed for his role in this atrocity in
April 1946.

RICARDO TROTA JOSE

See also "Death Railway" (Burma–Siam
Railway); Japanese Occupation of Southeast
Asia (1941–1945); Sandakan Death March
References:
Falk, Stanley L. 1962. *Bataan: The March of
Death.* New York: Norton.
Knox, Donald. 1981. *Death March: The Survivors
of Bataan.* New York: Harcourt Brace
Jovanovich.

BATAKS

The cosmopolitan history of North Sumatra's
Batak peoples belies any attempt to classify
them in superficial ways as remote, isolated,
highland tribal societies. Indeed, the Bataks are
among the most literate and school-focused of
Indonesia's Outer Islands peoples beyond Java
and Bali. Throughout the 1920s and 1930s,
they were particularly active shapers of early
Indonesian nationalist debates, in Tapanuli's
then-thriving vernacular newspaper trade (Ahmat 1995).

After the 1945–1949 national revolution against the Dutch, Bataks again spoke loudly on the national political stage. They featured in the military contest on both sides of the failed Pemerintah Revolusioner Republik Indonesia (PRRI) separatist rebellion from 1957 to 1959. Bataks were also prominent in the politics of culture debates about the permissible limits of ethnic society autonomy and pride under former president Suharto's authoritarian, Java-centered New Order regime (1965–1998). And most recently, they were active in public discussions in highland rural areas and in diaspora, émigré Batak communities about local control of natural resource development during the nation's fitful transition to democracy. This degree of engagement with larger-scale political discourses between colony and metropole and between ethnic society and the Indonesian nation continues a much longer historical trend: for centuries, the Bataks were deeply enmeshed in Southeast Asian dynamics between the court center and the highland society, just as they were in regional and international trade and in world religious exchanges.

Sumatra's long string of upland volcanic lakes, including Lake Toba, anchor productive, terraced, rice-farming societies with settlement patterns dating to at least 2,000 years ago. Forest clearings for swidden agriculture near Mount Kerinci and also Lake Toba may date to 4,000 to 7,000 years before the present (Bellwood 1997, 1995). Austronesian speakers reached Sumatra from Taiwan about 2500 B.C.E. (Bellwood 1997). The Batak dialects, generally called Karo, Toba, Simelungun, Dairi-Pakpak, and Angkola-Mandailing, apparently can be traced to this southward Austronesian migration era. By contrast, Sumatra's Malayic languages (Malay itself, Minangkabau, and some South Sumatran tongues) seem to be more closely tied to court state development in South Sumatra; this Malayic language expansion may well have ties to the rise of the kingdom of Śrivijaya in the seventh century C.E. (Bellwood 1997). Interaction between Batak hill settlements and Sumatra's impressive Indic court states such as Srivijaya (influential until the eleventh century) and Minangkabau's Adityavarman kingdom (about 1340 to 1400 C.E.) may have been extensive, if indirect and mediated through long-distance trade networks. The Batak syllabic scripts (the *aksara*) are clearly cultural imports to highland villages from such states (Kozok 1996). Sanskrit-derived words for some religious ideas (for instance, *Debata,* meaning "high god") are found in many Batak areas and may betoken long-term exchange with Sumatra's Indianized kingdoms. The ruins of a Tantric temple from around the twelfth or thirteenth century in Padang Lawas apparently can be traced to the Panai kingdom, mentioned as early as the sixth century in Chinese annals (Schnitger 1989). Panai was strategically located astride trade routes leading to the Straits of Melaka—the gold trade from Mandailing and Minangkabau and the trade in aromatic forest resins (camphor, benzoin) upland from Barus in Dairi. Starting by at least the seventh century, kingdoms of this sort not only had religious ties to India but also regularized economic connections to China. Were these hill peoples self-consciously calling themselves "Batak" at this period? That is unlikely, at the level of overt folk views.

Islam also strongly shaped Batak societies, particularly in the south in Angkola and Mandailing. Trade links to states were again pivotal. By the early 1300s, river ports in northern Sumatra along the Straits of Melaka served as stopovers for ships from India and the Middle East (West Asia). These sites became the archipelago's pioneer Muslim footholds. Spending five months in 1292 in Sumatra, Marco Polo reported considerable conversion to Islam in the Peurlak (Perlak) kingdom. Yet the early coastal Muslim presence apparently had little direct impact on most Batak peoples: their introduction to the faith came in the 1820s and 1830s, when the reformist, Wahabhist Padri forces marched northward from West Sumatra into the southern Batak areas, making large-scale conversions. Mandailing today is entirely Muslim, and Angkola is approximately 90 percent Muslim. Southern Toba and Silindung near Tarutung are largely Protestant Christian, with a small admixture of Islam along Angkola's vague border (all geographic demarcations here are labile, given the instability of Batak identities [Kipp and Kipp 1983]).

The Protestant presence in the south and Toba is largely the result of the vigorous proselytizing of the Rhenish Mission of Barmen, Germany (the RGM), starting in the 1850s. The colonial state warily allowed Christian missionary work in the Batak regions at this time, with the veiled aim of fostering a Christian buffer zone between Muslim Aceh and Muslim Minangkabau, both fervently anti-Dutch. Sipirok, which was largely Muslim by the 1850s, was the RGM's first base of operations, resulting in early school construction there. The state was developing Sipirok for coffee production at the time, as an offshoot of the forced cultivation schemes of the West Coast Residency, where Dutch officials oversaw the colonial administration of Sumatra. The mission made some conversions in Sipirok, but since the southern highlands were distinctly Muslim by this period, the astute Rev. Ingewar Ludwig Nommensen (1834–1918) soon took leave of his mission colleagues to push northward into pagan territory in Silindung. From there, he was soon to become the "Evangelist to the Toba." By the 1890s, Christianity had made major inroads and was central to Toba identity. To Muslim Malay observers along Sumatra's eastern coast, in fact, to be Batak meant to be Christian. Protestantism spread in the early twentieth century to Dairi, Pakpak, and sections of Simelungun (which had extensive Muslim influence from eastern coast sultanates). Under the auspices of the Dutch Reformed mission, Karo conversions increased in the 1920s and 1930s, although that area remained in part unconverted to the world religions until the political cataclysm of 1965 (Kipp 1990, 1996). Then, it became distinctly dangerous to not "have a religion," an official *agama* (otherwise, one could easily be branded a communist and thus an enemy of the emerging New Order [Kipp and Rodgers 1987]).

"Batakness" began to consolidate in the indigenous public imagination, to a degree, during the harsh Dutch colonial period (Niessen 1993). This was a conflicted identity: indeed, some Mandailing migrants to east coast tobacco, tea, and rubber plantations denied Batak heritage, as it was connected to imageries of tribalism, pig eating, and Christianity. Mandailing and Angkola migration for salaried work in Deli on the eastern coast was notable by the 1910s. Formal education in these southern regions had arrived by the 1870s, producing school graduates who could compete for Deli clerical jobs. The schools offered instruction in both Malay and Mandailing Batak; Sumatra's second teacher-training institute was opened in Tano Bato, Mandailing, in 1862, led by the Mandailing schoolmaster Willem Iskander. He had been trained in pedagogy in The Netherlands (a remarkable circumstance then for the Outer Islands). Some of his students went on to prominent careers in education and journalism (Said 1976). Angkola and Mandailing writers authored an abundant literature protesting colonial control in subtle ways (Rodgers 1997).

Toba's dealings with the colonial state were more violent. Major Dutch incursions into the area came in 1878, and thirty years of guerrilla warfare ensued. This conflict in effect ended with the military defeat and death of the charismatic priest-warrior-king Si Singamangaraja XII in 1907 (Batara Sangti 1997). Based in Bakkara, he had sought to repel the Dutch via both magic and weaponry. A period of high colonialism in Toba followed, with road, school, and hospital construction (Sherman 1990).

By the 1930s, a passable road linked the highlands to Deli. The eastern coast tea, tobacco, and eventually rubber plantations had burgeoned between the 1880s and 1920s (Stoler 1985). Infused with foreign capital, these plantations served as labor magnets on Angkola and Mandailing. Some families also fled the uplands to escape heavy corvée labor demands.

School development proceeded apace in the highlands, which now had both Dutch- and Malay-language primary and secondary schools in some favored areas (Rodgers 1995). The rush toward school-based literacy in "the Dutch letters" (the Latin alphabet) and away from "village tradition" had several interlocking ideological consequences for Batak youth in the colonial era. Old Batak ways came to be counterposed to Indies modernities. Familiarity with the Malay language (then being promoted by nationalists as Bahasa Indonesia) intensified, which nurtured nationalist debates in towns such as Sibolga, Tarutung, and Padangsidimpuan. Social horizons expanded, as Batak schoolchildren came to discover that they themselves were one of the many constituent peoples of the Indies. And a Batak elite of schoolteachers and newspaper writers encountered Dutch and mission scholarship on "the Batak peoples," their customs, and their languages. The categorization schemes of the colonists for typing language and culture began to be appropriated and debated by the colonized.

The Japanese occupation during the Pacific War (1941–1945) was devastating for the uplands, bringing much privation. The national revolution saw guerrilla action in several parts of Tapanuli and also the forced departure of some of the old traditional aristocrats (accused of being in league with the Dutch).

Since the 1950s, any possibility of a politically viable Batak nationalism has been swamped by Indonesian nationalism. The public schools have once again been crucial for identity formation. The Batak urban diasporas have grown, with many individuals now working for the national government, the police, and the military (other economic niches are education, law, journalism, the ministry, and bus transportation).

The New Order was a time of political compromise and contestation in North Sumatra, as the state attempted to folklorize the Batak societies as "quaint and outmoded" whereas Bataks themselves often painted their histories in politically stronger hues. Much argument over Batak heritage and who should properly narrate it ensued (Steedly 1993).

SUSAN RODGERS

See also Education, Western Secular; Indonesian Revolution (1945–1949); Missionaries, Christian; Nationalism and Independence Movements in Southeast Asia; Netherlands (Dutch) East Indies; Newspapers and Mass Media in Southeast Asia; Orde Baru (The New Order); Padri Movement; Partai Komunis Indonesia (PKI) (1920); Sumatra

References:
Ahmat Adam. 1995. *The Vernacular Press and the Emergence of Modern Indonesian Consciousness (1855–1913)*. Ithaca, NY: Cornell University Southeast Asia Program.
Batara Sangti. 1997. *Sejarah Batak* [*Batak History*]. Balige, North Sumatra, Indonesia: Karl Sianipar.
Bellwood, Peter. 1995. *Austronesians: Historical and Comparative Perspectives*. Canberra: Research School of Pacific and Asian Studies, Australian National University.
———. 1997. *Prehistory of the Indo-Malaysian Archipelago*. Rev. ed. Honolulu: University of Hawai'i Press.
Kipp, Rita Smith. 1990. *The Early Years of a Dutch Colonial Mission: The Karo Field*. Ann Arbor: University of Michigan Press.
———. 1996. *Dissociated Identities: Ethnicity, Religion, and Class in an Indonesian Society*. Ann Arbor: University of Michigan Press.
Kipp, Rita Smith, and Richard Kipp, eds. 1983. *Beyond Samosir: Recent Studies of the Batak Peoples of Sumatra*. Papers in International Studies. Athens: Ohio University Press.
Kipp, Rita Smith, and Susan Rodgers, eds. 1987. *Indonesian Religions in Transition*. Tucson: University of Arizona Press.
Kozok, Uli. 1996. "Bark, Bones, and Bamboo: Batak Traditions of Sumatra." Pp. 231–246 in *Illuminations: The Writing Traditions of Indonesia*. Edited by Ann Kumar and John McGlynn. Jakarta, New York, and Tokyo: Lontar and Weatherhill.
Niessen, Sandra. 1993. *Batak Cloth and Clothing: A Dynamic Indonesian Tradition*. Oxford in Asia Series. Kuala Lumpur: Oxford University Press.
Rodgers, Susan. 1995. *Telling Lives, Telling History: Autobiography and Historical Memory in Modern Indonesia*. Berkeley and Los Angeles: University of California Press.
———. 1997. "*Sitti Djaoerahital*": *A Novel of Colonial Indonesia*. Translated by M. J. Soetan Hasoendoetan. Madison: University of Wisconsin Southeast Asia Studies Program.
Said, Mohammad Haji. 1976. *Sejarah Pers di Sumatera Utara* [*History of Pers in North Sumatra*]. Medan, Indonesia: Waspada.
Schnitger, F. M. 1989 [1939]. *Forgotten Kingdoms of Sumatra*. Oxford in Asia Series. Singapore: Oxford University Press. First published in 1939 by E. J. Brill, Leiden, The Netherlands.
Sherman, George. 1990. *Rice, Rupees, and Ritual*. Ithaca, NY: Cornell University Press.
Steedly, Mary M. 1993. *Hanging without a Rope: Narrative Experience in Colonial and Postcolonial Karoland*. Princeton, NJ: Princeton University Press.
Stoler, Ann 1985. *Capitalism and Confrontation in Sumatra's Plantation Belt, 1870–1979*. New Haven, CT: Yale University Press.

BATAVIA (SUNDA KELAPA, JACATRA, DJAKARTA/JAKARTA)

The history of names introduces us to the history of a place. Jakarta is the capital of Indonesia, but the record of human habitation there is

Canal at Batavia, Indonesia. (Bettmann/Corbis)

much older than the name. Excavations have uncovered tools and a stone bearing, in Sanskrit, the record of the fifth-century C.E. King Purnavarman and his kingdom of Tarumanagara.

The site, under the name Sunda Kelapa, served the Hindu kingdom of Pajajaran (1344–1570s) as its principal outlet for pepper. In 1527, the sultan of Cirebon sent militias to conquer Sunda Kelapa. They renamed it Jayakerta, meaning "Great Victory." A hundred years later, Dutch shippers found in Jayakerta a port with about 2,000 Sundanese and Chinese residents. Jayakerta's ruler styled himself sultan, acknowledged the king of Banten as his suzerain, and used Javanese as the language of his administration. Dutch scribes rendered the port's name in Roman script as Jacatra.

Jayakerta had a good harbor and was conveniently sited for ships sailing archipelago water highways. In 1618, armed bands from Banten attacked the Dutch compound there. By May 1619, Dutch forces had repelled the attack, conquered the town, deposed Jayakerta's sultan, and burned down his palace and mosque. A European administration, acting for Holland's United East India Company (VOC), replaced Javanese rule and renamed the port Batavia to honor the Germanic tribe from whom the Dutch considered themselves descended. The new government promoted Protestant Christianity as the religion of Batavia's ruling class. It introduced the Christian calendar and workweek and set up Dutch municipal institutions.

Batavia Castle was built at the water's edge to control the harbor and house the headquarters of the VOC. International ships anchored in the bay and unloaded travelers and goods onto small sailing boats operated by Malays, Javanese, and Chinese. The walled town that grew around the castle was laid out like a

Southeast Asian port city. Each ethnic group was assigned its own quarters and lived under a headman (*kapitan*). Markets were located throughout the town. Land surrounding the walls was cleared for vegetable gardens and rice and sugar crops. These businesses were pushed from the walls as the town grew, and suburbs were laid outside the walls.

When the Dutch conquered Jayakerta, they declared the region between the sultanates of Banten and Cirebon to be under Dutch suzerainty. District heads now owed allegiance to the Dutch. They paid taxes to the Batavia authorities in products harvested from forest trees fringing the clearings where farmers sowed their crops. In the eighteenth century, farmers began planting coffee seedlings, obtained through the company, and they paid their taxes in harvested beans. Some of the lands were sold to Dutch, Javanese, and Chinese individuals, who ruled them as private fiefdoms.

Batavia was the major trading center in the archipelago for Chinese merchants. It had diplomatic relations with its principal neighbor, the Javanese sultanate of Mataram, and with most archipelago states. It obtained paramount privileges in Java's north coast ports from Amangkurat I (r. 1646–1677) in return for supplying Mataram with mercenaries from its own army. In the archipelago, Batavia was the seat of government for Dutch settlements and the site of a commercial power that was aggressively expanding its territorial and political reach into archipelago states.

Batavia was always a multiethnic town. From its polyglot population, there emerged a distinctive community identifying itself as the *Kaum Betawi* (Batavians). They were Muslim and speakers of a Malay that incorporated words from the Chinese and Balinese languages.

In the nineteenth century, a colonial government accountable to Holland's Parliament replaced rule by the VOC, which was primarily a private commercial company. Batavia became the capital of the Netherlands East Indies, and Dutch rule expanded north, east, and west in the period from 1850 to 1940. Batavia was the hub of the archipelago's commerce and transport networks, the headquarters of its businesses, the site of high schools and university colleges, and a rival to Indonesian sultanates in

setting fashions. From the 1890s, its steamship and telegraph services connected Indonesians to The Hague and Mecca.

In 1942, Japan defeated the colony's armed forces. Batavia became the headquarters for the Sixteenth Japanese Army, under the name Djakarta. It ceased to be the capital of an archipelago-wide state, shrinking to become only a principal city of Java. Separate Japanese army and navy administrations controlled Sumatra and eastern Indonesia until the end of the Pacific War (1941–1945).

Sukarno (1901–1970) proclaimed the independence of the Indonesian people in Djakarta on 17 August 1945. He envisioned the city as the capital of a republic that would extend to the boundaries of the former Dutch colony. In 1946, Dutch troops retook the city and revived the name Batavia. Sukarno led the struggle for independence from Yogyakarta. The Federal Republic of Indonesia achieved international recognition in December 1949 and named Djakarta its capital. Djakarta remained the capital following the transformation of Indonesia into a unitary state in August 1950. In 1972, the city became known as Jakarta when Indonesian spelling was revised.

In modern Indonesian life, Jakarta is the site of a new national culture. It exports Javanese settlers, soldiers, and administrators across the archipelago to hold together a multiethnic state. Jakarta represents both the nation's triumph and its exertion of power over Indonesia's regions and ethnic cores.

JEAN GELMAN TAYLOR

See also Amangkurat I (Sunan Tegalwangi) (r. 1646–1677); Banten (Bantam); Chinese in Southeast Asia; Coffee; Hindu-Buddhist Period of Southeast Asia; "Indonesia"; Indonesian Revolution (1945–1949); Java; *Kapitan China* System; Mataram; Netherlands (Dutch) East Indies; Pepper; Vereenigde Oost-Indische Compagnie (VOC) ([Dutch] United East India Company) (1602); Yogyakarta (Jogjakarta)

References:

Abeyasekere, Susan. 1987. *Jakarta, a History.* Singapore: Oxford University Press.
Blusse, Leonard. 1986. *Strange Company: Chinese Settlers, Mestizo Women, and the Dutch in VOC Batavia.* Dordrecht, The Netherlands: Foris.

Grijns, Kees, and Peter J. M. Nas, eds. 2000. *Jakarta-Batavia: Socio-Cultural Essays.* Leiden, The Netherlands: KITLV Press.

Heuken, S. J. Adolf. 1982. *Historical Sites of Jakarta.* Jakarta: Cipta Loka Caraka.

Taylor, Jean Gelman. 1983. *The Social World of Batavia: European and Eurasian in Dutch Asia.* Madison: University of Wisconsin Press.

BATIK

See Textiles of Southeast Asia

BATTAMBANG

Battambang, Cambodia's second largest city, is the capital of Battambang Province, bordering Thailand in Cambodia's northwest area. Its population was estimated at 80,000 in 1998. The region has long been productive agriculturally, and for most of the twentieth century, Battambang provided the bulk of Cambodia's rice exports.

Battambang has had a rich and often tumultuous history. In medieval times, when the kingdom known as Angkor dominated much of the region (ninth through fifteenth centuries), Battambang was the site of numerous Hindu and Buddhist temples. After the decline of Angkor in the sixteenth century, Battambang remained under the jurisdiction of the Cambodian king, whose capital was in the vicinity of Phnom Penh.

In 1794, the king of Thailand demanded that the Cambodian king, Ang Eng (ca. 1774–1797), who had just been crowned by Thai authorities, relinquish control of Battambang and the neighboring province of Siem Reap, in exchange for being allowed to return to Cambodia, which he had fled as a child. The provinces remained under Thai control until 1907, when French colonial authorities pressured the Thai to return them to Cambodian jurisdiction. During the Pacific War (1941–1945), Thailand occupied the provinces again, relinquishing them in 1946.

During the early years of independence, Battambang regained its position as Cambodia's rice bowl, and the city prospered. Along with other Cambodian cities, it was forcibly evacuated by the Khmer Rouge regime that governed Cambodia from 1975 to 1979. Hundreds of thousands of urban dwellers from Phnom Penh and elsewhere were relocated into the province at that time, and tens of thousands of them died of starvation or overwork and by execution. After the Khmer Rouge fell following a Vietnamese invasion in 1979, thousands of residents sought refuge in Thailand. In the 1980s and early 1990s, the province was the scene of an ongoing civil war. Battambang became a prosperous province in the 1990s, and the city benefited from extensive private investment from nearby Thailand.

DAVID CHANDLER

See also Ang Eng (ca. 1774–1797); Angkor; Angkor Wat (Nagaravatta); Cambodia (Eighteenth to Mid-Nineteenth Centuries); Cambodia under French Colonial Rule; Democratic Kampuchea (DK); French Ambitions in Southeast Asia; French Indochinese Union (*Union Indochinoise Française*) (1887); Khmer Rouge; Rama I (Chakri) (r. 1782–1809); Siem Reap

References:
Chandler, David. 2000. *A History of Cambodia.* 3rd ed. Boulder, CO: Westview Press.

BAYINNAUNG (r. 1551–1581)
"World Conqueror"

As the third ruler of the First Toungoo dynasty, Bayinnaung, in a series of wars with Burma's neighbors, established Burmese hegemony over mainland Southeast Asia from Manipur to Laos. His administration was patterned on a core area around the capital governed directly by the high king (*chakravartin,* meaning "world conqueror") and a periphery of surrounding appanages governed by royal relatives, or *bayin,* who were allowed usage of the five royal regalia (umbrella, fly whisks, betel box, golden slippers, and gongs). Autonomous, they often rebelled in attempts to take over the throne. Beyond these royal appanages was an outer circle of vassals among the ethnic groups in the uplands— Shan, Kachin, Chin, Kayah—over whom Bayinnaung established Burmese suzerainty.

Bayinnaung's conquest of Siam in 1569 continued this pattern. The conquered territory was not laid waste but was incorporated in the empire as part of the *mandala,* or circle of federated states owing allegiance to the chakravartin, whose righteousness was attested to by his possession of numerous White Elephants. A Siamese princess, sister of Prince Naresuan (later king, r. 1590–1605), was presented to Bayinnaung. A key element of his policies was to increase manpower beyond that available from the Burmese heartland. Chiang Mai came under Burmese suzerainty in this period and remained within the Burmese sphere of influence for two hundred years. Bayinnaung appointed his son ruler in Chiang Mai, a tradition that continued throughout the First Toungoo dynasty.

European travelers considered Pegu the foremost trading city in mainland Southeast Asia. From this base, Bayinnaung drew the profits of the Asian spice trade around the coasts of Siam and Burma and across the transpeninsular routes, as well as the luxury goods from the hinterland areas of the T'ai states. At Mergui and Tavoy, he made detailed administrative arrangements for the supervision of merchant shipping and envoys from India. In the 1570s, he had a fleet of seven oceangoing ships built for commercial ventures (Lieberman 1984: 31). By the end of the sixteenth century, some 18 percent of eastward trade from India passed through Mergui and Pegu. A devout Buddhist, Bayinnaung adorned the pagodas of Pegu with the wealth from international trade. But what the father won, the son lost, and by 1599, the empire was in disarray, with the rich delta lands laid waste and depopulated by the ravages of civil and external wars.

HELEN JAMES

See also Buddhism, Theravada; Burma-Siam
Wars; *Cakkavatti/Setkya-min* (Universal
Ruler); Chiang Mai; Economic
Transformation of Southeast Asia
(ca. 1400–ca. 1800); Pegu; Toungoo
Dynasty (1486–1752)

References:
Lieberman, Victor B. 1980. "Europeans,
Trade and the Unification of Burma, c.
1540–1620." *Oriens Extremus* 27, no. 2:
203–226.
———. 1984. *Burmese Administrative Cycles:
Anarchy and Conquest, c. 1580–1760.*
Princeton, NJ: Princeton University Press.
Reid, Anthony. 1993. *Southeast Asia in the Age of
Commerce, 1450–1680.* Vol. 2, *Expansion and
Crisis.* New Haven, CT: Yale University
Press.

BEJALAI

The Iban term *bejalai* means "to walk" or "to go on a journey." Traditionally, Iban men, especially unmarried men, were expected to leave home for a time and venture out into the world for adventure and to seek their fortunes. These journeys, or bejalai, frequently lasted for several years and often took parties of men far from home.

One Iban commentator (Datuk Amar Linggi) described the role of bejalai for Iban youth as a traditional "requirement for the transition from childhood to manhood, [which] our ancestors selected . . . as a test of character and an education for life" (Kedit 1993: vii–viii). By leaving home and journeying to other places, young men displayed courage and resolve, and in the course of their travels, they were expected to develop resourcefulness and gain experience and knowledge; they were also to bring home foreign goods, ideas, and a sense of the wider world beyond their local communities. Such travels contributed to Iban restlessness, giving men the self-confidence and planning abilities needed to undertake what became, at times, large-scale territorial migrations. Mobility itself was and continues to be culturally valued, and most Iban even today regard journeying as part of their cultural heritage. For young men, a further motive was *ngiga' bini* (meaning "to seek a wife"), travel being considered an enhancement to marriageability, while at the same time expanding the opportunities for courting.

Bejalai, however, has not always been seen in such positive terms. During the Brooke (1841–1941) era (while English gentleman-adventurer James Brooke was raja of Sarawak) and the later British colonial (1946–1963) period, European officers viewed Iban traveling as a matter of concern. Traveling parties of young men were frequently suspected of troublemaking and, during the nineteenth century, of clandestine headhunting. Bejalai was also thought to be a labor drain. In the contemporary situation, politicians blamed the practice of bejalai for the failure of rural development schemes and as a cause of family desertion. During the last quarter of the nineteenth century, bejalai played an important part in drawing the Iban into a monetized economy. Today, however, economic need tends to overshadow the lure of adventure, and many rural families depend on labor migration and the remittances of family members working in towns or timber camps to survive. Today, Iban men on *bejalai* may be found on North Sea oil rigs; in the dockyards of Singapore; and in logging camps in Cambodia, Papua New Guinea, Fiji, and Vanuatu.

CLIFFORD SATHER

See also *Adat;* Borneo; Brooke, James, and Sarawak; Dayaks; Ibans; Sarawak and Sabah (North Borneo)

References:
Freeman, J. D. 1974. *Report on the Iban.* London: Athlone Press.
Kedit, Peter M. 1993. *Iban Bejalai.* Kuching: Sarawak Literary Society.
Sandin, Benedict. 1994. *Sources of Iban Traditional History.* Edited by Clifford Sather. *Sarawak Museum Journal* Special Monograph no. 7. Kuching, Malaysia: Sarawak Museum.
Sather, Clifford. 1996. "'All Threads Are White': Iban Egalitarianism Reconsidered." Pp. 70–110 in *Origins, Ancestry and Alliance.* Edited by James J. Fox and Clifford Sather. Canberra: Research School of Pacific and Asian Studies, Australian National University.

BENGKULU (BENCOOLEN, BENKULEN)

Bengkulu is a town and region in West Sumatra. In the early seventeenth century, it was under the influence of both Banten and Minangkabau. The Dutch East India Company (VOC) established a trading post in the area in 1633. After the Dutch forced the English East India Company (EIC) to leave Banten, the English established Fort Marlborough along the beach in Bengkulu in 1685. This was long the only British stronghold in the Malay Archipelago. Consequently, Bengkuku was the only major region of British influence in the archipelago until the temporary demise of Dutch rule in the area between 1795 and 1811. Bengkulu had a port (or rather an anchoring place) about 9 kilometers off the coast. Through this port, mainly pepper was traded. However, the trade was only marginally profitable for the English. The areas surrounding Bengkulu were under Dutch influence. The VOC supported the rulers of Minangkabau against an expansionist Aceh, which yielded them the right to establish

trading posts all along Sumatra's western coast, with the main office in Padang.

After his stint as lieutenant governor in Java (t. 1811–1816), Stamford Raffles became governor of Bengkulu in 1818 and sought to expand the production of nutmeg, cloves, and cassava in the region. The Anglo-Dutch Treaty of 1824 revised the British and Dutch holdings in the Malay Archipelago, with the Dutch ceding Melaka and receiving Bengkulu. However, although Bengkulu was under Dutch influence, effective colonial government was not established there until 1868. At that stage, the area had little going for itself. Pepper production had waned, and other spices were ailing. Efforts to revive pepper production were unsuccessful, as was the promotion of coffee cultivation. The replacement of compulsory cultivation with a regular taxation system proved an incentive for the production of spices. The development of both the town and the region took off, and the Dutch turned Bengkulu into a separate residency in 1878. It became a province of Indonesia after the Pacific War (1941–1945).

PIERRE VAN DER ENG

See also Aceh (Acheh); Anglo-Dutch Relations in Southeast Asia (Seventeenth to Twentieth Centuries); Banten (Bantam); East India Company (EIC) (1600), English; Melaka; Minangkabau; Pepper; Raffles, Sir (Thomas) Stamford Bingley (1781–1826); Spices and the Spice Trade; Sumatra; Vereenigde Oost-Indische Compagnie (VOC) ([Dutch] United East India Company) (1602)

References:
Jaspan, M. A. 1974. "Bencoolen (Bengkulu): 136 Years after the Ending of the British Settlement." *Berita Kajian Sumatera* 4, no. 1: 19–30.
Marschall, W. 1995. *Menschen und Markte: Wirtschaftliche Integration im Hochland Sudsumatras* [*People and Markets: Scientific Integration in the Highlands of South Sumatra*]. Berlin: Reimer.

BHINNEKA TUNGGAL IKA ("UNITY IN DIVERSITY")

On the state crest of the Indonesian nation, the words *Bhinneka Tunggal Ika* are featured prominently. The language is old Kawi Javanese, and the words mean "Unity in Diversity." Bhinneka Tunggal Ika is the Indonesian motto, adopted on 17 August 1950. Indeed, it is a very logical motto, given that Indonesia consists of more than 13,000 islands spanning the seas from the Indian Ocean to Australia.

The origins of the motto are steeped in mystic tradition. According to legend, passed down to posterity from the fifteenth century or even earlier, a king called Purushada fed on human flesh. His victims were chosen from among the common folk, who were naturally terrified. A knight by the name of Sutasoma decided to help the people by offering up himself to be devoured. The king was furious that a mere knight would try to change his dietary preferences, and he attempted to kill the knight. A major fight ensued in which the celestial powers participated. Lord Śiva entered the body of the king, and Lord Buddha entered the knight's body. When the fight became supernatural, neither side could win. Brahmin priests intervened. They appealed to the combatants to stop fighting, arguing that the king and the knight were one, though their forms were different: the Brahmins used the phrase *Bhinneka Tunggal Ika* to describe the oneness of Śiva and Buddha. Thereupon, Śiva and Buddha left the bodies of the king and the knight, respectively, and the king gave up his habit of eating human flesh. This legend was recorded in a poem written by Mpu Tantular, the famous poet of the Majapahit court.

Bhinneka Tunggal Ika is a reflection of the challenges facing Indonesia. When the Netherlands East Indies became Indonesia, the nation consisted of many ethnic groups, with divisions existing even within those groups. And Dutch colonialism only also accentuated the differences. Consequently, working toward unity in accordance with the motto Bhinneka Tunggal Ika was imperative.

YONG MUN CHEONG

See also Borneo; East Indonesian Ethnic Groups; Ethnolinguistic Groups of Southeast Asia; "Indonesia"; Java; Netherlands (Dutch) East Indies; *Nusantara*; Sulawesi (Celebes); Sumatra

References:
Hitchcock, Michael, and Victor T. King. 1997. *Images of Malay-Indonesian Identity.* Kuala Lumpur: Oxford University Press.

BHUMIBOL ADULYADEJ (RAMA IX) (r. 1946–)
Beloved Monarch of Thailand

The most popular, revered, and respected monarch of his land, King Bhumibol (1927–) has become the highest symbol of Thailand and has successfully revitalized the Thai monarchy, transforming it in a way that had not been done since the death of King Chulalongkorn (Rama V) in 1910. Enthroned in the post–Pacific War (1941–1945) period, King Bhumibol has adroitly maneuvered the role of the monarchy so that it can function meaningfully in the rough political transition Thailand has experienced. Under his reign, the Thai monarchy has changed from the old center of power to the new center of loyalty, redefining the relationship between the institution and the people. More significantly, the monarchy has become a unifying force in a country divided and factionalized by the forces of political democratization and economic development. As a spiritual leader of the nation, he has instilled discipline to regulate the people so that the country can preserve its unity. The king has played many crucial roles in shaping the country's path to constitutional democracy.

King Bhumibol Adulyadej was born on 5 December 1927 in Cambridge, Massachusetts, where his father, Prince Mahidol, was studying medicine at Harvard University. He was the grandson of King Chulalongkorn. He ascended the throne on 9 June 1946 following the sudden death of King Ananda Mahidol (Rama VIII), his elder brother, on the same day. He was officially crowned King Rama IX of Thailand on 5 May 1950.

King Bhumibol began his primary school education in Bangkok before he and his family went to Switzerland. He finished his secondary education at the École Nouvelle de la Suisse Romande, Chailly sur Lausanne, and received a baccalaureate from the Gymnase Classique Cantonal of Lausanne. At Lausanne University, he chose to study political science and law instead of pursuing his interest in science. He was married to M. R. Sirikit in 1950 in Bangkok, shortly before his coronation. King Bhumibol is a gifted musician and composer, especially in jazz music. He is accomplished in the fields of painting, photography, and engineering, as well as languages and cultures. He is fluent in three European languages. The king has four children:

Princess Ubol Ratana (1951–), Crown Prince Maha Vajiralongkorn (1952–), Princess Maha Chakri Sirindhorn (1955–), and Princess Chulabhorn (1957–).

Since the Revolution of 1932, which overthrew the absolutist monarchy, questions about the proper role of the monarch in the constitutional regime have not been satisfactorily resolved. Generally, it is believed that the monarch should be a ceremonial head of state and is in a position of revered worship. He is above partisan affairs and should not be involved in any government decisions; nor should the monarch be disrespected. However, such principles are difficult to apply in an emerging nation-state like Thailand, where the traditional forces and support for the monarchy have been cultivated for a long time and the new democratic forces are relatively recent inventions. It is obvious to the king and royalists that in the twenty-first century, the only group that is capable of overthrowing the monarchy is the military. The most important question for the king during his active reign involves how to balance various political groups and parties so that the institution of the monarchy is able to exist safely while maintaining its spiritual leadership for the nation.

The immediate task of King Bhumibol was how to maintain good relations with the military in power, even though the monarch might find it more convenient to work with civilian governments, which are more divided and easier to deal with. Such political realities and conditions of the monarchy in relation to the political system determined, to a certain degree, the role of the monarchy in politics.

From 1946 to 1951, the king saw tumultuous political situations created by coups and factional conflicts between civilians and the military. By 1951, when he returned from abroad to stay permanently in Thailand, there had already been eleven governments installed, three constitutions abrogated, and four elections held, along with five coups and attempted coups.

By the mid-1950s, the royalists and conservatives were on the rise, and the monarchy began to see the role it could play in national life again. From their trip up-country and their regular radio broadcasts, the king and queen received an enthusiastic response from the people. Accordingly, they assumed more active roles in national life. The first break with the military-led government under Field Marshal Plaek Phibunsongkhram (Phibun) (1897–1964), the leader of the army faction of the People's Party, came in the late 1950s. In the symbolic celebration of the 2,500th anniversary of the death of the Lord Buddha, Phibun assumed the role of patron of Buddhism, a role previously played by monarchs. At the grand opening of the state ceremony in 1957, the king was conspicuously absent. In 1957, General Sarit Thanarat (d. 1963), a powerful army commander, launched a coup against Phibun and proclaimed that his legitimacy was derived from the throne.

From then on, the monarchy and its traditional ideology of a paternal king was revived, and the institution once again was identified closely with the nation and the people. To promote a good understanding of Thailand under the Sarit regime (1957–1963), the king and queen visited many foreign countries, especially Western European nations and the United States. Later on, the king also made many visits to provinces in Thailand, particularly the remote and less developed areas, after which came the royal development projects. By the 1970s, a version of Thai nationalism centered on the monarchy had become predominant. The popular support the monarchy gained from the people and university students in urban centers proved central in ending the period of military dictatorship.

The testing time for the monarchy came when the military establishment was crumbling under attacks by students and urban groups in the famous uprising of 14 October 1973. To restore peace and order, the king put an end to the riot and asked Field Marshal Thanom Kittikachorn (1911–), General Prapat Jarusathien (Praphas Charusathian), and Colonel Narong Kittikachorn to leave the country. The king's intervention forced the military to share power with civilian politicians; more significant still was the reversal of the relationship between monarch and government. The monarchy was no longer manipulated by the government in power but had become a center of authority in its own right.

Political radicalism from 1973 to 1976 was viewed by the king as threatening to the unity and proper order of the nation; thus, the palace actively supported the village scout movement,

Thailand's King Bhumibol Adulyadej at a state dinner he hosted for U.S. President George W. Bush at the Royal Grand Palace in Bangkok. (Jason Reed/Reuters Newsmedia Inc./Corbis)

a right-wing mass organization created and led by government agencies to fight against the student-labor-peasant movement. The coup of 6 October 1976 terminated leftist politics and the civilian government of Prime Minister Seni Pramoj (1905–1997), ostensibly to save the country from communism. The military-led government installed Thanin Kraivixien, a former Supreme Court justice and later a member of the Privy Council who was also the king's choice as prime minister.

The attempted coup led by Young Turks on April Fool's Day (1 April) in 1981 was another occasion on which the king took action. He left the Bangkok palace to join General Prem Tinsulanond (1920–) in Nakorn Rajasima, the northeastern headquarters of Army Region 2,

to fight against the coup party that had temporarily controlled key areas of Bangkok. However, the military coup in 1991 that was led by the National Peace Keeping Council (NPKC) against the civilian elected government of Chatichai Choonhavan was not openly opposed by the king. When protesters took to the streets and violence erupted from the attempted suppression by the military government in May 1992, the king called in the two leaders of the conflicting parties—the prime minister, General Suchinda Kraprayoon, and the protest leader, Major General Chamlong Srimuang. He told both of them to quit the fight and restore peace. Generally, the king has chosen order and stability rather than conflict, even when that meant he had to identify himself with a government that allowed a preeminent role for the military.

By nature, the monarchy is oriented toward conservatism, based on the idea of social organicism. Ideologically, King Bhumiphol emphasizes the primacy of the common good over the good of the individual. In times of crisis, he believes, authority, discipline, duty, and allegiance to an objective national interest should take precedence over any claim based on personal desire or personal interest. Given this Buddhist political worldview, coupled with the instability of elected governments, the king has urged that democracy in Thailand should not be defined according to foreign terms but should be modified to fit Thai culture and tradition. Thus, constitutionalism was not as crucial to the survival of the country as the preservation of unity and the old institutions of the nation.

THANET APHORNSUVAN

See also Constitutional (Bloodless) Revolution (1932) (Thailand); Constitutional Monarchy of Malaya/Malaysia; Military and Politics in Southeast Asia; National Peace-Keeping Council (NPKC); Plaek Phibunsongkhram, Field Marshal (1897–1964); Prem Tinsulanond (1920–); Student Revolt (October 1973) (Thailand); Thanom Kittikachorn, Field Marshal (1911–)

References:
Hewsion, Kevin. 1997. "The Monarchy and Democratization." Pp. 58–74 in *Political Change in Thailand: Democracy and*

Participation. Edited by Kevin Hewsion. London and New York: Routledge.

Keyes, Charles F. 1987. *Thailand: Buddhist Kingdom as Modern Nation-State*. Boulder, CO, and London: Westview Press.

Stevenson, William. 1999. *The Revolutionary King: The True-Life Sequel to the King and I*. London: Constable.

BINH XUYEN

The Binh Xuyen was not a religious group and therefore differed from other movements in South Vietnam, notably the Cao Dai and Hoa Hao. Named after a hamlet in South Cholon, the Binh Xuyen first emerged in the early 1920s as a criminal gang of about 200 individuals. Most of the early Binh Xuyen members came from marginal strata. Armed with rough weapons, the group relied on extortion and robbery in Saigon and Cholon.

The Binh Xuyen leader, Le Van Vien (Bay Vien), was born in 1904 in Cholon and served several prison terms. In August 1945, he aligned himself with the Vietnamese communists (Viet Minh) against the French. However, in June 1948, he rallied to the French, and four years later, the French promoted him to the rank of general.

At its height in the early 1950s, the Binh Xuyen group was believed to have up to 25,000 troops and paramilitary forces. Among the most important Binh Xuyen economic assets were gambling and lottery concessions, prostitution operations, opium-boiling plants, and retail shops in Saigon. The French also assigned the Binh Xuyen to collect a number of taxes, notably the coal tax.

By 1954, the Binh Xuyen military commander, Lai Van Sang, became director-general of Saigon's police. The Binh Xuyen troops controlled the Saigon region and the 100-kilometer strip between Saigon and Vung Tau, where they became notorious for their so-called road safety taxes. Once sought as a bandit, the Binh Xuyen chief—the illiterate Le Van Vien—was eyeing the post of prime minister by 1954.

However, in March and April 1955, the Binh Xuyen lost a violent confrontation with Prime Minister Ngô Đình Diệm (1901–1963) and his team. In September, Le Van Vien fled to France, and in October 1955, the last Binh Xuyen units halted their resistance. Following their military defeat in 1955, the Binh Xuyen ceased to exist as an organized force.

SERGEI A. BLAGOV

See also Ngô Đình Diệm; Viet Minh; Vietnam, South (post-1945)

References:

Darcourt, Pierre. 1977. *Bay Vien: Le maître de Cholon* [*Bay Vien: The Master of Cho Lon*]. Paris: Hachette.

Fall, Bernard. 1955. "The Political-Religious Sects of South Vietnam." *Pacific Affairs* 28, no. 3: 235–253.

Savani, A. M. 1955. *Visage et images du Sud Viet-Nam* [*Faces and Images of South Vietnam*]. Saigon: Imprimérie Française d'Outre-Mer.

BIRCH, J. W. W. (1826–1875)
First British Resident of Perak

John Woodford Wheeler Birch was the first British resident sent to the peninsular Malay state of Perak late in 1874 under the Pangkor Engagement. His zealous haste to effect changes exasperated the ruler and leading chiefs of Perak, and the conflict that ensued led to his assassination in November 1875, followed by British military intervention. Although his British contemporaries regarded Birch as a martyr to the cause of reform, present-day Malaysian historians and public opinion see his Malay opponents as champions of independence and Birch as an unworthy public figure.

After a brief stint in the Royal Navy, Birch joined the Ceylon (Sri Lanka) colonial government service in 1846 as a road overseer; subsequently, in 1853, he was transferred to the administrative service. He held a sequence of district and magistrate posts and made his reputation as an active and able official, with useful experience in the improvement of irrigation works. In May 1870, he was transferred to the Straits Settlements as colonial (chief) secretary, where he was judged to be efficient but rather domineering. He showed a keen interest in the western Malay States, which he visited on official missions in 1871 and 1874. He was not, however, included among the advisers who accompanied Governor Sir Andrew Clarke (t. 1874–1875) to the meeting at Pangkor in January 1874. The outcome of that meeting was that

Raja (later Sultan) Abdullah and some of the Perak chiefs were induced to sign the Pangkor Engagement, an ambiguous document whose purpose they probably did not fully grasp. Birch applied for the new post of resident to Perak, in which his function would be to advise the ruler on the improvement of the state government. Birch, however, believed that to achieve that end, he needed to act with a strong hand.

The inevitable conflict centered on Birch's determination to take control of the collection of taxes and to abolish "debt bondage," under which members of the Malay ruling class obtained domestic and personal services from followers who were nominally their debtors. Birch, like other British officials, regarded debt bondage as a form of slavery. In thus seeking to deprive Malay aristocrats of traditional privileges and their customary revenues, Birch appeared to them to undermine their status and authority. The British-installed Sultan Abdullah (r. 1874–1875) and his deposed predecessor, Sultan Ismail, together with the leading chiefs, were able to delay and frustrate Birch to some extent. Further complicating matters, Birch gave asylum in his household to runaway bondswomen, which led to Malay accusations of sexual impropriety on his part.

William F. D. Jervois (t. 1875–1877), who had succeeded Clarke as governor in May 1875, decided to adopt more drastic measures. Accordingly, Birch would become a commissioner with executive powers (for which the Pangkor Engagement made no provision). Sultan Abdullah was coerced into accepting this change, and Birch began a tour of Perak villages to post a proclamation announcing his new status. He arrived at Pasir Salak, where the local chief, the Maharaja Lela, was so embittered against Birch that he had him killed on 2 November. Jervois overreacted to the news and brought in from abroad a military force of several thousands, with naval support, to deal with a Malay opposition that, in reality, posed no serious threat, for it had neither purpose nor leadership.

The official inquiry that followed found that there had been much discussion, though inconclusive, between Abdullah and some chiefs (although others were at odds with him) and that the Maharaja Lela had received authority from Abdullah to take unspecified action. The Maharaja Lela and those directly involved in killing Birch were convicted of murder and hanged. Abdullah and three leading Malay chiefs were exiled to the Seychelles, and Ismail was exiled to Johor.

Frank Swettenham (1850–1946), who had narrowly escaped death along with Birch, argued that the result of these events was immediate Malay acquiescence instead of continuing resistance to necessary reforms. But Birch's death was also a warning to his successors that they needed to carry out their duties with patience, tact, and an understanding of the Malay point of view, which Birch entirely lacked. The choice of Birch to promote better government in Perak was a disastrous misjudgment, but it also reflected the more general British failure to understand the nature of the problems they faced and how to deal with them satisfactorily.

As a man, Birch had other faults. He drank too much, without being a drunkard, and allowed his personal finances to become an embarrassment. His confidence in his ability to perform his task in Perak was misplaced; among other failings, he lacked an adequate command of the Malay language. The allegations of sexual relations with refugee bondswomen and earlier suspicions during Birch's time in Singapore that he was corrupt are not supported by adequate evidence, but they formed part of the contemporary picture of a controversial figure.

JOHN MICHAEL GULLICK

See also Clarke, Sir Andrew (1824–1902); Low, Sir Hugh (1824–1905); Pangkor Engagement; Straits Settlements (1826–1946); Swettenham, Sir Frank (1850–1946); Western Malay States (Perak, Selangor, Negri Sembilan, and Pahang); "White Man's Burden"

References:
Birch, James Wheeler Woodford. 1976. *The Journals of J. W. W. Birch, First British Resident to Perak, 1874–1875.* Edited by P. L. Burns. Kuala Lumpur: Oxford University Press.
Cheah Boon-Kheng. 1998. "Malay Politics and the Murder of J. W. W. Birch, British Resident in Perak, in 1875: The Humiliation and Revenge of the Maharaja Lela." *Journal of the Malaysian Branch of the Royal Asiatic Society* 71, no. 1 (June): 75–106.
Khoo Kay Kim. 1965–1966. "J. W. W. Birch: A Victorian Moralist in Perak's Augean Stable?" *Journal of the Historical Society of the University of Malaya* 4: 33–47.

Parkinson, Cyril. 1960. *British Intervention in Malaya, 1867–1877.* Singapore: University of Malaya Press.

Swettenham, Frank. 1895. "James Wheeler Woodford Birch." Pp. 227–247 in *Malay Sketches.* London: John Lane Bodley Head.

Winstedt, Richard, and Richard Wilkinson. 1934. "The First British Resident." Pp. 102–114 in *A History of Perak,* by Richard Winstedt and Richard Wilkinson. Kuala Lumpur: *Journal of the Malayan Branch of the Royal Asiatic Society* 12, no. 1 (1974). (MBRAS Reprint No 3.)

BLITAR

The town of Blitar lies in the upper Brantas Valley of East Java. Religious sites in the Blitar region belong to the second half of the fourteenth century, the last of the three phases of classical art in this region.

The main site of the Blitar phase is Panataran, most of which was built between 1345 and 1375. The complex appears to have developed somewhat haphazardly, rather than according to an overall plan. The group of structures is divided into three courtyards, reminiscent of Balinese temple complexes. Though inscriptions imply that Panataran was sponsored by the highest levels of the court of the kingdom of Majapahit (1293–ca. 1520s), the trip to the shrines here would have required a pilgrimage of several days. The principal structure in the compound farthest from the entrance was a Viṣṇu shrine that consisted of a three-story stone base bearing *Râmâyana* reliefs, supporting a wooden structure that vanished long ago. Winged mythical creatures supporting its foundation symbolically bore it aloft, recalling a palace floating in heaven above Mount Meru. In the second courtyard stands the Candi Naga (Serpent Shrine), decorated with heavenly beings that carry serpents, perhaps recalling the churning of the elixir of immortality. The first courtyard that visitors enter contains a shrine with the date 1369 carved over its doorway. This temple at one stage contained a statue of Ganesha, the elephant-headed Hindu god who is the patron of learning. Also in the entrance courtyard are low foundations for wooden structures, probably open-sided. One of these has elaborate reliefs; many of them are undeciphered, but they include the story of Sri Tanjung and a princely figure, which may allude to one of the stories of the indigenous Panji cycle, a series of legends revolving around a prince who loses contact with his beloved and has to go through numerous trials before being reunited with her. In the environs of Blitar, there are several other sites, including a well-known statue of Ganesha at a site called Bara that probably once guarded a river crossing and several bathing places.

The Blitar area lies in the upper reaches of the Brantas watershed, near the foot of Mount Kelud, one of the most destructive volcanoes in Indonesia. In its vicinity lie numerous remains of the fourteenth-century kingdom of Majapahit, including the largest monumental complex of that kingdom, located at Panataran. This site apparently served as a kind of ceremonial center for the kingdom, and various structures were built there over the span of a century. Blitar's modern importance stems from the fact that the tomb of Indonesia's independence leader Sukarno (1901–1970) is located there, near the site of his birth. The tomb has become a major shrine visited by hundreds of thousands of Javanese each year, mainly during the Muslim fasting month of Ramadan. The pilgrims are drawn by a combination of reverence for his nationalist philosophy and his reputation as having supernatural spiritual power.

JOHN N. MIKSIC

See also *Candi*; Hindu-Buddhist Period of Southeast Asia; Hinduism; Indianization; Indonesian Revolution (1945–1949); *Mahâbâratha* and *Râmâyana;* Majapahit (1293–ca. 1520s); Monumental Art of Southeast Asia; Pancasila (Pantja Sila); Soekarno (Sukarno) (1901–1970)

References:
Brandes, Jan Laurens Andries, ed. 1909. *Beschrijving Van Tjandi Singasari en de Wolkentooneelen Van Panataran* [*Description of Candi Singasari and the Cloud Scenes of Panataran*]. The Hague: Martinus Nijhoff.

Sukarno. 1965. *An Autobiography, as Told to Cindy Adams.* Indianapolis, IN: Bobbs-Merrill.

BOAT PEOPLE

The term *boat people* refers to the more than 1 million Vietnamese refugees who fled from

A Vietnamese refugee with his belongings secured between his teeth climbs a cargo net to the deck of the combat store ship USS White Plains, *on 30 July 1979 in the South China Sea. (U.S. National Archives)*

their country by sea between the fall of Saigon in 1975 and the 1980s. More than 800,000 fled in the first six years, and altogether, perhaps 1.5 million escaped or tried to escape the newly reunified Vietnam. The original flow occurred after the communist takeover in South Vietnam and was composed of families linked in some way with the former regime. But the exodus grew in the following years with the worsening situation—the transformation of the South to socialism to the detriment of the private economy and the deterioration in relations with Cambodia and China, which ended in war in the early part of 1979. The composition of the refugees changed, too, by then including a large portion of ethnic Chinese (called Hoa), who for generations had prospered in trading and banking; other Hoa fled at this time from the North, through the Chinese border. The flow from the South continued after the 1979–1980 peak.

More or less illegal, the exodus encouraged corruption among officials who turned a blind eye to those leaving the country. The refugees embarked on various boats through the Gulf of Thailand and the South China Sea for perilous journeys, especially if they crossed pirates, who robbed, raped, and sometimes killed them. The neighboring countries—Malaysia, Hong Kong, Thailand, Singapore, Indonesia, and the Philippines—did not warmly welcome them. During the 1979 crisis, these countries announced that they would no longer accept refugees. Those who landed were housed in asylum camps pending relocation to third countries. For example, Pulau Bidong, an island off the northeast coast of Peninsular Malaysia, was a center for boat people for many years. After the June 1979 UN Geneva Conference, the UN High Commissioner for Refugees (UNHCR) got involved in resettlement projects, and Vietnam, for its part, accepted official emigration.

During the 1990s, as the domestic situation in Vietnam improved, the flow of boat people gradually receded. UNHCR encouraged a small relocation movement. The last camps were closed in the late 1990s when the refugees were relocated, mostly to North America, Western Europe, and Australasia.

HUGUES TERTRAIS

See also Indochina War (1964–1975), Second (Vietnam War); Sino-Vietnamese Relations; Sino-Vietnamese Wars; Vietnam, South (post-1945)

References:
Cargill, Mary Terrell, and Jade Quang Huynh, eds. 2000. *Voices of Vietnamese Boat People: Nineteen Narratives of Escape and Survival.* Jefferson, NC: McFarland.
Condoninas, Georges, and Richard Pottier. 1983. *Les réfugiés originaires de l'Asie du Sud-Est* [*Origins of the Refugees of Southeast Asia*]. Paris: La Documentation Française.

BOEDI OETAMA (BUDI UTOMO) (1908)
Harbinger of the Indonesian Nationalist Movement

Boedi Oetama (Budi Utomo in Javanese, meaning "high endeavor") was colonial Indonesia's first significant political association. Its focus was the strengthening and rejuvenation of Javanese aristocratic culture, but before being taken over by more radical organizations, it engaged seriously with the question of how Indonesian society should develop under colonialism.

In May 1908, Wahidin Soedirohoesodo founded Boedi Oetama. It was initially a student organization, but it soon became dominated by the lower echelons of the *priyayi,* Java's aristocratic-bureaucratic elite. The organization especially attracted people who were interested in the relationship between Eastern and Western culture and in the possibilities for some kind of synthesis that would reinvigorate Eastern society. Although it never challenged colonial rule and indeed was welcomed by some Dutch leaders as a sign of engagement between East and West, its aims implied an eventual end to the tutelary relationship between the Dutch and the Javanese. Its call to extend Western education in the Indies suggested that the Javanese would eventually replace the Dutch in at least some posts.

Boedi Oetama reached its membership peak of 10,000 in late 1909 and never developed a mass base. The later nationalist leader Tjipto Mangoenkoesoemo (1885–1943) was briefly a member of Boedi Oetama and argued unsuccessfully within it for a focus on mass education and for attention to the Netherlands Indies as a whole, rather than just Java. Short of funds and thoroughly outflanked by newer nationalist parties, Boedi Oetomo dissolved itself in 1935.

The anniversary of Boedi Oetomo's founding is celebrated in Indonesia as National Awakening Day, but the organization's focus on Java and its lack of a clear political platform have led many observers to describe it as a precursor to the nationalist movement rather than that movement's first expression.

ROBERT CRIBB

See also Colonialism; Education, Traditional Religious; Education, Western Secular; Ethical Policy (*Ethische Politiek*); Java; Nationalism and Independence Movements in Southeast Asia; Netherlands (Dutch) East Indies; *Priyayi*

References:
Nagazumi, Akira. 1972. *The Dawn of Indonesian Nationalism: The Early Years of the Budi Utomo, 1908–1918.* Tokyo: Institute of Developing Economies.

O'Malley, W. J. 1980. "Second Thoughts on Indonesian Nationalism." Pp. 601–613 in *Indonesia: Australian Perspectives.* Edited by J. J. Fox et al. Canberra: Australian National University.

BOMBAY BURMAH TRADING CORPORATION (BBTC)
Partner of British Imperialism

The Bombay Burmah Trading Corporation (BBTC) was a British-owned timber and trading firm derived from a company established in 1862. In that year, King Mindon (r. 1853–1878), whose government had recently been forced to abandon Lower Burma to the victorious troops of the British Indian Empire in 1856, gave the firm timber extraction rights in the Pyinmana area north of British-administered Lower Burma. In 1885, following years of suspicions and accusations, the king's government accused the BBTC of illegally exporting logs to avoid paying export duty owed to the Burmese state. The Hlutdaw, the king's council, imposed a fine on the company of 23 lakhs of rupees in August of that year. This prompted the corporation to seek the assistance of the British government's authorities in Rangoon and London. Pressure was then applied to reduce the fine, but before negotiations ended, the British imposed an ultimatum on the Burmese, to which they did not have time to respond. The result was war, and the BBTC entered Burmese nationalist historiography as the capitalist-imperialist engine of the country's colonialization and the ending of the Burmese monarchy. During the colonial period, the BBTC was one of many British firms that, in addition to dealing in timber, traded in other commodities, such as oil, rice, and various pulses for export abroad. The BBTC's operations in Burma were nationalized at independence in 1948, but the company continued to operate in other parts of Southeast Asia.

R. H. TAYLOR

See also Agency Houses, European; Anglo-Burmese Wars (1824–1826, 1852, 1885); British Burma; British India, Government of; Burma under British Colonial Rule; Colonialism; Hlutdaw; Imperialism; Konbaung Rulers and British Imperialism; Mindon (r. 1853–1878)

References:

Cady, John F. 1958. *A History of Modern Burma.* Ithaca, NY: Cornell University Press.

Pointon, A. G. 1964. *The Bombay-Burmah Trading Corporation, 1863–1963.* Southampton, UK: Millbrook Press.

BONIFACIO, ANDRES (1863–1897)
Proletarian Leader of the Philippine Revolution

Andres Bonifacio was the founder, organizer, and later supreme head of the Katipunan movement that started the revolution against the Spanish colonial regime in the Philippines. Filipinos venerate him as a national hero, the "Father of the Revolution," and more specifically as a plebeian hero, "the Great Plebeian," who epitomized the proletarian and mass character of the Revolution of 1896 (Agoncillo 1963: 1). When Bonifacio lost the leadership of the rebel forces to General Emilio Aguinaldo (1869–1964) in March 1897, it meant, in the words of a prominent Filipino historian, "the end of a share for the lower and non-ilustrado classes in the directing of the Revolution" (Corpuz 1989, 2: 204).

Andres Bonifacio was born in Tondo, Manila, on 30 November 1863. His parents were poor, and he had to work to earn his living. He attended primary school and one year of high school, but when his parents died, he had to quit school. He earned his livelihood first as a peddler and later as a clerk-messenger for a commercial firm and as a salesman. Bonifacio, who was largely self-educated, was reportedly fond of reading and had read José Rizal's (1861–1896) novels and books about the French Revolution (1792–1802). He married twice; his first wife died of leprosy, and in 1892, he married Gregoria de Jesus, daughter of a local official in Kaloocan.

When the Spanish government arrested Rizal and deported him to Mindanao in July 1892, Bonifacio, together with others, founded the Katipunan. Its aims were, to some extent, the same as those of Rizal's Liga Filipina, namely, fighting religious fanaticism, defending the poor and oppressed, and morally uplifting the people. But in addition, the organization intended to separate the Philippine Islands from Spain by means of a revolution. The Katipunan was a secretive society with a cellular organiza-

tional structure. In 1893 or 1894, Bonifacio became the *supremo* (supreme leader) of the Katipunan. Initially, the members were of lower-middle-class background, and during the first two years, only a few dozen people were initiated as members. But after January 1896, the number of followers increased, running into the thousands.

In August 1896, after the Spaniards had discovered the existence of the Katipunan and started a reign of terror, Bonifacio and his fellow leaders fled to the town of Balintawak in the province of Bulacan. During a mass meeting, the *katipuneros* decided to raise the flag of revolution. In Manila and the surrounding provinces, thousands of people joined the movement. Groups of revolutionaries attacked Spanish garrisons in and around Manila, but they were repelled and, during a Spanish counteroffensive, defeated. In December 1896, Bonifacio went to the province of Cavite, where the revolutionaries under the military leadership of Aguinaldo had been much more successful against the Spanish forces.

The revolutionary movement in Cavite had evolved out of several Katipunan town chapters, two of which had become the strongest—notably, the Magdalo group in the town of Kawit, led by Aguinaldo, and the Magdiwang group in the town of Noveleta, led by a relative of Bonifacio. Soon after Bonifacio's arrival in Cavite, tension arose between him and leaders of the Magdalo group, especially General Aguinaldo. The two men were basically competing for the leadership of the revolution. Bonifacio still clung to the organizational structure of the Katipunan, of which he was the head, whereas Aguinaldo had become the leader of a much larger revolutionary movement.

In late March 1897, when a Spanish army was marching against Cavite, the revolutionary leaders held a meeting in a house in Tejeros. During this meeting, they decided to replace the Katipunan by a revolutionary government, and they elected Aguinaldo as president of the new government. Bonifacio refused to accept these decisions, and he withdrew with his followers. Fearing a plot against the new government, Aguinaldo ordered Bonifacio's arrest. A trial was held, and Bonifacio was found guilty of treason and sentenced to death. He was executed on 10 May 1897.

Historians have interpreted and portrayed Bonifacio in different ways, and the discussion persists. Teodoro Agoncillo (1954) considered him the proletarian leader of the revolution—the leader of the masses who was tragically defeated in a competiton for power with Aguinaldo. Renato Constantino (1975) interpreted the Bonifacio-Aguinaldo conflict in terms of a class struggle between the lower classes and the landowning *ilustrado* (indigenous intelligentsia; lit. Spanish: "enlightened one") elite, depicting Bonifacio's execution as the victory for the elite. Reynaldo Ileto (1979) saw Bonifacio as the heir to an older religious folk tradition—the *pasyon,* or story of the suffering and redemption of Christ—with which the Catholic Filipinos had strongly identified themselves. He argued that Bonifacio and the katipuneros expected that independence for the Philippines would mean more than political liberation, that it would usher in a new era in which the world would become "whole" again. Glenn May (1997) pointed out that very little is known about Bonifacio, that publications attributed to him are surrounded with numerous doubts, and that it is probable they were forged. He saw much of the early-twentieth-century Philippine literature about Bonifacio as a conscious attempt to bolster the man's stature as a national hero. He argued that historians had to admit that little is known with certainty about the man behind the heroic myth. May's analysis, however, has been strongly contested by nationalistic Filipino historians (Reyes Churchill 1997).

WILLEM WOLTERS

See also Aguinaldo, Emilio (1869–1964); Katipunan; La Liga Filipina; *Noli Me Tangere* (1887) and *El Filibusterismo* (1891); Peasant Uprisings and Protest Movements in Southeast Asia; Philippine Revolution (1896–1898); Philippine War of Independence (1899–1902); Philippines under Spanish Colonial Rule (ca. 1560s–1898); Rizal, José (1861–1896)

References:
Agoncillo, Teodoro A. 1954. *The Revolt of the Masses: The Story of Bonifacio and the Katipunan.* Quezon City: University of the Philippines.
Constantino, Renato C., with the collaboration of Letizia R. Constantino. 1975. *The Philippines: A Past Revisited.* Quezon City, the Philippines: Renato C. Constantino.
Corpuz, O. D. 1989. *The Roots of the Filipino Nation.* 2 vols. Quezon City, the Philippines: Aklahi Foundation.
Ileto, Reynaldo Clemeña. 1979. *Pasyon and Revolution: Popular Movements in the Philippines, 1840–1910.* Quezon City, the Philippines: Ateneo de Manila University Press.
May, Glenn Anthony. 1997. *Inventing a Hero: The Posthumous Re-creation of Andres Bonifacio.* Quezon City, the Philippines: New Day Publishers.
Reyes Churchill, Bernardita, ed. 1997. *Determining the Truth: The Story of Andres Bonifacio.* Manila: Manila Studies Association.

BORNEO

The island of Borneo, the third largest island in the world, lies at the heart of Southeast Asia. Covering an area of some 750,000 square kilometers, the island is divided politically among the three states of Malaysia, Indonesia, and Brunei—the Malaysian states of Sabah and Sarawak; Brunei Darussalam; and the Indonesian states of East, Central, South, and West Kalimantan. The island is renowned for its important ecological zones, in particular the expanses of tropical rain forest. Except in certain coastal zones, the population is light and densities are low; recent estimates suggest a total population of about 16 million (Cleary and Eaton 1995). Ethnically and culturally diverse, the indigenous Dayak communities have been augmented by the in-migration of Malays, Europeans, Javanese, and Chinese groups over the centuries. Alongside traditional systems of shifting cultivation ("slash-and-burn" farming), overexploitation of the island's forest reserves through logging, coupled with the search for hydrocarbons and other minerals, has created rapid economic growth as well as serious environmental degradation. Such problems, together with political conflict, have meant that the island displays an uneasy coexistence between the apparent simplicity and stability of native groups and the rapacious pace of economic and environmental change.

Most of the island lies within the broad equatorial monsoon belt, and three broad ecological zones have historically dominated patterns of settlement, migration, and historical development—the coastal and estuarine zone, the river valleys, and the interior. The coastal and estuarine zone, often flanked by mangrove swamps, provides the location for the chief cities of Borneo—Kota Kinabalu, Bandar Seri Begawan, Kuching, Pontianak, and Samarinda. The coastal trade was vital for the early growth of such cities, and the wide river estuaries provided important means of access to the interior. This coastal zone was a prime area of settlement and colonization for the powerful Malay groups of Borneo. Settlement, trade, and economic development penetrated inland along the great river valleys of the Rajang, Kapuas, and Kayan. Colonization was focused along the rivers, especially at river confluences, with longhouse communities of groups such as the Ibans and Kayans extending along their banks. The interior of the island is dominated by tropical rain forest. Rich and diverse flora and fauna have long provided a livelihood for the range of indigenous tribal groups (known collectively by anthropologists as Dayaks) who practice shifting cultivation and trade in a range of jungle products with coastal peoples. Isolated groups of hunter-gatherers (the Penan are perhaps the best known) are interspersed with rich tablelands dominated by wet-rice cultivation.

The early peopling of Borneo is not easy to reconstruct because of the relative paucity of archaeological research that has been done. The Niah Caves system in Sarawak has provided evidence of human occupation dating back to at least 40,000 B.P., and subsequent research suggests a mixing of Austronesian and Austro-Mongoloid groups in the early settling of the island. Stone Age findings are concentrated in the coastal areas, and it is unlikely that metal came to be widely used on the island before the sixth or seventh century C.E. By the end of the first millennium C.E., the coastal regions were well settled, and there is plenty of evidence of trade between Borneo and the rest of Southeast Asia, notably China. It is the development and amplification of that trade from about 1000 C.E. that gives us an insight into how the economies and societies of Borneo developed. Archaeological finds, coupled with documentary records from Chinese sources, suggest that a range of jungle products from Borneo found their way onto the international market. The Chinese and Malays traded with coastal communities, who in turn sourced their products from the river and interior communities of the island. We know that the maritime empires of Majapahit and Melaka traded with groups on Borneo, and as Islam moved westward in the region onto the coast of Borneo, religious and trading connections were strengthened. Although the coast was the main focus, traders and their goods found their way deep into the interior.

When Antonio Pigafetta (b. 1480), the chronicler of Ferdinand Magellan's round-the-world voyage, visited the city of Brunei in northwest Borneo in 1521, he found a rich, socially diverse, and prosperous trading state that thrived as an entrepôt port. Skilled in the collection and processing of a range of products from the interior of Borneo—rattans, camphor, precious stones—traders exchanged these on the international market for textiles, ceramics, and metalwork and built the city's prosperity on that trade. Other cities followed a similar pattern, and the maps of the island that appear from the sixteenth century onward show the emergence of cities such as Brunei, Succadana, and Bandjarmasin as trading cities that thrived on their ability to control and channel the products of the interior. Their command of the coasts and estuaries of Borneo, as well as the cohesive influence of Islam, resulted in a rich and diverse set of Malay-Muslim city-states adept at trading, negotiating, and forming alliances to further their ends. This was the scenario that greeted the first European traders and explorers in the region: Borneo was not a primitive and undeveloped island.

In addition to general maritime trade, the search for minerals was an important catalyst for change. Gold in particular proved an important attraction for many Chinese miners, especially in western Borneo. In the early nineteenth century, the region was the largest gold producer in Asia, and the mining population in the goldfields between Sambas and Pontianak may have exceeded 30,000 (Jackson 1970). There, the powerful Chinese *kongsi* created a distinctive cultural and social landscape linked to specifically Chinese systems of organization and extraction. Many Chinese miners would later migrate into Sarawak, where the Bau goldfields were to contribute to the local economy.

European traders and explorers had sought commercial and military success on the island from the early seventeenth century onward, but their real interest lay elsewhere in the region. The Dutch, taking time from their activities in Java, established trading factories episodically on the island, as did the English, but met with only limited success. It was not until the nineteenth century that more concerted European intervention on the island developed. In essence, in the course of the nineteenth century, Borneo was divided up between the British and the Dutch. For many Europeans, it appeared to be an exotic, rich, and captivating land. As an island of wealthy Malay potentates, of "noble savages," of rich, diverse, and captivating natural treasures, it attracted a whole range of merchants and adventurers seeking their fortunes in the East. James Brooke (1803–1868) was one of the most powerful and successful of such individuals. From his arrival in Kuching in 1839, he expanded his personal fiefdom, taking over the lands of the moribund Bruneian empire and expanding northward to create Sarawak. By the 1880s, the establishment of a chartered company to govern North Borneo, together with the consolidation of British influence in Brunei, meant that much of northwest Borneo fell within the orbit of the British Empire. The Dutch, alarmed by this expansion of British interests, moved to consolidate control over their territories in Kalimantan and sought to strengthen their tenuous hold in central and eastern Borneo. By the early twentieth century, imperial powers controlled most of the island, albeit without any especially strong military presence.

The economic and social impact of European colonial authority on Borneo was mixed. Although the political power and authority of traditional leaders was compromised, the huge size and geographic difficulties of the island meant that colonial authority was, at best, only partial. Native rebellions in the early years of the twentieth century, notably the Mat Salleh revolt in North Borneo between 1895 and 1905, were crushed, but such armed revolt was exceptional. The expansion of mining (particularly the search for oil in eastern Kalimantan and Brunei), the development of plantation crops (notably rubber and tobacco), and attempts to open up communications both on the island and with neighboring regions (the steamship companies, for example, on both coast and river) gave some impetus to economic development. Attempts to develop schooling and health facilities also were made in the colonial period, although the extent to which such efforts penetrated much beyond the coastal and estuarine regions is difficult to estimate. The number of Europeans on the island was always tiny; the impress of the colonial government was relatively light. The much fabled wealth of Borneo turned out to be largely illusory given the huge costs of development, especially in the interior. For both the Dutch and British, the priority was to govern as lightly and, ultimately, as cheaply as possible.

Demands for independence elsewhere in Southeast Asia were especially strong, but in Borneo, ethnic and social diversity, coupled with the constraints of geography, meant that concerted independence parties faced numerous obstacles. With the establishment of the Republic of Indonesia in 1949, the Kalimantan states became four provinces of Indonesia. In Sarawak and North Borneo, the move toward independence was more complex. Both became Crown Colonies in 1946, as their previous regimes—Sarawak under the Brookes and North Borneo administered by the chartered company—were anachronistic and became untenable after the Pacific War (1941–1945). The concept of associating the British territories in Borneo with Malaya had been a part of postimperial strategy for some years. The independence of Malaya in 1957 made the position of Brunei, North Borneo, and Sarawak increasingly acute. A 1962 coup in Brunei, seeking to link together Sarawak, North Borneo, and Brunei, failed, and in 1963, North Borneo (renamed Sabah) and Sarawak joined the newly created Federation of Malaysia. Brunei remained outside the federation and became a fully independent state in 1984.

Today, the island of Borneo remains a place of striking contrasts. Although large areas of the interior remain characterized, as they have been for hundreds of years, by extensive tropical rain forests and traditional indigenous cultures, the pace of both economic and environmental change in recent decades has been rapid. International logging companies have made major inroads, bringing wealth and employment as well as environmental damage and cultural change. International scientific interest in the consequences of tropical deforestation has put Bornean research high on the international agenda. In-migration from the densely populated provinces of Indonesia, accelerated through the transmigration program, has brought indigenous Borneans into conflict with their Javanese, Madurese, or Sumatran compatriots. The island is the scene of major international investment in resource extraction. Like the timber business, the hydrocarbon industry has been a catalyst for change. The pace of change on the island has never been greater, and the conflicts between traditional and modern, between the old and the new, have never been sharper.

MARK CLEARY

See also Anglo-Dutch Relations in Southeast Asia (Seventeenth to Twentieth Centuries); Bajau; Bandjarmasin (Banjermasin) Sultanate; Brooke, James, and Sarawak; Brunei (Sixteenth to Nineteenth Centuries); Brunei Ethnic Minorities; Brunei Malays; Brunei Oil and Gas Industry; Brunei Rebellion (December 1962); Chinese Gold-Mining Communities in Western Borneo; Dayaks; East Malaysian Ethnic Minorities; Ecological Setting of Southeast Asia; Human Prehistory of Southeast Asia; Islam in Southeast Asia; Jungle/Forest Products; Kutai (Koetei); Majapahit (1293–ca. 1520s); Malays; Malaysia (1963); Mat Salleh Rebellion (1894–1905); Melaka; Metal Age Cultures in Southeast Asia; Neolithic Period of Southeast Asia; Niah Caves (Sarawak); Oil and Petroleum; Sambas and Pontianak Sultanates; Sarawak and Sabah (North Borneo); Swidden Agriculture

References:
Amarjit Kaur. 1997. *Economic Change in East Malaysia: Sabah and Sarawak since 1850.* London: Macmillan.
Borneo Research Bulletin. Annual publication of the Borneo Research Council, Williamsburg, VA.
Cleary, Mark, and Peter Eaton. 1995. *Borneo: Change and Development.* Kuala Lumpur: Oxford University Press.
Cranbrook, Earl of, and David Edwards. 1994. *A Tropical Rainforest: The Nature of Biodiversity in Borneo at Belalong, Brunei.* London: Royal Geographical Society.
Heidhues, Mary Somers. 2003. *Gold Diggers, Farmers, and Traders in Pontianak and the "Chinese Districts" of West Kalimantan, Indonesia.* Ithaca, NY: Cornell University Southeast Asia Program.
Jackson, James C. 1970. *Chinese in the West Borneo Goldfields: A Study in Cultural Geography.* Occasional Papers in Geography no. 15. Hull, England: University of Hull Press.
King, Victor. 1992. *The Best of Borneo Travel.* Singapore: Oxford University Press.
———. 1993. *The Peoples of Borneo.* London: Routledge.
King, Victor, and Michael Parnwell, eds. 1990. *Margins and Minorities: The Peripheral Areas and Peoples of Malaysia.* Hull, England: University of Hull Press.
Lindblad, J. Thomas. 1988. *Between Dayak and Dutch: The Economic History of Southeast Kalimantan, 1880–1942.* Vol. 134 of Verhandelingen van het Koninklijk Instituut voor Taal-, Land- en Volkenkunde. Dordrecht, The Netherlands, and Providence, RI: Foris Publications.
Ooi Keat Gin. 1997. *Of Free Trade and Native Interests: The Brookes and the Economic Development of Sarawak, 1841–1941.* Kuala Lumpur: Oxford University Press.

BOROBUDUR
A Buddhist Prayer in Stone

Borobudur, on the island of Java (near the town of Magelang), is a monument with a complex architectural history. It was primarily designed between the reign of the Sanjaya dynasty (732–ca. 882 C.E.) and the end of the eighth century, as a pyramid to support a Hindu temple. Meanwhile, a Buddhist dynasty, the Sailendra (752–ca. 832 C.E.), was set up in the south of the island. Initially practicing mainly the rituals of the Lesser Vehicle (the belief that each individual is responsible for his or her own salvation), the dynasty adopted the cult of the five Jina (Buddhas who were never born but have existed for all eternity) from about 790 C.E. This new doctrine was a great success and probably was accompanied by a military campaign against the Sanjaya that was also highly successful. When the Sailendra took over the site of Borobudur, the monument was in an unfinished state, having only two lower terraces of the pyramid that was intended to support the temple. These two stages were built with perspective effects meant to increase the apparent height of the building; in addition, the width of the staircase leading to the

Borobudur Temple, Java, Indonesia. (Corel Corporation)

third level was narrower than the width of the next lowest level.

The Sailendra decided to resume the work but changed the character of the temple, which would become Buddhist. One of the first acts of the new master of works was to suppress the perspective effects, which in various forms were the mark of Hindu architecture of the period (the temples of Dieng and Gedong Songo comprised such forms). The worksite experienced several collapses that necessitated important alterations in the architectural program, leading to the present monument.

Staircases were cut into the axes of the base, and they were modified several times because of the relative fragility of the structure. In a second phase—which was never finished (like the first phase left incomplete by the Sanjaya)—the edifice had at the center of its summit a rather rude structure. Since this structure collapsed several times, the base had to be significantly enlarged, completely obliterating the already partially sculpted reliefs illustrating the Buddhist text *Karmavibhanga*.

On top of the base stood four galleries enclosed on their exteriors by balustrades supporting niches, in which were placed statues depicting one or another of the five Jinas; they corresponded to the cardinal directions with the fifth and more important considered to reside in the center. The retaining walls on each of these galleries were decorated with reliefs, which, on the first gallery, were divided into two registers. On the upper register, beginning at the eastern staircase and proceeding in a southerly direction, the reliefs illustrate the life of the historical Buddha until his arrival at Bénares; the lower reliefs, readable in the same direction, depict previous lives of the Buddha.

The reliefs of the second and third galleries illustrate a text, the *Gandavyuha,* that recounts the quest for enlightenment undertaken by Sudhana, the son of a rich merchant. These reliefs do not imply that they should be read consecutively, since they contain numerous repetitions; it is thus probable that they were intended for something other than the education of pilgrims. These images contributed to the overall significance of the edifice (a practice that was the rule from the fourteenth century onward in East Java). Some reliefs illustrating the earlier lives of the Buddha (with numerous gaps) were added between the ground level and the lower cornice of the balustrade of the first gallery; their addition certainly had a goal quite distinct from simply being read, for that cannot be done unless one bends over. The reliefs of the fourth gallery illustrate another text, the *Samantabhadrapranidhana,* also with some repetitions and omissions.

The upper level supports the superstructure of the edifice, consisting of three nearly circular terraces on which have been built 72 latticed stupas, each containing a Buddha statue. There are 32 with lattices in lozenge form on the first terrace, 24 with lozenge-shaped lattices on the second, and 16 with square lattices around the central stupa on the third terrace. This latter edifice, which seems to be solid but in fact contains two empty chambers or hollow spaces in its interior, was first thought to contain a statue of an unfinished Buddha, but when other unfinished Buddha images were found in the fill of the monument, this hypothesis was abandoned. It is probable that the crowning structure symbolizes the essence of Buddhism, the 72 Buddhas are those of the future, and the hollow spaces in the central stupa represent the true essence of the world.

In 1955, a serious cave-in took place on the north wall. Fortunately, the incident occurred at night and without injuries, but it revealed the instability of the monument. The director of the Archaeological Service, Soekmono, launched an appeal that led to several meetings in 1965 and resulted in a restoration project that the UN Educational, Scientific, and Cultural Organization (UNESCO) entrusted to C. Voûte.

This project only restored the four quadrangular galleries. The upper terrace, which had been restored by the Netherlander Theodoor Van Erp in 1911, was judged to be in sufficiently good condition that it did not need to be redone. Project managers decided to interfere with the nearby section of the base as little as possible, electing instead to simply dismantle some rainwater drains. The four galleries were disassembled and rebuilt on reinforced concrete foundations. One difficulty was experienced in this reconstruction: Van Erp had already dealt with this part of the structure, preserving defor-

mities caused by such factors as the leaning of the walls of the ruin. It was possible through research to attempt to restore them to their original form, however, thereby considerably reducing the width of the galleries and making it less convenient to walk through them; also, the galleries had been restored according to the layout that Van Erp had provided. The dismantled stones were a given complex treatment that consisted of drying each stone and setting the facing on a sheet of lead, but the most important task was the installation of two vertical layers of waterproofing behind the facing.

Borobudur is perhaps the finest Buddhist monument representing the architectural genius of the Sailendra dynasty. Although the reliefs are based on Indian models, the sculpturing work clearly reflects Javanese artistic traditions.

JACQUES DUMARÇAY
TRANSLATED BY JOHN N. MIKSIC

See also Buddhism; Buddhism, Theravada; Hindu-Buddhist Period of Southeast Asia; *Jatakas;* Java; Monumental Art of Southeast Asia; Sailendras

References:
Bernet-Kempers, A. J. 1959. *Ancient Indonesian Art.* Amsterdam: C. P. J. van der Peet.

De Casparis, J. G. 1956. *Selected Inscriptions from the Seventh to the Ninth Century A.D. (Prasasti Indonesia II).* Bandung, Indonesia: Masa Baru.

De Vink, J. 1912. *Report on an Excavation on the East Side of the Borobudur.* Leiden.

Krom, N. J. 1927. *Archeological Description of Barabudur.* 2 vols. The Hague: Martinus Nijhoff.

Stutterheim, T. 1956. *Studies in Indonesian Archaeology.* The Hague: Martinus Nijhoff.

Van Erp, T. 1931. *Barabudur Architectural Description.* The Hague: Martinus Nijhoff.

BOSCH, JOHANNES

See Van den Bosch, Count Johannes (1780–1844)

BOSE, SUBHAS CHANDRA (1897–1945)

Indian Nationalist Hero

Hailed as the "Netaji," or Great Leader, at the height of his political career, Subhas Chandra

Bose was regarded by his admirers as almost an equal to Mahatma Gandhi (1869–1948) in the hierarchy of Indian nationalist heroes. According to a biographer, Bose was a charismatic man who provoked extreme reactions. His admirers idolized him for his style of leadership and fiery oratorical skills; his detractors regarded him as an ambitious man with authoritarian inclinations.

In 1942, he took the reins of leadership and revitalized the deflated Indian National Army (INA, Azad Hind Fauj). His involvement with the INA was motivated by both idealistic and pragmatic reasons. The INA not only served as a vehicle for Bose's burning ambition to prize India from British imperial rule, it was also supposedly formed (as revealed in the INA trials in 1946) to save thousands of Indian prisoners of war who faced starvation unless they organized themselves to fight on the side of the Japanese in the Pacific War (1941–1945). In the early 1940s, with prominent nationalist leaders placed in jail following the abortive Quit India movement, Bose became the most visible symbol of the Indian nationalist resistance to British rule.

Born in Cuttack, Bengal, Bose received his early education in Calcutta. He was influenced very early on by the philosophical teachings of Vivekenanda and Aurobindo Ghosh. He proceeded to England in 1919 and earned a place to read a tripos in moral sciences at Cambridge University. However, he was soon influenced by political developments in India. He abandoned his studies in 1921 to return home to participate in the nationalist movement spearheaded by Gandhi. During the 1920s, Bose was to spend several years in jail for his revolutionary activities. But as he got deeply involved in the nationalist movement, he became increasingly disillusioned with the nonviolent Gandhian approach.

His political differences with Gandhi cost him the presidency of the Bengal Provincial Congress Committee in 1939, where he was subsequently barred from holding elective office for three years. In 1941, while under house arrest, Bose escaped his British jailers and surfaced in Berlin. Having secured the support of Adolf Hitler (1889–1945), dictator of Nazi Germany, Bose then traveled to Southeast Asia, where, with the help of the Japanese, he entrenched himself as the leader of the Indian Independence League (IIL) and the INA. Under his stewardship, both the civilian arm (represented by the IIL) and the military arm (the INA) were reorganized and expanded. The prime objective of the INA, as envisioned by Bose, was to launch a "second front" in India's struggle for independence. Aided by the Japanese, Bose went on to organize and head the Free India Provisional Government in 1943.

The political career of Subhas Chandra Bose came to an abrupt end in August 1945 when he was fatally wounded in a plane crash in Taiwan. Despite the brevity of his political life, Bose was remembered as the man who offered an alternative approach to the Indian independence movement through his convictions and the way in which he went about realizing them.

TAN TAI YONG

See also Imphal-Kohima, Battle of (1944); Indian National Army (INA); Nationalism and Independence Movements in Southeast Asia

References:

Bhargava, Moti Lal. 1982. *Netaji Subhas Chandra Bose in South-East Asia and India's Liberation War 1943–1945*. Kerala and New Delhi: Vishwavidya Publishers.
Netaji Research Bureau. 1962. *Crossroads, Being the Works of Subhas Chandra Bose*. Calcutta and London: Asia Publishing House.

BOURBON REFORMS

The establishment of the Bourbon dynasty in Spain with the accession of Philip V (r. 1700–1746), grandson of Louis XIV (r. 1643–1715) of France, opened the country to the ideas of the Enlightenment. It heralded a prolonged period of reform under his successors, particularly during the reign of Charles III (r. 1759–1788). In the Philippines, the eighteenth century was distinguished by attempts to diversify trade, develop domestic resources more intensively, and overhaul public administration. Reforms were aimed at increasing economic productivity through state-directed enterprise and fostering commerce by a more liberal stance toward foreign merchants. In his General Economic Development Plan of 1779, Governor-General José Basco y Vargas (t. 1778–1787) proposed incentives for developing the islands' natural resources, favored further Chinese immigration, and recommended changes to the "galleon trade." The Plan for Reforming the Government of the Philippines, devised by his successor, Felix Berenguer de Marquina (t. 1788–1793), advocated opening Manila to foreign shipping, a policy that was effectively accomplished under the administration of Rafael María de Aguilar y Ponce de León (t. 1793–1806). In fact, the archipelago did not lack either readily exploitable resources (including gold, silver, and base metals) or suitable land for the cultivation of commercial crops (such as pepper, nutmeg, clove, cinnamon, sugarcane, tobacco, dyewoods, and timber). Rather, their neglect was due more to a merchant class grown rich and complacent on the easy profits of the monopolistic Manila-Acapulco trade. And just as the economic recovery of eighteenth-century Spain was greatly facilitated by the state's role in supporting the activities of joint-stock companies and economic societies, so these institutions similarly played a part in the development of the Philippines.

Proposals for a joint-stock company to initiate trade between Spain and the Philippines had first been raised at the beginning of the century, but it was not until 10 March 1785 that the Real Compañía de Filipinas was established. The company was granted an exclusive charter to sail directly to Manila and other Asian ports, and it had permission to carry merchandise to and from the Americas; its first vessel sailed from Cádiz on 1 October 1785. In the Philippines, the company attempted to develop agriculture by purchasing local products such as sugarcane, cotton, and indigo; planting mulberry trees; and introducing skilled labor to cultivate pepper. Most of these ventures, however, proved unsustainable, and the company's activities were already seriously in decline by 1789.

The company was finally dissolved in 1834. The reasons for its failure were almost as varied as its activities: the chaotic conditions in Spain from 1808 to 1814; the uncertainties of the American trade during the War of Independence (1775–1783); the opposition of competitors; and the complications of simultaneously being a product's investor, producer, and carrier. In its final years, growing debts, internal dissension, the continuing hostility of galleon traders, and disputes in Spain further hampered its activities. Yet the company did provide a new sense of direction for Philippine agriculture, drawing attention away from the Pacific to Europe, breaking the monopoly of the Manila galleon, and linking the archipelago to the contemporary commercial world.

Equally instrumental to the development of the Philippine economy was the Sociedad Económica de Amigos del País de Manila, established on 26 April 1781 and modeled after similar organizations in Spain and England. Composed of a small group of educated people, it established committees to investigate the natural history of the country and to promote local agriculture, industry, and trade. In particular, it organized the translation and publication of the latest scientific literature from Europe; convened regular meetings to disseminate such material; and offered prizes to cultivators, farmers, and inventors. Despite the society's promising start, however, interest soon began to flag, and it was dissolved in 1809. Revived by royal orders in 1811 and 1813, it played only a minor role during the nineteenth century. In the long run, however, the society was much more successful in making a wider public aware of the potentialities for economic enterprise in the archipelago. It was only after the colony's integration into the world commodity market in the 1820s that such ventures became more viable commercial propositions.

The colonial administration was also a target of reform during that period. Finances were placed on a sounder footing with the introduction of an *intendencia* (monitoring) system in 1784, the overhaul of government monopolies, and the creation of new ones. The most significant measure concerned the establishment of a tobacco monopoly in 1782 that confined cultivation to designated regions where no alternative crop could be grown and where even producers were forbidden from consuming their own products. Monitoring all these monopolies required the concomitant creation of a custom's agency, but that agency's troopers were often ill paid and easily bribed. The result was rampant smuggling. However, these reforms did generally prove effective in raising revenues, and the tobacco monopoly in particular became the colony's single most important source of funds after the loss of the *situado* (the yearly subsidy sent to the Spanish colonial administration in the Philippines from the Spanish treasury in Mexico) with Mexican independence (1821).

Despite the more modern character of many of these measures, however, mercantilism remained the governing paradigm of the Bourbon monarchy, and colonies were only considered to exist for the benefit of the metropolis. Overlooking the interests of the indigenes in the pursuit of enriching the metropolis sowed the seeds of discontent that subsequently evolved into nationalistic aspirations for independence toward the closing years of the nineteenth century.

GREG BANKOFF

See also Galleon Trade; Manila; Philippines under Spanish Colonial Rule (ca. 1560s–1898); Tobacco

References:

Cunningham, Charles. 1919. *The Audiencia in the Spanish Colonies; as Illustrated by the Audiencia of Manila (1583–1800).* Berkeley: University of California Press.

Cushner, Nicholas. 1971. *Spain in the Philippines: From Conquest to Revolution.* Quezon City: Institute of Philippine Culture, Ateneo de Manila University.

De Jesus, Edilberto. 1980. *The Tobacco Monopoly in the Philippines: Bureaucratic Enterprise and Social Change, 1766–1882.* Quezon City, the Philippines: Ateneo de Manila University Press.

Legarda, Benito. 1999. *After the Galleons: Foreign Trade, Economic Change and Entrepreneurship in the Nineteenth-Century Philippines.* Center for Southeast Asian Studies Monograph 18. Madison, WI: Center for Southeast Asian Studies.

Schurz, William. 1939. *The Manila Galleon.* New York: Dutton.

BOWRING TREATY (1855)

See Bowring, Sir John (1792–1872)

BOWRING, SIR JOHN (1792–1872)
Advocate of Free Trade

Sir John Bowring was a British diplomat who succeeded in negotiating with King Mongkut (Rama IV, r. 1851–1868) of Siam (Thailand) to sign a treaty opening Siam to Western commerce and culture in the middle of the nineteenth century. Bowring was a journal editor in the 1820s. During the 1830s and 1840s, he served as a member of Parliament and supported a free trade policy. In 1849, he took up a diplomatic career and was appointed British consul at Canton (Guangzhou) and superintendent of trade in China. In 1854, he assumed the governorship of Hong Kong.

Bowring was chosen by the British government to travel to Bangkok in 1855 as head of a government mission, rather than as a representative of the British East India Company (EIC). The main purpose of his mission was to persuade King Mongkut to open up Siam to Western trade after the British had failed to persuade King Rama III (r. 1824–1851), Mongkut's predecessor, to adopt a liberal trade policy.

Bowring was very well received by Mongkut, who recognized the power of Western colonialism and realized that Siam had to change its foreign policy if the kingdom was to avoid the same fate as Burma (Myanmar), defeated by the British in the war of 1824 to 1826. In the Bowring Treaty, signed in 1855, Siam agreed to adopt a free trade policy and allow the British to do business without intervention. Import and export taxes were levied at a fixed low level; in addition, British subjects were given extraterritorial rights (Wyatt 1984: 183–184). Even though the Bowring Treaty put Siam in a disadvantageous position vis-à-vis the Western powers, it undoubtedly helped save the kingdom from colonization and enabled Siam to develop into a modern state in terms of foreign trade and relations.

SUD CHONCHIRDSIN

See also Anglo-Burmese Wars (1824–1826, 1852, 1885); British Interests in Southeast Asia; Free Trade; French Ambitions in Southeast Asia; Konbaung Rulers and British Imperialism; Nguyễn Emperors and French Imperialism; Preservation of Siam's Political Independence; Reforms and Modernization in Siam

References:

Tarling, Nicholas, ed. 1992. *The Cambridge History of Southeast Asia.* Vol. 2. Cambridge: Cambridge University Press.

Wyatt, David K. 1984. *Thailand: A Short History.* New Haven, CT: Yale University Press.

BRIGGS PLAN
Cutting the Lifeline

The Malayan Emergency in British-ruled Malaya was declared in June 1948 in response to attempts by the mainly Chinese-dominated Malayan Communist Party (MCP) to overthrow British colonial rule. The communists launched a campaign of terror and sabotage with a spate of murders and destruction of rubber trees and tin mine equipment; the communists' objective was to cripple the colonial economy (rubber and tin) and, in the ensuing economic collapse and social chaos, to seize power. When the state of Emergency entered its third year in 1950, the British government announced the appointment of Lieutenant General Sir Harold Briggs to plan, coordinate, and direct the anticommunist operations. The Briggs Plan was but one of a variety of strategies—military, political, socioeconomic, and psychological warfare—employed by the British colonial government in countering the communist insurgency. One of the major features of these operations, which had already been implemented before Briggs arrived, was the resettlement of thousands of Chinese squatters who lived near the jungle fringes and were thought to provide the communist insurgents with their primary source of food, assistance, and information. Briggs restructured the plan more thoroughly by coordinating the civil, army, and police authorities. But before he had completed two years of service, ill health forced him to return to Britain. Ultimately, however, the plan that he drafted succeeded in disrupting the communists' "masses organizations" (min yuen) and isolating resettlement areas (later known as New Villages) from the communist insurgents.

At the height of the resettlement program in 1954, some 500,000 men, women, and children, 85 percent of whom were Chinese, were resettled in the New Villages (Stubbs 1989: 102). In 1952, expenditures on the New Villages amounted to $43.6 million Malayan; in 1954, the figure rose to $49.4 million (Stubbs 1989: 109–110). The sites of the New Villages were carefully surveyed and developed. They were located near main roads and were formed by extending the limits of existing towns; they were also enclosed by protective barbed-wire fences. The lands were provided by state governments and were usually surrounded by valuable estates or smallholdings. The New Villages looked like concentration camps, and each had its own police barracks, stations, and watchtowers. The movements of the New Villagers and their visitors were carefully checked at the gates each time they entered or exited. A curfew was imposed from 7:00 P.M. to 6:00 A.M. For those residents who gained their livelihood by working outside the New Villages on rubber estates, smallholdings, or tin mines, the curfew restrictions were rather frustrating, as they had to endure long delays each day caused by security checks at the gates. The New Villagers were allowed to form their own home guards to help the police protect and defend their areas, and by the end of 1952, more than 150,000 Chinese and Malay home guards were defending over 2,000 settlements (Stubbs 1989: 158). Many of these home guard troops were armed with shotguns.

The New Villagers were provided with normal social services. Roads and drains were laid out, wooden houses were built, wells were dug, and latrines were erected. Force was initially used to remove squatters from their land. Police screened these individuals, and then their huts were demolished and burned down. The squatters were transported in trucks to the new sites, escorted by British soldiers or local police. Gradually, shops and schools were opened and medical services were provided in the New Villages. Chinese-speaking officers were put in charge of the settlements, and even Christian missionaries helped in resettlement work.

Since the squatters were illegal occupants of the land, and since the communists sought out squatter farmers as a source of recruits, information, and food and medical supplies, attempts were made to provide each family with legally authorized land and thus to sever the lifeline of the communists. But this plan ran into trouble. The Malay-dominated state governments that exercised constitutional jurisdiction over land were not supportive. They had seen the large amount of money and attention being lavished on the New Villages and the Chinese, whom they considered to be responsible for the lawlessness and the persistent trouble with the communists, even as the largely law-abiding rural Malays were being neglected. They were, therefore, reluctant to alienate more land for New Village agriculture.

Undoubtedly, the resettlement of the squatters under the Briggs Plan did succeed in its aim of severing the close ties between the squatters and the communist insurgents. It also put pressure on the insurgents to come out into the open in search of food, where they could be attacked by the security forces. And over time, the resettlement program changed the demographic picture of Malaya, as many of the New Villages grew and developed into the large townships that exist today along the main trunk roads of Peninsular Malaya (West Malaysia).

CHEAH BOON-KHENG

See also Malayan Communist Party (MCP); Malayan Emergency (1948–1960); "New Villages" (Malaya/Malaysia); Strategic Hamlet Program (Vietnam); Templer, General Sir Gerald (1898–1970)

References:
Purcell, Victor. 1955. *Communist or Free?* Stanford, CA: Stanford University Press.
Stubbs, Richard. 1989. *Hearts and Minds in Guerrilla Warfare: The Malayan Emergency, 1948–1960.* Kuala Lumpur: Oxford University Press.

BRITISH BORNEO

The term *British Borneo* referred to the northwestern Bornean territories of Sarawak and North Borneo (Sabah) (present-day East Malaysia) and the Malay kingdom of Brunei that came into being in 1888 when all three territories became protectorates of Britain. Until the mid-nineteenth century, the sultanates of Brunei and Sulu held vague overlordship over Sarawak and North Borneo. The chance intervention of an English gentleman-adventurer—James Brooke (1803–1868), who became the raja of Sarawak in 1841—led to the establishment of a dynasty of White Rajas. Brooke and his successors expanded Sarawak's frontiers eastward until 1905 with the acquisition of Lawas.

The British East India Company (EIC) secured the cession of Labuan from Brunei in 1846, and Labuan remained a Crown Colony until 1890, when it was administered as part of British North Borneo. In the late 1870s, private Western entrepreneurs negotiated the cession of territories in North Borneo from the sultanates of Brunei and Sulu. In 1881, the territory of North Borneo (Sabah) was established and administered by the British North Borneo Chartered Company.

Throughout the Pacific War (1941–1945), British Borneo was occupied by the Japanese Imperial Army. In the postwar period, from 1946 to 1963, Sarawak and British North Borneo were Crown Colonies. In 1963, Sarawak and North Borneo joined the Federation of Malaysia and became East Malaysia. (Thereafter, North Borneo resurrected its ancient name of Sabah.) Brunei remained a British protectorate until its independence in 1984.

OOI KEAT GIN

See also British Interests in Southeast Asia; British North Borneo Chartered Company; Brooke, James, and Sarawak; Brunei (Sixteenth to Nineteenth Centuries); Labuan (1847); Sarawak and Sabah (North Borneo); Sulu and the Sulu Archipelago

References:
Irwin, Graham. 1955. *Nineteenth-Century Borneo: A Study in Diplomatic Rivalry.* The Hague: Martinus Nijhoff; reprinted in 1965 by Donald Moore, Singapore.
Tarling, Nicholas. 1971. *Britain, the Brookes and Brunei.* Kuala Lumpur: Oxford University Press.
Wright, L. R. 1970. *The Origins of British Borneo.* Hong Kong: Hong Kong University Press.

BRITISH BURMA

British Burma, which encompassed the area now known as the Union of Myanmar (Burma), was created as a result of three wars between the British East India Company (EIC) and the Burman Konbaung dynasty, whereby the latter was subsequently liquidated. After the first conflict (1824–1826), the British were ceded Arakan and Tenasserim; Pegu was annexed following the second war (1852). Initially, Arakan, Tenasserim, and Pegu (collectively referred to as Lower Burma) were known as British Burma. The Konbaung rulers continued to rule over Upper Burma. The third and final Anglo-Burmese War (1885) witnessed not only the annexation of Upper Burma but also the abolishment of the Konbaung monarchy. The whole country of what is today Myanmar became British Burma, and until the late 1890s, it was administered as part of the Presidency of Bengal of British India. British Burma dissociated itself from the Bengal government in 1897; thereafter, it became a province in itself administratively but remained part of British India. Rangoon (present-day Yangon) was the seat of government. In 1937, British Burma ceased to be part of British India and became a British colony. During the Pacific War, Imperial Japanese forces invaded and occupied the country (from 1942 to 1945). In 1948, Britain granted the colony independence, and the Union of Burma came into being.

OOI KEAT GIN

See also Anglo-Burmese Wars (1824–1826, 1852, 1885); East India Company (EIC) (1602), English; Konbaung Rulers and British Imperialism

References:

Cady, John F. 1960. *A History of Modern Burma.* Ithaca, NY: Cornell University Press.

Pollak, Oliver B. 1979. *Empires in Collision: Anglo-Burmese Relations in the Mid-Nineteenth Century.* Wesport, CT: Greenwood Press.

BRITISH INDIA, GOVERNMENT OF

The British encounter with India began in the early seventeenth century when the merchants and traders of the East India Company (EIC) steadily established a series of factories—warehouses—around the coast of the subcontinent, notably in Madras (Chennai), Bombay (Mumbai), and Calcutta. From its coastal settlements, the EIC, driven by the desire to protect its trade and other vested interests, gradually extended political control over large tracts of Indian territories. The expansion of British power in the subcontinent was, to a large extent, facilitated by a divided and weakened India as well as a power vacuum created by the declining Mughal Empire (1526–1857). By the mid-nineteenth century, the EIC had become the dominant political power in India, and most of the subcontinent soon came under direct or indirect British rule.

Having acquired political control over large parts of India, the British had to decide on the best way of governing their empire. From the capture of Calcutta in the mid-eighteenth century to the annexation of the Punjab nearly a century later, the stabilization of land revenue in the territories they held became a critical feature of EIC administration. The business of expansion exacted heavy resources, and money was needed to finance expensive wars of conquests and annexation and also to maintain the ever-growing military machinery. In the first instance, the EIC sought to institutionalize revenue collections based on local practices. In and around Bengal, a permanent settlement was effected with the established local order—the large landed magnates—to secure land revenue. In the west and south, the EIC adopted the *ryotwari* system, whereby payment of land revenue was arranged with individual proprietors, not collectively through headmen or chiefs, on the basis of the assumed value of the fields.

As the EIC transformed itself from a mere trading company to a territorial power and a political body responsible for the collection of revenue in many parts of India, it found that it had to expand its increasingly lucrative trade with China to meet its growing administrative costs in India. And as interests in the China trade increased, the EIC found a renewed interest in the Southeast Asian trade as well. This prompted the search for a strategic foothold along the Straits of Melaka that could be used to safeguard the company's trade route to the market in China as well as to counter Dutch influence (and trade monopoly) in the region. The need for a suitable base east of the Bay of Bengal had long been evident to EIC servants in India, who were concerned that India's eastern flank was especially vulnerable to a naval foe operating from the east.

In the late eighteenth century, Capt. Francis Light (1740–1794) had acquired a settlement in the island of Penang at the northern tip of the Straits of Melaka. But the island settlement was located too far north to be of strategic importance in the ensuing Anglo-Dutch rivalry. As it turned out, from their base in Penang, the British could hardly challenge the Dutch in the archipelago. In 1819, the lieutenant governor of Benkulen, Stamford Raffles (1781–1826), obtained permission from Lord Hastings (t. 1774–1785), governor-general at Calcutta, to search for a base farther south in the Straits of Melaka. This led to the founding of Singapore. By 1824, following the Anglo-Dutch Treaty, the EIC further entrenched its monopoly in the

Straits of Melaka by securing Melaka to add to Penang and Singapore. Two years later, the three port cities were amalgamated into the Straits Settlements (with Singapore as its headquarters from 1832) and governed from Calcutta. In 1851, the Straits Settlements were transferred from the Bengal Presidency to the direct supervision of the governor-general and the supreme government of India. The interests of the Straits Settlements and the government of India at Calcutta soon diverged, however, and in 1867, control of the Straits Settlements was transferred to the Colonial Office in London, thereby severing India's legislative and judicial control over British territories in peninsular and insular Southeast Asia.

During the nineteenth century, the government of India's concern to secure its northeastern borders against an ambitious Burmese empire, compounded by commercial designs and Anglo-French imperial rivalry, led to three separate Anglo-Burmese wars, culminating in the annexation of Burma to the British Indian Empire in 1886. The first war started in 1824 and concluded two years later with the Treaty of Yandabo, which placed Arakan and Tenasserim under British control. In 1852, Governor-General Lord Dalhousie, James Ramsay (t. 1847–1856), anxious to secure a continuous British-dominated eastern Indian coastline up to Melaka and Singapore, acquired Pegu after a brief conflict with the Burmese kingdom. Then, in 1885, suspicions that the Burmese king was consorting with the French against British interests led to a third war, which eventually resulted in the annexation of Upper Burma in 1886. Burma would be part of the British Empire in India until 1935, when the Government of India Act of the same year excluded the administration of the Burmese territories from the Indian Federation.

During the process of expansion and consolidation, the nature and objective of the British government in India became subjects of intense debate in London and India. The traditionalists argued that the EIC should not interfere too directly in the lives of its Indian subjects, who should, under British patronage, be tutored in their own culture and great traditions. The reformers (the utilitarians and evangelicals), by contrast, insisted that Britain had a "moral duty" to "civilize" India according to the modern British model. In the 1820s and 1830s, the

reformers held sway, and India went through an "age of reform." During this period, the wages and budgets of EIC servants were curtailed, Indians were brought into the lower rungs of administration, and the English penal code and education were introduced into the system. Historians have argued that the reforms had only a limited impact on Indian society and that the experience existed mainly in the minds of the British, who were concerned with India but not with the Indians. Nonetheless, British reforms unified India through a centralized administrative, political, and legal structure in which the apex at Calcutta (and later Delhi) was integrated with the provincial, district, and village administrations. The "steel frame" of empire consolidated British rule in India. This was particularly apparent after the revolt of 1857, when EIC rule was replaced by Crown rule, creating a centralized system of governance that permeated to the provincial and district levels.

To a very large extent, the administrative and judicial structures that were created in the British Empire in Southeast Asia were based on the British India model of governance, particularly when key administrative and military positions were regularly dominated by former members of the Bengal service as well as officers of the Bengal and Madras armies. But as in India, even with an elaborate administrative structure, effective British government continued to depend on strategic alliances forged between the rulers and the ruled.

Under British rule, the Indian economy was developed to serve Britain's industrial and imperial interests. India provided a vital market for British products and was a key supplier of raw materials to Britain and other markets in Europe and the United States. It also became a great recipient of British capital, and by the outbreak of World War I (1914–1918), about one-fifth of British capital overseas was invested in India. By the middle of the nineteenth century, with the abolition of slavery in the British Empire and the French colonies, India, too, became a major supplier of labor to various parts of the British Empire. Large numbers of people from India moved into Southeast Asia as indentured laborers, service workers, or merchants, taking advantage of the opportunities offered by an imperial labor market and trading network. From the third quarter of the nineteenth century, many from British India moved to Burma to take up employment opportunities when the latter came to be administrated as part of the Indian Raj after 1886. A similar exodus occurred when Indian immigrants went to Malaya to work in the rubber plantations there from the early decades of the twentieth century. On the eve of the Pacific War (1941–1945), there were an estimated 1 million Indians in Burma and about 750,000, mainly Tamils, in Malaya.

By the late nineteenth century, as Indian nationalism slowly gained momentum in the subcontinent, the British started to draw in the moderate, Western-educated Indian elite as political allies in a bid to deflect increasingly strident criticisms of and organized opposition to colonial rule. Indians were gradually brought into decision-making bodies by political reforms to the legislative mechanisms, as well as the "Indianization" of the civil service and military. By the twentieth century, the British government in India responded to the challenge of mass-based nationalist politics mainly by promoting containment through constitutional changes.

During the Pacific War, India was spared the ignominy of defeat that befell the rest of the British Empire in Southeast Asia, but the threat of a Japanese invasion through Burma remained throughout. The nationalist movement picked up momentum during the war years with the Quit India movement in India in 1942 and the mobilization of Indian prisoners of war (POWs) in Southeast Asia into the Indian National Army (INA), whose objective was to liberate India through a military invasion with Japanese help. Neither movement achieved its objectives: the Quit India movement was suppressed by British troops within weeks of being launched, and the INA turned out to be nothing more than a paper tiger that hardly threatened the British forces that engaged INA troops at the Imphal-Kohima front.

By the end of the war, the British were ready to relinquish their empire in the subcontinent. With the exception of Burma, which shared a similar constitutional experience with the rest of India until 1935, political changes and the nationalist movements in the British Empire in Southeast Asia did not keep pace with their Indian counterparts. And though the subcontinent and Burma achieved their respective independence a few years after the end of the Pacific War, the rest of the British Empire in Southeast Asia remained as colonies until the mid-1960s.

TAN TAI YONG

See also Anglo–Burmese Wars (1824–1826, 1852, 1885); Anglo–Dutch Relations in Southeast Asia (Seventeenth to Twentieth Centuries); Bose, Subhas Chandra (1897–1945); Chettiars (Chettyars); East India Company (EIC) (1602), English; Imphal-Kohima, Battle of (1944); Indian Immigrants; Indian National Army (INA); Konbaung Rulers and British Imperialism; Penang (1786); Singapore (1819); Straits Settlements (1826–1941); Yandabo (1826), Treaty of

References:

Bayley, C. A. ed. 1989. *An Atlas of the British Empire: The Rise and Fall of the Greatest Empire the World has Ever Known*. New York: Facts on File.

Bose, Sugata, and Ayesha Jalal. 1998. *History, Culture and Political Economy*. New York: Oxford University Press.

Chaliand, Gerard, and Jean-Pierre RAGEAU. 1995. *The Penguin Atlas of Diaspora*. New York: Viking Press.

Khoo Kay Khim. ed. 1977. *The History of Southeast, South and East Asia: Essays & Documents*. Kuala Lumpur: Oxford University Press.

Masselos, J. C. 1975. *Nationalism on the Indian Subcontinent: An Introductory History*. New Delhi: Sterling Press.

Murphy, Rhoads. 1996. *A History of Asia*. 2nd ed. New York: Harper Collins.

Osborne, Milton. 1997. *Southeast Asia: An Introductory History*. 7th ed. St. Leonards, Australia: Allen and Unwin.

Robinson, Francis. gen. ed. 1989. *The Cambridge Encyclopaedia of India, Pakistan, Bangladesh, Sri Lanka, Nepal, Bhutan and Maldives*. Cambridge: Cambridge University Press.

Tan Tai Young and Andrew J. Major. 1995. "India and Indians in the Making of Singapore." Pp. 1–20 in *Singapore-India Relations: A Primer*. Edited by YONG Mun Cheong and V. V. Bhanoji RAO. Singapore: Singapore University Press.

Turnbull, C. M. 1989. *A History of Singapore, 1819–1988*. 2nd ed. Singapore: Oxford University Press.

Wolpert, Stanley. 1982. *A New History of India.* 2nd ed. New York: University of California Press.

BRITISH INTERESTS IN SOUTHEAST ASIA

In Southeast Asia, as in other parts of the world, the nature of British interests varied over time, reflecting a variation in the relative importance of commercial, economic, political, strategic, religious, cultural, and demographic concerns. There was a regional variation as well, so that, although security of the homeland was necessarily always the prime interest, the relative importance of British interests in other parts of the world, of whatever kind, might fluctuate. There were also questions of hierarchy, questions of coordination, and questions of perception. The definition of British interests was contested among the groups involved—merchants and manufacturers, politicians and administrators, church and state, private groups and individuals and public opinion, local and metropolitan authorities. The mode in which the definition was contested also varied over time, given the growth of communications, the advance of literacy, and the development of democracy.

In no period did Southeast Asia enjoy a priority among British interests. Its importance to the British was often the result of factors extraneous to the region, such as its position in relation to its great neighbors, India and China. Nor was Southeast Asia always seen as a region, though it was recognized that significant interests in one part of the region might make another part of it important as well. And if the importance of the region to British interests was often indirect, so was the importance of some states or territories within the region.

Britain may be regarded as having been constituted, or reconstituted, when two of the "three kingdoms," England and Scotland, were drawn into the Union of 1707. That was part of a yet wider reconstruction that followed the Revolution of 1688 and that included, for example, the creation of the Bank of England. The reconstruction marked a further step in the emergence of the British islands from the division and conflict of the seventeenth century and the assertion of a wider role. Britain was not yet an industrial power, nor did it possess an empire in India. Its trade there—monopolized by the East India Company (EIC), chartered in 1600—was expanding, however, as a result of the fashion for Indian textiles. So, too, was its trade in China, then the source of the tea that became first a fashionable and then a popular drink, as well as a source of revenue.

Southeast Asia, particularly the area around the Straits of Melaka, became important to the British because it flanked the route to and from Canton (Guangzhou), the only port the Manchu dynasty opened to the British. The emergence of this interest concerned the Dutch, for it was a potential source of disruption for their empire in Java and the straits. They were concerned, too, by the commercial penetration of the Indies by the "country traders" based in India. The (Dutch) United East India Company (VOC), predominant in the seventeenth century, failed to compete effectively in textiles and tea. Its more old-fashioned monopoly of the spice trade therefore seemed all the more important. Indeed, the British were unwilling to accept the Dutch monopoly in the spice trade, since the fine spices were still confined to Maluku. To that point, however, they offered no open challenge. Good relations with the Dutch in Europe were a priority.

Britain's interests in Southeast Asia changed again when the East India Company became a territorial power in India. That outcome was precipitated by the transfer to the subcontinent of the bitter rivalry between the two main Western European powers, Britain and France, and the attempts of the commercially weaker player to gain advantage over the stronger by intervening in Indian politics. The Battle of Plassey (1757) can be regarded as a turning point. After that, the dominion of the British—still represented by the company, though from 1773 increasingly regulated and controlled from London—advanced. Threats from the French were still a factor, intensified with the new series of wars with France following the Revolution in 1789 and the rise of Napoleon (1769–1821). So, too, however, were the profits of conquest and acquisition, public and personal, though attempts were made—most famously with the 1788 trial of Warren Hastings (1732–1818)—to limit the corruption found in their connection.

Territorial dominion in India gave Britain additional resources. Commercially, it facilitated the expansion of the trade with China, providing opium as a means of paying for China tea at a time when British manufactures failed to penetrate the market; politically, it helped by providing the revenue and labor needed for maintaining or expanding ventures in the subcontinent and beyond. But this territorial dominion also imposed new responsibilities. The security of India became a factor in Britain's foreign policy. Indeed, India had security needs of its own, not entirely compatible with the needs of Britain itself. In India, Britain was a "continental" power, concerned that no state on its frontiers should be in a position to challenge it. Such states had to be kept clear of foreign European powers, such as the French and the Russians. They also had to demonstrate a degree of submission, so as not to set a bad example to the states on the subcontinent that entered what were called "subsidiary alliances" with the company. These requirements were not those of a commercial power, yet such was increasingly the nature of Britain's preferred relationship with the world.

It is easy to antedate the impact of the Industrial Revolution on Britain and its place in the world. But contemporaries clearly recognized that the creation of the first industrial society was a revolution. In the second quarter of the nineteenth century, if not sooner, the British came to recognize that they would gain more by promoting free trade than by adhering to the mercantilist regulation of the past. Furthermore, that approach would serve them better in promoting relations with other parts of the world on the basis of free trade rather than on a colonial basis. At the same time, they sensed that their advantages might be temporary, as others emulated and caught up with them. A small country on the fringe of Europe should not build a world empire. The "imperialism of free trade" was a striking but somewhat misleading description of Britain's policy at midcentury. The British were determined, for example, not to make China "another India." The "unequal treaties" were not a colonial relationship. Nor did the British believe that other powers—even the French—should be deprived of all opportunity overseas.

Their security at this time was enhanced by political as well as economic success. France had been defeated at sea at the Battle of Trafalgar (1805) and on land at Waterloo (1815). Those victories met Britain's prime interest, security in Europe. It was sustained in the subsequent decades by what is sometimes called the balance-of-power policy but what is better seen as an attempt to avoid the dominance of the Continent by any one power. The creation of a new kingdom of the Netherlands—initially including the Belgian provinces of the Hapsburgs as well as the old Dutch Republic—was an attempt to check the French. It was also designed to secure the independence of that part of Europe from which Britain was most vulnerable to attack.

The position of Southeast Asia in this phase reflected the nature of Britain's interests and the priorities among them. Despite its great power, Britain made no attempt to secure dominion over the region as a whole. Indeed, at least until the First Anglo-China War (1840–1842), it adopted a cautious policy on the mainland, lest it alienate the Chinese and damage the company's trade at Canton. It made a conciliatory treaty with Siam in 1826 and vainly sought to make one with Nguyễn Vietnam, accepting failure without any punitive action. When the break with China came and the victorious British acquired Hong Kong and made the first unequal treaties, no real break occurred in the relationship with the states to the south. Siam, in fact, made its own unequal treaty, the Bowring Treaty of 1855. Again, Vietnam failed to follow its example. The British did not, however, oppose the expedition that Napoleon III (1808–1873) sent against Vietnam from 1858 to 1859, ostensibly to support the cause of the Catholic missionaries. Their ambassador in Paris was instructed to ascertain the "ulterior object" of the expedition, if any, but "not to convey the impression that the French operations are viewed with any jealousy or suspicion" (Letter from Malmesbury 1858).

In Burma, however, Britain's policy differed, for it was an Indian policy, determined not by commercial interests at home or indeed abroad but by the security interests of the new subcontinental dominion. It was imperative that no foreign power establish itself in Burma, and beyond that, Burma itself had to accept a measure of subordination if it was to retain its independence. It refused. The First Anglo-Burmese War (1824–1826) was the result. Apparently, the only way to mark British supremacy was through the acquisition of Arakan and Tenasserim, yet that was not the object of the war, and it did not put Anglo-Burman relations on a secure footing. A second war followed in 1852, again less the result of the commercial disputes that were its ostensible cause than of the incompatible political objectives of the two states. Viceroy James Ramsay Dalhousie's (t. 1847–1856) answer was to acquire Pegu. But there is good reason to contend that he had not, in the radical Richard Cobden's (1804–1865) phrase, "got up" a war for that purpose. Dalhousie argued strongly against trying to secure a new treaty: it would only be a further source of dispute and lead to further territorial expansion. That should, he believed, be absolutely avoided.

In archipelagic Southeast Asia, the British demonstrated their ability to dislodge the other colonial powers but did not, in the event, do so. The need to provide for India's security gave the British a new interest not only in Burma but also in the western parts of the archipelago, from which the Bay of Bengal and thus the Coromandel Coast were vulnerable. The company's sole remaining settlement—at Bencoolen (Bengkulu) in West Sumatra—was too remote to be useful. That fact was an argument for acquiring Penang from the sultan of neighboring Kedah in 1786. However, in doing so, the company intended both to avoid a clash with Siam, to which Kedah owed tribute, and to avoid a challenge to the Dutch. Kedah was beyond the fringe of their empire in the Malay world, now focused on Maluku, Java, and Melaka.

Britain's concern for its own security put a premium on friendly relations with the Dutch Republic. Only when the republic came under French influence did the British move against the Dutch in the Indies. That had happened during the American Revolution (1775–1783). At its conclusion, however, the republic remained under the patronage of the French, which was one reason indeed for Britain to acquire Penang. In the peace treaty of 1784, the British had had to restore the acquisitions they had made, though to protect the country traders, they had secured the assurance of a right of free navigation in the "Eastern Seas," that is, Southeast Asian waters. The overthrow of the pro-French Patriots in 1787 was followed by a British attempt to reconcile the interests of the British and the Dutch. The former hoped to secure Trincomalee (Ceylon/Sri Lanka) as a naval base. They were no longer prepared to challenge the spice monopoly in Maluku, but they wanted a settlement at Riau. That would enable them to protect the route to China and provide an entrepôt for country trade with the archipelago, without directly challenging the position of the Dutch. The proposals looked toward an Anglo-Dutch compromise. But not even a friendly Dutch regime could, at that time, accept those terms. The compromise followed after the new sequence of French wars, in particular in the Anglo-Dutch Treaty of 17 March 1824.

That agreement affirmed that the British would accept Dutch predominance in the archipelago, provided that the Dutch levied only limited customs on Britain's trade. In addition, the Dutch, though taking over Bencoolen, had to transfer Melaka to the British and to accept that Singapore, occupied by Stamford Raffles (1781–1826) in 1819, should remain in British hands. With what became the Straits Settlements, the British could protect the route to China and secure a share of the trade of the archipelago, from which Bugis and other traders came. India helped to meet the expenses of the settlements, making it easier to free them from customs duties and all the more commercially attractive. The treaty created a kind of divide between peninsula and archipelago but not a frontier: the removal of the Dutch from the peninsula did not mean the insertion of the British. The treaty did, however, warn off other powers. At times, the two powers were at odds, particularly over the commercial clauses of the treaty, but overall, their compromise endured.

In the 1840s, a time of bad relations with the Dutch and, more generally, of commercial recession, the British government offered some support to the venture James Brooke (1803–1868) undertook in Sarawak and Brunei, though Borneo had arguably been left to the Dutch in 1824. Britain played down its commitments in the following decade, as prosperity returned and the Brooke venture became more controversial. But it did not endorse his policy in Sulu, where, in 1849, he had made a treaty with the sultan. That treaty challenged the claims of Spain, and Spain protested. Once more, European concerns prevailed at the British Foreign Office. The question of the Sulu treaty was to "sleep," said the foreign secretary. Pressing it would only promote French influence at Madrid.

The British had restored Manila to Spain after capturing it in 1762 during the Seven Years' War (1756–1763). The Spaniards sought to avoid antagonism—and, after the loss of Mexico and Peru, to gain revenue—by opening the Philippines to foreign trade in the new century. That gave the British a further stake in the continuance of their rule.

The 1870s saw a revival of the rivalry among European powers, promoted by the spread of the Industrial Revolution and the movement for national unification; this rivalry would be extended beyond Europe in the subsequent decades by an industrializing United States and a modernizing Japan. At the same time, non-European states felt the effects of that political rivalry and also of the economic and social changes promoted by the industrial and communications revolutions, and they generally found it difficult to respond.

In Southeast Asia, the changes threatened the arrangements that protected the interests of the British during the days of their primacy. The changes they made were reactive. They entered a third Burmese war in 1885 and abolished the kingdom of Burma on their victory. They established residents in a number of west coast Malay states in 1874, chartered the British North Borneo Company in 1881, and made the Borneo territories what they called "ordinary protectorates" in 1888. But those moves were designed to sustain a number of British interests in a changing world—in particular, the security of the route to China—and not to change the world. They did not, moreover, simply involve moving from informal dominance to formal empire: even where the British decided to strengthen their position, they sought to do so without provoking others. Burma was again an exception. There, a French threat, intended, it now seems clear, to give the Third Republic leverage over Siam and Laos, was met by war and acquisition. When the partition of Southeast Asia turned to repartition, the British were clear that they could not intervene in the Philippines. If the Spaniards could not remain, it was better that they should be replaced by the Americans rather than by the Germans. With that, too, the United States recruited itself, somewhat uncertainly, to the ranks of the colonial powers and placed an obstacle in the way of the Japanese, who had acquired Taiwan in 1895.

One theme in the world history of the early twentieth century was the question of the succession to Britain's primacy. Two potential superpowers were emerging, Russia and the United States. Could a powerful Germany then share world power? That notion lay behind the reckless policies of the kaiser and the yet more extreme policies of Adolf Hitler (1889–1945). The world wars, for which they bore prime responsibility, brought about the predominance of the two superpowers. Germany was defeated, but Britain, though on the victorious side, was greatly weakened, economically and politically.

That fact was reflected in Southeast Asia. One part of it gained a priority among British interests that it had not previously enjoyed, but in a sense, that outcome reflected weakness rather than strength. After intervention, the Peninsular Malay States had been a major source of tin. The development of the automobile industry spawned a rubber boom in the early twentieth century. That made Malaya a dollar-earner, and the Great War (1914–1918) made dollar earnings significant for Britain and the "sterling area" as a whole. Postwar, too, Singapore gained a new strategic importance, marked by the laborious and expensive creation of a naval base. But again, this was a sign of weakness as much as strength. It reflected Britain's commitment, under the Washington treaties of 1921 and 1922, not to modernize Hong Kong. It also reflected Britain's attempt to meet commitments in Asia as well as Europe with a one-ocean navy. No substantial fleet would be permanently based in Singapore; a major fleet would be sent there in case of crisis. In other parts of Southeast Asia in the interwar period, the British generally pursued cautious policies designed to avoid upsetting the status quo. Burma was, as ever, an exception and, as ever, because of its connection with India. Pressed by Burmese nationalism, the British accepted that Burma, as well as India, should advance to self-government.

Challenged by the Americans' decision to build a two-ocean fleet and by their embargoes, the Japanese abandoned their notion that, given time, Southeast Asia would fall into their hands. They dislodged the colonial regimes by a dramatic invasion in 1941 and 1942. Like the other colonial powers, the British nevertheless intended to return when the Japanese had been overthrown. Malaya and Singapore, they believed, would be no less important to them in the postwar world. But it was necessary to put their interests in Southeast Asia (and those of the Europeans in general) on a new, postimperial footing. In particular, they had to come to terms with the nationalists to whom the Japanese had given new opportunities and accept the concept of a Southeast Asia made up of nation-states. It was important, too, that those states be viable and able, with assistance, to defend themselves. The policy met only limited success. The Dutch and the French found it difficult to accept. In Malaya, Singapore, and Borneo, it was difficult to pursue. Exceptional yet again, Burma secured complete independence in 1948 and became the only country to leave the Commonwealth.

NICHOLAS TARLING

See also Anglo-Brunei Relations (Nineteenth Century to 1980s); Anglo-Burmese Wars (1824–1826, 1852, 1885); Anglo-Dutch Relations in Southeast Asia; Bengkulu (Bencoolen, Benkulen); Bowring, Sir John (1792–1872); British Borneo; British India, Government of; British Malaya; British Military Administration (BMA) in Southeast Asia; British North Borneo Chartered Company; Brooke, James, and Sarawak; Bugis (Buginese); Colonialism; Constitutional Developments in Burma (1900–1941); Country Traders; East India Company (EIC) (1600), English; Formosa (Taiwan); "Fortress Singapore"; Free Trade; French Ambitions in Southeast Asia; Germans (Germany); Great War (1914–1918); Hong Kong; Imperialism; India; Japan and Southeast Asia (pre-1941); Japanese Occupation of Southeast Asia (1941–1945); Java; Johor; Johor-Riau Empire; Maluku (The Moluccas); Manila; Missionaries, Christian; Nguyễn Emperors and French Imperialism; Opium; Penang (1786); Preservation of Siam's Political Independence; Residential System (Malaya); Rubber; Sarawak and Sabah (North Borneo); Singapore (1819); Spices and the Spice Trade; Straits of Melaka; Straits Settlements (1826–1941); Sulu and the Sulu Archipelago; Tin; Yandabo (1826), Treaty of

References:
Letter from Malmesbury to Cowley. 21 November 1858. Foreign Office 1071. FO 27/1240, Public Record Office (PRO), London.

Sardesai, D. R. 1977. *British Trade and Expansion in Southeast Asia, 1830–1914.* Colombo: South Asia Books.

Tarling, Nicholas. 1993. *The Fall of Imperial Britain in South-East Asia.* Singapore: Oxford University Press.

———. 1996. *Britain, Southeast Asia, and the Onset of the Pacific War.* Cambridge: Cambridge University Press.

Webster, Anthony. 1998. *Gentlemen Capitalists: British Imperialism in South East Asia.* London and New York: Tauris.

BRITISH MALAYA

The term *British Malaya* came into being after 1914 in reference to the Malay Peninsula (present-day West or Peninsular Malaysia) and Singapore. In formal and legal terms, British Malaya did not officially exist; however, administratively, the peninsular Malay States, Penang, and Singapore were under British control. British Malaya consisted of the Crown Colonies of the Straits Settlements (Penang, Melaka, and Singapore), the British protectorates of the Federated Malay States (Perak, Selangor, Negri Sembilan, and Pahang), the former Siamese Malay States until 1909 (Kedah, Perlis, Kelantan, and Terengganu), and Johor.

Penang was established as a British outpost in 1786. Melaka was under British control from 1795 to 1815 during the Napoleonic Wars (1803–1815) but was restored to the Dutch in 1816. The British acquired Province Wellesley in 1800 and Singapore in 1819. The entire Malay Peninsula came under the British sphere of influence in accordance with the Anglo-Dutch Treaty of 1824. In that year, the Dutch handed Melaka to the British in exchange for Bencoolen (Bengkulu). In 1826, Penang, Melaka, and Singapore formed the Straits Settlements, which were administered as part of British India until 1867; they then became a separate Crown Colony governed directly by the Colonial Office in London. Under the terms of the Burney Treaty of 1826, Britain acknowledged Siamese suzerainty over the northern Malay States of Kedah, Perlis, Kelantan, and Terengganu. The British expanded control over the central Malay States of Perak and Negeri Sembilan in 1874 and Pahang in 1888. These four Malay States became the Federated Malay States in 1896. Then, in 1909, under the terms of the Treaty of Bangkok, Siam ceded the four northern Malay States of Kedah, Perlis, Kelantan, and Terengganu to Britain. The southern Malay State of Johor (Johore) accepted a British adviser in 1914, thereby bringing to a conclusion the establishment of British political power over the entire Malay Peninsula and Singapore.

Imperial Japan occupied British Malaya from 1941 to 1945, during the Pacific War. In 1946, Penang and Melaka joined the Peninsular Malay States to form the Malayan Union. Singapore remained a Crown Colony. The Federation of Malaya replaced the Malayan Union in 1948, and Malaya became an independent nation in 1957.

OOI KEAT GIN

See also Anglo-Dutch Relations in Southeast Asia (Seventheenth–Twentieth Centuries); British Interests in Southeast Asia; Federated Malay States (FMS) (1896); Federation of Malaya (1948); Johor; Malayan Union (1946); Melaka; Pahang; Pangkor Engagement (1874); Penang (1786); Residential System (Malaya); Rubber; Siamese Malay States (Kedah, Perlis, Kelantan, Terengganu); Singapore (1819); Straits Settlements (1826–1941); Tin; Western Malay States (Perak, Selangor, Negri Sembilan, and Pahang)

References:

Andaya, Barbara Watson, and Leonard Andaya. 2000. *A History of Malaysia*. 2nd ed. London: Palgrave.

Chai Hon-chan. 1967. *The Development of British Malaya, 1896–1909*. 2nd ed. Kuala Lumpur: Oxford University Press.

BRITISH MILITARY ADMINISTRATION (BMA) IN SOUTHEAST ASIA

British Military Administration (BMA) was imposed on territories in the Southeast Asian theater under the military responsibility of the South-East Asia Command (SEAC), headed by Admiral Lord Louis Mountbatten (1900–1979), the supreme Allied commander (SAC). SEAC was entrusted with the unenviable task of reoccupying and establishing the military administration of a vast region of more than 160 million people, the majority of whom had suffered the worst ravages of war.

In Burma (Myanmar), BMA operated from January 1944 to October 1945; it commenced later in British Malaya, operating from September 1945 to April 1946, and in British Borneo—Sarawak, Brunei, and British North Borneo (Sabah)—it was implemented from January to July 1946. No formal BMA operated in Indochina or in Indonesia. However, British forces were compelled by circumstances in the aftermath of the Japanese surrender (15 August 1945) to undertake similar responsibilities in territories under BMA. The task of BMA was most trying in Burma, as it had to function in the midst of military operations against the Japanese.

Toward the closing months of 1942, work had commenced on planning for the reestablishment of military governments in territories of Southeast Asia under Japanese occupation. The planning for the postwar period focused on the formulation of future policy and the preparation for reoccupation and the establishment of military administration. The responsibility for Burma rested with the Government of Burma in exile in Simla, India. The Colonial Office in London undertook this task for Malaya and British Borneo, in consultation with the representatives of Raja Charles Vyner Brooke (r. 1917–1941, 1946) of Sarawak (who was then in Australia) and the Court of Directors of the British North Borneo Company in London.

Priorities and Challenges

BMA's chief priorities were to disarm and remove Japanese troops from the reoccupied territories and, at the same time, to liberate and relieve the hundreds of thousands of prisoners of war (POWs) and civilian internees in camps scattered throughout Southeast Asia. The functions of BMA were undertaken at two levels, administrative and political. At the administrative level, the functions involved providing transportation; supplying various types of equipment, clothing, accommodations, and housing; handling the importation of supplies (mainly rice, other foodstuffs, and basic consumer goods) for the civil population; and conducting relief work related to refugees and displaced individuals. Such BMA administrative duties were the responsibility of the Civil Affairs Service (CAS) headed by the chief civil affairs officer (CCAO). On the political level, BMA personnel were faced with the difficult task of handling local political interest groups, composed of ardent nationalists and militant resistance organizations with left-wing elements. The clarion call of these vocally assertive groups was the independence of their colonized countries. The SAC directly dealt with political issues.

Rice and independence posed the most acute challenges to BMA. Rice, the staple food of Southeast and East Asia, was the single most important and basic commodity of trade. Prewar Burma, Siam (Thailand), and Indochina were major exporters of rice. As a consequence of the Allied blockade, rice exports dwindled down to a trickle during the Japanese occupation of Southeast Asia. Moreover, wartime conditions severely retarded rice production, as producers reverted to subsistence in the absence of markets. BMA not only had to deal with rice shortages but also had to undertake the distribution of available supplies under an increasingly deteriorating situation of widespread lawlessness following the Japanese capitulation. Equally threatening to BMA operations were the activities of militant nationalists, with their unceasing clamor for independence. Facing BMA and at times even disrupting its operations was a strong and militant nationalist movement—left-wing inspired, fairly organized, well armed (ironically with guns and munitions supplied by the Allies during the war), and possessing a new self-confidence fostered by wartime experiences. In Indochina and Indonesia, nationalist elements were highly provocative, uncompromising in their stance, and ever raring for a fight.

Burma, British Malaya, and British Borneo

SEAC assumed the administration of liberated Burma from January 1944. The Civil Affairs Service (Burma), known as CAS (B), under Major General C. F. B. Pearce, established BMA in reoccupied Burma. Immediately, CAS (B) under SAC found itself in a predicament. Although entrusted with the immediate responsibility for restoring law and order, it had no authority in political matters; such authority resided with the Government of Burma in Simla. Further complicating matters, CAS (B) had to contend with the clandestine activities of operatives of Force 136, a unit of the Special Operations Executive (SOE) based at Kandy, Ceylon (Sri Lanka). In fostering guerrilla resistance movements, there were political implications in the activities of Force 136, which neither referred to nor conferred with SAC or CCAO.

A monumental task confronted CAS (B) in running BMA in Burma. Among all the countries of Southeast Asia, Burma had experienced the worst destruction of the war. The country had the most unfortunate fate of having been fought over from south to north in 1942 and again from north to south from 1944 to 1945. Furthermore, CAS (B) had to face the nationalist Anti-Fascist People's Freedom League (AFPFL), led by Aung San (1915–1947). In May 1945, a British government White Paper proposed a delay in Burma's constitutional development toward self-rule. AFPFL rejected outright all such proposals and insisted upon immediate and complete independence and swift dissociation from the British Commonwealth. By then, Pearce had been replaced by Major General H. E. Rance as CCAO for Burma.

At the time of the Japanese surrender, CAS (B) had control over the entire country except for the area east of the Sittang River. The surrender hastened the handover to the civil government that formally assumed control in October 1945. Although the governor of Burma, Sir Reginald Dorman-Smith (t. 1941–1946), took office in mid-October 1945, it was another five months before the transfer of all responsibility was effected. CAS (B) managed to restore the railway and inland water transport system, but acute shortages in consumer goods persisted and prices remained astronomical.

Unlike Burma, British Malaya was spared the wrath of Allied bombings; however, physical conditions reflected dilapidation and gross neglect. The human suffering due to wartime conditions was acute and widespread. Serious shortages of rice coupled with malnutrition among the inhabitants of some districts beset Major General H. R. Hone, CCAO (Malaya). The immediate and urgent tasks of BMA in Malaya were the relief of the thousands of POWs and civilian internees and the rehabilitation of the country's economy. BMA performed commendably in addressing both these tasks. The smooth implementation of the Key Plan for British Military Administration in Malaya (approved in March 1945) enabled BMA to be ready to hand over responsibility even before the civil authorities were in a position to assume control. On the political front, however, BMA had to contend with deteriorating Sino-Malay relations that erupted in armed clashes and several leftist-led industrial strikes. During October 1945, as a consequence of food shortages, riots broke out. Widespread lawlessness and banditry in some areas seriously threatened BMA authority. Meanwhile, plans for the Malayan Union, a new political-administrative scheme, was under way. This new setup envisaged the union of the nine Malay States and the Straits Settlements of Penang and Melaka. Singapore was excluded and would remain a British Crown Colony. Citizenship under the new arrangement offered equal rights to all, irrespective of ethnicity or creed. There was also a provision for dual citizenship. The Malayan Union was constituted on 1 April 1946 and ended the tenure of BMA in British Malaya.

Initially, British Borneo was within the theater of operation of the U.S. forces under General Douglas MacArthur (1880–1964). But when plans were being made for the reoccupation, the Australian Ninth Division was assigned the task. Following a brief but momentous six-month stewardship under the Australian British Borneo Civil Affairs Unit (BBCAU) from June to December 1945, SEAC took responsibility for British Borneo. Brigadier C. F. C. Macaskie, CCAO, headed the British 50 Civil Affairs Unit (50 CAU) and BBCAU. Although 50 CAU remained behind at Ingleburn, Australia, Macaskie and BBCAU, operating from Labuan after the Australian landings at Brunei Bay on 10 June 1945, established the initial military administration. Several British officers served with the Australians in BBCAU. When SEAC assumed responsibility for British Borneo, these British officers reverted to 50 CAU, which was then redesignated as British Military Administration (British Borneo), or BMA (BB). Most of the major towns in North Borneo and, on a lesser scale, in Brunei had been all but obliterated by preinvasion Allied naval bombardments. Sarawak escaped both aerial bombings (Allied or Japanese) and land battles.

By January 1946, when BMA (BB) began operations, active hostilities had ceased. BB-CAU, in fact, had attended to most of the pressing and major tasks, including containing epidemics, clamping down on occasional disturbances, bringing relief to European POWs and civilian internees, and redistributing foodstuffs. BMA (BB) thus continued and improved upon these tasks and at the same time concentrated on the major undertaking of rejuvenating the economy.

Raja Charles Vyner Brooke (1874–1963) of Sarawak and the Court of Directors of the British North Borneo Chartered Company had agreed to cede their respective domains to Colonial Office administration. The sultanate of Brunei was to retain its prewar status as a British protectorate. The British Crown Colonies of Sarawak and North Borneo came into being on 1 June 1946 and 15 July 1946, respectively. In respect to the handover by BMA (BB) to civil government, the case of Sarawak was unique. First, the transfer of authority to the raja's government was made on 15 April 1946; then, on 1 June, the raja ceded Sarawak to the British government. Thereafter, BMA (BB) continued to attend to the distribution of civil supplies, until its dissolution on 15 July. On the same date, the handover was effected in North Borneo. The handover in Brunei had been completed a week earlier, on 6 July 1946.

Indochina and Indonesia

In Indochina and Indonesia, no BMA structure was established. But SAC was entrusted with the tasks of enforcing the surrender and disarmament of the Japanese forces and liberating the POWs and civilian internees in these two territories. British forces operated in Indochina, specifically in Saigon, from September to December 1945; in Indonesia, they served for more than a year, from September 1945 to November 1946. In both cases, British troops confronted volatile and highly tense situations.

British ground troops were instructed to assist the small French contingent in the reoccupation of Indochina. Major General D. D. Gracey, commanding the Twentieth Indian Division, was assigned the mission of flying a British force into Saigon to reoccupy the headquarters of the Japanese Southern Armies. Accordingly, on 13 September 1945, Gracey and his British-Indian troops arrived in Saigon and swiftly secured certain key sections in the city and its immediate environs. Vulnerable points were protected by the British, and Japanese forces were deployed to maintain order elsewhere within the designated zones of Saigon-Cholon, Thudau Mot–Bien Hoa–Lai Taien, and Mytho.

The Viet Minh had declared the Democratic Republic of Viet Nam in August 1945. A public proclamation to this effect was made on 17 September 1945, and Viet Minh forces were poised for a confrontation with British troops. When his warning to the Viet Minh went unheeded, Gracey issued a statement asserting that he was under instructions from SAC to ensure law and order not only within the designated key areas of Saigon but also in all of Indochina south of sixteen degrees north latitude. This pronouncement actually went beyond his original instructions: theoretically, British forces assumed no governmental responsibility other than maintaining the peace. But due to prevailing conditions, they had to keep in operation essential public utilities and at the same time maintain an orderly food distribution system for the civil population. On 20 October, Gracey succeeded in convening a meeting between the French and the Viet Minh; no agreement, however, materialized.

Preempting an outbreak of hostilities, Gracey seized all the key areas of Saigon. The British commander had full authority over military and civil matters within the extended occupied area. This situation continued until the French administration and military forces assumed responsibility for the preservation of order. The handover to the French came in March 1946.

In comparison, Lieutenant General Sir P. A. Christison, commander of British forces in Indonesia, faced a more difficult situation. At the time British troops landed at Batavia in late September 1945, there were no Dutch forces on hand to offer assistance. Christison was instructed to receive the Japanese surrender and to prepare, through officers of Netherlands Indies Civil Affairs (NICA), for the eventual handover to Dutch civil authorities. Although these tasks appeared straightforward initially, developments in Indonesia had adversely changed in regard to the reinstatement of Dutch colonial rule.

On 17 August 1945, just two days after the Japanese surrender, Sukarno had proclaimed the Republic of Indonesia. Indonesian nationalists, armed with Japanese weapons, jealously guarded the six-week-old independent republic when British troops appeared on the scene. Notwithstanding republican armed opposition, Christison set out to secure key areas, namely, Batavia (29 September), Bandoeng (10 October), Semarang (17 October), and Surabaya (25 October). Despite landing in late October, British troops did not effectively secure control of Surabaya until 19 November. Likewise, armed clashes broke out with republican forces in Batavia, Bandoeng, and other towns where the British landings were contested. Ironically, British forces had to wage battles with the Indonesians they had come to liberate.

The presence of NICA staff was met with violent hostility from nationalists as well as the local population. Under such tense conditions, it was decided to replace NICA with the Allied Military Administration, Civil Affairs Branch (AMACAB). The takeover was achieved toward the end of October 1945. Fortunately, AMACAB received greater acceptance and cooperation from the Indonesians.

Dutch troops began to arrive in force in mid-1946, which enabled the withdrawal of British forces except in Java, Sumatra, and Riau. By July, British forces had transferred responsibility for Surabaya, Semarang, and Bandoeng to their Dutch counterparts. In the Outer Islands, the Dutch were in effective control, as republican influence was weaker.

It was no easy task for the British forces to disarm the Japanese (nearly 300,000) and relieve the POWs and civilian internees (about 200,000). And the situation was only aggravated by the republican opposition and open attacks on British operations. In retaliation for what they called transgression by Allied troops, republican authorities announced the cessation of all evacuations of POWs and internees effective 24 July 1946. Hence, the fate of 30,000 European men and women hung in the balance. Lord Killearn, the British special commissioner in Southeast Asia, intervened directly, and despite all odds and in a precarious situation, he succeeded in negotiating the resumption of the evacuation, which began in late September.

In October, Lord Killearn convened a conference between the republicans and the Dutch. This fruitful face-to-face meeting resulted in the declaration of a cease-fire on 4

October. On 15 November, the two parties penned the Linggadjati Agreement. Two weeks thereafter, the last British troops left Indonesia, thus concluding SEAC's responsibilities.

Sterling Performance

BMA was entrusted with wide-ranging responsibilities, encompassing the diverse areas of finance (currency control, custody of property), relief supplies (food, medical, and other supplies), trade and industry (facilitation and rejuvenation), the legislation of law and administration of justice, and the relief of POWs and internees and handling of refugees. Besides these heavy tasks, it had to deal with the political dimensions of an emerging nationalism characterized by militant resistance and violent opposition to the reinstatement of colonial regimes.

In terms of its overall performance in Burma, British Malaya, and British Borneo, BMA succeeded in attaining its general objectives despite trying conditions, particularly in the case of Burma. Moreover, in Burma as in British Borneo, BMA undertook its responsibilities in the midst of military operations. It was a daunting challenge in terms of the organizational skills, resources, and expertise required. Nonetheless, BMA earned accolades for its efficiency and professionalism, to the extent that in Sarawak, the Ibans regarded BMA as the government they would most like to have, thanks to the efficient food distribution network it implemented. In Indochina and Indonesia, there was no formal establishment of BMA, and the chief responsibility of the British commanders was political rather than administrative in nature, yet the rapidly changing circumstances ensured that British forces assumed a greater role in the administration of the reoccupied areas. Notwithstanding a tougher challenge, British forces in Indochina and Indonesia managed to give a sterling performance in carrying out their varied tasks amid a provocative and hostile situation.

Without undermining the achievements of BMA, it should also be noted that from the psychological standpoint, gratitude was owed to the fighting men of the Allied forces. "They indeed brought relief and the opportunity for freedom to the people whose countries had been darkened by the invasions of 1941 and 1942. All that the military governments could do was to try to make fruitful the gift offered by these men" (Donnison 1956: 443).

OOI KEAT GIN

See also Anti-Fascist People's Freedom League (AFPFL); Aung San (1915–1947); Dorman-Smith, Sir Reginald (t. 1941–1946); Force 136; Indochina War (1946–1954), First; Indonesian Revolution (1945–1949); Japanese Occupation of Southeast Asia (1941–1945); Linggadjati (Linggajati) Agreement (1947); MacArthur, General Douglas (1880–1964); Malayan Communist Party (MCP); Malayan People's Anti-Japanese Army (MPAJA); Malayan Union (1946); Mountbatten, Admiral Lord Louis (1900–1979); Nationalism and Independence Movements in Southeast Asia; Saigon (Gia Dinh, Hồ Chí Minh City); Soekarno (Sukarno, 1901–1970); South-East Asia Command (SEAC); Việt Minh (Việt Nam Độc Lập Đồng Minh Hội) (Vietnam Independence League); Vietnam, South (post-1945)

References:

Anderson, Benedict R. O'G. 1972. *Java in a Time of Revolution: Occupation and Resistance, 1944–1946.* Ithaca, NY: Cornell University Press.

Cheah Boon-Kheng. 1983. *Red Star over Malaya: Resistance and Social Conflict during and after the Japanese Occupation, 1941–1946.* Singapore: Singapore University Press.

Collis, Maurice. 1956. *Last and First in Burma.* London: Faber and Faber.

Dennis, Peter. 1987. *Troubled Days of Peace: Mountbatten and South East Asia Command, 1945–46.* Manchester, England: Manchester University Press.

Donnison, F. S. V. 1956. *British Military Administration in the Far East, 1943–46.* London: Her Majesty's Stationery Office.

Kahin, George McT. 1952. *Nationalism and Revolution in Indonesia.* Ithaca, NY: Cornell University Press.

Marr, David. 1981. "Vietnam: Harnessing the Whirlwind." Pp. 163–207 in *Asia: The Winning of Independence.* Edited by Robin Jeffrey. London: Macmillan.

Ooi Keat Gin. 1999. *Rising Sun over Borneo: The Japanese Occupation of Sarawak, 1941–1945.* London and Basingstoke, England: Macmillan; New York: St. Martin's Press.

Short, Anthony. 1989. *The Origins of the Vietnam War.* London and New York: Longman.

Smail, John R. W. 1964. *Bandung in the Early Revolution, 1945–6: A Study in the Social History of the Indonesian Revolution.* Ithaca, NY: Cornell University Press.

Stockwell, A. J. 1979. *British Policy and Malay Politics during the Malayan Union Experiment, 1942–1948.* Kuala Lumpur: Malaysian Branch of the Royal Asiatic Society.

Tinker, Hugh, ed. 1983–1984. *Burma: The Struggle for Independence, 1944–48.* 2 vols. London: Her Majesty's Stationery Office.

Tregonning, K. G. 1965. *A History of Modern Sabah (North Borneo, 1881–1963).* 2nd ed. Kuala Lumpur: University of Malaya Press.

BRITISH NORTH BORNEO CHARTERED COMPANY (1881–1946)

The British North Borneo Chartered Company was created toward the end of 1881 when the British monarch granted a royal charter for the administration of a territory known as North Borneo on the northwestern corner of the island of Borneo. The company administration lasted for more than six decades, and what was once a practically unknown land inhabited by a diversity of people constituting more than thirty ethnic communities was gradually transformed into a nascent modern state.

The genesis of North Borneo (renamed Sabah in 1963) as a modern state featured several players, all with material wealth in mind. Claude Lee Moses, the U.S. consul general to Brunei, obtained in mid-1865 the cession of territory in northern Borneo from the Brunei sultan in return for cash. Shortly thereafter, in September 1865 in Hong Kong, Moses sold the cession rights to two American businessmen—Joseph W. Torrey and Thomas B. Harris—and their two Chinese partners—Lee Assing and Pong Ampong. On the Kimanis River, a settlement named Ellena was established as the base of the newly formed American Trading Company. Both company and settlement were closed within a year for want of funds. Torrey was anxious to sell the concession, and his offer to do so was readily taken up by Baron Gustav von Overbeck (d. 1894). Overbeck, the Austrian consul in Hong Kong, was interested in brokering a sale to the Austrian government.

When Vienna showed no interest, Overbeck wooed Alfred Dent (1844–1927), a businessman based in London. Overbeck also attempted, albeit in vain, to attract German interest in this venture. At the same time, he discussed the possibilities of obtaining a royal charter from the British government with William H. Treacher (1849–1919), the governor of the British colony of Labuan. The Overbeck-Dent partnership renegotiated a new cession from the sultan of Brunei in December 1877. (Torrey's cession had expired in 1875.) This new cession covered the present-day outline of Sabah. Realizing that the eastern portion of the cession territory was under the jurisdiction of the sultan of Sulu, Overbeck proceeded to Sulu and obtained the sultan's agreement to cede the eastern half of Sabah in exchange for cash payment in January 1878. As a means of exhibiting their presence, Overbeck and Dent sent three Englishmen to North Borneo: William Pryer, based in Sandakan on the east coast; W. Pretyman, in Tempasuk; and H. L. Leicester, at Papar on the west coast.

On the matter of the charter, Julian Pauncefote, the permanent undersecretary in the British Foreign Office, was sympathetic to the Overbeck-Dent proposal. But it was a long (three-year) and uphill process for Pauncefote to convince his superiors of the advantages of granting a charter for North Borneo. He utilized a dual thesis, stressing the commercial aspect of the proposal and the *real* danger of a rival Western power colonizing North Borneo. There was, after all, Otto von Bismarck's Germany, which had shown interest in the region during the 1870s. Thanks to protests and objections raised by The Netherlands, the United States, and Spain, the Foreign Office as well as the Colonial Office became convinced of Pauncefote's strategic argument.

In September 1880, Overbeck sold off his share to Dent. Early the next year, Dent established a provincial association and transferred all of his share and control to it in exchange for a substantial cash payment. The association's chairman was Sir Rutherford Alcock, and several prominent personalities were members of the board. This association would cease once the charter was granted and once its assets had been transferred to the British North Borneo Chartered Company, which would undertake to administer North Borneo. Accordingly, on 1

November 1881, the royal charter was granted, and the British North Borneo Chartered Company came into existence.

A court of directors based in London governed the overall policy decisions of the company in its administration of North Borneo. The court appointed a governor to be its representative and head the administration of North Borneo. North Borneo was administratively divided into the West and East Coast Residencies, with Jesselton and Sandakan as the headquarters, respectively. Each residency (province) was under the direction of a resident and was further subdivided into districts under the charge of district officers. During the early decades of company rule, fewer than ten Englishmen governed a territory the size of Scotland. Due to the lack of personnel and the paucity of knowledge about local conditions, the company administration relied on the cooperation and assistance of native chiefs and headmen. Consequently, a native system of administration at the grass roots complemented the duties of the European district officers and residents.

The company administered North Borneo along the lines of a private business corporation in which profitmaking and producing handsome dividends for London shareholders were the chief objectives. Although the interests and the welfare of the indigenous inhabitants were kept in mind, the company generally approved capitalist ventures, knowing that such operations might impinge on native concerns. Large tracts of land concessions were granted to loggers, against the interests of native swidden rice cultivators. Commercial agriculture (tobacco, rubber) was enthusiastically promoted, with fair success, but mineral extraction (gold, manganese, coal) failed to meet expectations. Exports included timber, jungle products (damar, rattan, birds' nests, camphor, gutta-percha), and, on a lesser scale, sea produce (trepang [sea slugs], pearls). Roads were confined to urban networks; bridle paths greatly increased cross-country travel, and telegraph lines enhanced communication. A railway ran along the western coast from Jesselton to Tenom.

After North Borneo suffered through three years and eight months under occupation by the Japanese Imperial Army during the Pacific War (1941–1945) as well as wartime devastation, the Court of Directors was moved to consider transferring sovereignty to the British Crown in July 1946. Thus, North Borneo became a Crown Colony, and the British North Borneo Chartered Company ceased to exist.

OOI KEAT GIN

See also Bajau; Brunei (Sixteenth to Nineteenth Centuries); East Malaysian Ethnic Minorities; Jungle/Forest Products; Labuan (1847); Marine/Sea Products; Mat Salleh Rebellion (1894–1905); Sarawak and Sabah (North Borneo); Sulus and the Sulu Archipelago; Tausugs and the Sulu Sultanate

References:
Black, Ian. 1983. *A Gambling Style of Government: The Establishment of the Chartered Company's Rule in Sabah, 1878–1915.* Kuala Lumpur: Oxford University Press.
Ranjit Singh, D. S. 2000. *The Making of Sabah, 1865–1941: The Dynamics of Indigenous Society.* Kuala Lumpur: Penerbit Universiti Malaya.
Wright, L. R. 1970. *The Origins of British Borneo.* Hong Kong: Hong Kong University Press.

BROOKE, SIR CHARLES ANTHONI JOHNSON (1829–1917)
Protector of Native Interests

As the second white raja of Sarawak from 1868 to 1917, Charles Brooke laid the foundation of a modern state. He strongly adhered to the paternalistic tenets of the Brooke tradition, as advocated by his uncle, James Brooke (1803–1868), the first white raja, whereby the interests and the well-being of the indigenous inhabitants of Sarawak were paramount, surpassing even capitalist gain.

Charles Anthoni Johnson was the youngest son of Emma Johnson, the sister of James Brooke. After leaving the Royal Navy, he joined his uncle's service in 1852 at age twenty-three. His decade-long stewardship as a Brooke officer—spent in the heartland of the Iban region in the thickly forested valleys of the Lupar, Skrang, Saribas, and Krian Rivers—made him knowledgeable and respectful of the native culture and way of life. His formative experiences were recorded in his two-volume memoirs, *Ten Years in Sarawak,* published in 1866. He established himself as a consummate leader of Iban warriors, guiding them into countless expeditions. He was also instrumental in eliminating Chinese (1857), Iban (1850s), and Malay-Brunei (1860–1861) opposition to Brooke rule. Upon his uncle's insistence, Charles adopted the name Brooke in 1863.

Notwithstanding his position as an absolute ruler, Charles, like his predecessor, sought the advice and opinion of native chiefs. In complementing the Supreme Council (1855), an advisory body of Malay *datu* (nonroyal chiefs), Charles inaugurated the General Council (the present-day Council Negri) in 1867, with the goal of increasing interaction between the raja and his senior officers, on the one hand, and leaders and chiefs of the various ethnic communities, on the other. The General Council was more a public relations exercise than a functional advisory committee. Charles made it imperative that all European Brooke officers consult with native chiefs to keep abreast of native public opinion, although the advice the chiefs offered was considered nonbinding. Charles reorganized his uncle's makeshift administration with European residents and district officers, assisted by Malay native officers, Chinese and Eurasian court writers, and clerical personnel.

Believing the Brunei sultanate was in the last stages of collapse and considering himself the appropriate successor, Charles expanded the territorial boundaries of Sarawak eastward, ending in 1905 with the transfer of Lawas. He was apprehensive of Brunei's cession of the territory that subsequently became British North Borneo, administered by a stockholding company (the British North Borneo Chartered Company).

Having pride in the Brooke tradition of prioritizing the interests of the indigenous peoples over other concerns, Charles was highly critical of British imperialism, which he took to task in a 1907 pamphlet entitled *Queries: Past and Present*. He reluctantly accepted the protectorate status granted by Britain in 1888.

Charles greatly encouraged trade (jungle products, sago), promoted the exploitation of mineral resources (gold, coal, mineral oil), and supported the development of commercial agriculture (pepper, gambier, rubber, sago, coconut). Infrastructure facilities were developed, particularly land, sea, and river transport and the telegraph. Putting faith in the Chinese in regard to the development of the country's economy, Charles realized the ambition of his uncle in implementing the immigration of Foochow and Cantonese agriculturalists to the Lower Rejang (1900–1901). Although the original intention was to increase domestic rice production, the Chinese farmers, in the face of failures, turned their attention to rubber smallholdings and achieved much success.

Charles did not look favorably on speculative Western capitalist enterprises. Consequently, only a handful of European companies operated in Sarawak, notably the Borneo Company Limited (BCL), the oil companies, and a few other businesses in commercial agriculture.

Emphasizing food crop and commercial small-scale agriculture, Charles urged the native inhabitants to rely on the land for sustenance. He reminded his native subjects that their lands were their heritage or *darah daging* (blood and flesh) and that they should value and never lose possession of them. Fearing that natives could be left landless in their own homeland, Charles decreed in 1910, at the height of the rubber boom, that no land was to be sold or transferred to any European firm or individual.

In promoting agriculture, Charles set up an experimental farm at Matang near Kuching (the state capital), where various crops were cultivated and, if proven viable, promoted. Having faith in coal, he invested in the Simunjan colliery and bought the Muara Damit (Brooketon) mines. The auriferous (gold-rich) region of Upper Sarawak (gold, antimony, cinnabar) was left to the Chinese and BCL to exploit. The oil strike at Miri in 1910 placed Sarawak on the world map.

Although, like his predecessor, Charles sought to maintain the traditional way of life of the various ethnic inhabitants, age-old practices such as headhunting and Iban migration were proscribed and discouraged, respectively, and slavery was gradually abolished. Ironically, the Brooke government's punitive expeditions, which pitted downriver Ibans against recalcitrant upriver Ibans, Kayans, and Kenyahs, served as an impetus to headhunting.

Western-style schooling was introduced by Christian missionaries and the Brooke government, but Charles had reservations about the benefits that such an education could bring to the indigenous peoples. He favored miscegenation and encouraged it among his European officers; he himself had a child with a Malay woman. He believed the mixed-blood offspring would make better citizens and enlightened rulers of lands in the East.

Charles's pronative policies, designs toward Brunei, and anti-imperialistic views, coupled with his reserved personality and his aversion to mingle with European society whether in Britain or in Singapore, made him few friends. His wife, Ranee Margaret (1849–1936), lamented his maverick and isolated position, which distanced him from British official circles and the business community.

Charles died in 1917. His eldest son, Charles Vyner Brooke (r. 1917–1941, 1946), became third white raja of Sarawak. However, Raja Charles did not totally trust this son, and therefore, in his political will (1913), he established a joint rajaship between Vyner (1874–1963) and another son, Bertram (1876–1965).

OOI KEAT GIN

See also British Interests in Southeast Asia; Brooke, James, and Sarawak; Brunei (Sixteenth to Nineteenth Centuries); Colonialism; East Malaysian Ethnic Minorities; Ibans; Miscegenation; Rentap (d. ca. mid-1860s); Sarawak and Sabah (North Borneo)

References:

Crisswell, Colin N. 1978. *Rajah Charles Brooke: Monarch of All He Surveyed.* Kuala Lumpur: Oxford University Press.

Ooi Keat Gin. 1996. *World beyond the Rivers: Education in Sarawak from Brooke Rule to Colonial Office Administration, 1841–1963.* Hull, England: Department of South-East Asian Studies, University of Hull.

———. 1997. *Of Free Trade and Native Interests: The Brookes and the Economic Development of Sarawak, 1841–1941.* Kuala Lumpur: Oxford University Press.

Pringle, Robert. 1970. *Rajahs and Rebels: The Ibans of Sarawak under Brooke Rule, 1841–1941.* London: Macmillan.

Reece, R. H. W. 1991. "European-Indigenous Miscegenation and Social Status in Nineteenth Century Borneo." Pp. 455–488 in *Female and Male in Borneo: Contributions and Challenges to Gender Studies.* Edited by Vinson H. Sutlive. Williamsburg, VA: Borneo Research Council.

BROOKE, JAMES, AND SARAWAK
Maverick Colonialist

In 1841, James Brooke (1803–1868), an English gentleman-adventurer, established a dynasty of white rajas in a territory called Sarawak on the northwestern corner of the island of Borneo. The Brooke white rajas, who governed Sarawak for more than a century, were guided by principles that emphasized the protection and promotion of the rights and interests of the multiethnic indigenous inhabitants.

Born of an East India Company (EIC) official, Brooke spent his childhood in India and completed his early education in England. After sustaining an injury while serving as a cavalry officer in the First Anglo-Burmese War (1824–1826), Brooke returned to England. He made two voyages to China (1830–1831, 1834), visiting the Straits Settlements en route. Convinced of Stamford Raffles's vision of a greater role to be played by Britain in the Malay Archipelago, Brooke published a prospectus in 1838 wherein he advocated territorial possession in place of treaty arrangements as the basis for developing free trade and promoting British commerce and interests.

Utilizing the inheritance from his late father's estate, Brooke acquired the 142-ton schooner *Royalist* to undertake a geographic and scientific expedition to Marudu Bay at the northern tip of Borneo, the Celebes (Sulawesi), and New Guinea. He made his initial call at Kuching, the river port capital of Sarawak, in 1839 to convey a letter to Pengiran Bendahara Pengiran Muda Hassim (d. 1846) from the mercantile community of Singapore, thanking him for assisting shipwrecked British seamen. Sarawak was then a fiefdom of the sultanate of Brunei and was in the midst of a rebellion (1836–1840). On his journey home, Brooke again visited Kuching. Hassim was unable to end the rebellion and turned to Brooke for assistance, granting him the title of "Raja (Governor) of Sarawak" in return. Brooke succeeded and was conferred as the first white raja in 1841 by Sultan Omar Ali Saifuddin II (d. 1852) of Brunei.

Initially, Brooke attempted to realize the Rafflesian vision of a British commercial empire in the Malay Archipelago, but his hopes were dashed when the pro-British Hassim and his family were massacred in 1846. He then shifted his attention to Sarawak, where he laid the foundation of an enlightened, paternal despotism in which the raja ruled in consultation with the native chiefs by incorporating the Sarawak Malay *datu* (nonroyal chiefs) into his administration as advisers.

The principles of Brooke's rule emphasized the development of free trade, the protection of native interests, and the promotion of native welfare. In upholding native interests, the population's traditional way of life was maintained as far as possible; if change was necessary, its introduction was to be gradual, allowing the indigenous peoples to adopt and adapt at their own pace. Brooke objected to the large inflow of European capitalist investment and the concomitant influx of Europeans into the country, concerned that indigenous interests would be compromised in favor of Western interests and that native labor would be exploited for foreign capitalist gains. The principles of prioritizing native interests above all else became enshrined in the so-called Brooke Tradition, which was steadfastly adhered to by Brooke's successors— his nephew Charles Anthoni Johnson Brooke (r. 1868–1917) and the latter's son, Charles Vyner Brooke (r. 1917–1941, 1946).

Sir James Brooke, raja of Sarawak. (Hulton-Deutsch Collection/Corbis)

During his tenure as raja (1841–1868), James Brooke eliminated the piratical menace along the northwestern Bornean coast with the assistance of the Royal Navy, thereby facilitating trading activities. He also proscribed exploitative traditional native practices, such as *serah dagang* (forced trade), that Malay datu and Brunei *pangeran* (nobles) impressed on the weaker indigenous communities, including the Bidayuhs (Land Dayaks) and the Melanaus. Furthermore, the gory practice of head-hunting by the Ibans (Sea Dayaks) and other interior peoples was proscribed.

In 1857, the Hakka Chinese gold miners of Upper Sarawak attacked Kuching in an attempt to overthrow his regime, yet Brooke nonetheless maintained his faith in the ability of the Chinese to develop the economic resources of the country, especially in mining and trade. His goal of encouraging Chinese immigration was realized by his successor in the early 1900s when Foochow and Cantonese farmers were brought to settle in the Lower Rejang.

Brooke successfully overcame opposition to his rule from the Hakka Chinese (1857), the Brunei-backed Malays of Mukah (ca. mid-1850s–1860), and the upriver Ibans led by Rentap (1850s–1861). At the same time, he pushed Sarawak's borders eastward to the Rejang (1853) and the Bintulu (1861) Rivers at the expense of Brunei. However, he attempted in vain to secure recognition and protectorate status for Sarawak from Britain or from other European nations (The Netherlands, Belgium, France, and Italy). Although Sarawak was recognized as an independent state by the United States in 1850, it was not ceded by Britain until 1863.

Brooke was investigated for wrongdoing in the 1847 massacre of "pirates" at Batang Maru, but he was vindicated both in the British Parliament and at an inquiry in Singapore in 1854. Despite this vindication, however, Brooke remained disappointed about failing to gain recognition and protection for Sarawak, and he left for England in 1863 in poor spirits and failing health. He passed away in 1868. Brooke left a legacy whereby Sarawak's multiethnic indigenous inhabitants continued with their traditional subsistence-based livelihood, for the most part undisturbed by either European or Chinese capitalistic influence and exploitation.

OOI KEAT GIN

See also Borneo; Brooke, Sir Charles Anthoni Johnson (1829–1917); Brunei (Sixteenth to Nineteenth Centuries); Colonialism; East Malaysian Ethnic Minorities; Free Trade; Imperialism; Piracy; Raffles, Sir (Thomas) Stamford Bingley (1781–1826); Rentap (d. ca. mid-1860s); Sarawak and Sabah (North Borneo)

References:
Ooi Keat Gin. 1997. *Of Free Trade and Native Interests: The Brookes and the Economic Development of Sarawak, 1841–1941.* Kuala Lumpur: Oxford University Press.
Pringle, Robert. 1970. *Rajahs and Rebels. The Ibans of Sarawak under Brooke Rule.* London: Macmillan.
Saunders, Graham. 1973. "James Brooke and Asian Government." *Brunei Museum Journal* 3, no. 1: 105–117.
Tarling, Nicholas. 1982. *The Burthen, the Risk, and the Glory: A Biography of Sir James Brooke.* Kuala Lumpur: Oxford University Press.
———. 1992. "Brooke Rule in Sarawak and Its Principles." *Journal of the Malaysian Branch of the Royal Asiatic Society* 65, no. 1: 15–26.

BRUNEI (SIXTEENTH TO NINETEENTH CENTURIES)

The history of Brunei prior to the mid-nineteenth century reveals rare beacons of light within an ocean of darkness. Source materials are vestigial. Brunei was not a bureaucracy; government records and statistics hardly exist. Archaeology, coinage, and maps are of minimal assistance. Personal papers are wanting. Indigenous sources, particularly royal genealogies, yield valuable insights but little solid fact. Considerable reliance has to be placed, therefore, on European (mostly Iberian) reports. It is not known how many sultans there have been, nor can the reigns of many of them be dated accurately. The present monarch (Hassanal Bolkiah) is claimed officially to be the twenty-ninth of his dynasty; no serious historian accepts this. With regard to secondary sources, one or two Western writers suffer from a lingering colonialist mind-set, and some indigenous historians have succumbed to the imperatives of nation building and the glorification of Islam.

An eyewitness account reveals that the Muslim sultanate was definitely in existence by 1521; the exact date of its foundation remains unproven. The Brunei royal family certainly incorporated Bornean, Malay, Chinese, and Arabic elements. In 1521, Brunei's sway extended northward to Luzon and at least as far south in Borneo as the Kapuas Delta. The capital, built mainly over the river but also with a land section, had a settled court with an established protocol and was defended by land and naval forces.

Although Brunei gave its name to Borneo, it is doubtful whether the sultanate ever exercised sway over the whole island. During the sixteenth century, moreover, rival Muslim dynasties were established elsewhere around the coast. Brunei was not a territorial state with clearly defined frontiers. Its outer limits waxed and waned; its control of the interior was limited. The main method of control was to station an official at a river mouth to tax the trade going up and down the waterway.

Wealth was derived from products such as camphor, pepper, and fish; cloth was imported via Melaka. Europeans were prone to regard Brunei as of negligible commercial importance, but for the Portuguese, it provided a staging post between the Malay Peninsula and the Moluccas (Maluku). By 1580, when Portugal was brought under the Castilian throne, Spain had begun to make good its hold of the Philippines, which cut off Brunei's archipelagic empire. The Spaniards occupied the capital of Brunei from April to June 1578, razing the national mosque. They returned in March 1579 but sailed away without accomplishing anything. The upshot was that Brunei lost control of Sulu, and the activities of its Muslim missionaries in the archipelago were curtailed. Relations between Brunei and Manila steadied after 1588, but between 1577 and 1787, only seven trading vessels went to Manila from the Bornean kingdom.

The "despotic" reign of Sultan Hassan, which probably fell within the first two decades of the seventeenth century, has been called "the last high point in Brunei fortunes before the mid-twentieth century" (Saunders 1994: 62). Hassan is reported to have boosted the complement of viziers from two to four and to have reasserted Brunei domination of Sambas and Sulu.

Although Raja Bongsu, son of Sultan Hassan, was nominally Brunei's *adipati* (viceroy) in Sulu for about four decades until 1650, this did not preclude open warfare between the two Muslim regimes. In 1650, Raja Bongsu's illegitimate son, Raja Bakhtiar, took over and later styled himself Sultan Salah-ud-Din Bakhtiar, the "first authentic Sultan of Sulu." Sulu was strong and warlike and established its own zone of domination, including northern and northeast Borneo, its economy being based on slavery and piracy. Sulu was not warlike enough, however, to subjugate Brunei's heartland.

In the seventeenth century, Brunei was prone to civil war, connected with disputed successions to the throne. Such internal strife split the royal family into factions and weakened Brunei's dominion over its outlying territories. Seagoing Bajaus increasingly preyed on Brunei.

The eighteenth century is a particular problem in deciphering the historical record. Sultan Muhammad Aliuddin, whose reign had marked a rapprochement with Manila, died in 1690. The speculation is that his illegitimate son elbowed aside the nominated heir and called upon Buginese support to keep a "usurper dynasty" in power for several decades. The legitimate line was restored in the person of Sultan Omar Ali Saifuddin I, who was certainly reigning by 1762.

British reports indicate that in the late eighteenth century, there was still a junk trade between Brunei and China and that a Chinese community was settled locally. An ineffectual commercial treaty was signed in 1774 with the English East India Company (EIC) in return for protection against pirates.

Brunei remained beyond colonial control at the end of the eighteenth century, largely because it offered few economic prospects and was in a strategic backwater. The foundation of Singapore (1819), the growth of the India-China trade, and the involvement of ambitious individuals (such as James Brooke) would transform this situation. Meanwhile, Brunei's cause was not helped by further succession disputes within the royal family in the early decades of the nineteenth century.

From the 1840s onward the story of Brunei was one characterized by weakness, internal disunity, poverty, and massive territorial losses, first to the Brooke White Rajahs of Sarawak and subsequently to the British North Borneo

Company. The island of Labuan, which commands Brunei Bay, was acquired by Britain in 1846. By 1905–1906, when the situation had stabilized thanks to the appointment of a British Resident, the sultanate had been reduced to a rump state, comprising two separate wings detached from each other by the Limbang district of Sarawak. Political rescue was followed by economic salvation, thanks to the discovery of the Seria oil field in 1929.

A. V. M. HORTON

See also Anglo-Brunei Relations (Nineteenth Century to 1980s); British North Borneo Chartered Company (1881–1946); Brooke, Sir Charles Anthoni Johnson (1829–1917); Brooke, James, and Sarawak; Brunei Ethnic Minorities; Brunei Malays; East India Company (EIC) (1600), English; Manila; Piracy; Sarawak and Sabah (North Borneo); Slavery; Sulu and the Sulu Archipelago; Tausugs and the Sulu Sultanate

References:

Bassett, D. K. 1964. "The Historical Background, 1500–1815." Pp. 113–127, 415–420 in *Malaysia: A Survey*. Edited by Wang Gungwu. London: Pall Mall Press.

Brown, Donald E. 1971. "Brunei and the Bajau." *Borneo Research Bulletin* 3, no. 2 (December): 55–58.

Low, Sir Hugh. 1880. "Selesilah (Book of the Descent) of the Rajas of Bruni." *Journal of the Straits Branch of the Royal Asiatic Society* 5: 1–35.

Nicholl, Robert. 1975. *European Sources for the History of the Sultanate of Brunei in the Sixteenth Century*. Special Publications no. 9. Bandar Seri Begawan: Brunei Museum.

———. 1989. "Some Problems of Brunei Chronology." *Journal of South-East Asian Studies* 20, no. 2 (September): 175–195.

Saunders, Graham. 1994. *A History of Modern Brunei*. Kuala Lumpur: Oxford University Press.

Sweeney, P. L. Amin. 1968. "Silsilah Raja-Raja Berunai." *Journal of the Malaysian Branch of the Royal Asiatic Society (JMBRAS)* 41, no. 2: 1–82, with supplement in *JMBRAS* 42, no. 2 (1969): 222–224.

Tarling, Nicholas. 1978. *Sulu and Sabah: A Study of British Policy towards the Philippines and North Borneo from the Late Eighteenth Century*. Kuala Lumpur: Oxford University Press.

BRUNEI ETHNIC MINORITIES

The Brunei sultanate is dominated by the Brunei Malay, but its population also comprises several native ethnic minorities who have played important roles in the history of the state. Indeed, in oral traditions, the Brunei Malay and the ruling family are said to have descended from local pagan peoples who converted to Islam and "became Malay." The process of identifying with the politically and culturally dominant Malay, intermarrying with them, and converting to Islam continues to this day.

For constitutional and census purposes, the Brunei government classifies most of the indigenous ethnic groups in the country together with the Brunei Malay as Malay or as constituents of the Malay race, and their languages are identified as Malay dialects (King 1994: 178–179). The Brunei Nationality Enactment of 1961 and the national ideology of the "Malay Islamic Monarchy" both have the long-term aim of assimilating other groups into the Malay culture and polity (Braighlinn 1992: 19–20). The "Malay" category includes those people in Brunei called Dusun (or Bisaya), Murut (or Lun Bawang/Lun Dayeh), Kadayan, Tutong, and Belait. It excludes such groups as the Iban and the nomadic Penan, who are classified as "other indigenous" in government publications.

Historically, the constituent Malay ethnic groups of the Brunei sultanate were administered through their own leaders, designated *menteri darat* (land chiefs), who were granted Malay-derived titles by the state, such as *penghulu* (government-appointed district headman), *temenggong* (official responsible for defense and policing the city), and *pemancha* (a traditional title for a chief) (King 1993: 227). At the very bottom of the hierarchy were the village headmen (*ketua kampong*), who were responsible for the primary constituent units of the polity: the village and longhouse communities. These non-Malay populations were usually classified as subjects, dependents, or clients (*hamba*); some of them were also acquired as slaves (*ulun*) or concubines by members of the royal family, nobles, and nonnoble officials through capture, purchase, or indebtedness (Brown 1976: 187–189). With the gradual reduction in the extent of Brunei territories following European intervention in the mid-nineteenth century, several of these communities are now found in politically separate territories in Malaysian Sarawak and Sabah and even in Indonesian Kalimantan.

The group most closely associated with the Brunei Malay comprises the Kadayan—so much so that some observers have suggested they are complementary segments of the same society (Maxwell 1996). In the Malay language, *kadayan/kedayan* means "attendants," "followers," or "prince's retinue." These people were traditionally farmers and suppliers of rice and other food crops in the Brunei sultanate, and they occupied the land extending out on either side of the Brunei River and Brunei Bay; they are also now found in the district of Temburong, where they began to settle after 1918, as well as in the Miri and Lawas areas of Sarawak, in Sipitang in Sabah, and on the island of Labuan. They entered into economic relationships with the Brunei Malay, who comprised administrators, traders, craftspeople, and fishermen. The Kadayan are Muslims and speak a Malay dialect, and therefore, over time, they have tended to identify with the dominant Brunei Malay, intermarry with them, and assimilate to their culture. They appear to have acted as a buffer population between the Brunei Malay and the other pagan ethnic minorities, and there is evidence of Lun Bawang, Tutong, and Belait being absorbed into Kadayan communities.

The term *Murut* is an externally imposed word used by the Malay to refer to interior pagan populations in Brunei, adjacent parts of Sarawak, western Sabah, and East Kalimantan. They are not to be confused with the Murut of interior Sabah, who are culturally very different (King 1994: 190–191). The people (particularly those in Sarawak) call themselves *Lun Bawang,* which means "people of this place" or "people of the country" (in Sabah, the name *Lun Dayeh* is used, meaning "people of the interior"). In the past, the Lun Bawang had been subject to Brunei overlordship and subject to tribute and taxes. Their local leaders from the upper rank (*lun do'*) were appointed to offices in the sultanate and given titles. Some Lun Bawang were also absorbed into Malay society.

The term *Dusun* was also externally imposed; it is a Malay term meaning "[people of the] orchards" or "[people of the] gardens" and is still in use in Brunei. The internally accepted name is *Bisaya,* which is more frequently used in those communities in Sarawak. The

Dusun/Bisaya are found in the Tutong and Belait regions of Brunei and in the Limbang area of Sarawak (King 1994: 190–193). As with the Kadayan, the Bisaya traditionally supplied rice to the Brunei polity. Brunei officials were given special rights to tax the Dusun, and they in turn granted titles to selected Bisayan leaders, who periodically had to deliver tribute at special Brunei ceremonial occasions.

The Tutong and Belait are remnant populations who have been subject to processes of conversion to Islam and assimilation by the Malay and Kadayan. Their original culture and language have now largely disappeared. They are part of a much larger, submerged cultural complex of peoples scattered in the lower Baram River basin in Sarawak and western Brunei, and they demonstrate the consequences of the considerable pressures on local communities to identify with and assimilate to Brunei Malay culture.

VICTOR T. KING

See also Brunei (Sixteenth to Nineteenth Centuries); Brunei Malay; East Malaysian Ethnic Minorities; Ibans; Malays; Melayu Islam Beraja (MIB, Malay Islamic Monarchy); Sarawak and Sabah (North Borneo)

References:

Braighlinn, G. 1992. *Ideological Innovation under Monarchy: Aspects of Legitimation Activity in Contemporary Brunei*. Comparative Asian Studies 9. Amsterdam: VU University Press, Centre for Asian Studies.

Brown, D. E. 1976. *Principles of Social Structure, Southeast Asia*. London: Duckworth.

King, Victor T. 1993. *The Peoples of Borneo*. Oxford: Blackwell.

———. 1994. "What Is Brunei Society? Reflections on a Conceptual and Ethnographic Issue." *South East Asia Research* 2: 176–198.

Maxwell, Allen R. 1996. "The Place of the Kadayan in Traditional Brunei Society." *South East Asia Research* 4: 157–196.

BRUNEI MALAY

The Brunei Malay (or Barunay) are the politically, economically, and culturally dominant population of the sultanate of Brunei, the only surviving Muslim Malay monarchy on the island of Borneo. Until recently, the focus of their settlement was the famous Kampong Ayer (meaning "Water Village"), which traditionally surrounded the sultan's palace and the main mosque. In effect, it comprises several villages or parishes of wooden family dwellings raised on stilts above the waters of the Brunei River, upstream from Brunei Bay. Although Kampong Ayer is still a thriving settlement, many of its former inhabitants have now been resettled on dry land.

The origins of the Brunei Malay as a separately defined ethnic group are obscure. The Brunei Malay oral epic poem *Sya'ir Awang Simawn* provides an account of the origins and historical development of Brunei in the deeds of the founding heroes (Maxwell 1995: 178–206). The culture hero, Awang Simawn, is also well-known to other native, non-Muslim communities in the Brunei Bay area, including the Bisaya (Dusun), Kadayan, and Lun Bawang (Murut). There are several versions of these oral traditions, but the most likely interpretation of them is that at some unspecified time, local pagan populations converted to Islam; it is these who are the ancestors of today's Brunei Malay. Various versions of the epic have Simawn as an older brother of Awang Alak Batatar, a pagan Bisaya or Lun Bawang who converted to Islam and became Sultan Muhammad, the first Muslim ruler of Brunei. Stories of Awang Simawn therefore connect the Brunei Malay with the neighboring non-Muslim natives in a common cultural and historical heritage.

Although one Brunei authority has the conversion of their first ruler to Islam in 1363 and another puts it in 1405, European sources suggest that the conversion did not take place until the early sixteenth century (Nicholl 1975: 3–7). Brunei's roots as a trading emporium go back as far as the sixth century C.E. when a Hinduized state on the northwest coast of Borneo, which the Chinese referred to as P'o-ni, sent tribute to the imperial court. Following conversion to Islam, Brunei became a powerful trading center from the sixteenth to eighteenth centuries, claiming suzerainty over the whole island of Borneo and parts of the southern and central Philippines. However, the extent of its authority existed more in name than in substance, and Brunei power rarely penetrated the vast hinterlands of the island. The sultanate instead controlled strategic coastal and riverine locations and the flow of the luxury forest product trade. Brunei power was progressively weakened as Europeans began to intervene in local political and economic relations, and by the early twentieth century, the sultanate had lost most of its territories and retained only two small enclaves of land amounting to some 5,765 square kilometers (Leake 1990).

The focus of the realm was the Malay sultan, or *raja,* a hereditary ruler who could confer titles and appanages on his appointed administrators. The royal family and the nobility (*pengirans*) were highly stratified and status conscious, operating within an elaborate system of administrative, ceremonial, and ritual offices and a complex hierarchy of honorific titles, linguistic usages, and etiquette. The system was Hindu in origin, with subsequent Islamic modifications (Brown 1970: 11, 19, 87, 89). The main distinction was between the nobility and the commoners. The nobility comprised a "core," which was "descended from current or recent Sultans or other high officials" (Brown 1976: 186–187). The most important officials next to the sultan were the four viziers (*wazir*), who had ministerial functions. These comprised the *pengiran bendahara* (responsible for the administration of the land or the interior), the *pengiran di-gadong* (finance and treasury, particularly taxation), the *pengiran pemancha* (mediator of the State Council), and the *pengiran temenggong* (military leader) (Brown 1970: 106). Below the core nobility were the commoner nobles (*pengiran kebanyakan*); these were appointed as officials with the title *cheteria,* a Hindu-derived term for the warrior caste. They, too, had appanages assigned to them. Then came those of nonnoble rank, including the aristocrats (*awang*) who undertook much of the day-to-day administration of the state on behalf of the nobles and as officials were termed *menteri.* Finally, there were the commoners (*ra'ayat*), some of whom also had official positions.

Most of the Malay wards in the state capital performed specialist functions: fishing, strand collecting, palm weaving, woodworking, textile manufacturing, rice processing, and trading. Of special importance were the blacksmiths, silversmiths, and brass-smiths. Specialist smiths made high-quality items for the court, and their tasks were often associated with aristocratic households and handed down from parents to children.

Given the wealth generated in Brunei following the discovery of oil and gas in the 1930s, the present-day Brunei Malay enjoy a relatively high standard of living; they pay no income taxes and are provided with free schooling, health, and other services. The continuation of monarchical rule after achieving full independence from Britain on 31 December 1983 has also meant that many of the traditional offices, ranks, and titles of Brunei Malay society have survived into the modern era.

VICTOR T. KING

See also Borneo; Brunei (Sixteenth to Nineteenth Centuries); Brunei Ethnic Minorities; East Malaysian Ethnic Minorities; Kampong Ayer (Brunei); Malays; Melayu Islam Beraja (MIB, Malay Islamic Monarchy); Miscegenation; Sarawak and Sabah (North Borneo)

References:
Brown, D. E. 1970. *Brunei: The Structure and History of a Bornean Malay Sultanate.* Bandar Seri Begawan, Brunei: Brunei Museum Monograph.
———. 1976. *Principles of Social Structure, Southeast Asia.* London: Duckworth.
Leake, David, Jr. 1990. *Brunei: The Modern Southeast Asian Islamic Sultanate.* Kuala Lumpur: Forum.
Maxwell, Allen R. 1995. "Who Is Awang Simawn?" Pp. 178–206 in *From Buckfast to Borneo. Essays Presented to Father Robert Nicholl on the 85th Anniversary of His Birth, 27 March 1995.* Edited by Victor T. King and A.V. M. Horton. Hull, England: Centre for South-East Asian Studies, University of Hull.
Nicholl, Robert. 1975. *European Sources for the History of the Sultanate of Brunei in the Sixteenth Century.* Bandar Seri Begawan, Brunei: Brunei Museum.

BRUNEI NATIONAL DEMOCRATIC PARTY (BNDP) (1985–1988)

The Partai Kebangsaan Demokratik Brunei (Brunei National Democratic Party, BNDP) was the first political party to operate legally in the sultanate of Brunei after the Brunei People's Independence Front (BAKER) fizzled out in the early 1970s. Nonetheless, BNDP attracted minimal support from an apathetic populace and lasted for only three years (1985–1988). No legislature existed during that period.

The BNDP was registered in May 1985, with Haji Abdul Latif bin Abdul Hamid (d. 1990), former secretary-general of BAKER, as president and Awang Mohamad Hatta bin Haji Zainal Abidin as vice-president. Membership was confined to Malays. The party's objective was to establish parliamentary democracy under a constitutional monarchical system. It also compaigned for the sultanate to take control of the Brunei Shell Petroleum Company and for antipoverty measures to be activated. On the eve of its official launch in September 1985, a setback was suffered when the government prohibited civil servants (then comprising nearly half the sultanate's entire workforce) from engaging in political activity.

No sooner had the BNDP been founded than it split, apparently because its executive rejected calls for a congress to vote on the party's leadership. In November 1985, some 150 members resigned and set up the rival Brunei National Solidarity Party (BNSP), leaving the rump BNDP with fewer than 50 members. Nevertheless, the BNDP continued to hold press conferences abroad and to urge the government to hold elections. By early 1988, Sultan Hassanal Bolkiah (1946–) had begun to fear that party political activity would upset the stability of the nation. The BNDP was deregistered on 27 January 1988 on the grounds that it had contravened the Societies Act.

The party's president and its secretary-general, Abdul Latif Chuchu (b. 1946), were held without trial for two years. Amnesty International adopted them as "prisoners of conscience." Abdul Latif Hamid died in May 1990, at the age of fifty, shortly after his release from internment. Five years later, Abdul Latif Chuchu joined the BNSP, of which he was briefly president.

A. V. M. HORTON

See also Brunei National Solidarity Party (BNSP) (1985); Brunei Oil and Gas Industry; Brunei Rebellion (December 1962); Hassanal Bolkiah, Sultan of Brunei (1946–); People's Independence Front (Barisan Kemerdekaan Rakyat, BAKER) (1966)

References:

Amnesty International. *Annual Reports.*

Bartholomew, James. 1989. *The Richest Man in the World: The Sultan of Brunei*. London: Viking.

Eusoff Agaki Haji-Ismail. 1991. "Brunei Darussalam: Its Re-emergence as a Sovereign and Independent Malay-Muslim Sultanate (1959–1983)." M.Phil. thesis, University of Hull.

Ranjit Singh, D. S., and Jatswan S. Sidhu. 1997. *Historical Dictionary of Brunei Darussalam*. Lanham, MD, and London: Scarecrow Press.

Southeast Asian Affairs. Singapore: Institute of Southeast Asian Studies (annual).

BRUNEI NATIONAL SOLIDARITY PARTY (BNSP) (1985)

The Partai Perpaduan Kebangsaan (PPKB), usually translated as the Brunei National Solidarity Party and known by the acronym BNSP, appeared toward the end of 1985. It became largely inactive after 1988 but was revived in 1995 and again in 1998; in 2001 and 2002, it was cited from time to time in the local press, it held a party congress, and it was intending to set up a website, although none had appeared by the end of 2003. Press reports reveal that the party has both a women's section and a youth wing; even so, total BNSP membership remains limited to a few hundred persons at most.

Founded by breakaway members of the Brunei National Democratic Party (BNDP), the organization pledged support for all government policies executed within the framework of the Malay Islamic Monarchy concept (*Melayu Islam Beraja*, MIB). Unlike the BNDP, membership was open to Malays and those of other indigenous ethnic groups regardless of religion. After the dissolution of the BNDP in 1988, the BNSP became the sole legal political party in the country.

From 1988 to 1995, the political atmosphere in Negara Brunei Darussalam was quiet: "People had learned the futility of anti-government opposition," Graham Saunders remarked, "and on the whole accepted the secure but bland life offered to them" (1994: 189). In 1995, however, the BNSP sprang back into life, holding a general assembly attended by about fifty people. The BNSP hoped for a revival of the Legislative Council, which had been abolished in 1984. Forty-nine-year-old Haji Abdul Latif Chuchu (b. 1946), a businessman and former teacher, was elected president, with Haji Mohd Hatta Zainal Abidin, the founding party president, as vice-president. Haji Abdul Latif Chuchu resigned shortly afterward, however, reportedly as a condition of his release from detention five years earlier. In May 1998, the BNSP held a further congress, at which Haji Mohd Hatta was elected president.

Any serious political party would have made hay out of contemporary scandals in the sultanate; the BNSP, however, has failed to do so. In the meantime, the royal-led Brunei government is more than capable of upholding the MIB system without any assistance from the BNSP.

A. V. M. HORTON

See also Brunei National Democratic Party (BNDP) (1985–1988); Melayu Islam Beraja (MIB, Malay Islamic Party)

References:
Abu Bakar Hamzah. 1989. "Brunei Darussalam [in 1988]: Continuity and Change." *Southeast Asian Affairs:* 91–104.
Ranjit Singh, D. S., and Jatswan S. Sidhu. 1997. *Historical Dictionary of Brunei Darussalam.* Lanham, MD, and London: Scarecrow Press.
Saunders, Graham. 1994. *A History of Modern Brunei.* Kuala Lumpur: Oxford University Press.

BRUNEI OIL AND GAS INDUSTRY
A Sultanate's Treasure Trove

The wealth derived from hydrocarbons, beginning in 1932, transformed Brunei from a debt-ridden backwater into one of the richest countries in the world. Exports increased from Straits dollars 543,707 in 1915 (*Brunei Annual Report 1915:* 4) to B$6,733.5 million in 2000 (HSBC 2002: 8), government revenue from less than Straits dollars 29,529 in 1915 (*Brunei Annual Report 1915:* 1) to B$5,084.4 million in 2000 (HSBC 2002:7). In 2001 hydrocarbons accounted for 90 percent of all export receipts and 40 percent of gross domestic product (GDP).

Before 1922, several companies had prospected for oil in the country, but by the early 1920s, the British Malayan Petroleum Company (BMPC), a Shell subsidiary, had the field to itself. On 5 April 1929, oil was struck at Seria, but production was delayed pending more favorable market conditions. By the 1930s, Brunei had quickly become the third largest oil producer in the British Commonwealth. All the oil was exported via a pipeline to Lutong (Sarawak), completed in 1932. The BMPC, which soon acquired a major role in the sultanate, was reformed in 1957 as the Brunei Shell Petroleum Company (BSPC), the head office being in the sultanate itself. In 2000, BSPC oil production averaged 190,000 barrels a day, the highest level achieved by the company in more than twenty years. Under the Eighth National Development Plan, production of 212,000 barrels per day (bpd) was planned for 2001 and 207,000 bpd for 2002 to 2005. Proven reserves in 1999 stood at 1,400 million barrels; one source claims that Brunei's oil and gas reserves are currently estimated to last for twenty-five years and forty years respectively. Markets include countries of the Association of Southeast Asian Nations (ASEAN), Japan, South Korea, China, and Australasia.

During the first decade of the oil era (1932–1941), government revenue increased fourfold, the national debt was repaid, and substantial credit balances were amassed. A less inefficient standard of administration became possible; greater attention was paid to infrastructure and social services. The limited gains of the 1930s, however, went to waste during the period of Japanese military administration (1941–1945).

Following the postwar rehabilitation of the oil field, terrestrial production expanded rapidly, peaking at an average of 115,000 bpd in 1956. A new field was discovered at Jerudong in 1955, but production there fizzled out after a few years. Meanwhile, Brunei annexed its continental shelf in 1954, and several offshore strikes were made, initially at Southwest Ampa in 1963. Offshore production was inaugurated on 28 October 1964, and as output from Seria declined, Southwest Ampa rapidly became the oil industry's center of gravity. Overall, crude oil output hit 261,000 bpd in 1979, of which only 20 percent was derived from land-based wells. Although Brunei was not a member of the Organization of Petroleum Exporting Countries (OPEC), its coffers benefited massively from the rapid rise in global oil price during the 1970s. A conservation policy was then introduced, resulting in a phased reduction in output to 150,000 bpd by 1988. In the wake of the Gulf War (1990–1991), production crept up again to 182,000 bpd in 1992. Some 3 percent of Brunei's crude oil is retained for domestic use: for this purpose, there is an oil refinery at Seria with a capacity of 10,000 bpd, but actual output in 1990 was half that amount. The sultanate is seeking an expansion locally of "downstream" activities.

Liquefied natural gas (LNG), processed at Lumut since 1972 and 1973, is another lucrative source of income, with several million tons being shipped annually. LNG contracts are settled on the basis of government-to-government negotiation. Initially, Japan was the sole buyer; a second twenty-year deal was concluded in 1993. However, in the mid-1990s, a new customer was found in Korea Gas. In 1990, LNG exports were valued at B\$1,606.4 million, compared with crude oil shipments of around B\$2,336.1 million. In the mid-1970s, Brunei was the leading exporter of LNG in the world, although that status was not retained for long. According to the government newspaper *Pelita Brunei* (30 January 2002: 10), Brunei currently supplies less than 7 percent of the world market and is only the fifth largest producer, well behind Indonesia (26.76 percent). Proven reserves of natural gas in 1999 (390,000 million cubic meters) were sufficient to last thirty-five years at current rates of output. Prior to the LNG industry coming onstream, there was a gas plant at Seria, opened in 1955.

A new player in the oil industry, Jasra Elf, sells its oil to Brunei Shell. Another competitor, Fletcher Challenge Energy of New Zealand, was bought out by Shell in 2000–2001, thereby adding a further 35 million barrels of oil equivalent to the latter's reserves in NBD (*Daily Telegraph*, London, 11 October 2002: 38).

The hydrocarbon industry was originally taxed in the form of royalties (from 1932 to 1949), then royalties plus income tax (from 1950 onward). The state acquired a 25 percent stake in BSPC in 1973, doubled to 50 percent in 1975. A government minister chaired the BSPC board of management. Similarly, the Brunei Oil and Gas Authority (BOGA), set up in 1993 to supervise production levels and the granting of concession rights, had a government minister as chair. BOGA was superseded by the government-owned Brunei National Petroleum Company (officially abbreviated PetroleumBRUNEI), formed on 6 November 2001, which aims to play a major role in oil and gas policy and to accelerate the development of

a domestic industrial base in Brunei. The Brunei Oilfield Workers' Union was registered on 17 July 1962.

The need for economic diversification has been imperative almost since the inception of the oil industry. Future hopes for broadening the sultanate's economic base rest on the development of tourism and financial services. Thus far such efforts have met with limited success.

A. V. M. HORTON

See also Borneo; Economic Development of Southeast Asia (post-1945 to early 2000s); Oil and Petroleum; Sarawak and Sabah (North Borneo); Trade and Commerce of Southeast Asia (ca. Nineteenth Century to the 1990s)

References:
Borneo Bulletin (Kuala Belait; weekly newspaper).
Brunei Annual Report 1915. 1916. London: His Majesty's Stationery Office.
Cleary, Mark, and Peter Eaton. 1992. *Borneo: Change and Development*. Singapore, Oxford, and New York: Oxford University Press.
Cleary, Mark, and Wong Shuang Yann. 1994. *Oil, Economic Development and Diversification in Brunei Darussalam*. New York: St. Martin's Press; London and Basingstoke, England: Macmillan.
Economist Intelligence Unit (London). Quarterly reports on Malaysia/Negara Brunei Darussalam.
Europa World Yearbook 2000, Vol. 1. 41st ed. London: Europa.
Harper, G. C. 1975. *The Discovery and Development of the Seria Oilfield*. Bandar Seri Begawan: Brunei Museum Special Publication.
Hongkong and Shanghai Banking Corporation Limited (HSBC). 2002. *Brunei Darussalam*. Hong Kong: HSBC Business Profile Series; Public Affairs Department, HSBC, 11th ed., 4th quarter 2002. (Note: Copy seen by courtesy of HSBC, London.)
Ong Teck Mong, Timothy. 1983. "Modern Brunei: Some Important Issues." *Southeast Asian Affairs*: 71–84.
Pelita Brunei: Akhbar Rasmi Kerajaan Negara Brunei Darussalam [Official Government Newspaper of Negara Brunei Darussalam]. Bandar Seri Begawan: Government of Brunei.

BRUNEI REBELLION (DECEMBER 1962)

A Cry for Change

The revolt of December 1962 is the seminal event of Brunei's post–Pacific War (1941–1945) history: although the back of the attempted revolution was broken within a week, its ramifications persist to this day. In a coordinated maneuver, armed rebels seized control of much of the sultanate, along with parts of adjacent territories. Police were rushed in from North Borneo to hold the fort on the first day. Then, armed forces from Singapore (Gurkhas, Royal Marines, Green Jackets, Queen's Own Highlanders) recaptured the main towns, releasing rebel-held hostages in the process. No significant damage had been done to economic installations. The monarch was safeguarded, and a curfew was imposed. In the years since that tumultuous December, the deeper meaning of these events has been much debated. The whole truth has not yet emerged, particularly regarding the role played by Sultan Omar Ali Saifuddin III (1914–1986).

The late 1950s and early 1960s—part of a global age of transition between colonialism and independence—were times of political, economic, and social instability in Brunei. A climate of regional uncertainty had been generated by Malayan premier Tunku Abdul Rahman's (t. 1957–1970) proposal in May 1961 for the creation of a federation of Malaysia, which he expected Brunei to join. Domestic political weakness had been heightened by the ineptness of a new governmental system inaugurated after the end of the British Residential Era in 1959, by the failure of the sultan's government to honor its pledge to hold elections within two years of September 1959, and by the unpopularity of administrators seconded to Brunei from Malaya. Economic instability was occasioned by the gap between the completion of the first national development plan (1953–1958) and the commencement of the second (1962–1966), by the interval between the Seria oil field passing its peak (1956) and news of the discovery of deposits offshore (1963), and by an unemployment problem. Social instability arose out of a greater democratic spirit and waning deference by the common people toward monarchy.

When the elections were eventually held in late August 1962, the anti-"Malaysia" Brunei People's Party (Partai Rakyat Brunei, PRB) won a crushing victory; but power still eluded its members. The immediate pretext for their insurrection was a postponement of the first meeting of the Legislative Council. There was also a fear that the authorities had discovered their plans to stage a rebellion. Revolt erupted on the morning of Saturday, 8 December 1962. Led by the PRB and its military wing, the Northern Borneo National Army (Tentera Nasional Kalimantan Utara, TNKU), the aim was to establish a unitary state to be known as Kalimantan Utara, comprising Brunei, North Borneo, and Sarawak. Furthermore, a desire for eventual inclusion within Indonesia was hinted at in the name of the proposed new territory. For the time being, Sheikh Ahmad Azahari (1928–2002) was to be prime minister, with Sultan Omar Ali Saifuddin III (r. 1950–1967) as head of state. By the first evening of the insurrection, most of the country was in rebel hands, as were neighboring parts of Sarawak and North Borneo. However, the government still controlled the capital, including the telecommunications network, the radio station, and, crucially, the airport. Meanwhile, a message had been received in Singapore through the chief minister, saying that the sultan wished to invoke the protection of the British as enshrined in the 1959 agreements between Brunei and the United Kingdom.

A state of emergency, proclaimed on 12 December 1962, subsisted even as of 2004. In the short term, an emergency council including the sultan (as president) and the British high commissioner governed the sultanate. The PRB was proscribed. In addition, the Legislative and District Councils were suspended (until July 1963). Military mopping-up operations continued for some months, and the rebellion was not declared officially over until the rebel commander, General Muhammad Yassin Affandy bin Abdul Rahman, was arrested at Serdang on 18 May 1963.

TNKU casualties amounted to forty persons killed by 20 December 1962. The British suffered seven fatalities and twenty-eight wounded, many of them during an action at Limbang (Sarawak) on 12 December 1962 (James and Sheil-Small 1971: 42–43). Great bravery was shown by the police (many were from Malaya), particularly in defending the Panaga and Kuala Belait police stations; the former held out throughout the siege, and the latter was not surrendered until the last round had been fired, which meant that much-needed arms were denied to the insurgents. Overall, the rebellion was poorly led (Azahari was absent in Manila) and insufficiently provisioned. Effective outside support failed to materialize, particularly anticolonial intervention by the United Nations (as had happened in Indonesia in the late 1940s). Furthermore, at the height of the uprising, Sultan Omar Ali made a broadcast denouncing the outbreak, which led to the surrender of the many rebels who supposedly thought that they were fighting on his behalf. After the security forces had reestablished control, there were mass arrests, denuding many government departments of personnel, but all except the hard-core rebels were soon released. The last of the rebels, none of whom had ever been tried in court, were set free in 1990.

The Brunei Rebellion sparked a *Konfrontasi* (confrontation or low-intensity war) between Indonesia and Malaysia (1963–1966). Although Brunei opted to remain outside Tunku Abdul Rahman's federation in 1963, it would be dubious to argue that this decision was *caused* by the revolt. The sultanate's relations with both Kuala Lumpur and Jakarta remained strained until the late 1970s.

A. V. M. HORTON

See also Anglo-Brunei Relations (Nineteenth Century to 1980s); Azahari bin Sheikh Mahmud, Sheikh (1928–2002); Konfrontasi ("Crush Malaysia" Campaign); Malaysia (1963); Omar Ali Saifuddin III, Sultan of Brunei (1914–1986); Partai Rakyat Brunei (PRB)

References:
Borneo Bulletin. (Kuala Belait; weekly newspaper).
Braighlinn, G. 1992. *Ideological Innovation under Monarchy: Aspects of Legitimation Activity in Contemporary Brunei.* Comparative Asian Studies Series, no. 9. Amsterdam: VU University Press.
Eusoff Agaki Haji-Ismail. 1991. "Brunei Darussalam: Its Re-emergence as a Sovereign and Independent Malay-Muslim Sultanate (1959–1983)." M.Phil. thesis, University of Hull.
Hussainmiya, B. A. 1995. *Sultan Omar Ali Saifuddin III and Britain: The Making of Brunei Darussalam.* Kuala Lumpur: Oxford University Press.
James, Harold, and D. Sheil-Small. 1971. *The Undeclared War: The Story of Indonesian Confrontation, 1962–1966.* London: Leo Cooper.
Poulgrain, Gregory John. 1998. *The Genesis of "Konfrontasi": Malaysia, Brunei, Indonesia, 1945–1965.* Foreword by Pramoedya Ananta Toer. Bathurst: Crawford House Publishing; London: C. Hurst.
Saunders, Graham. 1994. *A History of Modern Brunei.* Kuala Lumpur: Oxford University Press.

BUDDHISM

Buddhism dates back to the sixth to fifth century B.C.E., when a man known as Siddhartha Gautama (ca. 563–ca. 483 B.C.E.) awakened (*buddha*) to the truth and became the most recent in a long series of Buddhas. From that moment on, the Buddha was no longer subject to *samsara,* the round of rebirth.

Buddhist thought holds that beings are trapped in samsara because of their greed, hatred, and ignorance. The term *nirvana* means the "extinction" of these vices. They or the opposite virtues inform all our intentional actions, or *karma.* Everyone's current and future experiences and rebirths as humans, animals, or inhabitants of the various Buddhist hells and heavens are determined by previous karma.

Although the ultimate truth is regarded as experiential and beyond the understanding of ordinary, unenlightened individuals, it is given a variety of formulations. Phenomena have three characteristics: impermanence, lack of an enduring self or soul, and suffering. The concept of the "four noble truths" formulates Buddhist teaching along the lines of a medical diagnosis. The first truth identifies the symptoms and asserts that everything is suffering or unsatisfactory; the second diagnoses the cause of this suffering, identified as craving; the third offers the prognosis that there can be an end or cure; the fourth presents the course of treatment to end the suffering, the "noble eight-fold path." This path includes virtuous action, correct understanding, and meditation. There are many types of Buddhist meditation, the principal mechanism through which one can transform one's mental and emotional re-

A Buddhist monk at a temple in Phnom Bok, Cambodia, 1993. (Corel Corporation)

sponses and attitudes. Other important practices include generosity, particularly in supporting the sangha (institution of the Buddhist monkhood living in monasteries, also including nuns in separate monasteries), undertaking pilgrimage, practicing rites, and participating in religious festivals. The role of the sangha includes preserving and providing religious teachings handed down from the Buddha, performing rituals, and providing a source of religious power and sanctity.

There are, therefore, two main sources of authority in Buddhism, the sangha and the texts, which consist of three collections. These are the *Vinaya Pitaka,* containing the rules for the sangha; the *Sutra/Sutta Pitaka,* which contains the Buddha's teachings; and the *Abhidharma/Abhidhamma Pitaka,* which systematizes those teachings, or *dharma.* Not all forms of Buddhism accept this third collection.

Buddhism spread throughout Asia from the third century B.C.E., under the patronage of the Indian emperor Asoka (ca. 271–238 B.C.E.). Its spread along the silk routes reflects the hegemony of India; the value of universal (rather than community or caste-specific) ethics; and its appeal to merchants and foreign rulers, in its authorization for the spiritual value of their occupations. Legends about its spread emphasize the meaningfulness of its teachings, the magical power of its teachers, and the close relationship between Buddhist monks and local kings.

KATE CROSBY

See also Borobudur; Buddhism, Mahayana; Buddhism, Theravada; Buddhist Institute of Phnom Penh; Buddhist Socialism; Hindu-Buddhist Period of Southeast Asia; I-Ching (I-tsing) (635–713 C.E.); Monumental Art of Southeast Asia; Palembang; Sri Lanka (Ceylon); Srivijaya (Sriwijaya); *Tam Giao;* Unified Buddhist Church (1963) (Vietnam)
References:
Marr, David G., and A. C. Milner, eds. 1986. *Southeast Asia in the 9th to 14th Centuries.* Singapore: Institute of Southeast Asian Studies; Canberra: Research School of Pacific Studies, Australian National University.
Skilton, Andrew. 1997. *A Concise History of Buddhism.* 2nd ed. Birmingham, UK: Windhorse.
Tambiah, S. J. 1976. *World Conqueror and World Renouncer: A Study of Buddhism and Polity in Thailand against a Historical Background.* Cambridge: Cambridge University Press.

BUDDHISM, MAHAYANA

Mahayana, meaning the "great way" or "great vehicle," is a collective term referring to a group of traditions in Buddhism. These traditions have a number of features in common, including an emphasis on the ideal of the altruistic spiritual hero, the *bodhisattva.* In addition to the three collections of texts at the core of Buddhism, scriptures such as the *Lotus Sutra* and *Perfection of Wisdom Sutra* are accepted, as well as the belief in many Buddhas existing at the same time. So, too, is the concept of having faith in "celestial" bodhisattvas and in one of a range of philosophical systems.

The origins of Mahayana are obscure. Quite commonly, it is regarded as a movement that validated the spiritual potential of laypeople in reaction to the perceived selfishness of the monastic life dedicated to personal enlightenment. However, Mahayana has, to a great extent, been preserved and pursued by monks and nuns. Furthermore, recent research shows that early Mahayana texts emphasized renunciation, meditation, and ascetic practices. They criticized more moderate or "lapsed" forms of monasticism. It is not known whether Mahayana began within the mainstream tradition or at the margins of the Buddhist world. The term *Mahayana* itself is polemical. It occurs in texts that claim that their version of Buddhism is great, or superior—*maha*—in contrast to the preexisting Buddhism, which is characterized as *hina* (inferior).

There are three main philosophical schools within Mahayana. Madhyamaka is associated with the doctrine of emptiness. Yogacara or Cittamatra (meaning "mind-only") is associated with theories of relativity in epistemology, the three "inherent natures," and the use of *alayavijnana* (storehouse consciousness) to explain memory and karmic causality. Tathagatagarbha emphasizes the potential, or embryo (*garbha*), to become a Buddha (*Tathagata*). Each school seeks to restate the original truth of Buddhism in such a way as to defend it from possible misinterpretation or misapplication, yet each is also criticized as straying from true Buddhism.

The bodhisattva ideal is the commitment to become a Buddha and save all beings from the sufferings of samsara. In Mahayana practice, a distinction is made between "the path of the perfections" (*paramitayana*) and the "path of sacred formulae" (*mantrayana*). The former is the long path pursued over many thousands of rebirths in which the bodhisattva, the person destined to become a Buddha, perfects the necessary set of virtues, including generosity, patience, and wisdom. The latter, *mantrayana,* is the fast route to enlightenment through the manipulation of inherently powerful sounds (*mantra*) and symbols. This path is often referred to as Vajrayana (meaning "diamond path or vehicle") or Tantric Buddhism. It is the Mahayana form of tantra, the pan-Indian religious phenomenon, that employs empowerment through initiation, the ritual manipulation of powers through microcosm-macrocosm identifications, and sometimes transgression of societal norms to acquire spiritual or worldly powers. Other key practices include the mental or visual creation of mandala, that is, patterns representing the macrocosm at the microcosmic level; the summoning of Buddhas and different deities; and the practitioner achieving Buddhahood through ritually identifying the Buddha with him- or herself. The ideology of all three philosophical schools underpins the interpretation of Buddhist tantra.

In modern Southeast Asia, Mahayana Buddhism has only been present among small minorities, with the exception of Chan (Zen) Buddhism in Vietnam under Chinese influence. From the eleventh through thirteenth centuries, Theravada replaced Mahayana as the dominant form of Buddhism in the rest of mainland Southeast Asia. This in part reflects developments in neighboring regions: the eclipse of the Mahayana dynasties of Bengal and Theravadin Sri Lanka's victory over the Hindu Cola (Chola) empire of south India. Islam largely replaced Indian religions in Indonesia from the thirteenth century. However, in the early medieval period, Mahayana flourished throughout Southeast Asia. Its former importance is reflected in the monumental architecture of the period, which is still impressive today. In mainland Southeast Asia during the twelfth century, King Jayavarman VII (r. 1181–ca. 1220) built the magnificent Bayon temple at Angkor Thom toward the end of the Angkor period. In the Indonesian archipelago, Borobudur—an enormous, terraced, and three-dimensional mandala decorated with scenes from Mahayana texts—was built under the Sailendra dynasty in central Java (eighth to ninth centuries). The Sailendra dynasty's more powerful ally, the Śrivijaya kingdom, centered in Sumatra (seventh to eleventh centuries), also embraced Buddhism and was a major patron. The kingdom even funded buildings at the Buddhist university of Nalanda in northern India. The Indian monk Atisa, who studied tantra in Sumatra in the eleventh century, became highly significant in Tibetan Buddhism.

That insular Southeast Asia adopted both Buddhism and forms of Hinduism, especially Saivism, is reflected in the close relationship between these religions as they survive in Java and Bali to this day. The significance of forms of Avalokitesvara, the bodhisattva of compassion,

throughout Southeast Asia and Sri Lanka reflects his importance as the patron saint of travelers at the height of the period when Buddhist
culture dominated the silk routes.

KATE CROSBY

See also Angkor Wat (Nagaravatta);
    Borobodur; Buddhism; Buddhism,
    Theravada; Hindu-Buddhist Period of
    Southeast Asia; I-Ching (I-tsing) (635–713
    C.E.); Jayavarman VII (r. 1181–1220?);
    Monumental Art of Southeast Asia; *Sangha;*
    Sri Lanka (Ceylon); Srivijaya (Sriwijaya)

References:

De Casparis, J. G., and I. W. Mabbett. 1992.
    "Religion and Popular Beliefs of Southeast
    Asia before c. 1500." Pp. 276–339 in *The
    Cambridge History of Southeast Asia.* Vol. 1,
    From Early Times to c. 1800. Edited by
    Nicholas Tarling. Cambridge: Cambridge
    University Press.
Williams, Paul. 1989. *Mahayana Buddhism.*
    London: Routledge.

BUDDHISM, THERAVADA

The term *Theravada* means "doctrine of elders,"
that is, senior monks, and is applied to the
dominant form of Buddhism in Sri Lanka
(Ceylon) and mainland Southeast Asia. It has
probably been present in these regions from the
third century B.C.E., when Buddhism spread
along trade routes partly because of the power
of the Mauryan empire (321–185 B.C.E.), centered in the heartland of Buddhism. Theravada
has been the state religion of Sri Lanka, Burma
(Myanmar), Thailand (Siam), Laos, and Cambodia in various periods, and all these countries
have myths describing visits made to them by
the Buddha. Theravada has also been present in
south India historically and in Bangladesh and
among Khmer and T'ai minorities in Vietnam
into the modern period.

Adherents regard Theravada as the purest
form of Buddhism. They claim it has preserved
the fullest form of the *Vinaya Pitaka* at the division between Mahasamghikas and Sthaviras at
the Second Council of the sangha in the fourth
century B.C.E. The *Vinaya Pitaka* is a Buddhist
text that espoused the discipline of the sangha
(institution of the Buddhist monkhood) in the
form of rules and decisions laid down by the
Buddha. At the second council of the sangha,

there was a split between the orthodox Sthaviravadins (Sthaviras), who were the Pali Ther-
avadins (followers of the "doctrine of the Elders") and the Mahasamghikas, the members of
the Great Community (Mahayana Buddhism).
In the first century B.C.E. a schism occurred
between the sects in the division into two sacred languages: the Sthaviravadins adopted Pali
and the others used the Sanskrit canon. Consequently the two sects evolved separately, each
developing divergent ideas that subsequently
formed the basis for the division into Mahayana
(Greater Wheel or Vehicle) and Hinayana
(Lesser Vehicle) Theravada. Theravada is then
associated with the form of Buddhism purified
of "heretics" by the Mauryan emperor Asoka
(Ashoka) (r. 264–238 B.C.E.) in the third century B.C.E. At the Third Council immediately
after this purification, the *Kathavatthu* ("Points
of Controversy"), a text of the Theravadin *Abhidhamma Pitaka* (a catechism-style exposition
of the *dhamma*), was compiled. This work discussed and rejected rival doctrines and revealed
some of the key doctrinal differences between
Theravada and other Buddhist schools at that
time. Doctrines rejected include the existence
of more than one Buddha at a time and the
concept of *dharmanairatmya,* that is, the notion
of no-self of *dhammas* into which the constituents of Theravada Abhidhamma analyze the
individual and the world, a doctrine pro-
pounded in *Perfection of Wisdom* literature and
Madhyamaka Buddhist philosophy. Theravada in
different regions was partly localized through
the incorporation of local deities into the pantheon of gods who support Buddhism. However, the doctrine that there is only one Buddha at a time means that the pantheon of
Theravada Buddhas is relatively limited, with
the only future Buddha being Metteyya
(Maitreya). The concept of the altruistic hero,
the *bodhisattva,* is present but not much emphasized in Theravada.

The chronicle literature of Sri Lanka and
mainland Southeast Asia associates the arrival of
Buddhism in Sri Lanka and mainland Southeast
Asia with missionaries sent by Asoka, Sona and
Uttara. They went to Burma, and Asoka's own
son, Mahinda, and daughter, Sanghamitta, be-
came the first monk and nun to go to Sri
Lanka. Mahinda is believed to have taken the
Buddhist canon to Sri Lanka immediately after
the Third Council, as well as the commentaries,

which are attributed to the Buddha's immediate disciples. Theravada tradition further authenticates the validity of its canon and commentaries as the original teachings of the Buddha and his enlightened disciples through the figure of the Indian monk Buddhaghosa. Buddhaghosa went to Sri Lanka in the fifth century, where he produced two types of work. One, a handbook called the *Visuddhimagga* ("Path of Purity"), systematizes the teachings of the canon under the tripartite division of moral conduct, meditation, and wisdom. To prove the perfection of this treatise, deities confiscated the text each time Buddhaghosa finished it. Only when he had finished it for the third time did the deities restore the first two copies, each of which was identical to the third, word for word. The other task attributed to Buddhaghosa is the composition of the commentaries on the canon—or rather, redressing them in the original language of the canon, Pali. This notion reflects the belief that Mahinda had translated the preexisting commentaries in local languages from Pali originals brought by him from India. Although scholars might regard the commentaries as showing historical development since the canon, Theravada orthodoxy does not accept this. Buddhaghosa is regarded by many as the representative of true Theravada orthodoxy.

The language in which Buddhaghosa composed, Pali, is treated as a sacred language in Theravada. It is regarded as the original, unchanging language in which the Buddha spoke but also the universal language spoken in heavens and hells or by a child if left abandoned in the wilderness. As such, Pali has been used in sacred texts and rituals. Local languages are also used for Buddhist texts or their interpretation.

The historical diversity of Theravada is difficult to assess because of the dominance of the Mahavihara school as well as the demise of Buddhism in mainland South Asia. In the twelfth century, King Parakkamabahu I of Sri Lanka unified different Buddhist monastic lineages under the Mahavihara school. The ascendancy of the Mahavihara school is associated with a period of Buddhist literary revival and a reemphasis on the strict adherence to Vinaya rules. With Sri Lanka's defeat of the south Indian Cola (Chola) empire and the defeat of the Buddhist rulers of north India by Muslim powers, Sri Lanka became dominant in the Buddhism of mainland Southeast Asia. The histories that we have come either from the Mahavihara school or from schools heavily influenced by it in mainland Southeast Asia, as Buddhists there sought to import the prestigious Buddhism of Sri Lanka.

KATE CROSBY

See also Buddhism; Buddhism, Mahayana; Hindu-Buddhist Period of Southeast Asia; *Sangha;* Sri Lanka (Ceylon)
References:
De Casparis, J. G., and I. W. Mabbett. 1992. "Religion and Popular Beliefs of Southeast Asia before c. 1500." Pp. 276–339 in *The Cambridge History of Southeast Asia.* Vol. 1, *From Early Times to c. 1800.* Edited by Nicholas Tarling. Cambridge: Cambridge University Press.
Swearer, Donald. 1995. *The Buddhist World of Southeast Asia.* Albany: State University of New York.

BUDDHIST INSTITUTE OF PHNOM PENH

The Buddhist Institute is a Cambodian learned society formed in 1931 under French colonial auspices in an effort to diminish Thai influence on the Buddhist sangha, or monastic community. In its early years, under the direction of the Buddhist scholar Suzanne Karpeles, the institute became a meeting place for Cambodian monks and laypeople interested in Buddhism and Cambodian culture. The institute sponsored a Khmer-language journal, *Kampuchea Surya* ("Cambodian Sun"), that contained learned articles and translations from Buddhist texts, as well as original Cambodian poems, folktales, novels, and short stories. The institute also became a forum for a group of young Cambodian nationalist intellectuals, led by Son Ngoc Thanh (1907–1976?). In 1936, the group began publishing a weekly Khmer-language newspaper, *Nagara Vatta* ("Angkor Wat"), which printed mildly nationalistic, development-oriented articles and gained a wide audience among Cambodia's small but influential intelligentsia, dominated by schoolteachers and Buddhist monks. Following the fall of France in 1940, the journal became stridently nationalistic, and many of its issues were censored. In the wake of an anti-French demonstration in July 1942, led by *Nagara Vatta*'s editor, Pach Chhoeun, the paper ceased publication.

During World War II (1939–1945), inspired by the French anthropologist Madeline Poree-Maspero, workers at the institute began collecting documents relating to Cambodian folklore, rituals, and popular religion. This archive was maintained until 1975 when the Khmer Rouge seized power, and it has never been recovered.

The institute remained closed under the Vietnamese protectorate (1979–1989) but re-opened in 1990. With funding from Germany and other countries, the institute again began publishing *Kampuchea Surya* in the 1990s, and it has resumed its position as a powerful force in Cambodia's intellectual life.

DAVID CHANDLER

See also Buddhism; Buddhism, Theravada; Cambodia under French Colonial Rule; Khmer Rouge; Newspapers and Mass Media in Southeast Asia; Son Ngoc Thanh (1907–1976?)

References:

Chandler, David. 2000. *A History of Cambodia.* 2nd ed. Boulder, CO: Westview Press.

BUDDHIST SOCIALISM

The official program of Buddhist socialism was initiated in 1960 by U Nu (1907–1995), the first prime minister of independent Burma, as part of his election platform. The ruling democratic party, the Anti-Fascist People's Freedom League (AFPFL), had split into two factions. The Stable group, led by U Kyaw Nyein and U Ba Swe, was based on the educated or college socialist groups within the AFPFL, and the Clean group, led by Thakin Kyaw Tun, was based on the uneducated or monastery school socialists. U Nu supported the Clean faction, which considered agriculture as the primary sector in the economy, whereas the Stable faction aligned itself with industrialization.

In 1954, U Nu launched his Pyidawtha Program for the Buddhist welfare state, which was to give practical expression to traditional Burmese cultural millenarianism anticipating the Metteyya (Maitreyea), or the coming Buddha; Metteyya would make a utopian society in the present world, long expected as the outcome of independence. In 1960, U Nu's Buddhist socialism drew on Burmese folklore to declare that the remedy for the poverty that had come on the people with the appearance of private property was for the fruits of their labor to be shared according to the toil needed to produce them. He evoked the legend of Mahathammada, the Yaza or Raja, who came to ease social unrest when the people's Wishing Tree, the Padeytha Tree, on which grew all the necessities of life, was destroyed after private property was introduced in society. He looked to the reintroduction of property in common in a utopian society without oppression, where Buddhist nirvana would replace samsara, the world of suffering. Drawing on the Buddhist doctrine of impermanence, U Nu explained that freeing oneself from suffering required one to realize that acquisition of property arose from ignorance and prolonged suffering.

His appeal to Burmese folk beliefs and incorporation of Buddhist social ethics led to a landslide victory at the polls in 1960. He also received major support from the Burmese Buddhist abbots at the monasteries at Sagaing, Ava, Amarapura, and Mandalay. The support for U Nu was impressive, indeed, to the extent that he was perceived as a *bodhisattva,* or a future Buddha, himself.

U Nu's platform of Buddhist socialism evoked one of the deepest cultural beliefs of Burmese people: to be Burmese is to be Buddhist. His platform encapsulated the ideals of the Burmese who had regretted the displacement of the monarchical state and the undermining of the Buddhist sangha, or monastic community, during the sixty years of British colonial rule. On being reelected, U Nu moved to make Buddhism the state religion of Burma, in accordance with the wishes of the Buddhist sangha. During his first term in office, from May 1954 to May 1956, he convened the Sixth Buddhist Synod at Kaba Aye Pagoda, evoking the actions of the great King Mindon in 1871, who had convened the Fifth Buddhist Synod in Mandalay. By a vote of 324 to 28, the State Religion Bill was passed in August 1961, ending the separation of church and state. Burma was once again a Buddhist nation, promoting Buddhism as the Burmese monarchs had done. At the instigation of Attorney General U Chan Htoon, the Buddha Sasana Council was established. Buddhism was to be taught in state schools. The Buddhist sabbath, based on the lunar calendar, was decreed the official holiday for government offices, schools, and markets, and no liquor was to be served that day. The Department of Religious Affairs initiated the building of 60,000 sand pagodas to support peace and tranquillity in the country.

However, the passage of the State Religion Act incensed the minorities and non-Buddhists, leading to serious civil unrest in the country. The measure appeared to fan the cause of federalism and minority aspirations for autonomy; to the army, it seemed to prepare the way for extended Chinese Communist influence in the northern states of Burma. Thus, on 2 March 1962, the army, led by General Ne Win (1910–2002), launched a coup. In the military takeover, Parliament and the constitution were prorogued, the State Religion Act was repealed, the Buddha Sasana Council was abolished, and the secular state was again affirmed, as Ne Win stated the new policy was to separate "*pongyis* [lit. "great glory," referring to a Buddhist monk in Burma] from politics."

HELEN JAMES

See also Anti-Fascist People's Freedom League (AFPFL); Buddhism, Theravada; Burma under British Colonial Rule; Military and Politics in Southeast Asia; Ne Win, General (1911–2002); Nu, U (1907–1995); *Sangha; Thakin* (Lord, Master)

References:
Harris, Ian. 1999. *Buddhism and Politics in Twentieth-Century Asia.* London and New York: Pinter.
King, Winston. 1976. "Contemporary Burmese Buddhism." Pp. 81–98 in *Buddhism in the Modern World.* Edited by Heinrich Dumoulin. New York: Macmillan.
Lester, Robert C. 1973. *Theravada Buddhism in Southeast Asia.* Ann Arbor: University of Michigan Press.
Ling, Trevor, ed. 1993. *Buddhist Trends in Southeast Asia.* Singapore: Institute of Southeast Asian Studies.
Mendelson, E. Michael. 1975. *State and Sangha in Burma.* Edited by John P. Ferguson. Ithaca, NY: Cornell University Press.
Sarkisyanz, E. 1965. *Buddhist Backgrounds of the Burmese Revolution.* The Hague: Martinus Nijhoff.
Schecter, Jerrold L. 1967. *The New Face of Buddha: Buddhism and Political Power in Southeast Asia.* New York: Coward-McCann.
Smith, Donald Eugene. 1965. *Religion and Politics in Burma.* Princeton, NJ: Princeton University Press.
Spiro, Melford. 1982. *Buddhism and Society.* 2nd ed. Berkeley and Los Angeles: University of California Press.
Sulak Sivaraksa, ed. 1999. *Socially Engaged Buddhism for the New Millennium.* Bangkok: Munlanithi Suthiankoset Nakhaprathip Foundation.
Taylor, Robert H. 1987. *The State in Burma.* Honolulu: University of Hawai'i Press.

BUGIS (BUGINESE)

The Bugis are the dominant ethnic group of South Sulawesi and occupy much of its fertile lowland. The Austronesian ancestors of the South Sulawesi peoples entered the area after 2500 B.C.E., bringing with them horticulture, pottery, weaving, polished stone axes, a tripartite cosmology, and hereditary leadership. The Bugis evolved as a separate linguistic group around the central lakes and in the long, narrow Soppeng Valley to the south.

Little is known of the Bugis during the Neolithic (ca. 2500 B.C.E.–ca. 300 B.C.E.): only one large site, Bulu Baku, in the upper Soppeng Valley has been discovered. From the Bronze Age through the Iron Age (ca. 300 B.C.E.–1200 C.E.), the Bugis were organized into a large number of small chiefdoms (*wanua*) practicing dry-field and shifting agriculture, with some wet-rice cultivation. A lively megalithic tradition flourished in Soppeng and other Bugis areas during the late Bronze Age through the Iron Age and continued into the early historical period (ca. 1200–1600).

Agricultural settlements centered on wet-rice farming appear in the archaeological record of the upper Cenrana Valley around 1200. The pace of change accelerated during the thirteenth century as a result of the incorporation of South Sulawesi in a trading network extending to India and China via the eastern Javanese kingdom of Singhasari-Majapahit. The next four hundred years saw the establishment of large, loosely unified kingdoms based on wet-rice cultivation. It is in this period of increasing social stratification, growing cultural sophistication, and rising population that much of the present-day Bugis "high culture" has its roots.

Oral traditions and cultural practices point to influence from Java: the Javanese-style cremation of the corpse and burial of the ashes in expensive, imported porcelain jars became standard practice after about 1300. The transvestite ritual priests called *bissu* who guarded the kingdoms' regalia and acted as intermediaries with the upper and lower worlds probably developed from an earlier shamanistic tradition.

The earliest kingdom was Luwu (or Ware') in the Gulf of Bone, which was established by Bugis settlers to control the trade in iron ore carried down from the Rongkong Valley. The iron was smelted at the principal Bugis settlement of Malangke and was a key element in the expansion of agriculture across the forested southern peninsula. The Luwu Bugis united the disparate hill tribes of the interior into a powerful, predatory kingdom that established itself as the regional overlord. Luwu was eclipsed after about 1500 by the rising power of the southern agricultural kingdoms that had expanded to their present borders. Wars between kingdoms became frequent, but several peace treaties between kingdoms endured for long terms.

The sixteenth century saw the rise of the Makassar kingdom of Gowa and its union with neighboring Tallo'. Gowa's trading ships plied the waters of Maluku and controlled a sizable part of the trade in nutmeg, cloves, and mace. The port of Makassar became an international entrepôt, attracting traders from India, Europe, China, mainland Southeast Asia, and other parts of the Indonesian archipelago. Cultural and technological development was rapid: guns and cannon were imported, and settlements were fortified with 3-meter-thick brick or stone walls and flanking defenses.

The Luwu Bugis converted to Islam in 1605, followed shortly by the ruling elites of other kingdoms. The Dutch arrived in Makassar the same year and attempted to impose control over the spice trade. They enlisted the aid of the Bone Bugis and defeated Gowa in 1669 after a protracted civil war. In exchange for a Dutch monopoly on trade, Bone became the effective overlord of South Sulawesi. The following decades saw a diaspora of Bugis who had sided with Gowa, with important consequences for the Malay world. The eighteenth century was a period of instability, with a contested succession to the throne of Gowa in 1739 and an uprising in 1776 led by a commoner: both drew on deep resentment of the Dutch presence in Makassar. The British replaced the Dutch in Makassar between 1811 and 1816 and invaded Bone, sacking the palace and seizing its library. Uneasy relations continued when the Dutch returned; Bone was invaded again in 1865 and 1905, when the king was deposed and exiled to Batavia.

Dutch colonial rule made use of traditional Bugis and Makassar hierarchies, and in the 1930s, a limited form of kingship was reintroduced. After the Japanese surrender in 1945, the notorious Dutch captain "Turk" Westerling directed a brutal repression of nationalist forces. From the early 1950s to the mid-1960s, the countryside was laid waste by the quasi-Islamic rebellion led by Kahar Muzakkar, a disaffected Bugis army officer from Luwu. The rebels controlled much of the countryside, and attempts were made to wipe out all non-Islamic elements, resulting in the burning of traditional houses and manuscripts. Recent years have seen increased prosperity, political stability, and a development of regional identities based on local histories, in which Bugis have a great interest.

IAN A. CALDWELL

See also Dutch Interests in Southeast Asia from 1800; Economic Transformation of Southeast Asia (ca. 1400–ca. 1800); Johor; Johor-Riau Empire; Majapahit (1293–ca. 1520s); Maluku (The Moluccas); Spices and the Spice Trade; Western Malay States (Perak, Selangor, Negri Sembilan, and Pahang)

References:

Andaya, L.Y. 1981. *The Heritage of Arung Palakka: A History of South Sulawesi (Celebes) in the Seventeenth Century.* The Hague: Nijhoff.

Bulbeck, D., and I. Caldwell. 2000. *Land of Iron: The Historical Archaeology of Luwu and the Cenrana Valley.* Hull, England: Centre for South-East Asian Studies.

Bulbeck, F. D. 1996–1997. "The Bronze-Iron Age in South Sulawesi." Pp. 1007–1076 in *Ancient Chinese and Southeast Asian Bronze Age Cultures,* vol. 2. Edited by N. Barnard. Taipei: SMC Publishing.

Caldwell, I. 1995. "Power, State and Society among the Pre-Islamic Bugis." *Bijdragen tot de Taal-, Land- en Volkenkunde* 151, no. 3: 394–421.

Noorduyn, J. 1972. "Arung Singkang (1700–1765): How the Victory of Wadjo' Began." *Indonesia* 13: 61–68.

Roessingh, M. P. H. 1986. "A Pretender on Gowa's Throne: The War of Batara Gowa—pt. 1, Singkilang in South West Celebes, 1776–c. 1790." Pp. 151–177 in *All of One Company: The VOC in Biographical Perspective.* Edited by L. Blusse. Utrecht, The Netherlands: Rijksuniversiteit Leiden.

Sutherland, H. 1980. "Political Structure and Colonial Control in South Sulawesi." Pp. 230–245 in *Man, Meaning, and History: Essays in Honour of H. G. Schulte Nordholt.* Edited by R. Schefold, J. W. Schoorl, and J. Tennekes. The Hague: M. Nijhoff.

BUMIPUTERA (BUMIPUTRA)

Bumiputera, literally meaning "son(s) of the soil," is a modern Malay word that was first used in the Malay Peninsula during the second and third decades of the twentieth century. The term came into current usage when the Malays were beginning to be conscious of the political threats that immigrants (namely, the Chinese and, to a lesser extent, the Indians) posed to their presumed ownership of the country. *Bumiputera* refers to the indigenous person(s), or people of Malay (*Melayu*) stock, and the native communities of the country. It is often interchangeable with *peribumi* (native, indigenous) and sometimes with *anak negeri* (son[s] of the country). A daily paper called *Bumiputera* was started in Penang in January 1933 but had ceased publication by the middle of 1935. In response to the constitutional commission in the mid-1950s, Partai Islam Se Malaysia (PAS), a party that adopts the viewpoint of Islam as not only a religion but also a political ideology, among others, repeatedly pointed out that the Peninsular Malays are the original and sovereign bumiputera of the country and should be respected and treated as such.

With the formation of Malaysia in 1963, the term *bumiputera* was entrenched in the Malaysian Federal Constitution to also refer to the natives of Sabah and Sarawak, who were accorded a "special position" previously granted to the Malays in the peninsula (West Malaysia). In daily life, it soon became a generic term to refer to all indigenous peoples of Malaysia, namely, the Malays, the peninsular Orang Asli (meaning "original people" or "aborigines"), and all the ethnic minorities of East Malaysia (Sabah and Sarawak). The Partai Bumiputera appeared in Sarawak in 1966, and early in 1973, it was enlarged to become the Partai Pesaka Bumiputera Bersatu (PBB), a political party that continues to be dominant in the state.

As provided for by Article 153 of the Malaysian Federal Constitution, affirmative measures were taken by the Malaysian government to uplift the social and economic conditions of the bumiputera, which were lagging behind those of the non-bumiputera, particularly the Chinese. Public institutions were set up to improve the lot of the bumiputera. Organizations such as the Bank Bumiputra (for credit and banking), the Perbadanan Nasional Berhad (PERNAS, for trading and employment), and the Majlis Amanah Rakyat (MARA, for training and education) were established as recommended by the 1965 and 1968 bumiputera economic congresses. Though only halfway successful, the New Economic Policy (NEP, 1971–1990) had, to some extent, improved bumiputera participation in banking, commerce, and industry. The NEP had greatly improved bumiputera access to education, in particular at the tertiary level.

ABDUL RAHMAN HAJI ISMAIL

See also Abdul Razak, Tun (1922–1976); East Malaysian Ethnic Minorities; Mahathir bin Mohamad, Dr. (1925–); Malayan/Malaysian Education; Malays"; "May 13th 1969" (Malaysia); Nationalism and Independence Movements in Southeast Asia; New Economic Policy (NEP) (Malaysia) (1971–1990); Orang Asli; Partai Islam Se Malaysia (PAS); Sarawak and Sabah (North Borneo); United Malays National Organization (UMNO) (1946)

References:

Means, Gordon P. 1991. *Malaysian Politics: The Second Generation.* Singapore: Oxford University Press.

Milne, R. S., and Diane K. Mauzy. 1978. *Politics and Government in Malaysia.* Singapore: Times Books International.

Shamsul, A. B. 1986. *From British to Bumiputera Rule: Local Politics and Rural Development.* Singapore: Institute of Southeast Asian Studies.

BUNGA EMAS (BUNGA MAS) (GOLD FLOWERS)

Bunga emas was a form of gift given by the Malay sultans of Kedah, Kelantan, Terengganu, and Patani to the ruler of Siam. In return, the Siamese ruler would give valuable gifts to the sultans and promise to protect their states from external threats. The tradition of sending *bunga emas* started in the fourteenth century and was first practiced by Kedah, as mentioned in the famous Kedah annal *Hikayat Merong Maha Wangsa* ("The Tale of Merong Maha Wangsa"). Initially, the gift was sent to the ruler of Siam, the older brother of the Kedah sultan, to mark the latter's happiness upon the birth of his first son. Thereafter, a bunga emas was sent to Siam after the birth of each child. This tradition began to be emulated by the other sultans. Some scholars, however, interpreted the giving of bunga emas from the Malay States as a show of allegiance from vassal states to their sovereign.

The bunga emas was made in the form of a tree, which was about 1.8 meters high. The trunk was made of teak wrapped in fine gold. The tree consisted of four boughs that were tiered upward. Each bough had three little branches, with five golden leaves about 2.5 centimeters in size on each. At the end of each branch was a golden flower with four petals, and on top of the tree, a golden bird was perched. The bunga emas was sent to Siam with much splendor. A special boat, called the *Perahu Bunga Emas* (Bunga Emas Boat), was used. Besides the bunga emas, other gifts were sent, such as silver flowers, four spears with golden handgrips, and two gold rings. Local specialists normally took six months to finish making one bunga emas, and because this and the other gifts were so important, the sultans personally supervised their creation.

The cost of making the bunga emas was borne by the people through the head tax imposed by the states. However, the value of each offering differed from state to state. It was reported that the Kedah bunga emas was the most costly.

Kedah claimed that the sending of bunga emas was a gesture of its friendship with Siam, but Kelantan sent one as a show of gratitude after Siam recognized Muhammad II as the sultan of the state. Terengganu claimed that bunga emas was sent to Siam in return for gifts sent by the Siamese king in recognition of the help the former had rendered in defeating Ligor. Patani, by contrast, sent bunga emas to Siam as a show of allegiance.

BADRIYAH HAJI SALLEH

See also Chinese Tribute System; Ligor (Nakhon); Patani (Pattani), Sultanate of; Siamese Malay States (Kedah, Perlis, Kelantan, Terengganu)

References:
Bonney, R. 1971. *Kedah, 1771–1821: The Search for Security and Independence.* Kuala Lumpur: Oxford University Press.
Ismail, Bakti. 1960. "'Bunga Emas'—Golden Flowers: Gift or Tribute (Kelantan)." *Malaya in History* 6, no. 1 (July): 40–42.
Kobkua Suwannathat-Pian. 1988. *Thai-Malay Relations: Traditional Intra-regional Relations from the Seventeenth to the Early Twentieth Centuries.* Singapore: Oxford University Press.
Shaharil Talib. 1984. *After Its Own Image: The Terengganu Experience, 1881–1941.* Singapore: Oxford University Press.
Sharom Ahmat. 1984. *Tradition and Change in a Malay State: A Study of the Economic and Political Development of Kedah, 1878–1923.* MBRAS Monograph no. 12. Kuala Lumpur: Malaysian Branch of the Royal Asiatic Society (MBRAS).

BUNNAG FAMILY
A Persian-Siamese Influential Lineage

The Bunnag family, one of the most powerful families of Siam (Thailand), played a vital role in administering the kingdom from the early Chakri period until the 1880s. Thereafter, King Chulalongkorn (Rama V) (r. 1868–1910) undertook administrative reforms—reforms that would ultimately lead to the decline in political and economic control exercised by the Bunnag family.

The ancestors of the Bunnag family were of Persian descent and settled in Ayutthaya during the reign of King Ekathotsarot (r. 1605–1610). The years of his reign saw an increasing volume of foreign trade, and the king needed foreign expertise to handle it. In 1602, the Persian brothers Sheik Ahmad and Muhammad Said arrived in Ayutthaya. They were very successful in conducting business in the capital city, and Sheik Ahmad served the bureaucracy as an official in a trade department dealing with Muslim merchants from India and Arab. During the two following reigns, Sheik Ahmad rose to power, first through his appointment as minister of trade and later as prime minister; his nephew, Muhammad Said, also served as a court official of King Songtham (r. 1610–1628). As a result, this Persian family established very firm roots in the Siamese bureaucracy from the middle of the Ayutthaya period.

One of the children of the Persian family, named Bunnag, spent his childhood with Thongduang, who later became King Rama I during the period prior to the fall of Ayutthaya in 1767. When Rama I founded Bangkok and established the Chakri dynasty in 1782, Bunnag served in the bureaucracy and established very close ties with the king through marriage (Wyatt 1994: 114, 117). During the reign of Rama I (1782–1809), Bunnag's power and influence steadily increased, and he was appointed *kalahom* (minister of defense). Thus, from the beginning of the new dynasty, the Bunnag family members gradually established their political and economic power with the royal family. These ties were strengthened during the reign of King Rama II (r. 1809–1824) because the king's mother was closely related to the Bunnag family. Her sister was the mother of two Bunnag members, who were appointed minister of defense and minister of the capital (responsible for Bangkok and its environs).

Another Bunnag, Dit, was appointed *phrakhlang* (minister of finance and foreign affairs) in 1822. When Rama II died in 1824, a grand assembly was called to choose the new monarch. (Rama II had not named the son who was born to the queen as his successor.) The Bunnag family, who by then controlled the most powerful ministries, supported Prince Chetsadabodin, King Rama II's son by a concubine, and he was duly named King Rama III (r. 1824–1851). During his reign, a younger brother of Dit, called That, was appointed kalahom. It is evident that by the third reign of the Chakri dynasty, members of the Bunnag family were the most powerful and influential among all courtiers.

Their political and economic power rose dramatically during the reign of King Rama IV, also known as King Mongkut (r. 1851–1868). King Rama III had died without directly naming his successor, even though he

favored Mongkut, who was still in monkhood at that time. A grand assembly was called again, under the chairmanship of the phrakhlang (Dit Bunnag), and it was decided to name Mongkut as the new king. King Mongkut rewarded the Bunnag family, and during his reign, members of the family filled a good number of important administrative positions (Wyatt 1984: 182). For instance, when Dit retired, he was replaced by his two sons, Chuang and Kham. Chuang took on the official title of Chaophraya Sri Suriyawong, the minister of defense, and Kham was appointed as a new finance minister. Once again, the Bunnag family was responsible for the most important ministries of the kingdom.

The family's rise in power culminated in October 1868 after Mongkut died without clearly naming his successor, even though he would have liked Chulalongkorn, his son born to the queen, to be the new king. But Chulalongkorn's ascension to the throne was based upon the condition that Sri Suriyawong would serve as a regent until the young king came of age (Wyatt 1984: 191). Sri Suriyawong had very close ties with Prince Wichaichan, the son of King Pinklao (who was known as the second king during the reign of King Mongkut). However, when a council was called, Sri Suriyawong named Chualalongkorn the new king, and the council agreed. As a result, Chulalongkorn became Rama V and ruled under the regency of Sri Suriyawong until 1873, when he came of age. During his regency, Sri Suriyawong took good care of the young king, and although many courtiers were afraid that he would usurp the throne, he never expressed any interest in doing so. Chulalongkorn rewarded him by giving him a princely title.

The power of the Bunnag family declined after the death of Sri Suriyawong in 1883 and after King Chulalongkorn undertook drastic administrative reforms in the 1880s in order to centralize the political and economic power with the king.

SUD CHONCHIRDSIN

See also Khaw Family; Reforms and Modernization in Siam; Trịnh Family (1597–1786)

References:
Girling, John L. S. 1987. *Thailand: Society and Politics.* Ithaca, NY: Cornell University Press.

Tarling, Nicholas, ed. 1994. *The Cambridge History of Southeast Asia.* Vol. 2. Cambridge: Cambridge University Press.

Trocki, Carl A. 1992. "Political Structures in the Nineteenth and Early Twentieth Centuries." Pp. 79–130 in *The Cambridge History of Southeast Asia.* Vol. 2, *The Nineteenth and Twentieth Centuries.* Edited by Nicholas Tarling. Cambridge: Cambridge University Press.

Wyatt, David. 1984. *Thailand: A Short History.* New Haven, CT: Yale University Press.

———. 1994. *Studies in Thai Histories.* Chiang Mai, Thailand: Silkworm Books.

BURMA COMMUNIST PARTY (BCP)

The Burma Communist Party (BCP) was the major armed opposition to the government of Burma (Myanmar) from the time it went underground in 1948 until its surrender to the army in 1989. The BCP was founded by a small group of intellectuals, including its two most prominent leaders, Thakins Than Tun and Soe, in Rangoon (Yangon) in 1939. It reached its popular apogee at the end of the Pacific War (1941–1945) when it combined with the Japanese-trained Burma National Army to form the Anti-Fascist People's Freedom League (AFPFL). However, the party soon split (in 1946) over the question of whether Burma could achieve independence without violence. The minority radical faction led by Thakin Soe, whose members called themselves the Red Flag Communists, then went underground, leaving the majority White Flag faction retaining the BCP title, with Thakin Than Tun at the helm.

Before long, though, the BCP fell out with its non-Communist associates in the AFPFL and was expelled from the government. Within three months of independence, the party went underground and began the long-running civil war. It was joined by a number of troops from the army and posed the major threat to the central government at Rangoon. However, the army slowly gained ground, and following the 1962 military coup, the BCP entered into peace talks with the government. When these failed, the party then went through a period of internal feuds, leading to the death of Thakin Than Tun. In 1971, the party established its base in the Shan State near the Chinese border. Ethnically still led by Burmans, its troops were composed primarily of minorities such as the Wa and Shan, many of whom had been involved in the drug trade. In 1989, when the People's Republic of China (PRC) withdrew its support for the BCP, the troops mutinied against their commanders, and the party collapsed.

R. H. TAYLOR

See also Anti-Fascist People's Freedom League (AFPFL); Burma during the Pacific War (1941–1945); Burma Independence Army (BIA); Ne Win, General (1911–2002); Shan Nationalism; Shan United Revolutionary Army; Thakin (Lord, Master)

References:

Linter, Bertil. 1990. *The Rise and Fall of the Communist Party of Burma (CPB).* Southeast Asia Program Series no. 6. Ithaca, NY: Cornell University Southeast Asia Program.

Smith, Charles B. 1984. *The Burmese Communist Party in the 1980s.* Singapore: Institute of Southeast Asian Studies.

BURMA DURING THE PACIFIC WAR (1941–1945)

The Pacific War had dramatic consequences for the future of Burma. The country was fought over twice, once as the Japanese invaded in December 1941 and again as the British returned in 1944. The economy was badly damaged, and the country has never regained the level of per capita income that had been achieved by 1939. During the war itself, many people suffered great privation as the export-oriented agricultural economy crumbled, and clothing and medicines became very scarce. The authoritarian behavior of the Japanese Imperial Army also caused much individual suffering. Thousands of Indian immigrants walked out of the country and back to India to flee the advancing Japanese. Politically, the ordered world of the colonial regime was upended. Those who had enjoyed power and privilege under the British were stripped of all their authority, whereas political radicals, many of whom had been imprisoned by the British, were able to assume the mantle of office, if not the power of government, under Japanese tutelage. When the British returned at the end of the war, they had lost the capacity to re-create the prewar order in the face of the torrent of nationalist and radical sentiment that had been engendered during the war years.

Thirty young Burmese nationalists who had fled the country in 1940 and 1941 to receive military training on Hainan Island under Japanese tutelage readily joined the latter in their invasion of Burma. Led by Thakin Aung San (1915–1947) and known as the Thirty Comrades, they included men who would become some of the most prominent leaders of the country for the next fifty years. Among them was Thakin Shu Maung, who, as General Ne Win (1911–2002), came to dominate Burma until the 1990s. The Thirty Comrades, entering Burma through the southern provinces of Tenasserim in 1942, organized a Burmese nationalist army in the wake of the Japanese, known as the Burma Independence Army (BIA). The BIA has now entered into the historiography of Burma as one of the greatest achievements of the nationalist era. Led by Thakin Aung San, the BIA soon became a group of approximately 30,000 young men who had been mobilized in the belief that the Japanese were about to restore their country's independence. The formation of the BIA was also a great boost to national morale, for the British had, until just prior to the war, refused to recognize the modern military prowess of the Burman population. The British military regularly recruited primarily from the ethnic minorities in the hill areas, namely, the Karens, Chins, Kachins, and Shans.

The war had the effect of increasing the political differences between the hill peoples and the lowland Burma population. Although the Burmans rallied to the BIA and their Japanese sponsors, many of the minority communities cleaved to the British. A number of Karen, Chin, and Kachin troops were organized into anti-Japanese guerrilla units and served behind the lines throughout the war, harassing the occupiers. Because of their loyalty to the British, many came to believe that Britain would not abandon them in the future. Toward the end of the war, a group of Burman troops massacred a number of Christian Karens, and this gory incident became a symbol of the growing strains between the ethnic communities. Also, the Shan Sawbwas were not included under the new administrative order the Japanese created but swore their allegiance directly to the Japa-

nese emperor in Tokyo. Moreover, the Shan States east of the Salween River were ceded to Thailand during the war years.

Within two weeks of the British departure from Rangoon, the Japanese installed Thakin Tun Oke as the chief administrator of the Burma *baho* (central) government. This was a government more in name than in reality, and the management of the country was effectively in the hands of the Japanese Imperial Army and the newly formed units of the BIA. A number of these troops lacked discipline, and disorder, accompanied by looting and banditry, soon became rife. In June, the Japanese ordered the BIA to cease its involvement in administrative and political affairs and to regroup for training as a more disciplined military force under General Aung San's command. The discredited baho administration was soon superseded by a preparatory committee established to create some degree of political order out of the chaos. The Japanese turned to the prewar leader Dr. Ba Maw (b. 1893) to spearhead this effort, and he brought together his own followers from the Hsinyeitha (Poor Man's) Party, as well as a number of young thakins and former student leaders, to begin to form a new government. The new joint organization, the Dobama-Hsinyeitha Party—renamed the Maha Bama (Greater Burma) Party in 1944—included a number of individuals of prominence. It featured Thakin Nu (1907–1995), who would be the first prime minister of Burma after independence in 1948, and Thakin Than Tun, who became the leader of the Burma Communist Party.

On 1 August 1943, Japan formally announced the independence of Burma under a government headed by Dr. Ba Maw. Ba Maw took the title of "*Naingngandaw Adipadi*" (State Leader), and later he was referred to as "*Anashin Mingyi Kodaw*" (King). Thakin Nu became the foreign minister in the new government, but since the only independent government that recognized the regime was Japan, he had little to do. Thakin Than Tun, however, as minister for agriculture and subsequently for transport, traveled the country widely and learned a great deal about the conditions of the peasantry, the vast majority of the population. Many other members of the government had been politically active under the British. From the start, however, many Burmese nationalists doubted the genuineness of Tokyo's promise of independence and refused to cooperate with the Japanese. Their views came to be more widely shared as the war progressed and the conditions of the country deteriorated. By 1944, when the once seemingly invincible Japanese began to suffer defeats, the tide of opinion ran very strongly against them.

While developing this new administration for Burma, the Japanese regrouped the BIA and opened an officer training school at Mingaladon. A number of officers who later served in the postwar Burma army received their military training there. The BIA had its manpower greatly reduced, and it was renamed the Burma Defense Army. It was renamed again, in September 1943, as the Burma National Army (BNA), under the command of Defense Minister Aung San and General Ne Win. The BNA was never used by the Japanese in battle but quickly became a political instrument at the disposal of its leaders.

Prior to the war, a number of thakins and other left-wing students took the view that it was inappropriate for nationalists to collaborate with the "fascist" Japanese even if doing so would speed Burma's independence. This was the position advocated by the followers of the budding communist movement within the nationalist ranks. Led by Thakin Soe, the leading theoretician of Burmese Marxism, this group held that Aung San and the Thirty Comrades had made a strategic error in cooperating with the Japanese. They argued that in the circumstances, it was better to cooperate, even if temporarily, with the British and other Allied forces against fascism. So, as the Japanese invasion commenced, a number of these individuals went underground and began to organize a resistance movement.

Thakin Thein Pe Myint, with another youth, walked out of the country to India, where he met with members of the British military intelligence and the Special Operations Executive (SOE), Force 136. They worked to organize anti-Japanese propaganda within Burma as well as an alliance with the Chinese and Indian Communist Parties. In so doing, they paved the way for the eventual (but temporary) reconciliation of the underground communists and Aung San and the BNA. By late in 1943, the beginning of what became the Anti-Fascist People's Freedom League (AFPFL)

had been formed, led by Aung San and his brother-in-law Thakin Than Tun, the agriculture minister and secret leader of the Burma Communist Party. During 1944, they worked covertly through bodies such as the East Asia Youth League and peasant and worker organizations to develop a resistance movement. Then, as the Japanese were weakening, Aung San led the BNA out of Rangoon on 27 March 1945 to join the Allied cause against their erstwhile Japanese benefactors.

Because of his role as leader of the BNA as well as general secretary of the AFPFL, Aung San was flown to Kandy, Ceylon (Sri Lanka), to negotiate the future of the indigenous army with Lord Louis Mountbatten (t. 1943–1946), the supreme Allied commander, South-East Asia Command (SEAC). Aung San sought to have the BNA recognized as an Allied armed force of a provisional government organized by the AFPFL. However, the British refused to countenance this proposed recognition, and eventually, Aung San had to accept that the BNA would become a subordinate element of the British forces in Burma.

The British returned to Burma in force in 1945 but were never able to assume the authority that they had possessed before the war. The country's infrastructure was in tatters, and for many months, the government was in the hands of the Civil Affairs Service (Burma), or CAS (B), under Major General Hubert Rance. Rance returned a few years later following the removal of Sir Reginald Dorman-Smith as the civilian governor (t. 1946–1948) appointed by the Labour government of Prime Minister Clement Attlee (t. 1945–1951). Mountbatten remained the dominant figure in shaping British policy toward Burma during that time. As viceroy of India, he eventually realized that the military forces necessary to hold Burma within the British Empire were evaporating as Indian independence loomed; an orderly departure from Burma was the best that could be achieved.

The AFPFL eventually came to cooperate with the British and led the country to independence in 1948. Before that happened, however, the communist and noncommunist factions of the league became estranged over strategy and tactics in the nationalist movement, paving the way for the civil war that engulfed Burma within three months of independence. Also, the rift between the Karens and the Burmans had not healed, and that, too, led to years of bloodshed. And in July 1947, Aung San and other members of the Governor's Executive Council were assassinated. The architect of Burmese independence was killed before his goal had been achieved.

R. H. TAYLOR

See also Anti-Fascist People's Freedom League (AFPFL); Aung San (1915–1947); Ba Maw, Dr. (b. 1893); British Military Administration (BMA) in Southeast Asia; Burma Independence Army (BIA); Collaboration Issue in Southeast Asia; Force 136; Japanese Occupation of Southeast Asia (1941–1945); Mountbatten, Admiral Lord Louis (1900–1979); Nationalism and Independence Movements in Southeast Asia; South-East Asia Command (SEAC); Thakin (Lord, Master); Thirty Comrades; U Saw and the Assassination of Aung San

References:

Ba Maw. 1968. *Breakthrough in Burma*. New Haven, CT: Yale University Press.

Collis, Maurice. 1956. *Last and First in Burma (1941–1946)*. London: Faber and Faber.

Guyot, Dorothy. 1966. "The Political Impact of the Japanese Occupation of Burma." Ph.D. diss., Yale University.

Nu. 1954. *Burma under the Japanese*. Translated by J. S. Furnivall. London: Macmillan.

Taylor, Robert H. 1980. "Burma in the Anti-Fascist War." Pp. 159–190 in *Southeast Asia under Japanese Occupation*. Edited by Alfred W. McCoy. Monograph Series no. 22. New Haven, CT: Yale University Southeast Asia Studies.

———. 1984. *Marxism and Resistance in Burma, 1942–1945: Thein Pe Myint's Wartime Traveler*. Athens: Ohio University Press.

Tun Pe. 1949. *Sun over Burma*. Rangoon: Rasika Ranjani Press.

BURMA INDEPENDENCE ARMY (BIA)

The Burma Independence Army (BIA) was the forerunner of the armed forces of Burma (Myanmar) after the country regained its independence in 1948. The BIA was formed in 1942, initiated by Burmese nationalist students who had become disillusioned with the parliamentary politics of the British Burma government and sought a revolutionary route to independence. The initial officer corps grew from the nucleus of the famous Thirty Comrades who, led by Thakin Aung San (1915–1947), had fled Rangoon (Yangon) in 1940. Aung San was intercepted by the Japanese in Amoy (Xiamen) and taken to Japan; there, the Japanese convinced him that they would support the Burmese nationalists in their independence struggle.

Returning from Japan to Rangoon in early 1941, with the assistance of colleagues in the Dobama Asi-ayone, a nationalist association led by students at the University of Rangoon, Aung San gathered the Thirty Comrades for eventual officer training on Hainan Island. The BIA was formed from Burmese in exile in Bangkok and subsequently from the southern peninsula of Burma during December 1941 and January 1942, in the wake of the Japanese Imperial Army's invasion of the country at that time. Riding the nationalist wave sweeping through Burmese youth, the BIA grew rapidly in the first months of 1942; by May, it was a force of about 23,000 ill-trained and ill-equipped men. Though used by the Japanese primarily behind the lines, engaging in only one major battle with British forces, the BIA played a significant role during 1942 by establishing effective, if short-lived, administrations in many areas as the British withdrew. These self-appointed local governments often clashed with the Japanese as well as with non-BIA Burmese politicians and administrators. During its rapid growth, the BIA had attracted adventurers and opportunists as well as patriots, and its reputation in some areas was tarnished by the high-handed, autocratic, and self-serving behavior of some of its members.

Because of the BIA's unwieldy size, slack discipline, and political pretensions, the Japanese ordered the force's reduction and consolidation in July 1942, and the BIA was regrouped as the Burma Defense Army (BDA). It was from the BDA, more than the BIA, that the bulk of the post-1948 officer corps was developed. The overwhelming majority of the Thirty Comrades eschewed subsequent military careers for politics and business, with the significant exception of General Ne Win (1911–

2002). Simultaneously with the formation of the BDA, the Japanese opened a military academy at Mingaladon near Rangoon to train regular officers and sergeants. In 1943, the BDA was renamed once again, becoming the Burma National Army (BNA).

In terms of social background, the officers of the Burmese force reflected the hierarchy of social rank and status in valley Burma at that time. The higher-ranking officers came from larger towns, and most had more formal education than the bulk of the population. Ethnically, the majority of the officers were Burman, though a few Karens, several from the former British Burma army, were also recruited. The BNA never penetrated and recruited from the hill areas, where the British continued to draw troops throughout the war.

Frustrated by the limitations placed on their nominally independent government and the arrogant behavior of some Japanese officers, a number of junior BNA officers began to plot in 1943 to rebel against the Japanese and side with the British. In this, they were advised and guided by a number of civilian politicians, many of whom were identified with the underground anti-Japanese resistance led by the Burma Communist Party (BCP). As the tide of the war turned against the Japanese, more and more officers came to believe that a revolt against the Japanese was essential. The military was prompted to act by the deteriorating economic conditions of the country, which were severely impacting the army's popularity. Furthermore, many believed that if the army were to have a role in postwar Burma, it would have to make itself useful to the British in the final defeat of the Japanese.

In August 1944, the BNA leadership entered into a united front, the Anti-Fascist People's Freedom League (AFPFL), with the Burma Communist Party to prepare for an eventual anti-Japanese rising. In February 1945, BNA troops attacked Japanese forces near Mandalay, and the following month, on 27 March, the remainder of the Burmese army under General Aung San marched out of Rangoon to attack the Japanese. That date has been celebrated as Army Day or Resistance Day in Burma (Myanmar) ever since.

Though some British officials felt that the leaders of the BNA, including Aung San, should have been tried as war criminals after the war, the supreme Allied commander for Southeast Asia, Admiral Lord Louis Mountbatten (1900–1979), took a different view. He and Lieutenant General William Joseph Slim (1891–1970) determined that it would be possible to work with the BNA in the final defeat of the Japanese. At Kandy in Sri Lanka (Ceylon) in 1945, Mountbatten and Aung San reached an agreement to incorporate a proportion of BNA troops, now renamed the Patriotic Burmese Forces (PBF), into the British Burma army. The remainder were organized into the People's Volunteer Force, which played a political role in the subsequent negotiations between the AFPFL and the British, leading to Myanmar's eventual independence. Aung San resigned from the army at that time, leaving General Ne Win as the senior Burman officer from the BIA and the Thirty Comrades in charge of the Burma army.

R. H. TAYLOR

See also Anti-Fascist People's Freedom League (AFPFL); Aung San (1915–1947); British Burma; Burma Communist Party (BCP); Burma during the Pacific War (1941–1945); Military and Politics in Southeast Asia; Mountbatten, Admiral Lord Loius (1900–1979); Nationalism and Independence Movements in Southeast Asia; Ne Win, General (1911–2002); South-East Asia Command (SEAC); Thakin (Lord, Master); Thirty Comrades

References:

Guyot, Dorothy Hess. 1966. "The Political Impact of the Japanese Occupation of Burma." Ph.D. diss., Yale University.

Taylor, Robert H. 1980. "Burma in the Anti-Fascist War." Pp. 159–190 in *Southeast Asia under Japanese Occupation*. Edited by Alfred W. McCoy. Monograph Series no. 22. New Haven, CT: Yale University Southeast Asia Studies.

Yoon, Won Z. 1973. *Japan's Scheme for the Liberation of Burma: The Minami Kikan and the "Thirty Comrades."* Southeast Asia Program Paper no. 27. Athens: Ohio University Center for International Studies.

BURMA RESEARCH SOCIETY (BRS) (1909)

For seventy-one years, the Burma Research Society (BRS) was an independent organization for the sponsorship and dissemination of research on the history, culture, economics, and natural sciences in Burma. Burma, now known as Myanmar, was colonized by Britain in the last quarter of the nineteenth century, but the colonial government did very little to understand the history and culture of the colony, which was then administered as a province of British India. The society originated in 1909 as the inspiration of John Sydenham Furnivall (1878–1960), a Cambridge University graduate and a member of the Indian Civil Service, the elite administrative corps of the British Indian Empire, as well as a Fabian socialist. His keen interest in all things Burmese grew from his study of the reasons why British institutions and ideas seemed to result in such socially divisive and politically destabilizing consequences when transferred to Burma. Having a deep knowledge of the Burmese language and (unusually for an Englishman in colonial Burma) being married to a Burmese woman, he had an intense and respectful interest in all aspects of Burmese culture.

It was in the spirit of Furnivall's broad intellectual interests that the BRS held its first formal meeting in Rangoon (Yangon) on 29 March 1910. The society attracted as members the leading British figures in Burma studies of the first half of the twentieth century—outstanding scholars such as C. O. Bladgen, C. Duroiselle, D. G. E. Hall, G. H. Luce, U Pe Maung Tin, and Htin Aung. The BRS published a number of monographs and texts on matters relating to Burmese history and culture, and biannually from 1911, it produced the *Journal of the Burma Research Society* in both Burmese and English. The society and its scientific aims were often considered subversive by the government, whether British or Burmese. British officials prior to the Pacific War (1941–1945) frequently considered the work of the society antithetical to the maintenance of colonial rule. Ironically, the BRS was closed down in 1980 by the Burma Socialist Programme Party government of General Ne Win (1911–2002).

R. H. TAYLOR

See also British Burma; British India, Government of; Burma Socialist Programme Party (BSPP); Ne Win, General (1911–2002)

References:
Journal of the Burma Research Society. 1911–1980.

BURMA ROAD
A Lifeline to China
The Burma Road, also known as the Lashio-Kunming Highway, was built in the late 1930s, primarily at the behest of the Chinese Nationalist government, to provide a southern route for the receipt of war supplies during the Second Sino-Japanese War (1937–1945). Running 1,120 kilometers (700 miles), it was opened in 1938. The Burma Road connected the town of Lashio in the Shan State of Burma (Myanmar) to the Chinese border at Muse and then continued on to Kunming, the capital of Yunnan Province in China. The southern terminus at Lashio connected with the single rail line that ran down to Mandalay and thence on to the port city of Rangoon (Yangon). This route was closed to the Chinese in 1941, when Japan invaded Burma and then occupied the country militarily for the next four years.

After the closure of the Burma Road and the broadening of China's war with Japan to include Britain and the United States, the U.S. Army Air Force (USAF) and the Royal Air Force (RAF) opened an alternative route to supply China via the air. However, the limited capacity of airplanes to fuel an army, especially in the difficult flying conditions encountered at high altitudes over the eastern Himalayan range, led the Allies to open another route later in the war. Known as the Ledo Road, it commenced at Ledo in India's Assam Province and ran across Burma to Myitkyina in the Kachin State where it connected with the Burma Road, a distance of about 800 kilometers (500 miles). This strategic stretch was also referred to as "Stillwell Road" in honor of the rough and tough U.S. commander Joseph "Vinegar Joe" Stillwell (1883–1946).

R. H. TAYLOR

See also Burma during the Pacific War (1941–1945); Highways and Railways; Japanese Occupation of Southeast Asia (1941–1945)
References:
Kirby, Stanley Woodburn. 1957–1969. *The War against Japan.* 5 vols. London: Her Majesty's Stationery Office.

Aerial view of the Burma Road, taken by a U.S. Army Signal Corps photographer in the China-Burma-India Theater in June 1944. This section of the Burma Road contains twenty-four switchbacks. (Bettmann/Corbis)

BURMA SOCIALIST PROGRAMME PARTY (BSPP)

The Burma Socialist Programme Party (BSPP), or Lanzin Party, was the ruling political institution in Myanmar (then known as Burma) from 1974 until 1988. The members of the Revolutionary Council military government that had seized power the previous March formed the BSPP in July 1962 as a small cadre party. Led throughout its existence by one man, General Ne Win (1911–2002), it was very much the instrument of his creation. In March 1964, the BSPP became the only legal party in Myanmar following the failure of talks between the Revolutionary Council and the previous legal political parties that had emerged from the Anti-Fascist People's Freedom League (AFPFL). The party's major ideological doctrines were drawn from the Revolutionary Council's policy statements, entitled "The Burmese Road to Socialism" (April 1962) and the "System of Correlation of Man and His Environment" (1963). Drawn from a blending of Buddhist and Marxist philosophical concepts, the party's ideology attempted to encapsulate the major political traditions in modern Myanmar political thought.

In 1971, the BSPP expanded to become a mass party. With the introduction of a new constitution in 1974, which was intended to pave the way to a civilian regime, General Ne Win and other senior officers resigned their military commissions but carried on in office. The BSPP government continued to pursue policies of economic autarky that were similar to those of its predecessor. Between 1971 and 1988, the party held several congresses to address the growing economic and political problems in the country. But by 1988, the socialist one-party model had lost what little viability it had ever had, and Chairman Ne Win resigned while calling for the abandonment of socialism and a return to multiparty democracy. His plans for a peaceful transition were thwarted, however, by public demonstrations that led to a military coup in September 1988.

R. H. TAYLOR

See also Anti-Fascist People's Freedom League (AFPFL); Buddhist Socialism; Military and Politics in Southeast Asia; Ne Win, General (1911–2002); State Law and Order Restoration Council (SLORC); Suu Kyi, Daw Aung San (1945–)

References:
Taylor, Robert H. 1987. *The State in Burma.* London: C. Hurst.

BURMA UNDER BRITISH COLONIAL RULE

Britain colonized Burma as the consequence of three wars fought in the nineteenth century against the armies of the Konbaung kings. The effects of colonial rule varied in different parts of the country, and some areas had a lengthier experience under colonialism than others. The British held the Tenasserim coast in the far south and Arakan, adjacent to Bengal, longer than any other area—more than one hundred and twenty years—whereas the Irrawaddy Delta (or what the British often referred to in the nineteenth century as Pegu or Lower

Burma) was held just over ninety years. The center of the country, the heartland of Burmese civilization in the previous centuries, was held by the British a mere sixty years, though the traumatic effects of the loss of the monarchy and its support for the Buddhist faith had profound consequences there. Farther north—in the region the British referred to as the Frontier Areas Administration, home to a variety of tribal peoples who had acknowledged the suzerainty of the Konbaung monarchy—the consequences of colonialism were by far the least profound. The differential political, economic, and social consequences of the colonial era contributed to the complexities of postcolonial Burmese society.

A review of the early consequences in each of the major regions of the country clarifies the initial differential effects. Arakan, or Rakine State, which bordered Indian Bengal, was opened to immigration from the Muslim population of that region, a fact that generated a degree of resentment among the Buddhist people who believed that their land and religion were being taken away from them. Antipathy to Muslims, who make up less than 5 percent of the current population of Burma (now known as Myanmar), is derived in part from this experience. Tenasserim, the other region colonized in 1824, was sparsely populated at the time and was a zone of contention between the Burmese and Siamese kings. Many of the people who resided in this region were from animist hill tribe minorities, and though Christian missionaries who accompanied the British merchants and soldiers found few converts among the Buddhist population, they had greater success among the hill tribes, particularly in the Karen community. Nearly a quarter of the Karen population became Christians and strongly identified their community with Britain, which was seen as their protector. Karen converts normally became Baptists, whereas Catholicism became the faith of a number of smaller tribes. The introduction of Christianity among the hill tribes then spread farther north; today, approximately 5 percent of the people of Myanmar consider themselves to be Christians.

Although the annexation of Arakan and Tenasserim generated ethnic and religious issues for Burmese society, the annexation of Lower Burma had profound economic consequences. The delta of the Irrawaddy River was largely unpopulated when the British assumed authority over it in 1852. As they had in the earlier annexed territories, they applied the rules and regulations of British India. The fundamental purpose of British rule was to ensure that trade and commerce could operate largely unfettered by government monopolies and constraints. But this goal was antithetical to the principles of statecraft of the Burmese kings, whose administrative system was buttressed by the concept of the monarch as the leading trader and organizer of economic life. The application of the principles of free trade and relative low levels of taxation by the British proved attractive to many Burmese peasants living in the north under the king's rule, and there was a large migration of families to open up new rice fields in the delta. They were facilitated in this by large-scale engineering works undertaken by the British to control the water levels of the delta and increase productivity.

Soon, Lower Burma became the rice bowl of not only Burma but also India. Prior to the Pacific War (1941–1945), Burma was the largest rice exporter in the world. But the new prosperity sought by the Burmese peasants under British rule proved illusory. The system of agriculture they established was heavily dependent on agricultural credit. Farmers borrowed funds at the beginning of each growing season to buy seeds and other materials and, in some cases, the labor they needed to plant and nurture their crops in the expectation that when they sold them after the harvest, they could repay their debts and have a profit for themselves. However, when crops failed or international rice prices fell below their production costs, the farmers fell into arrears, and eventually their land was confiscated by the moneylenders who had made loans to them.

Initially, many of the moneylenders were Burmese, but they were soon replaced by a caste of moneylenders from South India, known as Chettiars. The Chettiars were members of a banking caste and had no intention of becoming landlords. But like the peasant farmers with whom they did business, they were subject to world economic forces beyond their control. At times of economic crisis and particularly during the Great Depression of the late 1920s, the Western banks that they had borrowed from called in their loans, forcing the Chettiars to take possession of the lands of the Burmese peasants. By the 1930s, more than 25 percent of the best delta lands were no longer owned by owner-cultivators but were in the hands of alien landlords (Adas 1974: 188). Resentment at this situation, coupled with an increasing tax burden and the lack of alternative forms of employment, caused widespread disaffection among the peasant population of the delta. This expressed itself in the so-called Hsaya San Rebellion from 1930 to 1932, which was suppressed only after more than 10,000 troops were transferred into Burma from India.

The Hsaya San Rebellion was a manifestation not only of peasant economic grievances but also of one of the other major consequences of British rule in Burma—the development of modern nationalism. Nationalism in Burma came to be expressed in a Buddhist image—to be Burmese is to be Buddhist—for when the British annexed Upper Burma in 1885, they removed the king, who personified the Buddhist faith, and ignored the indigenous social institutions they found there. The Burmese interpreted this action as an attack on their faith, and the country was largely in revolt for the next ten years. The British were able to pacify the country, as they described it, by establishing a military occupation, but soon the Burmese began to organize their resistance through non-violent political means. The first such organization was the Young Men's Buddhist Association (YMBA), which became the General Council of Buddhist Associations after World War I (1914–1918) and later was known as the General Council of Burmese Associations (GCBA). The GCBA, with a related organization for Buddhist monks, led the nationalist movement until the early 1930s.

When the British introduced electoral politics to all the country except the frontier areas in the 1920s, some members of the GCBA formed political parties and entered into the colonial legislature. Others, however, refused, and they received encouragement from the peasantry, which organized at the village level to boycott the elections and refuse to pay taxes and rents. Hsaya San, a former Buddhist monk, provided a focus for these groups, and he rallied many of them to join his doomed revolt.

Students had been involved in Burmese nationalist politics from the start. Rangoon University students organized a boycott of the institution before it opened its doors in 1921. In the 1930s, students became involved in nationalist agitation in other ways. The Rangoon University Students Union became a focus of protest, and in the 1930s, it organized nationwide strikes of both university and high school students to protest what they referred to as the "slave education" provided by the British. Students also became involved in the Dobama Asiayone (DAA), or We Burmans Association. The DAA argued for more radical policies than those advocated by the politicians who cooperated with the British in the legislative politics of the day. Influenced by the ideas of Friedrich Nietzsche (1844–1900) and Karl Marx (1818–1883), as well as by British Fabianism and Burmese Buddhism, the DAA sought ways of overthrowing the British and regaining Burma's independence. DAA members were attracted to left-wing ideologies, yet when the Japanese offered to assist them in pursuing the goal of independence, many of those who subsequently came to power proved willing to work with "fascists."

While most of Burma was undergoing massive political, economic, and social changes during the colonial era, the areas in the far north that now make up the Shan, Kachin, Chin, and Kayah States remained largely untouched by the full effects of the modern world. There, the British, rather than uprooting the existing political order as they did in Burma proper, kept in place the traditional rulers, the Shan and Kayah *Sawbwas,* the Kachin *Duwas,* and the Chin headmen. There was very little economic change, other than that stemming from isolated pockets of mining for lead, zinc, and silver. Many of the poorer parts of the population were attracted to service in the colonial army, and having been identified by the British as "martial races," large numbers of Kachins, Chins, and Karens joined the military. They remained loyal to the British during the Pacific War, creating one of the great fissures in modern Burmese political life.

The colonial period saw the development of much of the infrastructure of modern Burma (Myanmar). The railways, roads, and inland navigation systems that were developed by British capital and Burmese and Indian labor tied the country together in ways unimaginable a hundred years earlier. Burma was also linked to the outside world through trade and immigration.

In the 1920s and 1930s, Rangoon was the busiest immigration point in the world after New York City, as thousands of Indian laborers entered and left the country each year to seek economic opportunities. But the rewards of the economic growth that colonialism had created were not equitably distributed, and the majority of the population—the Burmese peasants—felt that they were losing control of their lives and their livelihoods. The Burmese nationalist slogan captured their dilemma: in essence, it said that under the Burmese kings, they had been poor people in a poor country, but now they were the poorest people in a rich country. This sense of economic unfairness, coupled with the attack on Buddhism that colonial policies directly and indirectly fostered, generated a nationalist reaction, which took shape in the militant, autarkic nationalism that dominated Burmese thought and action after colonialism had passed.

R. H. TAYLOR

See also Anglo-Burmese Wars (1824–1826, 1852, 1885); Arakan; British India, Government of; Buddhist Socialism; Burma during the Pacific War (1941–1945); Chettiars (Chettyars); Chins; Constitutional Developments in Burma (1900–1941); General Council of Burmese Associations (GCBA) (1920); Kachins; Karens; Konbaung Rulers and British Imperialism; Nationalism and Independence Movements in Southeast Asia; Peasant Uprisings and Protest Movements in Southeast Asia; Rangoon (Yangon); Rice in Southeast Asia; Shans; Tenasserim; Young Men's Buddhist Association (YMBA) (1906)

References:

Adas, Michael. 1974. *The Burma Delta: Economic Development and Social Change on an Asian Rice Frontier, 1852–1941.* Madison: University of Wisconsin Press.

Cady, John F. 1958. *A History of Modern Burma.* Ithaca, NY, and London: Cornell University Press.

Donnison, F. S.V. 1953. *Public Administration in Burma: A Study of Development during the British Connexion.* London: Royal Institute of International Affairs.

Furnivall, J. S. 1948. *Colonial Policy and Practice: A Comparative Study of Burma and Netherlands India.* Cambridge: Cambridge University Press.

Maung Maung. 1980. *From Sangha to Laity: Nationalist Movements in Burma, 1920–1940.* New Delhi: Manohar.

Taylor, Robert H. 1987. *The State in Burma.* London: C. Hurst.

Thant Myint U. 2001. *The Making of Modern Burma.* Cambridge: Cambridge University Press.

BURMANS

The Burman people are the largest ethnic group in the modern state of Burma, which was renamed the Union of Myanmar in 1989. They make up one of the principal ethnic groups of Southeast Asia and have had a significant impact on the cultural, religious, and political development of the region. The Burmese language is part of the Sino-Tibetan language family. In the absence of significant archaeological research, linguistic classifications such as this have had considerable influence on attempts to write the early ethnohistory of the Burman people.

The beginning of the Burmese era is traditionally traced to 638 C.E. This date refers to the myth of a brother and sister who lived at Tagaung, a town in the upper Irrawaddy Valley. They died at the hands of Popa Sawrahan, an early king of the small city-state of Pagan in the dry zone in the central part of Burma, and they became significant in the distinctively Burman spirit, or *nat,* cults approved by the early Burman kings. This area in the dry zone is the historical and cultural heartland of the Burman people. Archaeologists believe that Burmans migrated into this region from the northeast in the seventh to tenth centuries. The ethnography of this region was already complex. Ethnic Pyu governed the principal city-states of the central zone as well as Upper Burma at that time, and to the south were the Mon kingdoms. Significant numbers of T'ai (Shan) people were also migrating down the Shweli, Irrawaddy, and Chindwin River valleys; other communities, such as the Karen, also seem to have been long established. The decline of Pyu power enabled the Burman kings to establish themselves as the dominant political authority in the central zone by the eleventh century.

Burman ethnohistory proper starts around 1044, when the Burman king Anawrahta (r. 1044–1077) took control of the small city-state of Pagan. This king also annexed Arakan to the west and subdued the Mon kingdoms in Lower Burma, including Thaton. A complete set of Mon Theravadan Buddhist scriptures, the *Tripitaka,* was taken to Pagan. Following this, a distinctly Burman political, cultural, and Theravadan Buddhist religious identity emerged. This identity incorporated elements of local popular nat homage and also contained elements of Mahayana Buddhism. During the next two centuries, a huge complex of pagodas and temple buildings developed around Pagan, which helped to establish a specifically Burman style of religious architecture. It was also in the Pagan period that the Burmese script developed, with the first inscriptions being dated to around 1100. These religious and literate identities are of importance in helping to define a specifically Burman ethnohistory.

The fall of Pagan, which resulted from Mongol invasions, is usually dated to 1287. Since the British colonial period (1824–1948), it has been customary to identify the Ava dynasty that followed not with ethnic Burman rulers but with three Shan brothers, who would thus be ethnic T'ais. These ideas have recently been challenged. Much more research is needed, but it is clear that the early Ava dynasty did not take on a Shan character, and it can thus still be identified as socially, culturally, and politically Burman. The periodization of Burman ethnohistory focuses on the establishment of dynasties that took their names from the places where their central authorities were established. Although kingship was hereditary, lineages were frequently overturned in the violent power struggles that ensued upon the death of a monarch. The main dynasties are known as the Ava, Taungoo (Toungoo), Shwebo, Konbaung, and Mandalay or Yadanapon. Some of these dynasties overlapped chronologically, reflecting the extremely unstable political situation of the region as Mon, Arakanese, and T'ai kingdoms all sought to expand their influence.

There were periods in which Burmese political control was very extensive, notably under King Bayinnaung (r. 1551–1581) and the Konbaung kings Alaungpaya (r. 1752–1760) and Bodawpaya (r. 1782–1819). From 1754 to 1757, Alaungpaya (Alaung-hpaya) retook most of Lower Burma from the Mons, raided Manipur, ousted the British from their factory trading post at Negrais, and sacked the Siamese capital of Ayuthaya. Alaungpaya's sons continued their father's expansionist policy, particularly westward through Arakan and Manipur. In 1824, this policy brought Burma into conflict with the British imperial administration in northeast India. In 1852, Lower Burma was annexed, and in 1885, the whole of Burma came under British rule and the last Burmese monarch, Thibaw (r. 1878–1885), was deposed. It was not until 1948 that independence was granted to Burma. Independent Burma, however, had a much more complex political structure ethnographically, as areas were now under the direct control of the majority Burman center that had previously been independent or only tributary to Burmese monarchs.

The British colonial period created many problems in the political, social, and economic relations between ethnic Burman peoples and other ethnic groups with whom they were in contact. These difficulties have not been resolved since independence. In this situation, the historical periods of expansion cited earlier, sometimes referred to as the era of "Burman empires," have gained significance in the attempt by Burman nationalists to give historical justification to the control over non-Burman peoples exercised by a Burman political center. Many non-Burman ethnic minority communities feel that the identification of the state of Burma (Myanmar) with majority Burman ethnohistory and Burman culture also challenges their right to cultural and political autonomy. As evidence, they cite policies that have been introduced by the country's military regime that encourage the hegemony of majority Burman culture. There are also a number of Burman subgroups with very strong linguistic identities who are vulnerable in this context. In reality, a great deal more social, anthropological, and historical research is needed to understand the relationships between ethnic Burmans and other communities in the country, as well as to understand the complexities of ethnic Burman identity and ethnohistory, which have considerable regional variation.

MANDY SADAN

See also Alaung-hpaya (r. 1752–1760); Anawrahta (Aniruddha) (r. 1044–1077); Bayinnaung (r. 1551–1581); Buddhism, Mahayana; Buddhism, Theravada; Burma under British Colonial Rule; First Ava

Dynasty (1364–1527 C.E.); Konbaung Dynasty (1752–1885); Konbaung Rulers and British Imperialism; Mon; Mons; Pagan (Bagan); Pyus; T'ais; Toungoo Dynasty (1531–1752)

References:
Aung-thwin, Michael. 1998. *Myth and History in the Historiography of Early Burma: Paradigms, Primary Sources and Prejudices.* Athens: Ohio University Press.
Pe Maung Tin and G. H. Luce. 1960. *The Glass Palace Chronicle of the Kings of Burma.* Rangoon: Rangoon University Press.
Scott, J. G. 1989. *The Burman: His Life and Notions.* Whiting Bay, UK: Kiscadale Publications.
Smith, Martin. 1999. *Burma: Insurgency and the Politics of Ethnicity.* London: Zed Press.
Than Tun. 1998. *Essays on the History and Buddhism of Burma.* Whiting Bay, UK: Kiscadale Publications.
Thant Myint U. 2001. *The Making of Modern Burma.* Cambridge: Cambridge University Press.

BURMA-SIAM WARS

Begun in the 1500s, the Burma-Siam wars extended until 1809. The period of conflict was launched by Tabinshweihti (r. 1531–1550) of Burma's First Toungoo dynasty (1486–1599) and Bayinnaung (r. 1551–1581), and it was pursued by Alaung-hpaya (r. 1752–1760), the first king of the Konbaung dynasty (1752–1885), and his sons Hsinbyushin (r. 1763–1776) and Bodawpaya (r. 1782–1819). These wars originated in economic rivalry over control of the revenues from international trade that traversed the trade routes of the upper Malay Peninsula and around the Gulf of Siam. From 1767 to 1809, Siam was continuously at war with Burma. From the destruction of the Siamese capital at Ayutthaya by the Burmese in 1767 to the founding of the new capital at Bangkok in 1782, the Siamese armies under the generals Phya Taksin (King Taksin, r. 1767–1782) and Phya Chakri (Rama I, r. 1782–1809) fought eleven campaigns against the Burmese. These wars were primarily struggles for regional and dynastic supremacy and were neither national nor ethnic conflicts.

Founded in 1350, the Siamese kingdom of Ayutthaya grew quickly to become a major commercial entrepôt in mainland Southeast Asia. In the late 1400s, Ayutthaya captured the trade routes on the Malay Peninsula that passed through Mergui, Martaban, and Tavoy, thus positioning itself to profit from the growing Indian Ocean trade based on Melaka. After the fall of Melaka to the Portuguese in 1511, the cities on the transpeninsular routes became alternative centers for the Muslim traders. In 1539, to capture this trade, Tabinshweihti moved the capital from Toungoo to Pegu in the Irrawaddy Delta, a convenient base from which to launch military offensives against Siam. Tabinshweihti unsuccessfully attacked Siam in 1548.

Under the pretext of gaining the propitious white elephants of the king of Siam that had been denied to him, Tabinshweihti's successor, Bayinnaung, succeeded in subduing Siam in 1569. Ayutthaya became a tributary kingdom until King Naresuan (r. 1590–1605) and his brother, Prince Ekathotsarot (r. 1605–1610), reestablished Siamese independence by defeating the Burmese armies at the Battle of Nong Sarai in 1593. King Naresuan killed the Burmese crown prince in a duel on elephant-back. Mergui reverted to Siamese control, the profits from the Indian Ocean trade again flowing to Ayutthaya. Burmese unity crumbled under King Nandabayin (r. 1581–1599), a fact that became apparent following the destruction of Pegu in 1599 by the Arakanese and their Portuguese allies. King Anauk-hpet-lun (r. 1606–1628) tried to recapture the transpeninsular trade, gaining Ye and Tavoy; however, the Siamese retained control of Mergui, destroying the Burmese fleet in 1614. Anauk-hpet-lun's successor, King Thalun (r. 1629–1648), recognized Ayutthayan independence and moved the Burmese capital north to Ava in 1635.

In the seventeenth century, Siam expanded its international linkages, revenues, and influence, attracting Dutch, English, French, Japanese, Arab, Persian, Chinese, and other Asian merchants to its burgeoning markets. The palace revolution of 1688 at the death of King Narai (r. 1656–1688), when the usurper, King Phetracha, seized the throne, did not interrupt Ayutthaya's commercial activities for long. At the death of King Borommakot in 1758, Ayutthaya was the wealthiest city in mainland Southeast Asia.

To capture this wealth and redirect trade to the newly established port city of Rangoon (Yangon), Alaung-hpaya launched his 1760 campaign against Ayutthaya. A subsidiary motivation may have been related to Siamese attacks on Burmese shipping around Tavoy and tacit Siamese support for the Mons during the civil war fought between 1740 and 1757. According to the *Burmese Annals,* Alaung-hpaya left Rangoon in January 1760 with an army of forty regiments, headed for Pegu and Martaban, sending a contingent to attack Tavoy, where he killed the governor, and his remaining forces were transported to Moulmein. At Tavoy, he waited seven days for reinforcements to arrive by ship from Rangoon and Martaban before proceeding to take Mergui and Tenasserim. His forces consisted of 300 horses and 3,000 men under Mingaung Nawrahta and 500 horses and 5,000 men under his son, the Myedu prince. To counter the advancing forces, the Siamese king assembled an army of five regiments (300 horses and 7,000 men) under Bya Tezaw and fifteen regiments (200 elephants, 1,000 horses, and 20,000 men) under Aukbya Yazawunthan. They met the invading force outside Kui but were forced to retreat. The Burmese took Phetburi and Ratburi, and despite a spirited Siamese stand at Ban Lwin, the Burmese, thanks to the timely arrival of the Myedu prince, captured Supanburi. The Siamese king defended the capital. A force of 300 elephants, 3,000 horses, and 30,000 men engaged the Burmese at the Talan River to prevent them from crossing it. Despite heavy losses, the Burmese pressed on, taking five senior Siamese commanders and their war elephants. On 11 April 1760, the Burmese army arrived in the environs of Ayutthaya, burning the outer suburbs and bombarding the city itself from 14 to 16 April 1760. Having defeated the new Siamese force of 15,000, the Burmese were on the brink of victory when they suddenly withdrew. Alaung-hpaya had fallen ill from scrofula. He died on 11 May 1760 at the village of Kinywa, a three-day march from Martaban, and was cremated at the family seat of Moksobo.

Renewing the attack in 1765, Hsinbyushin's three armies caught Ayutthaya in a pincer movement, cutting the communication routes and taking manpower from Ayutthaya's neighboring states and outlying provinces. One army came from the south through Tavoy, Mergui, and Tenasserim; a second came from the southeast through Three Pagodas Pass; and a third arrived from the north through Chiang Mai and Laos. Well prepared, they commenced the campaign at the start of the rainy season, had boats with them, and grew their own rice throughout the siege. Maha Nawrahta, one of two senior Burmese commanders, was killed; the other, Neimyo Thihapate, finished the campaign on his own. Chinese attacks in the north prompted Hsinbyushin to direct his commander on 9 January 1767 to sack the city and kill or deport the inhabitants; the Burmese forces were needed to defend the homeland. Ayutthaya fell through subterfuge. The Burmese dug tunnels under the walls, and those tunnels collapsed. The *Annals* describe courageous Siamese efforts to storm the forts protecting the tunnels. The city was plundered, the king was killed, and 2,000 members of the Siamese royal family were taken captive to Burma. The king's brother, Prince Uthumphon, found in chains, was freed and taken to Burma, where he lived out his life in a monastery at Sagaing. The First Anglo–Burmese War (1824–1826) finally ended the Burmese attempt to gain economic hegemony in mainland Southeast Asia.

HELEN JAMES

See also Alaung-hpaya (r. 1752–1760); Anglo-Burmese Wars (1824–1826, 1852, 1885); Ava; Ayutthaya (Ayuthaya, Ayudhya, Ayuthia) (1351–1767 C.E.), Kingdom of; Bayinnaung (r. 1551–1581); Chiang Mai; Economic Transformation of Southeast Asia (ca. 1400–ca. 1800); Elephants; First Ava (Inwa) Dynasty (1364–1527 C.E.); Hsinbyushin (r. 1763–1776); Konbaung Dynasty (1752–1885); Ligor (Nakhon); Melaka; Mons; Narai (r. 1665–1688); Patani (Pattani), Sultanate of; Pegu; Penang (1786); Phra Naret (King Naresuan) (r. 1590–1605); Phya Taksin (Pya Tak [Sin], King Taksin) (r. 1767–1782); Rama I (Chakri) (r. 1782–1809); Rangoon (Yangon); Siamese Malay States (Kedah, Perlis, Kelantan, Terengganu); Singapore (1819); Straits of Melaka; Tabinshweihti (r. 1531–1550); Toungoo Dynasty (1531–1752)

References:

Chutintaranond, S. 1995. *On Both Sides of the Tenasserim Range: A History of Siamese-Burmese Relations.* Institute of Asian Studies Monographs, no. 50. Bangkok: Chulalongkorn University Press.

James, Helen. 2000. "The Fall of Ayutthaya: A Reassessment." *Journal of Burma Studies* 5: 75–108.

Koenig, W. J. 1990. *The Burmese Polity, 1752–1819.* Ann Arbor: University of Michigan Press.

Lieberman, Victor B. 1984. *Burmese Administrative Cycles: Anarchy and Conquest, 1580–1760.* Princeton, NJ: Princeton University Press.

Mills, J. 1997. "The Swinging Pendulum: From Centrality to Marginality—A Study of Southern Tenasserim in the History of Southeast Asia." *Journal of the Siam Society* 85, nos. 1–2: 35–58.

Wyatt, David K. 1997. "King Borommakot, His Court, and Their World." Pp. 53–60 in *In the King's Trail: An 18th Century Dutch Journey to the Buddha's Footprint.* Edited by Remco Raben and Dhiravat na Pombejra. Bangkok: Sirivattana Interprint.

C

CABECILLA SYSTEM

The term *cabecilla* (meaning "boss" or "foreman") was used in the Philippines under the Spanish colonial administration in the first half of the nineteenth century to denote the headmen of occupational groups in the Chinese community. After about 1850, the term acquired a more general meaning as "head of a Chinese firm," particularly a Manila-based wholesaler of imported goods and export products dealing with foreign merchant houses, as has been pointed out by historian Edgar Wickberg (2000).

These wholesalers maintained a network of agents in the rural areas, through whom they distributed import goods and collected agricultural produce. The cabecilla-agent relationship was largely built on credit. A foreign merchant house would advance cash or credit to the cabecilla-wholesaler, enabling him to purchase import goods; he sent these goods on a consignment basis to his agents in the province, who in turn sold them to farmers in exchange for agricultural products; then, these products were shipped to the cabecilla in Manila, who delivered them to an exporting firm. The cabecilla-agent relationship was a way to avoid the Spanish "shop" tax, as the cabecilla did not maintain a store and did not sell his products to independent retailers but delivered them to his agents. The parties in these transactions usually kept their relationship secret.

As money circulation was very limited in the Philippines in the nineteenth century, the system of exchanging import goods against export produce within the cabecilla-agent network was a way to economize on the use of coins. Rather than paying in cash and having to ship large amounts of heavy metal coins back and forth between Manila and the provinces, participants used bookkeeping money and a mutual clearing system to carry out their business. This business practice—in the institutional economic literature known as interlinked transactions—was widely used in the Chinese trading community in Southeast Asia, and it has been extensively described for Sarawak and the Outer Islands of Indonesia. Trading import goods for export products worked best for crops that had a year-round production, such as Manila hemp (*abaca*), coconuts, and, from the beginning of the twentieth century, rubber.

WILLEM WOLTERS

See also Chinese in Southeast Asia; Philippines under Spanish Colonial Rule (ca. 1560s–1898); *Towkay*

References:

Wickberg, Edgar. 2000. *The Chinese in Philippine Life, 1850–1898.* Quezon City, the Philippines: Ateneo de Manila University Press. First published in 1965 by Yale University Press, New Haven, CT.

CACIQUES

The term *cacique,* though its specific etymology relates to the Arawak people of the Caribbean, was widely employed within the Spanish Empire to denote a local ruling class of chieftains. In this sense, it is sometimes used interchangeably in the Spanish Philippines with the indigenous word *datu* to denote an incumbent ruler, one who commands vassals, and all members of a chiefly class of either sex. Although a datu's authority arose from his descent, his actual power was dependent more on his reputation and personal prowess. The office was made hereditary under Spanish rule, confirming the chief's political power and transforming him into an agent of colonial authority as a municipal mayor (*gobernadorcillo*) or village headman (*cabeza de barangay*). However, such people were more commonly referred to in the Spanish colloquial to the archipelago as *principales,* and persons who belonged to this class were termed *principalia* rather than caciques.

Only in the latter part of the nineteenth century does the term *caciques* gain more widespread currency to refer specifically to a newly emergent rural elite composed from the remnants of the old indigenous principalia and commercially oriented Chinese mestizos. This group's ability to dominate local politics was known as *caciquismo,* and if anything, it became even more pronounced during the U.S. colonial administration (1898–1946), when the phenomenon was known by a corruption of the Spanish word as *caciquism* and *caciqueism* or more prosaically as *bossism.* Under this latter characterization, the term (and condition) is still prevalent in many rural areas of the contemporary Philippines.

GREG BANKOFF

See also *Barangay;* Chinese in Southeast Asia; Hispanization; *Inquilino;* Mestizo; Philippines under Spanish Colonial Rule (ca. 1560s–1898); Philippines under U.S. Colonial Administration (1898–1946); Spanish Philippines

References:
May, Glenn. 1984. *Social Engineering in the Philippines: The Aims, Execution, and Impact of American Colonial Policy, 1900–1913.* Quezon City, the Philippines: New Day Publishers.

Robles, Eliodoro. 1969. *The Philippines in the 19th Century.* Quezon City, the Philippines: Malaya Books.

Scott, William. 1994. *Barangay: Sixteenth-Century Philippine Culture and Society.* Quezon City, the Philippines: Ateneo de Manila University Press.

Sidel, John. 1999. *Capital, Coercion, and Crime: Bossism in the Philippines.* Stanford, CA: Stanford University Press.

Wickberg, Edgar. 2000. *The Chinese in Philippine Life, 1850–1898.* Quezon City, the Philippines: Ateneo de Manila Press. First published in 1965 by Yale University Press, New Haven, CT.

CAKKAVATTI/SETKYA-MIN (UNIVERSAL RULER)

The concept of the *cakkavatti,* or universal ruler, derives from the Buddhist principles of kingship as discussed in three long sermons (*dighanikaya*) of the early canonical texts. It is in the importance given to *dhamma* (*dharma*), or righteousness, that the Buddhists distinguished themselves from other contemporary writings on kingship, such as the *cakravartin* of the Sanskrit *Dharmasastras.* The Buddhist political dharma was a theory of royal conduct, which stated that *cariya* or *vidhana* (procedure or method) made the king a moral being, and this was the ultimate objective of early Buddhist political thought. Thus, by emphasizing righteous behavior, Buddhism provided a new meaning to the role of the king in society.

Historians have debated whether this concept was practiced or if it was merely a normative notion. Part of this debate derives from an implicit assumption that Buddhism was an apolitical religion and one that addressed itself largely to those who renounced social obligations, namely, the Buddhist monks and nuns. In recent years, this issue has been rethought.

It is being suggested that, though not referring to himself as a cakkavatti in his inscriptions dated to the third to second centuries B.C.E., the Mauryan ruler Asoka (ca. 271–238 B.C.E.) did adopt many of the Buddhist concepts of a righteous ruler—concepts that later found favor with several Southeast Asian dynasties. From around the ninth to tenth centuries C.E. onward, there is evidence for the direct attribution of qualities of the cakkavatti to pre-Aniruddha kings in Pagan and Sinhala rulers.

The concept underwent further adaptation and change in Southeast Asia under the Khmers. In 802 C.E., a *brahmana* priest (one well versed in the *Brahmanas*) performed the *cakravartin* ceremony for Jayavarman II (r. 802?–834 C.E.), who declared his independence from Javanese domination and proclaimed himself a *devaraja,* or god-king.

HIMANSHU PRABHA RAY

See also Buddhism; *Devaraja;* Hindu-Buddhist Period of Southeast Asia; Hinduism; Indianization; Indigenous Political Power; Jayavarman II (r. 770/790/802?–834 C.E.)

References:

Senevirante, A., ed. 1994. *King Asoka and Buddhism: Historical and Literary Studies.* Kandy, Sri Lanka: Buddhist Publication Society.

Tambiah, S. J. 1976. *World Conqueror, World Renouncer: A Study of Buddhism and Polity in Thailand against a Historical Background.* Cambridge: Cambridge University Press.

CAMBODIA (EIGHTEENTH TO MID-NINETEENTH CENTURIES)

Between the 1750s and the middle of the nineteenth century, Cambodia almost disappeared. The beleaguered kingdom was frequently a battleground between the Vietnamese and the Thai. Both of these powers sought to dominate Cambodian political life. The kingdom's internal politics in this period were particularly fragmented and full of rivalries, the monarchy was weak, its people were decimated in war, and over the years its territory became depleted.

Following the Burmese sacking of the Thai capital of Ayutthaya (Ayudhya) in 1767, a newly established Thai dynasty, led by a former provincial governor, sent invading armies into Cambodia several times in search of loot and prisoners. Vietnamese rebel forces and government troops sent against them also swept into the kingdom. In 1772, a Thai army sacked Phnom Penh, and soon afterward, in the wake of a Vietnamese incursion, several members of the Khmer royal family, including a young prince named Ang Eng (ca. 1774–1797), fled to Bangkok to seek the protection of the Thai court. A Thai general staged a coup against the throne in 1781 and became king himself, as Rama I (r. 1782–1809), in the following year. In 1794, the Thai court in Bangkok crowned Prince Ang Eng, who was then barely twenty years old. The young king was sent back to Cambodia to govern under Thai patronage. In exchange for placing him on the Cambodian throne, Siam assumed control of two prosperous Cambodian provinces, Siem Reap (which contained the ruins of the medieval city of Angkor) and Battambang. When Ang Eng died in 1797, his four sons were underage, and a Thai regent assumed the day-to-day administration in the Cambodian capital of Udong.

Over the next sixty years or so, rivalries between the Vietnamese and Thai royal houses, exacerbated by factional divisions in Cambodia, led to repeated invasions of Cambodia by Thai armies and to many years of enforced Vietnamese protection. This situation foreshadowed the French protectorate in the late nineteenth century, as well as the Vietnamese-installed Cambodian government in the 1980s.

This turbulent period bequeathed two legacies to Cambodians. One was a widespread resentment toward Vietnam and a distrust of Vietnamese intentions, which contrasted with a naive failure to admit the destructive aspects of Thai policies toward Cambodia. Another was awareness on the part of Cambodian monarchs and political actors that to survive and flourish, they needed patrons who could protect them against their rivals and against hostile foreign powers. Such patrons were often hard to locate, and in any case, their commitment to Cambodia was seldom deep. After ninety years of French colonialism, history came close to repeating itself when Cambodia's ruler Norodom Sihanouk (1922–), seeking a neutral position in the Cold War, sought protection from China against what he saw as the U.S.-backed hostility of the regimes in power in Thailand and southern Vietnam.

The period also saw a decline in the power and prestige of the Cambodian monarchy as an institution. The reign of Ang Eng's son, King Ang Chan (r. 1797–1835), was disastrous for Cambodia. Although the reign of his younger brother, Ang Duang (r. 1848–1860), was an improvement, the monarchy came under French control soon afterward, and Cambodian kings never regained the luster or freedom of maneuver that they had enjoyed in the 1700s.

One reason for the decline of the monarchy was Chan's unfortunate decision to resist Siamese patronage by seeking support from the Nguyễn emperors in Vietnam. Chan's rationale for seeking the friendship of Vietnam is unclear and probably had several aspects. The *Cambodian Chronicles* indicate that Chan may have offended the Thai monarch, Rama II (r. 1809–1824), by failing to attend his coronation. He certainly resented the loss of the northwestern provinces to the Thai. Economic links between Chan's court and entrepreneurs in Saigon might also have been important. In any case, after a brief Siamese invasion of Cambodia in 1811, Chan moved his capital to Phnom Penh and began to send tributary gifts on a regular basis to the Vietnamese emperor in Huế. Three of his brothers, with Thai encouragement, had sought refuge in Bangkok. Chan feared, correctly, that the Thai wished to place one of his brothers on the throne, and this fear probably forced him into an alliance with Vietnam. For several years, like Norodom Sihanouk in the 1950s and 1960s, Chan managed to play the two hostile powers off against each other to maintain a fragile independence.

Vietnamese protection became more systematic after a large-scale Thai invasion in 1833 that was possibly instigated by Chan's wife but also came in response to an antidynastic rebellion in southern Vietnam. Retreating from an unsuccessful campaign in Vietnam, the Thai army sacked Phnom Penh and drove thousands of Cambodians into captivity in Thailand, foreshadowing the forced evacuation of the city under the Khmer Rouge in 1975. Chan, meanwhile, had been hastily evacuated to Vietnam. Soon after returning to his devastated capital in 1834, Chan died, with his kingdom more or less in ruins. Vietnamese officials at his court, wishing to buy time and to strengthen their administrative grip on Cambodia, quickly named one of Chan's daughters (the deceased king had no sons) as Cambodia's queen but allowed her almost no independence.

Over the next few years, the Vietnamese proceeded with what the French would later call, referring to their own regime, a full-scale "civilizing mission" that was intended to turn Cambodia into a submissive and prosperous appendage of Vietnam. Vietnamese settlers, teachers, and bureaucrats were sent into the country; a local militia was raised; and the Vietnamese emperor, Minh Mang (r. 1820–1841), sought to reform Cambodian culture to fit Vietnamese Confucian norms. "Let . . . good ideas seep in," he wrote to a Vietnamese official in Cambodia, "turning the barbarians into civilized people" (Chandler 2000: 126).

The civilizing mission failed primarily because Cambodian provincial officials were unwilling to exchange their royal titles and capricious patron-client networks for Vietnam-dependent, supposedly meritocratic positions. Ordinary Khmer resented Vietnamese taxes and Vietnam's interference with Buddhism and other aspects of their lives. Vietnamese disdain for the Khmer and their harsh treatment of dissidents also increased local animosities toward them. Local uprisings against Vietnamese rule soon broke out in different parts of the kingdom, and a larger one, probably backed by Siam, occurred in 1840 after the Vietnamese had decided to tax Cambodians directly, bypassing what they considered to be corrupt and disloyal local officials.

Suspecting the queen of disloyalty, the Vietnamese imprisoned her, and rumors soon spread that she had been killed. In the following year, Siam invaded Cambodia for the third time since 1811. For the next five years, the kingdom was a battlefield, with the advantage seesawing between the Thai and the Vietnamese and with the casualties largely Khmer, in an eerie foreshadowing of the proxy wars fought by larger powers in Cambodia in the 1970s and 1980s. Minh Mang had died in 1841, and his successor, Thieu Tri (r. 1841–1847), was less interested than his father had been in dominating and "civilizing" every aspect of Cambodian life. The war dragged on nonetheless. In 1847, the Vietnamese finally withdrew their forces and allowed the Thai to install Chan's youngest brother, Ang Duang, on the Cambodian throne. Duang had lived in Siam, as well as briefly under Thai protection in Cambodia, since 1811.

The renewal of Thai patronage depended on Cambodian acquiescence and also on Vietnam's loss of interest in the kingdom. The Cambodian countryside was devastated, and the Khmer people, who preferred Thai patronage to Vietnamese protection, were happy to live in peace. Over the next thirteen years, King Ang Duang turned out to be a talented and popular ruler who presided over the kingdom's return to normal life. He sponsored the restoration of several Buddhist temples in Udong, helped to revive Cambodian literature (he was a talented poet), and was assiduous in performing the rituals that his subjects associated with the welfare of the kingdom. Duang also welcomed French Catholic missionaries to Cambodia. With the encouragement of one of them, he wrote to the French monarch, Napoleon III (r. 1852–1870), asking for his friendship, clearly a euphemism for protection. The presents accompanying the letter were lost en route, and the French court did nothing to protect the unknown, unimportant king. In the late 1850s, a second attempt on Duang's part to make contact with French emissaries was foiled by his patrons in Bangkok.

During Duang's reign, two Frenchmen, the naturalist Henri Mouhot and the missionary Edouard Bouillevaux, visited the ruins at Angkor. Both men claimed later to have "discovered" them. Mouhot's report fired the imagination of European scholars and of readers entranced by the notion of a "lost" city hidden in impenetrable jungle. Although the ruins were deserted and in bad repair, they were well-known to local people, and a Buddhist monastery on the grounds of Angkor Wat housed more than 100 Thai and Cambodian monks. The ruins did not come under Cambodian jurisdiction, however, until the early 1900s, when the Thai abandoned their claims to the province of Siem Reap.

When Duang died in 1860, his eldest son, Norodom (1836–1904), was unable to take the throne because of a revolt led by Cambodia's Muslim minority, descendants of the Chams who had been driven from Vietnam two centuries before. In the meantime, French forces had landed in southern Vietnam, and France began to be interested in what was later to become French Indochina. In 1863, Norodom, still uncrowned, agreed to accept French protection, assuming that this would involve military assistance and might relieve him from the patronage of Bangkok. Instead, he unknowingly ushered in nine decades of French colonial rule.

DAVID CHANDLER

See also Ang Chan (1781–1835); Ang Duong (Ang Duang) (1796–1860); Ang Eng (ca. 1774–1797); Angkor Wat (Nagaravatta); Battambang; Cambodia under French Colonial Rule; *Cambodian Chronicles;* Khmer Rouge; Nguyễn Dynasty (1802–1945); Norodom (1836–1904), King; Rama I (Chakri) (r. 1782–1809); Siem Reap; Sihanouk, Norodom (1922–)

References:

Chandler, David. 2000. *A History of Cambodia.* 3rd ed. Boulder, CO: Westview Press.

Chandler, David P. 1974. *Cambodia before the French: Politics in a Tributary Kingdom.* Ann Arbor, MI: University Microfilms.

Khin Sok. 1991. *Le Cambodge entre le Siam et le Vietnam* (Cambodia between Siam and Vietnam). Paris: École Française d'Extrême-Orient.

CAMBODIA UNDER FRENCH COLONIAL RULE

Although French missionaries had worked in Cambodia in the eighteenth and nineteenth centuries, France did not become politically interested in the Cambodian kingdom until after the French conquest of southern Vietnam in the early 1860s. In 1863, the Cambodian king, Norodom (1860–1904), fearful of Thai and Vietnamese intentions, secretly signed a treaty establishing a French protectorate over Cambodia. The Thai court pressured the king to break the treaty, but diplomatic negotiations between France and Siam soon led to the withdrawal of Thai patronage over the Cambodian court, leaving the French nominally in command. French control over Cambodia remained light. Laissez-faire economic policies, limited French investment, and relatively friendly relations between French authorities and the Cambodian court characterized the first two decades of the protectorate.

In 1884, however, Charles Antoine Francis Thomson, the French governor of Cochin China (t. 1883–1885) (the southern portion of present-day Vietnam), visited Phnom Penh without warning and at night. With a French gunboat moored opposite the royal palace, Thomson delivered a harsh ultimatum to Norodom. The French demanded the abolishment of what they considered to be slavery in

Cambodia, removed the king from day-to-day power, established a system of French resident governors, and opened the gates for the intensification of French investment and control. An anti-French rebellion broke out soon afterward, and it took the French and Cambodian forces nearly three years to suppress the uprising.

Norodom and the French became estranged in the closing years of the nineteenth century, but French control over Cambodia and Cambodian cooperation increased when Norodom's brother, Sisowath, handpicked by the French, took the throne in 1904. Sisowath, then in his sixties, reigned for twenty-three years. In 1907, the northwestern provinces of Battambang and Siem Reap were returned to Cambodia by Siam, which had held them since the 1790s. Over the next two decades, increased French investment brought economic prosperity and some modernization to the country in the form of urbanization, roads, and provincial towns, as well as increased exports of rice, rubber, and timber. Because the kingdom was at peace, Cambodia's population quadrupled in the colonial era; health care also improved, and the rudiments of a national school system were established, although Cambodia's first high school did not open until the 1930s (soon after the construction of its first railway). Yet few industries developed, no representative political bodies were formed, and no elections were ever held. Until the 1950s, there was no talk of Cambodia being granted its independence.

As a component of French Indochina (along with Laos and three sectors of what is now Vietnam), Cambodia was a backwater that attracted little sustained attention from the French. One area of exception was the field of archaeology. French scholars, inspired by the grandeur of Cambodia's medieval civilization popularly known as Angkor, examined its history in detail. They translated over 1,000 Angkorian inscriptions from Sanskrit and Old Khmer, restored dozens of Angkorian temples, built a museum to house Cambodian classical sculpture, and established the chronology of Angkor's artistic styles and its twenty-seven kings. In doing so, they presented Cambodia with a glorious past that had been more or less forgotten. The impact of the gift on Cambodia's intellectuals and ordi-

nary people was mixed, but an image of the most famous Angkorian temple, Angkor Wat, has appeared on every Cambodian flag since independence.

Cambodia prospered in the boom conditions of the 1920s and was badly hit by the Great Depression (1929–1931), when the prices for its export crops, rice and rubber, fell dramatically. In Vietnam, severe economic conditions provoked a series of violent rebellions led by the Vietnamese Communist Party, but no unrest occurred in Cambodia, where political activity of any sort was rare and where, despite high taxation, French rule was relatively benign. Meanwhile, Cambodian nationalism was slow to develop. The sluggishness was partly due to the fact that respected Cambodian institutions such as the court and the Buddhist monastic order remained in place and partly due to the innate conservatism of the Cambodian elite. In addition, many Cambodians believed that French colonization protected them against the encroachments of the Vietnamese and the Thai.

In the 1930s, nonetheless, a small Cambodian intellectual elite began to emerge, primarily in Phnom Penh. It was made up of civil servants, Buddhist monks, schoolteachers, and graduates of Cambodia's only high school, the Lycee Sisowath. The elite included several young men who were affiliated with the Buddhist Institute in Phnom Penh and with the mildly nationalist newspaper *Nagara Vatta* ("Angkor Wat"), founded in 1936. Some French officials referred to these encouraging developments as a national awakening, and Cambodians in the 1930s were gradually given a greater role in provincial governance.

After the fall of France in 1940, Indochina was isolated from Europe, and after 1941, Japanese troops were stationed there, but French administration of the region continued in force. In Cambodia, following the death of King Sisowath Monivong in 1941, the French crowned his grandson, Norodom Sihanouk (1922–), a nineteen-year-old student, as king. They expected him to be a pliant instrument of their policies.

In March 1945, fearful of an Allied invasion, the Japanese imprisoned French officials throughout Indochina and persuaded Sihanouk, along with other Indochinese rulers, to declare Cambodia's independence. The nationalist leader Son Ngoc Thanh (1907–1976?) was brought back from exile in Japan and briefly became prime minister. The government lasted until the French returned in strength in October 1945, arrested Son Ngoc Thanh, and imprisoned him for several years in France.

Because they faced serious military opposition in Vietnam, the French bought peace in Cambodia in 1946 and 1947 by offering the country's largely Francophile elite the chance to write a constitution, establish political parties, and elect a national assembly. These offers, although eagerly taken up, were almost meaningless because financial, diplomatic, and military affairs remained firmly in French hands. At the same time, Cambodians in the late 1940s and early 1950s regained an appetite for partisan politics that had been muffled for nearly ninety years. During these years, Sihanouk became aware of his political skills and popularity. He also chafed at the idea of being subordinated, constitutionally, to other politicians.

In 1949, France bestowed greater autonomy on Cambodia. Three years later, King Sihanouk dissolved the National Assembly and embarked on what he called a royal crusade for independence. The move embarrassed the French, who swiftly caved in and granted Cambodia its independence before similar arrangements could be made with Vietnam and Laos.

French scholar Paul Mus has called the French era in Cambodia a "painless colonialism," and the contrast between French conduct and local responses in Cambodia and those in Vietnam is very sharp. Most writers would agree that had the French not offered their protection in the 1860s, larger neighbors would probably have annexed Cambodia. The Cambodian elites were much more pro-French than their Vietnamese counterparts, and the population at large followed the lead of the Francophile rulers and civil servants. The aftermath of colonialism was almost as painless as the colonial era had been. Until the early 1970s, French was still Cambodia's official language, French investment in the country remained high, and government institutions, established under French control, remained essentially unchanged.

DAVID CHANDLER

See also Angkor Wat (Nagaravatta); Battambang; Buddhist Institute of Phnom Penh; French Ambitions in Southeast Asia; Norodom (1836–1904), King; Siem Reap; Sihanouk, Norodom (1922–); Son Ngoc Thanh (1907–1976?);Vietnam under French Colonial Rule

References:
Chandler, David. 2000. *A History of Cambodia.* 3rd ed. Boulder, CO: Westview Press.
Forest, Alain. 1980. *Le Cambodge et la colonisation française [Cambodia under French Colonialism].* Paris: L'Harmattan.
Osborne, Milton. 1969. *The French Presence in Cambodia and Cochinchina: Rule and Response.* Ithaca, NY: Cornell University Press.
Taboulet, G. 1956. *La Geste française en Indochine: Histoire par les textes de la France en Indochine des origines à 1914 [France's Heroic Achievement in Indochina: A Documentary History of France in Indochina from Its Beginnings to 1914].* Paris: Maisonneuve.
Tully, John A. 1996. *Cambodia under the Tricolour: King Sisowath and the "Mission Civilisatrice" 1904–1927.* Clayton, Australia: Monash Asia Institute.

CAMBODIAN CHRONICLES

The *Cambodian Chronicles* are historical documents originally written on specially prepared strips of palm leaves. Those still extant were begun at the outset of the nineteenth century. Most of them begin their stories in the mid-fourteenth century, just when the Angkor inscriptions end, and they seem to continue, in a different style, the history that may be constructed from those inscriptions.

It is impossible, however, to make a connection between the last rulers and events of Angkor and the first kings of the *Chronicles.* The *Chronicles* show no knowledge of Angkor, and the names of the kings are of an entirely different type. Therefore, the authenticity of the *Chronicles* for any time before they are corroborated with other evidence, that is, before the sixteenth century, is now being questioned. Internal evidence in the extant *Chronicles* shows that there had been a chronicle of the kings of Lovek (a sixteenth-century capital) starting at that time.

In the early nineteenth century, Cambodian scholars were under strong Thai influence, and they apparently wished to write new Cambodian chronicles beginning at about the same time as the Thai chronicles that started with the founding of Ayutthaya in 1351. They took the first king of the historical Lovek chronicle, Ang Chan (d. 1566), and inserted his posthumous title, *Nibbanapada* (pron. Nipean Bat), into the new composition in the mid-fourteenth century. Then, for the intervening two hundred years, they invented kings based on Cambodian and Thai folklore and semihistorical traditions.

Although they included some true information—an Ayutthayan occupation of Angkor in the mid-fifteenth century and a King Yat who developed a new Cambodia after that foreign occupation—the dates are misplaced, and the *Chronicles* are of no use in reconstructing the history of Cambodia between the end of Angkor and the middle of the sixteenth century (Vickery 1977; 1979).

MICHAEL VICKERY

See also Angkor; Ayutthaya (Ayuthaya, Ayudhya, Ayuthia) (1351–1767), Kingdom of; Cambodia (Eighteenth to Mid-Nineteenth Centuries); Hindu-Buddhist Period of Southeast Asia

References:
Coedes, G[eorge]. 1918. "Essai de classification des documents historiques cambodgiens conservés à la Bibliothèque de l'École Française d'Extrême-Orient." *Bulletin de L'École Française d'Extrême-Orient* 18, no. 9: 15–28.
Vickery, Michael. 1977. "Cambodia after Angkor: The Chronicular Evidence for the Fourteenth to Sixteenth Centuries." Ph.D. diss., Yale University.
———. 1979. "The Composition and Transmission of the Ayudhya and Cambodia Chronicles." Pp. 130–154 in *Perceptions of the Past in Southeast Asia*. Edited by Anthony Reid and David Marr. Asian Studies Association of Australia Southeast Asia Publications Series 4. Singapore: Heinemann Educational Books (Asia).

CẦN VƯƠNG (AID THE KING) MOVEMENT

Rebelling against the imposition of the French protectorate, the regent Tôn Thất Thuyết fled from Huế in July 1885 with the young king Hàm Nghi to seek refuge in the mountains and stimulate an anti-French resistance movement. An edict was issued, calling on all patriotic elements to take up arms in support of the king (*Cần Vương*, meaning "Aid the King"). Thus were precipitated the "righteous uprisings" known as the Cần Vương movement. From various parts of the country, scholar-gentry and peasants responded, but the most determined reaction came in the central provinces of Nghệ An, Hà Tĩnh, and Thanh Hóa, where Phan Đình Phùng, a former official of the imperial Censorate, created a guerrilla force around Vu Quang, west of the coastal city of Vinh.

The Cần Vương movement attested to the strength of the commitment of the Vietnamese at the time to the Confucian concept of dynastic loyalty (*trung quân*), which stood then for national consciousness. Having no real notion yet of Vietnam as a nation-state in competition with other nation-states, its partisans went to battle with the cry "Kill all heterodox people and drive out the French," the former objective being accomplished by the indiscriminate slaughter of Vietnamese Catholics. Their struggle was therefore not quite nationalistic but was rather a compound of xenophobia and Confucian loyalism. It never materialized on a nationwide scale but found expression only in disparate movements, heavily dependent upon regional leaders, none of whom gained enough prestige to unite their followers under a single command. And the Cần Vương fighters continued to nurture a disembodied monarchism six or seven years after 1888, when Hàm-Nghi's capture by the French deprived the movement of a physically present king to serve as a focus of loyalties. The December 1895 death of Phan Đình Phùng, the most obstinate of the fighters, put an end to their insurrection. With the total extinction after 1896 of the Cần Vương movement, the first stage of Vietnamese opposition against French control had clearly failed.

The Cần Vương movement was also, in a sense, a popular, religious movement. Ordinary villagers who responded to this royalist, scholar-gentry movement could be seen as fulfilling their traditional duties toward their social betters. However, the scholar-gentry also represented, at the local level, the link between the human and divine planes of existence. The political situation after 1885 would have been construed by many as the imminent end of the dynastic cycle, precipitating a tumultuous period during which the mandate of heaven might shift. And this was precisely one of those times when the scholar-gentry assumed leadership of popular movements. But the scholar was only one type of figure around whom the peasantry gathered. After the definitive suppression of the last focal points of the armed resistance that mobilized the Confucian literati on behalf of reestablishing the legitimate sovereign of Vietnam, traditionalist ideologies of resistance seemed to survive in sudden, short-range movements that would still stir up the countryside now and then. However, unlike the Cần Vương movement, those insurrections were no longer prompted by any clearly defined political doctrine. Rather, there was only a vague belief in the providential mission of leaders guided by supernatural forces in their struggle to restore the country's independence, either under a new heaven-sent king or under a descendant of the founder of the reigning dynasty; such an individual would restore the harmony between heaven and society that was so crucial for prosperity and happiness. The rebels were inspired by healers, fortune-tellers, or mediums, who had acquired some local notoriety through their allegedly magical power and who presented themselves as reincarnations of tutelary spirits of the country. These would-be messiahs were able to impress the peasants with magical practices and predictions. Promising to offer exactly what the Nguyễn dynasty was no longer capable of providing—solidarity, justice, and salvation—those messianic movements obviously indicated that people experienced intense crises for which traditional authority no longer seemed an adequate solution. Although they would in no way ever be able to seriously threaten the colonial order, such movements emphasized the state of disarray following upon the dire shock that the consolidation of the colonial regime had inflicted on the traditional sociopolitical structures.

NGUYỄN THẾ ANH

See also Confucianism; Nguyễn Emperors and French Imperialism; Peasant Uprisings and Protest Movements in Southeast Asia

References:
Fourniau, Charles. 1989. *Annam-Tonkin, 1885–1896: Lettrés et paysans vietnamiens face à la conquête coloniale* [*Annam-Tonkin, 1885–1896: Vietnamese literati and peasants facing the colonial conquest*]. Paris: L'Harmattan.

Marr, David G. 1971. *Vietnamese Anticolonialism, 1885–1925.* Berkeley: University of California Press.

Nguyễn Thế Anh. 1998. "The Vietnamese Confucian Literati and the Problem of Nation-Building in the Early Twentieth Century." Pp. 231–250 in *Religion, Ethnicity and Modernity in Southeast Asia.* Edited by Oh Myung-Seok and Kim Hyung-Jun. Seoul: Seoul National University Press.

CANDI

The Indonesian word *candi* means both "Hindu temple" and "Buddhist temple." Due to this double meaning, the word designates structures that are very different in form and function, from Candi Borobudur to Candi Prambanan. Although the Malay language is known to have existed from the seventh century, it is difficult to give a date for the first use of this term. However, it appears several times in a Javanese text, the *Nâgarakertâgama,* of the fourteenth century, with the sense of "monument."

The meaning of a Hindu temple has also evolved considerably over time. Although a "Candi Bima" was described in the eighth century and a "Candi Pari" was mentioned in the fourteenth century, these edifices certainly were not constructed according to the same basic principles. In epigraphic texts, the monuments are called *caitya, vihara,* and *prasada,* but none of these terms are well defined.

One cannot, therefore, give a precise definition of the term *candi* that would cover all these diverse structures. At best, it can be defined as a temple associated with a religion of Indian origin; accordingly, a mosque, for example, could not be considered a candi.

JACQUES DUMARÇAY
TRANSLATED BY JOHN N. MIKSIC

See also Blitar; Borobudur; Hindu-Buddhist Period of Southeast Asia; Malang Temples;

Mendut Temple in central Java, Indonesia. (Wolfgang Kaehler/Corbis)

Monumental Art of Southeast Asia;
Prambanan

References:

Bernet-Kempers, A. J. 1959. *Ancient Indonesian Art*. Amsterdam: C. P. J.Van der Peet.

Bosch, F. D. K. 1961. *Selected Studies in Indonesian Archaeology*. The Hague: Martinus Nijhoff.

Klokke, M. J. 1993. *Tantric Reliefs on Javanese Candi*. Leiden, The Netherlands: KITLV.

CANTONESE

See Chinese Dialect Groups

CAO ĐÀI

Cao Đài is an indigenous religion of Vietnam that emerged in 1925. Its full official name is Đài Dao Tam Ky Pho Do (The Third Great Universal Religious Salvation). Cao Đài, or Caodaism (literary translated as "High Palace"), denotes a heavenly palace where the Supreme Being reigns above the universe. Ngo Van Chieu (1878–1932), a district head in the French administration of Cochin China who is also known by the name Ngo Minh Chieu, was regarded as the first adept of Caodaism. In 1921, he saw the vision of a Divine Eye (*Thien Nhan*) and received messages from the Cao Đài God (*Duc Cao Đài*). Consequently, he adopted the Divine Eye as a symbol for worship.

In December 1925, the Cao Đài God identified Himself during a table-moving séance to three Vietnamese civil servants (Pham Cong Tac, Cao Hoai Sang, and Cao Quynh Cu). These were the first Caodaist mediums to be entrusted by the Cao Đài Spirit to propagate the religion. One of the early messages these men received (in 1926) went as follows: "Formerly people of the world lacked means of transportation, therefore they did not know each other. . . . Nowadays, all parts of the world are explored: humanity, knowing itself better, aspires to real peace. But because of the very multiplicity of religions, humanity does not always live in harmony. That is why I decided to unite all these religions into One to bring them back to the primordial unity." They were also directed to see Ngo Van Chieu for instructions.

The founders of Caodaism drew their ideas of salvation, spirituality, hierarchy, and organization from other religious philosophies (Confucianism, Buddhism, Taoism, the cult of ancestors, and Catholicism). However, the Caodaist religious banner has three colors only: red, yellow, and blue, representing the unity of the three religious traditions and beliefs that are widespread in Vietnamese society at large: red is associated with Confucianism, yellow with Buddhism, and blue with Taoism. In addition, the Cao Đài places much emphasis on performance of the spirit séance, unity between Heaven and Earth, direct communication with God, and the brotherhood of humankind. Inside every Cao Đài temple is a representation of a Divine Contract between Heaven and Earth written in French: Dieu and Humanité; Amour et Justice; and in Chinese: Tian Shang Tian Xia Bo Ai Gong Pinh. The Cao Đài pantheon of Great Spirits includes many famous personalities of the past, of which the most revered are Jesus, Kuan Yin, Li Bo, Sun Yat-sen, Victor Hugo, and Joan of Arc.

The organizational structure of Caodaism largely reflects its characteristics as transmitted by God and the Great Spirits. Within the structure, there are three powers: the Council of the Holy Spirits (Bat Quai Đài), directed by the Cao Đài God; the Medium Branch of the religion and the Legislative Body (Hiep Thien Đài), headed by the Protector of the Laws and Justice (Ho Phap); and the Executive Body (Cuu Trung Đài), headed by the Pope (Giao Tong).

The guiding texts of the religion are the Religious Constitution of Caodaism (Phap Chanh Truyen), a collection of divine messages that contain information on the election of officials, their powers, and ritual dresses; and the New Canonical Codes (Tan Luat), approved by the Spiritual Realm. The latter serve as laws regulating religious, secular, and monastic life. Both men and women play essential parts in the administration and priesthood of the religion. All positions, except that of the pope, are open to women. There are a few distinct denominations in Cao Đài, but the Tay Ninh group is regarded as the strongest. The charismatic and messianic appeal of Ho Phap Pham Cong Tac (1890–1959) contributed greatly to the popularity of Cao Đài.

It is estimated that there are between 2 and 3 million Cao Đài followers (U.S. Department of State 2002: 3). Following the fall of South Vietnam to the communist forces of North Vietnam in 1975, many Cao Đài families moved overseas, where they continue to adhere to Cao Đài teaching. They have established the U.S.-based Cao Đài Overseas Mission and new temples around the globe. Within Vietnam, despite years of communist suppression, Cao Đài remains strong, and its Holy See in Tay Ninh Province is a major center of pilgrimage as well as a tourist attraction.

TRAN MY-VAN

See also Buddhism; Buddhism, Mahayana; Buddhism, Theravada; Catholicism; Confucianism; Religious Development and Influence in Southeast Asia

References:

Blagov, Sergei. 1999. *The Cao Đài: A New Religious Movement.* Moscow: Institute of Oriental Studies.

Dong, Tan. 1998. *Tim Hieu Dao Cao Đài hay Giai dap 310 cau phong Van cua gio tri thuc dai hoc quoc te [Understanding Caodaism, or responses to questions posed by international academics].* Victoria, Australia: Cao Hien.

Oliver, Victor. 1972. *Caodai Spiritism: A Study of Religion in Vietnamese Society.* Leiden, The Netherlands: E. J. Brill.

Smith, Ralph. 1970. "An Introduction to Caodaism—pt. 1, Origins and Early History; pt. 2, Beliefs and Organisation." *Bulletin of the School of Oriental and African Studies* 33: 2–3.

Tran My-Van. 2000. *Vietnam's Caodaism, Independence and Peace: The Life and Work of Pham Cong Tac (1890–1959).* PROSEA Research Paper no. 38. Taipei: Academia Sinica.

U.S. Department of State. 2002. *International Religious Freedom Report 2002.* Washington, DC: U.S. Department of State.

Werner, Jayne. 1981. *Peasant Politics and Religious Sectarianism: Peasant and Priest in the Cao Đài in Vietnam.* New Haven, CT: Yale University Press.

CATHOLICISM

Catholicism arrived in Southeast Asia as a rival and competitor not only to tribal religions but also to the world religions—Buddhism, Confucianism, Hinduism, and Islam—that had arrived earlier. It appeared together with the various Western trading and colonizing nations, although missionaries often tried to distance themselves from the colonial regime. Today, an overwhelming majority of the people in the Philippines and East Timor are Catholics, but in other parts of the region, Catholics are a small minority.

The first Catholics to arrive in Southeast Asia were the Portuguese (1511), who made Melaka a vibrant Catholic center. Melaka had a bishop of its own from 1557 until 1641 when the city was taken over by the Dutch, who banned all priests from their territories. The Portuguese Catholics had arrived about one century after Melaka had accepted Islam. The race between Islam and Christianity was even closer in the Moluccas, where the sultanates of Ternate and Tidore accepted Islam about 1470. After some unlucky experiences of cohabitation between the fanatic Catholic Portuguese and the outspoken Muslim rulers of the Moluccas, the Portuguese founded the city of Ambon in 1576 as a Catholic realm in a nearly empty space. Portuguese traders also carried Catholicism to the southeastern parts of Indonesia, where it found adherents on Flores and Timor. Between 1602 and 1808, all Catholic priests were banned from the territory of the Dutch East India Company (VOC), and native Catholics (already comprising about 20 percent of the Moluccas population in 1600) were summoned to embrace Protestantism (Latourette 1937–1944, 3: 302). Catholicism only experienced a rebirth in Indonesia in the nineteenth century.

In the Philippines, the Spaniards were the first to propagate the Catholic faith, arriving from the east (through Mexico) in 1521. The first regular missionaries started work in 1565. Under Spanish rule, Catholicism was supported against native religions and against Protestantism and Islam. Consequently, the Philippines became the most Catholic nation of Southeast Asia (about 83 percent Catholic, according to national statistics in 2000) (Barrett 2001: 657). Catholicism, however, continued to be mixed with animist practices. In many respects, the Catholic Church was the human face of colonialism. The church offered education and health care. Only in the eighteenth century were Eurasians allowed to enter the priesthood; native Filipinos had to wait until the nineteenth century. The number of priests, both foreign and native, has remained low until the present day. In 1840, a first independent church developed as result of a schism within the Catholic Church: the Confraternity of St. Joseph. In the aftermath of the turmoil of the revolution of the 1890s, the Philippine Independent Church (PIC) was founded in 1902 by the Catholic priest Gregorio Aglipay (1860–1940) and the nationalist leader Isabelo de los Reyes (1864–1938). In this period, Catholicism lost its privileges and many of its possessions. After the imposition of U.S. rule in 1898, Catholicism gradually transformed and regained its power, but since then, a formal separation of church and state has been maintained. In 1906, church property was restored, and many of the Filipinos who had joined the PIC (half the population) returned to the Catholic Church (Sunquist 2001: 656). In 1905, the first Filipino was consecrated a bishop.

In Indonesia, Catholicism resumed its race with Islam after 1860, when more and more regions were subjected to colonial rule and opened to outside trade. The Dutch colonial administration kept some regions, such as Aceh, West Java, and Bali, closed to missionaries until the 1930s. Other regions were divided between Catholics and Protestants. "Double mission," overlapping of Catholic and Protestant missionaries working in the same field, was prevented. Flores and the eastern section of West Timor became Catholic strongholds, especially after all education in these regions was entrusted to the Catholic mission. West Papua was divided along the sixth degree north latitude: land to the south of this line became Catholic territory after 1900 (with Merauke as the center), and that north of the line was entrusted to Protestant missions. After 1905, the Catholics made quick and quite spectacular progress in central Java, where many nominal Muslims from the sultanates of Yogyakarta and Solo attended the schools of priests and nuns and converted to Catholicism. This region also produced the first Indonesian bishop, Soegijopranoto (1940), a staunch defender of independence in the period from 1945 to 1950. With about 3.5 percent of the population, the Catholics are a small minority in Indonesia, but thanks to their unity and their excellent schools and hospitals, they have more social, cultural, and political influence than would be expected from their modest numbers (Sunquist 2001: 374–382).

The temporary integration of East Timor into Indonesia brought prominence to Catholicism in that region. This last Portuguese territory was about 35 percent nominal Catholic in 1975, but since then, the Catholic Church has become one of the sources of opposition to Indonesian rule and oppression. Bishop Belo of Dili received the Nobel Peace Prize in 1996, at a time when nearly 90 percent of the people were baptized and considered themselves Catholic (Barrett 2001: 737–738).

In Vietnam, the first missionaries arrived from the Philippines in 1580. In 1668, there were already four Vietnamese priests. Though it had some quick successes, the mission also caused much opposition. The Edict of Tu Duc, banning Christianity in 1851, is said to have caused 90,000 deaths (Neill 1964: 415–417). This was the most serious of many persecutions that followed. In 1882, French colonial rule was imposed, in part because of the Nguyễn emperor's persecution of the Catholics. In 1933, the first Vietnamese native was ordained a bishop. In 1945, the four Vietnamese bishops supported independence, but after the struggle continued, most priests fled the communist north. Currently, about 3.5 percent of the population of Vietnam confess the Catholic faith.

In other Southeast Asian countries, Catholicism is the religion of a tiny fraction, for the most part ethnic minorities. In Malaysia, the 3.5 percent of the people who are Catholics are mostly Chinese, Indians, or ethnic minorities of Sarawak and Sabah (Barrett 2001: 474). In Thailand, Laos, and Cambodia, the 1 percent who are Catholics are by and large of Vietnamese or Chinese origin (Barrett 2001: 163, 439, 734).

KAREL STEENBRINK

See also Missionaries, Christian; Philippines under Spanish Colonial Rule (ca. 1560s–1898); Portuguese Asian Empire; Spanish Expansion in Southeast Asia

References:

Barrett, David B., ed. 2001. *World Christian Encyclopedia*. Oxford: Oxford University Press.

Latourette, Kenneth. 1937–1944. *A History of the Expansion of Christianity*. New York: Harper.

Neill, Stephen. 1964. *Christian Mission*. Pelican History of the Church Series. London: Hodder and Stoughton.

Reid, Anthony J. S. 1988. *Southeast Asia in the Age of Commerce, 1450–1680*. Vol. 1, *The Lands below the Winds*. New Haven, CT: Yale University Press.

———. 1993. *Southeast Asia in the Age of Commerce, 1450–1680*. Vol. 2, *Expansion and Crisis*. New Haven, CT: Yale University Press.

Sunquist, Scott, ed. 2001. *A Dictionary of Asian Christianity*. Grand Rapids, MI: Eerdmans.

CAVITE MUTINY

The Cavite Mutiny was staged in 1872 by a group of Filipinos employed in the Spanish arsenal at Cavite. Although it was more of a local expression of anger against specific actions of the Spanish colonial government, the uprising served as an excuse for Spanish friars to suppress the growing clamor for a more liberal administration. Ultimately, this led to a reign of terror that further entrenched anti-Spanish sentiment; it also aided in the development of nationalism in the Philippines.

The Cavite Mutiny was caused by the abolition, by Governor-General Rafael de Izquierdo y Gutierrez (t. 1871–1873), of privileges enjoyed by Filipinos in the service of the Spanish military and naval forces, as well as workers in the arsenal of Cavite. Around 250 of these Filipinos seized Fort San Felipe on the naval base at Cavite on the evening of 20 January 1872. The Spaniards responded quickly and sent troops from Manila, including two Filipino infantry regiments. The Spanish forces retook the fort the following day. Leaders of the mutiny were tried and executed, and the other rebels were imprisoned.

The Cavite Mutiny was defeated within three days, but the Spanish friars and conservative government officials saw it as an excuse to crack down on the growing number of Filipino priests, businessmen, and intellectuals who were calling for a more liberal and less discriminatory administration. The friars claimed that the mutiny was part of a large-scale conspiracy against Spain and that the real leaders were Filipino priests who had been campaigning for equal treatment.

The night after the mutiny began, Governor-General Izquierdo ordered the arrest of the three leading Filipino priests, Frs. Jose Burgos, Mariano Gomez, and Jacinto Zamora, together with other prominent Filipino professionals and businessmen. This was the first time the Spaniards had resorted to a reign of terror after an uprising. The three Filipino priests were subjected to a court-martial as leaders of the conspiracy but were denied a chance to defend themselves. They were executed in public on 17 February 1872, to serve as an example to other Filipinos should they continue to challenge Spain. The execution had the opposite effect, however, and served to further incite Filipinos to seek changes if not outright independence.

RICARDO TROTA JOSE

See also Friars, Spanish (The Philippines); Nationalism and Independence Movements in Southeast Asia; Peasant Uprisings and Protest Movements in Southeast Asia; Philippine Revolution (1896–1898); Philippine War of Independence (1899–1902); Philippines under Spanish Colonial Rule (ca. 1560s–1898)

References:

Artigas y Cuerva, Manuel. 1996. *National Glories: The Events of 1872.* Translated by O. D. Corpuz. Quezon City: University of the Philippines Press.

Corpuz, O. D. 1989. *The Roots of the Filipino Nation.* 2 vols. Quezon City, the Philippines: Aklahi Foundation.

CELEBES

See Sulawesi (Celebes)

CERAMICS

The term *ceramics* applies to items made predominantly of clay, which, in its wet state, can be molded into virtually any desired shape before setting as moisture is expelled through drying and firing. Vessels are the most important of Southeast Asia's ceramics, but clay figurines, architectural elements, and metalworking aids have also been made since ancient times, not to mention tobacco pipes and indus-

trial products introduced to Southeast Asia in recent centuries. Ceramics are divided into earthenware, stoneware, and porcelain objects. As the firing temperature increases, the color of the clay changes from russet to gray to white, the porosity and proportion of inclusions decrease, and the technological sophistication required to produce the ceramics rises from part-time cottage operations to factories staffed by craft specialists. When the technology needed for higher firing temperatures was introduced, thin glass coats (glazes) could replace or be used in conjunction with earlier developed surface treatments, such as slips of clay, resin coats, painting, and burnishing.

Regardless of the aspect of technology under consideration, China has been the ultimate source of inspiration in the field of ceramics, with minor contributions being made by India, the Arabic world, and, most recently, Europe. Of course, numerous traditions peculiar to Southeast Asia have developed over the millennia as Southeast Asian potters learned to utilize their natural and cultural resources and to blend the medley of exotic influences into products that met local needs. However, the penetration of Chinese advances in ceramic technology through Southeast Asia has been uneven. Derivative stoneware industries had spread across Thailand and Indochina by 600 years ago but not as far as island Southeast Asia. China jealously guarded the secret of its perfectly white, translucent porcelain until the last couple of centuries, when expatriate Chinese established porcelain factories at industrial centers across Southeast Asia.

Earthenware pottery constitutes the oldest ceramic tradition in Southeast Asia. Potshards appeared in archaeological sites in North Vietnam and northern Thailand by 8,000 years ago, Cambodia and Taiwan by 6,000 years ago, the Malay Peninsula and Borneo by 5,000 years ago, and the islands from the Philippines to Timor and Java by 4,000 to 3,500 years ago. Earthenware potting persists as a significant cottage industry across island Southeast Asia and Malaya, where, until very recent times, most households relied on these local wares for their water-storage jars and much of their crockery. Numerous field studies have recorded the details of forming the vessels and firing them in a bonfire or underground hearth, as well as information on the distribution network for the finished wares and, especially, the deployment and significance of local decorative motifs. Some progress has been achieved in identifying production locations from chemical analysis of the fabric (clay), and this can be useful in tracing the movement of mariners through the South Seas. An example in this regard is the confirmation of the South Sulawesi homeland of the Macassan traders who left potshards at their campsites in northern Australia, where they collected sea cucumbers between about 1700 and 1900 C.E.

Earthenware vessels, in particular those of high quality, have been widely trafficked across the archipelago. During the late nineteenth century, Kei Islanders, in the Moluccas, achieved regional fame for the quality of their pots. Earlier examples include the sixteenth-century to seventeenth-century wares, stamped with Islamic motifs, that were manufactured in Banten in West Java. Between the late first and middle second millennia C.E., "fine paste wares" could be found at various trading centers in Java, Sumatra, Malaya, and the Philippines. In fact, their shards are so common at Trowulan, the capital of the fourteenth-century to fifteenth-century empire of Majapahit in East Java, that they are sometimes referred to as Majapahit ware. East Java is the suspected source of most of the Sumatran examples. Indeed, the refined quality of Majapahit ware and Trowulan's production of lead-glazed architectural elements suggest that the Trowulan potters had access to kiln technology.

During late prehistoric to protohistorical times, vessels of exceptional quality were produced widely across mainland Southeast Asia. The painted Bronze Age wares from Ban Chiang, in northeast Thailand, are among today's most sought-after antiques of Southeast Asian origin. The ancient, locally established skills in pottery production undoubtedly facilitated the entry of more advanced ceramic techniques from China over the last two millennia, leading to numerous distinctive traditions among the subcontinent's major ethnolinguistic groups. Earthenware production has survived, particularly among certain hill tribe minorities, but only as a lesser ceramic tradition.

During the Han dynasty (202 B.C.E.–220 C.E.), when China established direct rule over the Dai Viet, Chinese artisans set up shop in northern Vietnam. Archaeological excavations in the Red River delta have documented the kilns used in making the bricks, tiles, model houses, and glazed pottery necessary to build Han-style tombs and furnish them to a standard appropriate for deceased members of the local bureaucracy. These kilns also produced comparable items for local household consumption and may have spawned the establishment of other factories to the south. At the Buu Chau site in central Vietnam, archaeologists have recovered numerous mold-impressed tiles and stamped-pottery shards of Han Chinese inspiration in contexts dated to the early centuries C.E. China's millennium-long rule over northern Vietnam firmly entrenched this region as Southeast Asia's leader in ceramic production. Glazed architectural elements were produced in abundance to build ornate religious structures as Buddhism blossomed in the region after the fifth century C.E. And large stoneware jars of export quality, sent to island locations in Southeast Asia by the eighth century, are very similar whether they derive from southern China or northern Vietnam.

The eviction of the Chinese in 979 allowed the Dai Viet to expand their repertoire of fine, whitish stonewares made from high-grade local clays. A wide range of celadons and other monochromes (single-colored wares) were exported in large numbers from Vietnam from the fourteenth to sixteenth centuries. A distinctive class of wares featured calligraphic scrolls and floral sprays, initially in iron black beneath a straw-colored glaze. Black was replaced by underglaze cobalt blue when this technology was introduced to East Asia from West Asia in the late fourteenth century. (Blue-and-white wares were not produced elsewhere in Southeast Asia until modern times.) China's brief reoccupation of northern Vietnam in the early fifteenth century, during the late Yuan dynasty, introduced a tradition of Yuan-style motifs, whose popularity persisted in Vietnam even after they fell out of fashion in China. They formed the high point in Vietnam's history of export tradewares, which included blue-and-white wares and small vessels with red and green enamels painted on the glaze, from the fifteenth to early seventeenth centuries. Vietnam was the chosen supplier for the blue-and-white tiles found at Trowulan and several other Majapahit sites. Even more remarkable is Vietnam's plethora of ornate, Buddhist statuary and ritual vessels, often embellished with multiple glaze colors, produced for domestic consumption over the centuries.

Massive stoneware jars, broadly similar to their Chinese counterparts and frequently bedecked with dragons, continued to be shipped from northern Vietnam for overseas destinations during the second millennium C.E. Particularly at around the fifteenth century, Cham potters based in central Vietnam added "Go Sanh Red" to the Southeast Asian trade in martavan (martaban) jars, along with minor quantities of the smaller vessels produced primarily for local consumption. Martavans in the "Sawankhalok" style were also a major export ware from Sisatchanalai in central Thailand, a specialist pottery center attached to the Thai kingdom of Sukhotai throughout the fifteenth and sixteenth centuries. Similar jars were concurrently produced in kilns throughout northern and central Thailand, but very few of these reached international markets.

The Thai tradition was influenced, to some degree, by the Khmer tradition, particularly as a result of Angkor's domination over much of mainland Southeast Asia from the ninth to fifteenth centuries. Khmer wares are characterized by a notably coarse body, which is often a high-fired earthenware; a limited range of black and brown glazes; a distinctive assortment of *kendi* (kettles), water droppers, covered bowls, and jars of massive architectonic structure; and more reminders of Indian influence than can be found in Southeast Asia's other main ceramic traditions. Recent work in Burma suggests that Burmese jars enjoyed a secondary currency on international markets, similar to that already recorded for Khmer wares. Also worthy of note is the production of "dragon jars" and other martavans by expatriate Chinese in Borneo and elsewhere during recent centuries.

The ceramic industry in Thailand has been treated to particularly intensive study. Its earliest known stonewares are heavily potted and sparsely decorated monochromes. Their local name, Mon wares, is probably correct in associating them with the Mon speakers who originally ruled much of Thailand. By the fourteenth century, "fish and flower" wares with iron decorations beneath a pale celadon glaze had appeared. These plates and bowls formed the blueprint for Thailand's mature export period during the fifteenth and sixteenth centuries. Sawankhalok celadons retained the fine stoneware body, open vessel form, and greenish glaze; Sawankhalok iron-painting techniques moved into small, covered vessels and a clear glaze over an array of geometric motifs similar in style to the Jizhou decorations of northern China; finally, Sukothai wares differed from the fish and flower wares principally in that they were made of much coarser stoneware. During the fifteenth and sixteenth centuries, Sisatchanalai was replete with kilns of various construction types, where martavans, smaller vessels, and Buddhist statuary were mass-produced in a range of monochrome and brown-and-white colors.

China's trade of its ceramics to and through Southeast Asia essentially paralleled the development of Southeast Asia's stoneware traditions. Han dynasty ceramics are claimed to have reached Java, Sumatra, and Borneo, but definite finds are restricted to Vietnam. Tang dynasty ceramics, dating to the late first millennium C.E., are known from major centers and transport nodes along the trunk route to the Indian Ocean, especially in Sumatra, Java, and Malaya. The Philippine register began slightly later, with Five Dynasties pieces found at Butuan in Mindanao. As the Song dynasty proceeded, increasing numbers of Chinese wares reached an ever wider set of destinations on the mainland and in the archipelago, achieving a temporary crescendo during the Yuan dynasty. A lull in China's fifteenth-century exports evidently spurred the peak period of trade in wares from Vietnam and Thailand. As of the sixteenth century, Chinese ceramics reentered the world market in full force, with an increasing array of monochromes and polychromes, until the "age of plastic" seriously eroded the market for ceramics beginning in the twentieth century.

Ceramics offer a unique insight into lifestyle changes and craft skills in Southeast Asia over the long term; during the historical period, they reveal patterns in commerce, technological exchange, and the transmission of ideas. Textiles have undoubtedly been more important in all of these aspects, but their survival as heritage pieces and archaeological debris has fared far worse, and textile workshops have rarely left a spectacular imprimatur like those of ceramic kilns. Southeast Asia's ceramics combine a strong showing in textual sources, vibrant long-term traditions, and remarkable archaeological preservation in helping to chart Southeast Asia's socioeconomic advances over the last two thousand years.

DAVID BULBECK

See also Archaeological Sites of Southeast Asia; Ban Chiang; Ban Kao Culture; Economic History of Early Modern Southeast Asia (Pre-Sixteenth Century); Economic Transformation of Southeast Asia (ca. 1400– ca. 1800); Hoabinhian; Human Prehistory of Southeast Asia

References:
Barbetti, Mike, and Don Hein. 1989. "Palaeomagnetism and High-Resolution Dating of Ceramic Kilns in Thailand: A Progress Report." *Journal of World Archaeology* 21, no. 1: 51–70.

Bellwood, Peter. 2001. "Southeast Asia Neolithic and Early Bronze." Pp. 287–306 in *Encyclopedia of Prehistory*. Vol. 3, *East Asia and Oceania*. Edited by Peter N. Peregrine and Melvin Ember. New York: Kluwer Academic/Plenum Publishers.

Bulbeck, David. 1996–1997. "The Bronze-Iron Age of South Sulawesi, Indonesia: Mortuary Traditions, Metallurgy and Trade." Pp. 1007– 1076 in *Ancient Chinese and Southeast Asian Bronze Age Cultures,* vol. 2. Edited by F. David Bulbeck and Noel Barnard. Taipei: Southern Materials Center.

Bulbeck, David, and Barbara Rowley. 2001. "Macassans and Their Pots in Northern Australia." Pp. 55–74 in *Altered States: Material Culture and Shifting Contexts in the Arafura Region*. Edited by Clayton Frederickson and Ian Walters. Darwin, Australia: Northern Territory University Press.

Glover, Ian, Mariko Yamagata, and William Southworth. 1996. "The Cham, Sa Huynh and Han in Early Vietnam: Excavations at Buu Chau Hill, Tra Kieu, 1993." *Bulletin of the Indo-Pacific Prehistory Association* 14: 166–176.

Guy, John S. 1990. *Oriental Trade Ceramics in South-East Asia, Ninth to Sixteenth Centuries.* Singapore: Oxford University Press.

Harrisson, Barbara. 1990. *Pusaka: Heirloom Jars of Borneo.* Singapore: Oxford University Press.

Higham, Charles. 1989. *The Archaeology of Mainland Southeast Asia.* Cambridge: Cambridge University Press.

Miksic, John N., and C. T. Yap. 1990. "Fine-Bodied White Earthenwares of South East Asia: Some X-Ray Fluorescence Tests." *Asian Perspectives* 28, no. 1: 45–60.

Scott, Rosemary, and John Guy, eds. 1995. *South East Asia & China: Art, Interaction & Commerce.* Colloquies on Art & Archaeology in Asia no. 17. London: University of London.

Soegondho, Santoso. 1995. *Tradisi gerabah di Indonesia dari masa prasejarah hingga masa kini [Earthenware Tradition in Indonesia from Prehistoric Times to the Present]*. Jakarta: Himpunan Keramik Indonesia.

CHAMPA

Champa is a general term used to denote a se-ries of small kingdoms along the coastline of what is now central Vietnam. The first of these kingdoms was founded at the end of the sec-ond century C.E., whereas the last was absorbed into the modern state of Vietnam during the first half of the nineteenth century.

The earliest recorded kingdom on this coastline was formed from the southernmost outpost of the Chinese Han dynasty (206 B.C.E.– 220 C.E.). Known to the Han as Xianglin, this outpost is thought to have been located in the region of the modern city of Hué. A rebellion around 192 C.E. succeeded in Xianglin's break-ing free from Han control, and an independent kingdom known as Linyi was formed there. During the third century, Linyi was known to have been a close ally of Funan, located in the lower Mekong Delta of modern Cambodia and southern Vietnam. Almost continuous warfare and piracy along the southern borders shared with China during the fourth and early fifth centuries, however, culminated in the sacking and looting of the capital of Linyi by a Chinese army in 445 C.E.

After this destruction, political and eco-nomic power in central Vietnam apparently shifted south to the Thu Bon Valley, near mod-ern Hoi An. This region had an active trade with southern China from at least the first cen-tury B.C.E., and inscriptions written in Sanskrit record the foundation of a Hindu temple by King Bhadravarman in the fifth century C.E.

This temple was founded at My Son, in the foothills of the upper Thu Bon Valley; the political center lay at Tra Kieu, some 15 kilometers downstream. The economy was largely based on trade. At the mouth of the river near Hoi An, an active port thrived. The name *Champa* first occurs in an inscription at My Son dated to around 600 C.E., but it may, in fact, relate only to this single valley system. This geographic and political pattern probably recurred along the whole coastline of central Vietnam, with small states developing within individual river valley deltas.

The wealth of these coastal kingdoms depended largely on maritime commerce with China, and the kingdoms flourished during the peak periods of the South China Sea trade under the early Tang (618–907 C.E.), Song (960–1279), and early Ming (1368–1644) dynasties of China. During the early Tang period, trade remained concentrated in the Thu Bon Valley, where Sanskrit inscriptions, brick temples, and sandstone sculpture attest to a flowering of Hindu and Buddhist cultures. After the decline of the coastal kingdoms' main trading counterpart of Guangzhou (Canton) in the mid-eighth century, however, the primary maritime trade routes transferred to the south. The kingdoms of Kauthara (based on the port of Nha Trang) and Panduranga (located around the modern town of Phan Rang) both appeared in this period.

With the return of trade to Guangzhou in the late ninth century, the Thu Bon Valley again became economically dominant, and it remained commercially important until at least the thirteenth century. From the eleventh century onward, however, political power in Champa became increasingly centralized under the kingdom of Vijaya, in modern Binh Dinh Province. From there, the most powerful kings were able to control and leave inscriptions at the main religious sites of My Son in the north and Nha Trang in the south.

The dominance of Vijaya on the central coastline led to increasing conflict with the neighboring powers of Dai Viet, based at Thanh Long (modern Ha Noi) to the north, and the kingdom of Yasodharapura (Angkor) to the west. Dai Viet won a series of major victories against Champa during the tenth and eleventh centuries, and in the mid-twelfth cen-

tury, Champa was again invaded by the Khmer king Sūryavarman II (r. 1113–1145?). Vijaya sacked Angkor in retaliation in 1177, but this in turn led to a series of military campaigns in Champa sponsored by Jayavarman VII (r. 1181–ca. 1220) from the end of the twelfth century onward.

Despite these political setbacks, Vijaya remained an important power in the region, successfully deflecting a Mongol invasion at the end of the thirteenth century and sacking Ha Noi three times at the end of the fourteenth century, under a king known to the Vietnamese as Che Bong Nga. However, the demographic dominance of northern Vietnam and its increasing administrative and military organization eventually overcame the politically fragmented and personality-based system of the Champa kingdoms. Vijaya itself fell to Dai Viet in 1471 and was followed by Kauthara in 1653. Panduranga retained some independence until 1832, when it finally became absorbed into the modern state of Vietnam. The most comprehensive history of Champa remains that written by Georges Maspero (1928), but Keith Taylor (1992) and Kenneth Hall (1992) provide a modern historical perspective.

WILLIAM A. SOUTHWORTH

See also Angkor; China, Imperial; Dai Viet (939 C.E.–1407); Funan; Hanoi (Thanglong); Jayavarman VII (r. 1181–1220?); Sūryavarman II (r. 1113–1145?)

References:

Boisselier, Jean. 1963. *La statuaire du Champa* [*Sculpture of Champa*]. Paris: École Française d'Extrême-Orient.

Hall, Kenneth R. 1992. "Economic History of Early Southeast Asia." Pp. 183–275 in *The Cambridge History of Southeast Asia*. Vol. 1, *From Early Times to c. 1800*. Edited by Nicholas Tarling. Cambridge: Cambridge University Press.

Maspero, Georges. 1928 [1988]. *Le Royaume de Champa* [*The Kingdom of Champa*]. Paris and Brussels: G. Van Oest. Reprinted in 1988 by École Française d'Extrême-Orient, Paris.

Taylor, Keith W. 1992. "The Early Kingdoms." Pp. 137–182 in *The Cambridge History of Southeast Asia*. Vol. 1, *From Early Times to c. 1800*. Edited by Nicholas Tarling. Cambridge: Cambridge University Press.

CHAMPASSAK

Bordering Cambodia and Thailand in south-western Laos astride the Mekong River, Champassak emerged in the early period as an independent kingdom separated by geography and tradition from the northern Laos kingdoms. With its origins reaching back to the fifth century and occupying the territory of the ancient state of Chenla, historical Champassak entered Khmer lore as the fount of the Angkorian kingdom from the ninth to the twelfth centuries. This correlation is attested to by Sanskrit inscriptions and other evidence associated with the Vat Phu temple of Hindu provenance and the hill flanking the sacred mountain of Bassak.

Champassak was eclipsed by Vientiane under Souligna Vongsa (r. 1637–1694), and its status under Vientiane was in turn reduced by vassalage imposed by King Taksin (r. 1767–1782) of Siam in 1778. Such dynastic and historical differences were well understood by the French, who juridically separated Champassak from the protectorate they imposed upon Luang Prabang in the late nineteenth century. The French abolishment of the monarchy in Champassak in 1912, notwithstanding the royal lineage of the court, continued under French-educated Prince Boun Oum (1912–1980), twelfth in the line of the royal family of Champassak. In 1941, with Japanese blessing, Champassak was ruled by Thailand, and it was only retroceded to Laos at the end of the Pacific War (1941–1945). An anti-Japanese fighter, Boun Oum of Champassak, emerged as the foremost personality and traditional leader of the southerners in the postwar period. Despite a secret protocol concluded with the French in 1946, he renounced his ambitions to the throne of Champassak. Although removed from the picture in 1975, the pro-Western Boun Oum never entirely relinquished his ambitions for southern autonomy vis-à-vis Vientiane and especially the court in Luang Prabang.

Champassak was known to the French as Bassac Province. Today, under the Lao People's Democratic Republic (LPDR), it is recognized as a territorially enlarged province, with its capital at Pakse.

GEOFFREY C. GUNN

See also Angkor; Chenla; French Indochina; French Indochinese Union (*Union Indochinoise Française*) (1887); Indochina during World War II (1939–1945); Lao People's Democratic Republic (LPDR); Laos (Nineteenth Century to Mid-1990s)

References:

Coedès, G. 1969. *The Making of South East Asia*. Berkeley: University of California Press.

Stuart-Fox, Martin, and Mary Kooyman. 1992. *Historical Dictionary of Laos*. Metuchen, NJ, and London: Scarecrow Press.

CHEA SIM (1932–)
A Party Stalwart

Chea Sim, a Cambodian political figure, was born into a peasant family in Svay Rieng Province. He studied for several years as a Buddhist monk. He joined the anti-French Khmer Issarak movement in 1951 and the Kampuchea Peoples' Revolutionary Party, a communist front, soon afterward. Chea Sim was active as a regimental commander during the Cambodian civil war that was fought from 1970 to 1975. Under the Khmer Rouge regime (1975–1979), he worked as a political commissar in eastern Cambodia, before seeking refuge in Vietnam in late 1978 following an unsuccessful uprising in eastern Cambodia against the Khmer Rouge. In early 1979, Chea Sim returned to Cambodia as part of the Vietnamese-sponsored Cambodian government established in Phnom Penh, in the Peoples' Republic of Kampuchea. He served briefly as minister of the interior and, after 1981, as chairman of the National Assembly. In 1991, following the withdrawal of Vietnamese troops, he became president of the Cambodian Peoples' Party (CPP), the formerly communist group that dominated Cambodian politics. He became president of the National Assembly again in 1993 and president of the newly established Senate in 1998.

Chea Sim's half century as a party stalwart and skillful infighter enabled him to build a strong base of support, especially in the Ministry of the Interior, eastern Cambodia, and the CPP. Although he was seen by some as a potential rival to the younger and more dynamic prime minister, Hun Sen (1951–), Chea Sim seemed content with the trappings of office, while nourishing his support base and his nationwide patronage networks.

DAVID CHANDLER

See also Democratic Kampuchea (DK); Hun Sen (1951–); Khmer Issarak (Free Khmer); Khmer People's National Liberation Front (KPNLF); Khmer Rouge; *Killing Fields, The*; Paris Conference on Cambodia (PCC) (1989, 1991); Sihanouk, Norodom (1922–); United Nations Transitional Authority in Cambodia (UNTAC)

References:
Chanda Nayan. 1986. *Brother Enemy.* New York: Harcourt Brace.
Evans, Grant, and Kelvin Rowley. 1990. *Red Brotherhood at War.* London:Verso.
Gottesman, Evan. 2002. *Cambodia after the Khmer Rouge: Inside the Politics of Nation Building.* New Haven, CT:Yale University Press.
Vickery, Michael. 1986. *Kampuchea.* Boulder, CO: Lynne Rienner.

CHENG HO (ZHENG HE), ADMIRAL (1371/1375–1433/1435)
The Foremost Chinese Navigator

Cheng Ho is commonly regarded as the greatest Chinese navigator in history. Between 1405 and 1433, he undertook seven expeditions from China to various places throughout the South Pacific Ocean, Indian Ocean, and Persian Gulf and as far as the eastern coast of Africa—an epic that took place eighty years before the voyages of Christopher Columbus (1451–1506).

Cheng was a Muslim eunuch in the early Ming dynasty (1368–1644). He was selected to command the voyages because of his knowledge of foreign countries, acquired from his father and grandfather, both of whom had been to Mecca on pilgrimage. His fleet called at major ports, including Champa, Kelantan, Pahang, Java, Melaka, Semudera, Lambri, Ceylon, Quilon, Cochin, and Calicut. Parts of his subsidiary fleets even reached Hormuz, Dhufar, Aden, Mogadishu, and Brava on the Somali coast of East Africa. His ships, known historically as "treasure ships," had facilitated cultural and economic interaction, carrying Chinese products (including tea, ironwares, porcelains, silks, and other luxurious items) to exchange for ivory, spices, and exotic animals (such as lions and leopards) as cargoes of tribute to the Ming emperor.

Cheng's expeditions proved to be among the most adventurous and costly navigational experiences in human history. The extraordinarily large fleet (sixty-two ships in the first expedition) employed huge ships (the biggest had nine masts and was 133 meters long and 56 meters wide) that were manned by a crew of about 27,000. Although Cheng's fleet was successful in spreading the Ming Empire's influence across half the earth, the adventures were stopped, as they had seriously drained the national coffers. Instead of maintaining a maritime empire, the Ming government opted to divert its dwindling financial resources to a defense against the revival of Mongol influence along the northern border.

Cheng's adventures impacted Southeast Asia in two major ways. First, they enhanced the spread of Chinese culture, including the lunar calendar and poetry, to the region. Second, Cheng himself grew to be a kind of patron saint of the Chinese sojourners who migrated to Southeast Asia in increasing numbers following his expeditions. Temples worshiping him can still be found in Java and Melaka; in the latter, he is revered among the Hokkien community as the deity Sam Poh Kong.

HANS W. Y. YEUNG

See also Chinese in Southeast Asia; Chinese Tribute System; Folk Religions; Melaka; Ming Dynasty (1368–1644)

References:
Levathes, Louise. 1994. *When China Ruled the Seas: The Treasure Fleet of the Dragon Throne, 1405–1433.* New York: Simon and Schuster.

CHENLA

The term *Chenla,* a Chinese name, was used from the seventh century C.E. to refer to the territory of modern Cambodia and northeast Thailand. Modern historians have also applied the term to the period of Cambodian history from the seventh to early ninth centuries C.E.

The origin of the name is unknown. According to *Sui shu* (*History of the Sui Dynasty,* 581–618 C.E.), Chenla was a former vassal of the kingdom of Funan, and it gradually grew in power until King She-to-ssu-na of Chenla was able to assert his independence and conquer Funan. She-to-ssu-na is generally identified with King Citrasena Mahendravarman, whose reign dates from around 600 C.E. and whose inscriptions have been found in many areas of modern

Cambodia and northeast Thailand. *Sui shu* first mentioned Chenla in its description of an embassy sent to the Chinese court in 616 or 617 C.E.; the embassy was likely that sent by Isanavarman I, the son of Citrasena Mahendravarman. His reign is known from inscriptions found at Sambor Prei Kuk in the present-day Kompong Thom Province of Cambodia and in many areas of the lower Mekong Valley. During the Tang dynasty (618–907 C.E.) that followed, embassies were also received in 623 and 628 and were perhaps sent by the same king.

Although *Chenla* is used as a general term in the Chinese histories of that period, it is important to note that the inscriptions found within Cambodia never mention this name. Territories were designated according to the most important political centers, such as Bhavapura or Isanapura, the latter name being identified with Isanavarman's capital at Sambor Prei Kuk. The ritual heart of this capital consisted of two sacred enclosures surrounding a complex series of brick temples or shrines, perhaps constructed over the course of two centuries, from the late sixth to late eighth centuries C.E. Despite some damage from bombing and the effects of long neglect, much of this ritual site remains intact.

At the beginning of the eighth century, in 711 and 717 C.E., two embassies from Chenla were received at the court of the Tang dynasty, together with embassies from a kingdom named Wentan. The *Chiu T'ang shu* (*Old History of the Tang Dynasty*) stated that from 706 C.E., Chenla was divided into two parts: Water Chenla and Land Chenla. Land Chenla was also called Wentan, and this kingdom sent three further embassies in 753 or 754, 771, and 799 C.E. An itinerary has survived from the end of the eighth century, describing an overland voyage to Wentan across the mountains from the region of modern Hà Tĩnh in north-central Vietnam. The precise route of this journey is uncertain, but one of the destinations may have been the ancient city and temple site at Vat Phu in southern Laos. It is probable that the story of the division of Land and Water Chenla originated from the realization by the Tang court that the territory of Chenla comprised at least two major kingdoms—one that could be reached by sea, the other reached overland.

Although the Chinese histories mentioned two distinct kingdoms in the eighth century, the

The crocodile stone, a boulder with a crocodile carved into it, which possibly was used for human sacrifice by the Chenla culture. Wat Phu, Champasak, Laos. (Nik Wheeler/Corbis)

study of Sanskrit and Old Khmer inscriptions has revealed a far more complex political structure, with largely autonomous city-states controlling particular areas of rice-growing land or particular stretches of the Mekong Valley. The rulers of these city-states were only the most conspicuous and sometimes arbitrary representatives of a highly stratified and largely permanent local bureaucracy, whose members enjoyed inherited status and performed particular duties within the society. It was clearly exceptional for a large number of city-states to be combined under one ruler, and only rarely were embassies sent to China as a mark of this status (or of the ambition to achieve it).

Between 806 and 820, a further embassy was sent from Chenla to China, possibly by King Jayavarman II (r. 770/790/802?–834 C.E.). This king is thought to have placed his capital in the region of Angkor, on the north bank of the Tonle Sap, and the Angkorian period is usually dated from the year of his consecration, 802. It is remarkable that no further embassies were sent to China for the next three hundred years. Consequently, historians often used Chenla as a convenient heading for the period of Cambodia's history from the seventh to early ninth centuries. It should be noted, however, that when King Sūryavarman II (r. 1113–1145? C.E.) renewed diplomatic contact with China in 1116 and 1120, his kingdom was again recorded under the name Chenla.

WILLIAM A. SOUTHWORTH

See also Angkor; Funan; Hindu–Buddhist Period of Southeast Asia; Jayavarman II (r. 770/790/802?–834 C.E.); Sūryavarman II (r. 1113–1145?)

References:

Briggs, Lawrence Palmer. 1999 [1951]. *The Ancient Khmer Empire*. Bangkok: White Lotus Press. First published in 1951 as *Transactions of the American Philosophical Society,* New Series 41, pt. 1.

Coedes, George. 1968. *The Indianized States of Southeast Asia*. Honolulu: East–West Center Press/University Press of Hawai'i.

Jacques, Claude. 1979. "'Funan,' 'Zhenla': The Reality Concealed by These Chinese Views of Indochina." Pp. 371–379 in *Early South East Asia: Essays in Archaeology, History and Historical Geography*. Edited by R. B. Smith and W. Watson. Oxford: Oxford University Press.

Pelliot, Paul. 1904. "Deux itinéraires de Chine en Inde a la fin du VIIIe. siècle" [Two Routes from China to India at the End of the Eighth Century]. *Bulletin de l'École Française d'Extrême-Orient* 4: 131–413.

Vickery, Michael. 1998. *Society, Economics, and Politics in Pre-Angkor Cambodia: The 7th–8th Centuries*. Tokyo: Center for East Asian Cultural Studies for UNESCO/Toyo Bunko.

CHETTIARS (CHETTYARS)

The Chettiars were a South Indian moneylending caste and played a decisive role in the expansion of Lower Burma's rice industry in the late nineteenth century. The Chettiars were ubiquitous and found in virtually every region of economic importance during the colonial period (ca. 1800–ca. 1960s) in Southeast Asia. Chettiar firms in Malaya and Burma borrowed from European banks in the region to relend, at a higher rate of interest, either to local cultivators or to indigenous moneylenders. Each Chettiar business concern, sustained by caste and kinship ties, was part of a network with links across the Southeast Asian region and India. Like the Chinese financial and commercial intermediaries, the Chettiars linked the rural Southeast Asian communities to the expanding Western economy.

The Burmese rice industry serves as an important example to highlight the role of Chettiar capital in export expansion in Southeast Asia. From around 1880, Chettiar moneylenders made mortgage loans to Burmese cultivators needing capital for land clearance and plow animals and to pay migrant workers. Indeed, it has been asserted that Chettiar credit was fundamental to the growth of the industry. When the Burmese cultivators suffered a reversal, they lost their land, which the Chettiars then sold to other cultivators; the process was repeated within a few years. The Chettiars were thus regarded as the cause of Burmese landlessness and impoverishment. They also played an important role in financing Malay agriculturalists in smallholder rubber production in Malaya. In Malaya, however, an amendment to the Malay Land Reservation Enactment in 1933 prevented Chettiars from gaining land through default in Malay reservations.

During the interwar period, the Chettiars made a significant transition. Once primarily short-term moneylenders, they became bankers, long-term creditors of trade and manufacturing concerns, and land and property owners.

AMARJIT KAUR

See also Banks and Banking; Burma under British Colonial Rule; Indian Immigrants; Rice in Southeast Asia; Rubber; Western Malay States (Perak, Selangor, Negri Sembilan, and Pahang)

References:

Adas, Michael. 1974. *The Burma Delta: Economic Development and Social Change on an Asian Rice Frontier, 1852–1941*. Madison: University of Wisconsin Press.

Brown, Rajeswary Ampalavanar. 1994. *Capital and Entrepreneurship in South-East Asia.* Basingstoke, England: Macmillan.

Lim Teck Ghee. 1977. *Peasants and Their Agricultural Economy in Colonial Malaya, 1874–1941.* Kuala Lumpur: Oxford University Press.

CHIANG MAI

Chiang Mai, with a population of about 300,000, is a vibrant and historical city that has been a major political, religious, and economic hub of the Salween, Chao Phraya, and Mekong River basins since the thirteenth century. As the capital of Lan Na—the "Kingdom of a Million Rice Fields"—it was a relative and rival of the Lao kingdom of Lan Chang—the "Kingdom of a Million Elephants" at Luang Prabang. Both were on the networks of the caravan trade routes between the mountains of Yunnan and the Andaman Sea and the Gulf of Thailand. As a hinterland polity, Chiang Mai based its wealth on wet-rice farming, forest products, and handicrafts production. At its height in the fifteenth century, it was the home to new Theravada Buddhist sects and Pali scholarship unrivaled in the Buddhist world. Yet it never lost its animistic roots and multiethnic, cosmopolitan character.

Chiang Mai did, however, lose its political preeminence and independence during the political turmoil and wars that took place from the mid-fifteenth century to the end of the eighteenth century. The new political ties forged in the nineteenth century with the Thai regime in Bangkok marked the beginning of its revival and eventual integration into the new Siam under King Chulalongkorn (Rama V) (r. 1868–1910). New territorial demarcations and administrative arrangements turned Chiang Mai into a border province of Thailand in the twentieth century. Yet its historical legacies, which include architecture, handicrafts, and cultural traditions, make it a unique Thai city and a hub for the trades and tourism of the Greater Mekong Subregion of the twenty-first century.

Origins, Expansion, and Disintegration (Thirteenth to Nineteenth Centuries)

Local written and oral historical records suggest that Chiang Mai was, in effect, an extension of a group of small city-states, or *muang,* a type of political community that was prevalent among the T'ai-speaking peoples. These clusters of city-states were scattered throughout the areas of present-day northern Thailand, northern Vietnam, Lao People's Democratic Republic, southern Yunnan, and eastern Myanmar (Burma), known as Yonok. These polities depended on wet-rice agriculture and the caravan trade, whose routes crisscrossed the mountainous river valleys. The Mekong, the Red River, the Salween River, and their tributaries were the main sources of water and aquatic food, as well as the arteries for navigation and access links with the neighboring communities. The leaders were related through a common ancestral family, possibly linked through marriage to one of the Wa or Lua groups. The Yuans of Yonok were based in Chiang Rung, Chiang Saen, and Chiang Rai. A prince named Mangrai moved from Chiang Rai to capture Haripunchai or Lamphun, the major center of another group of Mon city-states with links to Thaton on the Gulf of Martaban and Lopburi near the Chao Phraya River. Mangrai gradually moved out of Lamphun to build the walled city of Chiang Mai in 1296 between the Ping River and the sacred Suthep Mountain.

From the thirteenth to the sixteenth centuries, the Mangrai dynasty established a circle of power over more than fifty cities and towns stretching from Chiang Tung east of the Salween to Nan on the western bank of the Mekong. Chiang Mai's success mainly stemmed from its commitment to the rule of law, as reflected in the law code of King Mangrai, the *Mangraisat.* Further, its webs of matrimonial alliances and kinship ties, its dedication to reformed Buddhist sects and their Sri Lankan–educated scholars, and its support for easy flows of economic exchanges in a multiethnic context also contributed to its prosperity. Chiang Mai was at the center of a cultural zone identifiable by its common language and scripts; architectural styles; bronze Buddha images; beliefs and rituals that combined Buddhism with animism; and special music, cuisine, silver works, lacquerware technique, and textiles.

The political decline of Chiang Mai coincided with the arrival of European firearms and trading opportunities in the fifteenth century, which changed the balance of power in the region and tempted local rulers and the nobility to seek new status and autonomy. The entangled web of matrimonial alliances was now producing both male and female claimants to the Chiang Mai crown. The reformed Buddhist sects were in open, bitter feuds and competed for political favors. Chiang Mai also found itself in the middle of the Ayutthaya-Ava contest, which resulted in its annexation by the Ava-Pegu kingdom under Bayinnaung (r. 1551–1581) in 1558.

Nineteenth-Century Revival and National Integration

Chiang Mai became a tributary state of Bangkok in the early nineteenth century and was gradually absorbed into the modern state of Siam built by King Chulalongkorn. It was open to economic penetration by Western teak business interests as well as Protestant missionary activities that introduced modern medicine and education. Chinese merchants populated the city and dominated the regional market, where imported goods from China and Europe were exchanged for forest products and opium. A Bangkok bureaucratic and middle-class lifestyle became prevalent, as did Bangkok language, scripts, and tastes in music, food, and attire. In recent years, road building and pressure on forestland has forced the highland groups to adapt to the social and environmental changes, albeit with difficulty. National cultural homogeneity is the norm, but the cultural diversity these groups represent is an asset to the tourist industry.

Although over 700 kilometers from the sea, Chiang Mai has occupied a strategic and mediating position between southwestern China and northern Southeast Asia, on one hand, and between the eastern and western regions of the Mekong, on the other. Its economic and cultural strength offsets its loss of political autonomy since the nineteenth century.

Chiang Mai has not received much attention in Southeast Asian historiography because of its fringe location and the lack of experts who can read the northern Thai language and scripts. The few studies that have been produced include the translation of *The Chiang Mai Chronicle* by David Wyatt and Aroonrut Wichienkeeo (1998) and works by Hans Penth (1994) and Saratsawadi Ongsakun (2000).

RUJAYA ABHAKORN

See also Bayinnaung (r. 1551–1581); Buddhism, Theravada; Burma-Siam Wars; Chiang Rai; Luang Prabang; Reforms and Modernization in Siam; Sri Lanka (Ceylon)

References:
Freeman, Michael. 2001. *Lanna Thailand's Northern Kingdom*. Bangkok: River Books.
Penth, Hans. 1994. *A Brief History of Lan Na*. Chiang Mai, Thailand: Silkworm Books.
Renard, Ronald D. 2000. "The Differential Integration of Hill People into the Thai State." Pp. 63–83 in *Civility and Savagery*. Edited by Andrew Turton. London: Curzon.
Rujaya Abhakorn and David K. Wyatt. 1995. "Administrative Reforms and National Integration in Northern Thailand." Pp. 68–81 in *Regions and National Integration in Thailand, 1892–1992*. Edited by Volker Grabowsky. Wiesbaden, Germany: Harrassowitz Verlan.
Saratsawadi Ongsakun. 2000. *Prawatsat Lanna* [*History of Lan Na*]. Bangkok: Amarin Printing.
Wyatt, David K., and Aroonrut Wichienkeeo, trans. 1998. *The Chiang Mai Chronicle*. Chiang Mai, Thailand: Silkworm Books.

CHIANG RAI

Located on the Kok River, a western tributary of the Mekong River, Chiang Rai was founded in 1262 by King Mangrai of Ngoen Yang, a T'ai state associated with Yonok, or the Yuan country. Chiang Rai was probably already a small settlement in the region, based at present-day Chiang Saen on the Mekong. It has been suggested that Mangrai moved away from the banks of the Mekong in response to the Mongols' advance. He continued moving south to found another major city, Chiang Mai, over thirty years later, in 1296. Chiang Rai became secondary in status to the new center but continued to be ruled by senior princes of the Mangrai dynasty. Chiang Rai and Chiang Saen were important Myanmar (Burma) garrisons during the Pegu-Toungoo occupation of the Chiang Mai or Lan Na kingdom from the sixteenth to eighteenth centuries. The peoples from Chiang Rai and the neighboring region were moved to populate Chiang Mai after its reconstruction by the Kawila dynasty, which joined forces with Bangkok in driving out the Myanmar troops in the late eighteenth century.

Chiang Rai was rebuilt in 1843 with the population from the region east of the Salween River. When the north was integrated into the new Siam, Chiang Rai became a fourth-grade province in 1910. Its location on the crossroads between present-day Thailand, Yunnan, Myanmar, and the Lao People's Democratic Republic highlights its multinational nature, in which all kinds of commodities are exchanged.

Cultural Incubator

Chiang Rai and its region west of the Mekong is perhaps best viewed as the "cultural incubator" of northern Thai civilization before the thirteenth century. Stone chopping tools associated with Hoabinhian hunter-gatherers have been found near Chiang Rai and Chiang Saen. Aerial photographs show the existence of over 100 settlements with moats or earthen walls, 55 of them near Chiang Rai city. As the Kok River extends west into Myanmar and an overland northern route leads directly to the western towns of Sipsong Pan Na in Yunnan, Chiang Rai was an important center linking the Mekong, Salween and Ping Rivers. When considered as part of a fertile subregion, Chiang Rai and the communities on the Kok, Fang, Lao, and Ing Rivers and the western bank of the Mekong north of Luang Prabang formed a pre-thirteenth-century T'ai-Yuan civilization. Archaeological evidence, written records, and social traditions suggest that the people had basic knowledge in wet-rice cultivation and irrigation, means of providing for basic needs, and sustainable sociopolitical institutions. Legendary accounts of the exploits of heroic kings suggest a tradition of ancestral worship that unified the various scattered communities. As the political domains included a number of upland groups, particularly the Mon-Khmer-speaking peoples such as the Lua or Lawa, they were included in the state through rituals and probably marital relations. Local chronicles contain references that point to early practices of T'ai governmental and political polities, with their emphasis on tutelary spirits, fictive and real kinship association, the maintenance of social order, political legitimacy, and hegemony through descent. The Buddhism that came from the Mon country through Hariphunchai (present-day Lamphun) and Pagan was still in its formative stage.

Center of Buddhist Arts

It was during the Mangrai dynasty from the thirteenth to sixteenth centuries that the Chiang Rai-Chiang Saen region, combined with the Chiang Mai-Lamphun-Lampang area, prospered as a center of Buddhist arts—in particular, the design and casting of Buddha images and architecture and handicrafts such as lacquerware, silverware, textiles, and ceramics. Some of these artistic and cultural developments seem to have resulted from cross-cultural exchanges. For example, according to certain accounts, Mangrai made political advances into Pagan and brought back gong makers who were sent to Chiang Saen. The Emerald Buddha presently in Bangkok was said to have been first discovered in Chiang Rai before it was taken to Chiang Mai in 1486 and subsequently to Vientiane in the sixteenth century.

Chiang Rai continued to be part of the later development of the Chiang Mai–based polity and cultural zone, which was characterized by a literary society and adherence to a new and localized form of Theravada Buddhist tradition. However, the mass migrations of the twentieth century, caused by major conflicts and socioeconomic dislocations around the region, transformed Chiang Rai into an international border zone that reflected those upheavals, even as it attempted to maintain its Yuan roots.

RUJAYA ABHAKORN

See also Buddhism, Theravada; Burma-Siam Wars; Chiang Mai; T'ais; Yunnan Province

References:
Freeman, Michael. 2001. *Lanna Thailand's Northern Kingdom.* Bangkok: River Books.
Grabowsky, Volker. 1994. "Forced Resettlement Campaigns in Northern Thailand during the Early Bangkok Period." *Oriens Extremus* 37, no. 1: 45–107.
Kunstadter, Peter, and Sally Lennington Kunstadter. 1992. "Population Movements and Environmental Changes in the Hills of Northern Thailand." Pp. 17–56 in *Patterns and Illusions: Thai History and Thought.* Edited by Gehan Wijeyewardene and E. C. Chapman. Canberra: Australian National University.
Penth, Hans. 1989. "On the History of Chiang Rai." *Journal of the Siam Society* 77, no. 1: 11–32.

———. 1994. *A Brief History of Lan Na*. Chiang Mai, Thailand: Silkworm Books.

Renard, Ronald D. 2000. "The Differential Integration of Hill People into the Thai State." Pp. 63–83 in *Civility and Savagery*. Edited by Andrew Turton. London: Curzon.

Rujaya Abhakorn and David K. Wyatt. 1995. "Administrative Reforms and National Integration in Northern Thailand." Pp. 68–81 in *Regions and National Integration in Thailand, 1892–1992*. Edited by Volker Grabowsky. Wiesbaden, Germany: Harrassowitz Verlan.

Sarasawadee Ongsakul. 1993. "Chiang Rai Chronicle." Pp. 38–55 in *Lan Na Historical Sources from Palm Leaf and Paper Manuscripts*. Edited by Sarasawadwee Ongsakul. Chiang Mai, Thailand: Chiang Mai University Social Science Research Institute.

———. 2000. *Prawatsat Lanna* [*History of Lan Na*]. Bangkok: Amarin Printing.

———. 2002. "'The Chiang Saen Chronicle' (History of Chiang Saen)." Pp. 223–249 in *Studies of History and Literature of Tai Ethnic Groups*. Edited by Sarasawadee Ongsakul and Yoshiyuki Masuhura. Bangkok: Amarin Printing.

Shigeharu Tanabe. 2000. "Autochthony and the Inthakhin Cult of Chiang Mai." Pp. 294–318 in *Civility and Savagery*. Edited by Andrew Turton. London: Curzon.

Tun Aung Chain. 1996. "Chiang Mai in Bayinnaung's Polity." Pp. 65–72 in *Proceedings of the 6th International Conference on Thai Studies Theme VI—Chiang Mai, 1296–1996: 700th Anniversary, Chiang Mai, Thailand, 14–17 October 1996*. Chiang Mai, Thailand: Chiang Mai University.

Wyatt, David K., and Aroonfurt Wichienkeeo, trans. 1998. *The Chiang Mai Chronicle*. Chiang Mai, Thailand: Silkworm Books.

CHIN PENG (ONG BOON HUA/HWA) (1922–)
A Communist Guerrilla Leader

Chin Peng was the secretary-general of the Malayan Communist Party (MCP), which launched an armed uprising against British rule in Malaya in 1948. He remained the undisputed leader of the MCP until it called off its armed struggle and disbanded in 1989. By then, the British government had granted Malaya—the present-day West/Peninsular Malaysia—independence (in 1957) and allowed its Bornean colonies of Sarawak and Sabah to merge with Malaya, together with Singapore, to form the enlarged Federation of Malaysia (in 1963).

Chin Peng took over the post of secretary-general in 1947 from a Cantonese-speaking Vietnamese, Lai Tek, to whom he was a close companion. Lai Tek was exposed as a secret agent who had been planted in the party by the British police since 1934. Chin Peng and those who took over the leadership had not dared to tell party members about the traitor Lai Tek, who had absconded with the organization's funds, but kept the information to themselves for nearly a year until they had established their leadership.

It was, in part, this internal crisis that forced Chin Peng to take the party underground, to renounce the "soft and cooperative" policy adopted by Lai Tek toward the British authorities, and to adopt a militant line. It was not long before the British authorities enacted tough measures to curb communist activities such as strikes and demonstrations. Confrontations with the British authorities pushed the party toward armed revolution.

Chin Peng has been fondly remembered as a sincere communist ally in several memoirs by British intelligence officers who worked with him in the resistance war in the jungles of Malaya against the Japanese Imperial Army during the Pacific War (1941–1945). He was responsible for organizing food supplies and other services for British groups stranded behind enemy lines. In recognition of his wartime services, he was among the party's top guerrillas who were invited to London to attend the great victory parade at the conclusion of the conflict. He was later awarded a British decoration—Officer of the Order of the British Empire (OBE)—although that was rescinded when the MCP began its revolt.

Chin Peng's real name is Ong Boon Hua (Ong Boon Hwa); Chin Peng was his party nom de guerre. He was born in the coastal town of Sitiawan in Perak state, where his father owned a small bicycle repair shop. After an early education in Chinese, Chin Peng went to an English school. He was eighteen when he joined the MCP, cutting stencils for the group's propaganda department; there, he met his wife, who also worked in the department. His wife followed him into the jungles when the party launched its revolt in 1948. They have two children, one of whom is a lawyer.

A soft-spoken, courteous, and bookish man, Chin Peng wielded tremendous power over his small, highly trained, and efficient army of some 5,000 guerrillas (Coates 1992: 73, n. 46). The British government put a price of $200,000 on his head, but Chin Peng managed to elude capture. In 1955, the Malayan public and the world press witnessed him emerge from his jungle hideout to broker a deal with the Alliance Party leader, Tunku Abdul Rahman Putra Al-Haj (1903–1990), of the preindependence government of Malaya at Baling town in Kedah state near the Thai-Malayan border. But the talks collapsed due to Tunku's refusal to recognize the MCP as a legitimate political party and to allow surrendered communist guerrillas to return to society without police screening.

In 1960, as the communist forces were nearly routed militarily, they withdrew to the Thai-Malayan border, where they established base camps. The Malayan government declared an end to the state of emergency. As the party feared that an attempt would be made on his life, Chin Peng was ordered to leave for China; he sought refuge there because the Chinese Communist Party (CCP) had established cordial and fraternal ties with the MCP. He remained in China until 1989, all the while running his party's struggles from afar.

In 1989, Chin Peng was among several top MCP leaders who initiated a peace agreement between the party and the Malaysian government, which marked the end of their armed struggle. More than 1,000 party members accepted the Thai government's offer of land to set up homes in villages near the Malaysian border. However, Chin Peng and others waited in Thailand to be allowed to return to Malaysia and resettle. The latest press reports suggest that after a long and fruitless wait, they might now also decide to seek Thai citizenship.

On 3 April 2002, the seventy-six-year-old Chin Peng announced that he had just completed writing his memoirs, recounting the successes and mistakes committed by the pro-Beijing MCP, providing analyses on why the communist bloc collapsed in 1990, and detailing how the event affected communist parties globally. He also said that although the MCP had failed to grab power from the state, it was responsible for the country achieving independence in 1957. The memoirs were published in 2003.

CHEAH BOON-KHENG

See also Abdul Rahman, Tunku (1903–1990); Baling Talks (1955); Force 136; Malayan Communist Party (MCP); Malayan Emergency (1948–1960); Malayan People's Anti-Japanese Army (MPAJA)

References:
Barber, Noel. 1971. *The War of the Running Dogs.* London: Collins.
Chin Peng. 2003. *Alias Chin Peng: My Side of History.* Singapore: Media Masters.
Coates, John. 1992. *Suppressing Insurgency: An Analysis of the Malayan Emergency, 1948–1954.* Boulder, CO: Westview Press.
Miller, Harry. 1954. *Menace in Malaya.* London: George G. Harrap.

CHINA, IMPERIAL

Imperial China began in 221 B.C.E. when Emperor Qin Shihuangdi (r. 259–210 B.C.E.) unified North and Central China and ended when the Qing (Ch'ing/Manchu) dynasty (1644–1912) was overthrown. For more than two thousand years, Imperial China's relations with Southeast Asia were determined by the rate at which the native peoples of South and Southwest China became its subjects and their territories were settled by immigrant Chinese from the north. Maritime trade flourished and centered on ports now known as Guangzhou (Canton, the capital of modern Guangdong [Kwangtung] Province) and Hanoi (the capital of modern Vietnam), but Imperial China did not expand beyond what is today the northern half of Vietnam. During the tenth century, Vietnam became an independent kingdom. Imperial China reached its present land borders with Burma (Myanmar) and Laos only after the Mongol conquest of the kingdom of Dali (937–1253). Since the thirteenth century, the overland southern limits of China have been more or less firm until the present day.

Trade and diplomacy under the Han dynasty (206 B.C.E.–220 C.E.) were conducted through a tributary system, whereby countries bordering on China and countries that wanted to trade with China acknowledged China's imperial status by sending tribute. In return, Chinese emperors would send gifts to the respective rulers. This arrangement provided the framework for Sino–Southeast Asian relations until the nineteenth century.

The earliest chronicles of the Qin and Han dynasties described an ancient trade in rare luxury goods from the south. The first mission recorded (in the year 2 C.E.) came from India. Others that followed were sent by rulers of port kingdoms along the coasts of Indochina (modern Vietnam and Cambodia) and the Malay Archipelago (mainly the islands of Java and Sumatra). One purported to have come from Andun, the ruler of Daqin (the Roman Orient at the time of Marcus Aurelius, 161–180 C.E.).

The trade with the kingdoms of Linyi (later Champa, now central Vietnam) and Funan (later Zhenla, now Cambodia and Thailand [Siam]) was the most important down to the Tang dynasty (618–907 C.E.). It provided all that Imperial China needed from the region and from the Indian Ocean. In the Malay world (contemporary Malaysia, Indonesia, and the southern Philippines), the flow of trade between China and India was vital to the wealth and stability of the dynastic houses of Java and Sumatra. Notable were those of Moloyou (Melayu or Jambi) and later Sanfoqi (Śri Vijaya/Śrivijaya), both in eastern Sumatra, and Holing in Java. But no less significant was the fact that these and other Indianized kingdoms were centers where Chinese Buddhist monks sojourned to prepare for study in India.

Chinese traders were not themselves active in Southeast Asia until the tenth century, when independent Chinese kingdoms were established in the south after the fall of the Tang empire in 907. The most notable was the kingdom of Nan Han (917–971 C.E.), based in the modern province of Guangdong and Guangxi (Kwangsi). Also important was the empire of Min (907–945), based in modern Fujian (Fukien) Province, which, after 945, was conquered by the Yangzi Delta kingdom of Nan Tang (917–971 C.E.) and became its southernmost prefectures. Cut off from the north, the peoples of this region turned to the sea. This was a major turning point for the South China Sea trade. Even after these kingdoms were incorporated into the Song (Sung) empire (960–1279), the merchants of Guangdong and Fujian Provinces continued to be active in that trade. When the Song emperors lost their territories in northern China in 1127 and moved their capital to Hangzhou (Hangchow), Zhejiang (Chekiang), they became even more dependent on the revenues derived from that trade. This was the first time a Chinese imperial center was located at a coastal port, and the needs of the capital provided great stimulus to maritime relations with Southeast Asia.

Overland trade from India and Burma through the tribal areas of modern Yunnan Province had begun in the Han dynasty and become prominent during the Tang. Goods were transported north across Yunnan, carried down the Yangzi (Yangtze) River to Sichuan (Szechuan), and then either transported farther north to the ancient capital of Changan (now Xian) or east down the Yangzi Valley to the rich provinces of the delta region. This was also the route of Buddhist missions to the Burman and Shan, or Thai-Dai, peoples that carried the faith to the tribes within Yunnan. Although there was intermittent warfare among the tribes, trade and culture contact marked the cross-border relationships. The Chinese did not play a prominent role along these borders until the Southern Song dynasty (1127–1279) was cut off from its overland trade routes to the west via Central Asia.

The Mongols were the first nomads of the steppes to have conquered all of China and thus come into contact with Southeast Asia. They did so when they destroyed the kingdom of Dali (also known as Nanchao) in 1253 and reached the borders of Burma. Later, after they replaced the Song as the Yuan dynasty of China (1279–1369), they tried to subdue both Burma and Vietnam. The momentum of their empire building, however, did not stop at the coasts, as had happened with the Chinese during the earlier centuries. The Mongol Yuan sent expeditionary forces to invade Burma, Vietnam, and Champa (1281–1303) as well as Java (1292–1293). For the first time in history, a large part of both mainland and maritime Southeast Asia faced a colossal threat from a powerful empire in China.

None of the Mongol expeditions was successful, and the invasions across the South China Sea were aberrations in Chinese history. After Chinese rebels drove out the Mongols and established the Ming dynasty (1368–1644), the founder of the dynasty, Zhu Yuanzhang (Emperor Hongwu, r. 1368–1398), reverted to traditional policies. He adopted a strategy that focused on defending North China from nomadic enemies and coastal China from Japanese pirates. He used the tributary system both as a diplomatic instrument and as a means to control all external trade. His son, Zhu Di (Emperor Yongle, or Yung-lo, 1402–1424), then sent Admiral Zheng He (Cheng Ho, 1371–1435) on his famous naval expeditions to Southeast Asia and across the Indian Ocean to South and West Asia as well as East Africa. The seven expeditions lasted from 1403 to 1433. But though these were demonstrations of China's wealth and power, there was no reversal of imperial policy. Not only was there no intention to expand territory, there was also no commitment to continue the naval show of force. After 1433, the Chinese navies withdrew, and Imperial China never sent them out again.

Thus, over the following six centuries, the region we now call Southeast Asia was a relatively minor concern for Imperial China. From 1433 to the fall of the Ming dynasty in 1644, its emperors paid little attention to the south except to fight off pirates of both Chinese and Japanese origins and manage the armed traders sent by the kings of Portugal and Spain during most of the sixteenth century. By the early seventeenth century, internal rebellions from within and Manchu invaders in North China from without troubled the dynasty; consequently, maritime activities were neglected. The Portuguese in Melaka and Macao (Macau) and the Dutch in Java and Taiwan became the major players in Southeast Asia. They were joined by Chinese private navies off the Fujian coast led by Zheng Zhilong (d. 1661) and his son Zheng Chenggong (better known as Koxinga, 1624–1662), who had both learned from the Portuguese and Dutch experience. By the time the Ming dynasty fell in 1644, armed Chinese merchants had become active protagonists in the region.

On the mainland, Vietnam recovered from the war with Emperor Yongle that lasted from 1406 to 1428, but it continued to have an uncomfortable relationship with China. Burma, too, felt the pressure of Ming control of the borders to its north as Chinese settlers and armies moved into the new province of Yunnan. This presence grew when remnants of the Ming armies that were defeated by the northern Manchu invaders in the 1640s escaped into Burma. The situation fostered determined efforts by the Burmese kings to strengthen their control over the territories bordering China.

During this period, the kingdoms and port cities of Southeast Asia were only aware of China as a powerful neighbor that normally stayed aloof from their regional affairs. Following the decline of the Javanese empire of Majapahit at the end of the fifteenth century and the flourishing of Melaka throughout the fifteenth century with Chinese support, Chinese traders defied imperial policy to extend their trading ventures throughout the region. Several books recording their interest in the region had appeared during the fifteenth and sixteenth centuries, but it was not until the beginning of the seventeenth century that a full account was published. This was Zhang Xie's *Dongxi yang kao* [*On the Eastern and Western Oceans*] (preface dated 1617), the most important book on maritime affairs since the end of the Zheng He expeditions. It captured the growing freedom in the private trade with Southeast Asia on the eve of the Zheng family's dominance during the sixty years up to 1683. By that time, Portuguese, Spanish, and Dutch records were providing the world with glimpses of where in the region the Chinese were most active and how these Chinese merchants were contributing to new kinds of trading networks dominated by Europeans.

Imperial China continued to keep a tight control over foreign trade during the eighteenth century, and that policy was retained until the 1840s. In Chinese terms, this was a century and a half of peace and stability. The only external threats came from the Mongol and Turkic nomads of Inner Asia, and the Qing armies fought several fierce wars that reinforced China's dominance over modern Xinjiang (Sinkiang) and Tibet. A few local rebellions were troubling, but they were all crushed with relative ease. In short, on the eve of the British East India Company's Opium War with China in 1840, there were no reasons for Imperial China to feel threatened by enemies coming by sea. In turn, Southeast Asia noted China's indifference to its southern neighborhood. Each country in the region had to adjust, as best it could and in its own way, to the coming of the Europeans for over three hundred years. In so doing, the region was increasingly tied to European interests in India and the Middle East (West Asia). But private Chinese merchants and, following the opening of China and the advent of the Industrial Revolution, cheap Chinese labor for the mines and plantations of Southeast Asia together kept the region close to developments in China. The relationship was a relatively passive one until the end of Imperial China and the emergence of Nationalist China.

WANG GUNGWU

See also Angkor; Buddhism, Mahayana; Champa; Cheng Ho (Zheng He), Admiral (1371/1375–1433/1435); Chenla; Chinese in Southeast Asia; Chinese Tribute System; East India Company (EIC) (1600), English; Economic History of Early Modern Southeast Asia (Pre-Sixteenth Century); Economic Transformation of Southeast Asia (ca. 1400–ca. 1800); Formosa (Taiwan); Funan; Galleon Trade; Hong Kong; I-Ching (I-tsing) (635–713 C.E.); Java; Jungle/Forest Products; Macau (Macao); Majapahit (1293–ca. 1520s); Manila; Marine/Sea Products; Melaka; Ming Dynasty (1368–1644); Nam Viet (Nan Yue); Nan Chao (Nanchao) (Dali/Tali); Qing (Ching/Manchu) Dynasty (1644–1912); Sino-Vietnamese Relations; Sino-Vietnamese Wars; Śrivijaya (Śriwijaya); Sumatra; Tin; Vereenigde Oost-Indische Compagnie (VOC) ([Dutch] United East India Company) (1602); Yuan (Mongol) Dynasty (1271–1368); Yunnan Province

References:
Chang T'ien-tse. 1973 [1934]. *Sino-Portuguese Trade from 1514 to 1644: A Synthesis of Portuguese and Chinese Sources.* New York: AMS Press.
Fitzgerald, C. P. 1972. *The Southern Expansion of the Chinese People: "Southern Fields and Southern Ocean."* London: Barrie and Jenkins.
Leonard, Jane Kate. 1984. *Wei Yuan and China's Rediscovery of the Maritime World.* Cambridge, MA: Council on East Asian Studies, Harvard University.
Levanthes, Louise. 1994. *When China Ruled the Seas: The Treasure Fleet of the Dragon Throne, 1405–1433.* New York: Simon and Schuster.
Ma Huan. 1970 [1433]. *Ying-yai Sheng-lan: The Overall Survey of the Ocean's Shores.* Translated and edited by J.V. G. Mills. Cambridge: Cambridge University Press.
Ng Chin-keong. 1983. *Trade and Society: The Amoy Network on the China Coast, 1683–1735.* Singapore: Singapore University Press.
Wang Gungwu. 1981. *Community and Nation: Essays on Southeast Asia and the Chinese.* Singapore and Sydney: Heinemann Educational Books (Asia) and George Allen & Unwin Australia for the Asian Studies Association of Australia.
———. 1998. *The Nanhai Trade: The Early History of Chinese Trade in the South China Sea.* Singapore: Times Academic Press.
Wolters, O. W. 1967. *Early Indonesian Commerce: A Study of the Origins of Sri Vijaya.* Ithaca, NY: Cornell University Press.

CHINA, NATIONALIST

Nationalist China's origins were closely associated with Southeast Asia. The first Chinese Nationalist leader, Sun Yat-sen (1866–1925), turned for help to the Chinese in Singapore, Penang, and the Malay States in 1900. Sun Yat-sen's impact lasted until his death in 1925 and several years thereafter. The last political party he established, in 1921—the Guomindang (Kuomintang, KMT, or Nationalist Party)—expanded on these early links, especially after it became the party in government in 1928. His successor, Chiang Kai-shek (Jiang Jieshi, 1887–1975), was controversial because many overseas Chinese did not respect his assumption of power over the country. Nevertheless, the Guomindang's external connections remained strong because the party was projected as identical with the national government and with the fate of the Chinese republic. The party's influence thus continued after 1949, notwithstanding the Nationalist government's defeat at the hands of the Chinese Communist Party (CCP) and the fact that the Republic of China was forced to move to Taiwan. Although the circumstances were less favorable, KMT still retained the loyalties of its older members. Even after the European colonies of Southeast Asia gained their independence in the 1950s and 1960s, the government in Taiwan remained active in encouraging many Chinese school graduates of the region to study in universities in Taiwan. And despite the fact that the political links have diminished in significance, some Taiwan business firms still depend on their overseas Chinese supporters for facilitating start-ups in Southeast Asia.

When Sun Yat-sen first visited Singapore in August 1900, the Manchu Qing court had put a price on his head. He had led a rebellion against the dynasty five years earlier and was briefly incarcerated in the Chinese Legation in London in 1896. His dramatic escape made him an international figure, and thereafter, he saw himself as a revolutionary. But the British banned him from Hong Kong, his original political base, so he had to turn to his compatriots overseas in Japan and Southeast Asia for support. In 1905, he established a coalition of political parties, the Tongmeng Hui. He set up its South Seas headquarters the next year in Singapore and then moved it to Penang in 1909. By that time, he had become a symbol of the anti-Manchu movement among overseas Chinese everywhere. From 1906 to 1907, he personally traveled through the Western Malay States of the Malay Peninsula to collect funds for uprisings in South China. For the next five years, his followers, many of them students from China who had joined his party in Japan, were sent to do the same in other cities of the region, notably Penang, Bangkok, Rangoon (Yangon), Manila, Batavia (Jakarta), Medan, Saigon, and Hanoi. From the Chinese community of these Southeast Asian cities, he received enough help to launch a series of six uprisings between 1906 and 1911. Although every one of these failed, his prestige remained high among younger Chinese, especially those from the laboring classes. The most spectacular support from them came in 1911, when a large number volunteered for the rebellion in Guangzhou and sacrificed their lives. Of the "Seventy-Two Martyrs" of the Huanghua gang uprising, over twenty came from Southeast Asia.

The Qing dynasty was overthrown after the Wuchang Uprising in late 1911, and the Republic of China was proclaimed in Nanjing (Nanking) in 1912. Sun Yat-sen returned from North America and Europe via Southeast Asia to become its provisional president. Many of his Southeast Asian supporters followed him to serve the revolution in China. For the next thirteen years, through the many vicissitudes in his political struggle for the republic against a series of warlords in both North and South China, Sun Yat-sen continued to receive help from the party branches that he had set up in

the region. In particular, the party newspapers in various cities gave him sustained support. Also, his ideas were spread among the hundreds of modern Chinese schools that were set up wherever there were communities large enough to support them. And businesspeople who had first been encouraged to invest in the economic development of China by the Qing court were exhorted to a new patriotism toward the republic, and most of them responded readily.

The governments of Siam (Thailand) and the various European colonies in Southeast Asia viewed this development among their Chinese residents with growing concern. The British in the Straits Settlements had accepted Chinese consular representation in Singapore and Penang during the last decades of the Qing dynasty, and they watched the anti-Manchu movement grow from the start. After allowing dissidents such as Kang Youwei (K'ang Yu-wei, 1859–1927) and Sun Yat-sen to take refuge in British territory, they became very alert to the strong feelings aroused among the Chinese residents and sojourners under their jurisdiction. As a result, they were well prepared to deal with the revolutionary groups that would use the colonies to recruit supporters. The French authorities in Saigon and Hanoi were also sensitive to such activities because these Chinese rebels had inspired young Vietnamese to embrace nationalism and oppose French colonial rule. The Dutch, too, became increasingly troubled by the warm response to patriotic calls among the Chinese in the Netherlands East Indies, notably in the Sumatran areas close to British Malaya, and in the cities of Batavia and Surabaya. Indigenous reactions against Chinese business successes after 1900 were turned against colonialism itself. This only made the Dutch authorities more determined to place Chinese nationalist sentiments under tight control.

From 1916 to 1928, the new Republic of China was engulfed in a civil war among the warlords. Its seat of government in Beijing was weak. The Western powers that dominated the trade and politics along its southern and eastern coasts had little to fear from the republic. But when the Nationalist government in Nanjing replaced the ineffectual Beijing government in 1928, the situation changed. The new military leader, Chiang Kai-shek, continued to fight to try to unify all of China, and he encouraged strong Nationalist voices to be raised to rid China of Western dominance. These voices found their echoes among the overseas Chinese all over Southeast Asia.

Japan's ambitions in Shandong (Shantung) Province, where the Japanese had replaced the Germans after World War I (1914–1918), provoked even stronger emotions. The Shandong (Jinan) incident in 1928 was the beginning of a series of actions that heightened anti-Japanese patriotism throughout the 1930s. The Japanese invasion of Manchuria in 1931 alarmed all the Western powers, but international reaction was ineffective, and the Japanese pushed on into North China. Thus, the overseas Chinese in Southeast Asia were increasingly drawn into the vortex of China's politics, as it became inevitable that China and Japan would go to war. At the time, Chiang Kai-shek was fighting a civil war against his communist rivals and several surviving warlords, and he had tried to avoid an open war against the Japanese. His position became increasingly unpopular, including among the Southeast Asian Chinese. This situation was changed in 1936 by the Xian mutiny, led by the Manchurian leader Zhang Xueliang (Chang Hsueh-liang, 1898–2001). The mutineers forced Chiang Kai-shek to stand up against the Japanese, and the overseas Chinese responded with bursts of patriotic activities. In every city and town in the region, the Chinese organized themselves to express their approval.

When the Second Sino-Japanese War broke out in July 1937, the Chinese in Southeast Asia were ready to act. Young men were encouraged to volunteer for military service to fight in China. But the most effective strategy was to raise funds for the war-against-Japan effort. Activities encouraged and managed by the Nationalist government mobilized concerted efforts throughout the *Nanyang* (as the Chinese called maritime Southeast Asia). Under the leadership of Tan Kah Kee (Chen Jiageng, 1874–1961) in British Malaya, the South Seas China Relief Fund Union was established in October 1938, marking the first time a region-wide organization in support of the war in China was widely accepted.

The Nationalist leaders never succeeded in unifying the country. They had to fight the warlords until 1928. And at the same time, the Chinese Communist Party, their erstwhile partner (during the "united front" period from 1936 to 1945), continually contested the Nationalists' leadership of the revolution. When Chiang Kai-shek turned against the Communists, he concentrated on destroying them before tackling the remaining warlords and resisting Japanese advances into China. This decision was unpopular with both patriots and left-wing intellectuals. Rival groups formed in opposition to Chiang Kai-shek appeared, not least among the Chinese in Southeast Asia who wanted to see more resistance against Japanese encroachments in China. Of these, the Communists gained the sympathy of many schoolteachers and journalists. Through sections of the Chinese press and the students in Chinese schools, political radicalization began to take place.

In this way, Guomindang-Communist rivalry in China was reproduced in various parts of the region, notably in urban centers where the overseas Chinese were numerous. And where there was a sizable proletariat, as in British Malaya, left-wing movements critical of both the colonial and the Guomindang governments found growing support for their revolutionary cause. Although this phenomenon was a common threat to all governments, the British were the most concerned because, by the late 1930s, about half the population of British Malaya was Chinese; urban areas such as Singapore and Penang were literally "Chinatowns." The fact that there were deep divisions within these communities was not reassuring. Neither the nationalist call for patriotism toward the home country by the Guomindang nor the internationalist call against imperialism and colonialism by the Chinese Communists was acceptable to British interests. With the onset of war in Europe (in September 1939) and the threat of a Japanese invasion in Southeast Asia, however, the colonial powers found themselves on the same side as the Chinese. In the Philippines, Malaya, and the Netherlands East Indies, both Chinese Nationalists and Chinese Communists fought a common enemy, Japan, together with the Allied forces.

After World War II (1939–1945), Nationalist China fought a bitter civil war (1945–1949) against the Communists. For the first time, it found it had lost the support of major sections of the overseas Chinese. This was partly because local Chinese were adapting to new developments that replaced colonial regimes with indigenous Nationalists all over Southeast Asia but also because the younger generation of Chinese were sympathetic to the criticisms of widespread incompetence and corruption among Guomindang leaders. The Nationalists' loss of the war coincided with the establishment of new nation-states that demanded a new kind of loyalty from resident Chinese. The Sun Yat-sen heritage of the patriotic *huaqiao* (overseas Chinese) was thereafter no longer defensible.

Nationalist China asked Southeast Asian Chinese to look more toward their country of origin, but it also educated them to understand the world beyond China—the world of science, international economics, and national sovereignty. Thus, it was itself the source of the paradox that made some Chinese more Chinese and others more ready to adapt themselves to become the nationals of the new states of Southeast Asia.

WANG GUNGWU

See also China Relief Fund; Chinese in Southeast Asia; Chinese Revolution(1911); Kuomintang (KMT); Sun Yat-sen, Dr. (1866–1925)

References:

Akashi, Yoji. 1970. *The Nanyang Chinese National Salvation Movement, 1937–1941.* Topeka: Center for East Asian Studies, University of Kansas.

Eastman, Lloyd E. 1974. *The Abortive Revolution: China under Nationalist Rule, 1927–1937.* Cambridge, MA: Harvard University Press.

Hicks, George, ed. 1996. *Chinese Organisations in Southeast Asia in the 1930s.* Singapore: Select Books.

Tan, Antonio S. 1972. *The Chinese in the Philippines, 1898–1935: A Study of Their National Awakening.* Quezon City, the Philippines: Garcia Publishing.

Tan Kah Kee. 1994. *The Memoirs of Tan Kah Kee.* Edited and translated by A. H. C. Ward, Raymond W. Chu, and Janet Salaff. Singapore: Singapore University Press.

Williams, Lea E. 1960. *Overseas Chinese Nationalism: The Genesis of the Pan-Chinese Movement in Indonesia, 1900–1916.* Glencoe, IL: Free Press.

Yen Ching-hwang. 1976. *The Overseas Chinese and the 1911 Revolution.* Kuala Lumpur: Oxford University Press.

Yong, C. F. 1987. *Tan Kah-kee: The Making of an Overseas Chinese Legend.* Singapore: Oxford University Press.

CHINA RELIEF FUND

The China Relief Fund was a fund-raising effort among the Chinese sojourners in Southeast Asia from 1937 to 1942, with the goal of assisting China in its fight against Japanese aggression. After the outbreak of the Sino-Japanese War in July 1937, patriotic Chinese sojourners formed committees in different places in Southeast Asia to raise money for the resistive Chinese armies. In mid-1938, representatives of these groups urged the establishment of a federation to supervise the relief-fund committees. Primarily due to the efforts of Tan Kah Kee (1874–1961), a Chinese industrialist and educator in Singapore, a convention of over 180 representatives met in Singapore on 10 October 1938, China's National Day, and resolved to establish the Federation of China Relief Funds of Southern Asia. Tan was elected chairman.

The fund-raising activities were tolerated by the Straits Settlements and other Indochinese governments on the understanding that the money raised would not be used to pay the costs of the war but only to relieve the wounded soldiers and refugees, a restriction that was regarded as necessary to avoid agitating Japan. This restriction was sound only on paper, however, as all the donations were handed over to the Executive Yuan, the highest administrative organ of the Republic of China, which naturally directed the money to war purposes. With the patronage of the Executive Yuan, the federation actually served as a propaganda organ among the Chinese sojourners; for example, it denounced Wang Jingwei's betrayal of China in forming a pro-Japanese government in Nanjing and supported Britain in its war against Germany.

There is no accurate figure on the total donations remitted to China via the funds. According to Tan, the amount raised in 1939 and 1940 totaled $140 million in Chinese currency. By early 1942, all activities of the federation ceased when much of Southeast Asia fell into the hands of the Japanese army.

HANS W. Y. YEUNG

See also China, Nationalist; Chinese in Southeast Asia; Japanese Occupation of Southeast Asia (1941–1945); Sun Yat-sen, Dr. (1866–1925)

References:

Tan Kah Kee. 1994. *The Memoirs of Tan Kah Kee.* Edited and translated by A. H. C. Ward,

Raymond W. Chu, and Janet Salaff.
Singapore: Singapore University Press.

CHINA SINCE 1949

The swift victory of the Chinese Communist Party (CCP) led by Mao Zedong (1893–1976) in China's civil war (1945–1949) surprised contemporaries both in China and in Southeast Asia. That 1949 victory highlighted the threat communism posed to colonial governments as well as to the emerging nationalist leaders of Southeast Asia. Marxist-Leninist ideas had been introduced in the 1910s into Vietnam and the Netherlands East Indies, about the same time they reached China. But for forty years, communist movements had been overshadowed by the anticolonial struggles for freedom and independence. The fact that China became communist just when new nations were being established led to volatile relationships between China and the region. As a partner of the Soviet Union in the Cold War against the capitalist West in the 1950s, the Beijing regime put strong pressures on its southern neighbors to accept communism. In response, the local nationalist leaders turned to the West for help. They also became particularly wary of their residents and citizens of Chinese descent.

Throughout the Cold War era, Communist China was the source of the tension that colored the lives of all the Chinese who had decided to make their homes in the new nations. But even before the Cold War ended in 1990, China had embarked on systematic economic reforms that brought unforeseen changes to the country. In the early years of the twenty-first century, China under the Communist Party may still be called Communist China, but what remains of its communism no longer threatens its neighbors. Thus, two distinct periods may be distinguished: the period before the reforms (1949–1978) and the period after 1978.

In the first period, Communist China gave military support to communist forces in the Indochina states and Burma (Myanmar) and at least propaganda and moral support to those in Singapore and Malaysia, Indonesia, and the Philippines. Western powers helped those governments that sought their assistance. For most of the postwar years, the region was divided roughly between mainland Southeast Asia, where governments leaned toward the Soviet Union and China, and maritime Southeast Asia, where countries depended for their national security on the United States and its allies. Indonesia under Sukarno (1901–1970) was an exception in island Southeast Asia, but Sukarno's policies came to an end following a coup in September 1965. Thailand, by contrast, faced both the mountains and the seas and sought U.S. assistance in order to function as the pivot of the embattled region.

This was a time of particular difficulty for new nations. None was economically independent after long periods of colonial rule, and each had plural societies that had yet to give shape to a national identity. All had concerns whether their population of Chinese ancestry would give their loyalty to the adopted homes that offered them citizenship rights. The local Chinese had been drawn into the politics of China for more than half a century, and China was now divided between a communist regime on the mainland and a nationalist one on Taiwan. With both sides seeking legitimacy and financial support among the overseas Chinese (*huaqiao*), Southeast Asian governments treated their resident Chinese with varying degrees of suspicion. For their part, most Chinese had chosen to settle down in their adopted lands, and increasing numbers of them made firm commitments to the future of the new nations. During the critical years of the 1950s, the continuing rivalry between Beijing and Taipei to win their support did not sway them and may even have persuaded many to confirm their commitments.

More significant was Communist China's policy of weaning the new Southeast Asian countries away from the former imperial powers by encouraging them to be neutralist. To this end, the Bandung Conference in 1955 was a milestone in Southeast Asian history. The communists believed that the conference advanced their cause among the neutralist countries. But those against communism were alarmed that the neutralist positions taken by the new governments would undermine their influence in the region. President Sukarno had led Indonesia on the road to neutralism, with the support of Burma and Cambodia, whereas Britain, France, and the United States and its allies Thailand and the Philippines tried to find ways to counter this trend. The Southeast Asia Treaty Organization (SEATO) was an example of an early effort to contain Communist China's reach into the region through an international alliance.

As for the overseas Chinese, the message from Premier Zhou Enlai (1898–1976) in 1955 was clear: they should settle down to become good citizens of their adopted countries. Although the rhetoric was unambiguous, there was still skepticism about China's motives and the sincerity of the overseas Chinese response. The departing colonial government and its successor in Kuala Lumpur depicted the Malayan Communist Party (MCP) as a Chinese operation fighting a jungle guerrilla war against a legitimate authority. The Indonesian military was convinced that the Partai Komunis Indonesia (PKI, Communist Party of Indonesia) was financed and supplied by its comrades in China. Thus, tensions between "sons of the soil" and "immigrant Chinese" were aggravated by China's efforts to support its revolutionary friends throughout the Malay Archipelago.

By the early 1960s, China's troubled relationship with the Soviet Union provided relief for the region. The situation had begun to split the communist forces in Asia, and with the exception of Vietnam, it reduced the pressures on the new national governments in Southeast Asia. Also helpful were the internal power struggles within the CCP itself. Matters came to a head during China's Great Proletarian Cultural Revolution from 1966 to 1976. That self-destructive series of events coincided with two major developments in the region: the U.S. intervention in the Vietnam War (1964–1975) and the abortive coup by left-wing forces in the Indonesian military. Together with China's failure to win the Vietnamese communist leaders over to its side, these events led to China's final break with the Soviet Union (ca. 1970).

China's growing diplomatic isolation gave the United States the opportunity to revamp its policy toward Mao Zedong. Although the Kissinger-Nixon initiative in 1971 to open up relations with China could not prevent U.S. failures in Vietnam, it did encourage America's allies to refocus their policies with regard to China. After the fall of Saigon in 1975, three members of the Association of Southeast Asian Nations (ASEAN), which had been formed in 1967 to defend the region from the growing communist threat, decided to establish official relations with China and cut down on their

Chinese poster from 1968 encouraging the people to "respectfully wish Chairman Mao eternal life." Mao Zedong's image dominated the landscape of Chinese life for decades.
(Stefan Landsberger)

links with the rival Republic of China in Taiwan. It was a time when the Communist Parties in their respective countries were in disarray because of the intensifying Sino-Soviet rivalry, but it was the fear of a Soviet-Vietnamese partnership to advance communism in the region that led these Southeast Asian countries to review their policies toward Communist China.

The first period thus ended with a People's Republic of China (PRC) enfeebled by the Cultural Revolution and fearful of Soviet intervention. The Chinese leaders therefore sought to make friends in Southeast Asia in order to minimize the danger of isolation and encirclement. And because the excesses of the Cultural Revolution had antagonized the majority of the Chinese overseas, most of whom had turned away from communism altogether, their adopted countries were more comfortable in establishing formal ties with China.

Following the death of Mao Zedong in 1976 and the return of Deng Xiaoping (1904–1997) two years later to introduce radical economic reforms, the region began to face a "new China" that systematically began to look outward. This was an unexpected development, and even more surprising was the speed at which the Chinese people responded to the complete change of policy direction. Some doubted whether there was a rejection of communism in favor of capitalist ways. Others focused on the role that a reformed China might play in the region. For most Southeast Asian governments, China's cooperation with ASEAN, Australia, and the United States in settling the Cambodia problem and its efforts to restrain Vietnam's control of the Indochina area were encouraging developments. All of this prepared the way for China to be invited to join the ASEAN Regional Forum. At the same time, ASEAN could move forward to invite Laos, Burma, and Cambodia to join the organization; all ten countries of Southeast Asia are now in the alliance.

The export-led East Asia model of rapid growth had made the key countries of ASEAN confident that peace and security would be better secured by bringing in partners from beyond the region. The changing mood was a cautious one. The hard facts of China's size and potential power had to be acknowledged. If China's economy continued to grow at an annual rate of over 10 percent, as it had, on average, for twenty years, the only way to avoid its future dominance over the region would be for Southeast Asia to sustain the growth of its more advanced members. No one predicted the 1997–1998 financial crisis that undermined the progress of future "tigers" such as Malaysia, Indonesia, and Thailand, just as no one expected China to come out of that crisis almost unscathed. From 1997 to 2000, China strengthened its economy while the whole region struggled to free itself from heavy debts. This fact underlined the growing importance of China. Thus, steps were taken to draw China closer to the region in order to advance the security and prosperity of a larger East Asia in which Southeast Asia would be a vital part. It is in this context that the group known as "ASEAN plus Three" (the three being China, Japan, and South Korea) held special meetings between ASEAN and China that led to talks about a free trade agreement. When that finally comes about, a new era for the region will have dawned.

WANG GUNGWU

See also Asian-African (Bandung) Conference (April 1955); Association of Southeast Asian Nations (ASEAN) (1967); Chinese in Southeast Asia; Cold War; Democratic Kampuchea (DK); Economic Development of Southeast Asia (post-1945 to ca. 1990s); Formosa (Taiwan); Gestapu Affair (1965); Indochina War (1946–1954), First; Indochina War (1964–1975), Second (Vietnam War); Kuantan Principle (1980); Malayan Communist Party (MCP); Paris Conference on Cambodia (PCC) (1989, 1991); Partai Komunis Indonesia (PKI) (1920); Peoples' Republic of Kampuchea (PRK); Sino-Soviet Struggle; Sino-Vietnamese Relations; Sino-Vietnamese Wars; Soekarno (Sukarno) (1901–1970); Southeast Asia Treaty Organization (SEATO) (1954); Suharto (1921–); United States Involvement in Southeast Asia (post-1945)

References:
Brimmell, J. H. 1959. *Communism in South East Asia: A Political Analysis.* London: Oxford University Press.
Evans, Grant, Christopher Hutton, and Kuah Khun Eng, eds. 2000. *Where China Meets Southeast Asia: Social and Cultural Change in the Border Regions.* New York and Singapore: St. Martin's Press and Institute of Southeast Asian Studies.
Fitzgerald, Stephen. 1972. *China and the Overseas Chinese: A Study of Peking's Changing Policy, 1949–1970.* Cambridge: Cambridge University Press.
Gurtov, Melvin. 1971. *China and Southeast Asia—The Politics of Survival: A Study of Foreign Policy Interaction.* Lexington, MA: Heath Lexington Books.
Simon, Sheldon. 1968. *The Broken Triangle: Peking, Djarkarta and the P.K.I.* Baltimore, MD: Johns Hopkins University Press.
Wang Gungwu. 1977. *China and the World since 1949: The Impact of Independence, Modernity and Revolution.* New York: St. Martin's Press.
———. 1991. *China and the Chinese Overseas.* Singapore: Times Academic Press.
Zheng Yongnian. 1999. *Discovering Nationalism in China: Modernization, Identity, and International Relations.* Cambridge: Cambridge University Press.

CHINDITS
"Boldest Measures Are the Safest"

The Chindit Special Forces were a group of Allied servicemen from the United Kingdom, Burma, Hong Kong, India, Nepal, West Africa, and the United States who carried out guerrilla operations behind enemy lines in Burma in 1943 and 1944. They were led and trained by Major General Orde Charles Wingate (1903–1944). Wingate's brainchild was the concept of using long-range penetration groups backed by air support, a concept demonstrated with outstanding success in his first sortie into Burma in 1943 (Operation Loincloth). The name *Chindits* was derived from the word *chinthe,* a mythical lion-beast that guarded Burmese temples. The Chindits' motto was "Boldest Measures Are the Safest."

With experience in Ethiopia and Palestine, Wingate caught the eye of the British wartime prime minister, Winston Churchill (t. 1940–1945). Churchill took Wingate and his wife to the Quebec Conference in 1943, which developed plans for the liberation of Southeast Asia under Admiral Lord Louis Mountbatten (1900–1979). An unorthodox military man who was an inspirational leader, Wingate was killed along with eight others in the crash of a U.S. Army Air Corps transport plane in India on 25 March 1944. The remains of those killed were interred in Arlington National Cemetery, Virginia, on 10 November 1950.

The son of Colonel George Wingate and Mary Ethel Stanley Wingate (née Orde Brown), Wingate married Lorna E. M. Wingate (née Moncrieff Paterson). He was a well-decorated soldier, innovative and unorthodox, and a passionate Zionist. Wingate was awarded the Distinguished Service Order (DSO) and the Lawrence of Arabia Memorial Medal.

The sabotage operations of the Chindits, supported by the U.S. Army Air Corps, the forerunner of the U.S. Air Force, are credited with having thwarted the planned Japanese invasion of India in March 1944. Echoing the U.S. Army Air Corps motto, Wingate sent the Chindits a message stating, "We will go with you boys anyplace, anytime, anywhere." With six months of training in jungle warfare and survival techniques, the Chindits were launched into history. On the night of 5 March 1944, Operation Thursday saw over 500 men and 15 tons of supplies delivered behind Japanese lines to Landing Zone Broadway by means of C-47 cargo aircraft and gliders. On the night of 7 March 1944, ninety-two planeloads of men and supplies, one every four minutes, were safely deposited in a small jungle clearing as part of the successful effort to stop the Japanese invasion of India.

At the 1943 Quebec Conference, the Allied High Command had decided to utilize Wingate's strategy and planning. Accordingly, some 10,000 Chindits, 1,000 mules, artillery, and bulldozers were flown over the 8,000-foot (2,400-meter) mountains to the Indaw area of northern Burma in support of the American and Chinese forces commanded by the U.S. general Joseph "Vinegar Joe" Stilwell (1883–1946) in a concerted operation to drive the Japanese out of Burma. A new road was to be built from Ledo in India to the "old Burma Road" near Myitkyina in Kachin State, northern Burma. In a series of daring operations from strongholds Wingate had reconnoitered in 1943, the Chindits harassed Japanese forces in the Imphal and Kohima areas and along the Mandalay-Myitkyina railway. Fighting continued through the monsoon season. After Wingate's death, Major General Walter David Alexander Lentaigne led the Chindits.

Important engagements were fought at the Myitkyina airfield in May 1944, where the Japanese general Tanaka held out for seventy-six days against 15-to-1 odds while General Stilwell flew in reinforcements. The Chindits of the Seventy-seventh Brigade attacked close to Mogaung to prevent reinforcements from reaching Tanaka. In the Indaw area, where Tanaka had hoped to overcome the Chindits' "White City" stronghold, some 200 Chindits of the Black Watch ambushed 1,200 Japanese troops to enable the successful evacuation of the White City units, in what was recognized as the largest single action of the Burma campaign. In August 1944, the last Chindit operation occurred in the Padiga hills, where the Black Watch Corps overran closely defended Japanese positions and held them against counterattacks. On 8 August 1944, the Allied forces of the Thirty-sixth Division advancing from India met up with the remaining Chindits. Losses had been heavy.

One measure of the daring and courage of the Chindits is the score of Victoria Crosses awarded by King George VI. At Taukkyan War Cemetery and Rangoon Memorial in Myanmar, and Digboi and Gauhati War Cemeteries in India, the rolls of honor to some of the fallen from the Black Watch bespeak the lost youth of these daring commandos, most of whom were in their early twenties. Their exploits are commemorated at the Chindit Special Forces Memorial at the Westminster Embankment in London.

HELEN JAMES

See also Burma during the Pacific War (1941–1945); Burma Road; Force 136; Imphal-Kohima, Battle of (1944); Mountbatten, Admiral Lord Louis (1900–1979); Services Reconnaissance Department (SRD); South-East Asia Command (SEAC)

References:
Calvert, Michael. 1974. *Chindits: Long-Range Penetration*. London: Pan Books.
O'Brien, Terence. 1984. *Out of the Blue: A Pilot with the Chindits*. London: Collins.
Rooney, David. 1994. *Wingate and the Chindits: Redressing the Balance*. London: Arms and Armour.

CHINESE DIALECT GROUPS

Although the Chinese in Southeast Asia came mainly from the southeastern provinces of Guangdong (Kwangtung) and Fujian (Fukien), the immigrants originated from various districts within the provinces where the spoken languages were distinctly different from one another. The major dialect groups include the Hokkien, Cantonese, Teochew (Teochiu), and Hakka (Kheh). Other smaller speech groups are the Foochow (Hock Chiu), Hainanese (Hailam), and Henghua. There are also pockets of northern Chinese dialect groups from Tianjin (Tientsin) and Shandong (Shantung) and natives from Shanghai. Moreover, within each dialect, there are further divisions based on geographic origins, with slight variants in speech patterns. The Hakka, for instance, are differentiated into Taipu, Kaying, Hopo, and other groups. Interestingly, though Hokkien and Teochew dialects might share some similarities, Hakka is as unintelligible to a Foochow speaker as Dutch is to an Italian speaker.

The various dialect groups also harbored traditional animosity toward one another, which accompanied the immigrants to Southeast Asia; there, the strained relations might even be aggravated due to rivalry over economic activities. During the mid-nineteenth century, for instance, there was intense Hokkien-Cantonese rivalry over the control of the tin-mining industry in the peninsular Western Malay States. Consequently, business partnerships and also marriages across dialect lines were unknown and unacceptable during the prewar (pre-1941) period.

Chinese immigration to Southeast Asia occurred in trickles for several centuries. However, from the mid-nineteenth century, there was a mass exodus of people from southeastern Chinese provinces, most of them going to the *Nanyang* (Southeast Asia) and to areas such as North America, the Caribbean, South Africa, and Australia. Although earlier immigration involved traders and merchants mainly from the Hokkien and Teochew dialect groups, those in the mass migration that began in the 1840s were generally of peasant coolie stock and largely of Cantonese and Hakka origins.

Within Chinese communities throughout Southeast Asia, the various dialect groups are represented, but in certain localities and occupational niches, a particular dialect group predominates. In general, mercantile communities of Hokkien and Teochew tend to predominate in urban centers such as Rangoon (Yangon), Bangkok, Saigon-Cholon (Hồ Chí Minh City), Singapore, Penang, Surabaya, Kuching, and Manila. Mining areas such as those in the Malay Peninsula (West Malaysia) and southwestern Borneo (Kalimantan Indonesia) have a high density of Cantonese and Hakka communities.

The widespread use of vernacular Mandarin in Chinese schools throughout Southeast Asia after the May Fourth Movement (1919) gradually closed the dialect cleavage. Furthermore, the assimilation of Chinese minorities within the dominant indigenous host population in Myanmar (Burma), Thailand, Cambodia, Laos, Vietnam, Indonesia, and the Philippines diminished the usage and importance of dialects among these Chinese communities.

OOI KEAT GIN

See also Chinese in Southeast Asia; Education, Overseas Chinese; *Kongsi*

References:
Heidhues, Mary F. Somers. 1974. *Southeast Asia's Chinese Minorities*. Hawthorne, Australia: Longman.

Mak Lau Fong. 1995. *The Dynamics of Chinese Dialect Groups in Early Malaya*. Monograph no. 1. Singapore: Singapore Society of Asian Studies.

Purcell, Victor. 1965. *The Chinese in Southeast Asia*. 2nd ed. London: Oxford University Press.

Tan, Thomas T. W., ed. 1990. *Chinese Dialect Groups: Traits and Trades*. Singapore: Opinion Books.

CHINESE GOLD-MINING COMMUNITIES IN WESTERN BORNEO

Independent Chinese gold-mining communities existed from the mid-eighteenth century until 1884 in northwestern Borneo. Often described as democracies or republics, they demonstrated many attributes of a modern state—minting coins, dispensing justice, maintaining communications and public security, using religious traditions to cement mutual loyalties, and so forth. The Dutch saw these communities as states within the (colonial) state and determined to eliminate them.

The island of Borneo had widespread but not rich gold deposits. For centuries, local people had worked the gold as a sideline to hunting and agriculture, trading the gold dust they panned from rivers and streams to their rulers or using it to pay tribute. In the eighteenth century, however, Chinese miners, probably invited by the Malay rulers of Sambas and Mempawah, began mining gold. The immigrants worked in well-organized groups called *kongsis,* sharing the labor, electing a boss from among their number, and dividing the profits after the cost of food, supplies, and other items was deducted. They used simple machines, opened larger sites, and worked more continuously than the native people. The rulers expected to see their revenues increase.

The kongsis of Borneo soon grew larger and more powerful, and they escaped the control of the Malay rulers. They joined together into federated groups, partly for self-defense in a hostile environment. By the early nineteenth century, there were three federations, as well as a number of smaller, independent operations. The big three were the Fosjoen (*heshun*) Kongsi in Monterado, whose most important member

organization was the Thaikong (Malay, *dagang*) Kongsi; the Samtiaokioe (*santiaogou*) Kongsi, which was part of Fosjoen but in 1819 quarreled with Thaikong and moved north (Thaikong and Samtiaokioe remained enemies); and the Lanfang (*lanfang*) Kongsi in Mandor, not far from Pontianak.

If the small miners' kongsis were nominally democratic, the large kongsis were often under the influence of those who provided capital for mining. Only if new immigrants came from China and money was available for provisions could they continue to operate. Although Thaikong elected its headmen regularly and submitted policies to a vote of the miners, Lanfang had a fairly autocratic structure, especially after its peace with the Dutch in 1823, depending in its final years on the headman himself.

By the early nineteenth century, quarrels were common. Decades of mining had depleted many deposits, and miners fought over good sites and/or water supplies. They also quarreled with the Malay rulers, refusing to pay tribute to them. When the Dutch tried to establish their authority in the area after 1818, levying taxes on the miners, more conflicts ensued. As a result, the three so-called Kongsi Wars broke out from 1822 to 1824, 1850 to 1854, and 1884 to 1885.

In the first war, the Dutch managed to subdue Lanfang. They would ratify its choice of headman, and the kongsi promised to pay taxes regularly. They cowed Thaikong into submission as well (but only temporarily) and soon withdrew most of the colonial troops from the region.

In 1850, the Dutch took on the kongsis again, partly because they feared that Raja James Brooke in Sarawak would utilize the unrest to extend his influence into what they regarded as their territory. After a series of incidents involving tax evasion and smuggling, the Dutch took the side of the Samtiaokioe Kongsi against Thaikong and its smaller allies. They were determined to eliminate Thaikong and establish direct rule over the Chinese in the kongsis. Attacked by strong Thaikong forces, most Samtiaokioe people fled to Bau in Sarawak, effectively removing that kongsi from Dutch territory. The Dutch finally took Monterado in 1853 and declared Thaikong disbanded, although resistance continued for some months.

Because its headman maintained good relations with the Dutch, the Lanfang Kongsi survived until his death in 1884. Then, Lanfang was dissolved, eliminating the last independent Chinese community. Nevertheless, some kongsi elements resisted, and troops had to be sent in from Java to put down the resistance.

Thaikong and Lanfang had been heavily indebted, and their mines were depleted. Former miners and their descendants were turning to agriculture; many migrated to the coast. Others moved inland, seeking new gold sites. From the late nineteenth century, Chinese also went up-country to trade with the indigenous Dayak people. The former kongsi territories, called the "Chinese Districts" in colonial times, had a large, rural Chinese population until 1967, when Chinese villagers and farmers were driven from the area in a violent attack by Dayaks organized by the Indonesian military. They were accused of supporting procommunist and anti-Malaysia guerrillas in West Kalimantan, as the province is known to Indonesians. The Chinese population, over 350,000 (or about 10 percent of the total), is now concentrated along the coast and in larger towns (Suryadinata, Arifin, and Ananta 2003: 81).

MARY SOMERS HEIDHUES

See also Borneo; Brooke, James, and Sarawak; Dutch Borneo; Dutch Interests in Southeast Asia from 1800; Gold; *Hui; Kongsi;* Sambas and Pontianak Sultanates

References:

Heidhues, Mary Somers. 2003. *Gold Diggers, Farmers, and Traders in Pontianak and the "Chinese Districts" of West Kalimantan, Indonesia.* Ithaca, NY: Cornell University Southeast Asia Program.

Jackson, James C. 1970. *The Chinese in the West Borneo Goldfields: A Study in Cultural Geography.* Occasional Papers in Geography no. 15. Hull, England: University of Hull Publications.

Suryadinata, Leo, Evi Nurvidya Arifin, and Aris Ananta. 2003. *Indonesia's Population: Ethnicity and Religion in a Changing Political Landscape.* Singapore: Institute of Southeast Asian Studies.

Yuan Bingling. 2000. *Chinese Democracies: A Study of the Kongsis of West Borneo (1776–1884).* Leiden, The Netherlands: Research School of Asian, African, and Amerindian Studies, Universiteit Leiden.

CHINESE IN SOUTHEAST ASIA

The Chinese in Southeast Asia were known as *huaqiao,* or Chinese sojourners, until the 1950s because most of them were Chinese nationals living temporarily in foreign countries. Today, these Chinese are a minority, for most Chinese abroad have become nationals of the countries in which they now live. The common estimate is that there are 25 million *haiwai huaren,* or Chinese overseas, spread around the world, and about three-quarters of them live in Southeast Asia.

The 20 million domiciled in Southeast Asia include a great variety of people, but most of them are second- or third-generation local citizens and nationals, and many are only partly Chinese. In countries such as Thailand, the Indochinese states, Myanmar, the Philippines, and Indonesia, there are also many of Chinese ancestry who no longer identify themselves as Chinese. Thus, only the census figures from Singapore, Brunei, and Malaysia are relatively accurate.

China was an importer of immigrants until the Song dynasty (960–1276 C.E.), when records show that small numbers of Chinese trading overseas settled there and did not return to their homeland. These numbers grew slowly during the Ming dynasty (1368–1644), and after the sixteenth century, the Chinese merchants also took artisans and peasant workers with them. But it was not until the middle of the nineteenth century that large-scale emigration from China occurred.

That emigration was related to the growth in China's population in the coastal provinces, where people had access to the sea. The first rapid growth in South China had begun in the tenth to thirteenth centuries, and this accelerated during the fifteenth and sixteenth centuries. When the Manchu Qing dynasty (1644–1912) brought a century of peace to the empire during the 1700s, the total population reached nearly 400 million. Increasingly, the search for agricultural land or urban employment led to massive internal migrations. In addition, many of the migrations were forced on the people by war and by floods, droughts, locusts, and other natural disasters. It is difficult to calculate how many were actually involved, as these people movements happened under turbulent conditions and records were not properly kept. There is little doubt, however, that millions of people moved from their homes during every major dynastic change in Chinese history. Yet few ventured beyond the natural boundaries along the coasts.

These few were largely merchants who traveled around the empire in search of business and also reached out to overseas markets. Theirs was always a precarious profession, and only those who saw good profits and were willing to take great risks would leave the country to trade abroad. In addition, there were, from the beginning, official restrictions about who could or could not trade with foreigners. Furthermore, both family and community were disapproving of long absences from home that could end in the itinerants never returning.

The rise in the numbers of such merchants often resulted in some disorder at the ports, and security concerns led to an imperial monopoly of foreign overseas trade after 1368 that was to last for nearly two hundred years. In this period, although it was impossible to stop the trade altogether, private trading overseas was prohibited. When the Europeans arrived on the China coast, the ban was replaced by specific controls designed to regulate the number of Chinese traders. The Europeans found Chinese traders ready to cooperate with them, and they opened up many trading centers to which the Chinese were made welcome. By the seventeenth century, this situation had led to the amassing of Chinese ships and sailors who not only supported commercial activities but also established merchant fleets to compete with the Europeans. The most notable were those of the Zheng family—the family of the famous Zheng Chenggong (1624–1662) (Koxinga). The Zheng fleets were strong enough to delay the Manchu conquest of the coastal province of Fujian and able to harass the Qing armies for several decades after 1644.

Ultimately, the Qing rulers restored controls over foreign trade along the coasts and inhibited the Chinese traders' freedom to travel abroad. It was not until the nineteenth century, when the Qing empire was poorer and much weakened, that Chinese people left the country in large numbers to find work in distant lands. This new phenomenon of emigration marked the beginning of agrarian China's response to the Industrial Revolution in Europe. The Qing emperors were slow to realize what this involved, but a series of defeats, from the 1840–1842 Opium War to the 1894–1895 Sino-Japanese War, made it inevitable that China would have to join the race for modernization in order to survive.

All migrations involve pull or push factors. China experienced some of the cruelest forms of both during the nineteenth century. War and famine within the country drove many abroad, and the dire need for cheap labor in the newly industrializing powers opened up opportunities for China's poor. Thousands of coolies were transported around the world, including Southeast Asia. This emigration offered life and hope, and the Chinese met the challenge with a fortitude and enterprise that confounded their own governments and elites back in China. Their story is closely linked to the responses the sojourners made to the conditions they found abroad. The experiences that led many of them to decide to settle and not return to China shaped the kinds of communities they established. This in turn determined the future they hoped their descendants would have in their adopted countries.

The earliest of the Chinese who settled in Southeast Asia were assimilated over time and are no longer identifiable as Chinese. They were descended mainly from individuals who had traded there before the sixteenth century. After that, however, those sailing to Southeast Asia developed a regular sojourning pattern. As merchants and merchants' workers, they used their distinctive family, religious, and other customary ties at home to ensure that their small communities survived in foreign lands. Many Chinese men did marry local women and raise their families abroad, but sojourning remained the pattern, underlining the idea that the settlements were meant to be temporary.

After the middle of the nineteenth century, large numbers of urban and rural laborers were transported to work in mines and plantations. Most of them worked hard to save enough money to return home. Many, however, sojourned for longer periods. In this way, they strengthened the resistance to assimilation among those who had chosen to settle. By the beginning of the twentieth century, new waves of such sojourners followed. They included not only single women sent out to marry the men overseas but also families of women and children. In addition, there were educated teachers, journalists, students, and political refugees. Many of these individuals had communication and organizational skills that connected the emergent communities with a modernizing China.

Thus, the new sojourners of the early twentieth century carried with them changing political and cultural values from China—values that influenced the way Southeast Asian Chinese responded to new economic opportunities both within China and in their host countries. The successful ones relied on the economic roles they could play in relations with China. They saw that if they performed such roles successfully, they could ensure a continued political, social, and cultural position among the people they had chosen to live with. In regions where ports and cities traded closely with China, the importance of Chinese residents for the region's commercial success was more obvious, confirming how key China's proximity to the region had always been.

With a few exceptions, it had long been a habit of mind among sojourning Chinese to treat every place outside China as only a temporary home. This changed after World War II (1939–1945). From the 1960s, the majority of Chinese abroad decided to settle down permanently and accept foreign citizenship and nationality. Their integration into local societies has been marked by great progress ever since. Nevertheless, sojourning remains an option because education and travel today have contributed to the notion that settlement is no obstacle to regular contacts with China and Chinese communities anywhere in the world. Distance means much less than it used to now that facsimiles, diskettes, videos, e-mail, and other forms of modern communications are available. Given their trading origins, the sojourners cannot resist the immense business opportunities that such communications equipment can provide.

The sojourning tradition is still strong among the small and newer communities that were formed during the twentieth century. Although prone to assimilate or remigrate if their populations are not augmented by new immigration, the Chinese in these communities use their trading skills to sustain themselves. Most of them steer clear of political activity and, for their social and cultural life, depend on new technologies to reduce the distances between them and similar communities elsewhere. The recent economic transformation of Hong Kong, Taiwan, and then the mainland has made it possible for these communities, however small, to expand their trading role and strengthen their links with people in China.

The sojourner mentality is not simply the product of mere convenience and profit. It has deep roots in Chinese culture. It used to tie the Chinese intimately with their home villages or towns, their ancestral graves, and their extensive kinship connections. Sojourning today still draws strength from family relationships, but it has a more diffuse sense of Chinese identity. Thus, the Chinese who go abroad now are attracted to countries where there is less pressure to assimilate and where the laws protect minorities.

In an era of expanded global relationships, many of the Chinese communities around the world are now less likely to develop in isolation. The Southeast Asian Chinese are no exception. As they become more articulate and confident, this ability to keep in regular contact could lead them in several different directions. At one end of the spectrum, the political leaders in China might ask them to emphasize their Chinese identities and welcome them back to China. At the other, the settled communities might choose to give their total loyalty to their adopted homelands, the ten countries of the Association of Southeast Asian Nations (ASEAN). Between these extremes will be many positions along the spectrum, determined largely by local needs, the possibilities of remigration, and the place of China in the people's lives.

Unlike their predecessors in the nineteenth century and the first half of the twentieth, recent Chinese emigrants are primarily from the business and professional classes. Attracting most attention are the Chinese entrepreneurs who have adapted fully to the globalized world. Their achievements are remarkable because they come from a society where merchants did not have any place in the power and status structures. Traditionally, the merchants' wealth depended on official favor and was never secure. They invested their fortunes in land and property and sought respectability by giving away significant sums of money to support charities or show their appreciation of Chinese culture. If they were lucky, their sons would be able to choose either to follow in their footsteps or to study for the imperial examinations to become scholar officials.

Outside China, such merchants succeeded without the support of their government. They depended instead on their own daring, their skills, and, most of all, their entrepreneurship. For this, they needed a keen understanding of the power relationships in the country they lived in and a readiness to link up with the power that foreign rulers wielded in order to achieve their commercial ends. They learned how to be wealthy without seeking political power. This was a lesson reinforced by what they had already learned before leaving China. The conditioning they had received served them in good stead. By not seeking power, they were more acceptable to regimes that wanted them to help produce wealth for their lands. They thus laid the foundations that enabled later arrivals to succeed in commerce and industry.

Most Chinese in the region today aspire to hone their entrepreneurial and professional skills. They appreciate having the freedom to earn while living their own lives and becoming accepted in their adopted country. They can still promote trading and financial relations with enterprises in China. Some also send funds to their ancestral homes in China in order to build schools and clan temples, to support relatives, and even to help family members in local construction and housing ventures. This represents a symbolic return through philanthropic duty and proxy investments. Many maintain their obligations to relatives in China, and they keep the links alive to enable their families abroad to stay culturally Chinese.

The Chinese understand local power systems and national cultures, and they have learned to work effectively in such environments. They do not have to be totally assimilated to local cultures or neglect their links with other Chinese. Furthermore, Chinese values concerning business methods and responsibilities continue to be helpful. Young Chinese with modern educations are well attuned to the needs of business organizations and are better oriented than their predecessors to help their adopted countries develop

economically. Also, many governments have recognized the advantages of allowing the Chinese to use their own business connections and methods, which have proven invaluable for maintaining the extensive networks that Chinese entrepreneurs now control.

Entrepreneurs of Chinese descent have found it profitable—and in the host country's interests—to promote trade and investment in the economies of China, Taiwan, and Hong Kong. In this way, they demonstrate the value of cultural links. The bridges they are able to build between their adopted countries and the three Chinese territories have been fortified by their familiarity with Chinese values and commercial ways. There are signs now that an increasing number of such entrepreneurs are consciously playing a role in this process and that local nationalist leaders have come to accept that these entrepreneurs may prove invaluable to peace and prosperity in the region.

Chinese entrepreneurs have shown that they can adapt business skills to modern political and cultural changes. They understand how significant cultural factors are in their commercial and industrial enterprises, as well as in their dealings with other entrepreneurs and with powerful officials everywhere. Some exercise a wide range of options in a larger trading framework and a more open international system. The world has grown smaller, and the role of these entrepreneurs in helping to strengthen such economies has become potentially important. No study of the Chinese overseas can afford to neglect this phenomenon.

The importance of these Chinese for Southeast Asia is linked to changes in Greater China—that is, the Chinese mainland, Hong Kong–Macau, and Taiwan. Since Deng Xiaoping (1904–1997) implemented his reforms, the commitment to China's economic growth has been surprisingly successful. That growth has highlighted the need for Southeast Asia to be more competitive to prevent it from falling behind China's new centers of dynamism and entrepreneurship.

The Chinese in Southeast Asia have a role to play in this competitive struggle. They have come a long way, from adventurous merchants and desperate laborers to successful and respected sojourners and from new citizens of foreign nations to global entrepreneurs. Today, their networks centered on Asia and spreading toward the West have caught the imagination of business communities everywhere. The links these networks have with China have often intertwined both with their ties to their adopted homes and with their new national loyalties. This process has made the modern overseas Chinese multifaceted and complex: old stereotypes cannot be sustained. Perhaps the most important features that distinguish them from their predecessors are their dependence on the goodwill of their respective host nation-states and their readiness to serve the national interests of these countries. They also possess a sophisticated understanding of modern technology and an ability to skillfully use the international marketing system.

WANG GUNGWU

See also Baba Nyonya; Bangkok; Batavia (Sunda Kelapa, Jacatra, Djakarta/Jakarta); China, Imperial; China, Nationalist; China since 1949; Chinese Dialect Groups; Chinese Gold-Mining Communities of Western Borneo; Economic Development of Southeast Asia (Post-1945 to Early 2000s); Economic History of Early Modern Southeast Asia (Pre-Sixteenth Century); Economic Transformation of Southeast Asia (ca. 1400–ca. 1800); Education, Overseas Chinese; Education, Western Secular; Hong Kong; Macau (Macao); Malayan/Malaysian Chinese Association (MCA) (1949); Manila; Ming Dynasty (1368–1644); Miscegenation; Penang (1786); Peranakan; Qing (Ch'ing/Manchu) Dynasty (1644–1912); Saigon (Gia Dinh; Hồ Chí Minh City); Singapore (1819); Straits Settlements (1826–1941); Yunnan Province

References:

Cushman, Jennifer, and Wang Gungwu, eds. 1988. *Changing Identities of the Southeast Asian Chinese since World War II.* Hong Kong: University of Hong Kong Press.

Lim, Linda Y. C., and L. A. Peter Gosling, eds. 1983. *The Chinese in Southeast Asia.* Vol. 1, *Ethnicity and Economic Activity;* Vol. 2, *Identity, Culture and Politics.* Singapore: Maruzen Asia.

Pan, Lynn, ed. 1999. *Encyclopedia of the Chinese Overseas.* Cambridge, MA: Harvard University Press.

Purcell, Victor. 1965. *The Chinese in Southeast Asia.* Rev. ed. London: Oxford University Press.

Reid, Anthony, ed. 2000 [1996]. *Sojourners and Settlers: Histories of Southeast Asia and the Chinese.* Honolulu: University of Hawai'i Press. First published in 1996 by Asian Studies Association of Australia with Allen & Unwin, St. Leonards, Australia.

Skinner, William G., ed. 1979. *The Study of Chinese Society: Essays by Maurice Freedman.* Stanford, CA: Stanford University Press.

Suryadinata, Leo, ed. 1989. *The Ethnic Chinese in the ASEAN States: Bibliographical Essays.* Singapore: Institute of Southeast Asian Studies.

———. 1997. *Ethnic Chinese as Southeast Asians.* Singapore and London: Institute of Southeast Asian Studies.

Wang Gungwu. 1991. *China and the Chinese Overseas.* Singapore: Times Academic Press.

———. 2000. *The Chinese Overseas: From Earthbound China to the Quest for Autonomy.* Cambridge, MA: Harvard University Press.

CHINESE REVOLUTION (1911)

The Chinese Revolution of 1911 was the culmination of a decade-long endeavor aimed at overthrowing the Manchu dynasty in China. It achieved its purpose after a successful uprising in Wuchang, Central China, in October 1911. For the numerous uprisings that took place in the interim, Southeast Asia played an important role as a logistical base, where support in various forms was provided by Chinese sojourners there.

After China's defeat in the Arrow War (1856–1860), the Manchu court introduced some Western-style reforms to improve China's material strength. Unfortunately, such reforms, implemented beginning in the 1860s, could not prevent another Chinese defeat in a foreign war (the 1894–1895 Sino-Japanese War), this time by a former tributary state, Japan. The impotency of China in combating a small and presumably less advanced Asian country convinced some Chinese intellectuals that overthrowing the alien regime of the Manchu dynasty by force was the only alternative available to save China. Province-based revolutionary organizations thus sprang up, and small-scale rebellions occurred all over the empire.

Among the various revolutionaries, Sun Yat-sen (1866–1925) soon earned greater credit than others, both for his efforts in shaping a modern Chinese revolutionary ideology and especially for his perseverance in spreading the principles to the overseas Chinese (*huaqiao*) communities and seeking support from them. The revolutionary ideology that Sun propagated was known as *Sanmin Zhuyi* (Three Principles of the People): nationalism, democracy, and people's livelihood. Although all the uprisings planned by Sun broke out in South China, most of them were planned and organized abroad. He formed his first revolutionary body, the Xingzhonghui (Revive China Society), in Honolulu in 1895. The Tongmenghui (Chinese United League), a union of several revolutionary bodies that were organized along the lines of Xingzhonghui, was founded in Japan in 1905. Japan, a popular destination for overseas Chinese students, was made into an important center for training revolutionary cadres, and Southeast Asia gradually gained momentum as a revolutionary base for soliciting material support for the uprisings. Before 1900, there was no trace of revolutionary activity among the Chinese sojourners there, who were then under the strong influence of the royalist reformists, notably Kang Youwei (1858–1927). But in the 1900s, the efforts to spread revolutionary ideas by Sun and his colleagues, particularly Wang Lie (1866–1936), provided a kind of alternative patriotism, attracting the admiration and support of prominent local Chinese leaders such as Teo Eng Hock (1871–1957), Tan Chor Nam (1884–1971), Lim Nee Soon (1879–1936), and others.

Led by Tongmenghui branches in Indochina, such local Chinese made remarkable contributions to the ultimate success of the Chinese Revolution in many ways. They turned Southeast Asia—and Singapore in particular—into a center of propaganda, which worked closely with Tongmenghui branches in Hong Kong and Japan. Singapore actually served as the revolutionary headquarters from 1906 to 1911, when nearly all revolts in South China were planned there. Papers such as *Thoe Lam Jit Poh* and *The Chong Shing Press* were published as the revolutionary organs. Penang was another planning base, as well as a site for fund collection and the publication of revolutionary literature. Participants of uprisings in the Chinese mainland, after being suppressed, fled to Southeast Asia to seek refuge. The Tongmenghui branches in Indochina rendered indis-

pensable financial resources, usually comprising handsome donations from local Chinese sojourners, for the funding of such Chinese uprisings.

Bordering three Chinese provinces—Guangdong, Guangxi, and Yunnan—Vietnam was the only Southeast Asian territory that was directly involved in the operation-level preparations of the uprisings, primarily in the shipment of arms and ammunitions. Hanoi and Haiphong were two transshipment points. Ammunitions were shipped to China either across the Sino-Vietnamese border or via Hong Kong by commercial liners. The geographic advantage of South China, making it a convenient location for receiving such military supplies, partially explained why Sun chose it as the field for all ten of his major uprisings.

Chinese sojourners in Southeast Asia did not only act behind the scenes in the revolution. They also took part physically in the uprisings. For example, in the Guangzhou Uprising in April 1911 (the largest rebellion before the successful Wuchang Uprising), about one-third of the famous "Seventy-Two Martyrs" executed by the local Manchu authorities after the uprising failed were identified as Chinese revolutionaries from Southeast Asia.

Strictly speaking, the success of the 1911 Chinese Revolution was limited. Although it succeeded in overthrowing the Manchu dynasty and replacing the monarchy with a republic, the urgent need to avoid a potential civil war induced Sun to make a political compromise by shifting the presidency to Yuan Shikai (1859–1916). A prominent ex-Qing official and commander of a modern army, Yuan was regarded, especially by the foreign diplomats, as the only person capable of controlling the anarchic situation following the collapse of the Qing. However, this decision sowed the seeds of political struggle in the post-Qing era, as Yuan, a monarchist instead of a republican, used his presidency (1912–1916) in an attempt to restore the monarchy. His efforts to establish a new dynasty, with himself as the new "Son of Heaven," were strongly opposed by the Kuomintang (KMT, Nationalist Party), the successor to the Tongmenghui.

In his struggle against Yuan and the subsequent warlords, Sun implemented what he had learned from his previous revolutionary experiences in seeking support from the overseas

Chinese, who were acclaimed by him as "the Mother[s] of the Chinese Revolution." In turn, the Chinese people, both from the mainland and from overseas, proclaimed Sun "the Father of Modern China."

HANS W. Y. YEUNG

See also Education, Overseas Chinese; Hong Kong; Kuomintang (KMT); Newspapers and Mass Media in Southeast Asia; Penang (1786); Qing (Ching/Manchu) Dynasty (1644–1912); Singapore (1819); Sun Yat-sen, Dr. (1866–1925); Vietnam under French Colonial Rule

References:
Fairbank, John K., and Kwang-Ching Liu. 1980. *The Cambridge History of China: Late Ching, 1800–1911.* Vols. 10 and 11. Cambridge: Cambridge University Press.
Spence, Jonathan D. 1999. *The Search for Modern China.* 2nd ed. New York: Norton.
Yen Ching-hwang. 1976. *The Overseas Chinese and the 1911 Revolution, with Special Reference to Singapore and Malaya.* Kuala Lumpur: Oxford University Press.
Zhongguo Shehui Kexueyuan Jindaishi Yanjiusuo Jindaishi Ziliao Bianjizu, ed. 1981. *Huaqiao yu Xinhai geming* [*Overseas Chinese and the 1911 revolution*]. Beijing: Zhongguo Shehui Kexueyuan.

CHINESE TRIBUTE SYSTEM

The rhetoric and rituals of the Chinese emperor receiving tribute from a lesser ruler were rooted in the political structure of China from ancient times. This idea of the less powerful paying tribute to superior rulers was common to all known interstate relations in some form, but the Chinese developed it to its fullest extent for the longest period of time. After a unified empire was established in 220 B.C.E., the Chinese extended what had originally been feudal obeisance within the country into a tribute system that was applied to all others who wanted relations with China. Thus, the system reached well beyond Chinese boundaries and ultimately became one that was more elaborately evolved than all other tributary practices. With occasional breaks when China was weak and in disorder, the system was maintained for over twenty-five hundred years. And because of the relative accuracy of Chinese records from the Han dynasty (206 B.C.E.– 220 C.E.) to the Qing dynasty (1644–1912), the uses and refinements of the system are well documented. In fact, over the centuries down to the Ming dynasty (1368–1644), its institutions grew increasingly sophisticated, and the rationale for the system became better defined. It was so impressive and dominant by the fifteenth century that it has led to the idea that the system had been the basis for a Chinese "world order."

The tributary system may have been used mainly as an instrument of defense and diplomacy in China's overland relations. But, where Southeast Asia was concerned, it functioned more as a regulator of foreign trade. The controversy as to whether the system was more adapted for political purposes or for commercial purposes has been difficult to resolve. This is because tribute and trade were, in Chinese eyes, inseparable for so long that much of the documentation is ambivalent on this point. It was clearly a flexible institution that could be adapted to defense and diplomatic use when needed and be made to serve commercial ends if it was in the interest of the empire to do so.

The countries of Southeast Asia posed no serious military threat to the Chinese rulers, so the defense function was precautionary and rarely needed in that context. For the first thousand years, until the tenth century, the Chinese utilized tribute to manage border relations with the kingdom of Linyi and its successor state, Champa. The latter, at the peak of its power, covered the territory between the counties north of Hue and ports east of the Mekong Delta. Similarly, the tribute system was applicable to the kingdoms of Funan and Zhenla (modern Cambodia and southern Vietnam). During the Song dynasty (960–1279), a unique relationship was developed with the independent kingdom of Vietnam. This area was carved out of colonial territory that had been administered by Chinese and local commanders and mandarins since the Han dynasty. Unlike all others in the region, tribute from Vietnam was regular and primarily political. The Vietnamese rulers saw this special relationship as essential to their sovereignty and adapted the Chinese rhetoric to serve their own purposes. To that extent, Vietnamese tribute served a Chinese political order.

For the rest of Southeast Asia, however, trading and cultural relations were the key features of the tributary records kept by the Chinese. These were desultory during the Han and the Jin dynasties (from 2 to 420 C.E.). But following the establishment of the southern kingdom of Liu Song in 420 C.E., tributary records for the region were more systematic. This change had been stimulated by the role of Buddhism in the Chinese courts, by the need for Chinese and Vietnamese monks to get to India via the Buddhist kingdoms in the region, and by the growing market for incense and spices that came with the advent of the Buddhist connection. From then until the end of the Tang dynasty (618–906), regional trade from port cities and kingdoms on the western side of the South China Sea, mostly carried by Indian, Persian, and Arab merchants, was largely conducted through tribute missions. The tribute missions from various parts of the region during the seventh century marked one of the most prosperous periods of the *Nanhai* (or *Nanyang*, referring to Southeast Asia) trade. In the early eighth century, this led to the establishment in Guangzhou (Canton) of the office of superintendent of the shipping trade. In this way, the close links between tribute and trade where Southeast Asia was concerned were confirmed.

This kind of tribute-trade was intended to protect the foreign traders, whether they led or accompanied the missions, from rapacious Chinese officials. It also helped to ensure that, after the tributary goods were accounted for, the actual trade conducted between Chinese and foreign merchants yielded revenues for the emperor. However, the system was in the hands of protocol officials from the court who were given special powers, and they often harassed the traders on both sides. Thus, despite the practice of tribute, foreign trade at the ports was disrupted from time to time. This was particularly true after Tang imperial control was weakened beginning in the latter half of the eighth century. After 758 C.E., when the city of Guangzhou was sacked by Persian and Arab merchants, fewer tribute missions arrived. Private trading became more common over the next two hundred years.

The records on the tributary system during the decades of division in the tenth century are not well preserved, but in that period, the system was focused much more on trade than on defense. South China had freed itself from the imperial courts of the Five dynasties (907–960).

The independent kingdoms in Fujian, Guangdong, and Vietnam conducted their own relations with Southeast Asia. In particular, the Nan Han based on Guangzhou and the Min in Fuzhou encouraged overseas trade. The extent to which these kingdoms used the tribute system is not clear because their histories were written later from the records of the Song dynasty. It is likely that after Song Taizu (r. 960–976) conquered South China, references to tribute to these lesser kingdoms did not survive.

The Song (Sung) dynasty (960–1279) reaffirmed many Tang practices. Tribute missions from Southeast Asia arrived regularly, but the unified empire that was not fearful of the kingdoms to its south encouraged foreign trade and opened a new era for tributary trade. The rise of maritime commercial empires, such as Śrivijaya, that benefited from good diplomatic relations with the Song rulers was a major factor in the growing numbers of Chinese traders who were commercially active in Southeast Asia. They did not wait for official missions but financed their own shipping to sail to the coasts of Indochina, Siam (Thailand), the Malay Peninsula, and the island world of Java and Sumatra.

During the next two centuries, private overseas trade expanded at the expense of tribute. Song China was militarily on the defensive in the north and spent most of its imperial revenues pacifying enemies such as the Khitan Liao dynasty (907–1125) and then the Jurchen Jin dynasty (1115–1234). The latter drove the Song court out of its capital in Kaifeng in North China, forcing it to seek shelter in Hangzhou. The Song court was also cut off from the overland trade with the West by the Tangut Xi Xia kingdom (1032–1227). In this critical condition, the authority to insist on tribute was considerably weakened. As tribute became less relevant, Chinese traders were encouraged to venture out to sea and tap the markets of Southeast Asia themselves. Although official protocol remained in place where tribute missions were concerned, revenues derived from foreign trade had become significant. By the early thirteenth century, when the *Record of Foreign Nations* (*Zhufan zhi*) by Zhao Rugua (Chao Ju-kua) was compiled, the interaction among Chinese and Muslim traders became a vital part of the Southern Song (1127–1279) economy. It is interesting to observe that when the Chinese Empire really needed overseas trade, tribute was set aside.

Even more interesting was what the Mongols (the Yuan dynasty, 1279–1368) did with the tributary system after conquering the Song. They adapted it to their own vision of world conquest, in which tribute represented submission to a great power. Trade would continue to be important, but that could be left in private hands, including the foreign traders who regularly arrived on China's southern shores. Thus, the system was revived without reference to trade but employed to assert political power in the region. The rulers of kingdoms in Vietnam, Champa, Burma (Myanmar), and later Java were deemed not to have shown sufficient respect to the Mongol emperors. Therefore, expeditionary forces were sent to destroy them. Trade might have been affected because Chinese vessels were gathered to support the naval expeditions, but foreign merchants from the Indian Ocean retained their share of the China trade.

The Mongols reinterpreted the Chinese traditional tributary system in this way for nearly a century, which would have its effect on the Ming dynasty (1368–1644) that followed. Although the Ming founder Zhu Yuanzhang (Emperor Hongwu, r. 1368–1398) claimed to have returned to the institutions of the Han and Tang dynasties when he ousted the Mongols and restored China to Chinese rule, his adoption of a formal tributary trade system was unique. It was quite different in spirit not only from that of the Han and Tang but also from that of his Song and Yuan predecessors. In his struggle to gain imperial power, he encountered challenges from rivals whose power was based, to some extent, on the thriving maritime trade, including that with venturesome Japanese operating close to the Yangzi Delta and along the southern coasts. This experience confirmed him in his belief that it was not in the empire's interest to have much to do with maritime kingdoms. On coming to the throne, he therefore decreed that no more private overseas trade would be permitted.

From the end of the fourteenth century to the middle of the sixteenth century, the administration of tributary relations clearly emphasized political and security concerns. The seven expeditions of Zheng He (Cheng Ho, 1371/1375–1433/1435) conveyed the message about

Chinese power and reaffirmed that all relations had to be conducted through tribute. This tribute was not a financial burden for the missions, for they were well compensated for behaving appropriately, and their members were allowed to trade with the Chinese waiting at the designated ports, notably Guangzhou. Also, records indicate that trade was encouraged more for some than for others, and the details about how the missions were received and rewarded were carefully recorded. What was clear was that the relaxed conditions that existed for merchants during the late Tang dynasty, the Five dynasties, the Song dynasty, and the Yuan dynasty were now over.

The formal tributary system was steadily subverted after the arrival of the Europeans in Southeast Asia. By the end of the eighteenth century, only a few countries, such as Vietnam and Siam and the lands of some of the Shan rulers in Burma and Laos, still presented tribute regularly. Although much has been made of the British mission led by Lord Macartney in 1793, its failure actually marked how irrelevant the tribute system had become for the growing maritime trade. The hollow shell of the system would be preserved for another half century thereafter, but the time had clearly come for a new system of diplomacy and trade to help defend China.

WANG GUNGWU

See also Champa; Cheng Ho (Zheng He), Admiral (1371/1375–1433/1435); Chenla; China, Imperial; Economic History of Early Modern Southeast Asia (Pre-Sixteenth Century); Economic Transformation of Southeast Asia (ca. 1400–ca. 1800); Funan; I-Ching (I-tsing) (635–713 C.E.); Jungle/Forest Products; Majapahit (1293–ca. 1520s); Marine/Sea Products; Melaka; Ming Dynasty (1368–1644); Polo, Marco (1254–1324); Qing (Ching/Manchu) Dynasty (1644–1912); Sino-Vietnamese Relations; Śrivijaya (Śriwijaya); Yuan (Mongol) Dynasty (1271–1368)

References:

Fairbank, John K., ed. 1968. *The Chinese World Order: Traditional China's Foreign Relations.* Cambridge, MA: Harvard University Press.

Fairbank, John K., and Teng Ssu-yu. 1960 [1941]. "On the Ch'ing Tributary System." Pp. 107–218 in *Ch'ing Administration: Three*

Studies. Vol. 19. Cambridge, MA: Harvard-Yenching Institute.

Viraphon, Sarasin. 1977. *Tribute and Profit: Sino-Siamese Trade, 1652–1853.* Cambridge, MA: Harvard University East Asian Monographs.

Wade, Geoffrey Philip. 1994. "The *Ming Shi-lu* (Veritable Records of the Ming Dynasty) as a Source for Southeast Asian History: Fourteenth to Seventeenth Centuries." Ph.D. diss., University of Hong Kong.

Wang Gungwu. 1998a. "Ming Foreign Relations: Southeast Asia." Pp. 301–332 in *The Cambridge History of China.* Vol. 8, *The Ming Dynasty, 1368–1644, Part 2.* Edited by Denis Twitchett and Frederick W. Mote. Cambridge: Cambridge University Press.

———. 1998b. *The Nanhai Trade: The Early History of Chinese Trade in the South China Sea.* Singapore: Times Academic Press.

CHINS

The Chin peoples reside in the west and northwest of Burma (Myanmar). However, Chin communities also exist in the west portion of India in Mizoram and in the hill regions of Chittagong in Bangladesh. The term *Chin* is typically used only in reference to those living inside Burma. The origins of the term are uncertain. Some claim that it was derived from the Burmese word for "basket," possibly a reference to the handwoven baskets that Chin people would carry. Until recently, there appeared to be a consensus that the term *Chin* was not an identity that any of these peoples would choose to describe themselves, and for many, it was (and is) considered derogatory. However, some Chin nationalist historians have tried to claim authority for this term as an indigenized form of self-reference.

Although not invented by the British, the word was consolidated as an administrative term with the introduction of the Chin Hills Regulation in 1896. Following this, it became administrative ethnographic shorthand to refer to a broad range of socially, politically, and culturally complex communities. This usage continued after Burmese independence in 1948 with the establishment of the Chin Special Division. In 1974, a new constitution in Burma created the Chin State. However, a lingering awareness of the negative associations of the term historically have led some Chin nationalists to attempt to replace it with an ethnonym of their own. Some promote the terms *Zo* and *Zomi,* stating that they are derived from the name of the mythic common ancestor of all the Chin peoples. However, not all Chin groups accept this interpretation. There have also been concerns within the Burmese government about the development of a pan-Zo political movement, which might seek to unite "Zo Land" in Burma with Mizoram in India.

The Chin are divided into many subgroups, and the historical ethnographic literature on these peoples often uses a bewildering array of terms. Some subgroups are identified by their place of origin, some by a specific clan or lineage term, and others by dialect. Some of the largest Chin subgroups, based on linguistic and geographic definitions, are the Thado, Tiddim, Lushai, Falam, Haka, Asho, and Khumi. These communities have other ethnonyms by which they call themselves. A common Chin identity is asserted through linguistic links (although there is no common Chin tongue); similar customs, myths, and traditions; and a common understanding of the significance of Chin lineage and clan groups.

The Chin area is very diverse geographically, ranging from the high mountains near Mount Saramati in the north to the lowland-dwelling Asho Chin villages in Arakan (Rakhine State) and the Irrawaddy Valley, about 560 kilometers (350 miles) to the south. Some anthropologists have identified a north-south divide, with the northern groups having a more elaborate social, cultural, and political organization. Today, many Chin people are Christian, and our anthropological understanding of these complex communities is very out-of-date. A great deal more anthropological and historical research needs to be carried out.

The Chin people claim to have an ethnohistory of great length, with a major migration into the region traced from the tenth to the thirteenth centuries. Accounts are derived from Chin oral traditions and chronicles from neighboring cultures. The sixteenth to eighteenth centuries seem to have been turbulent times, with much infighting among the various Chin lineages. These disputes could also involve nearby Shan and Manipuri centers of authority. However, when the Burmese king Bodawpaya (r. 1782–1819) annexed Manipur in 1810, this led to increased conflict with the British, who were expanding into northeast India. Subsequent conflicts over the Kabaw Valley between the British and Burmese also involved Chin chiefs, who sought to establish advantageous positions for themselves.

The Chin chiefs and elders retained a high degree of independence throughout the nineteenth century, and it was not until 1894 that the British disarmed the Chin people and set about establishing their own authority through the medium of the hereditary chiefs. Yet there were always dangers of emergent nationalist discontent. For example, there was a widespread Chin uprising from 1917 to 1919, brought about by the enforced quota conscription of Chin men into the Burma Rifles during World War I (1914–1918). The British period saw control but little development of the region, leading some administrators, such as H. N. C. Stevenson, openly to lament the colonial administration's failure to prepare the "Hills regions" adequately for independence after the Pacific War (1941–1945). Representatives from parts of the Chin Hills were present at the Panglong Conference in 1947, where issues relating to independence were discussed with the main Burmese leaders, such as General Aung San (1915–1947). Since independence, many of these issues concerning the rights of minority nationalities such as the Chin within the Burmese state have not been resolved. A number of armed Chin nationalist organizations have opposed the Burmese government since the 1960s, such as the Chin Democracy Party, the Chin National Front, the Chin National Liberation Party, and the Chin National Unity Organization. The fragmented nature of the Chin ethnic political front partly reflects the historical lack of unitary political structures in this region, as well as the diversity of local ethnohistories among the Chin peoples themselves.

MANDY SADAN

See also Burma under British Colonial Rule; Burmans; Kachins; Mons; Shans

References:
Carey, B. S., and H. N. Tuck. 1896. *The Chin Hills: A History of the People, Our Dealings with Them, Their Customs, Manners and a Gazetteer of Their Country.* Rangoon, Burma: Government Printing Press.
Lehman, F. K. 1963. *The Structure of Chin Society: A Tribal People of Burma Adapted to a Non-*

Western Civilisation. Urbana: University of Illinois Press.
Lian Sakhong. 2000. *Religion and Politics among the Chin People in Burma (1896–1949).* Uppsala, Sweden: Uppsala University Press.
Stevenson, H. N. C. 1943. *The Economics of the Central Chin Tribes.* Bombay: Times of India Press.
Vum Son. N.d. *Zo History.* Mizoram, India: N. T. Thawnga.

CHULALONGKORN UNIVERSITY
A Bastion of Conservative and Royalist Traditions

Chulalongkorn University was founded in Bangkok on 26 March 1917 by King Vajiravudh (Rama VI) (r. 1910–1925) in memory of his father, King Chulalongkorn (Rama V) (1868–1910). The idea of an institution for higher learning that would be open to a wider group of citizens was conceived during the reign of King Chulalongkorn, spawned by the urge for the regime to modernize its kingdom. At that time, education was not an institution but was transmitted through home and monastery. In 1871, King Chulalongkorn initiated a series of formal schools in Bangkok, in particular the Suankularb, the Army Cadet School, the Cartographic School, the School for Princes, and the School for Dhamma Studies.

After the administrative reform in the 1890s, the focus was on training for the civil service, which led to the birth of the Royal Pages School in 1902. The focus expanded in 1911 to include more disciplines, such as law, international relations, commerce, agriculture, engineering, medicine, and teacher education. The Civil Service College operated for six years before it became a full university, with a huge plot of land donated by King Vajiravudh. The idea was that it should educate not only those who would become civil servants but also anyone who wanted to receive a higher education.

In the beginning, Chulalongkorn University had four faculties—in medicine, public administration, engineering, and arts and science. After the 1932 Revolution, the government transferred the Faculty of Law and Political Science (formerly Public Administration) to the newly founded Thammasat University. Chulalongkorn University continued developing undergradu-

Portrait of Chulalongkorn, or Rama V, King of Siam (present-day Thailand) (1868–1910). (Library of Congress)

ate programs until 1961, when it started to provide graduate studies and set up research centers and institutes.

As the first state university founded by the monarch, Chulalongkorn University became a bastion of conservative and royalist traditions. But this did not prevent its students from participating in political activism, especially in the demonstration against the rigged election of 1957 and the student uprising in 1973. Ironically, one of its arts students, Jit Phumisak, became a revolutionary hero of the student movement after the 1973 uprising.

THANET APHORNSUVAN

See also Constitutional (Bloodless) Revolution (1932) (Thailand); Education, Indigenous and Religious; Education, Western Secular; Reforms and Modernization in Siam;

Student Revolt (October 1973) (Thailand); Thammasat University; Vajiravudh (Rama VI) (r. 1910–1925)

References:

Amphon Namatra, ed. 1994. *A Pillar of the Kingdom: The Birth of Chulalongkorn University.* Bangkok: Chulalongkorn University Press.

Reynolds, Craig J. 1987. *Thai Radical Discourse: The Real Face of Thai Feudalism Today.* Ithaca, NY: Southeast Asia Program, Cornell University.

CLARKE, SIR ANDREW (1824–1902)
British Imperialist

As governor of the Straits Settlements (1873–1875), Andrew Clarke convened the Pangkor Engagement (1874) that introduced the Residential System in the Peninsular Malay States. Through his decisive actions, he ushered in a new epoch in Anglo-Malay relations that subsequently established British colonial rule over the Malay Peninsula (present-day West Malaysia).

Educated at Canterbury, England, Clarke joined the colonial service and spent the major part of his career in New Zealand. The earl of Kimberley, who served as the secretary of state for the colonies, designated Clarke as governor of the Straits Settlements in 1873 and instructed him to study the situation and to report on the advisability of appointing a British officer to reside in the then-anarchic Peninsular Malay States, entrusted with the task of restoring peace and protecting British trade and commerce. Taking the initiative to act first and report later, Clarke boldly convened a meeting of the warring factions in Perak at Pangkor. The Pangkor Engagement restored the peace in Perak. He conducted similar meetings in other troubled areas, such as Selangor and Sungai Ujong, whereby Pangkor-style treaties were signed with the contending groups.

In the Pangkor Engagement, Clarke widened Kimberley's suggestion relating to the responsibility of the British officer–styled resident. The resident was expected to give advice on all matters except those touching on Malay customs and traditions and the Islamic faith, in which the Malay ruler was obliged to take action. British residents were accredited to the court of the rulers of Perak, Selangor, and Sungai Ujong in 1874 and to Pahang in 1888. The Malay court paid the residents' salaries.

Clarke stood down as governor in May 1875 and proceeded to British India to serve on the Viceroy's Council. Despite the brevity of his governorship, Clarke was instrumental in introducing the Residential System to the Peninsular Malay States, which proved to be an innovative, practical, and economical method of exerting British political and economic influence on indigenous rulers.

OOI KEAT GIN

See also British Interests in Southeast Asia; Pangkor Engagement (1874); Residential System (Malaya); Western Malay States (Perak, Selangor, Negeri Sembilan, and Pahang)

References:
Cowan, C. D. 1961. *Nineteenth Century Malaya: The Origins of British Political Control.* London: Oxford University Press.
Gallagher, John, and Ronald Robinson. 1976. "The Imperialism of Free Trade." Pp. 53–72 in *The Robinson and Gallagher Controversy.* Edited by William Roger Louis. New York and London: Newviewpoints.
Khoo Kay Kim. 1972. *The Western Malay States, 1850–1873: The Effects of Commercial Development on Malay Politics.* Kuala Lumpur: Oxford University Press.
Vetch, R. H. 1905. *Life of Lieutenant General Sir Andrew Clarke.* London: Murray.

COCHIN CHINA

Cochin China is the term used to refer to southern Vietnam. Portuguese priests and merchants who arrived there in the middle of the sixteenth century coined the term, deriving *Cauchin* from *Giao Chi* (the Chinese name for Vietnam) and then adding *China* in order to distinguish the area from Cochin, a Portuguese colony in India (Karnow 1994: 70). When the French colonized southern Vietnam in the 1860s, Cochin China became the official name of the region as part of the French Indochinese Union.

Before it was attached to Vietnam, Cochin China was the border area under Cambodian rule. The Vietnamese began their "march to the south" (*nam tien*) in the early fifteenth century, and Huê soon fell under Vietnamese rule. However, it was under the Nguyễn family (which became the Nguyễn dynasty in the early nineteenth century) that the Vietnamese began a vigorous expansion southward. Vietnamese settlers from the center and the north had been sent to open and occupy the land in the south. By about 1700, the area around Saigon was occupied by the Vietnamese, and by 1750, the entire Mekong Delta was under Vietnamese rule (Fairbank, Reischauer, and Craig 1978: 268–269; Steinberg 1987: 234–235). After Nguyễn Anh of the Nguyễn family established the Nguyễn dynasty in 1802 C.E., he and his immediate successor, Minh Mang (r. 1820–1840), took it as their overriding task to develop the southern region. This they did by sending more people from the north and center to clear the land and settle in the south. Under the early Nguyễn dynasty, the south was divided into six provinces. It became the most important rice-producing area of the kingdom.

By the middle of the nineteenth century, the French were interested in expanding their colonial power to Vietnam. They were hoping to use Vietnam (especially the Red River in the north and the Mekong River in the south) as a gateway to southern China and also to proselytize the local people. However, their attempt to occupy the port of Đà Nẵng in central Vietnam in 1858 was not successful, and as a result, they moved toward the south. In February 1859, French forces entered and besieged Saigon, a major province in the south. The fighting lasted until 1861, when the French overcame Vietnamese resistance and were able to occupy the three eastern provinces of the south. The court of Huê appointed Phan Thanh Gian, the governor of the south, to negotiate with the French. In 1862, both parties concluded a treaty in which defenseless Vietnam had to cede to France the three eastern provinces, pay an indemnity of 20 million francs, and allow the French to use three ports (Nguyễn Khac Vien 1987: 149–150). The occupation of the three eastern provinces led to local resistance, which gave the French a pretext to resume the war in order to occupy the rest of the south, and in 1867, they conquered the three western provinces in the Mekong Delta. Phan Thanh Gian, who was still the governor, was humiliated and committed suicide. Thus, by 1867, Vietnam for the first time had lost its southern region to French colonialism. The treaty of 1872 between Vietnam and France confirmed the cession to France of the entire southern region of the kingdom and made the south a French colony under direct rule. Under French colonialism, the southern part of Vietnam became widely known as Cochin China, and the northern and the central regions were called Tonkin and Annam, respectively.

Since the Mekong Delta of Cochin China had the potential to become one of the major rice producers of the world, the French developed the entire area by building an intensive network of irrigation canals to exploit fully this fertile land. Under French rule, Cochin China became the major rice-producing competitor of British Burma and Siam. By the beginning of the twentieth century, French colonists developed rubber plantations in the south. Saigon (renamed Hồ Chí Minh City after the unification of the country in 1975) became the capital city of Cochin China.

Out of the five components constituting the French Indochinese Union created in 1887—the colony of Cochin China plus the four protectorates of Tonkin, Annam, Cambodia, and Laos—Cochin China became the most prosperous. It was the center of economic activity that generated income for the French administration in Indochina. This fact partly explains why the French tried to return and reoccupy the south after the Pacific War (1941–1945).

Cochin China was a de facto independent state (South Vietnam) during the period from 1954 to 1975, before being defeated by the communist regime from the north in April 1975. Thereafter, it became the southern region of reunified Vietnam.

SUD CHONCHIRDSIN

See also French Ambitions in Southeast Asia; French Indochina; French Indochinese Union (*Union Indochinoise Française*) (1887); Nam Tien; Nguyễn Anh (Gia Long Emperor) (r. 1802–1820); Nguyễn Dynasty (1802–1955); Nguyễn Emperors and French Imperialism; Saigon (Gia Dinh, Hồ Chí Minh City); Vietnam under French Colonial Rule; Viets

References:

Buttinger, Joseph. 1973. *A Dragon Defiant: A Short History of Vietnam.* Devon, UK: David and Charles.

Fairbank, John K., Edwin O. Reischauer, and Albert M. Craig, eds. 1978. *East Asia: Tradition and Transformation.* Boston: Houghton Mifflin.

Karnow, Stanley. 1994. *Vietnam: A History.* London: Pimlico.

Li Tana. 1998. *Nguyen Cochinchina: Southern Vietnam in the Seventeenth and Eighteenth Centuries.* Ithaca, NY: Cornell Southeast Asia Program.

Nguyễn Khac Vien. 1987. *Vietnam: A Long History.* Hanoi: Foreign Languages Publishing House.

Steinberg, David Joel, ed. 1987. *In Search of Southeast Asia.* Rev. ed. Honolulu: University of Hawai'i Press.

COCOA

Although cocoa had been introduced in Southeast Asia in the seventeenth century, the region did not become a world-class cocoa player until the 1980s. After fluctuating fortunes, the great 1970s price spike sparked a major boom, with Sulawesi smallholders emerging as the largest producers. Filipinos were the only Asians to become major consumers of chocolate, but they were rarely able to meet their own needs and had to import cocoa until the opening-up of Mindanao in the 1980s. Originally a lower-story tree of the Upper Amazon rain forests, cocoa needs fairly high heat and humidity throughout the year and can only be grown at elevations up to about 500 meters. It is thus more or less limited to lowland maritime Southeast Asia.

The Spaniards became acquainted with cocoa after seizing Mesoamerica in the early sixteenth century, and they spread the habit of drinking a newly concocted hot chocolate beverage to the Philippines. Cocoa seeds soon lost their ability to germinate, and it was hard to keep seedlings alive during the long journey across the Pacific, but eventually, a fine Criollo type of cocoa was successfully acclimatized in the Philippines. A vague assertion that Spaniards planted cocoa in North Sulawesi in 1560 is almost certainly legendary. A Jesuit probably planted the first cocoa in Leyte, in the eastern Visayas, around 1665, although a ship's pilot in the Bicol peninsula around 1670 also claimed this honor. Moreover, it is possible that the Dutch carried cocoa the other way around the world to Indonesia, via Ceylon (Sri Lanka), at about the same time.

Despite eighteenth-century attempts by the Dutch East India Company (VOC) to develop cocoa as an alternative to cloves in Maluku, cultivation long remained confined to meeting the needs of individual households. The Philippines could not even meet Manila's requirements, possibly because the islands lay in the typhoon belt and cocoa trees are sensitive to strong winds. Cocoa was thus one of the few commodities to be transported with silver on the yearly voyages of the Acapulco galleons across the Pacific. After ties with Mexico were cut in the early 1820s, some beans were sent directly from Ecuador, but supplies were erratic and Ecuador's Forastero cocoa was disliked. Indonesian smallholders and small Dutch planters in North Sulawesi and Maluku thus became Manila's main foreign suppliers. However, the pod borer moth, only found in Southeast Asia, ravaged aging groves of delicate Criollo trees from the 1850s. Consequently, Java and Ceylon became the mainstays of Manila's imports in the 1880s.

The trade to Manila was overshadowed by a burst of Javanese exports to The Netherlands from the 1880s. However, the Dutch discriminated against smallholders, backed European estates producing Criollo and Criollo-Forastero hybrids, and forced cocoa beans to be sent to The Netherlands. They were almost entirely re-exported, as their quality was unsuited to the needs of Dutch manufacturers. This expensive system could not withstand the sharp fall in the real-world price of cocoa from around 1910, especially as the pod borer moth spread in Java. The real price of cocoa remained extremely depressed in the interwar years, and cocoa was almost forgotten in Southeast Asia.

Southeast Asian interest in cocoa waxed and waned after the Pacific War (1941–1945), depending on erratic price swings and political problems. Postindependence chaos in Indonesia ensured that Malaysia got a head start in cocoa cultivation, but the Malaysians made the error of banking on estates in Sabah, which proved unable to make a profit when prices plummeted. The Philippines similarly backed large estates in Mindanao. By default rather than through any clear policy, a more politically stable Indonesia after 1965 gave smallholders their head start. There were both estates and smallholdings in various parts of the country, but the real dynamism lay with Bugis farmers, many of whom acquired planting material and a knowledge of cocoa cultivation by migrating to work on Sabah estates. An efficient chain of private commercial intermediaries, Bugis and Chinese, contributed to their success, as did successive currency devaluations. Sulawesi smallholders mainly grew the hardy Amelonado variety of Forastero, although they also experimented with faster-maturing Upper Amazon hybrids.

Despite its venerable history, cocoa cultivation has attracted little attention from historians of Southeast Asia, and chocolate consumption has been even less studied. The colonial bias in favor of estates is still widespread, despite the weight of historical evidence that smallholders are the most efficient producers. The shadow on the horizon remains the dreaded pod borer moth, and yet colonial research into this plague has been neglected, perhaps because so much of it is written in Dutch. A better grasp of cocoa's long history in Southeast Asia could thus help to boost rural prosperity.

WILLIAM G. CLARENCE-SMITH

See also Bugis (Buginese); Chinese in Southeast Asia; Cultivation System (*Cultuurstelsel*); Galleon Trade; Java; Maluku (The Moluccas); Manila; Mindanao; Sarawak and Sabah (North Borneo); Sulawesi (Celebes); Vereenigde Oost-Indische Compagnie (VOC) ([Dutch] United East India Company) (1602); Visayan Islands (Bisayan Islands, the Bisayas, the Visayas)

References:

Clarence-Smith, William G. 1998. "The Rise and Fall of Maluku Cocoa Production in the Nineteenth Century: Lessons for the Present." Pp. 113–142 in *Old World Places, New World Problems: Exploring Resource Management Issues in Eastern Indonesia.* Edited by S. Pannell and F. Von Benda-Beckmann. Canberra: Centre for Resource and Environmental Studies.

———. 2000. *Cocoa and Chocolate, 1765–1914.* London: Routledge.

Durand, Frédéric. 1995. "Farmer Strategies and Agricultural Development: The Choice of Cocoa in Eastern Indonesia." Pp. 315–338 in *Cocoa Cycles: The Economics of Cocoa Supply.* Edited by F. Ruf and P. S. Siswoputranto. Cambridge: Woodhead Publishing.

Pushparajah, E., and Chew Poh Soon, eds. 1986. *Cocoa and Coconuts, Progress and Outlook.*

Kuala Lumpur: Incorporated Society of Planters.

Putzel, James. 1992. *A Captive Land: The Politics of Agrarian Reform in the Philippines.* London: Catholic Institute for Race Relations.

Ruf, François, Pierre Ehret, and Yoddang. 1996. "Smallholder Cocoa in Indonesia: Why a Cocoa Boom in Sulawesi?" Pp. 212–228 in *Cocoa Pioneer Fronts: The Role of Smallholders, Planters and Merchants.* Edited by William G. Clarence-Smith. London: Macmillan.

Wood, G. A. R., and R. A. Lass. 1985. *Cocoa.* Harlow, UK: Longman.

COEN, JAN PIETERSZOON (1587–1629)
Architect of the Netherlands (Dutch) East Indies

Jan Pieterszoon Coen was born to a strict Calvinist family on 8 January 1587 in Hoorn, The Netherlands. He received his merchant's training in a Flemish company in Rome before joining the Dutch East India Company (VOC) as assistant merchant in 1607. He traveled extensively in the East Indies and returned to The Netherlands in 1610. Coen submitted a report on the trade opportunities throughout Southeast Asia to the VOC's directors. Consequently, he was sent to the Indies as chief merchant in 1612. Upon returning from a trip to the Moluccan islands in August 1613, he became head of the VOC's trading post in Banten (West Java); he was made general accountant of all VOC posts in October 1613 and then director-general of the company's operations in Asia in November 1614.

Coen was skillful in establishing alliances with local rulers against their rivals or against the Portuguese and English. In return for this support, the VOC received commercial monopolies. The most lucrative involved cloves in the Moluccan islands and nutmeg in the Banda islands. In this way, the VOC gradually increased its hold over trade in the archipelago. Coen's appointment as governor-general of the Dutch East Indies on 25 October 1617 (to 1623) was an acknowledgment of his skills.

When the sultan of Banten resisted his attempts to control the pepper trade, Coen transferred the VOC's headquarters to neighboring Jakatra (Jacatra), where the company had established a trading post in 1610. When the ruler of

Jakatra also opposed the presence of the VOC in 1618, Coen had a fortress constructed, despite disruptions both from the ruler and from the English. After an inconclusive sea battle against the English, Coen left for the Moluccan islands in January 1619 to seek naval reinforcements. On his return trip in May 1619, he lay waste to Japara, where Dutch residents had been killed the previous year. At Jakatra, he discovered that the forces of the sultan of Banten had subdued the Jakatran ruler, had forced the English to withdraw, and were besieging Fort Jakatra. Coen ended the siege, and on the ruins of Jakatra, he founded the city of Batavia, which became the center of Dutch power in Asia.

In 1620, the Dutch and English trading companies reached an agreement. Each would allow the other to conduct trading in existing trading posts, and both would contribute to a joint fleet against mutual foes. The English took up residence in Batavia but refused to accept VOC rules. Coen was dismayed. He curtailed the behavior of the English by organizing and implementing VOC rule in Batavia and its surroundings.

In January 1621, Coen left with a fleet for the Banda islands, where the rulers had started to supply spices to the English despite the VOC monopoly. After a short battle, the islands were brutally subdued. When this became known in The Netherlands, the VOC's board of directors reprimanded Coen.

In 1622, Coen sought to establish the VOC's influence in East Asia. He sent a fleet to China but only succeeded in establishing a Dutch settlement on the island of Formosa (Taiwan). This became the stepping-stone for the VOC's trade with China and Japan.

With the VOC's position in the East Indies consolidated and with the VOC maintaining trading posts from India to Japan, Coen believed that the time had come for the company to send Dutch colonists to the Indies. They could be involved in the intra-Asian trade while the VOC concentrated on trade between Asia and Europe. He left in February 1623 for The Netherlands to convince the VOC's directors of his plans.

Coen's appointment as governor-general was renewed on 3 October 1624 (to 1629). However, his travel back to the Indies was obstructed when details became known about the arrest and execution of some Englishmen in

Ambon on suspicion of hatching a plot to take the Dutch settlement. Coen was held responsible for their execution. The Dutch government wanted to maintain the friendly relations it then enjoyed with the English, so Coen was forbidden to return to the Indies. This suited the English, who regarded him as a formidable opponent in the Indies.

Coen returned incognito in 1627 and resumed his position. However, his colonization plans were stalled after the VOC directors decided not to grant colonists exemptions from the VOC's trade privileges. In 1628 and 1629, Batavia was besieged by Sultan Agung (r. 1613–1645) of Mataram, the most powerful ruler in Java, but the sultan was not successful. During the second siege, Coen masterminded the destruction of the sultan's supplies. However, he died suddenly on 21 September 1629 during the siege, probably of dysentery.

As a military commander and economic organizer, Coen established the foundations of the empire of the Dutch in the East Indies for the next three hundred and fifty years. He founded a chain of trading fortresses throughout the archipelago. In doing so, he forced the Portuguese to withdraw and prevented the further expansion of the English. However, Coen's military and administrative prowess was overshadowed by his harsh treatment of the indigenous peoples of Indonesia, particularly his cruelty toward the population of Banda.

PIERRE VAN DER ENG

See also Agung, Sultan of Mataram (r. 1613–1645); Ambon (Amboina/Amboyna) Massacre (1623); Anglo-Dutch Relations in Southeast Asia (Seventeenth to Twentieth Centuries); Banten (Bantam) (1526–1831); Batavia (Sunda Kalapa, Jacatra, Djakarta/Jakarta); British Interests in Southeast Asia; Dutch Interests in Southeast Asia from 1800; East India Company (EIC) (1600), English; Formosa (Taiwan); Java; Maluku (The Moluccas); Mataram; Netherlands (Dutch) East Indies; Portuguese Asian Empire; Spices and the Spice Trade; Vereenigde Oost-Indische Compagnie (VOC) ([Dutch] United East India Company) (1602)

References:
Colenbrander, H. T. 1934. *Jan Pietersz. Coen: Levensbeschrijving* [*Jan Pietersz. Coen: Biography*]. The Hague: M. Nijhoff.

Kohlenberg, K. F. 1978. *Ijzeren Jan: Jan Pieterszoon Coen, grondlegger van de koloniale macht van Nederland* [*Iron Jan: Jan Pieterszoon Coen, Founder of Dutch Colonial Power*]. Baarn, The Netherlands: Hollandia.

COFFEE

Southeast Asia was a major player in the world coffee market from the 1720s to the 1870s and became so again in the 1980s. The ravages of a fungus and the consequences of forced cultivation doomed the first boom, limited to Arabica varieties. The boom of the last decades of the twentieth century was based on hardier Robusta varieties, but land shortages and the falling popularity of instant coffee became worrisome.

The Arabica variety of coffee, originating in Ethiopia, was first cultivated in Yemen, whence the Dutch claimed to have introduced it into West Java in the 1690s. The Dutch signed contracts for the delivery of coffee at fixed prices with regents who forced their subjects to grow the crop, making West Java the chief source of Asian exports to Europe in the eighteenth century. However, Muslim pilgrims had already smuggled Yemeni seed to western India, the real source of Dutch seedlings, and probably introduced it into Sumatra. West Sumatran coffee was sold to British interlopers and to Americans from the 1790s. Catholic missionaries spread coffee further, notably to the Philippines in the eighteenth century. Southeast Asia's own consumption of coffee grew slowly, most closely associated culturally with Islam.

After the collapse of the Dutch East India Company (VOC) in 1800, forced coffee cultivation reached new heights. It persisted in West Java, even during the British interregnum from 1811 to 1816, and was imposed on North Sulawesi in the 1820s. After the inclusion of coffee in the Cultivation System (under which farmers were forced to cultivate cash crops, the sale of which would enable them to pay land tax to the Dutch colonial government) in 1832, the compulsory cultivation of coffee spread across Java and to West Sumatra. The Javanese preferred to grow coffee either as hedges or in forests, merely clearing the undergrowth and thinning the trees. However, Dutch officials insisted on the rapid felling and burning of primary forest and the laying out of

Vietnamese workers manually pick out foreign matter, such as tree branches and crushed stones, mixed in with beans at the Thang Loi Coffee Company, the biggest state-run producer in Vietnam's key growing province of Daklak, 16 May 2003. Vietnam rapidly emerged in the 1990s as the world's biggest producer of Robusta coffee, an expansion other producers partly blamed for leading global prices in the early 2000s to their lowest levels in thirty years. (Reuters NewMedia Inc./Corbis)

"regular plantations." These so-called plantations were divided among individual families, who transported dried beans to government storehouses and were paid in cash at the fixed price. As the world price rose in the nineteenth century, Dutch profits ballooned. The Portuguese in East Timor and the Spaniards in the Philippines attempted to copy Dutch methods, albeit with less rigor and more emphasis on European estates.

These prosperous days did not last. The 1870 Dutch abolition of the Cultivation System was gradually applied to coffee from the 1880s, and peasants quickly opted out of the hated crop. Coffee vanished in West Sumatra, North Sulawesi, and parts of Java. Clearing upland forest was prohibited in Java, as devastating erosion silted up lowland irrigation works. Leaf blight struck in the 1880s, caused by the

fungus *Hemileia vastatrix,* and the world coffee price collapsed in the mid-1890s, hastening the exodus from coffee by planters and smallholders across Southeast Asia. British planters fleeing leaf blight in Ceylon (Sri Lanka) carried coffee to Malaya but turned to rubber when the fungus caught up with them. The Philippines even became a net importer of coffee, as estates in southern Luzon gave up the crop. The New World, spared by *Hemileia vastatrix,* consolidated its supremacy on the world coffee market.

Nevertheless, coffee persisted in Southeast Asia. Arabica crops retreated to relatively high and dry areas, where leaf blight did less damage and other cash crops did poorly. Indigenous smallholders clung to Arabica in central Sulawesi, Timor, South Sumatra, central Vietnam, and southern Laos. They were joined by a few small, subsidized European planters who bene-fited from forced labor in the French and Por-tuguese territories. At lower elevations, some planters and smallholders grew hardy African Robusta and Liberica varieties as a catch crop, to be uprooted when the rubber trees, oil palms, or coconut palms matured. However, consumers disliked the taste of these varieties.

The situation was transformed after 1945 by better prices and cheap instant coffee, for which Robusta was suitable. The price spike of the late 1970s led to an export boom, and Southeast Asia replaced Africa as the world's main supplier of Robusta. Indonesia was at the fore, joined by Vietnam and Thailand. How-ever, coffee does best on cleared primary for-est, which is in increasingly short supply. Moreover, Robusta prices are low, due to a drift away from instant coffee by discerning Western consumers as well as increasing African competition.

The history of coffee cultivation suggests that estates suffer from high overhead costs and a lack of economies of scale, problems wors-ened by state ownership. Free smallholders are more efficient and better stewards of the envi-ronment. (Thus, they preferred agroforestry methods when the Dutch insisted on clear felling, with devastating ecological effects.) Moreover, smallholders are better positioned to serve niche markets in the West with highly valued organic Arabica brands, such as those from Timor, the Toraja country, and the Suma-tra Barisan.

WILLIAM G. CLARENCE-SMITH

See also Cultivation System (*Cultuurstelsel*); Java; Sumatra; Timor; Torajas; Vereenigde Oost-Indische Compagnie (VOC) ([Dutch] United East India Company) (1602); Western Malay States (Perak, Selangor, Negri Sembilan, and Pahang)

References:

Clarence-Smith, William G. 1992. "Planters and Smallholders in Portuguese Timor in the Nineteenth and Twentieth Centuries." *Indonesia Circle* 57: 15–30.
———. 2001. "The Spread of Coffee Cultivation to Asia, from the Seventeenth to the Early Nineteenth Century." Pp. 371–384 in *Le Commerce du café avant l'ère des plantations coloniales* [*The Coffee Trade before the Era of Colonial Plantations*]. Edited by Michel Tuchscherer. Cairo: Institut Français d'Archéologie Orientale.
Donner, Wolf. 1978. *The Five Faces of Thailand: An Economic Geography.* London: C. Hurst.
Elson, R. E. 1994. *Village Java under the Cultivation System, 1830–1870.* Sydney, Australia: Allen & Unwin.
Jackson, J. C. 1968. *Planters and Speculators: Chinese and European Agricultural Enterprises in Malaya, 1786–1921.* Kuala Lumpur: University of Malaya Press.
McStocker, Robert. 1987. "The Indonesian Coffee Industry." *Bulletin of Indonesian Economic Studies* 23, no. 1: 40–69.
Robequain, Charles. 1944. *The Economic Development of French Indochina.* London: Oxford University Press.
Wrigley, G. 1988. *Coffee.* Harlow, UK: Longmans.

COINAGE AND CURRENCY

As economies develop, they rely increasingly on the exchange of goods and services, for which money is required as a medium. Currency in Southeast Asia long consisted of an amalgam of imported silver coins and locally produced coins and ingots of various denominations, metals, shapes, and purity. These had to be weighed and assayed at every transaction. Mer-chants preferred silver as the unit of account.

The amount of silver in circulation ex-panded gradually after major silver mines were opened in Central and South America begin-ning in the sixteenth century. Silver minted as Spanish reals, or dollars, and, in the nineteenth century, as Mexican dollars reached Asia via the London silver market. European importers of Asian produce purchased dollars, which were the main goods that they traded in return for the products of Asia. Mexican dollars were pre-ferred because of their reputation for constant silver purity and weight (25.5 grams). They were accepted increasingly by unit rather than weight. The circulation of silver coins grew as a consequence of the development of interconti-nental trade, although Spanish reals leaked out of Southeast Asia into China, where the de-mand for reliable silver currency was insatiable. When reals were in short supply, the British East India Company (EIC) and the Dutch East India Company (VOC) minted additional silver coins.

Southeast Asia during the course of the nineteenth century faced a shortage of silver currency. The supply of dollars increased with trade between Europe and Asia, but intra-Asian trade drained dollars away to China and India. The money shortage constrained economic development. Governments, for instance, found it difficult to raise tax revenues. In Java, the Dutch colonial government issued currency notes, but these were accepted reluctantly and circulated at a discount. It also issued copper subsidiary coins, but the intrinsic and nominal values of such coins varied. Copper coins disappeared when copper appreciated relative to silver and vice versa.

To address the dollar shortage, British authorities in the Straits Settlements tried to introduce the Indian rupee as legal tender. Authorities in other parts of Asia imported their own dollars, which were similar in size, weight, and silver content to the Mexican dollar. The Dutch rix dollar was used in parts of Indonesia under Dutch colonial control. In 1867, the British introduced the Hong Kong dollar and later the British Trade dollar in the Straits Settlements and Hong Kong. The French in Indochina introduced a silver trade piastre in 1885, and the Spanish in the Philippines introduced a new peso for domestic circulation in 1887.

Although legislation specified only one currency as legal tender, foreign silver coins were widely accepted by weight. Throughout Southeast Asia, silver coins of various denominations could be found: Mexican dollars, Indian rupees, Thai ticals (known as baht), and Japanese yen. Only subsidiary coins were restricted to the countries of issue. Governments issued currency notes, and various private banks in the region issued promissory banknotes, but paper currency was mainly used by foreign firms and in cities. The denominations were too big for most people, and bullion was generally preferred.

Silver coins suited Asian economies as the means of exchange. The borders between countries were not yet clearly drawn, and in many areas, central governments only exercised nominal authority. Even if governments wanted to do so, it would have been difficult to enforce monetary unity. All Asian economies still had large subsistence sectors; the low level of economic development caused a low opportunity

cost for labor, and therefore, prices of the same commodities and services in Asia were lower than in Europe. The purchasing power of silver currency was higher in Asia, and the same transaction incurred a smaller amount of silver. Most domestic and intra-Asian transactions were relatively small and were settled with cash. Gold was too valuable to suit such transactions.

Silver could also be used in international trade with Europe and North America because its value was stable relative to gold. However, after 1870, silver depreciated quickly as a consequence of the discovery of new silver ore deposits and a decline in world gold production. Countries in Europe and North America with a bimetallic or silver standard currency system terminated the free coinage of silver. Most embraced the gold standard. Silver depreciation turned their silver coins into token coins, which circulated for their nominal rather than their intrinsic value. Many countries sold excess silver as bullion on international markets or used it to cover trade deficits with silver standard countries.

Countries with silver standards, such as those in Southeast Asia, had to come to terms with the fact that most international trade and finance became denominated in gold-based currencies. The depreciation of their silver currencies meant that imports from gold countries became more expensive, at a time when many silver countries required capital goods from Europe for their development. However, devaluation encouraged exports to countries with gold-based currencies. Governments in Southeast Asia also acknowledged that volatile exchange rates in principle discouraged foreign investment in their countries because of the exchange rate risk. They found it more difficult to borrow abroad because devaluation increased the cost of debt servicing. The depreciation of silver generally furthered inflation, which in turn increased interest rates.

From 1870 to 1914, most governments of Asian countries chose to stabilize their currencies against gold. Dutch Indonesia (1877), British India (including Burma, 1893), the Philippines (1903), the Straits Settlements (1904), and Thailand (1908) embraced the "gold-exchange standard." Only French Indochina continued the silver standard until 1930 because changing to a gold-based currency would have had negative consequences for its trade contacts with Hong Kong and China, which continued the silver standard.

Governments stopped the free minting of silver currency and passed legislation to make only one currency legal tender: the guilder in Dutch Indonesia, the rupee in Burma, the peso in the Philippines, the Straits dollar in Malaysia, the baht in Thailand, and the piastre in French Indochina. The nominal value of the legal silver coins gradually exceeded their intrinsic value, and coins started to circulate for their nominal value in the designated areas. Thus, the currencies of Southeast Asia became national currencies.

The nominal value of the national currencies was kept at a stable level relative to gold through reserves of a gold-based currency overseas (the Dutch guilder for colonial Indonesia; the pound sterling in the case of Burma, Thailand, and the Straits Settlements; and the U.S. dollar in the case of the Philippines). These reserves handled overseas payments and receipts for each country. For instance, a reserve accepted local currency from importers in Southeast Asia and released pound sterling for the payment of overseas exporters and vice versa. For this system to work, the countries had to have a trade surplus to stock the reserve with gold-based currency in order to defend a stable rate of exchange of the local currency. Due to the disruption of world trade, most countries had to suspend the gold-exchange system during World War I (1914–1918), but they resumed it in the 1920s.

While the currency systems took shape, more and more paper currency became circulated as the need for larger denominations increased. These notes were generally issued by designated privately owned central banks, such as the Javasche Bank in colonial Indonesia and the Banque de l'Indochine in French Indochina, or by private trading banks, such as the Chartered Mercantile Bank of India, London and China in Singapore.

Under the gold-exchange system, economies were not shielded from such fluctuations in international prices through currency devaluation. These fluctuations were immediately imported through an adjustment of the domestic money supply. This became painfully clear during the global economic crisis after 1929 (the Great Depression). International commodity prices plummeted, prices in the region fol-

lowed, and all Southeast Asian countries experienced the negative consequences on output and employment of rapid deflation. One by one, they followed the gold-based currencies against which their currencies had been pegged: Burma, Thailand, and the Straits Settlements (1931); the Philippines (1933); and French Indochina and Dutch Indonesia (1936).

During the Pacific War (1941–1945), Japanese occupation authorities and the government of Thailand did not have access to foreign currency reserves to maintain realistic exchange rates. The public hoarded coins, which disappeared out of circulation. The Japanese authorities issued increasing amounts of paper money to finance public expenditure. The value of this currency soon eroded, as local economies came to a standstill and less and less could be purchased. Inflation was rampant throughout the region. One of the first tasks of the governments that returned after the Japanese surrender in August 1945 was to reestablish monetary order by reintroducing prewar currencies and guaranteeing their value.

Despite decolonization, countries continued their monetary regimes. Only North Vietnam introduced a new currency, the dong (in 1947). Burma's rupee was renamed the kyat after 1947, and Indonesia's guilder was renamed the rupiah after 1949. Indochina's piastre became the South Vietnamese piastre, the Cambodian riel, and the Laotian kip after 1954. The Straits dollar became the Malayan dollar in 1957 and then the Brunei, Singapore, and Malaysian dollars in 1967. The Malaysian dollar was renamed the ringgit in 1975. The dong became Vietnam's national currency after monetary reunification in 1978. In all countries, central banks were either nationalized or established and put in charge of monetary policy and the issuing of banknotes.

Except for North Vietnam, all countries became members of the International Monetary Fund (IMF), promising to keep their currencies at a realistic rate of exchange relative to the gold-based U.S. dollar. Most countries experienced trade deficits that eroded the exchange funds available for the defense of realistic exchange rates. To avoid further erosion, the central banks of all countries strictly controlled the inflows and outflows of currency and gold. Such capital controls were used to allocate scarce foreign exchange. Subsequently, black markets for Southeast Asian currencies emerged.

In part due to superior export performance, controls were not a major obstacle in the case of Malaysia, Singapore, and Thailand, where the discrepancy between official and black market exchange rates remained minimal. For Burma, Indonesia, North and South Vietnam, Cambodia, Laos, and the Philippines, the discrepancy remained significant. The value of their currencies eroded in line with inflation fueled by budget deficits. Improved export performance and reduced inflation in Indonesia and the Philippines in the 1970s (and in the late 1980s, also in Vietnam) allowed the authorities to establish realistic official exchange rates.

In the 1980s, the members of the Association of Southeast Asian Nations (ASEAN) opened up to foreign trade and investment. Their growing dependence on foreign trade and investment required more flexible exchange rate regimes. One by one, they liberalized their foreign exchange controls and allowed international markets to determine the exchange rates of their currencies. Their central banks assumed an active role in currency markets, buying and selling local currency through open market transactions in order to dampen exchange rate fluctuations or defend a peg relative to the U.S. dollar or to an index of key international currencies.

In the early 1990s, high economic growth in Thailand, Malaysia, and Indonesia increased the need for investment capital. These countries opened up to short-term capital in the form of foreign investment in the shares of local companies and company debentures. In the light of sustained exchange rate stability, foreign lenders and local borrowers perceived a low exchange risk. Short-term debt denominated in international currencies increased quickly in the 1990s.

This development ended in mid-1997, when foreign investors and lenders learned about the difficulties firms had in servicing their debts. They rushed to sell shares and call in short-term debt, putting depreciating pressure on the currencies of the ASEAN countries. Central banks ceased defending their own currencies, which went into a tailspin. Malaysia stabilized its currency by reimposing capital controls and fixing the exchange rate to the U.S. dollar. Thailand and Indonesia applied for IMF support to stabilize the exchange rates of their currencies.

Throughout the 1990s, Burma, Vietnam, Laos, and Cambodia continued capital controls. The Vietnamese dong was stabilized after 1991, but the depreciation of the Cambodian riel and the Laos kip continued in line with inflation in these countries. The official value of the Burmese kyat remained unrealistic, and the gap between its black market and official rate surged after 1995 to 100 to 1 in 2001.

PIERRE VAN DER ENG

See also Ancient Coinage in Southeast Asia; Banks and Banking; Economic Development of Southeast Asia (post-1945 to early 2000s); Economic Transformation of Southeast Asia (ca. 1400–ca. 1800); Great Depression (1929–1931); Japanese Occupation of Southeast Asia (1941–1945); Trade and Commerce of Southeast Asia (ca. Nineteenth Century to the 1990s)

References:

Chiang Hai Ding. 1965. "Silver Dollars in Southeast Asia." *Asian Studies* 3: 459–469.

Klein, P. W. 1990. "Dutch Monetary Policy in the East Indies, 1602–1942: A Case of Changing Continuity." Pp. 419–453 in *Money, Coins and Commerce*. Edited by E. H. G. Van Cauwenberghe. Leuven, Belgium: Leuven University Press.

COLD WAR

An American columnist, Walter Lippman, coined the term *Cold War* to refer to the state of tension, hostility, competition, and conflict that characterized Soviet-Western relations, particularly those between the Soviet Union and the United States. It is conventional to date the Cold War as lasting from the mid-1940s to 1991, when the Union of Soviet Socialist Republics (USSR), or Soviet Union, disappeared from the political arena. Two main features of the Cold War were bipolarity and ideological competition. The most overt aspect of the Cold War was the division of the world into two competing camps—liberal-democratic and communist, each with its respective allies and satellites.

The Cold War appeared as a consequence of the power realignment after World War II (1939–1945). Only the United States and the USSR emerged with enough power to determine postwar settlement. The Cold War bore many features of a traditional geopolitical power struggle among nation-states. Americans could not understand why the Soviet Union did not accept the preeminence of the United States, and the Soviets could not understand why the Americans refused to treat them as equals. The two great empires competed without engaging in direct conflict.

The competition for preeminence in the postwar period was aggravated by ideological differences. The USSR wanted to advance socialism on a worldwide scale. The Soviet leadership was eager to provide a favorable context for the revolutionary struggle for socialism in the capitalist and newly independent countries—a struggle that Moscow would aid ideologically, politically, and materially. Leaders in the United States regarded communism as antithetical to their most basic values and principles and feared the Soviet Union's commitment to world revolution. America's goal was to create a world order conducive to the interests of the United States, in which the values Americans treasured would be carried around the world.

There was a security dilemma, too. Each step the Soviet leaders took to add to the security of their country was viewed by American leaders as detracting from the security of the United States. Each nation defined its own policies as defensive but saw the other's as threatening.

The Cold War began with the division of Europe into socialist and capitalist camps. The victory of communist forces in North Korea (1948) and China (1949) took the Cold War into Asia. As the Soviet and American positions in Europe and East Asia stabilized, the great powers turned their attention to the Third World—the newly independent nations in Asia and Africa, which were struggling to develop viable economies and to establish national identities. The USSR and the United States came to regard these new nations, including those in Southeast Asia, as testing grounds in the contest between their two systems and as pawns in the global struggle for power. Both vigorously competed for their allegiance by massive propaganda campaigns and generous offers of economic and military assistance. Containment denoted the American effort by military, political, and economic means to resist communist expansion throughout the world, particularly in Southeast Asia. That was the be-

ginning of confrontation and polarization in the region.

In Southeast Asia, a communist regime was created with Soviet and Chinese assistance in North Vietnam, where the Democratic Republic of Vietnam (DRV) was proclaimed in 1945. The Soviet Union and the People's Republic of China (PRC) supported communist parties and left-wing organizations in the region and instigated the anticolonial and anti-imperialist struggles of peoples in Southeast Asian countries. The USSR greeted the proclamation of independence in Indonesia and gave political, moral, and diplomatic support to the republican government in the United Nations during the Indonesian people's fight against Dutch and British imperialists. It welcomed the creation of an independent Burma and established friendly relations with it. At the same time, the communist powers tried to draw newly independent states into their orbit of influence.

The growth of communist and Soviet influence in Southeast Asia aroused great concern in the United States. American officials feared that the Soviet influence in North Vietnam would represent only the first stage of a broader pattern of Soviet and communist expansion in the region—the so-called domino theory. The policy of containing communism policy was extended to Southeast Asia. Washington also responded with policies to enhance U.S. influence in Southeast Asia. It supported anticommunist and right-wing nationalist forces in the countries of the region, as well as the establishment of authoritarian anticommunist regimes in Thailand, the Philippines, and South Vietnam, and it succeeded in drawing these nations into the orbit of its foreign policy. Southeast Asia split into two opposing camps: the pro-Soviet camp included the DRV and later was joined by the Lao People's Democratic Republic (LPDR) and, for a short period, by Cambodia, and the pro-American camp consisted of Thailand, the Philippines, and South Vietnam.

The 1954 formation of a military anticommunist bloc known as the Southeast Asia Treaty Organization (SEATO), which included Thailand and the Philippines and extended its control to South Vietnam, Laos, and Cambodia, completed the division of Southeast Asia. SEATO became a mutual defense alliance to deter communist aggression. As the Cold War in Southeast Asia intensified, the USSR and the United States rebuilt the military machines that had been demobilized after World War II and initiated an arms race in conventional, nuclear, and other sophisticated weapons of growing destructive capacity. The United States provided assistance to military regimes in Thailand and built a number of American navy and air bases in this country as well as in the Philippines. Meanwhile, the U.S. Navy roamed the seas in the region. The Soviet Union was escalating its assistance, including military aid, to the DRV, which was, in its turn, undermining anticommunist regimes in the region. A Soviet navy was also present in Southeast Asian seas.

Several great international crises of the Cold War era—the Korean War in 1950–1953, the Cuban crisis of 1962, the American involvement in Vietnam (1964–1973), the Soviet involvement in Afghanistan (1979–1988)—at times seemed to threaten the outbreak of a new world war.

The Vietnam War stands out among Cold War crises for its scale, length, intensity, and global repercussions. It claimed more than 58,000 American lives and more than 3.2 million Vietnamese lives ("The Cold War in Asia" 1995-1996: 232). The escalation of the conflict in Vietnam began soon after two incidents. The Tonkin Gulf incident in August 1964, naval exchanges involving American warships in the Gulf of Tonkin, was followed by the February 1965 attack by armed units of the National Front for the Liberation of South Vietnam (NFLSV) on the base of American military advisers in Pleiku, which triggered U.S. aerial bombardment on North Vietnam in retaliation. Fearing a loss of Soviet influence in the region, particularly in the context of the mounting differences between Beijing and Moscow, the USSR leaders pursued a policy of confrontation with the United States, which in turn facilitated President Lyndon Johnson's (t. 1963–1969) escalation of U.S. involvement in Vietnam. In the Cold War context, Soviet leaders could hardly react indifferently to the Vietnam conflict and the intensification of American military activity in Southeast Asia. Moreover, U.S. support for an unpopular neocolonial Saigon regime offered a target for condemnation and undermined Washington's international stature. Meanwhile, the USSR could pose as a consistent fighter for the triumph of a just cause. Moscow acted in the spirit of proletarian internationalism—as evidenced by its moral-political, economic, and military assistance to North Vietnam—and also as a potential mediator in the forging of a peaceful settlement.

Yet the Vietnam War also presented long-term difficulties and dangers for both Moscow and Washington because there was a real threat that it could escalate from a local fight into a world war. As sharp and intense as the tensions between the USSR and the United States were, both sides had an interest in constraining the Cold War; in limiting and controlling the rivalry and competition; and in achieving a degree of stability, order, and predictability in world politics. One of the most compelling reasons for containing the conflict was the existence of nuclear weapons—which threatened mutual annihilation in the event of the outbreak of a "hot war" between the great powers.

In fact, the hope for a peaceful settlement of the Vietnam War was shared by both Soviet and American leaders. Richard Nixon's victory in the 1968 elections marked a turning point in U.S. policy toward the USSR. The incoming Nixon administration (t. 1969–1974) made every effort to obtain greater Soviet involvement and cooperation in the process of achieving a peaceful settlement in Vietnam. And for its part, the USSR managed to make a considerable contribution to the peaceful settlement of the Vietnam conflict. Ultimately, in 1973, a bilateral agreement was signed by the DRV and the United States on ending hostilities and restoring peace in Vietnam. American military forces were withdrawn from Indochina.

An apparent victory for the Soviet side in the Cold War in Southeast Asia was signified by several happenings. The first was the end of the Vietnam War and the creation in 1976 of the Socialist Republic of Vietnam, which united the North and the South. Then came the establishment of the Lao People's Democratic Republic, the overthrow of the Khmer Rouge regime in Cambodia, and the creation of a pro-Vietnamese government, which seemed to signify a Soviet victory. The military presence of the USSR in the region grew from year to year. The key element was the strong Soviet naval presence, for the airpower of the USSR's naval forces in the Pacific and Indian Oceans became a challenge to the regional balance of power that had once favored the United States. Further, the civil government that came to power in Bangkok in 1973 pushed for an accelerated withdrawal of American military forces from the country. The withdrawal started in 1974 and ended by 1976, and all the bases were turned over to the government of Thailand. The military bloc SEATO disintegrated. The USSR acquired for its fleet the former American naval base in Cam Ranh Bay.

But at the end of the 1980s, the Soviet economy, overstrained by the arms race and by the competition with the United States, was in trouble. Soviet society was on the verge of crisis, and the political system was not working. The new communist leadership in the USSR, which came to power in 1985, became aware of the need for deep and urgent reforms. The new leaders required a respite from the Cold War to be able to devote their energies and the nation's resources toward building a more modern and efficient Soviet state. They rejected the ideological implication of Soviet foreign policy.

The USSR modified its military doctrine, reduced its armed forces, and concluded a number of agreements with Washington on strategic arms reduction and limitation. The Soviet Union and the United States had ceased to be enemies. In 1991, the USSR officially ceased to exist. Its successor, the Russian Federation, withdrew from Southeast Asia.

In the Southeast Asian region, this led to the end of ideological conflict and confrontation. Vietnam and Laos started their transitions to market economies. A coalition government was established in Cambodia, freed from Vietnamese influence. The Association of Southeast Asian Nations (ASEAN), an economic and cultural alliance that previously had included only nonsocialist countries, was opened for all Southeast Asian nations, regardless of ideology. This ended the division of Southeast Asia.

LARISSA EFIMOVA

See also Asian-African (Bandung) Conference (April 1955); Association of Southeast Asian Nations (ASEAN) (1967); China since 1949; Domino Theory; Indochina War (1964–1975), Second (Vietnam War); Korean War (1950–1953); Lao People's Democratic Republic (LPDR); Ngô Đình Diệm (1901–1963); Non-Aligned Movement (NAM) and Southeast Asia; Russia and Southeast Asia; Sino-Soviet Struggle; Southeast Asia Treaty Organization (SEATO) (1954); U.S. Involvement in Southeast Asia (post-1945); U.S. Military Bases in Southeast Asia; Vietnam, North (post-1945); Vietnam, South (post-1945); Zone of Peace, Freedom, and Neutrality (ZOPFAN) (1971)

References:
Brzezinski, Zbigniew. 1983. *Power and Principle: Memoirs of the National Security Adviser, 1977–1981.* New York: Farrar, Straus and Giroux.
Cohen, Warren I., ed. 1995. *The Cambridge History of American Foreign Relations.* Vol. 4, *America in the Age of Soviet Power, 1945–1991.* Cambridge: Cambridge University Press.
"The Cold War in Asia." 1995–1996. *Cold War International History Project Bulletin,* nos. 6–7 (Winter). Woodrow Wilson International Center for Scholars, Washington, DC.
Duiker, William J. 1994. *US Containment Policy and the Conflict in Indochina.* Stanford, CA: Stanford University Press.
Gaddis, John L. 1987. *The Long Peace.* Oxford: Oxford University Press.
Garthoff, Raymond L. 1985. *Detente and Confrontation.* Washington, DC: Brookings Institution.
———. 1994. *The Great Transition: American-Soviet Relations and the End of the Cold War.* Washington, DC: Brookings Institution.
Roberts, Geoffrey. 1999. *The Soviet Union in World Politics: Coexistence, Revolution and Cold War, 1945–1991.* London and New York: Routledge.

COLLABORATION ISSUE IN SOUTHEAST ASIA

Directly after the surrender of the Japanese in September 1945, the "collaboration issue" was widely discussed among the Allied powers. The Americans, who had already promised independence to the Philippines before the Pacific War (1941–1945), refused to bring into power representatives of the ruling class who, in their eyes, had collaborated with the Japanese. They believed such individuals should be removed from authority and arrested and tried for treason against the United States. This was one of the most radical interpretations at the time. The policy of the British and Dutch colonial powers toward indigenous ruling elites who had cooperated with the Japanese during the occupation, like that of the Americans, was directed toward removing them from power. But the collaboration issue was not a prime priority for the French in Indochina. Like their counterparts in Europe who had collaborated with the German Nazis, the French colonial authorities in Indochina had themselves collaborated with the Japanese military regime.

The Allied views, based on Western ideas about collaboration, were not apposite in the far more complex Asian context. Their views relating to *collaboration* were strongly connected to Western ideas about collaboration and resistance in the European context. With such concepts inspiring the policies of the Allies on the handling of the collaboration issue in their colonies in Asia, conflict between the colonial powers and the nationalists who had fought for independence was inevitable. The nationalists had quite different views on the issue of collaboration. In order to attain freedom for their people, they had decided to cooperate with the Japanese. They used the Japanese for their own means to liberate their countries from the colonial powers. When the colonial powers strove to restore their colonial regimes after the capitulation of Japan, the nationalists made it quite clear that they wanted independence for their respective countries. Most of the former colonial powers refused to negotiate with the nationalists and marked them as collaborators. Not only the nationalists but also many other people had cooperated with the Japanese by various means. However, little is known about the collaboration of the common people as compared with what is known about the different elites throughout Southeast Asia. To understand how the issue of collaboration influenced the postwar political debate in the countries of Southeast Asia, we must consider the issue in the historical context of each nation.

In the Philippines, the collaboration issue lay at the core of the political debate. In spite of the Commonwealth government's promise that, at the end of a prescribed period, an independent republic of the Philippines would be realized, many leading Filipinos chose to cooperate with the Japanese. The returning Americans saw the old elites who had been involved in the new administrative structure of the Japa-

nese military as traitors. They were viewed as leaders who had failed to discharge the demands of continuing loyalty to the Commonwealth government and to the United States. The case of José Paciano Laurel (1891–1959) and Jorge B. Vargas, two Philippine Commonwealth ministers in the prewar period, is a good example of the one-sided American policy. Laurel accepted the post of president in the nominally independent, Japanese-supported Philippine government, and Vargas was one of his closest colleagues. They followed a strategy of cooperating minimally while avoiding measures that actively helped the Japanese war effort. After the war, they were arrested on the orders of General Douglas MacArthur (1880–1964) and incarcerated in Sugamo Prison near Tokyo. The Americans demanded that the postwar Philippine government bring collaborators to trial. It was charged with investigating the conduct of those public officials or employees who had served during the enemy occupation and who might now be recalled to duty. In 1946, the José M. Sison trial was staged as a kind of test case. Sison belonged to the prewar elite and had served as minister of justice and home affairs in the Laurel government during the occupation. He was charged before the Peoples Court on twenty-six counts of treason. Sison's final defense before the judges was a fervent protestation of his innocence. He said that if it was a crime to have feigned collaboration with the enemy in order to be of service to his people, then he was ready to accept the penalty meted out to him by the tribunal of Philippine justice. He was sentenced to life imprisonment and fined 15,000 pesos. However, with the increasing threat of communism, the Americans abruptly changed their policy. To restore order and to lead the fight against communism, they advocated massive support of the traditional oligarchy. The collaboration issue faded, and a general amnesty was declared for those who had already been convicted (roughly 150 individuals).

The dream of Japanese-sponsored independence drove Sukarno (1901–1970), Aung San (1915–1947), and other nationalists to cooperate with the Japanese. They expected to gain concessions from the occupying force that had been denied them by their own colonial powers. Many of these nationalist leaders were released from detention by the Japanese armies.

In the Netherlands Indies, most of the nationalists cooperated with the Japanese throughout the occupation. Before the war, there were two groups of nationalists in the Netherlands Indies: the noncooperating and those who were still willing to work and cooperate with the Dutch colonial government. Faced with the refusal of the Dutch to make any political concessions that would lead to more autonomy, the latter changed their policy and cooperated with the Japanese in the hope of gaining independence for their country. The noncooperating nationalists who were imprisoned by the Dutch were released by the Japanese and used for anti-Allied propaganda and mass mobilization. From the beginning, however, it was clear that both the Japanese and the Indonesian nationalists had their own agendas for reaching their respective goals. Two of the most prominent leaders among them were Sukarno and Mohammad Hatta (1902–1980). The Japanese also tried to utilize Muslim influence, and Muslims consolidated among themselves while cooperating with the Japanese. They profited greatly from the opportunities offered by the Japanese. For the first time, the Muslims captured a position in the administrative structure. The independence of Indonesia was declared by Sukarno and Hatta two days after the Japanese surrender. Meanwhile, the Dutch, who had returned and wanted to restore their colony, accused Sukarno of being a Japanese collaborator and refused to negotiate with him. But the charge did not really bring him into disrepute, nor did it affect his political authority. The social revolution that swept throughout Java during the first three months after the Japanese surrender claimed many victims among people who were suspected of having profited from the wartime situation at the cost of others among them, in particular Chinese businesspeople and Indonesian officials.

In Burma (Myanmar), Aung San, the leader of one of the most important nationalist groups, fled his country before the war broke out to escape imprisonment by the British colonial government. He was offered military training by the Japanese and formed the Burma Independence Army (BIA). The BIA participated in the Japanese conquest of Burma, and the Burmese considered the invasion a liberation campaign. In July 1942, the BIA, which had taken over parts of the local government,

was forced to dissolve by the Japanese occupation regime. Yet despite the disbanding of the BIA, Aung San was willing to cooperate with the Japanese, who granted independence to Burma on 1 August 1943. When it emerged that the independence was purely nominal, Aung San changed his policy and turned to the British, fighting the Japanese with his Anti-Fascist Organization (AFO) until Tokyo surrendered in mid-August 1945. Aung San negotiated with the British, leading, in the end, to Burma's independence in 1948. The patterns laid down by the BIA in 1942 were the basis of his success after the war. The people's broad support for the movement convinced the British that independence could no longer be postponed. Aung San was assassinated in 1947 and did not experience independence himself. But Dr. Ba Maw (b. 1897), another prominent nationalist, who headed the Japanese-sponsored regime in Burma, remained politically active after the war. Like other well-known leaders, he viewed his own and other peoples' cooperation with the Japanese in the context of the nationalist movements to gain freedom for their countries.

In British Malaya, the prewar political allegiance with the British was divided along ethnic as well as social lines, affecting the choices people made for or against cooperation with the Japanese. On the one hand, Malays who belonged to the Malayan Civil Service (MCS) were pro-British but were not willing to oppose the Japanese fervently. On the other hand, Malay nationalists, who formed the Kesatuan Melayu Muda (KMM, Young Malay Union), welcomed the Japanese as liberators. The Japanese used them as community leaders without making any political concession for an independent Malayan state. By the outbreak of the war, Chinese formed the majority of the population in Malaya. Some of the locally born, British-oriented Chinese involved in business adapted to the Japanese regime. But among the Chinese migrants who were politically oriented toward their homeland, many were opponents of the Japanese due to Japan's invasion of China. These migrants were organized in the Kuomintang (KMT) and in the Malayan Communist Party (MCP), affiliated with the Chinese Communist Party (CCP) in China. During the Japanese occupation, the Communists were active in the Malayan Peoples' Anti-

Japanese Army (MPAJA). Indians, the third largest ethnic group, were organized in the Central Indian Association of Malaya. They cooperated with the Japanese, hoping to gain independence for India with Japan's support. Both the British and the Japanese tried to utilize these groups for their own aims. The British provided support for the Chinese guerrillas to fight the Japanese, and the Japanese maintained good relations with Malay nationalists and created a local defense force that was mainly used to combat the Chinese Communist–led guerrillas. After the restoration of British rule, it was clear that prosecutions for collaboration would be most unlikely. As an act of clemency in March 1946, the British government decided not to institute any action against people who would otherwise have been charged with collaboration with the enemy in British territories in Southeast Asia. This policy had been forced by the political situation in India, where it had been agreed that nationalists who had collaborated with the nationalist leader Subhas Chandra Bose (1897–1945) would not be punished.

Before the war, British Borneo had consisted of Sarawak, North Borneo (including Labuan), and the Malay kingdom of Brunei. Most of the inhabitants were in the first instance neutral or pro-Japan, but loyalties changed when the situation deteriorated under Japanese military rule. The Iban formed the largest ethnic group in Sarawak, and most of their leaders cooperated with the Japanese to survive the war. Many Chinese businesspeople benefited from the high demand for foodstuffs as the war turned against Japan. As elsewhere in occupied Southeast Asia, the Japanese supported the local branch of the Indian independence movement. The Borneo branch of the pro-Japanese Indian Independence League (IIL) was established in Kuching in mid-1942. British Borneo had been reoccupied by the Australians, with the ultimate task of reestablishing the British government. The prosecution of collaborators was not a priority for the Australians, but prominent members of the IIL and some of the native civil servants suspected of being collaborators faced the anger of the general public and were put in jail for their own safety. The only successful prosecution for collaboration took place in the Resident's Court in Kuching in early March 1946, when two Indians and a Chinese man were accused of various offenses involving assault. No further prosecution of collaborators was pursued, given the British clemency announcement in March 1946.

French Indochina was the only area under Japanese military influence in which a Western colonial regime was allowed to remain in place. The colonial authorities permitted Japanese troops to enter north Indochina in September 1940. Thereafter, the Japanese occupied northern Indochina but left the colonial regime intact until 9 March 1945 in accordance with their policy of maintaining tranquillity. The Japanese did not impose military rule as they had in other parts of Southeast Asia but instead granted the three nations of Indochina—Cambodia, Laos, and Vietnam—nominal independence. As elsewhere in occupied Southeast Asia, the choice between resistance and collaboration was related to aspirations for independence. Some Vietnamese politicians and intellectuals forged links with the Japanese using the political symbolism of Prince Cuong De (1882–1951). Ngô Đình Diệm (1901–1963) and other members of the Vietnamese Nationalist Party (Viet Nam Ai Quoc Dang or Viet Nam Quoc Dan Dang, VN-QDD) promoted Cuong De and even hoped to establish a government that would be approved of by the local Japanese military authorities. Their hopes were dashed in March 1945 when the Japanese army carried out a military coup and pushed the French aside. Instead of imposing military rule, the Japanese gave Emperor Bảo Đại (1913–1997) of Vietnam, King Sihanouk (1922–) of Cambodia, and King Sisavang Vong (1885–1959) of Laos the opportunity to declare the independence of their countries. In Vietnam, developments during this period contributed to the failure of the Japanese-supported Bảo Đại–Kim government to take the political initiative and led to the transfer of power to the Viet Minh under Hồ Chí Minh (1890–1969). After the war, the French who had initially collaborated themselves found their colony in great disorder, giving room to other power players such as the communists.

Thailand, the only independent nation in the prewar era, sought its own way through the war period. Just like indigenous leaders in the colonial situation, political figures changed sides according to the course of the war. One of the most prominent leaders at the outbreak of the Pacific War was Phibun (Plaek Phibunsongkhram, 1897–1964). In 1941, he was prime minister and chose to cooperate with the Japanese, using them to realize his dream of a greater Thailand. Phibun succeeded in expanding the territory of Thailand at the cost of Malaya and Burma. In July 1944, however, he was forced by other Thai politicians to resign as the war turned against Japan. His government was replaced by a more Allied-oriented one, which tried to repair Thailand's relationship with the Allied powers and at the same time maintained good relations with the Japanese. Not only the top political leaders but also larger groups of government officials had been pro-Japanese. Thanks to their position in the administrative structure, they had profited personally through the Japanese invasion and the subsequent seizure and confiscation of the property of enemy aliens in Thailand. After the Japanese surrender, Phibun and seven other political leaders were arrested. The British considered them collaborators and forced the Thai government to bring them to trial. But in 1946, the Thai Supreme Court decided that the 1945 War Criminal Acts were unconstitutional, and the charges against them were dropped. The collaboration issue did not damage Phibun's political career: in 1948, he returned to power, once again becoming prime minister.

In the wake of the immense political changes that took place directly after the end of the war in Southeast Asia, including the growing influence of communist-oriented groups that had fought the Japanese during the war, the collaboration issue faded away within a year. The Allied powers needed the support of the old elites who had collaborated with the Japanese to restore order and to form a bloc against communism. The Cold War had begun.

ELLY TOUWEN-BOUWSMA
TRANSLATED BY ROSEMARY
ROBSON-MCKILLOP

See also Anti-Fascist People's Freedom League (AFPFL); Aung San (1915–1947); Ba Maw, Dr. (b. 1893); Bao Đai (Vinh Tuy) (1913–1997); Bose, Subhas Chandra (1897–1945); Burma during the Pacific War (1941–1945); Burma Independence Army (BIA); Cold War; Constitutional Developments in the Philippines (1900–1941); Greater East Asia Co-prosperity Sphere; Hồ Chí Minh (1890–1969); Ibrahim Yaacob (1911–1979); Indochina during World War II (1939–1945); Kesatuan Melayu Muda (KMM) (Young Malay Union); Laurel, Jose Paciano (1891–1959); Malayan Communist Party (MCP); Mohammad Hatta (1902–1980); Nationalism and Independence Movements in Southeast Asia; Plaek Phibunsongkhram, Field Marshal (1897–1964); Sarawak and Sabah (North Borneo); Sihanouk, Norodom (1922–); Sisavang Vong (1885–1959); Soekarno (Sukarno) (1901–1970); Việt Minh (Việt Nam Độc Lập Đồng Minh Hội, League for the Independence of Vietnam)

References:

Abaya, Hernando J. 1946. *Betrayal in the Philippines.* Quezon City, the Philippines: Malaya.

Adams, C. 1965. *Sukarno: An Autobiography as Told to Cindy Adams.* New York: Bobbs-Merrill.

Agoncillo, Teodoro A. 1984. *The Burden of Proof: The Vargas-Laurel Collaboration Case.* Manila: University of the Philippines Press.

Cheah Boon-Kheng. 1983. *Red Star over Malaya: Resistance and Social Conflict during and after the Japanese Occupation of Malaya, 1941–1946.* Singapore: Singapore University Press.

Kahin, George McTurnan. 1952. *Nationalism and Revolution in Indonesia.* Ithaca, NY: Cornell University Press.

Kobkua Suwannathat-Pian. 1995. *Thailand's Durable Premier, Phibun through Three Decades, 1932–1957.* Kuala Lumpur: Oxford University Press.

Kurasawa Aiko. 1989. *Mobilization and Control: A Study of Social Change in Rural Java, 1942–1945.* Ann Arbor, MI: University Microfilms International.

Maung Maung. 1990. *Burmese Nationalist Movements, 1940–48.* Honolulu: University of Hawai'i Press.

McCoy, A. W., ed. 1985. *Southeast Asia under Japanese Occupation.* New Haven, CT: Yale University Southeast Asia Studies.

Reece, Bob. 1998. *Masa Jepun: Sarawak under the Japanese, 1941–1945.* Kuala Lumpur: Ampang Press for the Sarawak Literary Society.

Sata, S. 1998. "Japanese Occupation, Resistance, and Collaboration in Asia." Pp. 121–137 in *World War II in Asia and the Pacific and the War's Aftermath, with General Themes:*

A Handbook of Literature and Research. Edited by L. E. Lee. Westport, CT, and London: Greenwood Press.

Shiraishi, Takashi, and Motoo Furuta. 1992. *Indochina in the 1940s and 1950s.* Ithaca, NY: Cornell University Southeast Asia Program.

Steinberg, D. J. 1967. *Philippine Collaboration in World War II.* Ann Arbor: University of Michigan Press.

COLONIALISM

The term *colonialism* is often used more or less synonymously with *imperialism.* Similarly, *decolonization* is a word that covers the removal of the formal structures of European empire from the "colonial" world. *Neocolonialism,* like *neo-imperialism,* may be used to describe the external forces that appear to ensure the continued dependence of former "imperial" or "colonial" territories even after they have secured political independence. It is, however, possible to draw a distinction.

The word *colony* derives from a Latin word, *colonia,* which was applied to a settlement of Roman citizens in a hostile or newly conquered territory. *Colonization* thus implied settlement. *Empire,* again a word of Roman origin, did not necessarily do so: *imperium* implied a rule or sway over an extensive territory or collection of states. *Imperialism* was more apt than *colonialism* as a descriptive term for the creation of dependent territories in the nineteenth century. And but for the ugliness of the word, *de-imperialization* would be more apt than *decolonization* for the creation of independent states in the twentieth century.

Neither term truly encompasses one of the most extraordinary movements of the nineteenth century. Economic, social, and political change, coupled with the development of communications, contributed to worldwide migration on an altogether unprecedented scale—a movement of Asian people within and beyond Asia but even more a movement of European people to non-European parts of the world. In some cases, they built up what might properly be called colonies, though, rather confusingly, the British came to call them dominions. The great bulk of the emigrants went, however, to noncolonial territories, in particular to the former colonies of the United Kingdom, Spain, and Portugal in the Americas. They included people from European states that had little or no overseas territory. They also included vast numbers from states that did possess empires. Between 1871 and 1901, the grand total of German emigration was 2.75 million, but only about 21,000 Germans lived in the German colonies in 1911 (Knoll and Gann 1987: 160). Even more striking—since the German Empire was a Johnny-come-lately—were the British figures: two-thirds of the British emigrants for the period from 1843 to 1910 went to destinations outside the British Empire (*Times Literary Supplement,* 24 July 1987).

These mass movements have been reversed only to the most limited extent in the postcolonial period. In some cases, there have, however, been bitter struggles, and there may be more to come. One of the bitterest was in Algeria. There, after the French conquest, a substantial number of French *colons* (colonists) established themselves, without eliminating or absorbing the existing population. They desperately opposed the breaking of the colonial link, bringing down the Fourth Republic that had managed to extricate France from Indochina only a few years before. One of the Fourth Republic's difficulties had been with the colons in Cochin China, far more influential than their numbers suggested.

The French, like the Germans, had talked of "colony" rather than "empire." Eugène Étienne's famous pressure group in the France of the late 1880s and 1890s was seen as the *parti colonial* (colonial lobby). What Otto von Bismarck (1815–1898) took up in the mid-1880s was the so-called colonial question. No doubt these two countries had an obvious reason to prefer the term *colonialism* to the term *imperialism,* which was accepted in Britain by supporters as well as detractors. France attached the word *empire* to the regime of the Bonapartes, whose focus had been on Europe. The Germans, having defeated France in 1870 and 1871, had established an empire in Europe, the Second Reich.

In the case of the French at least, there was a more crucial distinction. They had, in fact, no concept of empire overseas, and no constitutional provision was made for it. The emphasis was on the republic, one and indivisible, of which all Frenchmen were deemed citizens. That included the colons and the limited number of non-French people in the overseas territories who were admitted to French citizenship. These groups were represented in the French Parliament. It was only after World War II (1939–1945) that the French sought to redesign their empire in terms of states as well as citizens, setting up the French Union.

The British had taken a different stance. At the time of the American Revolution (1775–1883), they had decided against the admission of colonial representatives in Parliament. However, the monarchy they retained gave them the possibility of establishing an empire in the sense of a congeries of states and territories. One form such an entity could take was that of a colony. Labuan was annexed as a colony in 1847, and the Straits Settlements became a colony in 1867, as did Sarawak and North Borneo (Sabah) in 1946. They were not colonies of settlement, but that did not prove to be an obstacle to self-government.

NICHOLAS TARLING

See also British Borneo; British Burma; British Interests in Southeast Asia; British Malaya; Dutch Interests in Southeast Asia from 1800; East India Company (EIC) (1600), English; French Ambitions in Southeast Asia; Imperialism; Labuan (1847); Netherlands (Dutch) East Indies; Portuguese Asian Empire; Preservation of Siam's Political Independence; Sarawak and Sabah (North Borneo); Spanish Expansion in Southeast Asia; Spanish Philippines; Straits Settlements (1826–1941); Vereenigde Oost-Indische Compagnie (VOC) ([Dutch] United East India Company) (1602)

References:

Knoll, Arthur J., and L. H. Gann, eds. 1987. *Germans in the Tropics.* New York: Greenwood.

Marshall, D. Bruce. 1973. *The French Colonial Myth and Constitution-Making in the Fourth Republic.* New Haven, CT: Yale University Press.

"COMFORT WOMEN"
Sex Slaves of the Japanese Imperial Forces

Female prostitutes forced to serve the Japanese Imperial Forces (JIF) during the Second Sino-Japanese War (1937–1945) and the Pacific War (1941–1945) were referred to as "comfort women," and their brothels were known as "comfort stations." The first Japanese overseas comfort station was set up in Shanghai in January 1932 when the Shanghai Incident occurred. After the Sino-Japanese War began in 1937, comfort stations were established in most of the places occupied by the JIF. Soon after the Pacific War broke out on 8 December 1941, the JIF started to set up stations in the occupied areas in Southeast Asia. In Malaya, the first one was opened in Alor Star on 19 December 1941. As of September 1942, a total of 400 comfort stations had been established: 280 in China, 100 in Southeast Asia, 10 in the South Pacific islands, and 10 in Sakhalin. The total number of comfort women is estimated to have been between 50,000 and 200,000, consisting of Koreans, Chinese, Japanese, Philippines, Indonesians, Vietnamese, Malays, Indians, Burmese, overseas Chinese, and Dutch. In Southeast Asia, some comfort women were from East Asia, but the majority were procured locally. Though not strictly followed, Japanese wartime law prohibited the sending of Japanese women abroad, with the exception of professionals over the age of twenty-one. However, there were no such restrictions in regard to female inhabitants in the colonized or occupied areas.

Some of the comfort stations were administered directly by the Imperial Army or the Imperial Navy, and those that were managed by private operators were also by and large supervised by the JIF. The main objective of setting up comfort stations was to lessen the incidence of rape of local women by Japanese soldiers, though they were proven ineffective in this respect. The means employed to procure young women were mostly deceit, abduction, coercion, and purchase. Sometimes, the JIF forced the local community leaders to supply girls for the comfort stations. And some comfort women were taken to the battlefronts.

Beginning around 1990, former comfort women began to demand an official apology and compensation from the Japanese government. Claiming the system had been run privately, the government, for its part, obstinately rejected such demands at first. However, given the revelations of various official documents that recorded the direct involvement of the JIF, the Japanese government partially admitted its responsibility in 1992.

HARA FUJIO

See also Japanese Occupation of Southeast Asia (1941–1945); Miscegenation; Sexual Practices; *Sook ching;* Women in Southeast Asia

References:

Hicks, George. 1995. *The Comfort Women: Sex Slaves of the Japanese Imperial Forces.* Singapore: Heinemann Asia.

Yoshimi, Yoshiaki, and Hayashi Hirofumi, eds. 1995. *Nihongun Ianfu* [*Comfort Women of the Japanese Army*]. Tokyo: Otsuki Shoten.

COMINTERN

The Comintern was an association of national communist parties that was founded in 1919, with its headquarters in Moscow. The Comintern based its ideology upon the doctrine of Marxism-Leninism and declared that its primary goals were to promote the "World Communist Revolution" and establish a dictatorship of the proletariat.

The Comintern's second congress was held in Moscow in 1920 and featured the participation of delegates from Asia. The resolutions promulgated at that meeting called for communist parties to be established in each participating country in order to train the proletariat for the seizure of state power. The Comintern's "Twenty-One Conditions of Membership" urged "the whole-hearted support of the Soviet Republic as the base of the world revolutionary movement," which would become one of the primary aims of all communist parties. Notwithstanding its stated purpose of promoting the World Communist Revolution, the Comintern functioned chiefly as an organ of Soviet Russia's control over the communist movement across the globe and as an instrument of foreign policy for the Union of Soviet Socialist Republics (USSR).

One of the conditions of membership had a direct bearing on the colonial question, for it compelled those seeking affiliation with the Comintern to denounce all the methods of their own imperialists in the colonies and to support liberation movements in the colonies by practical means. The effect of this was to ensure that all communist parties throughout the world would play an active part in bringing about the overthrow of imperialism and the liberation of colonial and dependent territories. Communists in the colonies were encouraged to form "anti-imperialist united front" organizations with various social groups of native populations, including the national bourgeoisie. The second congress approved the structure of the ruling organs—the World Congress, the Executive Committee, and the International Controlling Commission. Only the communist parties affiliated with and supportive of Comintern made up its sections.

During the Comintern's third congress, in 1921, the Youth Communist League and Profintern, the trade union organization of the Comintern, were established. The fourth congress, in 1922, discussed the Comintern's national-colonial program. "To the masses!" was the slogan proclaimed at that meeting, alluding to world communism's immediate task of enlisting the masses in its global campaign. The Asian parties were called on to participate in any movement that would give them access to the people. The fifth Comintern congress in 1924 emphasized the need to increase work with the labor unions and to strengthen the proletarian orthodoxy. At the same time, the congress called on the communists in the countries of the East to solve national and agrarian questions in the spirit of Leninism. In order to intensify communist activities in the colonies, the Central Executive Committee of the Comintern established an Eastern section, known as the Far Eastern Bureau.

The sixth congress approved the Comintern program that was designed to replace the global capitalist economy with communism. The program obliged the world proletariat to promote the building of socialism in the USSR. The communist parties were also directed to carry out a ruthless struggle against social democrats (perceived as "the last reserve of bourgeois society") and fascism. The defense of the Soviet Union was stressed as the foremost task of the Comintern and of communist parties in all countries. On the colonial question, the Comintern position held that the national bourgeoisie could not play a progressive role in national liberation movements.

The seventh and last Comintern congress was held in 1935. It launched the "Popular Front" policy, which envisaged an agreement with bourgeois and other non-working-class organizations in a common struggle against fascism and entailed adopting a more cooperative attitude toward democratic governments and organizations. For the communists in the colonies, that meant cooperating with their colonizing countries. With this new policy—and as a consequence of it—the former stress on proletarian revolution receded into the background for the time being. This approach represented a radical departure from previous communist tactics and from the basic statutes of the Comintern's Twenty-One Conditions of Membership, which forbade communists from coalescing with bourgeois parties. Thereafter, the conflict between Soviet national interests and world revolutionary interests was resolved by subordinating the world revolutionary strategy to the USSR's security concerns, on the grounds that the Soviet Union was the base of the World Communist Revolution and therefore had to be made safe at all costs.

With the signing of the Soviet-Nazi Pact in 1939, fascism ceased being stigmatized as the enemy in communist propaganda, and the Popular Front phase came to an end. Less than two years later, the German invasion of the USSR brought about an equally abrupt termination of Soviet-German collaboration. Fascism again became the main target of communist fulminations, and the Western powers were restored to favor.

Then, on 15 May 1943, the Comintern was dissolved. The official reasons were that there was no longer a need for an international body to guide the communist parties throughout the world and that the leading cadres of the parties in various countries had become politically mature. The prime object, however, was to allay fears of communist subversion among the USSR's Western allies in World War II (1939–1945).

LARISSA EFIMOVA

See also Burma Communist Party (BCP); Colonialism; Communism; Hồ Chí Minh (1890–1969); Imperialism; Indochina Communist Party (1930); Malayan Communist Party (MCP); Nationalism and Independence Movement in Southeast Asia; Partai Komunis Indonesia (PKI); Russia and Southeast Asia; Vietnamese Communist Party (VCP)

References:
Anderson, K. M., and A. O. Chubaryan, eds. 1998. *Comintern i Vtoraya Mirovaya Voina* [*Comintern and the Second World War*]. Pts. 1 and 2. Moscow: Pamyatniki Istoricheskoy Mysli (Relics of Historical Thought), Pamyatniki Istorii Rossii (Relics of the History of Russia), RAN (Russian Institute of Sciences), Institut Vseobchskey Istorii (Institute of World History).

Brimmel, J. H. 1959. *Communism in South-East Asia: A Political Analysis.* London: Oxford University Press.

Chin, Aloysius. 1994. *The Communist Party of Malaya: The Inside Story.* Kuala Lumpur: Vinpress.

McVey, Ruth T. 1965. *The Rise of Indonesian Communism.* Ithaca, NY: Cornell University Press.

COMMUNISM

Communism is a system of economic and social organization whereby the community owns all property and all members of that community share in the enjoyment of the common wealth according to their needs. The origins of communism lie deep in Western thought. The mainstream of contemporary communist theory originates in Marxism—a complex of philosophical and sociopolitical doctrines formulated by European socialists Karl Marx (1818–1883) and Friedrich Engels (1820–1895) in the *Political Manifesto,* published in 1848, and other works. The main ideas of Marxism call for the destruction of capitalism through socialist revolution, the victory of the proletariat over the bourgeoisie, and the establishment of a new organization of society (socialism and its highest stage, communism) by the destruction of all class distinctions. Founders of the original Marxist system held that socialist revolution could only take place in urban centers in highly industrialized Western Europe, where a massive proletarian class "groaned" under the rule of the bourgeoisie. The East and the colonial question were peripheral in Marxist thought because a major part of the population in the backward and mostly feudal, colonial, and semicolonial countries of Asia and Africa was peasants, regarded by Marx and Engels to be petty bourgeoisie.

After Marx's death, his followers began to reinterpret his doctrine. One of the main interpreters was a Russian left-wing socialist named Vladimir Lenin (1870–1924). His interpretation of Marxism was adjusted to conditions in Russia and was known as Leninism. Lenin asserted that socialist revolution could be brought about in a single country as highly industrialized and semifeudal as Russia was. It was he who first recognized the peasantry's worth as the proletariat's ally. Lenin also emphasized the fundamental connections between imperialism and capitalism and linked the demands of subject races for the right of self-government with the anticapitalist campaign for a "World Socialist Revolution." He argued that the proletariat and the socialists of industrializd countries should advocate the struggle for the liberation of the colonial and semicolonial peoples. In this way, Asian nationalism could rally the peoples of the East to the cause of world revolution, and removal of those areas from control by the colonizing powers would mortally injure the capitalist system. Lenin stressed the importance of a revolutionary alliance—a revolutionary bloc formed by the proletariat of the advanced countries and the oppressed peoples of the enslaved colonies for the victory of the world revolution. The colonial question and revolution in the East were moved from the margins of Marxist thought to its very center.

In the 1920s, communist ideology in its Marxist and Leninist variations penetrated the East. The most well-known Asian interpreter of communism became the leader of the Chinese Communist Party (CCP), Mao Zedong (1893–1976). Mao tried to adjust Marxism and Leninism to conditions in China. His contribution to communist doctrine lay in the recognition that in backward countries of the East, where the major part of the population lived in the countryside, the industrial working class (the proletariat) was too small a base on which to mount a revolution. Consequently, he formulated a new doctrine based on the belief that in the East, the socialist revolution could not be brought about in urban industrial centers. Instead, Mao advocated the establishment of a rural base that was physically separate from urban industrial centers and that was defended by an armed force. From this rural base, the Communist Party could seek to extend its power and influence outward. Instead of working-class support, the revolution would have to depend on the peasants. And instead of swift insurrection, there would be protracted war. Though it was recognized that political power grew out of the barrel of a gun, the supremacy of the party over the armed forces and of the proletariat

over the peasantry was upheld as an absolute principle.

The term *communism* is also applied to revolutionary movements inspired by Marxist, Leninist, and Maoist ideas that seek to bring about a society based on principles involving the destruction of class and common property. A number of communist parties sprang up in the world, including in East and Southeast Asia. The 1920s witnessed the emergence of the Partai Komunis Indonesia (PKI, Communist Party of Indonesia) in 1920, followed by the Chinese Communist Party in 1921. The next decade saw the establishment of the Indochina Communist Party (ICP, 1930), the Malayan Communist Party (MCP, 1930), the Communist Party of the Philippines (1930), and the Burma Communist Party (BCP, 1939). In 1942, the Communist Party of Thailand was formed. Most of the parties in Southeast Asia were encouraged and supported by the Soviet and Chinese communists, as well as the metropolitan communist parties in Europe, either directly or through the Comintern (the Communist International).

Communism was declared the official ideology and the main target of development in Soviet Russia (1917–1922) and the Union of Soviet Socialist Republics (USSR, 1922–1991), as well as in a number of socialist countries in Eastern Europe and Asia where communist parties held the reins of state power.

LARISSA EFIMOVA

See also Burma Communist Party (BCP); Colonialism; Comintern; Imperialism; Indochina Communist Party (1930); Malayan Communist Party (MCP); Malaya Emergency (1948–1960); Nationalism and Independence Movements in Southeast Asia; Partai Komunis Indonesia (PKI) (1920)

References:
Brimmel, J. H. 1959. *Communism in South East Asia: A Political Analysis.* London: Oxford University Press.
Lenin, V. I. 1957. *The National Liberation Movement in the East.* Moscow: n.p.
Marx, Karl, and Friedrich Engels. 1955. *Selected Writings.* Moscow: n.p.
McVey, Ruth T. 1965. *The Rise of Indonesian Communism.* Ithaca, NY: Cornell University Press.

Scalpino, R. A., ed. 1965. *The Communist Revolution in Asia: Tactics, Goals and Achievements.* Englewood Cliffs, NJ: Prentice-Hall.

COMMUNIST PARTY OF KAMPUCHEA (CPK)

See Democratic Kampuchea (DK); Khmer Rouge; Pol Pot (Saloth Sar) (1925–1998)

COMMUNIST PARTY OF MALAYA (CPM)

See Malayan Communist Party (MCP)

CONFUCIANISM

Confucianism is a body of ethical thought mainly based on the teachings of Confucius (551–479 B.C.E.). Among Southeast Asian countries, only Vietnam embraced this thought. Confucianism regards the ancient times of the saints as ideal. Moralistic and ritualistic politics are advocated. According to Confucianism, the Son of Heaven, who has virtue and received the Mandate of Heaven, civilizes people with the ideal of moral and ritual order, which was thought to have existed in the golden ancient times. Hierarchy and harmony are the focus of social relationships. Three Bonds (between ruler and subject, father and son, and husband and wife) and Five Cardinal Principles (the Three Bonds plus those between elder brother and younger brother and between friend and friend) are thought to be the basis for human relationships. Rites dedicated to Heaven, deities, ancestors, and sages are valued. Among the Confucian virtues, *ren* (benevolence) and *yi* (justice) are supreme.

In China, Confucianism became a state religion by the proposal of Dong Zhong Shu (176? B.C.E.–104? B.C.E.) of the Western Han dynasty (202 B.C.E.–8 C.E.). Dong Zhong Shu advocated a correlation between Heaven's will and human affairs, and it was assumed that Heaven as a personified god gives a warning to a government mismanaging its affairs. Neo-Confucianism was invented under the Song dynasty (960–1279) and completed by Zhu Xi (Chu Hsi, 1130–1200) of the Southern Song (1127–1279). Opposing Buddhism and Taoism, neo-Confucianists added philosophical dimensions, such as the *li* (abstract principles) and *qi* (material forces) theory, to Confucianism. Explanatory notes of the Four Books and the Five Classics by Zhu Xi were officially recognized, and neo-Confucianism established its position as the official state orthodoxy. A reconstruction of the rites system was planned. Enlightenment by private intellectuals—for example, in family rites and village rites—was advocated, in addition to enlightenment by the emperor. During the Ming dynasty (1368–1644), the doctrines of Wang Yang Ming (known as *Xinxue,* or the School of Mind) emerged. The Ming dynasty promulgated the Six Lessons taught by the first emperor and advocated enlightenment by the emperor. Wang Yang Ming promoted the spread of village rites as a private enterprise.

Vietnam won its independence from China in the tenth century C.E. State institutions were constructed following the Chinese system, but Confucian influence was not as strong. The influence of Buddhism was stronger from the tenth century to the thirteenth century. In the fourteenth century, a civil service examination system was developed, and regional, metropolitan, and palace examinations began. The Le dynasty (1428–1789), which won its independence from the temporary rule of the Ming dynasty in the early fifteenth century, introduced the Chinese system more faithfully than preceding dynasties had. In the times of Emperor Le Thanh Tong (r. 1460–1497), the civil service examination system and a school system were developed, and many Confucian intellectuals were educated. Confucian moralities of the Three Bonds came to be emphasized by the dynasty. The Forty-Seven Articles of Enlightenment were promulgated in the latter half of the seventeenth century. In these articles, the Five Cardinal Principles and moralities in villages were regarded as important, and Buddhism and folk belief were severely criticized. That criticism demonstrated the prosperity of Buddhism and folk belief then. In the eighteenth century, cheating on the civil service examination became quite common. As for the Forty-Seven Articles of Enlightenment, periodical reading in villages was advocated, but such a practice did not take root. However, the Tho Mai Family Rites (Tho Mai Gia Le) were edited on the basis of Zhu Xi's Family Rites, demonstrating the deepening of enlightenment as a private enterprise.

The Nguyễn dynasty (1802–1945) was the first dynasty to unify the north and the south. It held examinations and developed the school system on a countrywide scale. Emperor Minh Mang (r. 1820–1841) promulgated the Ten Maxims, which preached Confucian moralities, and mandated the periodical reading of them in towns and villages. Emperor Tu Duc (r. 1847–1883) translated the Ten Maxims, originally written in Classical Chinese, into Vietnamese and transcribed them into *chu nom* (southern characters) for broad distribution. In the early twentieth century, the Four Books and the Five Classics were removed as examination subjects, and Confucianism was less emphasized. The last palace examination was held in 1919. Thus, Confucianism as a state orthodoxy ended, although Tran Trong Kim tried to reinstate it between 1930 and the 1940s. The argument on the significance of Confucianism continues today.

Several features distinguish Vietnamese Confucianism. First, there was little interest in philosophical dimensions such as *li qi* theory. Second, no influence of Wang Yang Ming's doctrines has been found in the Vietnamese context. Third, the argument regarding the correlation between God's will and human affairs appeared often in the Nguyễn emperor's discourses. Fourth, local teachers educated many intellectuals in the rural areas. Fifth, Confucian intellectuals often conducted Taoistic practice, as well. And sixth, in the years since ritual Confucianism was ended in the country, the Vietnamese-specific belief in spirits has persisted.

SHIMAO MINORU

See also Buddhism, Mahayana; Le Dynasty (1428–1527; 1533–1789); Le Thanh Tong (r. 1460–1497); Nguyễn Dynasty (1802–1945)

References:
Cooke, Nola. 1994. "Nineteenth-Century Vietnamese Confucianization in Historical Perspective: Evidence from the Palace Examinations (1463–1883)." *Journal of Southeast Asian Studies* 25, no. 2: 270–312.
Le Viet Chung, Cao Xuan Huy, The Hung, Chuong Thau, Phan Dai Doan, and Dinh Xuan Lam. 1979. "The Confucian Scholars in Vietnamese History." *Vietnamese Studies* (Hanoi) 56: 1–187.
Smith, Ralph B. 1973. "The Cycle of Confucianization in Vietnam." Pp. 1–19 in *Aspects of Vietnamese History.* Edited by W. F. Vella. Honolulu: University Press of Hawai'i.
Taylor, Keith W. 1987. "The Literati Revival in Seventeenth-Century Vietnam." *Journal of Southeast Asian Studies* 18, no. 1: 1–22.
Whitmore, John K. 1987. "From Classical Scholarship to Confucian Belief in Vietnam." *Vietnam Forum* 9: 49–65.
Woodside, Alexander B. 1988. *Vietnam and the Chinese Model.* Cambridge, MA, and London: Harvard University Press.

CONSTITUTIONAL (BLOODLESS) REVOLUTION (1932) (THAILAND)

The Constitutional Revolution of 24 June 1932, staged by a group of mainly junior military and civilian officials organized underground as the People's Party, overthrew the absolute monarchy of Siam (Thailand). The coup took only three hours and caused no casualties. The People's Party then set about creating a constitution based on the concept of popular sovereignty. The monarchy was not abolished, but it was made subject to constitutional rules. Consequently, this 1932 coup has retrospectively been known as the Bloodless Constitutional Revolution.

In historical perspective, it is clear that the coup was the outcome of political conflicts generated by the political and social changes initiated during the long reign of King Chulalongkorn (Rama V) (r. 1868–1910), in response to the impact of and pressure from Western colonial powers. Modeled after the "new" colonial policies and administration of the Netherlands East Indies and British India, Chulalongkorn's reforms succeeded in creating a large, new, functionally organized civil service that allowed the monarch to centralize power in an unprecedented manner. But these reforms were much less successful in effecting greater social equality and justice for the king's subjects. Gradually, members of the new bureaucracy, into which many able commoners were necessarily recruited, began to resent the monopoly of high office by royalty and aristocrats and to see advantages in a republican form of government. The impending internal political conflict at the end of Chulalongkorn's reign was thus over whether the ruling regime should continue or should be modernized and transformed into a democratic state, with or without the monarchy. Still in full control of the government and the newly modernized army, the monarchy and upper-class elite were convinced that the implementation of a democratic form of government in Siam, allowing the population full political participation, was not a serious issue. For them, democracy in Siam was inappropriate and even farcical.

The seeds of the successful revolt against the absolute monarchy were sown during the reign of Chulalongkorn's son, King Vajiravudh (Rama VI) (r. 1910–1925). As early as 1912, a coup was attempted by a group of junior military officials whose political goal, in part influenced by the Chinese Republican Revolution of 1911, was the establishment of a republican form of government. The monarchy reacted to the failure of the coup and the growing restiveness of a new generation of government officials by instituting repression. Not long afterward, however, King Vajiravudh built a miniature town that he called Dusit Thani, whose residents were members of the nobility and government officials, to conduct experiments in self-government and as a living showcase of "democracy already at work" in the kingdom. Yet the king continued to appoint his favorites to powerful positions at court and in the government, causing great dissatisfaction among the senior royal princes and criticism within the emerging public sphere and among commoner civilian and military officials.

By the time that King Prajadhipok (Rama VII) (r. 1925–1935) succeeded to the throne, newspapers and magazines had spread the call for a constitution widely among the urban and educated populace of the kingdom. King Prajadhipok tried to salvage the declining image of the monarchy and its administration by creating the Supreme Council of State, consisting of senior members of the royal family, many of whom had been made inactive in government affairs during the previous reign. Feeling the pressure of the times, the king inclined toward the idea of promulgating a constitution as a means to restore faith in the regime. But his American adviser and the high nobility, including the members of the Supreme Council of State, were not supportive. The king therefore postponed the proclamation of any constitution. Meanwhile, the world economic depression had set in (1929–1931), and Siam was seriously affected by the plummeting prices of rice

and rubber on the international market. The state's finances had already been badly strained by the extravagance of Rama VI's reign, and the depression increased pressure for steep cuts in government spending and more taxes with stiff penalties imposed upon the people. Many Thai were hurt by these policies, but those best positioned to express their resentment were the urban educated, many of whom had their salaries cut or were dismissed from the civil service.

The seeds of the revolution sprouted inside the country, but those seeds had been brought home by Thai students who had studied overseas. In 1926, a group of seven government scholarship students in their mid-twenties, led by Pridi Phanomyong (1900–1983), a student in law and political economy at the University of Paris, got together in a student's dormitory in the Latin Quarter to "promote" a new future for Siam. They agreed to set up a political group to push for a change of the government in Bangkok. Their underground activities continued after they returned home to serve in civil and military posts. The so-called Promoters' plan came closer to reality when Colonel Phraya Phahonphonphayuhasena (Phot Phahonyothin), a senior military officer in the Royal Artillery whose sincere and humble character earned him respect and trust from many military as well as civilian officials of the time, agreed to lead the group. He had graduated from a military academy in Germany and afterward was sent on tour to Japan to study the Japanese army.

The revolution finally broke out in Bangkok very early in the morning of 24 June with a swift military takeover of Government House. Shortly thereafter, a large group of officer cadets, soldiers, and sailors were ordered to attend and observe a supposed training session for the cadets on the grounds in front of the Ananta Samakhom Throne Hall. Standing atop a tank, Phot Phahonyothin declared to this surprised audience that the People's Party had seized the government from the absolute monarchy regime. The royal government and the senior princes were unable to make any effective resistance, not least because King Prajadhipok was on vacation at his seaside palace, "Klai Kangwol" (*Sans Souci,* or Far from Worries), several hours away from the capital by train. Proclamation No. 1 of the People's Party, which served as the manifesto of the coup group, strongly condemned the monarchy's favoritism toward princes of blood and accused the absolutist of exploiting the people in hard times. It also demolished the ruling myth behind centuries of the absolute power and the righteousness of the monarchy. Not the king, according to the People's Party, but the people were the true owners of the country, and they themselves should rule it. Issuing Proclamation No. 1 was probably the most radical act by the coup group. And had it then been acted upon consistently, something like a real revolution might have developed.

The announced policy of the People's Party was summed up in six principles:

- To maintain absolute national independence in all respects, including the political, the judicial, and the economic
- To maintain national security both externally and internally
- To promote economic well-being by creating full employment and by launching a national economic plan
- To guarantee equality for all
- To grant complete liberty and freedom to the people, provided that this did not contradict the preceding principles
- To provide education for the people

In fact, the Promoters quite quickly backed off from the republican radicalism of Proclamation No. 1: Pridi and other leaders of the People's Party apologized to the king for the proclamation's "defamatory" language about the royal family. Soon came a period of negotiation and compromise between the old order and its adversaries, resulting in the appointment of several former high-ranking nobles to an interim cabinet. Two important figures who played a crucial role at this juncture were Phraya Manopakorn and Phraya Srivisarnvaja. Manopakorn was a chief judge of the Court of Appeals and was named prime minister. Srivisarnvaja, former permanent secretary to the Ministry of Foreign Affairs, was appointed foreign minister. (Ironically, he had helped to deter Prajadhipok from granting a constitution.)

Subsequent negotiations between King Prajadhipok and the People's Party resulted in the promulgation of the supposedly permanent Constitution of 1932, replacing an interim constitution written solely by Pridi of the People's Party. The 1932 Constitution created a unicameral parliament consisting of two categories of representatives in equal numbers. Because of the political "immaturity" of the common people, it was declared that the first category of members of Parliament (MPs) would be elected not directly but by delegates of the people, whereas the second category of MPs were to be nominated by the People's Party with royal consent. Direct election by the people—and the elimination of the second category of MPs—would be instituted when more than half the population had completed four years of primary education, a process to be completed in not more than ten years. The first indirect election took place on 15 November 1933. The *tambon* (subdistrict) representatives gathered in the provincial governors' offices to cast their votes for the parliamentary candidates, who presented their policies in speeches that day. Most of the successful candidates were respected local figures.

But the Constitution of 1932 by no means settled the conflicts between the People's Party and the court. The former worked to exclude aristocrats from the new arenas of democratic politics; the king and his circle resisted, insisting on Prajadhipok's prerogatives as a constitutional monarch.

Nine months after "the change of government" (*kan plian plang kan pokkrong*)—the phrase commonly used today to describe the 1932 Revolution—the first crisis broke out. Pridi had drafted in outline form an economic plan designed to fulfill the People's Party's stated commitment to ending unemployment and promoting social equality. This plan called for comprehensive state planning for and management of the economy, including the nationalization of industries and services. Private property, however, was to be respected. Pridi's initiative allowed the court and its allies to go on the offensive. The king himself wrote a detailed, confidential critique of the plan, which was promptly leaked by Foreign Minister Phraya Srivisarnvaja. Prime Minister Phraya Manopakorn, together with a faction of senior army members of the People's Party led by Colonel Phraya Songsuradej, thereupon denounced the whole plan as a communist plot.

An uproar broke out during the debate in the National Assembly in reaction to this campaign and to the prime minister's transparent threats to the leaders of the People's Party. Phraya Manopakorn then threw down the gauntlet by proroguing the National Assembly and issuing, on his own authority, an anticommunist law. Pridi was forced to leave for voluntary exile in Europe. When the military group within the People's Party under Colonel Phahol and Lieutenant Colonel Phibul (Phibunsongkhram) discovered that Phraya Manopakorn's and Phrya Songsuradej's factions were moving to eliminate the People's Party and to restore the absolute monarchy, they reacted swiftly. They executed a preemptive counter-coup, taking over the government and declaring Parliament open once again. Colonel Phahol became prime minister and Phibul minister of defense. In 1934, Pridi returned from his exile in France, and over the next years, he became, successively, minister of the interior, minister of foreign affairs, and minister of finance.

This setback to the royalists and the consequent strengthening of the younger and more progressive Promoters in the new government engendered a violent reaction. In October 1933, on the eve of Siam's first elections, provincial military units under the command of Prince Boworadet, a former minister of war under the absolute monarchy, marched down to Bangkok. The heavy fighting took place north of the capital, resulting in many deaths and casualties on both sides. But the rebellion was eventually suppressed by government troops under Lieutenant Colonel Phibul. The Boworadet Rebellion thus reintroduced into the infant constitutional system the old practice of employing force to overthrow a government.

Phraya Manopakorn's authoritarian proroguing of the National Assembly in 1933, together with the Boworadet Rebellion in the same year, destroyed the fragile understanding between King Prajadhipok and the People's Party. Although the king was not directly involved in either case, he had been implicated by the use of his name. Further unresolved conflicts finally led the king to abdicate the throne in 1935 (while in England for medical attention).

From 1934 to 1938, political stability and national sovereignty came to the government and the country. The much abused traditional practices of poll taxes, forced labor, and confiscation of peasants' land and property to pay their debts were finally abolished. The structures of government and the development of

political democracy, as outlined in the constitution, were based on a three-stage program: a period of military rule, a period of political tutelage, and a period of full constitutional government. These ideas closely resemble Sun Yat-sen's (1866–1925) theory of a three-stage revolution for China.

Underlying this political theory was a strong emphasis on popular education as a prerequisite for attaining political democracy. Educational progress was a significant component of national policy in the first four years of the government led by the People's Party. But private initiatives were also encouraged, the most remarkable of which was Pridi's personal founding of Thammasat University, the country's first open university, in 1934, specifically intended to develop that culture of citizenship that democracy requires.

As self-proclaimed defenders of the people, the Promoters were necessarily also nationalists. Nothing grated on their nationalist sensibilities more than the extraterritorial privileges forced on the absolute monarchy through a series of unequal treaties with Western powers and with Japan. By 1937, thanks largely to Pridi's efforts, these treaties were all terminated, and Siam was, for the first time, able to stand as a visibly independent nation-state.

The important legacy of the 1932 Revolution thus was the termination of the absolute monarchy and its replacement by a constitutional government based on the sovereignty of the people. Thailand thereby entered the historical era of formal bourgeois democracy, along with other former colonial and semi-colonial states in Asia. But Thailand's entry into that era occurred only with hesitation. The People's Party, born inside the absolutist bureaucracy, proved unable to transcend its origins fully. In an overwhelmingly rural society with a high degree of illiteracy, it had no large and firm popular base. It was quite easy to seize and retain power once the royalists had been crushed, but it was much more difficult to transform and modernize society in a thoroughgoing way. In significant respects, then, the coup of 1932 was actually the replacement of one elite by a newer and more modern one, while large segments of Thai society continued much as before. In this sense, "the Revolution of 1932" is mostly a misnomer. At the same time, 24 June 1932 does mark a turning point in Siam's history. There would be no reversion to absolutism, the prestige of the aristocracy was permanently damaged, and institutions and policies were created that opened the way for democratic popular participation in the longer run.

THANET APHRONSUVAN

See also Chinese Revolution (1911);
Indigenous Political Power; Military
and Politics in Southeast Asia; Nationalism
and Independence Movements in Southeast
Asia; Plaek Phibunsongkhram, Field Marshal
(1897–1964); Prajadhipok (Rama VII)
(r. 1925–1935); Pridi Phanomyong
(1900–1983); Reforms and Modernization
in Siam; Sun Yat-sen, Dr. (1866–1925);
Thammasat University; Vajiravudh
(Rama VI) (r. 1910–1925)

References:
Batson, Benjamin A. 1984. *The End of the Absolute Monarchy in Siam*. Singapore and New York: Oxford University Press.
Landon, Kenneth P. 1939. *Siam in Transition: A Brief Survey of Cultural Trends in the Five Years since the Revolution of 1932*. Chicago: University of Chicago Press.
Nakharin Mektrairat. 1997. *Kan patiwat Siam, 2475 [The Revolution of 1932 in Siam]*. Bangkok: Amarin Academic Publishings.
Stowe, Judith A. 1991. *Siam Becomes Thailand: A Story of Intrigue*. Honolulu: University of Hawai'i Press.
Thawatt Mokarapong. 1972. *History of the Thai Revolution: A Study in Political Behaviour*. Bangkok: Chalermnit.

CONSTITUTIONAL DEVELOPMENTS IN BURMA (1900–1941)

Burma was an integral province of British India until 1937. Consequently, constitutional developments in Burma between the beginning of the twentieth century and the Japanese invasion of the colony in 1941 shadowed constitutional developments in British India. There, the intention of constitutional policy was, after World War I (1914–1918), the creation of a viable, self-governing, democratic state that would be managed by politicians who would be attracted by its institutions and would implement policies sympathetic to British economic and strategic interests. Creating India and Burma as integral parts of the British Commonwealth of Nations as it operated in the 1930s was the ultimate but distant goal. The internal form this was to take was the establishment of a political system that was modeled on British parliamentary democracy, with an elected parliament, a cabinet responsible to the parliamentary majority, and a nonpolitical civil service to administer the state.

In January 1886, British Burma (present-day Myanmar) was created as a unified province. This political entity included Arakan and Tenasserim (both captured in 1826), Lower Burma including the Irrawaddy Delta and Pegu (annexed in 1852), the remainder of what is now the country of Myanmar (that is, Upper Burma), and what was known as the Frontier Areas. This entity was formally under the charge of a chief commissioner who was responsible to the governor-general of India. In 1897, after peace had been established in the province, the chief commissioner was replaced by a lieutenant governor. Assisting him was the small and purely advisory Legislative Council of 9 appointed members, all British officials except for 2 European businessmen. The council was expanded to 15 members in 1909, with 4 Burmese, 1 Indian, and 1 Chinese, all appointed by the lieutenant governor. It was again expanded in 1920 to include 30 members—there were 10 Burmese, 2 Indians, and 1 Chinese, with the remaining positions filled by officials and businessmen, almost all of whom were British.

During World War I, the British government in London repeatedly stated that the intention of colonial policy in India after the war would be to create conditions conducive to development and democracy under British tutelage. However, initially, it was believed that Burma was not "ready" for the first steps in self-government, and accordingly, it was excluded from the reforms introduced in 1919. At that time, the Montagu-Chelmsford reforms, named after the viceroy and the secretary of state for India, were incorporated in the Government of India Act of 1919. That act established a system of government known as a dyarchy in the provinces of India proper but excluded Burma. Dyarchy allowed for elected Indians to be responsible for some government departments while ultimate power, especially over defense, financial affairs, and foreign policy, remained in the hands of British officials, including the governors of Indian provinces.

The consequence of excluding Burma from the constitutional advances in India at that time was a nationalist campaign demanding the introduction of a more democratic political system than the then governor, Sir Percy Reginald Craddock (t. 1917–1922), had been willing to contemplate. Soon, amid widespread political protests in Burma, two delegations of Burmese politicians arrived in London and demanded that the dyarchy be extended to the colony. The secretary of state relented, and the British Parliament passed legislation to that effect in 1921. Responsibility for education and forests was given to Burmese elected politicians from 1922 onward, but their powers were limited, and the change did not affect the running of the government. Nor did their powers extend to the entire country. The Frontier Areas remained exclusively under the control of the governor. The new system was not popular, and very few people bothered to vote in the elections held every three years after 1922.

In 1928, the British government established the Simon Commission to review how dyarchy was working and to make recommendations for the next stages of tutelary democracy. It was followed by the Indian Round Table Conference (November 1930–January 1931) and the Burma Round Table Conference (November 1931–January 1932), which were efforts to gain the consent of nationalist politicians for constitutional reforms that would retain ultimate powers in the hands of the British. The conclusions of these conferences were that India and Burma should be given a greater degree of self-government under revised constitutional structures. Over the objections of the government of India, it was also decided that Burma should be separated from India and established as a discrete entity under the secretary of state for India and for Burma.

A large number of people in Burma had been advocating such a separation for many years. It was argued that, culturally and administratively, Burma was sufficiently different from India to justify a separate government. The absence of immigration controls between the two regions angered many Burmese, who saw the proportion of Indians in the total population rise within a short period of time to nearly 10 percent. Moreover, extensive Indian ownership of agricultural land and many industries was seen as holding back the advancement of the Burmese nation. Most Burmese nationalist politicians concurred with the government of Burma that India was draining their country of much-needed revenues through a fiscal system that operated in India. The demand for separation was clearly popular, and the Legislative Council endorsed the conclusions of the Burma Round Table Conference in February 1932.

Separation was to be the major issue in the next elections for the Legislative Council, to be held in November 1932. Although it was widely expected that political parties that favored separation would easily dominate the new council, the power of money in politics was soon to change the balance of power. None of the proseparatist political parties were able to raise much in the way of funds to back their election campaigns. However, their opponents, the politicians who advocated federation with India, were well financed by Indian businesses that believed their interests would be harmed by a separate Burmese political authority with autonomous control over immigration, financial flows, and the like. A number of leading politicians who initially advocated separation switched sides toward the end of campaigning. The antiseparatists won the election but then immediately began to backtrack, as they realized that the result had not been in the interest of the Burmese.

To resolve the issue, the British government called another Burma Round Table Conference to consult Burmese political opinion. After long and inconclusive consultations, the British Parliament concluded in 1934 that Burma would be established as a separate entity with the power to regulate trade and immigration with India after a transitional period. This arrangement was established in the Government of Burma Act (1935), which, in effect, became the constitution of Burma until the Japanese invasion in 1942. The act provided for a two-house legislature. The lower house, known as the Legislative Assembly, was to be fully elected, whereas the upper house, or Senate, was appointed by the governor. The governor's cabinet, which would be formed with majority support from the Legislative Assembly, would have responsibility for all government matters in Burma proper except for defense, finance, and foreign affairs. Those areas remained the prerogative of the governor, as did all the affairs of the Frontiers Area Administration. The Legislative Council had 132 members. Although the majority of these members were elected at large, there was separate representation provided for ethnic minorities. Twelve seats were reserved for Karens, 8 for Indians, 2 for Anglo-Burmans, and 3 for Europeans. In addition, there were 12 seats set aside for the various ethnic communities' chambers of commerce and 4 for labor unions. One seat was reserved for Rangoon University.

In the first and only election held under the 1935 Constitution, no party won a majority of seats, so a great deal of jockeying for position ensued to put together a coalition government. The man who succeeded in forming the first cabinet and who became the first premier was Dr. Ba Maw (t. 1937–1939). He remained in power until his majority dissolved following widespread public demonstrations, including anti-Indian riots in Rangoon and elsewhere. U Pu formed the second government in 1939, but it fell in turn the following year as the coalition broke up over internal divisions. The last government was formed by U Saw, who had been the forest minister in Pu's government and had been instrumental in bringing down Ba Maw's government. The second elections, scheduled to take place in 1941, were postponed because of the Pacific War (1941–1945).

During the five years that the Government of Burma Act of 1935 was in force, Burmese politicians and British civil servants developed a new working relationship with each other. By establishing what the Burmese press referred to as the "91 Departments Government"—denoting the 91 government areas that were now under Burmese ministerial jurisdiction—the 1935 act gave Burmese politicians significant political power, something they did not have under the dyarchy. The tone for working under the new constitution was set both by the two British governors who operated it and by the exigencies that their governments faced. After 1937, both governors were themselves politicians. Sir Archibald Cochrane (t. 1936–1941), the inaugural governor, was a somewhat dour individual who kept power and information to himself. His successor, Sir Reginald Dorman-Smith (t. 1941–1946), favored a far more open style of government and was willing to enter into political negotiations with his ministers. U Saw proved to be a master in this arena, and he was in the process of achieving significant advances in terms of increasing the Burmese proportion of the civil service and gaining control over Indian immigration. The Pacific War ended this experiment in tutelary democracy. But had it not occurred, one can at least speculate that Burma would have developed a political system more like that of India or Malaysia today rather than the military domination that has existed for most of the years since independence in 1948.

R. H. TAYLOR

See also Aung San (1915–1947); Ba Maw, Dr. (b. 1893); British Burma; British India, Government of; Dorman-Smith, Sir Reginald (t. 1941–1946); Nationalism and Independence Movements in Southeast Asia; Thakin (Lord, Master); University of Rangoon

References:

Cady, John F. 1958. *A History of Modern Burma.* Ithaca, NY: Cornell University Press.

Collis, Maurice. 1956. *Last and First in Burma.* London: Faber and Faber.

Donnison, F. S. V. 1953. *Public Administration in Burma.* London: Oxford University Press for the Royal Institute for International Affairs.

Furnivall, J. S. 1956. *Colonial Policy and Practice.* New York: New York University Press.

Harvey, G. E. 1942. *British Rule in Burma, 1824–1942.* London: Faber and Faber.

Taylor, Robert H. 1974. "The Relationship between Burmese Social Classes and British-Indian Policy on the Behaviour of the Burmese Political Elite, 1937–1942." Ph.D. diss., Cornell University.

———. 1976. "Politics in Late Colonial Burma: The Case of U Saw." *Modern Asian Studies* 10, no. 2 (April): 161–194.

Tinker, Hugh. 1969 [1954]. *The Foundation of Local Self-Government in India, Pakistan and Burma.* London: Pall Mall Press.

CONSTITUTIONAL DEVELOPMENTS IN THE PHILIPPINES (1900–1941)

During the American colonial period (1898–1946), the Philippines did not have its own constitution until 1935. Instead, American laws specifically passed for the Philippines replaced the constitution that was framed by Filipinos in Malolos, Bulacan, in 1898. In general, the provisions of the Bill of Rights of the U.S. Constitution applied to the Philippines, except for the right to bear arms and the right to a trial by jury. Filipinos lobbied for independence early in the colonial period, and their efforts, together with anti-imperialist sentiment in the United States, resulted in passage of the Jones Law in 1916, which promised the Philippines independence once stable government had been achieved. No steps were taken by the Americans to have Filipinos prepare a constitution, however, until the 1930s. Filipinos formed an independence congress in 1930 to thrash out potential problems related to independence, and they made recommendations in regard to the framing of a constitution.

Formal steps to draft a constitution were to be taken after the passage of a definitive independence law in the U.S. Congress, a law that would have to be approved by Filipinos. In 1934, the Tydings-McDuffie Law was passed by Congress and accepted by the Filipinos. Immediately thereafter, a constitutional convention was created. The convention drafted a constitution that was ratified in 1935 and became known as the 1935 Constitution. It had to be approved by the U.S. president and thus was written partially to gain acceptance in Washington. This constitution became the basic charter for the Philippine Commonwealth government, a semiautonomous government that would prepare the Philippines for independence in 1946. The 1935 Constitution, minus the transitory provisions, was also intended to serve as the basic law of the Philippine Republic that would be established in 1946. It set up a republican state based on the American model, with governmental powers separated into the executive, judicial, and legislative branches. The 1935 Constitution was amended in 1940 to turn the unicameral legislature into a bicameral body, and the length of the president's term was changed. As amended, that constitution served as the basic law of the Philippines until 1973, when a new constitution was ratified during the period of martial law (from 1972 to 1981) under President Ferdinand E. Marcos (t. 1965–1986).

When the Americans formally acquired the Philippines in 1898, under the terms of the Treaty of Paris, the Philippines had already established a republican government with a con-

stitution that had been framed and adopted in Malolos, Bulacan. However, the United States recognized neither the Philippine Republic nor the 1898 Constitution; instead, the Americans implemented a military government from 1898 to 1901. Thereafter, a civil government was established, which, as noted, applied most provisions of the U.S. Bill of Rights. The Philippines was governed by policies set by the U.S. president as carried out by the War Department; this arrangement was formally approved by the U.S. Congress in the Philippine Act of 1902, which gave the president the power to govern the Philippines. The direct representative of the president was the governor-general, who was head of the Philippine Commission that acted as the legislative and executive body in the Philippines. In 1907, under the provisions of the Act of 1902, Filipinos were allowed to participate in the legislative process with the creation of an elective assembly. The Philippine Assembly served as the lower house of the Philippine legislature, but all its bills had to be approved by the U.S. governor-general and the U.S. president.

In 1916, in line with the American democratic policy of self-determinism and independence for the Philippines, the Jones Law was passed. The legislature was changed to the all-Filipino Senate and House of Representatives, following the U.S. model. The Jones Law did not have any provisions for framing a constitution, however, and all laws passed by Filipinos had to be approved by the American governor-general and the president. Filipinos lobbied for independence under the Jones Law, sending special delegations of political leaders to the United States to champion the cause. In 1924, the Fairfield Bill was filed in the U.S. Congress, advocating that the Philippines be granted independence after a thirty-year transition period. The bill did not pass due to opposition by Filipino politicians led by Manuel L. Quezon (1878–1944), on grounds that the transition period was too long.

With no acceptable independence bills in the U.S. Congress, the Philippine legislature passed a measure that would provide for a nationwide plebiscite on the independence question. The bill was vetoed by Governor-General Leonard Wood (t. 1921–1927), sustained by President Calvin Coolidge (t. 1923–1929). To further the cause of independence and show the Filipinos' readiness for it, the First Independence Congress was held in Manila in February 1930. The congress discussed various problems the Philippines faced in regard to independence and made recommendations preparatory to drafting a constitution.

The Americans passed the Hare-Hawes-Cutting Act in 1933, providing for Philippines independence, but it was rejected by the Philippine legislature. Subsequently, the Tydings-McDuffie Act was passed after Quezon went to the United States seeking a more acceptable independence measure. That act was passed in 1934 and was accepted by the Philippine legislature.

The Tydings-McDuffie Act provided for a constitutional convention to be called no later than 1 October 1934. It also set basic requirements for the constitution: that it be republican in form, that it include a bill of rights, and that it be approved by the president of the United States. The measure also stated that any amendments to the constitution would have to be approved by the U.S. president.

Special elections were called on 10 July 1934 for delegates to the convention. The 202 delegates met in an inaugural session twenty days later. The oldest delegate, Teodoro Sandiko, had signed the 1898 Constitution; the youngest, Wenceslao Q. Vinzons, a former provincial governor, was twenty-five years old. Elected president of the convention was Claro M. Recto, a former senator.

The convention worked for six months, finishing on 8 February 1935 with the formal approval of the draft constitution. The document was formally signed by the delegates on 19 February 1935 and was approved by U.S. president Franklin D. Roosevelt (t. 1933–1945) on 23 March 1935. The Filipino people ratified it in a plebiscite on 14 May 1935.

The 1935 Constitution had seventeen articles that covered the national territory, national principles, the bill of rights, citizenship, suffrage, the civil service, and the conservation and utilization of natural resources. Also included were transitory provisions related to the country's shift in status from a colony to an independent republic, as well as the framework for creating a democratic republican state following the U.S. model. The government would follow the principle of the separation of powers and have three separate and equal branches—the executive, legislative, and judiciary. An elected president would head the executive branch; a unicameral national assembly would comprise the legislative branch; and a supreme court, together with regional and other courts, would form the judiciary. The president would have one six-year term.

Transitory provisions provided for the establishment of an American high commissioner to represent the U.S. president in the Philippines. They also addressed trade and immigration relations between the United States and the Philippines, currency and security limitations, and the continuance of American military and naval bases even after independence.

The 1935 Constitution served as the basis of the Philippine Commonwealth government and was meant to remain in force for the Philippine Republic that would be inaugurated after a ten-year transition period, on 4 July 1946.

Pursuant to the provisions of the 1935 Constitution, national elections were held on 17 September 1935. Manuel L. Quezon won as president, with Sergio Osmeña (1878–1961) as vice-president. Representatives of the National Assembly were also chosen in the first elections held under the constitution. The Commonwealth government was inaugurated on 15 November 1935.

The ruling Nacionalista Party met in July 1939 to consider amendments to correct weaknesses in the 1935 Constitution and, ostensibly in reaction to popular demand, to extend Quezon's term as president. Under the original provisions for the presidency, Quezon's term was to end in 1941, so an amendment was necessary in order to extend his stay in office. After much discussion, three amendments were formulated to: (1) change the terms of the president and vice-president to four years, with reelection, thereby giving a maximum of eight straight years for any one person; (2) change the unicameral National Assembly into a bicameral legislature to consist of the Senate and the House of Representatives; and (3) establish the independent Commission on Elections to supervise all official elections.

The National Assembly approved the amendments on 11 April 1940, and the Filipino people ratified them in a plebiscite on 18 June 1940. After President Roosevelt approved the amendments on 2 December 1940, the 1935

Constitution as amended went into force. This constitution remained in force throughout the rest of the Commonwealth years, including the years of the Pacific War (1941–1945) and those of the Philippine Republic inaugurated on 4 July 1946. It would be superseded by a constitution drafted in another constitutional convention convened in 1971; the new constitution would be ratified under the martial law regime of President Ferdinand E. Marcos.

The constitutional developments during the American regime in the Philippines showed that the Filipino people had an active political capacity. And for its part, the United States proved to be a permissive colonial power. The 1935 Constitution was the first document of its type to be created by Southeast Asian people under colonial rule.

RICARDO TROTA JOSE

See also Marcos, Ferdinand (1917–1989); Martial Law (1972–1981) (The Philippines); Osmeña, Sergio, Sr. (1878–1961); Philippines under U.S. Colonial Administration; Philippines-U.S. "Special Relationship"; Quezon, Manuel Luis (1878–1944); U.S. Military Bases in Southeast Asia

References:

Aruego, José. 1937. *The Framing of the Constitution of the Philippines.* Manila: University Publishing.

Golay, Frank H. *Face of Empire.* Quezon City, the Philippines: Ateneo de Manila University Press.

Hayden, Joseph Ralston. 1955. *The Philippines: A Study in National Development.* New York: Macmillan.

Pacis, Vicente Albano, et al. 1971. *Founders of Freedom: The History of Three Philippine Constitutions.* Manila: Capitol Publishing House.

CONSTITUTIONAL MONARCHY OF MALAYA/MALAYSIA

Like Thailand and Cambodia, Malaysia has a constitutional monarchy. The idea of a Malay ruler being guided by a written law can be traced to the *Undang-Undang Melaka* or *Hukum Kanun Melaka,* the laws of Melaka, which became the basis for the written laws of the various Malay sultanates after Melaka fell to the Portuguese in 1511. The development of the modern Malay constitutional monarchy was enhanced by the Residential System introduced by the British in Perak, Selangor, Negri Sembilan, and Pahang beginning in 1874. When the Federated Malay States (FMS) was formed in 1896 to streamline the administration of the four states, the Durbar, or Conference of Rulers, was instituted as a forum for the sultans to meet and express views on issues pertaining to their states. In the meantime, to guarantee its independence and to avoid direct foreign (British) intervention, Johor promulgated its modern constitution (the *Undang-Undang Tubuh Kerajaan Johor*) in 1895, which expressly prohibited even the sultan himself from ceding any part of the Johor territory to a foreign power. In the same light, Terengganu introduced its modern constitution in 1911. In general, in addition to the British Resident or Adviser, Malay rulers shared power with their respective state councils.

The Federation of Malaya/Malaysia Constitution stipulates that the nine hereditary Malay rulers will elect from among themselves the *yang di-pertuan agong,* or supreme head of state/paramount ruler (king), who shall hold office for a maximum of five years and be succeeded by another ruler likewise elected. Seniority is an important criterion; however, some rulers have declined on the basis of advanced age. The nine Malay sultans of the peninsular Malay States (Perlis, Kedah, Kelantan, Terengganu, Pahang, Perak, Selangor, Negri Sembilan, and Johor) form the Majlis Raja-Raja (the postindependence term for the Conference of Rulers), where the election is held.

Article 40 of the constitution states that the king "shall act in accordance with the advice of the Cabinet," headed by the prime minister. The amended Article 66 (4A) rules that a bill shall automatically become law thirty days after it has been presented to the king.

The king is the head of state in Malaysia and ceremoniously convenes and dissolves Parliament upon the advice of the prime minister. As each Malay sultan is the head of the Islamic faith in his own state, the king assumes this role for Penang, Melaka, Sabah, and Sarawak. The king can grant a royal pardon to a death-row inmate's appeal.

ABDUL RAHMAN HAJI ISMAIL

See also Bhumibol Adulyadej (Rama IX) (r. 1946–); Constitutional (Bloodless)

Revolution (1932) (Thailand); Federated Malay States (FMS) (1896); Johor; Melaka; Melayu Islam Beraja (MIB, Malay Islamic Monarcy); Pahang; Penang (1786); Residential System (Malaya); Siamese Malay States (Kedah, Perlis, Kelantan, Terengganu); Sihanouk, Norodom (1922–) *Undang-Undang Laut* (Melaka Maritime Laws/Code); Western Malay States (Perak, Selangor, Negri Sembilan, and Pahang)

References:

Azlan Shah, Raja Tun. 1982. "The Role of Constitutional Rulers: A Malaysian Perspective for the Laity." *Journal of Malaysian and Comparative Law* 9: 1–18.

Malaysian Constitution. 1970. Kuala Lumpur: Jabatan Cetak Kerajaan.

Mohammad Suffian Bin Hashim. 1975. *An Introduction to the Constitution of Malaysia.* Kuala Lumpur: Jabatan Cetak Kerajaan.

Perlembagaan Malaysia [*Constitution of Malaysia*]. 2002. Petaling Jaya, Malaysia: International Law Book Service.

CONSULADO

Merchants within Manila and certain other cities of the Spanish Empire were authorized to form guildlike organizations (*consulados*) with an executive composed of a "prior" and two "consuls" indirectly elected annually or biennially by the entire membership. Among the Manila consulado's most significant responsibilities after 1769 was the apportionment of the vouchers, or *boletas*, that entitled Spanish residents to cargo space on the two galleons each year that were the only authorized vessels permitted to transport Asian luxury merchandise across the Pacific to Acapulco. In general, affairs of a commercial nature were dealt with by these merchants, who organized themselves into a special court known as the *tribunal de consulado* (tribunal of commerce), with a jurisdiction confined to Manila but covering questions of mercantile obligation, commercial rights, and contracts. Decisions were reached more in accordance with the provisions of equity than through strict conformity with the letter of the law. Officers and seamen involved in the galleon trade were also subject to the court's jurisdiction while it persisted (until 1811). Appeals were referred to the *tribunal de alzadas* (court of appeal), composed of a magistrate from the high court and two merchants, and in the final resort to the Council of the Indies. In 1834, the tribunal de consulado was replaced by the *real tribunal de comercio* (royal court of commerce), and its jurisdiction finally was merged with that of the ordinary courts by a royal decree of 1 February 1869.

GREG BANKOFF

See also Galleon Trade; Hispanization; Manila; Philippines under Spanish Colonial Rule (ca. 1560s–1898); Spanish Philippines

References:

Bankoff, Greg. 1996. *Crime, Society and the State in the Nineteenth-Century Philippines.* Quezon City, the Philippines: Ateneo de Manila University Press.

Cunningham, Charles. 1919. *The Audiencia in the Spanish Colonies as Illustrated by the Audiencia of Manila (1583–1800).* Berkeley: University of California Press.

Legarda, Benito. 1999. *After the Galleons: Foreign Trade, Economic Change and Entrepreneurship in the Nineteenth-Century Philippines.* Center for Southeast Asian Studies Monograph 18. Madison, WI: Center for Southeast Asian Studies.

Schurz, William. 1939. *The Manila Galleon.* New York: Dutton.

COUNTRY TRADERS

Country trade was the term used by the British East India Company (EIC) in the eighteenth and early nineteenth centuries to describe the external commerce of India conducted privately and not with its own ships. The company's royal charter granted a monopoly of trade east of the Cape of Good Hope, but by the early eighteenth century, the EIC acknowledged private trade as useful; from the middle of the century, it left the bulk of external trade to country traders. These individuals were either the EIC's own officials, who were permitted to trade on their own account outside India itself, or merchants based in India under license. The trade was recorded in the company's books, and taxes were paid on it.

Until the mid-eighteenth century, country traders rarely ventured beyond Tenasserim, Kedah, and Aceh but were attracted eastward, largely by the rapid expansion of the China trade. They collected tropical produce from the

Indonesian archipelago, and beginning in the 1780s, they turned to the opium trade, which the company preferred to leave in private hands. The country trade was stimulated by the foundation of Penang—which was acquired for the company in 1786 by a Madras-based country trader named Francis Light (1740–1794)—and by the occupation of Dutch Java, Melaka, and the Moluccas during the Napoleonic Wars (1803–1815).

Country trade agency houses, mainly based in Bengal or Madras, were initially financed almost entirely by company servants in their private capacity and were often staffed by former officials. The end of the company's Indian trade monopoly in 1813 attracted free traders from Britain, who were not welcomed at first by country traders and found it difficult to compete. But they had broken into the archipelago trade by the time Singapore was founded in 1819, and the loss of the company's monopoly of the China trade in 1833 ended the country trade.

C. M. TURNBULL

See also Aceh (Acheh); Agency-Houses, European; Anglo-Dutch Relations in Southeast Asia (Seventeenth to Twentieth Centuries); British India, Government of; East India Company (EIC) (1600), English; Jungle/Forest Products; Junk Ceylon (Ujung Salang, Phuket); Light, Captain Francis (1740–1794); Napoleonic Wars in Asia; Opium; Penang (1786); Raffles, Sir (Thomas) Stamford Bingley (1781–1826); Singapore (1819); Spices and the Spice Trade; Straits of Melaka; Straits Settlements (1826–1941); Vereenigde Oost-Indische Compagnie (VOC) ([Dutch] United East India Company) (1602)

References:

Bassett, D. K. 1964. "British Commercial and Strategic Interest in the Malay Peninsula during the Late Eighteenth Century." Pp. 122–140 in *Malayan and Indonesian Studies.* Edited by John Bastin and R. Roolvink. Oxford: Clarendon Press.

———. 1971. *British Trade and Policy in Indonesia and Malaysia in the Late Eighteenth Century.* Hull Monographs on South-East Asia no. 3. Zug, Switzerland: Interdocumentation.

Wong Lin Ken. 1960. "The Trade of Singapore, 1819–69." *Journal of the Malayan Branch of the Royal Asiatic Society* 33, no. 4: 1–315.

CRUZ, APOLINARIO DE LA (1814/1815–1841)
Nationalist *Avant-la-lettre*

Apolinario de la Cruz was the founder of a religious organization that attracted large numbers of followers in the provinces of Tayabas, Laguna, and Batangas in the Philippines in 1840 and 1841. He is generally regarded as a Filipino hero, a nationalist *avant-la-lettre* (forerunner).

Cruz was born in 1814 or 1815 to a relatively well-to-do peasant family in the town of Lucban, in what was then called the province of Tayabas (present-day Quezon). He was deeply religious and wanted to enter the monastic life. For this purpose, he went to Manila at the age of fifteen. However, as a native Filipino, an *indio,* he was not allowed to join one of the religious orders. He worked as a lay brother in the hospital of San Juan de Dios, a charitable institution in Manila. He also became a lay preacher and begged for alms. In 1832, he belonged to a group of people who founded a confraternity, the Cofradia de San José—an association focused on the worship of God, praying, promoting union among its members, and practicing charity.

In 1840, Apolinario de la Cruz, who had become known as *Kakang* Pule (Elder Brother Pule), returned to Lucban. There, he established a chapter of the Cofradia and sent representatives to towns in the surrounding provinces to spread the word. Cruz also submitted a request to the government to officially recognize the Cofradia. The local friar became jealous and suspicious of the popularity of the association, and he alerted the Spanish authorities. The Spaniards suspected the confraternity of being a political and subversive organization. What especially aroused suspicion among the Spaniards was the fact that the Cofradia accepted only pure-blooded *indios,* not Spaniards or mestizos, and that the leaders traveled around in the countryside, preaching and recruiting members to the movement. The request for recognition was rejected, and the Lucban friar urged the authorities to dissolve the association. Local officials undertook a halfhearted attempt to arrest some of the members.

To escape this harassment, Cruz and many of his followers moved to the neighboring province of Laguna, where they attracted large numbers of adherents. In September 1841, they established a camp in a village near the town of Bay, where followers from all sides responded to the call to join the movement. On 23 October 1841, a group of Spanish militia, police, and supporters of the friars, led by the governor of Tayabas, attacked the Cofradia camp, but they were repelled, and the governor was captured and killed by the *cofrades* (members of the *cofradia*). The Cofradia then moved its camp to a place called Alitao on the slopes of a hill known as San Cristobal. On 29 October, a much stronger Spanish expedition surrounded the camp, and the cofrades were attacked while dancing, singing, and praying. On 1 November, the Spanish soldiers overran the defenses and entered the camp, where they killed 300 to 500 followers and took about 500 as prisoners, including some 300 women. Cruz escaped, but the Spaniards captured him within a day. After a mock trial, he was executed by a firing squad on 4 November, and his head was cut off, stuck on a bamboo pole, and displayed on the road to serve as a warning to the population. On the same day, hundreds of prisoners were executed.

Historians have often found it difficult to place this seemingly irrational rebellion within the tradition of resistance movements in the country. David Sturtevant (1976) characterized the confraternity as a millenarian rebellion in a series of popular uprisings, a precursor of the nationalist movement at the end of the nineteenth century. Reynaldo Ileto (1979) placed the Cofradia within a broader Philippine tradition, namely, that of the *pasyon,* the story of Jesus Christ's suffering, death, and resurrection as the savior of humanity. Ileto showed that folk versions of the story were recited among the rural people and that images of the pasyon pervaded the thinking of the Cofradia. Cruz urged his followers to pray frequently, to participate in rituals, and to experience suffering in order to liberate the inner self and to remain steadfast. What the Spaniards found striking about the rebels was that they were fighting in a state of excitement, with a seeming disregard for death. When Apolinario de la Cruz was executed, Spanish observers noted that he "died serenely and showed unusual greatness of spirit" (Ileto 1979: 79).

WILLEM WOLTERS

See also Anti-Spanish Revolts (The Philippines); Friars, Spanish; Mestizo; Peasant

Uprisings and Protest Movements in Southeast Asia; Philippine War of Independence (1899–1902); Philippines under Spanish Colonial Rule (ca. 1560s–1898)

References:

Corpuz, O. D. 1989. *The Roots of the Filipino Nation.* 2 vols. Quezon City, the Philippines: Aklahi Foundation.

Ileto, Reynaldo Clemeña. 1979. *Pasyon and Revolution: Popular Movements in the Philippines, 1840–1910.* Quezon City, the Philippines: Ateneo de Manila University Press.

Sturtevant, David R. 1976. *Popular Uprisings in the Philippines, 1840–1940.* Ithaca, NY: Cornell University.

Sweet, David. 1970. "The Proto-political Peasant Movement in the Spanish Philippines: The *Cofradia de San José* and the Tayabas Rebellion of 1841." *Asian Studies* 8: 94–119.

CULTIVATION SYSTEM (*CULTUURSTELSEL*)
Keeping The Netherlands Afloat

The Cultivation System (CS), or *Cultuurstelsel,* was designed as a revenue system and implemented by the Dutch colonial government mainly in Java. It forced farmers to use part of their existing farmland or to bring land under cultivation for the production of cash crops, the sale of which would enable them to pay the land tax.

The system was a consequence of the poor financial situation of the Dutch East Indies after the Java War (1825–1830). It continued the prerogatives of indigenous rulers, who taxed their people in the form of forced deliveries. During the rule of Governor-General Herman W. Daendels (t. 1808–1811) and the British lieutenant governor Stamford Raffles (t. 1811–1816), these practices were largely abolished in parts of Java under direct colonial rule and replaced with a land tax. The reasoning was that the Javanese would themselves start to produce cash crops for export. However, tax revenues remained below expectations, and under the regimes of Governor-General Godert A. P. Van der Capellen (t. 1816–1825) and Commissioner-General Leonard P. J. Du Bus de Gisignies (t. 1826–1830), the financial situation of colonial Indonesia deteriorated.

Governor-General Johannes Van den Bosch (t. 1830–1834) introduced the Cultivation System in 1830. He had argued against Du Bus's proposal to open Java to European entrepreneurs and have them cultivate idle land with wage labor. Van den Bosch favored state-led development that would maximize the revenues of the colonial government. Consequently, private entrepreneurs were banned from rural areas of Java under direct colonial rule. In those areas, rural villages were compelled to use a maximum of one-fifth of their land to produce cash crops, and villagers had to deliver corvée labor for a maximum of one-fifth of the year (sixty-six days). Until 1836, villages were exempted from the land tax and other taxes in kind if a sufficient amount of produce was delivered. They would also be indemnified against crop failures beyond their control. After 1836, the land tax was levied in full, and farmers received full payment for their produce. Van den Bosch believed that the Cultivation System would encourage Javanese farmers to produce export crops beyond what they needed to pay the land tax.

Junior officials of the colonial government—the *controleurs*—implemented the system through the local rulers—the *bupati* (regents) and *camat* (district heads). They determined the crops that had to be grown and the land to be set aside (in the case of, for instance, indigo or sugarcane) or the amount of land that had to be newly cultivated (in the case of, for instance, tea or coffee). They also requisitioned the labor to maintain, harvest, and transport the crops. The orders were passed to village heads, who then secured the cooperation of villagers. These officials arranged payment for the deliveries at predetermined prices and levied the land tax at the time of crop payments. Any surplus from the sale of produce above the land tax was credited to the farmer. Both colonial and Javanese officials had an interest in making the system work because they received a percentage of the revenues.

Produce was delivered to government agents, who organized the transport of the produce to local ports for shipment to the main ports of Batavia or Surabaya. When processing was required, for instance, with sugarcane, the produce was sold to government contractors. They produced the final product, such as sugar, with requisitioned labor and arranged transport to local ports.

A further reason for the implementation of the Cultivation System was the fact that the Dutch company Nederlandsche Handel-Maatschappij (NHM) badly needed customers. The company had been established in 1824 by all Dutch merchants engaged in trade with the Dutch East Indies, with Dutch king Willem I (r. 1815–1840) serving in his private capacity as its chief shareholder. The NHM received a monopoly on transporting CS products to The Netherlands and on their sale. The net proceeds of the auctions—gross sales less the value of the purchases, the NHM fees, freight charges, insurance premiums, and so on—benefited the coffers of the Dutch colonial government. In fact, these proceeds were not remitted to Indonesia because the colonial government used them to purchase various goods and services in The Netherlands.

After establishing the CS, Van den Bosch became minister of colonial affairs (t. 1834–1839) and designed the positive net revenue (*batig slot*) policy. It decreed that the government of the Dutch East Indies would be expected to generate budget surpluses for remittance to the treasury in The Netherlands. This expectation was based on the fact that the Dutch government had taken responsibility for the assets and liabilities of the Vereenigde Oost-Indische Compagnie (VOC) when the bankrupt company was dissolved in 1800. The Dutch government urgently required a source of revenue after subventions from the southern Netherlands (now Belgium) stopped when the Belgians declared independence in 1830.

The Cultivation System achieved its goals. Indigo and sugarcane were the first crops to be produced with compulsory cultivation. Coffee, tea, tobacco, and pepper were later added. The value of all exports increased quickly from ƒ11 million in 1830 to ƒ60 million in 1850 and ƒ125 million in 1870. CS products dominated exports during the first few decades. Government revenues increased quickly after the implementation of the system in line with exports, from ƒ19 million in 1830 to ƒ74 million in 1850 and ƒ124 million in 1870. Not all revenues were derived from the sale of CS crops, however, because the government gradually diversified its revenue base. From 1832 to 1877, the colonial government remitted positive net revenues to The Netherlands. Total remittances amounted to ƒ823 million, or ƒ18 million per year, approximately one-third of the Dutch government's budget (Van Baardewijk 1993).

As a consequence of the CS, the colonial administrative system deepened. By making the *bupati* responsible for the delivery of CS products, the system elevated them and increased their access to an additional source of revenue. However, to acquire it, the bupati relied on Dutch colonial authority, rather than indigenous supremacy. The CS therefore accelerated the conversion of the loosely structured administrative aristocracy into a salaried civil service. In principle, the bupati became dependent on their salaries. They were aided by a controleur, who himself answered to a regional Dutch resident. By 1860, Java's administrative divisions had been established, and the system of indirect colonial rule would, in essence, be maintained until the end of the colonial period.

In The Netherlands, controversy surrounded the CS. Two groups criticized the system: those who considered it morally wrong because of the degree of compulsion it employed and those who felt aggrieved by the effective monopolization of the trade in cash crops by the colonial government and the NHM. Both groups cited various incidents of misuse and abuse that became public knowledge to advance their case.

The first group emphasized the burden the system placed on farm households in Java. Several of the crops were alien to farmers, and their cultivation often took more time and effort than anticipated. Transportation of the produce was difficult and time-consuming. It was argued that farmers often had to neglect the production of food crops, which in turn caused occasional food shortages. Among the allegations raised against the CS was that the system had been the cause of famines in Demak and Grobogan (Central Java) in 1849 and 1850.

Other allegations concerned the fact that colonial officials received a percentage of the proceeds of the CS and conspired in the abuse of farmers. For instance, sugar contractors would insist on the delivery of cane at particular times during the milling season, for which purpose they plotted with colonial and indigenous officials to commandeer villagers, carts, and oxen for transporting the cane. In some cases, more than the set maximum of farmland or of corvée labor was commandeered. In other cases, farmers who had produced CS crops were also required to supply corvée labor. Sometimes, the bupati abused their authority, secure in the knowledge the Dutch controleur and resident would support them, by imposing additional burdens upon their subjects.

The benefits that Dutch firms drew from the system were another source of controversy. Sugar contractors established ventures that operated with guaranteed and generous margins set by the colonial government. The NHM used its monopoly on the transport and sale of CS products to become the biggest private company in colonial Indonesia. It diversified its operations into general trade and finance, and after 1900, it was one of the biggest banks. Several Dutch shipping companies benefited from the system because they were engaged by the NHM for the transport of CS produce to The Netherlands. And both NHM and shipping companies benefited from the fact that they were tacitly allowed to charge above-market rates for their services involving CS produce (for example, transport and insurance services).

Private entrepreneurs had found the way to urban Indonesia and parts of the country that were still under indigenous princely rule. However, only those who managed to obtain a contract to process or handle CS products derived benefits from the system. As the economy of the Dutch East Indies evolved, private enterprises in The Netherlands started to object to the fact that they could not invest in ventures in most of rural Java. They mobilized public opinion and Liberal opposition members in Parliament in favor of opening Java up to private enterprise. In the 1860s, it was argued that the limits of state-orchestrated development had been reached and that private enterprise should take over.

The evidence for the charge that the CS was detrimental to economic development in Java is inconclusive, since the implementation of the system varied over time and between regions. The CS imposed obligations on the rural population that were often difficult to meet and sometimes led to the neglect of food crops. However, the total payments that farm households received for crop deliveries exceeded tax payments. The system therefore brought cash into the Javanese economy and spurred economic activity, albeit on a still-modest scale.

The consumption of meat, salt, opium, and cloth all increased. Only 40 percent of all farm households in the whole of Java were involved in the production of CS crops in 1840 and less than 25 percent in 1870. Likewise, the share of total cultivated land used under the CS was only 25 percent around 1840 and 13 percent around 1870 (Van Baardewijk 1993).

Changes were introduced in the 1860s. In 1867, the Dutch Parliament was granted the right to approve the budget of the Dutch East Indies. Previously, the Dutch king in theory approved the budget of the colonial government through the minister of colonial affairs. Parliament thus gained influence in colonial affairs, which led to the decision to phase out the CS. This effort led to the new 1870 Agrarian Law, which allowed foreign investors to acquire land under short-term leases from indigenous landholders or through the purchase of unoccupied land from the colonial government under long-term leases.

The CS was gradually phased out. The batig slot policy ended in 1877, after which CS revenues only benefited the treasury of the Dutch colonial government. The compulsory cultivation of sugarcane was abolished in 1870, leaving it to the owners of sugar mills to organize the local production of cane. Forced cultivation of perennial crops continued, although tea and coffee estates were gradually handed over to villages. In 1915, the last government-owned coffee plantations were abandoned.

PIERRE VAN DER ENG

See also Coffee; Du Bus de Gisignies, Viscount Leonard Pierre Joseph (1780–1849); Forced Deliveries; Java; Java War (1825–1830); Liberal Experimental Period (1816–1830); Max Havelaar; Netherlands (Dutch) East Indies; Sugar; Van den Bosch, Count Johannes (1780–1844); Van der Capellan, Baron Godert Alexander Philip (1778–1848)

References:
Elson, R. E. 1994. *Village Java under the Cultivation System, 1830–1870.* Sydney, Australia: Allen & Unwin.

Fasseur, C. 1992. *The Politics of Colonial Exploitation: Java, the Dutch, and the Cultivation System.* Ithaca, NY: Southeast Asia Program, Cornell University.

Van Baardewijk, F. 1993. *Changing Economy in Indonesia.* Vol. 14, *The Cultivation System, Java 1834–1880.* Amsterdam: Royal Tropical Institute.

CỬU QUỐC (NATIONAL SALVATION)

The term *Cửu Quốc* (National Salvation) appeared in early 1941, when the first platoon of the National Salvation Troops (*Cửu Quốc Quân*) was formed under the control of the Indochina Communist Party (ICP) in the area of Bắc Sơn, about 40 kilometers west of Lạng Sơn. Operating at no more than squad level on the Chinese border in the beginning, these guerrilla forces would gather enough strength by August 1943 to engage in the actions of "armed propaganda" that contributed to the building of the first bases of the Việt Bắc liberated zone. In April 1945, these troops merged with the Vietnamese People's Propaganda Unit for National Liberation, created in December 1944, to become the Liberation Army of Vietnam, the forerunner of the People's Army of Vietnam (PAVN).

By then, the ICP had been expanding its influence by forming several mass organizations, all of which incorporated the title National Salvation Association (*Cửu Quốc Hội*). Thus, in 1943, the National Salvation Cultural Association (*Hội Văn Hóa Cửu Quốc*) was established with the assistance of ICP cadres to recruit urban intellectuals to the cause of the Viet Minh (Vietnam Independence League) and find ways of insinuating anti-French and anti-Japanese propaganda into legally published newspapers and journals. Other associations followed: the Peasants' National Salvation Association, Students' National Salvation Association, Women's National Salvation Association, Teenagers' National Salvation Association, and so on. Together, these organizations acted as a shield for the Viet Minh. Individually, each association translated esoteric communist slogans into the language of its own members. In theory, then, the Viet Minh front was the coalition of these National Salvation Associations, through which it could give impetus to a broad national movement, uniting large numbers of Vietnamese regardless of their politics and reaching down into the masses. The theme of unity and national salvation (even the Viet Minh's main newspaper bore the title *Cửu Quốc*) thus enabled the Viet Minh to involve local populations in its cause and the socioeconomic reforms it proposed.

The famine raging in North Vietnam in 1945 provided further opportunities for the Viet Minh both to eliminate the anticommunist village elites who had been seizing requisitioned rice to store in guarded granaries and to build a mass movement of political and social salvation in the countryside. "National independence" and "Seize paddy stocks to save the people from starvation" became, like "Peace, bread, and land" in the Russian October Revolution, the slogans around which the people were mobilized. Villagers responded enthusiastically to the appeals for donations to the Independence Fund, the National Defense Fund, and Gold Week in order to finance basic administrative operations and the expansion of the armed forces for the cause of national independence. In early 1946, as the need arose for a broadened coalition and wider participation of all progressive elements in preparation for possibly protracted fighting with the French, additional Catholic and Buddhist Cứu Quấc associations were formed as a part of the larger Liên Viet front.

Attesting to the Viet Minh's well-polished mass organizational skills, the different Cứu Quấc associations had thus contributed to laying the groundwork for the formation of local communist party branches. They also helped to enhance the legitimacy of Hồ Chí Minh's (1890–1969) government in preparation for the Franco–Viet Minh war (the First Indochina War, 1946–1954), during which the support of local populations would prove critical for the success of Viet Minh guerrilla strategy.

NGUYỄN THẾ ANH

See also Hồ Chí Minh (1890–1969); Indochina Communist Party; Indochina during World War II (1939–1945); Indochina War (1946–1954), First; Nationalism and Independence Movements in Southeast Asia; Việt Minh (Việt Nam Độc Lập Đồng Minh Hội) (Vietnam Independence League); Vietnam under French Colonial Rule; Vietnam, North (post-1945); Vietnam, South (post-1945); Vietnamese Communist Party (VCP, Dong Cong San Viet Nam)

References:

Huynh Kim Khanh. 1982. *Vietnamese Communism, 1925–1945*. Ithaca, NY: Cornell University Press.

Hy V. Luong. 1992. *Revolution in the Village: Tradition and Transformation in North Vietnam, 1925–1988*. Honolulu: University of Hawai'i Press.

Marr, David G. 1995. *Vietnam 1945: The Quest for Power*. Berkeley: University of California Press.

D

ĐÀ NẴNG (TOURANE)

A port on the South China Sea giving access to the plains of central Vietnam (Viêt-Nam, Quảng Nam Province), Đà Nẵng is built upon the banks of the Hàn River, at the back and to the southeast of a horseshoe-shaped bay. Protected on the east by the Tiên Sa peninsula and the Đà Nẵng cape hanging over the sea at a height of 693 meters and thus offering a splendid shelter to ships, this harbor was the site of the first landing of European missionaries in Vietnam (in 1535). The Jesuit Alexandre de Rhodes (1591–1660), the main contributor to the romanization of the Vietnamese script, arrived there in 1625. Known to Western traders and navigators as Tourane (sometimes Turon), the port was a haven for goods transportation and ship repair; it gradually developed into the main harbor of the Nguyễn principality in the eighteenth century thanks to its bay, which was capable of receiving large, deep-draft ships. After the emperor Minh-Mang (r. 1820–1841) decreed in 1835 that foreign ships would be allowed to cast anchor only at the mouth of the Hàn River, Đà Nẵng became the largest commercial port in central Vietnam.

French intervention in Vietnam came, in the very beginning, in the form of three attacks on Đà Nẵng: in 1847, when a French squadron, sent with the mission of demanding an immediate end to the persecution and proscription of Christians throughout the Vietnamese empire, opened fire on the Vietnamese fleet stationed in the bay; in January 1857, when the French ship *Le Catinat* bombarded the forts guarding the harbor; and in 1858, when, as an initial step to the conquest of Vietnam, Admiral Rigault de Genouilly, commander of the French fleet in the Far East, captured the port and its neighborhood before deciding to move the bulk of the French forces south to Saigon. After the imposition of a French protectorate, in 1888, the city of Tourane was ceded to the French colonial administration as a concession distinct from the territory of Annam.

Located 80 kilometers from Huê to the southeast, Đà Nẵng assumed new importance after the partition of Vietnam in 1954. In the late 1960s, the United States established a large military base there, and in one decade, growing rapidly, Đà Nẵng became the second largest city in South Vietnam, next to Saigon. Linked presently to Hồ Chí Minh City (formerly Saigon) by road and by railway, the city is a market for local produce; textile mills and machinery plants have recently been added to old traditional crafts. Đà Nẵng is home to the Cham Museum, which holds a great number of Cham objects from the surrounding area. There are also Buddhist temples carved into the limestone hills around the city and the Marble Mountains to the northeast.

NGUYỄN THẾ ANH

Germany lending a hand in the Vietnam conflict. In this aerial view of the huge U.S. base at Đa Nẵng, South Vietnam, the German hospital ship Helicoland *is seen berthed in the Đa Nẵng River (background, left). At right is a U.S. vessel. (Bettmann/Corbis)*

See also French Ambitions in Southeast Asia; Nguyễn Emperors and French Imperialism; Rhodes, Alexandre de (1591–1660); U.S. Military Bases in Southeast Asia

References:

Vandermeersch, Léon, and Jean-Pierre Ducrest, eds. 1997. *Le Musée de Sculpture Cam de Đà Nẵng* [*The Cham Sculpture Museum of Đà Nẵng*]. Paris: Association Française des Amis de l'Orient.

Vũ Tư Lập. 1977. *Viêt Nam: Données géographiques* [*Vietnam: Geographical Data*]. Hanoi: Editions en Langues Etrangères.

DAI VIET (939–1407 C.E.)

Dai Viet was the formal name for the Vietnamese empire employed from the Early Ly dynasty (980–1009 C.E.) to the Tay Son periods (1771–1802). The name *Dai Viet* (Great Viet) connoted an empire that would rule all the *Viet* people (from the Chinese term *Yueh,* which originally indicated all non-Chinese peoples south of the Yangtze [Yangzi] River). This concept was legitimized with two seemingly contradictory claims: that every dynasty defeated Chinese invasions but that the state and society were well civilized after the Chinese model (in maintaining Viet customs).

Ly Thanh Tong (r. 1127–1138) first adopted the name Dai Viet to replace the former name *Dai Co Viet* (also meaning "Great Viet" but in a more vernacular form), which had been employed since 966 C.E. Dai Co Viet/Dai Viet inherited the territory of the T'ang protectorate of Annam, including the Red River delta as the center, its surrounding mountainous area, and the present Thanh Hoa–Nghe Tinh region. The rulers regularly sent tribute to China from 973, disguising their imperial titles. Nevertheless, Sung (Song) China (960–1279) first regarded Chiao-Chih (an old Chinese administrative name for northern Vietnam) as a colony, trying to make a reconquest of it in 980 and 1075, both times in vain. The borders between Dai Viet and China were diplomatically fixed in the 1080s. Ly Anh Tong (r. 1138–1175) was conferred the title King of the Nation of Annam in 1174, a title that meant China recognized Annam as a separate state although it was still expected to pay tribute to China. From that point until the eighteenth century, Dai Viet maintained a dual diplomacy. On the one hand, faced with China and other East Asian countries, it was a Chinese vassal state of Annam; on the other hand, with Southeast Asian neighbors such as Champa and Cambodia, it was a Chinese-styled empire to which all these countries should be subject.

Under the Tran dynasty (1225–1400), the national/imperial consciousness developed with the victory against the Mongol invasion. The compilation of Chinese-styled imperial annals entitled *Dai Viet su ky* (The History of Dai Viet) and the development of the legend of the national/imperial founders (the Hong Bang dynasty and Hung kings) also contributed to the consciousness, both tracing back the history beyond the period of Chinese dominion (the second century B.C.E. to the ninth century C.E.). Though the short regime of Ho Quy Ly (1400–1407) replaced the name Dai Viet with *Dai Ngu* (after the kingdom of the ancient Chinese sage-king Shun), the Le dynasty (1428–1789) restored the name Dai Viet. This dynasty was established after driving back the Ming army that had occupied northern Vietnam for twenty years. In the Le declaration of independence, the Binh Ngo dai cao (Great Imperial Edict of Pacification of the Ming), the "[Great] Viet Empire" was defined as an empire that shared a common civilization with China but had its own territory, customs, emperors, and history.

Beginning in the fourteenth century, Dai Viet expanded to the south, due to the development of Chinese-styled government and intensive agriculture in the Red River delta (resulting in an everlasting population pressure). Champa, located in present-day central Vietnam, was crushed in the fifteenth to seventeenth centuries. To the west, Laos had been under Dai Viet's pressure since the fifteenth century. Ironically, the expanded empire lost its unity. The sixteenth century witnessed civil war between the Mac dynasty in the Red River delta and the Le in Thanh Hoa. During the seventeenth and eighteenth centuries, Tonkin—or the Trinh government (controlling the restored but powerless Le emperors)—ruled the northern provinces, while Cochin China—or the Nguyễn (also nominally recognizing the Le sovereignty)—ruled in the south, extending as far as the Mekong Delta.

By the end of the Le period, the Chinese-modeled consciousness of the greatness of their civilization had developed to the extent that the Vietnamese people sometimes called themselves the Han or the Hoa, regarding the Tau, or Ch'ing Chinese, as less civilized under the Manchurian regime. The northerners often called their country Annam among themselves, whereas the southerners, who did not have diplomatic relations with China, tended to speak of Dai Viet. Simultaneously, however, China's demographic and cultural expansion appears to have let Vietnam's national consciousness develop, especially among the northerners. With a conception of national history and geomancy within the actual borders, they criticized the legendary founders who had claimed the territory south of the Yangtze River. Similarly, they rejected the old history that legitimized Trieu Da (the Chinese Chao T'o, who founded the Nan-yueh kingdom in Kuang-tung in 203 B.C.E.) as one of their own emperors.

Defeating the short-lived Tay Son dynasty (1771–1802), Nguyễn Phuoc Anh established the Nguyễn dynasty (1802–1945) and unified a territory that was wider than any prior dynasty's. He did not regard his empire as a mere successor of Cochin China or of Dai Viet. Instead, he adopted, in 1804, the new formal name of *Vietnam* (lit. Southern Viet), which might have indicated the unification of the south (Dai Viet) and the north (Annam).

MOMOKI SHIRO

See also Annam; China, Imperial; Cochin China; Le Dynasty (1428–1527, 1533–1789); Ly Dynasty (1009–1225); Nam Tien; Nam Viet (Nan Yue); Nguyễn Ánh (Emperor Gia Long) (r. 1802–1820); Nguyễn Dynasty (1802–1945); Sino-Vietnamese Relations; Sino-Vietnamese Wars

References:

Le Thanh Khoi. 1954. *Le Viet-Nam, l'Histoire et Civilisation* [*Vietnam: The History and Civilization*]. Paris: Les Éditions des Minuit.

Li Tana. 1998. *Nguyen Cochinchina: Southern Vietnam in the Seventeenth and Eighteenth Centuries.* Ithaca, NY: Cornell University Southeast Asia Program.

Momoki Shiro. 1998. "Dai Viet and the South China Sea Trade: From the 10th to the 15th Century." *Crossroads* 12, no. 1: 1–34.

Tarling, Nicholas, ed. 1992. *The Cambridge History of Southeast Asia.* Vol. 1, *From Early Times to ca. 1800.* Cambridge: Cambridge University Press.

Taylor, Keith W. 1998. "Surface Orientations in Vietnam: Beyond Histories of Nation and Region." *Journal of Asian Studies* 57, no. 4: 949–978.

DAMRONG, PRINCE (1862–1943)
Engineered Administrative Centralization

Prince Damrong, a son of King Monkut (r. 1851–1868) of Siam, was born on 21 June 1862. His birth name was Dissaworakuman. During the reign of Chulalongkorn (Rama V) (r. 1868–1910), who was Damrong's elder brother and born to Mongkut's queen, he served in many important positions in the bureaucracy and proved to be one of the most talented and capable bureaucrats who helped the king to modernize Siam.

At the age of fourteen, Damrong attended a military school, and he served the king in the royal scribes' department and the royal pages' bodyguard regiment after he graduated. In the late 1880s, Chulalongkorn started the modernization of the kingdom and appointed Damrong the head of the department of public instruction in 1887. Modern public education expanded considerably under his leadership; this was the first time that commoners had access to modern education, although primary schooling was not made compulsory until the following reign. Both Chulalongkorn and Damrong considered education an important tool for the modernization of the kingdom.

However, the most outstanding contribution Damrong made to the kingdom took place in the 1890s when King Chulalongkorn undertook drastic administrative reforms to allow him to centralize his power. In 1891, the king sent Damrong to visit Russia as his representative and instructed him to take the opportunity to visit other European countries and colonies and study the organization of European governments. In the following year, the king launched the reforms and appointed Damrong as minister of interior. The interior ministry was established to help the king centralize ruling power, which, until the early 1890s, had still been under the control of local chiefs or noble families. As a result, Damrong was given a great responsibility, since the drastic administrative reforms at the expense of local power might have led to resistance from local leadership. Damrong, however, carried out his task successfully, with little opposition from local leaders.

He began his work by traveling to many parts of the country to study situations and to find alternative forms of administration. During his provincial tours, he found loopholes in the traditional administration by which local leaders, most of them semihereditary, were allowed to take advantage of their status for personal benefit. Corruption, injustice, and overlapping administrations were not uncommon (Wyatt 1984: 209).

At the same time, the external threat posed by Western colonialism prompted the central government to find methods to safeguard and rule remote areas. In order to make the bureaucracy more efficient and to allow the king and the central government to exercise more direct control over local administration, Damrong introduced a new form of local administration termed *monthon thesaphiban* (circle administrative system). Under this system, a number of provinces were grouped together to make a single administrative unit called the circle, or *monthon,* which was to be supervised by a resident commissioner appointed directly by the king. The resident commissioners were Chulalongkorn's brothers or close cousins, whom he could trust. The new local administrative system also allowed the central government to have complete control over other local affairs—for example, revenue collection, justice, and the police.

Clearly, this newly reformed administration was achieved at the expense of local power, and resistance was inevitable. However, the more powerful and better-equipped armies of the central government were able to suppress rebellions. Eventually, the ministry of the interior under the leadership of Damrong was able to transfer local power to the central government under Chulalongkorn at the turn of the twentieth century (Tarling 1992: 122). Damrong's success in carrying out administrative reforms was highly appreciated by Chulalongkorn, and as a result, Damrong retained the post of minister of the interior until the king's death in 1910.

Damrong still headed the ministry in the following reign of his nephew Vajiravudh (Vachiravudh) (r. 1910–1925) until 1915. At that point, he sought the king's approval to resign due to "poor health," and the latter gave his approval, though it was known that Vajiravudh wished to work with his own political following more than with that of his father (Wyatt 1984: 227; Girling 1981: 55). The resignation allowed Damrong to have more time to work on archaeology and history, interests that were sparked when he was a monk in 1883 but that he had not had enough time to develop in the intervening years.

After the government changed to a constitutional monarchy in 1932, Damrong left Siam for the British colony of Penang, where he spent the next decade. During that time, he greatly expanded his knowledge of Thai history and archaeology. He returned to Bangkok in 1942 when the Pacific War (1941–1945) made it more difficult for him to live in Penang. Damrong died in 1943 at the age of eighty-one. His contributions to the modernization and administrative reforms of the kingdom laid a solid foundation for modern Thailand.

SUD CHONCHIRDSIN

See also British Interests in Southeast Asia; French Ambitions in Southeast Asia; Paknam Incident (1893); Preservation of Siam's Political Independence; Reforms and Modernization in Siam; Vajiravudh (Rama VI) (r. 1910–1925)

References:
Girling, John L. 1981. *Thailand: Society and Politics.* Ithaca, NY: Cornell University Press.
Tambiah, S. J. 1977. *World Conqueror and World Renouncer: A Study of Buddhism and Polity in Thailand against a Historical Background.* Cambridge: Cambridge University Press.
Tarling, Nicholas, ed. 1992. *The Cambridge History of Southeast Asia.* Vol. 2, *The Nineteenth and Twentieth Centuries.* Cambridge: Cambridge University Press.
Wyatt, David, K. 1984. *Thailand: A Short History.* New Haven, CT: Yale University Press.
———. 1994. *Studies in Thai History.* Chaing Mai, Thailand: Silkworm Books.

DARUL ISLAM MOVEMENT (DI)
Struggling for an Islamic State of Indonesia

The Darul Islam Movement (DI) aims for the establishment of an Islamic state of Indonesia. DI in Java was closely associated with Tentera Islam Indonesia (TII, Islamic Troops of Indonesia). A very significant DI-TII revolt had broken out in West Java in the late 1940s, led by Sekarmadji Maridjan Kartosuwiryo (1905–1965). Later on, several other uprisings occurred in other regions in Indonesia, with aims similar to those of Kartosuwiryo's movement. They were the DI-TII revolt of Kahar Muzakkar (1920–1965) in South Sulawesi, the DI revolt of Daud Beureu'éh in Aceh (Acheh), the DI revolt of Amir Fatah in Central Java, and the rebellion of South Kalimantan. The movements associated with these revolts used the name of Darul Islam and developed networks with Kartosuwiryo's movement. In the paragraphs that follow, the focus will be on the DI-TII movements of Kartosuwiryo, Kahar Muzakkar, and Daud Beureu'éh.

Several factors were responsible for the rise of DI Movements—specifically, socioeconomic, religious, and political issues and the gulf between guerrilla leaders and political elites. The political situation that split the nationalist, Islamic, and communist groups remained apparent. Some Muslim leaders felt that their proposal for the establishment of an Islamic state was not accommodated.

Kartosuwiryo, the former vice-president of Partai Serikat Islam Indonesia (PSII) who was expelled because of his policy of noncooperation, moved to Malangbong, in the eastern part of West Java, and founded a kind of *pesantren* (Islamic school) called Institut Supah. This institute then became the center for training his guerrilla forces, Hisbullah and Sabilillah. Before the proclamation of Indonesian independence, Kartosuwiryo had actually announced "Darul Islam Independence" on 14 August 1945, though he then adhered to the leadership of Sukarno (1901–1970) and Mohammad Hatta (1902–1980). However, Kartosuwiryo clashed with the republican Indonesian government because he did not agree with the Renville

Agreement (1948). In fact, the Hisbullah and Sabilillah troops were left behind by the Tentera Nasional Indonesia (TNI, Indonesian National Army) and fought against the Dutch. When the Dutch left Indonesian territories, Kartosuwiryo still appealed for the establishment of an Islamic state of Indonesia, after having failed to achieve it through constitutional means. The efforts made by Prime Minister Mohammed Natsir (t. 1950–1951) toward reconciliation came too late because on 7 August 1949, Kartosuwiryo had already, for the second time, announced the establishment of Darul Islam as Negara Islam Indonesia (NII, Islamic State of Indonesia). He was the imam and commander-in-chief of the TII. The territory of Darul Islam was the mountainous area of West Java to the east of Bandung, expanding to the border area of Central Java. For the decade from 1949 to 1959, his power was still strong when the central government tried to negotiate with him. However, after the 1960s, his movement started to lose its strength when some of his followers were caught. Kartosuwiryo himself was captured on 4 June 1962 and was killed in September. Thereafter, the West Java DI Movement came to an end.

Kahar Muzakkar's DI Movement was initially a protest of the former guerrillas of South Sulawesi, who insisted on being transformed into TNI as a separate battalion group. Since Kahar had formed this group of ex-guerrillas during the Indonesian Revolution (1945–1949), he was sent to South Sulawesi to resolve the issue in early 1950. However, he refused the assignment from the government. Instead, Kahar then became the leader of approximately 20,000 guerrillas, and on 5 July 1950, he joined them in the jungle that covered the mountainous areas from southern to southeastern Sulawesi. Kahar made contact with Kartosuwiryo and used the DI ideology for his movement. On 20 January 1952, he was appointed as TII's Sulawesi commander, and later, on 7 August 1953, his movement was accepted as a part of Negara Islam Indonesia. Kahar criticized nationalist and communist parties as hypocritical and godless and Islamic parties as counterrevolutionary; therefore, he believed all of them should be eliminated. He exercised Islamic law and commanded that a spiritual revolution take place. In 1955, he made contact with DI Aceh and also with the Permesta (the Common Struggle Movement) in North Sulawesi—where he received weapons and ammunition—and with the Pemerintah Revolusioner Republic Indonesia (PRRI, Revolutionary Government of the Indonesian Republic) in Sumatra. However, after 1960, his movement was weakened by the TNI. The movement ended after Kahar was shot and killed on 3 February 1965 in southeastern Sulawesi.

Unlike what had happened in Sulawesi and West Java, the Aceh DI Movement arose mostly because of conflicts between the central government and local leaders over the issue of possessing more regional autonomy without intervention from Jakarta. The movement began in 1945, enriched by the social revolution between traditional elites and religious leaders. As residents of an important Islamic region where Dutch colonial rule had little impact, the Aceh people felt that they had an extensive role to play in achieving Indonesian independence. They refused to be integrated into the North Sumatran province and demanded a separate province. In 1953, Daud Beureu'éh, an Acehnese governor (t. 1949–1950), proclaimed that Aceh was part of the Islamic State of Indonesia and launched a rebellion against the central government. This movement also got in touch with Kartosuwiryo's DI Movement but without the intention of being part of it. In 1959, the central government gave Aceh the status of a special administrative district (*daerah istimewa*) with special autonomy in religious matters, education, and *adat* (customary) law. Daud Beureu'éh ended his movement in May 1962 and was pardoned by Sukarno. However, the peace in Aceh lasted only for several years. Aceh Province is still struggling for independence through a movement known as Gerakan Aceh Merdeka (GAM, Aceh Movement for Independence).

AMELIA FAUZIA

See also Aceh (Acheh); Aceh (Acheh) Wars (1873–1903); Indonesian Revolution (1945–1949); Islam in Southeast Asia; Islamic Resurgence in Southeast Asia (Twentieth Century); Minangkabau; Mohammad Hatta (1902–1980); Nationalism and Independence Movements in Southeast Asia; Persatuan Ulama Ulama Seluruh Aceh (PUSA); Renville Agreement (January 1948); Republik Maluku Selatan (RMS, Republic of the South Moluccas); Soekarno (Sukarno) (1901–1970)

References:

Boland, B. J. 1982. *The Struggle of Islam in Modern Indonesia*. The Hague: Martinus Nijhoff.

Kahin, George McT. 1952. *Nationalism and Revolution in Indonesia*. Ithaca, NY: Cornell University Press.

Ricklefs, M. C. 1981. *A History of Modern Indonesia*. London: Macmillan.

DAYAKS

The term *Dayak* has become an accepted general term for the native, non-Muslim populations of Borneo; alternative forms are *Dyak, Daya,* or *Dya*. The word first came into general use in the nineteenth century, when it was increasingly employed by Europeans to refer to the pagan, head-hunting natives they were gradually pacifying and bringing under colonial administrative control. Dutch and German scholars used the term to distinguish all native pagans from Muslim Malays. English writers in Sarawak tended to restrict the term to the Land Dayaks (or Bidayuhs, as they are now called) in the western areas of Sarawak inland from the state capital, Kuching. Sea Dayaks (or Ibans) were found throughout the western and northern regions of Borneo, and at the time of the establishment of the rule of James Brooke (1803–1868) in the 1840s in Sarawak, they were expanding rapidly to the east and northeast; in the company of Malays, they were engaged in coastal piracy and head-hunting (King 1993: 29–30). The ethnic label Dayak was known by the Dutch as far back as the mid-eighteenth century and was used then as a general referent for inland or interior people (Pringle 1970: XVIII). Complicating matters is the fact that the term has sometimes been employed specifically for native settled agriculturalists, and the separate and general referent *Punan* has been adopted for the forest nomads or hunter-gatherers (Rousseau 1990: 20).

Although the derivation of the term *Dayak* is uncertain, the word (or some variant of it) is used in various local languages, and it might have been adopted by coastal populations such as the Malays and given a condescending or pejorative connotation, meaning something akin to *rustic* or *yokel*. Despite this circumstance, the non-Muslim natives of Borneo have more recently begun to use the term *Dayak* in a political sense to demarcate themselves from Muslim communities. The word has also been incorporated into the names of indigenous political parties in Sarawak and Kalimantan, following the development of modern politics after independence.

There are no exact population figures for the Dayaks of Borneo, though they currently probably exceed 3 million in number. They comprise a culturally diverse collection of populations, among them the Ibans and related groups including the Kantus; Kayans; Kenyahs; Bidayuhs; Malayic-Dayaks such as the Selakos and Kendayans; the Barito groups including the Ngajus, Ot Danums, and Ma'anyans; Dusuns; and Muruts. There are also numerous smaller groupings, including the Kelabits, Kajangs, and Punans. However, the Dayaks are all speakers of Austronesian languages, and some common cultural elements are found widely throughout Borneo. Among these common elements are large pile-houses or longhouses on stilts accommodating many families; fertility cults related to head-hunting, rice cultivation, and death ceremonies; patterns and symbols in material culture, bodily decorations, cosmology, and religion; and social and economic adaptations to a riverine and rain forest environment (Avé and King 1986).

Although the term *Dayak* is contrasted categorically with *Malay,* the boundaries between the two are not sharply defined in practice. The majority of present-day Malays are descended from members of the Dayak communities of Borneo who converted to Islam and over time gradually changed their ethnic affiliation to Malay; the process is called *masok Melayu* (meaning "to become Malay" or "to enter Malaydom"). The Malay language has also long been used as a lingua franca. At any one time, there have therefore been transitional communities in Borneo, such as the Pekaki Malays who, having converted to Islam, continued to observe various Dayak customary practices.

The ruling families of the Malay States depended on alliances and sometimes intermarriage with local Dayak chiefs and headmen to mobilize support against their enemies; they also levied taxes, tribute, and services from Dayaks under their authority (the "tied" or "bonded" Dayaks) and raided hostile communities for slaves. Those natives, usually living beyond Malay jurisdiction, were referred to as "free Dayaks" (King 1993: 129–130).

Following European intervention, these Malay-Dayak relations were disrupted. Headhunting and feuding were stamped out. Dayaks were gradually incorporated into colonial administrations, settlement patterns were regularized, physical migrations were restricted, and local leaders were employed as low-level intermediaries to collect taxes and administer customary law; many Dayaks were converted to Christianity and given access to mission education. Traditional religious beliefs and practices were transformed, and some disappeared. The Dayaks also began to grow cash crops such as rubber and pepper for the market, and some migrated to coastal towns and plantations in search of paid work.

Since the 1970s, the social, economic, and cultural changes affecting the Dayaks have accelerated in pace, particularly with the opening of the rain forests for commercial timber exploitation, road building, mining, plantation agriculture, hydroelectric projects, resettlement, and ecotourism.

VICTOR T. KING

See also *Adat;* Borneo; Brooke, James, and Sarawak; Brunei Ethnic Minorities; Brunei Malays; East Malaysian Ethnic Minorities; Malays

References:

Avé, Jan B., and Victor T. King. 1986. *The People of the Weeping Forest: Tradition and Change in Borneo.* Leiden, The Netherlands: Rijksmuseum voor Volkenkunde.

King, Victor T. 1993. *The Peoples of Borneo.* Oxford: Blackwell.

Pringle, Robert. 1970. *Rajahs and Rebels: The Ibans of Sarawak under Brooke Rule, 1841–1941.* London: Macmillan.

Rousseau, Jérôme. 1990. *Central Borneo: Ethnic Identity and Social Life in a Stratified Society.* Oxford: Clarendon Press.

"DEATH RAILWAY" (BURMA-SIAM RAILWAY)

The Death Railway was the rail line between Siam (Thailand) and Burma (Myanmar) that was constructed by the Japanese Imperial Army (JIA) during the Pacific War (1941–1945). Its macabre name reflected the belief that a life was sacrificed for every sleeper (railroad timber) that was laid. The Death Railway has come to symbolize the horrors of the war.

The plan to construct a railway between Siam and Burma was originally devised by the JIA Railway Corps on board a ship traveling from Osaka to Vietnam in October 1941, prior to the outbreak of the war. The main objectives were to expedite military operations and to transport soldiers as well as materials. The difficulty of marine transportation due to enemy attacks necessitated the implementation of this railway plan.

In March 1942, the Imperial General Headquarters (IGH) ordered crews to complete the 415-kilometer railway connecting Kanchanaburi in Siam and Thanbyuzayat in Burma by the end of 1943. Work started in July 1942. In February 1943, the IGH shortened the completion term by four months, but the project was actually completed only in October 1943. The line passed over sheer cliffs and through deep jungles.

More than 60,000 Allied prisoners of war (POWs)—British, Australian, New Zealand, Dutch, U.S., and Canadian—worked on the project, together with 200,000 Southeast Asian *romushas* (laborers) comprising Siamese (all were Chinese residents in Thailand), Burmese, Malayans (the majority were Indian rubber tappers), Indonesians, and Vietnamese. Due to heavy workloads, maltreatment, lack of food, inadequate clothing and medicines, and harsh climates, some 40 percent of them perished. Though small numbers of Thai and Burmese laborers managed to abscond, laborers from other countries could not. They were unfamiliar with the terrain and faced severe difficulty in surviving should they escape and elude recapture. By contrast, of the more than 20,000 Japanese soldiers who were engaged in the work (some Korean civilian employees were included in their ranks), the number of deaths was something over 1,000.

After completion, the railway could not be effectively used due to frequent bombardment by the Allies. Although some of the remnant laborers stayed on to maintain and repair the railway, others were taken elsewhere. After the end of the war, more than 100 Japanese soldiers (and some of the Koreans) who had mistreated the POWs were prosecuted at the war crimes courts. (The ill treatment of the romushas, however, did not receive the attention of Allied prosecutors.) Of these, 36 were sentenced to death. Korean civilian employees who were compelled to directly mistreat the POWs tended to be subjected to unduly harsh punishment. Today, some 120 kilometers of track from the Death Railway in Thailand are still in use.

HARA FUJIO

See also Bataan Death March; "Comfort Women"; Japanese Occupation of Southeast Asia (1941–1945); Sandakan Death March; *Sook ching*

References:
McCormack, Gavan, and Hank Nelson, eds. 1993. *The Burma-Thailand Railway*. Sydney: Allen & Unwin.

DECOLONIZATION OF SOUTHEAST ASIA

Decolonization in Southeast Asia was the process whereby formerly colonized territories discarded their colonial controls and influences. Some of these territories assumed new forms of governance and often borrowed extensively from their colonial experience. Others retreated into the past to revive age-old forms of governance that predated colonial rule. The process of decolonization thus involved considerable change, and this change was peaceful, gradual, ugly, or violent depending on the circumstances.

In Southeast Asia, all societies experienced decolonization, including Thailand. Thailand was never formally placed under colonial rule but was nevertheless subjected to political pressures from nearby colonial powers.

The period normally associated with the process of decolonization started with the establishment of independent Southeast Asian governments after the Pacific War (1941–1945). However, there is as yet no terminal point to the process. Indeed, decolonization is an open-ended business, since the effects of the century of Western colonial rule are still not fully known.

The decolonization process brought together the transient and the durable. Governments continuing former colonial processes were established, but not all such governments lasted for long. Although national elections, the secret vote, the establishment of political par-

ties, modern armies, and police were embraced, these practices—many of them with colonial roots—were soon absorbed by and modified within the local cultures.

The decolonization process also did not occur in isolation. Rather, it took place in conjunction with other global processes occurring at the same time. In the postwar world, new power relationships developed, and decolonization came to be subsumed within these new developments. More specifically, decolonization in Southeast Asia must also be viewed in terms of the British liquidation of the Indian empire; the emergence of separate independent states such as India, Pakistan, and Ceylon (Sri Lanka); and the unification of China (minus Taiwan) by the communists under Mao Zedong (1893–1976). The reemergence of Japan as a major economic power following its defeat by the United States was also a global factor for consideration.

Decolonization is not the simple account of the withdrawal or retreat of Western colonial powers from Southeast Asia, although it cannot be too far wrong to start from that point. Most accounts of decolonization in Southeast Asia begin with the Japanese occupation (1941–1945).

In Vietnam, the struggle against the Japanese provided the stage on which previous enemies could coalesce around a common cause. Thus, the Chinese nationalist wartime government collaborated with the Vietnamese communist leader, Hồ Chí Minh (1890–1969), to fight the Japanese. Using their bases in China, the Vietnamese communists formed the Viet Minh, a united front of sympathizers mobilized against the Japanese. Because of their anti-Japanese role, the Viet Minh received assistance from the British and U.S. intelligence organizations. Hồ Chí Minh was able to consolidate his power, not least because he also suppressed all opposition. By 1945, the Viet Minh were unchallenged, what with the Japanese army in retreat, the Chinese supporters in disarray, and the French authority still not firmly reestablished. On 2 September 1945, Hồ Chí Minh proclaimed the Democratic Republic of Vietnam (DRV) in Hanoi.

By early 1946, with the withdrawal of the Chinese occupation forces from northern Vietnam, Hồ was left in undisputed control except in the south, where the French army returned in strength. It only remained to resist any further consolidation of the French, and this began with the Battle of Dien Bien Phu (1954) where the Viet Minh achieved a decisive victory over the French-led army. Then followed peace negotiations in Geneva that led to the division of Vietnam into north and south along the seventeenth parallel. The peace was short-lived. Massive migrations took place as anticommunists fled south to escape from the communists who now controlled the government in Hanoi. Meanwhile, American interests were further involved as the United States took on the job of fighting communism worldwide. It was only in 1975 that American troops were finally defeated and forced to leave, ignobly.

In Burma (Myanmar), the Thakins led by General Aung San (1915–1947) made the strategic decision to turn against the Japanese authorities once it was clear the British had succeeded in spoiling Japanese plans to invade India. The Thakins formed the Anti-Fascist People's Freedom League (AFPFL), a united front to drive out the Japanese. When the British were firmly reestablished at Rangoon (Yangon), they had to decide whether to punish Aung San for his wartime collaboration with the Japanese. The advice of Admiral Lord Louis Mountbatten (1900–1979), the Allied military commander of the South-East Asia Command (SEAC), prevailed. Aung San was recognized as the leader of the Burmese and designated prime minister. The road to decolonization was thus opened.

Thailand was the only state that was not colonized, although it still faced the pressures of Western colonialism. Making full use of its independence, Thailand presented itself as an ally to the Japanese and thus escaped occupation. In return, it declared war against the former Western colonial powers. However, when the tide turned against the Japanese, Thailand deftly exploited its independence to mend fences with the United States. With American support, it escaped almost unscathed the wrath of the Western colonial powers for having sided with the Japanese. A civilian politician emerged as the national leader after the succession of military commanders who controlled the country after 1932. It would thus appear that the impact of decolonization did not affect Thailand to any great extent, but in reality, the process had just begun. Surrounded by hostile neighbors, especially Vietnam and China, Thailand sought close ties with the United States. It was drawn into supporting the Americans in the Vietnam War from 1954 onward, aligning itself with a partner that was viewed as the dominant hegemonic power replacing the former Western colonial authorities. Thus, though Thailand escaped colonization during the colonial era and therefore did not experience decolonization as such, its subsequent history showed its inability to avoid entanglement with the regional conflicts that were a legacy of decolonization.

Cambodia and Laos were not critical players in the Japanese strategies to occupy Southeast Asia. The Cambodian leadership under King Norodom Sihanouk (1922–) continued intact from the colonial era through the Japanese occupation period to independence. Sihanouk successfully outmaneuvered his political opponents and was able to maintain Cambodia's neutrality in the regional conflicts. Generally, the decolonization process appeared to have given Cambodia a miss until the country was drawn into the maelstrom of war in neighboring Vietnam. From 1970, Cambodia became an essential part of Vietnam's decolonization process to get rid of foreign intervention and reestablish a reunified Vietnam.

Laos was another backwater state during the colonial era. Its borders were arbitrary. Various rival states were merged, and these continued to maintain uneasy relationships with other regional powers beyond Laos. As long as the French were able to impose an artificial unity, peace prevailed. However, as French control receded, rivalries resurfaced. The Laotian princes were encouraged and abetted by their regional neighbors, and the decolonization era was marked by conflicts among these princes, of whom there were three main players. One was allied with Thailand and the Americans. The second depended on Hanoi for support. The third sought to be neutral. Factional fighting with the armed forces and discontent among minorities further complicated the rivalries.

The decolonization process in Malaya (Malaysia) can be easily contrasted with the earlier period of colonial rule by the occurrence of near anarchy. As happened in other states in Southeast Asia, the weakness of British authority was revealed under the Japanese occupation in Malaya. The Malayan Communist Party (MCP), led mainly by Chinese cadres, launched a revolt in 1948 to prevent the restoration of British rule after the Japanese surrendered. This revolt, the so-called Emergency, lasted twelve years. It compelled the British to consider granting independence to Malaya earlier than was scheduled in order to counter the MCP propaganda that the British would only leave if forced to do so. It compelled the Malay elites to adopt multiracial political strategies to confront the communal threat of the MCP, consisting as it did mainly of Chinese followers. The outcome was the establishment of a federation of Malay States and the colonies of Penang and Melaka in 1948, with privileges entrenched for the indigenous Malays and citizenship extended to other immigrant races. The Federation of Malaya subsequently attained independence in 1957.

In the Philippines, plans for decolonization were already firmly in place by the 1910s. American colonial rule in the first decade of the twentieth century operated on the assumption that a tutelage process was necessary to train Filipinos in the art of democratic government. Many Filipino leaders therefore viewed the Japanese occupation as an interruption of this process. Thus, it was only in 1946 that the Philippines finally became independent. As in the United States, a two-party system with elections and four-year terms was established. However, this system remained rooted in the Filipino culture of family networks and patron-client relationships. The two-party system also faced the challenge of overcoming a third-party challenge in the form of the (Huk) communist revolt in central Luzon from the late 1940s until the early 1950s. The image of an independent Philippines was also somewhat marred by the agreement concluded with the departing Americans, stipulating that U.S. firms would be granted parity rights similar to those available to Philippine companies. In all, extraterritorial rights were granted to Americans within two military bases. These concessions, despite political decolonization, were issues that plagued the Philippine political scene for a few decades after independence because they suggested that the Philippines was not truly independent.

Some of the most detailed studies on the process of decolonization in Southeast Asia have been devoted to Indonesia. In 1942, the Japanese ripped apart the thin veneer of Dutch colonial rule. Then came three years of Japanese occupation, followed by surrender. The Dutch failed to restore their erstwhile colonial authority immediately, and in the ensuing vacuum of power, Indonesian nationalists proclaimed the independent Republic of Indonesia. The Dutch challenged this republic by establishing a federal state in which the republic would be incorporated as one of the constituent states, thus diluting its influence. Four years of dispute with the Dutch led nowhere, and in 1949, the Republic of Indonesia agreed to join the federal United States of Indonesia. After securing independence from the Dutch, the next step in the decolonization process was to rid the country of the Dutch-imposed federal structure. This task was successfully completed in 1950 and was followed by a campaign to wrest control over West Irian (which the Dutch retained after granting independence). Meanwhile, Sukarno (1901–1970), as president of the republic, attempted to restore more indigenous political practices, such as consensus seeking, rather than "Western democracy," which he disparaged as "50% + 1 democracy." In this vein, "guided democracy" was established in 1959. The decolonization process in Indonesia was thus multifaceted and multipronged.

The Wider Context of Decolonization

Decolonization impinged on Southeast Asia in different ways simply because the degree of colonization varied from region to region. Although lines were drawn on maps to delineate the spheres of influence of the British, Dutch, and French, these lines were set arbitrarily, without reference to the ethnic realities on the ground. As long as the Western colonial powers were strong, the lines served as boundaries. Once the Western colonial powers retreated, however, precolonial rivalries revived. Thus, Thailand, Laos, and Cambodia were involved in tussles over territories, while Vietnam interfered in Laotian affairs. Further south, the separation of the Malay Peninsula from the Indonesian archipelago was never a neat solution for the indigenous people living in both those regions. In short, one outcome of decolonization was the emergence of interstate disputes over boundaries.

This arbitrary separation of ethnically related peoples by boundaries inherited from the colonial past also resulted in the problem of minorities. Shan people were now distributed between the borders separating Burma and Thailand. In Vietnam, mountain people straddled the divide between Vietnam and Laos, constituting minorities when compared with the lowland Vietnamese. The Lao people were actually a minority in Laos, and most Lao people lived in Thailand. In every corner of Southeast Asia, minorities could be found, with the significant exception of Cambodia.

The migration of Chinese and Indians to settle in various parts of Southeast Asia during the colonial period further complicated matters when decolonization took place. The Indians formed important population groups in Burma and Malaya, and the Chinese were ubiquitous in practically all the Southeast Asian states that proclaimed independence in the late 1940s and 1950s. Both the Chinese and Indians became targets of nationalist agitation against further colonial intervention.

It will be useful to set the process of decolonization of Southeast Asia within a wider context of the end of empire. The discussion on the dynamics of decolonization described earlier merely related the story of the colonial dimension, namely, the domestic and, at best, regional factors that led to the overthrow of colonial rule. In the case of Southeast Asia, the primary focus fell on the period after 1945. There was also a global dimension at work—the changing international environment that emerged around 1945. This environment was not conducive to the continuance of colonial rule, principally because the Japanese occupation had demonstrated beyond doubt that Western colonial rule was an anachronism. It can also be argued that for Southeast Asia, the decision by the British to grant independence to India set the momentum for changes further east. There was also a metropolitan dimension, in terms of the changes taking place in the empire capitals such as London, Paris, and The Hague. New groups had emerged, questioning the basis and value of colonial subjugation of far-flung territories.

Unresolved Issues

If the causes of decolonization can be categorized and set in context, the next task is to ask when the process began and when it ended. This discussion has used 1945 as the starting point, but actually, a case can be made that the process began in the 1930s, signaled principally by the onset of the worldwide economic depression. The depression hit Southeast Asia unevenly, but it set in motion measures to decentralize government authority, and it raised issues that challenged the competency of Western colonial powers to continue their rule. When did the decolonization process end? It certainly did not end with the establishment of independent nation-states. If it were possible to identify a closing stage, then that stage would only take place in consonance with the ideological perspective of the observer. One who feels that a Southeast Asian state had returned to its original roots would argue that decolonization had completed its course. This, of course, begs the question of whether it is possible to discover these original roots. Another who feels that decolonization was a search for liberalization and democracy would argue that a Southeast Asian state had decolonized when the search was successful. This, of course, begged more questions than the answers provide. What, for example, is the definition of liberalization or democracy?

Then there are issues such as the geographic location within which the processes of decolonization took place. Was decolonization to be studied only within the confines of the nation-state that eventually emerged, that is, by reading history from the present back to the past with the benefit of hindsight? Was decolonization entirely a land-based event? Was there such an event as maritime decolonization? Should decolonization be studied in terms of peoples rather than nation-states? It seems to be easier to ask questions than to provide answers.

YONG MUN CHEONG

See also Anti-Fascist People's Freedom League (AFPFL); Aung San (1915–1947); British Military Administration (BMA) in Southeast Asia; Constitutional Developments in the Philippines (1900–1941); Dutch Police Action (First, Second); Federation of Malaya (1948); Geneva Conference (1954); Great Depression (1929–1931); Guided Democracy (*Demokrasi Terpimpin*); Hồ Chí Minh (1890–1969); Hukbalahap (Hukbo ng Bayan Laban Sa Hapon) (1942); Indochina War (1946–1954), First; Indochina War (1964–1975), Second (Vietnam War); Indonesian Revolution (1945–1949); Japanese Occupation of Southeast Asia

(1941–1945); Laos (Nineteenth Century to Mid-1990s); Laotinization; Malayan Communist Party (MCP); Malayan Emergency (1948–1960); Nationalism and Independence Movements in Southeast Asia; Paris Conference on Cambodia (PCC) (1989, 1991); Philippines-U.S. "Special Relationship"; Preservation of Siam's Political Independence; Sihanouk, Norodum (1922–); Soekarno (Sukarno) (1901–1970); United Nations Transitional Authority in Cambodia (UNTAC); U.S. Involvement in Southeast Asia (post-1945); U.S. Military Bases in Southeast Asia; Việt Minh (Việt Nam Độc Lập Đồng Minh Hội) (Vietnam Independence League); Vietnam, North (post-1945); Vietnam, South (post-1945)

References:

Cady, John F. 1974. *The History of Post-war Southeast Asia.* Athens: Ohio University Press.

Corpuz, Onofre D. 1965. *The Philippines.* Englewood Cliffs, NJ: Prentice-Hall.

Holt, Claire, ed. 1972. *Culture and Politics in Indonesia.* Ithaca, NY: Cornell University Press.

McAlister, John T., Jr., ed. 1973. *Southeast Asia: The Politics of National Integration.* New York: Random House.

Mohamad Noordin Sopiee. 1974. *From Malayan Union to Singapore Separation: Political Unification in the Malaysia Region, 1945–65.* Kuala Lumpur: Universiti Malaya Press.

Morrell, David L., and Chai-Anan Samudavanija. 1981. *Political Conflict in Thailand: Reforms, Reaction, Revolution.* Cambridge, MA: Oelgeschlager, Gunn & Hain.

Pluvier, J. M. 1964. *South-East Asia from Colonialism to Independence.* Kuala Lumpur: Oxford University Press.

Reid, Anthony. 1974. *The Indonesian National Revolution, 1945–1950.* Hawthorn, Victoria, Australia: Longman.

Silverstein, Josef. 1980. *Burmese Politics: The Dilemma of National Unity.* New Brunswick, NJ: Rutgers University Press.

Smith, Roger M., ed. 1974. *Southeast Asia: Documents of Political Development and Change.* Ithaca, NY: Cornell University Press.

Tarling, Nicholas, ed. 1992. *The Cambridge History of Southeast Asia.* Vol. 2, *The Nineteenth and Twentieth Centuries.* Cambridge: Cambridge University Press.

Tarling, Nicholas. 1993. *The Fall of Imperial Britain in South-East Asia.* Singapore: Oxford University Press.

DEMAK

Demak was the greatest Islamic kingdom of Java in the sixteenth century C.E., with a role that was very important for the development of Islam—religiously, politically, and economically. The political expansion that was motivated by religion and economic affairs made Demak a strong Islamic kingdom not only in Java but also in Indonesia and Southeast Asia. In Java, Demak's influence was ensured through the establishment of Cirebon and Banten on the north coast of West Java, which enabled the control of all ports along the north coast, including those of East Java. Close relationships between Demak and kingdoms in South Sulawesi, Maluku, and Aceh created the hegemony in defending against the political power of the Portuguese based in Melaka, the prime international trading center of Southeast Asia at the time. Rulers of Demak often launched offensives on Melaka in attempts to unseat the Portuguese.

Before the emergence of Demak as an Islamic kingdom, there were Muslim communities along the north coast of Java, then under the political control of the Hindu-Buddhist kingdom of Majapahit. The process of Islamization gained momentum in the face of a declining Majapahit, which prompted some aristocrats and the common people to readily embrace the new faith.

Against this backdrop, Raden Patah, together with his followers at Bintara in 1479, proclaimed Demak as an Islamic kingdom a year after the fall of the capital of Majapahit at Trowulan to Girindrawardhana, ruler of Kadiri. The Javanese *Chronicles* mentioned that the establishment of the kingdom of Demak was in accordance with the advice of Raden Rahmat, the pioneer *Wali Sanga* (the *Wali Songo,* the Nine Saints, were reputedly the nine founders of Islam on Java). Raden Patah, who was also called Dipati Jimbun, was the son of Brawijaya, the ruler of Majapahit, who married a Chinese princess. When the princess was pregnant, she was presented to Aria Damar, the governor of

Palembang. Demak consequently maintained close ties with Palembang.

After Raden Patah's ascension, Bintara was developed as the capital city of Demak. He erected the palace, the square, the mosque, and the market. The great mosque played an important function in the preaching of Islam undertaken by the Nine Saints. Under the reigns of Raden Patah (r. 1479–1513) and his successors Pate Unus (Sabranglor, r. 1513–1518) and Pangeran Trenggana (r. 1518–1546), Demak flourished as a city-state. The Portuguese traveler Tomé Pires mentioned that the city of Demak had about 8,000 or 10,000 houses and that Pate Rodim (which may have been a corruption of the name Raden Patah) was lord of the country. The international trade was conducted via Japara, as the harbor town of the kingdom. Persians, Arabs, Gujaratis, Bengalis, Malays, and other nationalities traded at this harbor town.

Demak's political influence spread to the western and eastern parts of the north coast of Java. Cirebon, one of the vassals of the Sunda-Pajajaran kingdom that had had a Muslim ruler since 1475, was under the political control of Demak. In 1526, Syarif Hidayatullah (Sunan Gunung Jati), one of the Nine Saints, established Banten as an Islamic kingdom. According to *Sajarah Banten* (Chronicle of Banten), Maulana Hasanuddin reigned over Banten from 1526 to 1552 under the supervision of his father, Syarif Hidayatullah, who lived at Cirebon until his demise in 1568.

Meanwhile, the Malay Islamic sultanate of Melaka under Sultan Mahmud Syah (r. 1488–1511) fell to the Portuguese Afonso de Albuquerque (1453–1515) on 10 August 1511, following a siege that lasted more than a month. Sultan Mahmud Syah and his son, Sultan Ahmad Syah, fled into the interior. Bentan (Bintang), Mahmud Syah's new capital, was also destroyed by the Portuguese in 1526. Sultan Mahmud Syah fled to Kampar on the eastern coast of Sumatra, where he died in 1528.

Albuquerque's political alliance with Ratu Samiam (Surawisesa), the ruler of Sunda, from 1511 to 1512 posed a threat to Demak. Consequently, in 1513, Demak launched a naval assault on Melaka, led by Pate Unus with the assistance of the Pate of Palembang. The Javanese armada was defeated, and Pate Unus was killed. Subsequently, on 21 August 1522, Albuquerque

signed a political and commercial treaty with the regent of the Sundanese kingdom, Ratu Samiam (perhaps Prabu Surawisesa). In 1527, a Portuguese armada under Francisco de Sa arrived at the harbor city of Kalapa (Kelapa). The armada was suddenly surrounded by Muslim forces from Demak and Cirebon, commanded by Fadhillah Khan (Falatehan). The Portuguese were defeated; on 22 June 1527, the victorious Fadhillah Khan renamed Kalapa as Jayakarta. Consequently, the Portuguese severed contact with the Hindu-Buddhist kingdom of Sunda-Pajajaran.

The Hindu-Buddhist kingdom in the hinterland of East Java, Daha-Kadiri, came under the control of Demak in 1527. During the reign of Pangeran Trenggana, the third sultan, Demak reached the zenith of its power. Cordial relations with the kingdoms of Aceh, Jambi, Palembang, South Kalimantan, and Maluku had been maintained against the expansion of Portuguese political and economic power.

Demak began to decline after Pangeran Trenggana waged a war against Panarukan. He was killed in battle in 1546. Thereafter, Demak witnessed a violent struggle within the royal family. Pangeran Adiwijaya (Jaka Tingkir), the son-in-law of Trenggana, emerged the winner after killing Aria Penangsang. But the Demak that he inherited was greatly weakened. The capital of Demak shifted to Pajang, in the hinterland, during the reign of Pangeran Adiwijaya (r. 1568–1586). Demak itself was reduced to the status of a regency, or *kadipaten*.

UKA TJANDRASASMITA

See also Aceh (Acheh); Albuquerque, Alfonso de (ca. 1462–1515); Banten (Bantam); Batavia (Sunda Kelapa, Jacatra, Djakarta/Jakarta); Hindu-Buddhist Period of Southeast Asia; Islam in Southeast Asia; Java; Kadiri (Kediri); Mahmud, Sultan of Melaka (r. 1488–1511); Majapahit (1293–ca. 1520s); Maluku (The Moluccas); Melaka; Palembang; Pires, Tomé (ca. 1465–ca. 1520s); Portuguese Asian Empire; Sulawesi (Celebes); *Wali Songo*

References:
Andaya, Barbara Watson, and Leonard Y. Andaya. 2000. *A History of Malaysia*. 2nd ed. London and Basingstoke, England: Palgrave.

Cortesao, Armando. 1967. *The Suma Oriental of Tome Pires: An Account of the East from the Red Sea to Japan, Written in Malacca and India in 1512–1515*. Vol. 2. Nendeln, Liechtenstein: Kaus Reprint.

Damais, L. Ch. 1957. "Études Javanaises I: Les Tombes Musulmanes datées de Tralaya" [Study on the Javanese I: The Date of the Moslem Tombs at Tralaya]. *Bulletin de l'École Française d'Extrême-Orient* 48: 353–415.

Djajadiningrat, Hoesein. 1913. "Critische beschouwing van de Sadjarah Banten terkenschet sing van de Javaanshe Historiografie" [Critical Observations on the "Chronicle of Banten": The Contribution to the Characters of Javanese Historiography]. Ph.D. diss., University of Leiden.

Graaf, H. J. de. 1970. "Southeast Asian Islam to the Eighteenth Century." Pp. 123–154 in *The Cambridge History of Islam*. Vol. 2, *The Further Islamic Society and Civilization*. Edited by P. M. Holt-Annk, S. Lambton, and Bernard Lewis. Cambridge: Cambridge University Press.

Hall, D. G. E. 1981. *A History of South-East Asia*. London and Basingstoke: Macmillan.

Robson, S. O. 1981. "Java at the Crossroads: Aspects of Javanese Cultural History in the 14th and 15th Centuries." *Bijdragen Koninklijk Instituut voor Taal-, Land- and Volkenkunde* 137: 259–292.

Schrieke, B. 1955. *Indonesian Sociological Studies: Selected Writings of B. Schrieke*. Pt. 1. The Hague and Bandung, Indonesia: W. van Hoeve.

Uka Tjandrasasmita. 1978. "The Introduction of Islam and the Growth of Moslem Coastal Cities in the Indonesian Archipelago." Pp. 141–160 in *Dynamics of Indonesian History*. Edited by Haryati Soebadio and Carine A. du Marchie Sarvaas. Amsterdam, New York, and Oxford: North-Holland Publishing.

———. 2000. *Pertumbuhan dan perkembangan kota-kota Muslim di Indonesia dari abad XIII sampai XVIII Masehi* [The Growth and the Development of Muslim Cities in Indonesia from the 13th to the 18th Century]. Jakarta: P. T. Menara Kudus.

van Leur, J. C. 1955. *Indonesian Trade and Society: Essays in Asian Social Economic History*. The Hague and Bandung, Indonesia: W. van Hoeve.

DEMOCRATIC ACTION PARTY (DAP)

The Democratic Action Party (DAP), the most dominant non-Malay opposition party in Malaysia since 1966, was formed when the People's Action Party (PAP) based in Singapore was deregistered in Malaysia after Singapore became a separate and independent nation in 1965. Headed by C. V. Devan Nair, the sole PAP representative in the Malaysian Parliament and a Malaysian citizen by birth, DAP, which was officially registered in March 1966, adopted the "Malaysian Malaysia" strategy of the PAP. From its beginnings, the DAP positioned itself as a vigorous critic of the Alliance Party government, which it accused of discriminatory practices against the non-Malays.

The DAP openly declared itself committed to the principle of racial equality in all fields, political, social, economic, cultural, and educational. Thus, it opposed the classification of the population into *bumiputera* (sons of the soil), referring to the Malays and other indigenous inhabitants, and non-bumiputera, or non-Malays and nonindigenous people, and demanded equal treatment and equal opportunities for all citizens, irrespective of racial origins. It openly attacked the special position of the Malays as provided for in the Malaysian Constitution and harped on the plurality of the nation and the use of the Chinese and Tamil languages on a par with Malay for official purposes. Like the PAP, DAP accused the Malaysian Chinese Association (MCA) of not doing enough for the Chinese and of being subservient to the United Malays National Organization (UMNO). It offered itself as the alternative to the MCA as well as to the Malaysian Indian Congress (MIC).

This confrontational style of the DAP and other radical non-Malay-based parties such as the People's Progressive Party (PPP) and Gerakan (Gerakan Rakyat Malaysia, the Malaysian People's Movement) was attractive to the younger generation of non-Malays. But the DAP was seen as a threat by the Malay political parties from within and without the government. The tense political atmosphere thus created contributed to the outbreak of the May 13, 1969 incident.

ABDUL RAHMAN HAJI ISMAIL

See also Alliance Party (Malaya/Malaysia); *Bumiputera* (*Bumiputra*); Federation of Malaya (1948); Malayan/Malaysian Chinese Association (MCA) (1949); Malayan/Malaysian Education; Malayan/Malaysian Indian Congress (MIC); "May 13, 1969" (Malaysia); New Economic Policy (NEP) (Malaysia) (1971–1990); People's Action Party (PAP); United Malays National Organization (UMNO) (1946)

References:

Means, Gordon P. 1976. *Malaysian Politics.* London: Hodder and Stoughton.

———. 1991. *Malaysian Politics: The Second Generation.* Singapore: Oxford University Press.

Milne, R. S., and Diane K. Mauzy. 1980. *Politics and Government in Malaysia.* Singapore: Times Books International.

Vasil, R. K. 1980. *Ethnic Politics in Malaysia.* New Delhi: Radiant Publishers.

DEMOCRATIC KAMPUCHEA (DK)

Democratic Kampuchea (DK) was a radical Marxist-Leninist regime that ruled Cambodia between April 1975 and January 1979, when it was driven from power by a Vietnamese invasion. The Cambodian Communists, known outside Cambodia as the Red Khmers (or Khmer Rouge), were led by Saloth Sar (1925–1998), better known as Pol Pot, and drew much of their inspiration from Maoist China.

Saloth Sar and his colleagues (who included Son Sen, Ieng Sary [1927–], and Nuon Chea) had developed their plans for a socialist Cambodia when they were hiding in guerrilla camps in the forested northeast in the late 1960s. During the civil war that swept through Cambodia from 1970 to 1975, the leaders gained valuable military and organizational skills and continued to believe that revolutionary zeal, top-down management, and the collectivization of property could solve Cambodia's social and economic problems and provide a luminous example for other developing countries.

The Khmer Rouge came to power in April 1975 when their forces seized Cambodia's capital, Phnom Penh. For several months, the leaders of the movement claimed that power was in the hands of the mysterious "Revolutionary Organization" whose affiliations, leadership, and membership were kept secret from outsiders. In January 1976, after its leaders had drafted a constitution, DK emerged as a state onto the international scene. The existence of the Cambodian Communist Party, however, and the names of its leaders remained concealed.

DK's leaders boasted that their revolutionary program owed nothing to foreign precedents or advice. However, it was clear to outside observers as information filtered out of the country that the program drew inspiration from Maoist China. Like Mao Zedong (1893–1976), DK's leaders based their ideology on continuous class warfare. They admired China's Great Leap Forward (1958) (which they probably thought had been a success) and the ongoing Cultural Revolution (1966–1976). They believed, like Mao, in the empowerment of the peasantry and in the importance of revolutionary will. Some DK policies, however, such as the abolition of money, markets, and private property and the wholesale evacuation of towns, were more radical than anything that had been attempted in China.

In July 1976, DK's leaders unveiled a utopian four-year plan, borrowing its name from China's Great Leap Forward, that envisaged tripling rice production throughout the country almost overnight, without material incentives or sufficient machinery and in the wake of a ruinous civil war. The foreign currency earned from rice exports, it was thought, would be used to buy agricultural machinery and to lay the basis for further industrialization. The plan was couched in pleasing revolutionary rhetoric but bore little relation to Cambodian realities and made no provision for the people's health or welfare. It was a colossal, overreaching failure. As it went into effect, hundreds of thousands of men and women, attempting to meet impossible agricultural goals, died of undernourishment and overwork. Thousands more, especially those evacuated from the towns, were executed summarily as enemies of the state. The DK leadership, unwilling to accept responsibility for what had happened, claimed that enemies from within wrecked the plan. Purges soon swept through the ranks of the party, the army, and the regions that had failed to reach their quotas. In a secret interrogation facility in the capital known by its code name, S-21, over

Cambodian Sam Vishna, age twenty-eight, looks at a mixture of brown and white skulls that make up a map of Cambodia at Tuol Sleng (S-21 prison) Museum in Phnom Penh, 9 December 1998. The former high school was turned into a prison by the Khmer Rouge during the Pol Pot regime. More than seventeen thousand men, women, and children were held there before they were taken to the "killing fields" to be executed. Sam Vishna's father, older brother, and sister were all killed in 1976. (AFP/Corbis)

14,000 men and women, accused of counter-revolutionary crimes, were questioned, tortured, and put to death. Those killed included many high-ranking members of the party. The purges continued until the demise of DK in January 1979.

In 1977, just before embarking on a state visit to China, Pol Pot revealed the existence of the Cambodian Communist Party. In China, he obtained political support and military aid for the growing conflict between Cambodia and Vietnam, which was allied with the Soviet Union and by implication hostile to China. Full-scale warfare broke out between Cambodia and Vietnam in early 1978, and although the Khmer Rouge forces were courageous, they were no match for the seasoned and well-equipped troops arrayed against them. Vietnam invaded Cambodia at the end of the year, driving Pol Pot and his colleagues into exile in Thailand.

A Vietnamese protectorate established in 1979 labeled DK a "fascist" regime and condemned Pol Pot and Ieng Sary to death in absentia. As data emerged from refugees, survivors, and archives over the next ten years, it became clear that DK had presided over the deaths of perhaps 2 million Cambodian citizens, or one in five, making it one of the cruelest, most misguided, and most horrific governments in recent times.

DAVID CHANDLER

See also Association of Southeast Asian
   Nations (ASEAN) (1967); China since 1949;
   Cold War; Ieng Sary (1927–); Khmer Rouge;
   Killing Fields, The; Kuantan Principle (1980);
   Peoples' Republic of Kampuchea (PRK); Pol
   Pot (Saloth Sar) (1925–1998); Sihanouk,
   Norodom (1922–); Sino-Soviet Struggle;
   Sino-Vietnamese Relations; Sino-
   Vietnamese Wars

References:
Becker, Elizabeth. 1986. *When the War Was Over.*
   New York: Simon and Schuster.
Chandler, David. 1999a. *Brother Number One: A
   Political Biography of Pol Pot.* 2nd ed. Boulder,
   CO: Westview Press.
———. 1999b. *Voices from S-21: Terror and
   History in Pol Pot's Secret Prison.* Berkeley and
   Los Angeles: University of California Press.
Jackson, Karl, ed. 1989. *Cambodia 1975–1978:
   Rendezvous with Death.* Princeton, NJ:
   Princeton University Press.
Kiernan, Ben. 1995. *The Pol Pot Regime.* New
   Haven, CT: Yale University Press.
Ponchaud, Francois. 1978. *Cambodia Year Zero.*
   New York: Henry Holt.

DEMOGRAPHIC TRANSITION IN SOUTHEAST ASIA

Demographic Transition in Perspective

The term *demographic transition* is used for the
process whereby high levels of mortality and
fertility—in other words, high death and birth
rates—slowly but irreversibly drop to much
lower levels. It is a long and drawn-out process
that can take many decades, even a century or
more.

The process is rather well documented for
Western Europe, and the general trend can be
summarized in a few sentences. From the late
eighteenth century onward, mortality figures
started to drop in a number of countries. From
death rates of between 25 and 50 or more per
thousand (the crude death rate, or CDR), they
fell to below 10 per thousand at the end of the
twentieth century. This mortality transition
(also called *epidemiological transition*) was accompanied by a fertility decline of similar proportions, from 40 or even 45 per thousand (crude
birth rate, or CBR), to 10 and below (Livi-
Bacci 1992: 101, 108).

At the beginning of the transition process,
the annual average rate of natural increase of

the population (births minus deaths) was often
fairly low. Between 1600 and 1750, most Western European countries experienced average
annual growth rates of 0.15 to 0.2 percent per
year (Livi-Bacci 1992: 69). As the death rate
usually started to drop quite some time before
the birth rate did, the rate of natural increase
went up considerably, easily reaching rates of 1
percent per year and over. Then, however, fertility started to fall as well, while the mortality
figures began to stabilize at a low level. Thus,
the rate of natural increase started to drop,
reaching zero growth. That moment had arrived when the so-called Total Fertility Rate
(TFR, or the average number of children per
woman) dropped below 2.1 or 2.15. In what
has been termed Europe's Second Demographic Transition, fertility rates dropped even
further after the mid-1960s, leading to a negative rate of natural increase.

Southeast Asia was and is going through the
same or at least a very similar process. However,
in most regions of Southeast Asia, the (first)
transition started much later, the growth rates
of the population were much higher, and it
would appear that the duration of the fertility
transition would be shorter.

The Transition in Action

Conventional wisdom has it that the fertility
decline did not start in Southeast Asia before the
1960s. Scholars are less sanguine about the beginning of the mortality transition, but most apparently agree that in many Southeast Asian
countries, the death rate started to drop at the
beginning of the twentieth century and that the
downward trend accelerated in the 1950s. In the
short run, this led to very high annual rates of
natural increase. However, around the year
2000, the total fertility rate had dropped in
some cases below replacement level (Singapore,
Thailand), and it was coming close to that in
others (Indonesia, Vietnam). In countries such as
Cambodia and Laos, with TFRs in 2000 of 4.77
and 4.80, respectively, the demographic transition still has a long way to go. Rates of natural
increase in the region are now 1 to 2.5 percent
per year (*The Future of Population in Asia* 2002:
132–135). This is, in a nutshell, the demographic
transition in Southeast Asia.

The remainder of this section is dedicated to
a more detailed discussion of the factors influ-

encing the demographic transition process. As the drop in mortality preceded the fall in fertility, the death rate will be discussed first.

As population statistics on most Southeast Asian areas are either absent or rather unreliable prior to 1900, it is virtually impossible to formulate statements on the development of the death rate in the whole region in the nineteenth century. There is mounting evidence, however, that in a number of areas, the death rate may have been dropping slightly, particularly during the latter half of the nineteenth century. The three most frequently mentioned factors behind this modest drop in mortality are vaccination against smallpox, the so-called *pax imperica* (lit., "imperial peace," the peace resulting from the establishment of Western colonial regimes), and improved transportation networks.

Vaccination was a technique discovered in Europe on the eve of the nineteenth century and already introduced in Asia shortly after 1800. It was not immediately implemented effectively on a large scale, but by 1850, it was a success in many areas in Southeast Asia. As smallpox was one of the big killers around 1800, successful vaccination campaigns ushered in lower mortality. In many areas, however, vaccination on a meaningful scale had hardly been started around 1900. Such differences were largely related to the presence or absence of a colonial state.

The colonial state was also the key factor in the pax imperica. In most areas where it was present, the colonial state put an end to constant "tribal" warfare, civil war, and other forms of intergroup violence, such as head-hunting. The number of direct victims of such violence may have been low, but the number of people killed by diseases and famine as a consequence of these conflicts appears to have been considerable, as the destruction of the means of production was often a side effect of conflict. Of course, colonial armies brought violence of their own, but it would seem that on balance, at least in the nineteenth century, the pax imperica meant lower death rates.

The nineteenth century also saw the construction of more and better roads and, in the last half of the century, the creation of railways and steamship connections. This made it much easier to send food to areas hit by harvest failures, thereby preventing local famines.

Be that as it may, the drop in the death rate is well documented for the twentieth century. After the medical revolution of the late nineteenth century, during which the causative agents of many lethal diseases were discovered, researchers were finally able to come up with effective cures for many killers. Apart from quinine, a drug that had been available in impressive quantities since the late nineteenth century, salvarsan (1909) and the sulpha drugs (1930s) were the first "chemical" treatments that brought mortality rates down slightly. This effect was greatly strengthened by the so-called miracle drugs (antibiotics) that came on the market after World War II (1939–1945). Other successes were to be found in the preventive sphere. Quinine had been an effective cure against some types of malaria, initially through species sanitation (elimination of the disease-carrying mosquitoes) and then, after the war, dichlorodiphenyltrichloroethane (DDT) did much to fight the vectors of the malaria plasmodium, the *Anopheles* mosquitoes. Of course, later on, DDT had to be abandoned when it turned out to be harmful to other life-forms as well, but it did bring down the rate of infection with malaria and therefore the CDR. Thus, the drop in the CDR accelerated in the 1950s. Steadily improving hygiene, primary health care, and a stream of new drugs and treatments coming from the Western world ensured that the death rate dropped slowly but surely and constantly.

Finally, the better quality of the diet of large sections of Southeast Asian populations since the 1970s, due to sustained rates of economic growth per capita, did much to reinforce the downward trend of the death rate. Whereas in the 1950s CDRs from 20 to 30 had been the rule, by the year 2000, mortality rates ranged from 5 to 15 per thousand (*The Future of Population in Asia* 2002: 132–135).

The drop in the birth rate came much later than that in the death rate. In fact, in the nineteenth century and even in the first half of the twentieth century, fertility appears to have increased among specific groups and during particular periods. We know even less about the details of this phenomenon than we do about the drop in mortality rates in the nineteenth century, but a number of factors are often quoted in the scholarly literature. The transition from foragers and shifting cultivators, often in tandem with conversion to Islam or Christianity, may have played a role. Also mentioned is a drop in the age of marriage, probably related to increased economic opportunities and/or increased labor burdens, in addition to shorter lactation periods. Both factors may lead to higher birth rates.

However, there are indications for dropping birth rates in the nineteenth century as well. This may have been related to locally deteriorating economic circumstances in high-population-density areas (density-dependent reaction). It may have been also influenced by the incipient drop in the death rate, which was strongly reflected in the rate of infant mortality. With fewer deaths among breast-fed children, the average period of lactation increased, thus influencing fecundity.

Almost all factors mentioned here imply that women were willing and able to manipulate their levels of fertility. There are, indeed, many indications that prior to the period of modern birth control methods, which started in the 1960s in Southeast Asia, traditional ways of family limitation had been known and used for ages. Generally speaking, it is now accepted by many scholars that "tribal" peoples, often engaged in foraging or shifting cultivation and often living in extended families, had low rates of fertility, much lower than the rates of "natural fertility" they were formerly assumed to have had.

Around 1960, rates of natural increase in most developing countries were so high that terms such as *population explosion* were used to describe this phenomenon. Rates from 2.5 to 3.5 percent per year—much higher than they had ever been in the developed world—were normal. In the 1950s, crude birth rates in Southeast Asia varied from 40 to almost 50. In the late 1990s, the extremes varied from just over 10 (Singapore) to around 35 (Cambodia, Laos), but most rates are now below 25 per thousand (*The Future of Population in Asia* 2002: 132–135).

What are the factors behind this amazingly rapid fertility transition? The "proximate factors" affecting the process are clear. Women marry later, and their marital fertility is lower than it used to be because they are using methods of family limitation, which they can do because reliable methods of birth control are readily available. For the search for the "ulti-mate" or "underlying factors," we have to look at things such as economic development, modernization, and mass communication.

Not so long ago, demographic orthodoxy insisted that in order to achieve lower rates of fertility, all that was needed was economic development. Even though it is now recognized that other factors have contributed to this process, it is still rather obvious that economic growth is the real motor behind the demographic transition. But the first step is to look at the proximate factors.

One of the most obvious factors is, of course, the use of modern methods of contraception, including the pill, condoms, sterilization, and intrauterine devices (IUDs). Singapore, Thailand, and Indonesia are good examples of countries where the acceptance of modern birth control methods has been increasing steadily. In Indonesia and Singapore, this has been strongly stimulated by the state. In the Philippines, where the influence of the Roman Catholic Church is strong, antinatalist policies are far less popular. This seems to be reflected in the Philippines' fairly high total fertility rate (TFR of 3.24 in 2000) (*The Future of Population in Asia* 2002: 134–135). Increased use of modern methods of birth control is reflected in lower rates of marital fertility. Early termination of pregnancies (induced abortions) may play a role as well, as is shown in the case of Singapore, where the law, originating in Victorian Britain, was changed in 1970. This brief discussion illustrates the potential importance of the state in these matters. It also suggests that variation between regions is to be expected, based on differences in culture, religion, and ethnic reproductive patterns.

The effects of family planning are reinforced by the increasing age of women at first marriage. In 1960, the proportion of women in Thailand aged twenty-five to twenty-nine who were married was 87; it had dropped to 75 by 1990. For Indonesia, these figures are 96 and 89. If experiences in East Asia are anything to go by (and they seem to be), this proportion might drop as low as 60 (Japan in 1990) (Westley and Mason 1998). Generally speaking, past experience has shown that a higher age at first marriage leads to lower numbers of children per woman.

Later age at marriage is generally assumed to be related to a drop in arranged marriages and to higher proportions of women being educated beyond primary school. Education for women also had other implications for the birth rate. Educated women were, at least in an early stage of the fertility transition, quicker to accept modern family-planning methods. More education for girls and young women also implies that they are no longer available to their parents as cheap labor. On the contrary, they are now costing money. It is assumed by many scholars that these considerations have played and still are playing an important role in the declining birth rate, as children are turning from being an economic asset into a liability, at least in the short run. However, the role of education for women varies from country to country. Whereas Singapore, the leader in fertility transition, shows the expected combination of low TFR and high proportion of women in secondary education, the runner-up, Thailand, combines a low TFR with a low rate of female participation in education.

But how do we explain the sudden interest of the state in birth control, the success in the adoption of family-planning methods, the growing interest in education, and the postponement of marriages? The keywords here are *modernization, economic development,* and *mass communication.*

Economic growth, in the sense of an almost continuous increase in real income per capita, is probably the most important driving force behind the success story of the demographic transition in (parts of) Southeast Asia. Economic development was largely responsible for the lower rate of mortality (through better diet and better medical care); it is also one of the main forces behind the fertility transition. Economic development implies, among other things, urbanization and a shift from agriculture to industry and the service sector, with young women migrating temporarily to urban areas. This may have influenced the age of marriage and the arrival of a first child, as children could be combined with agricultural activities but far less easily with working in the factory. Economic development also implies schooling.

Modernization, admittedly a rather vague notion, follows in the wake of economic growth. Notions of individual choices and destinies, of better education, of higher aspirations, particularly for women, are all part of the "Western" ideology that is more or less identical with the modern way of life, which has been globalized during the last few decades.

The enormous impact of modernization and the rapid adoption of methods of birth control would have been unthinkable without the spread of radio and television. It would appear that this goes a long way toward explaining why the fertility transition could have taken place so quickly in a number of countries.

About international and interregional migration, some thoughts are in order. In various Southeast Asian countries, large numbers of (young) people leave their region or country for many months or even years, in search of better-paid employment. However, this is temporary migration; the migrant is supposed to return to the home village eventually and start a family. This is somewhat different from the situation in Europe during the demographic transition, when many people left their countries in order to establish themselves permanently abroad. Temporary migration, particularly of women, might have some effect on the age at marriage, but it will probably be slight. The numbers involved seem to be huge, but as a proportion of the relevant cohorts, they are not impressive.

Consequences and Prospects

One of the positive effects, often referred to as the "demographic bonus," is the drop in the dependency ratio in countries where the fertility transition is well under way. As the proportion of young children in the population drops and the dependency ratio therefore falls, the number of workers per capita increases. This facilitates increased savings per household, leading to higher capital-to-labor ratios and thus increased productivity. At a later stage, the dependency ratio will go up again, when the proportion of elderly increases significantly, a situation now being witnessed in East Asia.

However, for the time being in many countries in the early stages of the demographic transition, the proportion of adolescents and young adults, sometimes indicated by the term *youth bulge,* has been increasing. This group is less likely to get married early and represents an increased demand for education (and, of course, jobs). In a stagnating economy, this poses an even more serious problem than is usually the case. It is a group that is, in several respects, at risk in a period in which the threat of HIV/AIDS looms as large as it does. It is difficult to believe that behavioral changes related to this threat will leave reproductive behavior unaffected.

The demographic transition process in Southeast Asia does not follow one trajectory, nor does it show one rhythm from one area to another. Nevertheless, it is to be expected that, within a few decades, the region as a whole will have emulated East Asia, the second region in the world where the (first) demographic transition was completed.

PETER BOOMGAARD

See also Diseases and Epidemics; Education, Western Secular; Highways and Railways; Newspapers and the Mass Media in Southeast Asia; Sexual Practices; Women in Southeast Asia

References:

Boomgaard, Peter. 1989. *Children of the Colonial State: Population Growth and Economic Development in Java, 1795–1880.* Amsterdam: Free University Press.

Coale, Ansley J., and Susan Cotts Watkins, eds. 1986. *The Decline of Fertility in Europe.* Princeton, NJ: Princeton University Press.

Doeppers, Daniel F., and Peter Xenos, eds. 1998. *Population and History: The Demographic Origins of the Modern Philippines.* Madison: Center for Southeast Asian Studies, University of Wisconsin.

The Future of Population in Asia. 2002. Honolulu, HI: East-West Center.

Hirschman, Charles, and Philip Guest. 1990. "The Emerging Demographic Transitions of Southeast Asia." *Population and Development Review* 16, no. 1: 121–152.

Hugo, Graeme J., Terence H. Hull, Valerie Hull, and Gavin Jones. 1987. *The Demographic Dimension in Indonesian Development.* Singapore: Oxford University Press.

Leete, Richard. 1996. *Malaysia's Demographic Transition: Rapid Development, Culture, and Politics.* Kuala Lumpur: Oxford University Press.

Livi-Bacci, Massimo. 1992. *A Concise History of World Population.* Cambridge, MA, and Oxford: Blackwell.

Mason, Andrew, Thomas Merrick, and R. Paul Shaw, eds. 1999. *Population Economics, Demographic Transition, and Development: Research and Policy Implications.* Washington, DC: World Bank.

Owen, Norman G., ed. 1987. *Death and Disease in Southeast Asia: Explorations in Social, Medical and Demographic History.* Singapore: Oxford University Press.

Saw Swee-Hock. 1999. *The Population of Singapore.* Singapore: Institute of Southeast Asian Studies.

van de Kaa, Dirk J. 1999. "The Past of Europe's Demographic Future." Uhlenbeck Lecture 17. Wassenaar, The Netherlands: Netherlands Institute of Advanced Studies (NIAS).

Westley, Sidney B., and Andrew Mason. 1998. "Women Are Key Players in the Economies of East and Southeast Asia." *Asia-Pacific Population & Policy,* no. 44: 1–4.

DEVARAJA

Throughout Southeast Asia, religion has been used to sanction kingship, be it a local religion or a religion that has spread to Southeast Asia from other regions, such as Buddhism, Confucianism, Vaisnavism, or Saivism. The degree of sanctity has ranged widely: from validating God's or the Buddha's sanction of the king's rule, via ritual, religious acts, or personal practice for the king, to associating the ancestors of the current ruler with deities, to identifying the king himself as a deity. In this, the holy men of the relevant religion, such as Brahmins or Buddhist monks, were involved in authenticating the king's sanctity. In the Angkor kingdom (present-day Cambodia), a series of kings had images and *lingas* consecrated, including portable lingas, each given a different name of the god Siva; his name was then also reflected in the king's own. A linga is a phallic representation of Siva, usually made of stone. A particularly famous but little understood association of the ruling monarch with the god Siva is found in the so-called *devaraja* cult, associated with Jayavarman II (r. 770/790/802?–834), who founded the Angkor empire at the beginning of the ninth century C.E.

The French scholar George Coedès interpreted the Sanskrit compound *deva-raja* literally, following the word order, as "god-king" and interpreted it to mean that Jayavarman and his successors were claiming to be God on earth. In other words, Jayavarman was supposedly creating a cult of himself and his successors. However, the grammatically correct interpretation of this Sanskrit compound is "king of the gods"—that is, the term should be read from right to left, as pointed out by the French Indologist Jean Filliozat in 1966. He reinterpreted the term to refer not to Jayavarman but to Siva as the king of the gods, an unremarkable epithet.

Hermann Kulke (1974) confirmed Filliozat's correction of Coedès's work. Reexamining the inscriptions, he suggested that the term refers to a transportable image of Siva being moved to the different Angkor capitals. A distinction is clearly made between "the king of the gods" and the earthly rulers he is said to accompany. In being taken by the kings to their different capitals, the statue acted as a centralizing palladium, located with the king even when the king moved. The significance of this particular Siva statue appears to have declined in the tenth century. There is therefore no such thing as the devaraja cult but rather just another instance of the Siva worship then widespread in mainland Southeast Asia.

There were two main difficulties in Coedès's understanding of references to devaraja. The first was that he had only a handful of Sanskrit and Khmer inscriptions. The second was that Coedès was involved in the process of making grand statements about the culture of Southeast Asia at an extremely early stage in the academic study of the region's history. This was fashionable in his day and perhaps necessary for a pioneer in the field.

That such a possibly insignificant cult has received so much attention is due to the fact that the works of Coedès were groundbreaking at the beginning of the twentieth century and, although now much revised, have remained seminal in the study of mainland Southeast Asia.

KATE CROSBY

See also Angkor; Hindu-Buddhist Period of Southeast Asia; Indianization; Indigenous Political Power; Jayavarman II (r. 770/790/802?–834 C.E.)

References:

Coedès, George. 1968. *The Indianized States of Southeast Asia*. Edited by Walter Vella, translated by Susan Brown Cowing. Honolulu: East-West Center Press/University Press of Hawai'i. Published in French in 1944, 1948, and 1964.

Kulke, Hermann. 1974. "Der Devaraja-Kult: Legitimation und Herrscherapotheose im Angkor-Reich" [The Devaraja-Cult: Legitimation and Ruler Apotheosis in the Angkor Kingdom]. *Saeculum* 25, no. 1: 24–55.

Mabbett, Ian W. 1969. "Devaraja." *Journal of Southeast Asian History* 10 (September): 202–223.

DEWAWONGSE, PRINCE (1858–1923)
Preserver of Siam's Independence

Prince Dewawongse was born on 27 November 1858 as Prince Dewan Uthaiwongse to Lady Piem, a consort of King Mongkut (Rama IV) (r. 1851–1868). He was appointed the minister of foreign affairs in 1885 and held this position until his death in 1923, thus becoming Thailand's longest-serving foreign minister. His most outstanding contribution was the development of a sophisticated and articulate foreign policy, which helped save the kingdom from Western colonialism.

As a child, Dewawongse already showed great intelligence and a particular aptitude at English and mathematics. When King Chulalongkorn (Rama V) (r. 1868–1910), whose three queens were younger sisters of Prince Dewawongse, undertook financial reforms by transferring to the royal audit office control of all the financial work of the kingdom, he appointed Dewawongse as chief of staff of the office. When the office of royal secretariat was founded, Chulalongkorn chose Dewawongse to be head of that office. While working at the royal secretariat, the prince also served as the king's adviser for foreign affairs. In 1882, on his advice, Siam for the first time appointed ambassadors to be posted in European countries.

In 1885, after considerable hesitation, Chulalongkorn appointed Dewawongse minister of foreign affairs, when the latter was only twenty-seven years old. Elderly and senior men traditionally held ministerial positions; Chulalongkorn's reluctance to make this appointment therefore reflected his desire to avoid conflict with his conservative courtiers. However, Dewawongse's talents and experience in giving advice on foreign affairs were indisputable, and most senior officials agreed that he was the most suitable person to hold the post. In 1887, he was sent to London as Chulalongkorn's representative, to attend the celebrations of the fiftieth anniversary of Queen Victoria's rule. The king also asked him to study the organization of European governments while abroad, for the purpose of implementing Siamese governmental reforms. Upon his return, Dewawongse recommended the establishment of a modern administration in Siam, comprising a cabinet and twelve ministries (Wyatt 1984: 200). Eventually, in 1892, the king undertook a major governmental reform and established the twelve ministries. The cabinet council was also founded, and Dewawongse was appointed chairman, a position he held for thirty-one years.

Dewawongse became the minister of foreign affairs at a time when Siam was facing the most serious threat from both France and Britain, who were competing in expanding their colonial rule in Southeast Asia. By the 1880s, France had already colonized Vietnam and some parts of Laos and Cambodia, but it wanted to extend its rule to cover Laos east of the Mekong River and western Cambodia, which were still under Siamese sovereignty. In Kedah, Kelantan, Perlis, and Terengganu in the Malay Peninsula, the British were seeking to have power transferred to them from Siam (Wyatt 1984: 203, 206). The first major confrontation with colonialism took place in July 1893 when the French sent gunboats to the Chaophraya River to demand that the region of Laos to the east of the Mekong River be ceded to France. The French also planned to blockade the Gulf of Siam and make Siam a French protectorate if the latter did not accede to their demands. The confrontation led to skirmishes between French and Siamese forces in the Chaophraya, which are referred to as the Paknam Incident (1893). Dewawongse had to handle the situation with great care because the independence of the kingdom was at stake. Even though he would have liked to use force to respond to the French threat, he chose a peaceful and compromising approach once he discovered how weak the Siamese forces were and how lukewarm the British response was during the crisis (Tuck 1995: 109, 114–115). Thanks to his diplomatic

finesse during the negotiations, the French withdrew, and the independence of the kingdom was saved, even though Siam had to accept the French demand to cede the region of Laos east of the Mekong River.

The Paknam Incident was only the beginning of colonialist threats. After the incident, the French and the British continued to demand that Siam cede territories under its sovereignty. For example, territories opposite Luang Prabang, Champasak, and Manophrai were ceded to France in 1904. Three years later, the Siamese court abolished its claims over western Cambodia, and the right to rule was transferred to France. And in 1909, after long negotiations, Bangkok agreed to cede the four Malay States to the British (Wyatt 1984: 206). Dewawongse played vital roles in these negotiations with the purpose of saving the independence of the kingdom, and he achieved that goal. Dewawongse died in 1923 after serving thirty-eight years at the Ministry of Foreign Affairs. Thanks to his brilliant diplomatic skills, Siam was able to preserve its independence.

SUD CHONCHIRDSIN

See also British Interests in Southeast Asia; French Ambitions in Southeast Asia; Paknam Incident (1893); Preservation of Siam's Political Independence; Reforms and Modernization in Siam

References:
Tambiah, S. J. 1976. *World Conqueror and World Renouncer: A Study of Buddhism and Polity in Thailand against a Historical Background.* Cambridge: Cambridge University Press.
Tarling, Nicholas, ed. 1992. *The Cambridge History of Southeast Asia.* Vol. 2, *The Nineteenth and Twentieth Centuries.* Cambridge: Cambridge University Press.
Tuck, Patrick. 1995. *The French Wolf and the Siamese Lamb.* Bangkok: White Lotus.
Wyatt, David K. 1984. *Thailand: A Short History.* New Haven, CT: Yale University Press.

DEWEY, COMMODORE GEORGE (1837–1917)
An American Imperialist

George Dewey was the commodore in command of the U.S. Asiatic Squadron and gained fame on 1 May 1898 when he won the Battle of Manila Bay against the Spanish fleet in the early days of the Spanish-American War (1898). That battle established the United States as a new Asiatic imperial power and paved the way for the American colonization of the Philippines.

Dewey was a professional U.S. Navy officer, born on 26 December 1837 in Montpelier, Vermont. He graduated from the U.S. Naval Academy at Annapolis, Maryland, and was commissioned as a regular navy officer. He saw action in the American Civil War (1861–1865) as executive officer of the USS *Mississippi.* Dewey was a supporter of Capt. Alfred Thayer Mahan's views on projecting national strength by sea power and naval bases, and he favored the U.S. acquisition of a naval base in Asia in the 1890s. He was in command of the Asiatic Squadron, based in the British colony of Hong Kong, when the Spanish-American War broke out and immediately prepared the squadron to attack the Spanish fleet in the Philippines. Leading the ships into Manila Bay on board his flagship, the USS *Olympia,* he caught the Spaniards by surprise, and with little opposition and the loss of only one man, his force totally destroyed the Spanish fleet. The Battle of Manila Bay was the first modern naval battle, and it made the United States a major world power. Dewey favored the American takeover of Luzon from the Spaniards, even as he reportedly promised to assist Filipino revolutionary forces in their war against Spain. He held off attempts by other powers to assert power over Manila Bay and assisted U.S. ground troops in the capture of Manila in August 1898.

For his victory over the Spanish fleet, Dewey was made an admiral of the navy, the highest rank in the U.S. Navy. He was given a hero's welcome on his return to the United States and continued to serve in the navy as president of the navy's General Board until his death on 16 June 1917. Americans remembered Dewey as the victor of Manila Bay and the man responsible for bringing the United States to empire status. To Filipinos, however, he is seen as an imperialist who broke his promise to aid the Filipino revolutionary forces.

RICARDO TROTA JOSE

See also Aguinaldo, Emilio (1869–1964); "Manifest Destiny"; Manila; Philippine Revolution (1896–1898); Philippine War of Independence (1899–1902); Philippines under U.S. Colonial Administration

(1898–1946); Spanish-American Treaty of Paris (1898); Spanish-American War (1898)

References:

Spector, Ronald. 1988. *Admiral of Empire: The Life and Career of George Dewey.* Columbia: University of South Carolina Press.

DIEN BIEN PHU, BATTLE OF (MAY 1954)
A Vietnamese Victory

On 7 May 1954, the Vietnamese Popular Army defeated the French forces at Dien Bien Phu, putting an end to the First Indochina War (1945–1954). The battle took place within the framework of French strategy. It was part of the Navarre Plan—named after the French commander-in-chief, General Henri Navarre—a two-year plan (1953–1955) intended to allow the French Union troops, which were supposed to hold back the armed forces of the Democratic Republic of Vietnam (DRV, under Hồ Chí Minh [1890–1969]), to progressively win back territory for the so-called national army of the State of Vietnam (headed by Bảo Đại [r. 1925–1955]) supported by France and the United States.

The occupation of the basin of Dien Bien Phu, situated in enemy territory near the Laotian border, served two purposes: first and most important, to immobilize the regular troops of the adversary that would be attracted by this entrenched camp and possibly be neutralized by it, and second, to protect Laos, where the valley was considered to be the birthplace of the T'ai people that the Lao belonged to. On 20 November 1953, Operation Castor enabled French parachutists to occupy the valley and to airlift the soldiers and matériel necessary to make it impregnable. This included an airstrip and a military defense system, defended by powerful artillery and protected by operational bases, mainly in the surrounding hills. Everybody seemed to be sure of themselves, with only a few exceptions. Roger Guillain, journalist for *Le Monde,* published the following description of the famous basin: "The true image would be that of a stadium, but of an immense stadium, at least 20 km long and 7 or 8 km wide. The bottom of the stadium is controlled by us, the slopes of the surrounding mountains by the Viet Minh" (*Le Monde,* 14–15 February 1954).

Supplies are delivered by parachute to French troops in Indochina during the Battle of Dien Bien Phu in 1954. French forces, led by General Henri Navarre, greatly underestimated the Viet Minh. The fall of Dien Bien Phu was not only the death knell of the French in Asia, it was also the beginning of U.S. involvement in the region. (U.S. National Archives)

The Viet Minh were determined to take up the challenge. It is difficult to know exactly who had more influence in making this decision, whether it was General Vo Nguyễn Giap and his staff or their Chinese advisers, whose role was crucial. Nevertheless, in spring 1954, the military effort of the Popular Army met this challenge by organizing a momentous mobilization to transport men and matériel from the other end of the north. The image of the endless columns of bicycles converted to transport heavy loads is well-known. In addition, trucks made their way down the mountains from the Chinese border. Thus, thousands of men and their artillery were discreetly deployed around the entrenched camp. The stakes were high because even as the battle was brewing, the decision had been made to hold an international conference in Geneva to reach a settlement of the Korean and Indochinese conflicts, which took place on 26 April 1954. It was therefore important for the DRV to achieve the best possible bargaining position.

Apparently in order to profit from the advantages of his own artillery and against the advice of his Chinese counselors, General Giap at the last moment renounced the decision to at-

tack early. The battle proper finally began on 13 March when a powerful bombardment destroyed the airstrip, thus immediately destabilizing the French system of defense. The concept of the French camp was, in fact, based upon the idea of an airlifted umbilical cord. The air force now had to proceed, subject to bad weather and to the long distance from its home bases, to parachuting reinforcements, ammunition, and other materials. Some 12,000 soldiers of the French Union endured the enemy bombardments under difficult conditions while the enemy was digging an entire network of trenches to approach them.

Would it have been possible for the United States—already involved financially in the conflict, to the extent of almost 80 percent of its cost—to intervene? The French government asked it to do so on 5 and 23 April. An American contingency plan, an air operation named Vulture, was readied in vain, as President Dwight Eisenhower (t. 1953–1961) decided not to put this plan into action, thereby condemning the French expeditionary corps to a predictible defeat. On 7 May 1954, after fifty-five days of bitter fighting, the entrenched camp was overrun by the Popular Army and the French garrison captured. The very next day, as part of its two-pronged goal, the Geneva Conference would tackle the Indochinese question, thus consecrating the French defeat.

The name *Dien Bien Phu* remains a synonym for *trap*. Those who conceived the battle plan fell into their own trap, and the fatal outcome caused them to lose the war. The end of the First Indochinese War sounded the knell of the French Empire, and the battle became a symbol for the irrevocable victory of a dominated country over an imperial power.

HUGUES TERTRAIS

See also Bảo Đại (Vinh Tuy) (1913–1997); China since 1949; French Indochinese Union (*Union Indochinoise Française*) (1887); Geneva Conference (1954); Hồ Chí Minh (1890–1969); Indochina War (1946–1954), First; Sino-Vietnamese Relations; U.S. Involvement in Southeast Asia (post-1945); Việt Minh (Việt Nam Độc Lập Đồng Minh Hội) (Vietnam Independence League); Vietnam, North (post-1945); Vo Nguyễn Giap, General (1911–)

References:

Gardner, Lloyd C. 1988. *Approching Vietnam: From World War II through Dien Bien Phu.* New York and London: W. W. Norton & Co.

Karnow, Stanley. 1983. *Vietnam: A History.* New York: Viking Press.

Navarre, General Henri. 1956. *Agonie de l'Indochine (1953–1954)* [*The Agony of Indochina, 1953–1954*]. Paris: Plon.

Rocolle, Col. Pierre. 1968. *Pourquoi Dien Bien Phu?* [*Why Dien Bien Phu?*] Paris: Flammarion.

Vietnamese Studies. 1975 [1965]. *Dien Bien Phu.* Nos. 3 and 43. Hanoi: Vietnamese Studies.

Vo Nguyễn Giap. 1994 [1954]. *Dien Bien Phu.* Hanoi: Gioi Publishers.

DIPONEGORO (PANGERAN DIPANEGARA) (CA. 1785–1855)
Nationalist Javanese Prince

The Javanese prince Diponegoro is one of those historical personages who still speak to the imagination. He was probably born in 1785, the eldest son of Hamengkubuwana III (r. 1810–1811, 1812–1814) and a woman of low birth. This fact would have exerted a decisive influence on his life, certainly when a younger brother was born to another of his father's wives who was from the aristocracy. It would be he and not Diponegoro who would be the heir apparent to the throne. Diponegoro grew up at some distance from the Javanese court of Yogyakarta in the village of Tegalreja. There, he lived with his grandmother, the Ratu Ageng, wife of Hamengkubuwana II (r. 1792–1810, 1811–1812). His relative isolation does not mean that he was not involved in the gossip and quarrels common to the court society of his time. He took the side of his father when the latter was appointed prince regent by the Dutch governor-general, Herman W. Daendels (t. 1808–1811), in 1811, and his grandfather, Hamengkubuwana II, in that same year was compelled to step down in favor of his son.

At an early stage in his life, according to the chronicle *Babad Diponegara* (Chronicle of Diponegara), Diponegoro had already devoted himself to Islam. It was his custom to pray in his own prayer house, where he could also recite endlessly from the Koran. The prayer house was situated in a garden with beds of flowers of all kinds and a pond full of goldfish. He roamed regularly through the countryside, where he visited the graves of his ancestors of the Mataram dynasty. He sojourned at these holy places, fasting and praying, and had visions in which it was foretold that he would be the one to purify Java from all iniquity. During his wanderings, he also visited the mosques in the region, where he talked with the local religious leaders. Soon, the common people in the region thought of him as a holy man, favored by Allah. When he was about twenty years old, he underwent a religious experience that convinced him that he was the one chosen to become the future king of Java. He would be the *Ratu Adil* (the just king) who, according to Javanese legend, would reign justly over the land after a short period of war.

In 1814, his father, Hamengkubuwana III, died unexpectedly, and his younger brother was appointed by the British lieutenant governor Stamford Raffles (t. 1811–1816) to take the throne as Hamengkubuwana IV (r. 1814–1822). In contrast to his elder brother Diponegoro, the new king led a carefree, dissolute life. The Javanese court increasingly adapted itself outwardly to the European lifestyle. This exorbitant court lifestyle had to be paid for by the people, who were subjected to extortion by the leaseholders of the aristocracy. Discontent grew among the common people and the aristocracy alike during the reign of Hamengkubuwana IV, who was increasingly confronted with the interference of the Dutch in internal court affairs. Two measures taken by the Dutch governor-general, Godert A. P. Van der Capellen, in 1822 and 1823 caused a growing part of the Javanese aristocracy to look to Diponegoro as the leader to free them from Dutch domination. The first action was a direct blow to Diponegoro. Upon the death of Hamengkubuwana IV in 1822, his three-year-old son was appointed as his successor instead of Diponegoro, who had hoped to succeed his brother. The second was the decision to abolish the private leasing of land to Chinese and Europeans. As a consequence, most of the Javanese aristocracy suffered great financial difficulties.

Mindless actions on the part of the Dutch authorities were the direct cause of the outbreak of the Java War (1825–1830). Without Diponegoro being informed, the colonial government had planned a road cutting across his land in Tegalreja. Skirmishes broke out, and Diponegoro was forced to flee. In the beginning, he and his troops were very successful at harassing the Dutch forces using guerrilla warfare. Diponegoro soon assumed the title of sultan and behaved as such. But in the course of 1827, the tide turned against Diponegoro. His troops were defeated time after time, and people began to desert him. At the beginning of 1830, Diponegoro decided to commence negotiations with the Dutch commander, General Hendrik Merkus de Kock. He was invited to meet the general in Magelang. When Diponegoro arrived, the fasting month of Ramadan had begun, where *puasa* (fasting) was observed, and Diponegoro refused to start the negotiations. The first talk took place after the fasting month. Diponegoro demanded that he be recognized by the Dutch as sultan as well as the leader of Islam in Java. This was unacceptable to the Dutch. Despite being guaranteed safety, Diponegoro was arrested and exiled to Makassar, where he died in 1855.

For the Indonesians, Diponegoro is still considered one of the first champions of independence. In Indonesian historiography, he marks the beginning of a new era that led into the breakdown of the Dutch colonial power and freedom for Indonesia. As such, he is a symbol for each generation of Indonesians who fought and continue to fight against oppression and injustice.

ELLY TOUWEN-BOUWSMA

TRANSLATED BY ROSEMARY ROBSON-MCKILLOP

See also Islam in Southeast Asia; Java War (1825–1830); Liberal Experimental Period (1816–1830); Mataram; Netherlands (Dutch) East Indies; Peasant Uprisings and Protest Movements in Southeast Asia; Raffles, (Thomas) Stamford Bingley, Sir (1781–1826); *Ratu Adil* (Righteous King/Prince); Van der Capellan, Baron Godert Alexander Philip (1778–1848); Yogyakarta (Jogjakarta)

References:
Carey, Peter. 1976. "The Origins of the Java War (1825–30)." *English Historical Review* 91: 52–58.
Carey, Peter, ed. 1981. *"Babad Dipanagara": An Account of the Outbreak of the Java War*

(1825–30). Kuala Lumpur: Oxford University Press.
Ricklefs, M. C. 1974. "Dipanagara's Early Inspirational Experience." *Bijdragen Taal-, Land- en Volkenkunde* 130, nos. 2–3: 227–258.
van der Capellan, G. A. G. P. H. 1860. "Aanteekeningen vanden Gouverneur Generaal van der Capellen over den opstand van Dipo Negoro in 1825" (Notes of G. G. van der Capellen about the rebellion of Dipo Negoro). *Tijdschrift van Nederlands-Indië* 22: 360–387.

DISEASES AND EPIDEMICS

Serious research on long-term disease patterns in Southeast Asia remains in its infancy, and much of what we know about the subject before 1800 is a matter of deduction from fragmentary reports of so-called plagues or extrapolation both backward from the last two centuries and laterally from better-documented patterns in Europe, China, and India. Nevertheless, in seeking to understand the long-term disease patterns of the world's humid Tropics, there is no better source of potential data for the seventeenth and eighteenth centuries than the copious reporting of Spanish and Dutch agents in Southeast Asia.

Southeast Asia in the Disease Pools of Eurasia

The heavily forested environment and year-round high temperatures and rainfall of Southeast Asia allowed a wide variety of human and animal parasites to flourish—parasites that would not have withstood the rigors of a northern winter. But as William McNeill (1995: 70–77) pointed out, the abundant diseases and parasites of the rain forest may have helped protect scattered Southeast Asian rural populations against their expanding urban enemies. This is in contrast to the biological advantage that enabled civilizations (in the sense of dense urban populations with antibodies against endemic diseases) in temperate Eurasia to defeat their rural enemies.

Nevertheless, these populations were never wholly isolated from broader Eurasian disease pools, such as the peoples of Australia, the Americas, or the Pacific islands. From at least the dawn of the common era, there were entrepôts in the region serving the long-distance trade of the Indian Ocean and the South China Sea and in turn interacting with hinterland forest populations. Two Eurasian diseases are likely to have played a particularly powerful role in keeping Southeast Asian populations low (in comparison with China and India). Smallpox has been in India and China for almost two millennia and must therefore also have reached Southeast Asia. The earliest records suggest it or related diseases such as measles were the most feared. In most settled agricultural areas and trading ports, it became endemic, affecting chiefly children every seven to ten years. Many more isolated populations, however, lost immunity and continued to be devastated by new exposure to it as late as the nineteenth century.

Malarial plasmodia, the parasites carried back and forth between the bloodstream of monkeys and humans by mosquitoes, were the principal reason why the lowlands of Southeast Asia were sparsely inhabited before the fourteenth century. The deltas of the Irrawaddy, Mekong, and Chaophraya and the swampy lowlands of eastern Sumatra and southern Borneo were forbidding for humans because they were havens for the *Anopheles* mosquito. Only when the forest was turned into continuous paddy fields where the mosquitoes were exposed to harsh sunlight did such areas become safe for humans. Viet cultivators appear to have achieved this in the Red River delta in the first millennium C.E., as did Thais in the lower Chaophraya in the fourteenth century and Javanese in the Surabaya-Gresik area in the fifteenth century. With these exceptions, the largest population concentrations were on higher ground beyond the reach of the *Anopheles* until the nineteenth century.

Crisis Mortality of the Early Modern Era

If, in general, Southeast Asian populations rose only very slowly and spasmodically before 1750, there appears to have been a particularly serious period of diseases from the fifteenth to seventeenth centuries. The new epidemics were not, as in the Americas, exclusively derived from Europeans; the European arrival in 1509 was part of a broader pattern of increasing commercial contacts throughout maritime Eurasia.

What the Europeans did bring was an increasing availability of census data at regular intervals for specified populations. These show, notably, a decrease of one-third in the population of much of the lowland Philippines from 1591 to 1655 and even more dramatic declines in Dutch-dominated areas of the Moluccas and northern Sulawesi from the 1630s to 1670s. Indigenous data for the larger population centers are more questionable. Nonetheless, it does seem that major rice bowls of the Red River and Irrawaddy deltas (present-day northern Vietnam and southern Burma [Myanmar]) both lost substantial population during periods of intense warfare (usually accompanied by disease and famine) in the late sixteenth century. Similarly, the Javanese heartland appears to have lost population in the century after 1650.

We cannot know whether this was simply a continuation of long-standing patterns of growth in stable periods and decline in unsettled ones or if it was really something new. If there was an increase in crisis mortality in this period, there are five rival explanations for the cause—urbanization, warfare, economic crisis, climate, and exposure to new epidemic diseases.

Southeast Asia's "age of commerce" from the fifteenth to seventeenth centuries was undoubtedly a period of exceptional preindustrial urbanism, perhaps 5 percent overall at the peak around 1650 and significantly more in highly commercial areas around the Straits of Melaka. As was the case everywhere before the introduction of clean water in the late nineteenth century, cities were breeding grounds of disease. Cities such as Pegu, Surabaya, Banten, and Makassar suffered drastic population losses in the seventeenth century primarily because of warfare, which always prompted epidemics that did most of the killing. Major urban epidemics not directly related to war occurred in Banten in 1625, when one-third of the population reportedly died in five months, and in Makassar in 1636, when 60,000 reportedly died in forty days (Reid 1988: 60–61). The most reliable data we have about urban crisis mortality, however, come from Dutch Batavia (Jakarta), which sustained an astonishing annual death rate equivalent to about half its roughly 100,000 population throughout the period from 1730 to 1752 (Reid 2001: 49–50; Van der Brug 1995). Recent research has shown that Batavia's notorious mortality at that time was a result of malaria, which overwhelmingly affected the great influx of new immigrants to the city (Dutch soldiers and Chinese immigrants and slaves), about half of whom died within a year of arrival (Van der Brug 1995).

Warfare does appear to have been the greatest variable in mortality. The decline in the northern Vietnamese population, for example, occurred during the ferocious civil war between Trinh and Mac from 1545 to 1592, whereas the population of Pegu was almost wiped out during the siege and warfare of the 1590s. The introduction of firearms, initially by Chinese and Muslim traders but much more murderously by Europeans after 1511, probably increased the human costs of warfare. But since these costs were greatest in terms of the famine and disease that always accompanied wartime dislocations, we might seek more fundamental reasons in the economic competition for Indonesia's valuable spices, which peaked with the Dutch quest for monopoly in the seventeenth century.

The notion of a seventeenth-century climatic crisis being the cause of increased mortality in Europe and China is still controversial. Trends over time in the Tropics are much less well understood, and the data for Southeast Asia are too sparse for more than speculation. The most persuasive piece of data is a tree-ring sequence from Java, supported by historical evidence of droughts and crop failures. This sequence shows exceptionally dry seasons in the two periods from 1633 to 1638 and 1643 to 1675, which correlate with unusually widespread and severe epidemics.

Evidence for new diseases reaching Southeast Asia with the Europeans is not very persuasive. Syphilis was once thought to have been carried by Europeans from the Americas, but there were reports of something very like it well before this contact. More likely is that the increasing mobility of European, Chinese, and Muslim traders and warriors in the age of commerce brought more frequent reinfections with smallpox, measles, and perhaps plague in areas where these had not yet become endemic.

Modern Epidemics

Despite the considerations that have been mentioned thus far, European observers of the six-teenth and seventeenth centuries generally considered Southeast Asians to be relatively healthy. They observed fewer crippled and disfigured people and reported fewer catastrophic epidemics than they were familiar with in the fetid cities of Europe. High rainfall, a habit of frequent bathing, and a diet low in meat except when animals were freshly slaughtered at feasts may, indeed, have given some protection against the diseases that were prevalent in Europe. Once conditions of political stability were established, as happened in Java, the Philippines, Vietnam, and Siam in the nineteenth century, populations rose at rates in excess of 1 percent a year.

Better data in the nineteenth and twentieth centuries and the beginnings of medical services enable us to track some major epidemics in the region. The first securely documented pandemic of Asiatic cholera began in Bengal in 1817 and reached Bangkok via Penang in May 1820. It may have caused upwards of 30,000 deaths there and a similar number in the then much smaller city of Saigon, within only three weeks. It reached Java in 1821, and the Dutch recorded with precision that 1,255 people died in Semarang and 778 in Batavia, each within a span of eleven days (Boomgaard 1987: 53). Total mortality from the disease in Java in 1821 has been estimated at 125,000 (Boomgaard 1987: 50). Cholera remained a recurrent feature of nineteenth-century Southeast Asia but subsequently became devastating only during times of severe warfare.

Plague is another disease once thought to have spared Southeast Asia until the modern epidemic of 1910, but as with cholera, this assumption was based principally on ignorance. Mortality from plague was not demographically weighty, with only 215,000 deaths attributed to this cause in Java between 1911 and 1939 (Hull 1987: 211). But countering the dreaded disease became a major preoccupation of the Dutch administration in the years after 1911, with a million and a half houses refurbished to make them rat-proof and tiled roofs replacing thatch as the norm of Javanese villagers.

Since 1950, a number of diseases have been reduced markedly in intensity through control measures, vaccination, and better nutrition and sanitation. Smallpox was the most spectacular success and was largely eradicated by inoculation by 1970. Malaria has been eliminated from urban areas in Singapore, Malaysia, Indonesia, and the Philippines, but the forests remain a prolific breeding ground for mosquito vectors.

Rising levels of welfare in most countries of the region after 1970 also dramatically reduced the incidence of waterborne diseases. Singapore and Malaysia by the 1980s reflected a pattern of disease not unlike those of developed countries in temperate areas, with the traditional "tropical" diseases no longer major killers. Thailand, Indonesia, Vietnam, and the Philippines were moving rapidly in a similar direction.

ANTHONY REID

See also Aceh (Acheh) Wars (1873–1903); Age of Commerce; Bangkok; Batavia (Sunda Kalapa, Jakatra, Djakarta/Jakarta); British Military Administration (BMA) in Southeast Asia; Burma during the Pacific War (1941–1945); Burma under British Colonial Rule; Burma-Siam Wars; Cambodia under French Colonial Rule; Ethical Policy (*Ethische Politiek*); Famines; Hanoi (Thanglong); Kuala Lumpur; Laos (Nineteenth Century to Mid-1990s); Indochina during World War II (1939–1945); Indochina War (1946–1954), First; Indochina War (1964–1975), Second (Vietnam War); Japanese Occupation of Southeast Asia (1941–1945); Manila; Penang (1786); Philippines under Spanish Colonial Rule (ca. 1560s–1898); Philippines under U.S. Colonial Administration (1898–1946); Rangoon (Yangon); Saigon (Gia Dinh; Hồ Chí Minh City); Singapore (Nineteenth Century to 1900s), Entrepôt Trade and Commerce of; Surabaya; Surakarta; Vietnam under French Colonial Rule; Western Malay States (Perak, Selangor, Negri Sembilan, and Pahang)

References:

Boomgaard, Peter. 1987. "Morbidity and Mortality in Java, 1820–1880: Changing Patterns of Disease and Death." Pp. 48–69 in *Death and Disease in Southeast Asia: Explorations in Social, Medical and Demographic History*. Edited by Norman G. Owen. Singapore: Oxford University Press for Asian Studies Association of Australia.
Hull, Terence H. 1987. "Plague in Java." Pp. 210–234 in *Death and Disease in Southeast Asia: Explorations in Social, Medical and Demographic History*. Edited by Norman G. Owen. Singapore: Oxford University Press for Asian Studies Association of Australia.
Liu T'sui-jung, James Lee, David Sven Reher, Saito Osamu, and Wang Feng, eds. 2001. *Asian Population History*. Oxford: Oxford University Press.
McNeill, William H. M. 1995. *Plagues and Peoples*. Harmondsworth, England: Penguin.
Owen, Norman G. 1987. *Death and Disease in Southeast Asia: Explorations in Social, Medical and Demographic History*. Singapore: Oxford University Press for Asian Studies Association of Australia.
Reid, Anthony. 1988. *Southeast Asia in the Age of Commerce, 1450–1680*. Vol. 1, *The Lands below the Winds*. New Haven, CT: Yale University Press.
———. 2001. "South-East Asian Population History and the Colonial Impact." Pp. 45–62 in *Asian Population History*. Edited by Liu T'sui-jung, James Lee, David Sven Reher, Saito Osamu, and Wang Feng. Oxford: Oxford University Press.
Van der Brug, P. H. 1995. *Malaria en malaise. De VOC in Batavia in de achttiende eeuw* [*Malaria and Malady: The VOC in Batavia in the Eighteenth Century*]. Amsterdam: De Bataafse Leeuw.

DOBAMA ASIAYONE (WE BURMANS ASSOCIATION)

See Aung San (1915–1947); Burma under British Colonial Rule; Burmans; General Council of Burmese Associations (GCBA) (1920); Nu, U (1907–1995); Thakin (Lord, Master)

DOMINO THEORY

In its broadest and most general meaning, the "domino theory" pertained to a chain reaction, a succession of events set in motion by a single force. The theory was announced in 1954 as the rationale for the U.S. policy in Southeast Asia. The immediate force behind the domino theory was the struggle that had developed between the United States and the Union of Soviet Socialist Republics (USSR) at the end of World War II (1939–1945), a contest for predominant political and strategic position as well as ideological influence in Southeast Asia. This competition was enhanced and sharpened with the communists' victory in China in 1949.

President Dwight D. Eisenhower (1890–1969) had introduced the term *domino theory* on 7 April 1954 in explaining why Indochina should not be allowed to come under communist control. The fall of Indochina, it was argued, would likely lead to the collapse of nearby states—Burma (Myanmar), Thailand, Malaya, Indonesia—and eventually all of Asia would stand in the path of an advancing communist menace.

But although many prominent resistance leaders of national liberation movements in Southeast Asia were communists, the movements usually had self-determination as an objective and not the fostering of Soviet, Chinese, or international communism. The major error of U.S. policy during the Cold War stemmed from a conviction that communist movements were the same everywhere, that all were subservient to the Soviet Union or China, that all were imposed upon the native populations, and that all were inherently hostile to American interests. Consequently, the administrations of John F. Kennedy (1961–1963) and Lyndon B. Johnson (1963–1969) reaffirmed the commitment to the domino theory. But gradually, Americans began to understand that the status of countries in Southeast Asia depended not on events in neighboring states or on command from Moscow or Peking (Beijing) but on conditions and problems within each nation. With the armistice of 1973 in the Vietnam War, the domino theory lapsed into limbo. Nevertheless, American governments have not discredited the idea itself.

LARISSA M. EFIMOVA

See also Cold War; Comintern; Indochina War (1964–1975), Second (Vietnam War); Malayan Emergency (1948–1960); Nationalism and Independence Movements in Southeast Asia; U.S. Military Bases in Southeast Asia; United States Involvement in Southeast Asia (post-1945)

References:
Barnet, Richard J. 1968. *Intervention and Revolution: America's Confrontation with Insurgent Movement around the World.* New York: World Publishing.

Encyclopedia of American Foreign Policy. 1978. Vol. 1. New York: Scribner.
The Pentagon Papers. 1971. Gravel Edition. Boston: Beacon.
Podhoretz, Norman. 1982. *Why We Were in Vietnam.* New York: Simon and Schuster.

DONG-SON

The term *Dong-son* has multiple meanings, standing for a major archaeological site in North Vietnam and the roughly two-thousand-year-old culture of the Bac-bo region in the far northeastern portion of Vietnam. It also refers to the famous bronze drums made by the Dong-son people, as well as the art style found on these drums and certain other antiquities. At the time they were occupied, sites belonging to the Dong-son culture were probably the largest in Southeast Asia and supported a standard of wealth and material sophistication that could not be found anywhere farther south. The several meanings of the term *Dong-son* testify to the importance of this culture in laying a substratum foundation for early civilization in North Vietnam and absorbing the brunt of ancient Chinese interest in, and occupation of, Southeast Asia. Scholars can claim considerable knowledge of the Bac-bo region some two thousand years ago because of the riches of the archaeological record, the brilliant depictions of Dong-son society on the drums, and early written accounts after the Chinese established an official presence on the Red River delta in 111 B.C.E.

The site of Dong-son introduced colonial French archaeology to the splendors of ancient Vietnam through the amateur collections of Louis Pajot in the 1920s and the systematic excavations by Olav Janse in the 1930s. More recent work, which was resumed at the site by Vietnamese archaeologists beginning in the 1960s, now suggests that it was first occupied around 1000 B.C.E. during the Go-mun phase, by which time bronze metallurgy and rice farming were entrenched in the region. By the Dong-son phase, after 500 B.C.E., iron implements (forged according to procedures prevalent in India at the time) and wet-rice agriculture were evidently standard features of daily life, as were spindle whorls, fishing equipment, pottery of ordinary quality, earrings of stone, and an enormous bronze repertoire. Bronze objects included axes of various shapes, dagger handles, spearheads, bracelets, apparel, bells, sickles, spittoons, plowshares, and blades of digging tools, as well as the kettledrums. Many of these items were found as though arranged around an extended corpse whose vestiges had long since disappeared, allowing the identification of cemetery areas. Habitation areas are equally detectable from traces of piles that would have elevated the houses above ground level, as are manufacturing areas from discarded blanks of bronze and stone. The site may have had a significant role in local commerce, as it occupied a defensible location on the banks of the Song-ma River at a point that could be reached from the coast by large watercraft.

The heart of Dong-son culture focused on the Red River delta, where most of the 100 or so recorded Dong-son sites lie. Opulent burials in boatlike coffins, with up to 100 funerary goods in a single coffin, demonstrate the existence of a wealthy elite, who were most probably hereditary chiefs. The fact that some sites are much larger than others and have more extensive cemeteries points to the operation of powerful centers that exercised authority over smaller, attached communities. Depictions on the kettledrums include a warrior class of well-armed individuals with sweeping headdresses who were presumably charged with maintaining the social order. The images depicted on the drums vividly display many other features of Dong-son life that are suggested from the study of habitation debris. The features included houses on piles, sometimes with granaries attached; large watercraft, sometimes defended by archers with crossbows; water buffaloes plowing the fields; farmers pounding their crops in mortars; elaborate dress; and the important role of the drums themselves as musical instruments and the insignia of authority. When the Chinese finally annexed the Bac-bo region as the southernmost province of their empire in 43 C.E., they confiscated the drums owned by the local chiefs to deprive them of these regalia.

Friezes of flying birds and intricate, curvilinear motifs provide further insight into the high culture of the paramount chiefs who headed Dong-son society and its numerous occupational divisions. Symbols of nature—deer, lizards, and fish—also occur occasionally on Dong-son panels. The middle of the drum's tympanum invariably features a bas-relief design with six to twelve engraved triangles pointing toward the center, leaving a star-shaped embossment. The exquisite decorations on the drums were achieved through the "lost wax" technique, in which wax was used to coat an inner core of clay. After the wax had been decorated, an outer casing of clay was packed around the wax, chaplets were positioned to hold the outer casing in place, the wax was removed by heating it, and molten bronze was poured into the resultant cavity. Removal of the outer casing revealed the finished drum. This technique and the drums themselves may have originated in Yunnan in southern China, where early Dong-son drums are quite common, rather than in the Bac-bo region.

Spearheads with bronze hafts and iron blades have so far been recorded only at Dong-son and the northeast Thailand site of Ban Chiang, suggestive of trade or technological transfer from Bac-bo to Thailand. Occasional gold and silver ornaments, beads of glass, and the bronze swords and halberds found at Dong-son were probably imported from sources beyond Southeast Asia. This would certainly apply to the Han Chinese mirror, coins, and stamped earthenware shards, which, as a group, show that habitation at Dong-son continued after 43 C.E. Han-style graves at the site reflect direct Chinese influence over its residents or even Chinese occupation. Dong-son drums continued to be produced in the Bac-bo region until around 300 C.E. but with increasing signs of Chinese influence, including occasional inscriptions in Chinese characters. Confucianism, Taoism, and Buddhism all began to make inroads into the Bac-bo region at around that time, spelling the end of the aristocratic warrior traditions and other homegrown beliefs that had evidently furnished Dong-son culture with its ideological inspiration. Dong-son culture receded in the face of the development of a true urban culture in the Red River delta, as exemplified by the fortified site of Co-loa that grew to an area of 600 hectares.

The Viennese scholar F. Heger classified the Dong-son kettledrums as Type I in his system, defined by their angular contours, wide bases, and equally wide tympana. His Types II to IV refer to derivative kettledrums produced in later times. Heger III drums, associated with the Karen people who live in the hills between

Burma and Thailand, are still made for the tourist trade. As well as being generally smaller than Heger I drums, they have narrower bases and more rounded contours and a simpler array of motifs dominated by frogs on the tympanum and elephants on the side. Heger II drums resemble Type III in their general shape and predilection for frogs on the tympanum but are restricted to the region between southern China, northern Laos, and central Vietnam (where they were still made into the early nineteenth century). Heger IV kettledrums are known in the thousands but are restricted to southern China; their simplified shapes and decorations betray their lack of great antiquity.

Also related to the Dong-son drums (but possibly descended from a different prototype) are the Pejeng drums, cast in Bali for use there and in East Java. These were among the first bronze kettledrums to be noticed in Western scholarship when Georgius Everhardus Rumphius recorded the enormous "Moon" drum at the village of Pejeng in Bali in the late seventeenth century. These hourglass-shaped drums stand up to 2 meters high and were decorated with bands of triangles and human faces with prominent eyes. The site of Sembiran in Bali yielded a production stamp in the Pejeng style that would date to the early centuries C.E., and a similar age is likely for a Pejeng drum that villagers found there. Although the Pejeng style is sufficiently distinct from the Dong-son style to warrant its own name, the intricate looping motifs found on rare ceremonial bronzes to the north—clapperless bells in Malaya and bronze flasks in Madura, southern Sumatra, Cambodia, and central Thailand—are conventionally referred to as the Dong-son style.

In support of this association, Dong-son drums made in Bac-bo have been recorded widely across Southeast Asia and, indeed, as far eastward as the Bird's-Head Peninsula of New Guinea. Their find locations are dispersed evenly across mainland Southeast Asia to the south of Bac-bo before coming to particular concentrations in the middle third of West Malaysia, the western half of Java, and the islands east of Sumbawa in southeastern Indonesia. Several drums are also known from southern Sumatra, as is a famous rock frieze of an armed warrior carrying one of these drums on his elephant. Conceivably, these ninety or so known cases of kettledrums transported over long distances could have underwritten the occurrence of geometric and curvilinear motifs similar to those on Dong-son drums, as found on early pottery (as well as bronzes) widely across Southeast Asia. Alternatively, the kettledrums could stand out as the spectacular markers of a vigorous trade in other, usually smaller bronzes from Bac-bo to regions to the south; this trade would have spread the Dong-son style over much of Southeast Asia.

However, other observations suggest that the so-called Dong-son style has deeper roots. Much of the pottery decorated in this style is older than the Dong-son culture; indeed, all of the Dong-son drums found in Indonesia could have been produced after Bac-bo had been incorporated within the Han empire. Nor have Dong-son drums been found in coastal central Vietnam, Borneo, the Philippines, or the main body of Sulawesi, where assemblages of pottery with lavish geometric and curvilinear motifs, referred by William Solheim as the "Sa-huynh Kalanay" tradition, are most prevalent. A case in point involves the ceramics from Kalumpang, in western Sulawesi, whose decorations are frequently compared to the Dong-son style but date back to at least 500 B.C.E. and possibly 1000 B.C.E. Similarities between the Dong-son and Sahuynh Kalanay decorative motifs would presumably extend back further in time and possibly reflect descent from early Neolithic southern China. Many of the same geometric motifs can be found on the ceramics from Hemedu, an ancient village site in southern China that dates to around 5000 B.C.E.

In addition, many of the objects depicted on Dong-son drums, such as houses on piles, large circular earrings, and various domesticated animals, would have been widely distributed across southern China and/or Southeast Asia around two thousand years ago. Olav Janse had preferred the term *Indonesian* for mortuary features at Dong-son that he considered indigenous to Southeast Asia, and his term underlines the similarities in material culture between Bac-bo and a good number of contemporary societies to the south. Thanks to the complexity of Dong-son society and its capacity to support highly skilled artisans, Dong-son imagery provides a unique insight into conditions that prevailed to varying degrees throughout Southeast

Asia on the eve of concerted attention from Chinese and Indian emigrants.

DAVID BULBECK

See also Archaeological Sites of Southeast of Asia; Human Prehistory of Southeast Asia
References:
Bellwood, Peter. 1978. *Man's Conquest of the Pacific.* Auckland, New Zealand: Collins.
———. 1997. *Prehistory of the Indo-Malaysian Archipelago.* Rev. ed. Honolulu: University of Hawai'i Press.
Bernet-Kempers, A. J. 1988. "The Kettledrums of Southeast Asia." *Modern Quaternary Research in Southeast Asia* 10.
Bulbeck, David. 2001. "Island Southeast Asia Late Prehistoric." Pp. 82–116 in *Encyclopedia of Prehistory.* Vol. 3, *East Asia and Oceania.* Edited by Peter N. Peregrine and Melvin Ember. New York: Kluwer Academic/ Plenum Publishers.
Higham, Charles. 1989. *The Archaeology of Mainland Southeast Asia.* Cambridge: Cambridge University Press.
Loofs-Wissowa, Helmut. 1991. "Dongson Drums: Instruments of Shamanism or Regalia?" *Arts Asiatiques* 46: 39–49.
Puig, Patricia, and Ian Walters. 2001. "The Vietnam War and Two Heger III Drums in Darwin." Pp. 95–120 in *Altered States: Material Culture and Shifting Contexts in the Arafura Region.* Edited by Clayton Fredericksen and Ian Walters. Darwin, Australia: Northern Territory University Press.
Stark, Miriam. 2001. "Mainland Southeast Asia Late Prehistoric." Pp. 160–205 in *Encyclopedia of Prehistory.* Vol. 3, *East Asia and Oceania.* Edited by Peter N. Peregrine and Melvin Ember. New York: Kluwer Academic/ Plenum Publishers.
Wheatley, Paul. 1983. *Nagara and Commandery: Origins of the Southeast Asian Urban Traditions.* Chicago: University of Chicago Press.

DORMAN-SMITH, SIR REGINALD
(t. 1941–1946)
The Last British Governor of Burma

Sir Reginald Dorman-Smith was the penultimate governor of British Burma from 1941 to 1946. A former president of the National Union of Farmers in Great Britain and a Conservative Party member of the House of Commons, he served as minister of agriculture in Prime Minister Neville Chamberlain's government (1937–1940) prior to World War II (1939–1945). When Chamberlain's government fell and was succeeded by Sir Winston Churchill's wartime government (1940–1945), Dorman-Smith was appointed in 1941 to succeed Sir Archibald Cochrane (t. 1936–1941) in Rangoon (Yangon). An extrovert, Dorman-Smith thoroughly enjoyed the political intrigues of the various Burmese politicians he worked with prior to the Pacific War (1941–1945). As colonial governor, he presided over a political system that gave Burmese politicians wide powers in all areas except defense, foreign affairs, finance, and the so-called Frontier Areas. Much of his time was spent in reaching compromises with the elected politicians over their respective spheres of authority.

His period of office was, however, interrupted in 1942 when he was forced to flee to Simla in India to establish a government-in-exile following the Japanese invasion. There, he laid elaborate plans for the reconstruction of Burma after the war. Constitutionally, he had agreed with the British government that he would take complete power during the reconstruction period, setting aside the democratic aspects of the Government of Burma Act until order and prosperity had been restored. This arrangement was unacceptable to the new generation of Burmese nationalist politicians he met on his return to Rangoon in October 1945. Led by General Aung San (1915–1947) and the Anti-Fascist People's Freedom League (AFPFL), they refused to compromise with him, and when the British Labour government under Clement Attlee (t. 1945–1951) recognized that the political stalemate in Burma was unsustainable, Dorman-Smith was recalled as governor.

R. H. TAYLOR

See also Anti-Fascist People's Freedom League (AFPFL); Aung San (1915–1947); Ba Maw, Dr. (b. 1893); British Burma; Burma during the Pacific War (1941–1945); Burma under British Colonial Rule; Constitutional Developments in Burma (1900–1941); Nationalism and Independence Movements in Southeast Asia
References:
Collis, Maurice. 1956. *Last and First in Burma.* London: Faber and Faber.

DU BUS DE GISIGNIES, VISCOUNT LEONARD PIERRE JOSEPH (1780–1849)

Fiscal Reformer of the Dutch East Indies

In 1825, Viscount Du Bus was appointed as commissioner-general of the Dutch East Indies to replace Governor-General Godert A. P. Van der Capellen (t. 1816–1825), during whose reign the cost of Dutch administration of the Indies had increased. Du Bus had to reorganize the colony's finances and investigate what system of government would be most appropriate. He reduced public expenditure by dismissing a number of public servants and lowering the salaries of those he retained. He also studied ways of increasing public revenue. His report of May 1827 advocated the development of Java by issuing unused land to private entrepreneurs for agricultural production. In addition, he lifted restrictions on the settlement of Europeans in Java. However, Du Bus's proposals were not implemented. The Dutch king, under the influence of Count Johannes Van den Bosch (1780–1844), did not expect instant financial benefits from the plan and advocated the Cultivation System (*Cultuurstelsel*).

Du Bus worked closely with Lieutenant Governor-General H. M. de Kock, who was in charge of ongoing affairs. Military exploits and monetary reforms marked Du Bus's tenure in the Indies. De Kock subdued the Diponegoro uprising during the Java War (1825–1830). Matan in southwest Kalimantan was conquered, and the sultanate of Sukadana was established there. Tanette in South Sulawesi was subdued, but an attempt to establish Fort Du Bus in New Guinea in 1828 failed.

Monetary reform was urgent. Previous governments had increased the circulation of copper doits and paper money. Silver and gold coins were in short supply, flowing out of the system due to the colony's trade deficit. Fluctuations in the exchange rates of the currencies caused monetary chaos. In an effort to encourage the use of silver, Du Bus decreed in 1826 that copper doits would be legal tender up to É10. He withdrew all paper currency, exchanging it for silver, gold, copper currency, and government bonds. He oversaw the establishment of the Java Bank in 1828, which received a monopoly on the issue of banknotes. Although encouraging, these efforts were insufficient to end the monetary chaos.

PIERRE VAN DER ENG

See also Cultivation System (*Cultuurstelsel*); Diponegoro (Pangeran Dipanagara) (ca. 1785–1855); Java War (1825–1830); Van den Bosch, Count Johannes (1780–1844); Van der Capellen, Baron Godert Alexander Philip (1778–1848)

References:

Van der Wijck, H. 1866. *De Nederlandsche Oost-Indische Bezittingen onder het Bestuur van den Kommissaris Generaal Du Bus de Gisignies (1826–1830)* [*The Dutch Possessions in the East Indies during the Government of Commissioner-General Du Bus de Gisignies (1826–1830)*]. The Hague: Nijhoff.

DUAL ECONOMY

The "dual economy" was an analytical concept first formulated by Julius H. Boeke (1884–1956) to explain sustained underdevelopment in Indonesia. Boeke never provided an unambiguous definition of the concept. He basically maintained that ethnic Indonesians were imbued with a different economic rationale compared with Western people. Rather than economic inducements such as relative wages, rents, and prices, Indonesians were largely motivated by mutual social obligations. They were inclined to work less if their income increased because they valued leisure. Western economic theory would therefore not apply to Asian societies. This different rationale made Indonesian farmers less susceptible to technological change.

Reflecting widely shared perceptions of the timeless social organization of rural villages in Indonesia, Boeke's term *static expansion* described a process by which more and more people were accommodated in Java's agricultural sector, without any dynamic changes in agricultural productivity or in the economy at large. Boeke argued that Dutch efforts to promote economic development would only hasten the disintegration of traditional society, without another social system taking its place. The Dutch could best serve the interests of native Indonesians by protecting and restoring what he perceived as traditional communal village life.

Boeke published most of his work after 1929 as an academic at the University of Leiden. He had little influence on economic policy formulation in colonial Indonesia. Contributions in *Indonesian Economics: The Concept of Dualism in Theory and Practice* (1961) indicated that many Dutch contemporaries rejected his pessimism about Indonesia's development prospects.

The economist Benjamin Higgins (1912–2001) criticized Boeke. He also used the term *dual economy,* but his version was grounded on the difference in production technology in the "modern" and "traditional" sectors. With reference to Indonesia, Higgins argued that the modern sector produced on the basis of capital-intensive technologies and that the traditional sector produced with labor-intensive technologies. The modern sector produced for export, and its expansion had little impact on the traditional economy, whereas development in the traditional sector was restricted by a shortage of investment capital.

PIERRE VAN DER ENG

See also Burma under British Colonial Rule; Cambodia under French Colonial Rule; Laos (Nineteenth Century to Mid-1990s); Netherlands (Dutch) East Indies; Patron-Client Relations; Philippines under U.S. Colonial Administration (1898–1946); Sarawak and Sabah (North Borneo); Vietnam under French Colonial Rule; Western Malay States (Perak, Selangor, Negri Sembilan, and Pahang)

References:
Boeke, J. H. 1953. *Economics and Economic Policies of Dual Societies as Exemplified by Indonesia.* Haarlem, The Netherlands: Tjeenk Willink.
Higgins, B. 1955–1956. "The 'Dualistic Theory' of Underdeveloped Areas." *Economic Development and Cultural Change* 4: 99–115.
Wertheim, W. F., ed. 1961. *Indonesian Economics: The Concept of Dualism in Theory and Policy.* The Hague: Van Hoeve.

DUPLEIX, JOSEPH FRANÇOIS (1696–1763)
Aspirant to a French Indian Empire

Joseph François Dupleix, whose dream had been to create in India a French empire to confront British imperialism, prefigured the type of colonial administrator often encountered in the history of French colonization in the nineteenth century. Although an agent of the French East India Company (Compagnie des Indes Orientales), he distinguished himself with his individual initiatives, his independence, and his propensity to act as an omnipotent proconsul. Spurred on by increasing international rivalry and interested only in the expansion of commerce and not at all in religious diffusion, he conceived from the outset the idea of inland expansion in India, which he persistently carried out.

He arrived in India in 1721 as an officer of the French East India Company, and ten years later, he was appointed governor of Chandernagor, where he acquired a considerable fortune. In 1742, he became governor of Pondichéry and was thus the chief official of the French establishments in India. He wished then to make the Compagnie des Indes Orientales not only a commercial but also a territorial power, and he began to devise an ambitious policy of territorial domination in order to develop French influence and to check the British control of India. In the First Carnatic War (1740–1748), part of Europe's War of the Austrian Succession (1740–1748), which brought the French and English East India Companies into conflict, he supervised the capture of the English company's territory of Madras (1746), but it was returned to the British by the Treaty of Aix-la-Chapelle (1748). Dupleix nevertheless continued to take advantage of the confused situation in South India to establish a real protectorate over southern Deccan. Integrated into the Mogul political and economic system (he obtained a *jagir*—a feudal concession and the title of *nabob* in 1750) and helped by his wife, "Begum Jeanne," who spoke several local languages, he intervened actively in native political intrigues and warfare (the Second Carnatic War, 1751–1754). Above all, he expected to use the taxes of the dependencies of his jagir to provide regular subsidies to the French company, the commerce of which he knew would be greatly at risk in the event of a war. Much at ease in his role as a Hindu prince, he interceded in succession quarrels: he helped Muzaffer Jing to become the *nizam* (the title accorded native rulers) of Hyderabad; he backed the claimant to the throne of the Carnatic, Chanda Sahib; and he assured the

Marathas of his support. Through the cleverly combined use of diplomacy and war and with a force of 2,000 European soldiers leading Indian sepoys, he conquered the coastal Andhra and gradually controlled nearly the entire Deccan.

Furthermore, Dupleix was eager to extend eastward the scope of the French company's activities. Aware of the importance of the Burmese ports in the naval strategy of the Bay of Bengal, he suggested as early as 1727 the establishment of a dockyard at Syriam, which began to function two years later under the management of experienced shipwrights. Approached by the Mons in revolt against the Burmans under King Alaung-hpaya (r. 1752–1760), he sent an envoy in 1751 to negotiate with the Mon government at Pegu and craft a treaty by which, in return for commercial concessions, the Mons were to receive substantial French aid. Convinced of the advantages that an armed intervention in the Mon-Burman struggle would bring to the French, he commanded a military expedition to gain control over the Mon kingdom. But the directors of the French company, who feared that anything involving military commitments would provoke a further contest with the British, rejected Dupleix's proposal.

Dupleix also turned his attention to Vietnam. In 1748, he sent a representative to Tourane to investigate the commercial possibilities, and in 1753, he obtained from the Nguyễn the authorization to set up a factory. This project, however, was abandoned following the outbreak of the Seven Years' War between England and France in 1756 because the French lacked the naval resources to defend the sea-lanes to such remote outposts. French interest in Vietnam, largely maintained by Dupleix, soon dwindled away after his departure from India in 1754.

Indeed, in India, the British regained ground under the leadership of Robert Clive (1725–1774), who repelled the troops of Chanda Sahib, Dupleix's ally, at the siege of Arcot. Anxious to avoid war and to negotiate peace with England, the French king Louis XV (1710–1774), apparently uninformed of Dupleix's grandiose schemes, recalled the governor in 1754. Dupleix's successor, Charles Godeheu, signed a truce with Thomas Saunders, the president of the English company at Madras, whereby the two companies committed themselves to abandoning their respective conquests in India. As a result, the hope of establishing a French empire in India vanished.

Dupleix's original initiative was a challenge that perhaps was impossible for France to take up, entangled as it was at the time in its European quarrels. In any case, such a policy went against the interests of the shareholders, who looked for immediate profit and would not care for colonization, and the French East India Company lacked the working capital that would enable it to embark on great undertakings. Its directors, who, by contrast, dreaded a policy of counterintervention on the part of the British, would limit themselves to a mercantile conception of expansion: "no power on land" but "many goods and some increase in dividends" (Moreel 1963). As for Dupleix, he spent the rest of his days pleading against the company in order to recuperate the sums he had advanced for it. He died in poverty and neglect.

NGUYỄN THẾ ANH

See also Alaung-hpaya (r. 1752–1760); British India, Government of; East India Company (EIC) (1600), English; French Ambitions in Southeast Asia; Mon; Nguyễn Emperors and French Imperialism; Pegu

References:

Dodwell, Henry. 1968. *Dupleix and Clive: The Beginning of Empire.* Hamden, CT: Archon Books.

Moreel, Léon. 1963. *Dupleix, marquis de fortune et conquérant des Indes, 1697–1763* [*Dupleix: Makeshift marquis and conqueror of the Indies, 1697–1763*]. Rosendaël, France: Éditions Le Port de Dunkerque.

Thompson, Virginia M. 1933. *Dupleix and His Letters, 1742–1754.* New York: R. O. Ballou.

Vincent, Rose, ed. 1993. *Pondichéry 1674–1761: L'Échec d'un rêve d'empire* [*Pondichéry 1674–1761: The failure of a dream of empire*]. Paris: Autrement.

DUPRÉ, MARIE JULES (1813–1880)
A French Imperialist in Vietnam

An activist governor of Cochin China, France's colony in southern Vietnam, from 1871 to 1874, Marie Jules Dupré is remembered for his failed attempt to gain control of northern Vietnam. He was born at Albi in southern France on 25 November 1813, the son of an army officer. After attending the French naval academy, he served in a wide range of appointments, including as governor of Réunion Island in 1864. He was promoted to rear admiral in 1867.

When Dupré became governor of Cochin China in April 1871, France was recovering from its defeat in the Franco-Prussian War (1870–1871), and policymakers in Paris were skeptical about the value of France's colony in Vietnam and opposed to further colonial expansion. Dupré took a very different view on both these issues. In Cochin China, he worked hard to entrench the French administration, strengthening the Native Affairs Service, introducing compulsory vaccination, and promoting primary education. But it was Dupré's attempt to adopt a forward policy of expanding France's colonial presence into northern Vietnam (Tonkin) that has most interested historians.

In 1873, at a time when relations between the French authorities in Saigon and the Vietnamese court at Hué were strained, Vietnamese officials in Hanoi prevented a French trader and adventurer, Jean Dupuis, from conducting commerce up the Red River into China. Dupuis appealed to Saigon for assistance, and Admiral Dupré seized on this appeal to send Francis Garnier (1839–1873) to northern Vietnam to extricate Dupuis. It also seems certain that he gave Garnier secret instructions to take the opportunity to establish a new colonial position in Hanoi and the surrounding region. Dupré never put these instructions in writing, and he would later deny authorizing Garnier to act as he did. In any event, Garnier was killed, and the small force that accompanied him to Tonkin was withdrawn in ignominy. Dupré was recalled from Cochin China in semidisgrace, but he was subsequently promoted to vice-admiral and ended his official career as the prefect of Toulon. He died in Paris in 1880.

MILTON OSBORNE

See also French Ambitions in Southeast Asia; French Indochina; Garnier, Francis (1839–1873); Hué; Lagrée-Garnier Mekong Expedition (1866–1868); Nguyễn Emperors and French Imperialism; Saigon (Gia Dinh, Hồ Chí Minh City); Tonkin (Tongking)

References:
Osborne, Milton. 1997 [1969]. *The French Presence in Cochinchina and Cambodia: Rule and Response (1859–1905)*. Ithaca, NY: Cornell University Press; Bangkok: White Lotus.

Taboulet, Georges. 1956. *La Geste française en Indochine: Histoire par les textes de la France en Indochine des origines à 1914* [*France's Heroic Achievement in Indochina: A Documentary History of France in Indochina from Its Beginnings to 1914*]. Vol. 2. Paris: Adrien Maisonneuve.

DUTCH BORNEO

Dutch Borneo encompassed the area of present-day Kalimantan Indonesia, covering the western, central, and eastern portions of Borneo. Not until the early decades of the twentieth century was Dutch political hegemony established over the several native principalities of Western and Central Borneo and the sultanates of Bandjarmasin and Kutai. The various small native states of Western Borneo include Sambas, Monterado, Mempawah, Mandor, Pontianak, Kubu, Landak, Sanggau, Sukadana, Sintang, Semitau, Tojan, Melawi, and Matan. The sultanate of Bandjarmasin claimed suzerainty over the southern portion of Borneo from Kotawaringin in the west to Pasir in the east. The sultanate of Kutai dominated the eastern half of Borneo and the area along the Mahakam River. Pockets of independent principalities were found in the northeastern region—Gunung Tabur, Sambaliung, and Bulungan.

Prior to the nineteenth century and despite contracting treaties with native rulers, the Dutch established no effective control over Western Borneo. However, by a combination of new treaties and expeditionary campaigns, they succeeded in establishing their authority over the Chinese *kongsi* (associations) of Sambas, Monterado, and Mempawah (ca. 1850s); Sintang (1846); Semitau (1858); and Melawi (1864). The interior Dayak territories in Semitau were finally brought under Dutch control in 1916.

Notwithstanding the fact that Bandjarmasin ceded Kotawaringin to the Dutch in 1787, it was only in 1824 that effective control was established. Likewise, it was only with the conclusion of the Bandjar War (1861–1865) that Bandjarmasin bowed to Dutch authority. In 1905, the Dutch finally exercised control over the Muaratewe area.

On the eastern coast, Kutai and Pasir submitted to the Dutch in the mid-1840s. In 1906, Gunung Tabur, Sambaliung, and Bulungan became Dutch vassal states. And from 1906 to 1908, the Dutch managed to subdue the Upper Mahakam and Upper Pasir.

During the Pacific War (1941–1945), Japanese Imperial forces occupied Dutch Borneo from 1942 to 1945. From 1945 to 1949, Dutch Borneo was a component state of the Dutch-created federation known as the United States of Indonesia. It formed part of the unitary setup of the independent Republic of Indonesia in 1949 and came to be referred to as Kalimantan Indonesia.

OOI KEAT GIN

See also Bandjarmasin Sultanate; Borneo; British Borneo; Chinese Gold-Mining Communities in Western Borneo; Kutai (Koetai); Netherlands (Dutch) East Indies; Sambas and Pontianak Sultanates

References:

Irwin, Graham. 1955. *Nineteenth-Century Borneo: A Study in Diplomatic Rivalry.* The Hague: Martinus Nijhoff; reprinted in 1965 by Donald Moore, Singapore.

Lindblad, J. Thomas. 1988. *Between Dayak and Dutch: The Economic History of South-East Kalimantan, 1880–1942.* Dordrecht, The Netherlands: Foris Publications.

DUTCH EAST INDIES

Although the term *Dutch East Indies* (or *India*)—alternatively, *Netherlands East Indies* (or *India*)—was widely adopted during the nineteenth century in reference to the Dutch realm in Southeast Asia (the area of present-day Indonesia), it was only in the early decades of the twentieth century that such an entity was an actuality.

Java was the main focus of the Vereenigde Oost-Indische Compagnie (VOC) ([Dutch] United East India Company). Founded in 1602, the VOC concentrated on securing the political hegemony of Java. The establishment of Batavia in 1619 gave the VOC a base for expansion during the next two centuries. Combining diplomacy and force of arms, the VOC progressively acquired control over West and East Java, the northern coastal periphery, and Madura at the expense of the Javanese empire

of Mataram. Subsequently, in the mid-eighteenth century, the decaying empire of Mataram fractured into two states—Surakarta and Jogjakarta—that between them controlled Central Java. With the dissolution of the VOC in 1799, Java came under the authority of the Dutch state—the Batave Republic, the Kingdom of Holland, and the Kingdom of the Netherlands. During the Napoleonic Wars (1803–1815), the English East India Company (EIC) administered Java from 1811 to 1816. The EIC encroached on territories in Central Java and eliminated the sultanate of Banten. Upon their return in 1816, the Dutch reasserted control over Java. The conclusion of the Java War (1825–1830) established Dutch supremacy over the entire island.

The exertion of Dutch suzerainty over Sumatra, begun in the mid-seventeenth century, was accomplished only in 1911. Over a period of three centuries, the Dutch had to contend with various native sultanates—Aceh (Acheh), Asahan, Deli, Siak-Indrapura, Indragiri, Djambi, Langkat, Palembang (including Bangka and Billiton), Riau-Lingga, Lampung (controlled by the West Javanese sultanate of Banten [Bantam]), the Minangkabau areas, and the Batak regions around Lake Toba. Padang was under Dutch control after 1659; the British assumed jurisdiction from 1795 and restored control to the Dutch in 1816. Under the terms of the Anglo-Dutch Treaty of 1824, Bencoolen (Bengkulu), a British outpost since 1685, was transferred to the Dutch, and in return, the British obtained Melaka. The Dutch annexed Bangka and Billiton in 1806; both were occupied by the British from 1812 to 1816 during the Napoleonic Wars and returned to the Dutch thereafter. Palembang bowed to Dutch suzerainty in the early 1820s. A decade later (in the early 1830s), Lampung fell to the Dutch. The end of the Padri Wars in the late 1830s witnessed the establishment of Dutch control over the Minangkabau territories and Indragiri. Siak submitted to Dutch authority in 1857, as did Djambi in the following year. But the interior of Djambi only acknowledged Dutch power in the first decade of the twentieth century. The Dutch subdued the Batak territories, beginning with Angkota and Mandailing (1832); Tapanuli (1841); Slindung (1859); Toba-Batak (1869); and Karo-Batak, Pakpak-Batak, and Dairi-Batak (1904–1907). Offshore islands,

A Dutch house in Melaka. The Dutch East India Company (VOC) received its charter in 1602, and the Dutch gained control of Melaka in 1641. (North Wind Picture Archives)

such as Siberut and Nias, came under effective Dutch control in 1905 and 1906, respectively. Although the Dutch offensive against Aceh began in 1873, the entire region only accepted Dutch overlordship from 1903 to 1904. The Galo-Alas territories, dependencies of Aceh, bowed to Dutch authority in 1907. Finally, with the annexation of Riau in 1911, the whole of Sumatra was under Dutch control.

The Dutch began to assert control over Borneo in the nineteenth century. Utilizing treaty arrangements coupled with military force, the various native sultanates and Chinese gold-mining *kongsi* (associations) of West Borneo—Sambas, Monterado, Sintang, Semitau, and Melawi—were brought under effective Dutch administration by the mid-1860s. The interior regions of Semitau were finally subdued in

1916. The Bandjar War (1861–1865) decisively eliminated any resurgence of the Bandjarmasin sultanate. In 1844, Pasir and Kutai bowed to Dutch authority. Nonetheless, the Dutch only succeeded in annexing the Upper Mahakam and Upper Pasir areas from 1906 to 1908 and the interior of Apokajan in 1911.

Dutch authority in Sulawesi (Celebes) was established over Makassar following the Treaty of Bongaya (1667); thereafter, the Dutch assumed control of Manado (1679), Gorontalo (1681), and the island of Salajar (1675). Butung had been a Dutch ally since the seventeenth century. Manado and Makassar were under the British from 1810 to 1816 during the Napoleonic Wars. Treaties were signed with Sopeng, Bone, and Luwu in the early 1860s and with Wadjo and Poso in 1888. Despite treaty relations, effective Dutch control had to be attained through military campaigns in the first decade of the twentieth century that finally brought into the fold Bone, Gowa, and Luwu, as well as the various confederacies of Mandar, Masenrempulu, and Adjatapparang. The sultanate of Ternate ceded Banggai, Laiwui-Kendari, and Bungkus to the Dutch in 1907, and only after that was Dutch sovereignty established over all of Sulawesi.

Effective Dutch authority over the Lesser Sunda Islands commenced toward the end of the nineteenth century and in the first decade of the twentieth century. Lombok acknowledged Dutch control after 1894, whereas Flores, Sumba, Sumbawa, and Timor did so from 1905 to 1908. Meanwhile, the Balinese kingdoms of Badung and Klungkung were subdued from 1906 to 1908.

In Maluku (the Moluccas), Dutch suzerainty was acknowledged by the sultanates of Tidore (1657), Batjan (1667), and Ternate (1683). By the early 1780s, the Dutch directly controlled Ternate, Tidore, Obi, Ambon (Amboina), Uliasser, the Huwamahal peninsula of Ceram, the Banda islands, and Halmahera. During the Napoleonic Wars, British authority was established over Ambon and Banda (1796) and Ternate (1799), but these territories were returned to the Dutch in 1816 and 1817. Ceram and Buru finally bowed to Dutch authority in 1905 and 1907, respectively.

By virtue of the sultanate of Tidore's status as a vassal to the VOC, the territories in its possession also came under Dutch authority. They included those in New Guinea such as the Onin peninsula; Bird's Head; the islands of Waigeo, Misool, Salawati, and Batanta; and the Radja IV archipelago. In 1900, the Dutch acquired all of Tidore's rights over New Guinea. But effective Dutch control was only established during the late 1890s and the early 1920s, with the submission of Fakfak and Manokwari (1898), Merauke (1902), Hollandia (1910), Biak (1916), and Waigeo and Misool (1921).

OOI KEAT GIN

See also Anglo-Dutch Relations in Southeast Asia (Seventeenth to Twentieth Centuries); Borneo; Coen, Jan Pieterszoon (1587–1629); Dutch Interests in Southeast Asia from 1800; Java; Maluku (The Moluccas); Melaka; Napoleonic War in Asia; Netherlands

(Dutch) East Indies; Spices and the Spice Trade; Sumatra

References:

Hall, D. G. E. 1981. *A History of South-East Asia.* 4th ed. London and Basingstoke, England: Macmillan/St. Martin's Press.

Irwin, Graham. 1955. *Nineteenth-Century Borneo: A Study in Diplomatic Rivalry.* The Hague: Martinus Nijhoff; reprinted in 1965 by Donald Moore, Singapore.

Ricklefs, M. C. 1982. *A History of Modern Indonesia.* London: Macmillan.

Tarling, Nicholas. 1962. *Anglo-Dutch Rivalry in the Malay World, 1780–1824.* Cambridge: Cambridge University Press.

DUTCH INTERESTS IN SOUTHEAST ASIA FROM 1800

For most of their history, the Dutch had no particular interest in or indeed concept of Southeast Asia. The commercial ventures in which the Dutch Republic, its chartered companies, and its citizens engaged in the seventeenth and eighteenth centuries were not only Asia-wide but also worldwide in scope. The focus of the Dutch monarchy and its subjects after the French Revolution (1789–1799) and the Napoleonic Wars (1803–1815) was on what they called "Netherlands India" and what nationalists were to call "Indonesia." What happened elsewhere in Southeast Asia—in fact, in Asia as a whole—interested them only in terms of its impact on Netherlands India.

Yet the striking feature of this phase is not that the Dutch lost so much but that they retained or gained so much. Their worldwide interests were depleted—though they still retained Surinam and remained the only Europeans with a toehold in Japan until the latter years of the Tokugawa—but for a small European state, their Indies realm was strikingly large and prosperous. What was it that enabled them to build up this impressive realm?

One of the most sophisticated of the Indonesian nationalists, the Sumatran Sutan Sjahrir (1909–1966), pointed to the answer. "For more than a hundred years now Dutch power over our country and our people has been a by-product of the calculations and decisions of British foreign policy." Since the beginning of the nineteenth century, the Dutch had remained in Indonesia "not on the basis of their own strength, but by favor of the English, on whose policies they have been wholly dependent" (Sjahrir 1968: 24–25).

Though the British had dislodged the Dutch from the Indies as well as the Cape of Good Hope and Ceylon (Sri Lanka) during the wars, they handed the Indies back in the convention of 1814. The aim was to consolidate the new monarchy and its friendship with the British, seen as a constraint on further threats from France. The acquisition of Singapore (1819) prompted a further adjustment—the Dutch left their settlements in India and on the Malay side of the straits, and the British left Sumatra—but the essence of the understanding was confirmed. Though the British would trade in the archipelago, they would not offer a political challenge to the Dutch. What was unspoken in the Anglo-Dutch Treaty of 1924 was no less important than what was openly said. Other powers also accepted the view of the predominant power of the day: territorially speaking, the Indies was for the Dutch.

Somewhat paradoxically, that enabled the Dutch to limit their establishment of formal political control over much of the Indies for some fifty years or more. Though the Dutch United East India Company (VOC) had established a measure of direct control in parts of Java during the late seventeenth and eighteenth centuries, it had, for the most part, continued to work through treaties and contracts with local rulers. The new colonial rulers adopted and adapted the practice. Indeed, throughout its history, Netherlands India remained a collection of directly ruled and "self-administering" territories.

Most colonial realms proceeded by securing collaboration from indigenous elites, backed up by infrequent demonstrations of effective and exemplary force. The Dutch were no exception: in fact, they were quite systematic in that regard. They had, after all, practical motives for the study of *adat* (custom or customary law), for the investigation of dynastic claims, and for the shaping of both. They had every reason, too, to be sparing in the use of force. Yet there were some conflicts they should not have entered into, for it was impossible to succeed. The notable one was, of course, the long war with Aceh.

The early years of the new realm had been marked by another major conflict, the Java War of the 1820s, brought to an end with difficulty

and deceit. Its challenge only intensified the problem the Dutch faced. How were they—their worldwide commerce finally destroyed by the French wars—to make the most of the empire to which they had been restored? How could that empire contribute to the new monarchy, itself challenged by the Belgian revolution of 1830 and the breakaway of an independent Belgium? The answers were found in the Cultivation System associated with Governor-General Johannes Van den Bosch (t. 1830–1833) and in the policy of "peace and order" associated with his successor, Jean C. Baud (t. 1833–1836). The former was designed to substitute Javanese labor for Dutch capital in developing exports from Netherlands India, and the latter was intended to avoid further disruption to a fragile realm. The concentration had to be, as Van den Bosch put it, on "profitable activity" (Graves 1971: 144).

These solutions would only work if they avoided alienating the British. They came near to doing so. The Cultivation System limited the role of British capital, and the differential duties imposed on foreign trade seemed to the British to breach the 1824 treaty. In view of the British protest to Dutch expansion in East Sumatra in the 1830s and 1840s, Baud withdrew the posts the Dutch had established, without dropping their claims. The dispute also led the British government to offer some support to James Brooke's venture in Borneo (1803–1868), though arguably Borneo had been left to the Dutch under the treaty. That worried the Dutch, who sought to back up their claims elsewhere in Borneo and in Bali. Essentially, however, the relationship with the British, though uneasy, remained positive. The security it offered made it possible to adopt *outhouding,* abstention from involvement in unprofitable areas.

Although the Dutch had become more prosperous by the 1870s—partly as a result of the success of the Cultivation System in boosting Indies exports and helping to create textile industries and infrastructure in The Netherlands—they had also become more nervous. Other powers were beginning to rival their patron, Britain, and the guarantee the British offered was thus less secure. The Dutch response was twofold. They extended to others the commercial opportunities they offered the British, indeed moving toward the abolition of differential duties and the creation of an "open-door" policy. They also moved toward asserting their control in parts of the archipelago where their rule was still informal or nonexistent—in Bali and Lombok, for example, as well as Aceh.

There was, of course, a larger threat, and the Dutch were unsure how to respond to it. The relationship with the British had helped to insulate the Indies from the outer world. But insulation was no longer possible. Even if the intervention of other powers could be precluded, new ideas penetrated. The development of the economy dislocated the relations with the elite established under the Cultivation System and required the introduction of at least a measure of modern education. A more sophisticated society could learn from newspapers what was going on elsewhere: that the Japanese had defeated the Russians in 1905, for example, or that the Manchu dynasty had been overthrown in 1911. Meanwhile, modernist Islam was gaining ground, despite Dutch colonial official Christiaan Snouck Hurgronje's (1857–1936) belief that it was a contradiction in terms. With the growth of democracy at home, the Dutch themselves had to find a new rationale for colonial policy.

The answer was the "Ethical Policy," an inflow of Dutch investment capital aimed at developing natural resources and increasing export production, associated with Dutch liberals C. Th. van Deventer and J. H. Abendanon (1852–1925) and several others. But this was an uncertain answer—even an ambiguous one— and was never fully adopted. Could the Dutch welcome or even encourage the Indonesian nationalism that developments were bringing about? Could they find new collaborators among the nationalists? Or did caution still have to prevail? Should the Dutch try to prevent the nationalists from making contact with the masses or even turn back to adat and to old elites? The unrest of the 1920s and the depression of the early 1930s largely destroyed the cause of the Ethical Policy.

During this period, the activities of the political information service (PID) made Netherlands India something of a police state. Its rulers acquired a new but negative interest in other parts of Southeast Asia. Singapore, thrust into the islands and always a source of commercial jealousy simply because it was a commercial convenience, now harbored nationalist opponents. The Americans, too, were setting a bad example in the Philippines. Manuel Quezon (1878–1944), soon to be the first president of the Philippine Commonwealth, visited Surabaya in 1934. Dutch officials thought him "more subversive . . . than Marx, Lenin, Trotsky and Stalin rolled into one" (Friend 1965: 170).

In fact, the British-backed colonial framework in Southeast Asia was dissolving, and it was upon that framework that the Dutch ultimately relied. The more immediate threat came, however, from the Japanese. The Dutch had been nervous when Britain allied with Japan in 1902. A Japan unrestrained by alliance was more worrying still, and its descent upon Manchuria in 1931 seemed a possible precedent, especially as Sumatra and Borneo had oil and the Japanese had none. Britain could make no promises and was of little help when the Japanese invaded Netherlands India in 1942.

The Dutch returned to the Indies once more after the defeat of the Japanese in 1945. They now faced a republic, proclaimed by Indonesian nationalists at the very end of the interregnum. Their patrons, the British—on whom, as Sjahrir saw, so much had depended and still depended—urged them to collaborate with nationalism. They could not, however, find nationalists with whom they were prepared to collaborate, and the use of force without a context of collaboration necessarily failed.

Netherlands India, they had proclaimed, extended from Sabang to Merauke. Yet when they accepted the independence of Indonesia in the Round Table Agreements of 1949, they were not prepared to make over West New Guinea to their successors. The Dutch States-General could not accept the disappearance of the Dutch flag from Asia: the Agreements were acceptable only if the transfer excluded West New Guinea. Yet for the Indonesians, West New Guinea was part of their inheritance, sanctified, moreover, by the sufferings of nationalists exiled there in the interwar years.

In the course of the dispute, which ended only in 1962, the Indonesians moved to eliminate Dutch economic interests in the republic. Those interests were, however, no longer deemed vital by the Dutch. "The transfer of sovereignty to Indonesia has opened the way for the Netherlands to resume the traditional position in the International economy," Dirk Stikker, the Dutch minister of Foreign Affairs, wrote in 1950 (Baudet 1984: 274). His colleague, the minister for economic affairs, had, on the very eve of the Round Table Agreements, offered the States-General an industrialization plan that did not mention Indonesia. That plan, new markets, the growth of services, and the European Economic Commission (EEC) offered the Dutch and their state new sources of wealth. Growth was "spectacular": 3.5 percent a year between 1950 and 1970 (Wesseling 1980: 128). There was no need for a flag.

NICHOLAS TARLING

See also Aceh (Acheh); Aceh (Acheh) Wars (1873–1903); *Adat;* Anglo-Dutch Relations in Southeast Asia (Seventeenth to Twentieth Centuries); Bali; British Interests in Southeast Asia; Brooke, James, and Sarawak; Cultivation System (*Cultuurstelsel*); Ethical Policy (*Ethische Politiek*); "Indonesia"; Indonesian Revolution (1945–1949); Islamic Resurgence in Southeast Asia (Twentieth Century); Japanese Occupation of Southeast Asia (1941–1945); Linggadjati (Linggajati) Agreement (1947); Lombok; Mohammad Hatta (1902–1980); Nationalism and Independence Movements in Southeast Asia; Netherlands (Dutch) East Indies; Padri Movement; Padri Wars (1820s, 1830s); Renville Agreement (January 1948); Singapore (1819); Singapore (Nineteenth Century to 1990s), Entrepôt Trade and Commerce of; Snouck Hurgronje, Professor Christiaan (1857–1936); Soekarno (Sukarno) (1901–1970); Sumatra; Van den Bosch, Count Johannes (1780–1844); Vereenigde Oost-Indische Compagnie (VOC) ([Dutch] United East Indies Company) (1602)

References:

Baudet, H. 1984. "Reflections on the Dutch Economists in the East Indies." Pp. 263–277 in *Enterprise and History.* Edited by D. C. Coleman and P. Matthias. Cambridge: Cambridge University Press.

Friend, Theodore A. 1965. *Between Two Empires: The Ordeal of the Philippines.* New Haven, CT: Yale University Press.

Graves, Elizabeth E. 1971. "The Ever Victorious Buffalo: How the Minangkabau of Indonesia Solved Their Colonial Question." Ph.D. diss., University of Wisconsin.

Ricklefs, Merle C. 1981. *A History of Modern Indonesia.* London: Macmillan.

Sjahrir, Sutan. 1968. *Our Struggle.* Translated by B. Anderson. Ithaca, NY: Cornell University Press.

Wesseling, H. L. 1980. "Post-imperial Holland." *Journal of Contemporary History* 15: 125–142.

DUTCH POLICE ACTIONS (FIRST AND SECOND)
A Clash of Wills

The First and Second Dutch Police Actions were military confrontations between the Dutch and the Republic of Indonesia. The Dutch believed the first action was necessary to enhance the conditions required to implement the terms of the Linggadjati Agreement (1947), a pact between the Netherlands government and the Republic of Indonesia whereby both agreed to the creation of a federal state to be known as the United States of Indonesia (USI). Similarly, the second action was launched by the Dutch to enforce compliance with the Renville Agreement (1948), an agreement between the Netherlands government and the Republic of Indonesia over recognition of the authority of the Republic over Java and Sumatra. The Republic of Indonesia regarded both police actions as undisguised aggression against its sovereignty.

The First Police Action was launched in July 1947. The field of operations encompassed Java and Sumatra. The tactical aim was twofold: first, to destroy the armed units operating in the name of the Republic of Indonesia, and second, to capture the export commodities in Dutch-owned estates that were located in republican-controlled territories. The republican response was guerrilla warfare. Of the two tactical aims, only the second was achieved. Estate products were recaptured, but the military units of the republic simply melted away.

The Second Police Action was launched in December 1948. The political aim was to force the republican government to participate in a federal government that the Dutch claimed was provided by the Renville Agreement concluded earlier in the year. The military operations centered on the capture of Jogjakarta, the republican capital. In one fell swoop, almost all of the top republican leaders were arrested and sent into exile. However, an emergency republican government was proclaimed in Sumatra, and the republican military units again melted into the countryside to resume their guerrilla warfare. Thus, the Second Police Action failed to extinguish the Republic of Indonesia.

YONG MUN CHEONG

See also Indonesian Revolution; Linggadjati (Linggajati) Agreement (1947); Mohammad Hatta (1902–1980); Nationalism and Independence Movements in Southeast Asia; Renville Agreement (January 1948); Soekarno (Sukarno) (1901–1970); United Nations and Conflict Resolution in Southeast Asia; Van Mook, Dr. Hubertus Johannes (1894–1948); Yogyakarta (Jogjakarta)

References:

Kahin, G. McT. 1952. *Nationalism and Revolution in Indonesia.* Ithaca, NY: Cornell University Press.

Reid, Anthony. 1974. *The Indonesian National Revolution, 1945–1950.* Hawthorn, Victoria, Australia: Longman.

Yong Mun Cheong. 1982. *H. J. van Mook and Indonesian Independence: A Study of His Role in Dutch-Indonesian Relations, 1945–48.* The Hague: Martinus Nijhoff.

DVARAVATI
A Mon Polity in Thailand

Dvaravati was the name given to a city or kingdom located in Central Thailand during the first millennium C.E. as well as to a wider archaeological or art historical culture in Central and Northeast Thailand. Both the kingdom and the culture are often identified with the Mon ethnic group, who are thought to have occupied much of Central Thailand during that period. The polity of Dvaravati appears to have been centered on the lower Menam or Chao Phraya River, and it is particularly associated with the Buddhist site of Nakhon Pathom and the walled citadel of U Thong. The name Dvaravati also survived into later periods of Thai history, appearing among the official names of both Ayutthaya and Bangkok.

Scholars in the nineteenth century originally reconstructed the name of the early state of Dvaravati in accordance with Chinese historical texts that mentioned a kingdom named To-lo-po-ti or Tu-ho-lo-po-ti. This country sent embassies to the Tang court of China in 638, 640, and 649 C.E. and was also mentioned by the Chinese Buddhist pilgrims Hsuan Tsang (ca.

596–664 C.E.) and I-tsing (635–713 C.E.), who traveled through Southeast Asia during the second half of the seventh century. However, there was no further record of this kingdom in Chinese sources after that date. Both Hsuan Tsang and I-tsing described To-lo-po-ti as lying east of Sri Ksetra, a kingdom of the Pyu people located in the central Irrawaddy Valley of present-day Burma (Myanmar) and west of Isanapura in modern Cambodia. To-lo-po-ti (Dvaravati) therefore seemed to have been located in the lower Menam Valley of modern Thailand.

These conclusions were supported by information published in 1964 about two silver medals found in the region of Nakhon Pathom in Central Thailand, which bore inscriptions reading "the meritorious act of the lord of Dvaravati." Two further medals with the same inscription were discovered in the 1970s (the first at U Thong and the second at Ban Ku Muang, north of Lopburi), and other examples have since been found at a number of early Buddhist sites in Central Thailand. Coins bearing the symbol of a conch shell (*sankha*) and the outline of a temple or shrine are known to have been minted at U Thong and Nakhon Pathom from the sixth to ninth centuries C.E. (Mitchiner 1998: 179–200).

Archaeological investigations at Nakhon Pathom and U Thong have revealed a distinct cultural level dating from the sixth to ninth centuries. This evidence has led to the definition of a Dvaravati culture, characterized by urban settlements protected by extensive earthen ramparts and moats and above all by Buddhist votive tablets, sculpture, and religious foundations. Among the most elaborate sculptural elements are stone *dharmacakras,* or "wheels of the laws," erected as symbols of Buddhist teaching, and carved *sema* stones, used to mark the sacred boundary of Buddhist monastic foundations. Both have been discovered in many areas of modern Thailand, although some particularly fine series of dharmacakras have been collected at Nakhon Pathom, as were sema stones at Muang Fa Daet in Northeast Thailand.

It is unclear, however, whether this cultural distribution suggests the territory of a wider kingdom or simply the pattern of local trade issuing from one or two major commercial, political, or religious centers. David Wyatt (1982: 21–24) has emphasized the commercial importance of the Central Plain of Thailand in commanding the overland trade routes leading westward into Burma, to the north up the Chao Phraya (Menam) Valley, and to the northeast into the Khorat Plateau. It is probable that the spread of Dvaravati culture was the result of this trade and that the polity of Dvaravati itself was localized in the lower Menam Valley.

Almost all of the sites associated with the Dvaravati culture are distinguished by the presence of inscriptions in the Mon language. This has encouraged the Thai art historian Piriya Krairiksh to suggest that the art forms associated with Dvaravati should preferably be described as "Mon art," as the geographic extent of the kingdom of Dvaravati remains unknown. However, the ethnic or linguistic composition of Central and Northeast Thailand at that time is also uncertain, and the term *Mon* may therefore be equally deceptive.

What is beyond doubt, however, from both the historical and the art historical material, is the importance of Theravada Buddhism in that culture. Small clay tablets bearing an image of the Buddha and sometimes a Buddhist formula in Pali on the obverse have been found in large numbers at many Dvaravati sites and also in cave sites in southern Thailand. It is clear that towns such as Nakhon Pathom must have played an important role in the propagation of Buddhism across much of mainland Southeast Asia. These towns formed part of a Buddhist network linking the ancient pilgrimage sites of northern India and Sri Lanka in the west to the new Buddhist dynasties in China, Korea, and Japan.

WILLIAM A. SOUTHWORTH

See also Buddhism, Mahayana; Buddhism, Theravada; Economic History of Early Modern Southeast Asia (Pre-Sixteenth Century); Hindu-Buddhist Period of Southeast Asia; I-Ching (I-tsing) (635–713 C.E.); Mon; Mons

References:

Brown, Robert L. 1996. *The Dvaravati Wheels of the Law and the Indianization of Southeast Asia.* Leiden, The Netherlands: E. J. Brill.

Dupont, P. 1959. *L'Archéologie Mône de Dvaravati* [*The Archaeology of Mon Dvaravati*]. Paris: École Française d'Extrême-Orient.

Krairiksh, Piriya. 1977. *Art Styles in Thailand: A Selection from National Provincial Museums and an Essay in Conceptualization.* Bangkok: Fine Arts Department, National Museum, Thailand.

Mitchiner, Michael. 1998. *The History and Coinage of South East Asia until the Fifteenth Century.* London: Hawkins Publications.

Wyatt, David K. 1982. *Thailand: A Short History.* New Haven, CT, and London: Yale University Press.

E

EAST INDIA COMPANY (EIC) (1600), ENGLISH
Transformer of Southeast Asian Trade and Commerce

The English East India Company (EIC) was a joint-stock firm founded by royal charter in 1600, with exclusive rights to trade between England and Asia. Its goal was to develop the spice trade of the eastern Indonesian archipelago. Unable to compete with the Dutch East India Company (VOC), it withdrew to India, maintaining only one outpost in Southeast Asia after 1685. A century later, it returned to establish the ports of Penang (1786) and Singapore (1819). The British government disbanded the EIC in 1858.

For its first twenty years, the EIC attempted to trade with the Moluccas and Bandas, the islands where cloves and nutmegs grew. But the VOC forestalled these efforts, and English forays in the area led to conflicts. The EIC lost out to the better-funded Dutch. Local events undermined attempts by the directors in London and Amsterdam to compel their employees in Indonesia to cooperate. (Their efforts included the transfer of the EIC's headquarters from Bantam [Banten] to the Dutch-controlled port of Batavia in 1619.) Finally, all was shattered when the Dutch governor of Ambon in the Moluccas executed ten English merchants in 1623, an incident known as the Amboina Massacre. After that, the EIC concentrated on its trade to India.

The factory in Bantam remained, collecting pepper, ginger, sugar, and (until the Dutch captured Makassar in 1667) cloves smuggled by Malay traders from the Moluccas. From Bantam, new voyages were made to Japan and China, Siam (Thailand), and Cambodia. But competition was severe—in Makassar, from Portuguese, Spanish, and Asian traders, and in Bantam, from Indians, Portuguese, and Danes. By 1670, Bantam was largely a supply station for the China trade, and when the VOC captured Bantam (1682), the English withdrew their pepper trade to Benkulen (Bengkulu), on the western coast of Sumatra.

But as the China trade grew, so did the EIC's need for Southeast Asian products, such as pepper, tin, and spices. These goods were smuggled from the Dutch-held territories to the Malay ports of Kedah, Selangor, and especially Riau by Malay and Bugis traders and taken to India by private English merchants (the "country traders," who were often financed by employees of the EIC).

In the 1760s, the China trade and the need for a safe haven on the windward side of the Bay of Bengal prompted the EIC to search for a new base in Southeast Asia. Various places were tried (Negrais, Manila, and Balambangan). In 1784, following the Dutch capture of Riau, the main port of the country trade, an English country trader named Francis Light (1740–1794) persuaded the sultan of Kedah to cede

Pulo Pinang (Penang) to the EIC (which he did in 1786).

By 1786, the EIC was more an organ of the British government, ruling an empire in India, than a commercial enterprise. In 1813, its monopoly of Asian trade was canceled, except for the trade to China. During the Napoleonic Wars (1803–1815), the EIC occupied the Dutch possessions in the archipelago, including Melaka, Batavia, and Ambon. By 1814, when these ports were returned to Dutch rule, it was apparent that Penang, at the western end of the Straits of Melaka, was no substitute for those ports or for Riau. The governor of Benkulen, Thomas Stamford Raffles (1781–1826), acquired Singapore, at the southern end of the Straits of Melaka, from a Johor prince who had been passed over in his claim to the throne. The Dutch disputed the legality of Raffles's 1819 treaty, but the port flourished, and the English were reluctant to give it up. Negotiations led to the Anglo-Dutch Treaty of 1824, which divided English and Dutch spheres of influence in the archipelago by a line through the Straits of Melaka. Benkulen was exchanged for Dutch Melaka.

The EIC administered Penang, Melaka, and Singapore (the Straits Settlements) as free ports until 1858. This was a period of commercial growth, encouraged by immigration from China. The peninsular Malay States, by contrast, were in political collapse because of a threatened invasion by Siam (Kedah was overrun in 1821) and economic recession. There was an upsurge of violence in the Straits of Melaka, as Malay princes battled to acquire power. Though the Straits government had been ordered to avoid direct intervention in the affairs of its neighbors, the peninsular Malay States viewed such actions as piracy and acted accordingly, laying the groundwork for British intervention and colonial rule later in the century.

The EIC helped to shape the face of modern Southeast Asia economically, socially, and politically. Together with the VOC and other European traders, the EIC at first brought an era of economic expansion, "which remade Southeast Asia and enabled it to play a leading role in global commerce" (Reid 1993: 326). But later, it brought decline and decay, as Penang and Singapore diverted trade from the Malay ports.

The Anglo-Dutch Treaty of 1824 set up a political division in the archipelago, and the EIC's encouragement of Chinese immigrants to its ports foreshadowed a policy in the British-governed Malay States that played an important role in shaping the demography of modern Malaysia.

DIANNE LEWIS

See also Ambon (Amboina/Amboyna) Massacre (1623); Anglo-Dutch Relations in Southeast Asia (Seventeenth to Twentieth Centuries); Banten (Bantam); Batavia (Sunda Kalapa, Jacatra, Djakarta/Jakarta); Bengkulu (Bencoolen, Benkulen); British Interests in Southeast Asia; China, Imperial; Country Traders; Dutch Interests in Southeast Asia from 1800; Economic Transformation of Southeast Asia (ca. 1400–ca. 1800); Light, Captain Francis (1740–1794); Maluku (The Moluccas); Netherlands (Dutch) East Indies; Penang (1786); Pepper; Singapore (1819); Singapore (Nineteenth Century to 1990s), Entrepôt Trade and Commerce of; Spices and the Spice Trade; Straits Settlements (1826–1941); Vereenigde Oost-Indische Compagnie (VOC) ([Dutch] United East India Company) (1602)

References:
Bassett, D. K. 1990. *The British in South-East Asia during the Seventeenth and Eighteenth Centuries.* Occasional Papers no. 18. Hull, UK: Centre for South-East Asian Studies.

Chaudhuri, K. N. 1965. *The English East India Company: The Study of an Early Joint-Stock Company, 1600–1640.* London: Frank Cass.

Keay, John. 1991. *The Honourable Company: A History of the English East India Company.* New York: Macmillan.

Reid, Anthony. 1993. *Southeast Asia in the Age of Commerce, 1450–1680.* Vol. 2, *Expansion and Crisis.* New Haven, CT, and London: Yale University Press.

Tarling, Nicholas. 1969. *British Policy in the Malay Peninsula and Archipelago, 1824–1871.* Kuala Lumpur: Oxford University Press.

Tarling, Nicholas, ed. 1992. *The Cambridge History of Southeast Asia.* Vol. 1, *From c. 1500 to c. 1800.* Cambridge and New York: Cambridge University Press.

EAST INDONESIAN ETHNIC GROUPS

Historically, eastern Indonesia has been variously defined. Here, it is considered to include the islands of Sulawesi, Maluku, and East and West Nusa Tenggara, including the whole of the island of Timor, half of which now (since August 2002) comprises the new nation of Timor Leste (East Timor).

Language is a useful starting point for any ethnic classification. The overwhelming majority of the population of eastern Indonesia speaks a language that belongs to the Austronesian family of languages. This places most eastern Indonesian ethnic groups among the large group of linguistically related populations that stretch from Madagascar in the west to Easter Island in the east and from Taiwan in the north to Timor in the south.

All of the Austronesian languages outside Taiwan are classified as Malayo-Polynesian. Within this grouping, linguists distinguish between Western Malayo–Polynesian and Central Malayo–Polynesian. The dividing line for this classification occurs within eastern Indonesia. All of the languages of Sulawesi and those on the western half of Sumbawa belong to the Western Malayo–Polynesian grouping. The language of Bima on Sumbawa and all of the languages of East Nusa Tenggara and North and South Maluku are considered to be Central Malayo–Polynesian. This Central Malayo–Polynesian grouping is a large and as yet provisional categorization that still lacks sufficient subgrouping criteria. It does, however, point to a long history of regional differentiation and linguistic interaction among language speakers in eastern Indonesia.

Eastern Indonesia, however, is also notable for its scattering of non-Austronesian languages. The largest number of these languages are found on the islands of Alor and Pantar. The languages are related to other languages found in central and eastern Timor as well as to one language on the island of Kisar. All of these languages are considered to belong to the Trans–New Guinea phylum of languages, most of whose members are found in New Guinea. Other non-Austronesian languages spoken on Ternate, on Tidore, and on Halmahera in northern Maluku belong to the West Papua family of languages. Long contact and interaction between speakers of Austronesian and

non-Austronesian languages have led to significant borrowings across these language families. This historical interaction is probably responsible for some of the social and cultural differences between the eastern and western halves of the Indonesian archipelago.

For a critical period in the 1930s, anthropologists associated with Leiden University, in particular J. P. B. de Josselin de Jong and his eminent pupil, F. A. E. van Wouden, looked upon eastern Indonesia, especially Flores, Timor, and the islands of Maluku, as a privileged field of study. In their view, this area preserved elements of the oldest forms of Indonesian society, particularly in various encompassing systems of marriage exchange and in the reliance on complex dual cosmologies. These views led to a somewhat exaggerated emphasis on the differences between these societies and other societies of the archipelago. Currently, greater attention is given to locating the majority of societies of eastern Indonesia within a more general comparative Austronesian framework and to tracing similarities as well as differences among these societies and other Austronesian-speaking populations.

Historically, the societies of eastern Indonesia have long been open to trade with the outside world. Nutmeg and clove from the islands of Maluku and sandalwood from Timor were traded as valued commodities for many centuries. These islands were also a principal location for the trade of bird of paradise feathers, marine products such as bêche-de-mer (*trepang*, or sea slug), and rare woods that originated from New Guinea. Trade in captured slaves was also widespread. These commodities provided a source of wealth in the creation of local polities and eventually attracted Europeans to the region. The sultanates of Ternate in Maluku, Makassar in Sulawesi, and, to a lesser extent, Buton on the island of Buton and Bima on Sumbawa were important trading ports and became political and religious centers of influence. Islam, which began to spread in eastern Indonesia in the fifteenth century, together with the increasing use of Malay as a lingua franca, was a crucial ingredient in the formation of trading networks.

The Portuguese were the first to arrive in eastern Indonesia in the sixteenth century, soon followed by the Spanish, British, and Dutch. The Europeans, particularly the Portuguese, fostered the spread of Christianity. Through the seventeenth century, the (United) Dutch East India Company (VOC) gradually gained monopoly control over most of the islands of eastern Indonesia, signing contracts with local rulers that recognized their local sovereign authority in return for support and the exclusive right of trade. Only in central and eastern Flores and on Timor were the Dutch unsuccessful in driving out the Portuguese. During the seventeenth and eighteenth centuries, control over these islands was strongly disputed. Some local rulers acknowledged Portuguese authority, others acknowledged Dutch authority, and some acknowledged both as was expedient. The allegiance of rulers and of their local populations was also linked to religion, both Islam and Christianity.

The Dutch maintained five main trading centers, or "factories": at Ternate, Ambon, and Banda in Maluku; at Bima on Sumbawa; and at Kupang on Timor. After a long struggle, the Dutch also managed to gain monopoly control of Makassar. In addition to a presence in these port centers, it was VOC practice to station Europeans as "interpreters" (often with a few soldiers) on many of the islands where they maintained contracts of trade.

Unlike the regulated Dutch VOC organization, the Portuguese presence in eastern Indonesia was organized through independent traders and missionaries, primarily Jesuits and Dominicans. This Portuguese presence was most notable at Larantuka in eastern Flores and at Lifao on the north coast of Timor. In 1769, the Portuguese officially transferred their authority from Lifao to Dili, leaving much of central Timor to the control of an independent group of Portuguese-speaking mestizo traders who were collectively referred to as "Topasses" or as "Black Portuguese."

After the Dutch colonial government took over from the VOC at the end of the eighteenth century, it continued to recognize the local polities of eastern Indonesia and to maintain a form of indirect rule through a complex structure composed of hundreds of local rajas and sultans. The preaching of Christianity by Dutch missionaries in the nineteenth century spread the Christian religion into the interior of many of the larger islands of eastern Indonesia. Local schooling in Malay was generally linked to this mission effort. The "pacification"

of some areas on Sumba, Flores, and Timor continued into the twentieth century, when the efforts began to consolidate the patchwork of local polities and crosscutting patterns of allegiance in a more ordered colonial structure. After independence, the government of Indonesia continued the process of establishing bureaucratic uniformity over a diversity of social groups with complex historical roots in widely varying environments.

By rough count, there are more than 300 linguistically distinct ethnic groups in eastern Indonesia (130 in Maluku, 110 in Sulawesi, and 60 in Nusa Tenggara). The majority of these groups are of relatively small size, consisting of fewer than 10,000 to 20,000 individuals. Only a few groups number more than 1 million, notably the Bugis (Ugi), Makassarese, Gorontalo, and Atoni. The Bugis and Makassarese of South Sulawesi have historically migrated widely and can now be found in large numbers in Maluku as well as in Kalimantan. The Gorontalo are prominent in North Sulawesi, whereas the Atoni (Atoni Pah Meto/Dawan) constitute the dominant population of West Timor and of the East Timorese enclave of Oecussi. Groups with populations of over half a million include the Sadan Toraja of Sulawesi, the Bimanese of Sumbawa, the Manggarai of west Flores, and the Tetun of Timor.

The Butonese present an interesting case. Those identified as Butonese include speakers of different languages from various islands of Southwest Sulawesi, all of which were once part of the sultanate of Buton. Together, these Butonese also constitute a major group in eastern Indonesia. The Bajau present another interesting case. Although by no means as large a group as the Butonese, the Bajau (sometimes known as the "sea gypsies") can be found scattered in small coastal settlements throughout the region. The sea, rather than the land, defines their social life and provides their means of livelihood.

Given the diversity of these groups and their complex histories, a simple characterization of the region is impossible. Social identities are closely entwined with local ideas of origin. These ideas uphold status distinctions of long standing. Disputes over precedence in matters of origin are prominent in social life and give scope for considerable social mobility. Houses—in a social as well as a physical sense—are a focus of identity and provide the basis for the reckoning of descent relationships. Religious allegiances, whether Muslim, Catholic, or Protestant, are another critical component of local social identity. Many groups continue to maintain elaborate registers of dual symbolic categories that emphasize spiritual complementarity, and most groups perform engaging rituals associated with marriage, house building, and death. Exchange between groups at such rituals is fundamental to defining individuals within society and joining generations, including the ancestral dead.

In a modern context, education is seen as highly desirable and a means of gaining status. Local, national, and increasingly international migration affects most communities in the region. This migration is, in many ways, a continuation of a long-standing historical pattern. Conflict has been a part of this pattern and has, in recent years, come to the fore in Maluku, parts of Sulawesi, and Timor. Traditionally, countervailing local relationships have limited such conflicts, and it is likely that this will continue to be the case in the years ahead.

JAMES J. FOX

See also Bajau; Bugis (Buginese); Dutch Interests in Southeast Asia from 1800; Ethnolinguistic Groups of Southeast Asia; Jungle/Forest Products; Maluku (The Moluccas); Marine/Sea Products; Missionaries, Christian; Netherlands (Dutch) East Indies; Portuguese Asian Empire; Republik Maluku Selatan (RMS, Republic of the South Moluccas); Slavery; Spices and the Spice Trade; Sulawesi (Celebes); Timor; Torajas; Vereenigde Oost-Indische Compagnie (VOC) ([Dutch] United East Indies Company) (1602)

References:

Andaya, Leonard Y. 1993. *The World of Maluku: Eastern Indonesia in the Early Modern Period.* Honolulu: University of Hawai'i Press.

Fox, James J. 1977. *Harvest of the Palm: Ecological Change in Eastern Indonesia.* Cambridge, MA: Harvard University Press.

———. 1980. *The Flow of Life: Essays on Eastern Indonesia.* Cambridge, MA: Harvard University Press.

———. 1988. *To Speak in Pairs: Essays on the Ritual Languages of Eastern Indonesia.* Cambridge: Cambridge University Press.

Hoskins, Janet. 1993. *The Play of Time: Kodi Perspectives on Calendars, History, and Exchange.* Berkeley: University of California Press.

Lewis, E. Douglas. 1988. *People of the Source: The Social and Ceremonial Order of Tana Wai Brama on Flores.* Providence, RI: Foris Publications.

McKinnon, Susan. 1991. *From a Shattered Sun: Hierarchy, Gender, and Alliance in the Tanimbar Islands.* Madison: University of Wisconsin Press.

McWilliam, Andrew. 2002. *Paths of Origin, Gates of Life: A Study of Place and Precedence in Southwest Timor.* Leiden, The Netherlands: KITLV Press.

Molnar, Andrea Katalin. 2000. *Grandchildren of the Ga'e Ancestors.* Verhandelingen van het Koninklijk Instituut voor Taal-, Land- en Volkenkunde, vol. 185. Leiden, The Netherlands: KITLV Press.

Traube, Elizabeth G. 1986. *Cosmology and Social Life: Ritual Exchange among the Mambai of East Timor.* Chicago: University of Chicago Press.

Van Wouden, F. A. E. 1968. *Types of Social Structure in Eastern Indonesia.* The Hague: Martinus Nijhoff.

EAST MALAYSIAN ETHNIC MINORITIES

In a very real sense, minorities and their identities are created, and the native populations of the Malaysian Borneo territories of Sarawak and Sabah (formerly British North Borneo) were incorporated into and became minorities in the expanding empire of Britain from the nineteenth century onward. At that time, Britain was in intense competition with The Netherlands for control of the trade in profitable tropical commodities and the sources of production, although European merchants had been arriving on the coasts of Borneo and had established relatively precarious footholds there since the seventeenth century. Competition in Asian trade, in which the British were increasingly establishing a dominant position, also led to the European powers gradually taking control over territory and drawing local populations into colonial administrations. Nevertheless, the British were, in some respects and certainly in some circumstances, reluctant imperialists. It is in this connection that the form of Western control established in northern Borneo and the particular ways in which local minorities were administered are of special interest.

One significant consequence of the Anglo-Dutch rivalry in Borneo was that ultimately the island was divided into two separate colonial spheres of influence. The political boundaries that were agreed upon and drawn between the British-dominated north and the Dutch-administered south arbitrarily cut across the distribution of ethnic groups, and as a result, culturally and linguistically related populations found themselves in separate political units subject to different kinds or styles of European administration. However, the carving up of territories and the drawing of fixed lines on maps did not prevent the physical movements of local people across borders for the purposes of trade, warfare, and settlement.

For Britain, the northwest coasts of Borneo were of strategic importance to protect shipping along the great sea routes between India and China and between the Malay Peninsula, the Straits Settlements (especially Singapore), and the eastern Indonesian spice islands. The coastal Bornean trading settlements along these routes, which were under the sovereignty of the sultanates of Brunei and Sulu, also channeled valuable tropical forest products and marine resources into Asian commercial networks. In establishing control in northern Borneo, the British wanted to secure these northern coasts without being encumbered with an expensive civil administrative apparatus (Irwin 1967: 10). They were also engaged in combating coastal piracy and head-hunting, which were causing considerable problems for the safe and profitable conduct of trade. With great good fortune, the British were able to accomplish their strategic and commercial objectives by working through two surrogates rather than establishing a system of direct rule. In 1839, the English adventurer James Brooke (1803–1868) arrived at the Sarawak River and was subsequently installed as the governor of Sarawak (the "White Raja") by the sultan of Brunei. Over the next sixty years or so, Brooke and his successor and nephew, Charles Brooke (1829–1917), extended their domains at the expense of the weakened Brunei sultanate (Crisswell 1978). In northern and northeastern Borneo, what was to become the British North Borneo Company was ceded territory by the sultans of Brunei and Sulu, and in 1881, it was granted a royal charter to administer these regions (Black 1983: 30–79). The British granted Sarawak, North Borneo, and Brunei protectorate status in 1888, assuming responsibility for the three territories' external affairs but leaving internal government in the hands of the Brookes, the chartered company, and the sultan of Brunei in their respective domains.

Therefore, the local populations were administered by and through British "representatives." Over time, a distinction came to be drawn between the Muslim communities of northern Borneo, the majority of whom were designated by the term *Malay*, and the native non-Muslim communities, delineated by "tribal" or subgroup names, although commonly referred to by Europeans by the general referent *Dayak;* alternative forms are *Dyak, Daya,* and *Daya*. One important exception in this regard was the forest nomads, or hunter-gatherers of the interior rain forests, who were referred to either by their group names or by the separate cover term *Punan,* although they are related culturally to various neighboring Dayak farming communities (Rousseau 1990: 20). The coastal and riverine Malays were part of loosely organized states based on the control of trade, and leading members of Malay communities served as intermediaries between Europeans and Dayaks and were recruited as low-level administrators in colonial regimes. Nevertheless, prior to European intervention, the ethnic boundaries between the Malays and Dayaks were not sharply drawn. Many Malays traced their descent from local pagan peoples who had converted to Islam and over time had increasingly adopted Malay customs and language and "become Malay" (*masok Melayu,* meaning "to enter Malaydom") (King 1993: 30–34).

There is still much dispute about the derivation of the term *Dayak*. It was known by the Dutch as far back as the mid-eighteenth century and was used by them as a general term for inland or interior people (Pringle 1970: xviii). Yet it is likely that the term was coined by coastal Malays to refer pejoratively to the "less civilized" rural inhabitants of the upriver and hinterland regions of the island. Early on, the Brooke government in Sarawak confined the term *Dayak* to two major groups—the Sea Dayaks (who later came to be called Ibans) and the Land Dayaks (subsequently referred to as

Bidayuhs). At the time of the establishment of Brooke's rule (around the 1840s), the Ibans were expanding aggressively and rapidly eastward and northeastward into the territories that came to be known as Brooke Sarawak. In the company of Malays, the Ibans were engaged in coastal piracy from the Skrang and Saribas areas of the lower Batang Lupar basin. In search of fertile areas of virgin forest to occupy and then to clear, burn, and plant with rice and other crops, the Ibans were also involved in headhunting raids against those who stood in their way. In some cases, they took captives in war, and they formed alliances with, intermarried with, and ultimately assimilated with other native groups. By contrast, the Land Dayaks, living in the hilly, upriver regions of the Sarawak and Sadong River basins, were a much more settled and peaceable people and often the victims of Iban headhunters.

The term *Dayak* also embraces several other non-Muslim groups in Sarawak, including the Selako Dayaks of western Sarawak; the Kayans and Kenyahs of Central Borneo, traditional enemies of the Ibans, and several smaller neighboring groups, usually considered together as Kajangs (some of the coastal groups called Melanau and related to interior Kajangs have mainly embraced Islam); the Kelabits-Muruts of the easternmost parts of Sarawak (Muruts are now referred to as Lun Dayehs or Lun Bawangs); and the Berawans and several small related groups of the Baram River basin. In Sabah, most of the Dayak groups have close linguistic affinities with native populations of the Philippines. Significant numbers are known as Dusuns, apparently a coastal Malay–derived term to refer to farmers or "orchard" people. They comprise several named subgroups that reside along the northwest coasts of Sabah, including the Kadazan, Rungus, Ranau, and Tambunan, and on the east coasts, there are Islamized Dusuns referred to as Idahans. The other major population comprises Muruts, culturally different from the Murut of Sarawak, who are found in the lowlands from Keningau through the interior uplands and southward and eastward from there (King 1993: 36–57).

Despite the diversity and complexity of the ethnic category Dayak, some social, cultural, and ecological commonalities are relatively widespread and can be traced back to the settlement of the island by Austronesian speakers. There are similarities in worldview, cosmology, and symbolism; funeral practices and fertility cults, such as head-hunting and rice rituals; material culture; and kinship organization. Many but not all of the settled agriculturalists live in longhouses—large pile-houses on stilts accommodating several household or family units. Finally and with the exception of the forest nomads, their dominant mode of subsistence is the shifting cultivation of hill rice, supplemented by forest hunting, gathering, and fishing.

Although elements of Dayak traditional culture are still in evidence, these native populations have been subject to dramatic changes set in train by the colonial powers. However, it is well to remember that transformations such as the conversion to Islam, physical migrations, and environmental adaptations had taken place prior to European intervention and were to continue during it. One of the major changes introduced by the British regimes in the north was the elimination of head-taking, intervillage feuding, slavery, and human ritual sacrifice. Another was the incorporation of the scattered populations into a formal administration. Pacification was accomplished by the use of punitive expeditions (in Sarawak, for instance), often employing mercenaries drawn from among friendly Dayaks. Other methods included military patrols, fines, imprisonment, the conclusion of treaties, and the institution of intertribal peace-makings. Taxation systems were developed, population censuses organized, ethnic classifications formulated, land registered, and village headmen and regional chiefs employed as local representatives and administrators to ensure that law and order were maintained and taxes were collected. Traditional or customary law was gradually undermined.

Pacification and administrative incorporation were also accompanied by the expansion of Roman Catholic and Protestant Christian missions and the conversion of natives to Christianity, along with the introduction of Western schools and education, using English and Malay as the main languages of instruction. These changes quite naturally led to the elimination or at least the modification and adaptation of traditional pagan beliefs and practices. In addition, Europeans promoted the cash economy, with the gradual displacement of subsistence production along with the expansion of urban and market centers; they introduced cash crops such as rubber, coffee, cocoa, and pepper; developed a transport infrastructure; and encouraged the migration of Chinese to Borneo as miners, commercial farmers, traders, and shopkeepers. In Sarawak, the emphasis remained on smallholding cultivation, but under much more commercially minded chartered company rule in North Borneo, large-scale rubber and tobacco plantations using imported labor were established along the east coast. The colonial powers were also especially concerned about reducing the practice of shifting cultivation, which they considered wasteful of natural resources, and progressively restricting native migrations and promoting the permanent settlement of land.

With the transfer of sovereignty over Sarawak and North Borneo to the British Crown in 1946, followed by the political independence of British Borneo (with the exception of Brunei) within the wider Federation of Malaysia in 1963, the pace of change among the native peoples has, if anything, increased. Three of the most prominent transformations have been the founding of political parties and the involvement of Dayaks in modern political activity, the rapid development of education and the increasing contribution of Dayaks to the state bureaucracy and the market economy, and the accelerating displacement of traditional modes of livelihood by the widespread exploitation of the rain forests for commercial timber and the development of large-scale plantation agriculture (Avé and King 1986: 65–80, 103–117). Nevertheless, despite these changes, the sense of identity among the various Dayak groups remains strong, and with the growth of tourism and an increasing interest in Dayak culture both from within and beyond Dayak communities, there has been considerable innovation and adaptation of Dayak arts, crafts, performance, and rituals in the modern era.

VICTOR T. KING

See also *Adat;* Bajau; Borneo; British North Borneo Chartered Company (1881–1946); Brooke, Sir Charles Johnson (1829–1917); Brooke, James, and Sarawak; Brunei Ethnic Minorities; Brunei Malay; Dayaks; Iban; Jungle/Forest Products; Kadazan-Dusuns; Marine/Sea Products; Sarawak and Sabah (North Borneo)

References:

Avé, Jan B., and Victor T. King. 1986. *The People of the Weeping Forest: Tradition and Change in Borneo.* Leiden, The Netherlands: Rijksmuseum voor Volkenkunde.

Black, Ian. 1983. *A Gambling Style of Government: The Establishment of Chartered Company Rule in Sabah, 1878–1915.* Kuala Lumpur: Oxford University Press.

Crisswell, Colin N. 1978. *Rajah Charles Brooke: Monarch of All He Surveyed.* Kuala Lumpur: Oxford University Press.

Irwin, Graham. 1967 [1955]. *Nineteenth-Century Borneo: A Study in Diplomatic Rivalry.* Singapore: Donald Moore Books. First published in 1955 by Martinus Nijhoff, The Hague.

King, Victor T. 1993. *The Peoples of Borneo.* The Peoples of South-East Asia and the Pacific. Oxford and Cambridge, MA: Blackwell.

Pringle, Robert. 1970. *Rajahs and Rebels: The Ibans of Sarawak under Brooke Rule, 1841–1941.* London: Macmillan.

Rousseau, Jérôme. 1990. *Central Borneo: Ethnic Identity and Social Life in a Stratified Society.* Oxford: Clarendon Press.

ÉCOLE FRANÇAISE D'EXTRÊME-ORIENT, L'

On 15 December 1898, a decree signed by Paul Doumer (t. 1897–1902), Indochina's governor-general, founded the Archaeological Mission of Indochina. Then, on 20 January 1900, the mission took its present name of L'École Française d'Extrême-Orient (EFEO) in order to specify the role it was assigned in collecting, inventorying, and analyzing the archaeological and cultural data of Indochina. It did not take long, though, for this research organization to widen its exploratory activities to the neighboring civilizations of India, China, Japan, and insular Southeast Asia. However, installed in Hanoi since 1902 after a short stay in Saigon, it naturally favored studies of the country where it was established: practically half of the first eleven works published during the first years of the EFEO's existence related to Vietnam, be they on numismatics, on linguistics and philology, on history, or on archaeology.

A learned institution placed under the patronage of France's Académie des Inscriptions et Belles-Lettres, the EFEO had nonetheless been conceived as an appendage of the colonial system, which gave it life, and it was from the beginning confronted with the contradictions of its status and its vocation. Should its members be considered as scholars at the service of an administration to which they were to furnish the ruled peoples' secrets? Or should they be specialists devoted to applying European methods of investigation and analysis to exotic and unfamiliar subjects of study? In any case, the EFEO could not escape the political influences of its times. From 1907 to 1908, for instance, after having published in its *Bulletin* Phan Châu Trinh's (1871–1926) letter to the governor-general of Indochina requesting comprehensive reforms in Vietnamese society, the EFEO was called to order and to its initial vocation. Thereafter, it was careful to limit its researches to the fields least likely to harm the interests of the French authorities: social sciences were to be somehow ruled out for the benefit of archaeology, linguistics, textual criticism of ancient documents, history, and some cautiously conducted ethnology. These research fields have been thoroughly explored nevertheless, and the scope of the investigation is visible through the diverse published monographs and the very numerous and copious articles of the *Bulletin de l'École Française d'Extrême-Orient;* year after year, its issues (eighty-seven tomes to date) have supplied hundreds of printed pages of scholarly studies and reports. Determined to vie with the famous École d'Athènes and École de Rome, of which it is the Asiatic counterpart, the institution has been spreading its focal interest over the whole of Asia and has given to Orientalism many of its most distinguished names. Yet the public is more aware of the restorations it has carried out for the temples of Angkor in Cambodia and the Cham monuments in central Vietnam or the research it has conducted on the architecture of the site of Pagan in Burma, rather than the less perceptible in-depth processing of old texts and inscriptions accomplished by its members.

Departing from Hanoi in 1957 after the end of the First Indochina War (1946–1954), the EFEO has transferred its seat to Paris, at No. 22, Avenue du Président Wilson, where its library presently provides researchers on Asia with every facility. Its reorganization has led to the setting up of local centers at Pondichéry and Poona (India), Kuala Lumpur (Malaysia),

Jakarta (Indonesia), Bangkok and Chiang Mai (Thailand), Phnom Penh and Siem Reap (Cambodia), Vientiane (Laos), Hanoi (Vietnam), Beijing and Hong Kong (China), Taipei (Taiwan), and Kyoto and Tokyo (Japan), which attests to its physical presence at the foci of its activities.

NGUYỄN THẾ ANH

See also Buddhist Institute of Phnom Penh; Burma Research Society (1909); French Ambitions in Southeast Asia; French Indochina; Phan Châu Trinh (1871–1926); Sarawak Museum; Straits/Malayan/Malaysian Branch of the Royal Asiatic Society (MBRAS);Vietnam under French Colonial Rule

References:
Clementin-Ojha, Catherine, and Pierre-Yves Manguin. 2001. *Un siècle pour l'Asie: L'École Française d'Extrême-Orient, 1898–2000 [A Century for Asia:The French School of the Far East, 1898–2000]*. Paris: Les Éditions du Pacifique and EFEO.
Le Failler, Philippe, ed. 2000. *L'École Française d'Extrême-Orient à Hanoi, 1900–2000: Regards croisés sur un siècle de recherche [The French School of the Far East in Hanoi, 1900–2000: Intersecting Looks at a Century of Research]*. Hanoi: Nhà Xuât Ban Van Hóa Thông Tin.
Singaravelou, Pierre. 1999. *L'École Française d'Extrême-Orient ou l'institution des marges (1898–1956): Essai d'histoire sociale et politique de la science coloniale [The French School of the Far East or the Institution on the Sidelines (1898–1956): Essay on the Social and Political History of Colonial Science]*. Paris: L'Harmattan.

ECOLOGICAL SETTING OF SOUTHEAST ASIA

The ecological setting of Southeast Asia, its climate, relief, soils, and vegetation, has always been an important factor in the evolution of the landscapes, cultures, and peoples of the region. Its past and present cultural environment can be seen as a product of the interaction of human societies with their physical environment; that environment has played, and continues to play, an important role in shaping patterns of land and life. Human settlements; the patterns of farming, commerce, and trade; and the flow of goods, people, and ideas have reflected the diverse and complex interactions of physical ecology and human ingenuity. Any proper understanding of the history of the region must be rooted in an appreciation of its ecological character.

Much of the physical character of the region can be attributed to the effects of the geological structure on relief, orientation, and drainage patterns. Recent research into plate tectonics has shown that the region consists of a zone formed by the Eurasian plate to the north that is bounded by a series of deep-sea trenches where the Australian, Pacific, and Philippine plates to the south are submerged or subducted under the Eurasian plate. Along the line of that subduction is a broad arc of intense tectonic activity characterized by volcanoes and earthquakes produced by strong plate movement. Recent research has been focused on identifying both the rate of movement and the likely locations for the intense tectonic activity that might result. The relatively stable Sunda Shelf, on top of the Eurasian plate, forms a broad continental shelf in the region. Structurally then, the region is characterized by an older, relatively stable, and heavily weathered mountain range in the north; a wide, relatively shallow continental shelf fronting the coastline; and a tectonically active, relatively young set of landform assemblages running through the island region (see Map 1).

This physical structure is particularly important in understanding the broad character of mountain, valley, and coast in the region. The older mountain ranges in Indochina and Burma (Myanmar) constitute outliers of the great Himalayan massif and, historically, provided something of a barrier to the southward movement of peoples and goods. In terms of mineral wealth, the longer period of denudation in these uplands has sometimes exposed deep-seated ore deposits in regions such as Perak in northern Malaya, where tin deposits have been significant. By contrast, the more recent Tertiary deposits of the tectonic arc have proved less rich in minerals, with the exception of hydrocarbons. From the older mountain ranges to the north, major rivers flow southward—the Irrawaddy, Sittang, Salween, Mekong, and Song Koi (Red River)—bringing with them large quantities of eroded material and creating important valley and estuarine sites for farming and settlement.

The Sunda Shelf has been an important structural element in the human and physical geography of both the mainland and island Southeast Asia. During the Quaternary (from about 2 million to some 15,000 years ago), lower sea levels meant that much of the Sunda Shelf was above sea level. That had two important consequences. First, mainland and insular Southeast Asia would have been connected by a variety of land bridges, thereby facilitating flows of plants and animals through the region. Second, the relatively recent flooding of the coastal area has led to the drowning of river mouths and estuaries, with the consequent deposition of huge quantities of silt in those estuaries as rivers have adjusted to their changing base levels. That has produced ideal conditions for wet-rice farming in valley and estuary, and extensive low-lying areas of swamp and mangrove along the shallow shores of eastern Sumatra and western and southern Borneo. Rising sea levels in the contemporary period are likely to accentuate such characteristics.

The importance of the arc of tectonic activity running through the region is hard to overestimate. Along that arc, running through Sumatra, Java, the Outer Islands of Indonesia, and the Philippines, the danger of volcanic eruptions (from Krakatoa in 1883 to Mt. Pinatubo in 1990) and of earthquakes is ever-present, and human settlement has had to cope with the consequences of living in a tectonic shatter-belt. Equally, however, the predominance of geologically younger, less weathered acidic rocks there can produce astonishingly fertile soil conditions for intensive rice farming. Along with the estuaries of the great rivers to the north, the young soils of parts of Java and Bali, for example, produce prodigious yields of rice, and can support very high population densities. Elsewhere in the region, however, soils remain relatively poor, despite the apparent richness of the vegetation. This apparent paradox of lush vegetation coupled with poor soils can be explained in a number of ways. First, most of the nutrients in these tropical ecosystems are concentrated in the plant biomass above the ground, rather than in the soil. Thus the canopies of the tropical forest store large quantities of nutrients that tend to be recycled within the plant mass, rather than through decomposition on the forest floor. Biomass and nutrients that do become part of the soil are, in

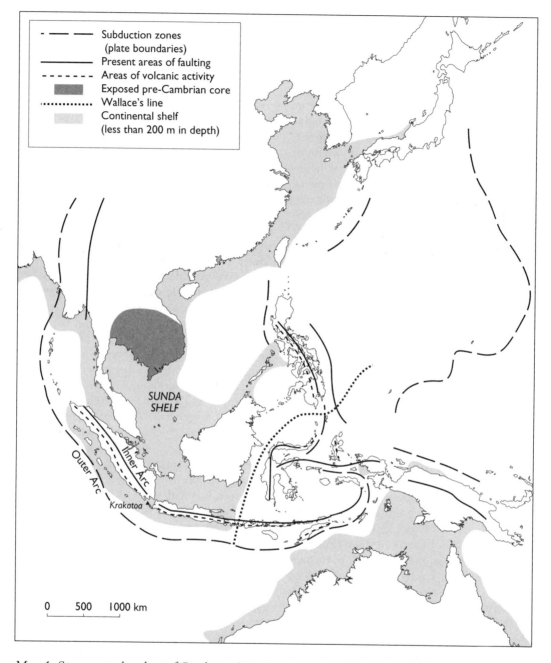

Legend:

- – – –   Subduction zones (plate boundaries)
- ———   Present areas of faulting
- - - - -   Areas of volcanic activity
- ■   Exposed pre-Cambrian core
- ·······   Wallace's line
- ░   Continental shelf (less than 200 m in depth)

SUNDA SHELF

Outer Arc

Inner Arc

Krakatoa

0   500   1000 km

Map 1. Structure and geology of Southeast Asia. Southeast Asia: A Region in Transition. *(Adapted by permission from Rigg, Jonathan, ed. 1991. London: Unwin Hyman, p. 4)*

any case, recycled very quickly because of the rapid rate of physical and chemical composition in the tropical climate. Second, high rates of rainfall, coupled with rapid chemical activity, can quickly leach minerals and nutrients out of the soil. This leaching impoverishes many tropical soils and can lead to a laterite layer in the soil horizon that makes cultivation very difficult. Failure to recognize the essential poverty of many soil types in the region can lead to overexploitation of what are essentially fragile soils.

The region has some of the richest and most diverse ecosystems in the world. Most of the great Indo-Malayan tropical rain forest formations are to be found in a region extending from northern Burma to the Outer Islands of Indonesia. These rain forests have attracted travelers, scientists, and settlers over many hundreds of years and provide a majestic setting. For the geographer Charles Ficher (1964: 42–43), the forest, "with its gigantic soaring trees and its wealth of shrubs and smaller plants is renowned for its remarkable stillness, broken only by the occasional chatter of monkeys and the sudden swish of a snake. . . . The buzzing of myriads of insects, the trilling of cicadas and the hideous croaking of frogs." There is a huge variety of flora and fauna in the rain forest, and the formations of the region are diverse. With increasing elevation, one can trace a shift from the mangrove formations in the flooded lowlands to the tropical lowland evergreen formations and semievergreen formations in the higher elevations.

For all its geographic and ecological diversity, the rain forest shares a number of common features that divide it from surrounding biogeographical zones. Thus, as Alfred Russel Wallace (1823–1913) argued more than a century ago, a floral and faunal division between Southeast Asia and Australia can be identified reflecting the broad tectonic lineaments of the region. Species diversity is the rule—a conservative estimate suggests at least 50,000 different plant species. Many more remain to be discovered, and this diversity is likely to provide an important gene pool for future biotechnological innovations. In their natural state, rain forests provide a stable, carefully balanced ecosystem that is often structured vertically into a series of distinctive ecological layers between forest floor and upper canopy. That diversity of ecological niches provides a wealth of flora and fauna, and has historically provided a vital resource, producing jungle products such as camphor, resins, and rattans as well as internationally traded timber products. That trade can be traced back to the earliest societies in the region.

For human settlement then, the forest has long offered huge potential. Indigenous peoples exploited the hunting and collecting possibilities of the forest. Shifting cultivators cleared through slash and burn, before moving on to other parts of the forest in order to allow the ecosystem some time for recovery. Such systems of cultivation, the mainstay for at least 15 percent of the population well into the late twentieth century, have now become increasingly vulnerable with population growth and the loss of indigenous lands to logging. Thus modern exploitation has focused on logging and clearing, with transnational corporations seeking out the especially valuable hardwoods—the *dipterocarps,* which are most in demand on the international timber market. The growth of population and increased intensity of shifting cultivation has resulted in extensive growths of secondary forest, or *belukar,* a degraded form of the original cover, while overburning has in some areas led to a savanna-type vegetation of *lalang,* which is difficult to cultivate. Today, the rain forests provide the arena for major conflicts between economic development and environmental protection, particularly in areas such as Borneo and Sumatra.

The region lies within the humid tropics and, while sharing in broad terms a climate that is hot, wet, and humid, does nevertheless show considerable geographic variations that are a function of both latitude and elevation. Temperatures are generally high, with annual averages of around 27–30° C and relatively little annual variation. Such variations as exist for both daily and annual temperature can be attributed largely to temperature changes with elevation. Rainfall provides the main climatic variant in the region. While few parts of the region receive less than around 1,500–2,000 mm of rain, there are important regional variations in the annual distribution of that total. Within about 10 degrees of the equator, rainfall is relatively evenly distributed through the year. Singapore, for example, does not have a marked wet or dry season but rather has only slight variations around a monthly mean.

However, as one moves away from the equator, seasonality of rainfall increases, primarily as a consequence of the monsoon regime. Thus the northeast monsoon that dominates from December to March forms the wet season in much of island Southeast Asia, while the southwest monsoon from July to September brings drier conditions. On the mainland, as one moves from the equator, rainfall can be slightly lower and more seasonally pronounced, and the effects of the monsoon on rainfall are reversed. The northeast monsoon brings drier air to

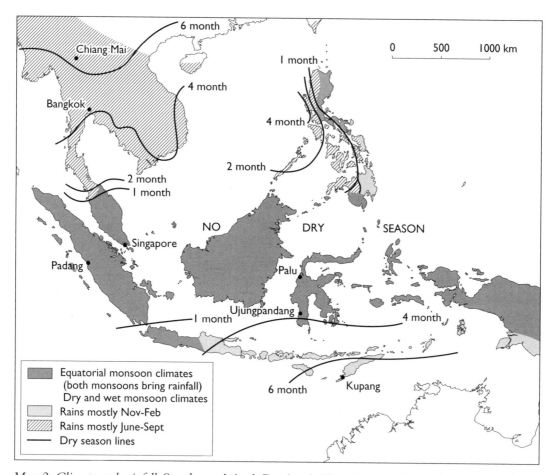

Map 2. Climate and rainfall. Southeast Asia: A Region in Transition. *(Adapted by permission from Rigg, Jonathan, ed. 1991. London: Unwin Hyman, p. 7)*

Thailand and Vietnam, and the southwest monsoon brings wetter conditions. With distance from the equator, variation in the climatic regime increases, the monsoon becomes more pronounced, and the length of the dry season increases (see Map 2).

From the point of view of human settlement and exploitation, it is seasonality and the variability of rainfall, rather than absolute totals, that are most important. Rainfall variability can have a major impact on rice cultivation systems. Rice varieties and cultivation techniques have traditionally been carefully adjusted to the climatic regime. Thus hill rice can prosper in regions where a marked dry season is evident, while irrigated rice systems, often producing very high yields, require a more even annual rainfall regime. The development of new varieties and techniques, often the product of the "green revolution" of the last few decades, has tended to accentuate, rather than reduce, the importance of such basic physical constraints.

In addition to influencing rainfall variability, the monsoon winds have an important effect on maritime communication. Generally, the seas of the region are warm, shallow, and easily navigable. The shallow continental shelf, only flooded since the Pleistocene, provides a long, indented, and navigable coastline in the region. Typhoons are locally significant—the Philippines and the Vietnamese coast are periodically subject to these storms—but their effect is fortunately localized. In the era of sail, the monsoon winds played an important part in determining sea travel, especially at the continental scale. The southwest monsoon tended to blow shipping away from the Straits of Melaka and Sunda Straits toward India and China, while the northwest monsoon blew shipping back to the Straits region. Historically, then, ships plying the Middle East–India–China routes would be forced to anchor somewhere in these "lands below the winds" to wait for the monsoon to "turn." Ports such as Melaka, Singapore, Palembang, and Batavia grew up largely to service this trade.

Ecological characteristics undoubtedly provide both constraints and advantages for the development of the region. Certainly the nature of the climatic regime does pose problems for human settlement and growth. While the direct effects on human health of a regime of high humidity, temperatures, and rainfall have perhaps been exaggerated, indirect effects are potentially severe. Climate and physical conditions create distinctive patterns of disease that, historically at least, have created difficult living conditions. Malaria thrives in many of the waterlogged coastal and swamp areas, as well as in the hill country of the mainland. Human settlement, drainage, and the use of spraying have dramatically reduced its incidence, but new and resistant strains continue to emerge as resistance to antibiotics grows. Equally important in terms of the geography of health is the incidence of diseases such as cholera and typhus. The former, in particular, can emerge in very sudden flare-ups and is especially significant in areas where irrigation, drainage, and sewage are under pressure.

In general, though, it would be difficult to argue that the ecology of the region has been a barrier to development and growth. Clearly the evidence of the tremendous historical achievements of the region argue against too deterministic a view of climatic and physical constraints. Thus while such conditions may have constrained development in some areas (some of the coastal mangrove areas, for example, have proved resistant to development), in general, physical conditions have been beneficial to development. The combination of fertile acidic soils, accented slope, and human skills has produced some of the most sophisticated and productive wet-rice systems, in regions such as Java and Bali; in the deltaic regions of the Red River, Irrawaddy, and Mekong, similar skills have harnessed the river waters and silts to produce highly sophisticated farming systems. Likewise, the sheer wealth and diversity of the rain forest environment have provided major opportunities for well-developed farming groups to evolve complex and sustainable farming systems based on shifting cultivation, communal farming, and involvement in trade in rain forest products.

The physical layout of the region has been a contributory factor to its growth and development. The importance of the sea cannot be overestimated. Maritime communication was fundamental to the power of both mainland and island Southeast Asia. The growth of a farming-fishing culture, the local and long-distance trade, and the flow of goods, ideas, capital, and peoples into the region were enhanced by the enormous area of coastline. The region has a longer coastline, area for area, than any other part of the world of comparable size, with most of the best agricultural land located within some 200 kilometers of tidal waters. That fact alone goes some way toward explaining the huge importance of the sea in the human and physical geography of the region. The ecological setting has also shaped the nature of external penetration into the region. The mountain barrier to the north, a barrier dividing China from the Indian Ocean, has been important both in shaping Chinese interest in Burma as a link to that ocean and in the encouragement that land barrier gave to Chinese maritime trade through the Straits of Melaka. It was through the sea-lanes of the region that precolonial empires such as those of Śrivijaya and Melaka were established. Power was measured in maritime rather than territorial control. Equally, European colonialism was channeled, in the early stages at least, through sea-lanes and maritime conquest rather than in outright territorial conquest.

Ecology then provides a framework, a set of constraints and possibilities, that has shaped many aspects of the history and human geography of Southeast Asia. The tectonic structure and geology have created important physical environments for human exploitation. The patterns of human settlement and exploitation of the "old" uplands of Indochina or the new, volcanically active lands of Java and Bali reflect both physical constraints and human ingenuity.

Equally, patterns of vegetation and soils have been important in the evolution of farming systems, patterns of settlement, and the evolution of intraregional and international trade. Finally climate has been important through its impact on developments in farming, settlement, trade, and, not least, disease pathologies. While the advances of modern technology have perhaps mitigated some of the more damaging aspects of the physical environment of the region, they have involved economic and social costs. Contemporary societies, no less than those in the past, are shaped in many ways by the ecological framework within which they have originated, flourished, and, ultimately, declined.

MARK CLEARY

See also Diseases and Epidemics; Historical Geography of Insular Southeast Asia; Historical Geography of Mainland Southeast Asia; Human Prehistory of Southeast Asia; Jungle/Forest Products; Marine/Sea Products; Monsoons; Straits of Melaka; Swidden Agriculture; Wallace Line

References:

Ficher, C. A. 1964. *South-East Asia: A Social, Economic and Political Geography.* London: Methuen.

King, V. T., ed. 1998. *Environmental Challenges in South-East Asia.* London: Curzon.

Rigg, Jonathan. 1991. *Southeast Asia: A Region in Transition.* London: Unwin Hyman.

Spencer, J. E. 1976. *Asia: East by South—A Cultural Geography.* New York: John Wiley.

Whitmore, T. C. 1990. *Tropical Rain Forests of the Far East.* Oxford: Clarendon.

———. 1998. *An Introduction to Tropical Rain Forests.* Oxford: Oxford University Press.

ECONOMIC DEVELOPMENT OF SOUTHEAST ASIA (POST-1945 TO EARLY 2000s)
Introduction: Enclaved Beginnings

A half-century ago, there were many theories concerned with how economic development of poor countries such as those in Southeast Asia should best proceed. These countries depended on agriculture for subsistence, and commodity exports were the only means for foreign-exchange earnings. Experts then believed that a whole new set of economic models and policies, very different from those in Western market economies, would be needed for the development of poor countries. Over the years, the various countries in Southeast Asia have followed different paths toward development, and with different results. Today, in contrast, economic policy prescriptions have become more uniform, regardless of country. Managing the economy well is now the same everywhere—that is, through higher levels of efficiency as dictated by market forces. This means prudent monetary as well as fiscal policies, coupled with increased liberalization that will pave the way toward tapping the world's markets to drive growth even further.

Of the countries in Southeast Asia, some are still being referred to as "mango republics"; five—Indonesia, Malaysia, the Philippines, Singapore, and Thailand—formed the regional economic alliance, the Association of Southeast Asian Nations (ASEAN), in 1967. These countries, which include a couple of "mini-tigers," have gained ground, albeit at different rates, over three of their neighbors. In Vietnam, the war has been over for nearly thirty years, and although it proclaimed itself a socialist republic in 1976, like China it has begun to tap into globalization for its growth. Cambodia, Myanmar (Burma prior to 1989), and Laos, on the other hand, choose instead to look inward, preferring to shield themselves from external interference, although funds from foreign sources essential for financing growth would be welcomed if under acceptable terms.

The most unusual case in Southeast Asia is perhaps Brunei, which is among the last bastions of absolute monarchy in the world. Citizens and residents of Brunei pay no taxes, and all public expenditures, whether social services or infrastructure, are at the pleasure of the sultan. Revenue in relation to the size of his highness's kingdom is plentiful, because of the rich oil resources that make it possible for the Brunei dollar to be pegged, one to one, with Singapore's dollar. Brunei became a member of ASEAN in 1984.

Southeast Asian countries once formed enclaves of Western domination even when they were never or no longer colonies. However, education, technology, information, source of financing, and the ability to do cross-border business deals all went through revolutionary changes during recent decades. As a result, Western and Eastern—or for that matter

Northern and Southern—interactions were forced to evolve and produced a world that is increasingly seamless in both time and space, leaving behind only the last remnants of archaic barriers that divide peoples despite common goals of better living standards and a safer environment. Once countries interacted one to one; the big dominated the small. Today the interaction is among many of varying sizes, possessing special core competencies that have the capability of offering a wide variety of niched products and services.

Postwar Reconstruction

Immediately after the Pacific War in 1945, Southeast Asia reverted to its status before the Japanese military occupation in 1941: Indochina returned to the French and Malaya and Singapore to Britain. The Philippines, which was increasingly granted self-government by the United States, became fully independent in 1946. Burma was a province of India until 1937, when it was given self-rule as a Crown colony, but after the Japanese withdrawal the country was liberated and proclaimed independence in 1948, as Indonesia did. Thailand, which had never been colonized, was again free.

However, political liberation was a far cry from economic independence, because integral to postwar reconstruction are the continuing presence and therefore influence of former colonial powers. In Indonesia, the Dutch, with superior wealth and education, controlled the economy. Indian investors continued to dominate the Burmese economy, as French investors did in Indochina. Economic presence by Americans continued in the Philippines. In Malaya and Singapore, British rule had been well entrenched without the visible uprising found among its neighbors, and thus political liberalization, despite the existence of local nationalistic ideologies, remains unlikely for an indefinite period. Thailand too was an open field for foreign investments.

Although foreign funds bore the bulk of postwar reconstruction in Southeast Asia, the intention was not to restructure the respective economies such that they could evolve along a path of development similar to those experienced by their colonial powers. Instead, the thinking then was that Southeast Asia could continue splendidly as a source of raw and semiprocessed materials. Industrialization, a key component of economic growth in the West, was thought unwise, because it would be best left to locations on the globe that have an abundance of bituminous coal, which is of insufficient supply in Southeast Asia. Furthermore, in largely agrarian subsistence societies there would be little demand in the local market for manufactured goods. Trade should thus be on the basis of comparative advantage—the West exporting manufactured goods and the East exporting commodities, since this is how the appropriate skills happen to be divided.

Technological Shifts

In retrospect, the experts erred when they decided on the thrust of postwar development in Southeast Asia. It was labor, not coal, that determined where manufacturing would be best located, and the size of the local market became irrelevant, because the only market is the entire globe (see Alonso 1975). Timing made all the difference in which country would succeed and which was passed over. The 1970s marked the beginning of large-scale production of integrated circuits, which at the time was highly labor intensive. Unlike other manufactures, electronics was light enough to exploit the age of intercontinental commercial transport by jet. It became possible to ship input components into Southeast Asia and return the assembled product to the markets of the world. Such shipment costs were lower than the difference in wage costs between production carried out within advanced countries and in the cheap labor markets in the East. The choice locations in Southeast Asia were the ASEAN countries, where foreign investors were enticed by further widening the cost savings through tax incentive packages.

This concept spawned the product life-cycle theory of trade. Before, countries in Southeast Asia were made to focus on commodity production because that was their comparative advantage. Later on, Linder's theory suggested that even if manufacturing were to be adopted as a natural sequence to economic development, on the basis of product quality, the only hope for exporting manufactures would be to countries at an even lower stage of development. Experts again erred. As it turned out, high-volume production in the attempt to reduce unit costs would require standardized production processes. Once that had taken place, the cheap labor markets gained the advantage, forcing high-tech goods to transfer their production to the less developed East. To remain in business, the North, from which these high-tech goods first originated, had to bring forth via research and development (R&D) activities yet another generation of high-tech goods that would eventually also transfer their production to the East. This iterative process considerably shortens product life cycles—that is, the time elapsed from invention and prototyping to full-scale production.

Countries in the East, for a long time the choice location for foreign direct investments (FDIs), became the world's major exporters of manufactured goods. During trade talks, the West wants intellectual properties protected so that investments in R&D do not merely end up profiting producers in the East (Speiss 2002). Nonetheless, before the issue is likely to be amicably solved the Internet will set forth yet another revolution in global production, as air transport and electronics did during the early 1970s. Broadband global communications would completely remove the isolation of any part of the world. While multilateral debates go on heatedly, the global village has more and more become reality. Somewhere in the world a keyboard is punched to invoke an order. The computer scans stock levels among different production locations across the world and existing inventory that will set prices minute by minute. Automated warehouses transfer the ordered items to the shipping floor. Planes take off and land, and bookkeeping entries take place to reflect the amount of funds transferred as payment. Economic textbooks talk about the perfectly competitive market of total knowledge and zero distance between seller and buyer. What is described is nearing that utopia in our real world.

Open Economies

Most Southeast Asian economies are very open economies. ASEAN member countries aggressively exploited the benefits of global trade, and for their efforts those economies enjoyed phenomenal economic expansion at rates well beyond what would have been achieved if growth were dependent only on domestic markets. To achieve this, however, many priorities in the domestic agenda have to be set aside, in preference to competition policy that is demanded in the more borderless world. As a result, exports and imports make up a substantial portion of the countries' gross domestic product (GDP) (see Basu et al. 2003; Davidson 2002; Hakim 2002).

Almost overnight, these countries were able to wean themselves out of their dependence on commodity exports to become major producers of manufactured goods and components. Producing for the world's markets means not only going high-tech but also doing so at low unit prices at huge production volumes. FDIs made this possible. However, contrary to widespread apprehensions during the sixties and seventies, FDIs turned out not to be postcolonial manufacturing versions of enclaves formed by foreign ownership of local plantations and mines, which occurred during colonial times. Instead, there is much evidence of closed business partnerships formed between foreign investors with domestic enterprises.

The opening-up of ASEAN economies was the result of export-oriented industrialization during the early 1970s. The more typical import-substitution industrialization adopted by developing countries was, however, not replaced. Instead, these economies practiced a dual regime system that enabled selected industries to undertake free trade alongside protectionism in other production sectors. Although import duties help keep local industries viable, they do not encourage global competitiveness. Therefore in the attempt to further foster trade, as well as to boost the scope and volume of interregional trade, ASEAN members have begun scheduling the abolishment and reduction of tariffs across a broad range of traded items among themselves under the ASEAN Free Trade Agreement (AFTA).

Closed Economies

ASEAN members saw the potential for growth that trade might bring even though they saw each other more as keen competitors than as strategic partners. Nevertheless, the need to compete likely made these countries more resilient than they would have otherwise been. Forty to fifty years afterward, the original ASEAN member countries are in stark contrast to the remaining countries of Southeast Asia. Population growth rates did not vary much among these countries, but over the course of development, income levels have deviated among them. Myanmar (formerly Burma) had long been under the rule of generals. While its open economy counterparts in Southeast Asia struggled with financial reforms and liberalization in order to further integrate into the global economy, Myanmar remained on guard against foreign imperialists thought to have the intention of destabilizing and then toppling its government. Three or four decades ago, such a call might have gained popular attention. Today, however, the thinking has changed.

Across the buffer that Thailand provides, Vietnam, Laos, and Kampuchea did not see an end to wars until at least a couple of decades later than the rest of Southeast Asia. Vietnam began mending the wounds of war after U.S. military withdrawal in 1973. Although tightly controlled by their communist government, the Vietnamese are highly entrepreneurial. Unfortunately, Vietnam was not as timely in catching the first waves of foreign investment during the 1970s as the founding members of ASEAN. Then again, timing may not have been as critical an issue when compared with the bureaucratic backlog caused by the maze of regulations to maneuver before business could be legitimately carried out. Vietnam was admitted into ASEAN in 1995.

In Kampuchea a fifth of the population lost their lives under the reign of the Khmer Rouge from 1975 until after its invasion by Vietnam in 1978. The United Nations sponsored elections in 1993 and again in 1998 that produced a fragile coalition government. Laos, like Myanmar, remains under the military, which controls the single party that makes up the government. Kampuchea, along with Laos, has attempted economic reforms to heighten business confidence and attract foreign investments. Faced with the current economic downturn, investment funds are sorely needed. However, just as important political reforms remain overlooked. Inspired by Vietnam's entry into ASEAN, the three remaining countries in Southeast Asia applied for admission in 1996. Myanmar and Laos gained membership the following year, but Kampuchea was finally admitted only in 1999. ASEAN stands to become the unifying factor that will bring all of Southeast Asia together into a caucus that will not only provide regional stability but also boost trade.

Market Integration

Although countries in Southeast Asia started out in much the same ways as did their developing country counterparts in most parts of Africa, the success in Southeast Asia of global trade has made the critical difference. Opening up the economy causes the ratio of trade to the gross national product to expand and helps drive economic growth, which averaged 5 percent per annum during the early nineties. In contrast, much of Africa has remained as impoverished as it was a half-century ago in absolute terms, worse still in relative terms compared with the technologically advancing world.

The original ASEAN members plus Brunei began the Asian Free Trade Agreement (AFTA) initiative in 1992, aimed at creating a free trade area among them by 2003. A common effective preferential tariff or CEPT scheme was introduced that would systematically reduce intra-ASEAN tariffs and abolish them altogether by 2010. With the introduction of Vietnam, Myanmar, Kampuchea, and Laos as members of ASEAN, their participation in AFTA means an intra–Southeast Asian market that contains a half-billion population.

Tariff reductions, aimed to boost trade, are but a means to market integration. Accompanying the CEPT scheme are other initiatives such as the ASEAN Investment Area, the ASEAN Industrial Cooperation, and the ASEAN Customs Initiatives that would foster industrial production linkages among manufacturers more seamlessly across Southeast Asia. For example, when these are fully implemented, a Thai manufacturer located in the Philippines would enjoy all the privileges of a local Filipino. The same would be true for any Southeast Asian national located anywhere in Southeast Asia.

In the meantime, talks are under way for an AFTA + 3 scheme that includes China, Korea, and Japan and will eventually extend to cover India—that is, eventually a total market size in excess of three billion people, the largest market in the world.

Funding Development

FDIs spared Southeast Asian countries a major portion of the badly needed development funding. Compared with Latin America, the external debt is thus much smaller, especially when the debt burden is considered in proportion to export revenues, the latter being the chief source of foreign exchange earnings useful for servicing the debt. This relatively lower debt position turned out to be quite useful: when the East Asian financial crisis, which has since extended into the current recession, occurred in 1997, it became possible for these countries to widen their external debts for funding economic recovery programs without seriously affecting their debt servicing capabilities.

The more remarkable development, however, is that Southeast Asian countries were able to develop domestic capital markets fairly successfully. The types of debt securities that are traded remain few, but those that do remain have received strong support by local private investors. These fledgling financial markets manage to attract short-term foreign capital as well. This means that economic growth is driven not entirely by public fiscal spending, but also by the expansion in commerce and industries funded by capital markets.

The subject of interest among economists is the question of how much economic growth can be mustered by making investments. One special feature of the rapid pace of growth experienced in much of Southeast Asia has been the very high rate of investments funded not only via FDIs but also through, by world standards, a massive amount of domestic savings. In Latin America capital inflows have tended to boost consumption, and growth has therefore been led mainly by capital. Up to a point, economic growth could easily be achieved by the injection of investment funds. But economies like those of Indonesia, Malaysia, Singapore, and Thailand are already investing some three- to four-tenths of their gross national products (GNP), such amounts being nearly twice the rate in most countries. Milking more growth in the future becomes increasingly difficult because it will require that citizens set aside an even greater portion of their income to raise even more investment funds.

The Workforce

The labor resource remains in good supply in Southeast Asia; it does not suffer from the aging population structure affecting most advanced economies. About half of the population in nearly all Southeast Asian countries are below the age of 25. Typical of emerging societies, labor is less organized. International organizations such as Amnesty International and the International Labor Organization (ILO) attempt to keep a keen watch over labor practices and working conditions, seeking ways to enforce labor standards through trade rules. However, until recent years, exports have been quickly expanding in most of Southeast Asia, resulting in full employment conditions. Competition for labor allowed Asian workers to be relatively well taken care of. Before long, however, wage pressures began to erode away the cost advantage that made Southeast Asia the choice industrial location. To remain competitive against alternative production sites worldwide, skills and labor productivity have to rise in relation to wage costs. That is why Southeast Asian countries put heavy emphasis on education in their development budgets, hoping to develop greater competence in the workforce. But in reality the task of human development is formidable because of the large numbers in the school-age population.

Competitiveness

Political stability is perhaps among the most important attributes that help Southeast Asia become a choice investment location for FDIs (Borner et al. 1995). The electorate in Singapore and Malaysia has returned the same political party to government throughout their postindependence histories. Thailand, on the other hand, has never been colonized. There were frequent shifts at the reins alternating between influential businessmen and army generals, but Thailand has always been politically stable. Thais are steadfastly loyal to their king, who becomes a powerful moderating force during political conflicts. In the Philippines, where there is a two-term limit to the presidency, the people continue to experience peaceful transitions of power through the exercise of their constitutional rights since the 1980s. Vietnam, on the other hand, remains tightly controlled as a socialist society. In the rest of Southeast Asia, the military has played a dominant role in the political structure and thus leaves very little behind by way of political discourse and the exercise of democratic rights. Indonesia has become the exception, as a new political leadership without ties to the military has finally come into existence.

One weakness of too much stability, however, is that governments become too powerful, leading to questionable policies and lack of transparency. The extent to which that is true depends on the degree of openness of the economies concerned, because if investor confidence is to be earned, regulations, policies governing money supply and the banking system, and other relevant controls must harness market forces, not stifle them. Southeast Asian economies, being very open, have had to be relatively free in the context of having policies that embrace the market. The relative success of these countries may be judged by scores given by independent assessors, such as those published by the World Economic Forum (WEF) and by the International Institute of Management Development (IMD) as follows:

	WEF	IMD
Singapore	1	2
Hong Kong	2	3
United States	3	1
Taiwan	9	18
Malaysia	10	23
Japan	13	4
Thailand	14	30
Britain	15	19
Germany	22	10

SOURCE: *The Economist,* 1 June 1996.

The WEF score depends on the ability of the country to achieve sustained high rates of growth, compared against the IMD's definition of competitiveness, which rates the country's ability to increase wealth by managing production factors integrated into an economic and social model.

Agricultural Production and Food Security

The inability to modernize the agricultural sector is a major failure among Southeast Asian countries. It may not be for lack of trying, but rather because of the large peasant population, distorted agricultural pricing, and shrinking land availability resulting from competing land uses. The greatest impact, however, was social mobility, involving the transition out of agriculture over the course of development. As a result, although the number of rural poor declined, living standards among them did not improve as much as for those who switched to other sectors of the economy. Policies aimed at retaining agricultural population while modernizing and significantly improving their living standards would have been better at keeping agriculture viable and ensuring better food security in the future.

Prospects and Conclusions

During the last half-century, Southeast Asia has emerged from its dismal past under foreign dominance to become a viable economic player within the international division of labor in the age of globalization. Singapore, for instance, is by per capita income standards well past the level that marks a developed nation. But at the close of the twentieth century, the age of miraculous growth appeared to be nearing its end for Southeast Asian economies as growth rates plummeted. For decades, Southeast Asia had been the recipient of the bulk of foreign investments. By the 1990s, four-fifths of the investment capital, along with the latest technologies, had instead gone to the People's Republic of China (PRC), leaving the remainder to be shared by the countries of Southeast Asia. This development would not have been as critical had Southeast Asia embraced its golden age of economic expansion with a little more emphasis on building up technocratic skills and with more robust capital markets. It would have had at least a couple of decades of a head start.

The time for yet another transition has come, because Southeast Asian countries can no longer continue to compete on the basis of cheap labor and resources. Instead they need to move up to become a global supplier that bridges the technology gap between the advanced North and those new entrants that have now joined the global production market. A half-century of growth in Southeast Asia has mostly been a disarray of strategies, policies, and priorities among its various countries. Today there is a refreshing hope that ideas and mind-sets will converge through the tested forum of ASEAN, whose membership list is now complete for all of Southeast Asia.

CHAN HUAN CHIANG

See also Association of Southeast Asian Nations (ASEAN) (1967); Banks and Banking; Brunei Oil and Gas Industry; Buddhist Socialism; Democratic Kampuchea (DK); Guided Democracy (*Demokrasi Terpimpin*); Lao People's Democratic Republic (LPDR); Laos (Nineteenth Century to mid-1990s); Martial Law (1972–1981) (The Philippines); New Economic Policy (NEP) (1971–1990); New Economic Zones (NEZs) (Vietnam); *Orde Baru* (The New Order); Singapore, Entrepôt Trade and Commerce of (Nineteenth Century to 1990s); State Law and Order Restoration Council (SLORC); Taxation; Trade and Commerce of Southeast Asia (ca. Nineteenth Century to the 1990s)

References:

Agenor, Richard, and Peter Montiel. 1996. *Development Economics*. Princeton: Princeton University Press.

Alonso, William. 1975. "Location Theory." Pp. 64–96 in *Regional Policy: Readings in Theory and Application*. Edited by John Friedman and William Alonso. Cambridge, MA, and London: MIT Press.

Andrus, J. Russel. 1946. *Basic Problems of Relief Rehabilitation and Reconstruction in South-East Asia*. Oxford: Oxford University Press.

Asian Development Bank. 1971. *Southeast Asia's Economy in the 1970s*. London: Longman.

Basu, Parantap, Chandra Chakraborthy, and Derrick Reagle. 2003. "Liberalization, FDI, Growth in Developing Countries: A Panel Cointegration Approach." *Economic Inquiry* 41, no. 3: 510–516.

Borner, Silvio, Aymo Brunetti, and Beatrice Weder. 1995. *Political Credibility and Economic Developement*. London: Macmillan.

Davidson, Paul. 2002. "Globalization." *Journal of Post-Keynesian Economics* 24, no. 3: 475–492.

The Economist. Various issues.

Gylfason, Thorvaldur. 2001. "Nature, Power and Growth." *Scottish Journal of Political Science* 48, no. 5: 558–588.

Hakim, Peter. 2002. "Two Ways to Go Global." *Foreign Affairs* 81, no. 1: 148–162.

Li, Rex. 1999. "The China Challenge: Theoretical Perspectives and Policy Implications." *Journal of Contemporary China* 8, no. 22: 443–476.

Mittelman, James H. 2000. "Globalization, Captors and Captive." *Third World Quarterly* 21, no. 6: 917–929.

Rosewarne, Stuart. 1998. "The Globalization and Liberalization of Asian Labor Markets." *World Economy* 21, no. 7: 963–978.

Speiss, Thomas J., III. 2002. "Sellers Proceed with Caution: The Far East Response to Western Concept of 'Intellectual Property Rights.'" *Orange County Business Journal* 25, no. 49: 12.

Wade, Robert. 1991. *Governing the Market: Economic Theory and the Role of Government in East Asian Industrialisation*. Princeton: Princeton University Press.

World Bank. 1995. *Social Indicators of Development*. Washington, DC: World Bank.

ECONOMIC HISTORY OF EARLY MODERN SOUTHEAST ASIA (PRE-SIXTEENTH CENTURY)

When did the early modern period in Southeast Asia begin? Some historians identify the middle of the fifteenth century as a time when rapid change began to affect Southeast Asia's economy and society. The spread of trade networks based on Islam and the incursions of Europeans beginning some fifty years later have been conventionally identified as two of the major factors responsible for the transition to the modern era. Other historians and some archaeologists suggest that the new economic institutions that became established during the fifteenth century, in some areas associated with early conversion to Islam, did not constitute discontinuity with the past. Instead, they formed part of a gradual transition that had begun one or even two centuries earlier.

Few records of everyday economic activities in early Southeast Asia have survived. It is therefore difficult to prove that the spread of Islam and European influence were correlated with important changes in the economic systems of the region, since the amount and types of documentation available changed greatly over the course of the sixteenth century. Evidence is, however, accumulating to show that another key factor in altering economic conditions in Southeast Asia—sizable communities of resident foreign merchants—was already present by the thirteenth century. Chinese immigrants may have begun to form enclaves by the twelfth century. They were not the first; Tamil groups may have been present in northern Sumatra and southern Thailand by the early eleventh century, but their influence in the economic sphere, as opposed to artistic and religious matters, seems to have been neither extensive nor lasting.

Chinese involvement in the region's trade therefore preceded both intensive Islamization and European influence. The role of Chinese communities in Southeast Asia's economy is still one of the principal features of that sphere of activity today. Effects of Chinese merchant communities in Indonesia include the introduction of a convenient, low-value coinage suitable for use in everyday market transactions. Southeast Asian coins were traditionally made of gold and silver, high-value materials, which restricted their usefulness in low-value trading. A Javanese document of 1300 C.E. shows that Chinese coinage was common enough that it had become the accepted legal tender of Majapahit, one of Southeast Asia's largest kingdoms. The existence of this mode of exchange would have led to a much greater volume of economic activity and would have encouraged occupational specialization. Archaeological discoveries indicate that Chinese coinage was used over an area stretching from East Java to northeast Sumatra. When Islamic kingdoms in fifteenth-century Southeast Asia, such as Melaka, began minting locally made low-value coins, the use of these coins would not have represented a new idea but rather an elaboration of a preexisting custom.

The monetization of mainland Southeast Asia's economy began in the fifth century. The oldest coin hoards have been found in a zone reaching from Myanmar (Burma) through Thailand to southern Vietnam. Although coinage existed both on the Southeast Asian mainland and in major islands of the archipelago by 800 C.E., the two regions followed different paths of development thereafter. Coinage disappeared from the archaeological record of the mainland, not to reappear until after Islamization and the arrival of Europeans. The large kingdoms of Pagan and Angkor abolished coinage and implemented a command economy in which the government regulated economic activity through taxation and redistribution. In Indonesia, by contrast, coinage continued to be produced, and it became more integral and/or essential to the functioning of several societies.

This dichotomy is correlated with differential involvement in long-distance trade. Indonesian kingdoms had been heavily involved with trade networks from China to the Persian Gulf since the beginning of the common era (C.E.). Mainland Southeast Asian societies, however, seem to have shifted their orientation away from the sea and toward elaborate, agrarian-based economies. By the fourteenth century, Chinese coinage had become a standard medium of exchange in kingdoms from North Sumatra to Bali. Thus, an economy based on coinage was already well developed in the insular realm of Southeast Asia before either Islamic or European models were introduced. However, data are lacking to draw inferences regarding the impact this means of exchange had on social structures. The most that can be said is that monetization was already well advanced when the new forms of documentation of the Southeast Asian economy became available.

The origins of Southeast Asian Islam are still a subject of inquiry. Many early Chinese immigrants may have been Muslims, as records of the Zheng He (Cheng Ho) voyages in the early Ming dynasty attest. But immigrants from India were almost certainly the most important group in this transition. In any case, Islamization, which primarily affected southern Southeast Asia, would have had an impact on two areas of economic history in particular: the use of wealth and the formation of new networks of relationships. In premodern times, much wealth (considered as liquid assets such as money or other readily exchangeable commodities, accumulated from taxation and trade) was probably expended on large-scale ritual performances, fulfilling a kind of redistributive function. The introduction of Islam must have had an important effect on the use of surplus wealth. Large ceremonies such as cremations when substantial amounts of wealth were burned or given out to the public were gradually abandoned. Court life would have become more somber and restrained. Although Bali is not a fossilized replica of premodern Southeast Asia, a comparison between the amount of resources expended on religious activity in (Hindu) Bali and (Muslim) Java today has to correspond to the reallocation of resources that must have occurred in Java during the conversion to Islam. The end result would have been to increase the amount of wealth theoretically available for reinvestment in productive enterprises rather than conspicuous consumption or gift giving.

Yet it would be a mistake to characterize pre-Islamic Southeast Asia as economically unsophisticated, concerned mainly with ritual and ceremony. One of the main reasons for the existence of royal courts may have been the organization of rituals involving large proportions of their subjects, but most of the population would still have had to obtain their means of livelihood from other sources. The amount of change that took place in the sixteenth century, when Islam attained its greatest extent and Europeans began to enter the region, is difficult to measure but would not have been very great.

When the Portuguese, the first European group to penetrate Southeast Asia, arrived in 1509, their own country was still comparatively underdeveloped economically in comparison with the more prosperous areas of Europe. Their motivations were to gain wealth and to make converts to Christianity. Their leader, Afonso de Albuquerque (ca. 1462–1515), had fought Muslims in northern Africa and considered himself a religious crusader rather than a merchant. The Portuguese incursion into Southeast Asia was also part of a grand strategy to outflank the greatest trading port in the Mediterranean at the time, Venice, and its Muslim partners, the Mamelukes of Egypt. The chosen tactic was the bold stroke of advancing straight to the heart of the region that provided the basis of Venice's wealth: the spice islands. By seizing Melaka in 1511, the Portuguese achieved what Christopher Columbus (1451–1506) had tried and failed to do in 1492. They succeeded in establishing a direct route from Europe to Maluku, the only source of the cloves and nutmeg, a route that played such a disproportionate role in Europe's balance of power relative to its utilitarian value. From Melaka, the Portuguese forced their way to Maluku, and through a combination of violence and negotiation, they sought to deflect the income that had built the grand structures of the Venetian lagoon to Lisbon.

Although the Portuguese strategy succeeded in attaining its physical objectives, it failed to make Lisbon the equivalent of Venice. One of the results of Portugal's policy was simply to shift the locus where most of the spices entered the main east-west trade route from Melaka to Banten (Bantam), West Java. Melaka languished under the Portuguese until 1641, when it was acquired by the Dutch, who intentionally prevented it from competing successfully with their own base in West Java, Batavia (Jakarta). Economically, the main lesson to be drawn from this sequence of events is that the spice trade network was flexible enough to make quick adjustments to unforeseen disturbances to its overall system.

The strength of trading connections forged by Islamic traders provided the flexibility of the spice trade network. From Gujarat, northwest India, to the Coromandel Coast and Bengal, the network passed through the Arakan coast where rulers were either Muslims or Buddhists whose culture had a strong Muslim element. Thereafter, the network went to Aceh at Sumatra's northern tip, to the Straits of Melaka, to Cambodia and southern Vietnam where Muslim Malays and Chams were predominant, and eventually to Quanzhou, Fujian, where a Muslim population had been established since the early Ming dynasty. Other important Muslim ports were found at Brunei in northwest Borneo and along the eastern rim of the South China Sea in the Philippines. Welded together by a common religion, traders all along this extensive network of ports enjoyed access to commercial intelligence and credit facilities that the overseas Chinese were only beginning to assemble.

Other than causing a slight repositioning of the trade routes, the Portuguese and later the Spanish had little effect on the Southeast Asian economy. They did not add a large new element of demand to the market, so prices remained largely the same. The Muslim network for the most part stayed intact. The seventeenth century tells a different story, however. The arrival of the English and especially the Dutch was correlated with a shift in dominance from the Muslim to the Chinese network. India became an area for competition among various European powers, and gradually, the hold of the Mughals over their mainly Hindu subjects was broken. Indian Muslim political and economic power declined in tandem with the introduction of more efficient north European military technology. Muslim groups in Southeast Asia found themselves increasingly fragmented and facing competition from several parties at once. Slowly but inexorably, the Sino-European alliance overcame the Muslim coalition. The climactic event in this transition was the transfer of control over Banten's economy to the Dutch in 1682. Banten was the last great Muslim trading port to survive; after its ruler ceded control in return for Dutch support in a civil war against his own father, indigenous shippers found themselves more and more hemmed in by Dutch restrictions. These regulations were intended to favor Dutch traders, but due to a combination of factors, the Chinese ended up as the main beneficiaries. The Dutch were physically unable to conduct all trade and transport themselves; the Chinese were able and willing to pay fees to the Dutch, thus guaranteeing them their profit, while still making enough additional money to accumulate their own capital. Thus was formed an alliance between two non–Southeast Asian groups. The Dutch were never entirely happy with this arrangement, and more than once, they turned on their Chinese subjects. Nonetheless, the Chinese traders managed to survive and resume their activities after periodic pogroms once the Dutch realized that they could not prosecute their economic plans without Chinese participation. Muslims from India and Arabs too continued to participate in the economy, but they were less influential or powerful than the Chinese.

Only in Sumatra, Borneo, and the southern Philippines did Muslim networks remain dominant through the early modern period. Aceh and Brunei and, to a lesser extent, the Johor-Riau area at the southern end of the Malay Peninsula and the Sulu sultanate represented significant concentrations of economic power in the hands of Muslim rulers with strong links to Islamic kingdoms across the Indian Ocean.

The economy of mainland Southeast Asia was much less intertwined with long-distance trade and therefore attracted less attention from outsiders. Cambodia experienced a brief era of involvement on the part of various foreign groups, from both Europe and other areas of Southeast Asia (particularly Malays), but it sank back into relative isolation due to a lack of large quantities of products in demand in international markets. Similarly, Europeans and other Asian groups made attempts to exploit the commercial possibilities of the Arakan and Martaban coasts of Myanmar, but they made no significant impact there during the early modern era. In Siam (Thailand/Ayutthaya), the Dutch, French, and English tried during the seventeenth century to reap commercial profits and gain political influence, but they were rebuffed.

The practices through which foreign trade was conducted during the early modern period incorporated both premodern and modern elements. And even within the same kingdom, policies might fluctuate between one pole and the other. An example is Aceh. Strong sultans such as Iskandar Muda (Mahkota Alam, r. 1607–1636) of the early seventeenth century attempted to monopolize all international trade throughout their realm, which, in his case, extended over much of North Sumatra and far down the west coast as well to pepper-producing regions in West Sumatra. Later, a system of rule by queens was adopted. This practice seems to have been favored by local merchants, who found the rule of women much less onerous. In most cases, international trade was conducted on the basis of the ideal of reciprocity and gift giving rather than hard bargaining. The Dutch eventually learned to turn this system to their advantage, usurping the rights of local rulers through treaties and instituting monopoly control over foreign trade as efficiently as any local rulers ever had succeeded in doing. The Dutch quickly gained the upper hand over other foreign groups in Southeast Asia, and from 1641 through 1800, they dominated most of the region's long-distance maritime trade.

Although many data exist for the study of the international trade of Southeast Asia during the early modern period, the agrarian economy is much less well documented. That economy was not of interest to the foreign traders, and local archives have not survived. On the mainland, coinage was only gradually introduced during the early modern period. In Thailand, the practice of using cowrie shells instead of coins persisted until modern times. This system was also very popular across the border in Yunnan, where the Chinese had to resort to threats of imposing the death penalty to suppress the use of cowries instead of Chinese coins in the late Ming dynasty (seventeenth century) among the T'ai linguistic groups of that region. According to an English visitor of the early seventeenth century, this shell money was used as far south as Kedah in the Malay Peninsula and at other places around the Bay of Bengal. In the absence of a widespread system of coinage, taxes and tribute were paid in produce and precious metal by weight rather than in a currency system.

In both mainland and island Southeast Asia, the very notion of "the economy" differed from that of the modern period in one important respect: control over labor was much more esteemed and emphasized than control over physical assets. The social structures of both parts of the region were predicated upon the notion that it was the fate of everyone to "belong" to someone else of higher status, in the sense of the need to uphold a set of mutual obligations. The lower-status person in most settled societies was expected to form part of the retinue of someone of higher status and to perform certain duties for that individual in return for the fulfillment of specific obligations, mainly protection. Early European sources refer to slaves as a major component of Southeast Asian population, but this single word does not do justice to the range of relationships that it described in early modern Southeast Asia. People could become enslaved for debt and as war captives, or they could sell themselves. As a result of accepting someone as a slave in some societies, however, the slave master in fact became responsible for ensuring the welfare of the slave. In this matter as in so much else having to do with early modern Southeast Asia, one cannot simply read the European sources as literal descriptions of reality. References to slavery have to be analyzed in the context of the place and specific period in which they are situated. The complexity of this set of institutions in determining the allocation of social and physical resources and in determining the economic choices of individuals suggests that the notion of the economy in early modern Southeast Asia is itself a concept in need of definition according to the local situation.

The early modern period can be conveniently considered to end in the early nineteenth century. The next decades saw the rapid spread of European administration from small enclaves to a large proportion of Southeast Asia. Economic activity was strongly influenced by imperial demands and administrative practices,

plantation agriculture, industrial expansion, and a host of other new factors. Yet even in the twenty-first century, one cannot understand Southeast Asian attitudes toward matters that Westerners may consider purely economic without recognizing that Southeast Asians often place higher priorities on matters of personal relationships than on principles of profit and loss. Continuity with aspects of the premodern and early modern periods is still an important phenomenon.

JOHN N. MIKSIC

See also Aceh (Acheh); Age of Commerce; Albuquerque, Alfonso de (ca. 1462–1515); Ancient Coinage in Southeast Asia; Angkor; Ayutthaya (Ayuthaya, Ayudhya, Ayuthia) (1351–1767), Kingdom of; Banten (Bantam); Batavia (Suanda Kelapa, Jacatra, Djakarta/Jakarta); British Interests in Southeast Asia; Brunei (Sixteenth to Nineteenth Centuries); Cheng Ho (Zheng He), Admiral (1371/1375–1433/1435); Chinese in Southeast Asia; Chinese Tribute System; Coinage and Currency; Dutch Interests in Southeast Asia from 1800; Economic Transformation of Southeast Asia (ca.. 1400–ca. 1800); Gujaratis; Indian Immigrants; Islam in Southeast Asia; Iskandar Muda, Sultan Mahkota Alam (r. 1607–1636); Johor-Riau Empire; Majapahit (1293–ca. 1520s); Maluku (The Moluccas); Mataram; Melaka; Ming Dynasty (1368–1644); Pagan (Bagan); Portuguese Asian Empire; Slavery; Spanish Expansion in Southeast Asia; Spices and the Spice Trade; Straits of Melaka; Sulu and the Sulu Archipelago; T'ais; Vereenigde Oost-Indische Compagnie (VOC) ([Dutch] United East Indies Company) (1600); Yunnan Province

References:
Allen, J. 1977. "Sea Traffic, Trade and Expanding Horizons." Pp. 387–418 in *Sunda and Sahul: Prehistoric Studies in Southeast Asia, Melanesia and Australia*. Edited by J. Allen, J. Golson, and R. Jones. London: Academic Press.

Bulbeck, D., Anthony Reid, Tan Lay Cheng, and Wu Yiqi. 1998. *Southeast Asian Exports since the 14th Century: Cloves, Pepper, Coffee and Sugar.* Singapore: Institute of Southeast Asian Studies for Economic History of Southeast Asia.

Christie, J. W. 1996. "Money and Its Uses in the Javanese States of the Ninth to Fifteenth

Centuries A.D." *Journal of the Economic and Social History of the Orient* 39, no. 3: 243–286.

Glover, I. C. 1989. *Early Trade between India and South-East Asia.* Occasional Papers no. 16. Hull, England: Centre for South-East Asian Studies, University of Hull.

Reid, A. 1988, 1993. *Southeast Asia in the Age of Commerce, 1450–1680.* Vol. 1, *The Lands below the Winds*; Vol. 2, *Expansion and Crisis.* New Haven, CT: Yale University Press.

Srisuchat, A., ed. 1996. *Ancient Trades and Cultural Contacts in Southeast Asia.* Bangkok: Office of the National Culture Commission.

Vogel, H. U. 1993. "Cowry Trade and Its Role in the Economy of Yünnan: From the Ninth to the Mid-seventeenth Century. Part II." *Journal of the Economic and Social History of the Orient* 36: 309–353.

Wang Gungwu. 1979. "A Comment on the Tributary Trade between China and Southeast Asia." *Southeast Asian Ceramics Society*, Singapore, Transaction 7.

Wicks, R. S. 1992. *Money, Markets, and Trade in Early Southeast Asia: The Development of Indigenous Monetary Systems to A.D. 1400.* Ithaca, NY: Cornell University Southeast Asia Program.

Wolters, O. W. 1967. *Early Indonesian Commerce: A Study of the Origins of Srivijaya.* Ithaca, NY: Cornell University Press.

ECONOMIC TRANSFORMATION OF SOUTHEAST ASIA
(ca. 1400–1800)

The humid Tropics, despite their abundance of water, are not easy to tame with settled agriculture. Southeast Asia was relatively lightly peopled until the nineteenth century; the majority of the population then consisted of mobile, shifting cultivators and fisherpeople. Pockets of irrigated rice agriculture became important in the drier areas from the ninth to thirteenth centuries and sustained the classic cultures of Angkor, Pagan, Java, and Dai Viet in that period.

Throughout the recorded history of the region, Southeast Asia was a place of exchange and interaction—between uplands and coasts, trading ports and hinterlands, specialist production centers and their clients. Because it lay athwart the maritime routes between China, the world's largest economy, and the rest of the known world, Southeast Asia was always home

to important ports, notably around the Straits of Melaka, the portages across the Malay Peninsula, and the Cham coast of what is today southern Vietnam. Rivers and sea-lanes provided ready access by water to populated parts of the region, compensating for the unusual difficulty of movement by land.

Cash Crops for the World

Until the fifteenth century C.E., the long-distance exports of the region were the product of foraging rather than agriculture—exotic spices; birds' nests; birds of paradise; woods and resins from the forests; and pearls, tortoiseshells, and seashells from the oceans. Even the cloves and nutmeg that found their way from the Maluku ("Spice") Islands of eastern Indonesia to the Roman Empire and Han China had been plucked from trees growing wild in these small islands.

In the decades before and after 1400, evidence suggests a more systematic production for the export of cloves in northern Maluku (especially Ternate and Tidore), nutmeg and its by-product mace in the Banda islands, and pepper in northern Sumatra. Venetian agents reported that about 30 tons of cloves and 10 tons of nutmeg annually were arriving in the Mediterranean ports of Europe, through Egypt, at that time. The growth was slow and spasmodic through most of the fifteenth century but rapid enough after 1570 to find about 200 tons of cloves and 100 tons of nutmeg arriving in Europe annually by the early 1600s. Prices paid in Maluku for the spices also grew about twenty-fold as competition mounted between 1500 and 1600 (Reid 1993: 13–24). Since these precious spices passed through many hands on their long journey from entrepôt to entrepôt, they were crucial to the growth of mercantile activity.

Piper nigrum, the true pepper vine, is native to India, and southwest India provided virtually all the world's needs for this commodity until around 1400. Likely stimulated by Chinese demand, pepper then began its remarkable career in Southeast Asia, beginning in northern Sumatra. Primary forest was felled to create the pepper gardens, and yields would decline after about the tenth year of production, leading to the opening of new tracts of forest and the abandoning of exhausted ones. Pepper cultivation therefore tended to shift, spreading around almost the whole of the coastal and riverine portions of Sumatra most accessible to trade and into the Malay Peninsula, coastal Borneo, southeastern Siam, and south-central Vietnam. By the early 1600s, Southeast Asia was exporting 4,000 tons of pepper a year and supplying the bulk of the world's needs. Around 6 percent of the population of Sumatra and the Malay Peninsula must have been living from pepper production for export in the seventeenth century (Reid 1993: 33).

Sugar began its career as a major Southeast Asian export in the seventeenth century. Chinese (mostly Teochiu) immigrants started growing it, primarily for export to Japan, in the Quang Nam area of central Vietnam, in Siam, and in Cambodia. Chinese migrants also began growing sugar in the outskirts of Banten, in Java, around 1600. The Dutch encouraged them to move to Batavia in the 1620s, and by the 1640s and 1650s, up to 1,000 tons a year were being shipped by the Dutch to Europe, Japan, and Persia (Bulbeck et al. 1998: 112).

Mention should also be made of tin, Southeast Asia's primary mineral export. Tin was extracted from flooded pits by part-time Thai and Malay miners, primarily in the river valleys of Perak and Kedah on the Malay Peninsula and Phuket. Production appears to have grown markedly from the time around 1500 when the Melaka sultanate controlled the export to India until the seventeenth century, when Dutch, Acehnese, and Thai authorities competed to control it. At its seventeenth-century peak around the 1630s, 1,000 tons may have been exported (Irwin 1970: 268–269).

An Age of Commerce

The growth in cash cropping around 1400 was likely stimulated by the extraordinary interest in Southeast Asia (and beyond) of the first three Ming dynasty rulers of China (1368–1424). In particular, the third, the Yung-lo emperor, sent six huge naval expeditions to the ports of the region and intervened militarily in Dai Viet and northern Burma. There is good evidence for the Chinese demand for Southeast Asian products such as pepper, sappanwood, and minerals, and Chinese migrants left behind by the expeditions greatly assisted the development of ports such as Japara, Demak, and Gresik (in Java); Ayutthaya (in Siam); Melaka; Brunei; and Manila.

Subsequent emperors lost interest in official contacts while continuing to ban private trade, and the Chinese commercial element merged with other traders to form a largely Malay- and Javanese-speaking trading class. Whereas earlier and later Chinese contacts proceeded both along the western route (Vietnam coast and Malay Peninsula) and the eastern route (Taiwan, Philippines, and Borneo), the eastern route appears to have died in the mid-fifteenth century. Manila, Brunei, and eastern Indonesia redirected their China trade through the major entrepôt of Melaka, presumably because goods traveling along the coastal routes linking that city to Chinese ports were easier to disguise as local trade. Around 1500, therefore, Melaka played a crucial role as the single privileged entrepôt for trade in cloth from India and spices from the archipelago, as well as metal goods and ceramics from China.

The arrival of Portuguese vessels in 1509 and their capture of Melaka two years later contributed to a major disruption to Southeast Asian trade and to Indian Ocean trade more generally. The predatory nature of their attacks on the large Javanese and Indian Muslim ships that dominated the trade appears to have set back the level of commerce by several decades. By the 1530s, however, Muslim traders had established new bases in ports such as Aceh (North Sumatra), Patani, Pahang and Johor (Malay Peninsula), and Banten (West Java), and they established a direct route for pepper and spices from Aceh to the Red Sea ports controlled by Turkey, avoiding the former stapling ports in India where the Portuguese had become dangerous. The Portuguese themselves adjusted to more peaceful forms of trade, and the oceanic trade networks continued to expand.

The height of Southeast Asia's age of commerce occurred in the period from 1570 to 1630, fueled by rising prices for most products, an abundant flow of silver, and intense competition for the key commodities. Three related events contributed to the increase in commerce. First, in 1567, the Ming emperor lifted the imperial ban on foreign trade, beginning a system of licensing junks for a dozen Southeast Asian ports. Second, silver production from both Peru and Japan increased rapidly beginning around 1570 as a result of new techniques of mercury extraction. And third, the Spanish established in Manila (1570) an entrepôt where

Chinese traders could obtain American silver as well as Japanese and Southeast Asian goods. Muslim and Portuguese traders competed in carrying silver and Indian cloth eastward to exchange for spices, pepper, and Chinese manufactures in Southeast Asian ports, with the result that prices and quantities both rose. The Japanese began sailing directly to Southeast Asian ports in the 1580s (chiefly to exchange with the Chinese, which they were forbidden to do directly), and the northern Europeans did so in the 1590s, adding to the competition and the buoyancy of mercantile ports.

Urban Life and Commerce

This age of commerce created large cosmopolitan cities, which, for more than a century, were the centers of cultural innovation and political power as well as commercial dynamism. In both Burma and Java, the political and cultural centers shifted to coastal ports roughly between 1450 and 1620, and Cambodia's capital also moved to the river port of Phnom Penh in the fifteenth century. Port cities such as Pegu, Ayutthaya, Aceh, Banten, and Makassar grew to the dimensions of contemporary European cities and dominated their agricultural hinterlands to an even greater extent. Most cities had a royal core, often fortified in the form of a citadel, and extensive suburbs in which the different national groups of traders would congregate in their respective quarters.

The growth of commercial transactions stimulated a relatively sophisticated pattern of commercial techniques, paralleling many of the capitalist institutions of Europe, India, and China in the period. The alternation of monsoon winds in the region favored a pattern of seasonal voyages, with traders from China, India, or Java remaining for several months in the main entrepôts before returning home on the favorable wind. Within the region, traders identified with Java, Banda, Makassar, Pegu (ethnically Mon), Melaka/Johor/Patani (ethnically Malay), and Champa owned and operated large rice junks as well as smaller vessels, whereas the trade to China and India was dominated by Indian and Chinese traders, respectively.

The key indigenous commercial actors were the *nakhoda* (supercargos) who traveled on each vessel and regulated the trade of the traveling merchants on it and the merchant-aristocrats (*orangkaya* in Malay) who regulated commerce in the ports and mediated with rulers, often also acting as port officials. These were frequently foreign-born individuals, since what autonomy and security of property they enjoyed rested largely on their mobility. In addition, resident Indian, Chinese, Arab, and Portuguese minorities played important mediating roles, often including the introduction of commercial or manufacturing techniques. Indian commercial castes, including Gujarati Sharafs and south Indian Chettiars, operated as money changers, moneylenders, and protobankers, with the capacity to send letters of credit (*hundi*) to their counterparts in distant cities. In the larger ports, an interest rate of 2 percent per month became common for reliable borrowers (Reid 1993: 110). Trading voyages were financed through established principles of profit sharing and bottomry (a credit system of lending to a ship owner on the security of his vessel).

If in these respects Southeast Asia was moving in a capitalist direction comparable to that in Europe, India, and Japan, it lagged behind in others. In the seventeenth century, there still were no impersonal banks or stock exchanges, as were starting to emerge in Europe. A more fundamental point was the lack of security of property against the whim or greed of a ruler. Power was diffuse in practice but unlimited in theory, in part because the new port-centered power bases adopted new ideologies of absolutism to justify using power to obtain wealth and vice versa. The orangkaya elite adopted a number of devices to curb arbitrary royal power, including a succession of female rulers in Aceh and Patani, child rulers in Banten, and supernaturally sanctioned pluralities in Makassar. Yet none of these became permanently institutionalized, as free cities, parliaments, and courts did in parts of Europe.

Crisis and Retreat in the Seventeenth Century

The Europeans traveled to Southeast Asia in pursuit of increasingly high-priced spices and at first contributed to the competition that drove local prices higher still. In the mid-seventeenth century, however, the Dutch East India Company (VOC) established an effective monopoly over cloves, nutmeg, and mace and a partial monopoly over pepper, cinnamon, and sandalwood. In pursuing these monopolies, the VOC also conquered two of the largest entrepôts—Makassar (1669) and Banten (1682)—and weakened a number of others. It has therefore often been blamed for reversing the healthy development of Indonesian commerce as well as urbanism, at least in Indonesia, and inaugurating a period when foreigners dominated all the high points of commerce.

Other parts of the world, however, such as the Hapsburg, Chinese, and Ottoman Empires, also experienced major crises in the mid-seventeenth century. Some of the factors that turned Southeast Asians away from an export-dependent path were global, notably, a worldwide cooling effect, which appears to have caused unusual climatic variation, and a downturn in world output of silver, which had been fueling price rises throughout the sixteenth century. In almost every part of Southeast Asia for which records are available, population dipped in the second half of the seventeenth century. It is more helpful to see the increasingly deadly competition for spices in the 1600s as a development in a time of crisis, in which there was room for only one winner.

For Southeast Asians, one major effect was a sharp decline in the influence that cosmopolitan port cities had in their lives. Capitals had fallen and shifted before, but there were to be no indigenous replacements when major port cities fell in this crisis, as Pegu did in 1599, Surabaya in 1623, Makassar in 1669, or Banten in 1684. The Javanese and Mon ethnic groups ceased to be identified particularly with maritime commerce, which became increasingly the business of minority diasporas—Chinese, Arab, European, Malay, Bugis. In the archipelago, the defeat of important port capitals led to a return to more diffuse systems of power, though on the mainland, such an effect was short-lived at best.

Euro-Chinese Cities

The Portuguese occupation of the Melaka entrepôt in 1511 dislocated trade to new centers but had little effect on urban life more broadly. The establishment of Manila in 1570, however, immediately proved very interesting to Chinese traders who had been newly authorized to trade to the *Nanyang* (South Seas, namely, Southeast Asia). By 1589, almost half of all junks that ac-

quired licenses were destined for Manila, where they could exchange the abundant manufactures of China (especially silk and porcelain) for Mexican silver. By 1603, there were about 20,000 Chinese living in the Chinese quarter (*parian*) of Manila and providing most of the city's needs for manufactures, construction, and foodstuffs (De la Costa 1967: 68, 205).

Founded by the VOC in 1619, Dutch Batavia set out to emulate this model by attracting Chinese settlers and traders through every means possible, including force. By 1630, the Chinese had become the most useful group in terms of urban services, manufacturing, and tax revenue, but they made up less than 20 percent of the population. Batavia was the headquarters of the Asia-wide network of the VOC, and slaves were introduced first from India and Arakan and then, after 1670, chiefly from South Sulawesi and Bali. They constituted about half of Batavia's population in the sixteenth century, and freed slaves (*mardijkers*) comprised another 20 percent (Raben 1996: 82–97). Batavia was even more attractive than Manila to both Chinese and Muslim (chiefly Indian Muslim and Malay) traders and settlers, since no demands were made for conversion or cultural assimilation. This model of a culturally plural entrepôt, with a valuable Chinese population of craftspeople and traders, was repeated in other Dutch ports, such as Padang, Melaka (after 1640), Semarang, Makassar, and Kupang.

The trade, which initially sustained the early Dutch, Spanish, and English operations in Southeast Asia, was gradually supplemented by the controlled cultivation of cash crops for export. The Dutch had begun with nutmeg after 1621, producing all the world's supply on slave estates in Banda. Company cloves and pepper were produced through binding contracts with producers in specified regions. The British also used a system of binding contracts with local chiefs to produce their share (about a quarter, at best) of the world's pepper needs after 1684. In 1707, the Dutch company began distributing coffee seedlings to the chiefs of the Priangan highlands above Batavia with such success that West Java became Europe's main supplier of coffee until West Indian slave production developed in the 1730s.

The eighteenth-century companies were as much producers of tropical produce under monopoly contracts as they were traders. In 1781, the Spanish took a similar route (about the time the VOC system was collapsing), declaring all tobacco cultivation in the Philippines a government monopoly. In the 1790s, a factory was built to produce the subsequently renowned Manila cigars, employing 5,000 women rollers (De Jesus 1980). This quickly became the Philippine government's primary source of revenue.

A Second Commercial Boom

In the latter part of the eighteenth century, European and Chinese free traders were visiting Southeast Asia in ever-increasing numbers, whereas the Dutch, English, and Spanish monopoly systems were in decay. The freeing of trade to competitive influences, coinciding with a period of global trade growth, inaugurated another phase of commercial expansion and urban growth roughly between 1780 and 1840.

China's population is thought to have doubled during the relatively peaceful and prosperous reign of the Qienlong emperor (1736–1795). Chinese trade and emigration to Southeast Asia increased throughout the reign but especially after 1754, when Chinese were officially permitted to return home with their foreign wealth. In the previous century, Manila and Batavia were the principal destinations, but now the Chinese made Asian-ruled centers such as Bangkok, Saigon, Ha Tien, Riau, Brunei, Sulu, and Terengganu their major destinations. Miners for tin and gold and planters of pepper, gambier, and sugar established relatively autonomous frontier settlements in lightly populated areas in Borneo, the Malay Peninsula, the Riau archipelago, and the Gulf of Thailand. In the decades before Singapore's foundation (1819), Bangkok became the largest base for Chinese trade and shipping outside China.

The Chinese may have been the most important single factor in the second boom. Nonetheless, the growing numbers of English and French country traders based in India after 1760, of New England pepper traders from 1793, and of Chulia and other Indian merchants also profited from the atrophy of the Dutch and English companies, which could no longer control effective monopolies. The Americans as a group were the biggest single buyer behind a huge expansion of pepper growing in Aceh from the 1790s, and Aceh's total exports increased about tenfold in value between the 1770s and the 1820s (Bulbeck et al. 1998: 66). Coffee escaped from the narrow world of Dutch forced cultivation in the Priangan to become the smallholder crop par excellence in much of Sumatra and Java. By the 1830s, Southeast Asia produced the bulk of the world's coffee as well as pepper. Shipping records for Singapore in the years after 1819 reveal that maritime trade in its hinterlands, from southern Vietnam and Siam to Bali and Borneo, increased severalfold between the 1790s and the 1830s.

This kind of expansion in trade, the most measurable dimension of economic performance, was matched by a growing commercialization within the larger states of the region. It is possible to see this second period of commercial growth, like the age of commerce two centuries earlier, as the harbinger of various types of modern sensibility in literature, art, and religion, as well as of more modern, centralized state forms. For instance, Nidhi Aeusrivongse has shown this scenario for Siam in the early Bangkok period; likewise Li Tana for Cochin China.

ANTHONY REID

See also Aceh (Acheh); Arabs; Ayutthaya (Ayuthaya, Ayudhya, Ayuthia) (1351–1767 C.E.), Kingdom of; Banten (Bantam); Batavia (Sunda Kelapa, Jakatra, Djakarta/Jakarta); British Interests in Southeast Asia; Chettiars (Chettyars); China, Imperial; Chinese in Southeast Asia; Chinese Tribute System; Coffee; Coinage and Currency; Country Traders; Dutch Interests in Southeast Asia from 1800; East India Company (EIC) (1600), English; Economic Transformation of Southeast Asia (ca. 1400–ca. 1800); Hanoi (Thang-Long); Indigenous Political Power; Islam in Southeast Asia; Java; Jungle/Forest Products; Manila; Marine/Sea Products; Melaka; Ming Dynasty (1368–1644); Penang (1786); Pepper; Portuguese Asian Empire; Saigon (Gia Dinh, Hồ Chí Minh City); Shipbuilding; Spanish Expansion in Southeast Asia; Spices and the Spice Trade; Sugar; Sumatra; Vereenigde Oost-Indische Compagnie (VOC) ([Dutch] United East India Company) (1602)

References:
Bulbeck, D., Anthony Reid, Tan Lay Cheng, and Wu Yiqi. 1998. *Southeast Asian Exports since*

the 14th Century: Cloves, Pepper, Coffee and Sugar. Singapore: Institute of Southeast Asian Studies for Economic History of Southeast Asia.

De Jesus, E. C. 1980. The Tobacco Monopoly in the Philippines: Bureaucratic Enterprise and Social Change, 1766–1880. Quezon City, the Philippines: Ateneo de Manila Press.

De la Costa, H. 1967. The Jesuits in the Philippines, 1581–1768. Cambridge, MA: Harvard University Press.

Irwin, G. W. 1970. "The Dutch and the Tin Trade of Malaya in the Seventeenth Century." Pp. 267–287 in Studies in the Social History of China and Southeast Asia. Edited by Jerome Ch'en and Nicholas Tarling. Cambridge: Cambridge University Press.

Kathirithamby-Wells, J., and John Villiers. 1990. The Southeast Asian Port and Polity: Rise and Demise. Singapore: Singapore University Press.

Lieberman, Victor, ed. 1999. Beyond Binary Histories: Re-imagining Eurasia to c. 1830. Ann Arbor: University of Michigan Press.

Lombard, Denys. 1990. Le Carrefour javanais: Essai d'histoire globale [A Javanese Crossroad: Essay in World History]. 3 vols. Paris: Éditions de l'École des Hautes Études en Sciences Sociales.

Raben, Remco. 1996. "Batavia and Colombo: The Ethnic and Spatial Order of Two Colonial Cities, 1600–1800." Ph.D. diss., Leiden University.

Reid, Anthony. 1988, 1993. Southeast Asia in the Age of Commerce, c. 1450–1680. Vol. 1, The Lands below the Winds; Vol. 2, Expansion and Crisis. New Haven, CT: Yale University Press.

Reid, Anthony, ed. 1997. The Last Stand of Asian Autonomies: Responses to Modernity in the Diverse States of Southeast Asia and Korea, 1750–1900. Basingstoke, England: Macmillan.

Tarling, Nicholas, ed. 1992. The Cambridge History of Southeast Asia. Vol. 1, From Early Times to c. 1800. Cambridge: Cambridge University Press.

EDSA REVOLUTION (1986)
"People Power Revolution"

EDSA is the acronym for Epifanio De los Santos Avenue, the major highway in metropolitan Manila, the national capital region of the Philippines. It was the site of the four-day "people power revolution" of 22 to 25 February 1986, where more than a million Filipinos gathered on the road to force a showdown with president-turned-dictator Ferdinand Marcos (1917–1989). Marcos had refused to resign from office after fourteen years at the helm of a repressive regime. The vast multitude responded to frantic calls by Manila's archbishop, Jaime Cardinal Sin, to go to EDSA to show their support for the defense minister, Juan Ponce Enrile, and the armed forces vice chief of staff, Fidel Ramos, who had forsworn Marcos and defected to the opposition, headed by Corazon (Cory) Aquino (1933–). In four days, EDSA swelled with crowds of Filipinos from all walks of life—rich, poor, young, old, professionals, executives, farmers, workers, laborers, students, women, children, religious, and so on. The phenomenon had a heavily religious atmosphere. Priests and nuns intoned prayers and chants; carried religious icons such as the Virgin Mary and Santo Niño (Child Jesus); and offered rosaries, flowers, and food to Marcos's soldiers, who were just waiting for orders to shoot into the crowd.

Some called the EDSA rebellion nothing short of a miracle because, with the presence of a million people and the full weight of Marcos's military arrayed against them, the potential for violence was extremely high but did not erupt. All that was needed was for someone in the crowd to throw a stone, and violence would have ensued. It was a very tense situation, yet the crowd remained disciplined but determined. They pleaded with rather than confronted or taunted the military. For their part, the troops could not fire on the crowds or drive their tanks into their midst because they knew some of their relatives and friends were there. They voluntarily returned to their barracks without firing a single shot.

The defection of various units of the military, especially the air force under Colonel Antonio Sotelo, sealed the fate of Ferdinand Marcos. Isolated in Malacanang, the presidential palace, with his family and loyal military, he underestimated the size of the EDSA crowd and continued ordering his troops not to shoot. Meanwhile, he was in constant touch with the administration of Ronald Reagan (t. 1981–1989), asking the U.S. president, whom he considered his friend, what to do. In turn, President Reagan (1911–2004) requested a U.S. senator, Paul Laxalt, to tell Marcos to "cut, and cut cleanly," to which the latter responded, "I'm so very very disappointed" (Kerkvliet and Mojares 1991: 160). In his delusion, if not arrogance, he had expected Reagan to support him to the very end.

On the night of the fourth day at EDSA, two helicopters from Clark Field Air Force Base in the Philippines arrived at the presidential palace to evacuate Marcos and company after the dictator was persuaded it was in his best interests to go into exile in Hawai'i. The U.S. Embassy in Manila had contacted incoming president Cory Aquino, who had said in very definite terms that it was best for Marcos to leave the Philippines to forestall any violence that might ensue if he remained. Marcos and his entourage of eighty-nine persons were put on a plane to Guam, en route to Hawai'i. A second plane carried 300 pieces of luggage, containing jewelry, Philippine currency, U.S. dollars, guns, medical equipment, clothing, Imelda Marcos's shoes, and other items too numerous to mention, which were later impounded by the U.S. Customs authorities in Honolulu.

The EDSA crowd reached Malacanang after the Marcos party had left, and the people celebrated the end of the dictatorship by throwing out and burning the portraits of Ferdinand and Imelda Marcos. They photographed themselves taking over the presidential desk and other parts of the palace. The incoming Aquino government had sent its couriers to retrieve whatever papers and documents were left behind, which could later be used in court cases against the Marcoses. Much jewelry had been left behind, as well as several dialysis machines, confirming long-standing rumors that Marcos had suffered from a kidney disease.

EDSA has since been reconstructed, with a massive statue at its heart symbolizing "people power." There is also a specially commissioned, towering icon of the Virgin Mary, to whom the crowd prayed during those tense days to bring a peaceful end to the Marcos regime. The site is a reminder of the unique Filipino contribution to the theory of modern revolution.

BELINDA AQUINO

See also Aquino, Corazon Cojuangco (1933–); Marcos, Ferdinand (1917–1989); Martial Law (1972–1981) (The Philippines); Ramos, Fidel Valdez (1928–)

References:
Kerkvliet, Benedict J., and Resil B. Mojares, eds. 1991. *From Marcos to Aquino: Local Perspectives on Political Transition in the Philippines.* Honolulu, HI, and Manila, the Philippines: Ateneo de Manila University Press.

EDUCATION, OVERSEAS CHINESE

The educational policies and provisions for immigrant Chinese and their descendants, Southeast Asia's most significant immigrant minority, changed as former colonies became independent countries striving for national unity and development in the 1950s and 1960s. The relations between China and the immigrants' countries of overseas residence influenced the educational changes that occurred. Across the region, there were variations in the minority status of the Chinese, including their numerical and economic importance. These differences affected government policies toward Chinese education—policies that had political as well as educational significance.

Extensive Chinese immigration to Southeast Asia in the nineteenth century led to the emergence of a settled Chinese population and a demand for local schools, as only a small proportion of the Chinese could afford to send their children to private tutors or to China for education. Some Chinese children gained an education in the few modern, Western-style schools established by colonial authorities and Christian missionaries. These schools used the colonial language and a curriculum designed to produce the colonies' future clerks and bureaucrats. As in the Straits Settlements, the Chinese children educated in these schools became a distinctive segment of the Chinese population—the English-educated Anglo-Chinese.

The inability of these schools to accommodate the demand spawned by the growing school-age population among the Chinese, especially those seeking a Chinese-language education, led local Chinese associations to found their own schools. Diversity characterized these early community-funded schools. There was no common curriculum or common language of instruction. Although some schools taught in Mandarin, the national language, many used the dominant local Chinese dialect, such as Hokkien, Teochew (Teochiu), or Cantonese.

Soon, these schools, begun as a response to the immediate educational needs of the emigrant Chinese families and employers, were influenced by the social and political reform movements in China, where education was emphasized as a key to modernization, including the replacement of the Qing (Ch'ing) dynasty (1644–1912). In Southeast Asia, local schools were urged to prepare citizens for the new China through a modern, Western-oriented curriculum that used the Chinese national language. The recruitment of teachers from China to overcome local shortages contributed to curriculum reform in Southeast Asia's Chinese schools, including an increased use of Mandarin. Colonial governments viewed the expansion of the schools and their orientation to China with suspicion. Accordingly, they introduced restrictions on size, curriculum, and teachers to ensure that the schools did not become promoters of a Chinese nationalism that would threaten colonial interests.

After the Pacific War (1941–1945), the Chinese schools played an important role in meeting the growing popular demand for education. But their perceived links to China, with its communist government that was supporting communist groups in Southeast Asia, strengthened the concerns of the colonial authorities. Many indigenous independence leaders also were hostile to the economic influence of the Chinese, which they wished to limit as their countries became independent.

With the growth of nationalism, Chinese schools became subject to even harsher controls in the 1950s and 1960s. The use of the Chinese language was either banned or severely curtailed. In the Philippines and Indonesia, schools were closed or restricted so that they could not provide a viable alternative to the national systems of education that had as a major objective the promotion of national unity. Even in Singapore, with its majority Chinese population, the government worked to establish a national system of education based on English, with a subsidiary role for Chinese, Malay, and Tamil.

These changes coincided with a declining demand for separate Chinese education, as the Southeast Asian Chinese increasingly saw that their long-term future lay in the region. Immigration from China ceased, and the idea of returning to China was less attractive to Southeast Asian Chinese. Among the growing numbers of locally born Chinese, there was a strong desire to become more fully integrated into the new homelands. One pathway was to be educated in the mainstream school system, following the national curriculum and using the national language. The merging of Nanyang University with the University of Singapore in 1980 deprived the region of its only Chinese-language tertiary institution. The closure, justified on the grounds of declining student numbers, symbolically ended more than a century of Chinese community-based education in Southeast Asia. Today, only in Malaysia, where the ethnic Chinese remain a significant minority, are there private as well as government schools making significant use of Chinese as their medium of instruction. The status of these schools and educational provisions for ethnic Chinese remains an important area of political debate.

By the end of the twentieth century, improving political relations between China and Southeast Asian countries and their growing economic links led to a lessening of hostility toward knowledge of the Chinese language and culture. Although there has been an easing of bans on the use and teaching of the Chinese language in countries such as Indonesia, it is difficult to envisage an extensive return to separate schooling for ethnic Chinese in Southeast Asia.

CHRISTINE INGLIS

See also China since 1949; China, Imperial; China, Nationalist; Chinese Dialect Groups; Chinese in Southeast Asia; Chinese Revolution (1911); Education, Western Secular; Malayan/Malaysian Education; Qing (Ch'ing/Manchu) Dynasty (1644–1912)

References:

Guerassimoff, Eric. 2003. *Chen Jiageng et l'éducation. Stratégies d'un émigré pour la modernisation de l'enseignement en Chine (1913–1938)* [Chen Jiageng (Tan Kah Kee) and Education. Strategies of an Emigrant for the Modernization of Teaching in China (1913–1938)]. Paris: L'Harmattan.

———. 2004. *Émigration et éducation. Les Écoles chinoises à Singapour (1819–1919)* [Emigration and Education. The Chinese Schools in Singapore (1819–1919)]. Paris: Les Indes Savantes.

Inglis, Christine. 1977. "Chinese Education in Southeast Asia." Pp. 108–136 in *Appetite for*

Education in Contemporary Asia. Development Studies Centre Monograph no. 10. Edited by Kenneth Orr. Canberra: Australian National University.

Loh Fook Seng, Philip. 1975. *Seeds of Separatism: Educational Policy in Malaya, 1874–1940.* Kuala Lumpur: Oxford University Press.

Murray, D. 1964. "Chinese Education in Southeast Asia." *China Quarterly* 20: 67–95.

Pan, Lynn, ed. 1998. *The Encyclopedia of the Chinese Overseas.* Singapore: Archipelago Press and Landmark Books.

Tan Liok Ee. 1997. *The Politics of Chinese Education in Malaya, 1945–1961.* Kuala Lumpur and New York: Oxford University Press.

EDUCATION, TRADITIONAL RELIGIOUS

Prior to European contact, Southeast Asia had strongly developed traditions of literacy and education. These traditions were built upon the region's diverse religious heritage and the Hindu, Buddhist, and Islamic institutions integral to the local societies. Buddhism, with an education system based on the monasteries, was firmly established in contemporary Myanmar (Burma), Thailand, Laos, and Cambodia. Islamic schools existed in Malaysia, Brunei, and Indonesia. In Vietnam, Confucian principles derived from China underpinned a highly systematized pattern of education. Only in the Philippines is there little evidence of such a tradition of religious education. The initial contacts between Western education, both Christian and secular, and these traditional patterns of education varied with religion and colonial policies and their reception in the traditional societies.

The contemporary survival and modification of these earlier patterns of traditional education have been affected in complex ways by the patterns of religious diversity that exist in today's nation-states. Another important factor is whether the nation-state is secular or has an official religion. Indonesia is a secular state, although most of its people are Muslims, with smaller numbers of Christians, Buddhists, Hindus, and animists. By contrast, Islam has an official role both in Brunei, an Islamic monarchy with an Islamic majority, and in Malaysia, where one of the attributes of a Malay is to be a Muslim. Yet Malaysia has a far smaller percentage of Muslims in its population than Indonesia, and there are substantial minorities of Buddhists, Hindus, and Christians. Thailand is a Buddhist monarchy and includes several Muslim provinces in its southern region. Vietnam, Cambodia, and Laos have all had periods of communist rule and, like Burma, have no state religion. The Philippines has a Christian (mainly Catholic) majority but also has provinces dominated by Muslims.

The extent to which religious education touched the lives of children in traditional society is difficult to determine precisely. Family-based education provided the skills needed for daily agricultural and domestic life and was probably the most common form of education available to boys as well as girls in traditional Southeast Asia. In those regions where animism was the major form of religious and spiritual belief, education could also include apprenticeships in magic and sorcery. Indeed, when Western-style schools were introduced in such areas, they were sometimes viewed as a form of these apprenticeships.

Buddhist Education

The traditional form of education in Buddhist societies was provided by monks attached to the monasteries (*wats*). The first stage of education was a prerequisite for young men to be ordained as monks, an important rite of passage in these societies. Typically at the age of five or six, boys were sent to the local monastery, where monks would teach them to read religious texts, do simple arithmetic, and learn religious principles. The instruction was individualized, as a monk would have no more than ten or twelve pupils, each working through his lessons at his own pace. There was no specific curriculum or formal examination, although there was progression through texts and tasks. Boys were free to come and go as they wished from the classes. Once they had been ordained as monks, only a few would remain to continue their studies in religious or secular knowledge.

For most young men, their education did not continue past their ordination. Although they had gained some secular knowledge, the educational outcome most frequently emphasized by Western observers was that they had gained a moral education that situated them within their community. With education considered a religious act, commentators suggest that this type of education was relatively common among young men. Girls were not part of this system; they learned to read or write either at home from members of the family or, in certain elite groups, with a tutor. The young men who continued with their education were the exception; the system did provide an avenue of social mobility for those from poorer backgrounds.

In Burma in 1866, the British had initially proposed to provide Western education by working in conjunction with the monasteries. Although slow to develop, 801 of these monastic schools existed by 1873, compared with only 112 secular schools. Later policies favored these Anglo-vernacular secular schools. They became the path to employment in the colonial economy and increasingly attracted pupils from the monastery schools. There was also a decline in the prestige of the monks. Some of the monks involved themselves in anti-British uprisings. Most significant, argued British administrator John Sydenham Furnivall (1878–1960), was that young men and their families were more interested in economic gain and opportunities for social mobility than in the moral education at the heart of Buddhist education. He also noted that the extensive changes affecting the society that monastic education had served further undermined its viability (Furnivall 1948).

In Laos, the French had a similar plan to build upon the monastic schools. Colleges were set up in 1909 and 1911 to retrain the monks to teach in the secular school system. Although welcomed by the local population, the scheme proved impractical, as the monks sought better-paying civil service posts when they completed their training. Efforts to modernize the monastic schools by adding subjects such as French and arithmetic encountered problems because of difficulties in finding monks with the appropriate training to teach them.

In Thailand, however, the strategy of using the monastic schools as a basis for the expansion of modern education was far more successful. After 1898, these schools underpinned the effort to extend modern education beyond Bangkok and into the provinces. Modern textbooks were provided to the schools, which also received limited government funding. Important for the success of this strategy was the active support provided by King Chulalongkorn (Rama V) (r. 1868–1910); indeed, his brother, head of an influential monastery, was in charge of its implementation. This situation contrasted with that in Burma and Laos, where the traditional power holders were not involved in the attempts to modify the monastic schools. The Thai monastic schools also complemented rather than competed with the lay school system in providing pathways to social mobility. The viability of the strategy was demonstrated by the fact that in the early 1970s, one-fifth of Thai primary schools were still these monastic schools. In the Muslim areas of southern Thailand, the government also allowed the operation of Koranic schools that combined Muslim education with parts of the national primary curriculum.

Islamic Education

In contrast to the organization of Buddhist education around individual monasteries, there was greater diversity in the patterns of Islamic education that developed in Southeast Asia. Apart from recitation centers associated with mosques, the major form of schooling was the village school (*pondoks, pesantren*), where students (*santri*) would gather around an individual scholar (*'ulama* or *kyai*). Often, these were boarding schools. The content of education followed patterns not too dissimilar from those found in Buddhist schools: rote learning was the method of instruction, and students would work their way through a series of religious texts. The schools also were intended for boys rather than girls. One significant difference, however, was that many of these schools used not the vernacular language but rather Arabic, the language of Islamic religious texts and rituals. Few students studied beyond the initial level, but for those who continued, educational opportunities were available outside Southeast Asia in the Middle East (West Asia) at institutions including al-Azhar University in Egypt, which played a major role in the development of modern forms of Islam. The existence of this alternative to higher education in the European metropoles was an important element that was absent from Buddhist education. It was also a factor of particular significance for the development of Islamic education in the Netherlands East Indies.

Most of the people of the Netherlands East Indies were Muslims, but there were significant differences in the nature of their involvement with Islam. Those from western Sumatra and Aceh were widely regarded as far more devout in their practice of Islam as compared with those from Java and other islands. Acehnese efforts to gain independence from the Dutch administration were intertwined with the work of Islamic opposition groups who derived much of their support from students inspired by their Islamic teachers. There was also considerable debate among Indonesian intellectuals about how and to what extent Islam and Islamic education should be modernized to operate more effectively within the changing world order. During the 1920s and 1930s, increasing numbers of *madrasahs* (traditional Islamic schools), which combined Islamic and modern, secular education, were set up. Changes also occurred in certain pesantren as they attempted to compete with the reformist Islamic schools. Debate about modernization was not unique to Indonesia, but it played a most important role in political, as well as educational and religious, developments. Among the movements that changed Islamic religious education in the first half of the twentieth century were Kaum Muda (young group) and Muhammadiyah ("Way of Muhammad"), which established pesantren based on modernist principles. Taman Siswa (Garden of Students) schools, with their combination of Javanese culture and a modernist, Western-oriented curriculum, provided an alternative to modernist Islam.

After the Pacific War (1941–1945), the newly independent Republic of Indonesia was constituted as a secular state that recognized the existence of different religious groupings. Nevertheless, its state-funded education system still supports both secular and Islamic systems of schooling. The Ministry of Education regulates the secular schools, whereas the Islamic schools are under the control of the Ministry of Religious Affairs. The government Islamic schools are recognized as an integral part of the state education system, and their structure parallels that of the secular schools at the primary and secondary levels. One of the challenges confronting educators responsible for these schools is their ability to successfully integrate a modern education and a religious education. The Ministry of Religious Affairs also is responsible for supervising the private pesantren or pondoks. Though these schools enjoy considerable independence, there is nevertheless a decline in their enrollments, and increasing control is exercised by the government, as they accept funding from it.

Like Indonesia, contemporary Brunei also has a parallel system of Islamic schooling; this voluntary schooling requires that students study at both the secular and the religious schools. Unlike Indonesia, however, Brunei is an Islamic state. The existence of a parallel system of Islamic religious schools in secular Indonesia seems somewhat paradoxical. But it should be viewed as an attempt by the state to maintain control over religious education that, in the past, provided a base for opposition to national unity and political leaders.

In British Malaya, Islamic schools never became the same focal point for opposition to the administration as occurred under the Dutch in Indonesia. In large part, this was because the traditional rulers retained effective political and religious control while working with, rather than against, the British administration. The divisions between advocates of modernism and more traditional approaches of Islam existed in the British colonies but did not result in the establishment of alternative systems of Islamic schooling. The growth of the government village schools was slow, as villagers saw little advantage in sending their children to them because the curriculum was based on Malay literacy and vocationally oriented schooling for the boys and girls. Attempts to overcome resistance to the village schools involved associating religious instruction with these schools in parts of British Malaya.

Following independence (1957), a priority for the Malaysian government was to unify the linguistically diverse colonial education system. This task was accomplished through introducing a common curriculum and making Bahasa Melayu the primary medium of instruction in all except the Chinese and Indian primary schools. Today, however, to meet pressures for greater diversity, the government allows private schools to operate. Although some cater to the Chinese-speaking population and those wanting English-language education, there is also a group of Islamic schools that operate alongside the regular state school system. They do not need a license to operate, but these schools are monitored and regulated by the Religious Affairs Department of the Ministry of Education. In allowing the operation of these schools, the government is accommodating stronger, more fundamentalist views of Islam. These schools exist in certain states of Peninsular Malaysia, where political parties with a strongly Islamic base oppose the national government led by the United Malays National Organization (UMNO). Recent years have also seen a growth of fundamentalist Islamic influences throughout Malaysia, paradoxically associated, in part, with Malay students studying in Western countries. The effectiveness of these controls has been called into question by evidence that Jemaah Ismaliah, an extremist group in Southeast Asia, used Islamic educational institutions to promote its course. In response, the Malaysian government temporarily suspended public funding to private Islamic schools in 2002. There are also proposals to closely regulate the content of private Islamic education and absorb the estimated 126,000 students studying in private Islamic schools into the government's national schools. Further, plans are being discussed to remove religious instruction from the national school curriculum, leaving its provision to special after-school classes with no political content.

Confucian Education

When the French administration was established in Vietnam in the 1880s, a highly developed national system of education based on the Chinese Confucianist model existed. Although more appropriately regarded as an ethical system rather than a religion, Confucianism provided the basis for a rigorous classical education in which successful exam candidates were appointed to administrative positions in the mandarinate. Like both Buddhist and Islamic schooling, Confucianist education catered to boys rather than girls. Like them, it also provided opportunities for social mobility independent of established elite status, although students from educated, official families began with better resources for success in the examination system. Where Confucian education differed was that the examination system ensured that students pursued a uniform pattern of education.

Instead of seeking to use Confucian education as a basis for introducing modern, Western

education, the French aim was to replace the whole system. The Confucianist schools taught Vietnamese literacy through the medium of Chinese characters; the French administrators replaced this with the romanized form of *quốc ngù* (lit., national language) in their own schools. Complementing practical reasons for this shift, there was also a view that the use of characters inhibited modernization. The French also hoped to remove a source of potential opposition by undermining the power of the Vietnamese mandarins. By the 1870s, the Confucianist schools were already losing their influence and role. The abandonment of the national system of examinations eliminated the employment rationale for the schools. To gain employment in the French administration, students now needed the newer education introduced by the French. It was also becoming difficult to find teachers able to use the Chinese characters needed to teach Vietnamese.

The Future of Traditional Religious Education

Examples exist of the incorporation and modification of traditional patterns of religious education in the colonial school systems and, in some cases, in the educational systems of contemporary Southeast Asian nations. However, in many cases, the continuity is more apparent than real. Extensive modernization of curricula has occurred in an effort by both government and religious leaders to ensure that the schools provide a meaningful pathway to modern life. The challenges involved in this "modernization" were evident in Singapore's attempts in the 1980s to introduce a moral education curriculum based on traditional Asian values and religions. Singaporean educators had to decide which version of Hinduism, Islam, or Buddhism was to be privileged in the curriculum. In the case of Confucianism, the task involved reformulating the key social relationships at the core of traditional Confucianism so that they neither ignored nor downplayed the role of women.

Many commentators have noted, with romantic regret, the loss of traditional values associated with these changes to traditional and religious education. This sentiment overlooks the way the traditional societies served by these schools have undergone irreversible changes as they have been drawn, over more than a century, into a modern world very different from that which existed before. When governments such as that of Myanmar speak of revitalizing monastic education to complement primary education, this does not mean a return to the older forms but an attempt to use them to meet contemporary needs. The Thai experience shows that the success of using the Buddhist monastic schools to extend the new, modern education depended on a very specific combination of factors. These factors were motivated by a concern to retain the schools' contribution to moral and ethical standards while expanding opportunities to learn the modern knowledge necessary to survive in a rapidly changing world. Islamic reformers in Indonesia had similar objectives. In other Southeast Asian countries, the diverse approaches of those seeking to introduce an Islamic dimension to contemporary education highlight the ways in which religious education may be used for directly political purposes hostile to existing governments. However, religious education can also be an important means of providing the ethical and moral dimension to education overlooked in many instrumental approaches to educational expansion and innovation.

CHRISTINE INGLIS

See also Aceh (Acheh); Boedi Oetama (Budi Utomo) (1908); Brunei (Sixteenth to Nineteenth Centuries); Buddhism; Buddhism, Mahayana; Buddhism, Theravada; Burma under British Colonial Rule; Cambodia under French Colonial Rule; Confucianism; Darul Islam Movement (DI); Education, Western Secular; Islam in Southeast Asia; Islamic Resurgence in Southeast Asia (Twentieth Century); *Kiai;* Laos (Nineteenth Century to Mid-1990s); Malayan/Malaysian Education; Muhammadiyah; Muslim Minorities (Thailand); Netherlands (Dutch) East Indies; Partai Islam Se Malaysia (PAS); *Quoc Ngu;* Reforms and Modernization in Siam; *Sangha; Santri;* Taman Siswa (1921); United Malays National Organization (UMNO) (1946); Vietnam under French Colonial Rule

References:

Aragon, Lorraine. 2000. *Fields of the Lord: Animism, Christian Minorities, and State Development in Indonesia.* Honolulu: University of Hawai'i Press.

Furnivall, J. S. 1948. *Colonial Policy and Practice: A Comparative Study of Burma and Netherlands India.* Cambridge: Cambridge University Press.

Keyes, Charles, ed. 1991. *Reshaping Local Worlds: Formal Education and Cultural Change in Rural Southeast Asia.* New Haven, CT: Yale University Southeast Asian Studies, Yale Center for International and Area Studies.

Mohd. Taib Osman, ed. 1997. *Islamic Civilization in the Malay World.* Kuala Lumpur: Dewan Bahasa dan Pustaka and the Research Centre for Islamic History, Art and Culture, Istanbul.

Osborne, Milton. 1997. *The French Presence in Cochinchina and Cambodia: Rule and Response (1859–1905).* Bangkok: White Lotus Press.

Postlethwaite, T. Neville, and R. Murray Thomas, eds. 1980. *Schooling in the ASEAN Region: Indonesia, Malaysia, the Philippines, Singapore, Thailand.* London: Pergamon Press.

Taufik, Abdullah. 1971. *Schools and Politics: The Kaum Muda Movement in West Sumatra (1927–1933).* Ithaca, NY: Cornell Modern Indonesia Project, Cornell University.

Tu, Wei-Ming, ed. 1996. *Confucian Traditions in East Asian Modernity: Moral Education and Economic Culture in Japan and the Four Mini-dragons.* Cambridge, MA: Harvard University Press.

Yegar, Moshe. 1979. *Islam and Islamic Institutions in British Malaya: Policies and Implementation.* Jerusalem, Israel: Magnes Press.

EDUCATION, WESTERN SECULAR

Colonialism underlay the introduction of Western education to the countries of Southeast Asia. The exception was Thailand, where King Chulalongkorn (Rama V) (r. 1868–1910) introduced Western education as a means to modernize his country. As colonies became independent after the Pacific War (1941–1945), colonial education systems were viewed as inappropriate for the needs of the new nations in pursuing national development and unity. Extensive educational restructuring and expansion characterized the period of independence, to be followed by efforts to improve the quality and relevance of education to meet emergent needs. Although these phases and the type of issues addressed are remarkably constant throughout Southeast Asia, each country's history and development dictated the specific forms of educational change and expansion.

The Colonial Period

Southeast Asian societies had long traditions of literacy, albeit restricted to the secular and religious elite. Patterns of elite education were also the norm in Europe until the late nineteenth century, and they influenced the earliest forms of European education introduced to Southeast Asia. Under the Spanish administration in the Philippines from the sixteenth century, the Catholic Church played a major role in education, including the foundation of Santo Tomas University in 1611. Although educational initiatives of this type were significant for the introduction of Western religion and knowledge, they touched only small sections of colonial society. The more extensive impact of Western education began in the latter half of the nineteenth century as the expansion of European colonization coincided with the European development of compulsory, secular systems of schooling. The focus of content then shifted from the classics toward new, scientific knowledge to meet the needs of an industrializing society for a suitably educated, literate, and compliant labor force. This type of Western education attracted rulers such as King Chulalongkorn. It was also the form familiar to European administrators. Nevertheless, not all administrators saw the content of European education as appropriate in the colonies, even if they were committed to bringing their colonial subjects the benefits of Western civilization.

Until the latter half of the nineteenth century, Christian missionaries played the major role in establishing schools for the small European population and local elite in Southeast Asia. These schools operated independently and did not provide a common system of education. This situation changed as the colonial powers established more formal control in the region and began to consider the role of schooling for the ethnically diverse and stratified populations under their administration. Their response was shaped by circumstances different from those in Europe, as they were operating in societies without sizable European populations but with established elites, large agricultural populations, and growing numbers of Chinese and other immigrant groups who played an important role in the colonial economies. Although the need for workers fluent in European languages was limited, other objectives of schooling included the maintenance of traditional lifestyles and inculcating loyalty to the colonial regime. Financial constraints also shaped colonial educational policies, since the colonies were intended to provide wealth to the metropole rather than to be an economic burden on it.

Debates about the language of education—whether teaching should be done in the local vernacular or in the colonial language—played an important part in the formulation of colonial education policies. In India and in Burma (Myanmar), British administrators had adopted policies based on extensive English-language education. However, British administrators in the Federated Malay States (FMS) and the Straits Settlements believed that this policy had led to a large, "overeducated" populace that was dissatisfied with the traditional lifestyle and unable to find employment in the relatively small, Western-oriented urban economies. As part of their policy of protecting the lifestyle of the Malay peasant, they thus settled on a policy of vocationally oriented, vernacular primary education for Malay students. However, for the Malay elite, who were to provide the core of the colonial administration, they established the Malay College at Kuala Kangsar, modeled on British boarding schools such as Eton, to groom the country's leadership. The government played only a limited role in establishing other schools. The Chinese set up their own schools, which were regulated by, but eligible for only limited funding from, the colonial administration. The children of Indian plantation workers were educated in vernacular primary schools funded by the plantation owners. However, the administration did establish a small number of English-language schools and offered grants to those English schools that were established by Christian churches. In doing so, they were addressing the need of the colonial administration and commerce for a relatively small number of English-educated local workers. These schools became extremely popular; Eurasians, Chinese, and Indians viewed the English-medium schools as avenues for social mobility. During the depression of the 1930s, the administration reduced funding to them, in part to limit the numbers of "unemployable" graduates.

The linguistically stratified systems of education in British Malaya were also replicated in French Indochina and the Netherlands East Indies after often lengthy consultations and debate. The Dutch Ethical Policy, emphasizing the need to uplift the Indonesian people through education and closer association with The Netherlands, led to increased opportunities for Dutch-language schooling, although the majority of children were educated in vernacular schools. In Indochina, the 1917 Code of Public Instruction was a key expression of educational policy and practice. Both colonies had schools, primarily for European students, that followed the metropole's education system and curriculum. In the rural areas, a system of vocationally focused village primary schools that used the vernacular evolved. In Vietnam, *Quốc Ngù,* or romanized Vietnamese, replaced the traditional Chinese characters for Vietnamese; this was a means to distance the new schools from the traditional ones. In the higher levels, French was introduced. Despite this innovation and despite the presence of Link schools (elementary schools "linked" to a particular secondary school) in the Netherlands East Indies, there was little scope for students from these schools to progress to secondary schooling that used French or Dutch as the medium of instruction.

The Philippines under U.S. control from 1898 followed a different path. Although the Spanish administration had promulgated educational decrees in 1863 and 1865 applying to primary and secondary schooling, little progress had been made to implement these policies. When the Americans seized control of the Philippines, they rebuilt the education system using English and patterning the organization, curriculum, and methods of instruction on those in the United States.

By the end of the 1930s, just prior to the Pacific War, the colonial systems of Western education had been in existence for little more than thirty years. Although schooling had been extended to many in the local population, primary education and literacy were far from universal. The 1925 Monroe Report in the Philippines highlighted the shortcomings that persisted in the education system despite substantial expenditure. Similar evaluations were made in other colonies. A lack of financing and

a low priority for education meant that little action was taken to redress problems of access and quality. Especially in rural areas, schooling opportunities were ignored by the local population as either irrelevant or in competition with more important priorities, such as the harvesting of crops and domestic chores. Western education did, however, provide an important means of social and economic mobility for a group of Western-educated individuals fluent in the colonial language.

The Pacific War and the Japanese occupation of many Southeast Asian countries were watershed events for educational development. Schooling was extensively disrupted, with many teachers and students displaced or killed. In Singapore and Penang, the Japanese introduced Japanese-language (*Nihon-go*) schooling, but few students attended, and, as elsewhere, the outcome was the collapse of the earlier school systems. When the colonial administrations returned after 1945, they faced major educational challenges, including the need to rebuild schools and satisfy the unmet demand for education. Even more significant were the strong pressures for independence, since it was evident that the earlier educational policies were unsuitable for modern independent nations.

Preparing for Independence

In Burma, Indonesia, and the Philippines, independence followed swiftly after the Japanese capitulation, so the colonial authorities had little opportunity to revisit educational policies. In Indochina, Cambodia, Laos, and Vietnam gained independence from the French in the early 1950s, but the conflict surrounding French withdrawal ensured that there was little educational preparation for independence. By contrast, in British Malaya, independence did not come for more than a decade. During this period, the British confronted the pent-up demand for education. Schools had to be rebuilt, teachers trained, and textbook and resource materials prepared. Similar pressures existed for the newly independent nations.

The more pressing political issue confronting educators in British Malaya was resolving the tensions associated with the linguistically stratified prewar schooling system. Indian and especially Chinese immigrant groups made up a substantial segment of the population, and they now sought a future alongside the Malays in an independent Malaya. How could this be accomplished under the existing educational policies? Compounding the difficulty was the fact that the predominantly Chinese Malayan Communist Party (MCP), which had played a major role in resisting the Japanese during the occupation period, was mounting an insurgency campaign against the British—the Malayan Emergency (1948–1960). Prewar British concerns about the loyalty of the Chinese and the role of Chinese schools again came to the fore. Early on, the British decided to separate predominantly Chinese Singapore from the rest of British Malaya. However, this move did not resolve the issue of linguistic diversity in Singapore's school system, since a substantial divide existed between Chinese educated in the English-medium schools and those from the Chinese-language schools. Not only were the latter viewed with political suspicion, they also faced barriers to employment in the English-language administration. Chinese schoolteachers also were alienated by the fact that they received less pay than their peers in English schools, who were considered better qualified. Dissatisfaction spilled into the streets in bloody rioting in 1955 and 1956 before the government set up the All Party Committee on Chinese Education. The report issued by this committee recommended that unity be encouraged through a policy of instituting a common curriculum and giving equal treatment to each of the four language streams of schooling: English, Chinese, Tamil, and Malay. Given the unequal resources available, this approach was never likely to be fully achievable. Nevertheless, it provided a respite while the administration and the Singaporean politicians charted a future federation with the other states of Malaya. Given the predominance of Malays in the short-lived Malaysia, which included Singapore (1963–1965), it was not surprising that the Malay language was declared the national language, although in Singapore, English remained the language of administration and Chinese and Tamil had the status of official languages. Elsewhere in Malaysia, educational issues surrounding the preparation for independence took a similar, although far less conflictual, course. As a result, it was acknowledged within the federation that the independent government should support the four separate strands of education.

The inherent instability of this policy became evident when Singapore broke from Malaysia in 1965 and further changes were made to education.

Postindependence Education

The independent states of Southeast Asia embraced Western mass education as a tool for achieving their sociopolitical objectives of developing national unity and ensuring the legitimacy of the new political regimes. All the countries inherited ethnically diverse populations through annexation and the immigration of groups such as the Chinese. The achievement of national unity was a major imperative for all the new states, and schooling was seen as capable of making a substantial contribution to that end. One way this was to be achieved was by teaching in a common language. The older colonial debates about the relative importance of the vernacular and the metropole's language took a new turn at independence as nations sought to unify around a single language. The selection of the common language was influenced by the linguistic composition of the population and debates about the advantages of a major international language such as English. In the Philippines, the debate was settled in favor of retaining English as the medium of instruction. However, in other colonies, the stratified schooling system worked against this approach. In Indonesia, Bahasa Indonesia was identified as the lingua franca to be developed in place of Dutch or a regional language. Bahasa Melayu played a similar role in Malaysia, although the government continued to fund Chinese and Tamil vernacular primary schools. In Singapore, Bahasa Melayu remained the national language and was taught with English in all schools, including those using Chinese and Tamil as the medium of instruction until 1979. In that year, reforms began, so that today, English is used in all schools, with students also studying their native Chinese, Malay, or Tamil. In Indochina, Laotian, Vietnamese, and Khmer replaced French as national languages, and Burmese replaced English in Burma. This issue also confronted Thailand, since it, too, had a diverse population, including Chinese who had developed their own schooling system. These schools were closed, and the Thai language became the medium of instruction in all schools. At the same time, English was introduced as a subject. Before independence in 1984, Brunei had separate English and Malay schools, but these were amalgamated to provide bilingual education in English and Malay.

Another means used by states to promote national unity was the introduction of curriculum content that promoted the national ideology, such as Pancasila ("Five Principles") in Indonesia, Rukunegara ("National Principles") in Malaysia, and civics and moral education. In doing so, they were highlighting the state's distinctive values and seeking to socialize the youth into them. This was especially important in states involved in revolutionary change, such as Cambodia and Vietnam. In Singapore, too, the moral education curriculum was emphasized as a means of promoting the society's underlying Asian values as a prerequisite to avoiding adoption of undesirable and alienating Western values associated with individualism. Asian values have been viewed as contributing to successful Singaporean social and economic development.

The potential of mass education to contribute more directly to economic development has also been embraced by national leaders. In doing so, they share the views of international experts on development and modernization who advocate the importance of basic levels of education and literacy as key to economic development and modernization, goals espoused by all the states. This agreement is particularly significant for those developing states unable to fund their educational expansion without international assistance, since many international agencies provide funding for projects that are congruent with their educational models. In addition to international agencies such as the United Nations Educational, Scientific, and Cultural Organization (UNESCO) and the World Bank, the Southeast Asian region has regionally based agencies with an educational focus, including the Asian Development Bank and the Southeast Asian Ministers of Education Organization (SEAMEO). Established in 1965, SEAMEO sponsors twelve specialist centers concerned with educational issues, including educational innovation and technology (INNOTECH), mathematics and science education (RECSAM), vocational and technical education (VOCTECH), language teaching (RELC), and history and tradition (CHAT).

The lack of substantial economic resources has been exacerbated by lengthy and debilitating periods of civil war and unrest, particularly in the countries of Indochina, Indonesia, and the Philippines. In addition to reducing funding for education, civil unrest directly affects the ability of schools to operate.

By the 1970s, although considerable resources had been invested by all states in developing universal primary education and achieving literacy, questioning arose in regard to the educational outcomes, which often fell far short of the high initial expectations for economic growth and social development. Concerns continue today and include whether the expansion has actually resulted in higher levels of literacy and whether educational access for women and regional and ethnic minorities has been substantially improved. Explanations for the educational outcomes focus on the quality of the education. Particular attention is given to the existence of adequately trained teachers, appropriate teaching methods, textbooks, and other classroom resource materials as well as suitable curricula. The emphasis in these explanations is on the technical nature of the problems confronting education.

Other criticisms are more concerned with underlying educational assumptions and strategies. They focus on the appropriateness of the curricula. These criticisms are bolstered by evidence that many students favor the more academic curriculum associated with higher education and social mobility despite indications that, with increasing levels of education, their aspirations may not be achievable. A related issue is that vocational training, seen as more important for economic development, is failing to attract a sufficient number of students. It is somewhat ironic in light of colonial rural educational policies that some people explain these trends by arguing that the "Western" curriculum is inappropriate for those in rural areas, as it is irrelevant to their needs and may dislocate them from their traditional lifestyles.

As this indicates, notions of what constitutes Western education have changed over the years of contact between Europe and Southeast Asia. Initially, Western education was distinguished by the way in which it introduced different belief systems and knowledge, which, in conjunction with other changes associated with colonialism, led to change in the traditional societies. By the nineteenth century, one of the distinguishing features of Western education in Southeast Asia was the development of education systems that offered a more homogeneous and centrally determined educational experience (albeit within diverse educational streams). Although there was also some shift in the content of education to include newer subject areas, attempts were made to ensure that change in traditional rural society was minimized. In the postindependence period, Western education has come to be associated with the further development of mass education systems involving extensive government control, even as the trend toward increasing privatization at the primary, secondary, and postsecondary levels has grown. This growth reflects a market response to unmet educational demand sanctioned by states for financial and/or ideological reasons. The challenge for Southeast Asian states in the years ahead will be to determine whether a modification of their control of education in the postindependence period will jeopardize the future achievement of their national objectives.

CHRISTINE INGLIS

See also Chulalongkorn University; Education, Overseas Chinese; Ethical Policy (*Ethische Politiek*); Federated Malay States (FMS) (1896); Japanese Occupation of Southeast Asia (1941–1945); King Edward VII College of Medicine; Malay College, Kuala Kangsar (MCKK); Malayan Communist Party (MCP); Malayan Emergency (1948–1960); Malayan/Malaysian Education; "Manifest Destiny"; Missionaries, Christian; *Mission Civilisatrice* ("Civilizing Mission"); Pancasila (Pantja Sila); Penang Free School (1816); *Quốc ngữ;* Raffles College; Reforms and Modernization in Siam; Rukunegara; Santo Tomas, University of; Straits Settlements (1826–1941); University of Malaya; University of Rangoon; "White Man's Burden"

References:

Ayres, David M. 2000. *Anatomy of a Crisis: Education, Development and the State in Cambodia, 1953–1998.* Honolulu: University of Hawai'i Press.

Kelly, Gail. 2000. *French Colonial Education: Essays on Vietnam and West Africa.* Edited by David Kelly. New York: AMS Press.

May, Glenn A. 1980. *Social Engineering in the Philippines: The Aims, Execution and Impact of American Colonial Policy, 1900–1913.* Westport, CT: Greenwood Press.

Postlethwaite, T. Neville, ed. 1995. *International Encyclopedia of National Systems of Education.* Oxford: Pergamon Press.

Postlethwaite, T. Neville, and R. Murray Thomas, eds. 1980. *Schooling in the ASEAN Region: Indonesia, Malaysia, the Philippines, Singapore, Thailand.* London: Pergamon Press.

SEAMEO. 2000. "Challenges in a New Millennium." *Journal of Southeast Asian Education* 1, no. 1.

Tan, Jason, S. Gopinathan, and Ho Wah Kam, eds. 2001. *Challenges Facing the Singapore Education System Today.* Singapore: Prentice-Hall.

Van der Veur, Paul. 1969. *Education and Social Change in Colonial Indonesia.* Papers in International Studies, Southeast Asian Series no. 12. Athens: Ohio University Center for International Studies, Southeast Asian Program.

Watson, Keith. 1980. *Educational Development in Thailand.* Hong Kong, Singapore, and Kuala Lumpur: Heinemann Asia.

ELEPHANTS
From the Sacred to the Mundane

The Asian elephant (*Elephas maximus*) has been worshiped as a god, served as the mount of royalty, suffered as a battle tank, and labored as the workaday helper of loggers, farmers, soldiers, and merchants throughout much of its history. It is smaller, more docile, and more adaptable to life among humans than its distant relative, the African elephant (*Loxodonta africana*). The Asian elephant is now an endangered species.

The range of the Asian elephant once extended from present-day Syria east to Vietnam, north to China, and south to Sri Lanka. By the end of the twentieth century, the habitats of both wild and tamed elephants were limited to scattered locations in Sri Lanka, India, Pakistan, Bangladesh, and Nepal in South Asia. They were also confined to forested areas and preserves in Burma (Myanmar), Thailand, Laos, Cambodia, Malaysia, and the island of Sumatra in Indonesia. Elephants numbered in the hundreds of thousands as recently as the nineteenth century. Yet at the beginning of the twenty-first

Statue of Ganesh decorated with hibiscus flowers.
(Paul Seheult/Eye Ubiquitous/Corbis)

century, wild Asian elephants likely numbered under 50,000, and tame elephants approximate less than 20,000.

No historical or prehistorical record informs us when the elephant was tamed in Southeast Asia. The South Asia evidence is clear, however, that elephants were under human control during the Indus Valley civilization in the third millennium B.C.E. A Mohenjo-Daro steatite seal depicts an elephant with a saddle blanket, and others show elephants at feeding troughs. The idea of elephant control may have spread from India into the heavily forested areas of Southeast Asia, where wild elephant populations abounded. In Southeast Asia, the use of elephants in warfare may not have occurred until complex, stratified societies with chiefs and minor kings developed.

An early state or complex of chiefdoms now called Funan, dating to the first five centuries C.E., had the first record of Southeast Asian use of elephants. The Funan polities were located in the Mekong Delta and north into Cambodia. Chinese envoys to Funan in the fourth century

C.E. recorded tame elephants sent to the Chinese emperor as tribute. Elephants increasingly assumed important roles in work and in aristocratic society about the time South Asian cosmology and writing were adopted. The elephant in the form of the Hindu god Ganesh, an elephant-headed human, came to take a prominent place in Southeast Asian religion, a place still retained today.

The elephant was most clearly recorded during the Khmer empire dating from roughly 809 C.E. to 1431 C.E. During this time, the great temple of Angkor Wat and the Bayon were built. The frequent wars against the Thais and Chams involved use of large "tuskers," or superior male elephants, as well as elephants that carried men and goods. Elephants were important in moving the stones that built the temples, the logs that built the palaces, and the rice and other foods produced by the populace to feed the royalty and the priests. The war elephants are wonderfully illustrated in the reliefs on the gallery walls of Angkor Wat. Similarly, many elephants are found among the carvings on the walls of Borobudur, the great Javanese Hindu-Buddhist temple dating to about 800 C.E.

Elephants continued to play important roles throughout the historical period, in the colonial era, and into modern times. The sacred and royal "white elephant," a rare elephant with light skin color and special characteristics, was always the property of a king. Possession of the white elephants often figured in conflicts among kings. An important episode in Thai history featured King Mahachakrapat of Ayutthaya, who ascended the throne in 1549, facing the attacking Burmese army. The king rode his war elephant, as did Queen Suriyothai and Princess Tepsatri. In battle, Queen Suriyothai drove her elephant between those of her husband and the Burmese king, saving King Mahachakrapat's life but losing her own and her daughter's lives. This heroism has remained celebrated among the Thai, most recently in the 2002 feature film *Suriyothai.*

With the appearance of the Western colonial powers in Southeast Asia, teak logging became important, and elephant use shifted emphasis. Elephants and teak logging were especially important in British Burma, throughout the interior and upland forests of the region. Teak logging continued in the early twentieth century in Burma but was largely curtailed by the Pacific War (1941–1945) and by the postwar diminishing of the forests. The teak elephants did play an important role in the war, being used by both the Allies and the Japanese army to haul equipment, munitions, and men in the remote, inaccessible, and inhospitable interiors. Elephants continued their war efforts, although only for haulage, in the Indochina conflicts of the 1960s. Elephant populations suffered greatly in Vietnam and Cambodia, since U.S. pilots shot elephants to prevent their use by enemy forces.

At the close of the twentieth century, elephants no longer were held in large numbers in royal stables, they no longer logged (except in Burma and in occasional illegal logging), and they no longer served as war elephants. An endangered animal today, they increasingly play roles in tourism, carrying visitors around the temples of Angkor and into Thai forest on short excursions, and they are favorites in festivals and fairs. International elephant polo teams now compete, replacing the real battles of the past. The Asian elephant has lost much of its sacred status, although it is still loved as a symbol by millions. Its survival may depend on history—on the cultural heritage of its millennia of partnership with the Southeast Asian people.

BION GRIFFIN

See also Angkor Wat (Nagaravatta); Burma-Siam Wars; Borobudur; Funan; Hindu-Buddhist Period of Southeast Asia; Hinduism; Indianization; Indigenous Political Power

References:

Amranand, Ping, and William Warren. 1998. *The Elephant in Thai Life and Legend.* Bangkok: Monsoon Editions.

Gröning, Karl, and Martin Saller. 1999. *Elephants: A Cultural and Natural History.* Cologne, Germany: Könemann.

Lair, Richard. 1997. *Gone Astray: The Care and Management of the Asian Elephant in Domesticity.* Rome: Food and Agriculture Organization of the United Nations, Forestry Department, and Forestry Department Group, Regional Office for Asia and the Pacific.

U Toke Gale. 1974. *Burmese Timber Elephant.* Rangoon: Trade Corporation.

EMERGENCY (1948–1960) (MALAYA)

See Malayan Emergency (1948–1960)

ETHICAL POLICY (*ETHISCHE POLITIEK*)

The Ethical Policy was the stance adopted by the Dutch in their colonial administration after 1900. By the end of the nineteenth century, it seemed that Dutch policy in colonial Indonesia was not generating the effects expected from the demise of the Cultivation System thirty years earlier. With the phasing-out of the Cultivation System in Java and the inflow of Dutch private investment capital for the purpose of developing colonial resources, increasing export production was expected to gradually improve the lot of indigenous people in colonial Indonesia. However, in the late 1890s, foreign enterprise had not flooded into colonial Indonesia to the degree anticipated, and there were no clear signs that the lot of the Indonesian people was improving, particularly in Java. In fact, famines in 1900 and 1902 in Semarang suggested that the Javanese population was sliding into poverty.

In The Netherlands, criticism of the colonial policy was mounting. The lawyer Conrad Theodor van Deventer, later a Liberal Democratic member of the Dutch Parliament, gave such criticism particularly influential expression. In an 1899 article in the journal *De Gids,* he argued that The Netherlands had been draining wealth from Java during the nineteenth century and had therefore incurred a "debt of honour" of f200 million that had to be repaid. He suggested that the colonial policy be reformulated to include a program aimed at improving the welfare of the Indonesians, generously supported by the Dutch treasury. In 1901, the editor of the newspaper *De Locomotief* in Semarang, Pieter Brooshooft, maintained that colonial Indonesia required an "ethical policy." Such a policy, he proposed, would include altruistic measures by the Dutch government to further the prosperity of Indonesians in the main island of Java, where the indigenous population was widely believed to be experiencing a decline in living standards.

The leader of the Dutch Anti-Revolutionaire Partij (the Calvinist Christian Democrats), Abraham Kuijper, had long advocated an end to the economic exploitation of colonial Indonesia. In 1901, he came to lead a new coalition government that provided an opportunity for change in Dutch colonial policy along the lines suggested by van Deventer. In her annual speech to the Dutch Parliament, Queen Wilhelmina (r. 1880–1962) formally announced this change. She mentioned that it was the "moral duty" of The Netherlands to combat the causes of perpetual poverty in colonial Indonesia and improve the welfare of the people there.

The new stance became popularly known as the Ethical Policy. However, a clear definition of this policy, particularly its goals and means, has never been provided. The queen's announcement was only a reflection of an ongoing process of change in Dutch colonial policy. The term therefore meant different things to different people.

Its most fervent supporters saw the Ethical Policy as the Dutch version of the "white man's burden," a selfless experiment aimed at transforming Indonesian society, enabling a new elite to share in the riches of Western civilization, and bringing the colony into the modern world. For instance, van Deventer foreshadowed the emergence of a Westernized elite that would be grateful to The Netherlands for its material wealth and high culture and would work to cement a lasting bond between Indonesia and The Netherlands. Others hoped for the development of a new Indonesian society that would blend elements of Indonesian and Western cultures. Furthermore, this new society would enjoy a large measure of autonomy within the framework of the Dutch colonial empire. Brooshooft stressed decentralization of colonial administration and measures to spur the welfare of Indonesians. A widely used slogan summarized the practical implications of the Ethical Policy: "irrigation, migration and education."

The Ethical Policy comprised a complex of ideas and goals, all arising from a sense of ethical or moral responsibility for colonial Indonesia. In practical terms, it was associated with improvements in educational opportunities for Indonesians, a degree of tolerance for Indonesian nationalism, decentralization of the colonial administrative system in Indonesia, limited participation in local government for Indonesians, and a series of proactive policies aimed at furthering economic development, particularly in Java.

It was initially believed that economic change in Indonesia could be achieved with financial assistance from The Netherlands. In 1904, the Dutch Parliament approved a proposition that The Netherlands guarantee the repayment of the current debt of the Dutch colonial government, extending $f40$ million as grants-in-aid for development projects (Van der Eng 1996: 152). Although a sizable sum at the time, the grant was much less than van Deventer's debt of honor and small compared with sums required to further economic improvement in Indonesia. Hence, most policy initiatives were to be funded with revenues generated in colonial Indonesia. This imposed clear limits on the initiatives the colonial government could develop with the aim of furthering economic and social development. Still, during the late colonial period, the government developed and pursued a range of initiatives. In all cases, these measures involved the creation of public services and an expansion of the number of public officials—both Dutch and Indonesian.

From the start, improvements in irrigation works were at the forefront, possibly as a consequence of Dutch prowess in hydraulic engineering. Already in the 1890s but with more fervor after 1901, weirs and primary and secondary irrigation channels were improved with modern construction methods, schedules for water distribution and management were established in river systems, and schemes for the operation and maintenance of irrigation structures were put in place throughout Java. The aims of such measures varied, but they generally involved raising rice yields, increasing the area suitable for double cropping, and reducing crop failure. Despite some failures, such as the grandiose Solo Valley works in 1905, the irrigation effort contributed to the sustained growth of rice production in Java in the face of increasing population pressure.

In the nineteenth century, Dutch officials were concerned about the rising population density in Java. Orchestrated migration to sparsely populated parts of the country was entertained as a possible way to relieve population pressure. Government-sponsored migration schemes started in 1905 with a project in Lampung (South Sumatra), and later projects were initiated in Kalimantan and Sulawesi. But between 1905 and 1930, only 37,800 people migrated under these projects, while the population in Java increased by 9 million. The effort to enhance education involved the establishment of village schools after 1906, which brought larger numbers of indigenous children into the classrooms. However, the colonial government continued to favor educational facilities for European children. The enrollment of indigenous children increased quickly, but the quality of their educational facilities and of the education they received remained lower than that of European children and children of the indigenous aristocratic elite. Still, these changes created chances for bright Indonesian children to qualify for education at European primary and secondary schools and at institutions for tertiary education. This development nurtured the rise of a small but well-educated indigenous elite who, ironically, started to give expression to the growing popular anticolonial feelings. By the end of the 1930s, still only a small number of indigenous students graduated from high school, and the adult literacy rate was just under 19 percent (Van der Eng 1996: 120).

The Dutch colonial government introduced a range of other public services, including an agricultural extension service that propagated improved crops, superior farming methods, and the use of fertilizers. The Public Health Service disseminated knowledge of common diseases and how to prevent them through basic hygiene. A service for small-scale credit aimed to reduce widespread dependence for credit on usurers and crop forestallers (moneylenders who accept the pledge of the farmer's future crop as surety for credit), in an effort to combat the problem of rural indebtedness and the evil of usury. A system of village banks and district banks was established and became the predecessor of the current Bank Rakyat Indonesia.

Throughout the 1920s, Dutch colonial officials were involved in most aspects of indigenous agriculture. They assisted and advised the people on irrigation, selection and spreading of new crop varieties, improvement and demonstration of new cultivation procedures, prevention of pests and crop diseases, furthering fertilizer use, credit supply, agricultural education, rural cooperatives, and enforcing an agrarian legislation that protected the rights of small farmers. Before the Pacific War (1941–1945), several international observers of Dutch colonial policy considered that the Ethical Policy had been without precedent in the colonial world, and they praised the benevolence of the Dutch colonial regime.

The popular perception of the Ethical Policy involved more than furthering prosperity. Decentralization of government and greater political participation of Indonesians in political processes were other aspects of the approach. Developments in this regard took the form of the establishment of municipal and regency councils and a surrogate parliament (the *Volksraad*) in 1918, all with participation of indigenous Indonesians, and the subsequent establishment of three provinces with a degree of administrative autonomy in Java in the late 1920s. It is difficult to say whether all these measures were, in a strict sense, part of the Ethical Policy because neither the Dutch nor the colonial government ever defined the policy or made a formal announcement of the policy's abolishment. In addition, the phrase *Ethical Policy* was less commonly used in the early 1920s because it became associated with a budding Indonesian nationalism that took on more and more radical tendencies. Although initially perceived as a development effort that would help Indonesia achieve administrative self-sufficiency, the Ethical Policy became increasingly regarded as a politically neutral effort to enhance popular prosperity.

Despite the grandiose visions some may have entertained about the impact of the ending of the Cultivation System, the achievements of the Ethical Policy in the form of spurring indigenous prosperity were, on the whole, modest. The good intentions and genuine candor of colonial administrators were not in doubt, and evidence to conclude that there was a continued slide of greater numbers of people in Java into poverty was scant, but a very significant improvement in the living standards of Indonesians in Java was not achieved. A major reason was that, due to limitations of the budget of the colonial government, the development effort was simply not extensive enough. However, the seeds for the further development of the welfare services were sown. All were reestablished after Indonesia's independence, and they formed the basis for later efforts to improve prosperity through education, health care, agricultural extension, popular credit, and other means.

PIERRE VAN DER ENG

See also Boedi Oetama (Budi Utomo)
(1908); Cultivation System (*Cultuurstelsel*);
Dutch Interests in Southeast Asia from
1800; Education, Western Secular; Famines;
Java; "Manifest Destiny"; *Mission
Civilisatrice* ("Civilizing Mission");
Nationalism and Independence Movements
in Southeast Asia; *Volksraad* (Peoples
Council) (1918–1942); "White Man's
Burden"

References:

Cribb, R. 1993. "Development Policy in the
Early 20th Century." Pp. 225–245 in
*Development and Social Welfare: Indonesia's
Experiences under the New Order.* Edited by
Jan-Paul Dirke, Frans Hsken, and Mario
Rutten. Leiden, The Netherlands: KITLV
Press.

Dick, H., V. J. H. Houben, J. Th. Lindblad, and
Thee Kian Wie. 2002. *The Emergence of a
National Economy: An Economic History of
Indonesia, 1800–2000.* Honolulu:
University of Hawai'i Press.

Locher-Scholten, E. B. 1981. *Ethiek in
fragmenten: Vijf studies over koloniaal denken
en doen van Nederlanders in de Indonesische
Archipel, 1877–1942* [*Ethics in fragments:
Five studies of colonial thoughts and actions by
the Dutch in the Indonesian archipelago,
1877–1942*]. Utrecht, The Netherlands:
HES Publishers.

Otterspeer, W. 1989. "The Ethical Imperative:
C. Snouck Hurgronje and Dutch Ethical
Colonial Policy." Pp. 204–229 in *Leiden
Oriental Connections, 1850–1940.* Edited by
W. Otterspeer. New York: E. J. Brill.

Prince, G. H. A. 1999. "Landbouwvoorlichting
en Onderwijs als Onderdelen van de
Koloniale Welvaartspolitiek" [Agricultural
extension and education as part of the
colonial welfare policy]. *NEHA Jaarboek*
62: 211–230.

Van der Eng, P., ed. 1996. *Agricultural Growth
in Indonesia: Productivity Change and Policy
Impact since 1880.* New York: St. Martin's
Press.

Van Miert, H. 1991. *Benlongenheid en
Onvermogen: Mr. J. H. Abendanon
(1852–1925) en de Ethische Richting in het
Nederlandse Kolonialisme* [*Inspiration and
Incapacity: Mr. J. H. Abendanon (1852–1925)
and the Ethical Direction in Dutch Colonial
Policy*]. Leiden: KITLV Press.

ETHNOLINGUISTIC GROUPS OF SOUTHEAST ASIA

There is still considerable dispute among archaeologists, prehistorians, anthropologists, and ethnolinguists about the origins, differentiation, distributions, and migrations of the major ethnolinguistic groups of Southeast Asia and the interrelationships among them. However, what is certain is that the prehistory and early history of Southeast Asia must be seen in a much broader context, given that the region and its constituent nation-states are relatively recent creations and that ethnic and cultural relationships do not map neatly onto these political units. As Sandra Bowdler noted, "There is no particular reason to assume that south China was a separate entity from northern Vietnam, Laos and Burma in prehistoric times" (1993: 49). Indeed, there were considerable movements of people and traits across this mainland region, and there is evidence of shared cultural traditions and exchanges, as well as migrations by sea between what is now southern China and Southeast Asia. Thus, there are no sharply defined and bounded ethnolinguistic or human biological groupings either in prehistory or at the present time. Peter Bellwood has shown in some detail that it is "impossible to construct watertight categories"; specifically, "a cursory survey of the ethnographic record reveals that people who appear biologically to be quite different may speak languages in the same family, and peoples with strong physical similarities may be quite different in terms of language and cultural background" (1992: 56).

Research on the prehistory of Southeast Asia, including the neighboring and culturally related area of southern China, has made an important contribution to our knowledge about the development of human societies (Bellwood 1992: 54). It was from the Southeast Asian region that Australo-Melanesian populations made early sea-crossings to Australia and the western Pacific islands some forty thousand years ago. These early Australoid hunting-and-gathering communities were subsequently displaced by expansions of Southern Mongoloid agriculturalists in what were quite remarkable colonizations by Austroasiatic speakers into much of mainland Southeast Asia and by Austronesian speakers into the maritime regions and further afield into the Pacific. Northern mainland Southeast Asia and south-central

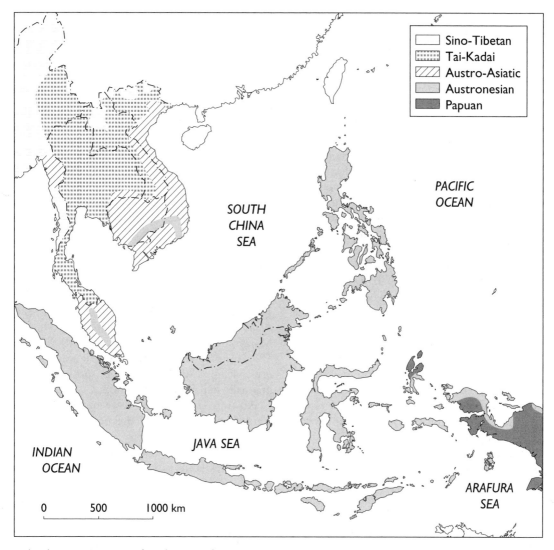

Ethnolinguistic pattern of modern Southeast Asia. The Modern Anthropology of South-East Asia: An Introduction.*(Adapted by permission from King, Victor T., and William D. Wilder. 2003. London: RoutledgeCurzon, p. xxv)*

China were also important sites for the development of early Neolithic cultures and the domestication of plants and animals.

The first clear evidence we have for the presence of *Homo sapiens* in Southeast Asia is the human skull found in the West Mouth of the Niah Caves limestone complex in northwestern Borneo. The skull was dated to the late Pleistocene period about forty thousand years ago, though there is still some debate about the accuracy of this dating, given the methods employed in the Niah archaeological excavations undertaken in Sarawak during the 1950s (King 1993: 65–67). Some archaeologists suggest that the skull may be more recent than originally supposed (Bellwood 1997: 84). What seems to be agreed is that it is of Australoid or Australo-Melanesian type and that Southeast Asia was populated at that time (and probably further back to fifty thousand years ago) by ancestors of the present differentiated Australian-Melanesian aboriginal populations of Australasia and New Guinea (Bellwood 1997: 91–92). Other more recent skeletal remains, also of Melanesian type, have been excavated in Niah burial sites; in addition, in Tabon Cave, on the Philippine island of Palawan, an excavated mandible, dated between 20,000 and 18,000 B.C.E., was also identified as Australo-Melanesian.

The Southeast Asian Australo-Melanesian economy was based on hunting, gathering, and fishing. Large forest animals were hunted, including cattle, pigs, and deer, as well as arboreal mammals such as monkeys and orangutans. These early communities made use of cave sites at or close to the coast or in more open sites along the lower courses of rivers, though there is evidence of some communities penetrating to inland lake sites and caves some distance from the sea. They used stone implements, and some were also "coastally adapted" and used watercraft (Bowdler 1993: 57). Early stone tools were probably multifunctional and comprised pebble and basic flake artifacts, which became more refined between twenty thousand and ten thousand years ago, with evidence of such processes as edge grinding. Many of the finds from the Niah excavations comprise burial artifacts of stone, bone tools, and ritual shells occurring in a range of different burial types, dated between about 15,000 B.C.E. and 4000 B.C.E. (King 1993: 68–72). No doubt, these early peoples also fashioned equipment and objects from perishable materials such as bamboo, wood, and other vegetable matter. There is also early evidence of hunter-gatherers in mainland Southeast Asia at the rock shelter of Lang Rongrien in Krabi Province, southern Thailand, with hearths, animal bones, and flaked stone implements dated from thirty-eight thousand to twenty-seven thousand years ago, at the Red River sites of Son Vi, which have been dated from about 18,000 B.C.E., and in the important Hoabinhian sites south of the Red River Valley, commencing from about 11,000 to 9000 B.C.E. (Higham and Thosarat 1998: 24–25, 64; Higham 1989: 35).

Up to about 8000 B.C.E., roughly at the commencement of the Holocene period, the climate was drier and cooler than it is today, vegetation was more open, and sea levels were lower; consequently, large areas of the Sunda Shelf comprised dry land, bridging what is now mainland and island Southeast Asia. However, postglacial warming, commencing from about eighteen thousand to six thousand years ago, resulted in gradually rising sea levels, increasing temperatures and rainfall, and denser and lusher vegetation, especially in the tropical, equatorial zones. Mainland Southeast Asia, once joined to what is now western Indonesia and permitting the movements by land of people and fauna, became separated from such present-day islands as Sumatra, Borneo, and Java by the South China Sea, the Gulf of Thailand, the Straits of Melaka, and the Java Sea. It is from the warmer, wetter Holocene period that we have evidence of marked cultural change, the domestication of plants and animals, and the movements of people by sea.

Again, the details are disputed. Bellwood and others argued that from about 3000 B.C.E., these early Australo-Melanesian populations, which were widespread in Southeast Asia, gradually gave way in the island world to Southern Mongoloid, Austronesian-speaking peoples, the ancestors of most of the present-day Southeast Asians in the Philippines and the Indo-Malaysian archipelago (Bellwood 1997: 96–127). In mainland Southeast Asia, it was Southern Mongoloid Austroasiatic speakers who gradually expanded southward.

Austronesian cultures were moving southward from Taiwan into the northern Philippines from about forty-five hundred years ago and are assumed to have settled much of the Philippines and eastern Indonesia between 2500 and 1500 B.C.E. and the western Indo-Malaysian archipelago between about 1500 and 500 B.C.E. The related Austronesian-speaking Polynesian and Micronesian populations began to settle the Pacific islands in about 2000 B.C.E., and with the exception of New Guinea and some neighboring islands, they had populated most of the Pacific islands by 500 C.E.

Nevertheless, this was not a straightforward replacement process, and neither were the boundaries between Australo-Melanesians and Southern Mongoloids sharply defined; migrations, interactions, and local evolutions were undoubtedly complex, and aside from migrations of people, there were movements of ideas and practices. Bellwood has also considered and to some extent accepted the view that "the postulated Southern Mongoloid migrants may have been settling amongst populations [Australo-Melanesians] who were also evolving in similar ways." Moreover, "many aspects of the present Southern Mongoloid phenotype have actually evolved within Southeast Asia from the

Late Pleistocene onward." Indeed, "many of the present Southern Mongoloid populations of Indonesia and Malaysia also have a high degree of Australo-Melanesian genetic heritage" (Bellwood 1997: 89, 92).

The Southern Mongoloids are usually distinguished from Northern Mongoloids, represented by the Chinese, Koreans, and Japanese, and these southern populations probably originated somewhere in present-day southern China before some of them began to move eastward and seaward to Taiwan and the Philippines. In physical type, Southern Mongoloids are generally short or medium in stature, with yellowish or brown skin, and most are straight-haired. By contrast, the remaining Australo-Melanesian peoples of Southeast Asia are generally small in stature and very dark-skinned, with tight curly or woolly hair (sometimes brown or red in color) and Australoid facial features.

Residual elements of earlier Australo-Melanesian settlement are represented today in the Negrito populations of central Peninsular Malaysia and in small pockets in the Philippine islands of Luzon, northern Palawan, Panay, Negros, and Mindanao; they are also in the Andaman Islands and in various Melanesian communities in the eastern Indonesian islands of the Lesser Sundas and the Moluccas. Of course, substantial numbers of Melanesians in western New Guinea (Irian Jaya, West Papua) were incorporated into the Netherlands East Indies, and following a Dutch postwar interregnum, these territories were eventually transferred to the Republic of Indonesia in 1962. Australoids have also intermixed with Mongoloid populations to give rise to phenotypically intermediate populations, such as the Senoi of Peninsular Malaysia (Bellwood 1997: 72). Moreover, the Philippine Negritos have adopted Austronesian languages from their neighbors, and Malaysian Negritos speak Austroasiatic languages related to Mon and Khmer. Prior to their contact with Mongoloid populations, we assume that they spoke Papuan-type languages distantly related to those of the present-day Australo-Melanesian groups.

Evidence from archaeological excavations in island Southeast Asia suggests a "cultural break" during the third millennium B.C.E. and the appearance of hand-molded, plain or red-slipped pottery in burial and other sites. But in mainland Southeast Asia in Hoabinhian and Bacson-ian sites, pottery remains are found in earlier hunting-gathering contexts, at least going back some seven thousand years ago (Bellwood 1992: 87). Bellwood and others have argued that cultural and other changes from about 2500 B.C.E. coincided with the expansion of Austronesian settlement in island Southeast Asia (Bellwood 1997: 119–124).

The Austronesians were agriculturalists who planted rice, millet, and sugarcane, though they also hunted, gathered, and fished. They kept domestic pigs, poultry, and dogs; used more sophisticated stone tools; lived in substantial timber houses; manufactured pottery; developed distinctive art styles; practiced a range of elaborate funerary rituals; and used canoes for sea transport. In their movements into the tropical regions, there was also increasing adoption of other crops, including taro, breadfruit, banana, yam, sago, and coconut. Nevertheless, small groups of Austronesians and surviving Australo-Melanesian communities were involved in forest hunting and gathering, and some Austronesian communities specialized in coastal marine fishing and strand collecting.

In mainland Southeast Asia, too, the Southern Mongoloid ancestors of Austroasiatic speakers had expanded their settlement from the north probably from about 4000 B.C.E. By 2000 B.C.E., the whole of the mainland region, extending through the Malaysian Peninsula and Sumatra (with a possible outlier in western Borneo), was occupied by Southern Mongoloid, Austroasiatic populations (Bellwood 1995: 105; 1997: 117). Austroasiatics and Austronesians increasingly came into contact in the western Malay-Indonesian archipelago as Austronesians expanded westward from about 1500 B.C.E. and also settled in coastal southern Vietnam. There is evidence of rice-cultivating, pottery-making Austroasiatic populations from excavations at Ban Kao in Kanchanaburi and Tha Kae in the Lopburi area and from the Red River Valley in Vietnam. The finds indicate that agriculture was known from about 2300 B.C.E. (Higham and Thosarat 1998: 76–89) and in the Khorat Plateau of northeast Thailand from about five thousand years ago (Bellwood 1992: 97–98). The use of metals came somewhat later, during what is termed the Late Neolithic. Archaeological evidence suggests bronze casting was known in Thailand and Vietnam soon after about 1500 B.C.E., and iron forging was known from about a thousand years later, associated subsequently with an increase in population and the size of settlements, political centralization, and trade with India and China (Higham 1989: 190–238). It was during this latter period that the Austroasiatic Dong-son bronze industry, with its manufacture of remarkable decorative bronze drums, flourished in the region around Hanoi in northern Vietnam, and the Austronesian Sa Huynh culture, especially skilled in iron manufacture, developed in central and southern Vietnam. Both bronze and iron appeared together in island Southeast Asia toward the end of the first millennium B.C.E.

Linguistic classification is a subject of much controversy in Southeast Asia, given that there have been both convergence and divergence of languages over a considerable period of time in Asia, and some of the interrelationships are still uncertain. However, it is generally maintained that there are four major language families in the region: Austronesian (with two major subgroups, Formosan and Malayo-Polynesian), Austroasiatic (or Mon-Khmer), Tai-Kadai, and Sino-Tibetan. This classification is based on genetic relationships; in other words, languages grouped together in the same overarching language family are assumed to share some common characteristics, which are attributed to a postulated common ancestor or protolanguage (Amara Prasithrathsint 1993: 76–77).

Austronesian is a nontonal language, and proto-Austronesian is said to have originated from a Taiwanese source about six thousand years ago and ultimately from southern China (Bellwood 1997: 117). Austronesian speakers then spread over the Indo-Malaysian archipelago from about 2500 B.C.E. onward.

They also populated the islands in the Pacific. They found their way to central and southern Vietnam, where the colonization eventually gave rise to the kingdom of Champa. (Austronesian languages are spoken by the Cham and by Vietnamese upland minorities such as the Rhade and Jarai.) Others traveled across the Indian Ocean to Madagascar in eastern Africa; Malagasy is an Austronesian language (Bellwood 1995: 98–101). It is estimated that this language family now comprises up to about 1,200 identifiable languages. Austronesian languages also constitute the national languages of Malaysia, Brunei, Singapore, Indonesia (Malay/Indonesian), and the Philippines (Taga-

log). The largest Austronesian-speaking community is the Javanese, whereas the major Austronesian-speaking minority populations are the Balinese; the Dayaks of Borneo; the Batak, Rejang, and Minangkabau of Sumatra; the Toraja of Sulawesi; and the Ifugao and Kalinga of northern Luzon.

In mainland Southeast Asia, the linguistic patterns are rather more complex. However, a major set of languages comprises the Austroasiatic family, consisting of about 150 separate languages spoken by the Vietnamese; the Khmers or Cambodians; the Mons of Burma; and certain hill groups of northern Burma, Assam, Vietnam, and Laos, including the Khasi, Palaung, Wa, Lawa, and Moi. Also included are most of the aboriginal groups of the Malay Peninsula and the Nicobarese. The Austroasiatic family also encompasses the Munda languages of Bihar, Orissa, and West Bengal. Prior to the movements into northern Southeast Asia of such ethnic groups as the Thais and the Burmese, there must have been a continuous distribution of Austroasiatic speakers over much of the mainland region and into eastern India.

The third language family is that of Tai-Kadai. The languages in this group are very widely spoken in Thailand; the Shan states of Burma; lowland Laos; the southern Chinese provinces of Guizhou (Kweichow) and Guangxi (Kwangsi); and on the northern fringes of Cambodia, Vietnam, and Malaysia. Major Tai-speaking populations, who began to expand from the borderlands of southern China into northern mainland Southeast Asia in the eleventh century C.E. and displaced Austroasiatic speakers, are the Thais, Laos, and Shans. The scattered Hmong-Mien (or Miao-Yao) languages, spoken by upland tribal minorities in southern China and northern mainland Southeast Asia, once thought to be separate from Tai-Kadai, have more recently been included within this language family (Bellwood 1997: 111).

Finally, there is the Sino-Tibetan language family, of which Chinese is a member. A major branch is Tibeto-Burman, and its speakers comprise the lowland Burmese or Burmans and various hill peoples in Burma and the neighboring mainland Southeast Asian countries, as well as in southern China, northern and northeastern India, Bangladesh, southern Tibet, and Nepal (Amara Prasithrathsint 1993; Burling

1992: 162–165). Important minorities in the borderlands from Assam through Burma, southern China, Laos, northern Thailand, and northern Vietnam include the Garo, Karen, Kachin, Lolo, Chin, Naga, Akha, Lisu, and Lahu. The language of the lowland Burmese became firmly established in central and lowland Burma following the expansion of the power of the Burmese kingdom of Pagan from the interior dry zone of Upper Burma from the ninth and tenth centuries C.E. At one time, this major language family was thought to include Tai-Kadai, but subsequently, Tai-Kadai was established as a separate family.

Although the matter is still a subject of contention among linguists, it has been suggested that there could be very remote connections among these four large Asian language families. Some linguists argue for distant connections between Tai-Kadai and Austronesian (together referred to as Austro-Tai), whereas others argue for remote or deep links between Austronesian and Austroasiatic (together known as Austric) (Bellwood 1997: 111–112). Bellwood has also suggested that the ancestors of all these four families, who were of Southern Mongoloid physical stock, inhabited contiguous areas of southern and central China, south of the Yangzi (Yangtze) River, from the early period of monsoon agricultural development about eight thousand years ago. However, it is uncertain whether these networks of linguistic connections were the result of common origins or borrowings or both, and there is still some uncertainty about the status of Sino-Tibetan (Bellwood 1995: 96–98). Bellwood has further suggested that these Neolithic revolutions then led to the expansion of settlement and, over a very long period of time, the complex movements of populations and cultural traits into other parts of Asia, including the regions to the south. Some thirty-five years ago, Robbins Burling, though suggesting that some of the "typological resemblances" among several of the mainland languages are likely to have been the result of contact and exchange, also posed the following question: "Could it be that all these languages are, even if only very remotely, related to each other in one great super-family?" (1992: 157).

Undoubtedly, a considerable amount of further social, cultural, political, and economic differentiation then took place, beginning in the early centuries of the first millennium C.E., when Southeast Asian peoples were adopting traits from both India and China and were becoming increasingly involved in far-flung Asian trade. Early Indian-influenced coastal states were identified from the second century C.E. along the sea routes between India and China, in southern and central Vietnam, around the margins of the Gulf of Thailand, in southern Thailand, in Sumatra, and in West Java. Northern Vietnam, however, was incorporated into a Chinese cultural sphere of influence. With the introduction of Indian court culture, particularly Hinduism and Mahayana Buddhism and subsequently, during the second millennium C.E., Theravada Buddhism and Islam, the lowland populations of Southeast Asia, which were part of large-scale political systems with more developed urban forms of settlement, became increasingly differentiated from upland tribal populations. This differentiation persisted between the lowland peoples and the upland communities despite their shared common linguistic and cultural roots. These divisions were further consolidated during the period of European colonialism and, in the Philippines, the conversion of the majority of the lowland communities in the northern two-thirds of the island to Roman Catholicism.

The contemporary cultural diversity of Southeast Asia is therefore the result of a progressive differentiation of populations originally of the same stock as they moved through and settled in different parts of the region. The diversity is also a consequence of the complex migrations of peoples and the displacement and assimilation of some by others, long-established exchanges of goods and cultural elements, and, subsequently, the adoption of cultural influences from India, China, the Middle East (West Asia), and the West.

VICTOR T. KING

See also Archaeological Sites of Southeast of Asia; Bajau; Ban Kao Culture; Bataks; Brunei Malay; Buddhism, Mahayana; Buddhism, Theravada; Bugis (Buginese); Burmans; Champa; Chins; Dayaks; Dong-son; East Indonesian Ethnic Groups; East Malaysian Ethnic Minorities; Hindu-Buddhist Period of Southeast Asia; Hinduism; Hmong; Hoabinhian; Human Prehistory of Southeast Asia; Iban; Ilanun and Balangingi; Indian

Immigrants; Indianization; Islam in Southeast Asia; Kachins; Kadazan-Dusun; Karens; Khmers; Lao; Malays; Metal Age Cultures in Southeast Asia; Minagkabau; Mons; Neolithic Period of Southeast Asia; Niah Caves (Sarawak); Orang Asli; Orang Laut; Pagan (Bagan); Pyus; Shans; Sulu and the Sulu Archipelago; Tabon Cave (Palawan); T'ais; Torajas; Viets

References:

Amara Prasithrathsint. 1993. "The Linguistic Mosaic." Pp. 63–88 in *Asia's Cultural Mosaic: An Anthropological Introduction.* Edited by Grant Evans. New York and Singapore: Prentice-Hall and Simon and Schuster (Asia).

Bellwood, Peter. 1992. "Southeast Asia before History." Pp. 55–136 in *The Cambridge History of Southeast Asia.* Vol. 1, *From Early Times to c. 1800.* Edited by Nicholas Tarling. Cambridge: Cambridge University Press.

———. 1995. "Austronesian Prehistory in Southeast Asia: Homeland, Expansion and Transformation." Pp. 96–111 in *The Austronesians: Historical and Comparative Perspectives.* Edited by Peter Bellwood, James J. Fox, and Darrell Tryon. Canberra: Australian National University, Research School of Pacific and Asian Studies, Department of Anthropology, Comparative Austronesian Project.

———. 1997. *Prehistory of the Indo-Malaysian Archipelago.* Rev. ed. Honolulu: University of Hawai'i Press.

Bowdler, Sandra. 1993. "Asian Origins: Archaeology and Anthropology." Pp. 30–62 in *Asia's Cultural Mosaic: An Anthropological Introduction.* Edited by Grant Evans. New York and Singapore: Prentice-Hall and Simon and Schuster (Asia).

Burling, Robbins. 1992 [1965]. *Hill Farms and Padi Fields: Life in Mainland Southeast Asia.* Monographs in Southeast Asian Studies. Phoenix: Arizona State University, Program for Southeast Asian Studies.

Higham, Charles. 1989. *The Archaeology of Mainland Southeast Asia: From 10,000 B.C. to the Fall of Angkor.* Cambridge: Cambridge University Press.

Higham, Charles, and Rachanie Thosarat. 1998. *Prehistoric Thailand: From Early Settlement to Sukhothai.* London: Thames and Hudson.

King, Victor T. 1993. *The Peoples of Borneo.* The Peoples of South-East Asia and the Pacific. Oxford: Blackwell.

EUROPEAN WAR (1914–1918)

See Great War (1914–1918)

F

FAMINES

Historically, hunger and malnutrition were common problems throughout Southeast Asia. Hunger often occurred before the main rice harvest when old stocks were depleted. Malnutrition was the plight of the poorest, who had no access to land for growing food crops or who lived in marginal areas with high crop-failure risks. But, unlike famines, hunger and malnutrition do not necessarily endanger survival. They are incidental situations in which the normal systems that ensure access to sufficient nutrients for survival break down, causing social disintegration. The community loses its ability to support marginal members, who migrate or die from starvation or starvation-induced diseases.

Southeast Asia did not suffer extensive famines as China and India did. Its population density was much lower. Access to land was, for a long time, sufficient to expand food production by rolling back the land frontier. Famines were generally caused by coincidence, such as natural disasters (drought or floods and subsequent crop failures), and/or acute man-made problems, such as war. For instance, the eruption of the Tambora volcano in Sumbawa (Nusatenggara, Indonesia) destroyed food crops in 1815 and caused 44,000 deaths from hunger (Stibbe and Uhlenbeck 1921: 254). Evidence of abandoned villages in the Red River delta in North Vietnam suggests that population growth was long constrained by crop failures and famines caused by floods in delta areas.

Densely populated Java suffered local famines in the nineteenth century. The operation of a rice mill by European entrepreneurs and the granting of padi purchase monopolies to them triggered the 1844–1847 famine in Cirebon Residency (West Java). The millers purchased padi without regard for local rice requirements. In the lean season, local supplies were insufficient, and Chinese rice traders, generally a source of credit to bridge the season, were no longer allowed to operate in the area.

The 1849–1850 famine in Demak and Grobogan (Central Java) was caused by four successive crop failures due to drought. Farmers had to sell buffaloes to pay the land tax. The demands on farmers to supply labor for the Cultivation System, local rulers, village elite, and colonial public works worsened the situation. A lack of action by colonial officials to bring relief also explains why this famine took the lives of 83,000 people (Elson 1985: 56).

The 1881–1882 famine in Banten Residency (West Java) was caused by cattle plague, which reduced the cattle stock by two-thirds, followed by a fever epidemic that killed 10 percent of the population (Hugenholtz 1986: 172). The 1900–1902 famine in Semarang Residency was the result of several crop failures, followed by a cholera epidemic that kept people at home and left the fields uncultivated. The colonial government mitigated both disasters by selling imported rice below cost.

The development of markets for imported and locally produced food products was effective famine mitigation. Areas suffering food deficits experienced an inflow of food products, organized by entrepreneurs to take advantage of high prices. The development of the intraregional trade of rice from Burma, Thailand, and South Vietnam to rice-deficit areas prevented starvation in times of adversity.

The Japanese occupation caused famine in Java and North Vietnam. In Java, the requisitioning of rice to feed Japanese troops amounted to modest demands compared with total production. However, Japanese authorities paid for rice purchases with money that quickly lost its value, and farmers became reluctant to sell. In 1943 and 1944, the Japanese imposed a quota from the highest to the lowest administrative levels and forbade all nonregulated trade of rice. Farmers sought to evade the quota, and rice production plummeted. A long dry season that delayed planting and harvesting for the 1944–1945 crop aggravated the situation. Insufficient rainfall caused widespread crop failures. Black market food prices increased quickly, and people not included in the official rice distribution system, such as migrant workers in urban areas, and those without assets to sell or barter were caught out. In 1944 and 1945, excess mortality was 2.4 million people (Van der Eng 2002: 503).

In the 1930s, North Vietnam was a rice-deficit area that depended on imports from South Vietnam. The Japanese obliged French Indochina to supply large amounts of rice for export to Japan and to troops in Asia. Most rice came from South Vietnam, but to meet the demands, the French introduced a system of compulsory requisitioning throughout the country, including North Vietnam. Inflation eroded purchase prices and increased the reluctance among farmers to produce a surplus. In 1944, the fifth-month harvest was poor. Insufficient rice was available until the main tenth-month harvest. When typhoons followed by strong tidal waves swept the country, flooding destroyed a large part of the tenth-month crop. Famine spread in North Vietnam, particularly among the landless. The cold 1944–1945 winter prevented the production of nonrice food crops. Estimates of the deaths during 1944 and 1945 range from 1 to 2 million people (Bui 1995: 575–576).

Other parts of Southeast Asia were also affected, particularly the areas that relied on food imports in times of production shortfalls. For instance, drought in 1944 affected the Nusatenggara region in East Indonesia, where at least 40,000 people died on Timor (Telkamp 1979: 75). A major famine struck East Timor in 1975 and 1976 as a consequence of the war in Timorese freedom fighters and Indonesian troops. The dislocation of farming communities and the destruction of food crops caused the death of possibly 100,000 people (Cribb 2001: 82–98).

In the mid-1970s, a famine emerged in Cambodia, which had been a rice-surplus area in the 1960s. In 1970, civil war broke out between Khmer nationalists and the U.S.-supported government. Warfare and American bombing drove more than a quarter of the population to the cities. Starvation started in Phnom Penh in 1974. The victorious Khmer Rouge forced people to join regimented rural cooperatives and work the land. Massive dislocation, widespread purges, and the shunning of foreign aid led to starvation. A Vietnamese invasion in 1978 toppled the brutal regime, but many people abandoned fields and fled toward Thailand. By 1979, Cambodia suffered a full-blown famine, requiring foreign food assistance. From 1975 to 1979, an estimated 1.5 million people died from malnutrition, illness, or overwork (Chandler 1999: 3).

Floods and drought caused occasional food shortages in the region, as in Irian Jaya in 1997 and 1998 and Vietnam in 1999. The specter of widespread famine has, however, disappeared. The Green Revolution in rice agriculture increased rice productivity. Growing numbers of people are no longer primarily dependent on food agriculture; their discretionary income is high enough to purchase food. Better communications encourage food to flow where the price is highest, including areas suffering shortages. Further, individual countries and international aid agencies now have famine prevention and relief mechanisms in place.

PIERRE VAN DER ENG

See also Cultivation System (*Cultuurstelsel*);
Democratic Kampuchea (DK); Diseases and
Epidemics; Great Depression (1929–1931);
Indochina during World War II (1939–1945);
Japanese Occupation of Southeast Asia

(1941–1945); Java; Khmer Rouge; Timor; Vietnam, North (Post-1945); Vietnam, South (Post-1945)

References:

Bui Minh Dung. 1995. "Japan's Role in the Vietnamese Starvation of 1944–45." *Modern Asian Studies* 29: 573–618.

Chandler, David. 1999. *Voices from S-21.* Berkeley and Los Angeles: University of California Press.

Cribb, R. 2001. "How Many Deaths? Problems in the Statistics of Massacre in Indonesia (1965–66) and East Timor (1975–80)." Pp. 82–98 in *Violence in Indonesia*. Edited by I. Wessel and G. Wimhöfer. Hamburg: Abera.

Elson, R. E. 1985. "The Famine in Demak and Grobogan in 1849–50: Its Causes and Circumstances." *Review of Indonesian and Malayan Affairs* 19, no. 1: 39–85.

Fernando, R. 1980. *Famine in the Cirebon Residency in Java, 1844–1850: A New Perspective on the Cultivation System.* Working Paper no. 21. Melbourne, Australia: Centre of Southeast Asian Studies, Monash University.

Hiebert, M., and L. G. Hiebert. 1979. "Famine in Kampuchea: Politics of a Tragedy." *Indochina Issues* (4 December): 1–6.

Hugenholtz, W. R. 1986. "Famine and Food Supply in Java, 1830–1914." Pp. 155–188 in *Two Colonial Empires*. Edited by C. A. Bayly and D. H. A. Kolff. Dordrecht, The Netherlands: Nijhoff.

Kratoska, P. H., ed. 1998. *Food Supplies and the Japanese Occupation in South-East Asia.* Basingstoke, England: Macmillan.

Napitupulu, B. 1968. "Hunger in Indonesia." *Bulletin of Indonesian Economic Studies* 3, no. 9: 60–70.

Stibbe, D. G., and E. M. Uhlenbeck, eds. 1921. *Encyclopaedie van Nederlandsch-Indië.* Vol. 4. The Hague: Nijhoff.

Telkamp, Gerard J. 1979. "The Economic Structure of an Outpost in the Outer Islands in the Indonesian Archipelago: Portuguese Timor 1850–1975." Pp. 71–89 in *Between People and Statistics: Essays on Modern Indonesian History Presented to P. Creutzberg.* Edited by Francien van Anrooij, Dirk H. A. Kolff, Jan T. M. van Laanen, and Gerard J. Telkamp. The Hague: Martinus Nijhoff,

under the auspices of the Royal Tropical Institute, Amsterdam.

Van der Eng, P. 2002. "Bridging a Gap: A Reconstruction of Population Patterns in Indonesia, 1930–1961." *Asian Studies Review* 26, no. 3: 487–509.

FEDERATED MALAY STATES (FMS) (1896)

The Federated Malay States (FMS) came into being in 1896, bringing the peninsular Malay States of Perak, Selangor, Negri Sembilan, and Pahang under a central federal administration based in Kuala Lumpur. Although the FMS created uniformity and greater administrative efficiency, it enhanced the role and status of the central federal government at the expense of the state authorities. The FMS eroded the power and authority of the Malay rulers, who were reduced to the status of constitutional monarchs without political influence.

The British Residential System, implemented after the Pangkor Engagement (1874), created four separate independent entities of the Malay States of Perak, Selangor, Negri Sembilan, and Pahang (from 1888), each under their own resident. There was a limited amount of mutual support and cooperation among the states. The tin-rich states of Perak, Selangor, and Negri Sembilan progressed and prospered by leaps and bounds. Pahang, however, despite its size and perceived potential mineral and agricultural resources, became a financial liability, with the Straits Settlements' government as its creditor. Federation appeared to be Pahang's salvation, as the richer partners would be obliged to assist in developing its resources.

Frank Swettenham (1850–1946), an ardent proponent of federation, stressed the advantages of administrative uniformity, greater administrative efficiency, and economy. Centralization would enhance coordination of services such as revenue, infrastructure development (in particular rail and road construction), public health, education, and law and justice. The agricultural and mining sectors would benefit from federation, as would matters relating to land.

Interestingly, although the issue of federation would significantly change the status of the Malay sultans and their country, the debate was confined within British colonial official circles. In a whirlwind tour of ten days in July 1895,

Swettenham secured the signatures of the Malay rulers to the Federation Agreement.

On 1 July 1896, FMS came into effect. Perak, Selangor, Negri Sembilan, and Pahang became British protected states, to be administered under the advice of the British government through its representative, the resident-general based in Kuala Lumpur. He would advise the four Malay sultans on all aspects of administration, apart from those dealing with the Islamic religion. Theoretically, the powers and authority of the Malay rulers remained intact but confined to their respective states.

Sir Charles B. H. Mitchell (t. 1894–1899), governor of the Straits Settlements and first high commissioner for FMS, presented a blueprint of how this new entity was to be administered. Centralization of authority dwelling on the resident-general was apparent. Federal heads of the various government departments, directly responsible to the resident-general, would direct and coordinate the work of his department in the four states. A *Durbar* (conference of Malay rulers) was constituted whereby the four Malay sultans would meet annually with British officials to discuss state affairs; the outcomes of these meetings were, however, nonbinding.

Although the resident-general was, in theory, subordinate to the governor, he could exert his independence through sheer force of personality, as demonstrated by Swettenham, who was the inaugural appointee. To prevent having a too-powerful resident-general, Governor Sir John Anderson (t. 1904–1911) created the Federal Council in 1909 to ensure that power and authority were centralized with the governor/high commissioner, who was its president. Furthermore, the title of resident-general was reduced to chief secretary in 1910. Although all resolutions passed in the Federal Council had to be sanctioned by the State Councils presided over by the sultans before they were enacted, this step was a mere formality, as all decisions made by the former had to be accepted. Consequently, the State Councils functioned as mere rubber stamps to the federal government.

Partly to assuage concerns about overcentralization and the erosion of the political authority of the Malay rulers and partly to induce the five other Malay States (Perlis, Kedah, Kelantan, Terengganu, and Johor) to join FMS, proposals for decentralization were initiated during the 1920s and 1930s. However, the decentralization proposals of Sir Lawrence Nunns Guillemard (governor/high commissioner, t. 1920–1927) and Sir Cecil Clementi (governor/high commissioner, t. 1930–1934), which were approved and implemented in 1927 and 1933, respectively, did not restore power to the Malay rulers. Instead, these rulers remained politically impotent despite being consulted more frequently. Toward the late 1930s, state governments regained control over certain departments (medical and public works), and State Councils could legislate on certain subjects and have some control over their revenue and expenditure. Efforts at decentralization failed to entice the other Malay States to participate in federation.

The creation of FMS brought prosperity to all its member states, including Pahang. Infrastructure development was efficiently undertaken, whereby a good rail and road network was established. The economy—in particular, the agricultural sector (mainly the rubber industry)—benefited tremendously from federation. Notwithstanding the socioeconomic benefits, however, FMS reduced the four Malay rulers to politically impotent constitutional monarchs and further strengthened the colonial clasp of the British over the most prosperous parts of the Malay Peninsula.

OOI KEAT GIN

See also Johor; Pahang; Residential System (Malaya); Siamese Malay States (Kedah, Perlis, Kelantan, Terengganu); Western Malay States (Perak, Selangor, Negri Sembilan, and Pahang)

References:

Chai Hon-chan. 1967. *The Development of British Malaya, 1896–1909.* 2nd ed. Kuala Lumpur: Oxford University Press.

Gullick, J. M. 1992. *Rulers and Residents: Influence and Power in the Malay States, 1870–1920.* Singapore: Oxford University Press.

Thio, Eunice. 1969. *British Policy in the Malaya Peninsula, 1880–1910.* Vol. 1, *The Southern and Central States.* Kuala Lumpur: University of Malaya Press.

Yeo Kim Wah. 1982. *The Politics of Decentralization: Colonial Controversy in Malaya, 1920–1929.* Kuala Lumpur: Oxford University Press.

FEDERATION OF MALAYA (1948)

The Federation of Malaya was officially established in February 1948. This was a new form of government in Malaya, replacing the much-criticized Malayan Union formed by the British in 1946. Under the federation, all the nine Malay States—Perlis, Kedah, Perak, Selangor, Negri Sembilan, Johor, Pahang, Kelantan, and Terengganu—as well as the former Straits Settlements of Penang and Melaka were placed under one government headed by a British high commissioner.

The high commissioner, who was the highest-ranking executive officer of the federal government, administered the federation with the help of two councils, the Executive and Legislative Councils. He had to ensure that Malay privileges and the rights of the different communities according to the constitution were safeguarded. The federal government was also responsible for matters concerning security, foreign affairs, civil laws and legislation, trade, transport, communication, and finance.

The position of the nine sultans as heads of their respective states was guaranteed. They headed the state governments with the help of the State Executive and Legislative Councils. The state governments had jurisdiction over matters concerning their own local governments, religious affairs, education, health, and land. The governments of Melaka and Penang, former members of the Straits Settlements, were headed by governors appointed by the high commissioner. The sultans and the governors formed the Rulers' Council to discuss matters concerning themselves and other crucial issues with the high commissioner. They met annually or whenever the need arose.

One very important factor that emerged under the constitution of the federation was the question of citizenship. Under the constitution, people could apply for citizenship by legal means or acquire it by birth. Citizenship was accorded to those who had been born in any one of the states, or alternatively whose parents (or at least one parent) had been born in the states and had been domiciled for a specific period of time. They were also required to know the Malay language or English and to be of good character. The Federation of Malaya placed all the states in Malaya under one constitution, and for the first time, non-Malays were given the opportunity to be citizens of the federation.

BADRIYAH HAJI SALLEH

See also Abdul Rahman Putra Al-Haj, Tunku (1903–1990); British Malaya; Decolonization of Southeast Asia; Federated Malay States (FMS) (1896); Johor; Malayan/Malaysian Chinese Association (MCA) (1949); Malayan Union (1946); Melaka; Onn bin Jaafar (1895–1962); Pahang; Penang (1786); Siamese Malay States (Kedah, Perlis, Kelantan, Terengganu); Straits Settlements (1826–1941); Tan Cheng Lock, Sir (1883–1960); United Malays National Organization (UMNO) (1946)

References:

Mohamed Noordin Sopiee. 1974. *From Malayan Union to Singapore Separation: Political Unification in the Malaysia Region, 1945–65.* Kuala Lumpur: University of Malaya Press.

Stockwell, Anthony J. 1984. "British Imperial Policy and Decolonization in Malaya, 1942–52." *Journal of Imperial and Commonwealth History* 13, no. 1: 68–87.

FILIPINIZATION

Filipinization was the process, during the American colonial period in the Philippines, of putting Filipinos in active positions in government, replacing U.S. officials. This was part of the American policy of creating a government for the Philippines and preparing the country for eventual independence. Filipinization peaked during the administration of Governor-General Francis Burton Harrison (t. 1913–1921), when Harrison made it his policy to place more administrative control in the hands of Filipinos.

Since the establishment of American civil government in the Philippines in 1901, U.S. policy toward the islands was to create a stable government and to build a Philippines for the Filipinos. In the first thirteen years of American rule, Filipinos were gradually given positions of increasing responsibility in government, including local government and the legislature. Those with sufficient educational attainment and economic means were given the right to vote; out of the three provincial board positions, Filipinos held two of them through election. The lower chamber of the legislature was

Filipino-controlled. Until 1913, however, Filipinos were a minority in the upper chamber of the legislature, the Philippine Commission. They were seldom appointed as executive division or bureau heads, and in the provincial governments, U.S. officials routinely checked up on local administration. The governor-general—always an American—had the final say in legislative, executive, and judicial matters.

Filipinization echoed the liberal policy adopted by the Democrat U.S. administration, headed by President Woodrow Wilson, from 1913 to 1921. In the Philippines, Governor-General Harrison endorsed the belief that the best way to prepare Filipinos for independence was to place them in government and in positions of responsibility and to grant them as much autonomy as possible. Hoping to encourage Americans who were working in government service in the islands to retire early or otherwise leave their posts, he approved legislation that offered attractive early-retirement benefits and lowered the salaries of those Americans who stayed on. As Filipinos replaced Americans who vacated such positions, the civil service was increasingly dominated by Filipinos.

In addition to appointing Filipinos as executive department and bureau heads, Harrison allowed the top Filipino political figures, led by Manuel L. Quezon (1878–1944) and Sergio Osmeña (1878–1961), to form the Philippine Council of State, an advisory body to assist the governor-general. Meanwhile, President Wilson increased the number of Filipinos in the Philippine Assembly, thereby giving them control of both houses of the legislature. The Harrison administration also made all provincial board positions elective, thus paving the way for an all-Filipino provincial administration.

The Jones Law (sponsored by William Atkinson Jones, a Democratic representative from Virginia), passed by the U.S. Congress in 1916, gave greater impetus to Harrison's Filipinization policy. The law provided that the United States would withdraw its sovereignty over the Philippines and recognize its independence when a stable government could be established. Harrison believed that a stable government would be one controlled by Filipinos who had been prepared for self-government by handling the government themselves. Toward that end, he also gave Filipinos greater leeway in administration by not actively exercising his powers as governor-general, thereby giving more initiative to the local political leaders. He also used his veto power sparingly and supported actions of the Filipinos in government.

Harrison's Filipinization policy reduced the number of Americans in the Philippine government from 2,623 in 1913 to only 614 in 1921, while increasing the number of Filipinos from 6,363 in 1913 to 13,240 in 1921 (Agoncillo and Alfonso 1967: 340). Filipino political power increased as that of the Americans waned.

The people of the Philippine Islands welcomed Filipinization, especially as undertaken by Governor-General Harrison. The policy was, however, criticized by Americans who wanted greater U.S. control over the Philippine insular government. Critics pointed out that the rapid pace of Filipinization resulted in inexperienced persons taking important posts and led to inefficiency and corruption. Governor-General Leonard Wood (t. 1921–1927), who succeeded Harrison, discontinued the Filipinization policy.

RICARDO TROTA JOSE

See also Constitutional Developments in the Philippines (1900–1941); Harrison, Francis Burton (1873–1957); Osmeña, Sergio, Sr. (1878–1961); Philippines under U.S. Colonial Administration (1898–1946); Quezon, Manuel Luis (1878–1944)

References:
Agoncillo, Teodoro A., and Oscar M. Alfonso. 1967. *History of the Filipino People.* 2nd ed. Quezon City, the Philippines: Malaya Books.
Gleek, Lewis E., Jr. 1998. *The American Half-Century.* Manila: Historical Conservation Society.
Harrison, Francis Burton. 1922. *The Cornerstone of Philippine Independence.* New York: Century Company.
Stanley, Peter W. 1974. *A Nation in the Making: The Philippines and the United States.* Cambridge, MA: Harvard University Press.

FILIPINO-AMERICAN WAR (1899–1902)

See Philippine War of Independence (1899–1902)

FIREARMS

When Portuguese and Spaniards first entered the seas of Southeast Asia, early in the sixteenth century, they often marveled at the quantity and the quality of the locally cast swivel-guns in use aboard boats and on the wooden palisades of fortified settlements. These were light, very mobile cannons, many of them carried and shot by a single man. The guns were mounted on a swivel yoke that could be set up almost instantly on stirrups cut into the rails of ships or on stockades, to absorb recoil. Most of the pieces were made of bronze, but some were cast in brass; it is known that both copper alloys often were obtained through the smelting of imported Chinese cash. Although most of the cannons that were made were muzzle-loading, there are also quite a few examples of breech-loading cannons in various collections, and these are probably the oldest. A piece of wood, or tiller, was inserted into the back handle and lashed to the cannon with rattan, which enabled it to be trained by the gunner. Most of these swivel-guns had small bores (30 to 60 millimeters). They were loaded with small cannonballs or hail shots and primarily used against people. Such firearms were still being cast and used until modern times, as they were best adapted to common Southeast Asian warfare techniques. Brunei was known for its foundries in the nineteenth century, and in 1904, the Americans often fought in the Philippines against "Moros" armed with such cannons.

Chinese are known to have built breech-loading swivel-guns in the sixteenth century. These, however, were considered, in China, to be of Turkish origin. This is a perfect illustration of the swift diffusion of firearms and gunpowder techniques in the Old World, after the invention of fast-burning gunpowder in thirteenth-century China. Southeast Asia came in regular contact with Chinese artillery shortly after this invention, during Kublai Khan's (1215–1294) late-thirteenth-century invasions, and there are a few other testimonies to the use of firearms in Southeast Asia during the fourteenth and early fifteenth centuries. At the crossroads of the transasian maritime route and in overland contact with both India and China, Southeast Asians quickly adopted the warring techniques they needed in military conflicts, whether internal or with the Europeans.

Larger cannons do not seem to have been in regular use in Southeast Asia before the second half of the sixteenth century. When they appeared in the region, they did so as part of a broader evolution of military techniques. At sea, small swivel-guns were ideally suited for the light and swift local boats that composed most of the war fleets of the Southeast Asian powers in the beginning of the sixteenth century. Later on, much larger, galley-type war vessels, influenced by Mediterranean techniques learned from Portuguese renegades and Turkish shipwrights, complemented these indigenous fleets. Sultan Iskandar Muda (r. 1607–1636) of Aceh built the largest of them all in the 1620s. These sturdier vessels were able to carry and absorb the recoil of much larger cannons that could be used in sieges for offshore bombardment.

As a by-product of sixteenth- and seventeenth-century developments in fortress construction, large land-based siege cannons were soon cast in most countries of Southeast Asia, with the help of Turkish and Portuguese foundries. Regardless of the actual efficiency of such unwieldy cannons in war tactics, local legends and literature point to the spiritual power that was attached to them and to the vested interest Southeast Asian rulers had in possessing as many as possible. Lighter guns, such as muskets, were also incorporated into the armament of Southeast Asian armies, whether locally produced or bought from Indians, Turks, or Europeans.

By the late seventeenth century, technological innovations and mass production meant European firearms became ever more efficient and prestigious among Southeast Asian rulers, leaving local productions in their wake. They became a trade commodity that European merchants could provide best, at a cost. The ability to purchase and resourcefully use European artillery was a decisive factor in conflicts internal to the region, such as the eighteenth- and early-nineteenth-century wars between Burma and Siam or between the warring lords of Vietnam.

PIERRE-YVES MANGUIN

See also Aceh (Acheh); Aceh (Acheh) Wars (1873–1903); Anglo-Burmese Wars (1824–1826, 1852, 1885); Anti-Spanish Revolts (The Philippines); Burma-Siam Wars; Elephants; Iskandar Muda, Sultan (Mahkota Alam) (r. 1607–1636); Java War

(1825–1830); Moros; Nguyễn Dynasty (1802–1945); Piracy; Shipbuilding; Sino-Vietnamese Wars; Trinh Family (1597–1786)

References:

Harrisson, Tom. 1969. "Brunei Cannon: Their Role in Southeast Asia." *Brunei Museum Journal* 1, no. 1: 94–118.

Manguin, Pierre-Yves. 1976. "L'Artillerie légère nousantarienne: À propos de six canons conservés dans des collections portugaises" [Light Artillery in the Malay World: On Six Cannons in Portuguese Collections]. *Arts Asiatiques* 32: 233–254.

———. 1993. "The Vanishing *Jong:* Insular Southeast Asian Fleets in War and Trade (15th–17th Centuries)." Pp. 197–213 in *Southeast Asia in the Early Modern Era: Trade, Power, and Belief.* Edited by A. Reid. Ithaca, NY, and London: Cornell University Press.

Reid, Anthony. 1969. "Sixteenth-Century Turkish Influence in Western Indonesia." *Journal of Southeast Asian History* 10, no. 3: 395–414.

———. 1988, 1993. *Southeast Asia in the Age of Commerce, 1450–1680.* Vol. 1, *The Lands below the Winds*; Vol. 2, *Expansion and Crisis.* New Haven, CT, and London: Yale University Press.

FIRST AVA (INWA) DYNASTY (1364–1527 C.E.)

Prelude to Modern Myanmar

The end of the Pagan kingdom in the early fourteenth century as a central and unifying authority ushered in a short period of political decentralization, with different centers of power struggling for paramountcy. By 1364, these contending powers had been unified under a new dynasty that was located at the city of Ava and hence was called the First Ava (or Inwa, in Burmese) dynasty, which lasted until 1527. Although the Ava period is conventionally known as the "period of Shan domination," there is little or no evidence to support such a contention, particularly since the significance of this age was more political, cultural, and religious than ethnic. Indeed, the structural principles and institutions that the Burmese kingdom of Pagan had established did not die; instead, the kingdom of Ava resurrected them to perpetuate the Pagan standard, the model for subsequent dynasties. The crucial difference between Pagan and Ava was quantitative, not qualitative: in size and scale, wealth and power, influence and image. Ava was, in effect, Pagan writ small.

The city of Ava was located on an island. On its north and west was the Irrawaddy River; on its east was the Myitnge River, which flowed into the former; and on its south was the Myittha River, a tributary of the Myitnge running east to west to which was joined a canal, both emptying into the Irrawaddy. Clearly, security and defense were on the minds of the new leaders when they made Ava the capital. The shift northeast from Pagan to Ava, over 128 kilometers (80 miles) away, addressed an important concern that all Upper Burma capitals faced: an invasion from the north coming down the Irrawaddy Valley. The kingdom of Nanchao invaded the Pyu kingdom in the ninth century from the north via this route. Pagan, likewise, had to fight unnamed forces from the north in the early twelfth century, only to be invaded again from the north in the late thirteenth century by Mongols using the same routes. Pagan's leadership seemed to have anticipated this problem early and addressed it during the eleventh century by building a line of 43 forts along that invasion path. (The Yuan sources actually mentioned 300 stockades built for that purpose.)

Ava's location revealed another concern: the city lay at a strategic point for control of Shwebo and Kyaukse, two of the most important rice-growing regions in Burma at the time. They were the economic mainstay of any Burma dynasty, especially one that had political ambition or visions of reunifying the country. Although Pagan was far from Kyaukse, it had been powerful enough to control the region from that distance. But the new dynasty was not as powerful and therefore had to move its capital right to its source of wealth, where the region could be better defended and utilized. By doing so, however, the seat of power was also moved farther away from the coasts of Lower Burma, which meant the dynasty lost control over that region (control that Pagan once had). The result was the rise of the first Lower Burma kingdom in Burma's history, led by kings who claimed Mon rather than Burman descent. Thus, the decision to build the new capital at Ava, next to the dynasty's main economic resources, revealed both defensive and offensive military and economic concerns and would have unanticipated consequences.

The style and configuration of the capital city revealed that traditional cosmological beliefs were also part of the dynasty's concern. The city of Ava represented heaven on earth and was designed to suggest that the king, while in his symbolic city, was the intermediary between this world and the heavenly realm. Culturally, the Ava period is best known for the further development (and in some cases, the birth) of Burmese literature. Pagan had clearly been a very literate society as well, and in many respects, it produced literature (especially Pali literature) that has not, in general, been surpassed. But certain genres of verse, some of the earliest chronicles, and several of the most exemplary treatises on legal and religious topics to have survived had their origins at Ava. Still, the principles, conceptualizations, and organization of court and king, provincial administration, military and Crown service groups, village society, the economy, the legal system and jurisprudence, and the sangha (Buddhist monkhood) and religious affairs were virtual replicas of Pagan's—only on a smaller scale.

Ava *did* break with the Pagan tradition in at least one respect: in its art and architecture. The city of Sagaing, across the Irrawaddy from Ava, represents Ava's field of merit, where most of its temples and other religious edifices were built. The majority of the monuments at Sagaing reflect a preference for the solid temple, or *stupa*. Although important at Pagan as well, the stupa was not a prevailing style like the hollow *gu* (cave-temple) had been, with its interior space, keystone arching, barrel vaults, double stories, interior stairways, and varied floor plans. Ava may have lost the technique of keystone arches and barrel vaults, the architectural principle fundamental to the hollow-style temples of Pagan. Indeed, there is some evidence of this, as the few Pagan-style hollow temples built during the immediate post-Pagan period at the city of Pinya, briefly the predecessor to Ava, showed signs of flawed and tiered design in their arches.

Perhaps it was also a matter of economic resources. Ava did not and could not recapture the wealth needed for this kind of expensive and technically demanding temple construction on the size and scale enjoyed by Pagan, especially since the latter had committed, in perpetuity, much of the available landed wealth to the tax-exempt sector. At the same time, Ava could no longer harness the commercial revenues of the Lower Burma coasts that Pagan had enjoyed, as that region saw the beginning of a new Lower Burma dynasty led by Mon speakers centered at Pegu, once a provincial capital under Pagan. Moreover, other areas that had once submitted to Pagan and had supplied it with human and material resources, such as Arakan on the western coast and the Shan polities located in the highlands, both north and east of Ava, were no longer reliable tributary regions.

The zenith of the Ava kingdom occurred during the hundred years between 1400 and 1500, when it was politically and militarily dominant in all of Upper Burma and exercised considerable influence over Lower and western Burma periodically. This was the time when Ava produced brilliant Burmese poetry and literature, when hundreds of temples and monasteries were built, and when religion was well patronized. It was also the time when the court was resplendent and when Crown soldiers were strong enough to repel invasions by powerful external forces such as the Ming, as well as internal competitors from Arakan, Pegu, and Prome. It was also a time when Ava was considered a model Buddhist state by its Buddhist neighbors. In short, it was an era when Ava was once more like Pagan but on a smaller scale. But this era was not to last.

In 1527, one of its Shan vassals, sensing the weakness at the center with court factionalism, marched on Ava and took it. The city's vulnerability was, in part, caused by the same kind of wealth flow experienced by Pagan from state to sangha, along with the untimely death of a brilliant young general who would have been king. However, without a larger vision to unite Burma, the conquerors only played the role of spoiler, and after appointing a titular head to hold the city, they returned to their home turf, leaving the heartland in limbo. With no central authority and no able leaders with the kind of vision needed to unify the "feudalistic" and anarchic situation, the population fled to another regional center farther south that was once under Ava's rule, Toungoo. And here began the next dynasty of Burma, the Toungoo, which was to reunify the country once more in the mid-sixteenth century under the militarily brilliant king Bayinnaung (r. 1551–1581). This dynasty was to become the largest, most far-reaching empire that the Burmese ever had, twice conquering Ayutthaya, the capital of Siam, and even taking Vientiane, now the capital of Laos. But the Toungoo was also the shortest dynasty, ruling for a mere seventy-seven years before it was brought down by internal factionalism, wealth flow to the religious sector, and the ambition of regional rivals.

The legacy of the First Ava dynasty lay in its contributions in developing Burmese literature and preserving many of the classical traditions begun and developed at Pagan, including the Burmese Theravada Buddhism (and its conceptual system) that has underpinned Burma's state and society to the present. But it did more than preserve traditions: it also preserved what was to become modern Burma. It did this by successfully forming a political, cultural, and military barrier at Ava against the movement of the T'ai speakers who had been migrating southward into the river valleys of western mainland Southeast Asia for several centuries. In doing so, it prevented that migration from going down the plains of the Irrawaddy River and establishing what might have been a T'ai polity in what is now Burma. And perhaps, therefore, it also prevented the formation of a modern Thailand that would have stretched from Assam on the Indian border in the west to Cambodia on the east.

MICHAEL AUNG-THWIN

See also Bayinnaung (r. 1551–1581); Buddhism, Theravada; Burmans; Ming Dynasty (1368–1644); Mon; Mons; Monumental Art of Southeast Asia; Nan Chao (Nanchao) (Dali/Tali); Pagan (Bagan); Pegu; *Sangha;* Shans; T'ais; Temple Political Economy; Yuan (Mongol) Dynasty (1271–1368)

References:

Aung-Thwin, Michael. 1996. "The Myth of the 'Three Shan Brothers' and the Ava Period in Burmese History." *Journal of Asian Studies* 55, no. 4 (November): 881–901.

Bennett, Paul J. 1971. "The 'Fall of Pagan': Continuity and Change in 14th Century Burma." Pp. 3–53 in *Conference under the Tamarind Tree: Three Essays in Burmese History.* Yale University Southeast Asia Monograph Series 15. New Haven, CT: Yale University Press.

Harvey, G. E. 1925. *A History of Burma: From the Earliest Times to 10 March 1824—The Beginning of the English Conquest.* London: Frank Cass.

Lieberman, Victor B. 1984. *Burmese Administrative Cycles: Anarchy and Conquest, c. 1580–1760.* Princeton, NJ: Princeton University Press.

Phayre, Sir Arthur. 1969 [1883]. *History of Burma.* New York: Augustus M. Kelley. First published in 1883 in London.

Than Tun. 1959. "History of Burma: A.D. 1300–1400." *Journal of the Burma Research Society* 42, no. 2: 119–133.

Tin Hla Thaw. 1959. "History of Burma: A.D. 1400–1500." *Journal of the Burma Research Society* 42, no. 2: 135–151.

FIRST WORLD WAR (1914–1918)

See Great War (1914–1918)

FOLK RELIGIONS

To speak of folk religions is, in the first place, to refer to what ordinary village people do in everyday practice rather than to ideals articulated by religious specialists or urban elites. As soon as Europeans, already conditioned by the print revolution of the Reformation (sixteenth century), encountered the peoples of what we call Southeast Asia, they registered differences between formal professions of faith and everyday practices. Most observers thought this meant that ordinary people did not really understand Islam or Buddhism, the prevalent formal religions, and that, in practice, locals were actually animists, or superstitious believers in magical powers and ancestral spirits.

More recently, students of the region were influenced by the anthropologist Robert Redfield's analysis of folk and civic traditions in Mexico and India. He suggested that the "great tradition" of urban written cultures always interacted dynamically with a "lesser tradition" of village oral customs—each shaping the other yet remaining distinct and coherent (Redfield 1956). Thus, although Burmese villagers bow to Theravada monks, they may be more focused on healing and connection to spirits, the *nats,* than on the Buddhist imagination of spiritual liberation. Similarly, committed Muslims in Java may spend more time making pilgrimages (*ziarah*) to sacred sites to connect with the goddess of the Southern Ocean (Nyai Loro Kidul) than practicing daily prayers (*solat*).

The keynotes of folk religion in villages throughout monsoon Asia are remarkably consistent. Villagers have generally held that all of existence, even stones and metals, is animate—alive and charged with specific, magical energies. In the Malay Archipelago, such ideas are evident in beliefs about the *kris,* or the wave-shaped daggers that were traditionally critical to war and manhood. Springs, caves, mountains, and trees (especially the banyan) are each thought to be alive with spirits that influence the human domain. The spirit of rice, named Nang Phrakosib in Thailand or Dewi Sri in Java and Bali, is seen as a goddess upon whom life depends.

Beyond shared awareness of a spiritually charged environment, villagers usually relate to nature through hierarchies of spirits inhabiting invisible planes accessible only to especially powerful people. Shamanic mediums and healers have often been female; the *datu* (rulers or chiefs) have usually been "big men," meaning important men in the society. In any case, every person is understood as being differently empowered rather than equal, and links with guardian (or tutelary) spirits are believed to underlie the power of the living. Thus, the founding ancestor of a community or kingdom would, upon death, move into the spirit world, becoming a bridge between human and natural realms and remaining accessible to living descendants. Usually, prayer or meditation at graves or other sacred sites would be undertaken to tap into spirit powers through contractual relationships, which ensured healing of the sick, the success of crops, or social power.

The past is knowable through living practices as well as through traces in texts, monuments, or artifacts. Since ethnography exposes such practices in a way archival research cannot, cultural archaeology is a crucial means to aid our understanding of local histories on their own terms. Insofar as prehistoric patterns persist into the present, they must have conditioned intervening transitions. Village rituals, divination, sexual magic, and the quest for powers through sacred sites relate at once to contemporary social contests and, as Anthony Reid (1988) showed, to early historical transitions. Because animistic folk religion remains a pervasive underlayer in village societies, the basic logic of this pattern must be original. Although this does not imply that the substratum is either singular in essence or unique to the region, it does mean that it is foundational in the same way that grammar is within language.

Focus on ancestral folk religion became a central feature in seminal works of French scholarship on Indochina. George Coedès (1968) termed it a "substratum," whereas Paul Mus (1975) stressed that contractual relations with tutelary spirits underpinned rice cultures throughout Asia. Their works helped shift attention from outside influences to indigenous forces, from elites to the foundations of subsistence and everyday life, to what Harry Benda (1962) later called the "infrastructure." We are now more likely to call the village substratum a Bakhtinian "chronotype," noting that folk religion carries a distinctive sense of time that speaks dialogically with subsequent discursive domains, thus producing the separate rhythms of social life in agricultural villages, trading ports, and dynastic kingdoms.

Distinct spheres, related at once to different historical phases and groups, coexist in the present, however transformed internally and through the gestalt that contextualizes them, rather than replacing each other in simple sequence. This relationship is suggested by the coexistence of oxcarts, horse carriages, bicycles, cars, and airplanes—each following a distinct rhythm and thus embodying a different sense of time yet moving together. Using this image and noting that peasant societies have focused, as Mercia Eliade (1954) suggested, on rituals that "regenerate time," we can imagine a sense in which folk religions maintain a literally timeless, because nonlinear, awareness from prehistory into the present.

In sociological terms, continuity of the substratum is stressed in the works of J. C. van Leur and B. J. Schrieke. Van Leur (1967: 95) held that "the sheen of the world religions and foreign cultural forms is a thin and flaking glaze; underneath it the whole of the old indigenous forms has continued to exist." Schrieke (1957) argued that the infrastructure of Java did not fundamentally change from 700 to 1700 C.E. And Mus (1975) noted that Vietnamese villagers were traditionally autonomous in their internal affairs. Symbolically, bamboo hedges marked their autonomy, bounding them socially just as they were insulated by the mediation of councils of notables that protected them from centralizing states. Later and in different ways Clifford Geertz's (1976) work on Java and S. J. Tambiah's (1970) on Thailand drew attention to the persistence of primal village religious patterns within present frames.

The formation of states in what would remain the core areas—the dominant centers of population and power in Southeast Asia—brought dynastic periodicity into the seasonal and life cycles of the folk religious substratum: villages counterpointed courts so that they came to define each other. Cosmopolitan contacts within early states brought not only increasing scale but also an imperative to conceptualize local forces in more universalized terms—as societies of millions replaced the kinship patterning of villages, scale called for specialization, for a new language to orchestrate energies. Indian (or in Vietnam, Chinese) written culture offered an instrument for this purpose.

There is no doubt that, in the process, folk religion was transformed. Through most of Southeast Asia, even most of what became the Philippines, Indian-derived terms for deities, *dewi* or *dewa,* became common. Mythologies derived from Indian cycles—the *Jatakas, Mahâbhârata,* and *Râmâyana*—found reenactment in oral village traditions such as the *wayang* (shadow play) in Java. Notions of karma and reincarnation became parts of a pervasive new frame for local imaginations of spirit realms.

Syncretism defined the process by which local beliefs found voice within, rather than being simply replaced by, Indian spiritual vocabularies. Syncretism arises naturally from folk religious ontologies because those usually register all as being one at root. This perspective predisposed locals to allow additions and new interpretations, to be received as supplements that enriched by elaboration rather than replacements for what went before. Localization provided new idioms relating to the same energies of spirits, shrines, caves, and ancestors. Spirit hierarchies continued to parallel social structures, as had earlier tutelary spirits. But with new kingdoms, kings, queens, princes, and armies fought in the spirit as well as the social realms.

Everywhere in these societies, external influences have been transformed, reworked, and used by local systems that have ancestral spirits at their heart. As the template world religions fitted into has been animistic, spirit cults still percolate below the surface. Richard Winstedt (1951) linked shamanism, Saivism, and Sufism to show how the main strands of Malay religious history wove into a pattern based on prehistoric systems. L. Golomb (1985) noted that animistic healing practices transcended boundaries between Buddhism and Islam or Thais and Malays. Because Muslims in Java meditate on graves seeking magical powers, Suharto's grave complex at Blitar was styled to enshrine him as the guardian ancestor of the modern state in the same way that earlier Indian-influenced rulers had themselves enshrined within massive stone temples.

When changes appear overwhelming on the surface, underlying continuity is obviously obscured. The substratum is now breaking down rapidly, yet it retains more power than we easily register. Only nocturnal ethnography opens this face of local practice, as in the daylight, little activity suggests any of the power present within sacred sites. As with the subconscious or the submerged portion of an iceberg, the surface evidence of folk religion—what may catch our eye and enter discourse—depends profoundly on what does not appear. Emphasis on it is analogous to the importance of the first years of life as recognized in psychology: we may not remember them, but we know that the patterns imprinted then nevertheless inform our subsequent paths. The spiritual substratum of the Southeast Asian region is especially hard to see because modern Europeans have suppressed or marginalized their analogues to it and cannot see in others what they can no longer imagine as existing in themselves.

PAUL STANGE

See also *Adat;* Buddhism; Buddhism, Mahayana; Buddhism, Theravada; Cao Dai; Catholicism; Darul Islam (DI) Movement; Hindu-Buddhist Period of Southeast Asia; Hinduism; Hispanization; Hoa Hao; Indianization; Islam in Southeast Asia; Islamic Resurgence in Southeast Asia (Twentieth Century); *Jatakas; Mahâbâratha* and *Râmâyana; Tam Giao; Wali Songo; Wayang Kulit*

References:
Benda, H. 1962. "The Structure of Southeast Asian History." *Journal of Southeast Asian History* 3, no. 1: 103–138.

Coedès, G. 1968 [1944]. *The Indianized States of Southeast Asia.* Honolulu, HI: East-West Center Press.

Eliade, Mircea. 1954. *Cosmos and History: The Myth of the Eternal Return.* New York: Harper & Row.

Geertz, C. 1976 [1960]. *The Religion of Java.* Chicago: University of Chicago Press.

Golomb, L. 1985. *An Anthropology of Curing in Multiethnic Thailand.* Urbana and Chicago: University of Illinois Press.

Mus, Paul. 1975 [1934]. *India Seen from the East: Indian and Indigenous Cults in Champa.* Translated by I. Mabbett. Papers on Southeast Asia no. 3. Clayton, Australia: Centre for Southeast Asian Studies, Monash University.

Redfield, Robert. 1956. *Peasant Society and Culture.* Chicago: University of Chicago Press.

Reid, A. 1988. *Southeast Asia in the Age of Commerce, 1450–1680.* Vol. 1, *The Lands below the Winds.* New Haven, CT: Yale University Press.

Schrieke, B. J. 1957. *Indonesian Sociological Studies: Selected Writings.* Pt. 2, *Ruler and Realm in Early Java.* The Hague and Bandung, Indonesia: W. van Hoeve.

Tambiah, S. J. 1970. *Buddhism and the Spirit Cults in North-East Thailand.* Cambridge: Cambridge University Press.

van Leur, J. C. 1967 [1955]. *Indonesian Trade and Society: Essays in Asian Social and Economic History.* The Hague: W. van Hoeve.

Winstedt, Richard. 1951. *The Malay Magician: Being Shaman, Saiva and Sufi.* London: Routledge & Kegan Paul.

Wolters, O. W. 1982. *History, Culture, and Region in Southeast Asian Perspectives.* Singapore: Institute of Southeast Asian Studies.

FOOCHOW (HOCK CHIU)

See Chinese Dialect Groups

FORCE 136
Promoting Anti-Japanese Armed Resistance

The India Mission of Britain's Special Operations Executive (SOE) was set up in May 1941 to counter subversion in India. In August 1942, its purpose changed to the promotion of in-digenous military resistance in Japanese-occupied Burma, Malaya, Siam, Indochina, and Sumatra. The mission was based at Meerut in India and then, from 1944, at Kandy, Ceylon (Sri Lanka). After coming under the control of the South-East Asia Command (SEAC), the India Mission changed its name in March 1944 to Force 136. European and Asian operatives of Force 136 armed and trained thousands of Southeast Asians, with the aim of eventually expelling the Japanese and reestablishing British dominance.

As well as operating with pro-British groups such as the Karen in Burma (Myanmar), Force 136 struck alliances with anticolonial and left-wing resistance groups. Consequently, in May 1945, Aung San's Burma National Army deserted the Japanese for the British. In Malaya, Force 136 gained the support of the Malayan Communist Party's Malayan People's Anti-Japanese Army (MPAJA).

Operations in Sumatra and Indochina were much less successful. In Sumatra, there was insufficient opposition to the Japanese to support armed resistance. And in Indochina, the Force 136 support of pro-French resistance proved too weak to withstand Japanese attacks.

There was often bitter operational rivalry between Force 136 and the U.S. Office of Strategic Services (OSS). The United States aimed to extend its political and economic influence in Southeast Asia and opposed the restoration of British, French, and Dutch colonies.

By the end of the Pacific War (1941–1945), Force 136's biggest military successes were in Burma, where it assisted British reoccupation. In Siam, the war ended before troops trained by Force 136 could make any significant military impact. In 1948, the communist forces, armed and trained by Force 136 in Malaya, commenced a twelve-year (1948–1956) insurgency against the British in the so-called Emergency.

IAN K. SMITH

See also British Military Administration (BMA) in Southeast Asia; Burma Independence Army (BIA); Japanese Occupation of Southeast Asia (1941–1945); Malayan Emergency (1948–1960); Malayan People's Anti-Japanese Army (MPAJA); Services Reconnaissance Department (SRD); South-East Asia Command (SEAC)

References:

Aldrich, Richard. 2000. *Intelligence and the War against Japan: Britain, America and the Politics of Secret Service.* Cambridge: Cambridge University Press.

Cruickshank, Charles Greig. 1983. *Special Operations Executive: SOE in the Far East.* Oxford: Oxford University Press.

Rasseur, C. 1992. *The Politics of Colonial Exploitation: Java, the Dutch, and the Cultivation System.* Ithaca, NY: Southeast Asia Program, Cornell University.

Van Baardewijk, F. 1993. *Changing Economy in Indonesia.* Vol. 14, *The Cultivation System, Java 1834–1880.* Amsterdam: Royal Tropical Institute.

FORCED DELIVERIES

The term *forced deliveries* refers to the compulsory deliveries of produce by farmers to rulers. The term is generally associated with the Cultivation System (*Cultuurstelsel*), which the Dutch colonial government maintained in Java between 1830 and 1870. Under this system, farmers were forced to produce cash crops such as coffee and take their produce to collection points supervised by Dutch colonial officials. Payment for the crops enabled the farmers to pay the land tax. However, the Dutch colonial government continued a prerogative of indigenous rulers in areas it had brought under direct colonial rule. Such deliveries to local rulers had generally been made in rice. The predecessor of the Dutch colonial government, the Dutch United East India Company (VOC), also demanded the delivery of produce. The VOC often exacted from subjugated indigenous rulers valuable cash crops such as coffee and spices as either a form of tribute or a tax in kind from farmers in areas under its direct rule. The Cultivation System was based on such precedents. The practice of forced deliveries existed in places other than colonial Java as well. For instance, in the surroundings of Padang, farmers were compelled to supply coffee in lieu of income tax.

PIERRE VAN DER ENG

See also Coffee; Cultivation System (*Cultuurstelsel*); Java; Java War (1825–1830); Max Havelaar; Netherlands (Dutch) East Indies; Sugar; Van den Bosch, Count Johannes (1780–1844); Van der Capellen, Baron Godert Alexander Philip (1778–1848); Vereenigde Oost-Indische Compagnie (VOC) ([Dutch] United East Indies Company) (1602)

References:

Elson, R. E. 1994. *Village Java under the Cultivation System, 1830–1870.* Sydney: Allen and Unwin.

FORMOSA (TAIWAN)

An island situated 160 kilometers off the coast of Fujian Province in China, Formosa (also known as Taiwan) was governed by the Republic of China from 1949. Due to its geographic proximity, it has, from time to time, played a part in the Southeast Asian network throughout its known history.

The word *Formosa* originated in the term *Isla Formosa* (Beautiful Island), expressing admiration for the island's beauty as experienced by sailors aboard a Portuguese ship in 1517. Nowadays, the term *Formosa* may connote the independent regime on the island that is objectionable to the Beijing Chinese leaders, who regard the island as an indivisible part of China. The Chinese first used the name *Taiwan* during the Ming dynasty (1368–1644). Neither the Portuguese nor the Chinese were indigenous to the island. Aborigines of Malay-Polynesian origin had lived on the island since the prehistoric era.

Though the island had been mentioned vaguely in Chinese texts since the Sui dynasty (581–618 C.E.), it was under the Dutch that Taiwan gained its first experience of being ruled by a regime, albeit briefly (from 1624 to 1662). The Dutch East India Company (VOC) then made Taiwan a transshipment center for China, Japan, and Batavia. Such trade continued after the Dutch were expelled by Zheng Chenggong (also known as Koxinga, 1624–1662), who established an anti-Manchu regime in Taiwan that existed from 1662 to 1683. To Zheng, the relationship with Southeast Asia was something beyond trade. He planned to stage an onslaught on the Manchus in China, manned by an army of Philippine Chinese. However, the effort was aborted, as the Spanish killed all the 10,000 Chinese in the Philippines upon learning of the plot.

Taiwan was incorporated institutionally as part of Fujian Province after the Manchus defeated Zheng's regime in 1683. Trade was maintained only with the Chinese mainland, and Taiwan's Southeast Asian connections were not renewed until the latter half of the nineteenth century. The Treaty of Tianjin (1858) opened Taiwan to foreign trade. Liners bound for Southeast Asia plied the waters between Taiwan and ports such as Singapore, Saigon, and Manila (Luzon). The enhanced economic and strategic importance of the island made the Qing court grant it provincial status in 1887.

After two hundred years of Chinese rule, Taiwan became a colony of Japan. The Treaty of Shimonoseki that concluded the Sino-Japanese War (1894–1895) ceded the island to Japan after China's defeat. Taiwan became an attractive market for Japanese products, although its exports, including tea, camphor, sugar, and opium, continued to go to Southeast Asia. During the Pacific War (1941–1945), Japan used Formosa as a military base for the expansion to Southeast Asia.

Taiwan was returned to China after Japan's defeat in 1945. Taiwan was portrayed as "Free China" after 1949 (as it continues to be), for it was planned to be an anticommunist stronghold under the Kuomintang (KMT), which still claimed legitimacy over the whole of China in spite of its defeat by the Chinese Communist Party (CCP). Anticommunism became a common interest for Taiwan in maintaining relations with Southeast Asian countries, but other factors hindered closer contact. The newly independent Southeast Asian states developed industries quite similar to those of Taiwan, and they became competitors. A further setback was suffered in the diplomatic sphere. In 1971, Taiwan, represented as the Republic of China, lost its seat to Beijing (that is, the People's Republic of China, PRC) in the United Nations. Vietnam, Cambodia, Laos, Malaysia, Thailand, and the Philippines recalled their ambassadors from Taiwan in the mid-1970s and recognized the PRC; the latter had, by then, become less threatening to its Asian neighbors after reaching rapprochement with the United States.

Taiwan's diplomatic setback was partially compensated by its "economic miracle." Toward the end of the 1970s, Taiwan was recognized as a successful newly industrialized country (NIC) and extolled as one of Asia's "Four Little Dragons," alongside Hong Kong, South Korea, and Singapore. In the 1980s, Southeast Asia had a new role to play in Taiwan's economic development. The rise of the middle class in Taiwan led to a huge demand for domestic helpers. Southeast Asians filled the need, and currently, their numbers total more than 200,000. In view of the mounting labor cost in Taiwan in the 1980s, Taiwanese entrepreneurs running labor-intensive industries turned to the Southeast Asian countries, which by then had adopted open-door policies and provided the much-needed cheap labor. This trend of southward investments culminated in the proclamation of the 1993 "go south policy" by President Lee Teng-hui (1923–), with a view to checking the multiplying investments to mainland China, a trend that may put Taiwan in a bewildered situation in a future political contest with Beijing.

To break its diplomatic isolation, Taiwan practiced "pragmatic diplomacy" in the 1990s, and Southeast Asia was considered important for relations at various levels. However, developments are not optimistic. On the one hand, Beijing will not tolerate any Taiwanese diplomatic activities conducted under the name Republic of China or Taiwan. And on the other hand, there are sovereignty conflicts over territories such as the Spratly Islands in the South China Sea, where Taiwan, China, Vietnam, Malaysia, Brunei, and the Philippines claim overlapping parts of these lands.

HANS W. Y. YEUNG

See also China, Imperial; China, Nationalist; China since 1949; Hong Kong; Kuomintang (KMT); Manila; Ming Dynasty (1368–1644); Qing (Ch'ing/Manchu) Dynasty (1644–1912); Saigon (Gia Dinh; Hồ Chí Minh City; Singapore (Nineteenth Century to 1990s), Entrepôt Trade and Commerce of; Spratly and Paracel Archipelagos Dispute; Vereenigde Oost-Indische Compagnie (VOC) ([Dutch] United East Indies Company) (1602)

References:

Chen, Jie. 2002. *Foreign Policy of the New Taiwan: Pragmatic Diplomacy in Southeast Asia.* Cheltenham, England, and Northampton, MA: Edward Elgar Publishing.

Chen, Tain-jy, et al. 1995. *Taiwan's Small- and Medium-Sized Firms' Direct Investment in Southeast Asia.* Taipei: Chung-hua Institution for Economic Research.

Copper, John F. 2000. *Historical Dictionary of Taiwan (Republic of China).* Lanham, MD, and London: Scarecrow Press.

Odgaard, Liselotte. 2002. *Maritime Security between China and Southeast Asia: Conflict and Cooperation in the Making of Regional Order.* Aldershot, England, and Burlington, Australia: Ashgate.

Rubinstein, Murray A. 1999. *Taiwan: A New History.* Armonk, NY: M. E. Sharpe.

"FORTRESS SINGAPORE"

Illusory Strategy

After World War I (1914–1918), Singapore became a focal point for the British military in Southeast Asia. Faced with U.S. objections to the continuation of the Anglo-Japanese Alliance, the British government in London decided in June 1921 that the interests of regional and empire defense would best be served by building a new, first-class naval base in Singapore.

Situated on the northern coast of the island at Sembawang less than a mile (about 1.6 kilometers) across the Strait of Johor from the Malayan shore, it was designed to become the largest base that the Royal Navy possessed east of Malta in the Mediterranean. However, it was never the British government's intention to station a substantial number of warships permanently at the Sembawang base. Nonetheless, the Admiralty envisaged that in times of grave emergency, such as the outbreak of war with Japan, the Royal Navy would send a large battle fleet to Singapore to defend British interests in the region. This plan (the "Singapore strategy") has often been derisively described as a strategic illusion. Starved of the funds necessary to build a first-class naval base, the Sembawang base could never hope to function as the British planners had originally hoped it would. Moreover, the growth of fascism and militarism in Germany, Italy, and Japan in the 1930s was to pose an ever-increasing problem for the British and reveal the improbable nature of their Singapore strategy. This was clearly a case of imperial overreaching, and no amount of wishful thinking would make Singapore become the fortress it was portrayed as the international media. Denied the aircraft and defensive measures in Malaya that it would have required if it was ever to have become an impregnable fortress, Singapore became a hostage to fortune once the Japanese had launched their invasion of Southeast Asia on 8 December 1941. By 31 January 1942, the Malay Peninsula had fallen, and Singapore became a temporary home for more than 100,000 British and Allied forces. Shortly thereafter, the island fell to General Tomoyuki Yamashita's (1885–1946) forces on 15 February 1942.

Fortress Singapore was little more than a mirage and the "Singapore Strategy" an unrealistic anachronism more suited to the Victorian heyday of *Pax Brittanica* than the turbulent epoch in which it was actually conceived and supposed to operate.

MALCOLM H. MURFETT

See also Great War (1914–1918); Japanese Occupation of Southeast Asia; Yamashita Tomoyuki, General (1885–1946)

References:

Hamill, Ian. 1981. *The Strategic Illusion: The Singapore Strategy and the Defence of Australia and New Zealand, 1919–1942.* Singapore: Singapore University Press.

Murfett, Malcolm H., John N. Miksic, Brian P. Farrell, and Chiang Ming Shun. 1999. *Between Two Oceans: A Military History of Singapore from First Settlement to Final British Withdrawal.* Singapore: Oxford University Press.

FREE THAI MOVEMENT

The Free Thai Movement (or Siamese Movement, as it was called by the British) was a national resistance group organized while Japanese troops occupied Thailand (Siam) from 1941 to 1945. Before the Japanese invasion on 8 December 1941, the Thai government, in anticipation of the coming of war, had instilled in the people's mind the duty to fight and sacrifice their lives to preserve the nation's independence. Quickly following the surprise invasion of the country, many Thai political and government leaders, both inside and outside of the country, began to formulate what would later become the Free Thai Movement. The movement's objectives were, first, to fight against the Japanese occupation of Thailand and, second, to be able to negotiate with the principal Allied countries in order to resolve Thailand's status in the war. Ultimately, the primary aim was to ensure the restoration of Thailand's sovereignty and establish an independent nation that would be regarded as an equal by the Allies.

By late December 1941, Pridi Phanomyong (1900–1983), the former foreign minister in Plaek Phibunsongkhram's government (1938–1944) who would shortly be appointed chairman of the regency, formed an underground organization to resist the Japanese occupation in Thailand. Operating from the regent's office, the underground movement quickly gained support and cooperation from members of Parliament, bureaucrats, and military officials. Meanwhile, Thais in the United States and Britain organized parallel resistance movements. The Free Thai Movement in the United States was initiated and led by M. R. Seni Pramoj (1905–1997), a prominent lawyer appointed by Phibun to be the Thai minister in Washington. Seni made clear from the beginning that the Thai legation in Washington would not follow the Bangkok government's collaboration with Japan, and he firmly sought U.S. support to fight against Japanese acts of aggression. Thai students in England organized, by themselves, the third resistance movement in July 1942, without support from the Thai officials there. The group, however, received support from the British government and high-ranking royalty who resided in England following the 1932 Revolution.

During the first phase of the movement, from 1941 to 1943, the three resistance groups in Thailand, the United States, and Britain operated independently from one another. There was no real and systematic cooperation in their efforts to resist Japanese occupation. Not until the second phase, from 1943 to 1945 during which Pridi assumed the official leadership of the Free Thai Movement, did all the resistance forces come under a unified command that directed concerted activities. This was the period when the Free Thai Movement finally established contacts with and joined the U.S. and British forces in fighting the Japanese.

By the end of the Pacific War (1941–1945), the Free Thai Movement had proved to be a very successful effort on the part of the Thais because it helped saved the country from becoming a defeated nation that would be subjected to harsh punishment and reparation for its war crimes. Furthermore, the Free Thai Movement was also the first grassroots political movement to give an opportunity to many local political activists. This opened the way for the development and growth of their organizations, including the Communist Party of Thailand (CPT), which was formed on 1 December 1942.

THANET APHORNSUVAN

See also Collaboration Issue in Southeast Asia; Japanese Occupation of Southeast Asia (1941–1945); Khmer Issarak (Free Khmer); Lao Issara; Plaek Phibunsongkhram, Field Marshall (1897–1964); Pridi Phanomyong (1900–1983); Seni Pramoj, M. R. (1905–1997)

References:
Charivat Santaputra. 1985. *Thai Foreign Policy, 1932–1946.* Bangkok: Charoen Wit Press.
Haseman, John B. 1978. *The Thai Resistance Movement during the Second World War.* De Kalb: Northern Illinois Center for Southeast Asian Studies.
Thamsook Numnond. 1977. *Thailand and the Japanese Presence, 1941–45.* Research Notes and Discussions Series no. 6. Singapore: Institute of Southeast Asian Studies.

FREE TRADE

Free trade is a phrase that has, over time, been widely used in public affairs, and like other such phrases, it has consequently been subjected to a diversity of meanings. They all call to mind the relationship between the state and the economy. In the contemporary phase of globalization and the nation-state, that relationship seems more important than ever. Are the governments going to promote the free trade that globalization calls for? Or is the relationship a more ambiguous one, depending on the relative position and interest of the states? Contemporary concerns may cast light on the past, just as study of the past may enhance an understanding of current problems.

Even before they avowed their interest in the welfare of the people, governments the world over were interested in the prosperity of their domains: only that, after all, could provide them with revenues for sustaining church and state and with the sinews of war. In the majority of states, the prime resource was agriculture, and trade was local or regional. For some states, foreign trade was more important, and for a few—such as Venice or Melaka—it was the state's very raison d'être.

Intensifying competition among the European states accompanied the disintegration of the Holy Roman Empire and the advent of the Renaissance. That was a powerful motive behind the voyages of "discovery" and the establishment of dependencies and trading posts outside Europe on the part of the Portuguese and the Spaniards initially and then others, such as the Dutch and the English. Though the world economy expanded—with the exploitation of Japanese silver mines and then with the mobilization of the wealth of Mexico and Peru—states still saw it in strictly competitive terms, and the recession that followed in the seventeenth century promoted a mercantilist approach. Trade was seen as a zero-sum game: what one had, another could not have. Commercial competition was thus accompanied by measures designed to reserve the colonial trade to the colonial power and to exclude others.

In the long period of expansion that ensued in the eighteenth century and that gathered momentum with the industrial and communications revolutions of the nineteenth century, such perceptions were undermined. The relationship of state and commerce remained important. Should a state cling to old-fashioned regulations or sacrifice the vested interests involved in them in favor of new interests that would profit by a new approach? Not all the states would answer the question in the same way, for their positions differed.

The keenest advocates of free trade had been the states whose economies were most likely to benefit. The Dutch East India Company (VOC) had used the argument of *mare liberum*—open seas—against the then much weaker English East India Company (EIC) in the early seventeenth century, though it also proceeded to argue that it could impose commercial monopolies by making agreements with the rulers in Southeast Asia. In the late eighteenth and nineteenth centuries, the British came to enjoy an economic advantage over other European states and became the advocates of free trade. Though it took some decades, they abandoned their navigation acts and accepted competition at home and overseas in the confidence that they could benefit from it. The lesson that Adam Smith had drawn from the struggle with the American colonies in *The Wealth of Nations* (1776) was adopted. "No nation ever voluntarily gave up the dominion of any province," he had argued, "how troublesome it might be to govern it. Such sacrifices . . . are always mortifying to the pride of every nation, and . . . contrary to the private interest of the governing part of it. . . . If it was adopted, however, Great Britain would not only be immediately freed from the whole annual expense of the peace establishment of the colonies, but might settle with them such a treaty of commerce as would effectually secure to her a free trade, more advantageous to the great body of the people, though less so to the merchants, than the monopoly which she at present enjoys" (quoted in Bennett 1962: 47).

Britain embarked on what Ronald Robinson and John Gallagher (1953) memorably but misleadingly called "the imperialism of free trade." The object was not to rule other lands—rather the reverse—but to remove the trade obstacles their governments put in the way of Britain's goods, which would otherwise, it was assumed, have been economically competitive. In the closing decades of the nineteenth century, those goods faced a new obstacle. Emulating Britain's industrialization, other Western states, including the United States as well as Germany and Russia, sought to protect their nascent industries by protective tariffs. Britain did not react by abandoning free trade until, under the impact of the depression (1929–1931), it adopted a strategy of "imperial preference" in 1931 and 1932. The United States, which was then the predominant economic power, criticized this British strategy. It was the United States that appeared to be the prime advocate of free trade in the postwar years.

In Southeast Asia, the French had initially adopted a free trade regime in Cochin China, designed to attract Chinese and other traders. The Meline Tariff of 1892 imposed a protectionist regime on Indochina, which was to stand in the way of industrialization in Vietnam. The Dutch, long pressed by the British and now anxious to avoid the intervention of others, dropped protectionism in Netherlands India in the 1870s, but in the depression, they reintroduced it as a means, above all, of limiting the competition of cheap Japanese goods.

NICHOLAS TARLING

See also Age of Commerce; British Interests in Southeast Asia; Dutch Interests in Southeast

Asia from 1800; East India Company (EIC) (1600), English; Economic Development of Southeast Asia (Post-1945 to ca. 1990s); Economic History of Early Modern Southeast Asia (Pre-Sixteenth Century); Economic Transformation of Southeast Asia (ca. 1400-ca. 1800); French Ambitions in Southeast Asia; Penang (1786); Portuguese Asian Empire; Raffles, Sir (Thomas) Stamford Bingley (1781–1826); Singapore (1819); Singapore (Nineteenth Century to 1990s), Entrepôt Trade and Commerce of; Spanish Expansion in Southeast Asia; Vereenigde Oost-Indische Compagnie (VOC) ([Dutch] United East India Company) (1602); Vietnam under French Colonial Rule

References:

Bennett, George, ed. 1962. *The Concept of Empire: Burke to Attlee, 1774–1947.* 2nd ed. London: A. & C. Black.

Robinson, R., and J. Gallagher. 1953. "The Imperialism of Free Trade." *Economic History Review,* 2nd series, 6: 1–15.

FRENCH AMBITIONS IN SOUTHEAST ASIA

Before the nineteenth century, the French made no attempt to establish a territorial empire in Asia. In the two previous centuries, French commercial and missionary interests in India, China, and Southeast Asia were sustained by *comptoirs* (stations, outposts, branches) and mission stations, protected by naval forces that were eventually based on Mauritius. From the mid-nineteenth century, the interventions of the French state in Asia became more systematic and culminated in the formation of a territorial empire principally located in mainland Southeast Asia. In the process, the ambitions of the French were both stimulated and constrained by rivalry with the British, whose large Eastern empire was seen both as a standing threat to French interests in Asia and as a model to emulate.

In Asia from 1669, the French presence consisted of a succession of short-lived royal-chartered trading companies. In 1720, the formation of the powerful new Compagnie des Indes inaugurated over forty years of direct competition with the English East India Company (EIC) for dominance of the India trade. The downfall of this company in 1769 left French influence diffused among mercenaries working for Indian rulers, individual traders operating from small settlements in India, and French missionary networks extending from India to China.

In Southeast Asia, political initiatives by the French government were rare. The Chaumont embassy to Siam, a major diplomatic mission sent by Louis XIV (r. 1643–1715) in 1687 and 1688 to implant French political and military influence and encourage Christianization, had been a disaster, precipitating the downfall of King Narai (r. 1656–1688) in a political coup. A later intervention in Vietnam was equally without success. In 1787, a French missionary, Msgr. Pierre Joseph Georges Pigneau de Behaine (1741–1799), negotiated a Franco-Vietnamese treaty and obtained material assistance for the reinstallation of the Nguyễn dynasty on the throne of Vietnam. The French state made nothing of this isolated adventure, which was of temporary benefit only to French missionaries in Vietnam until the persecutions of the 1820s.

The earliest signs of a systematic state policy to establish a significant French presence off the mainland of Southeast Asia began in the 1840s, when King Louis Philippe's (r. 1830–1848) premier, François Guizot, sanctioned a search for a naval station in the South China Sea. But the effort, intended to support French trade with China, produced no suitable point d'appui. The intensification of missionary appeals for protection from persecution in Vietnam in 1856 and 1857 spurred the beginnings of the French commitment to large-scale territorial annexation in Southeast Asia. Anti-Christian violence provided the occasion for intervention, but French military involvement plainly reflected an interest in pursuing economic and strategic advantages in the region. The Brenier Commission (1857), convened to report on the proposal for a Vietnam expedition, strongly emphasized the material benefits both of establishing some form of protectorate over Vietnam and of gaining a strategic foothold from which to protect French access to the China market. The proposal was controversial, and Napoleon III's (r. 1852–1870) cabinet balked at the likely cost. It was the emperor himself who made the final decision, influenced by Empress Eugénie's concern about Vietnamese persecution of missionaries.

The subsequent development of a new French colony in Vietnam was the product of initiatives by French expeditionary admirals. The first of these, Admiral Rigault de Genouilly, seemed reluctant to embark on wholesale conquest. He planned to impose a limited political and commercial treaty on the Vietnamese after a difficult assault on the port of Tourane (Danang), close to the capital. But the Vietnamese declined to capitulate, and his successor, Admiral Page, decided to shift the locus of French attack southward to Cochin China, the main source of Vietnam's food supply. In a peace treaty forced on him by Admiral Louis Adolphe Bonard in 1862, the Tu Duc emperor finally acknowledged French sovereignty over Saigon and the three eastern provinces. In June 1867, without prior authorization from Paris, Admiral-Governor Charles-Marie de La Grandière seized an opportunity provided by rebel cross-border infiltration to extend and consolidate French dominance over the rest of the Mekong Delta. Shortly afterward, a nominal French protectorate over the kingdom of Cambodia, previously agreed upon in secret between King Norodom (r. 1860–1904) and Admiral de La Grandière, was reluctantly acknowledged by King Mongkut (Rama IV, r. 1851–1868) of Siam, Norodom's overlord, in a formal treaty with France. In return for Siamese renunciation of suzerainty over Cambodia, the French foreign office, in the teeth of de La Grandière's protests, acknowledged Siamese sovereignty over two formerly Khmer provinces, Battambang and Siem Reap, held by Siam since 1794. Battambang, which bordered the Great Lake of Cambodia (Tonle Sap), was of considerable economic value, and Siem Reap, containing the ruins of Angkor, was the historical heartland of the Khmer people. These two Siamese-held Khmer provinces remained consistently high on the French colonialist agenda for future retrieval.

The historiography of the later stages of French expansion reflects considerable debate and forms part of the wider framework of controversy over the nature of later nineteenth-century imperialism as a whole. Most historians agree that there was a clear pattern of preemptive economic calculation behind French expansion over the following forty years. There is less agreement as to whether expansion was led by officials seeking to establish a raison d'être for this haphazardly assembled colony or whether business pressures alone were strong enough to account for it.

The early stages of growth took place under exclusively naval management. In the 1860s and 1870s, French entrepreneurs and banks had largely ignored Cochin China as a field of activity, but the navy's colonial administration pursued strategic control over the remainder of Vietnam's major river systems as a means of securing political dominance over the whole economy. Initially, Admiral de La Grandière had hoped to seize Siamese Laos in order to connect the Mekong Delta with the southwest China market. Draining Chinese goods out through the delta would help, in the governor's phrase, to turn Saigon into "the queen of the Far East," outperforming Shanghai, Hong Kong, and Singapore. When the Mekong River expedition under Captain Ernest Doudart de Lagrée (1823–1868) discovered in 1866 that the great river was blocked and unusable for this purpose, administrative attention shifted away from Laos and toward the northern Vietnamese province of Tonkin (Tongking). There, when a French trader discovered in 1872 and 1873 that the Song Koi, or Red River, was commercially usable as a link to the southwest China market, the naval administration in Saigon under Admiral Marie Jules Dupré acted. An unauthorized expedition was mounted, led by Lieutenant Francis Garnier (1839–1873), to seize the Song Koi and with it the rest of Tonkin. One of the major concerns driving Dupré had been the fear of intervention by British and German China coast business interests, which had shown excitement at the opening of the river. But when Garnier was killed on a sortie in December 1873, French forces were ignominiously withdrawn. In 1874, Dupré and his successor, Admiral Jules François Émile Krantz, sought to cover French embarrassment by imposing two treaties on Vietnam by which the French acquired a range of special commercial and political privileges in Tonkin and Annam. British diplomatic pressure, however, ensured that the term *protectorate* did not appear in these agreements, leaving French dominance in question.

The Garnier fiasco, a mission undertaken without authorization from Paris, had been a response to local crisis and opportunity. The subsequent decision to seize Tonkin by the government of Jules Ferry in the early 1880s was an outcome of a more complex process of political change in France itself, stimulating the revival of a state policy of colonial expansion in Africa, the Middle East (West Asia), and the Pacific.

Defeat at the hands of Prussia in 1870 had helped to inflame French nationalism, but German continental ascendancy made French colonial expansion a safer outlet than *revanche* (revenge) for the restoration of French prestige. Business interests were also becoming more evidently engaged in the process of colonial acquisition. Historians, however, are divided over whether French capitalism or French nationalism was the greater influence in French expansion. Charles Ageron (1978), C. M. Andrew and A. S. Kanya-Forstner (1981), and Patrick Tuck (1995) have developed, in relation to Southeast Asia and elsewhere, the argument of Henri Brunschwig that the nationalistic colonial party was the predominant force shaping French late-nineteenth-century imperialism. John Laffey (1969), Pierre Brocheux and Daniel Hémery (1995), and Dieter Brötel (1971) have argued that French expansion in Southeast Asia was fundamentally a business-driven process.

In the new climate of metropolitan commitment to expansion, the cabinet of Jules Ferry (t. 1883–1885) opted to monopolize control over the Song Koi route into southwest China. Ferry found himself engaged first in hostilities with the Vietnamese in 1883 and 1884 and then in a debilitating conflict with the Vietnamese monarch's overlord, China. By 1885, the increasing scale and cost of the Franco-Chinese war provoked revulsion among the French public, and Ferry was ejected from office. His successors were to take a further decade to pacify northern Vietnam, and the possession, renamed French Indochina, continued to disappoint French economic expectations. A belated effort by Governor Paul Doumer in 1899 and 1900 to galvanize the Indochina economy by organizing the seizure of the Chinese province of Yunnan was suppressed by the French foreign office, resulting in Doumer's removal. Not until after the start of World War I (1914–1918) did the economy begin to fulfill the aspirations of the 1880s.

As colonial expansion proceeded in the 1880s, French possessions in mainland Southeast Asia came to converge with those of the British in the vicinity of Siam, and the "Siam question" then emerged as an acute issue in Anglo-French diplomacy. Already at odds with Britain over Egypt and in tropical Africa, the French colonial interest in Paris and Indochina showed increasing concern at the possibility that Siam would become a British colony. Siam's economy, already closely linked to the trade of British India, Singapore, and Hong Kong, could only be wrenched into alignment with that of Indochina if the French imposed political control and forced the kingdom's economy into their new colonial protectionist system, formed in 1892. This became the objective of a powerful French colonial lobby, the *parti colonial,* which worked through official networks and through Parliament to promote the advance of French expansion across the Mekong Valley. French challenges to Siamese suzerainty over Lao principalities in the Mekong Valley eventually precipitated a crisis (the Paknam Incident) between France and Siam in 1893, marked by a French naval invasion of the Chaopraya River and the imposition of a humiliating treaty. But the crisis backfired on the French colonialists. In order to reduce ensuing diplomatic friction with the British, the French foreign ministry chose to sidestep the colonial party, and by the Declaration of London in 1896, France agreed with Britain to avoid pursuit of military measures or exclusive privileges in the central part of the kingdom. Debarred from pursuing French dominance, the colonial party aimed at joint Anglo-French exploitation of the kingdom, but this project was thwarted by Siamese exclusion of virtually all forms of French influence from the kingdom. Only in negotiations leading to the Entente Cordiale of 1904 did the French colonial party finally give up its ambitions for an Anglo-French "condominium" in Siam, in return for the prospect of British diplomatic support for the French dominance of Morocco. By the terms of a subsequent agreement with Siam in 1907, the colonial party agreed to sacrifice some French extraterritorial rights in return for the Siamese surrender of Battambang and Siem Reap to the French-protected state of Cambodia. This final acquisition brought French territorial expansion in Southeast Asia to a close.

PATRICK TUCK

See also Anglo-French Declaration of London (1896); Annam; Battambang; British Interests in Southeast Asia; Cochin China; Colonialism; Đà Nẵng (Tourane); French Indochina; Germans (Germany); Imperialism; Lagrée-Garnier Mekong Expedition (1866–1868); Laos (Nineteenth Century to Mid-1990s); Napoleonic Wars in Asia; Nguyễn Anh (Emperor Gia Long) (r. 1802–1820); Nguyễn Emperors and French Imperialism; Norodom (1836–1904); Paknam Incident (1893); Pigneau de Béhaine, Pierre Joseph Georges, Bishop of Adran (1741–1799); Preservation of Siam's Political Independence; Reforms and Modernization in Siam; Siem Reap; Tonkin (Tongking)

References:

Ageron, Charles Robert. 1978. *France colonial ou Parti Colonial?* [*Colonial France or Parti Colonial?*] Paris: Presses Universitaires de France.

Andrew, Christopher, and Sydney Kanya-Forstner. 1981. *France Overseas.* London: Thames and Hudson.

Brocheux, Pierre, and Daniel Hémery. 1995. *Indochine: La Colonisation ambigüe* [*Indochina: Ambiguous Colonialism*]. Paris: Éditions de la Découverte.

Brötel, Dieter. 1971. *Fransösischer imperialismus in Indochina* [*French Imperialism in Indochina*]. Freiburg, Germany: Atlantis.

Laffey, John. 1969. "Les Racines de l'impérialisme française en Extrême-Orient à propos des thèses de J. F. Cady" [The Roots of French Imperialism in the Far East with Regard to J. F. Cady's Theses]. *Revue d'Histoire Moderne et Contemporaine* 16: 282–299.

Tuck, Patrick. 1995. *The French Wolf and the Siamese Lamb: The French Threat to Siamese Independence, 1858–1907.* Bangkok: White Lotus

FRENCH INDOCHINA

The term *French Indochina* refers to the French-created Indochinese Union (1887), constituting the colony of Cochin China, the protectorates of Annam, Tonkin (Tongking), and Cambodia. When Laos became a French protectorate in 1893, it was incorporated in this administrative structure.

The imperialistic expansion of France into Indochina was begun in the late 1850s and was completed by 1893. The French occupied Tourane (Đà Nẵng) in 1858 and proceeded to capture Saigon, including the three surrounding provinces, from 1859 to 1862. Cambodia then became a French protectorate in 1863. Subsequently, in 1867, the French annexed three other provinces in lower Cochin China, situated west of the Mekong Delta to Pulo Condore. Annam and Tonkin became French-protected territories in 1883 and the French extended similar protectorate status to Laos in 1893.

During the Pacific War (1941–1945), French Indochina initially allied itself with the Japanese Imperial military authorities. However, in the early part of 1945, the French civil administration was terminated and replaced by Imperial Japanese military rule. The Indochinese Federation replaced the prewar Indochinese Union, whereby the components Vietnam, Cambodia, and Laos were constituted as quasi-independent "associated states" within the federation.

Full political independence was attained: Cambodia in 1953, Vietnam in 1954, and Laos in 1953 and 1954. Vietnam, however, was partitioned at the seventeenth parallel that split the country into two, with Tonkin and North Annam constituting the Democratic Republic of Vietnam (DRV) and Cochin China and South Annam forming the Republic of Vietnam (or South Vietnam).

OOI KEAT GIN

See also Cambodia under French Colonial Rule; Dien Bien Phu (May 1954), Battle of; French Ambitions in Southeast Asia; French Indochinese Union (*Union Indochinoise Française*) (1887); Indochina during World War II (1939–1945); Laos (Nineteenth Century to Mid-1990s); Vietnam, North (post-1945); Vietnam, South (Post-1945); Vietnam under French Colonial Rule

References:

Buttinger, Joseph. 1967. *Vietnam: A Dragon Embattled.* Vol. 2. London: Pall Mall.

Osborne, Milton. 1969. *The French Presence in Cochinchina and Cambodia.* Ithaca, NY: Cornell University Press.

Truong Buu Lam. 1967. *Patterns of Vietnamese Response to Foreign Intervention, 1858–1900.* New Haven, CT: Southeast Asia Studies, Yale University.

Tuck, Patrick. 1995. *The French Wolf and the Siamese Lamb.* Bangkok: White Lotus.

FRENCH INDOCHINESE UNION (*UNION INDOCHINOISE FRANÇAISE*) (1887)

Spread over some thirty-odd years, the French takeover of Indochina started with the absorption of southern Vietnam and its conversion into the Cochin China colony (1858–1867); it was completed with the establishment in 1893 of the French protectorate over the Lao principality of Luang Prabang. But as early as 1887, Cambodia, Cochin China, Annam, and Tonkin had been brought together to form the *Union Indochinoise,* placed under the ultimate authority of the French minister of marine and colonies in Paris. The administration was entrusted to a civilian governor-general assisted by a higher commander of the troops, a higher commander of the marine, a general secretary, a chief of the judiciary service, and a director of the customs and excise. The governor-general was advised but not controlled by a government council (called *Conseil Supérieur de l'Indochine*—Higher Council of Indochina—from 1887 to 1911, and *Conseil de Gouvernement*—Council of Government—after 1911), which sat each year to discuss general matters of public interest.

It was Paul Doumer, governor-general from 1897 to 1902, who made the Indochinese Union an actual administrative and financial unity. He centralized the civil services of the colony—customs, postal telegraph service, forestry, and commerce. He also introduced the common general budget funded by the proceeds of indirect taxes (customs, taxes on opium, alcohol, salt, etc.), while revenues from direct taxes (land and poll taxes) were assigned to the regional administrations. At the same time, he organized for Laos an entirely new state within borders formed by the amalgamation of territories that had never before been under a single administration. During Doumer's term of office, the Indochina Geographical Service was created, as well as the École Française d'Extrême-Orient, a scientific establishment whose mission was to collect and study the archaeological and cultural data of Indochina and to preserve its historical monuments.

The *Union Indochinoise* incorporated into a political, economic, and social federalism five separate administrative regions, under five regional heads, the governor of Cochin China and the *résidents supérieurs* of Annam, Tonkin, Cambodia, and Laos. It represented a complex supranational structure. If Cochin China was the colony in the narrow constitutional sense, a system of indirect government, similar to that applied by the British to certain parts of Burma, was put into practice in the protectorates of Cambodia and Laos. Local political structures based on the Cambodian provincial governors and the Laotian *chao müang* (heads of provinces) had been left intact. But it meant for Vietnam in particular the dismantlement of its territorial unity. Moreover, the bureaucracy of the "protected" Vietnamese emperor was merged into a highly centralized system dependent exclusively on the competence of France's representatives, who surrogated themselves to the authority of the monarch on the one hand, and his mandarins on the other, for the effective exercise of power. In such a regime of protectorate, the distinction between direct and indirect rule was legal rather than practical.

In fact, the actual movement was toward more direct rule—notwithstanding Governor-General Paul Beau's (t. 1902–1907) efforts after 1902 to restore a part of the local administration and set up a consultative assembly in Tonkin, and Albert Sarraut's (t. 1911–1914) promise in 1911 to revert to the policy of association, while reforming justice, developing public education, and enlarging political representation in consultative councils. Eventually, in 1928, Indochina was endowed with a *Grand Conseil des Intérêts Économiques et Financiers* (Great Council of Economic and Financial Interests). It was composed of a French section and a native section, with an advisory role for all financial and economic issues and the right of decision on the matters of taxation. At the regional level, the creation of indigenous assemblies with elected delegates seemed to indicate a liberal evolution. Nevertheless, the governor-general's authority remained absolute, and as far as his position was concerned the term *viceroy* could be used. If the policy of association was supposed to be guiding the French administration of the *Union Indochinoise* from 1907 until the suspension of direct French rule by the Japanese in March 1945, the powers of the governor-general were repeatedly exercised to overrule the nominal autonomy of the component territories. Although native sovereignties continued to be recognized in certain formalities, in practice they were considered to be overridden by the authority of the French state.

In any case, during most of its history, the *Union Indochinoise* was administered by governor-generals whose average term of office was less than two years, with the exception of Paul Doumer, who stayed in office for five years. Moreover, the men appointed to this paramount position were nearly proconsuls whose previous careers had brought them little experience relevant to the problems of colonial administration. Rare certainly were men of established professional standing whose names came to figure on the list of Indochina's governors-general.

The movement toward greater centralization, rationalization, and efficiency could be explained by metropolitan demands to reduce costs and to find local resources for colonial improvements and for European capitalist investments. The interest attached to the colonies was indeed related to the investments they represented and controlled by means of big financial groups: the principal mining or rubber companies in Indochina depended more or less directly on the Banque de l'Indochine (Bank of Indochina). The influx of private capital (more than 3 billion francs from 1924 to 1932) accelerated economic development, while colonial loans were allocated to the construction of the rail and road infrastructure (Nguyễn 1999: 350–351). But the new economy based on rich cultures, mining, and big commerce disturbed the balance between the forms of activity: efforts were concentrated on the exportation of raw materials and the importation of metropolitan manufactured articles. And, compared with the other products, rice was by far the most exported item. Thanks to the construction of new dykes in Tonkin and of irrigation canals in Cochin China, rice fields covered 4 million hectares in 1913, and 5.6 million in 1938 (ibid.: 354).

But the people did not live better because rice, coal, and rubber could now be exported. Indochina's apparent prosperity at the end of the 1920s was beneficial to less than 10 percent of the population, and first to the civil or military French population (36,000 in 1937) and to a thin class of well-off natives (ibid.: 356). The 1929–1930 economic crisis was going to show that the number of economic consumers in Indochina amounted to 1,800,000 persons, whereas more than 17 million were utterly destitute (ibid.).

NGUYỄN THẾ ANH

See also Annam; Cambodia under French Colonial Rule; Cochin China; Laos (Nineteenth Century to Mid-1990s); Nguyễn Emperors and French Imperialism; Tonkin (Tongking); Vietnam under French Colonial Rule

References:

Brocheux, Pierre, and Daniel Hémery. 2001. *Indochine: La Colonisation Ambigüé, 1858–1954* [*Indochina: The Ambiguous Colonization, 1858–1954*]. 2nd ed. Paris: La Découverte.

Dommen, Arthur. 2001. *The Indochinese Experience of the French and the Americans: Nationalism and Communism in Cambodia, Laos and Vietnam.* Bloomington: Indiana University Press.

Isoart, Paul. 1992. "La Création de l'Union Indochinoise" [The Creation of the Indochinese Union]. *Approches Asie* 11: 45–71.

Nguyễn Thế Anh. 1999. "Asie du Sud-Est" [Southeast Asia]. Pp. 311–405 in *L'Asie Orientale et Méridionale aux XIXe et XXe Siècles* [*East and South Asia in the 19th and 20th Centuries*]. Edited by Hartmut O. Rotermund et al. Paris: Presses Universitaires de France.

Thompson, Virginia. 1968 [1937]. *French Indochina.* New York: Octagon.

FRETILIN (FRENTE REVOLUCIONÁRIA DO TIMOR-LESTE INDEPENDENTE)

FRETILIN, the Revolutionary Front for an Independent East Timor (Frente Revolucionária do Timor-Leste Independente), was established on 12 September 1974 by members of the Timorese Social Democratic Association (Associacão Social Democrata Timorense, ASDT), which had been founded only a few months previously, on 20 May 1974. Initially, its founders considered FRETILIN as a united front directed by a central committee rather than as a unitary party.

During 1975, after conflict with rival parties, FRETILIN gained control of the Portuguese colony, and on 28 November 1975, it declared the country's independence as the Democratic Republic of East Timor. The first East Timorese government under FRETILIN included Francisco Xavier do Amaral as president, Nicolau

Lobato as prime minister, Mari Alkatiri as minister of state for political affairs, Abilio de Araujo as minister for economic and social affairs, Rogerio Lobato as defense minister, Vincente Sa'he as minister of labor and welfare, José Goncalves as minister for economic coordination, Alarico Fernandes as minister for internal affairs and security, and José Ramos Horta as minister of foreign affairs. Many of these founding members of FRETILIN went on to play significant roles in a long struggle to regain independence for East Timor.

On 7 December 1975, Indonesia invaded the country, and East Timorese resistance groups, under FRETILIN leadership, were forced to flee into the mountains. Key members of the Central Committee—Mari Alkatiri, Rogerio Lobato, and José Ramos Horta—were overseas. As a consequence, the Central Committee established two fronts, an armed front and a diplomatic front, to maintain its struggle. The Armed Forces for the Liberation of East Timor (Forças Armadas da Libertação de Timor Leste, FALINTIL) carried out guerrilla warfare within East Timor, whereas the diplomatic efforts were pursued at the United Nations and in countries that supported FRETILIN's struggle, in particular Portugal and Mozambique.

In the year after the invasion and under heavy pressure from Indonesian forces, party stalwarts in the mountains adopted a Marxist-Leninist stance, which resulted in internal disputes. Xavier do Amaral, the head of FRETILIN and the country's former president, was expelled from FRETILIN and was later captured by the Indonesians in September 1977; he was replaced by Nicolau Lobato, who would be killed on 31 December 1978. José Alexandre "Kay Rala Xanana" Gusmão replaced Lobato as the head of FALINTIL and began a process of restructuring the resistance forces in the interests of national unity. As part of this process, FALINTIL was formally detached from FRETILIN on 7 December 1986, to become the army of national resistance. One year later, Gusmão formally resigned from FRETILIN and was joined in this move by Ramos Horta.

The Central Committee of FRETILIN agreed to work with the broader resistance bodies established under Gusmão's leadership. The first of these was the Revolutionary Council of National Resistance (CRRN), formed in 1981; this was followed by the National Council of Maubere Resistance (CNRM), formed in 1987, and the National Council of Timorese Resistance (CNRT), which was established in Peniche, Portugal, in April 1998. During this period, a third, "clandestine" front was established to carry the struggle from the countryside into the towns and villages of East Timor.

During the 1980s, FRETILIN was headed by a succession of guerrilla leaders, two of whom, Ma Huno (Antonio Gomes) and Hudo Ran Kadalak (José da Costa), were captured by Indonesian forces, as was Xanana Gusmão in 1992. For a brief period thereafter, Konis Santana assumed command of both FALINTIL and FRETILIN.

In 1999, East Timor was given the right to a UN-supervised vote on whether to accept autonomy within Indonesia. Activists under the umbrella of the National Council of Timorese Resistance rallied the population, which voted overwhelmingly for independence. Following this vote, the UN Transitional Administration of East Timor assumed responsibility from Indonesia for preparing the country for independence.

For a period, the CNRT acted as the principal representative of the East Timorese population. Key political figures returned from detention, from the diaspora, or from the mountains where they had maintained guerrilla struggle.

In preparation for elections to the Constituent Assembly that was to draft a constitution for the country, FRETILIN—as well as its rival, União Democrática Timorense (UDT)—withdrew from CNRT to operate independently. Other parties were also established or reconstituted until, in the end, there were sixteen parties in the election for the eighty-eight-member Constituent Assembly.

Francisco Xavier do Amaral formed his own party, the Timorese Social Democratic Association (ASDT), using the name of the 1974 organization that was transformed into FRETILIN; Abilio de Araujo, who had been expelled from FRETILIN for cooperating with Indonesia, established the Timorese National Party (PNT).

In the elections held on 30 August 2001, FRETILIN obtained over 57 percent of the vote, giving it an allocation of forty-three nationally determined seats and another twelve district seats in the new assembly. It was thus able to form a government on 20 May 2002 when the United Nations officially handed over authority to East Timor.

The new government included Mari Alkatiri as prime minister, Rogerio Lobato as minister of internal affairs, and José Ramos Horta as foreign minister. Lu Olo (Francisco Guterres), the head of FRETILIN, became the speaker of the National Assembly, and Xanana Gusmão, who had been elected by an overwhelming majority in a contest with Xavier do Amaral, became the president of the revived Democratic Republic of East Timor. It had taken twenty-seven years of work by a committed group of East Timorese, all of whom were at one time or another associated with FRETILIN, to achieve this goal.

JAMES J. FOX

See also Nationalism and Independence
    Movements in Southeast Asia; Portuguese
    Asian Empire; Suharto (1921–); Timor
References:
Dunn, James. 1983. *Timor: A People Betrayed.*
    Milton, Brisbane, Australia: Jacaranda Press.
Fox, James J., and Dionisio Babo Soares, eds.
    2000. *Out of the Ashes: Destruction and
    Reconstruction of East Timor.* Adelaide,
    Australia: Crawford House Publishing.
Joliffe, Jill. 1978. *East Timor: Nationalism and
    Colonialism.* St. Lucia, Australia: University of
    Queensland Press.
Nicol, Bill. 2002. *Timor: A Nation Reborn.*
    Singapore and Jakarta: Equinox.
Taylor, John. 1999. *East Timor: The Price of
    Freedom.* London: Zed Books.

FRIARS, SPANISH
(THE PHILIPPINES)

The friar orders played a crucial role both in the evangelization of the Philippines and in the maintenance of Spanish colonialism in the islands for over three hundred years. The close relationship between ecclesiastical mission and secular authority had its basis in the *patronato real* (royal patronage), whereby the Spanish Crown assumed the financial support of the Roman Catholic Church in the New World, including the cost of sending missionaries, in return for the privilege of nominating ecclesiastical benefices. This arrangement was extended to the Philippines with the arrival of Miguel López de Legazpi (1505–1572) to-

gether with five members of the Augustinian order in 1565, an event that constitutes the origins of missionary endeavor in the archipelago. Many religious came from Spain, a journey that involved sailing to Vera Cruz on the Caribbean coast of Mexico, traveling overland to the Pacific port of Acapulco via Mexico City, and finally taking a ship to Manila. Sending just one missionary from Spain to the Philippines is said to have cost 129,526 maravedis or about 1,012 pesos, a truly fabulous sum for the period (Cushner 1971; Roth 1977). Despite an unfavorable start to the mission, reflecting the tenuousness of the Spanish settlement's early days, there were 134 religious in the archipelago by 1595. Apart from the Augustinians, these included the Franciscans arriving in 1578, the Jesuits in 1581, and the Dominicans in 1587. Other orders subsequently arrived: the Augustinian Recollects (1606), the Fathers of San Juan de Dios (1641), the Vincentians or Paúles (1862), the Capuchins (1886), and the Benedictines (1895). By 1896, there were a total of 1,124 friars in the archipelago (Cushner 1971; Roth 1977). Nor should the good works of the female religious be overlooked. Notable for their contributions to charity, education, and health were the Beaterio of the Society of Jesus, established in 1684 (presently the Religious of the Virgin Mary); the Beaterio of Santa Catalina in 1696; and the Daughters of Charity in 1852. The Philippines also functioned as a base for missionary endeavors to the rest of Asia and the Pacific; missionaries set forth from the archipelago to evangelize neighboring peoples in Japan, China, Formosa (Taiwan), Indochina, Siam (Thailand), the Moluccas, the Marianas, and the Caroline and Palau islands.

The religious retained houses in and around Manila, though each of the four main orders had definite districts or missions assigned to them by the king (royal decree of 27 April 1594). Augustinians were mainly in northeastern Luzon and the central Visayas; Franciscans in southern and eastern Luzon, Mindoro, and Marinduque; Jesuits (before their expulsion in 1768) in the Visayas; and Dominicans in Pangasinan and northwestern Luzon. The Augustinian Recollects also played an important role in evangelizing Romblon, Bohol, and Negros. Members of the missionary orders enjoyed a great deal of freedom to evangelize in their own ways. The *Omnimodam auctitatem,* first granted by Pope Adrian VI to the Franciscans in 1522 and subsequently extended to the other orders, gave friars permission to perform every episcopal faculty as occasion demanded for the conversion of pagans and the preservation of the faith. Their independence was further strengthened by the papal brief *Exponi nobis* in 1567, which effectively authorized members of the missionary orders to act in the capacity of parish priests throughout the archipelago. Friars were only supposed to administer *doctrinas*— communities of the recently converted—as a temporary stage in preparing these communities to become established parishes or curacies, at which point they were to be handed over to the care of the secular clergy. However, due to the shortage of the latter in the Philippines, this transfer was never completed, and many doctrinas effectively became regular parishes administered by the religious orders.

Evangelization was carried out in the vernacular despite the difficulties often encountered in finding appropriate equivalents for Christian concepts; it was considered easier for a friar to learn the local language than for a community to learn Spanish. The colonial government's repeated orders to establish local schools in which the Spanish language was taught were stubbornly ignored. Instead, the friars' main missionary endeavors were directed at the principal inhabitants of a village, as such conversions often encouraged others in the community to follow suit. These first baptisms were conducted with great pomp to impress upon people the solemn nature of the sacrament being received, and they were accompanied by choirs and brass bands and followed by other festivities. The fact that many friars were accomplished physicians able to dispense medicine and cure the sick also greatly facilitated their activities. Nor should the distinct social advantages of conversion in terms of legal status, tributary payments, and labor requirements be underestimated in this respect. For most of the colonial period, these friars constituted the only European presence to be found in most native pueblos; Spanish settlers did not become a significant factor until the second half of the nineteenth century with the opening of the Suez Canal in 1869, and even then, they came only in small numbers. As such, the religious often paid dearly for their mission, being seized or murdered by nonsubdued tribespeople and

marauding pirates. Jesuits in the Visayas proved particularly tempting prizes for Muslim raiders due to both their geographic vulnerability and the ransoms they commanded. Still, this missionary endeavor was ultimately responsible for the gradual evangelization of most of the archipelago, from the northernmost islands off Luzon to the tip of the Zamboanga peninsula in Mindanao.

Relations were often strained among the friar orders, the colonial governments, and episcopal authorities. Enforcement of the royal patronage resulted in friar-secular clashes. For instance, the Augustinians and the Jesuits objected to the action of governors-general in appointing or removing the religious from parishes; the friar orders claimed that only their superiors in Rome possessed such a prerogative. The orders successfully opposed in 1637, 1650, and 1682 the efforts of the colonial governments to impose the Crown's right of *presentación* (the right to offer an ecclesiastical benefice). In this struggle with the secular authorities, the orders turned to the simple threat of relinquishing their parishes amidst an acute shortage of secular clergy. Likewise the orders relied on the same strategy when they resisted the efforts of the Archbishop of Manila during the seventeenth and eighteenth centuries to exert control over the friar orders by vetting those acting as parish priests and carrying out episcopal visitations. However, in 1773 Archbishop Basilio Sancho de Santa Justa y Rufino bravely called the Augustinians' bluff and expelled them from their parishes in Pampanga. Rufino replaced them with Filipino clergy who were hastily ordained and largely unprepared. The dire consequences of this policy considerably weakened the development of a native clergy vis-à-vis the religious, who returned to their parishes and attained a stronger position than they had possessed previously. Although the Crown generally supported the policy of episcopal visitation, as any claim to perpetual parish jurisdiction seriously compromised the royal patronage, it was also mindful of the important role friars played in maintaining allegiance and order in rural areas and so sought to mediate in these disputes.

Many friars destined for the Philippines were those who were "exiled" there for one reason or another, with consequent repercussions for both the clerics involved and the proper evangelization of native peoples. Regular complaints about their abuse of office had been partly responsible for attempts at enforcing episcopal visitation in the first place. Friars were frequently accused of exacting excessive fees for burials and weddings (supposedly free or voluntary offerings), illegally using indigenous labor, and requisitioning food supplies. Still others were charged with openly flaunting their vows of celibacy and living in concubinage with indigenous women who acted as their so-called housekeepers. Many of these women also played important roles as the priests' agents or factotums, helping them with their financial and trade transactions. Specific orders were known for particular transgressions: Augustinians were continually admonished for engaging in local commerce, Jesuits for usurping lands and engaging in the galleon trade, and Dominicans for excessive rigor and the use of corporal punishment at the slightest provocation. A particular cause of much resentment was the growth of the religious-owned estates, or *haciendas,* often acquired by means of fraudulent surveys and the illegal incorporation of village lands. Anger and frustration culminated in the agrarian revolt of 1745, one of the most serious uprisings against Spanish colonialism prior to the Philippine Revolution (1896–1898). Attacks on haciendas occurred in the provinces of Cavite, Tondo, Bulacan, and Batangas, during which granaries and irrigation works on disputed lands were burned down or destroyed, cattle were stolen or slaughtered, and administrators were forced to flee. The rebellion was only suppressed by an adroit mixture of firmness and redress, which involved restoring much of the disputed lands to the municipalities in question. Despite limitations on growth, the religious orders still had extensive landholdings by the nineteenth century, from which they derived a substantial income.

The influence and material assets of the religious orders grew accordingly in a colony where they played such an important role in upholding the regime, though much of this wealth was directed toward the maintenance of schools, hospitals, orphanages, asylums, and universities. In particular, the expansion of the export economy proved an incentive to develop the friar-owned haciendas during the nineteenth century. Undeveloped portions of estates were often leased out to Chinese mestizo or indigenous tenant farmers (*inquilinos*), who generally hired sharecroppers (*kasamahanes*) to work the land. Attempts to raise rents in line with increasing productivity were bitterly resented and a major cause of the widespread anticlericalism found among the *ilustrado* (intelligentsia) sector of society. Some 40 friars were killed during the Philippine Revolution, and a further 403 were taken prisoner, though virtually all of these were later released (Cushner 1971; Roth 1977). Still, only 472 religious were left in the Philippines by 1900, and their numbers continued to decline, falling to 246 in 1902 (Cushner 1971; Roth 1977). Appropriation of friar lands was called for under the Malolos Constitution (1899) but was not realized until 1903 when the new U.S. colonial administration purchased approximately 166,000 hectares for redistribution, farmed by some 60,000 tenants (Cushner 1971; Roth 1977). However, the subsequent resale of these estates to members of the upper class did much to consolidate a landed elite in the Philippines and proved the root cause for a continuing agrarian unrest that persists today.

GREG BANKOFF

See also Anti-Spanish Revolts (The Phillippines); Catholicism; Cavite Mutiny; *Ilustrados;* Friar-Secular Relationship; Galleon Trade; Missionaries, Christian; Patron-Client Relations; Philippine Revolution (1896–1898); Philippines under Spanish Colonial Rule (ca. 1560s–1898); Rizal, José (1861–1896); Spanish Expansion in Southeast Asia

References:

Bankoff, Greg. 1992. *"In Verbo Sacerdotis": The Judicial Power of the Catholic Church in the Nineteenth-Century Philippines.* Monograph Series no. 2. Darwin, Australia: Northern Territory University, Centre for Southeast Asian Studies.

Connolly, Michael. 1992. *Church Lands and Peasant Unrest in the Philippines: Agrarian Conflict in 20th-Century Luzon.* Quezon City, the Philippines: Ateneo de Manila Press.

Cushner, Nicholas. 1971. *Spain in the Philippines: From Conquest to Revolution.* Quezon City: Institute of Philippine Culture, Ateneo de Manila University.

Fernandez, Pablo. 1979. *History of the Church in the Philippines (1521–1898).* Manila: National Book Store.

Phelan, John Leddy. 1959. *The Hispanization of the Philippines: Spanish Aims and Filipino Responses, 1565–1700*. Madison: University of Wisconsin Press.

Roth, Dennis Morrow. 1977. *The Friar Estates of the Philippines*. Albuquerque: University of New Mexico Press.

FRIAR-SECULAR RELATIONSHIP

Relations between the religious orders and the colonial and episcopal authorities of the secular clergy in the Philippines under Spanish colonialism were seldom harmonious. The *Omnimodam auctitatem* ("Enlargement of any kind," meaning extension of power) of Pope Adrian VI (t. 1522–1523) in 1522 granted the missionary orders the freedom to evangelize in their own way, and the papal brief *Exponi nobis* ("It is expounded to us," meaning provide a detailed explanation) of 1567 effectively allowed them to act as parish priests in the archipelago. Friars were only supposed to administer communities of the recently converted (known as *doctrinas*), as a preparatory stage to becoming established parishes that were then to be surrendered to the secular clergy. Despite Philip II's (r. 1556–1598) confirmation in 1583 that parochial administration belonged to the latter except where dire necessity had prompted papal concessions, the transfer of parishes was never completed in the Philippines. An acute shortage of secular clergy, occasioned by the reluctance to ordain Filipinos, meant that many doctrinas effectively became regular parishes administered by friars. The subsequent history of the colonial state in the islands was largely determined by the various attempts of both royal and episcopal officials to limit the influence of these orders and exert their own authority over rural populations.

Enforcement of the royal patronage led to much bitter controversy as governors-general tried to remove or appoint the religious from parishes, which the latter claimed was the sole prerogative of their superiors in Rome. The colonial governments' attempts to impose the Crown's right of nomination were successfully resisted in 1637, 1650, and 1682. The simple expedient of threatening to relinquish their parishes in the face of an acute shortage of secular clergy gave the orders the upper hand in any such contest of wills. A further attempt by Ferdinand VI (r. 1746–1759) to relieve the orders of their parishes in 1753 was never put into effect in the Philippines. Similarly, efforts by the archbishops of Manila to exert episcopal control over the friar orders by vetting religious acting as parish priests and carrying out visitations failed for much the same reasons during the seventeenth and eighteenth centuries. The most serious confrontation occurred in 1773 when Archbishop Basilio Sancho de Santa Justa y Rufino called the Augustinians' bluff and expelled them from their parishes in Pampanga, replacing them with hastily ordained and unprepared native clergy. The disastrous results of this policy led the king to rescind his actions and restore the friars to their ministries. Although the Crown vigorously resisted all claims that might compromise the royal patronage, it was also mindful of the important role the religious played in maintaining allegiance and order in rural areas.

Secularization assumed more overtly political dimensions during the nineteenth century as an issue between a largely Spanish regular clergy and an increasingly native secular one. The shortage of regular clergy due to the expulsion of the Jesuits (1768), together with the fact that there were fewer arrivals from Spain during the Napoleonic Wars (1803–1815), ensured that secularization continued as parishes were turned over to native clergy on an interim basis. The question was raised once again in 1803 when three new parishes were assigned to the regular orders, prompting a petition to the king to assign them to the secular clergy. The subsequent royal consent, however, was simply ignored by colonial authorities in the Philippines. Prior to the independence of Spain's American colonies, successive governments in Madrid had been in favor of further secularization to relieve the state of the high costs of sending religious to the colonies. After the loss of the Americas, however, Ferdinand VII (r. 1808–1833) moved swiftly to prevent any further moves of that type and even called for the restoration of the religious orders to their former parishes on the death or retirement of their secular incumbents (royal order of 8 June 1826).

The last half century of Spanish rule was one of increasing hostility between a largely secular native clergy deemed to have separatist aspirations and a colonial administration bent on restoring the influence of the religious orders.

Matters were only exacerbated by subsequent royal orders that granted friars parishes that were formerly in the possession of the secular clergy and by the return of the Jesuits in 1859. Events further degenerated after the recall of the liberal governor-general Carlos Maria De La Torre y Nava Cerrada (t. 1869–1871) and his replacement by the much less sympathetic Rafael Izquierdo (t. 1871–1873). Subsequently, three secular native priests—Frs. José Burgos (1837–1872), Mariano Gomes (1799–1872), and Jacinto Zamora (1835–1872)—were implicated in the abortive Cavite Mutiny of 1872 and executed. Others were sentenced to varying terms of exile in Guam. It is now generally considered that the friars seized upon this incident to preserve their influence and discredit the native clergy. Though the latter played a much less prominent role in subsequent developments, José Rizal (1861–1896) dedicated his second novel, *El Filibusterismo,* to the memory of the executed priests, and still others were arrested for circulating revolutionary material. The complete secularization of the parishes was only effected during the Philippine Revolution (1896–1898), when many of the religious were forced to abandon their parishes and subsequently prevented from returning.

GREG BANKOFF

See also Catholicism; Cavite Munity; Friars, Spanish (The Philippines); Missionaries, Christian; *Noli Me Tangere* (1887) and *El Filibusterismo* (1891); Philippine Revolution (1896–1898); Philippines under Spanish Colonial Rule (ca. 1560s–1898); Rizal, José (1861–1896)

References:

Corpuz, Onofre. 1989. *The Roots of the Filipino Nation.* 2 vols. Quezon City, the Philippines: Aklahi Foundation.

Cushner, Nicholas. 1971. *Spain in the Philippines: From Conquest to Revolution.* Quezon City: Institute of Philippine Culture, Ateneo de Manila University.

De La Costa, Horacio. 1969. "The Development of the Native Clergy in the Philippines." Pp. 65–104 in *Studies in Philippine Church History.* Edited by Gerald H. Anderson. Ithaca, NY: Cornell University Press.

Fernandez, Pablo. 1979. *History of the Church in the Philippines (1521–1898).* Manila: National Book Store.

Schumacher, John. 1978. "Eighteenth-Century Filipino Clergy: A Footnote to De la Costa." *Philippine Studies* 26: 157–173.

———. 1981. *Revolutionary Clergy: The Filipino Clergy and the Nationalist Movement, 1850–1903.* Quezon City, the Philippines: Ateneo de Manila University Press.

FUJIWARA KIKAN (F. KIKAN)

Harnessing Indigenous Nationalist Support

Fujiwara Kikan (known as F. Kikan) was the Japanese military intelligence organization headed by Major Fujiwara Iwaichi (1908–1986) (who was promoted to lieutenant colonel in August 1944). The *F* stands for Fujiwara as well as "Freedom" and "Friendship"; *Kikan* means "organization."

The Japanese Imperial General Headquarters (IGH) formed F. Kikan in September 1941. Originally, the organization consisted of six officers (excluding Fujiwara) and an interpreter; later, it increased to more than twenty members. At the end of September 1941, members were sent to Bangkok to contact and garner the cooperation of the various nationalist movements—Indian, Malay, Indonesian, and Chinese—in preparing for the war. They were most successful with the Indian Independence League (IIL). Fujiwara met its leader, Pritam Singh, in October 1941 and secured his agreement to cooperate with the Japanese Imperial Army (JIA). (Pritam Singh died in a plane crash in Japan in March 1942.) When the Pacific War (1941–1942) started, F. Kikan, with the help of some seventy IIL members who followed the JIA, succeeded in persuading many British Indian army soldiers to switch allegiance without fighting. While advancing southward in the Malay Peninsula, the Indian National Army (INA), which had been formed on 31 December 1941, recruited troops from among surrendered British Indian soldiers. In the main cities, IIL branches were established.

After reaching agreement with Fujiwara, Captain Mohan Singh, who was skeptical of the real intention of the Japanese, became commander of the INA; in February 1942, he was promoted to major general. The agreements with both Pritam Singh and Mohan Singh stated that the Indian organizations were independent and were to be treated as Japanese allies. These agreements were, however, regarded by the IGH as personal matters and ignored. The IGH staffers tended merely to utilize the Indian organizations as their subordinates. Though 25,000 of the 65,000 British Indian army soldiers who had surrendered to the Japanese ultimately joined the INA, the superior attitude exhibited by the Japanese increasingly irritated their organization (Allen 1977: 261).

F. Kikan also contributed largely in the Sumatran campaign. Twenty Sumatra Youth League members recruited by F. Kikan penetrated into Sumatra and succeeded in mustering tens of thousands of local people to drive out the Dutch. F. Kikan also played a part in gaining the support of the Young Malay Union (Kesatuan Melayu Muda) of Malaya, headed by Ibrahim Yaacob (1911–1979).

In April 1942, Fujiwara was transferred to the Southern Army Headquarters, and F. Kikan was replaced by Iwakuro Kikan, headed by Colonel Iwakuro Hideo (1897–1965). After this replacement, Mohan Singh was arrested in December 1942. A paramount nationalist leader, Subhas Chandra Bose (1897–1945), arrived in Singapore from Berlin in July 1943 to lead the IIL as well as the INA.

HARA FUJIO

See also Bose, Subhas Chandra (1897–1945); Collaboration Issue in Southeast Asia; "Death Railway" (Burma-Siam Railway); Ibrahim Yaacob (1911–1979); Imphal-Kohima, Battle of (1944); Indian National Army (INA); Japanese Occupation of Southeast Asia (1941–1945); Kesatuan Melayu Muda (KMM) (Young Malay Union)

References:

Allen, Louis. 1977. *Singapore 1941–1942.* Newark, NJ: University of Delaware Press.

Fujiwara, Iwaichi. 1983 [1966]. *F. Kikan: Japanese Army Intelligence Operations in Southeast Asia during World War II.* Translated by Akashi Yoji. Hong Kong: Heinemann Asia. Originally published in Japanese in 1966.

FUNAN
An Early Maritime Power

Funan is the name applied in Chinese dynastic histories to a maritime kingdom located in the lower Mekong Valley of modern Cambodia and Vietnam, dated from the third to seventh centuries C.E. At the height of its power in the mid-third century, Funan is also thought to have controlled some of the major ports on the Malay Peninsula and to have been influential in the development of maritime trade between India and China.

Archaeological excavations in 1944 at the town of Oc Eo in the western Mekong Delta have demonstrated close contact with the Indian subcontinent during the first centuries C.E. It may well have been a manufacturing site for the nearby city of Angkor Borei, where archaeologists from Hawai'i University have recently excavated the remains of a substantial ceremonial center.

Much of our knowledge of Funan is derived from a Chinese embassy led by K'ang T'ai and Chu Ying in the mid-third century C.E. Their original writings have not survived but are quoted in later Chinese histories. They include a description of the founding of Funan by a man named Hun-t'ien, who sailed to Funan and married a queen named Liu Ye or "Willow Leaf." This story is also recounted in a seventh-century inscription from Champa. There, however, the man is called Kaundinya and the queen, Soma.

The importance of Funan as a maritime power is attributed to the king Fan Man or Fan Shi Man, whose reign has been dated to around 200 C.E. He is said to have constructed a fleet of ships and to have attacked more than ten kingdoms. Only three kingdoms were individually named, but all have been identified with the Malay Peninsula. These raids appear to have been an attempt to take control of the maritime trade flowing from India through the Malay Peninsula to China.

The embassy of K'ang T'ai and Chu Ying was received by King Fan Chan, who also sent and received envoys from the country of Dayuezhi in northern India. Fan Chan sent a further embassy to the southern Wu kingdom of China in 243 and 244. However, relations with Wu gradually soured, and in 268, envoys were sent to the northern Chinese kingdom of Jin, together with representatives from the kingdom of Linyi in what is now central Vietnam. Between 270 and 280, Linyi and Funan continually harassed the southern Wu borders until the kingdom finally fell to the Jin in 280 C.E. King Fan Hsün thereafter sent three trade embassies to China from 285 to 287.

Little is known of Funan in the fourth century. In 357 C.E., a gift of trained elephants was sent to the Jin court by a king of Funan named T'ien Chu Chan-t'an. T'ien Chu was a common Chinese name for India at that time, and it has been argued that this king was of Indian origin (Coedès 1968: 46–47). Another king, named Kaundinya, is said to have come from the kingdom of Pan Pan on the Malay Peninsula and to have introduced Indian administrative reforms in the early fifth century. Little is really known, however, regarding either of these men. The first king of Funan with a recognizably Indian Sanskrit name was Shih-li-t'o-pa-mo (possibly Sri Indravarman), who sent three embassies to China between 434 and 438 C.E.

In 484 C.E., an embassy was sent by Kaundinya Jayavarman of Funan and delivered by a Buddhist monk named Nagasena. Kaundinya Jayavarman was granted the title of "General of the Pacified South, King of Funan" by the Chinese Liang emperor in 503, and he sent further embassies in 511 and 514. Two inscriptions have been attributed to his wife and son: the first, from the province of Takeo, was ordered by a Queen Kulaprabhavati; the second, from the Plain of Reeds, by Gunavarman. According to the Chinese histories, a king named Rudravarman succeeded Kaundinya Jayavarman. He sent six embassies to China between 517 and 539. The Chinese associated his reign with Buddhism; two monks named Sanghapala and Mandrasena were sent to China from Funan.

According to Chinese sources, after the reign of Rudravarman, Funan was conquered from the north by the kingdom of Zhenla (Chenla). However, three more embassies were received from Funan between 559 and 588, and further embassies were sent in the early seventh century. Funan was clearly an important maritime power during the third century C.E., and it was a center of Buddhist learning in the late fifth and early sixth centuries. It is widely regarded as an ancient, maritime precursor of the modern kingdom of Cambodia. Paul Pelliot (1903) pioneered the collection of information on Funan derived from Chinese sources; George Coedès (1968) added the evidence gleaned from inscriptions.

WILLIAM A. SOUTHWORTH

See also Buddhism, Mahayana; Champa; Chenla; China, Imperial; Chinese Tribute

System; Economic History of Early Modern Southeast Asia (Pre-Sixteenth Century); Elephants; Hindu-Buddhist Period in Southeast Asia; Hinduism; Indianization; Khmers; Oc-Èo

References:
Coedès, George. 1968. *The Indianized States of Southeast Asia.* Honolulu: East-West Center Press/University Press of Hawai'i.
Jacques, Claude. 1979. "'Funan,' 'Zhenla': The Reality Concealed by These Chinese Views of Indochina." Pp. 371–379 in *Early South East Asia: Essays in Archaeology, History and Historical Geography.* Edited by R. B. Smith and W. Watson. Oxford: Oxford University Press.
Mabbett, Ian, and David Chandler. 1995. *The Khmers.* Oxford: Blackwell.
Malleret, Louis. 1959–1963. *L'Archéologie du Delta du Mékong* [*The Archaeology of the Mekong Delta*]. 4 vols. Paris: École Française d'Extrême-Orient.
Pelliot, Paul. 1903. "Le Fou-nan." [In Funan] *Bulletin de l'École Française d'Extrême-Orient* 3: 248–303.
Stark, M., Bion Griffin, and P. and C. Phoeurn. 1999. "Results of the 1995–1996 Archaeological Field Investigations at Angkor Borei, Cambodia." *Asian Perspectives* 38, no. 1: 7–36.

FUNCINPEC (UNITED NATIONAL FRONT FOR AN INDEPENDENT, NEUTRAL, PEACEFUL AND CO-OPERATIVE CAMBODIA)

FUNCINPEC is the Cambodian royalist political party founded in Pyongyang, North Korea, by Prince Norodom Sihanouk (1922–) in March 1981. Its name is an acronym for its full French title, usually translated as United National Front for an Independent, Neutral, Peaceful and Co-operative Cambodia.

In the aftermath of the Khmer Rouge era (1975–1979) in Cambodia, Sihanouk was living in comfortable exile in North Korea. Cambodia was governed by a pro-Vietnamese regime, following the Vietnamese invasion that had driven the Khmer Rouge from power. Sihanouk's patrons in Pyongyang and Beijing pressed him to form a united front with the Khmer Rouge faction, which operated a guerrilla army on the Thai-Cambodian border and occupied Cambodia's seat at the United Nations. Sihanouk agreed reluctantly and designated his eldest son, Norodom Rannaridh, then a professor in France, as leader of the party. FUNCINPEC joined forces with the Khmer Rouge and with another anti-Vietnamese faction on the Thai-Cambodian border to confront the Vietnamese forces still occupying Cambodia. The three factions formed the Coalition Government of Democratic Kampuchea (CGDK) in 1982 and held Cambodia's UN seat until the early 1990s. FUNCINPEC candidates contested national elections sponsored by the United Nations in 1993 and won a majority of seats. But the incumbent former communist party forced the royalists into a coalition, which survived for several years but broke down in 1997 when Cambodia's prime minister, Hun Sen (1951–), carried out a *coup de force* (sudden successful strategy employed with overwhelming force/pressure) against his coalition partners. Under foreign pressure to reinstate the coalition, Hun Sen agreed, but new elections in 1998 confirmed the popularity of his party vis-à-vis FUNCINPEC, whose fortunes declined sharply over the next two years.

DAVID CHANDLER

See also Hun Sen (1951–); Paris Conference on Cambodia (PCC) (1989, 1991); Sihanouk, Norodom (1922–); United Nations Transitional Authority in Cambodia (UNTAC)

References:

Gottesman, Evan. 2002. *Cambodia after the Khmer Rouge.* New Haven, CT: Yale University Press.

FURNIVALL, J. S. (1878–1960)

See Burma Research Society (1909); Plural Society

G

GAJAH MADA (t. 1331–1364)
Javanese Empire-Builder

Gajah Mada's name is popular in post-Majapahit traditions, though in contemporaneous sources such as inscriptions and the literary work *Nâgarakĕrtâgama,* the name is also often spelled Gaja Mada. As the grand vizier (t. 1331–1364) of the kingdom of Majapahit during its heyday in the fourteenth century C.E., Gajah Mada served two sovereigns of Majapahit, namely Queen Tribhûvanatunggadewî (r. 1329–1350) and her successor son, King Râjasanegara Dyah Hayâm Wuruk (r. 1350–1389).

His career in serving the Majapahit kingdom began as a leader of the king's guard, when the king at the time was Tribhûvanatunggadewî's brother, King Sundarapandyadewa (r. 1309–1329)—more popularly known as King Jayanagara. The corps of the king's guard was called Bhayamkara (meaning "that generates fear" or "to be feared by the enemies"). (This name is presently used in the administration of the Republic of Indonesia as a denomination for the state police.) His praiseworthy achievement related to the incident of Badander, where he, as the chief guard, protected and hid King Jayanagara from the hazards of Kuti, the rebel Javanese nobleman. Kuti was then subjugated. That happened in the year śaka 1241 (the śaka years refer to the Burmese Era beginning in 78 c.e.), or around 1319 c.e. Presumably after these heroics, he assumed a position as rake mapatih ring Janggala Kadiri (head or chief minister of the

provinces Janggala and Kadiri); his name was mentioned (as Pu Mada) in an undated inscription of Walandit. His appointment as grand vizier (freely translated from the titles used, such as sang mantry-apatih, rakryan sang mapatih, or sang mantry-adhimantri, which is normally mentioned as the first among high dignitaries) was the pinnacle of his illustrious career.

The mention of *Janggala Kadiri* may mean just a territorial part of the great kingdom of Majapahit, which consisted of several other regions, such as Wurawan and Madhura (Madura). However, it may also be symbolic of the general idea of unification. As it is mentioned in a much later chronicle (ca. early seventeenth century), the *Pararaton,* Gajah Mada was said to take an oath that he would not partake of pleasures (*amukti palapa*) until (the entire) *Nusantara* (regions overseas) came under the domination of Majapahit. The names of places mentioned in that text, excluding the hinterland of Majapahit itself such as Kadiri and Janggala, are Gurun, Seran (in Maluku), Tanjungpura (in Kalimantan), Haru, Pahang, Dompo (in Sumbawa), Bali, Sunda, Palembang (in Sumatra), and Tumasik (Singapore).

Nine years after the rebellion of Kuti, Tañca, the royal physician, assassinated King Jayanagara. Gajah Mada killed Tañca in śaka 1250 (1328). A year later, Tribhûwanatunggadewî, the princess of Jîwana and Jayanagara's sister, was put on the throne of Majapahit. In 1331, Gajah Mada was sent to vanquish Sadeng and Keta, the enemies of Majapahit. Thereafter, his position was raised, and he became "the protector of the kingdom." According to the *Nâgarakĕrtâgama* in the year śaka 1265 (1343), Gajah Mada led an expedition to subjugate Bali. An inscription at the posterior of a statue of Mañjuśrî found at Candi Jago in East Java, from the year 1341, mentioned that in his campaigns to Bali, Gajah Mada was accompanied by Adityawarman, a prince of the Singhasâri-Majapahit line of descent who later became a king in Sumatra. From such evidence, it can be surmised that the conquest of Bali took several years; Bali was finally subjugated in 1343. An account of Gajah Mada's death in the year 1364 is noted in the *Nâgarakĕrtâgama*.

Gajah Mada's popularity in traditional historiography spills over into fictional literature. Works possibly written in the late seventeenth century, called the *Kidung Sunda* and the *Kidung Sundayana*, dramatically rendered, were supposedly based on a short account in the *Pararaton*. The chronicle related historical incidents in which Gajah Mada played a significant role, namely, the defeats of Dompo and Sunda in the year śaka 1279 (1357). Even in the twentieth century, a poetical work in Old Javanese composed in Bali, the *Kakawin Gajah Mada*, narrated Gajah Mada's story from his divine birth to the peak of his career in Majapahit. As P. J. Zoetmulder (1974) observed, there are many details in this fiction that are incongruous with historical accounts.

EDI SEDYAWATI

See also Bali; Hayâm Wuruk (Rajasanagara) (r. 1350–1389); Hindu-Buddhist Period of Southeast Asia; Java; Kadiri (Kediri); Madura; Majapahit (1293–ca. 1520s); *Nusantara;* Palembang; *Pararaton* (Book of Kings); Singhâsari; Tumasik (Temasek)

References:
Brandes, J. L. A. 1920. *Pararaton (Ken Arok) of Het Boek der Koningen van Tumapel en van Majapahit: Uitgegeven en Toegelicht* [*Pararaton (Ken Arok) or the Book of Kings from Tumapel and Majapahit: Published and Annotated*]. 2nd ed. Edited by N. J. Krom with the collaboration of J. C. G. Jonker, H. Kraemer, and R. Ng. Poerbatjaraka. The Hague: Martinus Nijhoff; Batavia: Albrecht & Co. (Verhandelingan van het Bataviaasch Genootschap van Kunsten en Wetenschappen, Deel LXII [Papers of the Batavia Society of Arts and Sciences, Vol. 32].)

de Casparis, J. G. 1940. "Oorkonde uit het Singosarische (Midden 14e Eeuw A.D.)" [Deed of the Singosarische (Mid-14th Century A.D.)]. Pp. 50–61 in *Inscripties van Nederlandsch-Indië* [*Inscriptions of the Dutch-Indies*], Aflevering 1 [Tract 1]. Koninklijk Bataviaasch Genootschap van Kunsten en Wetenshappen; Oudheidkundige Dienst in Nederlandsch-Indië [Royal Batavia Society for Arts and Sciences; Archaeological Commission in the Dutch-Indies]. Batavia (Jakarta): Drukkerij De Unie.

Pigeaud, Theodore G. Th. 1960, 1962, 1963. *Java in the 14th Century: A Study in Cultural History—The "Nâgara-kĕrtâgama" by Rakawi Prapañca of Majapahit, 1365 A.D.* Vols. 1–3 (1960), vol. 4 (1962), vol. 5 (1963). The Hague: Martinus Nijhoff.

Pradotokusumo, Partini Sarjono. 1986. *"Kakawin Gajah Mada": Sebuah karya sastra Kakawin abad Ke–20—Suntingan naskah serta telaah struktur, tokoh dan hubungan antarateks* [*"Kakawin Gajah Mada": A Kakawin Literary Work of the 20th Century—A Study of Structure, Character, and Intertext Relations*]. Bandung, Indonesia: Binacipta.

Robson, Stuart. 1995. *"Deśawarnana" ("Nâgarakṛtâgama") by Mpu Prapañca*. Leiden, The Netherlands: KITLV Press. (Verhandelingen van het Koninklijk Instituut voor Taal-, Land- en Volkenkunde [Papers of the Royal Institute on Linguistics and Anthropology] 169.)

Sumadio, Bambang, ed. 1993. "Jaman Kuna." Pp. 257–280 in *Sejarah Nasional Indonesia* [*National History of Indonesia*]. Vol. 2. Edited by Poesponegoro, Marwati Djoened, and Nugroho Notosusanto. Jakarta: Balai Pustaka.

Zoetmulder, P. J. 1974. *Kalangwan: A Survey of Old Javanese Literature*. The Hague: Martinus Nijhoff. (Koninklijk Instituut voor Taal-, Land- en Volkenkunde [KITLV] [Royal Institute of Linguistics and Anthropology] Translation Series 16.)

GALLEON TRADE
Spurring Asia-Pacific Commercial Links

Prior to the nineteenth century, the commerce of the Spanish colony in the Philippines was built around a single activity known as the galleon trade. The strategic location of Manila off the Chinese mainland and its colonial links with the Americas ensured that the port became an important entrepôt from the late sixteenth century onward. Manila merchants acted as middlemen in the exchange of New World silver brought by galleon across the Pacific for the luxury merchandise of East and South Asia. Initially, this trade was conducted by Manila together with the Viceroyalties of New Spain (Mexico) and Lima and proved highly lucrative. Effective lobbying by the merchants of Seville and Cádiz, who felt their commercial position in the American market was threatened, and mercantilist fears about the drain of silver to China led the Spanish monarch to end unrestricted shipping. Laws passed between 1591 and 1604 confined sailing between China and Manila to the Mexican port of Acapulco and restricted those able to engage in it to Spanish residents of the Philippines. Trade was further constrained to only two galleons of 300 tons a year (raised to 560 tons in 1729), and limits were placed on the value of the goods carried: America-bound merchandise was not to exceed 250,000 pesos in value and that of the return cargo of bullion 500,000 pesos. Reshipment of goods between New Spain and South America was strictly prohibited, but this rule was difficult to enforce. In the Philippines, the Spaniards' inability to discover workable mines of precious metals and their disinclination to engage in tropical agriculture largely confined economic activity in the colony to the galleon trade. Moreover, the duties levied on cargoes at Acapulco (10 percent ad valorem, subsequently raised to 16.6 percent) were returned to the Philippines, along with an annual subsidy known as the *situado* to cover the yearly administrative deficit of the Manila treasury.

All Spanish residents in the Philippines were theoretically considered to be merchants and thus able to engage in this trade. A galleon's hold was divided into parts equal to a bale, or *fardo,* with each bale being further subdivided into four *piezas* (packages). The right to ship merchandise was then allotted by a system of *boletas,* or vouchers, that corresponded to one pieza each with a nominal value of 125 pesos. Vouchers were supposedly distributed according to individual needs and resources as determined by the governor-general. In 1604, however, the governor-general was forced to share this privilege with a *junta de repartimiento* (board of apportionment) representing the principal interests of the Spanish community (royal government, church, "city and commerce"); it was subsequently replaced by a *consulado* (the executive of a mercantile guild) of merchants in 1769. However, as the governor and board members were also the chief beneficiaries of any such apportionment and wielded inordinate influence in colonial society, the system was open to abuse. Charges of fraud and nepotism were commonplace; governors-general reserved up to 45 tons of a vessel's cargo for themselves, and in one instance, a governor-general did not provide any space at all for citizens. The selling of vouchers also became common practice during the seventeenth century, as many of those who were allotted vouchers (such as common soldiers and widows) lacked the means to purchase exportable merchandise. Though such sales were forbidden by decree in 1638, vouchers continued to be illegally exchanged. Eventually, in 1734, the law was relaxed to permit widows and orphans to sell vouchers openly to active merchants.

The most flagrant circumvention of the restrictions occurred in regard to the issue of a cargo's value. Trade was supposedly highly regulated, with the governor-general of the Philippines providing the viceroy in New Spain with a report on the distribution of space. At the same time, a treasury official in Acapulco inspected the arriving cargo to ensure that it complied with the manifest and that the vessel did not carry contraband. In practice, though, the values of cargoes in both directions were regularly underestimated, and ships frequently carried the equivalent of 6,000, 12,000, or even 18,000 piezas in some years (the officially permissible number was 4,000). Nor were the tonnage restrictions strictly enforced, and some galleons were as large as 2,000 tons by the eighteenth century. Despite periodic incremental revisions of the *permiso* (the allowable value) from 300,000 pesos outgoing in 1702 to 500,000 pesos in 1734 and 750,000 pesos in 1776, with return cargoes double these amounts, galleons continued to regularly carry from 1.5 million to 3 million pesos during the galleon trade's last century of operation. Space was made by piling the decks high with chests and bales, stowing away the cannons, and depending on qualls at sea to replenish minimal water supplies. Officers, crew, and passengers also filled their chests of "personal" belongings with silks and other trade items. Additional cargo was often loaded during the ship's progress through the island-studded channels along the south coast of Luzon en route to Mexico. When the *Covadonga* was captured in 1742, for example, it was found to be carrying 1,313,843 pesos in pieces of eight and 35,632 ounces of bullion, with many of the coins secreted in the rind of cheeses and the silver stuffed into the vessel's beams and timbers. The accounting for cargoes was made even more difficult by a legal loophole that exempted Filipino goods and repatriated proceeds from previous voyages from the limits imposed by the permiso.

Much of the capital used in the Manila-Acapulco trade was supplied by the Obras Pías. These were pious foundations composed of lay brothers affiliated with religious orders such as the Hermandad de la Misericordia de Manila, a group of virtuous gentlemen originally formed to raise alms and provide charitable services. Granted space on the galleons from which to finance these activities, they grew immensely rich on the proceeds of trade. Moreover, the various legacies of the *hermanos* (brothers) and other wealthy benefactors often specifically apportioned a third part of their bequest for use in the Acapulco trade. The income derived from such ventures not only supported the foundations' good works but also was lent out at interest to others engaged in the galleon trade, the funds having the character of both bank loan and marine insurance. Over time, this commercial involvement would make the Obras Pías a powerful economic force in the colony, and by the end of the eighteenth century, they operated much in the capacity of a professional banking system run by salaried officials experienced in financial matters.

The galleon trade itself drew on the full spectrum of goods available in the East, attracting silks from the north (China and Japan), spices from the south (Southeast Asia), and cottons and ivory from the west (Indian subcontinent). More specifically, exports to Mexico included textiles, porcelain, ivory (especially carved religious images), furniture (inlaid and lacquered items), metalwork (from grills and delicate filigrees to cast-iron pots), various foods and plants (rice, tea, mangoes, orchids, and other flowering species), and occasionally slaves. Carpets from Persia, precious stones from India and Burma (Myanmar), rich hangings and bedcoverings from Bengal, cinnamon from Ceylon, pepper from Java and Sumatra, balsam from Cambodia, camphor from Borneo, civet from the Ryukyu Islands, and silverware from Japan also figured among the items transported. Domestic Philippine exports included gold dust, wax, cordage, various kinds of sheeting, and some textiles but never amounted to more than 10 percent of the total value of the shipment. Return cargoes constituted mainly silver (from 90 to 99 percent) in the form of irregular cob coins and minted dollars (after 1732), along with some American products (cochineal, cacao, leather bags) and transshipped Spanish products such as wine, olive oil, and woolen cloth. Of more importance was the transfer of New World plants, some of which enriched the diets of Filipinos (maize, papaya, cassava, tomatoes, eggplant, and potatoes); others subsequently became important commercial crops, such as tobacco, indigo, maguey, cacao, pineapple, and coffee.

The galleons were mainly constructed in the Philippines (except one built in Siam [Thailand] and another in Japan). They were made of native hardwoods (almost impervious to contemporary cannonballs), fitted with cordage prepared from local abaca, and had sails manufactured in the Ilocos; only the metal fittings were imported from China, Macao, Japan, or India. Filipinos also constituted the workforce employed in their construction (through the *repartimiento,* or *polo,* system of forty days' annual corvée labor) and between 50 and 80 percent of the crews that sailed in them.

Initially conceived of as a means to provide gainful livings for Spanish settlers in the islands, the trade gradually became concentrated in fewer and fewer hands as rich merchants monopolized the cargo space and bought up the vouchers of others. When the galleon *San Martín* sailed for Acapulco in 1586, the merchandise it carried belonged to 194 persons, but when the *San Andrés* sailed two centuries later, its cargo was the property of just 28 individuals. A law of 1769 that restricted trading to Spaniards with ten years of residence in the archipelago and in possession of 8,000 to 10,000 pesos in capital only further constrained participation. Moreover, even at the best of times, the galleons remained an erratic source of income for the colony, subject to the vagaries of weather, the arrival of junks from China, the state of the market in Mexico, and the deprivation of corsairs. The failure of a galleon could plunge Manila into a financial crisis, as happened when the *San Javier,* bound for Acapulco, sank with its entire cargo in 1705 or when the returning galleon of 1709 was wrecked. The distress was particularly acute when a succession of such events occurred, as was the case when the situado failed to arrive in the three years prior to 1721. In all, 30 of the 108 galleons that sailed between 1565 and 1815 (or nearly a third) were lost to shipwreck or capture (4 of them fell to the English).

It is estimated that in the span of more than two hundred years of the galleon trade, more than 250 million pesos in silver and 50 million in gold were carried from Acapulco to Manila. Cyclical analyses of trade reveal five discernible periods: expansion between 1580 and 1620, severe contraction from 1620 to 1670, recovery between 1670 and 1720, mild recession between 1720 and 1750, and brief expansion again after 1750. In 1773, the galleons were allowed to call at Californian ports for the first time, but despite such new initiatives, there was a gradual overall decline in the trade during the eighteenth century, leading to the gradual immiseration of even formerly wealthy Spanish families. Many factors contributed to this deterioration. They included embezzlement, corruption, overtaxation, the loss of ships, the British seizure of Manila (1762–1764), and the inroads made by English and French merchants. The drain of silver to China, the increased competition of industrial products from Western Europe, the establishment of the Royal Philippine Company (1785), and the outbreak of the Mexican War of Independence in 1810 further contributed to the overall decline. By 1790, the decline was irreversible, and the last galleon, aptly called the *Magallanes,* set sail for Mexico in 1811.

In the context of East Asian commerce, however, the galleon trade was an innovative one, stimulating increased traffic between China and the Philippines, linking the archipelago to a world economy based on Seville and the Atlantic, and making Manila the first primate city (large urban center) in Southeast Asia.

GREG BANKOFF

See also *Consulado*; Economic History of Early Modern Southeast Asia (Pre-Sixteenth Century); Economic Transformation of Southeast Asia (ca. 1400–ca. 1800); Manila; Philippines under Spanish Colonial Rule (ca. 1560s–1898)

References:
Bernal, Rafael. 1965. *México en Filipinas: Estudio de una transculturación* [*Mexico in the Philippines: A Study in Transculturalism*]. Mexico City: Universidad Autónoma de México.
Cushner, Nicholas. 1971. *Spain in the Philippines: From Conquest to Revolution.* Quezon City: Institute of Philippine Culture, Ateneo de Manila University.
Legarda, Benito. 1999. *After the Galleons: Foreign Trade, Economic Change and Entrepreneurship in the Nineteenth-Century Philippines.* Center for Southeast Asian Studies Monograph 18. Madison, WI: Center for Southeast Asian Studies.
Obregon, Gonzalo, et al. 1971. "El galeón de Manila" [The Galleon of Manila]. *Artes de México* 17: 143.
Perez, Gilbert. 1954. "Manila Galleons and Mexican Pieces of Eight." *Philippine Social Sciences and Humanities Review* 19, no. 2: 193–215.
Schurz, William. 1939. *The Manila Galleon.* New York: Dutton.
Wimer, Javier, ed. 1992. *El galeón del Pácifico: Acapulco-Manila, 1565–1815* [*The Pacific Galleon: Acapulco-Manila, 1565–1815*]. State of Guerrero, Mexico: Gobierno Constitucional del Estado de Guerrero.

GAMA, VASCO DA (1459–1524)
Precursor of Portuguese Imperialism

Vasco da Gama's fame rests on his discovery of the sea route to India, which made possible the foundation of the Portuguese Empire in Asia. Da Gama was born in Sines about 1459 into a family of minor Portuguese nobility. As a young man, he had some experience as a seafarer, but little is known about his life before 1497. The Portuguese king Manuel I (1495–1521) gave him the command of a fleet of four ships, with instructions to sail to India. His mission was to complete the work begun by Bartolomeu Dias, the first Portuguese to sail around the Cape of Good Hope (1487–1488). He was to identify the principal spice markets and to persuade any

Christian rulers he might encounter to join an alliance of Christian powers against Islam. On 20 May 1498, he landed near Calicut, India. He was coolly received by its Hindu ruler, the *samorin,* whom he believed to be a Christian, and soon incurred the hostility of the powerful Muslim traders in the city. He left Calicut, with a small cargo of spices, at the end of August 1498 but did not reach Lisbon until September 1499.

In 1500, Manuel I dispatched another, larger fleet to India, commanded by Pedro Álvares Cabral. Cabral also soon fell out with the Muslim merchants in Calicut and so bombarded the city and made alliances with the rulers of Cochin and Cannanore, who were opposed to the samorin. In 1502, Vasco da Gama, now ennobled as conde da Vidigueira, was again sent to India, with an even larger fleet, to punish Calicut—which he did with appalling ferocity—and to establish the Portuguese permanently as a naval and military power in India capable of wresting control of trade in the Indian Ocean from Muslim hands. In 1503, he returned to Portugal and remained there until 1524, when he went once more to India as viceroy. He died in Cochin on Christmas Day in that year.

JOHN VILLIERS

See also Albuquerque, Afonso de (ca.
1462–1515); Portuguese Asian Empire;
Spices and the Spice Trade

References:

Fonseca, Luís Adão da. 1998. *Vasco da Gama: O Homem, a Viagem, a Época* [*Vasco da Gama: The Man, the Voyage, the Age*]. Lisbon: Parque Expo 98, Sociedade Anónima.

Ravenstein, E. G. 1898. *A Journal of the First Voyage of Vasco da Gama, 1497–1499.* London: Hakluyt Society.

Subrahmanyam, Sanjay. 1997. *The Career and Legend of Vasco da Gama.* Cambridge: Cambridge University Press.

GARNIER, FRANCIS (1839–1873)
Explorer of the Mekong

A naval officer, a colonial official, and, most important, an explorer of the Mekong River, Francis Garnier typified the generation of convinced and energetic French colonialists who served in Vietnam and Cambodia in the 1860s and 1870s. Second in command of the 1866–1868 French Mekong River expedition, he became its leader after the death of Ernest Doudart de Lagrée (1823–1868) and was later responsible for the publication of the expedition's official report. In 1873, he was killed while heading an unofficial attempt to establish a new French colonial position in northern Vietnam.

The son of a retired army officer, Garnier was born on 25 July 1839 at Saint-Étienne in central France. Baptized as Marie Joseph François (Francis) Garnier at birth, he was known by his shorter name throughout his brief but adventurous life. Entering the French naval college at Brest against the wishes of his family in 1848, he participated in the French conquest of southern Vietnam (Cochin China) in 1860. After recuperating from a tropical illness, he returned to France's new colony in Vietnam as an inspector of native affairs in 1862 and took up his post in Cholon, Saigon's twin city. In this position, Garnier was among a small group of officials who lobbied the French government to explore the Mekong River, arguing that this would open up the possibility of profitable trade with China using the river as a transportation route.

As second in command of the Mekong Commission, as it was called, Garnier displayed great energy and personal courage, among other things overcoming serious illness in the expedition's early stages. In terms of French hopes that the Mekong would be navigable and that commercial opportunities would be found in China, the expedition was a failure. From the point of view of exploring previously unknown territory, however, the expedition was of the greatest importance. Throughout the expedition, which lasted for more than two years, Garnier played a major part in surveying and mapping more than 6,000 kilometers (3,759 miles) of the river and surrounding territory. He also compiled a mass of information on political and ethnographic aspects of the regions through which the expedition traveled. Assuming leadership of the expedition when Lagrée died in China in March 1868, he led it to its conclusion in June of that year.

Returning to France, Garnier was the principal author of the magnificent official account of the expedition, contained in two volumes of text and another two devoted to maps and illustrations. Yet his achievements excited remarkably little interest in France, a fact that Garnier resented deeply. However, he shared an award with the famous Scottish explorer and missionary David Livingstone (1813–1873) at the 1869 Geographical Congress in Antwerp. The following year, he was honored by the Royal Geographical Society of London and awarded the society's Patron's Medal for an expedition that was described as "the happiest and most complete of the nineteenth century" (Osborne 1997 [1975]: 186).

Concerned for his financial future and bitter about France's defeat in the Franco-Prussian War (1870–1871), the recently married Garnier returned to the East in 1872 with the hope of beginning a commercial venture importing silk and tea from China. Nothing came of these plans. Instead, in October 1873, he answered an appeal for assistance from the French governor of Cochin China, Admiral Marie Jules Dupré (1813–1881), to extricate a French trader, Jean Dupuis, who was in difficulties with the Vietnamese authorities in Hanoi. The weight of evidence strongly suggests Dupré authorized Garnier to try to establish a new colonial position in northern Vietnam, but he was careful not to include this direction in the written orders he gave Garnier, since such action was contrary to the policy of the government in Paris.

Despite being briefly successful in gaining control over an area around Hanoi, Garnier was soon threatened by a combined force of Vietnamese troops and Chinese Black Flag bandits. Characteristically making a bold advance against these adversaries, Garnier was killed on 21 December 1873. The French authorities wholly disavowed his actions in Hanoi. It was only after a decade that his reputation was rehabilitated. A statue honoring Garnier was eventually erected in Paris in 1896.

A man of passionate beliefs and strong convictions, Francis Garnier was a loyal friend if sometimes a difficult companion for those who did not share his views. A firm supporter of France's advance in the Indochinese region, his association with the Mekong River prefigured the later French advance into the Lao territories at the end of the nineteenth century. Likewise, his actions in northern Vietnam set the stage for France's subsequent occupation of the

Portrait of Francis Garnier. (Milton Osborne)

whole of Vietnam in the 1880s. Above all, his role as a member of the Mekong River expedition ensured Garnier's status as one of the great explorers of the nineteenth century.

MILTON OSBORNE

See also Annam; Cochin China; Dupré, Marie Jules (1813–1881); French Ambitions in Southeast Asia; Hanoi (Thang-long); Lagrée-Garnier Mekong Expedition1866–1868); Nguyễn Emperors and French Imperialism; Saigon (Gia Dinh; Hồ Chí Minh City); Tonkin (Tongking);Travelers and Sojourners, European;Yunnan Province

References:

Delaporte, Louis, and Francis Garnier. 1998. *A Pictorial Journey on the Old Mekong: Cambodia, Laos and Yunnan.* Bangkok:White Lotus Press.

Garnier, Francis.1996a [1873]. *Travels in Cambodia and Part of Laos:The Mekong Exploration Commission Report (1866–1868).* Vol. 1. Bangkok:White Lotus Press.

———. 1996b [1873]. *Further Travels in Laos and Yunnan:The Mekong Exploration Commission Report (1866–1868).* Vol. 2. Bangkok:White Lotus Press.

Osborne, Milton. 1995. "Francis Garnier (1839–1873): Explorer of the Mekong River." Pp. 51–107 in *Explorers of South-East Asia: Six Lives.* Edited by Victor T. King. Kuala Lumpur: Oxford University Press.

———. 1996/1997 [1975]. *River Road to China: The Search for the Source of the Mekong, 1866–73.* London and New York: Allen & Unwin and Liveright. New editions published in 1996 by Archipelago Press, Singapore, and in 1997 by Atlantic Monthly Press and Allen & Unwin, New York and Sydney.

———. 2000. *The Mekong: Turbulent Past, Uncertain Future.* New York and Sydney: Atlantic Monthly Press and Allen & Unwin.

GENERAL COUNCIL OF BURMESE ASSOCIATIONS (GCBA) (1920)

Crystallizing the Burmese Nationalist Movement

The General Council of Burmese Associations (GCBA) succeeded the Young Men's Buddhist Association (YMBA) in 1920, as the earlier association was split by disagreement between those who were uncomfortable with the overt political focus the association was taking and those who wished to pursue more radical measures against the British colonial administration. Within the GCBA, the General Council of Sangha Samettgi (GCSS) became the vehicle for politically conscious Buddhist monks, or *pongyis,* concerned at the decline of monastic education and discipline within the Burmese Buddhist sangha (term denoting the Buddhist monkhood). They sought to unite the urban-based, Western-educated nationalist leadership with the rural masses in protest actions against the foreign domination of Burmese cultural and political life. There were precedents for this in the monk-led uprisings in Tenasserim, Toungoo, and Tharrawaddy against the British in Lower Burma after Pegu was annexed in 1852. One of the politically active monks, U Ottama (1897–1939), had participated in the Indian National Congress Party's independence movement. Returning to Burma in 1921, he preached self-rule for Burma and urged monks to leave their monasteries to take up the national struggle.

In its 1921 conference in Mandalay, the GCBA had 12,000 affiliated associations, led by the council's president, U Chit Hlaing. The split in the GCBA between those who advocated cooperation (led by U Ba Pe) and those who urged boycotting the Legislative Council elections resulted in a triumph for the latter group, which was led by U Chit Hlaing. At the first elections, twenty-eight members were elected to the Legislative Council. Sir Harcourt Butler (t. 1923–1927), the new governor in Burma, however, chose only one of these individuals for his Council of Ministers. Others, such as U Maung Gyi, were chosen from among the loyalists in the Twenty-One Party. Another group, the Golden Valley Party, supported the government. Thereafter, the GCBA was referred to as the Hlaing-Pu-Gyaw Party, reflecting the names of its leaders. The fragmentation in the GCBA after its sixteenth conference marked the end of the first phase of the nationalist movement. The Dyarchy reforms initiated by the British administration in India soon failed due to internal dissent within the nationalist group, leaving a suspicion of Western institutions and those who supported them (Maung Maung 1980: 35).

The GCBA drew support for its policy of noncooperation from younger monks, in particular the martyred U Wizara (1888–1929), whom U Ottama had sent to the Indian National Congress at Gaya. From 1927 to 1929, he was imprisoned by the British for his political activities, and he died on 19 September 1929 as a result of a 166-day hunger strike. As political dissent grew following the Rangoon University strike of 1920, the government's persecution of monks and leaders of village *wunthanu* (anticolonial rural societies) increased. From 1928 to 1929, the colonial authorities imprisoned some 120 monks for political activities. Political agitation by the pongyis on 17 February 1939 led to a tragic massacre of monks, part of the concerted program of dissent that had gathered pace since the 1930 Hsaya San peasant revolt in Tharrawaddy District.

The Hsaya San revolt (1930–1931) and the formation of the Dobama Asiayone (We Burmans Association) by student activists at Rangoon University marked the transition from nonviolent to violent agitation, culminating in a series of labor and race riots during the late 1930s. Arising from economic hardship and repression, the Hsaya San rebellion quickly spread to other districts in the Pegu Yomas. From

Theyetkan village in Shwebo District, Hsaya San had been a member of the district GCBA. In August 1931, he was betrayed when he sent a local guide to a village for food; he was then tried by a special tribunal and hanged on 28 November 1931. The Hsaya San rebellion was the most serious challenge to the colonial authorities since 1886.

At Rangoon University, student leaders who gained experience in organizing nationwide mass protests advanced the nationalist cause. Under the tutelage of the Thakin movement (composed of members of Dobama Asiayone, including Aung San [1915–1947]), the cooperative government of Dr. Ba Maw (b. 1893), which had been formed following elections in November 1935 based on the new constitution and the Government of Burma Act of 1935, was undermined. This process began with the 1936 student strike at Rangoon University and was furthered by the oil field labor strike in Chauk, initiated on 8 January 1938, in the period leading up to the Pacific War (1941–1945).

Known as the BE 1300 Revolution, the thirty-four strikes affecting the oil industry, foundries, dockyards, steamer services, manufacturing plants, plantations, port labor, rice mills, and offices were a measure of how far the nationalist movement had come since the debating days of the YMBA. Marxist literature had begun circulating among the nationalist groups after the Hsaya San revolt in 1930. Thakin Thein Maung brought back more such works from the London Round Table Conference in 1932, where he had met Ashin Kyaw Sein, a member of the British Communist Party who introduced him to the League against Imperialism and for National Independence. (Established in 1919 in London, the League Against Imperialism and for National Independence was an ultranationalist, leftist group, comprising left-leaning elements, communists, and nationalists with close ties to international Marxism. It was closely allied to the Burma Reform League.) J. S. Furnivall (1878–1960) introduced further sources through his Burma Book Club (Trager 1959: 21). Steeped in such literature, the nationalist movement within the Dobama Asiayone soon split into communists and socialists, a legacy that would continue past independence on 4 January 1948 into the history of postcolonial Burma.

At the beginning of the Pacific War, the Burma Freedom Bloc had begun calling for the Burmese right to self-determination. The political agitation of the 1930s, the various associations and parties, and exposure to new ideologies provided a foundation for the leaders of the independence movement, mostly students at Rangoon University, to prepare to lead the nation. The achievement of the 1930s nationalist movement, inaugurated by the GCBA, was to bring together the urban and the rural, the educated and the working class, and the peasant and the office clerk in a genuine mass movement for Burmese independence. By the end of the 1930s, several Burmese political groups in addition to the Dobama Asiayone were actively seeking political change, among them the Sinyetha Wunthanu Aphwegyi of Dr. Ba Maw and the Myochit Party led by U Saw. The reforms of 1937 granted by the British colonial administration were too little, too late, as signified by the burning of the Union Jack at the high court by those who became the leaders of independent Burma (Myanmar).

HELEN JAMES

See also Aung San (1915–1947); Ba Maw, Dr. (b. 1893); Burma under British Colonial Rule; Decolonization of Southeast Asia; Great Depression (1929–1931); Nationalism and Independence Movements in Southeast Asia; Peasant Uprisings and Protest Movements in Southeast Asia; *Sangha;* Thakin (Lord, Master); University of Rangoon; *Wunthan Athin;* Young Men's Buddhist Association (YMBA) (1906)

References:

Adas, Michael. 1998. *State, Market and Peasant in Colonial South and Southeast Asia.* Aldershot, England: Ashgate Variorum Collected Studies Series.

Bobilin, Robert. 1999. "Buddhism, Nationalism and Violence." Pp. 297–306 in *Socially Engaged Buddhism for the New Millennium.* Edited by Sulak Sivaraksa. Bangkok: Munlanithi Suthiankoset Nakhaprathip Foundation.

Maung Maung. 1980. *From Sangha to Laity: Nationalist Movements of Burma, 1920–1940.* ANU Monographs on Southeast Asia, no. 4. Delhi, India: Manohar Publications.

———. 1989. *Burmese Nationalist Movements, 1940–1948.* Edinburgh: Kiscadale.

Moscotti, Albert D. 1974. *British Policy and the Nationalist Movement in Burma 1917–1937.* Honolulu, HI: University of Hawai'i Press.

Pye, Lucian W. 1962. *Politics, Personality and Nation Building: Burma's Search for Identity.* New Haven, CT, and London: Yale University Press.

Silverstein, Josef. 1980. *Burmese Politics: The Dilemma of National Unity.* New Brunswick, NJ: Rutgers University Press.

Tinker, Hugh. 1957. *The Union of Burma: A Study of the First Years of Independence.* New York: Oxford University Press.

Trager, Frank, ed. 1959. *Marxism in Southeast Asia: A Study of Four Countries.* Stanford, CA: Stanford University Press.

GENEVA CONFERENCE (1954)
Birth of Two Vietnams

The Geneva Conference, which took place in the Swiss city from April to July 1954, was an outgrowth of a meeting among the United States, the Soviet Union, Britain, and France in Berlin in January and February. It was intended to seek a settlement of the war in Korea, in which the Chinese had introduced troops that they called "volunteers," hoping to thus avoid all-out war, and thus follow up the truce of July 1953. It failed in this regard, but it succeeded in bringing an end to the war in Indochina, which had been added to its agenda.

Whether in so doing it also averted a major war is less certain, though there was much apprehension about the possiblity of a large-scale conflict at the time, especially in Britain—a fear that was only increased by news of the unexpected power of the hydrogen bomb. In retrospect, it seems unlikely, but the negotiations were conducted against that background. The attempts of Anthony Eden (t. 1951–1955), the British foreign secretary, to bring about a settlement were the more persistent, and his success is the more widely admired. But the United States saw his achievement as a defeat, not strictly in line with their goals of containment, and the process soured the Anglo-American relationship.

In Indochina, the Viet Minh, backed by Chinese aid and advice, had won striking successes against the French: these climaxed, after the conference had started, at Dien Bien Phu. Support for the war in France had never been wholehearted, and by late 1953, leaders in the Joseph Laniel (1889–1975) government (1953–1954) were committed to peace without dishonor—a goal they hoped might be secured through international negotiation. But though the People's Republic of China (PRC), like the Soviet Union, had switched to a policy of coexistence, it was not prepared to abandon Hồ Chí Minh (1890–1969). Nor did it want a colonial power to remain on its southern frontier.

What kind of deal, if any, was possible in these circumstances? The British believed it had to be some kind of partition of Vietnam. That would leave the Viet Minh with a north Vietnamese state, establish an independent Laos and Cambodia, and leave the Bảo Đại regime (t. 1949–1955) in the south. The British recognized that the division of Vietnam might only be temporary.

Such a deal accorded with the British desire for peace and Britain's pragmatic foreign policy. The United States, however, could not endorse the "loss" of territory to communism. It had no intention of introducing troops nor, indeed, of using the bomb. Its main objective was to keep the French fighting, while pressing them to complete the independence of the Indochina states.

A settlement was reached in July. A new French premier, Pierre Mendès-France (t. 1954–1955), had set himself a deadline for achieving one. The Chinese wanted a settlement in Indochina all the more because they had not gotten one in Korea, and the PRC's premier and foreign minister, Zhou Enlai (1898–1976), was ready to accept an independent Laos and Cambodia. The deal over Vietnam that Zhou impressed on Hồ effected a kind of partition based on military regrouping but envisaged unification elections in 1956. The Americans did not endorse the settlement but did not undertake any overt military action to oppose it.

The Americans' fear that the "loss" of the north would be followed by the "loss" of the south encouraged them to support the regime Ngô Đình Diệm (1901–1963) created in the south, which lasted from 1955 to 1963. So, too, did their experience in Korea: they drew a mistaken parallel between South Korea and South Vietnam.

NICHOLAS TARLING

See also Bảo Đại (Vinh Tuy) (r. 1925–1945);
China since 1949; Cold War; Decolonization
of Southeast Asia; Dien Bien Phu (May
1954), Battle of; Domino Theory; Hồ Chí
Minh (1890–1969); Indochina War, First
(1946–1954); Korean War (1950–1953);
Ngô Đình Diệm (1901–1963); Sino-Soviet
Struggle; Sino-Vietnamese Relations; Việt
Minh (Việt Nam Độc Lập Đồng Minh Hội)
(Vietnam Independence League); Vietnam,
North (Post-1945); Vietnam, South (Post-
1945); U.S. Involvement in Southeast Asia
(Post-1945)

References:

Cable, James. 1986. *The Geneva Conference of
1954 on Indochina*. Basingstoke, England:
Macmillan.

Gurtov, Melvin. 1967. *The First Vietnam Crisis*.
New York: Columbia University Press.

Joyaux, Francois. 1979. *La Chine et le règlement
du premier conflit d'Indochine* [*China and the
Settlement of the First Conflict in Indochina*].
Paris: Sorbonne.

Randle, Robert F. 1969. *Geneva 1954: The
Settlement of the Indochinese War*. Princeton,
NJ: Princeton University Press.

Tarling, Nicholas. Forthcoming. *Britain,
Southeast Asia and the Impact of the Korean War*.

GERMANS (GERMANY)

If they did not invent the term *Southeast Asia*,
Germans and Austrians gave it a scholarly usage, even before the Pacific War (1941–1945)
and before the creation of Admiral Lord Louis
Mountbatten's allied South-East Asia Command (SEAC) gave it popular and political currency. Franz Heger may have been the first to
use the term in the title of a book—*Alte Metall-
trommeln aus Sudostasien* [*Ancient Metaldrums
from Southeast Asia*] (1902)—and the 1923
monograph entitled "Sudostasien" [Southeast
Asia] gave Robert Heine-Geldern a claim to be
the founder of Southeast Asian studies. Neither
Germans nor Austrians possessed colonies in
the area, and they could more readily adopt a
regional approach, "not hampered," as Donald
K. Emmerson (1984: 5) put it, "by the geographic limits that preoccupation with a specific possession tended to place on the perspectives of land-controlling colonizers."

Their lack of possessions did not mean that
the Germans were without political effect, particularly after the creation of the Second Reich
in 1871. The colonial powers were bound to
consider that a major new European state might
become a colonial rival, despite the disclaimers
of the German chancellor, Otto von Bismarck
(1815–1898). "For us in Germany," he had said,
"this colonial business would be just like the
silken sables in the noble families of Poland who
have no shirts on their backs" (quoted in Henderson 1993: 32). Action matched rhetoric: in
1871, he took Alsace-Lorraine from France but
not Cochin China. "We are not rich enough to
be offered the luxury of colonies," he explained
(quoted in Taboulet 1956: 579). Yet apprehension about Germany was a factor in Britain's decision
to protect the security of the Straits by appointing residents in Perak and Selangor in 1874.

The presence of German ships and traders
in Sulu alarmed the Spaniards and concerned
the British. The British ambassador in Berlin
was, however, assured in 1873 that Germany
had "no wish or intention . . . to acquire
transatlantic possessions in the Sulu Archipelago, or indeed in any other portions of the
Globe" (Tarling 1978: 132). Refraining from a
colonial policy, however, meant that it was "urgently . . . bound to secure German commerce
from unjustifiable encroachments on the freedom of its movements." Such were presented
by the "paper claims" of other powers (Tarling
1978: 132, 147).

Bismarck's domestic politics shifted in 1879
when he offered the industrialists a protective
tariff. That had its effect on the free-trading
British, giving Lord Kimberley, secretary of
state for the colonies, for example, an additional
argument for granting a charter to the British
North Borneo Company. Bismarck's adoption
of a "colonial policy" should, however, be seen
less as a further gesture to industrial interests
than as a means of co-opting right-wing support. "All this colonial business is a fraud, but
we need it for the elections" (quoting Winfried
Baumgart, in Knoll and Gann 1987: 157). Bismarck tried to adopt a limited policy of "protection" that would not alienate other powers.

In 1884 and 1885, Bismarck took up the
idea of a conference on the Congo; that conference was held in Berlin and was designed to
prevent antagonism to Germany as a colonial
power but also to gain it recognition as a world
power. The conference was, in theory, confined
to Africa, but in renewing the opposition to

"paper claims," it was enunciating a principle of "effective occupation" that might be used elsewhere. The Dutch became more determined to round out their claims in eastern Indonesia, and the British established protectorates in Borneo. British premier William Gladstone (1809–1898) welcomed Germany's colonial endeavor, however, and New Guinea was divided.

After the fall of Bismarck, the kaiser's government adopted a more vigorous "world policy," especially from 1897. The extension of the Spanish-American War (1898) to the Philippines the following year aroused the interest of all the powers. Prince Heinrich, then in command of the Asiatic squadron, cabled that the Filipinos were ready to place themselves under German protection. Bernhard von Bulow, the secretary of state, advised against allying with revolutionaries. But after the Peace of Paris, Germany agreed to pay Spain U.S.$4.2 million for the Caroline, Pelew, and Mariana islands, except Guam, and the United States accepted the deal. These islands were to become Japanese mandates after the Great War (1914–1918).

German competition in trade and shipping aroused some jealousy in Singapore, and in the war, the interned Germans were connected with the mutiny of 1915. German expertise had, however, been welcomed in Siam, which sought to utilize a mix of foreign experts, including some from noncolonial states. Germans were particularly prominent in railway construction. Other states welcomed them, too. Lord Dalhousie, governor-general of India, appointed Dietrich Brandis as superintendent of forests in the newly acquired Pegu, Lower Burma, in 1855, and his first order became the basis for forest administration in India as a whole.

NICHOLAS TARLING

See also British North Borneo Chartered Company (1881–1946); Colonialism; Imperialism; Reforms and Modernization in Siam; Residential System (Malaya); South-East Asia Command (SEAC); "Southeast Asia"; Spanish-American Treaty of Paris (1898); Straits Settlements (1826–1946); Sulu and the Sulu Archipelago; Western Malay States (Perak, Selangor, Negri Sembilan, and Pahang)

References:

Emmerson, Donald K. 1984. "'Southeast Asia': What's in a Name?" *Journal of Southeast Asian Studies* 15, no. 1: 1–21.

Henderson, W. O. 1993. *The German Colonial Empire, 1884–1919.* London: Cass.

Knoll, Arthur, and L. H. Gann, eds. 1987. *Germans in the Tropics.* New York: Greenwood.

Taboulet, Georges. 1956. *La Geste française en Indochine: Histoire par les textes de la France en Indochine des origines à 1914* [*France's Heroic Achievement in Indochina: A Documentary History of France in Indochina from Its Beginnings to 1914*]. Vol. 2. Paris: Adrien Maisonneuve.

Tarling, Nicholas. 1978. *Sulu and Sabah.* Kuala Lumpur: Oxford University Press.

GESTAPU AFFAIR (1965)
Annihilation of the Left

The Gestapu Affair was an ambiguous coup launched by junior military officers in Jakarta and Central Java on 1 October 1965, ostensibly to forestall a coup by senior officers that was allegedly scheduled for 5 October. The coup was thwarted by General Suharto (Soeharto) (1921–), who blamed it on the Partai Komunis Indonesia (PKI, Communist Party of Indonesia) and used it as the pretext for a bloody purge of communists in which perhaps 500,000 people died.

Early on 1 October, military units arrived at the houses of seven conservative generals to arrest them. Three generals, including the army commander General Ahmad Yani (1922–1965), were shot while resisting arrest; three more were captured, and the seventh, Defense Minister General A. H. Nasution (1918–2000), escaped, though his daughter was killed. The survivors were taken to the Halim air force base in south Jakarta, where they were killed; their bodies were dumped in an unused well. Other troops seized important positions in central Jakarta, and both President Sukarno (1901–1970) and the PKI leader, D. N. Aidit (1923–1965), were taken to Halim. The ostensible leader of the coup, Lieutenant Colonel Untung, who was commander of President Sukarno's palace guard, the Tjakrabirawa Regiment, then announced that the action had been launched to prevent a coup by a "council of generals" on 5 October. He also announced the formation of a revolutionary council to rule Indonesia as an interim government. A similar seizure of power took place in Central Java.

Untung, however, appeared to do little to consolidate his coup, and his forces were soon outmaneuvered by those of General Suharto, commander of Komando Cadangan Strategis Angkatan Darat (KOSTRAD, Army Strategic Reserve). The coup in Jakarta was crushed within twenty-four hours, and that in Central Java was put down within three days. The immediate leaders of the coup were tried in a special military tribunal (*Mahmillub*) and were sentenced to death or long prison terms. Suharto's forces, however, quickly claimed that the coup had been masterminded by the PKI, and on this basis, he launched a campaign of extermination against the party. The character of the killings varied widely from region to region. In some places, they were mainly the work of army units, especially Resimen Para Komando Angkatan Darat (RPKAD, Army Paracommando Regiment). In other places, the army trained and armed civilian militias to carry out the killings, and in still other locations, social antagonisms were so strong that news of the coup and clear indications that killing would not be punished were enough to start massacres. The military further encouraged the killings by circulating false stories that the murdered generals had been sexually tortured by communist women before they were killed. The name Gestapu (from the acronym for the 30 September Movement) was adopted to link the coup with the methods of the Gestapo in Nazi Germany. There is almost no evidence on the number of people killed, but many scholars suggest that the figure was close to half a million.

The question of who organized the coup remains deeply contested, and reliable evidence is still scanty. The New Order maintained that the PKI organized the coup through a "Special Bureau" set up to infiltrate the military and that the actions in Jakarta and Central Java were only the first phase of a planned nationwide seizure of power in which the enemies of the PKI were to be massacred on a vast scale. Evidence of this broader plan is virtually nonexistent. The Special Bureau appears to have existed, but whether it instigated, encouraged, or simply observed the coup plans is unclear. As later events proved, the PKI was highly vulnerable to military suppression and would have had great interest in an action to weaken the military's power.

Sukarno's presence at Halim compromised him in the eyes of many people, and shortly after the coup, there was speculation that he might have instigated it to remove Yani and other obstructive generals. Little evidence has emerged to back this view. Further speculation has focused on General Suharto, for several reasons: because he was the most senior general not on the list to be kidnapped, because he was a friend of Untung and is known to have met one of the plotters a few hours before the coup, and because the incompetence of the plotters in consolidating the coup raises the suspicion that it was intended to fail. This theory attracted much attention in Indonesia after the fall of Suharto in 1998. It has also been suggested that the U.S. Central Intelligence Agency (CIA) used agents in the PKI Special Bureau to instigate an unsuccessful coup as a pretext for destroying the party. Although this speculation cannot be dismissed, the evidence is perhaps more consistent with Suharto and/or the CIA having had some inkling of a plot and having seized the opportunity it presented rather than having engineered the affair.

The alleged treason of the PKI in 1965 became an important source of legitimacy for Suharto's New Order, and the anniversary of the coup was commemorated each year as Sacred Pancasila Day.

ROBERT CRIBB

See also Military and Politics in Southeast Asia; *Orde Baru* (The New Order); Nasution, Abdul Haris, General (1918–2000): Pancasila (Pantja Sila); Partai Komunis Indonesia (PKI) (1920); Soekarno (Sukarno) (1901–1970); Suharto (1921–); U.S. Involvement in Southeast Asia (Post-1945)

References:

Anderson, Benedict, and Ruth T. McVey. 1971. *A Preliminary Analysis of the October 1, 1965, Coup in Indonesia.* Ithaca, NY: Modern Indonesia Project, Cornell University.

Cribb, Robert, ed. 1990. *The Indonesian Killings of 1965–1966: Studies from Java and Bali.* Clayton, Australia: Monash University Centre of Southeast Asian Studies.

Crouch, Harold. 1978. *The Army and Politics in Indonesia.* Ithaca, NY: Cornell University Press.

Dake, Antonie C. A. 1973. *In the Spirit of the Red Banteng: Indonesian Communists between*

Singapore prime minister Goh Chok Tong speaks to the media surrounded by supporters of his ruling People's Action Party after voting in national elections, 3 November 2001. (Reuters NewMedia Inc./Corbis)

Moscow and Peking, 1959–1965. The Hague: Mouton.

Elson, R. E. 2001. *Suharto: A Political Biography.* Cambridge: Cambridge University Press.

U.S. Central Intelligence Agency. 1968. *Indonesia, 1965: The Coup That Backfired.* Washington, DC: Central Intelligence Agency.

GISIGNIES, DU BUS DE

See Du Bus de Gisignies, Viscount Leonard Pierre Joseph (1780–1849)

GOH CHOK TONG (1941–)
Leading the "Second Generation"

Goh Chok Tong is the second person to have held the office of prime minister of Singapore, having succeeded Lee Kuan Yew (1923–) on 28 November 1990. He was born on 20 May 1941 in Singapore. After studying at Raffles Institution, he read economics at the University of Singapore, graduating with first-class honors in 1964. He then joined the premier administrative service and was sent to Williams College in Massachussetts, where he graduated at the top of his class with an M.A. in developmental economics in 1967. Two years later, he was seconded to Neptune Orient Lines, the newly established national shipping company, as its planning and projects manager. Within four years, he became its managing director and was credited with having put the company back on its feet. In 1976, he was recruited by the finance minister, Hon Sui Sen (t. 1972–1983), to enter electoral politics. Within nine months of being elected to Parliament in the general elections of December 1976, Goh was promoted to senior minister of state for finance in 1977. In 1979, he became Singapore's first trade and industry minister, a post he held until 1981, when he moved to other portfolios in the Health and Defense Ministries. After the general elections in December 1984, Goh was picked by his cabinet colleagues to be first deputy prime minister and leader of the younger team to succeed the "first-generation" leaders. Though not Lee Kuan Yew's first choice, Goh succeeded him as prime minister in November 1990. He is distinguished from Lee, who remained in the cabinet as senior minister, by his more consultative political style. But like his predecessor, he is not averse to making tough and controversial decisions to ensure Singapore's sovereignty, political stability, social unity, and continual economic progress. One of the urgent tasks that he sets for himself is that of party and leadership renewal: to find a new group of men and women to lead Singapore in the twenty-first century.

ALBERT LAU

See also Lee Kuan Yew (1923–); Singapore (Nineteenth Century to 1990s), Entrepôt Trade and Commerce of; Singapore-Malaya/Malaysia Relations (ca. 1950s–1990s)

References:
Ho Khai Leong. 2000. *The Politics of Policy-Making in Singapore.* Oxford: Oxford University Press.

GOLD
All That Glitters

Gold, one of the most easily worked of all metals, is found in varying amounts (often along with silver, copper, lead, tin, and zinc) in various parts of mainland and island Southeast Asia. It appears in Myanmar (Burma), Vietnam, the Philippines, the Malay Peninsula (West Malaysia), the islands of Sumatra, eastern and southern Kalimantan (Borneo), western and southern Sulawesi (Celebes), and eastern Indonesia. On Java, there are virtually no deposits of modern economic significance. Gold, though rarely found in large quantities, has been of economic importance for centuries and was one of the earliest exports from the region, along with spices, aromatics, and other forest products. With silver, it played a major role in the medieval and later trading systems of East and Southeast Asia and was an important part of early tribute systems throughout the region.

Early Indian sources refer to *Suvarnabhumi* (the land of gold) or to *Suvarnadvipa* (the gold islands) of Southeast Asia. The Romans knew of the Malay Peninsula. Pliny mapped it as *Aurea Chersonea* (the Golden Chersonese)—a source of gold, though its gold may have come from Sumatra. For centuries, India has had an insatiable demand for gold. Indeed, the earliest Indianizing influences in the archipelago are associated with the polities of Kutei in eastern Kalimantan, thought to have been established by the fifth century C.E., and the slightly later Tarumanegara in the Sundalands of western Java, both polities being founded in close proximity to alluvial gold sources. Those in Kalimantan are extensive and gave rise to the Busang gold hoax of the 1990s. In western Java, alluvial sources at Ponggol along the upper reaches of the Cikaniki River, which rises in the hills of Banten, may have been worked during the early Hindu period. These were lost, however, for centuries due either to earthquakes or landslides that covered the workings, only to be rediscovered in the 1980s. In Sulawesi, the Kalumpang Buddha, dated to the sixth century C.E., was discovered at a riverine settlement site on a route that leads to gold deposits in the interior. Although the arrival of outsiders may have stimulated a demand for gold, the metal apparently was appreciated by indigenous peoples in Southeast Asia long before the arrival of Indian and other traders.

By the early medieval period, the Hindu Buddhist polities of Central Java generated a strong demand for gold for use in rituals. Although Java is mentioned in historical records as a source of gold, the precious metal would have been imported there in exchange for rice. The advanced skills of the Javanese gold workers are reflected in the magnificent jewelry and ritual utensils recovered in the ninth-century Wonoboyo hoard found near Yogyakarta, now in the National Museum in Jakarta. Cambodia also imported gold, having none of its own.

In Sumatra, Hindu and Buddhist images made from gold-washed copper-bronze appear to have produced in preference to those of pure gold, possibly reflecting the relative difficulty in obtaining the metal. In medieval Kalimantan and Java, by contrast, images were made of pure gold.

Gold foil impressed with Chinese characters was recovered at Kota Cina, a medieval Tamil trading site in northeast Sumatra. China exported gold in preference to silver, and Chinese gold artifacts have been found in medieval shipwrecks. Unfortunately, in the past, most recoveries of earlier gold artifacts seem to have been simply melted down and reworked. Traditional gold-working methods exist among most peoples of the archipelago, with some very fine filigree jewelry made by the Acehnese and Malays. A large part of the modern gold trade is in the hands of Chinese goldsmiths.

Although almost all gold procured in the Malay Peninsula and the Indonesian archipelago came from alluvial sources, gold was mined on a relatively large scale in Vietnam from the twelfth century on. In the archipelago, Pasai, Melaka, and Aceh produced small gold coins known as *mas* (gold). Gold dust would appear, however, to have been the most usual medium of exchange.

By the latter half of the eighteenth century and into the nineteenth, immigrant Chinese exploited alluvial deposits in the Sambas region of western Kalimantan. Apart from a minor operation at the Salida mine under the Dutch East India Company (VOC) in western Sumatra between 1669 and 1735, there was little European interest in commercial gold exploitation in the Indonesian archipelago until the end of the nineteenth century. Western-style commercial gold exploitation has had a very checkered history.

In the Malay world, gold was panned from alluvial deposits that produce *mas urai* (loose gold) using a *dulang* (wooden pan). The Rejang people of the interior of Bengkulu in southwest Sumatra used chicken feathers to extract gold dust from streams. Alluvial deposits do, however, tend to run out, and signs of earlier workings are no guarantee of any present-day presence of the metal. Modern indigenous, small-scale, alluvial gold-mining operations are often associated with acute mercury and cyanide poisoning.

E. EDWARDS MCKINNON

See also Borneo; Chinese Gold-Mining Communities in Western Borneo; Hindu-Buddhist Period of Southeast Asia; Java; Sumatra; *Suvarnabhumi* (Land of Gold)

References:
Meilink-Roelofsz, M. A. P. 1962. *Asian Trade and European Influence, 1500–1620.* The Hague: Martinus Nijhoff.
Whitmore, John. 1983. "Vietnam and the Monetary Flow of Eastern Asia, Thirteenth to Eighteenth Centuries." Pp. 363–393 in *Precious Metals in the Later Medieval and Early Modern Worlds.* Edited by J. F. Richards. Durham, NC: Carolina Academic Press.

GOLKAR
Harnessing Loyalty

Golkar, a shortened form of Golongan Karya (Functional Groups), is a political party in Indonesia. Golkar was dominant under the regime of President Suharto (Soeharto) (t. 1967–1998).

After Indonesia's general elections of 1955, a large number of parties in Parliament kept the country politically divided. In reaction, President Sukarno (t. 1945–1967) established "guided democracy" in 1959 and furthered the establishment of an increasing number of "functional groups" that would replace political parties. In an effort to consolidate the political power base of the Indonesian army, senior army personnel established the Joint Secretariat of Functional Groups (Sekretariat Bersama Golongan Karya) in October 1964. It was intended to be the coordinating body for almost 100 anticommunist social organizations but later became a federation of these organizations. In theory, Golkar was a nonpartisan organization representing the functional groups.

Under President Suharto's New Order, military men were appointed in administrative positions, and the military started to use Golkar as

its political vehicle. Effectively, Golkar became the government party and drew its strength from the fact that promotions, assignments, and appointments in the public service depended on the loyalty of public servants to Golkar.

In 1971, Golkar secured 236 of the 360 seats in the Indonesian Parliament. It supported the government's forced amalgamation of the remaining nine political parties into two parties. These opposition parties could not prevent Golkar from scoring overwhelming majorities in the subsequent parliamentary elections in 1977, 1982, 1987, 1992, and 1997. Each of these elections was followed by the unopposed reelection of Suharto to the office of president.

Golkar's electoral success owed much to the pressure exerted on voters during elections by the various government agencies, particularly the regional public service. Polls were also managed to ensure its success. At least initially, Golkar's success was also due to the fact that the party was genuinely popular in several sections of society and willingly accepted in many others. When Golkar was opened to individual membership in 1983, it soon had around 9 million individual members (Reeve 1985: 220).

Golkar obtained 21 percent of the votes during the free elections in 1999 and became the biggest opposition party. It has since sought to cast off its reputation as Suharto's political machine. It remains a significant player in Indonesian politics because, unlike other parties, it has extensive resources and an organizational network that spans the entire nation.

PIERRE VAN DER ENG

See also Guided Democracy (*Demokrasi Terpimpin*); Military and Politics in Southeast Asia; Orde Baru (The New Order); Soekarno (Sukarno) (1901–1970); Suharto (1921–)

References:
Reeve, D. 1985. *Golkar of Indonesia: An Alternative to the Party System.* Singapore: Oxford University Press.

GREAT DEPRESSION (1929–1931)

Economies are subject to business cycles. The more they are integrated in the international economy through trade and investment, the more the business cycles of various countries will be synchronized. For that reason, the so-called Great Depression of the early 1930s reverberated more strongly in the Western world, where it originated, than in the rest of the world, including Southeast Asia.

The Depression was triggered by the bursting in October 1929 of an asset bubble caused by extensive speculation on the U.S. stock market. The deeper causes of the crisis were overproduction in various economic sectors, such as the automotive industry and in real estate, in the 1920s. Overproduction reduced the profitability of U.S. firms, but that was hidden by the sustained inflation of stock prices fueled by misguided optimism. The stock market crash brought underlying problems into the open and forced companies to reduce production and costs by dismissing workers and reducing wages. The severe macroeconomic contraction decreased U.S. imports from overseas. The crisis was first felt in Europe in 1930, after stock markets followed the U.S. trend and companies started to experience difficulties in exporting to the United States. European firms also started to lay off workers and reduce wages. The macroeconomic contraction in Western Europe was less severe than in the United States.

The gold standard made it impossible to use exchange rate devaluation as a buffer against having to import deflation, until some countries ceased gold-parity—for instance, the U.K. devalued in September 1931, the United States in April 1933, and France in September 1936. The crisis was also combated through severe trade restrictions to reduce imports and encourage import-substituting production. World trade was drastically reduced and became subject to stifling bilateral trade agreements.

The impact of the crisis in Southeast Asia was exacerbated by the buildup of excess production capacity in various export commodities such as rubber, sugar, copra, tobacco, tea, rice, and tin during the 1920s. For instance, Java achieved record sugar output levels as a consequence of the development of high-yielding cane varieties and the success of sugar factories in achieving economies of scale. But that happened at a time when various Western countries imposed restrictions on sugar imports. Rice production for export in Burma (Myanmar), Thailand (Siam), and South Vietnam reached record levels in the 1920s, and rice prices started to fall after 1928. Rubber trees that had been planted when rubber prices peaked in the late 1910s were ready for tapping by the early 1920s, thereby increasing production. Consequently, the prices of the region's main export commodities fell during the late 1920s.

The price decrease accelerated in 1930 and 1931, when firms in the United States and Europe scaled back imports of primary commodities. Particularly the contraction of overseas automobile production caused a decline in the demand for rubber for car tires, affecting rubber producers in Indonesia, Malaya, and Vietnam. Their initial reaction was to increase output for export in an effort to beat declining prices, thus exacerbating the price drop. In particular, rubber producers with low marginal costs of production increased output. The initial reaction of other producers of primary commodities was the same. However, orders decreased, and access to foreign markets became more restricted. Consequently, the deterioration of the terms of trade was much worse for commodity-exporting nations than for exporters of manufactures. The decline in both the volume of exports and commodity prices led export revenues to reach rock bottom in 1932 throughout Southeast Asia, as the accompanying table shows.

The crisis in the United States and Europe also affected Southeast Asia in the monetary sphere. Preceding the 1929 crisis, the speculative stock market boom had led to increases in interest rates as well as reduced lending to less developed parts of the world, including Southeast Asia. The onset of the crisis led to bank collapses in North America and Europe, which intensified international credit scarcity, including in Southeast Asia. Higher interest rates were difficult to absorb in the region's export industries, because by the late 1920s they were already operating with small profit margins. Falling export revenues caused firms to default on their debts, which in turn reduced the international creditworthiness of Southeast Asia.

Colonial governments in the region (except for Thailand) were to different degrees dependent on taxing foreign trade. They saw their revenues decline. Although some governments increased borrowing, all had to cut expenditure drastically, mainly by dismissing public servants. Export revenues and reserves were insufficient to sustain imports. Limited reserves also made it difficult to qualify for loans to sustain imports.

The macroeconomic contraction was worsened by the monetary regimes of countries in Southeast Asia. When the crisis hit, all had a gold exchange standard according to which the value of their currencies was fixed relative to a gold-based international currency. Such monetary regimes made it difficult to use currency devaluation as a buffer to reduce the overseas cost of their export products. The regimes forced countries to import deflation. Some relief came for Burma, Thailand, and Malaya when the U.K. devalued the pound in September 1931 and for the Philippines when the United States devalued the dollar in April 1933. In contrast, French Indochina and colonial Indonesia had to wait until September 1936.

An earlier devaluation of the guilder would have relieved the plight particularly of Indonesia. Given the small size of the Dutch market, Indonesia could not benefit from preferential trade agreements with The Netherlands. Devaluation would have been possible, because Indonesia effectively had its own currency—the guilder—which was kept at par with the Dutch guilder in The Netherlands. On the other hand, devaluation might not have had much effect. Indonesia's access to commodity markets for sugar and rubber had been severely restricted. Indonesia had the highest level of foreign debt in the region, largely denominated in the gold-based Dutch guilder. A devaluation of the guilder in Indonesia would have increased the cost of servicing that debt and would have made it difficult for the colonial government to borrow on the Dutch capital market in order to dampen the fall in public expenditure in Indonesia.

International import restrictions meant that goods were traded on the basis of bilateral trade agreements rather than price, quality, and delivery terms. Thus the recovery in Southeast Asia was assisted by the preferential trade arrangements that the Philippines, Malaya, Burma, and Indochina had with, respectively, the United States, the British Commonwealth, and France.

The Philippines suffered less from the crisis, because of the preferential access for Philippine sugar to the protected U.S. market. In fact, sugar production in the Philippines increased during the 1930s. In contrast, sugar from Java suffered severely from declining free-market prices and rising protectionism in Japan, India, and Europe following the 1931 Chadbourne Agreement. Sugar producers in Java did not have a benefactor, as the Dutch market was too small to absorb Java sugar. Sugar production had to be scaled back dramatically in Indonesia.

Rice producers in Burma benefited from lower import duties in India and Malaya on Burmese rice than for Thai rice, while rice producers in South Vietnam were supported by the fact that France and its colonies gave preferential treatment to Vietnamese rice and significantly increased rice imports after 1930. In contrast, Thai rice producers faced depressed international prices.

At the micro level, the crisis started to take its toll in 1932. Increasing numbers of firms were unable to find sufficient markets for their produce or were unable to meet production costs. The initial reaction had been to reduce production costs by lowering wages and dismissing workers, but by 1932 more were forced to close down. In particular, the labor-intensive plantations and mines in Malaya and Sumatra released hundreds of thousands of migrant workers from China, India, and Java.

Small indigenous producers of products such as rice, rubber, and copra chose instead to increase production in an effort to offset lower prices. For instance, rubber farmers in Sumatra and Kalimantan increased production until the colonial government in Indonesia entered the 1934 International Rubber Regulation Agreement and imposed a production quota system to curtail output and stabilize prices. Thai rice producers also maintained high levels of export production. Thai rice found ready markets throughout Southeast Asia, particularly in Indonesia, where imports of cheap Thai rice—and also cheap Japanese manufactures such as textiles—increased quickly as a consequence of the fact that the Indonesian guilder remained linked to gold until September 1936.

The literature on the crisis in Southeast Asia is dominated by concern about the consequences for the standard of living. It was argued that the crisis exacerbated the plight of the rural poor, leading them to resist payment of land taxes to governments and of debt to moneylenders. That led to peasant uprisings and a heightened level of political radicalization that preluded later calls for independence. However, the available evidence reveals a mixed experience. In Indochina, the colonial government insisted on land tax payments, while the colonial administration in the Philippines and In-

Crisis and Recovery of Exports and Government Revenues, 1929–1938

	Burma	Thailand	Indochina	Malaya	Indonesia	Philippines
A. Commodity exports from Southeast Asia (million U.S.$)						
1929	249	97	125	378	588	164
1932	115	54	43	76	217	100
1935	201	70	85	226	301	102
1938	183	90	82	238	360	147
Crisis: fall 1929–1932	-54%	-44%	-66%	-80%	-63%	-39%
Recovery: 1932–1938	59%	67%	91%	213%	66%	47%
B. Government expenditure in Southeast Asia (million U.S.$)						
1929	92	47	42	121	369	42
1932	64	26	24	88	253	40
1935	96	41	37	86	324	38
1938	60	59	26	143	355	70
Crisis: fall 1929–1932	-30%	-45%	-43%	-27%	-31%	-5%
Recovery: 1932–1938	-6%	127%	8%	63%	40%	75%

SOURCE: Calculated/compiled from export and government expenditure data from Mitchell, B. R. 1993. *International Historical Statistics: Africa, Asia & Oceania.* London: Macmillan.

donesia turned a blind eye to tax evasion. In Burma rising rural indebtedness indeed led to increased landlessness as Chettyar (Chettiar) moneylenders foreclosed on land that marginal farmers had put up as collateral. Rural indebtedness increased in Indonesia as well, but it did not lead to a similar degree of increased landlessness because Chinese moneylenders were prohibited from owning agricultural land and would not accept it as collateral.

Recent research has emphasized that the impact of the crisis varied across Southeast Asia, depending on the dependence of income earners on export production. For instance, urban wage laborers experienced an increase in their standard of living as retail prices fell faster than wages. In rural areas, farmers changed to the production of nonexport crops for domestic markets where technically possible and economically feasible.

Perhaps the crisis was more important for its long-term impact. In particular, it instilled among local nationalists a sense of lasting mistrust of economic forces and of colonialism. Reflecting international trends, governments in the region implemented trade policies that furthered domestic industrial production in an effort to reduce dependence on international commodity markets and to diversify economies. Such remedies established the foundations for inward-looking development policies that became prominent after the Pacific War (1941–1945).

PIERRE VAN DER ENG

See also Banks and Banking; Chettiars (Chettyars); Cocoa; Coffee; Labor and Labor Unions in Southeast Asia; Peasant Uprisings and Protest Movements in Southeast Asia; Rice in Southeast Asia; Rubber; Sugar; Taxation; Tobacco; Trade and Commerce of Southeast Asia (ca. Nineteenth Century to the 1990s)

References:

Azmi Khalid, A. 1989. "Reassessing Malaya during the Depression: A Response to Brown." *Sarjana* 4: 149–154.

Baker, C. J. 1981. "Economic Reorganization and the Slump in South and Southeast Asia." *Comparative Studies in Society and History* 23: 325–349.

Boomgaard, P., and I. Brown, eds. 2000. *Weathering the Storm: The Economies of*

Southeast Asia in the 1930s Depression. Singapore: Institute of Southeast Asian Studies (ISEAS).

Brown, I. 1986. "Rural Distress in South East Asia during the World Depression of the Early 1930s: A Preliminary Reexamination." *Journal of Asian Studies* 5: 995–1025.

———. 1999. "Tax Remission and Tax Burden in Rural Lower Burma during the Economic Crisis of the Early 1930s." *Modern Asian Studies* 33: 383–403.

De Moll, J. Th., and A. Neytzell de Wilde. 1936. *The Netherlands Indies during the Depression: A Brief Economic Survey.* Amsterdam: Meulenhoff.

Korthals Altes, W. L. 1979. "De Depreciatie van de Nederlands-Indische Gulden in 1936" [The Depreciation of the Dutch East Indies guilder in 1936]. Pp. 157–175 in *Between People and Statistics: Essays on Modern Indonesian History Presented to P. Creutzberg.* Edited by F. van Anrooij et al. The Hague: Nijhoff.

Owen, N. G. 1989. "Subsistence in the Slump: Agricultural Adjustment in the Provincial Philippines." Pp. 95–114 in *The Economies of Africa and Asia in the Inter-War Depression.* Edited by I. Brown. London: Routledge.

Van Laanen, J. T. M. 1982. *The World Depression (1929–1935) and the Indigenous Economy in the Netherlands Indies.* Southeast Asian Studies Committee Occasional Paper no. 13. Townsville, Australia: James Cook University of North Queensland.

GREAT WAR (1914–1918)
Conflict between Imperialists

Southeast Asia was involved in the 1914–1918 Great War only indirectly, whereas it was twice fought over in the 1941–1945 Pacific War. Yet it was, inevitably, affected by the Great War, which is also referred to as World War I or the European War.

Controversy over the origins of the war dates back to its outbreak but was intensified by the horrors of the trench warfare into which it rapidly descended and by its unexpected length. The victorious Allies (mainly Britain and France, and the United States) were to pin guilt upon the Germans, though they did not, as after World War II (1939–1945), proceed with the trial of war criminals. Historians are less confident about attributing guilt, but the investigations and reconsiderations that have continued to take place have led to something of a consensus that the German leaders bore a predominant share of responsibility for the deterioration in international relations that preceded the war and for the outbreak itself.

After the accession of Kaiser Wilhelm II (1859–1941) in 1890 and especially after 1897, the Germans had spoken of achieving "world power" and pursued *Weltpolitik* (playing a role in world affairs and politics). What they meant was not always clear, though not the less alarming to other powers in consequence. Perhaps the best definition relates German aspirations to those of the British, the predominant nineteenth-century power, and those of the Americans and the Russians. The potential of the United States and Russia seemed so great that they were likely to dominate the world of the twentieth century, territorially and economically. The Germans could not wait for the achievement of economic success, which would certainly take them past Britain, though not the United States. To be sure of obtaining a share of world power, moreover, they believed they would need a secure base in Europe, and since Europe could, at most, sustain only one power with worldwide influence, the British had to see the wisdom in stepping aside and accepting German leadership in Europe. What Britain perceived, however, was a threat to its security and even its independence, and it sought to uphold the resistance of other powers to German hegemony.

Baffled and frustrated, the Germans attempted an open challenge to "encirclement." At most, they expected a short war; it would quickly resolve a diplomatic impasse, and the troops would be home by Christmas. They failed, however, to secure the rapid victory they anticipated. Nor did they admit defeat. The war extended, drawing in other powers—even, in 1917, the United States itself. It also challenged the organization of the individual states and their capacity to mobilize their human and material resources. The weakest of the Great Powers (though the most populous)—Russia—could not meet the challenge. The czarist regime was overthrown in Russia, and in October 1917, the Bolsheviks seized power. At the end of the war, the German and Austrian monarchies were also overthrown. At the same time, the victorious European powers had themselves been profoundly challenged. The involvement of the Americans on their side had committed them to a more idealistic approach to international affairs, set out, for example, in U.S. president Woodrow Wilson's (1856–1924) Fourteen Points (which called for greater liberalism in international affairs and supported national self-determination) and the creation of the League of Nations.

The extension of the war to Asia was more indirect than direct. Germany was deprived of its colonial possessions, but those were mostly in Africa and the Pacific. Its Turkish ally was dismantled, though by no means without conflict or without effect on Islam. One way in which Turkey sought to fight back was by supporting Indian revolutionaries, particularly the Ghadr movement, radical and militant Indian nationalists of the Ghadr (Mutiny) Party. The future of India was, however, more affected by the concessions the British felt they had to make, given their increasing use of the Indian army. Those culminated in the Montagu declaration of 1917, which made it clear that India was destined for self-government within the empire.

In the first war, unlike the second, Japan was the ally, not the opponent, of Britain. Tokyo took advantage of its position to secure the German concessions in Shandong (Shantung) and to exert pressure on divided postrevolutionary China while the Europeans were otherwise occupied, presenting the so-called Twenty-One Demands in 1915. It also enjoyed major economic opportunities, becoming a creditor rather than a debtor nation in this phase. The British needed Tokyo's friendship, but they also wanted to restrain Japan, feeling that the help Japan offered in the Singapore mutiny of 1915 was too demonstrative. The British felt that the efficient and powerful force of the Japanese should be concentrated on China rather than on British territory.

In Southeast Asia, the colonial structure was unaffected by the war. In the Great War, unlike the Pacific War, the Dutch were neutral. The British consul general thought that the government in Batavia leaned toward the German side, but the Foreign Office gave no support to his suggestion that Japan should be given part of eastern Indonesia. Britain's object was to maintain the status quo for as long and as far as

possible. That remained its postwar policy: though victorious, it had been greatly weakened by the war.

The ideologies the war promoted were also to have their effect in the longer term. Burma was to seek the self-rule Britain had promised India. Even the Dutch were moved to set up the *Volksraad* (People's Council). They and, to a lesser extent, the other colonial powers faced an upsurge in communism after 1917. Nationalists did not have the opportunity they found in the Pacific War—to secure independence out of a worldwide struggle—but the struggles among their metropolitan powers suggested the possibility of change. Some Southeast Asians were directly involved in the conflict. Though they made no political concessions in Indochina, the French recruited seventeen Indochinese battalions to fight in the Balkans and on the western front. Siam declared war in 1917 in the hope of enhancing its status and ending the unequal treaties.

NICHOLAS TARLING

See also Constitutional Developments in Burma (1900–1941); Germans (Germany); Japan and Southeast Asia (pre-1941); Preservation of Siam's Political Independence; Russia and Southeast Asia; *Volksraad* (Peoples Council) (1918–1942)

References:

Hinsley, F. H., ed. 1977. *British Foreign Policy under Sir Edward Grey.* Cambridge: Cambridge University Press.

Kennedy, Paul. 1980. *The Rise of the Anglo-German Antagonism.* London: Allen & Unwin.

Kuwaijima, Sho. 1991. *Indian Mutiny in Singapore (1915).* Calcutta, India: Ratna Prakshan.

Tarling, Nicholas. 1993. *The Fall of Imperial Britain in South-East Asia.* Singapore: Oxford University Press.

GREATER EAST ASIA CO-PROSPERITY SPHERE
Imperial Japan's Aspiration

Establishing the "Greater East Asia Co-prosperity Sphere" was the official goal of the Japanese government when it waged the war in Asia and the Pacific that began on 8 December 1941. The concept implied that Japan would liberate

East and Southeast Asia from Western colonial rule and create a co-prosperity sphere under its leadership. In reality, however, it was a pretext for Japan to invade, occupy, and rule Asian countries. The term was first announced by the Japanese foreign minister, Matsuoka Yosuke (1880–1946), on 1 August 1940. Previously, a few cadres of the military proposed to establish the "East Asia Co-prosperity Sphere" around 1938. The sphere was to contain Japan, Manchuria, North China, and Mongolia as the "self-relying" sector; Siberia, central and southern China, and the parts of Southeast Asia located east of Burma (Myanmar) as the defense sector; and India and Australia as the economic sector.

According to Matsuoka, the sphere would encompass Japan, Manchuria, and China as the basic unit, with the South Sea area, consisting of Dutch East Indies (Indonesia), French Indochina, and Thailand, as the supplemental unit. In September 1940, British Malaya, Borneo, Burma, and India were added (India could be put in the Soviet survival bloc). Originally, the decisive objective was proclaimed to be securing the important strategic resources in East and Southeast Asia. However, from around September 1940 on, liberation of the area was advocated. The second objective was apparently to procure Asian peoples' support for Japan's war against the Western powers. In Japan, there are still individuals who insist that as a result of this policy, Asian countries were able to attain independence much earlier. Few Asians, however, concur with this thesis.

HARA FUJIO

See also "Asia for the Asiatics"; Japan and
    Southeast Asia (pre-1941); Japanese
    Occupation of Southeast Asia (1941–1945)
References:
Gibney, Frank, ed. 1995. *Senso: The Japanese
    Remember the Pacific War.* Translated by Beth
    Cary. Armonk, NY: M. E. Sharpe.
Lebra, Joyce C., ed. 1975. *Japan's Greater East
    Asia Co-prosperity Sphere in World War II:
    Selected Readings and Documents.* Kuala
    Lumpur and New York: Oxford University
    Press.

GUANGZHOU (CANTON)

See China, Imperial; Chinese Tribute System

GUIDED DEMOCRACY (*DEMOKRASI TERPIMPIN*)
Indonesian Style of Governance

Guided Democracy was a semiauthoritarian regime introduced by President Sukarno (t. 1945–1967) in Indonesia from 1957 to 1959. The system led to economic decay and sharp political tension, and it collapsed in late 1965 in the aftermath of the Gestapu Affair.

Guided Democracy was a confluence of four processes. First, it was an expression of Sukarno's drive to place his person at the center of Indonesian politics. He had been the most important nationalist leader since 1927 and president since 1945, but he was only a figurehead under the parliamentary system from 1950. Guided Democracy placed him once more in the center of politics as the arbiter of political power and the main source of ideology. During 1957 and 1958, he teased the Indonesian public with hints about the kind of system that he believed would suit Indonesia. In 1959, he sidestepped the Constituent Assembly, which had been elected in 1955 to prepare a new national constitution, and unilaterally restored the provisional 1945 constitution that gave the president sweeping powers. He became president-for-life in 1963 and took grandiloquent titles such as "Extension of the People's Tongue." He paid little attention, however, to administration, and the government of the country decayed disastrously, especially after the death of his nonparty chief minister Djuanda Kartawidjaja (1911–1963), who had headed a series of "business" or "working" cabinets on Sukarno's behalf. By 1965, Indonesia was suffering from high inflation, administrative disintegration, infrastructure collapse, and impending famine.

Second, Guided Democracy was an intellectual response to the problems of applying Western democratic forms to a large and diverse developing country. Many Indonesians, especially Sukarno, felt that the party system encouraged division rather than unity and that a majoritarian system would necessarily oppress minorities. Sukarno described a process of *musyawarah* (exhaustive discussion) and *mufakat* (consensus articulated by wise leaders), allegedly followed in village Indonesia, as more appropriate to Indonesian culture. Guided Democracy also rested on a long-standing intellectual tradition of corporatism in Indonesian thought that emphasized the harmonious interaction of different functional groups within society, rather than competition based on individual, class, or other particularist interests. Sukarno also stressed *gotong royong* (mutual self-help) as preferable to competition, and in 1959, he appointed 200 functional group representatives (representing workers, peasants, women, intellectuals, youth, and so on) and 94 presidential nominees to sit alongside the existing 281 members of Parliament in the new Provisional People's Deliberative Council (Madjelis Permusyawaratan Rakjat–Sementara, MPRS), which formally became the central legislative body of Guided Democracy.

Third, Guided Democracy was a major step toward military domination of Indonesian politics. In March 1957, Sukarno responded to a series of regional military rebellions by declaring martial law, effectively ending parliamentary rule and legalizing those rebellions. The army also took over management of former Dutch-owned enterprises, which were seized by workers in December 1957 in protest against the Dutch retention of West New Guinea (Irian Barat), which Indonesia claimed as an integral part of its territory. The army was active in sponsoring mass organizations as representatives of the various functional groups. Although martial law formally ended in 1963, Guided Democracy greatly expanded the military's economic resources and established it as the clear leader of a broad coalition of anticommunist forces.

And fourth, Guided Democracy was an unsuccessful attempt to overcome the political conflict of the 1950s by creating a structure in which parties and social groups would be forced to cooperate. Until Indonesia received international recognition in 1949, deep disagreements over the appropriate nature of the independent state had been partly controlled by the need for national unity. From 1950, however, the deep divisions over regional autonomy, social and economic reform, and the place of Islam raised the stakes in Indonesian politics.

By 1957, several regions were in revolt, discontented with their treatment by Java, and the elected Constituent Assembly was deadlocked over whether Islam was to have a place in the constitution. At the same time, a major Islamic revolution, the Darul Islam, was under way in the countryside in West Java and South Sulawesi. Moreover, the strong performance of the communists (Partai Komunis Indonesia, PKI) in the 1955 national elections and their even stronger performance in 1957 regional elections raised the prospect of communist participation in government after the elections scheduled for 1959. Under these circumstances, Guided Democracy initially seemed to offer a moratorium on political change.

Quickly, however, it became apparent that change had only been postponed. Observers commonly described the real political structure of Guided Democracy as a triangle, in which Sukarno balanced the army (with the Muslims) against the communists. Sukarno, however, was ailing and aging, and he would be succeeded either by the PKI or by an army-led coalition. Bitter antagonism developed between the two sides, often spilling over into violence when the PKI pursued issues such as land reform. The external campaign to recover West Irian (West New Guinea), which succeeded in 1963, as well as the subsequent *Konfrontasi* ("Crush Malaysia" campaign launched by Sukarno's Indonesia against British plans to create a new Federation of Malaysia) and Sukarno's general espousal of Third World anti-imperialist causes, provided only limited distraction from internal divisions. The perception that the PKI had launched a preemptive coup against the army high command in Jakarta on 1 October 1965 (the Gestapu Affair) gave the military grounds to destroy the party and to remove Sukarno from power.

The military-dominated Suharto regime that succeeded Guided Democracy described itself as the New Order, in contrast to Sukarno's Old Order. However, it inherited from the Sukarno era an authoritarian presidential constitution, a doctrine of military engagement in politics, and a system of military finance through enterprises separate from the state budget. It also assumed a suspicion of democracy, a sympathy for political corporatism, and a preference for removing conflicts by repressing them and defining them out of existence. In this respect, the legacy of Guided Democracy persisted until the late 1990s.

ROBERT CRIBB

See also Aceh (Acheh); Darul Islam Movement (DI); Gestapu Affair (1965); Islamic Resurgence in Southeast Asia (Twentieth

Century); Konfrontasi ("Crush Malaysia" Campaign); Military and Politics in Southeast Asia; Mohammad Hatta (1902–1980); *Orde Baru* (The New Order); Partai Komunis Indonesia (PKI) (1920); Republik Maluku Selatan (RMS, Republic of South Moluccas); Soekarno (Sukarno) (1901–1970); Suharto (1921–)

References:

Crouch, Harold. 1978. *The Army and Politics in Indonesia.* Ithaca, NY: Cornell University Press.

Feith, Herbert. 1967. "Dynamics of Guided Democracy." Pp. 39–409 in *Indonesia.* 2nd ed. Edited by Ruth T. McVey. New Haven, CT: Southeast Asian Studies, Yale University.

Feith, Herbert, and Lance Castles, eds. 1970. *Indonesian Political Thinking, 1945–1965.* Ithaca, NY: Cornell University Press.

Legge, J. D. 1973. *Sukarno: A Political Biography.* Harmondsworth, England: Pelican.

Lev, Daniel S. 1966. *The Transition to Guided Democracy: Indonesian Politics, 1957–1959.* Ithaca, NY: Modern Indonesia Project, Cornell University.

McVey, Ruth T. 1971, 1972. "The Post-revolutionary Transformation of the Indonesian Army." *Indonesia* 11: 131–176; 12: 147–181.

Mohamad Goenawan. 1988. *The "Cultural Manifesto" Affair: Literature and Politics in Indonesia in the 1960s—A Signatory's View.* Clayton, Australia: Centre of Southeast Asian Studies, Monash University.

Oey Hong Lee. 1971. *Indonesian Government and Press during Guided Democracy.* Zug, Switzerland: Inter Documentation.

Sundhaussen, Ulf. 1982. *The Road to Power: Indonesian Military Politics, 1945–1967.* Kuala Lumpur: Oxford University Press.

Tan Tjin-kie, ed. 1967. *Sukarno's Guided Indonesia.* Brisbane, Australia: Jacaranda Press.

Weatherbee, Donald E. 1966. *Ideology in Indonesia: Sukarno's Indonesian Revolution.* New Haven, CT: Yale University Press.

GUJARATIS

Of the Indian trading groups that conducted international trade throughout Southeast Asia, the most widespread and important was the Gujarati. The Gujaratis, from their base at Gujerat on the west coast of India, were skilled shippers and traders and formed part of the vast trading network that linked western Indian ports with ports on the eastern shores of the Bay of Bengal. These included the Burmese ports of the Irrawaddy Delta, Thai ports, and Malay ports. The Gujaratis plied routes linking West Asia, the Mediterranean, Southeast Asia, Japan, and China. They were specialist textile traders, distributing silk and cotton textiles from Ahmedabad and Baroda to the Southeast Asian region in exchange for rice and teak from Burma, pepper and tin from western Indonesia and Malaya, and spices gathered in the Straits of Melaka from the neighboring region. Gujarati shipowners controlled the interisland trade and parts of the international trade with western Asia and Europe.

Like the Chettiars, the Gujaratis also developed a financial trading system throughout the region. They operated as bankers and merchant bankers, and their letters of credit (*hundi*) issued in one region could be cashed in another. The arrival of the Europeans in the sixteenth century resulted in the dispersal of the spice trade and forced the Gujarati and Malabar Muslim networks to disperse into other areas as well.

In the nineteenth and twentieth centuries, the Gujaratis became increasingly important as compradors (*shroffs*) to Western banks in Southeast Asia, securing credit for large urban textile firms or opium traders, with networks extending from Persia (Iran) to China. The Gujaratis also provided short-term credit to the Chettiars. Their dominance in the Indian textile trade in the urban areas of Singapore, West Malaysia, Sabah and Sarawak, Indonesia, and Bangkok continues to this day.

AMARJIT KAUR

See also Age of Commerce; Arabs; Banks and Banking; Chettiars (Chettyars); Economic History of Early Modern Southeast Asia (Pre-Sixteenth Century); Economic Transformation of Southeast Asia (ca. 1400–ca. 1800); Indian Immigrants; Singapore (Nineteenth Century to 1990s), Entrepôt Trade and Commerce of; Spices and the Spice Trade; Textiles of Southeast Asia; Trade and Commerce of Southeast Asia (ca. Nineteenth Century to the 1990s)

References:

Brown, Rajeswary Ampalavanar. 1994. *Capital and Entrepreneurship in South-East Asia.* Basingstoke, England: Macmillan.

Reid, Anthony. 1988. *Southeast Asia in the Age of Commerce, 1450–1680.* Vol. 1, *The Lands below the Winds.* New Haven, CT: Yale University Press.

———. 1993. *Southeast Asia in the Age of Commerce, 1450–1680.* Vol. 2, *Expansion and Crisis.* New Haven, CT: Yale University Press.

GULF OF TONKIN INCIDENT (AUGUST 1964)

Prelude to the Vietnam War

The Gulf of Tonkin Incident involved the August 1964 naval exchanges in which U.S. warships faced smaller North Vietnamese naval units in the Gulf of Tonkin. It was the main event preceding the massive involvement of U.S. forces in Vietnam, and it served as the pretext for the United States to escalate its intervention.

To this day, the facts surrounding the incident remain controversial, as does the background to the event. On 2 August, there was a twenty-minute skirmish between Hanoi patrol boats and the destroyer USS *Maddox* off the North Vietnamese coast. Washington decided not to act. In a tense context between North and South Vietnam, ten years after the Geneva cease-fire, the juxtaposition of two American naval operations near the Democratic Republic of Vietnam (DRV, North Vietnam) would prove explosive—the OPLAN-34A commando raids on coastal islands (covert operations from South Vietnam) and the U.S. naval patrols near DRV territorial waters (DeSoto program for electronic surveillance). But on 4 August, in very bad weather, a second alleged naval incident occurred, involving the *Maddox* and another U.S. destroyer, the *Turner Joy,* which apparently was attacked by DRV torpedo boats. Did this last Vietnamese attack really happen? Decades later, former U.S. defense secretary Robert McNamara himself apparently was not sure (McNamara 1996).

Regardless of what actually did or did not happen on 4 August, the consequences of the incident are clear. Only a few hours later, Washington authorized reprisal raids on four North Vietnamese patrol boat bases and an oil depot. Thereafter, events unfolded quickly: sixty-four sorties were made from aircraft carriers cruising nearby, and Lieutenant Everett Alvarez Jr. be-

U.S. president Lyndon B. Johnson signs the Gulf of Tonkin Resolution on 10 August 1964. The congressional resolution authorized the president to take whatever measures he deemed necessary to deal with communist aggression in Vietnam. The resolution was repealed at the end of 1970. (U.S. National Archives)

came the first U.S. pilot to be shot down and imprisoned in Hanoi. Even more important, on 7 August 1964, the U.S. Congress voted almost unanimously for the Gulf of Tonkin Resolution that had been submitted by Lyndon B. Johnson's administration (1963–1969): "the Congress approves and supports the determination of the President, as Commander in Chief, to take all necessary measures to repel any armed attack against the forces of the United States and to prevent further aggression" (quoted in Galloway 1970: 167). The idea incorporated in the resolution had been percolating for a few months, and the Gulf of Tonkin incident gave the opportunity for its execution. The time had arrived for the Vietnam War.

HUGUES TERTRAIS

See also Cold War; Domino Theory; Indochina War, Second (Vietnam War) (1964–1975); U.S. Involvement in Southeast Asia (post-1945); Vietnam, North (post-1945); Vietnam, South (post-1945)

References:

Galloway, John. 1970. *The Gulf of Tonkin Resolution.* Rutherford, NJ: Fairleigh Dickinson University Press.

Karnow, Stanley. 1983. *Vietnam, a History: The First Complete Account of Vietnam at War.* New York: Viking Press.

McNamara, Robert S. 1996. *In Retrospect: The Tragedy and Lessons of Vietnam.* New York: Vintage Books.

Porter, Gareth. 1993. "Coercive Diplomacy in Vietnam: The Tonkin Gulf Crisis Reconsidered." Pp. 9–22 in *The American War in Vietnam.* Edited by Jane Werner and David Hunt. South East Asia Program Series no. 13. Ithaca, NY: South East Asia Program Series, Cornell University.